1832   First Reform Bill in Britain: victory of middle-class liberalism

1846   Repeal of British Corn Laws: another liberal victory

1848   Wave of liberal and nationalistic revolutions in Europe

        The Communist Manifesto, by Marx and Engels

1851   (December 2) *Coup d'état* by Louis Napoleon in France

1853   "Opening" of Japan by United States Commodore Perry

1859   *Origin of Species,* by Darwin

        On Liberty, by J. S. Mill

1861   Civil War in the United States

        Emancipation of serfs by Tsar Alexander II

1867   British North America Act: Canada a dominion

        Ausgleich: Habsburg Empire reorganized as Dual Monarchy

1870   Franco-Prussian War: leading to completion of German and Italian unification and
        to Third French Republic

1882   Triple Alliance: Germany, Austria-Hungary, Italy

1891   *Rerum Novarum*, by Pope Leo XIII: basis of modern Catholic social philosophy

1898   *J'Accuse*, by Zola: agitation over Dreyfus in France

        Spanish-American War: United States emerging as world power

1899   Boer War in South Africa

1904   *Entente Cordiale* of Britain and France: Triple Entente in formation

1905   Japan victorious in Russo-Japanese War: partly successful revolution in Russia

A History of Civilization

A History

Crane Brinton

McLean Professor of Ancient and Modern History, Harvard University

John B. Christopher

University of Rochester

Robert Lee Wolff

Archibald Cary Coolidge Professor of History, Harvard University

# of Civilization

VOLUME TWO   1715 to the Present

Third Edition

Prentice-Hall, Inc.,   Englewood Cliffs, New Jersey

A History of Civilization

Volume Two: 1715 to the Present

Brinton, Christopher, and Wolff

Maps by Vincent Kotschar

Picture Editor: Gabriele Wunderlich

Design by Walter Behnke

C

Current printing (last digit):
15   14   13   12   11   10   9   8   7   6   5   4   3

Preface

In preparing this third edition of *A History of Civilization* we have sought to record and interpret the fast-moving and often bewildering events that have occurred since the publication of the second edition in 1960, and we have also sought to profit by the new discoveries that continue to revolutionize man's knowledge of the past, especially the remote past. The text incorporates suggestions for improvement made by readers of the second edition, and the maps and illustrations have undergone a complete revamping. The result represents not a mere tinkering with the second edition but a thorough revision and, we hope, a more attractive and more useful book.

In particular, we have recast sections of Volume I treating the first civilizations (Chapter 1), the Minoans and Mycenaeans (Chapter 2), the Etruscans (Chapter 3), and the Ottoman Turks (Chapter 9) to bring them abreast of recent scholarship. In Volume II we have reorganized Chapters 30 and 31, which cover events since 1945, to stress the interaction of developments in the Western democratic world, the communist world, and the emerging states of the nonwestern world. Both the mounting tide of paperbound editions and the flow of new scholarly works have necessitated extensive changes in the reading suggestions at the conclusion of each chapter. New maps have been added, old ones redrawn, and all have been printed in two-colors to make the cartographical work at once more appealing and more instructive. The great majority of the illustrations, both in color and in black and white, are new and have been selected with an eye to their freshness and their appropriateness in reflecting the changing climates and "styles" of human culture.

A revision of these dimensions would scarcely have been possible without the help of many people. We thank all the students and teachers who have taken the trouble to write us. We wish to express special appreciation to the following gentlemen for their critiques of the third edition: William F. Allen, University of Bridgeport; Ralph H. Bowen, Northern Illinois University; Gene Brucker, University of California at Berkeley; Elmer Louis Kayser, the George Washington University; Robert G. Lunde and Gerard E. Silberstein, University of Kentucky; and Bernard C. Weber and David B. McElroy, University of Alabama. And, as this edition goes to press, we thank again the expert readers whose comments contributed so substantially to the quality of the first two editions. Finally, we wish to record our heavy debt to those with whom we have worked most closely: to the members of the Project Planning Department of Prentice-Hall, who have applied their skills and energies most generously and effectively; to Miss Gabriele Wunderlich, for her taste and resourcefulness in obtaining illustrative materials; to Vincent Kotschar, for his clear and painstaking revision of the maps; and to our colleagues and our families whose sympathy, understanding, and aid mean that the authors' salute to them is no mere gesture but a response from the heart.

CRANE BRINTON   JOHN B. CHRISTOPHER   ROBERT L. WOLFF

A Note on the Tables of Historical Dates

Some day psychologists may be able to tell us just what and how to remember. But at present we know little more than this: though a few exceptional people can absorb and tap at will large stores of systematically arranged facts — say, the list of popes from St. Peter on — most human beings cannot remember great systems of facts for very long unless they make fairly regular use of them. The average educated American does not remember such a relatively short list as that of the presidents of the United States. Indeed, if we never did any figuring at all, most of us would forget the multiplication table. Few of us make any regular use of history. Fortunately, the modern world is admirably supplied with works of ready reference that can free our minds for more useful work than just memorizing. The engineer, for example, does not need to keep in mind all the formulas and equations he might need; he has his engineer's handbook. So anyone using history has a host of reference books available in libraries, and on his desk he may have for immediate use such a storehouse of information as the one-volume *Encyclopaedia of World History* (Houghton Mifflin, 1948), edited by W. L. Langer.

Yet we do need something like a historian's equivalent of the multiplication table, if only to give us a frame of reference. The trouble with most historical tables, however, is that they are much too long and contain far too many facts for the average person. It is as if our multiplication table, instead of stopping with twelve times twelve, or even ten times ten, went on to fifty times fifty. The lists of dates to be found on the endpapers of the books are an attempt to construct the historian's equivalent of the multiplication table. It is a simple list of approximately a hundred dates, a kind of rough map of historic time. It is worth memorizing bit by bit and keeping in memory.

The list is not necessarily meant to include all the "hundred great dates." It is meant rather to assist the reader to keep his mind on the course of history by focusing on two threads that serve to put an order, a pattern, into a complex set of facts.

First, there is the concept of recorded history as a series of streams which have different sources on this earth, but which finally flow together in the One World of the present. Of course, some of the streams — the Chinese, the East Indian, the African, for example — have by no means wholly mingled, and are still present as separate currents. We take as the main stream in the endpapers, as we do in this book, our western civilization with its sources in the river valleys of the ancient Near East.

Second, there is the concept of a specific region or nation as a leader, a center, a focal point of historic change in our own western civilization at a given period. Periclean Athens, the Rome of the Caesars, and Victorian Britain are classic examples. Very broadly speaking, these centers of leadership have since 3000 B.C. swung westward and northward in a huge arc, from Egypt and Mesopotamia to Greece, Rome, western and central Europe, the United States. But the metaphor is imperfect. As we have taken pains to point out in this book, in the thousand years after the "fall" of the western Roman Empire, the Byzantines, the Slavs, and even perhaps the Moslems were in some ways quite as focal to western history as the medieval westerners. Moreover, leadership, especially in politics, may pass from one region to another, and former leaders like ancient Athens may fall almost to the status of ghost towns. Yet on the whole the area of western civilization constantly widens. Those parts left behind in the march of history do not lapse into an entirely separate existence; they remain a part, though only a subsidiary part, of the West.

A Note on the Reading Suggestions

A list of reading suggestions is appended to each chapter of this book. Almost all historical bibliographies nowadays begin with the statement that they are highly selective and do not, of course, aspire to be exhaustive. This apology is hardly necessary, for the fact is that in most fields of history we have outrun the possibility of bringing together in one list all the books and articles in all languages on a given topic. There are for the wide fields of this book, and in English alone, thousands of volumes and hundreds of thousands of articles in periodicals. The brief lists following each chapter are simply suggestions to the reader who wishes to explore a given topic further.

Each list attempts to give important and readable books, with special attention to paperbacks, which are often the editions most available in a college community. A useful guide is *Paperbound Books in Print*, a monthly review of new paperbacks, with encyclopaedic cumulative issues published three or four times a year. In addition, good readings in original sources, the contemporary documents and writings of an age, are sometimes listed, though the reader can supplement these listings from the text itself and from the footnotes. In addition, there are many good collections of sources for European history, notably the *Introduction to Contemporary Civilization in the West* (1954), prepared by faculty members at Columbia University; this begins with the Middle Ages and gives much longer selections from the sources than such compilations usually do. Other good collections are to be found in the Portable Readers (published by Viking). There are also many source books and pamphlets on central or controversial problems in

European history. A good example is K. M. Setton and H. R. Winkler, eds., *Great Problems in European Civilization*, rev. ed. (Prentice-Hall, 1965). Another is the series of pamphlets edited by R. W. Greenlaw under the general title "Problems in European Civilization" (D. C. Heath).

Our lists also include historical novels and, occasionally, dramas. Professional historians are likely to be somewhat severe in their standards for a historical novel. They naturally want its history to be sound, and at bottom they are likely to be somewhat prejudiced against the form. The historical novels listed here are all readable and all reasonably good as history. But note that historical novels, like historical films, though accurate on such material matters as authentic settings and appropriate costumes, often fail to capture the immaterial aspects — the psychology, the spirit — of the age they are written about. Many such novels motivate their characters, especially in love, as if they were modern Europeans and Americans. Exceptions to this rule are noted in the lists.

It is easy to assemble more material on a given topic than is furnished by our reading lists. American libraries, large and small, have catalogues with subject and title listings, as well as a section of reference books with encyclopaedias and bibliographies. Many libraries have open shelves where, once a single title is discovered, many others may be found in the immediate area. Perhaps the first printed list of books to be consulted is *A Guide to Historical Literature* (Macmillan, 1931) and its sequel, *The American Historical Association's Guide to Historical Literature* (Macmillan, 1961). For more recent books one can turn, for American history, to the *Harvard Guide to American History* (Belknap, 1954), edited by O. Handlin and others. And for the history of Europe and other areas there are many good bibliographies; see, for example, those in "The Rise of Modern Europe" series edited by W. L. Langer (Torch); in the multivolumed *Oxford History of England;* and in R. R. Palmer and J. Colton, *A History of the Modern World* (Knopf, 1965). For historical fiction, one may consult two older specialized guides: E. A. Baker, *A Guide to Historical Fiction* (Macmillan, 1914) and J. Nield, *A Guide to the Best Historical Novels and Tales* (Elkins, Mathews, and Marrot, 1929). The more recent *Fiction Catalogue* (Wilson, 1951) while covering much besides historical fiction, does furnish keys to books that cover particular countries and particular historical eras.

What is much more difficult than assembling titles is securing an evaluation of individual books. For older books the *Guide to Historical Literature*, already mentioned, gives the most useful references to critical reviews of the titles it discusses. *The Book Review Digest* gives capsule reviews and references to longer ones. For current books the weekly book section of *The New York Times* and *The Times Literary Supplement* (published in London) usually provide informative reviews of historical works soon after they are published. Later — sometimes as much as three years later — full scholarly appraisals are published in the *American Historical Review*, its British equivalent, the *English Historical Review*, and in more specialized reviews, such as the *Journal of Modern History, Speculum* (for medieval studies), *The Middle East Journal*, and many others. A new American scholarly journal, *History and Theory,* covers a field of great interest to historians today. By reading a few reviews of a book one can usually get a fair indication of its scope and quality. In our reading suggestions we have tried, within a very brief compass, to give comparable indications.

Contents

The Old Régime and the International Balance, 1715–1789   *1*

16

I INTRODUCTION: THE PROSPECT IN *1715*.   II THE WESTERN POWERS. *The Commercial Revolution. The Mississippi and South Sea Bubbles. The Agricultural Revolution. The Beginnings of the Industrial Revolution. The Assets of Britain. Cabinet Government. The Liabilities of France. The Other Western States.*   III ITALY AND GERMANY. *Disunited Italy. Divided Germany: The Habsburg Dominions. The Rise of Prussia. Frederick William I.*   IV THE EASTERN POWERS. *The Early Years of Peter the Great. The Western Trip. Peter's Wars. The Machinery of Peter's Government. Other Innovations of Peter the Great. Peter the Great: A Final Evaluation. Poland and Turkey.*   V WAR AND DIPLOMACY, 1713–1789. *Main Characteristics. The Turkish and Polish Questions. 1716–1739. The War of Jenkins' Ear. The War of the Austrian Succession, 1740–1748. The Uneasy Peace, 1748–1756. The Seven Years' War, 1756–1763. The International Balance in Review.*

The Enlightenment   *43*

17

I BASIC PRINCIPLES AND TRAITS. *The Inheritance from Locke and Newton. Eighteenth-Century Science. French Leadership.*   II THE REFORM PROGRAM OF THE PHILOSOPHES. *Laissez-Faire Economics. Justice. Education. Attitudes toward Religion. Political Thought: Montesquieu. Political thought: Rousseau. Enlightened Despotism.*   III THE ENLIGHTENED DESPOTS. *Prussia: Frederick the Great. Austria: Maria Theresa and Joseph II. Other Despots. Limitations of Enlightened Despotism.*   IV RUSSIA, 1725–1825. *The Fate of the Autocracy. 1725–1762. Nobles and Serfs, 1730–1762. Catherine the Great (1762–1796). Paul (1796–1801). Alexander I (1801–1825). Russian Foreign Policy, 1725–1796.*   V GEORGE III AND THE AMERICAN REVOLUTION. *George III. Background of the Revolution. Implications of the Revolution.*   VI THE CULTURE OF THE EIGHTEENTH CENTURY. *The Limitations of Reason. The Evangelical Revival. Literature. Art. The Great Musicians.*

The French Revolution and Napoleon   89

18

I CAUSES OF THE REVOLUTION. *The Monarchy. The First and Second Estates. The Third Estate. The Financial Crisis. The Estates General.* II THE DISSOLUTION OF THE MONARCHY. *Popular Uprisings, July – October, 1789. The National Assembly, 1789 – 1791. The Constitution of 1791. The Legislative Assembly, October, 1791 – September, 1792.* III THE FIRST REPUBLIC. *The September Massacres, 1792. Gironde and Mountain. The Reign of Terror, June, 1793 – July, 1794. The Record of the Terror. The Thermidorean Reaction. The Directory, October, 1795 – November, 1799.* IV NAPOLEON AND FRANCE. *The First Coalition, 1792 – 1795. Napoleon's Early Career. Brumaire. Napoleonic Government. Law and Justice. Religion. Education. Economics.* V NAPOLEON AND EUROPE. *The War, 1800 – 1807. The Empire at Its Height, 1807 – 1812. The Continental System. The Peninsular War. German Resistance. The Russian Campaign. The Downfall.* VI THE LEGACY OF THE REVOLUTION AND NAPOLEON.

Revolution and Counter-Revolution, 1815–1850   135

19

I INTRODUCTION. II THE ROMANTIC PROTEST. *The Revolt against Reason. The Return to the Past. Music. The Arts. Religion and Philosophy. The Romantic "Style."* III THE CONSERVATIVE OUTLOOK AND THE VIENNA SETTLEMENT. *Burke and Metternich. The Congress of Vienna. The Quarantine of France.* IV THE REVOLUTIONS OF THE 1820's. *The Revolutionary Credo. The Iberian States and Naples. The Greek War of Independence. The Decembrist Revolt in Russia.* V THE REVOLUTIONS OF 1830. *France: The July Revolution. Belgium. Poland. Italy and Germany. The Lessons of 1830.* VI THE REVOLUTIONS OF 1848. *Common Denominators. France. Italy. Germany. The Habsburg Domains. The Lessons of 1848.*

The Impact of the Economic Revolutions   177

20

I THE INDUSTRIAL REVOLUTION. *Preparation and Take-off. Coal and Iron. Transport and Communication. Banking and Capital. The Timetable of Industrialization.* II ECONOMIC AND SOCIAL CONSEQUENCES OF INDUSTRIALIZATION. *The Agricultural Revolution. Changes in Population. The Aspirations of the Middle Class. The Grievances of the Working Class.* III THE RESPONSES OF LIBERALISM. *The Classical Economists. Utilitarianism: Bentham. Democratic Liberalism: Mill.* IV THE SOCIALIST RESPONSE — THE UTOPIANS. *Saint-Simon and Fourier. Owen. The Early Utopians Appraised.* V THE SOCIALIST RESPONSE — MARX. *Basic Principles. The Communist Manifesto. The Later Career of Marx.* VI OTHER RESPONSES. *The Anarchists. Proudhon. The Christian Socialists. The Catholic Response.*

The Western Democracies in the Nineteenth Century   *211*

21

I BRITAIN, *1815–1914. The Process of Reform. Parliamentary Reform. The Two-Party System: Liberals and Conservatives. The Two-Party System: An Explanation. Reforms of the Utilitarians. Free Trade. Labor and Factory Legislation. Education. Chartism. Foreign Policy. Imperial Policy. The Irish Problem. The Threat to Free Trade. The Welfare State. The Labor Party.* II FRANCE—SECOND EMPIRE AND THIRD REPUBLIC. *The Coup d'Etat of 1851. The Second Empire, 1852–1870: Domestic Developments. The Second Empire: Foreign Policy. The "Liberal Empire." The Birth of the Third Republic. The Constitution of 1875. Boulanger and Panama. The Dreyfus Case. The Republic after Dreyfus.* III ITALY, *1848–1914. Cavour and the Completion of Unification. Assets and Liabilities of United Italy.* IV THE UNITED STATES. *The Federal Union. Civil War and Reconstruction. Economic and Social Development. The Myth of Isolation.*

Central and Eastern Europe   *253*

To the Outbreak of World War I

22

I INTRODUCTION. II GERMANY, *1850–1914. Prussia and the German Confederation, 1850–1859. Bismarck Comes to Power. The Schleswig-Holstein Question, 1863–1865. War with Austria, 1866. The North German Confederation. Showdown with France. The German Empire. Domestic Developments, 1871–1878. Domestic Developments, 1878–1890. William II. Domestic Tensions, 1890–1914.* III THE HABSBURG MONARCHY, *1850–1914. Character of the Empire. Political Experiments, 1850–1867. Dual Monarchy, 1867. The Czechs. Poles and Ruthenians. Other Minorities in Austria. Minorities in Hungary: Slovaks, Rumanians, South Slavs. Croatia. Bosnia-Herzegovina. Austrian Society and Politics, 1867–1914. Hungarian Society and Politics, 1867–1914.* IV RUSSIA, *1825–1914. Character of the Empire. Nicholas I (1825–1855). The Crimean War. Alexander II and Reform. Russian Intellectual Life. Nihilism, Populism, Terrorism. Foreign Policy under Alexander II. The Reaction, 1881–1904. The Russo-Japanese War. The Revolution of 1905. The Dumas, 1906–1914.* V CONCLUSION.

The Intellectual Revolution   *297*

23

I DARWINISM. *The Origin of Species. Darwin's Theories. The Effect on Theology. The Effect on Social and Economic Attitudes. Eugenics. "Racism." The New Historical Determinism.* II LITERATURE AND THE ARTS. *The Victorian Age. The Realistic Novel. The Naturalistic Novel: Zola. The Literature of Pessimism and Protest. Poetry. Painting. The Other Arts. Music. The Arts in Review.* III PHILOSOPHY. *Idealism and Realism. Dynamism and the Cult of the Will. The Revolt against Reason. The Chastened Rationalists. The Extreme Anti-Rationalists.* IV POLITICAL AND SOCIAL THOUGHT. V THE CENTURY OF HOPE.

Nineteenth-Century Imperialism   *327*

24

I THE MOVEMENT IN GENERAL. *The Economic Aspect. The Powers Involved. The Areas Involved.*
II THE BRITISH EMPIRE. *South Africa. The Boer War and After. Egypt. The Rest of British Africa.*
Other British Spheres. India: Political Organization. India: "The Meeting of East and West." III THE
OTHER EMPIRES. *The French: North Africa. The French: Tropical Africa. The French: Asia. The Ger-*
mans. The Italians and Belgians. The Americans. The Japanese. IV THE DEBATE OVER IMPERIALISM.
Pro: The Argument from Social Darwinism. Pro: The Argument of Duty. Pro: The Defensive Argument.
Con: Anti-Imperialist Arguments. V THE COLONIES OF WHITE SETTLEMENT. *Canada: Back-*
ground of Revolt. Canada: Durham and a New Status. The Extension of Dominion Status. The Common-
wealth in Review. VI THE RESULTS OF IMPERIALISM.

The First World War   *357*

25

I INTRODUCTION. II CAUSES OF THE WAR. *The Shift in the Balance of Power. The Role of Public*
Opinion. German Aspirations. British Aspirations. The Other Belligerents. The Era of Bismarck, 1871–
1890. Formation of the Triple Entente, 1890–1907. A Decade of Crises, 1905–1914. The Final Crisis,
July–August, 1914. The Entry of Other Powers. III THE COURSE OF THE WAR. *Resources of the*
Belligerents. The Western Front: German Offensive. The Eastern Front. The Italian Front. The Dar-
danelles. The Balkan Fronts. The Near East and the Colonies. The War at Sea. The Western Front: Allied
Victory. Morale on the Fighting Fronts. The Home Fronts. The Role of Propaganda. Political Repercussions.
IV THE PEACE SETTLEMENTS. *The Aftermath of World War. The Fourteen Points. Opposing Hopes*
and Promises. The Process of Peacemaking. The Territorial Settlement. The Mandates. The Punishment
of Germany. The Settlement Evaluated.

Communist Russia, 1917–1941   *397*

26

I INTRODUCTION II THE RUSSIAN REVOLUTION OF *1917. The Immediate Background. The*
March Revolution. The Provisional Government. Lenin and Bolshevism. The Coming of the November Revo-
lution. The Constituent Assembly. III WAR COMMUNISM AND NEP, *1917–1928. War Communism.*
Civil War. Why the Counter-Revolution Failed, NEP ("The New Economic Policy"). The Struggle for Power:
Stalin versus Trotsky. The Struggle for Power: Stalin's Victory. IV STALIN'S SUPREMACY: RUSSIAN
INTERNAL AFFAIRS, *1928–1941. Collectivized Agriculture. Industrialization. The Social Impact. The*
Purge Trials. The Authoritarian State. The Russian Thermidor? V SOVIET FOREIGN POLICY,
1918–1941. Foreign Office and Comintern, 1918–1928. Stalin and the West, 1928–1939. Stalin and
the Second World War. VI CONCLUSION.

The Rise of Fascism, 1918–1939   *437*

27

I INTRODUCTION.   II ITALY AND FASCISM. *The Setting. Mussolini: Early Career. Mussolini: Rise to Power. The "March" on Rome. The Fascist Dictatorship. The Corporative State. Other Fascist Domestic Policies. Fascist Foreign Policy and its Consequences.*   III GERMANY AND THE WEIMAR REPUBLIC, *1918–1933. The Impact of Defeat. Postwar Political Alignments and Activities. The Weimar Constitution, 1919. Right and Left Extremism, 1920–1922. Hitler: Early Career. The Inflation, 1922–1923. The Consequences of Inflation. The End of Inflation, 1923–1924. Recovery at Home, 1924–1929. "Fulfillment" Abroad, 1924–1930. The Impact of the Depression, 1929–1931. The Republic in Danger, 1931–1932. Hitler: Rise to Power, 1932–1933.*   IV GERMANY UNDER HITLER, *1933–1939. The Nazi Dictatorship. Racism and Political Theory. The Bases of Foreign Policy. Legal and Economic Policies. Religion and Culture.*   V THE FAILURE OF PARLIAMENTARISM IN SPAIN AND EASTERN EUROPE, *1918–1939. Spain: The Background. Birth of the Spanish Republic. Crisis of the Spanish Republic, 1933–1936. The Spanish Civil War, 1936–1939. Eastern Europe. Austria. Hungary. Yugoslavia. Other Authoritarian Régimes. Fascism in Review.*

The Democracies and the Colonial World   *479*

Domestic and Imperial Problems, 1919–1939

28

I INTRODUCTION.   II GREAT BRITAIN. *The Postwar Depression. The Conservative and Labor Programs. Postwar Politics. Settlement of the Irish Question. The Commonwealth of Nations.*   III FRANCE. *The Impact of the War. Social and Political Tensions. The Stavisky Case and the Popular Front. Divided France.*   IV THE UNITED STATES. *Isolationism. The Road to Internationalism. Boom—and Bust. The New Deal. Confident America.*   V THE LOOSENING OF IMPERIAL TIES. *Japan. China: The Revolution of 1911–1912. China between the World Wars. The Chinese Communists. Southeast Asia. India. The Middle East.*

The Second World War   *511*

29

I INTERNATIONAL POLITICS, *1919–1932. The "Era of Fulfillment." The Failure of "Fulfillment." The Aggressors.* II THE ROAD TO WAR, *1931–1939. The First Step: Manchuria, 1931. The Second Step: German Rearmament, 1935–1936. The Third Step: Ethiopia, 1935. The Fourth Step: The Spanish Civil War, 1936–1939. The Fifth Step: "Anschluss," 1938. The Sixth Step: Czechoslovakia Dismembered, 1938–1939. The Final Step: Poland, 1939. Democratic Policy in Review.*   III THE NATURE OF THE WAR.   IV EARLY SUCCESSES OF THE AXIS. *Polish and Finnish Campaigns. "Phony War" and Blitzkrieg in the West. "The Fall of France." The Battle of Britain. Mediterranean and Balkan Campaigns. The Invasion of Russia. American Policy. Pearl Harbor and After.*   V THE VICTORY OF THE UNITED NATIONS. *The Turning Points. The Battle of Supply. The Axis on the Defensive. The Defeat of Germany. The Defeat of Japan. The Allied Coalition. Political Issues.*

The Post-War World, 1945–1953   545

30

I   THE COLD WAR. *Atomic Weapons. A Divided World: Germany and China. The Two Coalitions. The United Nations.*   II   THE MAJOR FREE-WORLD STATES: *1945–1953. The United States. Canada. Western Europe. Great Britain. France. West Germany. The Other Western Countries.*   III   THE COMMUNIST BLOC, *1945 TO 1953. Soviet Government and the Economy. Soviet Intellectual Life. Soviet Foreign Policy: Europe. The Yugoslav Rebellion. Soviet Foreign Policy: Asia.*   IV   THE REVOLT AGAINST IMPERIALISM. *Causes of the Revolt. The Far East. Southeast Asia. India and Pakistan. The Middle East. Latin America.*

The Contemporary World since 1953   581

31

I   THE COMMUNIST WORLD SINCE THE DEATH OF STALIN: THE U.S.S.R. AT HOME. *The Soviet Succession. The Denunciation of Stalin and its Consequences. The Khrushchev Era. The Bureaucratic Problems. The Khrushchev Era and Beyond: Industry and Agriculture. Education and the Art*   II   SOVIET CONFRONTATION WITH THE WEST. *Berlin. U-2, The Wall, Testing, Cuba. The Test-Ban Treaty. Rumania Disengages. The "Bloc" in 1966.*   III   THE U.S.S.R., CHINA, AND AMERICA IN ASIA. *The Soviet-Chinese Quarrel: Ideology. Southeast Asia: Vietnam and Laos. Khrushchev's Fall: Kosygin and Brezhnev.*   IV   THE EMERGING NATIONS. *East Asia. Southeast Asia. South Asia. The Middle East. Africa. Latin America and the West Indies.*   V   THE FREE WORLD SYSTEM. *NATO and the other American Alliance-Systems. The United Nations. The United States. Canada. Western Europe. Great Britain. West Germany. France. Italy.*

Man's Fate in the Twentieth Century   641

32

I   THE INTELLECTUAL REVOLUTION CONTINUES. *Psychology: Freud. The Implications of Freudianism. Psychology: Behaviorism. Socio-political Thought. Pareto. The Planners and Persuaders. Philosophy. The Sciences. Literature and the Arts. High Art: Literature. High Art: The Fine Arts.*   II   THE TEMPER OF OUR TIMES. *The Optimism of the Enlightenment. Repudiation or Revision of the Enlightenment.*

Illustrations   669

Index   671

Maps

Europe in 1715,   2–3

Growth of Prussia, 1740 to 1795,   19

Russian Expansion in Europe, 1689–1796,   25

North America and the Caribbean, 1763,   38

Partitions of Poland, 1772, 1793, 1795,   72

Napoleonic Europe, 1812,   124–125

Europe after 1815,   150–151

Centers of Revolution, 1820–1830, 1848–1849,   152

Latin America, 1828,   154

Industrialization in Europe and the United States, 1860,   182–183

Europe in the mid-Nineteenth Century,   213

Unification of Italy, 1859–1870,   240

Growth of the United States,   244

Unification of Germany, 1866–1871,   255

Nationalities in Central and Eastern Europe,   269

Africa and the Middle East, 1910,   329

Asia and the Pacific, 1910,   331

North America and the Caribbean, 1910,   344

Diplomatic Alignments before 1914,   364

Europe and the Near East, 1914–1918,   375

Territorial Settlements in Europe, 1919–1926,   389

The Balkans and the Middle East, 1878–1921,   392–393

Russia in Revolution, 1917–1921,   409

Europe on the Eve, August, 1939,   522

European and Mediterranean Theaters, 1941–1945,   526

Asian and Pacific Theaters, 1941–1945,   539

The World, 1953,   550–551

Europe, 1953,   558–559

The Soviet Union, 1953,   564

Asia, 1967,   606

The Middle East, 1967,   612

Africa, 1967   617

Caribbean America, 1967, 621

South America, 1967,   623

16

The Old Régime

and the International Balance,

1715–1789

I Introduction: The Prospect in 1715

Long years of peace and quiet appeared to be in prospect for Europe in 1715. In the West, the Utrecht settlement of 1713 had ended Louis XIV's prolonged threat to the balance of power, and in the Baltic, as we shall see, the protracted Great Northern War between Russia and Sweden was nearing a settlement. The death of Louis XIV himself in 1715 gave fresh promise of international stability, for the crown of France passed to his great-grandson, Louis XV, a boy of five. During the long regency now ahead, France would probably be too preoccupied with internal matters to attempt adventures abroad. Finally, the great conflicts of Louis XIV had exhausted his own state and had also brought his victorious opponents to the edge of bankruptcy. Europe needed an extended period of convalescence.

Europe in 1715

Brandenburg-Prussia
Austrian Habsburg Lands
Swedish possessions
Venetian possessions
Ottoman Empire

Boundary of the Holy Roman Empire

■ Battle sites

NORWAY

Oslo

Stockho...

SW...

S...

W...

SCOTLAND

Edinburgh
Berwick

North Sea

DENMARK

Copenhagen

Baltic

SWEDISH POMERANIA

ULSTER

IRELAND

Drogheda
Boyne R.
Dublin

Limerick

KINGDOM OF GREAT BRITAIN

Hamburg

Bremen
Elbe R.

Fehrbellin
Berlin

THE

BRANDENBURG

Oder R.

ENGLAND

London

Dover

Ryswick

Utrecht
Nimwegen

WEST-PHALIA

EMPIRE

SAXONY

SILES...

Tor Bay

C. La Hogue

Atlantic Ocean

UNITED NETHERLANDS

AUSTRIAN NETHERLANDS

Oudenarde
Ramillies

Aachen

Rhine R.

Prague

BOHEMIA

MORAVIA

Malplaquet

Verdun

Metz

Blenheim

Augsburg

AUSTRIA

Seine R.

Paris

LORRAINE

Toul

Rastadt

Strasbourg

Vienna

STYRIA

Versailles

ALSACE

Nantes

Blois

Orléans

Loire R.

FRANCE

FRANCHE COMTÉ

BAVARIA

CARINTHIA

SWITZERLAND

TYROL

CARNIOLA

Geneva

Bordeaux

Rhône R.

SAVOY

MILAN

Po R.

Venice

VENETIAN REPUBLIC

Avignon (to the Papacy)

Genoa

Ra...

Marseilles

Florence

Adriatic Sea

PORTUGAL

Burgos

Ebro R.

PAPAL STATES

SPAIN

Tagus R.

Madrid

Lisbon

Barcelona

CORSICA (to Genoa)

Rome

NAPLES

Valencia

BALEARIC IS.

MINORCA (Br.)

Naples

Guadalquivir R.

Seville

Granada

SARDINIA (to Austria, 1714; to Savoy, 1720)

Gibraltar (Br.)

Mediterranean Sea

Palermo

SICILY

(to Savoy, 171...
to Austria, 172...

ALGERIA

TUNIS

MALTA

0   500

Miles

FINLAND

L. Onega

L. Ladoga

Nystadt

Gulf of Finland

St. Petersburg

Narva

INGRIA

Novgorod

ESTONIA

LIVONIA

Pskov

Volga R.

COURLAND

W. Dvina R.

Vilna

Moscow

Oka R.

Königsberg

LITHUANIA

Smolensk

PRUSSIA

R U S S I A

Warsaw

POLAND

Kiev

Vistula R.

Dnieper R.

Poltava

Dniester R.

TRANSYLVANIA

MOLDAVIA

Don R.

Volga R.

UNGARY

CRIMEA

Caspian Sea

Karlovitz

WALLACHIA

Black Sea

rade

Passarovitz

Danube R.

MONTE-
NEGRO

O T T O M A N

Vardar R.

E M P I R E

Salonika

Constantinople

Aegean Sea

Tigris R.

NIS.

Athens

RHODES

CYPRUS

Euphrates R.

CRETE

Growth of France 1559-1769 (inset)

ENGLAND

Calais

Rhine R.

ARTOIS
1659

ALSACE
1648–1681

THE EMPIRE

Paris

LORRAINE
1766

FRANCHE COMTÉ
1678

1601

FRANCE

Rhône R.

1601

55

Avignon

ROUSSILLON
1659

CORSICA
1768

Growth of France
1559-1769
—— Boundary of the Empire, 1559

Historians use the term "Old Régime" to describe the institutions prevailing in Europe, especially France, before 1789: It was the Old Régime of the eighteenth century in contrast to the "new" régime of the French Revolution. In many respects the Old Régime resembled the still older régime of the Middle Ages. Its economic foundations were agrarian, for most Europeans lived in farming villages and retained the parochial outlook of the peasant. In Western Europe—particularly in Britain, France, the Low Countries, and Germany west of the Elbe River—the great majority of peasants had long been free of the bonds of serfdom. In Eastern Europe, however—notably in Germany beyond the Elbe, and in Hungary, Poland, and Russia—the majority were still serfs.

The social foundations of the Old Régime rested firmly on the medieval division of society into the first estate of the clergy, the second estate of the nobility, and the third estate of commoners, who included the urban bourgeoisie as well as the peasantry. Within the third estate, only the men at the top exerted much political influence—well-to-do businessmen in England and Holland, French lawyers or merchants wealthy enough to purchase government office. Generally, bourgeois influence diminished as one moved eastward. Almost everywhere the titled nobles and the landed gentry of the second estate still wielded substantial power and wanted to regain some of that assumed by the "vile bourgeois," in the phrase of the aristocratic Duc de Saint-Simon. As the present chapter will show, every government in Europe tended to represent the interests of the few, whether it was an absolute monarchy, like France or Prussia, a constitutional monarchy, like Britain, or a republic, like the Dutch United Provinces.

Europe had long been oligarchical, agrarian, and parochial, and in 1715 it seemed likely to remain so forever. The Old Régime, however, did not last forever; its apparent stability was deceptive. By the middle of the eighteenth century, its social and economic foundations were beginning to crumble under the pressure of revolutionary economic changes. Leaders of the intellectual movement called the Enlightenment (see Chapter 17) were voicing the demands for institutional reform that culminated in the revolution of 1789.

The international stability promised by the Utrecht settlement also faded relatively soon. The defeat and death of Louis XIV did not end the world-wide rivalry of Britain and France, who began another round of their long conflict in 1740. Meanwhile, the rapid emergence of two new states caused shifts in the balance of power. Russia was moving out of semi-isolation to take an active and often aggressive part in international affairs, and the once-obscure German electorate of Brandenburg-Prussia was developing into a first-class military power, intent on expansion.

II   The Western Powers

The changes in commerce, agriculture, and industry that helped to undermine the Old Régime were most evident in Western Europe, especially in France, the Low Countries, and, above all, Britain. They were in fact economic revolutions, though some historians shy away from the term because it may suggest a more sudden discharge of economic energy or technological inventiveness than actually occurred. The commercial, agricultural, and industrial revolutions, while slower and less dramatic than political revolutions, were in the long run perhaps even more revolutionary in their effects upon human history.

The Commercial Revolution

In the eighteenth century, the commercial revolution was more advanced than the other two. Its basic institutions had been developed before 1715, banks and insurance firms in the Renaissance, for example, and chartered trading companies in the sixteenth century. Mercantilism, the rather ill-defined set of principles determining governmental policies toward commerce, had matured in the Spain of Philip II and the France of Louis XIV and Colbert. The steady growth of trade in the eighteenth century, however, quickened the pace of the commercial revolution.

For example, it increased the demand for insurance on ships and cargoes. Early in the century the insurance brokers of London often gathered in coffee houses to discuss business, news, and politics. Specialists in marine insurance gravitated to Edward Lloyd's coffee house in Lombard Street and continued to meet there after Lloyd died in 1713. Thus was born Lloyd's of London, the firm that developed the standard form of policy for marine insurance and published *Lloyd's List*, the first detailed and accurate shipping newspaper. Another great London institution to emerge from the informal atmosphere of the coffee house was the stock exchange. As the buying and selling of shares in joint-stock companies increased, traders began to gather at Jonathan's; in 1773 the name was changed from Jonathan's to the Stock Exchange Coffee House.

Marine insurance prospered in part because improved charts and the installation of lighthouses and buoys made navigation safer. At sea, captains could determine their geographical position by using two new instruments, the sextant and the chronometer. The sextant, an elaboration of the telescope, showed the altitude of the sun at noon and thus indicated the ship's latitude. The chronometer, a clock unaffected by the motion of the ship, was kept on Greenwich Mean Time (the time at the meridian running through Greenwich near London). The two new instruments made it possible to calculate the ship's longitude, which represented the difference between Greenwich Mean Time and the local time aboard ship calculated with the sextant.

On land, the improvements in communication and transport came much more slowly. Except for the good highways of France, Euro-

pean roads were scarcely better than paths or trails. The shipment of goods overland remained slow, unsafe, and expensive until after 1750, when the construction of turnpikes and canals gradually eased the situation. The pioneer English canal, built in 1759–1761 by the Duke of Bridgewater, cut in half the cost of moving coal from the mines on his estate to the new factory town of Manchester.

Businessmen also faced the handicaps imposed by restrictive guild regulations and by the abundance of coins, weights, measures, and local tolls. Sweden, for example, minted only copper money, including a monstrosity weighing 43 pounds. Baden, one of the smaller German states, had 112 separate measures for length, 65 for dry goods, 123 for liquids, and 163 for cereals, not to mention 80 different pound weights! A German merchant who shipped timber down the Elbe from Dresden in Saxony to Hamburg had to pay so many tolls to the towns and principalities along the way that of 60 planks floated at Dresden only six would reach Hamburg. Even in France, the land where uniformity and centralization were supposedly the rule, all sorts of local taxes and other obstacles to internal trade persisted.

The survival of local vested interests showed the limitations of the power of the mercantilist state. Mercantilism required the regulation of trade on the national, rather than the local, level. But no eighteenth-century government possessed the staff of officials needed to make national regulation effective; states had to rely heavily on private companies and individuals to execute most of their policies. Thus the English and Dutch East India Companies exercised not only a trading monopoly in their colonial preserves but also virtual sovereign powers, including the right to maintain soldiers and conduct diplomacy. Inventors worked on their own, not in government laboratories, although the state occasionally offered prizes on matters of critical importance to the business community. Although the English Parliament promised £20,000 for the invention of a reliable "seagoing" clock, the inventor of the chronometer had to wait twenty-five years to collect his prize money. Private initiative, not sluggish governments, made the commercial revolution advance at a swift pace in the eighteenth century. The fact was underlined by two speculative booms that occurred early in the century —the Mississippi Bubble in France and the South Sea Bubble in England.

The Mississippi and South Sea Bubbles

In 1715, hardly a state in Europe could manage the large debts that had piled up during the recent wars. Yet all of them had to find some way of meeting at least part of the large annual interest on bonds and other obligations, or else go bankrupt. The governments of France and England chose the way of experiment. They transferred the management of state debts to joint-stock companies, which they rewarded with trading concessions. The commerce of the companies, it was hoped, would prove so lucrative that their profits would easily cover the interest charges on government bonds.

John Law (1671–1729), a Scottish mathematical wizard and an inveterate gambler, presided over the experiment in France. He studied monetary problems and banking methods in Amsterdam, at that time the commercial capital of Europe. Law was a mercantilist, but with a difference. He agreed with the doctrine that the strength of a state depended upon the quantity of money it possessed. But, he asserted, the limited supply of silver and gold made it difficult to increase the amount of specie circulating in any country and therefore difficult to promote business. Paper money, Law concluded, was the solution—paper money backed by a nation's wealth in land and in trade. The quantity of paper money in circulation could easily be raised or lowered in accordance with the needs of business. Trading companies would prosper as never before, the whole country would prosper, and, in the general prosperity, government debts would be paid off.

The death of Louis XIV gave Law the opportunity to try his "system." The regent for Louis XV, the Duke of Orléans, who was a gambling crony of Law, permitted him to set up a central bank in Paris. Whereas the value of French money had been sinking lower and lower because of the government's debasing the coinage, Law's bank, following the practice of the Bank of Amsterdam, issued paper notes of stable value. Business activity at once increased. Next, Law set up the Mississippi Company, which received a monopoly of commerce with the Louisiana colony and soon absorbed the other French colonial trading companies.

Law's system now reached to almost every corner of the French economy, and Law himself, appointed controller-general, became the economic dictator of the kingdom. His company took over the government debt and agreed to accept government bonds in partial payment for shares of Mississippi stock. Many bondholders responded enthusiastically to Law's offer, because the bonds had depreciated to 20 per cent or less of their face value. Law, however, had to sell additional shares of Mississippi stock in order to obtain sufficient working capital for his company. To attract cash purchasers, Law promoted a boom in Mississippi stock, painting the company's prospects in brightest colors. Investors, large and small, caught the fever of speculation, and by the close of 1719 Mississippi stock was selling at forty times its par value.

The Mississippi Bubble soon burst, for Law's paper money could not stand the pressure. As the price of Mississippi shares rose higher and higher, cautious investors decided to cash in. They sold their shares, received payment in banknotes, then took the notes to Law's bank and demanded their redemption in specie. The bank exhausted its reserves of gold and silver and suspended specie payments in February, 1720. Law was forced to relinquish the post of controller-general in May, 1720; he fled France shortly thereafter.

The explosion of the Mississippi Bubble had international repercussions, for within a few weeks of Law's resignation the South Sea Bubble burst in London. It might have been expected that management of the English government's debt would devolve upon the Bank of England. Founded in 1694 as a private institution (it was fully nationalized only after

World War II), the Bank of England issued banknotes and rendered other valuable services to the government during the last wars against Louis XIV. The debt, however, was taken over not by the Bank but by the new South Sea Company, which paid the government the exorbitant sum of more than seven and a half million pounds. The resources of the South Sea Company were slim, consisting largely of the right to exploit the trading concessions that Britain obtained under the Asiento agreement at the end of the War of the Spanish Succession. These privileges were limited to furnishing Spain's American colonies with 4800 slaves annually and to sending one ship a year to Panama for general trade.

The South Sea Company, like the Mississippi Company, invited government creditors to transfer their bonds into company stock. The directors of the company bought and sold shares in secret to create a more lively market for them, encouraged purchases of stock with a down payment of only 10 per cent in cash, and spread reports of forthcoming sailings by the company's ships on voyages of unparalleled promise. In short, like Law, they created a speculative boom. South Sea shares, with a par value of £100, sold for £129 in January of 1720, and for £1050 in June. Dozens of other promoters sprang into action, advertising schemes for wheels of perpetual motion, for making salt water fresh, "for carrying on an undertaking of great advantage, but nobody to know what it is." The gullibility of the investing public was remarkable, but it was not inexhaustible. South Sea shares fell to £880 in August, 1720, and to £150 in September. Parliament ordered an investigation and, to protect the company's creditors, seized the estates of its directors, who had meantime destroyed the company's books and fled the country.

The two bubbles produced some unfortunate results. The collapse of the Mississippi scheme ruined Law, whose talents, if used more discreetly, might have revitalized the French economy. In England, the South Sea fiasco long impeded the development of new stock companies, which were henceforth required to buy costly charters. It tarnished the reputations of many in high places. The mistresses

London during the South Sea Bubble. The hunchback is hiring himself out as a desk.

of George I and the King himself had been "let in on the ground floor" in return for endorsing the venture enthusiastically, and more than a hundred members of Parliament had borrowed money from the company in order to buy its shares on the installment plan.

The bubbles were by no means total misfortunes. They were an acute instance of the economic growing pains suffered as the states of Europe groped for solutions to baffling financial problems. Voltaire later correctly observed that Law's "imaginary system gave birth to a real commerce," and released French business from the torpor induced by the defeats of Louis XIV. The Mississippi Company, reorganized after 1720, consistently made a handsome profit. In England, the South Sea Bubble scarcely affected the strongest institutions. The East India Company continued to pay an annual dividend of 5 to 10 per cent. The Bank of England, no longer competing with the South Sea Company for government favors, became more than ever the financial mainstay of the realm. In the political shake-up following the Bubble, the Whig statesman, Robert Walpole (see pp. 12–13), came to power with a program of honoring the debt as a *national* debt. This was a novel concept and a great step forward in fiscal morality in an age when most states still treated their debts as the monarch's personal obligation, to be acknowledged or repudiated as he saw fit.

The Agricultural Revolution

The agricultural revolution, the second of the forces transforming the modern economy, centered on improvements that enabled fewer farmers to produce more crops. The application of technological discoveries to agriculture was an old story, as old as the irrigation ditches of ancient Mesopotamia and the improved plows and horse-collars of the Middle Ages. What was new and revolutionary in the eighteenth century was the accelerating tempo of the advance in farming techniques.

The leaders of the movement were the "improving landlords" of England, who often owed much to innovators on the Continent. Jethro Tull (1674–1741), for example, studied French truck-gardens and vineyards, where farmers obtained heavy yields from small plots by planting seeds individually and by carefully hoeing the soil around each plant and vine. Tull adapted French methods to the much larger grain fields of England. In place of the inefficient custom of scattering seed broadcast, he planted it deeply in regular rows with a horse-drawn "drilling" machine, and he cultivated his crops with a horse-drawn hoe. Viscount Townshend (1674–1738) experimented with two new crops brought in from Holland, turnips and clover. The former made it possible to feed all the livestock until the arrival of the spring pasturing season, and thus to avoid the customary slaughter of stock

at the onset of winter. Clover, by fixing nitrogen in the soil, increased the fertility of the land and curtailed the old practice of letting fields lie fallow every third year. "Turnip" Townshend's four-year rotation—planting the same field to turnips, barley, clover, and wheat, in successive years—soon became standard on many English estates.

The improvements of Tull and Townshend won enthusiastic praise from Arthur Young (1741–1820), the articulate publicist of the new agriculture, who reported at length on his frequent trips throughout the farming districts of the British Isles and part of the Continent. Young won an international following that included George III, George Washington, the Marquis de Lafayette, and Catherine the Great. Before 1789, however, the new agriculture gained the support of only the most enterprising landlords, and even in Britain it appealed chiefly to the holders of large estates.

The agricultural revolution of the eighteenth century, uneven though it was, marked an important stage in the long, gradual shift from the largely self-sufficient manor of the Middle Ages to the modern capitalist farm producing specialized crops. The improving landlords needed large amounts of capital, and they also needed large plots of land that were not subdivided into long narrow strips for individual cultivators or otherwise used in common by many individuals. Since these old ways hampered the new agriculture, there was a mounting demand that common fields be fenced off as the private lands of single proprietors. Enclosures, which in Tudor days were introduced to extend sheep pastures, were now aimed to increase crop land. The new enclosure movement reached its peak in the last decades of the eighteenth century and the first decades of the nineteenth, when Parliament passed hundreds of separate enclosure acts affecting several million acres. Rural England was assuming its modern aspect of large fields fenced by hedgerows.

Enclosures, then, created large farms well suited to the application of drill-planting, horse-hoeing, and crop rotation. They enabled Britain to feed her growing population by increasing her agricultural output. But they also created widespread social misery. In Georgian England, as in ancient Greece and Rome, the development of capitalistic estates ruined many small farmers, or yeomen, who could not get along without their rights to use common lands and who could not afford to buy tools, install fences, and become improving landlords themselves. Many of them became hired hands on big farms or sought work in the expanding towns.

The Beginnings
of the Industrial Revolution

By increasing productivity and at the same time releasing part of the agricultural labor force for jobs off the farm, the agricultural revolution was assisting the industrial revolution. Industry also required raw materials, markets for its manufactures, and capital

to finance the building and equipping of factories. The raw materials and the markets were supplied in part by the colonies overseas, and the capital in part by merchants. Thus the commercial revolution, too, assisted the industrial revolution.

In textiles, the making of yarn and cloth had long been organized under the "domestic system." Spinners or weavers worked at home on simple wheels or looms; often they did not buy their own raw materials or market their finished products but worked as wage-laborers for an entrepreneur who furnished the raw materials and sold the finished yarn and cloth. In some industries, however, production was organized not under the domestic system but in primitive factories, which assembled many laborers in a large workshop, though still relying on hand processes rather than on machines. These early factories were particularly common in enterprises utilizing expen-

Eighteenth-century grinders at work, as illustrated in the *Encyclopedie.*

sive materials, like gold or silver threads for luxury cloth, or requiring close supervision for reasons of state, like cannon foundries.

The industrial revolution made the domestic system obsolete and transformed the factory system. Machines superseded simple hand tools, like the spinning-wheel and the home loom, and water or steam replaced human muscles and animal energy as the source of power. Because power-driven machines were often big, complicated, and costly, larger factories were needed to house them. By 1789, these revolutionary changes had affected only a few industries, but they were key industries — mining, metallurgy, munitions, and textiles.

Coal-mining was becoming a big business, largely because of the increased demand for coke by iron-smelters. Smelters had always used charcoal to make iron from ore, and they continued to do so in countries like Sweden that had abundant wood for charcoal. But in England, where most of the great forests had been cut down, the price of charcoal rose so high that it constituted 80 per cent of the cost of producing iron. By 1750, despite the abundant native supply of ore, the output of English smelters was declining rapidly, and the country was using more and more imported iron. Ordinary coal could not replace charcoal as smelter fuel because the chemicals in coal made the iron too brittle. Here necessity mothered invention, as the Darby family of Shropshire discovered how to remove the chemical impurities from coal by an oven process that converted it into coke, which was almost pure carbon.

In England, the Darbys and other private firms were the pioneers in metallurgy. On the Continent, governments took the lead — a significant exception to the rule about the inability of states to solve economic problems. Warfare required weapons and munitions in large quantities; France and Prussia met the demand by setting up state-financed and state-operated foundries and arms factories.

The revolution in textiles was focused on the cheaper production of cotton cloth. The "flying shuttle," a technical device first applied to the hand loom in England (1733), enabled a single weaver to do work that had

previously required the services of two. Looms equipped with the flying shuttle used up the supply of hand-spun thread so rapidly that the London Society for the Encouragement of Arts, Manufactures, and Commerce offered a prize for improvement of the spinning process. James Hargreaves won the prize in 1764 with his "spinning jenny," a series of spinning wheels geared together which made eight threads simultaneously. Soon the jenny was adapted to water power, and its output was increased to a hundred or more threads at once. The eventual emancipation of industry from dependence on unreliable water power was foreshadowed in the 1760's when the Scotsman, James Watt, introduced the steam engine.

Although Britain had nearly 150 cotton mills in 1789, woolens and dozens of other basic commodities were still made by hand. Full industrial development would not take place until the canal and railroad permitted cheap transport of heavy freight and until the shortages of capital and skilled labor were overcome. A Swedish inventor of the early 1700's designed excellent machines for cutting wheels and files but could not raise the money to put them into operation. And in Britain the difficulty of making precise parts for Watt's engine delayed its production in large quantities. While the eighteenth century had taken many of the initial steps in the industrial revolution, it remained for the next century to apply them on a truly revolutionary scale (see Chapter 20).

The Assets of Britain

Leadership in the economic revolutions was making Britain the wealthiest nation in the world. British bankers, buttressed by the Bank of England and by the careful management of the national debt, extended credit to business enterprises at the relatively low interest rate of 5 per cent. The City, the square mile comprising the City of London proper and including the financial district, recovered quickly from the South Sea Bubble and challenged Amsterdam's position as the international capital of trade and finance. In the course of the eighteenth century, British merchants outdistanced their old trading rivals, the Dutch, and gradually took the lead over their new competitors, the French. Judged by the three touchstones of mercantilism—commerce, colonies, and sea power—Britain was the strongest state in Europe.

The British colonial empire, however, was not a mercantilist undertaking in the full sense. Supervision of the colonies rested with a government department, the Board of Trade, which followed an easygoing policy contrasting with the rigid controls exerted by other colonial powers over their possessions. This was the famous policy of "salutary neglect." In the long run, as the American Revolution was to show, "salutary neglect" did not satisfy the colonists, but in the short run it worked reasonably well by promoting the colonists' prosperity and self-reliance.

The Royal Navy enjoyed the assets of a superior officer corps and greater size. Future captains went to sea at the age of sixteen, or even younger, and passed through long practical training before receiving commissions. The ships they commanded in the mid-century wars were inferior in design to those of France and Spain; but there were more of them. Britain had a 2 to 1 advantage over France in number of warships, a 6 to 1 lead in merchant ships, and a 10 to 1 lead in total number of experienced seamen, merchant and naval. In wartime, the fleet could draw on the merchant marine for additional sailors and auxiliary vessels. Service in the Royal Navy had its grim aspects. Food was monotonous and unhealthy, and punishments included flogging and keelhauling, in which the victim was dragged the length of the barnacle-encrusted keel. Since these were the common afflictions of all sailors in the eighteenth century, however, they did not put the British navy at a comparative disadvantage.

The British army, by contrast, was neither large nor impressive. Its officers were reputed to be the poorest in Europe, and its soldiers were in part mercenaries from the German state of Hesse-Cassel, the Hessians of the American Revolutionary War. Neglect of the army was a deliberate policy. The British Isles were relatively safe from invasion; moreover, statesmen feared that a standing army might become an instrument of potential absolutism, for they remembered the uses that Cromwell and James II had made of this weapon.

The Glorious Revolution, which had done so much to confirm distrust of the army, had also confirmed Britain's unique and greatest asset—the supremacy of Parliament over the King. Parliament had approved the accession of William and Mary in place of James II; when Anne, Mary's sister and the last Stuart monarch, died in 1714, Parliament had already arranged for the succession of the House of Hanover. Under the first kings of the new house—George I (1714–1727) and George II (1727–1760)—the institution that was to assure the everyday assertion of parliamentary supremacy was undergoing steady development. This was the cabinet.

Cabinet Government

Today the British cabinet is a committee of the majority party of the House of Commons, headed by the prime minister, and it remains in office as long as it can continue to enlist the support of a majority in Commons. It is "Her Majesty's Government," while the chief minority party forms "Her Majesty's Opposition," a loyal opposition whose leader receives an official salary. The cabinet rules because it controls the executive branch of the government; the monarch merely reigns.

Under the first two Hanoverian kings the cabinet was only starting to accumulate this immense authority. George I and George II by no means abdicated all the old royal prerogatives. They took a direct interest in the South Sea Bubble and other financial matters, and they intervened in the conduct of war and diplomacy to a degree that would be regarded as highly improper today. George II was the last English monarch to command troops in person on the battlefield—in 1743 during the War of the Austrian Succession. The two Georges chose their cabinet ministers from the Whig party, then in control of the Commons. They did so, however, not because they were obliged to, which would be the case to-day, but because it suited their convenience, and, even more, because they really had no choice. They thoroughly distrusted the other party, the Tories, some of whom were involved in futile Jacobite plots to restore to the throne the descendants of James II (Jacobite from Jacobus, Latin for James). The Whigs, on the other hand, had engineered the Glorious Revolution and had arranged the Hanoverian succession.

For two decades after the collapse of the South Sea Bubble, from 1721 to 1742, Robert Walpole, who led the Whigs in the Commons, headed the cabinet; he was in fact prime minister, although the title was not yet official.

The House of Commons in the eighteenth century, by Hogarth. Walpole is at the left.

Walpole was a master politician who maintained his majority in the Commons by skillful manipulation of the Whigs. The task was not easy, for party discipline of the modern kind did not exist; the terms "Whig" and "Tory" referred to informal and shifting interest groups, not to parties in our sense. In 1733, when Walpole forced the resignation of ministers opposed to his plan for radical fiscal reform, he took a major step toward establishing the principle of cabinet unanimity on a crucial issue.

Under the first two Georges the Whigs were a coalition of landed gentry and "funded" gentry; that is, of nobles and squires from the country and of businessmen from London and provincial towns. Thus the Whigs renewed a political alliance that had first appeared in the later Middle Ages when the knights of the shire had joined the burgesses to form the Commons. In the Whig parliaments the country gentlemen predominated by sheer numbers; in 1754, for instance, they outnumbered by 5 to 1 the merchants and lawyers sitting in the House of Commons. Family ties, common political aims, and a common reverence for property bound together the rural and urban Whigs. In order to consolidate the gains of the Glorious Revolution, the Whigs opposed Jacobite schemes and supported the unprepossessing Hanoverians. To protect their property, they passed legislation making death the penalty for stealing livestock, for cutting down cherry trees, and for other relatively minor offenses.

Exactly what did terms like "gentry," "gentlemen," and "squire" mean in the eighteenth century with respect to social class? Historians are still debating the question, but it is generally agreed that they referred to a class just below the titled nobility. The ranks of the gentry included the younger sons of nobles, technically not nobles themselves since the title and a seat in the House of Lords passed to the eldest son. They also included other owners of landed estates, all of whom were addressed verbally as "sir" and in writing as "Esquire," originally a shield-bearer, the lieutenant of the feudal knight. Historically, the gentry lived off the revenues of landed property, but by the eighteenth century many of them also had a stake in the commercial revolution. Indeed, successful businessmen sometimes bought country estates, set themselves up as gentlemen, and were accepted as such by the local gentry. The intermingling of country gentlemen with men of business and intermarriage of the two classes demonstrated that Britain enjoyed more social mobility than did the states of the Old Régime on the Continent.

Robert Walpole himself exemplified the Whig fusion of landed and funded elements. He inherited his manners and his tastes from his father, a country squire. A heavy drinker, and an inveterate teller of bawdy stories in mixed company, he fixed the English politician's tradition of the long country weekend in order to indulge his passion for hunting. Like many Whig squires, Walpole married into the aristocracy of trade; his wife was the daughter of a timber merchant and former Lord Mayor of London. As prime minister, Walpole, the country gentleman, promoted the interests of the City. His basic policy supported the City's program of financial stability through the gradual retirement of the national debt, and political stability through Whig cabinets.

In social and political structure, the Britain of Walpole was, of course, oligarchical rather than democratic. Only gentlemen could hope to rise in the professions, to become army and navy officers, lawyers, clergymen, and physicians. In local affairs, the landed gentry alone supplied the justices of the peace, who not only presided over courts, but also fixed wage scales, superintended the relief of the poor, provided for the maintenance of bridges and highways, and were in general the despots of the English countryside. Fanatic defenders of the propertied classes, the justices of the peace inspired the saying that "You may as well be hanged for [stealing] a sheep as a lamb."

In the main, only gentlemen had the right to vote for members of Parliament. The small number of voters in many constituencies encouraged corruption, particularly in the "rotten" or "pocket" boroughs, which had such a tiny electorate that control of their vote reposed in the pocket of some wealthy lord. Politicians often bribed voters outright or else promised them places on the government payroll. An immensely rich Whig, the Duke of Newcastle, controlled the outcome of elections in four counties and in seven pocket boroughs.

In Britain, as on the Continent, the ruling classes governed the voteless masses. But the British ruling classes, selfish and narrow-minded though they often were, had at their best a sense of *noblesse oblige,* of public spirit and civic-mindedness. Within the aristocracy of land and trade there were fewer social barriers than on the Continent, and the English gentry were on the whole more responsive than their continental counterparts to the need for changes and reform. Disraeli, the great nineteenth-century Tory, dubbed the Whig cabinets of the first two Georges a "Venetian oligarchy," by which he meant that the wealthy ran the country for their private benefit, like the merchants of Renaissance Venice. And so they did; yet the Whigs, for all their oligarchy and corruption, provided the most enlightened government in eighteenth-century Europe.

The Liabilities of France

Where Britain was strong, France was weak. In the France of Louis XV (1715–1774), barriers to social mobility were more difficult to surmount, though commoners who were rich or aggressive enough did overcome them. France suffered particularly from the rigidity of its colonial system, the inferiority of its navy, and the very mediocre abilities of most of its statesmen. The Ministry of the Navy, which ruled the overseas empire, regarded these possessions as so many warships permanently at anchor. It refused to sanction steps toward self-government and applied the same regulations to colonies as different as the sugar islands of the West Indies and the wilderness of Canada. Under these policies, the mother country prospered, but the colonies languished. Commercial activity doubled in Nantes, Bordeaux, and other ports; refineries grew up to process the raw sugar imported from the plantations of Guadeloupe and Martinique. Overseas, the plethora of controls, however, stifled the initiative of the colonists, and the French imperial system lacked the elasticity to meet the test of war.

The French navy needed greater resources and better leadership. Its warships, though admirably designed, were inadequate in number. Since Dutch and British vessels carried much of French commerce, the merchant marine was too small to supplement the fleet. French naval officers, though rigorously trained in the classroom, lacked the experience gained by British captains in a lifetime at sea. Moreover, in a fashion characteristic of the Old Régime at its worst, officers from the aristocracy devoted much of their energies to thwarting the rise of those from the middle class.

French rulers were almost bound to neglect the navy in favor of the army, since France was above all a land power, and its vulnerable northeastern frontier, lying across the Flemish plain, invited invasion. Except in size, however, the army of Louis XV scarcely lived up to the great traditions of Louis XIV. The troops were poorly trained, and the organization was top-heavy. There was one officer to fifteen men, as compared with one to thirty-five in the more efficient Prussian army. Many aristocratic officers regarded a commission simply as a convenient way of increasing their personal wealth.

Both the navy and the army underwent important reforms after 1763 and the defeats suffered by France in the Seven Years' War (see p. 38). The number of warships was increased, the officer corps of the army was cleared of much dead wood, and more aggressive military tactics were introduced. These improvements accounted in part for the excellent showing made by France in the American Revolutionary War and in the military campaigns resulting from her own revolution. They came too late, however, to save the vanishing prestige of the Old Régime.

The Old Régime was weakest at its head, the monarchy itself. There were no "sun kings" in France after the death of Louis XIV, and few ministers who approached the caliber of Richelieu or Colbert. The Duke of Orléans, the Regent from 1715 to 1723, was a gambler,

drunkard, and pervert, who popularized the word "roue" by remarking that his friends deserved to be broken on the wheel (*roué* is French for wheel). The Regent, however, did attempt two important experiments. He allowed John Law to try out his "system," as we have seen, and, in place of Louis XIV's method of ruling through individual bourgeois ministers, he set up a series of ministerial councils staffed by men from the most distinguished noble families of the realm. Although the first experiment produced some beneficial results, the second failed, after a three-year trial, in part because of the endless squabbles among the noble councillors. The French second estate had outlived its usefulness. The Regency proved that the nobles were no longer able to govern; the mid-century wars proved that they were no longer able to lead French armies to victory.

Soon after the regency of Orléans, power passed to one of the few statesmen of pre-revolutionary France, Cardinal Fleury, the tutor of Louis XV and the chief minister from 1726 until his death in 1743 in his ninetieth year. Without attempting basic reforms, the aged Cardinal, in the words of Voltaire, "treated the state as a powerful and robust body which could cure itself." Fleury did not remedy the chronic and deep-seated injustice and inefficiency of French fiscal methods. But he did stabilize the coinage, and he put the farming of taxes on a more businesslike basis by restricting tax-farmers to the comparatively modest profit of 7½ per cent. To make loans more readily available, he established state pawnshops in the chief cities of France. Fleury's success impressed Lady Mary Montagu, the observant wife of an English diplomat, who wrote in 1739:

France is so much improved, it is not . . . the same country we passed through twenty years ago. Everything I see speaks in praise of Cardinal Fleury; the roads are all mended . . . and such good care taken against robbers, that you may cross the country with your purse in your hand. . . . The French are more changed than their roads; instead of pale, yellow faces, wrapped up in blankets, as we saw them, the villages are filled with fresh-coloured lusty peasants, in good cloth and clean linen. It is

The Marquise de Pompadour, by Quentin de la Tour. The range of her interests is indicated by the sheet music in her hands and by the books on the table, including Montesquieu's *Spirit of the Laws* and a volume of the *Encyclopédie*.

incredible the air of plenty and content that is over the whole country.*

The administrative stability achieved by Fleury soon vanished after Louis XV began his personal rule in 1743. Intelligent but timid, lazy, and debauched, Louis XV did not have the interest or the patience to supervise the details of government in the manner of Louis XIV. He appointed and dismissed ministers on a personal whim or at the bidding of his mistresses and favorites. In thirty years he had 18 different foreign secretaries, and 14 different controllers-general (the chief fiscal officer). Each change in personnel meant a shift in policy, and Louis aggravated the instability by conspiring against his own appointees.

*Letters, Everyman ed. (New York, 1906), 271–272.

France had two conflicting foreign policies: that of the diplomatic corps; and the "King's Secret," conducted by royal agents who operated at cross purposes with the regular diplomats. Louis XV, while allowing the reins of government to go slack, yet refused to give them over to firmer hands.

Nevertheless, France remained a great power. Still the most populous country in Europe, she contained almost inexhaustible reserves of strength. Her army, though enfeebled, was the largest in the world, and her navy was the second largest. She led the world in overseas trade until Britain forged ahead of her in the last quarter of the eighteenth century. French tastes, French thought, and the French language retained the international pre-eminence won in the age of Louis XIV. The misgovernment and the other weaknesses of the Old Régime were relative rather than absolute.

The Other Western States

Spain was the only other state in western Europe with a claim to great-power status. War and its aftermath had put an end to the major international roles played by Sweden and the Dutch Republic during the seventeenth century. The Great Northern War (see pp. 25–26), ruined the Baltic empire of Sweden and killed off the flower of Swedish manhood. The Dutch, exhausted by their wars against Louis XIV, were losing their commercial leadership and could no longer afford a large navy or an independent foreign policy. Eighteenth-century Holland, in the phrase of Frederick the Great, was often a "cockboat in the tow of the English frigate."

Spain, by contrast, suffered comparatively little damage from the great war over the succession to her throne that was fought in the early 1700's. The loss of Belgium and parts of Italy at the Utrecht settlement of 1713 reduced the unwieldy Spanish domains to more manageable size. The new Bourbon kings were a marked improvement over the last Spanish Habsburgs. Philip V (1700–1746), the first of the Spanish Bourbons, infused fresh life into the country's fossilized institutions by importing French advisers schooled in the system of Louis XIV. He also enlisted the aid of two able adventurers. Alberoni and Ripperdá,

whose fantastic careers almost outdid John Law's. Alberoni, the son of an Italian gardener, was successively a cook, a diplomat, the chief minister of Spain, and a cardinal. Ripperdá, a Dutch business expert and diplomat, ultimately lost the favor of Philip, entered the service of the Sultan of Morocco, and, after a lifelong alternation between the Protestant and Catholic faiths, died a Moslem. Philip and his remarkable advisers cut down the excessive formalities and endless delays of Spanish administration. They reasserted the authority of the monarchy over the traditionally powerful nobility and clergy. They improved the tax system, encouraged textiles and other industries, built up the navy, and fortified strategic points in the Spanish empire in America.

The new dispensation, however, did not strike at the root causes of Spanish decline. The greed of governors and the restrictions of mercantilism still checked the progress of the colonies. The mother country remained impoverished, burdened with reactionary noble and clerical castes, and hampered by inadequate resources. Philip V himself was neurotic, refusing, for instance, to cut his toenails which grew so long that he limped. He was dominated by his strong-willed second wife, Elizabeth Farnese, the patroness of Alberoni. Since Philip's son by his first marriage would inherit Spain, Elizabeth was determined to find thrones for her own two sons. Her persistent attempts to secure the succession of Italian states for them repeatedly threatened the peace of Europe.

III   Italy and Germany

Disunited Italy

By 1715, the Italian states had lost much of the political and economic power they had enjoyed during the Renaissance. It is easy to see why. The opening of new worlds overseas

and the rise of Spain, England, and the other Atlantic powers had diminished the importance of the Mediterranean. In the Mediterranean itself, the Ottoman Turks and their satellites in North Africa long menaced Italian shipping and trade. Moreover, beginning with the French invasion of 1494, Italy had been threatened with conquest by one of the new national monarchies.

The Spanish Habsburgs made the conquest. For almost two centuries Spain ruled Milan, Naples, and Sicily directly, and dominated the rest of the peninsula. In the readjustment of the European balance in 1713, Italy exchanged one foreign master for another, as the Austrian Habsburgs took over the Italian possessions of their Spanish cousins. On the completion of the readjustment in 1720, the political map of the peninsula showed Austria established in Lombardy, flanked by the decaying commercial republics of Venice and Genoa. In the mountainous northwest was the small but rising state of Piedmont-Savoy, technically the Kingdom of Sardinia after its acquisition of that island in 1720. Farther down the peninsula were the Grand Duchy of Tuscany (formerly the Republic of Florence), the Papal States, and the Austrian Two Sicilies. None of these states was more than a minor power.

Yet Italy could not be written off as a negligible quantity in the eighteenth century. Rome remained the capital of Catholicism, Venice still produced fine painters, and Naples was the schoolmaster of European musicians. Lombardy, Tuscany, and Naples all contributed to the economic and intellectual advances of the century. Meantime, Italy was a major stake in balance-of-power politics, a perennial source of dissension and spoils. In 1720, to counter the ambitions of the Spanish queen, Elizabeth Farnese, the Austrian Habsburgs took over the island of Sicily, which had gone to Piedmont in the Utrecht settlement; in return, Piedmont secured Sardinia, originally assigned to Austria. In the 1730's, a series of exchanges gave the Two Sicilies to Elizabeth's elder son, "Baby Carlos," while the Austrians gained some minor bits of territory and the succession of Tuscany. In 1768, Genoa sold the island of Corsica to France. Italy was, in the old phrase, merely "a geographical expression," not a political whole but a series of parts to be shifted and exchanged by ambitious dynasts and empire-builders from outside the peninsula.

Divided Germany: The Habsburg Dominions

In some ways Germany deserved even more to be called a geographical expression, for it was divided into three hundred states, large, small, and minute. The Thirty Years' War had caused wide devastation, and the Peace of Westphalia ending the war in 1648 had enhanced the sovereign rights of the individual German states and reduced virtually to zero the authority of their nominal overlord, the Holy Roman Emperor. Unlike Italy, however, Germany did include two considerable powers, Austria and Prussia.

The Austrian Habsburgs won a series of military and diplomatic victories in the two decades before 1715. In 1699, by the peace of Karlovitz, they recovered Hungary from the Ottoman Turks, thereby advancing their own *Drang nach Osten*. In 1713, though they failed to keep the old Habsburg crown of Spain from going to the Bourbon Philip V, they received handsome compensation in Belgian and Italian territories. Yet these last acquisitions were distant from the main bloc of Habsburg lands in central Europe.

Charles VI (1711–1740), aware that his title of Holy Roman Emperor conferred little real authority, concentrated on the Habsburg family possessions. He spent much of his reign persuading his own noble subjects to ratify the Pragmatic Sanction, a constitutional agreement whereby, in the absence of sons, his daughter Maria Theresa would succeed him in all his lands. A good deal of scorn has been directed at Charles for devoting so much time and energy to a scrap of paper, but recent historians have noted that the Pragmatic Sanction did indeed establish the principle of linking together the scattered family territories. Much, however, remained to be done to consolidate Habsburg rule over an assemblage of lands which represented many different nations and could never be forged into a single national monarchy. In three key national areas

—German Austria, Czech Bohemia, and Magyar Hungary—the nobles still kept most of their medieval prerogatives and, by controlling local estates and diets, controlled grants of taxes and the appointment of officials. The financial and military weakness of the Habsburg regime is suggested by the fact that when Charles VI died, in 1740, the pay of the army and of the civil service was more than two years in arrears. Small wonder that the army fell short of its paper strength of 100,000 men as it faced the great test of strength with Prussia that came in 1740.

The Rise of Prussia

Whereas Austria enjoyed the appearances rather than the realities of great-power status, Prussia possessed few of the appearances but a great many of the realities. Its territories were scattered across North Germany from the Rhine on the west to the Vistula and beyond on the east; consisting largely of sand and swamp, these lands had meager natural resources and carried on relatively little trade. With less than three million inhabitants, Prussia ranked only twelfth among the European states in population. Her capital city, Berlin, located on the unimportant River Spree, had few of the obvious geographical advantages enjoyed by Constantinople, Paris, London, and the other great capitals. A wise prophet in 1600 might well have foreseen that Catholic Austria would never unite a Germany in which Protestantism was so strong. But he would probably have predicted that a new Germany would center in Frankfurt in the heart of the Rhine country, or in Saxon Leipzig or Dresden; he would hardly have chosen the unpromising town of Berlin and the minor house of Hohenzollern.

The Hohenzollerns had been established since the fifteenth century as Electors of Brandenburg, which lay between the Elbe and Oder rivers. A Hohenzollern was the last Master of the Teutonic Knights, a crusading order which in the thirteenth century had pushed the Germanic frontier beyond the Vistula to

a land called Prussia at the southeast corner of the Baltic Sea. In 1618, when this Prussian area fell to the Hohenzollerns, it was separated from Brandenburg by Polish territory and was still nominally a fief held from the Polish king. In western Germany, meantime (1614), the Hohenzollerns acquired Cleves, Mark, and some other parcels in the lower Rhine valley. Thus, when Frederick William, the Great Elector (1640–1688), succeeded to the Hohenzollern inheritance as the Thirty Years' War was drawing to a close, his lands consisted of a nucleus in Brandenburg with separate outlying regions to east and west. With extraordinary persistence, the rulers of Brandenburg-Prussia for the next two hundred years devoted themselves to the task of making a solid block of territory out of these bits and pieces.

The Great Elector was the first in a line of able Hohenzollern rulers. In foreign policy, he won recognition from Poland as the full sovereign of Prussia, no longer subject to Polish overlordship. He also tried, with less success, to dislodge the Swedes from the Pomeranian territories, between Brandenburg and the Baltic, which they had acquired in 1648. Though he won military renown by defeating the Swedes at Fehrbellin in 1675, he made few practical gains because of his own tortuous diplomacy. In the wars against Louis XIV, he shifted repeatedly from the French to the anti-French side and back.

In his domestic policy, he made more substantial accomplishments. He had found his domains largely ruined by war, the farms wasted, the population cut in half, the army reduced to a disorderly rabble of a few thousand men. The Great Elector repaired the damage thoroughly. To augment the population, he encouraged the immigration of Polish Jews and other refugees from religious persecution, notably 20,000 French Huguenots to whom he gave partial exemption from taxation. He built a small but efficient standing army that enabled Prussia to command large foreign subsidies for participating in the campaigns for or against Louis XIV. In peacetime, he assigned the soldiers to the construc-

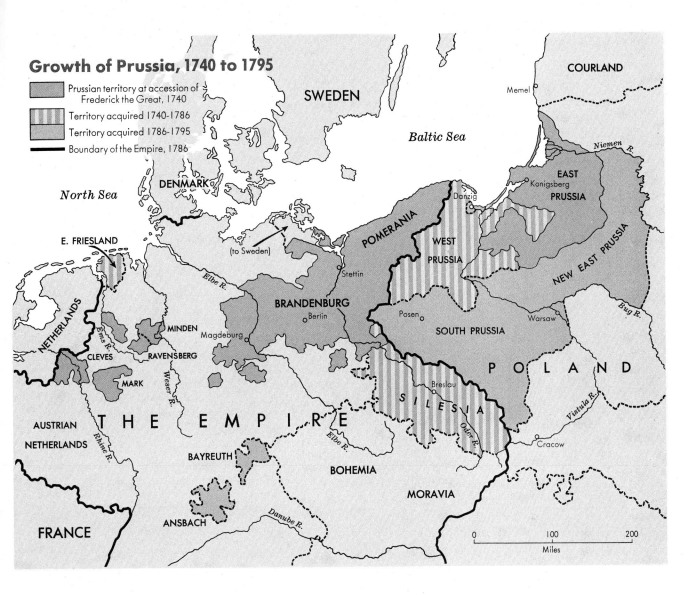

Growth of Prussia, 1740 to 1795

- Prussian territory at accession of Frederick the Great, 1740
- Territory acquired 1740-1786
- Territory acquired 1786-1795
- Boundary of the Empire, 1786

tion of public works like the canal between the Elbe and the Oder.

In administration, the Great Elector fixed the Hohenzollern pattern of militarized absolutism, a policy in which he was assisted by an educational tradition and a Lutheran state church that taught the virtues of obedience and discipline. On his accession, he found that in all three territories—Prussia, Brandenburg, and Cleves-Mark—the authority of the ruler was limited by Estates, medieval assemblies representing the landed nobles and the townspeople. In all three territories he battled the Estates for supremacy and won, thereby delaying for two centuries the introduction of representative government into the Hohen-

zollern realm. He gradually gathered into his own hands the crucial power of levying taxes. Much of the actual work of collecting taxes and performing other administrative functions was done by the War Office and the army; even policing was executed by the military. Like Louis XIV, the Great Elector reduced the power of the aristocracy; unlike Louis, however, he relied not on bourgeois officials but on a working alliance with the landed gentry, particularly the celebrated Junkers of Prussia proper. He confirmed the Junkers' absolute authority over the serfs on their estates and their preponderance over the towns, and he encouraged them to serve the state, especially as army officers. In contrast to other mon-

19

archies, the absolutism of the Hohenzollerns rested on the co-operation of the sovereign and the aristocracy, not on their mutual antagonism.

Under the Great Elector's son, Frederick I (1688–1713), Prussia played only a minor role in the great wars that humbled Louis XIV and made few territorial gains in the Utrecht settlement. But in 1701 the Elector Frederick made a significant gain in prestige by assuming the title "King in Prussia" and insisting on international recognition of his new status as the price for his entry into the War of the Spanish Succession. Though technically Frederick was king only in Prussia proper, which lay outside the boundaries of the Holy Roman Empire, even a limited royal title conferred new dignity on the Hohenzollerns. In living up to his new eminence, however, King Frederick I nearly bankrupted his state by lavish expenditures on the trappings of monarchy. Since he thought that a suggestion of marital infidelity enhanced the majesty of a king, he maintained an official mistress with whom he took decorous afternoon promenades. Actually, he was happily married, and his talented queen enlivened the provincial Hohenzollern court by inviting intellectuals and artists to Berlin. As Frederick the Great later remarked, under Frederick I Berlin was the "Athens of the north."

Frederick William I

But as Frederick the Great also remarked, under the next king, Frederick William I (1713–1740), Berlin became the "Sparta of the north." The flirtation with luxury and the finer things of life proved to be a passing exception to the usual Hohenzollern rule of austerity. Frederick William I returned with a vengeance to the policies of the Great Elector and devoted himself entirely to economy, absolutism, and the army. As soon as he had given his father a lavish funeral, he dismissed most of the officials of the court, converted a large portion of the royal palace into offices, and reduced governmental expenses to a

One of the giant soldiers of Frederick William I of Prussia.

fraction of what they had been. He reiterated the order *Ein Plus Machen* (make a surplus), and he bequeathed a full treasury to his son. His frugality enabled him to undertake the occasional project that he thought really worth while. Thus he financed the immigration of 12,000 South German Protestants to open up new farm lands in eastern Prussia.

To strengthen royal control over the apparatus of state, Frederick William I instituted a small board of experts, with the wonderful German title of *Generaloberfinanzkriegsunddomänendirektorium* (General Superior Finance, War, and Domain Directory). The members of the General Directory were charged both with administering departments of the central government and with supervising the provinces. The arrangement, while cumbersome, did detach provincial administration from local interests and bring it under closer royal control. The King insisted on hard work and punctuality. He treated the counselors of the General Directory as he treated lesser officials, paying them meanly and belaboring them with his cane for slovenly performance of their duties. A late arrival at one of the daily sessions of the General Directory paid a severe fine; an unexcused absentee faced six months in jail.

Frederick William I doubled the size of the standing army, but he maintained the strength of the laboring force of his underpopulated state by furloughing troops for nine months a year to work on farms. To secure guns and uniforms, he established state factories. The army also prompted his sole extravagance—a regiment of tall grenadiers, all six feet or over, who wore special caps more than a foot high to increase the impression of size. In recruiting his beloved "giants," the king threw economy to the winds, employing scores of scouts in other German states, paying exorbitant prices, and even trading royal musicians and prize stallions for especially tall specimens. Frederick William cherished his army too much to undertake an adventurous foreign policy. His only significant military campaign was against Sweden in the last phase of the Great Northern War, whereby Prussia ob-

tained in 1720 part of Pomerania and also the important Baltic port of Stettin. Thus Frederick William advanced the Great Elector's old aim of liquidating the Swedish possessions in Germany.

Eighteenth-century observers rightly called the Prussia of Frederick William an "armed camp" and berated its army for being a "gigantic penal institution" in which minor infractions of regulations entailed the death penalty. The King himself, obsessed with military matters, showed scant concern for culture, neglected the education of his subjects, and despised everything French. He carried parsimony to the extreme of refusing pensions to soldiers' widows. The inadequate fees of judges and lawyers encouraged the corruption and lethargy that obstructed the course of justice in Prussia. Yet this régime worked and, in terms of power, worked extremely well. The Junkers, although feudal in outlook, were intensely loyal to the Hohenzollerns and made splendid officers. The army itself, though smaller than those of France, Russia, and Austria, was the best drilled and the most rigorously disciplined force in Europe. When Frederick William I died in 1740, the Prussian David was ready to fight the Austrian Goliath.

IV   The Eastern Powers

The Early Years of Peter the Great

Even more spectacular than the rise of Prussia was the emergence of Russia as a major power during the era of Peter the Great (1682–1725). In 1682, at the death of Tsar Fedor Romanov, Russia was still a backward eastern European country, with few diplomatic links with the West, and very little knowledge of the outside world. Contemporaries, Russians as well as foreigners, report on the brutality, immorality, drunken-

ness, illiteracy, and filth prevalent among all classes of society. Even the clergy, most of whom could not read, set no shining example by their mode of life. It is perhaps little wonder that students familiar with conditions in Russia before the advent of Peter the Great have saluted him as the great revolutionary who altered the face of his country. Yet the changes he made were neither so numerous nor so drastic as his admirers have often claimed. Moreover, the foundations for most of them were already present in the society he inherited, and Russia would no doubt eventually have become a power of international importance without Peter, although it would have taken longer. Even if we accept all these dilutions of the usual estimate of his contribution, however, the fact remains that Peter was an awe-inspiring—and terror-inspiring—figure.

Tsar Fedor died childless in 1682, leaving a fifteen-year old brother, Ivan, who was partly blind and almost an idiot, and an ugly and capable sister, Sophia, both children of Tsar Alexis (1645–1676) by his first wife. The ten-year-old Peter was the half-brother of Ivan and Sophia, the son of Alexis by his second wife, and as bright and vigorous as Ivan was debilitated. A major court feud quickly developed between the partisans of the family of Alexis' first wife and those of the family of the second. At first the old Russian representative assembly, the *zemski sobor*, elected Peter as Tsar. But Sophia, as leader of the opposing faction, won the support of the *streltsy*, or musketeers, a special branch of the military, many of whom belonged to the conservative religious schismatics known as the Old Believers. Undisciplined, and angry with their officers, some of whom had been cheating them, the *streltsy* were a menace to orderly government.

Sophia and her supporters encouraged the *streltsy* to attack the Kremlin, and the youthful Peter saw the infuriated troops murdering some of his mother's family and racing through the palace in pursuit of the rest, stabbing the furniture with swords and spears. For good measure, they killed many of the nobles living in Moscow and pillaged the archives where the records of serfdom were kept. But, though their movement obviously had some social content, it was primarily a successful effort by Sophia to gain power. Sophia now became regent for both Ivan and Peter, who were hailed as joint Tsars.

But before her power was stabilized, she had to deal with the ungovernable *streltsy*, who terrorized the capital until threatened with open war by the regular army. Once the *streltsy* were calmed, Sophia moved to punish the Old Believers and any revolting serfs that could be captured. The first woman to govern Russia

since Kievan times, Sophia was bound to face severe opposition. Even her supporters would not allow her to proclaim herself autocrat. And the maturing Peter, though out of favor and away from court, posed a threat to her position; in the end, the *streltsy* let her down. In 1689, Sophia was shut up in a convent, and Peter and Ivan ruled together until Ivan's death in 1696, although in practice Ivan never counted for anything.

The young Peter was almost seven feet tall, and extremely lively. Highly intelligent, he had learned to read and write (but never to spell) from a drunken tutor who was the only academic instructor the troubled times afforded. Even in his early years, Peter was fascinated by war and military games. He set up a play-regiment, staffed it with full-grown men, enlisted as a common soldier in its ranks (promoting himself from time to time), ordered equipment for it from the Moscow arsenals, and drilled it in war games with unflagging vigor, himself firing off cannon or pounding on a drum with equal enjoyment. He discovered a broken-down boat in a barn and unraveled the mysteries of rigging and sail with the help of Dutch sailors settled in the foreigners' suburb of Moscow. Sailing remained one of his keenest passions. Though he married at the age of sixteen, Peter neglected his wife and preferred working on his military maneuvers, sailing his boats, and relaxing with his peculiar circle of cronies.

This rowdy lot smoked huge quantities of tobacco (which horrified the conservative Muscovites, who believed that smoking was specifically forbidden by the Biblical text which says that what cometh out of the mouth defileth a man), and regularly got completely drunk. Then they would engage in obscene parodies of church services, or play elaborate and highly dangerous practical jokes on the unoffending citizenry, roaring about Moscow in winter late at night on sleighs and treating the sleeping populace to shrieking serenades. Masquerades and parties lasted for days; staid Moscow ladies, accustomed to almost harem-like seclusion, were commanded to put on low-necked evening dresses in the western style, and dance and engage in social chit-chat. They were literally forced to drink with the Tsar and his friends: If a lady refused, Peter simply held her nose, and poured the wine down her throat. Peter spent enormous sums of state revenue on this sort of party and richly endowed his boon companion Lefort, a young Swiss soldier of fortune who became Field Marshal, Grand Admiral, and "chief diplomat."

The almost frantic energy that Peter devoted to pleasure reflected only part of his appetite for new experience. Just as he served in the ranks of his own play-regiment and sailed his boats himself, so he eagerly learned any new technique that came to his attention. At various times he took up carpentry, shoe-making, cooking, clock-making, ivory-carving, etching, and—worst of all—dentistry. Once he had acquired a set of dentist's tools, nobody was safe, since Peter did not care whether the intended victim had a toothache or not; whenever he felt the need to practice, he practiced—and those were the days before anesthetics. Preferring to wear shabby work clothes, driving his own horses, neglecting formal obligations and paying little attention to court and church ceremony, Peter in his own person was a shock to the Muscovites, and not in the least in keeping with their idea of a proper tsar.

After Lefort died in 1700, Peter's favorite was Menshikov, a man of low birth, who received high offices, the title of Prince, and a huge fortune. Like many of the public servants of the period, he was an unscrupulous grafter. Peter wrote to Menshikov as "my brother," and, though he came to distrust him, he never ruined him as he did many other favorites. Meantime, Peter had his first wife shut up in a convent and made a nun. He later took on as mistress a girl from the Baltic region, who had already passed through the hands of Menshikov and others, and after some years of liaison with her, during which she gave birth to two of Peter's children, he finally married her in 1712. This was the Empress Catherine, a simple, hearty, affectionate woman, long devoted to her difficult husband, and able to control him as no other human being could. But again, one can understand the horrified reaction of the old-fashioned Russian noble.

The Western Trip

In 1695, anxious to try his hand at war, Peter led a campaign against the Turks at Azov in the area of the Black Sea. He failed, but in the next year, with the help of Dutch experts, he assembled a fleet of river-boats on the Don, sailed them downriver, and defeated the Turks at Azov. Since the Habsburgs at the time were waging a long war against the Turks, this rather surprising Russian contribution aroused much curiosity. The project of forming a league against the Turks with the states of western Europe now gave Peter the pretext for a trip outside Russia, the first undertaken by a Russian sovereign since the Kievan period.

Through ostensibly traveling incognito as a noncommissioned officer, Peter naturally failed to conceal his identity: After all, there were no other authoritarian seven-footers in the party. What fascinated him was western "know-how," especially naval. He planned to go to Holland, England, and Venice, where the best ships (in his opinion) were made, find out how they were made, and bring the knowledge back to Russia for the advancement of Russian aims. He hired several hundred technicians to work in Russia, raised money when he needed it by selling to an English peer the monopoly of tobacco sales in Russia, and visited every sort of factory or museum or printing press he could find. The huge Russian Tsar in all his vigor and crudity, emerging into the air of western Europe from his antiquated and stagnant country, made an unforgettable impression.

From this celebrated trip many well-known pictures emerge: Peter laboring as a common hand on the docks in Holland; Peter and his suite, drunk and dirty, wrecking the handsome house and garden of the English diarist, John Evelyn, near London: "There is a house full of people," wrote Evelyn's harassed servant, "and that right nasty." Less well known perhaps are the spectacles of Peter dancing with a German princess, mistaking her whalebone corsets for her ribs, and commenting loudly that German girls have devilish hard bones; of Peter receiving an honorary degree at Oxford; of Peter deep in conversation (Dutch) with William Penn about the Quaker faith; of Peter gobbling his food without benefit of knife or fork, or asleep with a dozen or so of his followers on the floor of a tiny room in a London inn with no windows open.

Before Peter could get to Venice, the western trip was interrupted by news that the *streltsy* had revolted again (1698). Peter rushed home and personally participated in the punishment of the alleged plotters; he and Menshikov rather enjoyed chopping off the heads of the victims. Though many innocent men suffered torture and death, Peter had broken the *streltsy* as a power in Russian domestic life.

From the West, Peter had returned more determined than ever to modernize his country and his countrymen. The very day of his return he summoned the court jester, and with his assistance went about with a great pair of shears, stopping his courtiers and clipping off their beards. Though this may seem a trivial joke, in fact it was an action full of symbolism. The tradition of the Orthodox Church held that God was bearded; if man was made in the image of God, man must also have a beard. Deprived of his beard, man was no longer made in God's image, and was a natural candidate for damnation. This was the way the Muscovite nobles and churchmen felt. Peter now decreed that Russian nobles must shave, or else pay a substantial tax for the privilege of wearing their beards. Bronze beard-tokens worn around the neck certified that the tax had been properly paid; without such a token a bearded man ran the risk of being clipped on sight.

Presently, Peter issued an edict commanding that all boyars, members of the gentry class, and the city population generally must abandon traditional Russian dress, which included long robes with flowing sleeves and tall bonnets, and adopt western-style costume. The manufacture of the old-fashioned clothes was made illegal, and Peter added point to his decree by taking up his shears again and cutting off the sleeves of all the people he met wearing the forbidden robes. The enactments on the beards and on dress were regarded by the victims as an assult on precious customs and a forcible introduction of hated foreign ways.

Peter's Wars

War was Peter's greatest interest. We can understand his policies at home only after we realize how closely related they were to the virtually constant warfare of his reign, and to the ever-mounting need for money for fighting. On his way back to Russia in 1698, he discovered that the Austrians, instead of being eager to join him in a full-scale crusade against the Turks, were anxious to end their Turkish war. Irritated by the Austro-Turkish Peace of Karlovitz in 1699, which he felt to be a betrayal of Russia, Peter made a separate peace of his own with the Sultan in 1700. By this time, his plans for new aggression were already formed.

The victim was to be Sweden. Peter's allies, already signed up in 1699, were Denmark and Poland, the latter under its elected king, Augustus the Strong, who was also Elector of Saxony and who had become an intimate of Peter after their first meeting in 1698. The real engineer of the alliance and moving spirit of the war against Sweden was a nobleman named Patkul from the Baltic shore, deeply resentful of measures taken by the Swedes against the feudal proprietors of that area. Patkul went from interview to interview, holding out to Augustus and Peter the prospect that after they had defeated Sweden they might divide her Baltic territories. In 1697, the Swedish throne had descended to a youth of fifteen, King Charles XII, whom Peter, Augustus, and Patkul hoped they might easily overcome. They might have reconsidered had they seen Charles strengthening his sword-arm by beheading at a single stroke apiece whole flocks of sheep driven down his palace corridors in single file.

The fact was that Peter the Great characteristically rushed unprepared into the Great Northern War (1700–1721). Charles knocked Denmark out of the war before Russia even got in. He then frustrated Augustus' effort to take the Baltic port of Riga and completely defeated a vastly larger Russian force at Narva (1700), capturing the entire supply of modern cannon of which Peter was so proud. Instead of taking advantage of Peter's helplessness, however, and marching into Russia, Charles detoured into Poland, where he spent seven years pursuing Augustus, sponsoring his own King of Poland, a noble named Stanislas Leszczynski, and eventually forcing Augustus to abandon the Polish crown to Leszczynski and to give up the Russian alliance. Charles then seized and executed Patkul.

In the interim, Peter had been busy rebuilding the Russian armies and had conquered from the Swedes the two Baltic provinces nearest to Russia, Ingria and Livonia. In the first he founded in 1703 a new city, St. Petersburg, soon to be the capital of Russia, and from the beginning the apple of Peter's eye. In 1708, Charles made the mistake of sweeping far to the south and east into the Ukraine in an effort to join forces with the Cossacks, whose leader Mazepa was an ally. Exhausted by the severe winter, the Swedish forces were finally defeated by the Russians in the decisive battle of Poltava (June 27, 1709). Charles managed to flee safely westward across the Dniester River and onto Turkish territory.

Peter was able to reinstate Augustus as King of Poland, but he was not able to force the Turks to surrender to him the refugee King of Sweden. Charles had embarked on intrigues to bring about a war between Turkey and Peter, and thus to avenge his defeat. So Peter in some dismay found himself embroiled in war against the Turks (1710–1711). For the first time in history the Russians made an appeal to the Balkan Christian subjects of the Turks on the ground of their common Orthodox faith. Bearing banners modeled on those of Constantine, first Emperor of Byzantium, and promising liberation from the Moslems, the Russian forces entered Turkish territory

by crossing the river Pruth westward into the Danubian province of Moldavia (now a part of Rumania). Here the Turkish armies trapped Peter and forced him to surrender (1711).

The Turks could have dragged Peter off in captivity to Istanbul had they wanted, but they proved unexpectedly lenient. They required the surrender of Azov and the creation of an unfortified "no-man's land" between Russian and Ottoman territory. Furious with the Turks for not taking full advantage of Peter's discomfiture, Charles worked to bring about still another Russo-Turkish war. Although he came

Russian Expansion in Europe, 1689-1796

very close to success, the Turks eventually tired of their firebrand visitor and expelled him. Their own peace with Russia was secure, and Charles went sadly home (1714).

Still the Great Northern War dragged on for seven more years of diplomatic intrigue and military and naval action, involving the Prussians (see p. 21) and affecting the interests of all the western European powers. As Russian forces seized Finland, inflicted naval defeats on the Swedes in the Baltic, and occupied islands only a few miles from the Swedish coast, the Swedish empire was obviously dissolving. To the last years of the Great Northern War belong a whole series of matrimonial and other alliances between Russia and the petty German courts, bringing the Russians deep into Central Europe and embroiling them in questions in which Russia really had no national interest. From a remote and little-known state somewhere behind Poland, Russia had emerged as a major military power with enough might to affect the destiny of European states.

The death of Charles XII in 1718 cleared the way for peace negotiations, but it took a Russian landing in Sweden proper (1719) to force a decision. At Nystadt (1721), Russia received all the former possessions of Sweden along the eastern shore of the Baltic. Peter returned Finland to Sweden and agreed to pay a substantial sum for the territories acquired. These Baltic lands were Peter's famous "window on the west," putting Russia into immediate contact with Europe and ending the curious situation by which all seaborne traffic to Russia had had to sail around the northern edge of Europe and into the White Sea. Next, Peter undertook a brief campaign (1722–1723) against the Persians. At his death in 1725, Russia had been at war for almost the entirety of his thirty-five-year reign.

The Machinery
Of Peter's Government

Constant warfare requires constant supplies of men and money. Since the enlistment of volunteers provided cannon fodder but not seasoned troops, Peter's government developed a crude form of draft system according to which a given number of households had to supply a given number of recruits. More men died of disease, hunger, and cold than at the hands of the enemy, and desertion was commonplace. But the very length of the Great Northern War meant that survivors served as a tough nucleus for a regular army. Though Peter built a Baltic fleet at the first opportunity, Russian naval tradition failed to strike deep roots. From 800 ships (mostly very small) at the moment of his death, the fleet declined to fewer than twenty a decade later. There was no merchant marine whatever. The apprehensions of the English and the Dutch that Russian emergence on the Baltic would create a new maritime nation proved unfounded.

To staff the military forces and the administration, Peter rigorously enforced the rule by which all landowners owed service to the state. He eventually decreed "civil death" for those who failed to register; this put them outside the protection of the law, and anyone could attack or kill them without fear of the consequences. State service became compulsory for life; at the age of fifteen, every male child of the service class was assigned to his future post, in the army, in the civil service, or at court. Peter often forced the gentry to do jobs they considered beneath them; he did not care whether they were interested in their work or even very much whether they had been trained for it. He filled their ranks with newcomers, who obtained grants of land, rank, and title. And he required that when a member of this class died he must leave his estate intact to one of his sons, not necessarily the eldest, so that it would not be divided anew in every generation.

Thus the class of service nobility—which now substantially included the survivors of the nobility of ancient birth, the old boyars—was brought into complete dependence upon the tsar. The system threw open the possibility of a splendid career to men with talent. A person without estates or rank who reached a certain level in any branch of the service (for example, major in the army) automatically received lands and a title of nobility. The nobility of ancient birth viewed this as a cheapening of their position and hated to see new recruits come into their own social order. But under Peter there was little they could do about it.

To raise cash, Peter tried all kinds of measures. He debased the currency; he taxed virtually everything—sales, rents, real estate, tanneries, baths, and beehives—and appointed special officials called "revenue-finders" to think up new levies. The government held a monopoly over a bewildering variety of important products, including salt and oil, coffins and caviar. The basic tax on each individual household was not producing enough revenue, partly because the number of households had declined as a result of war and misery, and partly because households were combining in order to evade payment. Peter's government therefore substituted a head tax on every male—the "soul tax," as the Russians called it—making it useless for individuals to conceal themselves in households. This innovation required a new census, which produced a most important, and unintended, social result: The census-takers now classified as serfs a large number of floaters on the edge between freedom and serfdom, who thus found themselves and their children eternally labeled as unfree. At the cost of human misery, Peter's government managed in its later years to balance the budget.

In the administration, new ministries (*prikazy*) were first set up to centralize the handling of funds received from various sources. A system of army districts adopted for reasons of military efficiency led to the creation of the first provinces, first eight, then nine, then twelve, embracing all Russia. Each province had its own governor, and many of the functions previously carried on inefficiently by the central government were thus decentralized. With the tsar often away from the capital, and many of the former *prikazy* abolished, decentralization had gone so far that Russia seemed at times to have little central government. But when Peter set out for the Pruth campaign in 1711, he created a nine-man "governing Senate" to exercise power in his absence. Later, Peter copied the Swedish system of central ministries to supersede the old *prikazy* and created nine "colleges" —for foreign affairs, army, navy, commerce, mines and manufactures, justice, income, expenditure, and control. Each "college" was administered not by a single minister but by a majority vote of an eleven-man board of directors or *collegium*. Corruption now became more difficult, because the conduct of any one member of a college could be checked by his colleagues. On the other hand, the lengthy deliberations of so many directors often delayed final decisions.

The total picture of Peter's efforts to increase the efficiency of government is one of mixed success at best. Attempts to model Russian local government on Swedish practice broke down because of the enormous difference between the two countries in literacy, size, tradition, and attitude toward civic responsibility. Corruption still continued in high places; savage punishments were inflicted on some of those who were caught, while others, like Menshikov, were apparently immune. And yet the cumbrous machinery that Peter gradually established, hit or miss, to meet the immediate needs of his wars, was superior to any that Russia had previously known.

Other Innovations of Peter the Great

Ever since 1703, Peter had been building a great city in the swamps he had seized from the Swedes. Thousands of men died in the effort to drain the marshes and create a seaport and a capital worthy of its imperial resident. Remote from the rest of Russia, St. Petersburg was frightfully expensive, because all food and building materials had to be transported great distances. It was also dangerous. When floods poured through the streets, Peter roared with laughter at the sight of furniture and household effects floating away. Wolves prowled the broad new boulevards and devoured a lady in front of Prince Menshikov's own house one fine day in June. But Peter made St. Petersburg his capital and commanded all members of the nobility to make it their home. Although palaces sprang up at the Tsar's command, the nobles complained bitterly about abandoning their beloved Moscow for this uncomfortable and costly town. Thus St. Petersburg became the symbol of Peter's war against his own gentry.

Peter also determined to disarm all possible future threats to his power from the Church. Knowing how the clergy loathed the new régime he was trying to impose, he simply failed to appoint a successor when the Patriarch of Moscow died in 1700. Eventually, in 1721, he extended the collegiate system of administration to the Church itself. He put it under an agency first called the "spiritual college," and later the Holy Directing Synod, headed by a Procurator who was a layman. Thus the Church became more than ever a department of state. Peter's own statement of his purpose is remarkably frank:

> From the collegiate government of the church there is not so much danger to the country of disturbances and troubles as may be produced by one spiritual ruler. For the common people do not understand the difference between the spiritual power and that of the autocrat; but, dazzled by the splendor and glory of the highest pastor, they think that he is a second sovereign of like power with the autocrat or with even more, and that the spiritual power is that of another and better realm. If then there should be any difference of opinion between the Patriarch and the Tsar, it might easily happen that the people, perhaps misled by designing persons, should take the part of the Patriarch, in the mistaken belief that they were fighting for God's cause.*

The educational advances of the period reflected Peter's technological and military interests. Naval, military, and artillery academies were established to educate future officers and also many civil servants. When the government tried to institute compulsory education by requiring the establishment of two schools in each province, it stressed mathematics and navigation, and the attempt failed. Part of the

*Quoted by E. Schuyler, *Peter the Great* (New York, 1884), II, 389.

difficulty came from the reluctance of parents to see their children "waste time" in school, and part from the government's inexperience and its unwillingness to begin with primary education. Primary education was left to the church schools, which were few and not very competent. At all levels, foreigners had to be summoned to provide Russia with scholars. An Academy of Sciences founded just before Peter's death began with seventeen imported fellows, and eight students, also imported. Probably the mere presence in the new capital of these exotic academies helped to stimulate the native intellectual developments that would characterize the next generation. Such tokens as the first Russian newspaper (1703) and the printing of occasional textbooks also augured well for the future.

Peter continued the practice, begun long before him, of importing foreign technicians and artisans to practice their crafts and teach them to Russians. Quite aware of the mercantilist ideas of the age, he offered such inducements as freedom from taxation and from government service, and all sorts of tariff protection, to develop manufacturing. Though sometimes employing a substantial number of laborers, industrial enterprise in Russia, chiefly textiles and iron, continued to be backward. The labor force was recruited among unwilling and badly treated serfs and criminals. Factory-owners were permitted to buy and sell serfs (otherwise a privilege restricted to the gentry), provided they were always bought or sold as a body together with the factory itself. This "possessional" industrial serfdom hardly provided much incentive for good work, and Russian produce continued inferior to comparable goods manufactured abroad. In the commercial field, Peter's heavy protective tariffs discriminated against foreign goods, encouraging smuggling and false registration of foreign agents as Russian nationals. The effort to make Russia a manufacturing nation exporting its own produce was a failure. But Peter's conquests in the Baltic did give Russia the great port of Riga, and he successfully bent every effort to make St. Petersburg into a great trading center.

Peter the Great: A Final Evaluation

The records of Peter's secret police are full of the complaints his agents heard as they moved about listening for subversive remarks. The wives and children of the peasantry found themselves deserted by their men, who were snatched away to fight on distant battlefields or to labor in the swamps to build a city that nobody but Peter wanted. The number of serfs increased with the imposition of the new soul-tax and the multiplication of land grants to service men. The tax burden was back-breaking. Service men found themselves in a kind of bondage of their own, condemned to work for the Tsar during the whole of their lives and seldom able to visit their estates. Nobles of ancient birth found themselves treated no differently from the upstarts who were flooding into their class from below. Churchmen of the conservative school were more and more convinced that Peter was the Antichrist himself, as they beheld the increase of foreigners in high places and saw the many innovations imported into the government and social life from the hated West. Rumors circulated that this was not the true Tsar at all, but a changeling somehow substituted for the real Peter by foreigners during the trip abroad, and sent back to persecute Russians and to ruin Russia.

Among the lower orders of society resistance took the usual form: peasant uprisings, punished with fantastic brutality. The usual allies of the peasant rebels, the Cossacks, suffered mass executions and sharp curtailment of their traditional independence. The leaders of the noble and clerical opposition focused their hopes on Peter's son by his first wife, the young heir to the throne, Alexis, who, they believed, would stop the expensive and (they felt) needless foreign wars, and move back to Moscow and comfortable Russian conservatism. Alexis, an alcoholic, was afraid of his father and was early estranged from him. Though not stable enough to lead a true conspiracy against Peter, he fanned the hopes of the opposition by letting them know he shared their views. Eventually he caused a scandal by fleeing abroad and asking asylum from his brother-in-law, the Austrian Emperor Charles

Peter I striding along the dikes during the building of St. Petersburg; a painting by V. A. Serov.

VI. Promising him fair treatment and forgiveness, Peter lured Alexis back to Russia and made him the show-piece of one of those horrible Russian investigations of nonexistent plots. Many were tortured, killed, and exiled; Alexis himself was tortured to death in his father's presence.

In the early nineteenth century, when the first self-conscious group of Russian intellectuals developed a keen interest in the past history of their country, they made a central figure of Peter. He had, they felt, intensified western influences on Russian society and had thus turned his back on Russia's peculiarly Slavic character and her Byzantine heritage. One group hailed these actions as necessary to put Russia on her proper course. Its opponents damned Peter for having forced an unnatural development upon his country, and for having warped its social and political life by imposing an alien pattern. But both his friends and enemies among these later intellectuals believed, as most scholars have since argued, that what he did was drastic and revolutionary.

Yet we can see that Peter simply intensified the chief characteristics of Russian society. He made a strong autocracy even stronger, a universal service law for service men even more stringent, a serf more of a serf. His trip abroad, his fondness for foreign ways, his worship of advanced technology, his mercantilism, his wars, all had their precedents in the period of his forerunners. The Church, which he attacked, had already been weakened by the schism of the Old Believers, itself the result of western influences. Where Peter was radical was in the field of everyday manners and behavior. The attack on the beards, the dress, the calendar (he adopted the western dating from the birth of Christ and abandoned the traditional dating from a hypothetical year of the Creation), his hatred of ceremony and fondness for manual labor—these things were indeed new. So too were the vigor and passion with which he acted. They were decisive in winning a revolutionary reputation for a monarch who in the major aspects of his reign was carrying out policies long since established.

Poland and Turkey

By the early eighteenth century, Russia was the only great power in eastern Europe. Poland and the Ottoman Empire still bulked large on the map, but their territories included lands they were soon to lose. Both states suffered from incompetent government, from a backward economy, and from the presence of large national and religious minorities. The Orthodox in Catholic Poland and Moslem Turkey were beginning to look to Russia for protection. In addition, the evident decay of both states stimulated the aggressive appetites of their stronger neighbors. Poland, consequently, was doomed to disappear as an independent power before the end of the century, the victim of partition by Russia, Austria, and Prussia. Turkey held on, but only just, and was already beginning to acquire the perilous reputation of being the "Sick Man of Europe."

The Polish government was a political curiosity shop. The monarchy was elective; each time the throne fell vacant, the Diet chose a successor, usually the candidate who had offered the biggest bribes, and sometimes a foreigner. Once elected, the king was nearly powerless, since he was obliged to transfer the royal prerogatives to the Diet when he accepted the crown. The Diet was dominated by the nobility and was celebrated for its *liberum veto*, whereby any one of its members could block any proposal by shouting "I do not wish it!" and then galloping off before his colleagues could catch up with him to make him change his mind. The Diet was not a parliament in the western sense of the term, but an assembly of aristocrats, each of whom thought of himself as a power unto himself; unanimity was therefore necessary for all decisions. This loosely knit Polish national state had no regular army or diplomatic corps or central bureaucracy. Unlike the English gentry or Prussian Junkers, the dominant nobles had no concept of service to the Crown or indeed any sense of loyalty except to their own social class. They helped destroy a once-flourishing urban middle class by persecuting Jewish shopkeepers and foreign merchants. On their estates, the lot of the serfs was harsher than it was in Russia.

Compared with Poland, the Ottoman Empire was still a functioning state, yet it was falling farther and farther behind the major European powers, particularly in economics and technology. It had no Peter the Great to attack traditional ways; with few exceptions, the sultans of the eighteenth century were captives of harem intrigue and could do little to discipline such powerful groups as the Janissaries, who exploited their privileges and neglected their soldierly duties. This retrograde and corrupt government did at least govern, however, and showed considerable staying power in war. So the "Sick Man" was to linger on throughout the century, kept alive in part by the still unexhausted Ottoman reserves of vitality, and in part by the rivalry between the two would-be heirs of the Turkish inheritance, Russia and Austria.

V   War and Diplomacy, 1713 – 1789

Main Characteristics

From the survey just concluded of the European states in the early eighteenth century, it is evident that the international balance was both fluid and precarious. Should the strong states decide to prey upon the weak, the balance was certain to be upset. One such upset resulted from the Great Northern War, which enabled Russia to replace Sweden as the dominant power in the Baltic. The expansion of Russia continued to threaten the balance during most of the eighteenth century; the chief victims, in addition to Sweden, were Poland and Turkey. A second major threat to the balance came from the expansion of Prussia at the expense of Austria, Poland, and Sweden. A third involved the colonial and commercial rivalry between Britain and the Bourbon monarchies of France and Spain.

These were not the only international issues of the day. The old competition between Austria and France, which dated back to the Habsburg-Valois wars of the 1500's, remained very lively. It was complicated by the already noted ambitions of Elizabeth Farnese, second wife of Philip V of Spain, who won the support of France and threatened the Austrian hegemony in Italy. The Austrian Habsburgs themselves were vigorous expansionists, aiming to drive the Turks from the Danube and extend their own domains southeast to the Black Sea.

While the interplay of all these rivalries led to frequent shifts in the international balance, the idea that there should be a balance of power was generally maintained. Indeed, eighteenth-century war and diplomacy are often cited as the classic case history of balance-of-power politics in operation. The limited financial resources of the governments of the Old Régime allowed only limited warfare; nobody could as yet afford the enormous armies or navies required for total war. On the battlefield, generals were reluctant to risk losing soldiers who represented a costly investment in training; they favored sieges and other formal maneuvers executed according to conventions well understood by all belligerents. At the peace table, diplomats were reluctant to destroy an opponent; according to another well-understood convention, they generally sought to award him a bit of territory or a minor throne as compensation for a greater loss. Like "total war," "unconditional surrender" was not an eighteenth-century concept.

The manner in which the century conducted war and diplomacy has often been likened to an elaborate game. It was a serious and sometimes a bloody game, but it was governed by extensive rules generally observed by the players and designed to minimize their losses and to keep any of them from being eliminated entirely from the play. The principal players —the monarchs, diplomats, generals, admirals —were for the most part aristocrats, who accepted a uniform code of behavior. Whatever their nationality, they usually understood and respected one another far more than they understood or respected the lower social classes in their own countries.

These generalizations, we shall find, did not always apply in practice. A few of the most successful players—notably Frederick the Great of Prussia and Pitt of England—did not always play the game according to the rules. And the custom of compensation was forgotten in the case of Poland, when it was partitioned out of existence late in the century. Earlier in the century, however, Poland, along with Turkey, provided a most instructive exhibit of the balance-of-power game in operation.

The Turkish and Polish Questions, 1716–1739

The Ottoman Empire suffered heavy losses in the Austro-Turkish War of 1716–1718. By the Treaty of Passarowitz (1718), the Habsburg Emperor, Charles VI, recovered the portion of Hungary still under Ottoman rule and secured other Danubian lands that form part of present-day Rumania and Yugoslavia. A second Turkish war, 1735–1739, reversed the outcome of the first and disclosed the growing infirmity of the Habsburg army. In this second war Austria was allied with Russia, but, in a fashion foreshadowing the later struggles of the two powers for control of the Balkans, they fell to quarreling over division of the prospective spoils. In the end there was little to divide, and Charles VI had to hand back to Turkey the Danubian lands annexed at Passarowitz. During the negotiations leading to the Austro-Turkish settlement of 1739, France gave the Ottoman Empire powerful support in order to redress the balance of power. This was one of many occasions on

which the French used their Turkish alliance to check Habsburg expansion.

Meantime, in the early 1730's, Bourbon and Habsburg were ranged on opposing sides in a crisis over the crown of Poland. In the early stages of the Great Northern War, as we have seen, Charles XII of Sweden had unseated the Polish king, the Saxon Augustus the Strong, and had given the crown to a Polish nobleman, Stanislas Leszczynski; then, thanks to the support of Peter the Great, Augustus recovered the Polish throne. Stanislas, however, had by no means completed his historical role, for he eventually gave his daughter, Marie, in marriage to Louis XV of France. When Augustus the Strong died in 1733, French diplomats engineered the election of Stanislas to succeed him. But both Austria and Russia disliked the prospect of a French puppet on the Polish throne, and Russia sent 30,000 troops into Poland and convoked a rump session of the Diet which elected a rival king, Augustus III, son of Augustus the Strong. The stage was set for the War of the Polish Succession, 1733–1735—Stanislas, France, and Spain versus Augustus III, Russia, and Austria.

After French and Austrian armies had fired away at each other for a while in the Rhine Valley and in northern Italy, hundreds of miles from Poland, the diplomats worked out a compromise settlement. To the satisfaction of Austria and Russia, Augustus III secured the Polish throne. From the French standpoint, Stanislas Leszczynski was well compensated for his loss. He acquired the duchy of Lorraine, on the northeastern border of France, with the provision that when he died Lorraine would go to his daughter, Marie, and thence to the French crown. France would thus move one step closer toward filling out her "natural" frontiers. To be sure, Lorraine already had a duke, Francis, husband of the Habsburg heiress, Maria Theresa, who moved to the Italian Grand Duchy of Tuscany, where the old line of rulers conveniently died out in 1737. Finally, as a by-product of the settlement, Elizabeth Farnese of Spain capped twenty years of maternal perseverance by procuring the Kingdom of Naples for "Baby

Carlos," her elder and now grown-up son.

The War of the Polish Succession may well seem futile and trivial, much ado about a kingship possessing no real power. And the postwar settlement, which affected chiefly Italy and Lorraine, may seem to be a striking case of diplomatic irrelevance. Yet the whole Polish crisis neatly illustrates the workings of dynastic politics and the balance of power. Certainly no great national issues were at stake, except for the rather nebulous ones of French, Russian, and Austrian prestige. The statesmen regarded thrones as the pawns of diplomacy, to be assigned without reference to the wishes of the populations involved. No politician of the Old Régime would have contemplated canvassing Neapolitan sentiment on Carlos or holding a referendum to see whether the Poles preferred Stanislas or Augustus.

The complicated arrangements of the 1730's preserved the balance of power by giving something to almost everybody involved. Although the diplomats could not prevent a little war over Poland, they did keep it from becoming a big one. The achievement showed the old international system at its best. Throughout the period from 1713 to 1739 the force of diplomacy operated to avert or at least to localize wars. Britain and France took the lead in the campaign to keep any one power from upsetting the international apple-cart. For example, the British sent a squadron to the Baltic during the last part of the Great Northern War so that Tsar Peter's gains would not be too great. To prevent the dismemberment of Ottoman territories in Europe, Britain intervened in the negotiations between Turkey and Austria at Passarowitz in 1718, and the French revived their Ottoman alliance in the 1730's.

The War of Jenkins' Ear

The diplomatic partnership of Britain and France in the 1720's and 1730's reflected the basic policies of Walpole and Fleury, both of whom sought stability abroad to promote economic recovery at home. The partnership, however, collapsed in the face of the competi-tion between the two Atlantic powers for commerce and empire. Neither Walpole nor Fleury could prevent the world-wide war between Britain and the Bourbon monarchies that broke out in 1739 and that lasted, with many intervals of peace, until the final defeat of Napoleon in 1815. This "Second Hundred Years' War" had, in fact, already begun half a century before 1739, in the days of Louis XIV. The Utrecht settlement of 1713 had not fully settled the rivalry between Britain and France (and France's Bourbon partner, Spain). Thus the war of 1739 was as much the renewal of an old struggle as the onset of a new one.

The specific issue behind the crisis of 1739 was the comparatively minor question of British chagrin at the disappointing results of the Asiento privilege. As the South Sea Company discovered, the Asiento gave Britain little more than a token share in the trade of the Spanish American colonies (see p. 7). What British captains could not get legiti-mately they got by smuggling. Spain retaliated by establishing a coast-guard patrol in Ameri-can waters to ward off smugglers. British merchants complained of the rough treatment handed out by the Spanish guards, and in 1738 they exhibited to Parliament Captain Jenkins, who claimed that Spanish brutality had cost him an ear, which he duly produced, preserved in salt and cotton batting. Asked to state his reaction on losing the ear, he replied, "I commended my soul to God and my cause to my country." Walpole retorted that the protec-tion of British smugglers against legitimate Spanish patrols did not give the government a very strong case. But Walpole could restrain neither the anti-Spanish fever sweeping the country to which Jenkins had commended his cause, nor the bellicose faction of "Boy Pa-triots" that had arisen within Walpole's own Whig party.

In October, 1739, to the joyful pealing of church bells, Britain began the War of Jenkins' Ear against Spain. "They are ringing their bells now," Walpole observed tartly. "They will be wringing their hands soon." As if to vindicate his prophecy, the British fleet lost the opening campaign in the Caribbean, and France showed every sign of coming to Spain's assistance. Dynastic ties had already brought the two Bourbon monarchies into alliance during the Polish war; now French economic interests were at stake, for France supplied the bulk of the wares which Spanish galleons carried to America, and which cheaper British contraband was driving out of the Spanish colonial market.

The War of the Austrian Succession, 1740–1748

In 1740, a chain of events linked the colonial war to a great continental conflict, the War of the Austrian Succession. On the death of the Emperor Charles VI in 1740, the Habsburg domains passed to his daughter, Maria Theresa, who was only twenty-three years old. Expecting to outwit Maria Theresa because of her youth, her sex, and her political inexperience, the German princes ignored the Pragmatic Sanction guaranteeing her succession and looked forward to the possible partition of the Habsburg lands. In addition, the Elector of Bavaria, a cousin of the Habsburgs, hoped to become Holy Roman Emperor, defeating Maria Theresa's candidate, her own husband, Francis of Lorraine and Tuscany. The first of the German princes to strike, however, was Frederick the Great (1740–1786), who had just inherited the Prussian throne from Frederick William I. In December, 1740, Frederick suddenly invaded Silesia, a Habsburg province located in the upper Oder valley to the southeast of Brandenburg. Though Frederick advanced a flimsy family claim to Silesia, Europe generally regarded his invasion as an act of simple aggression.

In the ensuing War of the Austrian Succession, England and Austria were ranged against France, Spain, Prussia, and Bavaria. Frederick won an emphatic victory in the campaigns on the Continent. The Prussian army astounded Europe by its long night marches, sudden flank attacks, and other tactics of surprise quite different from the usual deliberate warfare of sieges. Frederick, however, deeply antagonized his allies by repeatedly deserting them to make secret peace

arrangements with Austria. And he did little to support the imperial aspirations of the Bavarian Elector, who enjoyed only a brief tenure as "Emperor Charles VII."

The Anglo-Austrian alliance worked no better than the Franco-Prussian one. Many Englishmen felt that George II was betraying their true interests overseas by entangling them in German politics and the defense of Hanover. Nevertheless, the British preference for the Hanoverians over the Stuarts was evident when "Bonnie Prince Charles," the grandson of the deposed James II, secured French backing and landed in Britain (1745). He won significant recruits only among the chronically discontented Scottish highlanders, and in 1746 he was thoroughly defeated at Culloden. Jacobitism, never a very important political threat, was dead.

Outside Europe, the fighting of the 1740's was quite indecisive. The New England colonists took Louisburg, the French naval base on Cape Breton Island commanding the approach to the St. Lawrence. On the other side of the world, the French took the port of Madras from the English East India Company. The Treaty of Aix-la-Chapelle (1748) restored both Louisburg and Madras to their former owners, and Britain later agreed to give up the troublesome Asiento privilege. In Central Europe, on the other hand, the war was a decisive step in the rise of Prussia to the first rank of powers. The new province of Silesia brought not only a large increase in the Prussian population but also an important textile industry and large deposits of coal and iron. Maria Theresa got scant compensation for the loss of Silesia. Although her husband, Francis, won recognition as Holy Roman Emperor, she had to surrender Parma and some other territorial crumbs in northern Italy to Philip, the second son of Elizabeth Farnese.

The Uneasy Peace, 1748–1756

The peace made in 1748 lasted only eight years. Then another and greater conflict, the Seven Years' War of 1756–1763, broke out, caused partly by old issues left unsettled at

The Battle of Culloden, 1746, showing the rigid battle formations used in the eighteenth century.

Aix-la-Chapelle and partly by new grievances arising from the War of the Austrian Succession. The world struggle between Britain and the Bourbons kept right on in the undeclared warfare waged during the years of nominal peace after 1748. In Asia, the English and French East India companies fought each other once removed, so to speak, by taking sides in the rivalries of native princes in southern India. By 1751, the energetic French administrator, Dupleix, had won the initial round of this indirect fight. Then the English, led by the equally energetic Clive, seized the initiative, and in 1754 Dupleix was called back home by the directors of the French company, who were unwilling to back his aggressive policy. In North America, English colonists from the Atlantic seaboard had already staked out claims to the rich wilderness between the Appalachians and the Mississippi. But the French, equally intent

on appropriating the area, stole a march on them and established a string of forts in western Pennsylvania from Presqu'Isle (later Erie) south to Fort Duquesne (later Pittsburgh). In 1754, a force of Virginians under the youthful George Washington tried unsuccessfully to dislodge the French from Fort Duquesne.

In Europe, the dramatic shift of alliances called the Diplomatic Revolution immediately preceded the outbreak of the Seven Years' War. In the new war the fundamental antagonisms were the same as in the old — Britain versus France, Prussia versus Austria — but the powers reversed their alliances. Britain, which had joined Austria *against* Prussia in the 1740's, now paired off *with* Frederick the Great. And, in the most revolutionary move of the Diplomatic Revolution, France, which had sided *with* Frederick before, not only stood *against* him but also joined *with* her hereditary

35

enemy, Habsburg Austria. The Diplomatic Revolution reflected the resentment of the powers at the disloyal behavior of their old partners in the War of the Austrian Succession. The French had bitter memories of Frederick's repeated desertions and secret peace arrangements. Britain deplored Austrian reluctance to defend English continental interests, which included maintaining the territorial integrity of Hanover and excluding the French from the Austrian Netherlands. Austria, in turn, regarded Hanover and Belgium as peripheral to her main concern, the recovery of Silesia.

In 1755, the British almost unwittingly touched off the Diplomatic Revolution. In order to enlist a second power in the task of defending Hanover, they concluded a treaty with Russia, which had taken a minor part in the War of the Austrian Succession as an ally of England. The Anglo-Russian treaty alarmed Frederick the Great, who feared an eventual conflict between Prussia and Russia for control of the Baltic and Poland. In January, 1756, the Prussian king concluded an alliance with Britain which detached her from Russia. The alliance between England and Prussia isolated France and gave the Austrian chancellor, Kaunitz, the opportunity he had been waiting for. What Austria needed in order to avenge herself on Frederick and to regain Silesia was an ally with a large army; what Austria needed was the alliance of France, not Britain. Using the Anglo-Prussian alliance as an argument, Kaunitz convinced Louis XV and his mistress, Madame de Pompadour, to drop the traditional Bourbon-Habsburg feud in favor of a working partnership. The last act of the Diplomatic Revolution occurred when Russia joined the Franco-Austrian alliance. The Russian Empress Elizabeth (1741–1762) hated Frederick the Great and feared his aggression all the more now that he had deprived her of her English ally.

The Seven Years' War, 1756–1763

The new war, like its predecessor, was really two separate wars—one continental, the other naval and colonial. In the European campaigns of the Seven Years' War, Frederick the Great faced a formidable test. Prussia confronted the forces of Austria, France, and Russia, whose combined population was more than fifteen times larger than her own. She had almost no allies except for Britain, which supplied financial subsidies but little actual military assistance. The Spartan traditions of the Hohenzollerns enabled Prussia to survive. The King himself set the example; in 1757, he wrote to one of his French friends:

I am assaulted from every side. Domestic trials, secret afflictions, public misfortunes, approaching calamities—such is my daily bread. But do not imagine I am weakening. If everything collapses I should calmly bury myself beneath the ruins. In these disastrous times one must fortify oneself with iron resolutions and a heart of brass. It is a time for stoicism: the disciples of Epicurus would find nothing to say. . . .*

Frederick's "iron resolution" and "heart of brass" led him to adopt any expedient to gain his ends. To fill up the depleted ranks of his army, he violated international law by impressing soldiers from Prussia's smaller neighbors, Mecklenburg and Saxony. Since British subsidies covered only a fraction of his war expenses, he seized Saxon, Polish, and Russian coins, melted them down, and kept for Prussian use a large part of their precious metallic content.

A final factor in saving Prussia, perhaps the most important one of all, was the shakiness of the apparently formidable coalition arrayed against her. Most fortunately for Frederick, his enemies were never capable of exploiting their military successes to deliver a knockout blow. Russia's generals were timid, and those of France and Austria were sometimes downright incompetent. Moreover, the French, the strongest of the allies, had to fight a two-front war, in Europe and overseas, but did not have the financial resources to do both. The grand alliance created by Kaunitz suffered to an unusual extent from the frictions, mistrust, and cross-purposes that customarily beset war-

*Quoted in G. P. Gooch, *Frederick the Great* (London, 1947), 41.

time coalitions. Indeed, the coalition did not last out the war. When Elizabeth of Russia died in January, 1762, she was succeeded by Tsar Peter III, a passionate admirer of Frederick the Great, who at once deserted Elizabeth's allies and placed Russia's forces at Frederick's disposal. Although he occupied the Russian throne for only a few months (see Chapter 17), Peter's brief rule marked a decisive turning in the Seven Years' War. In 1763 Prussia won her war, and Austria agreed to the Peace of Huber-

Fredrick the Great, after the Seven Years' War.

tusburg confirming the Hohenzollern retention of Silesia.

Meanwhile, Frederick's British partner was gaining a smashing victory abroad. During the first year and a half of the fighting, the British suffered setbacks on almost every front. At sea, they lost the important Mediterranean base of Minorca in the Balearic Islands, a disaster to which the home government contributed by sending (too late) reinforcements (too few) under Admiral Byng (a poor choice).

Byng was unfairly saddled with the whole blame and was executed — "in order to encourage the others," Voltaire observed ironically. In North America, the British lost the outpost of Oswego on Lake Ontario and fumbled an attack on Louisburg, the key to French Canada. The most dramatic of Britain's misfortunes occurred in India. In June, 1756, the Nawab of Bengal, a native ally of the French, crowded 146 British prisoners into one small room with only two windows. The result was the atrocious "Black Hole" of Calcutta, thus described by an officer of the English East India Company:

It was the hottest season of the year, and the night uncommonly sultry. . . . The excessive pressure of their bodies against one another, and the intolerable heat which prevailed as soon as the door was shut, convinced the prisoners that it was impossible to live through the night in this horrible confinement; and violent attempts were immediately made to force the door, but without effect for it opened inward.

At two o'clock not more than fifty remained alive. But even this number were too many to partake of the saving air, the contest for which and for life continued until the morn. . . .

An officer, sent by the nawab, came . . . with an order to open the prison. The dead were so thronged, and the survivors had so little strength remaining, that they were employed near half an hour in removing the bodies which lay against the door before they could clear a passage to go out one at a time; when of one hundred and forty-six who went in no more than twenty-three came out alive. . . .*

William Pitt turned the tide in favor of Britain. This famous representative of the Whig oligarchy sat in Parliament for Old Sarum, a notorious "rotten" borough. The grandson of "Diamond" Pitt, a merchant prince who had made a fortune in India, he consistently supported the interests of the City. In the late 1730's he had led the Whig rebels, the "Boy Patriots" who forced Britain into the War of Jenkins' Ear, against Walpole's pacifistic policy. Now Pitt's great war ministry (1757–1761) at last ended the shilly-shallying policies of the cabinets that had held office since Wal-

*R. Orme, *A History of the Transactions of the British Nation in Indostan* (London, 1778), II, sec. 1, 74 ff.

pole's downfall in 1742. When deficits rose higher and higher, Pitt used his personal and business connections with the City to assist the successful placement of government loans. He strengthened the Anglo-Prussian alliance by sending Frederick substantial subsidies and placing English forces in Hanover under an able Prussian commander in place of the bungling Duke of Cumberland, a son of George II. Everywhere Pitt replaced blundering generals and admirals; everywhere his energetic measures transformed the character of the naval and colonial war. In 1759, the Royal Navy de-

North America and the Caribbean, 1763
Situation after the Seven Years' War

British Territory:
- Held before 1763
- Acquired from France
- Acquired from Spain
- —— Proclamation Line of 1763

feated both the Atlantic and Mediterranean squadrons of the French fleet.

Britain's command of the seas enabled her to continue trading abroad at a prosperous pace, while French overseas trade rapidly sank to one-sixth of the pre-war rate. Cut off from supplies and reinforcements from home and faced by generally superior British forces, the French colonies fell in quick succession. In Africa, Britain's capture of the chief French slaving station ruined the slavers of Nantes in the mother country. In India, Clive and others avenged the "Black Hole" by punishing the Nawab of Bengal and capturing the key French posts. In the West Indies, the French lost all their sugar islands, except for Santo Domingo. In North America, the 65,000 French, poorly supplied and poorly led, were helpless against the million British colonists, fully supported by their mother country. Fort Duquesne was taken at last, and renamed after Pitt, and the British went on to other triumphs in the war that the colonists called "French and Indian." In Canada, the English General Wolfe took Louisburg (1758) and in the next year, 1759, lost his life but won immortal fame in a great victory on the Plains of Abraham outside Quebec. When the remaining French stronghold, Montreal, fell in 1760, the doom of France's American empire was sealed.

This rain of victories led the British to expect sweeping gains in the postwar settlement; their expectation was soon disappointed. Pitt had won the war, but he did not make the peace: the accession of the obstinate and ambitious George III in 1760 led to the dismissal of the Prime Minister the next year. In the Peace of Paris, 1763, the successors of Pitt allowed the French to recover their islands in the West Indies, then highly prized as a major source of sugar. British planters in the Caribbean were much relieved, for their markets had been flooded by sugar from captured French islands during the war. But to outraged patriots it seemed as though Britain had let the grand prize slip through her fingers.

France, however, lost all her possessions on the mainland of North America. Britain secured both Canada and the vast disputed territories between the Appalachians and the

Mississippi. Moreover, she also obtained Florida from Spain, which had joined France in 1762 when the war was already lost. And, though the French were permitted to retain a few trading posts in India, they were not allowed to fortify them or to continue their old policy of manipulating the politics and rivalries of native states. For Britain, the Seven Years' War marked the beginning of a virtually complete ascendancy in India; for France it marked the virtual end of her "old Empire."

The International Balance in Review

The peace settlements of Hubertusburg and Paris ended the greatest international crisis that was to occur between the death of Louis XIV and the outbreak of the French Revolution. New crises were to arise soon after 1763, as the next chapter will show in detail—in 1768, a Russo-Turkish war (which Russia won); in 1772, the first partition of Poland; in 1775, the American War of Independence. The new crises in the East did not fundamentally alter the international balance; they accentuated shifts that had long been underway. And, although American independence cost Britain the thirteen colonies, the maritime and imperial supremacy she had gained in 1763 was not otherwise seriously affected.

The international balance established in 1763, then, remained largely unchanged down to 1789. In the incessant struggle for power during the eighteenth century, the victorious states were the strongest states—Britain, Prussia, and Russia. The states that were less fit—France, Spain, Austria, Turkey—survived, though they sometimes suffered serious losses. The weakest units, Poland and Italy—as a Spanish diplomat observed early in the century —were being "pared and sliced up like so many Dutch cheeses."

The Duke of Choiseul, the foreign minister of Louis XV during the Seven Years' War, remarked that the "true balance of power resides in commerce." Choiseul's remark held a large measure of truth, but not the whole truth. The world struggle between Britain and the Bourbon empires did much to justify the mercantilist view that conceived of international relations in terms of incessant competition and strife. According to the mercantilist doctrine of the fixed amount of trade, a state could enlarge its share of the existing supply only if it reduced the shares held by rival states, either through war or, in time of peace, through smuggling and retaliatory legislation. All this was borne out by the War of Jenkins' Ear and by British success, and French failure, in maintaining overseas trade during the course of the Seven Years' War. Yet the modern concept of economic warfare was only beginning to take shape. During the War of the Austrian Succession, London brokers supplied both insurance and information on naval movements to French shipowners.

Moreover, economic factors did not wholly explain all the changes in the international balance during the century. For example, efficient utilization of Prussian resources played its part in the victories of Frederick the Great. But his success depended still more on qualities that had little to do with economics—his own brilliant and ruthless leadership, and the discipline of the society that he headed. The case of Britain seemingly offers the most compelling evidence to support Choiseul's contention, as Pitt turned her formidable financial and commercial assets to practical advantage. Yet Pitt himself is not to be explained in simple economic terms. His accession as prime minister in the dark days of 1757, like that of Churchill in the dark days of 1940, was made possible by a political system that enabled the right man to come forward at the right time.

Finally, the eighteenth century, despite its wars, was an interlude of comparative calm between the age of religious strife that had preceded it and the storms of liberalism and nationalism that were to be loosed by the French Revolution. The prospect in 1715, the prospect of long years of peace and quiet, had not, after all, been wholly deceptive. The Seven Years' War of the eighteenth century, for example, did not begin to equal in destructive force the Thirty Years' War of the seventeenth. Much more was involved here than the relative shortness of the Seven Years' War. Few of the combatants had the feeling of fighting for a great cause, like Catholicism or Protestantism or national independence. The fighting itself was conducted in a more orderly fashion than it had been a hundred years before; soldiers were better disciplined, and armies were better supplied; troops lived off the land less often and no longer constituted such a menace to the lives and property of civilians. Even warfare indicated that this was the century of order and reason, the Age of the Enlightenment.

Reading Suggestions on the Old Régime and the International Balance

(*Asterisk indicates paperbound edition.)

General Accounts

The following volumes in the series, "The Rise of Modern Europe," (*Torch) provide a detailed introduction to eighteenth-century war and politics and have extensive and up-to-date bibliographies: P. Roberts, *The Quest for Security, 1715–1740*; W. L. Dorn, *Competition for Empire, 1740–1763*; and L. Gershoy, *From Despotism to Revolution, 1763–1789*.

M. S. Anderson, *Europe in the Eighteenth Century 1713–1783* (Holt, Rinehart & Winston, 1961). A very good introductory volume by a British scholar.

R. J. White, *Europe in the Eighteenth Century* (*St. Martin's). Another good introduction, at a less advanced level, by a British scholar.

The New Cambridge Modern History, Vol. VII: "The Old Regime, 1713–1763" and Vol. VIII, "The American and French Revolutions 1763–1793" (Cambridge Univ. Press, 1957, 1965). Wide-ranging essays by specialists; useful mainly for interpretations and reference.

Economics
and
Society

E. F. Heckscher, *Mercantilism*, 2 vols., rev. ed. (Macmillan, 1955). A famous and controversial work; a mine of information on eighteenth-century economic developments.

T. S. Ashton, *The Industrial Revolution, 1760–1830* (*Galaxy). Clear and informative introduction.

P. Mantoux, *The Industrial Revolution in the Eighteenth Century* (*Torch). Scholarly study of the factory system in England.

J. Carswell, *The South Sea Bubble* (Stanford Univ. Press, 1960). Excellent monograph.

A. Goodwin, ed., *The European Nobility in the Eighteenth Century* (Black, 1953). Very helpful essays arranged country by country.

D. Ogg, *Europe of the Ancien Régime* (*Torch). A social study, focused on Britain.

The Western
Powers

W. E. H. Lecky, *A History of England in the Eighteenth Century*, 8 vols. (Longmans, Green, 1883–1890). A celebrated detailed study.

B. Williams, *The Whig Supremacy, 1714–1760,* 2nd. ed., rev. by C. H. Stuart (Clarendon, 1962). A competent modern survey.

J. H. Plumb, *England in the Eighteenth Century* (*Penguin). A good brief account by an expert. Plumb has written several other studies of the period, notably *Sir Robert Walpole,* Vol. I, "The Making of a Statesman" (Houghton, Mifflin, 1956); *The First Four Georges* (Macmillan, 1957); and *Chatham* (Macmillan, 1953), an account of the elder Pitt.

C. G. Robertson, *Chatham and the British Empire* (*Collier). Brief, popular introduction to the achievements of the elder Pitt.

L. Kronenberger, *Kings and Desperate Men* (*Vintage). Lively essays on eighteenth-century English society and personalities.

A. Cobban, *A History of Modern France,* Vol. I, 1715–1799 (*Penguin). Good recent general survey by a British scholar.

J. Lough, *An Introduction to Eighteenth-Century France* (Longmans, Green, 1960). Clear and enlightening discussion of the Old Régime.

A. M. Wilson, *French Foreign Policy during the Administration of Cardinal Fleury* (Harvard Univ. Press, 1936). A sound monograph, and one of the relatively few good books in English on the France of Louis XV.

G. P. Gooch, *Louis XV* (Longmans, Green, 1956), and Nancy Mitford, *Madame de Pompadour* (*Pyramid). Entertaining and rather old-fashioned biographical studies.

F. Ford, *Robe and Sword* (*Torch). An instructive study of the French aristocracy in the eighteenth century.

The Eastern Powers

H. Rosenberg, *Bureaucracy, Aristocracy, Autocracy* (*Beacon). A somewhat opinionated analysis of Prussian history, 1660–1815.

S. B. Fay, *The Rise of Brandenburg-Prussia to 1786,* rev. by K. Epstein (*Holt). A lucid little volume, packed with information.

F. L. Carsten, *The Origins of Prussia* (Clarendon, 1954). A monograph that carries the story through the reign of the Great Elector.

F. Schevill, *The Great Elector* (Univ. of Chicago Press, 1947). A helpful study of the founder of the Hohenzollern despotism.

R. R. Ergang, *The Potsdam Führer* (Columbia Univ. Press, 1941). A splendid study of Frederick William I of Prussia.

E. Schuyler, *Peter the Great,* 2 vols. (Scribner's, 1884). An old but excellent account by an American diplomat and scholar.

V. Klyuchevsky, *Peter the Great* (*Vintage). Translation of a famous account by a pre-revolutionary Russian scholar.

B. H. Sumner, *Peter the Great and the Emergence of Russia* (*Collier). A very good introductory account.

The International Balance

A. Sorel, *Europe Under the Old Regime* (*Torch). A famous little essay on the eighteenth-century balance by a French expert.

L. Dehio, *The Precarious Balance* (*Vintage). Reflections on the shifts in the balance of power by a German scholar.

J. F. C. Fuller, *A Military History of the Western World,* 3 vols. (Funk and Wagnalls, 1954–1956). The second volume covers the seventeenth and eighteenth centuries.

C. T. Atkinson, *A History of Germany,* 1715–1815 (Methuen, 1908). An older account, particularly full on war and diplomacy.

B. H. Sumner, *Peter the Great & the Ottoman Empire* (Blackwell, 1949). A short and meaty monograph.

H. Dodwell, *Dupleïx and Clive* (Methuen, 1920). A balanced treatment of the imperial antagonists in Italy.

Sources

Arthur Young, *Tours in England and Wales* (London School of Economics and Political Science, 1932). A good selection from the reports of this prolific and perceptive agricultural expert.

Lady Mary W. Montagu, *Letters* (Everyman). Perhaps the best of the century's letter-writers; particularly valuable on the Habsburg and Ottoman empires.

G. P. Gooch, *Courts and Cabinets* (Knopf, 1946). A graceful introduction to the memoirs of some of the great personages of the era.

Historical Fiction

H. Fielding, *Tom Jones* (*several editions). The greatest of social novels on eighteenth-century England.

T. Smollett, *The Adventures of Roderick Random* (*Signet). A novel that provides a good contemporary account of life in His Majesty's Navy two centuries ago.

D. Merezhkovsky, *Peter and Alexis* (Putnam, 1905). Novel, dramatizing the conflict between the great Tsar and his son.

17

The Enlightenment

I Basic Principles and Traits

Reason, natural law, progress — these were key words in the vocabulary of the eighteenth century. It was the Age of the Enlightenment, when the belief became widespread that human reason could cure men of past ills and help them to achieve utopian governments, perpetual peace, and a perfect society. *Reason* would enable men to discover the *natural laws* regulating existence, and the *progress* of the human race would thereby be assured.

The intellectuals who professed this optimistic creed were known by the French name of *philosophes*, though some of them were not French and few of them were philosophers in the strict sense. The *philosophes* were critics, publicists, economists, political scientists, and social reformers. By no means all of them ex-

43

pressed their views in the naïvely simple and cheerful way formulated at the end of the last paragraph. The most famous *philosophe,* Voltaire, in his most famous tale, *Candide,* ridiculed the optimists who thought that all was for the best in the best of all possible worlds. Many intellectuals followed Voltaire in stressing the unreasonable aspects of human behavior and the unnatural character of human institutions. Nevertheless, though many pessimistic cross-currents eddied beneath the gleaming surface of the Enlightenment, the main current of the age was optimistic. Voltaire himself, for all his skepticism, carried on a life-long crusade against the unnatural and the unreasonable. On the whole, the Enlightenment relied on men's capacity to correct the errors of their ways, once they had been pointed out, and to move on to a better and brighter future. A perfect instance was the American Declaration of Independence, which listed "the pursuit of happiness" as a fundamental human right along with life and liberty. The idea that men could pursue happiness and might even attain it was indeed new and revolutionary, a profound departure from the traditional Christian belief that such joy could never be expected on earth.

The Inheritance
from Locke and Newton

The *philosophes* of the eighteenth century derived their basic principles from the men of the preceding "century of genius." Their faith in natural law came from Newton and their confidence in the powers of human reason in part from Descartes, who had deduced a whole philosophy from the fact that he reasoned at all, and still more from Locke. John Locke (1632–1704) wrote a celebrated defense of England's Glorious Revolution, the *Two Treatises of Government* (1690). Men are, he contended in the *Second Treatise,* "by nature all free, equal, and independent"; they submit to government because they find it convenient to do so and not because they acknowledge any divine right on the part of the monarchy. They

make a compact or contract to be governed, which they may break by revolutionary action if the monarch does not live up to his obligations as James II had not lived up to his.

The new psychology that Locke put forward strengthened his case against absolute monarchy. Defenders of political and religious absolutism contended that the inclination to submit to authority was present in men's minds when they were born. In the *Essay concerning Human Understanding* (1690), Locke denied the existence of such innate ideas. He called the new-born mind a *tabula rasa,* a blank slate:

Let us then suppose the mind to be . . . white paper, void of all characters, without any ideas. How comes it to be furnished? . . . To this I answer, in one word, from EXPERIENCE. . . . Our observation employed either about *external sensible objects, or about the internal operations of our minds perceived and reflected on by ourselves, is that which supplies our understandings with all the materials of thinking.* These two are the fountains of knowledge, from whence all the ideas we have, or can naturally have, do spring.*

In other words, the two "fountains of knowledge" were environment, rather than heredity, and reason, rather than faith. Locke's matter-of-fact outlook and his empiricism (reliance on experience) place him among the rationalists. He believed that human reason, though unable to account for everything in the universe, explains all that men need to know. "The candle that is set up in us," he wrote, "shines bright enough for all our purposes."

Locke pointed the way to a critical examination of the Old Régime. The *philosophes* read and admired both his political writings and the *Essay concerning Human Understanding.* They submitted existing social and economic institutions to the judgment of common sense and discovered many to be unreasonable and unnecessarily complex. Locke's psychology suggested to them that teachers might improve human institutions by improving the thinking of the rising generation. The *philosophes* sought what was in effect the right kind of chalk to use on the blank slates of impress-

Essay (New York, 1947), Bk. II, Ch. I.

ionable young minds; their search brought them to accept the view of the universe that has been aptly termed the "Newtonian world machine."

The Enlightenment seized on Newton's discoveries as revelations of ultimate truth. Newton had disclosed the natural force, gravitation, that held the universe together; he made the universe make sense. The *philosophes* believed that comparable laws could be found governing and explaining all phases of human activity. They pictured themselves as the Newtons of statecraft, justice, and economics who would reduce the most intricate institutions to formulas as neat as Sir Isaac's own mathematical laws and principles. The world, they argued, resembled a giant machine. Hitherto, men had hampered its operations because they did not understand the machinery; once they grasped the basic laws by which it ran, the "world-machine" at last would function as it should.

The optimistic implications of this credo were expressed most completely in *The Progress of the Human Mind* (1794) by the *philosophe* Condorcet and written, ironically enough, when he was in hiding as a victim of political persecution during the French revolutionary Reign of Terror. Condorcet asked:

If men can predict, with almost complete assurance, the phenomena whose laws are known to them . . ., why should it be regarded as a vain enterprise to chart, with some degree of probability, the course of the future destiny of mankind by studying the results of human history? Since the only basis of belief in the natural sciences is the idea that the general laws, known or unknown, regulating the phenomena of the universe are regular and constant, why should this principle be any less true for the development of the intellectual and moral faculties of man than for the other operations of nature?*

"Nature has placed no bounds on the perfecting of the human faculties," Condorcet concluded, "and the progress of this perfectibility is limited only by the duration of the globe on which nature has placed us."†

*Condorcet, *Esquisse d'un Tableau Historique des Progrès de l'Esprit Humain* (Paris, n.d.), 203. Our translation.
†*Ibid.,* 5.

Eighteenth-Century Science

The technological and scientific advances of the eighteenth century further buttressed the faith in natural law and progress. The *philosophes* hailed both the improvements in industry and agriculture and the rapid expansion of the pure sciences. Biology and chemistry were now beginning to assume a modern look. Linnaeus (1707–1778), a Swede, demonstrated the natural laws of family relationships in biology. He took every known plant and animal, classified it by species, then bracketed several species together in a genus—and so on up the hierarchy of classification from genus through order to class. Thus arose a practice that biologists still follow in assigning a specimen two Latin names, that of its genus and that of its species.

Modern chemical analysis started with Black and Lavoisier. Joseph Black (1728–1799), a Scottish professor, exploded the old theory that air was composed of a single element by proving the existence of several air-like substances or gases. Black's French contemporary, Lavoisier (1743–1794), continued his study of gases, invented the name "oxygen," and demonstrated that water was made up of oxygen and hydrogen. Lavoisier asserted that all substances were composed of a relatively few basic chemical elements, of which he identified twenty-three.

Meanwhile, astronomy and physics were consolidating the great advances they had made in the seventeenth century. Laplace (1749–1827), the "Newton of France," rounded out Sir Isaac's investigation of celestial mechanics and explained the movement of the solar system in a series of mathematical formulas and theorems. The versatile American, Benjamin Franklin (1706–1790), showed that electricity and lightning were really the same thing. He obtained an electrical charge in a key attached to the string of a kite flown during a thunderstorm in Philadelphia. This experiment, which aroused a lively interest across the

Atlantic, was repeated at Versailles for the French royal family.

Almost everybody who was anybody in the eighteenth century attempted experiments. Voltaire made a serious hobby of chemistry; Montesquieu studied physics; and a noble French lady reportedly kept a cadaver in her carriage so that she might employ her travels profitably in dissection and the study of anatomy. Almost every state in Europe had its *philosophes* and its royal society or learned society to promote the progress of knowledge. Intellectual life was by no means limited to the capitals and big cities; France, for example, by the middle of the eighteenth century, possessed many provincial academies, well equipped with reading rooms and lending libraries. In addition, intellectuals paid scant attention to national frontiers and, even when their countries were at war, continued to visit an enemy and correspond with its citizens. It was a striking example of the eighteenth century's disposition to keep warfare within strict limits and maintain business as usual.

French Leadership

The cosmopolitan qualities of the century appeared at their best in the Enlightenment, which had its roots in France and England and extended its branches to Scotland, Germany, Italy, Spain, and the New World. Yet the Age of Reason also marked the high point of French cultural hegemony, when, as the American *philosophe* Thomas Jefferson put it, every man had two homelands, his own and France. The French language endowed the Enlightenment with its medium of communication; the *salons* of Paris helped to set the tone of enlightened writing; the great *Encyclopédie,* edited and published in France, provided a vehicle for enlightened thought.

By the eighteenth century, French was the accepted international language. Louis XIV had raised it to supremacy in diplomacy; Racine and the other great seventeenth-century writers had made it pre-eminent in literature. There was much justice in the claim that "a dangerous work written in French is a declar-

ation of war on the whole of Europe." Almost everywhere, even in distant Russia, rulers, aristocrats, and intellectuals preferred French to their native tongues. In 1783, it was not a French society but the Academy of Berlin that conducted a competition for the best reply to the question, "What has made the French language universal?" According to the prize-winning essay, "Precise, popular, and reasonable, it is no longer just French; it is the language of humanity."

The Parisian *salons* taught writers precision, reasonableness, and the popular touch. The *salon* was the reception room of a large private home where guests assembled for an afternoon or evening of conversation under the guidance of the hostess, usually a wealthy woman from the nobility or the upper bourgeoisie. Here is a contemporary report of the way in which one of them conducted her *salon:*

. . . This circle was formed of people who were not linked together. She had taken them from here and there, but chosen so well that when they were together they harmonised like the strings of an instrument tuned by a cunning hand. . . . She played on this instrument with an art that was almost genius; she seemed to know what sound the string she was going to touch would give: I mean that so well were our characters and minds known to her, that she had only to say one word to bring them into play. Nowhere was conversation livelier, or more brilliant, or better controlled. . . . The minds she worked upon were neither shallow nor weak. . . . Her gift for throwing out an idea, and giving it to men of this type to discuss; her gift for discussing it herself, like them, with precision, and sometimes with eloquence; her gift for bringing in new ideas and varying the conversation . . ., these gifts, I say, are not those of an ordinary woman. It was not with fashionable trifles or self-conceit that, every day for four hours' conversation without weariness or emptiness, she knew how to make herself interesting to these brilliant minds.*

Although some *salons* were snobbish and superficial, most of them gave young *philosophes* the opportunity to receive a hearing — and to obtain a square meal; they welcomed

Memoirs of Marmontel, Brigit Patmore, trans. (London, 1930), 270.

and, if the need arose, protected new men and new ideas. Pressure from the *salons* determined the outcome of elections to the French Academy, which passed under the control of the *philosophes* in the 1760's.

The great organ of the *philosophes* was the *Encyclopédie,* which published the first of its many volumes in 1751. Its roster of 160 contributors included Voltaire, Montesquieu, Rousseau, Condorcet, Quesnay, and Turgot. For years the editor-in-chief, Denis Diderot (1713–1784), put in a fourteen-hour working day to advance his crusade for reason and progress. He commissioned the drawing of superb plates showing the details of the new industrial machines and even learned to operate some of the machines himself. Diderot and his colleagues did not intend to create an objective compendium of information. Their purpose was didactic: to expose the superstition and intolerance of the existing order and to instruct the public in the virtues of natural law and the wonders of science. As Diderot explained in the article on the word "encyclopedia," they aimed to assemble knowledge

. . . in order that the labors of past centuries should not prove useless for succeeding centuries; that our descendants, by becoming better informed, will at the same time *become happier and more virtuous. . . .**

While the *Encyclopédie* antagonized many defenders of the Old Régime, it accomplished its purpose and gained enough subscribers to prove a profitable business venture. Louis XV tried to prevent its being printed or circulated, the Church condemned it for its materialism and for its skepticism, and the publishers, without consulting Diderot, ordered the printers to cut out many passages likely to cause offense. But to no avail. The indignation of Diderot, the ridicule leveled by the *philosophes* at their enemies, the loyalty of the subscribers to the *Encyclopédie,* and the help given the editors by Choiseul, the foreign minister, and Madame de Pompadour, herself an enlightened spirit—all frustrated the censors. In the small provincial city of Dijon, for example, there were sixty copies of the *Encyclopédie* in 1768.

*(Our italics.)

II   The Reform Program of the *Philosophes*

Laissez-Faire Economics

Since the *philosophes* passed severe judgments on almost every facet of the Old Régime, the major reforms they proposed encompassed economic behavior, standards of justice, and quality of education, as well as religious and political practices. Their economic program was introduced in the articles written for the *Encyclopédie* by the versatile François Quesnay (1694–1774), biologist, surgeon, and personal physician to Louis XV and Madame de Pompadour. Quesnay headed a group of thinkers and publicists who adopted the name of Physiocrats, believers in the rule of nature. The name revealed the basic outlook of the school. The Physiocrats expected that they

would, as Quesnay claimed, discover natural economic laws "susceptible of a demonstration as severe and incontestable as those of geometry and algebra." And to arrive at such laws, the "sovereign and the nation should never lose sight of the fact that the land is the only source of wealth, and that agriculture increases wealth."*

This new Physiocratic concept of natural wealth clashed with the mercantilist doctrine of equating money and wealth. "The riches which men need for their livelihood do not consist of money," Quesnay argued, "they are rather the goods necessary both for life and for the annual production of these goods." Mer-

*Quesnay, "Maximes Générales du Gouvernement Economique d'un Royaume Agricole," in E. Daire, ed., *Physiocrates* (Paris, 1846), I, 82. Our translation.

cantilist states, therefore, committed a whole series of errors by placing excessive emphasis on specie. They tried to regulate commerce, when they should have freed it from controls. They made goods more expensive by levying tariffs and other indirect taxes, Quesnay concluded, whereas they should have collected only a single, direct tax on the net income from land. *"Laissez faire, laissez passer,"* the Physiocrats urged — live and let live, let nature take its course. They repudiated the controlled economy of mercantilism and enunciated the "classical" or "liberal" doctrine of the free economy. The state ought not to interrupt the free play of natural economic forces. Most of all, it ought not to interfere with private property, so necessary for the production of agricultural wealth.

The classic formulation of laissez-faire was made by the Scotsman, Adam Smith (1727–1790), in his *Inquiry into the Nature and Causes of the Wealth of Nations* (1776). Smith, too, leveled a vigorous attack on mercantilism. It was wrong to restrict imports by tariffs for the protection of home industries:

> It is the maxim of every prudent master of a family never to attempt to make at home what it will cost him more to make than to buy. The tailor does not attempt to make his own shoes, but buys them of the shoemaker. The shoemaker does not attempt to make his own clothes, but employs a tailor. . . .
>
> What is prudence in the conduct of every private family, can scarce be folly in that of a great kingdom. If a foreign country can supply us with a commodity cheaper than we ourselves can make it, better buy it of them with some part of the produce of our industry. . . .*

Like the Physiocrats, Adam Smith attributed the wealth of nations to the production of goods; but, as befitted a citizen of Britain, the leading commercial and industrial state of the day, he took a less agrarian view of the matter. For Adam Smith, production depended less on the *soil* (the Physiocratic view) than on the *labor* of farmers, craftsmen, and mill-hands. Again like the Physiocrats, he minimized the role of the state, claiming that men who were freely competing to seek their own

Wealth of Nations, Bk. IV, Ch. 2.

wealth would be led to enrich their whole society as if they were being guided by "an invisible hand" — that is, by nature. Thus, Smith claimed, government should merely be a passive policeman:

> According to the system of natural liberty, the sovereign has only three duties to attend to; . . . first, the duty of protecting the society from the violence and invasion of other independent societies; secondly, the duty of protecting, as far as possible, every member of the society from the injustice and oppression of every other member of it, or the duty of establishing an exact administration of justice; and thirdly, the duty of erecting and maintaining certain public works and certain public institutions, which it can never be for the interest of any individual, or small number of individuals, to erect and maintain.*

The mercantilists had raised the state over the individual and had declared a ceaseless trade warfare among nations. Adam Smith and the Physiocrats, reversing the emphasis, proclaimed both the economic liberty of the individual and free trade among nations to be natural laws. The laissez-faire program of the Enlightenment marked a revolutionary change in economic thought and was later used to justify the rugged individualism of nineteenth-century industrial pioneers (see Chapter 20). It did not, however, revolutionize the economic policies of the great powers, who long remained stubbornly mercantilist. Turgot, for instance, the chief practical exponent of Physiocratic doctrine, tried in vain to emancipate French agriculture and French business from traditional restrictions during his brief tenure as chief minister of Louis XVI in the 1770's (see Chapter 18). The Physiocrats neglected what so many *philosophes* neglected. They overlooked the difficulty of accommodating the simple and reasonable dictates of natural law to the complexity of politics and the irrationality of human nature.

Justice

The disposition to let nature take its course, so evident in laissez-faire economics, also

Ibid., Bk. IV, Ch. 9.

characterized the outlook of the *philosophes* on questions of justice. They believed that man-made legislation prevented the application of the natural laws of justice. They were horrified by the cumbersome judicial procedures of the Old Régime and by its unjust and antiquated statutes. New law-givers were needed to humanize and simplify legal codes, and a new science was needed to make the punishment of crime both humane and effective.

The new science, which laid the foundations of modern sociology, was promoted by Cesare Beccaria (1738–1794), an Italian *philosophe* and the author of the *Essay on Crimes and Punishments* (1764). Beccaria formulated three natural laws of justice, which are excellent examples of the Enlightenment's confident belief that common sense would enable men to formulate nature's truths. First, punishments should aim to

. . . prevent the criminal from doing further injury to society, and to prevent others from committing the like offence. Such punishments, therefore, . . . ought to be chosen, as will make the strongest and most lasting impressions on the minds of others, with the least torment to the body of the criminal.*

Second, justice should act speedily

. . . because the smaller the interval of time between the punishment and the crime, the stronger and more lasting will be the association of the two ideas of *Crime* and *Punishment*.†

And last:

Crimes are more effectively prevented by the *certainty* than by the *severity* of the punishment. . . . The certainty of a small punishment will make a stronger impression than the fear of one more severe. . . .**

Beccaria attacked both torture and capital punishment because they deviated so sharply from these natural laws. Torture, he claimed,

falsely assumed that "pain should be the test of truth, as if truth resided in the muscles and fibres of a wretch in torture." Jail sentences, not execution, should be imposed as punishments. Like many later reformers, Beccaria asserted that punishment alone was not enough. The best method of preventing crime was to "let liberty be attended with knowledge," to "perfect the system of education."

Education

In education, too, the Old Régime failed to pass the tests of reason and natural law. The *philosophes* deplored both the almost universal ecclesiastical control of education and the heavy emphasis on theology, Greek and Latin, and ancient history. They demanded more consideration of science, modern languages, and modern history. Diderot declared:

Under the name of rhetoric, is taught the art of speaking before teaching the art of thinking; and that of good expression before the students have any ideas to express.

. . .

Under the name of physics, are wearisome disputations about the elements of matter and the terrestrial systems; but not a word about natural history nor good chemistry, very little about the motion and fall of bodies, very few experiments, still less anatomy and no geography.*

Still more drastic changes were proposed by the great nonconformist of the Enlightenment, Jean-Jacques Rousseau (1712–1778). Rousseau rebelled against the strict and disciplined society of his birthplace, Calvinist Geneva. He rebelled against the intensive bookish studies he had been forced to pursue as a young boy, and against the polite conventions he later encountered in the Paris *salons*. The result was *Emile* (1762), half treatise and half romance, a long and fervent plea for progressive education. *Emile* had two heroes —Emile, the student, and Rousseau himself, the teacher. The training that Rousseau pre-

---

*Essay on Crimes and Punishments, Ch. 12.
†*Ibid.*, Ch. 19.
***Ibid.*, Ch. 27.

*Quoted in F. de la Fontainerie, *French Liberalism and Education in the Eighteenth Century* (New York, 1932), 208–209.

scribed for his pupil departed in every particular from eighteenth-century practice:

> Life is the trade I would teach him. When he leaves me, I grant you, he will be neither a magistrate, a soldier, nor a priest; he will be a man.*

Rousseau followed a policy of laissez-faire toward his pupil. He did not argue with Emile, or discipline him, or force him to learn reading at any early age. Emile observed the world of nature from first-hand experience, not in books. He learned geography by finding his own way in the woods (with his tutor's help), and agriculture by working in the fields. And when in his teens he was finally taught to read, his first assignment was Defoe's *Robinson Crusoe*, "the best treatise on an education according to nature."

Rousseau's educational program had many faults. It was impractical, for it assumed that every child should have the undivided attention of a tutor twenty-four hours a day. And it fostered the permanent dependence of pupil upon teacher; when Emile married and became a father, he implored his tutor to remain at his post: "I need you more than ever now that I am taking up the duties of manhood." And yet *Emile* was a most important book. Rousseau returned to some of the great ideas of the past—to the Renaissance concept of the universal man and to the ancient Greek ideal of the sound mind in the sound body. His theoretical program was adapted to the practical requirements of the classroom by the Swiss educator, Pestalozzi (1746–1827), who set an influential example by teaching geography, drawing, and other novelties in his experimental school. Still more influential was the reaction of Pestalozzi against the barracks tradition of drilling lessons into the pupil through a combination of endless repetition and bodily punishment. Students of the twentieth century may thank the educational reformers of the eighteenth for having discovered the natural law that children should be treated as children, not as miniature adults.

*Emile, Everyman ed. (New York, 1911), 9.

Attitudes toward Religion

Attacks on clerical teaching formed part of a vigorous and growing body of criticism against the role of the clergy in the Old Régime. In denouncing fanaticism and superstition, the *philosophes* singled out the Society Jesus, the symbol and the instrument of militant Catholicism. Pressure for the dissolution of the Jesuits gained the support of Catholic rulers, who had long been annoyed by Jesuit intervention in politics. In 1773, after the Jesuits had been expelled from several leading Catholic countries, Pope Clement XIV dissolved the Society. It was revived half a century later, when the political and intellectual climate had become less hostile.

As champions of tolerance, the *philosophes* showed a particular affinity for the religious attitude called deism (from the Latin *deus*, god). Deist doctrines arose in seventeenth-century England, the England of the civil war and Newtonian science, where the deists sought settlement of religious strife by the use of reason rather than by resort to arms. All men, they asserted, could agree on a few broad religious principles. Since the Newtonian world-machine implied the existence of a mechanic, the deists accepted God as the creator of the universe; they also believed that he would preside over the Last Judgment. But they limited his role to the distant past and the remote future, and they doubted that he had any concern with day-to-day human activities or would answer prayer and bestow grace.

The chief exponent of deism in France was Voltaire (1694–1778), a veritable one-man Enlightenment who poured forth a prodigious quantity of letters, plays, tales, epics, histories, and essays. Clear, witty, and often bitingly satirical, his writings were enormously popular, not least when they were printed under an assumed name or outside France to evade the censorship. It was Voltaire who made Frenchmen aware of great Englishmen like Locke, Newton, and Shakespeare (though Shakespeare was much more representative of the Renaissance than of the Enlightenment). And it was Voltaire who broadened the writing of history to include economics and culture as well as war and politics, thus foreshadowing the "new history" and "surveys of civilization" of the twentieth century.

Voltaire coined the anticlerical watchword *Ecrasez l'infâme*—crush the infamous thing, crush bigotry, superstition, perhaps the Church itself. Also, he had experienced political intolerance at first hand. As a young man he had spent a year as a prisoner in the gloomy Paris Bastille, and three years of exile in England because he had criticized the French government and had offended a member of the privileged nobility. The religious and political freedom of Britain made an immense impression on the refugee:

If there were just one religion in England, despotism would threaten; if there were two religions, they would cut each other's throats; but there are thirty religions, and they live together peacefully and happily.*

Back home, Voltaire carried on a life-long crusade for tolerance. In 1762, a Protestant merchant of Toulouse, Jean Calas, was accused of having murdered his son to prevent his conversion to Catholicism. Calas died in agony, his body broken on the wheel. Voltaire discovered that the accusation against Calas was based on rumor and that the court condemning him had acted out of anti-Protestant hysteria. He campaigned for three years until the original verdict was reversed, and the name of Calas was cleared.

The existence of evil—of injustices like that which broke Calas—confronted the Age of Reason with a major problem. Few of the *philosophes* accepted the traditional Christian teaching that evil arose from original sin,

Lettres Philosophiques, Letter No. 6. Our translation.

Table talk with Voltaire (hand raised); among those present are Diderot and Condorcet.

from the fall of Adam and Eve. If God were purely benevolent, they asked, why then had he created a world in which evil so often prevailed? Could a perfect God produce an imperfect creation? Alexander Pope, Voltaire's English contemporary, contended that this was the best of all possible worlds:

> All Nature is but Art, unknown to thee;
> All chance, direction which thou canst not
>   see;
> All discord, harmony not understood;
> All partial evil, universal good:
> And, spite of Pride, in erring Reason's spite,
> One truth is clear, *Whatever is, is right.*

Voltaire took his stand in *Candide*, which satirized the disasters abounding in the best of all possible worlds. A real disaster had inspired the writing of *Candide*—the great earthquake, tidal wave, and fire that engulfed the city of Lisbon on November 1, 1755, and killed upwards of 10,000 people.

Deism enabled Voltaire to effect a kind of reconciliation between a perfect God and the imperfect world. Voltaire believed that God was indeed the Creator:

> When I see a watch . . . , I conclude that an intelligent being arranged the springs of this mechanism so that the hand should tell the time. Similarly, when I see the springs of the human body, I conclude that an intelligent being has arranged these organs to be kept and nourished in the womb for nine months; that the eyes have been given for seeing, the hands for grasping, etc.*

But, Voltaire concluded, there was no way to determine whether or not God would attempt to perfect his creation. On one point Voltaire had no doubts: He never questioned the social usefulness of religion. "Man," he stated, "has always needed a brake." For the masses of people almost any religion, no matter how primitive, was better than atheism.

Baron d'Holbach (1723–1789), however, the most outspoken atheist of the Enlightenment, argued that men did not need the brake of religion; simple self-interest would suffice to make them behave morally. For

*Le Traité de Métaphysique, Ch. II. Our translation.

Holbach, organized religions were sinister institutions that thwarted the benevolent operations of reason and natural law, and God was merely a "phantom of the imagination," whose existence was denied by the evils and imperfections of the world that he was alleged to have created. A wealthy man, Holbach extended the hospitality of his *salon* to all, even to Jesuit refugees from anticlerical persecution. His tolerance impressed his contemporaries more favorably than his atheism did; most *philosophes* continued to profess deism, which was at least halfway between belief and disbelief.

Political Thought: Montesquieu

"In politics as in religion toleration is a necessity," decreed Voltaire. To him, therefore, tolerant Britain seemed utopia, and he paid the British constitution the most flattering compliment at the command of his age when he claimed that it "might have been invented by Locke, Newton, or Archimedes." Montesquieu (1689–1755), a French lawyer and *philosophe*, set out to analyze the political virtues of Britain. In his major work, *The Spirit of the Laws* (1748), Montesquieu laid down the premise that no one system of government suited all countries. Laws, he wrote,

> . . . should be in relation to the climate of each country, to the quality of its soil, to its situation and extent, to the principal occupation of the natives, whether husbandmen, huntsmen, or shepherds: they should have relation to the degree of liberty which the constitution will bear; to the religion of the inhabitants, to their inclinations, riches, numbers, commerce, manners, and customs.*

Montesquieu cautioned against supposing that old customs could simply be decreed out of existence, and he cited the telling example of Peter the Great's failure to impose western ways on Russia.

In spelling out the influence of tradition and environment upon forms of government,

*The Spirit of the Laws, Thomas Nugent, trans. (New York, 1949), Bk. I, Ch. 3.

Montesquieu concluded that republics were best suited to the small and barren countries, limited monarchies to the middle-sized and more prosperous, and despotisms to vast empires. Britain, being middle-sized and prosperous, was quite properly a monarchy limited by aristocracy. The hereditary nobility sat in the House of Lords; a kind of nobility of talent, the elected representatives, composed the Commons. All this was admirable in Montesquieu's view, for he pronounced the mass of people "extremely unfit" for government. If only the French monarchy had let the aristocracy retain their old political functions, France would never have sunk to her present low state.

Montesquieu found another key to the political superiority of Britain in the famous concept of checks and balances. In Parliament, Lords and Commons checked each other; in the government as a whole, the balance was maintained by means of *the separation of powers:*

When the legislative and executive powers are united in the same person, or in the same body of magistrates, there can be no liberty; because apprehensions may arise, lest the same monarch or senate should enact tyrannical laws, to execute them in a tyrannical manner.

Again, there is no liberty, if the judiciary power be not separated from the legislative and executive. Were it joined with the legislative the life and liberty of the subject would be exposed to arbitrary control; for the judge would be then the legislator. Were it joined to the executive power, the judge might behave with violence and oppression.*

Here Montesquieu failed to take into account a development that was not exactly obvious in the mid-eighteenth century, when *The Spirit of the Laws* appeared. He failed to see that the British constitution was moving, not toward the separation of powers, but toward their concentration in the House of Commons; the cabinet was becoming the instrument for the assertion of legislative supremacy over the executive.

Montesquieu likewise ran into trouble when he tried to derive specific corollaries from his general theorem about the influence

*The Spirit of the Laws, Bk. XXI, Ch. 6.

of climate and geography on human institutions. Autocracy and Catholicism, he asserted, flourish in the Mediterranean states where the climate is warm and natural resources abundant. Moderate government and Protestantism, conversely, are at home in the colder and harsher environment of northern Europe. The facts did not always confirm this rule about North and South. Freedom-loving Protestant Britain and Holland behaved in good northern fashion; but if Montesquieu were correct, barren, northern, Protestant Prussia should have been a citadel of liberty, not the stronghold of Hohenzollern absolutism. By jumping to conclusions from insufficient evidence, Montesquieu committed a fault common among the *philosophes.* But, unlike some of them, he had too firm a grasp on political realities to assume that governments either were or should be the same everywhere. Later political thinkers made good use of the comparative methods introduced by *The Spirit of the Laws* and refined Montesquieu's judgments on the interrelationship of geography, religion, and politics.

Political Thought: Rousseau

From the standpoint of American history, as we shall see, Montesquieu and Locke proved to be the most influential political thinkers of the Enlightenment. From the standpoint of European history, the most important was Jean-Jacques Rousseau, who inspired the radicals of the French Revolution. Rousseau's ideas proceeded from a sweeping generalization very typical of the Enlightenment. Whereas nature dignifies man, he contended, civilization corrupts him; man would be corrupted less if civilized institutions followed nature more closely. This theme ran through many of Rousseau's principal writings. In *Emile,* it was at the heart of his program for educational reform; earlier, it was enunciated in the *Discourse on the Moral Effects of the Arts and Sciences* (1750), which won a competition set by the Academy of Dijon. The Academy asked: Has the restoration of the arts and sciences had a purifying effect upon morals? Certainly not, the prize-winner answered; it has nearly ruined them.

In a second discourse, *On the Origin of the Inequality of Mankind* (1755), Rousseau blamed the vices of civilization on private property:

The first man who, having enclosed a piece of ground, bethought himself of saying, 'This is mine,' and found people simple enough to believe him, was the real founder of civil society. From how many crimes, wars, and murders, from how many horrors and misfortunes might not any one have saved mankind, by pulling up the stakes, or filling up the ditch, and crying to his fellows: 'Beware of listening to this imposter; you are undone if you once forget that the fruits of the earth belong to us all, and the earth itself to nobody.'*

Men accepted laws and governors in order to protect their property:

. . . They had too many disputes among themselves to do without arbitrators, and too much ambition and avarice to go long without masters. All ran headlong to their chains, in hopes of securing their liberty; for they had just wit enough to perceive the advantages of political institutions, without experience enough to enable them to foresee their danger.†

Government was evil, Rousseau concluded, but a necessary evil. "What, then, is to be done? Must societies be totally abolished? . . . Must we return again to the forest to live among bears?" No, civilized men could not return to a primitive existence, could "no longer subsist on plants or acorns, or live without laws and magistrates."**

Rousseau's major political work, *The Social Contract* (1762), attempted to reconcile the liberty of the individual and the institution of government through a new and revolutionary version of the contract theory of government. Earlier theories of contract, from the Middle Ages to John Locke, had hinged on the agreement between the people to be governed, on the one hand, and a single governor or small group of governors, on the other. Earlier theories postulated a political contract; Rousseau's contract was social in that a whole society agreed to be ruled by its *general will:*

Each of us puts his person and all his power in common under the supreme direction of the general will, and, in our corporate capacity, we receive each member as an indivisible part of the whole.*

"Each individual," Rousseau continued, "may have a particular will contrary or dissimilar to the general will which he has as a citizen." If the individual insists on putting self-interest above community interest, he should be obliged to observe the general will. "This means nothing less than that he will be forced to be free."† Thus, the general will was moral as well as political in nature, for it represented what was *best* for the whole community, what the community *ought* to do.

Formulating the general will, Rousseau believed, was the business of the whole people. The power of legislation, he argued, could never be properly transferred to an elected body:

The deputies of the people . . . are not and cannot be its representatives; they are merely its stewards, and can carry through no definitive acts. Every law the people has not ratified in person is null and void—is, in fact, not a law. The people of England regards itself as free; but it is grossly mistaken; it is free only during the election of members of Parliament.**

Executing the general will, however, could legitimately be the business of a smaller group. Like Montesquieu, Rousseau believed that the number of governors should vary inversely with the size and resources of the state— monarchy for the wealthy, aristocracy for the state of middling size and wealth, and democracy for the small and poor. Rousseau doubted, however, that any state was ready

---

*"Discourse on the Origin of Inequality," in *The Social Contract and Discourses*, Everyman ed. (New York, 1913), 192.
†*Ibid.*, 205.
**Ibid.*, 228

The Social Contract, Everyman ed. (New York, 1913), 13.
†*Ibid.*, 15.
**Ibid.*, 78.

for the absolute form of democracy in which the people actually execute the laws. "Were there a people of gods, their government would be democratic. So perfect a government is not for men."*

Rousseau was quite aware that *The Social Contract* was not a manual of practical politics. On another occasion, when he made suggestions for the reform of the Polish government, his counsels were decidedly more cautious. He admonished the Poles to renew their national spirit through education and patriotic festivals. While favoring the abolition of the *liberum veto* (see p. 30), he recommended that the elective monarchy be retained, that the nobles keep many of their privileges but acquire a new sense of duty, and that the serfs be liberated but only after they had been taught responsibility.

Although these suggestions were moderate enough, the influence of Rousseau has not been exerted on the side of moderation. Almost every radical political doctrine in the past two centuries has owed something to Rousseau. Socialists justify collectivism on the basis of his attacks on private property and of his insistence that "the fruits of the earth belong to us all." Patriots and nationalists hail him as an early prophet of the creed that nations do—and should—differ. Throughout his writings as well as in his advice to the Poles, he referred to "the dear love of country." *The Social Contract* concluded with a plea for the establishment of a "civil religion," which would displace the traditional faith. The moral code of early Christianity might be retained, Rousseau allowed, but the State should no longer have to compete with the Church for the allegiance of citizens.

Rousseau's concept of the general will has aroused conflicting interpretations. Because it is ethical in character, it seems to represent something more than the sum of individual wills—the whole appears to be more than the sum of its parts. Many, therefore, see in Rousseau a man who exalted the welfare of the nation over that of the citizens composing it, who indeed worshipped the state. Dictators

have justified their totalitarianism by asserting that they have a special insight into the general will; Hitler's celebrated "intuition" is an example. The police state can be justified on the grounds that it is doing its subjects a favor by "forcing them to be free."

The authoritarian interpretation indicates some of the possible consequences of Rousseau's ideas, but it overlooks both the strongly idealistic and democratic tone of his writings and his personal hostility toward the absolutism of the Old Régime. "Were there a people of gods, their government would be democratic." This declaration has moved the democratic disciples of Rousseau from the French Revolution on down to the present. The people are not gods? Then they must be trained in godliness, and Rousseau himself pointed the way. *Emile* showed how education could help, and *The Social Contract* at least implied that men might one day become so virtuous that they would follow the general will naturally and would no longer have to be "forced to be free."

Enlightened Despotism

Some *philosophes,* however, sought a short cut to utopia, a political prescription that was more practicable than the *Social Contract* and that could operate within the framework of existing monarchical insitutions. They found the answer in enlightened despotism. The Physiocrats, the chief theorists of enlightened despotism, had little sympathy with the concern of Montesquieu and Rousseau over the status of the legislative power. In the Physiocratic view, God was the legislator, nature preserved the divine legislation, and the sole duty of government was to administer these natural laws. Democracy and aristocracy alike had the fatal weakness of delegating administrative authority to individuals whose transient selfish aims clashed with the permanent welfare of the nation. By contrast, the Physiocrats explained, the personal interests of a hereditary monarch coincided with national interests through his "co-ownership" of the territories under his rule. Because the king was best qualified to work for the

---

The Social Contract, 56.

national interest, he should be a despot, not in any sinister sense but on the model of the tyrants of ancient Greece or the best of the Renaissance despots. Like a new Solon, the enlightened despot should unearth the natural laws decreed by God and clear away the accumulation of artificial, man-made law that was choking progress.

III   The Enlightened Despots

In the eighteenth century, self-styled "enlightened" or "benevolent" despots occupied many thrones — in Prussia, Frederick the Great; in Austria, Joseph II; in Russia, Catherine the Great; in Spain, Charles III; in Sweden, Gustavus III; and still others. The program of enlightened despotism won such wide endorsement from European monarchs because it gave them the opportunity to pose as the champions of reason and progress while pressing their age-old fight to make royal authority more absolute. Their mixture of motives made their kingdoms at best uncertain proving grounds both for the theory of enlightened despotism and for the practicality of the whole reform program of the Enlightenment.

Prussia: Frederick the Great

Of all the monarchs of eighteenth-century Europe, Frederick II, the Great, of Prussia (1740–1786), appeared best attuned to the Enlightenment. As a youth, he rebelled against the drill-sergeant methods of his father, Frederick William I (see Chapter 16). He delighted in music, and played the flute, which he took with him even on military campaigns. An attentive reader of the *philosophes*, he exchanged letters with them and brought Voltaire to live for a time as his pensioner in his palace at Potsdam near Berlin. He wrote a pamphlet, *Anti-Machiavel*, denouncing the immorality of *The Prince*. And he himself laid down the fundamental requirements for an enlightened despot:

Princes, sovereigns, kings are not clothed with supreme authority to plunge with impunity into de-bauchery and luxury. . . .[The prince] should often remind himself that he is a man just as the least of his subjects. If he is the first judge, the first general, the first financier, the first minister of the nation, . . . it is in order to fulfill the duties which these titles impose upon him. He is only the first servant of the state, obliged to act with fairness, wisdom, and unselfishness, as if at every instant he would have to render an account of his administration to his citizens.*

Frederick was indeed "the first servant of the state," shunning luxury, wearing stained and shabby clothing, and toiling long and hard at his desk. But did he also act with "fairness, wisdom, and unselfishness"? Despite his *Anti-Machiavel*, Frederick conducted foreign and military affairs in true Machiavellian style; his invasion of Silesia (see Chapter 16) would have aroused the envy of Caesar Borgia. At home, closeted in his Potsdam palace where he conducted the business of state by correspondence, he drove his subordinates like slaves. Viewed as a general, diplomat, and the master mechanic of Prussian administration, Frederick the Great was efficient and successful, but he was scarcely enlightened. His claim to be a benevolent despot must rise or fall on the record of his social and economic reforms.

No Physiocrat could have done more than Frederick to improve Prussian agriculture. From England he imported clover, crop rotation, and the iron plow, which turned up the soil more effectively than the old wooden share. He drained the swamps of the lower Oder Valley, opened up farms in Silesia and

---

*"Essai sur les Formes de Gouvenement et sur les Devoirs des Souverains." *Oeuvres Posthumes* (Berlin, 1788), VI, 64, 83–84. Our translation.

elsewhere, and brought in 300,000 immigrants to populate the new lands. After the ravages of the Seven Years' War, he gave the peasants tools, stock, and seed to repair their ruined farms. He nursed along the admirable German tradition of scientific forestry, then in its infancy.

Frederick, however, was hostile to the doctrine of laissez-faire and cut imports to the bone in order to save money for support of the army. His mercantilism stimulated the growth of Prussian industry, particularly the textiles and metals needed by the army. But it also placed a staggering burden of taxation on his subjects and produced several economic absurdities. For instance, Frederick tried to make Prussia grow its own tobacco, for which the climate was not suited. And, since the German taste for coffee required a large outlay of money abroad, he laid a heavy duty on imported coffee beans, and even established a special corps of French "coffee-smellers" to trap smugglers.

The religious and social policies of Frederick the Great likewise combined the Age of Reason at its most reasonable with the Old Régime at its least enlightened. A deist, Frederick prided himself on religious tolerance. He invited Jesuits to seek refuge in Prussia and protected the minority of Catholics in his predominantly Protestant kingdom, urging them to build their church steeples as high as they liked. He even boasted that he would build a mosque in Berlin if Moslems wanted to settle there. Yet the same Frederick alleged that Jews were "useless to the state," levied special heavy taxes on his Jewish subjects, and tried to exclude them from the professions and from the civil service.

Frederick rendered Prussians a great service by his judicial reforms. He reduced the use of torture; he put an end to the curious custom of taking appeals from the ordinary courts to university faculties and instituted a regular system of appellate courts. He mitigated the venal practice of bribing judges by insisting that "tips" received from litigants be placed in a common pool from which each judge should draw only his fair share.

Yet the same Frederick took a positively

Frederick the Great playing the flute in characteristically untidy surroundings.

medieval view of the merits of social caste. He did nothing to loosen the bonds of serfdom that still shackled much of the Prussian peasantry. When he gave the peasants material assistance and urged them to learn the "three r's," his aims were severely utilitarian. Peasants were to learn nothing beyond the rudiments of reading and writing; otherwise, they might become discontented with their station in life. Regarding the middle class, too, with disdain, Frederick respected only the landed nobility and gentry. And even the favored Junkers did not escape Frederick's penny-pinching. Although he appointed only Junkers as army officers, he discouraged their marrying to reduce the number of potential widows to whom the state would owe a pension.

While Frederick indulged his favorite dogs and horses, giving them special house privileges, he was temperamentally incapable of getting along with people. He despised and neglected his wife. Voltaire, that great French champion of toleration, could not tolerate the strain of prolonged daily association with Frederick. When the King requested him to edit his rather feeble French verses, Voltaire made a cutting remark about washing the dirty linen of royalty; Frederick retorted by comparing his guest to an orange, to be sucked dry and thrown away. The two men eventually renewed their friendship through the less demanding medium of correspondence.

Frederick's will directed that he be buried beside his pet dogs—"Such," remarked a French observer, "is the last mark of contempt he thought proper to cast upon mankind." The verdict has been sustained by many liberal historians, who pronounce Frederick's supposed enlightenment a mere device of propaganda, an attempt to clothe the nakedness of his absolutism with the decent intellectual garments of the age. This is, however, rather too harsh and one-sided, an attempt perhaps to fix on Frederick part of the guilt for the atrocities committed by Hitler and the Nazis almost two centuries after him. It would be fairer to argue that Frederick espoused two often conflicting philosophies—the Spartan traditions of the Hohenzollerns and the humane principles of the Enlightenment. He was an enlightened despot only so far as he could reconcile the precepts of the Age of Reason with the imperatives of Prussian kingship. He was a Hohenzollern, first and always.

Austria: Maria Theresa and Joseph II

Frederick's decisive victory in the War of the Austrian Succession (see Chapter 16) laid bare the basic weaknesses of the Habsburgs' dynastic empire. The Empress Maria Theresa (1740–1780) at once saw the need for reform and often took as her model the institutions of her hated but successful Hohenzollern rival. She and her capable ministers increased taxes, especially on the nobility, and strengthened the central government at the expense of local aristocratic assemblies, building up the still

rather sketchy departments of central administration. They obliged the non-German provinces to accept the hegemony of the German officials and German language of Vienna. Unlike Frederick the Great, Maria Theresa also took the first steps toward the abolition of serfdom. While personally very devout, she extended her policies to the Church, subjecting it to heavier taxation and confiscating some monastic property.

Maria Theresa employed both force and charm to get her way. The nobles of Hungary momentarily forgot their anti-German tradition when the beautiful and spirited empress, her infant son in her arms, personally appealed to their chivalry in the crisis of the War of the Austrian Succession. She was the first housewife of the realm as well as the first servant of the state. She was the mother of sixteen children, and she adored and respected Francis, her grasping, fickle husband. Francis' will provided a large bequest for his mistress; his widow executed its terms to the letter.

As a pious Catholic, Maria Theresa was fundamentally out of sympathy with the Age of Reason. "Lady Prayerful," as Catherine the Great called her, banned the works of Rousseau and Voltaire and even forbade the circulation of the Catholic *Index,* lest that list of forbidden books pique the curiosity of her subjects. History, therefore, has denied her the title of enlightened despot and chosen instead Joseph II, her eldest son, who became emperor after the death of Francis in 1765 and was co-regent with his mother until her death in 1780. Frederick the Great wrote Voltaire a glowing estimate of the new Emperor:

Born in a bigoted court, he has cast off its superstition; raised in magnificence, he has assumed simple manners; nourished on incense, he is modest; burning with a thirst for glory, he sacrifices his ambition to the filial duty which he executes scrupulously; and, having had only pedantic teachers, he still has enough taste to read Voltaire and to appreciate his merits.*

Frederick exaggerated only a little. Earnest,

*"Correspondance avec les Souverains," *Oeuvres Complètes de Voltaire* (Paris, 1828), LXXIV, 37. Our translation.

industrious, and puritanical in temperament, Joseph promised to make "philosophy the legislator of my empire." Thwarted and restrained by Maria Theresa during her lifetime, the impatient Emperor plunged into activity after her death. During his ten years as sole ruler (1780–1790), eleven thousand laws and six thousands decrees issued from Vienna. For the first time in the history of Catholic Austria, Calvinists, Lutherans, and Orthodox gained full toleration. And, with a generosity unparalleled in Habsburg annals, the Emperor took measures to end the ghetto existence of the Jews, exempting them from special taxes and from the requirement of wearing a yellow patch as a badge of inferiority.

Joseph intensified his mother's Catholic policies. While a faithful churchgoer, he insisted that he himself and not the Pope should be the arbiter of the Church's activities in Austria. He encouraged what he considered socially useful in Catholicism and dealt ruthlessly with what he judged superfluous and harmful. Thus he established hundreds of new churches and at the same time reduced the number of religious holidays. He called monks "the most dangerous and useless subjects in every state" and promised to convert "the monk of mere show into a useful citizen." He cut in half the number of monks and nuns and, of 2100 monasteries and nunneries, he suppressed 700, chiefly those run by the contemplative orders. Houses actively engaged in educational or charitable work were generally spared. The government sold or leased the lands of the suppressed establishments, applying the revenue to the support of the hospitals that were beginning to earn Vienna its reputation as a great medical center.

Unlike Frederick the Great, Joseph really believed in popular education and social equality. His government provided the teachers and textbooks for primary schools. More than a quarter of the school-age children in Austria actually attended school—the best record of any country in late eighteenth-century Europe. Everyone in Vienna, high and low, was invited to visit the Prater, the great public park of the capital, the entrance to which bore the inscription, "A place of pleasure for all men,

prepared for them by their friend." The new Austrian legal code followed the recommendations of Beccaria in abolishing capital punishment and most tortures and in prescribing equality before the law. Aristocratic offenders, like commoners, were sentenced to stand in the pillory and to sweep the streets of Vienna. Joseph's peasant policy marked the climax of his equalitarianism. He freed the serfs, abolished most of their obligations to manorial lords, and deprived the lords of their traditional right of administering justice to the peasantry. He also experimented with the collection of a single tax on land as recommended by the Physiocrats, a revolutionary innovation from the social as well as the economic point of view, because the estates of the aristocracy were to be taxed on the same basis as the farms of the peasantry.

Joseph's economic policies, however, often followed the traditions of mercantilism, notably in the erection of high protective tariffs and in the government's close supervision of economic life. In politics Joseph continued his mother's Germanizing program. He customarily spoke German, patronized German writers, and made the French playhouse in Vienna a German-language theater. He attempted to terminate the autonomous rights of his non-German possessions, such as Bohemia, Hungary, and Belgium.

Both Joseph's enlightened reforms and his Germanizing policies aroused mounting opposition. Devout peasants, almost oblivious of his well-meaning attempts to improve their social and economic status, keenly resented his meddling with old religious customs. The nobility clamored against his equalitarian legislation; in the case of the single-tax experiment their opposition was so violent that he had to revoke the decree a month after it was issued. Hungary and Belgium rose in open rebellion against his centralizing efforts and forced him to confirm their autonomous liberties. In foreign policy, too, his ambitious projects miscarried. By supporting Russian plans for the dismemberment of Turkey (see p. 73), Austria gained only a narrow strip of Balkan territory. Joseph also attempted to annex lands belonging to the neighboring South German state

Emperor Joseph II of Austria working a plow.

of Bavaria, where the death of the ruler opened another of those succession quarrels so common in the eighteenth century. But Frederick the Great was determined to check any advance of Habsburg power in Germany. In the half-hearted "Potato War" of the late 1770's, Austrian and Prussian troops spent most of their time foraging for food, and Joseph secured only a tiny fragment of the Bavarian inheritance.

Joseph II worked himself to death, as one of his friends observed, "by governing too much and reigning too little." Where his mother had often sought to flatter or charm her opponents out of their opposition, Joseph simply laid down the law. He defended his habit of interfering personally in almost every detail of government:

What else can I do in this country devoid of mind, without soul, without zeal, without heart in the work? I am killing myself because I cannot rouse up those whom I want to make work; but I hope I shall not die until I have so wound up the machine that others cannot put it out of order, even if they try to do so.*

*Quoted in Prince de Ligne, *His Memoirs, Letters, and Miscellaneous Papers* (Boston, 1902), II, 132.

Joseph never got the machine properly wound up; he could not implant in the Austrian bureaucracy the almost inhuman Prussian discipline that was needed to serve his purposes. Joseph II died unshaken in the conviction that he had pursued the proper course, yet believing that he had accomplished nothing. In the judgment of posterity, however, Joseph appears as the most truly enlightened despot. In ten years he attempted more than Frederick attempted in almost half a century. Though some of his major reforms, like the abolition of serfdom, were repealed soon after his death, others survived him, helping to transform the Habsburg lands into a more modern centralized state.

Other Despots

Prominent among the enlightened rulers of lesser states was Joseph's younger brother Leopold, Grand Duke of Tuscany from 1765 until he became emperor in 1790. Leopold tidied up the administration of his Italian duchy, which included the busy port of Leghorn in addition to the city of Florence. He introduced economic reforms along Physiocratic lines and judicial reforms following the recommendations of Beccaria on the abolition of torture and of the death penalty. Unlike his brother, Leopold actively enlisted the participation of his subjects in affairs of state, and, unlike any other enlightened despot, he contemplated establishing a representative assembly and studied the constitution of Virginia for guidance.

Sweden's benevolent despot, King Gustavus III (1771–1792), was the most theatrical monarch of the century. Like his uncle, Frederick the Great, Gustavus admired the French and French ideas, and, when he inherited the Swedish crown, he proclaimed in

King Charles III of Spain in hunting costume, by Goya.

ringing speeches his devotion to the Age of Reason. He also resolved not to be cramped by the oligarchical factions that had run the country since the death of the warrior king, Charles XII, early in the century. While he distracted Swedish party leaders at the opera one evening, his soldiers staged a *coup* that enabled him to revive the royal authority and to dissolve the factions. In economics and religion, his enlightenment outdistanced that of his uncle in Prussia, for he removed obstacles to both domestic and foreign trade and extended toleration to Jews as well as to the non-Lutheran Christian sects. Success, however, turned the head of Gustavus III. As he became more and more arbitrary, the nobles determined to recover their old power; in 1792, he was assassinated at a masquerade in Stockholm, and oligarchy resumed its sway.

One of the most remarkable features of enlightened despotism was its emergence in the Iberian Peninsula, so long the preserve of aristocratic and clerical influence. Its representative in Portugal was not a monarch but the Marquis of Pombal, the first minister of King Joseph I (1750–1777). Pombal secured his reputation by the speed and good taste he demonstrated in rebuilding Lisbon after the earthquake of 1755. The Portuguese economy depended heavily on income from the colonies, on the sale of port wine to Britain, and on the purchase of manufactured goods from Britain. Pombal tried to enlarge its base by fostering local industries and encouraging the growth of grain in addition to grapes. To weaken the grip of clericalism on Portuguese life, he expelled the Jesuits, advanced religious toleration, and modernized the curriculum of the national University of Coimbra. To weaken that of the nobles, he attacked their rights of inheritance. Pombal's methods were in every instance high-handed, and when he fell from power in 1777 the prisons released thousands of men whom he had confined years earlier for their alleged involvement in aristocratic plots.

The Spanish enlightened despot was Charles III (1759–1788), Elizabeth Farnese's "Baby Carlos." When he inherited the crown on the death of his half-brother, he had already been seasoned in the struggle against feudalism and clericalism by a long and successful apprenticeship as King of Naples. With the assistance of Italian advisers whom he brought from Naples and of lawyers from the lower ranks of the Spanish nobility, Charles III energetically advanced the progressive policies begun under his father, Philip V (see Chapter 16). Though a pious Catholic, he objected strongly to the political activities of the Church and expelled the Jesuits from the native country of their founder, Loyola. He reduced the authority of the aristocracy, extended that of the Crown, and made Spain more nearly a centralized national state. He curbed the privileges of the great sheep-ranchers, whose almost unlimited grazing rights blighted Spanish agriculture. To revivify the torpid economy, he undertook irrigation projects, reclaimed waste lands, and established new roads, canals, banks, and textile mills. The results were astonishing: Spain's foreign commerce increased fivefold during the reign of Charles III. His successors, however, abandoned many of his forward-looking policies, and Spain soon began to slip back into her old ways, though the influence of the Enlightenment at least remained alive.

Limitations
of Enlightened Despotism

The question of succession, in fact, vitiated the whole structure of enlightened despotism.

So long as monarchs came to the throne by the accident of birth, there was nothing to prevent the unenlightened or incapable mediocrity from succeeding the enlightened despot. This happened in Spain, where the well-meaning but feeble Charles IV (1788–1808), succeeded Charles III; it happened in Sweden, where the weak Gustavus IV (1792–1809), succeeded Gustavus III; and it happened in Prussia under Frederick the Great's unenlightened nephew, Frederick William II (1786–1797). The principal exception to the rule occurred in Austria, where Emperor Leopold II (1790–1792), with his long experience in Tuscany, managed to salvage some of the reforms of Joseph II.

Even the least of the enlightened despots deserve the credit for having improved a few of the bad features of the Old Régime. But not even the best of them could strike a happy balance between enlightenment and despotism. Joseph II was too doctrinaire, too inflexible in his determination to apply the full reform program of the Age of Reason. Pombal and Gustavus III, in particular, were too arbitrary. Frederick the Great, obsessed with strengthening the crown, entrenched the power of the Junkers, who were hostile to the whole Enlightenment. Finally, in Russia, events during the century after the death of Peter the Great, a forerunner of the enlightened despot, furnished another lesson in the difficulty of adjusting rational principles to political realities.

IV   Russia, 1725– 1825

The Fate of the Autocracy,
1725–1762

When Peter the Great died, he left a tangled family situation in which nobody could truly decide who was his legitimate successor. Over the course of the next thirty-seven years, the throne changed hands seven times. The suc-

cession zigzagged across the family tree of the Romanovs: first to Peter's widow, who ruled as Empress Catherine I (1725–1727); then to Peter's young grandson, son of the murdered Alexis (see p. 30), who became Peter II (1727 –1730); then to Peter's niece, who reigned as Empress Anne (1730–1740); then to Anne's great-nephew, Ivan VI, who was only eight weeks old when he began his one-year reign

(1740–1741); then to Peter's own daughter by Catherine I, the Empress Elizabeth (1741–1762); then to Elizabeth's nephew, Peter III, who reigned only for six months in 1762; and finally to Peter III's brilliant young widow, who became Catherine II, the Great (1762–1796), and dominated Russia as Peter I himself had done. More important than the individuals who governed Russia between Peter and Catherine the Great were the social forces contending for power, and the social processes at work in an autocracy suddenly deprived of its autocrat and for so long unable to produce a new one. In the series of palace overturns, the guards' regiments founded by Peter exercised a decisive influence. The service nobility, no longer restrained by the tsar, now entered into its era of dominance.

On the death of Peter the Great, his immediate circle, particularly Menshikov (see Chapter 16), had every reason to fear the passage of the throne to the nine-year-old Peter, son of Alexis, and possible heir to the loyalties of the old nobility who had hated Peter the Great. Menshikov therefore strongly supported his one-time mistress, the Empress Catherine I, and succeeded in rallying to her side members of the guards who had come to like her while on campaigns. Since Catherine herself took little interest in affairs of state, Menshikov ran Russia during the two years of her reign. He tried to make himself secure by appointing a six-man "Supreme Privy Council" at the top of the administration, and to perpetuate his power he even planned to marry his daughter to the young heir, the future Peter II. On the death of Catherine I in 1727, he took the eleven-year-old boy into his house, where he proceeded to make him an alcoholic, as his father had been.

But Menshikov's arrogance had alienated even his followers. By 1728, the old boyars, led by the families of Dolgoruky and Galitsyn, had captured the throne, and Menshikov was exiled. Two Dolgoruky princes put themselves on the Supreme Privy Council, and the young Peter was engaged to a member of their family. The ascendancy of boyar families marked the return to supreme influence of a group that had been losing power ever since the days of Ivan the Terrible. Their plans were brought into crisis by the sudden death of Peter II on the very day scheduled for his coronation (January 19, 1730).

Their program can be studied in the conditions they submitted to the new candidate for the throne, Anne, the widow of the Duke of Courland. Summoning her from her petty Baltic principality, the Dolgoruky and the Galitsyns demanded that she sign these "Articles" before she take the throne. By their terms, she undertook never to marry or name an heir, and to continue the Supreme Privy Council, which by now had eight members, including four Dolgoruky and two Galitsyns. She further swore not to make peace or war, levy taxes, confer ranks in the army above that of colonel, or spend state funds without the specific consent of the Council. Moreover, the Councillors claimed for themselves supervision over the guards' regiments. This insistence on limiting the power of the new Empress reflected the outraged feelings of the old boyars, who had long been claiming the right to be consulted on all matters of state. The entire program was the most explicit constitutional destruction of all that Peter the Great had striven for. Anne signed the "Articles." Had she kept to their provisions, Russia would have embarked on an era of boyar oligarchy.

But the military-service nobility looked with horror at the prospect of taking orders indefinitely from the small group of old boyars. And the service gentry had a powerful lever in the guards' regiments. What its members wanted was an autocrat who would loosen the bonds that Peter the Great had forged for them. And so, when one of the Supreme Privy Councillors, the clever German Ostermann, convinced Anne that she need not abide by the Articles, the gentry in its armed might supported him. Anne simply tore up the Articles; thus, the attempt to create an oligarchy of the two great families failed. The gentry now had the real power in Russia.

Anne allowed her lover, the German adventurer Biren, and a flock of Germans to obtain the most influential positions in the state. The secret police, abolished after the death of Peter the Great, was now revived, and many thousands suffered torture, exile, and death at its hands. When Anne died, the German favorites fell out among themselves. Ostermann, a man of real ability, together with an excellent soldier, Marshal Münnich, brought about Biren's downfall and exile; then Ostermann forced Münnich out. Meanwhile, the tsar was the infant Ivan VI, whose mother, a German princess, acted as regent, and was so lazy that she lounged in her bedroom without the energy even to put on her clothes. Foreign intrigue produced the next shift in the imperial title. The French were anxious to terminate the power of Ostermann, who had been instrumental in cementing an alliance between Russia and France's traditional enemy, Austria. A clever French ambassador played on the patriotic feelings of the guardsmen, disgusted with the behavior of the Germans at court. In 1741 a guards' *coup* brought to the throne the daughter of Peter the Great, Elizabeth. The infant Ivan VI vanished into a prison cell with his indolent mother.

Elizabeth inherited her father's lust for life but not his brains or interest in matters of state. A succession of lovers had kept her busy all her life, and her habits did not change when she came to the throne. Though owning thousands of splendid dresses, she lived rather sluttishly in grubby palaces and enjoyed most of all a rousing peasant banquet with plenty to drink and lots of rustic music. Important state papers languished for days because the Empress could not be bothered to read them, much less sign them. Though she proclaimed her intention of restoring her father's methods of rule, she had no clear conception of what these had been. In an autocracy the autocrat has to take an interest in the affairs of state and assume responsibility for them; this Elizabeth did not do, and Russia drifted.

Soon after her accession, Elizabeth proclaimed her nephew, the half-mad Peter, heir to the throne. In 1745 he married a clever little German princess, the future Catherine II. Peter III, as he became after his succession in January, 1762, has had a bad "press"; he surely was not unusually intelligent, but was hardly the utter lunatic portrayed in the memoirs of his celebrated wife, who loathed him. The chief trouble with Peter seems to have been his great admiration for Prussia and his dislike of Russia. His effort to introduce rigid discipline on the Prussian model into the Russian army and his hatred for the influential guards' regiments cost him the friends he needed most. He could have played his wargames with his toy soldiers, held court-martials on rats whom he convicted of gnawing cardboard fortresses, and swilled his favorite English beer with impunity, and he would not have been any worse than many another tsar. But to drill the guards in the Prussian manner was unforgivable. So a new palace revolution took place, and Peter was eventually murdered by one of Catherine's lovers. The Empress' own role in his overthrow is still obscure.

Nobles and Serfs, 1730–1762

A deeply dissatisfied social group that had the power to make and unmake autocrats naturally had a program for the redress of its own grievances. Once the gentry had enabled Anne to tear up the Articles in 1730, it began strenuous efforts to emancipate itself from the servitude riveted upon it by Peter. Anne repealed the law requiring the noble to leave his estate intact to one of his sons. She founded a military school for noblemen's sons, graduation from which entitled one to a commission; no longer did young gentlemen have to start their careers in the ranks, as under Peter. Anne shortened the terms of service from life to twenty-five years, and exempted one son of every family with at least two sons, so that there would be one member of each generation able to look after the estate.

Simultaneously came a deepening of the authority of the nobles over the serfs. The proprietors became the government's agents for the collection of the poll tax. Serfs could no longer obtain their freedom by enlisting in the army and could not engage in trade or purchase land without written permission from their masters. Masters could deport their serfs to Siberia and might punish them physically in any way they wished. Moreover, under Elizabeth, a series of laws restricted the right of owning serfs to those who were already nobles. Thus the class that had been open to new recruits under Peter was closed by his daughter.

In 1762, finally, Peter III decreed that the nobles no longer need serve at all unless they wished to do so; except in the midst of a war, they might resign any time they chose. It was little wonder that some of the nobles proposed to erect a solid gold statue of Peter III. To understand the revolutionary nature of this liberation of the nobles from a duty to serve, we must remember that they had historically obtained their lands and serfs only on condition that they would serve. Now they kept their lands and serfs but had no obligations. Yet the service that had been hated when it was compulsory became fashionable now that it was optional; there was really little else for a Russian noble to do except serve the state. In contemplating all this, a great Russian historian remarked that the logic of history would have properly required that all serfs be liberated the day after the nobles were released from their duty to serve. But nothing could have been further from the thoughts of Peter III or of any other Russian leader.

In these middle decades of the eighteenth century, successive waves of foreign influence affected the Russian nobility. It was not only the influx of foreigners that brought in western habits; it was also the involvement of Russia in the European wars of the period, and the increased travel abroad by Russians. Under Elizabeth, when the hated Germans disappeared from court, the way was clear for the French to exert their influence. With the French language came the literature, and many a Russian noble bought French books by the yard for his library because it was the thing to do. The champagne business boomed (the Russians liked the sweet kind that most Frenchmen despised); French styles of dress were copied by both men and women. Francomania took its extreme form among those Russians who were ashamed of being Russian and who would not fall in love with any girl unable to speak French. Indeed, the noble and the peasant no longer spoke the same language. This deep rift between the Frenchified nobles and the Russian people was to prove of critical importance for later Russian history.

Catherine the Great (1762–1796)

With the advent of Catherine II, we come to the most arresting personality to occupy the Russian throne since the death of Peter. Brought up in a petty German court, she found herself transplanted to St. Petersburg as a mere girl, living with a husband she detested, and forced to pick her way through the intrigues that flourished around the Empress Elizabeth. She managed to steer clear of trouble only by using her keen wits. Catherine fancied herself as an intellectual; she wrote plays, edited a satirical journal, and steeped herself in the literature of the Enlightenment. Both before and after ascending the throne she maintained a goodly supply of lovers, several of whom had important roles in affairs of state.

Catherine had a truly twentieth-century feeling for the importance of public relations, and cared deeply that leading spirits in the West should think well of her and of the state of Russia under her rule. Hence her voluminous correspondence with westerners. She invited Diderot to take up in Russia the task of editing the *Encyclopédie;* then she bought his library, but he kept his books, and received a pension—very favorable publicity for Russia and the Russian Empress. Diderot himself visited Russia in 1773; though he came back entranced with Catherine, who, he said, had the soul of Brutus and the charms of Cleopatra, the visit was not entirely a success. Catherine complained that in the excitement of conversation he pinched her legs until they were black and blue. Voltaire, though he judiciously stayed away from Russia, accepted Catherine's bounty, and in return poured out the praises that she yearned for, calling her "the north star" and "the benefactress of Europe."

Catherine would perhaps have liked to reform conditions in Russia; there was something of the enlightened despot about her "style." But as a woman and a foreigner and a usurper, owing the throne to a conspiracy, she could not act upon her inclinations. Depending

Catherine the Great, about 1762.

as she did upon the good will of the nobility, she could not lay a finger on the institution of serfdom. She had to reward her supporters with vast grants of state land, inhabited by hundreds of thousands of state peasants, who once could not be sold but who now became privately owned serfs who could be sold. Even in theory, Catherine felt, Russia was so large that the only possible form of government was an autocracy. As an autocrat she was as arbitrary as any of her predecessors.

Once firmly established on the throne, however, Catherine decided to convoke a commission to codify the laws of Russia, a task that had not been accomplished since 1649. Catherine herself, with the help of advisers, spent three years composing the *Instruction* to the delegates, a long, rather windy document, full of abstract argument drawn from Montesquieu's *Spirit of the Laws* and Beccaria's *Crimes and Punishments* but altered to conform with the Empress' own beliefs. Here one can discern no intention to meddle with the fundamental institutions of Russia, but some concern for eliminating their worst abuses. The 564 delegates to the commission were elected by organs of the central government and by every social class in Russia except the serf peasants. Each delegate — noble, townsman, crown peasant, Cossack — was charged to bring with him a collection of written documents from his neighbors presenting their grievances and demands for change.

Many of these survive and teach us a great deal about the state of public opinion in Catherine's Russia. Nobody seems to have been dissatisfied with the autocracy; at least we find no requests that it modify its power or consult its subjects. People did seek more rights and duties for local government and wanted their own obligations more clearly defined. Each class of representatives was eager to extend the rights of that class: The free peasants wanted to own serfs; the townsmen wanted to own serfs and be the only class allowed to engage in trade; the nobles wanted to engage in trade, and to have their exclusive right to own serfs confirmed. After 203 sessions lasting over a year and a half, devoted to inconclusive and sometimes heated debate, Catherine put an end to the labors of the commission in 1768. It had not codified the laws, but from Catherine's own point of view it had been a success; she knew that most of her subjects supported her as absolute autocrat. It is important to remember that the commission, with all its imperfections, was the last effort by the tsardom to consult the Russian people as a whole for 138 years — until revolution summoned the first duma into existence in 1906 (see Chapter 22).

Catherine turned the spadework of the legislative commission to good advantage in her later reforms, which resulted from the great rebellion of the Cossacks under the leadership of Pugachev, 1773–1775. Pugachev roused the frontiersmen to revolt against Catherine's cancellation of their special privileges. Pretending to be Tsar Peter III, and promising liberty and land to the serfs who joined his forces, Pugachev swept over a wide area of southeastern Russia and finally marched toward Moscow. Like the disturbances of the seventeenth century, Pugachev's revolt revealed the existence of bitter discontent in Russia, a discontent directed not at the supreme autocrat but at the landlords and local officials.

The ramshackle provincial administration almost collapsed under the strain of Pugachev's rebellion. Orders filtered down slowly to local officials, and the soldiers defending the government moved almost as slowly. When the rebels were finally suppressed, and Pugachev was traveling northward in an iron cage before being drawn and quartered, Catherine took action. Her reorganization of local government (1775) created fifty provinces where there had been twenty before. She thus replaced a small number of unwieldy units with a larger number of small provinces, each containing roughly 300,000 to 400,000 inhabitants. The reform of 1775 gave the nobles the lion's share of provincial offices but subjected them to the close direction of the central government, which had its own administrative, financial, and legal representatives in each province.

In the charter of 1785 the nobles received exemption from military service and taxation and secured absolute mastery over the fate of their serfs and their estates. A charter to the towns in the same year (1785) disclosed Catherine's sympathy with the tiny but growing middle class. It established the principle of municipal self-government, but the principle remained a dead letter because of the rigorous class distinctions maintained in the backward urban centers of Russia. For the serfs, needless to say, there was no charter. Indeed, besides adding almost a million to their number by the gifts of state lands to private persons, Catherine increased still further the power of the proprietors. Long accustomed to selling the serfs without their land, the landlords now received the right to make such sales legally. Serf families were broken up, violent punishments and even torture employed (one notorious lady tortured seventy-five of her own serfs to death, but she was imprisoned for it), serfs were gambled away at cards, given as presents, and mortgaged for loans. All serf-owners were not cruel any more than all slave-owners in our own slave states, but both institutions tended to degrade both master and man. As in the American South, there was a distinction in Russia between field hands and household servants. Great landowners often had hundreds of the latter, some of whom were formed into orchestras, gave dramatic performances, tutored the sons of the family, or acted as household poets and scientists.

The contrast between the climate of the Enlightenment which surrounded the court and the actual conditions in Russia was keenly felt by sensitive men. Foremost among them was a young noble, Alexander Radishchev, educated abroad and widely traveled. In his *Journey from St. Petersburg to Moscow,* Radishchev included vivid and horrifying vignettes of serfdom and the abuses of the administration. Moreover, Radishchev's poetry praised Cromwell, the regicide. It is possible that the author's truly western culture might have enabled him to get away with this in the early days of Catherine's reign. But by 1790 the French Revolution was under way, and Catherine had begun to hate the French and "their abominable bonfire" as much as she had formerly loved them. Proposing to burn the dangerous books of the Enlightenment, she could hardly overlook the subversive character of Radishchev's writings. Off he went into exile in Siberia. Similarly, the humanitarian Freemason, Nicholas Novikov, manager of the newly active Moscow University Press, editor of newspapers, and sponsor of campaigns to raise money and food for famine-stricken peasants, was also jailed on flimsy charges. Though Novikov had done nothing against the régime, it could not tolerate the continuance of any enterprise it did not dominate. The two enlightened intellectuals, Radishchev and Novikov, not only serve as an illustration of the contrast between Catherine's professed principles and her actual conduct but also provide the first real examples of thoroughly westernized individual Russians.

Paul (1796–1801)

Catherine's son Paul (who may or may not have been the son of Catherine's husband, Peter III) succeeded her in 1796 as a man of forty-two. All his life his mother had distrusted him, fearing that there might be a conspiracy to oust her and install Paul, ostensibly a legitimate Romanov. The best-educated Russian royal personage to date, active and eager to serve the state, Paul found himself given no duties, kept in the dark about the secrets of state, and even deprived of his two eldest children, Alexander and Constantine, whom Catherine insisted on educating herself. All he could do was drill a small garrison on his country estate and dress them in Prussian uniform.

Consequently, when Paul finally did succeed to the throne, he appeared to be motivated chiefly by a wish to undo his mother's work and act in every possible way contrary to the precedents she had set. He exiled some of Catherine's favorites, and released many of her prisoners, including Radishchev and Novikov. Paul believed in legality and system, and hoped to install a great deal more of both in Russia. He tried to restore more power and order to the central administration by putting the colleges (see p. 27) under single ministers in place of the former boards of directors. Paul's behavior, however, was spasmodic and eccentric. He forbade the importation of sheet-music because he feared that all music would be as revolutionary as the *Marseillaise.* He imposed a strict curfew on the capital. He issued a manifesto limiting to three the number of days per week a serf might be required to work on his master's land, but it is not clear whether this was a binding law or only a recommendation. In any case, he continued to give away state lands, and transformed some half a million state peasants into privately owned chattels.

What was probably fatal to Paul was his policy of toughness toward the nobility. A noble, he is said to have remarked, is the man I am talking to at the moment, and he ceases to be a noble when I stop talking to him. This definition could hardly be expected to appeal to the privileged masters of Russia. Paul exacted compulsory service again, and in the provinces he curtailed the powers of the nobility. Nobles found themselves forced to meet the bills for public buildings, paying new taxes on their lands, and subjected to corporal punishments for crimes. Paul, like Peter III,

wanted to Prussianize the army, and especially to inculcate in the officers a sense of responsibility for the men. In the guards' regiments such programs were detested, and a conspiracy of guardsmen ended in 1801 with Paul's murder and Alexander's succession. The forces behind the *coup* were the same as those that had engineered so many shifts of power during the preceding century. The precise degree to which Alexander was informed of the *coup* in advance is sometimes debated, but he knew at least that the conspirators intended to force his father's abdication.

Alexander I (1801–1825)

In Alexander I there came to the throne an emperor whom historians usually call "enigmatic." Educated by a liberal Swiss tutor, he absorbed so much of the new eighteenth-century doctrines that he actually blossomed out with a red-white-and-blue ribbon, the colors of revolutionary France, on hearing of the fall of the Bastille to the Paris mob. Yet the application of liberal principles in Russia would involve a direct challenge to the most powerful forces in society. So, although Alexander would occasionally say to his intimates that some day he would grant Russia a constitution and himself retire to a castle on the Rhine, in fact this was little but romantic twaddle. Tall and handsome, utterly devastating to the ladies, charming and cultivated, Alexander liked to please everybody; he vacillated, compromised, and in the end accomplished very little. Moreover, he loved power dearly, and always shied away from proposals to limit it.

The quarter-century of his reign was twice interrupted by major wars against Napoleon, in 1805–1807, and in 1812–1815 (see Chapter 18). In the first period of relative peace, 1801–1805, Alexander gathered round him a small group of young men which he called the "unofficial committee." One of the members, Stroganov, had been an active member of the Jacobin Club in Paris during the revolution; two others greatly admired the English system of government. Meeting regularly after dinner over coffee and brandy, the unofficial committee had as its self-appointed task the preparation of a constitution for Russia, after due study of all known constitutions. But its discussions were little more than the unsystematic talk of pleasant, well-born young men who had dined well. A decree sponsored by the committee did abolish the administrative colleges and created eight new ministries to take their place; but this in fact had largely been accomplished by Paul. When the committee stopped meeting in 1803, it had done nothing with regard to serfdom. The Tsar himself in these years passed two laws, whose very mildness shows how little he intended to disturb existing institutions. One of them forbade the public advertisement of sales of serfs without land, but the law was easily circumvented. The other created a new category of "free farmers," serfs who had been freed by their masters, and prescribed that if a proprietor freed an entire village of serfs he must confer their land upon them at the same time. Since this left the initiative for liberation entirely in the hands of the proprietor, fewer than 40,000 among all the millions of serfs in Russia actually received their freedom.

In the second period of peace, 1807–1811, Alexander had as his chief mentor a remarkable figure, Michael Speransky, son of a Russian priest, intelligent, well-educated, and conscientious. Utilizing Montesquieu's principle of the separation of powers, Speransky drafted for Alexander a constitutional project that would have made Russia a limited monarchy. A series of elected assemblies, beginning at the lowest level of administrative subdivision and continuing on up through district and province, would culminate in a great national assembly, the duma. A similar pyramid of courts and a new set of executive institutions was also planned. The duma would have to approve any law promulgated by the Tsar and would have been a genuine Russian parliament. It is true that the franchise Speransky proposed would have enormously favored the nobility, while the serfs of course would not have participated in government. It is also true that Speransky did not include emancipation of the serfs in his proposal. None

the less, the plan was decidedly advanced; Speransky knew that not everything could be accomplished at once. Indeed, as it turned out, Alexander balked at executing the plan that he himself had commissioned Speransky to draw up.

This is one of the most critical moments in all Russian history. Why did Speransky fail? He instituted a reform of the civil service, requiring examinations and a system of promotion by merit, which disturbed many of the almost illiterate and thoroughly incompetent men in high office. He even proposed that the nobility pay an income tax. Friends and intimates of the Tsar spread slander about Speransky, but at bottom Alexander himself was at fault and unwilling to act on his own alleged beliefs. Speransky's scheme was shelved, except for two elements that in no way diminished the power of the Tsar. A Council of State, which could advise the Tsar, was created, but he was not obliged to take its advice. Since he appointed and dismissed all members, the effect was simply to increase imperial effi-

Tsar Alexander I of Russia.

ciency, not to limit imperial authority. Further administrative efficiency was obtained through the reorganization of the ministries, whose duties were set out clearly for the first time, eliminating overlapping.

During the second war against Napoleon (1812–1815) Alexander fell under the influence of a Baltic Baroness named Madame de Krüdener, a mystical lady now repenting an ill-spent youth. She convinced the Tsar that he was a "man from the North" designed by destiny to overthrow Napoleon and institute a new order. At the Russian court an atmosphere of pious mysticism and conservatism replaced the earlier flashes of liberal views. Although the leading spirits of the new religiosity were all nominally Orthodox, its character was rather Protestant. It was based upon assiduous reading of the Bible, and it also included a mixture of elements from Freemasonry, Pietism (see p. 79), and the more eccentric Russian sects. It aimed at the union of all Christendom in one faith and thus aroused the fear and opposition of many Orthodox clerics. Its real importance lay in its impact on Alexander, who was now convinced that as the bearer of a sacred mission all he needed to do was follow the promptings of his inmost feelings.

During the last decade of Alexander's reign, 1815–1825, the most important figure at court was Count Arakcheev, a competent but brutal officer, who once bit off the ear of one of his men as a punishment. The chief innovation of the decade, accomplished under Arakcheev's direction, was the hated system of "military colonies," the drafting of the population of whole districts to serve in the regiments quartered there. When not drilling or fighting, the soldiers were to work their farms, and their entire lives were subject to the whims of their officers. Far from being model communities, the military colonies were virtual concentration camps. By the end of Alexander's reign, almost 400,000 soldiers were living in them.

Though Alexander gave Russia no important reforms, he did act on liberal principles outside Russia, in Poland and in Finland. Made King of Poland by the Vienna settlement of 1815 (see Chapter 19), Alexander gave the Poles an advanced constitution, with their own army, their own Polish officialdom, and the free use of their own language. He allowed the Finns, after their annexation by Russia in 1809, to preserve their own law codes and the system of local government introduced during the long preceding Swedish rule. But the "liberal Tsar" was liberal only outside his Russian dominions.

Russian Foreign Policy, 1725–1796

The motives of Russian foreign policy in the century between the death of Peter the Great and that of Alexander I were still the ancient ones of expansion against Sweden, Poland, and Turkey. But as a new member of the European power constellation, Russia found that pursuit of these old aims was now involving her in matters that had primary significance for western Europe. In 1726 Ostermann concluded an alliance with the Habsburg Empire which was to be a cornerstone of Russian foreign policy. Yet, especially in joint undertakings against the Turks, the Russians and Austrians found, as early as the 1730's, that they had conflicting ambitions in southeast Europe. This early conflict of interests was a cloud, still no larger than a man's hand, but destined to swell into the colossal thunderhead that exploded in the World War of 1914–1918. To the eighteenth century also belong the first regular Russian diplomatic service, the first Russian participation in international espionage and intrigue, and the first real Russian foreign ministers: Ostermann and his Russian successor Bestuzhev-Ryumin, men of enormous personal influence on the course of Russian diplomacy.

In the War of the Polish Succession (see p. 33) Russian forces took part in alliance with Austria in supporting Augustus III and helped to force the abdication of Stanislas Leszczynski. Immediately, the Russians and Austrians became allies in a new war against the Turks, 1735–1739 (see p. 32). Though Marshal Münnich successfully invaded the Crimea, Russian gains at the Treaty of Belgrade in 1739 were limited to Azov. The Austrians failed to co-operate satisfactorily in an invasion of the Danubian principalities and made it clear that they did not relish a Russian advance into the principalities and thus to the Habsburg frontiers.

At the opening of the War of the Austrian Succession in 1740, the Russians were preoccupied with the dynastic problem. We have already seen how the French ambassador worked to put Elizabeth on the throne and to bring about the downfall of the pro-Austrian Ostermann. But, since Bestuzhev-Ryumin continued Ostermann's policies, French hopes were largely disappointed. Prussian (and therefore anti-Austrian) influence manifested itself with the appearance of Peter III as heir, and with the choice of the future Catherine II as his bride. Thus, during the War of the Austrian Succession, there was a good deal of jockeying for Russian assistance. The advance of Frederick the Great along the Baltic shore alarmed the Russians, and so, as the war ended, a Russian corps was leisurely pushing westward, intending to join the fighting.

Anti-Prussian sentiment crystallized during the interval of peace before the outbreak of the Seven Years' War. Bestuzhev labored mightily to obtain an alliance with England, which he managed in 1755, the Russians accepting a large subsidy in exchange for a promise to keep troops in readiness against the Prussians. But the Diplomatic Revolution of 1756, making Prussia and England allies, negated this arrangement. The Russians thus remained loyal to Austria and fought the Prussians in the Seven Years' War. Once more Russian forces marched west, so slowly that there was suspicion of treason and the commander was removed. In 1758 the invasion of East Prussia began; and eventually in 1760 Russian forces entered Berlin. Elizabeth's death and the succession of the pro-Prussian Peter III led the Russians to change sides and join the Prussians briefly against the Austrians and French. Catherine, on her succession, withdrew the Russian forces, but

did not again attack the Prussians. Thus Russia found herself excluded from the peace conferences of 1763.

In foreign policy, Catherine the Great was as vigorous and unscrupulous as she was at home. She concentrated on the traditional anti-Polish and anti-Turkish aims of Russia. In 1763, only a year after she became Empress, the throne of Poland fell vacant, and Catherine secured the election of her protégé and former lover, a pro-Russian Pole, Stanislas Poniatowski. Frederick the Great joined with Catherine in a campaign to win rights for the persecuted Lutheran and Orthodox minorities in Catholic Poland. One party of Polish nobles, their national pride offended at foreign intervention, resisted, and secured the aid of France and Austria, which adopted the stratagem of pressing Turkey into war with Russia to distract Catherine from Poland.

In the first Russo-Turkish War (1768–1774), Catherine's forces won a series of victories. A Russian Baltic fleet, sent all the way around Europe and into the Mediterranean through the Straits of Gibraltar, destroyed the Turkish fleet in the Aegean (1770), largely owing to the superior seamanship of a few English officers who were advising the otherwise inefficient Russians. But the Russians failed to follow up their initial advantage by storming the Straits and attacking Istanbul, and operations shifted to the Crimea and the Danubian principalities. While the Russians and Turks were discussing peace terms, Frederick the Great had concluded that Russia had been too successful against the Turks and might seize most of Poland for herself unless he acted quickly.

So Frederick took the leading part in arranging the first partition of Poland (1772). Poland lost to Russia, Prussia, and Austria almost one-third of her territory and one-half of her population. Frederick's share of the loot—the lands immediately to the west of East Prussia—was the smallest but the most strategic. It included the region that had previously separated Brandenburg from East Prussia. Maria Theresa, the Empress of Austria, abandoned her Turkish and Polish allies to participate.

She did seem somewhat reluctant, yet, as Frederick the Great observed, "She wept, but she kept on taking." Russia received a substantial area of what is now known as Belorussia, or White Russia.

Two years later, the Russians imposed upon the Turks a most humiliating peace treaty, at Kutchuk Kainardji (1774). Catherine annexed much of the formerly Turkish stretch of Black Sea coast and two places in the Crimea; the rest of the Crimea was separated from the Ottoman Empire as an independent Tartar state.

She also obtained something the Russians had long coveted: freedom of navigation on the Black Sea and the right of passage through the Bosphorus and the Dardanelles. A vaguely worded clause gave her various rights to protect the Christian subjects of the sultan, thus providing a convenient excuse for Russian intervention in Turkish affairs later on.

Catherine now began to dream of expelling the Turks from Europe and reviving the Byzantine Empire under Russian protection. She saw to it that her younger grandson was christened

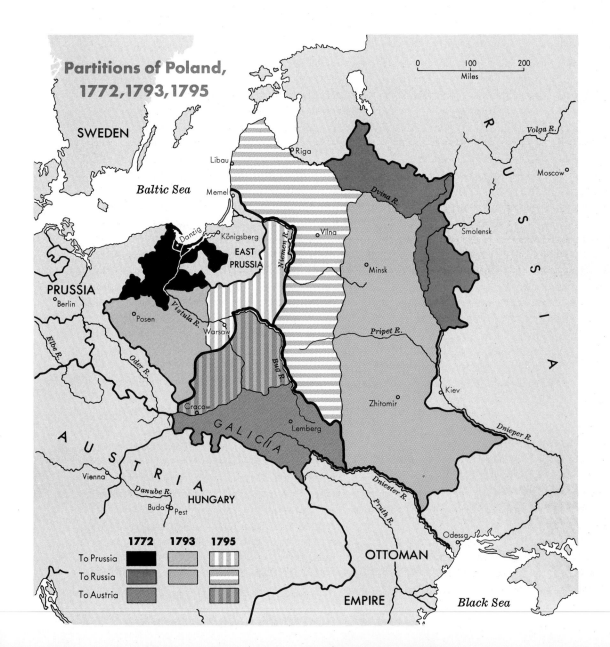

Partitions of Poland, 1772, 1793, 1795

	1772	1793	1795
To Prussia			
To Russia			
To Austria			

Constantine and imported Greek-speaking nurses to train him in the language. She also proposed to set up a kingdom of Dacia (the Roman name for the area) in the Danubian principalities to be ruled by her lover and general, Potemkin. By way of preparation, in 1783, Catherine annexed the Tartar state of the Crimea, where she built a naval base at Sebastopol. To achieve these grandiose designs, Catherine sought the consent of Austria and invited Joseph II on a famous tour by riverboat of the newly developed and annexed territories of the Russian southwest. On this tour, the Austrian Emperor was allegedly shown the famous "Potemkin villages," mere cardboard facades facing the river to look like settlements but with nothing behind them; like so many other good stories, this one is untrue. At Sebastopol, however, signs pointed across the Black Sea, saying, "This way to Byzantium." In a second Russo-Turkish war (1787–1791), Catherine's allies, the Austrians, once again provided feeble assistance and made a separate peace. Again, a conflict of interests over the European lands of the Sultan precipitated Austro-Russian disagreement. In the end, Catherine had to abandon her Greek project and content herself with annexing the remaining Turkish lands along the northern coast of the Black Sea and securing recognition of Russian sovereignty over the Crimea.

Before her death, Catherine participated in two more partitions of Poland. The second partition came as the result of a Polish constitutional movement, supported by the Prussians in opposition to Russian interest. Catherine intervened on the pretext of defending the established order in Poland and fighting the virus of revolution. In 1793, both the Russians and Prussians took large new slices of Polish territory; the Austrians did not participate in this second partition of Poland. An attempted Polish revolution against the reduction of their state to a wretched remnant dominated by foreigners was followed by the third and final partition of 1795, by which Poland disappeared from the map. This time Austria joined the other two powers and obtained Cracow; Prussia got Warsaw, and Russia secured Lithuania and other Baltic and east Polish lands.

The spectacular successes of Catherine meant the transfer to Russia of millions of human beings—Poles, Lithuanians, Belorussians—who loathed the Russians, and left a legacy of trouble. It also meant that Russia had destroyed useful buffers in the shape of the Polish and Tartar states, and now had common frontiers with her potential enemies, Prussia and Austria. The last two partitions of Poland had been made possible by the preoccupation of the western powers with their war against revolutionary France; the story of Russian foreign policy after Catherine forms part of the larger story of this great war (see Chapter 18).

V George III and the American Revolution

George III

Though Catherine the Great failed to apply the ideas of the Age of Reason, her name usually appears on lists of enlightened despots. Another name might possibly be added to the list—George III, King of Great Britain (1760 –1820). Actually, "Farmer George" showed very little enlightenment beyond taking an interest in the agrarian revolution and writing articles on turnips for Arthur Young's *Annals of Agriculture*. In politics, however, he did attempt a course that may be termed a dilute form of enlightened despotism, or, more exactly, a reassertion of the monarch's authority. The first of the Hanoverian monarchs born and bred in England, George III proposed to reassert some of the royal prerogatives that had lapsed under the first two Georges. He tried to wrest control of the House of Commons from the long-dominant Whig oligarchy and retain it by the Whig devices of patronage and bribery. He endeavored to beat the Whigs at their own parliamentary game.

Virtuous as a person and devoted to his family, George as a monarch was stubborn, short-sighted, and in the long run unsuccessful. It was easy for him at first to exploit the factional strife among the Whigs, maneuver Pitt out of office in 1761, and make his friend and tutor, Lord Bute, the head of the cabinet. Bute and the King, however, found it hard to justify their failure to deprive France of the sugar-rich West Indies in the Peace of Paris, which brought the Seven Years' War to a conclusion (see Chapter 16). The Commons ratified the treaty, but George dismissed Bute to appease the critics of British diplomacy.

The harshest criticism came from John Wilkes, a member of Commons, who dubbed the Peace of Paris "the peace of God, for it passeth all understanding." Wilkes' attack on the treaty in his paper, the *North Briton*, infuriated the King; bowing to the royal anger, the Commons ordered the offending issue of the *North Briton* to be burnt. Later, Wilkes ran for Parliament three separate times, and three times the Commons, under royal pressure, threw out his election. When Wilkes finally took his seat again in 1774, he was a popular hero, and riots had occurred in defense of "Wilkes and Liberty." A wise king would have reconsidered his course, but George III did not relax his determination to manage both Parliament and cabinet. After seven years of short-lived, unstable ministries (1763–1770), George finally found a man to fill Bute's old role and do the King's bidding—Lord North, who headed the cabinet for a dozen years (1770–1782). Under North, royal intervention in politics at first stiffened, then wavered, and at length collapsed. At home, the King unwittingly prepared the way for the increase of parliamentary authority; abroad, he lost the thirteen North American colonies.

Background of the Revolution

The breach between colonies and mother country first became serious at the close of the Seven Years' War when Britain began to retreat from the old policy of "salutary neglect" and to interfere more directly and more frequently in colonial matters. But, by 1763, the colonies had acquired the habit of regulating their own affairs, though the acts of their assemblies remained subject to the veto of royally appointed governors or of the King himself. The vast territories in Canada and west of the Alleghenies acquired in 1763 brought Britain added opportunities for profitable exploitation and added responsibilities for government and defense. When an uprising of Indians under Pontiac threatened frontier posts in the area of the Ohio Valley and the Great Lakes, colonial militias failed to take effective action, and British regulars were brought in. The continuing threat from the Indians prompted the royal proclamation of October, 1763, forbidding "all our loving subjects" to settle west of a line running along the summit of the Alleghenies. To His Majesty's "loving subjects" in the seaboard colonies, however, the proclamation seemed deliberately designed to exclude them from the riches of the West.

The colonies resented still more keenly the attempt by Parliament to raise more revenue in North America. The British government had very strong arguments for increasing colonial taxes. The national debt had almost doubled during the Seven Years' War; the colonies' reluctance to recruit soldiers and raise taxes themselves had increased the cost of the war to British taxpayers; now the mother country faced continued expense in protecting the frontier. Surely the Americans would admit the reasonableness of the case for higher taxes.

That, however, was precisely what the Americans did *not* admit. The first of the new revenue measures, the Sugar Act of 1764, alarmed the merchants of the eastern seaboard because the customs officers actually undertook to collect duties on molasses, sugar, and other imports. Here was a departure from the comfortable laxity of salutary neglect. And here was a threat to the colonial economy, for the import duties had to be paid out of the colonies' meager supply of specie (metal coin). The second revenue measure, the Stamp Act of 1765, imposed levies on a wide variety of items, including legal and commercial papers, liquor licenses, playing cards, dice, newspapers, calendars, and academic degrees. These duties, too, drained the supply of specie, which sank so low that some merchants faced bankruptcy.

The revenue measures touched off a major controversy. Indignant merchants in the New World boycotted all imports rather than pay the duties, and in October, 1765, delegates from nine of the thirteen colonies met in New York City as the "Stamp Act Congress." The Congress complained that the new duties had "a manifest tendency to subvert the rights and liberties of the colonists." The Congress resolved:

That His Majesty's liege subjects in these colonies are entitled to all the inherent rights and liberties of his natural born subjects within the kingdom of Great Britain.

That it is inseparably essential to the freedom of a people, and the undoubted right of Englishmen, that no taxes be imposed on them but with their own consent, given personally or by their own representatives.

That the people of these colonies are not, and from their local circumstances cannot be, represented in the House of Commons in Great Britain.

That the only representatives of these colonies are persons chosen therein by themselves, and that no taxes ever have been, or can be constitutionally imposed on them, but by their respective legislatures.*

The Stamp Act Congress thus proclaimed the celebrated principle of no taxation without representation. Britain surrendered on the

*Documents of American History, H. S. Commager, ed. (New York, 1940), 58.

practical issue, but did not yield on the principle. The appeals of London merchants, nearly ruined by the American boycott against British goods, brought the repeal of the Stamp Act in 1765. In 1766, however, Parliament passed the Declaratory Act asserting that the King and Parliament could indeed make laws affecting the colonies.

For the next decade, Britain adhered firmly to the principles of the Declaratory Act, and colonial radicals just as firmly repeated their opposition to taxation without representation. Parliament again tried to raise revenue, this time by the Townshend duties (1767) on colonial imports of tea, paper, paint, and lead. Again the merchants of Philadelphia, New York, and Boston organized boycotts. In 1770, Lord North's cabinet withdrew the Townshend

An English commentary on the Boston Tea Party and the tarring and feathering of a royal tax collector, who is forced to drink under a liberty tree.

duties except for the three-penny tariff on a pound of tea, retained as a symbol of parliamentary authority over the colonies. Three years later, the English East India Company attempted the sale of surplus tea in North America, hoping to overcome American opposition to the hated duty by making the retail price of East India tea, duty included, far cheaper than that of Dutch tea smuggled by the colonists. The result was the Boston Tea Party. On December 16, 1773, to the cheers of spectators lining the waterfront, a group of Bostonians, who had a large financial stake in smuggled tea, disguised themselves as Indians, boarded three East India ships, and dumped into the harbor chests of tea worth thousands of pounds.

Britain answered defiance with coercion, and the colonists met coercion with resistance. The Quebec Act (1774), incorporating the lands beyond the Alleghenies into Canada, bolted the door to the westward expansion of colonial frontiers. The "Intolerable Acts" (1774) closed the port of Boston to trade and suspended elections in Massachusetts. At Lexington and Concord in April, 1775, the "embattled farmers" of Massachusetts fired the opening shots of the War of Independence. At Philadelphia on July 4, 1776, the delegates to the Continental Congress formally declared the American colonies independent of Great Britain.

Implications of the Revolution

For the mother country, the American Revolution implied more than the secession of thirteen colonies. It involved Britain in a minor world war that jeopardized her dominance abroad and weakened the power and prestige of King George III at home. The most crucial battle in North America came early in the war—the surrender at Saratoga in 1777 of the British forces under Burgoyne, who had been marching south from Montreal with the aim of driving a wedge between New England and the other rebellious colonies. Burgoyne's surrender convinced the French that support of the American colonists would give them an excellent chance to renew their world-wide strug-

gle with Britain and avenge the humiliation of 1763. Entering the war in 1778, France soon gained the alliance of Spain and eventually secured the help, or at least the friendly neutrality, of most other European states. French intervention prepared the way for the victory of George Washington's forces and the final British surrender at Yorktown in 1781. In the peace signed at Paris in 1783, Britain recognized the independence of her former colonies. To Spain she handed back Florida, which she had taken in 1763, and the strategic Mediterranean island of Minorca. But she kept Gibraltar, which the Spanish had also hoped to recover, and she ceded only minor territories to France.

During the early years of the war, the British public had been inclined to agree with Dr. Samuel Johnson that the Americans were "a race of convicts" and "ought to be thankful for anything we allow them short of hanging." But the temper of opinion changed as the strength of American resistance became evident, as instances of British mismanagement piled up, and as most of Europe rallied to the rebellious colonies. By 1780, George III and his policies were so unpopular that the House of Commons passed a resolution declaring that "the influence of the crown has increased, is increasing, and ought to be diminished."

The influence of the Crown *was* diminished. In 1782, Lord North, who had been imploring the King for three years to accept his resignation, finally stepped down. In the next year, the post of prime minister fell to William Pitt the Younger, son of the heroic Pitt of the Seven Years' War. Though only twenty-five years old, he was a seasoned parliamentarian who was to head the cabinet for the next eighteen years. With the advent of Pitt, control of British politics shifted away from the King and back to the professional politicians. George III briefly contemplated abdication and then gradually resigned himself to the passive role of constitutional monarch. The British flirtation (it was really no more than that) with enlightened despotism had come to an end.

While American independence was a nationalist rather than a social revolution, the movement that produced it did have social implications. In the colonies, opinion was by no means unanimous in support of the revolution. Many well-to-do colonists, including southern planters and Pennsylvania Quakers, either backed the mother country or took a neutral position in the struggle; New York supplied more recruits to George III than to George Washington. Some of these "Loyalists" or "Tories" were to flee to Canada when independence became a fact. Scholars, however, now find that the traditional estimate—that only one-third of the colonists actively backed the Revolution—is too low. Revolutionary sentiment ran particularly high in Virginia and New England and among social groups who had the habit of questioning established authority—the pioneers living on the frontier, and the numerous Presbyterians, Congregationalists, and members of other strong-minded Protestant sects. Like adolescents everywhere, the colonists resented parental tutelage yet appealed to family precedent. They claimed that they were only following the example set by Englishmen in 1688 and defended by John Locke.

The ideas of Locke and Newton were as well known and as much respected in North America as they were in Europe. They underlay the Declaration of Independence:

When in the course of human events, it becomes necessary for one people to dissolve the political bands which have connected them with another, and to assume among the Powers of the earth, the separate and equal station to which the Laws of Nature and Nature's God entitle them, a decent respect to the opinions of mankind requires that they should declare the causes which impel them to the separation.

The opening paragraph of the Declaration thus expressed the concept of a world-machine ruled by the "Laws of Nature." The next paragraph applied to the colonies Locke's theory of contract and his justification of revolution:

We hold these truths to be self-evident, that all men are created equal, that they are endowed by their Creator with certain unalienable Rights, that among these are Life, Liberty and the pursuit of Happiness. That to secure these rights, Govern-

ments are instituted among Men, deriving their just power from the consent of the governed. That whenever any Form of Government becomes destructive of these ends, it is the Right of the People to alter or to abolish it, and to institute new Government. . . .

Another political idea of the Enlightenment congenial to the revolutionaries was the separation of powers proposed by Locke and by Montesquieu as a guarantee against tyranny. At the heart of the draft drawn up by the delegates to the constitutional convention at Philadelphia in 1787 was the separation of the executive, legislative, and judicial arms of government. Each of the branches had the power to check the other two. The President, for instance, could check the Congress by applying a veto; Congress could check the executive and the judiciary through impeachment and the right of confirming appointments; and one house of Congress exercised a check on the other by the requirement that both houses consent to legislation. Since these balancing devices were in part derived from Montesquieu, it may be argued that the recurrent tensions between President and Congress originated in the American adaptation of an eighteenth-century French misreading of British constitutional practice. The "Founding Fathers" of the American republic sought guidance not only from *The Spirit of the Laws* but also from the constitutions of the thirteen original states and from English precedents. The first ten amendments to the Constitution (1791), guaranteeing freedom of religion, freedom of the press, and other basic liberties, were taken mainly from the English Bill of Rights of 1689.

The Constitution abounded in compromises. It attempted a balance between states' rights and the central power of the federal government, and between the democratic principle of a directly elected House of Representatives and the aristocratic principle of an indirectly elected and conservative Senate. It was a compromise designed to win support from both rich and poor and from both the Tory opponents and the democratic supporters of the recent revolution. Like any compromise, it did not at first please all parties, but it worked well enough to make the new American republic a going concern. The "Founding Fathers" of the United States had succeeded perhaps better than any other statesmen of the century in adjusting the ideals of the *philosophes* to the realities of practical politics.

VI   The Culture of the Eighteenth Century

The Limitations of Reason

The Enlightenment, however, seldom produced such happy political results as it did in the United States. On the whole, the *philosophes* expected men to see reason when it was pointed out to them, to abandon the habits of centuries, and to revise their behavior in accordance with natural law. But men would not always see reason; as Joseph II discovered to his sorrow, they *would* cling perversely to irrational customs and unnatural traditions. The rationalism of the Enlightenment tended to omit the complexities of human nature from its calculations.

Responsibility for this major shortcoming lay partly with the "classical spirit" of the seventeenth century, inherited by the Enlightenment of the eighteenth. The writers of the Age of Louis XIV had found in their classical models, not a confirmation of existing standards, but a better, simpler set of standards that the eighteenth-century *philosophes* easily adapted to the concept of "nature's simple plan." The great writers achieve the miracle of giving life to these abstractions. But the lesser ones make only bloodless types, and encourage in their hearers and readers—the men and women who finally do work out social change—the belief that these easy mental images are somehow more real, and certainly more desirable, than the bewildering complexity of their concrete experiences. Like the "classical spirit," the spirit of natural science went too far when it was applied uncritically to problems of human relations. It gave men the illusion that what was going on in their minds would shortly go on in reality.

A minor *philosophe,* the Abbé Mably, got at this central problem when he asked: "Is society, then, a branch of physics?" Most of the *philosophes* and their followers believed that it was. They applied to the unpredictable activities of man the mathematical methods used in the physical sciences. The Physiocrats, for example, tried to reduce the complexities of human economic activities to a few simple agricultural laws. Like the stars in their courses, human beings were thought to fit neatly into the Newtonian world-machine.

A few eighteenth-century minds disagreed. David Hume (1711–1776), the skeptical Scottish philosopher, insisted on submitting principles to the test of factual observation. The *philosophes*, he said, failed to do this and thus deduced untested conclusions from two great abstract principles—faith in natural law, belief in reason. Hume made short work of the *philosophes'* appeals to nature. The laws of justice, he argued, were not absolute and inflexible natural laws:

. . . Suppose a society to fall into such want of all common necessaries, that the utmost frugality and industry cannot preserve the greater number from perishing, and the whole from extreme misery; it will readily, I believe, be admitted, that the strict laws of justice are suspended, in such a pressing emergence, and give place to the stronger motives of necessity and self-preservation. Is it any crime, after a shipwreck, to seize whatever means or instrument of safety one can lay hold of, without regard to former limitations of property?*

Nor, Hume argued, could human conduct be analyzed "in the same manner that we discover by reason the truths of geometry or algebra."

An Enquiry concerning the Principles of Morals, L. A. Selby-Bigge, ed. (Oxford, 1902), 186.

It appears evident that the ultimate ends of human actions can never, in any case, be accounted for by *reason*, but recommend themselves entirely to the sentiments and affections of mankind, without any dependance on the intellectual faculties. Ask a man *why he uses exercise:* he will answer, *because he desires to keep his health.* If you then enquire, *why he desires health,* he will readily reply, *because sickness is painful.* If you push your enquiries farther, and desire a reason *why he hates pain*, it is impossible he can ever give any. . . .*

David Hume was among the first and most profound critics of the Age of Reason. The Romantics of the next generation would repeat his warnings against reason and his pleas on behalf of the "sentiments and affections of mankind" (see Chapter 19). In Hume's own day, Rousseau and Kant were also worried by rather similar problems. Rousseau both represented the Enlightenment and foreshadowed the revolt against it. No *philosophe* defended natural law more ardently, yet no Romantic argued more powerfully on behalf of the irrational faculties of man. "Too often does reason deceive us," Rousseau wrote in *Emile.* "We have only too good a right to doubt her; but conscience never deceives us; she is the true guide of man; . . . he who obeys his conscience is following nature and he need not fear that he will go astray."†

Immanuel Kant (1724–1804), who taught philosophy at the University of Königsberg in Prussia, raised Rousseau's argument to the level of metaphysics. While advocating many of the doctrines of the Enlightenment, Kant also believed in a higher reality reaching ultimately to God. He called the eternal verities of the higher world "noumena," in contrast to the phenomena of the material world. Knowledge of the noumenal realm, Kant believed, reached men through reason—reason, however, not as the Enlightenment used the term, not as common sense, but as intuition. The highest expression of the Kantian reason was the "categorical imperative." This was the moral law within, the conscience implanted in man by God. It was the inescapable realization by the individual that, when confronted

with an ethical choice, he must choose the good and avoid the evil. Kant's redefinition of reason and his rehabilitation of conscience exemplified the philosophical reaction against the dominant rationalism of the Enlightenment. The popular reaction took the very different form of the evangelical revival, which began with the German Pietists.

The Evangelical Revival

The Pietists were the spiritual descendants of the sixteenth-century Anabaptists. Deploring alike the growing Lutheran concern with the formalities of religion and the deists' emphasis on natural law, the Pietists asserted that religion came from the heart, not the head. For the Pietists God was far more than the watchmaker, the remote creator of the world-machine. One of the chief leaders of Pietism was a German nobleman, Count Zinzendorf (1700–1760), founder of the Moravian Brethren, who set up a model community based on Christian principles. Moravian emigrants to America planted a colony at Bethlehem, Pennsylvania, helping to give the "Pennsylvania Dutch" their reputation for thrift, hard work, and strict living. In England, meanwhile, the example of Zinzendorf and other Pietists inspired Wesley.

Ordained a priest of the Church of England, John Wesley (1703–1791) at first stressed the ritualistic aspects of religion. But after the failure of his two-year ministry to the backward colony of Georgia (1736–1737), he felt his own faith evaporating: "I went to America, to convert the Indians: but Oh! who shall convert me! Who, what is he that will deliver me from this evil heart of unbelief?"* Pietism converted Wesley and taught him that he would find faith through inner conviction. For more than fifty years, Wesley labored tirelessly to share his discovery, traveling throughout the British Isles, and preaching in churches, in the fields, at the pitheads of coal mines, and even in jails. Angry crowds came to scoff but remained to pray. When Wesley died in 1791,

---

Ibid., 293.
†*Emile*, Everyman ed. (New York, 1911), 249–250.

*John Wesley, *Journal.* Everyman ed. (New York, 1907), I, 74.

his movement had already attracted more than a hundred thousand adherents. They were called Methodists, because of their methodical devotion to piety and to plain dressing and plain living. Though Wesley always considered himself a good Anglican, the Methodists eventually set up a separate organization—their nonconformist "Chapel" in contrast to the established Church of England. The new sect won its following almost entirely among the lower and middle classes, among people who sought the religious excitement and consolation that they did not find in deism or in the austere formalism of the Church of England.

Although the beliefs of the Methodists diverged entirely from those of the enlightened rationalists, both groups worked in their different ways to improve the condition of society. Where the *philosophes* advised public reform, the Methodists favored private charity; and where the *philosophes* attacked the *causes* of social evils, the Methodists accepted these evils as part of God's plan and sought to mitigate their *symptoms*. They had in full measure the Puritan conscience of the nonconformists. They began agitation against drunkenness, the trade in slaves, and the barbarous treatment of prisoners, the insane, and the sick. John Wesley established schools for coalminers' children and opened dispensaries for the poor in London and Bristol. While the Methodists' success came in part from their social activities, it also came from the magnetism of John Wesley and his talented associates. His brother Charles composed more than 6500 hymns, and in America Methodist missionaries flourished under the dynamic leadership of Francis Asbury (1745–1816). The number of colleges called Wesleyan and the number of churches and streets called Asbury testify to the significance of Methodism in American social history.

Literature

The middle-class public so strongly attracted to Methodism welcomed the novels of the Englishman, Samuel Richardson (1689–1761), who made a significant contribution to this emerging literary form. A printer by trade, Richardson turned to writing late in life and produced three gigantic novels in the form of letters by the chief characters. In *Clarissa Harlowe* (1748), for example, Richardson devoted 2400 pages of small print to the misfortunes of Clarissa, whose lover was a scoundrel, and whose relatives were a greedy pack, scheming to secure her considerable property. Whatever her plight, Clarissa never lost the capacity to pour out her miseries on paper. If anyone missed the point of the story, he had only to turn to Richardson's preface:

What will be found to be more particularly aimed at in the following work is—to warn the inconsiderate and thoughtless of one sex, against the base arts and designs of specious contrivers of the other—to caution parents against the undue exercise of their natural authority over their children in the great article of marriage—to warn against preferring a man of pleasure to a man of probity upon that dangerous but too-commonly-received notion, *that a reformed rake makes the best husband*—but above all, to investigate the highest and most important doctrines not only of morality, but of christianity, by showing them thrown into action in the conduct of the *worthy* characters; while the *unworthy*, who set these doctrines at defiance, are condignly, and, as may be said, consequentially punished.

Clarissa was read aloud at family gatherings, it is said, and whenever some new disaster overwhelmed the heroine, the members separated for a good solitary cry. In spite of Richardson's exaggerations, his descriptions of the struggles of passion and conscience carried conviction.

By no means all the masters of English fiction were as sentimental as Richardson. In *Roderick Random* (1748), Tobias Smollett drew an authentic picture of life in the navy, with all its cruelty and hardship. Henry Fielding introduced a strong leaven of satire and burlesqued the excesses of Richardson. Fielding covered a broad social scene in his masterpiece, *Tom Jones* (1749), depicting both the hard-riding country squires and the low characters of the city slums. Richardson gave the English novel emotional and moral earnestness; Smollet and Fielding gave it vigorous realism.

On the whole, the eighteenth century was an age of prose and produced few poets of stature. Its literary monuments were the novels of Richardson and Fielding, the tales and essays of Voltaire, Gibbon's *History of the Decline and Fall of the Roman Empire* (1788), and Dr. Johnson's *Dictionary* (1755). Edward Gibbon utilized history for a sustained Voltairian attack on Christian fanaticism and employed a Ciceronian prose style which, by its balance and discipline, perfectly suited the classical temper of the Enlightenment. Dr. Samuel Johnson's dictionary also expressed the "style" of the age. He declared in the preface:

When I took the first survey of my undertaking, I found our speech copious without order and energetick without rules: wherever I turned my view, there was perplexity to be disentangled, and confusion to be regulated; choice was to be made out of a boundless variety, without any established principle of selection; adulterations were to be detected, without a settled test of purity; and modes of expression to be rejected or received, without the suffrages of any writers of classical reputation or acknowledged authority.

Pedantry and prejudice sometimes overcame the autocratic doctor. His definition of a cough—"a convulsion of the lungs, vellicated by some sharp serosity"—revealed the dangers of employing little-known Latinisms. Whenever he could, he aimed a volley at his favorite target, the Scots. Thus he defined oats as "a grain, which in England is generally given to horses, but in Scotland supports the people." In the main, however, Dr. Johnson succeeded admirably in his aim of becoming a kind of Newton of the English language.

Art

The classicism of the century strongly affected its art. Gibbon's history, the researches of scholars and archaeologists, and the discovery in 1748 of the ruins of Roman Pompeii, well-preserved under lava from Vesuvius, raised the interest in antiquity to a high pitch. For the men of the Enlightenment, the balance and symmetry of Greek and Roman temples represented, in effect, the natural laws of building. Architects retreated somewhat from the theatricalism of the Baroque style and adapted classical models with great artistry and variety. We owe to them the elegance of the London town house, the monumental magnificence of the buildings flanking the Place de la Concorde in Paris, and the country-manor charm of Washington's Mount Vernon. The twentieth-century vogue of the "colonial" and the "Georgian" testifies to the lasting influence of this neoclassical architecture.

In painting, neoclassicism had an eminent spokesman in Sir Joshua Reynolds (1723–1792), the president of the Royal Academy and the artistic tsar of Georgian England. Beauty, Sir Joshua told the academy, rested "on the uniform, eternal, and immutable laws of nature," which could be "investigated by reason, and known by study." Sir Joshua and his contemporaries, though preaching a coldly reasoned aesthetic, gave warmth to the

Dr. Samuel Johnson, by Sir Joshua Reynolds.

Left: Eighteenth-century classical design: the Library at Ken Wood, near London, designed by Robert Adam.

Right: The Gothic revival in design: gallery at Horace Walpole's Strawberry Hill, near London.

portraits that they painted of wealthy English aristocrats. This was the golden age of English portraiture, the age of Reynolds, Lawrence, Gainsborough, and Romney. But it was also the age of William Hogarth (1697–1764), who cast aside the academic restraints of neoclassicism to do in art what Fielding did in the novel. Instead of catering to a few wealthy patrons, Hogarth created a mass market for the engravings that he turned out in thousands of copies, conveying with brutal frankness the vices of London—*Marriage à la Mode, The Rake's Progress, The Harlot's Progress,* and *Gin Lane.*

The realism of Hogarth was not the only exception to the prevailing neoclassicism. The fashions for the oriental, the natural, and the Gothic, which were to be so important in the Age of Romanticism were already beginning to catch on. The taste for the exotic produced Chinese wallpaper, the "Chinese" furniture of Thomas Chippendale, and the familiar Chinese pattern of "willowware" plates. Gardens were bestrewn with pagodas and minarets, and gardeners abandoned Louis XIV's geometrical landscaping for the natural English garden. Even the dominance of neoclassical architecture was challenged. At Strawberry Hill near London, Horace Walpole, the son of the great Robert, endowed his house with an abundance of Gothic "gloomth"—battlements in the medieval style, and "lean windows fattened with rich saints in painted glass."

82

The Great Musicians

Music was perhaps the queen of the arts in the eighteenth century, and music, too, transcended the boundaries of narrow classicism or rationalism. Early in the century Johann Sebastian Bach (1685–1750) brought to perfection the Baroque techniques of seventeenth-century composers. He mastered the difficult art of the fugue, an intricate version of the round in which each voice begins the theme in turn while the other voices repeat and elaborate it. Bach also composed a wealth of material for the organ, the most Baroque and the most religious of instruments. His sacred works included many cantatas, the Mass in B minor, and the two gigantic choral settings of the Passion of Christ according to St. John and St. Matthew. The religious music of Bach, dramatic and deeply felt, was a world apart from the anticlericalism of the Enlightenment.

In contrast to Bach's quiet career as composer and conductor in Germany was the stormy international experience of his contemporary, Handel (1685–1759). Born in Germany, Handel studied in Italy, then spent most of his adult years in England trying to run an opera company in the face of the intrigues, clashes of temperament, and fiscal headaches inevitable in artistic enterprise. Handel wrote more than forty operas, including *Xerxes*, famous for "Handel's Largo." He used themes from the Bible for *The Messiah* and other vigorous oratorios directed at a mass audience and arranged for large choruses. These elaborate works differed greatly from the original oratorios of seventeenth-century Italy, which had been written for the tiny prayer chapels called oratories.

While Bach and Handel composed many instrumental suites and concertos, it was not until the second half of the century that orchestral music really came to the fore. New instruments appeared, notably the piano, which greatly extended the limited range of the older keyboard instrument, the harpsichord. New forms of instrumental music also appeared, the sonata and the symphony, developed largely by Haydn (1732–1809). Haydn wrote more than fifty piano pieces in the form of the sonata, in which two contrasting themes are stated in turn, developed, interwoven, repeated, and finally resolved in a *coda* (the Italian for "tail"). Haydn then arranged the sonata for the orchestra, grafting it onto the Italian operatic overture to create the first movement of the symphony.

The operatic landmark of the early century was John Gay's *Beggar's Opera* (1728), a tuneful work caricaturing English society and politics in Hogarthian vein. Later, Gluck (1714–1787) revolutionized the technique of the tragic opera. "I have striven," he said,

to restrict music to its true office of serving poetry by means of expression and by following the situations of the story, without interrupting the action or stifling it with a useless superfluity of ornaments. . . . I did not wish to arrest an actor in the greatest heat of dialogue . . . to hold him up in the middle of a word on a vowel favorable to his voice, nor to make display of the agility of his fine voice in some long-drawn passage, nor to wait while the orchestra gives him time to recover his breath for a cadenza.*

Accordingly, Gluck's operas were well-constructed musical dramas, not just vehicles for the display of vocal pyrotechnics. He kept to the old custom of taking heroes and heroines from classical mythology, but he tried to invest shadowy figures like Orpheus, Eurydice, and Iphigenia with new vitality.

Opera, symphony, and chamber music all reached a climax in the works of Mozart (1756–1791). As a boy, Mozart was exploited by his father, who carted him all over Europe to show off his virtuosity on the harpsichord and his amazing talent for composition. Overworked throughout his life, and in his later years overburdened with debts, Mozart died a pauper at the age of thirty-five. Yet his youthful precociousness ripened steadily into mature genius, and his facility and versatility

*Preface to *Alcestis*, as translated by Eric Blom and quoted in Curt Sachs, *Our Musical Heritage* (New York, 1948), 287.

grew ever more prodigious. He tossed off the sprightly overture to *The Marriage of Figaro* in the course of an evening. In two months during the summer of 1788, he produced the three great symphonies familiar to concert audiences as No. 39 (E flat major), No. 40 (G minor), and No. 41 ("The Jupiter"). Mozart's orchestral works also included a long list of concertos, with the solo parts sometimes for piano or violin and sometimes, just to show that it could be done, for bassoon or French horn. In chamber music, Mozart experimented with almost every possible combination of instruments.

Three of Mozart's great operas were in the comic Italian vein—the farcical *Così Fan Tutte* ("Thus Do All Women"); *The Marriage of Fi-garo* based on Beaumarchais' famous satire of the caste system of the Old Régime, in which Figaro the valet outwits and outsings his noble employers; and, finally, *Don Giovanni*, depicting the havoc wrought by Don Juan on earth before his eventual punishment in hell. Mozart composed with equal skill mournful and romantic arias for the Don's victims, elegantly seductive ballads for the Don himself, and a catalog of the Don's conquests for his valet ("A thousand and three in Spain alone"). The instruments in the pit dotted the "i's" and crossed the "t's" of the plot—scurrying violins to accompany characters dashing about the stage, portentous trombones to announce the entrance of the Devil. For the ballroom scene of *Don Giovanni*, Mozart employed three or-

Mozart singing his Requiem, a painting by Thomas W. Shields.

chestras, playing simultaneously three different tunes for three different dances — a minuet for the aristocracy, a country dance for the middle class, a waltz for the lower orders. In his last opera, *The Magic Flute*, Mozart tried to create a consciously German work; but only the vaguest political significance emerged from the fantastic libretto, which apparently sought to vindicate the enlightened ideas of Joseph II and to decry the conservatism of Maria Theresa.

The Magic Flute was a rare exception to the cosmopolitanism of eighteenth-century music. The great composers with the German names had very little national feeling. Almost all of them felt equally at home in Vienna, Prague, Milan, Paris, and London, and they gratefully accepted patrons in any country. The fortunate Haydn moved from the princely estate of the Hungarian Esterhazy family to score an equal success with the paying public of the London concert-halls. Italian music was never totally eclipsed, nor was German dominance complete. Bach patterned his concertos on Italian models, Haydn borrowed Italian operatic overtures for his symphonies, and every oper-

atic composer of the century profited from the labors of his Italian predecessors. The great composers also borrowed freely from folktunes and ballads, the popular music of their day, and were rewarded by having their themes whistled in the streets. Mozart's operas, Haydn's symphonies, and the choral masterpieces of Bach and Handel retained the capacity to engage the listener's emotions.

Of all the arts, music probably came closest to resolving the great conflict in eighteenth-century culture, the tension beteen reason and emotion, between the abstractions of the Enlightenment and the flesh-and-blood realities of human existence. In other realms, however, as the century drew toward its close, the lines were drawn for the vigorous prosecution of the conflict. In thought, the ideas of Kant and Hume were challenging the optimistic rationalism of the *philosophes*. Romantic artists and writers were beginning to defy the defenders of classicism. And in politics, as the century ended, the European powers sought to thwart the supreme effort to realize on earth the Enlightenment's dream of reason, natural law, and progress — the French Revolution.

Reading Suggestions on the Enlightenment

(*Asterisk indicates paperbound edition.)

General Accounts

W. L. Dorn, *Competition for Empire, 1740–1763* (*Torch). Contains a meaty chapter on the Enlightenment and a full bibliography.

L. Gershoy, *From Despotism to Revolution, 1763–1789* (*Torch). A sympathetic study of the ideas of the Enlightenment, and a comprehensive and sometimes caustic analysis of the Enlightened Despots; with full bibliographies.

F. Manuel, *The Age of Reason* (*Cornell Univ. Press), and G. Bruun, *The Enlightened Despots* (Holt, 1929). Two helpful brief introductions.

R. R. Palmer, *The Age of the Democratic Revolution,* Vol. I (Princeton Univ. Press, 1959). A political history of Europe and America at the close of the Old Régime, stressing the parallel developments on the two continents.

New Cambridge Modern History, Vol. VIII: "The American and French Revolutions, 1763–1793" (Cambridge Univ. Press, 1965). Some chapters in this collaborative work are quite helpful.

Peter Gay, *The Enlightenment: The Rise of Modern Paganism* (Knopf, 1966). The first half of a projected two-volume study by a leading scholar; with a rich bibliographical essay.

**The Ideas
of the
Enlightenment**

G. R. Havens, *The Age of Ideas: From Reaction to Revolution in Eighteenth-Century France* (*Free Press). A most useful volume, fully abreast of modern research.

P. Smith, *The History of Modern Culture,* Vol. II (Holt, 1934). A mine of information on details often neglected in intellectual histories.

E. Cassirer, *The Philosophy of the Enlightenment* (*Beacon, 1955). An important study of the great principles of eighteenth-century thought.

P. Hazard, *European Thought in the Eighteenth Century* (*Meridian). A useful survey of some of the thinkers of the Enlightenment.

K. Martin, *French Liberal Thought in the 18th Century* (*Torch). A brilliant and opinionated survey of the *philosophes*.

C. Becker, *The Heavenly City of the Eighteenth-Century Philosophers* (*Yale Univ. Press). A delightful and influential essay, stressing the parallels between the medieval Age of Faith and the Age of Reason. May be coupled with R. O. Rockwood, ed., *Carl Becker's Heavenly City Revisited* (Cornell Univ. Press, 1958).

J. B. Bury, *The Idea of Progress* (*Dover, 1955). A famous old pioneering study of enlightened optimism.

L. I. Bredvold, *The Brave New World of the Enlightenment* (Univ. of Michigan Press, 1961). Controversial, basically hostile, but deserves attention.

L. G. Crocker, *An Age of Crisis: Man and World in Eighteenth Century French Thought* (Johns Hopkins Univ. Press, 1959). An informative recent study.

F. Manuel, *The Eighteenth Century Confronts the Gods* (Harvard Univ. Press, 1959); R. R. Palmer, *Catholics and Unbelievers in Eighteenth-Century France* (*Princeton Univ. Press). Informative studies on attitudes toward religion.

T. D. Kendrick, *The Lisbon Earthquake* (Lippincott, 1957). An instructive account of the social and intellectual ramifications of the catastrophe.

**Some
Individual
Thinkers**

A. Wilson, *Diderot: The Testing Years, 1713–1759* (Oxford Univ. Press, 1957). The first part of a definitive biography.

N. L. Torrey, *The Spirit of Voltaire* (Columbia Univ. Press, 1938). A thoughtful study.

Peter Gay, *Voltaire's Politics: The Poet as Realist* (*Vintage). By a leading expert on the subject.

A. Cobban, *Rousseau & the Modern State* (Allen & Unwin, 1934). A good introduction to the implications of Rousseau's thought.

J. L. Talmon, *The Origins of Totalitarian Democracy* (*Praeger). Another interpretation of Rousseau.

F. Manuel, *The Prophets of Paris* (Harvard Univ. Press, 1962). Turgot and Condorcet are among those considered.

The Arts

F. Fosca, *The Eighteenth Century* (Skira, 1953). Handsomely illustrated introduction to the painting of the era.

J. Reynolds, *Discourses on Art* (*Collier). By the great eighteenth-century champion of neoclassical painting.

M. Bukofzer, *Music in the Baroque Era* (Norton, 1947). Survey of the period before 1750.

E. M. and S. Grew, *Bach* (*Collier); A. Einstein, *Mozart: His Character, His Work* (*Galaxy); E. J. Dent, *Mozart's Operas* (*Oxford). Informative works on individual musicians.

The Enlightened Despots

G. P. Gooch, *Frederick the Great* (Knopf, 1947), and F. J. P. Veale, *Frederick the Great* (Hamish, Hamilton, 1935). Two reasonable and balanced assessments.

L. Reniers, *Frederick the Great* (Oswald Wolff, Ltd., 1960). A critical evaluation.

W. H. Bruford, *Germany in the Eighteenth Century* (*Cambridge Univ. Press). A descriptive study, stressing social and intellectual history.

C. L. Morris, *Maria Theresa, The Last Conservative* (Knopf, 1937). Informative and sympathetic.

S. K. Padover, *The Revolutionary Emperor* (Ballou, 1934). Warmly favorable account of Joseph II.

G. Scott Thomson, *Catherine the Great and the Expansion of Russia* (*Collier). A sound, brief introduction. Of the full biographies of Catherine, one of the best is K. Walizewski, *The Romance of an Empress* (Appleton, 1894); a recent one is Z. Oldenbourg, *Catherine the Great* (*Bantam).

R. Herr, *The Eighteenth-Century Revolution in Spain* (Princeton Univ. Press, 1958). A full account of the reign of Charles III and of the impact of the Enlightenment.

George III and the American Revolution

J. C. Miller, *Origins of the American Revolution* (*Stanford Univ. Press). Excellent study.

L. H. Gipson, *The Coming of the Revolution, 1763–1775* (*Torch); J. R. Alden, *The American Revolution, 1775–1783* (*Torch). Full accounts in the "New American Nation" series.

E. S. Morgan, *The Birth of the Republic, 1763–1789* (*Phoenix). Another good introductory account.

C. Becker, *The Declaration of Independence* (*Vintage). An admirable monograph, analyzing the Declaration sentence by sentence and examining its European roots.

M. Beloff, *Thomas Jefferson and American Democracy* (*Collier). A good introduction to one of the most versatile and intellectual of the Founding Fathers.

J. S. Watson, *The Reign of George III, 1760–1815* (Clarendon, 1960), Volume XII of *The Oxford History of England*. An up-to-date general account, incorporating recent scholarly reinterpretations of this important reign.

E. A. Reitan, *George III: Tyrant or Constitutional Monarch?* (*Heath). Excerpts from the diverse judgments passed on George.

L. B. Namier, *The Structure of Politics at the Accession of George III* (*St. Martin's), and *England in the Age of the American Revolution* (*St. Martin's). Detailed and controversial studies of politics in the 1760's.

G. Rudé, *Wilkes and Liberty* (*Oxford). Analysis of the unrest in Britain early in George's reign.

Sources

C. Brinton, ed., *The Portable Age of Reason Reader* (*Viking). A good cross-section of the writing of the Enlightenment.

F. Manuel, ed., *The Enlightenment* (*Spectrum), and I. Berlin, ed., *The Age of Enlightenment: the 18th-Century Philosophers* (*Mentor). Two other useful anthologies.

B. R. Redman, ed., *The Portable Voltaire* (*Viking, 1949). A well-chosen selection, prefaced by an informative introduction.

Montesquieu, *The Spirit of the Laws* (*Hafner).

Rousseau, *The First and Second Discourses* (*St. Martin's); *The Social Contract* (*Hafner).

F. de La Fontainerie, ed., *French Liberalism and Education in the Eighteenth Century* (McGraw-Hill, 1932). Proposals for educational reform by Diderot and others.

Beccaria, *On Crimes and Punishments* (*Liberal Arts).

B. Dobrée, ed., *The Letters of King George III* (Cassell, 1935).

M. Beloff, ed., *The Debate on the American Revolution, 1761–1783* (*Torch). Handy compilation of British speeches and writings for and against the rebels.

H. S. Commager, ed., *Documents of American History* (*Appleton-Century-Crofts).

W. F. Church, ed., *The Influence of the Enlightenment on the French Revolution* (*Heath). Selections from later historians, with a useful, brief, critical bibliography on the Enlightenment.

Historical Fiction

S. Richardson, *Clarissa* (*Riverside).

See also the works suggested for Chapter 16.

18

The French Revolution

and Napoleon

I   Causes of the Revolution

Opposite: NAPOLÉON À ARCOLE, by Antoine-Jean Gros, Versailles Chateau, 1796. Ektachrome Giraudon.

In France, as in the thirteen North American colonies, a financial crisis produced a revolution. There was not only a parallel but also a direct connection between the revolution of 1776 and that of 1789. French participation in the War of American Independence increased an already excessive governmental debt by more than 1,500,000,000 *livres*,* and the example of America fired the imagination of discontented Frenchmen. To them, Benjamin Franklin, the immensely popular American envoy to France, was the very

*It is impossible to set a very meaningful value on the pre-revolutionary *livre* in terms of present-day money. It has been estimated that the *livre* was worth a little over $1.00 in terms of the 1966 dollar, but the estimate is misleading because of the enormous increase in prices and the shifts in the proportionate cost of basic necessities during the two centuries since the Old Régime.

embodiment of the Enlightenment, and the new republic overseas promised to become the utopia of the *philosophes*. Yet it would be going too far to claim that the American Revolution actually caused the French Revolution; rather, it speeded up developments in France that had long been under way. The forces causing the upheaval of 1789 were almost fully matured in 1776. And, just as the reasons for revolution were more deeply rooted and more complicated in France than in America, so the revolution itself was to be more violent and more sweeping.

The *immediate* cause of the great French Revolution, then, was financial. King Louis XVI vainly tried one expedient after another to avert bankruptcy and finally summoned the Estates General, the central representative assembly that had last met 175 years earlier. Once assembled, the deputies of the nation initiated the reforms that were to destroy the Old Régime in France. The *basic* causes of the Revolution, however, reached deep into France's society and economy and into her political and intellectual history. Behind the financial crisis of the 1780's lay many decades of fiscal mismanagement; the government had been courting insolvency since the last years of Louis XIV. The nobles and clergy, jealously guarding their traditional privileges, refused to pay a fair share of the taxes. Resentment against inequitable taxation and inefficient government built up among the unprivileged —the peasantry, the workers, and, above all, the bourgeoisie. The ideas of the *philosophes* translated bourgeois resentment into a program of active reform.

The Monarchy

France, the home of the Enlightenment, was never ruled by an enlightened despot until the advent of Napoleon. King Louis XV had refused to take decisive steps to remedy the abuses of the Old Régime (see Chapter 16). What Louis XV would not do, his grandson and successor could not do. Louis XVI (1774–1792), unlike his grandfather, was earnest and pious, but he had a slow mind and

was both irresolute and stubborn. He also labored under the handicap of a politically unfortunate marriage. Marie Antionette, his wife, was frivolous and ignorant; worse still, she was a Habsburg, the daughter of Maria Theresa, a constant reminder of the ill-fated Franco-Austrian alliance during the Seven Years' War.

For want of a good mechanic, the machinery of centralized royal absolutism was gradually falling apart. The fact that it functioned at all could be credited to a relatively few capable administrators, notably the *intendants* who ran so much of provincial France. The best of the *intendants*, like the Physiocrat Turgot at Limoges, provided a welcome touch of enlightened despotism, but they could do little to stay the slow disintegration of the central government.

The whole legal and judicial system required reform. The law needed to be codified to eliminate obsolete medieval survivals and to end the overlapping of the two legal systems—Roman and feudal—that prevailed in France. The courts needed a thorough overhaul to make them swift, fair, and inexpensive. Many judges and lawyers purchased or inherited their offices and regarded them not as a public trust but as a means to private enrichment. Louis XV had permitted his ministers to attack the strongholds of these vested interests, the high courts known as Parlements which existed in Paris and in a dozen provincial centers. One of the last acts of his reign had been the suppression of the Parlements; one of the first moves taken by Louis XVI was their restoration. Many Frenchmen viewed the Parlements favorably as a constitutional check on the absolutism of the monarchy, but the Parlements were also a formidable obstacle to social and economic reform.

The First and Second Estates

Like the monarchy itself, the social and economic foundations of the Old Régime were beginning to crumble by the middle of the eighteenth century. The first estate, the clergy, occupied a position of conspicuous importance in France. Though forming less than one per cent of the total population, the clergy controlled extensive and lucrative properties and performed many functions that are normally undertaken by the state today. They ran schools, kept records of vital statistics and dispensed relief to the poor. The Gallican Church, however, was a house divided. The lower clergy came almost entirely from the third estate; humble, poorly paid, and generally hardworking, the priests resented the wealth and the arrogance of their ecclesiastical superiors. The bishops and abbots maintained the outlook of the noble class into which they had been born. Although some of them took their duties seriously, others regarded the Church as a convenient way of securing a large income. Dozens of prelates turned the administration of their bishoprics or monasteries over to subordinates, kept most of the revenue themselves, and took up residence in Paris or Versailles.

The wealth and the lax discipline of the Church aroused criticism and envy. Good Catholics deplored the dwindling number of monks and nuns and their growing tendency to stress the exploitation of their properties. Well-to-do peasants and townspeople coveted these rich ecclesiastical estates. Taxpayers hated the tithe levied by the Church, even though the full 10 per cent implied by the word "tithe" was seldom demanded. They also complained about the Church's exemption from taxation and about the meager size of the "free gift" voted by the clergy to the government in lieu of taxes. The peasants on the whole remained moderately faithful Catholics and regarded the village priest, if not the bishop, with esteem and affection. The bourgeois, however, more and more accepted the anticlerical views of the *philosophes*. They interpreted Voltaire's plea to "crush the infamous thing" as a mandate to strip the Church of wealth and power.

Like the higher clergy, the nobles of the Old Régime, the second estate, enjoyed privilege, wealth—and unpopularity. Although forming less than 2 per cent of the population, they held about 20 per cent of the land. They had virtual exemption from taxation; they monopolized army commissions and appointments to high ecclesiastical office. The French aristocracy, however, comprised not a single social unit but a series of differing groups. At the top were the hereditary nobles, a few of them descended from royalty or from feudal lords of the Middle Ages, but more from families ennobled within the past two or three centuries. These "nobles of the sword" tended to view most of their countrymen, including the lesser nobility, as vulgar upstarts. In spite of their failure during the regency of Orléans (see Chapter 16), they dreamed of the day when they might rule France again, as the feudal nobles had ruled in the Middle Ages. Many of them, clustered at Versailles, neglected their duties as the first landlords of the realm. Arthur Young, the English economic expert who made a tour of France in the late 1780's, commented on the uncultivated aristocratic lands he found:

Much of these wastes belonged to the Prince de Soubise, who would not sell any part of them. Thus it is whenever you stumble on a Grand Seigneur, even one that was worth millions, you are sure to find his property desert. The Duke of Bouillon's and this prince's are two of the greatest properties in France; and all the signs I have yet seen of their greatness, are wastes. . . . Oh! if I was the legislator of France for a day, I would make such great lords skip again!*

Below the nobility of the sword came the "nobility of the robe," including the robed justices of the Parlements and other courts and a host of other officials. The nobles of the robe, or their ancestors, had originally secured aristocratic status by buying their offices. But, since these dignities were then handed down from father to son, the mercenary origins of their status had become somewhat obscured with the passage of time. By the late eighteenth century, there was often little practical distinction between the gentry of the robe and their brethren of the sword; marriages between members of the two groups were common. On the whole, the nobles of the robe were richer than the nobles of the sword, and

*Travels in France, Constantia Maxwell, ed. (Cambridge, England, 1929), 62.

they exerted more power and influence by virtue of their firm hold on key governmental positions. The ablest and most tenacious defenders of special privilege in the dying years of the Old Régime were the rich judges of Parlement, not the elegant but ineffectual courtiers of Versailles.

Many noblemen, however, had little wealth, power, or glamor. They belonged to the lowest level of French aristocracy—the *hobereaux*, the "little falcons" or "sparrow-hawks." They vegetated on their country estates, since they could not afford the expensive pleasures of the court. In the effort to conserve at least part of their traditional status, almost all the *hobereaux* insisted on the meticulous collection of the surviving feudal and manorial dues from the peasantry. Their exhumation of old documents to justify levies sometimes long forgotten earned them the abiding hatred of the peasants and prepared the way for the document-burning that occurred during the Revolution.

Not every noble was a snobbish courtier or a selfish defender of the status quo. Some *hobereaux* drifted down the social ladder to become simple farmers. Some nobles of the robe, attracted by the opportunities for profit, took part in business ventures. Even the loftiest noble families produced enlightened spirits, like the Marquis de Lafayette, who returned from the American War of Independence to champion reform at home, or like the young bloods who applauded the ingenious valet, Figaro, when he outwitted his social superiors in Beaumarchais' satire on aristocracy, *The Marriage of Figaro,* first staged in 1784.

The Third Estate

The first two estates included only a small fraction of the French nation; 98 per cent of Frenchmen fell within the third estate in 1789. The great majority of these commoners were peasants. In some respects, the status of the peasantry was more favorable in France than it was anywhere else in Europe. Serfdom, which was still prevalent in central and eastern Europe, had disappeared almost entirely except in Lorraine and the Franche Comté (County of Burgundy). While enclosures were gradually pushing small farmers off the land in England, small peasant holdings existed by the millions in France. Three out of every four adult peasants, it is estimated, held some land. Nevertheless, the observant eye of Arthur Young noted many signs of rural misery in 1787 and 1788. In southwestern France, for example:

Pass Payrac, and meet many beggars, which we had not done before. All the country, girls and women, are without shoes or stockings; and the ploughmen at their work have neither sabots nor feet to their stockings. This is a poverty, that strikes at the root of national prosperity. . . . It reminded me of the misery of Ireland.*

Although the degree of agrarian distress varied greatly from province to province, the total picture was far from bright. The trouble came in part from three factors—backward methods of farming, the shortage of land, and overpopulation. The efficient techniques of the agricultural revolution made little headway in France before 1789. Vast areas were not cultivated at all or lay fallow every second or third year in accordance with medieval practice. The constantly increasing rural population simply could not find steady employment or a decent livelihood. Primitive farming required large tracts of land, but the property-holding three-quarters of the French peasantry controlled less than one-third of the land. The average holding was so small that even a propertied peasant might face starvation in poor crop years. The landless peasant turned to begging and sometimes to theft.

Rising prices and heavy taxes also oppressed the peasants. The upward trend of prices in France throughout the eighteenth century brought prosperity to many towns, but to the backward rural economy it brought the new hardship of inflation. The price of the products sold by the farmer rose less swiftly than that of the goods which the farmer had to buy. To the Church the peasants paid the

*Travels in France, 23–24.

tithe, and to the nobility they paid feudal and manorial dues. To the state they owed a land tax, an income tax, a poll tax, and a variety of other duties, of which the most widely detested was the *gabelle*, the obligatory purchase of salt from government agents, usually at an exorbitant price.

France had a long history of agrarian unrest, going back to the *jacquerie*, the savage peasant uprising during the Hundred Years' War. In the decades before 1789 there was no new *jacquerie*, but unemployment and poverty had created a revolutionary temper among the peasants. They did not want a change in the form of government; they were ignorant of the reform program of the Enlightenment. But they most emphatically wanted more land, if need be at the expense of the clergy and the nobility; they wanted an end to obsolete manorial dues; and they wanted relief from a system of taxation that bore hardest upon those who could least afford to pay.

The other members of the third estate, the urban workers and the bourgeoisie, had little reason to cherish the Old Régime. "Labor," in our modern sense of a large, self-conscious body of factory workers, hardly existed in pre-revolutionary France, where few large factories as yet existed. Almost every good-sized town, however, had its wage-earners and apprentices employed chiefly in small businesses or workshops. These urban laborers felt with particular sharpness the pinch of rising prices. They were not, however, to take the commanding role in the Revolution itself; geographically scattered, lacking in class cohesiveness, they were ready to follow the lead of the bourgeoisie.

The bourgeoisie included Frenchmen of very divergent resources and interests—rich merchants and bankers in the cities, storekeepers and lawyers in country towns and villages, doctors and other professional men, and thousands upon thousands of craftsmen running their own little businesses. Implacable hostility to the privileged estates and warm receptiveness to the propaganda of the *philosophes* cemented this sprawling middle class into a political force. The bourgeoisie suffered fewer hardships than the peasants and workers

did, but they resented the abuses of the Old Régime perhaps even more keenly. Though they paid a smaller proportion of their incomes in taxes, they violently denounced the inequality of assessments. While profiting by the rise in prices, the wealthier and more enterprising businessmen complained of guild regulations and other restrictions on free commercial activity. They found it galling to be snubbed by the nobility, treated as second-class subjects by the monarchy, and excluded from posts of power in government, Church, and army.

In sum, the men of the middle class fully realized their own growing economic importance, and they wanted social and political rights to match. Because they were wealthier, better educated, and more articulate than the peasants and wage-earners, they took the leading part in formulating the grievances of the entire third estate. These grievances were compiled in statements called *cahiers* and submitted to the Estates General in 1789.

The *cahier* of the third estate of the Longuyon district in Lorraine may serve as a sample of bourgeois attitudes toward reform.* While it dealt in part with purely local problems, like the destruction of the woods to supply fuel for iron-smelters, other portions showed a sharp awareness of the great issues of the day. The *cahier* pronounced the freedom of the press the "surest means of maintaining the freedom of the nation." It deplored the harshness of the criminal laws; they should conform to "the customs and the character of the French nation, the kindest people in the universe." It recommended "a social contract or act between the sovereign and his people," to safeguard "the personal freedom of all citizens" and "prevent the recurrence of those disastrous events which at present oppress the king and the nation." While insisting upon the sanctity of private property, the third estate of Longuyon advocated a large measure of equality. It proposed that "all Frenchmen should have the right and the hope of securing

*The full text of this *cahier* is printed in B. F. Hyslop, *A Guide to the General Cahiers of 1789* (New York, 1936), 318–326. The quotations that follow are in our translation.

any State office, of whatever grade, and all military and ecclesiastical dignities." Existing taxes should be swept away, to be replaced by levies on "all property without distinction as to owners, and on all persons without distinction of order and rank."

The Financial Crisis

The chronic financial difficulties of the French monarchy strengthened the hand of the middle-class reformers. The government debt, already large at the accession of Louis XVI, tripled between 1774 and 1789; about half the increase resulted from French participation in the American War of Independence. In 1789, the debt stood at 4,500,000,000 *livres*. The budget for 1788, the only one computed for the Old Régime, made alarming reading:

Estimated Expenses	(In *livres*)
For debt service	318,000,000
For the court	35,000,000
For other purposes	276,000,000
Total	629,000,000
Estimated Revenues	503,000,000
Estimated Deficit	126,000,000

Especially disturbing was the very high proportion of revenues consumed by interest payments on debts already contracted.

Louis XVI, in his feeble way, tried to cope with the growing emergency. On coming to the throne in 1774, he named as chief minister Turgot, who sympathized with the Physiocrats and had made a brilliant record as *intendant* of Limoges. Turgot temporarily reduced the deficit by imposing strict economies, particularly on the expenditures of the court. To promote the welfare of the third estate, he curtailed ancient guild monopolies, lifted restrictions on internal shipments of grain, and replaced the *corvée*, the work on highways demanded of peasants, with a tax affecting nobles and commoners alike. At this the vested interests rebelled and, seconded by Marie Antoinette, secured Turgot's dismissal in 1776. The ousted minister admonished Louis XVI: "Remember, sire, that it

was weakness which brought the head of Charles I to the block."

Louis ignored Turgot's warning. The government continued to raise new loans— 653,000,000 *livres* between 1783 and 1786 alone. Then in 1786 the bankers refused to make new advances. The French government was caught between the irresistible force of the third estate's demands for tax relief and the immovable object of the other estates' refusal to yield their fiscal exemptions. The monarchy had temporized and borrowed until it could afford neither fresh delays nor new loans. Calonne, the finance minister in 1786, proposed to meet the crisis by reviving Turgot's reforms. In the hope of persuading the first two estates to consent to heavier taxation, he convoked the Assembly of Notables, which included the chief aristocratic and ecclesiastical dignitaries of the kingdom. But the Notables declined to be persuaded.

Louis XVI dissolved the Notables and dismissed Calonne. Then, with unaccustomed firmness, he decided to levy a uniform tax on all landed property without regard to the social status of the holder. The clergy replied by reducing their "free gift" for 1788 to one-sixth of what it had previously been. The Parlement of Paris declared the new tax law illegal and asserted that only the nation as a whole assembled in the Estates General could make so sweeping a change. The King retreated and in the summer of 1788 announced that the Estates General would meet the following spring.

The Estates General

In summoning the Estates General Louis XVI revived a half-forgotten institution which did not seem likely to initiate drastic social and economic reforms. The three estates, despite their immense variation in size, had customarily received equal representation and equal voting power, so that the two privileged orders could outvote the commoners. The Estates General of 1789, however, met under unique circumstances.

In the first place, its election and subsequent meeting took place during an economic crisis that heightened chronic social and financial tensions. One difficulty was the continued gravitation of unemployed peasants to the cities, especially Paris, in search of work; another difficulty was the weather. Hail and drought had reduced the wheat harvest in 1788, and the winter of 1788–1789 was so bitter that the Seine froze over at Paris, blocking shipments of grain or flour by water. Half-starved and half-frozen, Parisians huddled around bonfires provided by the municipal government. By the spring of 1789 the price of bread had almost doubled—a very serious matter in an age when bread was the mainstay of the diet. It has been estimated that the average workingman normally spent almost half his wages on bread for his family; now he was obliged to spend a higher proportion.

France had survived bad weather and poor harvests many times in the past without experiencing revolution. This time, however, the economic hardships were the last straw. Starving peasants begged, borrowed, and stole, poaching on the hunting preserves of the great lords and attacking their game wardens. The turbulence in Paris boiled over in a riot (April, 1789), witnessed by Thomas Jefferson, then the American minister to France:

. . . The Fauxbourg St. Antoine is a quarter of the city inhabited entirely by the class of day-laborers and journeymen in every line. A rumor was spread among them that a great paper manufacturer . . . had proposed . . . that their wages should be lowered to 15 sous a day [three-quarters of a *livre*]. . . . They flew to his house in vast numbers, destroyed everything in it, and in his magazines and work shops, without secreting however a pin's worth to themselves, and were continuing this work of devastation when the regular troops were called in. Admonitions being disregarded, they were of necessity fired on, and a regular action ensued, in which about 100 of them were killed, before the rest would disperse.*

These disturbances increased the sense of critical urgency pressing on the deputies to the Estates General.

*Autobiography of Thomas Jefferson, P. L. Ford, ed. (New York, 1914), 133–134.

In the second place, the methods followed in electing the deputies aided the champions of reform. The suffrage was wide, especially in rural areas, where almost all adult males met the qualifications for voting. Indeed, it is probable that more Frenchmen actually voted in 1789 than in any subsequent election or referendum during the revolutionary era. In each district of France the third estate made its choice not directly by secret ballot but indirectly by choosing at a public meeting electors who later selected a deputy. Since this procedure greatly favored bourgeois orators over inarticulate farmers, middle-class lawyers and government administrators won control of the commoners' deputation. The reforming deputies of the third estate found some sympathizers in the second estate and many more in the first estate, where the discontented clergy had a large delegation. A majority of the deputies were prepared to make drastic changes in the Old Régime.

But in all past meetings of the Estates General each estate, or order, had deliberated separately, with the consent of two estates and of the Crown required for the passage of a measure. In 1789, the King and the privileged orders favored retaining this "vote by order." The third estate, on the contrary, demanded "vote by head," with the deputies from all the orders deliberating together, each deputy having a single vote. Pamphleteers invoked Rousseau's concept of the general will. "What is the third estate?" wrote Abbé Siéyès in an influential broadside of the same name. "Everything."

. . . If votes are taken by order, five million citizens will not be able to decide anything for the general interest, because it will not please a couple of hundred thousand privileged individuals. The will of a single individual will veto and destroy the will of more than a hundred people.*

The question of procedure became crucial soon after the Estates General convened on May 5, 1789, at Versailles. Siéyès, a priest, and Mirabeau, a renegade nobleman, both of them sitting in the third estate, led the cam-

*Emmanuel Siéyès, Qu'est-ce Que le Tiers Etat?, E. Champion, ed. (Paris, 1888), 82. Our translation.

paign for vote by head. On June 17, the third estate cut the Gordian knot of procedure by accepting Siéyès' invitation to proclaim itself the "National Assembly." It also invited the deputies of the other two estates to join its sessions. A majority of the clerical deputies, chiefly parish priests, accepted; the nobility refused.

The King then barred the commoners from their usual meeting place, whereupon they assembled at an indoor tennis court on June 20 and solemnly swore never to disband until they had given France a constitution. To the "Tennis-Court Oath" Louis replied by commanding each estate to resume its separate deliberations. The third estate and some deputies of the first disobeyed. Louis, vacillating as ever, now gave in and on June 27 directed the noble and clerical deputies to join the National Assembly. The nation, through its representatives, had successfully challenged the King and the vested interests. The Estates General was dead, and in its place sat the National Assembly, pledged to reform French society and give the nation a constitution. The revolution had begun.

II   The Dissolution of the Monarchy

Popular Uprisings, July–October, 1789

The National Assembly had barely settled down to work when a new wave of rioting swept over France, undermining further the position of the King. Economic difficulties grew more severe during the summer of 1789. Unemployment increased, and bread seemed likely to remain scarce and expensive, at least until after the harvest. Meanwhile, the commoners feared that the King and the privileged orders might attempt a counter-revolution. Large concentrations of troops appeared in the Paris area early in July—to preserve order and protect the National Assembly, the King asserted. But the Parisians suspected that Louis was planning the forcible dissolution of the Assembly. Suspicion deepened into conviction after Louis dismissed Necker, the popular financier who had been serving as the chief royal adviser.

The reaction to Necker's dismissal was immediate and revolutionary. On July 12 and 13, the men who had elected the Paris deputies of the third estate formed a new municipal government and a new militia, the National Guard, both loyal to the National Assembly. Paris was forging the weapons that made it the leader of the Revolution. Crowds were roaming the streets, demanding cheaper bread and parading busts of Necker draped in black. On July 14 they broke into government buildings in search of arms. They found one arsenal in the Invalides, the great military hospital in Paris, and they hoped to find another in the Bastille, a fortress in the eastern part of the city. An armed group, several hundred strong, stormed the Bastille, killing part of the garrison and suffering many casualties themselves.

The fall of the Bastille had immense significance. While the fortress housed only 7 prisoners, all of whom deserved to be there, it frowned like a monster sentry over a teeming quarter inhabited by woodworkers, cabinetmakers, locksmiths, cobblers, and other craftsmen and their assistants. Men of this modest social and economic background formed the bulk of the force that took the Bastille and demonstrated what could be done by an aroused people. The capture and subsequent demolition of the Bastille symbolized the destruction of the Old Régime. It is no wonder the Fourteenth of July became the great national holiday of Frenchmen, their counterpart of the American Fourth of July.

Rioting spread over much of France late in July, 1789, as the provincial population responded to the news from Paris or acted on its own. In town after town, mobs attacked the local version of the Bastille. Arthur Young, who was surveying the agriculture of Alsace, witnessed the scene at Strasbourg:

. . . The Parisian spirit of commotion spreads quickly; it is here; the troops . . . are employed to keep an eye on the people who shew signs of an intended revolt. They have broken the windows of some magistrates that are no favourites; and a great mob of them is at this moment assembled, demanding clamourously to have meat at 5 *sous* a pound.*

The countryside, in the meantime, was experiencing the "Great Fear," one of the most

Travels in France, 181.

extraordinary attacks of mass delusion on record. From village to village word spread that "brigands" were coming, aristocratic hirelings who would destroy crops and villages and force the National Assembly to preserve the status quo. There were in fact no bands of brigands, only an occasional starving farmhand trying to steal food. But the peasants in many districts went berserk, grabbing hoes and pitchforks, anything resembling a weapon. When the brigands did not materialize, they attacked chateaux and broke into other buildings that might house a hoard of grain or the hated documents justifying collection of manorial dues. Some nobles voluntarily gave the peasants what they wanted; others saw

Scene in front of the Paris City Hall, July 14, 1789. Bust of Louis XIV "witnesses the triumph of freedom."

VUE DE LA PLACE DE GREVE LE JOUR DE LA PRISE DE LA BASTILLE • NOUS CEDONS A L'AMOUR DE LA LIBERTÉ

Par Palloy Patriote

their barns and archives burnt, and a few were lynched. The Great Fear, beginning as a psychological aberration, ended as an uprising of the peasantry against its traditional oppressors.

By the end of July, 1789, then, four distinct sets of revolutionary events had taken place in France: (1) the constitutional revolution of June, resulting in the creation of the National Assembly; (2) the Paris revolution and the taking of the Bastille; (3) the comparable outbreaks in provincial cities and towns; and (4) the Great Fear. Each of the four drove another nail into the coffin of the Old Régime. The transformation of the Estates General into the National Assembly and the creation of new local governments undermined the traditional political advantages of the first two estates. The Great Fear began the destruction of their social and economic privileges. Everywhere, legally constituted officials were turned out, taxes went unpaid, and valuable records were destroyed.

The "October Days," the last crisis of a momentous year, demonstrated anew the impotence of Louis XVI and the power of his aroused subjects. The harvest of 1789 had been good, but a drought crippled the operation of water-mills for grinding flour from the wheat. Thus, as autumn drew on, Parisians still queued for bread and still looked suspiciously at the royal troops stationed in the neighborhood of their city. Rumors of the Queen's behavior at Versailles further incensed them. Marie Antoinette made a dramatic appearance at a banquet of royal officers, clutching the Dauphin (the heir to the throne) in her arms, striking the very pose that her mother, Maria Theresa, had employed so effectively to win the support of the Hungarians in the 1740's. And, on hearing that the people had no bread, she was said to have remarked callously: "Let them eat cake." This story was false, but it echoed and re-echoed in the lively new Paris papers that delighted in denouncing *l'Autrichienne* ("the Austrian hussy").

The climax came on October 5, 1789, when an array of determined women—rough market-women and fishwives, neatly dressed milliners, even middle-class "ladies with hats"—marched the dozen miles from Paris to Versailles in the rain. They disrupted the National Assembly, extracted kisses from Louis XVI, and later penetrated the palace, perhaps endangering the lives of Louis and, especially, Marie Antoinette. Although historians have not yet discovered who planned and organized this bizarre demonstration, it had very significant political consequences. On October 6, the women marched back to Paris, escorting "the baker, the baker's wife, and the baker's boy"—in other words, the royal family—who took up residence in the Tuileries Palace. More important, the National Assembly, too, moved to Paris. The most revolutionary place in France had captured both the head of the Old Régime and the herald of the new.

The National Assembly, 1789–1791

The outlines of the new régime were already starting to take shape before the October Days. The Great Fear prompted the National Assembly to abolish in law what the peasants were destroying in fact. On the evening of August 4, 1789, the Viscount de Noailles, a liberal nobleman, addressed the deputies:

The kingdom at this moment hangs between the alternative of the destruction of society, and that of a government which will be the admiration and the exemplar of Europe.

How is this government to be established? By public tranquillity. . . . And to secure this necessary tranquillity, I propose:

(1) . . . That taxation will be paid by all the individuals of the kingdom, in proportion to their revenues;

(2) That all public expenses will in the future be borne equally by all.*

The deputies voted the proposals of Noailles. In addition, the clergy gave up its tithes, and the liberal minority of the second estate surrendered the nobility's game preserves, manorial dues, and other medieval rights. The

Archives Parlementaires, Series 1, VIII, 343. Our translation.

assembly made it a clean sweep by abolishing serfdom, forbidding the sale of justice or of judicial office, and decreeing that "all citizens, without distinction of birth, can be admitted to all ecclesiastical, civil, and military posts and dignities." When the memorable session inaugurated by Noailles' speech ended at two o'clock on the morning of August 5, the Old Régime was dead.

Three weeks later, on August 26, 1789, the National Assembly formulated the Declaration of the Rights of Man. "Men are born and remain free and equal in rights," it asserted (Article 1). "These rights are liberty, property, security and resistance to oppression" (Article 2). Property it called "an inviolable and sacred right" (Article 17), and liberty "the exercise of the natural rights of each man" within the limits "determined by law" (Article 4). "Law," the Declaration stated, "is the expression of the general will. All citizens have the right to take part, in person or by their representatives, in its formation" (Article 6). "Any society in which the guarantee of rights is not assured or the separation of powers not determined has no constitution" (Article 16).*

The Declaration of the Rights of Man mirrored the economic and political attitudes of the middle class. It insisted on the sanctity of property, and it proclaimed that "Social distinctions may be based only on usefulness," thus implying that some social distinctions were to be expected. It committed the French to the creed of constitutional liberalism already affirmed by the English in 1688–1689 and by the Americans in 1776, and it incorporated the key phrases of the *philosophes*: natural rights, general will, and separation of powers. The National Assembly made a resounding statement of the ideals of the Enlightenment. Yet, as the subsequent history of the Revolution soon demonstrated, the Assembly found no magic formula by which to translate these ideals into practice.

The economic legislation of the National Assembly provided a case in point. Belief in the theory of the equal taxation of all Frenchmen did not solve urgent financial problems.

*G. Lefebvre, *The Coming of the French Revolution* (Princeton, 1947), Appendix.

Marie Antoinette and her children.

The new and just land tax imposed by the deputies simply could not be collected. Tax-collectors had vanished in the general liquidation of the Old Régime, and naive peasants now thought that they owed the government nothing. Once again, the French state borrowed until its credit was exhausted, and then, in desperation, the National Assembly ordered the confiscation of church lands (November, 1789). "The wealth of the clergy is at the disposition of the nation," it declared, explaining that ecclesiastical lands fell outside the bounds of "inviolable" property as defined in the Declaration of the Rights of Man because they belonged to an institution and not to private individuals.

The government thus acquired an asset worth at least 2,000,000,000 *livres*. On the basis of this collateral it issued *assignats*, paper notes used to pay the government's debts. So far, so good: The *assignats* had adequate security behind them and temporarily eased the financial crisis. Unfortunately, the Revolution repeated the mistake of John Law (see Chapter 16): It did not know when to stop. As the state sold parcels of confiscated land—that is, as it reduced the collateral securing its paper money—it should have destroyed *assignats* to the same amount. The temptation not to reduce the number of *assignats* proved too great to resist. Inflation resulted: The *assignats*, progressively losing their solid backing, depreciated until in 1795 they were worth less than 5 per cent of their face value.

The state sold at auction the property seized from the Church and from nobles who had emigrated from France. Well-to-do peasants profited by the opportunity to enlarge their holdings, and many bourgeois also bought up land, sometimes as a short-term speculation, sometimes as a long-term investment. The poor and landless peasants, however, gained nothing, since they did not have the money with which to buy. True to the doctrine of laissez-faire, the National Assembly made no move to help these marginal farmers. Following the same doctrine, it abolished the guilds and the irksome tariffs and tolls on trade within France. And deeming the few primitive organizations of labor unnatural restrictions on economic freedom, it abolished them too. In June, 1791, after an outbreak of strikes, it passed the Le Chapelier Law banning both strikes and labor unions.

Since the suppression of tithes and the seizure of ecclesiastical property deprived the Church of its revenue, the National Assembly agreed to finance ecclesiastical salaries. The new arrangement virtually nationalized the Gallican Church and made it subject to constant government regulation. The Assembly's decision to restrict monasteries and convents caused little difficulty; many of these establishments were already far gone in decay. But an uproar arose over the legislation altering the status of the secular hierarchy.

The Civil Constitution of the Clergy (June, 1790) redrew the ecclesiastical map of France. It reduced the number of bishoprics by more than one-third, making the remaining dioceses correspond to the new civil administrative units known as departments (see below). It transformed bishops and priests into civil officials, paid by the state and elected by the population of the diocese or parish; both Catholics and non-Catholics (the latter usually a small minority) could vote in these elections. A new bishop was required to take an oath of loyalty to the state, and the Civil Constitution stipulated that he might not apply to the pope for confirmation, though he might write to him as the "Visible Head of the Universal Church."

These provisions stripped the "Visible Head of the Universal Church" of effective authority over the Gallican clergy and ran counter to the whole tradition of the Roman Church as an independent ecclesiastical monarchy. Naturally the pope denounced the Civil Constitution. The National Assembly then required that every member of the French clergy take a special oath supporting the Civil Constitution, but only seven bishops and fewer than half of the priests complied. Thus a breach was opened between the Revolution and a large segment of the population. Good Catholics, from Louis XVI down to humble peasants, rallied to the non-juring clergy, as those who refused the special oath were termed. The Civil Constitution of the Clergy, supplying an issue for rebellion and civil war, was the first great blunder of the Revolution.

The Constitution of 1791

The major undertaking of the National Assembly was the Constitution of 1791. The Assembly devised a neat and orderly system of local government to replace the bewildering complex of provincial units that had accumulated under the Old Régime. It divided the territory of France into eighty-three departments of approximately equal size. Each department was small enough for its chief town to be within a day's journey of the outlying towns; each bore the name of a river, a mountain range, or some other natural landmark. The departments were subdivided into *arrondissements* or districts, and the districts into communes—that is municipalities. The commune-district-department arrangement resembled, on a reduced scale, the American hierarchy of town-county-state. In the communes and departments, elected councils and officials enjoyed considerable rights of self-government. The administration of the new France, on paper anyhow, was to be far more decentralized than that of the Old Régime.

The principle of the separation of powers guided the reconstruction of the central government. The Constitution of 1791 established an independent hierarchy of courts staffed by elected judges. It vested legislative authority in a single elected chamber. Although the king still headed the executive branch, his actions now required approval by his ministers, who were responsible only to him and not to the legislature, as they generally are in a "parliamentary" or "cabinet" government. The King did receive the power of veto, but it was only a suspensive veto, which could block legislation for a maximum of four years. Louis XVI, no longer the absolute "King of France," acquired the new constitutional title, "King of the French."

The new constitution subscribed to many other principles issuing straight from the Enlightenment. It promised to give France a new law code, and it declared marriage a civil contract, not a religious sacrament. The state took over the old ecclesiastical functions of keeping records of vital statistics and providing charity and education. Indeed, the Constitution promised a system of free public education. It also promised that the foreign policy of revolutionary France would be more virtuous than that of autocratic France:

> The French nation renounces the undertaking of any war with a view of making conquests, and it will never use its forces against the liberty of any people.[*]

The Constitution of 1791 went a long way

[*]J. H. Stewart, *A Documentary Survey of the French Revolution* (New York, 1951), 260.

toward instituting popular government, but it stopped well short of full democracy. It divided Frenchmen into two classes of citizens, "active" and "passive," and limited the right of voting to "active" citizens, who paid annually in taxes an amount equal to at least three days' wages for unskilled labor in the locality. The "passive" citizens, numbering about one-third of the male population, enjoyed the full protection of the law but did not receive the franchise. Moreover, the new legislature was chosen by a process of indirect election. "Active" citizens did not vote for their deputies but for a series of electors, who were required to be men of substantial wealth, and who ultimately elected the deputies. The French middle class evidently assumed that the amount of worldly goods a man possessed determined the degree of his political wisdom.

The decentralized and limited monarchy established by the Constitution of 1791 was doomed to fail. It was too radical to suit the King and most of the aristocracy, and not radical enough for the many bourgeois who were veering toward republicanism. The majority in the National Assembly supporting the Constitution suffered the fate commonly experienced by the politically moderate in a revolution: they were squeezed out by the extremists. Despite their moderate intentions, they were driven to enact some drastic legislation, notably the Civil Constitution of the Clergy, which weakened their own position. And they failed to develop an effective party organization at a time when the deputies of the radical minority were consolidating their strength.

These radicals were the Jacobins, so named because they belonged to the "Society of the Friends of the Constitution," which maintained its Paris headquarters in a former Jacobin (Dominican) monastery. The Jacobins were no true friends of the Constitution of 1791. They accepted it only as a stopgap until they might end the monarchy and set up a republic based on universal suffrage. To prepare for the millennium, the Jacobins used all the techniques of a political pressure group. They planted rabble-rousing articles in the press and manipulated the crowds of noisy and volatile spectators at the sessions of the National Assembly. Their network of political clubs extended throughout the provinces, providing the only nation-wide party organization in France. Almost everywhere, Jacobins captured control of the new department and commune councils. In local elections, as in the elections to the Estates General, an able and determined minority prevailed over a largely illiterate and politically inexperienced majority.

The defenders of the Old Régime played into the hands of the Jacobins. From the summer of 1789 on, alarmed nobles and prelates fled France, leaving behind more rich estates to be confiscated and giving Jacobin orators and editors a splendid opportunity to denounce the rats leaving a sinking ship. Many of these *émigrés* gathered in the German Rhineland to intrigue for Austrian and Russian support of a counter-revolution. The King's grave misgivings about the Civil Constitution of the Clergy prompted his disastrous attempt to join the *émigrés* on the Franco-German frontier. In June, 1791, disguised as a valet and governess, Louis and Marie Antoinette left the Tuileries. But Louis unwisely showed his face in public, and a local official along the route recognized the royal profile from the portrait on the *assignats*. The alarm was sent ahead, and at Varennes in northeastern France a detachment of troops forced the royal party to return to Paris. After the abortive flight to Varennes, the revolutionaries viewed Louis XVI as a potential traitor and kept him closely guarded in the Tuileries. The experiment in constitutional monarchy began under most unfavorable auspices.

The Legislative Assembly, October, 1791–September, 1792

On October 1, 1791, the first and the only legislative assembly elected under the new constitution commenced its deliberations. No one faction commanded a numerical majority in the new assembly:

POLITICAL COMPLEXION OF THE
LEGISLATIVE ASSEMBLY, 1791

	Approximate No. of Seats
Right	
(Constitutional Monarchists)	265
Center (Plain)	345
Left (Jacobins)	130

(In the practice followed by most continental European assemblies, the Right sat to the right of the presiding officer as he faced the assembly, the Left to his left, and the Center in between.)

The balance of political power rested with the timid and irresolute deputies of the Center, who were neither strong defenders of the Constitution nor yet convinced republicans. Since they occupied the lowest seats in the assembly hall, they received the derogatory nickname of the Plain or Marsh. The capable politicians of the Left soon captured the votes of the Plain, to demonstrate anew the power of a determined minority.

Leadership of this minority came from a contingent of Jacobins known as Girondins because some of them, though by no means all, came from Bordeaux, in the Gironde department. The Girondins specialized in patriotic oratory. They pictured revolutionary France as the intended victim of a reactionary conspiracy, engineered by the *émigrés*, aided at home by the non-juring clergy and the royal family, and abetted abroad by a league of monarchs under Leopold II, the Austrian emperor and the brother of Marie Antoinette. But Louis XVI, despite the flight to Varennes, was no traitor, and Leopold II cautiously limited his aid to the *émigrés*. The sudden death of Leopold in March, 1792, and the accession of his inexperienced and less cautious son, Francis II, at once increased the Austrian threat. At the same time, belligerent Girondins secured control of French diplomacy. On April 20, 1792, the Legislative Assembly declared war on Austria. In the eyes of Frenchmen the war was defensive, not the campaign of conquest that the nation had forsworn in the fine phrases of its constitution.

Partly because the emigration of many nobles had depleted the corps of French officers, the war went badly for France at the outset. Prussia soon joined Austria, and on July 25, 1792, the Prussian commander, the Duke of Brunswick, issued a manifesto drafted by an *émigré*. The manifesto stated the war aims of the allies:

. . . To put a stop to the anarchy within France, to check the attacks delivered against throne and altar, to re-establish legal authority, to restore to the king the security and freedom of which he has been deprived, and to place him in a position where he may exercise the legitimate authority which is his due.

A threat followed. "If the Tuileries is attacked, by deed or word, if the slightest outrage or violence is perpetrated against the royal family, and if immediate measures are not taken for their safety, maintenance and liberty"—then Paris would witness "a model vengeance, never to be forgotten."*

The Duke of Brunswick's manifesto did not frighten the French, as it was intended to do. On the contrary, it stiffened the already firm determination of republicans to do away with the monarchy. All through the early summer of 1792 the Jacobins of Paris had been plotting an insurrection. They won the support of a formidable following—army recruits; mem-

Le Moniteur Universel, August 3, 1792. Our translation.

bers of the National Guard from the provinces, who had come to Paris to celebrate the third anniversary of the fall of the Bastille; and the rank and file of Parisians, who were angered by the depreciation of the *assignats* and by the high price and short supply of food and other necessities. One by one, the forty-eight *sections* or wards into which the city was divided came under the control of Jacobins, who advertized their democratic sympathies by inviting passive citizens to take part in political activity. The climax came on the night of August 9–10, 1792, when the leaders of the *sections* ousted the regular municipal authorities from the Paris city hall and installed a new and illegal Jacobin commune.

The municipal revolution had immediate and momentous results. On the morning of August 10, the forces of the new commune attacked the Tuileries and massacred the King's Swiss guards, while the royal family took refuge with the Legislative Assembly. The uprising of August 10 sealed the doom of the monarchy and made the Assembly little more than the errand boy of the new Paris commune. With most of the deputies of the Right and the Plain absent, the Assembly voted to suspend the King from office, to imprison the royal family, and to order the election of a constitutional convention. Until this new body should meet, the government was to be run by an interim ministry staffed largely by Girondins. The birth of the First French Republic was at hand.

III   The First Republic

The September Massacres, 1792

The weeks between August 10 and the meeting of the Convention on September 21 were weeks of crisis and tension. The value of the *assignats* depreciated by 40 per cent during August alone. Rabble-rousing Jacob-

ins continually excited the populace of Paris, already stirred by the economic difficulties and by the capture of the Tuileries. Excitement mounted still higher when the news arrived that Prussian troops had invaded northeastern France. In the emergency, Danton, the interim minister of justice, won immortality by urging patriots to employ "*de*

l'audace, encore de l'audace, toujours de l'audace"
—boldness, more boldness, always boldness.

In Paris, boldness took the form of the "September massacres," lynchings of supposed traitors and enemy agents made possible by the collapse of normal police authority. For five days, beginning on September 2, bloodthirsty mobs moved from prison to prison. At each stop they held impromptu courts and summary executions. The number of victims exceeded one thousand and included ordinary criminals as well as aristocrats and non-juring priests, who were often innocent of the treason charged against them. The crowning horror was the mutilation of the Princesse de Lamballe, the Queen's maid of honor, whose severed head was paraded on a pike before the window of the royal prison so that Marie Antoinette might see "how the people take vengeance on their tyrants." The September massacres foreshadowed the terror in store for France.

Later in the month (September 20, 1792), a rather minor French victory, grandly styled "the miracle of Valmy," turned the Duke of Brunswick's forces back from the road to Paris; more solid French successes followed during the final months of 1792. Then the tide turned again, washing away the conquests of the autumn. By the summer of 1793 half-defeated France faced a hostile coalition including almost every major power in Europe. No wonder an atmosphere of perpetual emergency surrounded the Convention.

Gironde and Mountain

In theory, the election of deputies to the National Convention (August-September, 1792) marked the beginning of true political democracy in France. Both active and passive citizens were invited to the polls. Yet only 10 per cent of the potential electorate of 7,000,000 actually voted; the others abstained or were turned away from the polls by the watchdogs of the Jacobin clubs, ever on the alert against "counter-revolutionaries." The result was a landslide for the republicans:

POLITICAL COMPLEXION OF THE
CONVENTION, SEPTEMBER, 1792

	Approximate No. of Deputies
The Right (Gironde)	*165*
The Center (Plain)	*435*
The Left (Mountain)	*150*

The radicalism of the Convention was underlined by the Jacobin antecedents of both its Right and its Left. Many ties in common existed between the Gironde and the Mountain (so named because its deputies sat high up in the meeting hall). Both factions came from the middle class, both were steeped in the ideas of the *philosophes*, and both united to declare France a republic (September 21, 1792).

Bitter dissension, however, soon arose between the Gironde and the Mountain.

Danton (1759–1794), in a sketch by David.

The Girondins favored a breathing spell in revolutionary legislation, and they also defended provincial interests against possible encroachments by Paris. As one of their deputies told the Convention (and his allusion to classical antiquity was most characteristic of the Revolution):

I fear the despotism of Paris. . . . I do not want a Paris guided by intriguers to become to the French Empire what Rome was to the Roman Empire. Paris must be reduced to its proper one-eighty-third of influence, like the other departments.*

The Gironde, therefore, favored a large measure of "federalism," which meant decentralization in the Revolutionary vocabulary, and a national government limited by many checks and balances. The details were set forth in a draft constitution completed early in 1793 by the distinguished Girondin deputy, Condorcet, the prophet of human progress (see Chapter 17). In Condorcet's draft, the executive and the legislature would be independent of each other and separately elected, the results of elections would be adjusted according to proportional representation, projected laws would be submitted to a popular referendum, and voters would have the right to recall unworthy elected officials.

The leaders of the Mountain denounced federalism and advocated an all-powerful central government. Their chief spokesman was Maximilien Robespierre (1758–1794). This earnest young lawyer did not look like a revolutionary: He powdered his hair neatly and wore the light-blue coat and knee-breeches of the Old Régime. Yet Robespierre was a political fanatic whose speeches were lay sermons couched in the solemn language of a new revelation. He put his creed most forcefully in a discourse delivered in February, 1794:

What is the goal toward which we are striving? The peaceful enjoyment of liberty and equality: the rule of that eternal justice whose laws have

been engraved . . . upon the hearts of men, even upon the heart of the slave who ignores them and of the tyrant who denies them.

We desire an order of things . . . where our country assures the welfare of each individual and where each individual enjoys with pride the prosperity and the glory of our country; where the souls of all grow through the constant expression of republican sentiments; where the arts are the ornament of the freedom which in turn ennobles them; and where commerce is the source of public wealth, not just of the monstrous opulence of a few houses.*

Apparently Robespierre truly believed that he could translate the ideals of Rousseau's *Social Contract* into a practical political program. Like Rousseau, he had faith in the natural goodness of humanity, in "the laws engraved upon the hearts of men." He was sure that he knew the general will, and that the general will demanded a Republic of Virtue. If Frenchmen would not be free and virtuous voluntarily, then, as Rousseau had recommended, they would be "forced to be free."

Robespierre and the Republic of Virtue triumphed. The Mountain won out over the Gironde in the competition for the votes of the relatively uncommitted deputies of the Plain in the Convention. The first step came when, after one hundred hours of continuous voting, the Convention declared "Citizen Louis Capet" guilty of treason and by a narrow margin sentenced him to the guillotine without delay. Louis XVI died bravely on January 21, 1793. Although the majority of the French population disapproved of the King's execution, the majority did not control the Convention. The Girondin deputies made the political mistake of splitting their votes on the issue. Those who voted against the death penalty took a courageous stand in defense of the humanitarian principles of the Enlightenment, but they also exposed themselves to the charge of being "counter-revolutionaries."

A combination of events at home and abroad soon destroyed the Gironde. In February, 1793, the Convention rejected Condor-

Louis XVI, a moment before his execution.

cet's draft constitution, and in the same month it declared war on Britain, Spain, and the Netherlands. France now faced a formidable coalition of opponents, since Austria and Prussia remained at war with her. In March, the army under Dumouriez, a Girondin general, suffered a series of defeats in the Low Countries, and in April Dumouriez deserted to the enemy. At home, in the face of unemployment, high prices, and food shortages, the Gironde had little to offer except laissez-faire. The *sections* of Paris demanded price controls and food requisitioning; they also pressed for the expulsion of Girondins from the Jacobin clubs and the Convention. Finally, on June 2, 1793, a vast crowd of armed men from the *sections* of Paris, following the precedent of August,

1792, invaded the Convention and forced the arrest of twenty-nine Girondin deputies. Backed by these armed Parisians, the Mountain intimidated the Plain, and the Convention consigned the arrested Girondins to the guillotine. The Reign of Terror had begun.

The Reign of Terror, June, 1793 – July, 1794

How was it that the advocates of democracy now imposed a dictatorship on France? Here is Robespierre's explanation:

. . . To establish and consolidate democracy, to achieve the peaceful rule of constitutional laws, we must first finish the war of liberty against tyranny. . . . We must annihilate the enemies of the republic at home and abroad, or else we shall perish. . . .

If virtue is the mainstay of a democratic government in time of peace, then in time of revolution a democratic government must rely on *virtue* and *terror*. . . . Terror is nothing but justice, swift, severe and inflexible; it is an emanation of virtue. . . . It has been said that terror is the mainstay of a despotic government. . . . The government of the revolution is the despotism of liberty against tyranny.*

The Convention duly voted a democratic constitution, drawn up by the Mountain, granting universal manhood suffrage and giving supreme power, unhampered by Girondin checks and balances, to a single legislative chamber. The Constitution of 1793 was approved by a referendum, but its operation was then postponed indefinitely. As Robespierre explained, "To establish and consolidate democracy, we must first finish the war of liberty against tyranny."

The actual government of the Terror centered on a twelve-man Committee of Public Safety, composed of Robespierre and other stalwarts from the Mountain. Though nominally responsible to the Convention, the Committee of Public Safety exercised a large measure of independent authority and acted as a kind of war cabinet. Never under the dominance of a single individual, not even Robespierre, it really functioned as a committee — "The Twelve Who Ruled" is an appropriate description. A second committee, that of Public Security, supervised police activities and turned suspected enemies of the Republic over to the new Revolutionary Tribunal. To speed the work of repression, the sixteen judges and sixty jurors of the Tribunal were eventually divided into several courts.

The Mountain scrapped much of the local self-government inaugurated under the Constitution of 1791. Local Jacobin clubs purged department and commune administrations of political unreliables, while special local courts supplemented the grim labors of the Revolutionary Tribunal. To make sure that provin-

Le Moniteur Universel, February 7, 1794. Our translation.

cial France toed the line, the Mountain sent out trusted members of the Convention as its agents, the "deputies on mission." From the standpoint of administration, the Terror marked both an anticipation of twentieth century dictatorship and a return to the age-old French principle of centralization. The deputies on mission were the successors of the *intendants* of Richelieu, the *enquêteurs* of St. Louis, and the *missi dominici* of Charlemagne. The "Twelve Who Ruled" were more effective absolutists than Louis XIV himself.

The Record of the Terror

The "swift, severe, and inflexible justice" described by Robespierre took the lives of nearly 20,000 Frenchmen. Although the Terror claimed such social outcasts as criminals and prostitutes, its main purpose was military and political — to clear France of suspected traitors, including Marie Antoinette, and to purge the Jacobins of dissidents. It fell with the greatest severity on the clergy, the aristocracy, and the Girondins. Many of its victims came from the Vendée, a strongly Catholic and royalist area in western France which had revolted against the Republic's attempts to recruit soldiers. Many prisoners from the Vendée were among the 2,000 victims of the *noyades* (drownings) at Nantes, where the accused were set adrift on the River Loire in leaky barges. Equally grisly was the repression of an uprising of Girondin sympathizers at Lyons, which also claimed 2,000 victims.

The wartime hysteria that helped to account for the excesses of the Terror also inspired a very practical patriotism. On August 23, 1793, the Convention issued a decree epitomizing the democratic nationalism of the Jacobins:

From this moment, until the time when the enemy shall have been driven from the territory of the Republic, all Frenchmen are permanently requisitioned for the service of the armies.

Young men will go into combat; married men will manufacture arms and transport supplies; women will make tents and uniforms and will serve in the hospitals; children will make old linen into bandages; old men will be carried into the public squares to arouse the courage of the soldiers, excite hatred for kings and inspire the unity of the Republic.*

In an early application of universal conscription, the army drafted all bachelors and widowers between the ages of eighteen and twenty-five. Hundreds of open-air forges were installed in Paris to manufacture weapons. Since the war prevented the importation of the saltpeter needed for gunpowder, the government sponsored a great campaign to scrape patches of saltpeter from cellars and stables.

By the close of 1793, the forces of the Republic had driven foreign troops from French soil. Credit for this new shift in the tide of battle did not rest solely with the Jacobins. The military successes of the Republic reflected in part the improvements made in the army during the dying years of the Old Régime; they resulted still more from the weaknesses of the coalition aligned against France. Yet they could scarcely have been achieved without the new democratic spirit that allowed men of the third estate to become officers and that made the French army the most determined, the most enterprising— and, perhaps, the most idealistic—in Europe.

"Total" mobilization demanded an approximate equality of economic sacrifice. To exorcise the twin devils of inflation and scarcity, the Terror issued the "*maximum*" legislation, placing ceilings on prices and wages. In theory, at least, wages were checked at a maximum 50 per cent above the wage-rate of 1790, and prices were halted at 33 per cent above the price level of 1790. The government rationed bread and meat, forbade the use of white flour, and directed all patriots to eat *pain d'égalité*— "equality bread," a loaf utilizing almost the whole of the wheat. Finally, early in 1794, the Convention passed the "Laws of Ventôse," named for a month in the new revolutionary calendar. These laws authorized seizure of the remaining properties of the *émigrés* and other opponents of the Republic and recommended their distribution to landless Frenchmen.

Le Moniteur Universel, August 24, 1793. Our translation.

Socialist historians have sometimes found in the *maximum* and the Laws of Ventôse evidence that the Terror was moving from political to social democracy, that the Republic of Virtue was indeed beginning the socialist revolution. Actually the *maximum* regulations did not prove very effective. Attempts by the government to enforce wage ceilings made Parisian workingmen indignant. And, though the *maximum* on prices temporarily checked the depreciation of the *assignats*, many price-controlled articles were available only on the black market, which even the government had to patronize.

Moreover, the redistribution of property permitted by the Laws of Ventôse was never implemented. When the Laws were proposed, a spokesman for the Committee of Public Safety explained that no general assault on property was intended:

The revolution leads us to recognize the principle that he who has shown himself the enemy of

Robespierre, sketched during a meeting of the Convention.

Sketch of Marie Antoinette on her way to the guillotine, by David.

his country cannot own property. The properties of patriots are sacred, but the goods of conspirators are there for the unfortunate.*

To the thorough-going socialist not even the properties of patriots are sacred. The middle-class leaders of the Terror were not genuine socialists; only the emergencies of the Revolution forced them to abandon laissez-faire. They had to make food cheaper for townspeople—whence the *maximum*; and they had to promise men some hope of future well-being—whence the Laws of Ventôse.

The Terror presented its most revolutionary aspect in its drastic social and cultural reforms. The Convention abolished slavery in the French colonies; at home, according to Robespierre, "we desire to substitute all the virtues and all the miracles of the Republic for all the vices and all the nonsense of monarchy." When Robespierre said "all," he meant "all"—clothing, the arts, amusements, the calendar, religion. The Republic of Virtue could tolerate nothing that smelled of the Old Régime. Even the traditional forms of address, .

*Saint-Just, February 26, 1794, in *Le Moniteur Universel*, February 27, 1794. Our translation.

"Monsieur" and *"Madame,"* gave way to *"Cito-yen"* (citizen) and *"Citoyenne"* (citizeness).

Ever since 1789, revolutionaries had discarded elaborate gowns and knee-breeches (*culottes*) as symbols of idleness and privilege. With the exception of Robespierre, good republican men were *sans-culottes* (literally, without knee-breeches), attired in the long, baggy trousers of the humble peasant or workman. Women affected simple, high-waisted dresses, copied from the costumes of the ancient Romans. Rome became the model for behavior—the virtuous Rome of the Republic, of course, not the sordid Empire. Parents named their children Brutus or Cato or Gracchus, and the theater shelved the masterpieces of Racine and Corneille for stilted dramas glorifying Roman heroes. Cabinet-makers, deserting the graceful style of Louis XV, produced sturdy neoclassical furniture decorated with Roman symbols. "The arts," said Robespierre, "are the ornament of the freedom which in turn ennobles them." Playwrights, authors, and editors who failed to ornament freedom properly experienced censorship or even the guillotine. The Jacobins reduced the lively newspapers of the early revolution to dull semi-official organs.

They also instituted a sweeping reform of the calendar (October, 1793). The first day of the Republic, September 22, 1792, was designated the initial day of Year I, Roman numerals were assigned to the years, and the months received new and more "natural" names:

THE MONTHS OF THE
REVOLUTIONARY CALENDAR

Fall: Vendémiaire (Grape-Harvest)
        Brumaire (Misty)
        Frimaire (Frosty)

Winter: Nivôse (Snowy)
        Pluviôse (Rainy)
        Ventôse (Windy)

Spring: Germinal (Sprouting)
        Floréal (Flowering)
        Prairial (Meadow)

Summer: Messidor (Wheat-Harvest)
         Thermidor (Heat)
         Fructidor (Ripening)

Each month had thirty days, divided into three ten-day weeks. Every tenth day was set aside for rest and for the celebration of one of the virtues so admired by Robespierre—Hatred of Tyrants and Traitors, Heroism, Frugality, Stoicism, not to mention two anticipations of Mother's Day (Filial Piety and Maternal Tenderness). The five days left over at the end of the year were dedicated to Genius, Labor, Noble Actions, Awards, and Opinion. The revolutionary calendar, for all its sanctimonious touches, was worthy of the Enlightenment. Yet it antagonized workmen, who disliked laboring nine days out of ten, instead of six out of seven. It never really took root, and Napoleon scrapped it a decade later.

The Convention had better luck with another reform close to the spirit of the Age of Reason—the metric system. A special committee, including Condorcet, Laplace, Lavoisier, and other distinguished intellectuals, devised new weights and measures based on the uniform use of the decimal system rather than on the haphazard accumulations of custom. In August, 1793, a decree made the meter the standard unit of length, and supplementary legislation in 1795 established the liter as the measure of volume and the gram as the unit of weight. Even in some Anglo-Saxon countries, which, cling to older and less rational weights and measures, scientists have adopted the metric system of revolutionary France.

By and large, however, the forces of tradition proved too strong for the Terror. Nowhere was this fact more evident than in the attempts to destroy the old religion and legislate a new one. Many churches were closed and turned into barracks or administrative offices; often their medieval glass and sculpture were destroyed. Some of the Jacobins launched a "de-Christianization" campaign to make Catholics into *philosophes* and their churches into "temples of Reason." Robespierre, however, disliked the cult of Reason; the Republic of Virtue, he believed, should acknowledge an ultimate author of morality. The Convention therefore decreed (May, 1794) that "the French people recognize the existence of the Supreme Being and the immortality of the soul." At the festival of the Supreme Being, June 8, 1794, Robespierre set fire to figures representing Vice, Folly, and Atheism, and from the embers a statue of Wisdom emerged, but smudged with smoke because of a mechanical slip-up. The audience laughed. The deistic concept of the Supreme Being was too remote and the mechanics of the new worship too artificial to appeal to the religious emotions of Frenchmen.

The Thermidorean Reaction

Indeed, the Republic of Virtue was too abstract in ideals, and too violent in practice, to retain popular support. Like the Geneva of Calvin, the France of Robespierre demanded superhuman devotion to duty and inhuman indifference to hardships and bloodshed. During the first half of 1794, Robespierre pressed the Terror so relentlessly that even the members of the Committees of Public Safety and General Security began to fear they would be the next victims. Robespierre lost his backing in the Convention, as more and more deputies came to favor moderation. The crucial day was the ninth of Thermidor, Year II (July 27, 1794), when shouts of "Down with the Tyrant!" drowned out Robespierre's attempts to address the deputies. The Convention ordered Robespierre's arrest, and on the next day the great fanatic went to the guillotine.

The leaders of the Thermidorean Reaction, many of them former Jacobins, soon dismantled the machinery of the Terror. They disbanded the Revolutionary Tribunal, recalled the deputies on mission, and deprived the Committees of Public Safety and General Security of their independent authority. They closed the Paris Jacobin Club and invited the surviving Girondin deputies to resume their old seats in the Convention. They took the first step toward the restoration of Catholicism by permitting priests to celebrate Mass, though under state supervision and without state financial support. The press and the theater recovered their freedom, and pleasure-seekers again flocked to Paris, now liberated from the somberness of the Republic of Virtue. France was resuming a normal existence.

Normality, however, exacted a price. In southern and western France a counter-revolutionary "White Terror," equalling the great Terror in fury, claimed many lives, not only supporters of the Mountain but also purchasers of former church and noble lands. The men of Thermidor caused an acute inflation by canceling the economic legislation of the Terror. No longer checked even slightly by the *maximum*, the prices of some foods rose to a hundred times the level of 1790, and the *assignats* sank so low in value that businessmen refused to accept them. Desperate, half-starving Parisians staged several demonstrations against the Thermidoreans during 1795. Sometimes the rioters voiced their support of the discredited Mountain and its democratic Constitution of 1793, and sometimes they let themselves be used by royalist agents, but always they clamored for bread and lower prices.

The Thermidorean Reaction concluded with the passage of the Constitution of 1795, the last major act of the Convention. The men of Thermidor wanted both to retain the Republic and to assure the dominance of the propertied classes. The Constitution of 1795 therefore denied the vote to the poorest quarter of the nation and required that candidates for public office possess considerable property. It established two legislative councils, the Five Hundred and the Elders (who had to be at least forty years old and either married or widowed); both councils were to be elected piecemeal after the American practice of renewing one-third of the Senate every two years. Two-thirds of the initial members of the councils were to be drawn from the deputies of the Convention, who were therefore labelled *"les perpetuels."* The Council of Five Hundred nominated, and the Elders chose, five directors who headed the executive. Otherwise the Directory was almost totally independent of the legislative councils.

The Constitution of 1795 marked the third great effort of the Revolution to provide France with an enduring government. It followed in part a classical example, for the two councils were patterned on the Areopagus and the Five Hundred of ancient Athens; it also followed the American precedent of 1787 and the French precedent of 1791. It embodied the separation of powers and deferred to the aristocracy of wealth, though not to that of birth. By abandoning the political democracy of the still-born Constitution of 1793 and by reverting to the restricted suffrage of 1791, it demonstrated that the most radical phase of the Revolution had passed.

The Directory, October, 1795 – November, 1799

The new regime of the Directory made a vigorous attack on economic problems. It levied high protective tariffs, both as a measure of war against England and as a concession to French businessmen. Again responding to business pressure, it destroyed the plates used to print the *assignats* and in 1797 withdrew paper money from circulation. The return to hard money required stringent governmental economies. The Directory instituted these economies, and it eased the crushing burden of the national debt by simply repudiating two-thirds of it. In short, the Directory brought a semblance of order out of chronic financial chaos.

Political instability, however, plagued the Directory. It suppressed with ease the amateurish "Conspiracy of the Equals" (1796–1797) sponsored by Gracchus Babeuf, who dreamed of a more collectivist society. But it experienced more difficulty with the recurrent plots of royalists or Jacobins. Moreover, the directors and the legislative councils clashed repeatedly, each side seeking to turn the political balance in its own favor, and each, in consequence, violating the constitution. The councils sacked directors before their terms were finished; the directors refused to allow duly elected councilors to take their seats. Disgruntled politicians and apprehensive moderates, who feared that the Directory might be taken over by extremists, began to maneuver for the help of the army. The result of their maneuvering was the *coup d'état* of Brumaire in 1799 and the dictatorship of a general, Napoleon Bonaparte.

IV   Napoleon and France

Edmund Burke, the British political philosopher, foresaw very early the long process that culminated in Napoleon's dominance of France and Europe. In 1790, Burke warned the French—and his own countrymen—in his *Reflections on the Revolution in France:*

Everything depends on the army in such a government as yours; for you have industriously destroyed all the opinions, . . . all the instincts which support government. Therefore the moment any difference arises between your National Assembly and any part of the nation, you must have recourse to force. Nothing else is left to you. . . .

It is besides to be considered, whether an assembly like yours . . . is fit for promoting the discipline and obedience of an army. It is known, that armies have hitherto yielded a very precarious and uncertain obedience to any senate, or popular authority. . . . The officers must totally lose the characteristic disposition of military men, if they see with perfect submission and due admiration, the dominion of pleaders; especially when they find that they have a new court to pay to an endless succession of those pleaders. . . . In the weakness of one kind of authority, and in the fluctuation of all, the officers of an army will remain for some time mutinous and full of faction, until some popular general who understands the art of conciliating the soldiery, and who possesses the true spirit of command, shall draw the eyes of all men upon himself. Armies will obey him on his personal account. There is no other way of securing military obedience in this state of things. But the moment in which that event shall happen, the person who really commands the army is your master; the master . . . of your king, the master of your assembly, the master of your whole republic.*

In 1790, however, except for Burke, no one outside France paid much heed to the French army. It was widely believed that the very in-

*Everyman ed. (New York, 1910), 215–217.

tensity of domestic problems made France incapable of a vigorous foreign policy. Catherine the Great predicted as late as 1792 that ten thousand soldiers would be sufficient to conquer France. Liberals everywhere hailed the peaceful promise of the Revolution. The capture of the Bastille delighted Charles James Fox, a leading English Whig: "How much the greatest event it is that ever happened in the world! and how much the best!"

The First Coalition, 1792–1795

The war that broke out in the spring of 1792 soon destroyed the illusions of French military weakness and French liberal purity. The war was to last continuously, save for a few intervals of peace, down to the final defeat of Napoleon. It deserves to be called the World War of 1792–1815, for almost all the European powers eventually participated, and the fighting ranged far beyond Europe. By the time the war was a year old, Austria and Prussia, the charter members of the First Coalition against France, had been joined by Holland, Spain, and Great Britain. The British had both ideological and strategic interests at stake. They regarded the attack on the Tuileries, the September massacres, and the execution of Louis XVI as outrages against human decency and the institution of monarchy. And the French invasion of the Austrian Netherlands in the fall of 1792 raised the unpleasant prospect that this Belgian "cockpit of Europe" would fall under French control. The early campaigns of the war were indecisive. Late in 1792, the French followed up their success at Valmy by invading Belgium, only to lose ground again in 1793 after the defeat and desertion of Dumouriez (see p. 106). Then in 1794 the French definitely gained the advantage, and by 1795 French troops had occupied Belgium, Holland, and Germany west of the Rhine.

One reason for French success we have already seen—the Convention's energetic mobilization of national resources. Another reason, equally important yet easy to overlook, was the weakness of the First Coalition. The partners in the coalition lacked a first-rate commander; nor did they achieve effective co-ordination of their efforts. The Duke of Brunswick's failure to take Paris in 1792 resulted as much from his own deficient generalship as from the "miracle" of Valmy. Moreover, the partitions of Poland in 1793 and 1795 greatly assisted the French by distracting Prussia, Russia, and Austria. The pick of the Prussian army was diverted to occupation duty in newly annexed Polish provinces. By 1795 things had come to such a pass that the Prussians did not dare attack the French for fear of being assaulted from the rear by their nominal Austrian ally.

Prussia was the first member of the coalition to make peace. In the Treaty of Basel (1795) she ceded to France the scattered Prussian holdings west of the Rhine on the understanding that she might seek compensation elsewhere in Germany. Spain and Holland soon deserted the coalition also. In 1795, then, France at last secured her "natural frontiers." In addition to Belgium and the Rhineland she had also annexed Savoy and Nice, thereby extending her southeastern border to the crest of the Alps. These conquests, however, belied the ideals of the Revolution. In declaring war on Austria in 1792, France had sworn to uphold the promise of the Constitution of 1791: that she would never undertake a war of conquest. This was to be "not a war of nation against nation, but the righteous defense of a free people against the unjust aggression of a king." But the conquering armies of the First Republic brought closer the day when nation would fight nation—when the European nations would invoke "the righteous defense of a free people against the unjust aggression" not of a king, but of revolutionary France.

Napoleon's Early Career

At the close of 1795, only Britain and Austria remained officially at war with France. To lead the attack against Habsburg forces in northern Italy, the Directory picked a youthful general who was something of a *philosophe* and revolutionary as well as a ruthless, ambitious adventurer. He was born Napoleone Buonaparte on Corsica in 1769, soon after the French acquisition of that Mediterranean island from Genoa. He retained throughout his life the intense family loyalty characteristic of the rather primitive society of Corsica and bestowed on the members of the Bonaparte clan all the spoils of conquest, even thrones.

As a boy, Napoleon attended military school in France and, though he now spelled his name in the French style, was snubbed as a "foreigner" by some of his fellow cadets. He immersed himself in his studies and in reading (Rousseau was his favorite) and dreamed of the day when he might liberate his native island from French control. Later, however, his zeal for Corsican independence faded in consequence of the rupture between the Bonapartes and the hero of Corsican nationalism, Paoli, who was an ally of Britain. When the Revolution broke out, the young artillery officer helped to overthrow the Old Régime at home and then went back to France to resume his military career. He defended the Convention, but more out of expediency than from conviction, and commanded the artillery in December, 1793, when the forces of the Jacobin Convention recaptured the Mediterranean port of Toulon, which had fallen to the British earlier in the year. In October, 1795, he rescued the Thermidorean Convention in the last moments before the Directory took over by mowing down royalist rioters with the famous "whiff of grapeshot." Then he married Josephine de Beauharnais, a widow six years his senior and an intimate of the ruling clique of the Directory. Josephine's connections and Napoleon's own demonstrated talent gained him the Italian command in 1796.

In the celebrated Italian campaign Napoleon cleared the Austrians out of their strongholds in the space of a year and made them sue for peace. He showed a remarkable ability to strike quickly and by surprise before his opponents could consolidate their defenses. He also showed a gift for propaganda and "public relations," as this proclamation from the early phases of the campaign will illustrate:

Soldiers! In two weeks you have won six victories; you have made 15,000 prisoners; you have killed or wounded more than 10,000 men.

Deprived of everything, you have accomplished everything. You have won battles without cannon, negotiated rivers without bridges, made forced marches without shoes, encamped without brandy, and often without bread. Only the phalanxes of the Republic, only the soldiers of Liberty, would have been capable of suffering the things that you have suffered.

You all burn to carry the glory of the French people; to humiliate the proud kings who dared to contemplate shackling us; to go back to your villages, to say proudly: 'I was of the conquering army of Italy!'

Friends, I promise you that conquest; but there is a condition you must swear to fulfill: to respect the people whom you are delivering; to repress horrible pillaging.

Peoples of Italy, the French army comes to break your chains; greet it with confidence; your property, religion and customs will be respected.*

It was characteristic of Napoleon to promise all things to all men. He encouraged the nationalism of underpaid and underfed French soldiers; yet he appealed also to the nationalism of the Italians, promising them liberation from Austria and guaranteeing the orderly conduct of the French army. He did not, of course, tell the Italians that they might be exchanging one master for another, nor did he publicize the money that he seized from Italian governments and the art treasures that he took from Italian galleries and shipped back to France.

In the Treaty of Campoformio (1797) terminating the Italian campaign, Austria acknowledged the loss of Belgium and recognized the two puppet states that Napoleon set up in northwestern Italy, the Ligurian Republic (Genoa) and the Cisalpine Republic (the former Austrian possession of Lombardy). In return, the Habsburgs received the Italian territories of the Venetian Republic and a secret French assurance that Prussia, despite the specific promise made to her in 1795, would not be permitted to compensate for her losses in the Rhineland by taking lands elsewhere in Germany.

Only Britain remained at war with France. Napoleon decided to attack her indirectly through Egypt, then a semi-independent vassal of the Ottoman Empire. This would-be Alexander the Great, seeking new worlds to conquer, talked grandly of digging a canal at Suez, which would give French merchants the monopoly of a new short trade-route to India and exact belated retribution from Britain for Clive's victory in the Seven Years' War. Since Napoleon shared the passion of the Enlighten-

Napoleon, 1798; unfinished portrait by David.

*Abridged from *Le Moniteur Universel,* May 17, 1796. Our translation.

ment for science and antiquity, he invited archaeologists and other experts to accompany his army and thereby helped to found the study known as Egyptology. Frenchmen discovered the Rosetta Stone, later deciphered by Champollion, the first key to the translation of ancient Egyptian hieroglyphics. Napoleon's experts established in Egypt an outpost of French cultural imperialism that lasted until the twentieth century.

From the military standpoint, however, the campaign failed. Having eluded the British Mediterranean fleet commanded by Nelson, Napoleon landed in Egypt in July, 1798, and quickly routed the Mamluks, the ruling oligarchy. Then disaster struck. On August 1, 1798, Nelson discovered the French fleet moored at Abukir Bay along the Egyptian coast and destroyed it before its captains had time to weigh anchor. Nelson's victory deprived the French of supplies, of reinforcements, and even of news from home. After a year of futile campaigning in the Near East, Napoleon suddenly left Egypt in August, 1799, and returned to France.

Brumaire

Napoleon found the situation in France ripe for a decisive political stroke. The Directory was shaken by a strong revival of Jacobinism. Several hundred deputies in the legislative councils belonged to the "Society of the Friends of Liberty and Equality," essentially the old Jacobin club. Under their influence, the councils in 1799 decreed a forced loan from the rich and passed a Law of Hostages, designed to make the *émigrés* behave by threatening their relatives in France with reprisals if they engaged in activities hostile to the French Republic. Moderates feared that a new Reign of Terror would soon be unleashed.

Abroad, the Directory had established four new satellite republics with classical names — the Roman, the Parthenopean in Naples, the Batavian in Holland, and the Helvetian in Switzerland. But this new success of French imperialism upset the European balance and provoked the formation of the Second Coali-

tion, headed by Britain, Austria, and Russia. The Habsburgs resented the extension of French influence in their former Italian preserve, and Tsar Paul I (1796–1801) feared that Napoleon would damage Russia's Mediterranean interests. The eccentric Tsar was head of the Knights of Malta, a Catholic order dating back to the Crusades, whom Napoleon had expelled from their headquarters on the island of Malta. In the campaign of 1799, Russian troops fought in Italy and Switzerland, and the Russian General Suvorov, who defeated the French repeatedly, became the hero of western Europe. By August, 1799, the French had been expelled from Italy, and their puppet republics — Cisalpine, Roman, and Parthenopean — had been dismantled.

In these circumstances, Napoleon got a rousing reception on his return from Egypt. Soon he was engaged in a plot to overthrow the Directory, with the complicity of two of the five directors, Roger-Ducos and Siéyès, the old champion of the third estate. On November 9 and 10, 1799 (18 and 19 Brumaire by the revolutionary calendar), the plot was executed. The three directors not in the plot resigned, and the two legislative councils named Napoleon military commander of Paris. He was then to persuade the councils to entrust to the two remaining directors and himself the task of drafting a new constitution. The Elders agreed, but in the Five Hundred, where there were many Jacobin deputies, Bonaparte heard the ominous cry, "Down with the tyrant!," which had doomed Robespierre on the 9th Thermidor. He was jostled and fainted, but his brother Lucien, the presiding officer of the Five Hundred, saved the day until a detachment of troops loyal to Napoleon expelled the hostile deputies.

This almost comic *coup d'état* of Brumaire ended the Directory. The Bonapartist minority in the council vested full power in the victorious triumvirate of Roger-Ducos, Siéyès, and Napoleon, of whom only Napoleon really counted. It had all happened just as Edmund Burke had predicted:

In the weakness of authority, . . . some popular general shall draw the eyes of all men upon himself.

Armies will obey him on his personal account. . . .
The person who really commands the army is
your master.

Napoleonic Government

The Constitution of the Year VIII, drawn
up after Brumaire, was based on Siéyès' autocratic maxim, "Confidence from below, authority from above." It erected a very strong executive, the Consulate, named, like other bodies
set up by the constitution, after institutions
of republican Rome. Although three consuls
shared the executive, Napoleon as First Consul
left the other two only nominal power. Four
separate bodies had a hand in legislation: (1)
the Council of State proposed laws; (2) the
Tribunate debated them but did not vote; (3)
the Legislative Corps voted them but did not
debate; (4) the Senate had the right to veto
legislation. The members of all four bodies
were either appointed by the First Consul or
elected indirectly by a process so complex that
Bonaparte had ample opportunity to manipulate candidates. The core of this system was
the Council of State, staffed by Bonaparte's
hand-picked choices, which served both as a
cabinet and as the highest administrative court.
The three remaining bodies were intended
merely to go through the motions of enacting
whatever the First Consul decreed. Even so,
they were sometimes unruly, and the Tribunate
so annoyed Napoleon that he finally abolished
it in 1807.

Meantime, step by step, Napoleon increased
his own authority. In 1802, he persuaded the
legislators to drop the original ten-year limitation on his term of office and make him First
Consul for life, with the power to designate
his successor and amend the constitution at
will. France was now a monarchy in all but
name. In 1804, he took the next logical move
and prompted the Senate to declare that "the
government of the Republic is entrusted to an
Emperor." A magnificent coronation took
place at Notre Dame in Paris on December 2.
The Pope consecrated the Emperor, but, following Charlemagne's example, Napoleon
placed the crown on his own head.

Each time Napoleon revised the Constitution in a non-republican direction he made the
republican gesture of submitting the change to
the electorate. Each time, the results of the
plebiscite were overwhelmingly favorable: In
1799 – 1800, the vote was 3,011,107 for Napoleon and the Constitution of the Year VIII, and
1,562 against; in 1802, it was 3,568,885 for
Napoleon and the life Consulate, and 8,374
against; in 1804, 3,572,329 for Napoleon and
the Empire, and 2,579 against. Although the
voters were exposed to considerable official
pressure and the announced results were perhaps rigged a little, the majority of Frenchmen
undoubtedly supported Napoleon. His military triumphs appealed to their growing nationalism, and his policy of stability at home
insured them against further revolutionary
crises and changes. Confidence did indeed
seem to increase from below as authority increased from above.

If by any chance confidence failed to materialize below, Napoleon had the authority
to deal with the recalcitrant. He wiped out
the local self-government remaining from the
early days of the Revolution. In place of lo-
cally elected officials, he substituted those appointed by himself—prefects in departments,
sub-prefects in *arrondissements,* mayors in communes—and all were instructed to enforce
compliance with the Emperor's dictates. Napoleon brought the old French tradition of
centralization to a new peak of intensity.

Men of every political background staffed
the imperial administration. Napoleon cared
little whether his subordinates were returned
émigrés or ex-Jacobins, so long as they had ability. Besides, their varied antecedents reinforced the impression that narrow factionalism
was dead and that the Empire rested on a
broad political base. Napoleon paid officials
well and offered the additional bait of high
titles. With the establishment of the Empire
he created dukes by the dozen and counts and
barons by the hundred. He rewarded outstanding generals with the rank of Marshal and other
officers and civilian officials with the Legion of
Honor. "Aristocracy always exists," Napoleon
remarked. "Destroy it in the nobility, it re-
moves itself to the rich and powerful houses

of the middle class."* The imperial aristocracy gave the leaders of the middle class the social distinction that they felt to be rightfully theirs.

Law and Justice

Napoleon revived some of the glamor of the Old Régime but not its glaring inequalities. His series of law codes, the celebrated *Code Napoléon* (1804–1810), declared all men equal before the law without regard to their rank and wealth. It extended to all the right to follow the occupation, and embrace the religion, of their choosing. It gave France the single coherent system of law which the *philosophes* had demanded and which the revolutionary governments had been too busy to formulate.

The *Code Napoléon* did not, however, embody the full judicial reform program of the Enlightenment; it incorporated from the old Roman law some practices that strengthened the absolutism of the Empire. It favored the interests of the state over the rights of the individual, and it permitted some use of torture in trial procedure. Judges were no longer elected, as they had been under the Constitution of 1791, but appointed by the Emperor; jurors were selected by his prefects. Though Napoleon confirmed the revolutionary legislation permitting divorce by mutual consent, the code cancelled other revolutionary laws protecting wives, minors, and illegitimate children. The man of the family regained his old legal superiority. At times confirming the principles of 1789, and at times betraying them, Napoleonic law and justice offered a fair summary of the fate of the Revolution under the Empire.

A similar ambiguity clouded Napoleon's attitude toward civil liberties. He practiced religious toleration of a sort and welcomed former political heretics into his administration. But his generosity stemmed always from expediency, never from any fundamental belief in liberty. If he failed to get his way by conciliation, he used force. In the western departments, where royalist uprisings had become chronic since the revolt in the Vendée, he massacred the rebels who declined his offer of amnesty in 1800. In 1804, he kidnapped the Duke of Enghien from the neutral German state of Baden because the Duke was believed to be the choice of monarchist conspirators for the throne of France. Though Napoleon immediately discovered the Duke's innocence, he had him executed none the less.

Napoleon cared little for freedom of speech. In July, 1801, for example, he directed his librarian to read all the newspapers carefully and

. . . make an abstract of everything they contain likely to affect the public point of view, especially with regard to religion, philosophy, and political opinion. He will send me this abstract between 5 and 6 o'clock every day.

Once every ten days he will send me an analysis of all the books or pamphlets which have appeared . . .

He will take pains to procure copies of all the plays which are produced, and to analyse them for me, with observations of the same character as those above mentioned. This analysis must be made, at latest, within 48 hours of the production of the plays.*

And so on through "bills, posters, advertisements, institutes, literary meetings, sermons and fashionable trials" — no segment of public opinion escaped Napoleon's manipulation. He reduced by five-sixths the number of Paris newspapers and pestered theater managers with suggestions for improving the patriotic tone of plays. When he wanted to arouse French feelings, he simply started a press campaign, as in this instance from 1807:

A great hue and cry is to be raised against the persecutions experienced by the Catholics of Ireland at the hands of the Anglican Church. . . . Bishops will be approached so that prayers will be offered entreating an end to the persecutions of the Anglican Church against the Irish Catholics. But the administration must move very delicately and make use of the newspapers without their realizing

*Quoted in H. A. L. Fisher, *Napoleon* (New York, 1913), Appendix I.

*Quoted in J. M. Thompson, ed., *Napoleon's Letters* (London, 1954), 93–94.

what the government is driving at. . . . And the term 'Anglican Church' must always be used in place of 'Protestants,' for we have Protestants in France, but no Anglican Church.*

Religion

Political considerations colored all Napoleon's decisions on religion. "I do not see in religion the mystery of the incarnation," he said, "but the mystery of the social order. It attaches to heaven an idea of equality which prevents the rich man from being massacred by the poor."† Since French Catholics loathed the anticlericalism of the Revolution, Napoleon sought to appease them by working out a reconciliation with Rome.

The Concordat negotiated with Pope Pius VII (1800–1823) in 1801 accomplished the reconciliation. It canceled only the most obnoxious features of the Civil Constitution of the Clergy. The French state, while agreeing to pay clerical salaries, also agreed to suppress the popular election of bishops and priests. The bishops were to be nominated by the government and then consecrated by the Pope; the priests were to be appointed by the bishops. At this point, Napoleon's concessions stopped. By declaring that Catholicism was the faith of the "great majority of Frenchmen," rather than the state religion, the Concordat implicitly admitted the toleration of Protestants and Jews. Also by implication the Pope accepted such important measures of the Revolution as the abolition of the tithe and the confiscation of ecclesiastical lands.

Finally, the Concordat made the activities of the Church in France subject to the "police regulations" of the state. These regulations were spelled out in the Organic Articles, which Napoleon appended to the Concordat without consulting the Pope. The French government was to supervise the publication of papal bulls, the establishment of seminaries, the nature of catechisms, and a host of other details. The Articles also reaffirmed the principle of the

*Lettres Inédites de Napoléon (Paris, 1897), I, 93–94. Our translation.
†Quoted in H. A. L. Fisher, Napoleon (New York, 1913), Appendix I.

special autonomy enjoyed by the Gallican Church within Catholicism. Despite all this, the anticlericals opposed the Concordat, and it took all Napoleon's pressure to obtain ratification of the Concordat by the legislative bodies of the Consulate.

The Concordat, then, made the Church a ward of the French state. Though it antagonized anticlericals, it did conciliate large numbers of Catholics, and it remained in force until 1905. The Concordat, however, did not bring complete peace between France and the Vatican, for Napoleon insisted that the Pope should render to Caesar the things that were Caesar's. When Pius VII objected to Napoleon's making a French satellite of the Papal states, the new Caesar lectured him on the proper division of authority between the spiritual and temporal powers. Pius passed the last years of the Napoleonic regime as Bonaparte's prisoner, first in northern Italy and then in France.

Education

The Revolution and Napoleon cost the Church its monopoly over education. The Constitution of 1791 had promised France a system of state schools. The Convention, while doing little to apply this principle to primary education, did set up institutions for advanced training, like the famous *Ecole Polytechnique* in Paris for engineers. In each department it established a "central school" to provide secondary education of good quality at relatively low cost to students. Napoleon abolished these central schools in 1802 and replaced them with a smaller number of *lycées* open only to the relatively few pupils who could afford the tuition or who received state scholarships. The change had a political motive, for Napoleon intended the *lycées* to groom capable and loyal administrators. The students wore uniforms and marched to military drums and the curriculum, too, served the ends of patriotic indoctrination. To provide for the superintendence of all schools, lay and clerical, Napoleon founded in 1808 a body with the misleading name of the "University." He neglected primary schooling almost completely; yet building on the revolutionary base, he did advance the construction of secular schools. The educational competition of Church and State, so often a bitter issue in modern French life, dates back to the Revolution and Napoleon.

Economics

Political aims likewise governed the economic program of an emperor determined to promote national unity. The French peasants wanted to be left alone to enjoy the new freedom acquired in 1789; Napoleon did not disturb them, except to raise army recruits. The middle class wanted a balanced national budget and the end of revolutionary experiments with paper currency and a controlled economy. Napoleon continued the sound money of the Directory and, unlike the Directory, balanced the budget, thanks to the immense plunder that he gained in war. He greatly improved the efficiency and probity of tax-collectors and established the semi-official Bank of France (1800) to act as the government's financial agent. He strengthened the curbs placed on labor by the Le Chapelier Law of 1791 (see p. 100) and obliged every workman to carry a written record listing his jobs

and his general reputation. Though seaports suffered from the decline of overseas trade, rich war contracts and subsidies kept employment and profits generally high. As the war went on and on, however, Napoleon found it increasingly difficult to keep the peasantry and the bourgeoisie contented. Despite the levies on conquered countries, he had to draft more soldiers from the peasantry and increase the already unpopular taxes on salt, liquor, and tobacco.

In summary, the domestic policies of Napoleon I had something in common with the methods of all the celebrated one-man rulers. Like Caesar in Rome, Napoleon rendered lip-service to the Republic while subverting republican institutions; he used prefects to impose centralized authority as Louis XIV had used *intendants*; and, like modern dictators, he scorned free speech. Yet Napoleon was also a genuine enlightened despot. His law code and some of his educational reforms would have delighted the *philosophes*. He ended civil strife without sacrificing the redistribution of land and the equality before the law gained in 1789 and the years following. Abandoning some revolutionary policies, modifying others, and completing still others, Napoleon regimented the Revolution without wholly destroying it.

V   Napoleon and Europe

To many Frenchmen, Napoleon was the Man of Destiny, the most brilliant ruler in their country's long history. To most Europeans, on the other hand, Napoleon was the sinister Man on Horseback, the enemy of national independence, the foreigner who imposed French control and French reforms. As French conquests accumulated, and as nominally free countries became French puppets, Europe grew to hate the insatiable imperialism of Napoleon. Napoleonic France succeeded in building up a vast empire, but only at

the cost of arousing the implacable enmity of the other European nations.

The War, 1800–1807

Napoleon had barely launched the Consulate when he took to the field again. The Second Coalition, which had reached the peak of its success in August, 1799, was now falling to pieces. Tsar Paul of Russia alarmed Britain and Austria by his interest in Italy, and

Britain offended him by retaining Malta, the headquarters of his beloved Knights. The Tsar launched against Britain a Baltic League of Armed Neutrality linking Prussia, Sweden, and Denmark with Russia. He even contemplated joining with France to drive the British out of India; this fantastic scheme collapsed when he was murdered in 1801 and succeeded by his son, Alexander I. Meanwhile, in the spring of 1800 Napoleon crossed the Alps with much fanfare, acting as though no one had ever made the passage before. He defeated the Austrians in Italy and negotiated the Treaty of Lunéville (1801), whereby Austria recognized the reconstituted French satellites in Italy and agreed that France should have a hand in redrawing the map of Germany.

After Lunéville, as after Campoformio four years before, Britain alone remained at war with France. British taxpayers, however, wanted relief from their heavy burden; British merchants longed to resume trading with continental markets partially closed to them since 1793. Though Britain had been unable to check Napoleon's expansion in Europe, she had very nearly won the colonial and naval war by 1801. She had captured former Dutch and Spanish colonies, and Nelson's fleet had expelled the French from Egypt and Malta. The British cabinet was confident that it held a strong bargaining position and could obtain favorable terms from Napoleon. But in the Peace of Amiens (1802) the British promised to surrender part of their colonial conquests and got nothing in return. The French failed either to reopen the Continent to British exports or to relinquish Belgium, which remained, in Napoleon's phrase, "a loaded pistol aimed at the heart of Britain."

In 1803 Napoleon alarmed Austria and Prussia by promoting a major revision of the map of Germany. In that year the *Reichsdeputationshauptschluss* (a fine German word, "chief decree of the imperial deputation") abolished more than a hundred of the Germanies, chiefly city-states and small ecclesiastical principalities. The chief beneficiaries of this readjustment were the south German states of Bavaria, Württemberg, and Baden, which Na-poleon clearly intended to form into a "third" Germany, dominated by France, as opposed to the "first" and "second" Germanies of Austria and Prussia, respectively.

Meantime, the one-sided Peace of Amiens provided only a year's truce in the world-wide struggle of France and Britain. Napoleon aroused British exporters by a more stringent tariff law (1803) and jeopardized British interests in the Caribbean by a grandiose project for a colonial empire based on the island of Haiti (Santo Domingo) and on the vast Louisiana territory that Spain had returned to France in 1801. French soldiers wrested Haiti from the able Negro chieftain, Toussaint l'Ouverture; but the continued resistance of the Haitians and an outbreak of yellow fever took a fearful toll of French troops and forced Napoleon to abandon the American project. In 1803, he sold to the United States for about $15,000,000 all of Louisiana, which later formed the whole or part of 13 states.

When the Louisiana Purchase was completed, France and Britain were again at war. Napoleon interned many of the British tourists who had flocked to Paris since the Peace of Amiens, thus striking a new note of "total" war, contrasting with the eighteenth-century custom that permitted enemy citizens to circulate relatively freely even during hostilities. From 1803 through 1805, Napoleon actively prepared to invade England. He assembled more than a hundred thousand troops and a thousand landing barges on the French side of the Straits of Dover. In 1805, he sent Admiral Villeneuve and the French fleet to the West Indies to lure the British fleet away from Europe. Then Villeneuve was to return posthaste to convoy the French invasion force across the Channel while Nelson was still vainly combing the Caribbean. Villeneuve failed to give Nelson the slip; back in European waters, he put in at a friendly Spanish port instead of heading directly for the Channel as Napoleon had ordered. Nelson engaged the combined French and Spanish fleets off Cape Trafalgar at the southwest corner of Spain (October, 1805). He lost his own life but not before he had destroyed half of his adversaries' ships without sacrificing a single one of his own. The hapless Villeneuve, long aware of French naval inferiority, committed suicide. Trafalgar gave the British undisputed control of the seas and blasted French hopes of a cross-Channel invasion.

By the time of Trafalgar, Austria and Russia had joined with Britain in the Third Coalition. Bonaparte routed his continental opponents in the most dazzling campaign of his career. At Ulm, on the upper Danube (October, 1805), he captured 30,000 Austrians who had moved westward without waiting for their Russian allies. He met the main Russian force and the balance of the Austrian army near the Moravian village of Austerlitz. The ensuing battle (December 2, 1805) fittingly celebrated

the first anniversary of Napoleon's coronation as emperor. Bringing up reinforcements secretly and with great speed, Napoleon completely surprised his opponents; their casualties were three times greater than his own. Within the month he forced the Habsburg emperor, Francis II, to sign the humiliating Treaty of Pressburg, giving the Austrian Tyrol to Bavaria and Venetia to the Napoleonic puppet kingdom of Italy.

A still harsher fate awaited the Prussians, brought back into the war for the first time since 1795 by Napoleon's repeated interventions in German affairs. The fact that the inept Duke of Brunswick was still the Prussian commander indicated how much the army had

A supposed Napoleonic scheme for the invasion of England, by sea, air, and cross-Channel tunnel; the kites are Britain's anticipation of anti-aircraft defense.

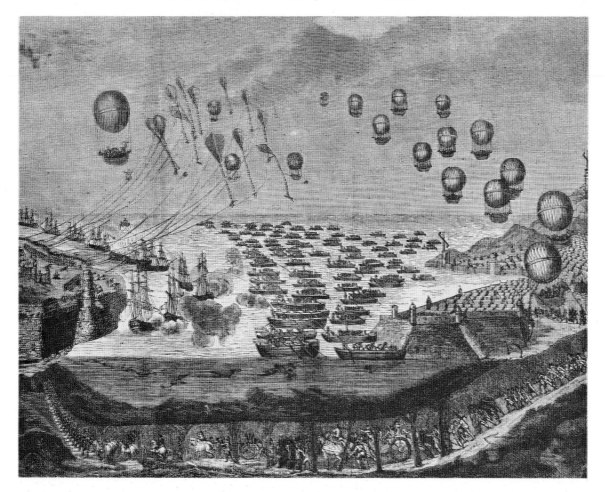

Napoleon's bivouac on the night preceding the Battle of Austerlitz, 1805.

deteriorated since the days of Frederick the Great. In October, 1806, the French pulverized the main Prussian contingents in the twin battles of Jena and Auerstädt, and occupied Berlin. Napoleon postponed a final settlement with Prussia until he had beaten his only remaining continental opponent. Russia went down at Friedland (June, 1807).

Napoleon's great string of victories against the Third Coalition resulted partly from the blunders of his enemies. The miscalculations of Austrian, Prussian, and Russian generals contributed to French successes at Austerlitz and at Jena. Furthermore, the French army was the most seasoned force in Europe. Its soldiers of every rank were well trained, and new recruits were quickly toughened by the French custom of the *amalgame*, assigning them in small batches to veteran units. Its officers were promoted because of ability rather than be-

cause of seniority or influence. Bonaparte seldom risked an engagement unless his forces were the numerical equal of the enemy's; then he staked everything on a dramatic surprise, as at Austerlitz. Yet even this French army had defects. The medical services were poor, the pay was low and irregular, and supplies were also irregular, since the French made a policy of having their soldiers live off the land to economize on time and expense. Though eventually serious in their impact, these shortcomings did not prevent Napolean's ascendancy over Europe in 1807.

The Empire at Its Height, 1807–1812

Napoleon reached the pinnacle of his career when he met Tsar Alexander I on a raft anchored in the Niemen River at Tilsit, on the frontier between East Prussia and Russia. There, in July, 1807, the two emperors drew up a treaty dividing Europe between them. Alexander acknowledged France's hegemony over central and western Europe and secured in return the recognition of eastern Europe as the Russian sphere. Napoleon pledged Russia a share in the spoils if the Ottoman Empire should be dismembered. He demanded no territory from the defeated Tsar, only a commitment to cease trade with Britain and to join the war against her. The Tilsit settlement, however, made Alexander bitterly unpopular at home, where Russian propaganda had been denouncing Napoleon as anti-Christ.

While the two emperors negotiated on the raft, Frederick William III (1797–1840), the Prussian king, nervously paced the banks of the Niemen. He had good cause to be nervous, for Tilsit cost him almost half his territory. Prussia's Polish provinces formed a new puppet state, the Grand Duchy of Warsaw, which Napoleon assigned to a French ally, the King of Saxony. Prussian territory west of the Elbe River went to Napoleon to dispose of as he wished. Napoleon also stationed occupation troops in Prussia and fixed the maximum size of its army at 42,000 men.

Under this latter-day Caesar almost all Europe could be divided into three parts. First came the French Empire, including France proper and the territories annexed since 1789. Second were the satellites, ruled in many cases by relatives of Napoleon. And third came Austria, Prussia, and Russia, forced by defeat to become the allies of France. The only powers remaining outside the Napoleonic system were Britain, Turkey, and Sweden. In 1810, Bernadotte, one of Napoleon's marshals, became Crown Prince for the childless Swedish king, but he, too, guided Swedish policy against France.

The frontiers of the French Empire at their most extensive enclosed Belgium and Holland; the sections of Germany west of the Rhine and along the North Sea; the Italian lands of Piedmont, Genoa, Tuscany, and Rome; and finally, physically detached from the rest, the "Illyrian Provinces," stretching along the Dalmatian coast of the Adriatic, taken from Austria in 1809, and named after an old Roman province. The annexed territories were usually subdivided into departments and ruled by prefects, just like the departments of France proper.

The satellites flanked the French Empire. The Kingdom of Italy, an enlarged version of the Cisalpine Republic, included Lombardy, Venetia, and the central Italian lands not directly annexed by France. Napoleon was the king, and his stepson, Eugène de Beauharnais, was viceroy. In southern Italy, Napoleon deposed the Bourbon king of Naples in 1805 and gave the crown first to his brother Joseph and then to Joachim Murat, the husband of his sister Caroline. Joseph moved from Naples to Madrid in 1808 when Napoleon deposed the Spanish Bourbons in order to force the Spaniards to remain in the war against Britain.

In Central Europe, Napoleon energetically pursued his project of a "third" Germany. He decreed a further reduction in the number of German states, and in 1806 aided the dissolution of that museum-piece, the Holy Roman Empire. Francis II, the reigning Habsburg, last of the Holy Roman Emperors, now styled himself Emperor of Austria. To replace the vanished Empire, Napoleon created the Confederation of the Rhine, which included almost every German state except Austria and Prussia. At the heart of this confederation, Napoleon carved out for his brother Jerome the Kingdom of Westphalia, which incorporated the Prussian holdings west of the Elbe seized at Tilsit. Two states completed the roster of French satellites—Switzerland and the Grand Duchy of Warsaw. Europe had not seen such an empire since the heyday of imperial Rome.

Napoleon longed to give dignity and permanence to his creations. It was not enough that his brothers and his in-laws should sit on thrones; he himself must found a dynasty, must have the heir so far denied him in fifteen years of childless marriage. He divorced Josephine, therefore, and in 1810 married Marie-Louise, the daughter of the Habsburg Francis II. In due time, Marie-Louise bore

Napoleonic Europe, 1812

Empire of France
States under French control
Allied with France
■ Battle sites

UNITED KINGDOM
OF GREAT BRITAIN
AND IRELAND

SCOTLAND

IRELAND

WALES

ENGLAND

London

North Sea

SWEDEN

Baltic

KINGDOM OF DENMARK AND NORWAY

Oldenburg   Hamburg

NETHERLANDS

K. OF
WESTPHALIA

CONFEDERATION

OF THE

RHINE

Berlin

SAXONY

P R U S S

D U

Prague

Austerlitz

Auerstädt   Leipzig

Jena

Atlantic Ocean

Antwerp
Waterloo
Amiens

Seine R.

Paris   Varennes
Versailles
Valmy

Nantes

Loire R.

FRANCE

Gironde R.

Limoges

Bordeaux
Payrac

Longuyon
Luneville
LORRAINE
ALSACE

Meuse R.
Rhine R.

Weser R.

BADEN

Strasbourg
Ulm

Basel

SWITZERLAND

PIED-
MONT

Lyons

Rhône R.

Marengo
Genoa

Nice

Danube R.

BAVARIA

Vienna
Pressburg

TYROL

Campoformio

Milan

Po R.

KINGDOM
OF ITALY

Venice

E M

A

ILLYRIAN PROVINCES

Adriatic Sea

PORTUGAL

SPAIN

Madrid

Ebro R.

Tagus R.

Guadalquivir R.

CAPE
TRAFALGAR

CORSICA

BALEARIC IS.

SARDINIA

ELBA

TUSCANY

PAPAL STATES

Rome

Naples

KINGDOM
OF
NAPLES

Palermo

SICILY

MALTA
(Br.)

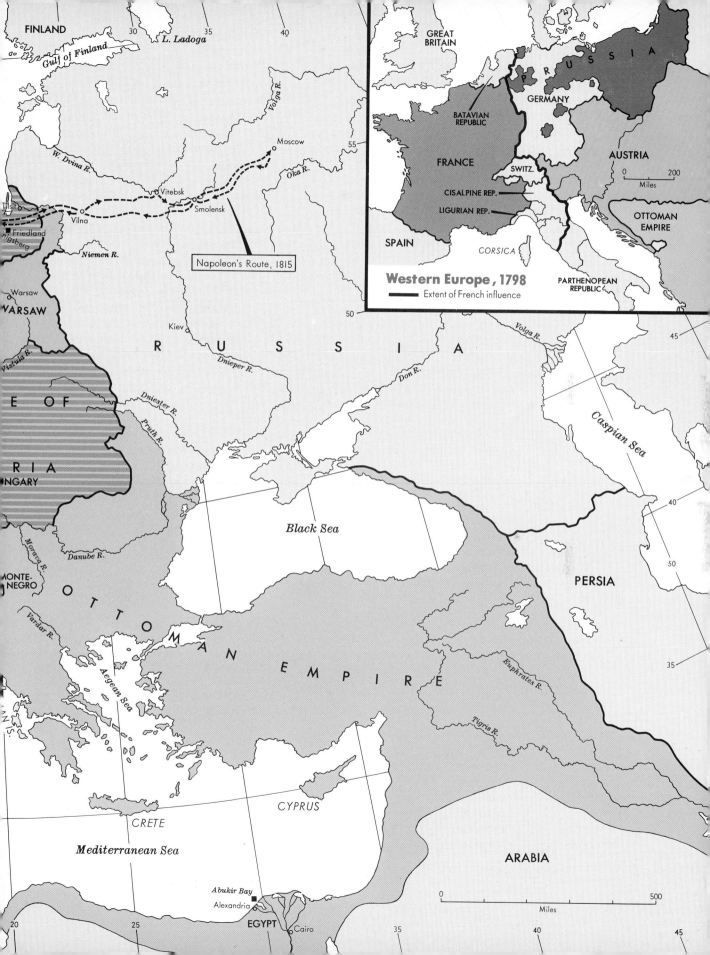

FINLAND
L. Ladoga
Gulf of Finland
W. Dvina R.
Volga R.
Moscow
Oka R.
Vitebsk
Smolensk
Tilsit
Vilna
Friedland
gsberg
Niemen R.
Napoleon's Route, 1815
Warsaw
WARSAW
Kiev
R   U   S   S   I   A
Vistula R.
Dnieper R.
E OF
Dniester R.
Don R.
RIA
Pruth R.
NGARY
Caspian Sea
Morava R.
Black Sea
MONTE-
NEGRO
Danube R.
Vardar R.
PERSIA
50
O   T   T   O   M   A   N   E   M   P   I   R   E
40
Aegean Sea
35
Euphrates R.
Tigris R.
CYPRUS
CRETE
Mediterranean Sea
ARABIA
Abukir Bay
0   500
Alexandria
Miles
EGYPT   Cairo
20   25   35   40   45

GREAT
BRITAIN
RUSSIA
GERMANY
BATAVIAN
REPUBLIC
FRANCE
AUSTRIA
SWITZ.
0   200
CISALPINE REP.
Miles
LIGURIAN REP.
OTTOMAN
EMPIRE
SPAIN
CORSICA
PARTHENOPEAN
REPUBLIC
Western Europe, 1798
Extent of French influence

a son, whom his father called "The King of Rome."

"Napoleon II," however, was never to rule in Rome or anywhere else. Throughout the new French acquisitions and the satellites Bonaparte and his relatives played the part of enlightened despots, curbing the power of the Church, abolishing serfdom, building roads, and introducing the metric system and the new French law codes. Everywhere, however, they exacted a heavy toll of tribute and subjection. In the Kingdom of Italy, for instance, Napoleon doubled the tax rate previously levied by the Austrians; half the revenues of the kingdom went to defray the expenses of the French army and the French government. Napoleon flooded his relatives with instructions on the government of their domains and brought them abruptly to heel whenever they showed signs of putting local interests above those of France. When Louis Bonaparte in Holland dared to disobey the imperial orders, his brother delivered a crushing rebuke:

> In ascending the throne of Holland, Your Majesty has forgotten that he is French and has stretched all the springs of his reason and tormented his conscience in order to persuade himself that he is Dutch. Dutchmen inclining toward France have been ignored and persecuted; those serving England have been promoted. . . . I have experienced the sorrow of seeing the name of France exposed to shame in a Holland ruled by a prince of my blood.*

Louis' boldness cost him his throne; his Dutch kingdom was annexed to France in 1810.

The Continental System

Nowhere was Napoleon's imperialism more evident than in his attempt to regulate the economy of the whole Continent. The Continental System had a double aim: to build up the export trade of France and to cripple that of Britain. The collapse of Napoleon's cross-Channel invasion plans led him to expand the earlier tariff measures against

*Lettres Inédites de Napoléon (Paris, 1897), I, 382–383. Our translation.

Britain into a great campaign to bankrupt the nation of shopkeepers. The defeat of the Third Coalition gave him the opportunity to experiment with economic warfare on a continental scale and to carry mercantilism to extremes.

The Berlin Decree, issued by Napoleon in November, 1806, forbade all trade with the British Isles and all commerce in British merchandise. It ordered the arrest of all Britons on the Continent and the confiscation of their property. Britain replied by requiring that neutral vessels wishing to trade with France put in first at a British port and pay duties. This regulation enabled Britain to share in the profits of neutral shipping to France. Napoleon retaliated with the Milan decree (December, 1807), ordering the seizure of all neutral ships that complied with the new British policy. The neutrals, in effect, were damned if they did and damned if they didn't.

Napoleon's vassals and allies had to support the Continental System or suffer the consequences. Of all the "un-French" activities countenanced by Louis Bonaparte in Holland, the worst, in Napoleon's view, was his toleration of Dutch smuggling of English contraband. The Emperor likewise expected the satellites to feed French industrial prosperity. When Italians objected to the regulation of their silk exports, Napoleon lectured his viceroy, Eugène, on the facts of economic life:

> All the raw silk from the Kingdom of Italy goes to England. . . . It is therefore quite natural that I should wish to divert it from this route to the advantage of my French manufacturers: otherwise my silk factories, one of the chief supports of French commerce, would suffer substantial losses. . . . My principle is: France first. . . .
>
> It is no use for Italy to make plans that leave French prosperity out of account; she must face the fact that the interests of the two countries hang together.*

The gigantic attempt to make "France first" failed almost totally. Only a few French industries benefited from the Continental System; the cessation of sugar imports from the

*Quoted in J. M. Thompson, ed., Napoleon's Letters, 241–242.

West Indies, for example, promoted the cultivation of native sugar beets. But the decline of overseas trade depressed Bordeaux and other French Atlantic ports, and the increasing difficulty of obtaining raw materials like cotton caused widespread unemployment and produced a rash of bankruptcies. The new French markets on the Continent did not compensate for the loss of older markets overseas; the value of French exports declined by more than one-third between 1805 and 1813.

The Continental System did not ruin Britain, although it did confront the British with a severe economic crisis. Markets abroad for British exports were uncertain; food imports were reduced; and, while prices rose sharply, wages lagged behind. Both farm workers, already pinched by the enclosure movement, and factory workers suffered acutely. Yet Britain, fortified by her leadership in the economic revolutions and by the overwhelming superiority of her navy and merchant marine, rode out the storm. Every tract of land at all capable of growing food was brought under the plow. Exporters not only developed lucrative new markets in the Americas, the Ottoman Empire, and Asia but also smuggled goods to old customers on the Continent. Napoleon lacked the vast naval force to apprehend smugglers at sea, and he lacked the large staff of incorruptible customs inspectors to control contraband in the ports. Moreover, since the French army simply could not do without some items produced only in British factories, Napoleon violated his own decrees by authorizing secret purchases of British cloth and leather for uniforms.

The Continental System antagonized both the neutral powers and Napoleon's allies. French seizure of American vessels in Euro-

Gillray, "Tiddy-Dolly, the great French Gingerbread-Baker, drawing out a new Batch of Kings—his Man, Hopping-Talley, mixing up the Dough"—a British comment on Napoleon's imperialism.

pean ports under the terms of the Milan Decree put a dangerous strain on Franco-American relations. But British restrictions likewise bore heavily on the Americans. British impressment of American seamen on the pretext that they were deserters from the Royal Navy, together with the designs of American expansionists on Canada, produced the indecisive Anglo-American War of 1812–1814.

The Peninsular War

In Europe, the political and military consequences of the Continental System formed a decisive and disastrous chapter in Napoleonic history. The chapter opened in 1807 when the Emperor decided to impose the System on Britain's traditional ally, Portugal. The Portuguese expedition furnished Napoleon with an excuse for the military occupation of neighboring Spain. In 1808 he lured the Spanish royal family away from Madrid and made his brother Joseph King of Spain. But every measure taken by Napoleon—the removal of the ineffectual Bourbons, the installation of a foreign monarch, the attempted enforcement of the Continental System, and, not least, the suppression of the Inquisition and the curtailment of noble and clerical privileges —violated Spanish customs and offended Spanish nationalism. The irreconcilable Spaniards began fighting Napoleon when the population of Madrid rose in revolt on May 2, 1808.

While the rising in Madrid was soon repressed, the Peninsular War (named after the Iberian Peninsula), rapidly grew from a minor irritation to a deadly cancer on the body of the Napoleonic Empire. The Spaniards employed ambushes and poisoned wells and used other guerrilla devices. The expedition that Britain sent to assist them upset all the rules about British inferiority in military, as opposed to naval, matters. It was ably commanded by Sir Arthur Wellesley (later the Duke of Wellington), generously supplied from home, and based on Portugal and on Britain's unshakable command of the seas. Napoleon poured more than 300,000 troops into the Peninsular campaign, but his opponents

gained the upper hand in 1812, when he detached part of his forces for the invasion of Russia. In 1813, King Joseph left Madrid forever, and Wellington, having liberated Spain, crossed into southern France.

German Resistance

Napoleonic imperialism also aroused a nationalistic reaction among the traditionally disunited Germans. Intellectuals launched a campaign against the French language and French culture, which had long exerted a powerful influence. Johann Grimm and his brother Wilhelm contributed not only their very popular—and very German—*Fairy Tales* (1812) but also philological researches designed to prove the innate superiority of the German language. The philosopher Fichte delivered at Berlin the highly patriotic *Addresses to the German Nation* (1807–1808), claiming that German was the *Ursprache*, the fountainhead of language. And the Germans themselves, Fichte continued, were the *Urvolk*, the oldest and the most moral of nations.

Napoleon began to feel the impact of German nationalism when Austria re-entered the war in 1809. For the first time, the Habsburg monarchy now attempted a total mobilization comparable to that decreed by the French Convention in 1793. While the new spirit enabled the Austrians to make a better showing, they were defeated by a narrow margin at Wagram (1809) and for the fourth time in a dozen years submitted to a peace dictated by Napoleon. The Treaty of Schönbrunn (1809) stripped them of the Illyrian Provinces and assigned their Polish territory of Galicia to the Grand Duchy of Warsaw. Francis II gave his daughter to Napoleon in marriage, and his defeated land became the unwilling ally of France. Leadership in the German revival passed to Prussia.

The shock of Jena and Tilsit jarred Prussia out of the lethargy that had overtaken her since the death of Frederick the Great in 1786. The new University of Berlin, founded in 1810, attracted Fichte and other prophets of German nationalism. Able generals and

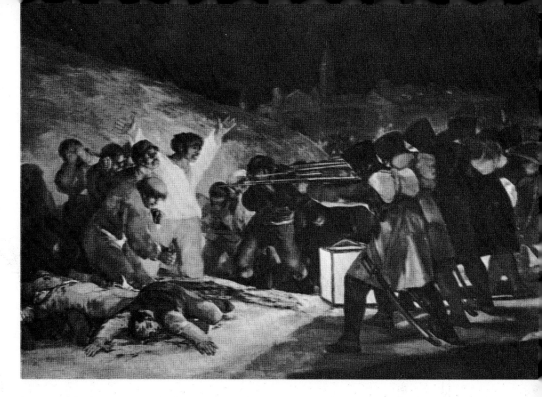

Goya, "The Third of May, 1808," now in the Prado Museum, Madrid; Spaniards being executed by Napoleonic troops.

statesmen, most of them non-Prussian, came to power. General Scharnhorst headed a group of officers who abolished the inhuman discipline of the army and improved its efficiency. The ceiling of 42,000 soldiers imposed by Napoleon was evaded by the simple device of assigning recruits to the reserve after a fairly brief period of intensive training and then inducting another group of recruits. By 1813, Prussia had more than 150,000 trained men available for combat duty.

The social and administrative reorganization of the Prussian state was inspired by the energetic Stein—Baron vom und zum Stein, an enlightened aristocrat from the Rhineland. Stein conciliated the middle class by granting towns and cities some self-government. To improve the status of the peasantry, he sponsored the edict of October, 1807, at long last abolishing serfdom in Prussia. The edict, however, did not break up the large Junker estates or provide land for the liberated serfs; nor did it terminate the feudal rights of justice exercised by the Junker over his peasants. Stein and the others eliminated only the worst abuses of the Old Régime and left authority where it had traditionally rested—with the king, the army, and the Junkers. The Hohenzollern state was not so much reformed as restored to the traditions of absolutism and ef-

ficiency established by the Great Elector and Frederick the Great.

The Russian Campaign

The event that enabled a developing German nationalism to turn its force against Napoleon was the French debacle in Russia. French actions after 1807 soon convinced Tsar Alexander that Napoleon was not keeping the Tilsit bargain and was intruding on Russia's sphere in eastern Europe. When Alexander and Napoleon met again at the German town of Erfurt in 1808, they could reach no agreement, though they concealed their differences by a show of great intimacy. French acquisition of the Illyrian provinces from Austria in 1809 raised the unpleasant prospect of French domination over the Balkans, and the simultaneous transfer of Galicia from Austria to the Grand Duchy of Warsaw suggested that this Napoleonic vassal might next seek to absorb the Polish territories of Russia. Meanwhile, Napoleon's insistent efforts to make Russia enforce the Continental System increasingly incensed Alexander. French annexations in northwest Germany completed the discomfiture of the Tsar, for they wiped out the state of Oldenburg, where his uncle was the reigning duke. All these factors caused the break between the Tsar and the Emperor, and the famous invasion of Russia by the French in 1812.

For the invasion Napoleon assembled the *Grande Armée* of nearly 700,000 men. A large proportion of the Grand Army, however, were not Frenchmen but unwilling conscripts in the service of a foreign master. The supply system broke down almost immediately, and the Russian scorched-earth policy made it very hard for the soldiers to live off the land. As the Grand Army marched eastward, one of Napoleon's aides reported:

> There were no inhabitants to be found, no prisoners to be taken, not a single straggler to be picked up. We were in the heart of inhabited Russia and yet we were like a vessel without a compass in the midst of a vast ocean, knowing nothing of what was happening around us.*

Napoleon marched all the way to Moscow without ever managing to strike a knockout blow. He remained in the burning city for five weeks (September-October, 1812) in the vain hope of bringing Tsar Alexander to terms. But Russian obduracy and the shortage of supplies forced him to begin a retreat that became a nightmare. Ill-fed and inadequately clothed and sheltered, the retreating soldiers suffered horribly from Russian attacks on stragglers and from the onslaughts of "General Winter." Less than a quarter of the Grand Army survived the retreat from Moscow; the rest had been taken prisoner or had died of wounds, starvation, disease, or the cold.

The Russian leaders had feared that Napoleon would liberate the serfs and turn them against their masters. Nevertheless, the peasants, despite the ill-treatment to which they had been subject for so long, formed guerrilla bands, harassed Napoleon's forces, and proved that their patriotic sentiments outweighed their class grievances. Kutuzov, the victorious Russian commander, now wanted to allow Russia's allies to prosecute the war. But Alexander insisted on pursuing the French,

*A. A. L. de Caulaincourt, *With Napoleon in Russia* (New York, 1935), 62.

and sent Russian armies westward beyond the Russian frontiers on the track of Napoleon's forces.

The Downfall

The British had been the first to resist Napoleon successfully, at Trafalgar and on the economic battlefields of the Continental System. Then had come Spanish resistance, then Russian. Now in 1813 almost every nation in Europe joined the final coalition against the French. Napoleon raised a new army, but he could not replace so readily the equipment squandered in Russia. In October, 1813, he lost the "Battle of the Nations," fought at Leipzig in Germany, and by April, 1814, the forces of the coalition occupied Paris. Faced also with mounting unrest at home, the Emperor abdicated. After attempting suicide by poison, which turned out to have lost much of its strength since he had procured it for the Russian campaign, he went into exile as ruler of the minute island of Elba not far from the western coast of Italy.

The statesmen of the victorious coalition gathered in the Congress of Vienna to draw up the terms of peace (see Chapter 19). The Bourbons returned to France in the person of Louis XVIII, a younger brother of Louis XVI. Realizing that he could not revive the Old Régime intact, the new king issued the Charter of 1814 establishing a constitutional monarchy. The returned *émigrés*, however, showed no such good sense. They unleashed a new "White Terror" against the Revolution and all its works. Then, on March 1, 1815, Bonaparte pulled his last surprise: He landed on the Mediterranean coast of France.

For a hundred days, from March 20, 1815, when Napoleon re-entered Paris, the French Empire was reborn. Once again the Emperor rallied the French people, this time by promising a truly liberal régime, with a real parliament and genuine elections. He never had time, however, to show whether his promise was sincere, for on June 18, 1815, the British under Wellington and the Prussians under

Blücher delivered the final blow at Waterloo, near Brussels. Again Napoleon went into ex-ile, to the remote British island of St. Helena in the South Atlantic. There, in 1821, he died.

VI   The Legacy of the Revolution and Napoleon

Bonapartism did not die in 1815 or 1821, any more than the Caesarism of ancient Rome had died on the Ides of March. A Napoleonic legend arose, fostered by the Emperor himself on St. Helena. It glossed over the faults and failures of its hero, depicting him as the paladin of liberalism and patriotism, and paved the way for the advent of another Napoleon in 1848 (see Chapter 19). This legend, with its hero-worship and belligerent nationalism, was one element in the legacy bequeathed by revolutionary and Napoleonic France. A second, and still more powerful, element was the great revolutionary motto — *Liberté, Egalité, Fraternité*. The motto lived on, to inspire later generations of Jacobins in France and elsewhere. And behind the motto was the fact that Frenchmen enjoyed a larger measure of liberty, equality, and fraternity in 1815 than they had ever known before 1789.

The Revolution founded a potent new tradition of liberty. True, the Mountain's deputies on mission and Napoleon's censors and prefects gave new force to the old traditions of absolutism and centralization, the middle class had won its freedom from obsolete restraints, and Protestants, Jews, and free-thinkers had gained toleration both in France and in French-dominated countries. While French institutions in 1815 did not measure up to the liberal ideals expressed in the Declaration of the Rights of Man, the ideals had been stated, and the effort to embody them in a new regime was to form the main theme of French domestic history in the nineteenth century.

The revolutionary and Napoleonic regimes introduced a large measure of equality. They established the principle of equal liability to taxation. They provided a greater degree of economic opportunity for large numbers of the third estate by breaking up the large landholdings of the clergy and nobility and by removing obstacles to the activity of businessmen, big and little. The *Code Napoléon* buried beyond all hope of exhumation the worst legal and social inequalities of the Old Régime. There was a good deal of truth in Napoleon's boast:

Whether as First Consul or as Emperor, I have been the people's king; I have governed for the nation and in its interests, without allowing myself to be turned aside by the outcries or the private interests of certain people.*

The Revolution and Napoleon promoted fraternity in the legal sense by making all Frenchmen equal in the eyes of the law. They advanced fraternity in a broader sense by encouraging nationalism, the feeling of belonging to the great corporate body of Frenchmen who were superior to all other nations. French nationalism had existed long before 1789; Joan of Arc, Henry IV, and Louis XIV had all been nationalists in their diverse ways. But it remained for the Convention to formulate a fervent new nationalistic creed in its decree of August 23, 1793, providing for total mobilization. The Napoleonic Empire then demonstrated how easily nationalism on an unprecedented scale could lead to imperialism of unprecedented magnitude. A century ago, Alexis de Tocqueville, the great French student of democracy, wrote:

The French Revolution was . . . a political revolution, which in its operation and its aspect resem-

*Quoted in Caulaincourt, *With Napoleon in Russia,* 364.

bled a religious one. It had every peculiar and characteristic feature of a religious movement; it not only spread to foreign countries, but it was carried thither by preaching and by propaganda.

It roused passions such as the most violent political revolutions had never before excited. . . . This gave to it that aspect of a religious revolution which so terrified its contemporaries, or rather . . . it became a kind of new religion in itself—a religion, imperfect it is true, without a God, without a worship, without a future life, but which nevertheless, like Islam, poured forth its soldiers, its apostles, and its martyrs over the face of the earth.*

*A. de Tocqueville, *The Old Régime and the Revolution,* Part I, Ch. 3. (London, 1888).

Its early adherents were fanatics—Robespierre and the Jacobins. Its later exponents—the men of Thermidor and Brumaire—modified the creed in the interests of practicality and moderation. Even in the hands of Napoleon, however, the Revolution remained a kind of religion, demanding political orthodoxy and punishing heretics, as Napoleon punished King Louis Bonaparte of Holland, by political excommunication. And after 1815, as we shall see in the next chapter, the "new religion" of the Revolution continued to pour forth "its soldiers, its apostles, and its martyrs over the face of the earth."

Reading Suggestions on the French Revolution and Napoleon

(*Asterisk indicates paperbound edition.)

General Accounts

C. Brinton, *A Decade of Revolution, 1789–1799* (*Torch), and G. Bruun, *Europe & the French Imperium, 1799–1814* (*Torch). Comprehensive volumes in the "Rise of Modern Europe" series, treating the whole of the Continent; with full bibliographies.

G. Lefebvre, *The French Revolution,* 2 vols. (Columbia Univ. Press, 1962, 1964). Another comprehensive treatment, ranging beyond France itself, by an eminent French scholar.

R. R. Palmer, *The Age of the Democratic Revolution,* 2 vols. (Princeton Univ. Press, 1959, 1964). Detailed exposition of the thesis that the French Revolution was part of a general democratic revolution in the West; by a first-rate American scholar, who examines revolutionary movements both in France and elsewhere.

Jacques Godechot, *France & the Atlantic Revolution, 1770–1799* (Free Press, 1965). A ranking French scholar comes to conclusions similar to Palmer's.

P. Amann, ed. *The 18th-Century Revolution, French or Western?* (*Heath). Selections from writings both hostile and sympathetic to the Palmer-Godechot interpretation.

L. Gershoy, *The French Revolution & Napoleon* (Appleton-Century-Crofts, 1964). Lucid textbook account, stressing events in France.

G. Rudé, Revolutionary Europe, 1783–1815 (*Meridian). A brief account by one of the younger generation of historians, with bibliography.

The French Revolution

P. Farmer, *France Reviews Its Revolutionary Origins* (Octagon, 1963). A history of French historical writing about the revolution.

A. de Tocqueville, *The Old Regime & the Revolution* (*Anchor). A celebrated essay of interpretation, more than a century old, stressing continuities between the old and new régimes.

A. Mathiez, *The French Revolution* (*Universal). Narrative treatment to 1794, by an eloquent French scholar sympathetic to the Jacobins.

G. Lefebvre, *The Coming of the French Revolution* (*Vintage). Masterly short study of the causes of the revolution and of its course to October, 1789.

G. Salvemini, *The French Revolution, 1788–1792* (*Norton). Colorful narrative by an Italian scholar of warm, liberal outlook.

J. M. Thompson, *The French Revolution* (*Galaxy). Good account by a British scholar.

A. Cobban, *The Social Interpretation of the French Revolution* (Cambridge Univ. Press, 1964). A critique of attempts to view the revolution as a class struggle.

N. Hampson, *A Social History of the French Revolution* (Univ. of Toronto, 1963). Well-balanced synthesis of recent scholarly work in the field.

G. Rudé, *The Crowd in the French Revolution* (Oxford Univ. Press, 1959). Fascinating study of the great revolutionary "days" and the demonstrators who took part.

R. B. Rose, *The Enragés: Socialists of the French Revolution?* (Melbourne, Australia Univ. Press, 1964). An excellent monograph.

A. Soboul, *The Parisian Sans-Culottes & the French Revolution, 1793–1794* (Clarendon, 1964). An important monograph, based on Paris police records; by a capable Marxian scholar.

C. Brinton, *The Jacobins* (Macmillan, 1930), and M. J. Sydenham, *The Girondins* (Oxford Univ. Press, 1961). Informative analyses of major political groupings.

R. R. Palmer, *Twelve Who Ruled* (*Atheneum). Highly readable collective biography of Committee of Public Safety; sympathetic in tone.

J. M. Thompson, *Robespierre & the French Revolution* (*Collier), and G. Bruun, *Saint-Just: Apostle of the Terror* (Houghton, Mifflin, 1932). Biographical sketches of particularly significant figures.

C. H. Tilly, *The Vendée* (Harvard Univ. Press, 1964). An original treatment by a sociologist well trained in historical research.

C. Brinton, *The Anatomy of Revolution* (*Vintage). Examines the common denominators of the Puritan English, the American, the French, and the Russian revolutions.

Napoleon

J. M. Thompson, *Napoleon Bonaparte: His Rise and Fall* (Oxford Univ. Press, 1952), and F. Markham, *Napoleon* (*Mentor). Readable biographies, based on up-to-date scholarship.

H. A. L. Fisher, *Napoleon* (Oxford Univ. Press, 1945), and A. L. Guérard, *Napoleon I* (Knopf, 1956). Good, shorter biographies.

F. Markham, *Napoleon & the Awakening of Europe* (*Collier). Brief account, arguing that European nationalisms, while aroused by Napoleon, were as yet underdeveloped.

E. Heckscher, *The Continental System: an Economic Interpretation* (Clarendon, 1922), Important monograph by a Swedish economist.

P. Geyl, *Napoleon, For and Against* (*Yale). Lengthy survey of judgments passed on Napoleon by historians from his own day to the mid-twentieth century.

H. A. L. Fisher, *Studies in Napoleonic Statesmanship: Germany* (Clarendon, 1903). A detailed evaluation of the impact of French reforms on some Napoleonic satellites.

O. Connelly, *Napoleon's Satellite Kingdoms* (Free Press, 1965). Analysis of Spain, Holland, Westphalia, Naples, and Italy.

Sources

J. H. Stewart, *A Documentary Survey of the French Revolution* (Macmillan, 1951). Ably edited collection of constitutional texts and other official documents.

E. Higgins, *The French Revolution as Told by Contemporaries* (Houghton, Mifflin, 1938). Handy compendium of reports by participants and eye-witnesses.

A. Young, *Travels in France,* C. Maxwell, ed. (Cambridge Univ. Press, 1929). Spirited diary of the English agricultural expert, who journeyed over much of France on the eve and during the early days of the revolution.

E. Burke, *Reflections on the Revolution in France* (*several editions). The celebrated indictment of the revolution.

J. M. Thompson, ed., *Napoleon's Letters* (Everyman). A most interesting collection, arranged chronologically.

J. C. Herold, ed., *The Mind of Napoleon* (*Columbia Univ. Press). Another most interesting collection, from his writings and conversations, arranged topically.

A. de Caulaincourt, *With Napoleon in Russia* (*Universal), and *No Peace with Napoleon* (Morrow, 1936). Vivid memoirs of the last campaigns by one of the Emperor's chief aides.

Historical Fiction

A. France, *The Gods Are Athirst* (Roy). Excellent brief novel about a fanatical Jacobin.

C. Dickens, *A Tale of Two Cities* (*many ed.). Famous, colorful — and inaccurate.

R. Sabatini, *Scaramouche* (*Bantam). Delightful yarn set in an authentic revolutionary background.

L. Tolstoy, *War & Peace* (*several editions, often abridged). The epic novel about the Russian campaign.

19

Revolution and Counter-Revolution, 1815–1850

I Introduction

While the half century after Napoleon recorded no crisis so momentous as that of 1789 and produced no personality so dominant as Bonaparte, it was still crowded with major developments. Between 1815 and 1870 the industrial revolution came of age, modern doctrines of socialism were born, and Darwin's evolutionary hypothesis revolutionized the social sciences as well as biology. In politics, Great Britain and the United States moved steadily, and France more erratically, toward the practical establishment of democracy; Italy and Germany at last achieved national unification. All these developments, though they were well under way by 1850, reached a climax after the mid-century mark and will therefore be discussed later (Chapters 20–23). The present chapter focuses on the interaction of cultural and political forces, particularly in continental Europe, during the post-Napoleonic generation from 1815 to 1850.

The terms "reaction" and "counter-revolution" are often applied to this generation. By 1815, Europe was reacting strongly both against the French Revolution, which had made Napoleon possible, and against the Enlightenment, which had made the Revolution possible. The reaction against the Enlightenment took the form of the Romantic movement. Romantic writers and artists protested against the omnipotent reason of the eighteenth century and championed faith, emotion, tradition, and other values slighted by many *philosophes*. The political counter-revolution came of age at the Congress of Vienna in 1814–1815, where the leaders of the last coalition against Napoleon re-established the European balance of power and repudiated the revolutionary principles, though not all the revolutionary achievements, that had shattered the eighteenth-century balance. Reason and natural law, in the judgment both of political leaders and of many Romantics, had led not only to progress but also to the Reign of Terror and Napoleonic imperialism.

But the spirit of 1789 did not die in 1815; revolution persisted, despite the ascendancy of counter-revolutionary forces. Liberal and nationalistic ideas and aspirations produced new outbreaks of revolution in the 1820's, in 1830, and in 1848. Although none of these revolutions proved to be as formidable as the great upheaval of 1789, all of them threatened the status quo. In addition, the revolutions of 1848 marked a critical turning point in the development of European liberalism and nationalism.

II   The Romantic Protest

The Romantic protest against reason rose to full force during the first third of the nineteenth century—the Romantic decades of 1800 to 1830 or 1840. Actually, as Chapter 17 has already shown, the reaction against the Enlightenment had set in much earlier. Before 1750, Wesley and the Pietists were challenging the deism of the *philosophes* and preaching a religion of the heart, not the head. Soon Rousseau proclaimed conscience, not reason, the "true guide of man"; Hume fastened on men's "sentiments and affections" as the mainsprings of their actions. Kant elevated intuition over the common-sense reason of the Enlightenment and restated, in very philosophical language, the Platonic belief in a noumenal realm of eternal verities beyond the world of transient phenomena. Then in 1790 Edmund Burke's *Reflections on the Revolution in France* neatly turned against the *philosophes* their favorite appeal to the simple mathematical laws of Newtonian science. Natural rights, Burke argued,

. . . entering into common life, like rays of light which pierce into a dense medium, are, by the laws of nature, refracted from their straight line. Indeed in the gross and complicated mass of human passions and concerns, the primitive rights of men undergo such a variety of refractions and reflections, that it becomes absurd to talk of them as if they continued in the simplicity of their original direction. The nature of man is intricate; the objects of society are of the greatest possible complexity. . . .*

The protest against the oversimplification of man and society, and the insistence on the intricacy and complexity of humanity, formed one common denominator of the Romantic movement. Romanticism, however, was much too complex and contradictory to be defined by a simple formula. Other common denominators will emerge from a survey of the achievements of the Romantics, beginning

Reflections on the Revolution in France, Everyman ed. (New York, 1910), 59.

with their most characteristic and productive realm of activity—literature.

The Revolt against Reason

Literary Romanticism may be traced back to the mid-eighteenth-century novels of sentiment and duty, like Richardson's *Clarissa.* Its immediate precursor was the German movement of the 1770's called *Sturm und Drang* ("Storm and Stress") after the title of a contemporary play. The hero of the drama, totally incapable of settling down, flees Europe to fight in the American Revolution:

Have been everything. Became a day-labourer to be something. Lived on the Alps, pastured goats, lay day and night under the boundless vault of the heavens, cooled by the winds, burning with an inner fire. Nowhere rest, nowhere repose. See, thus I am glutted by impulse and power, and work it out of me. I am going to take part in this campaign as a volunteer; there I can expand my soul, and if they do me the favour to shoot me down,—all the better.*

Yearning, frustration, and despair were also dominant emotions in the most popular work of the *Sturm und Drang* period, *The Sorrows of Young Werther,* a lugubrious short novel by the youthful Goethe (1749–1832). Even the seemingly hard-boiled Napoleon claimed to have read it seven times over, weeping copiously each time as the hero shoots himself to death because the woman he loves is already married. Self-pity, self-destruction, the sense of alienation, of being an "outsider" continued to be favorite themes of the Romantic writers. In contrast to the optimism of the *philosophes,* the Romantics sounded chords of pessimism and despair.

Goethe himself, however, whose career extended through the whole Romantic era, was no Romantic hero. In many respects he was a good eighteenth-century man of reason, interested in natural science, comfortably established at the enlightened court of a small

*Klinger, *Sturm und Drang,* quoted in Kuno Francke, *A History of German Literature as Determined by Social Forces,* 4th ed. (New York, 1931), 309.

German state at Weimar, and quite detached from the political passions sweeping Germany and Europe in the revolutionary and Napoleonic age. Yet Romantic values lie at the very heart of Goethe's greatest work—many would say the greatest work in the German language—*Faust.* Begun when he was in his twenties, and finished only when he was eighty, this long poetic drama was less a play in the conventional sense than a philosophical commentary on the main currents of European thought. According to the traditional legend, the aged Faust, weary of book learning and pining for eternal youth, sold his soul to the Devil, receiving back the enjoyment of his youth for an allotted time, and then, terror-stricken, went to the ever-lasting fires. Goethe transformed the legend. While Faust finds intellectual pursuits disillusioning and profitless and makes his infernal compact, he is ultimately saved through his realization that he must sacrifice selfish concerns to the welfare of others. A drama of man's sinning, striving, and redemption, Goethe's *Faust* is a reaffirmation of the Christian way that the Enlightenment had belittled. The return to Christian values was a striking feature of Romanticism.

By the early 1800's, Romantic writers decried what seemed to them the stilted and artificial verses of Racine and Pope and praised the color and vigor of the Bible, Homer, and Shakespeare. They called for a literary renaissance, a rebirth of imagination, feeling, and sensitivity. In consequence, the Romantic era was an age of poetry, in contrast to the eighteenth-century age of prose.

Britain produced a galaxy of Romantic poets—Byron, Shelley, Keats, Wordsworth, Coleridge, and still others. Of them all, Wordsworth (1770–1850) and Coleridge (1772–1834) perhaps pressed farthest in reaction against classicism and rationalism. In 1798, the two men published *Lyrical Ballads,* an early landmark in English Romanticism. As Coleridge later explained, their purpose was explicitly anti-classical:

In the present age the poet . . . seems to propose to himself as his main object . . . new and striking images; with incidents that interest the affections or excite the curiosity. Both his characters and his descriptions he renders, as much as possible, specific and individual, even to a degree of portraiture. In his diction and metre, on the other hand, he is comparatively careless.*

To *Lyrical Ballads* Coleridge contributed the *Rime of the Ancient Mariner,* a supernatural and very Romantic tale of the curse afflicting a sailor who slays an albatross. Among Wordsworth's contributions was *The Tables Turned,* notable less for its poetry than for its specific attack on conventional learning:

> Come forth into the light of things,
> Let Nature be your teacher.
>
> She has a world of ready wealth,
> Our minds and hearts to bless—
> Spontaneous wisdom breathed by health,
> Truth breathed by cheerfulness.
>
> One impulse from a vernal wood
> May teach you more of man,
> Of moral evil and of good,
> Than all the sages can.
>
> Sweet is the lore which Nature brings;
> Our meddling intellect
> Mis-shapes the beauteous forms of things:—
> We murder to dissect.
>
> Enough of Science and of Art;
> Close up those barren leaves;
> Come forth, and bring with you a heart
> That watches and receives.†

Wordsworth transformed the old concept of nature; nature was no longer something to be analyzed and reduced to laws but a mysterious, vitalizing force that had to be sensed and experienced. Here, from his long autobiographical *Prelude,* are two passages that express his beliefs more poetically:

> Ye Presences of Nature in the sky
> And on the earth! Ye Visions of the hills!
> And Souls of lonely places! can I think
> A vulgar hope was yours when ye
>   employed

*Biographia Literaria, Everyman ed., (New York, 1908), 173.
†*The Tables Turned,* lines 15–32.

> Such ministry, when ye, through many
>   a year
> Haunting me thus among my boyish
>   sports,
> On caves and trees, upon the woods and
>   hills,
> Impressed, upon all forms, the characters
> Of danger or desire; and thus did make
> The surface of the universal earth,
> With triumph and delight, with hope
>   and fear,
> Work like a sea?

. . .

> Dust as we are, the immortal spirit grows
> Like harmony in music; there is a dark
> Inscrutable workmanship that reconciles
> Discordant elements, makes them cling
>   together
> In one society.*

"Presences," "Visions," "Souls," "haunting" —this is truly Romantic language. In place of the light shed by Newton's laws, Wordsworth finds "a dark inscrutable workmanship," and in place of the *philosophes'* belief in the perfectibility of man through reason he puts his faith in the "immortal spirit" of the individual. Wordsworth in fact lived in France during the early years of the Revolution and was disillusioned by the failure of rational reform.

The Return to the Past

It may seem a long leap from the almost pantheistic universe of Wordsworth to the Romantics' enthusiasm for the Middle Ages in general and for the earlier history of their own nations in particular. And yet nationalism is an irrational, almost mystical force that—so its devotees believe—"reconciles discordant elements, makes them cling together in one society." The heightened sense of nationalism evident almost everywhere in Europe by 1815 was in part a matter of political self-preservation. In the crisis of the Napoleonic wars, for example, the Spaniards became more aware of their Spanish heritage and the Germans of

*The Prelude, Book I, lines 464–475, 340–344.

their Germanic one. The Romantic return to the national past, however, though intensified by French imperialism, had begun before 1789 as part of the general retreat from the Enlightenment. The pioneers of Romanticism tended to cherish what the *philosophes* detested, notably the Middle Ages and the medieval preoccupation with religion.

The German writer, Herder (1744–1803), provided intellectual justification for medieval studies with his theory of cultural nationalism. Each separate nation, he argued, like any organism, had its own distinct personality, its *Volksgeist* or "folk spirit," and its own pattern of growth. The surest measure of a nation's growth was its literature—poetry in youth, prose in maturity. Stimulated by Herder, students of medieval German literature collected popular ballads, and the brothers Grimm compiled their *Fairy Tales.* In 1782, the first complete text of the *Nibelungenlied* was published, a heroic saga of the nation's youth that had been much admired in the later Middle Ages only to be forgotten in succeeding centuries. By putting a new value on the German literature of the past, Herder helped to free the German literature of his own day from its bondage to French culture. Herder, however, was no narrow nationalist and asserted that the cultivated man should know cultures other than his own. So Herder also helped to loose the flood of translations that poured over Germany about 1800—translations of Shakespeare, of *Don Quixote,* of Spanish and Portuguese poetry, even of works in Sanskrit.

Some German Romantics, stirred by the patriotic revival after Jena and Tilsit, (see Chapter 18), carried national enthusiasm to an extreme that Herder would have deplored. Thus the Grimms claimed pre-eminence for the German language, and the dramatist Kleist (1777–1811), in his *Battle of Arminius,* boasted of the prowess of the ancient Germans in defeating the legions of Augustus, in 9 A.D. For the Romantic extremists, the mere fact of being German appeared to be a cardinal virtue. Yet many German writers struck Herder's happy balance between national and cosmopolitan interests; Goethe, for example, prided himself on being a good European, not simply a German.

Other nations, too, demonstrated that the return to the past meant veneration of the Middle Ages rather than classical antiquity. In Britain, Sir Walter Scott (1771–1832) assisted in collecting the vigorous medieval folk ballads and went on to write more than thirty historical novels, of which *Ivanhoe,* set in the days of Richard Lionheart and the Crusades, is the best known. In France, the home of the "classical spirit," the Romantic reaction gathered slowly but reached full strength after 1825 with the vivid historical dramas of Victor Hugo (1802–1885) and his famous novel of fifteenth-century France, *Notre Dame de Paris.* In Russia, to cite a third example, the poet Pushkin (1799–1837) deserted the archaic Slavonic language of the Orthodox Church to write the first major literary works in the national vernacular. He took subjects from Russia's past and introduced local color from its newly acquired provinces in the Crimea and the Caucasus. He also celebrated his own exotic grandfather, Hannibal, the African Negro slave of Peter the Great.

Music

Romantic musicians, like the poets, sought out the popular ballads and tales of the national past. They, too, were inventive and imaginative, seeking to make their compositions more dramatic and flexible, less constrained by classical rules. To achieve color and drama, composers of opera and song often turned for subjects to literature—Shakespeare's plays, Scott's novels, and the poems and tales of Goethe and Pushkin. Yet, although literature and music often took parallel paths during the Romantic era, the parallel was far from complete. Romantic musicians scarcely revolted against the great eighteenth-century composers in the way that Wordsworth and Coleridge revolted against their predecessors. Rather, Romantic music evolved peacefully out of the older classical school.

The composer who played the commanding part in this evolution was Beethoven

(1770–1827), a Fleming by ancestry and a Viennese by adoption. Whereas Coleridge had said that the Romantic artist might be careless in matters of diction and meter, Beethoven showed a classical concern for the forms and techniques that were the musical counterparts of diction and meter. Yet his experiments and innovations also enriched the great tradition that he inherited from Bach, Haydn, and Mozart. For example, where Mozart and Haydn had used the courtly minuet for the third movement in a symphony, Beethoven introduced the more plebeian and rollicking *scherzo*. Where earlier composers had indicated the tempo with a simple *allegro* (fast) or *andante* (slow), Beethoven added such designations as *appassionato* and "Strife between Head and Heart." Part of the color and passion of Beethoven's works derived from his skill in exploiting the resources of the piano, which was perfected during his lifetime. He also scored his orchestral compositions for a greater number of instruments, especially winds, percussion, and double-basses, than had been the practice of Mozart and Haydn.

After Beethoven, orchestral works took on increasingly heroic dimensions. The French composer, Berlioz (1803–1869), projected an orchestra of 465 pieces, including 120 violins, 37 double-basses, and 30 each of pianos and harps. Although this utopian scheme remained on paper, Berlioz was virtually the first to score his compositions for the full complement of instruments, especially winds and percussion, that make up the modern orchestra. His experiments with the theatrical potentialities of orchestral music created a series of landmarks in musical history, among them the "Fantastic Symphony" (1830), based, it is said, on Goethe's *Werther.*

Music for the human voice reflected both the increased enthusiasm for instruments, particularly the piano, and the general Romantic nostalgia for the past. In composing songs and arias, Romantic musicians devoted as much skill to the accompaniment as to the voice part itself. Franz Schubert (1797–1826), Beethoven's Viennese contemporary, made a fine art of blending voice and piano in more

than six hundred sensitive *Lieder* (songs), seventy of them musical settings of poems by Goethe. Meantime, Von Weber (1786–1826) was striving to create a truly German opera, taking an old legend as the libretto for *Der Freischütz* ("The Freeshooter," 1820). Its plot ran the good Romantic gamut of an enchanted forest, a magic bullet, and an innocent maiden outwitting the Devil, and its choruses and marches employed many folk-like melodies. Weber was by no means the only serious composer to utilize national folk tunes. In Russia, Glinka (1804–1857) cast aside the Italian influences that had previously dominated the secular music of his country. He based his opera, *Russlan and Ludmilla* (1842), on a poem by Pushkin and embellished it with dances and choruses derived from the native music of Russia's Asian provinces.

The Arts

In the fine arts, the forces of Romanticism gained no such triumph as they won in literature and music. The virtual dictator of European painting during the first two decades of the nineteenth century was the French neoclassicist, David (1748–1825), who was the official painter of the French Jacobins and then of Napoleon. David's canvases formed a capsule history of the rise and decline of revolutionary fervor—before 1789, Roman republican heroes and victims of aristocratic persecution like Socrates; after 1789, dramatic moments like the Tennis Court Oath and the death of Marat; and, still later, Napoleon's crossing of the Alps and his coronation. No matter how revolutionary the subject, David employed traditional neoclassical techniques, stressing form, line, and perspective.

The works of David's Spanish contemporary, Goya (1746–1828), were much less conventional and much closer to the Romantic temper with their warmth and passion and sense of outraged patriotism. No one could have any illusions about Spanish royalty after looking at Goya's revealing portraits of the enlightened Charles III and his successors. After viewing Goya's etchings on the Peninsular War, no one could doubt the horrors of warfare (see illustration on p. 129). Goya is said to have made the sketches for these etchings in the very blood of the executed Spanish patriots whose agonies he was portraying.

Romantic painting did not acquire formal recognition until the official Paris exhibition of 1824. Although many of the pictures hung in the salon of 1824 came from the school of David, the two leaders of Romantic painting were also represented—the Englishman, Constable (1776–1837) and the Frenchman, Delacroix (1799–1863). Constable took painting out of doors, studied nature afresh, and produced a series of landscapes that stressed light and color more than classical purity of line, and paved the way for the impressionists of the later nineteenth century (see Chapter 23). Delacroix, too, championed color and light and urged young painters to study the flamboyant canvases of Rubens, whom David had banished from the ranks of orthodox artists. The purpose of art, Delacroix claimed in a good Romantic definition, was "not to imitate nature but to strike the imagination." His painting of "The Massacre of Scio," a bloody episode in the Greek War of Independence (see p. 155), was denounced at the salon of 1824 as "barbarous, drunken, delirious"—the "massacre of painting." Today, however, the work of Delacroix seems conventional enough and less experimental than that of Goya. By the 1830's, French painters were divided into opposing schools: the still influential disciples of David, and the Romantic followers of Delacroix, with the master himself finding exotic new subjects in North Africa.

In architecture, also, two schools flourished during the first half of the nineteenth century—the neoclassical, looking to Greek and Roman antiquity, and the neo-Gothic, or Gothic revival, looking to the Middle Ages. Significantly, the label "Gothic" was no longer derogatory, as it had once been when employed by rationalist haters of things medieval. While there were obvious differences between the two schools, the contrast was not total. Many architects of the early 1800's mastered both styles; moreover, they did not so much copy ancient or medieval structures

outright as adapt them to the needs and tastes of the day. Generally, the basic design was classical in its proportions, even if the external shell and decoration were medieval. The Houses of Parliament in London, rebuilt in the 1830's and '40's after a disastrous fire, seem very Gothic at first glance with their spires and towers. But a longer look shows that they also embody classical principles of balance and symmetry. Romantic architecture anticipated the eclecticism, the wide range of inspiration and style, characteristic of the later nineteenth century.

As the nineteenth century began, the Roman vogue, so firmly set by the French Revolution, reached a peak in Napoleonic Paris with the *Arc de Triomphe* and with the Church of the Madeleine, patterned on an actual Roman temple (the *Maison Carrée* or "square house" at Nîmes). In America, the versatile Thomas Jefferson, who was a gifted designer, pronounced the *Maison Carrée* a perfect example of "cubical" architecture and adapted it to secular purposes for the Virginia capitol building at Richmond. At Charlottesville, about 1820, Jefferson provided the University of Virginia with a most distinguished group of academic buildings focused on a circular library, derived from the Roman Pantheon (the perfect example of "spherical" architecture). From the library, somewhat in the manner of a large Roman villa, he extended two rows of smaller structures, each recalling a different Roman temple and interconnected by colonnades. By the second quarter of the nineteenth century, neo-Roman was yielding place to the "Greek revival," stirred in part by the wave of Philhellenic enthusiasm then sweeping the western world (see p. 155). London's British Museum and Philadelphia's Girard College are two of many splendid examples of the Greek revival.

Meantime, especially in Britain, the Gothic revival was gaining ground, stimulated by the wealth of medieval architectural lore in Scott's novels, by the revival of religion, and by buildings like Fonthill Abbey, which had been started in 1797 and boasted an immensely long and high hall. Though it cost its owner, an eccentric millionaire, £500,000, it was so shoddily built that the central tower collapsed twenty-five years later. Undeterred, British architects applied the Gothic manner to every kind of structure after 1820, to public buildings like the Houses of Parliament, to churches, to elaborate villas, and modest cottages. Excessive "gloomth" often resulted, and the fad for "medieval" furniture, bristling with spikes, prompted one critic to warn that the occupant of a neo-Gothic room would be lucky to escape being "wounded by some of its minutiae." Though the Gothic revival prompted some monstrosities, it also fostered the preservation or restoration of medieval masterpieces half ruined by neglect or by anti-clerical vandalism.

Religion and Philosophy

Neo-Gothic architecture was one sign of the Christian revival that formed part of the Romantic movement; another sign was the

Delacroix: self-portrait.

The Houses of Parliament, London.

pope's re-establishment in 1814 of the Jesuit order, whose suppression in 1773 had been one of the great victories of the Enlightenment. Most of the Romantics were horrified by the religious skepticism of the *philosophes;* an outspoken atheist like Shelley was an isolated exception. In Germany, Catholicism gained many converts among Romantic writ-

pounded in Germany. Chief among these German philosophers was Hegel (1770–1831), a follower of Kant and a professor at the University of Berlin. Like his master, Hegel attacked the tendency of the Enlightenment to see in human nature and human history only what first met the eye. The history of mankind, properly understood, was the

Monticello, the house that Jefferson designed for himself in Virginia.

ers, and in England Wordsworth and Coleridge vigorously defended the established Church. Coleridge declared:

. . . that the scheme of Christianity, as taught in the liturgy and homilies of our Church, though not discoverable by human reason, is yet in accordance with it; that link follows link by necessary consequence; that Religion passes out of the ken of Reason only where the eye of Reason has reached its own horizon; and that Faith is then but its continuation. . . .*

Coleridge introduced his countrymen to the new Romantic philosophies being ex-

Biographia Literaria, Everyman ed., 334.

history of human efforts to attain the good, and this in turn was the unfolding of God's plan for the world. For Hegel, history was a *dialectical* process—that is, a series of conflicts. The two elements in the conflict were the *thesis,* the established order of life, and the *antithesis,* the challenge to the old order. Out of the struggle of thesis and antithesis emerged the *synthesis,* no mere compromise between the two but a new and better way, another step in man's slow progression toward the best of all possible worlds. The synthesis, in turn, broke down; a new thesis and antithesis became locked in conflict; the dialectic produced another synthesis—and so on.

The death throes of the Roman Republic

afforded Hegel an illustration of the dialectic at work. The thesis was represented by the decadent republic, the antithesis by oriental despotism, and the synthesis by the Caesarism of the early Roman Empire. Hegel explained that "This important change must not be regarded as a thing of chance; it was *necessary,*" a part of God's grand design. Julius Caesar himself Hegel called a "hero," one of the few "world-historical individuals" who "had an insight into the requirements of the time" and who knew "what was ripe for development." This concept of the hero as the agent of a cosmic process is another characteristic of the Romantic temper.

The dialectical philosophy of history was the most original and influential element in Hegel's thought, one antecedent, for example, of the dialectical materialism of Karl Marx (see Chapter 20). It is perhaps difficult for citizens of a twentieth-century democracy to appreciate that Hegel was once even more famous as a liberal idealist. His emphasis on duty, his choice of Alexander the Great, Caesar, and Napoleon as "world-historical" heroes, his assertion that the state "existed for its own sake"—all suggest a link with authoritarianism. Hegel himself, however, seems to have foreseen the final synthesis of the dialectic not as a brutal police state but as a liberalized version of the Prussian monarchy.

The Romantic "Style"

Thus Hegel, like the *philosophes,* believed in progress and the perfectibility of man, though he also believed that the process would require far more time and struggle than a man like Condorcet had ever imagined. Indeed, the "style" of Romanticism by no means contrasted in every particular with that of the Enlightenment. Not only a modified doctrine of progress but also eighteenth-century cosmopolitanism lived on into the nineteenth. Homer, Cervantes, Shakespeare, and Scott won appreciative readers in many countries; the giants of the age, men like Beethoven and Goethe, were not merely Austrian or German but citizens of the world.

These similarities and continuities notwithstanding, Romanticism did have a decided style of its own—imaginative, emotional, and haunted by the supernatural and by history. The Romantics could no longer view history in Gibbon's terms of a classical golden age followed by long centuries of benighted superstition. Rather history was, as Hegel and Herder had argued an organic process of growth and development, which was indebted to the Middle Ages for magnificent Gothic buildings, religious enthusiasm, folk ballads, and heroic epics. Just as the Romantics rejected the Enlightened view of the past, so they found the Newtonian world-machine an entirely inadequate interpretation of the universe. It was too static, too drab and materialistic, and in its place they put the neo-Gothic world of religious mystery, the Hegelian world of dialectic and heroes, the poetic and artistic world of feeling, color, an "impulses from the vernal wood." Perhaps the most conspicuous feature of the Romantic style was its insistence that society was more than a branch of physics and man more than a cog in a machine.

III   The Conservative Outlook and the Vienna Settlement

The usual image of the Romantic political figure is the rebel or the defender of a cause—Shelley preaching anarchism, Byron dying in the Greek War of Independence, revolutionaries protesting against the status quo. This image is, however, misleading. While it is true that Romanticism by its stress on the individual ultimately enriched the doctrines of liberalism and by its emphasis on the national community strengthened the force of nationalism, its immediate political influence was more frequently counter-revolutionary. More representative of the Romantics than Shelley and Byron were Wordsworth and Coleridge who, in their maturity, lost their youthful zeal for the French Revolution and adopted conservative views in politics as well as in religion.

Burke and Metternich

The man who set the tone of Romantic conservativism was Edmund Burke (1729–1797). Unlike the champions of revolution, Burke could not accept simple black-and-white assumptions about the goodness of man and the unmitigated evil of the Old Régime. He revered the social and political institutions so painstakingly built up over the centuries. He, however, did not believe that these institutions were petrified; they had developed gradually in the past, they would develop gradually in the future. Political change was possible but difficult, he concluded. Reforms had to be introduced so that "the useful parts of the old establishment" might be preserved; they had to be managed slowly and "with circumspection and caution"—in a word, conservatively.

Burke approved of the American Revolution, for it was not so much a revolution as a reaffirmation of the glorious tradition of 1688. The same reasoning drove Burke to violent condemnation in his *Reflections on the Revolution in France* (1790). The men of 1789 destroyed everything, good, bad, and indifferent. Rage and frenzy, he observed, "pull down more in half an hour, than prudence, deliberation and foresight can build up in a hundred years";* thereby society itself is jeopardized. "Society is indeed a contract," Burke wrote, but he did not mean what Rousseau had meant:

The state ought not to be considered as nothing better than a partnership agreement in a trade of pepper and coffee, calico or tobacco, or some such other low concern, to be taken up for a little temporary interest, and to be dissolved by the fancy of

the parties. It is to be looked on with other reverence, because it is not a partnership in things subservient only to the gross animal existence of a temporary and perishable nature. It is a partnership in all science; a partnership in all art; a partnership in every virtue, and in all perfection. As the ends of such a partnership cannot be obtained in many generations, it becomes a partnership not only between those who are living, but between those who are living, those who are dead, and those who are to be born.*

The force of tradition so revered by Burke bore heavily upon the politics of post-Napoleonic Europe. This was the Age of Metternich—Prince Clement Wenceslas Lothair Népomucène Metternich (1773–1859), Austrian foreign minister from 1809 to 1848 and the chief figure in European diplomacy during most of his long career. Handsome, dashing, an aristocrat through and through, Metternich retained some of the eighteenth century's belief in reform through enlightened despotism. But, he also believed, reform should proceed with Burkean caution, not at a revolutionary pace. His own family, living in the German Rhineland, had suffered directly from the French Revolution. Moreover, Metternich served a state that was particularly susceptible to injury by the liberal and nationalist energies released by the Revolution. Tradition, he knew, was the cement that held together the disparate parts of the Austrian Habsburg realm; it should be fortified as much as possible.

The Congress of Vienna

In 1814 and 1815, Metternich was host to the Congress of Vienna, which approached its task of rebuilding Europe with truly conservative deliberateness. For the larger part of a year, the diplomats indulged to the full in balls and banquets, concerts and hunting parties. "Congress dances," remarked an observer, "but it does not march." Actually, the brilliant social life distracted the lesser fry while the important diplomats settled things in private conference.

*Reflections, Everyman ed., 164.

*Ibid. 93.

Four men made most of the major decisions at Vienna—Metternich, Castlereagh, Talleyrand, and Tsar Alexander I. Viscount Castlereagh, the British foreign minister, shared the conservative outlook of Metternich. He was less concerned with punishing the French for their past sins than with preventing the appearance of new Robespierres and Bonapartes. Castlereagh announced that he went to Vienna "not to collect trophies, but to bring

Talleyrand in 1809.

the world back to peaceful habits." The best way to do this, he believed, was to restore the balance of power and keep any of the major states, including France, from becoming either too strong or too weak.

Talleyrand, the foreign minister of Louis XVIII of France, scored at Vienna the greatest success of his long career. Originally a worldly bishop of the Old Régime, he had in succession rallied to the Revolution in 1789, supported the Civil Constitution of the Clergy (one of the very few bishops to do so), served as Napoleon's foreign minister, and intrigued against him during the years after Tilsit. Now he was serving the restored Bourbon king, and in his old age he would take an important part in the Revolution of 1830. This supremely adaptable diplomat soon maneuvered himself into the inner circle at Vienna, and the representatives of the victorious powers accepted the emissary of defeated France as their equal. Talleyrand was particularly adept in exploiting his nuisance value—acting as the spokesman of lesser diplomats who resented being shoved aside, and making the most of the differences that divided the victors.

To these differences Alexander I contributed greatly. Metternich actually called the Tsar a Jacobin, although Alexander's reputation for enlightenment was only partially deserved (see Chapter 17). By 1814, the Tsar had acquired a thoroughly Romantic enthusiasm for religion. For hours on end, he prayed and read the Bible in the company of Madame de Krüdener and under her influence prepared a "Holy Alliance" whereby all states would regenerate their policies by following Christian teachings. In the first months at Vienna, it was not Alexander's Romantic scheme of a Holy Alliance but rather his Polish policy that nearly disrupted the Congress. He proposed a partial restoration of pre-partition Poland, with himself as its monarch. Austria and Prussia would lose the Polish lands they had grabbed late in the preceding century. Alexander won the support of Prussia by backing her demands for the annexation of Saxony, whose king had remained loyal to

The statesmen of Europe at the Congress of Vienna, 1814–1815. Metternich is standing prominently at left front, Wellington at extreme left. Talleyrand is seated at right with his arm resting on the table.

Napoleon. Metternich, however, did not want Austria's traditional Prussian rival to make such a substantial gain. Moreover, both Metternich and Castlereagh disliked the prospect of a large, Russian-dominated Poland.

The dispute over Saxony and Poland gave Talleyrand a magnificent chance to fish in troubled waters. Thus it was that in January, 1815, the representative of defeated France joined Metternich and Castlereagh in threatening both Prussia and Russia with war unless they moderated their demands. The threat produced an immediate settlement. Alexander obtained Poland but agreed to reduce its size and allow Prussia and Austria to keep part of their loot from the partitions. Prussia took about half of Saxony; the King of Saxony retained the balance.

Once the Saxon-Polish question was out of the way, the Congress achieved a fairly amicable resolution of other important dynastic and territorial questions. According to the doctrine that Talleyrand christened "the sacred principle of legitimacy," thrones and frontiers were to be re-established as they had existed in 1789. In practice, however, legitimacy was ignored almost as often as it was enforced, since the diplomats at Vienna realized that they could not undo all the changes worked by the Revolution and Napoleon. Although they restored Bourbon dynasties to the thrones of France, Spain, and Naples in the name of legitimacy, they did not attempt to resurrect the Republic of Venice or to revive all the hundreds of German states that had vanished since 1789.

In Germany, the Congress provided for thirty-nine states, loosely grouped together in a weak confederation. The German Confederation came close to reincarnating the impotent Holy Roman Empire; its chief organ, the diet, was to be a council of diplomats from sovereign states rather than a representative national assembly. Its most important members were Prussia and Austria, for the German-speaking provinces of the Habsburgs were considered an integral part of Germany. Both states obtained important new territories at Vienna. Prussia, in addition to her Saxon annexation, expanded the old scattered Hohenzollern lands in western Germany into the imposing new Rhine Province. Austria lost Belgium, which was incorporated into the Kingdom of the Netherlands in order to strenghten the northern buffer against France. But she recovered the old Habsburg territory of Lombardy in Italy, to which Venetia was now joined, and she also recovered the Illyrian Provinces along the eastern shore of the Adriatic.

In Italy, too, the Congress of Vienna confirmed the tradition of political disunity. It restored the Bourbon Kingdom of Naples in the south and the Papal States in the center. In the northwest it gave Genoa to the Kingdom of Piedmont-Sardinia. Austria was in a position to dominate Italy both by her possession of Lombardy-Venetia and by the close family ties between the Habsburgs and the ruling dynasties in the other Italian states.

Elsewhere in Europe, the Congress of Vienna restored to independence the Republic of Switzerland and enlarged it somewhat as another buffer against France. It sanctioned the transfer of Norway from the rule of Denmark, which had generally been pro-French, to Sweden. And it confirmed the earlier transfer of Finland from Sweden to Russia. Great Britain received the strategic little Mediterranean island of Malta and, outside Europe, the former Dutch colonies of Ceylon and the Cape of Good Hope plus a few insignificant French outposts.

The Quarantine of France

France at first was given her boundaries of 1792, which included the minor territorial acquisitions made during the early days of the Revolution. Then came Napoleon's escape from Elba and the Hundred Days. The final settlement reached after Waterloo assigned France the frontiers of 1790, substantially those of the Old Régime plus Avignon. In addition, the French were to return Napoleon's art plunder to its rightful owners, pay the victorious allies an indemnity of 700,-000,000 francs (roughly $140,000,000), and finance allied military occupation of 17 frontier fortresses on French soil for not more than five years.

The Vienna diplomats did not so much punish France as take measures to quarantine any possible new French aggression. Castlereagh conceived the policy of strengthening France's neighbors so that they would be able to restrain the troublemaker in the future. Thus to the north the French faced the Belgians and the Dutch combined in the single Kingdom of the Netherlands. On the northeast they encountered the Rhine Province of Prussia, and on the east the expanded states of Switzerland and Piedmont. The Quadruple Alliance, signed in November, 1815, constituted the second great measure of quarantine. The four allies—Britain, Prussia, Austria, and Russia—agreed to use force, if necessary, to preserve the Vienna settlement. At Castlereagh's insistence, the allies further decided on periodic conferences to consider the measures "most salutary for the repose and prosperity of Nations, and the maintenance of the Peace of Europe." The Quadruple Alliance was to be both a watchdog against France and an experiment in government by international conference, a modest step along the road leading to the League of Nations and United Nations of the twentieth century.

Public opinion, especially in the English-speaking countries, unfortunately confused the Quadruple Alliance with Alexander's Holy Alliance, which it identified with the blackest reaction. The Holy Alliance, signed in September, 1815, was actually a fairly harmless document dedicated to the proposition that "the policy of the powers . . . ought to be guided by the sublime truths taught by the eternal religion of God our Saviour." Although most of the major European rulers signed the Holy Alliance, only Tsar Alexander seems to have taken it seriously. Castlereagh called it "a piece of sublime mysticism and nonsense," and Britain declined to participate—the first sign of the rift that was to open between her and the continental powers. The pope, refusing an invitation to join, remarked tartly that the Vatican needed no new interpretations of Christian doctrine by the laity.

Together with Westphalia (1648), Utrecht (1713), and Versailles (1919), the Vienna settlement of 1814–1815 marked one of those rare attempts at the massive political reconstruction of Europe. Of the four, Vienna in many respects succeeded best. There was to be no major European war until the Crimean conflict of the 1850's, and none embroiling the whole of Europe until 1914. Most of the leading diplomats at Vienna could have said with Castlereagh that they acted "to bring the world back to peaceful habits." Seldom have victors treated the defeated aggressor more generously. Castlereagh, above all, deserved credit for his project of pacifying international disputes through conferences of the Quadruple Alliance. In operation, however, the Quadruple Alliance never fulfilled the noble aims of Castlereagh. Within five years of the Congress of Vienna, revolution broke out again in Europe, causing serious dissension within the Quadruple Alliance. And for these outbreaks the Congress of Vienna was itself responsible, at least in part because it attempted to stifle both liberal and nationalist aspirations.

IV   The Revolutions of the 1820's

The Revolutionary Credo

The revolutionary leaders of the early nineteenth century despised the traditions so revered by conservatives. Opposing the counter-revolutionary alliance of Throne and Altar, they stood for Liberty, Equality, and Fraternity. In the revolutionary credo, Liberty and Equality continued to signify the abolition of noble and clerical privileges in society and, with few exceptions, the application of laissez-faire to economics. They also involved the broadening of civil rights, the institution of representative assemblies, and the granting of constitutions, which would bring limited monarchy to most states but a republic to the truly advanced, like France. For these aspects of the revolutionary program, the best label is liberalism. Almost every leader of revolution proclaimed himself a liberal, although, as we shall soon see, the kind of liberalism actually practiced varied from the narrow to the sweeping.

The third word of the great revolutionary motto now came to have a more precise meaning. Fraternity, intensified by the Romantic cult of the nation, continued to evolve into the formidable doctrine of nationalism. The nationalists of the post-1815 generation dreamed of a world in which each nation would be free of domination by any other, and all nations would live together harmoniously. In terms of practical politics, this signified movements toward national unity and national independence. It meant growing pressure for the unification of Germany and Italy. And it inspired demands for freedom by peoples living under the control of a foreign power—by Belgians against their Dutch rulers, by Poles against Russians, by Greeks and Serbs against Turks, and by Italians, Hungarians, and Czechs against the Habsburgs of Vienna.

The Iberian States and Naples

The first revolutionary outbreaks after 1815 took place in Spain, Portugal and the Kingdom of the Two Sicilies. In all three states the return to legitimacy restored the Old Régime at its least enlightened. The great majority of the population responded to the restoration calmly, even enthusiastically. The aristocracy were delighted to recover their ancient privileges and the peasantry welcomed the return of familiar traditions; a small minority, drawn chiefly from the middle class, the intellectuals,

Europe after 1815

― Boundary of the German Confederation
■ Battle sites

FINLAND

L. Onega

L. Ladoga

Gulf of Finland

St. Petersburg

Volga R.

Königsberg

Moscow

Oka R.

W. Dvina R.

Niemen R.

R U S S I A

Warsaw

Don R.

OLAND

Kiev

Volga R.

EP. OF
ACOW

Dnieper R.

GALICIA

Dniester R.

O F

Pruth R.

Odessa

Caspian Sea

est

MOLDAVIA

ia

DANUBIAN
PROVINCES

CRIMEA

WALLACHIA

Black Sea

RBIA

Bucharest

Morava R.

Danube R.

MONTE-
NEGRO

Vardar R.

O

Adrianople

T

Istanbul

T

O

M

A

N

E

M

P

I

R

E

Aegean Sea

Euphrates R.

Tigris R.

NIAN IS.

CHIOS

Athens

Navarino

CYPRUS

CRETE

ARABIA

and the army, dissented. In Spain and Italy, they greatly regretted the abrogation of the *Code Napoléon,* and of the anti-feudal and anti-clerical legislation introduced by the French. In all three states the discontent of the liberal minority produced the revolutionary movement of 1820.

The trouble began in Spain. During the war against Napoleon, representatives from the liberal middle class of Cadiz and other commercial towns had framed the Constitution of 1812. Based on the French revolutionary Constitution of 1791, this document limited greatly the power of the monarchy, gave wide authority to a Cortes elected on a broad suffrage, and deprived the Spanish Church of some of its lands and privileges. This liberal constitution was doubtless too liberal to be very workable in traditionalist Spain, and the Bourbon Ferdinand VII soon suspended it after he assumed the Spanish crown in 1814. Ferdinand also restored the social inequalities of the Old Régime and re-established not only the Jesuits but also the Spanish inquisition. Army officers, alienated by his high-handedness and clericalism, and merchants, facing ruin because of the revolt of Spanish colonies in the New World, joined the political clubs and masonic lodges that formed the liberal opposition.

It was Ferdinand's attempt to subdue the rebellious colonies that triggered revolution at home. The independence movement in Spanish America was caused directly by the refusal of the colonial populations either to recognize Napoleon's brother Joseph as their king or to accept the closer ties between colonies and mother country proposed by patriots in Spain. Behind the Spanish-American independence movement lay several other factors: the powerful examples of the American and French revolutions; the sympathetic interest of Great Britain, anxious to release lucrative markets from Spanish mercantilist restrictions; and the accumulated resentment of colonial peoples at the centuries of indifferent rule by Spanish governors. The colonial rebels won their initial success at Buenos Aires in 1810, and their movement spread rapidly to Spain's other American possessions.

Ferdinand now determined to crush the rebels by force; to transport troops he augmented the small Spanish fleet with three leaky hulks purchased from Russia. At the end of 1819, this motley new armada, carrying 20,000 men, was about to sail from Cadiz. It never sailed, for on January 1, 1820, a mutiny broke out at Cadiz led by the liberal Colonel Riego. Uprisings soon followed in Madrid, in Barcelona, and in other Spanish cities.

Centers of Revolution

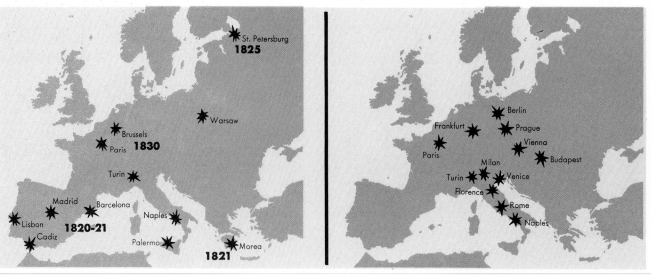

1820-1830   1848-1849

The revolutionaries sang "Riego's Hymn," with the refrain "Swallow it, you dog" (the "it" referred to the Constitution of 1812). Ferdinand surrendered.

The liberal minorities in Portugal and Naples followed the Spanish lead. An army faction seized control of the Portuguese government in 1820, abolished the Inquisition, and set up a constitution on the Spanish model of 1812. In Naples, the revolution was the work of General Pepe, backed by the *Carbonari* (charcoal-burners). This secret society, with a membership exceeding 50,000, had been opposed to the French and to reforms in the days of Napoleon's hegemony but now sponsored a vaguely liberal program inspired by the French Revolution. King Ferdinand I of the Two Sicilies, who was the uncle of the Spanish Ferdinand VII, gave in at the first sign of opposition in 1820 and accepted a constitution of the Spanish type.

The strength of the revolutionary movement of 1820 ebbed as quickly as it had risen. The reforms introduced precipitately by the inexperienced liberal leaders in Spain and Naples alienated the bulk of the population at home and so alarmed the conservative leaders of the great powers that they sponsored counter-revolutionary intervention. The Spanish revolutionaries were further weakened by a split between *moderados,* who wanted to restore the Constitution of 1812, and *exaltados,* led by Colonel Riego, who wanted to go much farther and set up a violently anticlerical republic. Only in Portugal did the revolutionary regime survive, and only because it had British protection. Even so, there was enough confusion to enable the great Portuguese colony of Brazil to declare itself independent of the mother country (1822).

The revolutions of 1820 tested both the stability of the Vienna settlement and the solidarity of the Quadruple Alliance of Britain, Prussia, Austria, and Russia. Legitimacy was again restored in Spain and Italy, but in the process the Quadruple Alliance was split in two. While the continental allies increasingly favored armed intervention to suppress revolution, Britain inclined more and more toward the principle of non-intervention.

The split became evident at the conference of the Quadruple Alliance meeting at Troppau in Silesia late in 1820. Castlereagh, the British foreign minister, knowing that the Neapolitan revolution threatened the Habsburg hegemony in Italy, was willing to see Austria intervene in Naples, but without the backing of the Alliance. The Alliance, Castlereagh declared, was never designed "for the superintendence of the internal affairs of other states," and Britain refused to participate formally in the Troppau meeting. Metternich, supported by Alexander, pressed for a blanket commitment from the Alliance, and the result was the Troppau Protocol (November, 1820), signed by Austria, Prussia, and Russia. It declared that

States which have undergone a change of Government, due to revolution, the results of which threaten other states, *ipso facto* cease to be members of the European Alliance, and remain excluded from it until their situation gives guarantees for legal order and stability. If, owing to such alterations, immediate danger threatens other states, the Powers bind themselves, by peaceful means, or if need be by arms, to bring back the guilty state into the bosom of the Great Alliance.*

Under the terms of the Troppau Protocol, an Austrian army duly toppled the revolutionary government of Naples in 1821. In 1823, a French army crossed the Pyrenees and restored the absolute authority of Ferdinand VII, who proceeded to execute Colonel Riego and hundreds of his followers.

French intervention in Spain provoked the strong opposition of Great Britain and ended the Quadruple Alliance. Canning, who had succeeded Castlereagh as British Foreign Minister in 1822, suspected that the continental powers might now aid Spain to recover her former American colonies. So also did the United States, which had recognized the independence of the Latin-American republics. But America also feared both a possible Russian move southward from Alaska along the Pacific coast and an attempt by Britain to

---

*Quoted in W. A. Phillips, *The Confederation of Europe* (New York, 1920), 208–209.

extend her sphere of control in the Caribbean. Therefore, when Canning proposed a joint Anglo-American statement to ward off any European interference in Latin America, the government of President Monroe refused the invitation.

In a message to the American Congress in December, 1823, the President included the statement that is known to history as the Monroe Doctrine:

In the wars of the European powers, in matters relating to themselves, we have never taken any part, nor does it comport with our policy so to do. It is only when our rights are invaded, or seriously menaced, that we resent injuries or make preparation for our defence. With the movements in this hemisphere, we are, of necessity, more immediately connected, and by causes which must be obvious to all enlightened and impartial observers. The political system of the allied powers is essentially different, in this respect, from that of Amer-

ica. . . . We owe it, therefore, to candor, and to the amicable relations existing between the United States and those powers, to declare, that we should consider any attempt on their part to extend their system to any portion of this hemisphere, as dangerous to our peace and safety. With the existing colonies or dependencies of any European power, we have not interfered, and shall not interfere. But with the governments who have declared their independence, and maintained it, and whose independence we have, on great consideration, and on just principles, acknowledged, we could not view any interposition for the purpose of oppressing them, or controlling, in any other manner, their destiny, by an European power, in any other light than as the manifestation of an unfriendly disposition towards the United States.

Although this document marked an important assertion of policy on the part of the youthful American republic, it had little immediate international significance. The European powers were not fully committed to the project of restoring Spain's American empire. And, so far as they were deterred from that venture, they were deterred not by President Monroe but by Canning and the possible actions of the British fleet.

The Greek War of Independence

The British fleet was soon to take an important role in the Greeks' bid for national independence. The Greek revolt was part of the general movement of the Balkan nations for emancipation from their Turkish overlords. During the last quarter of the eighteenth century, the Christian peoples of the Balkan peninsula began to awaken to their national identities under the impulse from French Revolutionary and Romantic ideas. They examined their national past with new interest and affection, and they put an especially high value on their native languages. The first outbreak against the Turkish authorities came in Serbia in 1804 and was led by a well-to-do pig-raiser named Karageorge. From the first, the Serb nationalists knew they would need outside help; some turned to Russia, others to Austria, thereby fixing a pattern of conflicting

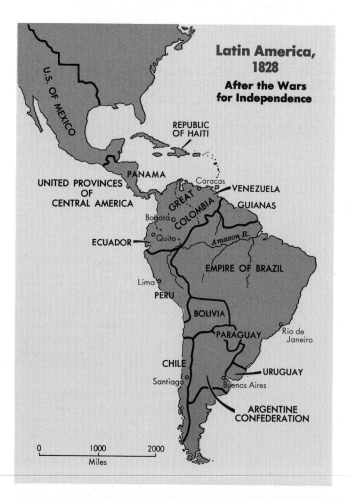

Latin America, 1828
After the Wars for Independence

interests that ultimately led to World War I. Napoleon's venture in the Illyrian provinces (see p. 123) further stimulated the south Slavic desire for independence. After Karageorge's defection in 1813, leadership of Serb nationalism passed to his rival, Milosh Obrenovich, who won Russian support and succeeded by 1830 in becoming prince of an autonomous Serbia. Although he still paid tribute to the Ottoman Emperor, and a Turkish garrison remained in the Serb capital of Belgrade, a major step toward eventual independence had been completed.

Meantime, the Greeks had launched a revolution. Leadership came from two groups —the Phanariot Greeks, named for the quarter where they lived in Istanbul, and the Island Greeks, merchants from the ports and islands of the Aegean. The Phanariots had long held positions of power and responsibility in governing the Orthodox subjects of the Ottoman Empire. The Island Greeks dominated the commerce of the Near East and had business outposts at Vienna, Marseilles, London, and Russia's Black Sea port of Odessa. The Island Greeks revived not only the old Greek trading tradition but also some of the old Greek zeal for self-government. From their home islands and from their merchant colonies abroad they poured forth a stream of patriotic exhortation. Greek nationalists sponsored a campaign to purge the modern Greek language of its Turkish and Slavic words and to return it to the classical tongue of the Age of Pericles. A revolutionary secret society was formed in Odessa, patterned after the *Carbonari* of Italy and headed by Ypsilanti, a Phanariot who was a general in the Russian army.

In 1821, Ypsilanti led an expedition into the Rumanian areas of the Ottoman Empire but failed in his aim to stir up a major revolt. The conspirators were more successful in the Morea (the ancient Peloponnesus) where they formented an uprising among the peasants. The ensuing war for independence was a ferocious conflict: the Morean peasants slaughtered every Turk they could lay their hands on; the Ottoman government retaliated by killing or selling into slavery thirty thousand Greeks from the prosperous Aegean island of Chios

(Scio), an atrocity that inspired Delacroix's famous painting. In the work of repression, the Ottoman emperor supplemented his own inadequate forces by those of his vassal, the governor of Egypt, Mehemet Ali. By 1827, it appeared likely that the Egyptian expedition would recapture the last rebel strongholds. Then Britain, France, and Russia intervened to save the Greek independence movement at its darkest hour.

The three-power action resulted from the combined pressures of public opinion and strategic interests. In Britain and France, and also in Germany and the United States, the Philhellenic (pro-Greek) movement had won legions of supporters. Philhellenic committees sent supplies and money and demanded that civilized governments intervene directly. Intervention hinged on the action of Russia, for Greek patriots had formed their secret society at Odessa, on Russian soil and with Russian backing. For a time, Metternich was able to restrain Russia by pointing out the dangers to the European balance in supporting revolution in one country and repressing it in others. Ultimately, however, Russia's Balkan aspirations won out over her concern for preserving the status quo, and she rallied openly to the Greek cause. Britain and France now felt obliged to take action because of Philhellenic pressure and, still more, because they feared to let Russia act alone lest she gain mastery over the whole Near East. A three-power intervention seemed the only course that would both rescue the Greeks and check the Russians.

Neither aim was fully achieved. In October, 1827, Russian, British, and French squadrons sank the Turkish and Egyptian vessels anchored at Navarino, on the southwest corner of the Morea, and thus destroyed the chief Ottoman base. The subsequent Treaty of Adrianople, 1829, while allowing Russia to annex outright only a little Turkish territory, arranged that the Ottoman Danubian provinces of Moldavia and Wallachia (the heart of present-day Rumania) should become a virtual Russian protectorate. After considerable wrangling, the European powers accorded formal recognition to an independent Greek

Delacroix, "The Massacre of Scio," in the Louvre, Paris.

kingdom of very modest size, which left many Greeks still within the Ottoman Empire. Neither nationalism nor liberalism had won a complete victory in the Greek war. Greek patriots now schemed for the day when they might enlarge the boundaries of their new kingdom. And Greek politicians were to threaten its stability and disillusion Philhellenists abroad by continuing the bitter feuds that had divided them even in the midst of their desperate struggle for independence.

The Decembrist Revolt in Russia

Russia, who did so much to determine the outcome of revolutions elsewhere, herself felt the revolutionary wave, but with diminished force. A brief uprising took place after the death of Tsar Alexander I (December, 1825), as the "Decembrists" vainly attempted to apply and extend the program of liberal reforms apparently promised by the Tsar but seldom implemented by him.

The last period of Alexander's reign, marked by the influence of the unpopular Arakcheev and by the establishment of the hated military colonies (see Chapter 17), had thoroughly disappointed Russian liberals. Liberal ideas, however, continued to penetrate the country. As in other European states, secret societies flourished in Russia after 1815. The introduction of Freemasonry during the eighteenth century, and the secret ritual connected with many of the lodges, had given jaded nobles a thrill and had also enabled them to meet on equal terms with men from other ranks of society. Masonry aroused humanitarian urges; it also afforded a cover of secrecy under which subversive ideas might be incubated. Moreover, the contrast between the relatively enlightened West and backward Russia made a deep impression on officers who had served in the campaigns against Napoleon. One of the future Decembrist leaders left this report of his reactions upon returning home:

> From France we returned to Russia by sea. The First Division of the Guard landed at Oranienbaum and listened to the *Te Deum.* . . . During the prayer the police were mercilessly beating the people who attempted to draw nearer to the lined-up troops. . . . Finally the Emperor appeared, accompanied by the Guard, on a fine sorrel horse, with an unsheathed sword, which he was ready to lower before the Empress. But at that very moment, almost under his horse, a peasant crossed the street. The Emperor spurred his horse and rushed with the unsheathed sword toward the running peasant. The police attacked him with their clubs. We did not believe our own eyes and turned away, ashamed for our beloved Tsar.*

High-ranking officers at St. Petersburg secretly formed the Northern Society, which aimed to make Russia a limited, decentralized monarchy, with the various provinces enjoying rights somewhat like those of the states in the American republic. The serfs would receive their freedom but no land, and the whole series of reforms would be achieved by peaceful means. A second secret organization, the Southern Society, with headquarters at Kiev, included many relatively impoverished officers among its members; its leader was Colonel Pestel, a Jacobin in temperament and an admirer of Napoleon. On every main issue the program of the Southern Society went beyond that of the Petersburg group. It advocated a highly centralized republic, the granting of land to liberated serfs, and the use of violence—specifically, assassination of the

*Quoted in Anatole G. Mazour, *The First Russian Revolution* (Berkeley, Calif., 1937), 55.

Tsar—to gain its ends. Pestel himself planned to install a dictatorship, supported by secret police, as an interim government between the overthrow of the tsardom and the advent of the republic.

Both the Northern Society and the Southern Society tried to profit by the political confusion following the death of Alexander I. Since Alexander left no son, the crown would normally have passed to his younger brother, Constantine, his viceroy in Poland. Constantine, however, had relinquished his rights to a still younger brother, Nicholas, but in a document so secret that Nicholas never saw it. On the death of Alexander, Constantine declared that Nicholas was the legal tsar, and Nicholas declared that Constantine was. While the two brothers were clarifying their status, the Northern Society summoned the Petersburg garrison to revolt against Nicholas. Throughout the day of December 26, 1825, the rebels stood their ground in Russia's capital city until Nicholas subdued them. Two weeks later, the Southern Society launched a movement that was doomed from the start because its leader, Pestel, had already been placed under arrest.

The Decembrist revolt, for all its ineffectiveness, was an important episode. It thoroughly alarmed Tsar Nicholas I (1825–1855), who now resolved to follow a severely autocratic policy (for details, see Chapter 21). Although Nicholas dismissed the unpopular Arakcheev and put an end to the military colonies, he also had five of the Decembrists executed and exiled more than one hundred others to Siberia, where many of them contributed to the advance of local government and education. The Decembrists were the first in the long line of modern Russia's political martyrs, and the program of Pestel's Southern Society may now be seen as a kind of early blueprint for the revolutionary dictatorship that came to Russia as a consequence of the Bolshevik uprising of 1917 (see Chapter 26).

V   The Revolutions of 1830

France: The July Revolution

The next revolutionary wave—that of 1830—swept first over the traditional home of revolution, France. King Louis XVIII (1814–1824) had given the Bourbon restoration a fairly promising start. By personal inclination he would have preferred to be an absolute ruler, but he was sensible enough to know that a full return to the Old Régime was impractical, especially since he was declining in years and in health and suffered from the additional political handicap of having been imposed on the French by their enemies.

The middle-of-the-road policies of Louis XVIII were well exemplified by the constitutional Charter that he issued in 1814. Its preamble asserted the royal prerogative: "The authority in France resides in the person of the King." But the Charter then proceeded to grant a measure of constitutional monarchy. There was a legislature, composed of a Chamber of Peers appointed by the king, and a Chamber of Deputies elected on a very restricted suffrage that allowed fewer than 100,000 of France's thirty millions the right to vote. "In the King alone is vested the executive power," the Charter stated, and the Chambers had no formal right to confirm the King's choices as ministers. Yet since Louis tended to select ministers acceptable to majority opinion in the legislature, this was a kind of back-handed parliamentary government. The Charter confirmed many of the decisive changes instituted in France since 1789. It guaranteed religious toleration, equality before the law, and equal eligibility to civil and military office; it likewise accepted the *Code Napoléon* and, still more important, the revolutionary property settlement.

The Charter, however, greatly irritated the ultra-royalist faction, drawn from the noble and clerical *émigrés,* who had returned to France after their revolutionary exile. These "Ultras," grouped around the King's brother and heir, the Count of Artois, were determined to recover both the privileges and the property they had lost during the Revolution. Louis XVIII held the Ultras at bay for five years. When the election of 1815 gave them control of the Chamber of Deputies, he dismissed the Chamber at the insistence of the allies, and held a new election, which returned a less fanatical majority. He chose moderate ministers who worked to pay off the indemnity to the victorious allies and, in general, to put French finances in good order. Events, however, soon strengthened the Ultras' hand. Anti-revolutionary fears swept France in the wake of the Spanish uprising of 1820 and of the assassination of the Duke of Berri, the King's nephew (February, 1820), stabbed by a fanatic who hoped to extinguish the Bourbon line (the widowed duchess, however, gave birth to a son seven months later). The Ultras won control of the Chamber of Deputies, clamped controls on the press, and obliged Louis XVIII to appoint a reactionary ministry, which sent French troops to aid Ferdinand VII against the Spanish revolutionaries.

The tempo of the reaction quickened when Louis died and the Ultra leader, Artois, became King Charles X (1824–1830). A charming and graceful man, Charles had little sense of political realities. He tried to revive some of the medieval glamor of monarchy by staging an elaborate coronation ceremony—and arranged a nine-month prison term for the witty poet who called it "The Consecration of Charles the Simple." He greatly extended the influence of the Church by encouraging the activities of the Jesuits, who were still legally banned from France, and by appointing clerics as principals and administrators in the state school system. The *émigrés,* in compensation for their lost property, were granted state annuities. It was widely, though not entirely correctly, believed that the reduction of the annual interest on government obligations from 5 per cent to 3 was designed to help finance the annuities. The indemnification of the *émigrés* could be defended as a sensible political move that lifted the last threat of confiscation from those who had acquired property during the Revolution. But the reduction of interest on government obligations, together with Charles' clericalism, infuriated many influential Parisian bourgeois.

The Ultras, therefore, lost ground in the elections of 1827, and Charles for a time endeavored to put up with a moderate ministry. But he wearied of the attempt and in 1829 appointed as his chief minister the Prince of Polignac, an Ultra of Ultras, who claimed to have had visions in which the Virgin Mary promised him success. Polignac hoped to bolster the waning prestige of his monarch by scoring a resounding diplomatic victory. He therefore attacked the Dey of Algiers (a largely independent vassal of the Ottoman emperor) who was notorious for his collusion with the hated Barbary Pirates and who had insulted the French consul by striking him with a fly-whisk. The capture of Algiers (June, 1830) laid the foundation of the French empire in North Africa. Meanwhile, the liberal majority in the Chamber of Deputies had attacked Polignac's ministry as unconstitutional because it did not command the approval of the legislature. In the hope of securing a more tractable chamber, Charles X held a new election in May, 1830, but the opposition won. On July 25, 1830, without securing the legislature's approval, Charles and Polignac issued ordinances muzzling the press, dissolving the newly elected Chamber, ordering a fresh election, and introducing new voting qualifications that would have disfranchised the bourgeois who were the mainstay of the opposition. The King and his chief minister believed that public opinion, mollified by the recent victory at Algiers, would accept these July Ordinances calmly. They miscalculated utterly.

Aroused by the protests of Thiers and other liberal journalists, and encouraged by the fine summer weather, the Parisians staged a riot that became a revolution. During *les trois glorieuses* (the three glorious days of July 27, 28, and 29) they threw up barricades, captured the Paris city hall, and hoisted the tricolor atop Notre Dame. When Charles X saw the revolutionary flag through a spyglass from his suburban retreat, he arranged to abdicate on behalf of his grandson, the posthumous son of the Duke of Berri, and sailed to exile in England. Contrary to an impression often held, the July Revolution was not bloodless: some 1,800 insurgents and 200 soldiers were slain.

Contrary to another widespread impression, the revolutionaries were not the poor and the downtrodden. Although there was unemployment, as a result of bank failures, and although poor harvests created high food prices, this suffering remained in the background. The revolutionary leaders of 1830 came mainly from the parliamentary opposition to Charles X, and the revolutionary crowds from the solid working class and from the lower bourgeoisie. The men of 1830 were very much like those of 1789 or 1792. Again like the men of the great revolution, they were not agreed on the kind of regime they wanted. The radicals, who rallied around that aged revolutionary symbol, Lafayette, wanted a democratic republic based on universal suffrage. The moderates wanted a safe and sane constitutional monarchy with a fairly narrow suffrage; they wanted France's 1830 to be the counterpart of England's 1688. The moderates were headed by the young Thiers, by the elderly but still astute Talleyrand, and by the banker Laffitte. They had the money, they had the brains, and they had the support not only of the parliamentary opponents of Charles X but also of veteran Napoleonic officials, who were weary of languishing in the political wasteland. And they had the perfect candidate for the throne—Louis Philippe, the Duke of Orléans.

Louis Philippe was a symbol of revolution at its most moderate. His father had participated in the Paris demonstrations of 1789, had assumed the revolutionary name of *Philippe Egalité*, and voted for the execution of Louis XVI, only to be guillotined during the Terror.

Louis Philippe himself had fought in the revolutionary army at Valmy in 1792, then had emigrated in 1793 before the worst of the Terror. He claimed to have little use for the pomp of royalty and dressed and acted like a sober and well-to-do businessman. Having deceived the gullible Lafayette into thinking he was a republican, he accepted the crown at the invitation of the Chamber that had been elected in May, 1830.

The July Monarchy, as the new regime was termed, retained many features of the Charter of 1814. It did, however, allow the legislature more initiative, delete references to royal absolutism, and call Louis Philippe not King of France but, following the precedent of 1791, King of the French. It also substituted the revolutionary tricolor for the white flag of the Bourbons. The suffrage, though doubled in size, was still highly restricted; in 1831 only 166,000 Frenchmen had the right to vote. The July Monarchy left France a long way from democracy and did little to fulfill the radical revolutionaries' concept of Liberty, Equality, and Fraternity.

Belgium

Within a month of the July uprising in Paris, a nationalistic and liberal revolution began in Belgium. The union of Belgium and the Netherlands, decreed by the peacemakers of 1815, worked well only in economics. The commerce and colonies of Holland supplied raw materials and markets for the textile, glass, and other manufactures of Belgium, at that time the most advanced industrial area of the Continent. In the very sensitive areas of language, politics, and religion, however, King William I of the Netherlands exerted arbitrary power where he might better have made tactful concessions. He made Dutch the official language throughout his realm, including the French-speaking Walloon provinces. He denied the pleas of Belgians for more equitable representation in the States-General, where the Dutch provinces, with their two million inhabitants, and the Belgian, with their three and a half million, were given the

same number of seats. He refused to grant special status to the Catholic Church in Belgium and particularly offended the faithful by insisting that the education of priests be subject to state supervision. All these grievances tended to create a Belgian nationalism and to forge common bonds between the Catholic Dutch-speaking Flemings of the provinces north of Brussels and the French-speaking Walloons of the highly industrialized southern provinces. The Flemish-Walloon partnership, however, has never been an easy one.

The revolution broke out in Brussels on August 25, 1830, at a performance of a Romantic opera which depicted a revolt in Naples. Headed by students, inspired by the example of Paris—and perhaps incited by French agents—the audience rioted against Dutch rule. By the end of September, Dutch troops had been driven out of Brussels, and Dutch rule was collapsing. The insurgents recruited their fighters chiefly from the industrial workers, many of whom complained of low pay and frequent unemployment. The better-organized middle-class liberals soon captured control of the revolutionary movement and predominated in the national Belgian congress that convened in November, 1830.

This congress proclaimed Belgium independent and made it a constitutional monarchy. The new constitution granted religious toleration, provided for wide local self-government, and put rigorous limits on the king's authority. Although it did not establish universal suffrage, the financial qualifications for voting were markedly lower in Belgium than they were in Britain or France, and the electorate was proportionately larger. The congress first chose as king the Duke of Nemours, a son of Louis Philippe. Britain protested violently, for this would have brought Belgium within the orbit of France. The congress then picked Leopold of Saxe-Coburg, a German princeling, and the widowed son-in-law of George IV of Britain. Leopold was admirably fitted for the exacting role of a constitutional monarch in a brand-new kingdom. He had already shown his political shrewdness by refusing the shaky new throne of Greece; he now demonstrated it by marrying a daughter of Louis Philippe, thus mitigating French disappointment over the aborted candidacy of the Duke of Nemours. Under his rule, the Kingdom of the Belgians became a model of laissez-faire liberal monarchy, early nineteenth-century style.

The Belgian revolution made the first permanent breach in the Vienna settlement. Although it aroused little enthusiasm among the great powers, Metternich and Tsar Nicholas were too distracted by revolutions in Italy and Poland to organize a crusade on behalf of King William. Representatives of Britain, France, Prussia, Austria, and Russia guaranteed both the independence and the neutrality of Belgium. (It was this guarantee that the German government called "a scrap of paper" when its forces invaded Belgium in 1914.) King William, stubborn as the proverbial Dutchman, tried to retake Belgium by force in 1831–1832. A French army and a British fleet successfully defended the Belgians, and negotiations finally resulted in Dutch recognition of Belgium's new status in 1839.

Poland

The course of revolution in Poland contrasted tragically with that of Belgium. In 1815, the Kingdom of Poland possessed the most liberal constitution on the Continent; twenty years later, it had become a mere colony of the Russian Empire. The constitution given to the Poles by Tsar Alexander I preserved the *Code Napoléon* and endowed the diet with limited legislative power. A hundred thousand Poles received the franchise, more than the total number of voters in the France of Louis XVIII, which had a population ten times greater. In practice, however, difficulties arose. Many of the men chosen for official posts in Poland were not acceptable to the Poles; indeed, one may doubt that any government imposed by Russia would have satisfied them. Censorship, unrest, and police intervention developed during the last years of Alexander I.

The advent of the highly conservative Nicholas I in 1825 increased political friction,

although the new tsar at first abided by the Polish constitution. Meantime, Romantic doctrines of nationalism made many converts at the Universities of Warsaw and Vilna (in Lithuania). Polish nationalists demanded the transfer from Russia to Poland of provinces that had belonged to the pre-partition Polish state—Lithuania, White Russia, and the Ukraine. Secret societies on the *Carbonari* model arose in these provinces and in the Kingdom of Poland.

A secret society of army cadets in Warsaw launched a revolution in November, 1830. The rebels soon split into the two hostile camps of "Whites" and "Reds," the former representing the highly conservative aristocrats, the latter the somewhat less conservative gentry. Neither "Whites" nor "Reds" gained the support of the peasants, whom both factions had long oppressed. The misery of the Poles increased with a terrible epidemic of cholera, the first outbreak of that Asian disease in Europe. Russian forces, at first taken off guard, had mastered the situation by 1833. Nicholas I then scrapped the constitution, imposed a regime of permanent martial law, and closed the universities of Warsaw and Vilna, the chief centers of Polish nationalist propaganda. To escape the vengeance of Nicholas, Polish intellectuals fled the country by the tens of thousands and Paris became a kind of capital for Polish exile groups.

Italy and Germany

The liberals and nationalists of Italy and Germany likewise suffered defeat in the early 1830's. In 1831, *Carbonari* insurgents in north central Italy briefly controlled the little duchies of Parma and Modena and a sizable part of the Papal States, including the city of Bologna. Among the participants was the youthful Louis Napoleon Bonaparte, nephew of Napoleon I, who was later to become Emperor Napoleon III. The revolutionaries counted on French assistance, but the July Monarchy had no intention of risking war with Austria by poaching on the Habsburg preserve. Again, as in 1821, Metternich sent troops to restore legitimacy in Italy.

Metternich did not require soldiers to preserve legitimacy in Germany; whenever a crisis arose, the Diet of the German Confederation obediently followed the Austrian lead. In Prussia, King Frederick William III (1797–1840) had never fulfilled his promise to grant a constitution, though he did set up provincial diets. Only Weimar and a few south German states enjoyed liberal constitutions, on the order of the French Charter of 1814. Political agitation came almost entirely from the small minority of intellectuals who had roused national resistance to Napoleon—journalists, Romantic writers, university professors, and students.

After 1815, German university students formed a new organization, the *Burschenschaften* ("Students' Union"). In October, 1817, students of the University of Jena held a rally on the Wartburg, where Luther had worked on his German translation of the Bible, to celebrate both the tercentenary of the Ninety-Five Theses and the fourth anniversary of the battle of Leipzig (see p. 120). During the rally the *Burschenschaften* burned a diplomat's wig, a Prussian officer's corset, and books by reactionary writers. In March, 1819, a demented theological student, apparently influenced by *Burschenschaften* ideas, assassinated one of the writers, Kotzebue, who was also a Russian agent. Metternich, already alarmed by the student prank of 1817, now got the Diet of the German Confederation to approve the Carlsbad Decrees (September, 1819), which stiffened press censorship, dissolved the *Burschenschaften*, and curtailed academic freedom.

Despite the Carlsbad Decrees, mild political ferment continued in Germany, and the *Burschenschaften* reorganized underground. In 1830 and the years following, a few rulers in northern Germany, notably in Saxony and Hanover, were forced to grant constitutions. Excited by these minor successes, twenty-five thousand revolutionary sympathizers gathered in May, 1832, to toast Lafayette and demand the union of the German states under a re-

public. Effective action for unification, however, was another matter. In 1833, the would-be republicans made a forlorn effort to seize Frankfurt, the seat of the Diet and capital of the German Confederation, and then relapsed into inactivity.

The Lessons of 1830

The revolutionary wave of the 1830's revealed two great facts of political life. First, it widened the split between the West and the East already evident in the wake of the Revolutions of 1820. Britain and France were committed to support mild liberalism both at home and in neighboring Belgium. On the other hand, Russia, Austria, and Prussia were more firmly committed than ever to the counter-revolutionary principles of the Troppau Protocol (see p. 153). In 1833, Tsar Nicholas I, Metternich, and King Frederick William III formally pledged their joint assistance to any sovereign threatened by revolution.

Second, revolution succeeded in 1830 only in France and Belgium, only where it enlisted the support of a large segment of the population. It failed in every country where the revolutionaries represented only a fraction of the people. In Poland, the peasantry viewed both "Whites" and "Reds" as oppressors. Italian revolutionaries still relied on their Romantic *Carbonari* tradition and on flimsy hopes of foreign aid. In Germany, revolution was a matter of student outbursts, toasts to Lafayette, and other gestures by a small minority. Liberal and nationalist intellectuals needed to make their doctrines penetrate to the grass roots of society; they needed to develop able political leaders and to mature well-laid plans for political reform. These were the tasks which they undertook after 1830; their success was to be tested in the most formidable and the most extensive chain of political uprising in the history of nineteenth-century Europe—the Revolutions of 1848.

VI   The Revolutions of 1848

Common Denominators

One of the common denominators of revolution in 1848 was nationalism. It prompted the disunited Germans and Italians to attempt political unification, and it inspired the subject peoples of the Habsburg Empire to seek political and cultural autonomy. The Romantic movement had stimulated a nationalistic renaissance among most peoples in central and eastern Europe. For the national minorities within the Habsburg Empire, as for the Christian nationalities within the Ottoman Empire, the new nationalism tended to be focused on language. The Czech language, for example, was on the verge of extinction in the later eighteenth century; the population of Bohemia increasingly used the German of their Austrian rulers. By 1848, however, a Czech linguistic and literary revival was in full swing. Patriotic histories of Bohemia and collections of Czech folk-poetry kindled a lively interest in the national past and fostered dreams of a Pan-Slavic awakening in which the Czechs would lead their brother Slavs.

The nationalists of 1848 were not necessarily generous or liberal. While some of them preached with Mazzini, the democratic Italian patriot, that each nation's "special mission" fulfilled the "general mission of humanity," others held less generous views. John Stuart Mill, the English liberal observer, deplored those who ignored the welfare "of any portion of the human species, save that which is called by the same name and speaks the same language as themselves."* There were many self-styled Chosen People in the revolutions of 1848.

Liberalism, the second common denominator of the revolutions, also encompassed a

*J. S. Mill, "The French Revolution and Its Assailants," *Westminster Review,* II (1849), 17.

wide range of programs. In central and eastern Europe, where much of the Old Régime survived, liberals demanded constitutions to limit absolute monarchy and to liquidate feudal rights and manorial dues. In France, where constitutional monarchy had already been achieved, many liberals sought to replace the July Monarchy with a democratic republic. French liberalism, in fact, shaded into socialism; the Paris radicals of 1848 demanded the guarantee of the right to work and other advanced measures.

Finally, in the Europe of 1848, as in the France of 1789, an economic crisis helped to catalyze discontent into revolution. A blight ruined the Irish potato crop in 1845 and soon spread to the Continent; the grain harvest of 1846 also failed in western Europe. The consequences were a sharp rise in the price of bread and bread riots; mass starvation occurred in Ireland, and widespread misery affected France, Germany, and Austria. The food crisis was compounded by an industrial depression, touched off in 1847 by the collapse of a boom in railroad construction. The number of unemployed mounted just as food prices were rising, thus intensifying popular suffering.

France

The economic crisis hit France with particular severity. Railroad construction almost ceased, throwing more than half a million laborers out of work; coal mines and iron foundries, in turn, laid men off. Unemployment increased the discontent of French workers already embittered by their low wages and by the still lower esteem in which they were held by the government of Louis Philippe. Under the July Monarchy, French agriculture experienced a golden age, while industrialization also began to develop. The government, however, appeared to be indifferent to the social misery that accompanied the new prosperity. In eighteen years, it took only two steps to improve the welfare of the industrial working class: an extension of state aid to primary schools in 1833, and a laxly enforced law in 1841 limiting child labor. There was a great deal of truth in the famous judgment passed by Alexis de Tocqueville, an acute political observer—that "Government in those days resembled an industrial company whose every operation is undertaken for the profits which the stockholders may gain thereby."

The "stockholders" of the July Monarchy were the Napoleonic veterans who emerged as prefects and diplomats after a wholesale overturn of official personnel, and the landowners,

Daumier, "The Fight of the Citizens of France against the Oppression of Louis-Philippe."

investors, and businessmen who had the right to vote and whose numbers never exceeded 200,000. They answered demands for liberalization of the suffrage with the curt reply of one of their leaders: *Enrichissez-vous!*—make yourself rich enough to meet the stiff fiscal qualifications for voting. The government banned labor organizations and repressed harshly the workmen of Paris and Lyons who

demonstrated in the early 1830's to demand a republic and higher wages. It imposed a censorship when the press caricatured the pear-shaped head and the inevitable umbrella of Louis Philippe.

Opposition to the July Monarchy, though stifled in the 1830's, revived rapidly during the 1840's, nourished in part by the fiasco of the French attempt to back the empire-building of the Egyptian governor, Mehemet Ali, whose ambitions alarmed both his Ottoman overlord and most of the great powers. The opposition in France, however, was far from united—a fact that does much to explain the hectic course of the revolution it set off. Heading one group was Adolphe Thiers, a principal architect of the July Monarchy, who was shelved by Louis Philippe in favor of Guizot, the chief minister from 1840 until 1848. Thiers continued to support the principle of constitutional monarchy, and cynics claim that the chief difference between him and Guizot was the fact that he was out of office while Guizot was in. The disappointed republicans of 1830 formed a second opposition group. The third, and smallest, group took in various socialists, who were to gain recruits from the economic depression of the late 1840's. Potentially more formidable than any of these, but as yet representing only a vague, unorganized sentiment, were the Bonapartists. The return of the Emperor's ashes from St. Helena to Paris in 1840 revived and renewed the legend of a glorious and warlike Napoleon, so different from the uninspiring Louis Philippe.

In the summer of 1847, constitutional monarchists of the Thiers faction joined with republicans to stage a series of political banquets throughout France calling for an extended suffrage and the resignation of Guizot. This campaign appeared comparatively harmless until a particularly huge banquet was announced for February 22, 1848, to be held in a radical quarter of Paris. When the Guizot ministry forbade the banquet, the Parisians substituted a large demonstration. On February 23, Louis Philippe dismissed Guizot and prepared to summon Thiers to the ministry. But his concessions came too late. Supported by workers, students, and the more radical republican leaders, the demonstration of February 22 turned into a riot on the 23rd. More than fifty of the rioters who attacked the residence of Guizot were killed or wounded. It has never been established who fired the first shots, but the casualties of February 23rd at once intensified the revolutionary atmosphere. On the next day, Louis Philippe abdicated.

Again, as in 1830, radicals and moderates competed to fill the political vacuum. In 1848, however, the radicals had a more pronounced working-class character, since their ranks had been swelled by laborers from new industries and their ideas had been influenced by the new doctrines of socialism. They demanded both a republic and the extensive social and economic reforms summed up in the formula, the right to work. The radicals, however, still lacked organization and hard-headed leadership; their spokesmen in 1848 were only slightly less gullible than Lafayette had been in 1830. The middle-class moderates were

ready to concede universal suffrage but were determined to protect the rights of property and to keep social and economic concessions to a minimum.

The moderates secured the direction of the provisional government formed on February 24. To calm the Parisian radicals, they promised to guarantee the right to work and authorized the establishment in Paris of National Workshops, apparently inspired by the socialist, Louis Blanc (1811–1882). Louis Blanc had long advocated "social workshops," which the workers themselves would own and run with the financial assistance of the state. The National Workshops of 1848, however, were simply a relief project organized along semimilitary lines, and enrolling more than 100,000 unemployed from Paris and the provinces. About 10,000 of the recruits received two francs (about 40 cents) a day for working on municipal improvements; the rest received a dole of one franc a day.

The moderates commanding the provision-

Daumier, "The Uprising, 1848," in the Phillips Memorial Gallery, Washington.

al government gained new strength as a result of the election of April, 1848—the first election in European history in which almost the entire adult male population of a country voted. Eight million Frenchmen elected members of the National Assembly that was to draw up a new constitution. The conservative peasants, who still made up the bulk of the population, approved the fall of the July Monarchy but dreaded anything resembling an attack on private property. Of the almost 900 deputies elected, therefore, only a hundred or so sympathized with the Paris radicals.

The latter, however, refused to accept the decision of the country. On May 15, a huge crowd of noisy but unarmed demonstrators invaded the meeting hall of the National Assembly and proposed the dissolution of the Assembly and the formation of a new provisional government at the Paris City Hall. The moderates, now thoroughly alarmed, arrested radical leaders and decided that the National Workshops threatened law and order because they concentrated so many economically desperate men in Paris. The Assembly therefore dissolved the Workshops and gave the recruits the alternative of enlistment in the army or accepting work in the provinces. The workers of Paris resisted. From June 23 to June 26, 1848, the radical districts of the capital rose in insurrection until they were finally subdued by the troops brought in by General Cavaignac, the energetic Minister of War.

These "June Days" were a landmark in modern history, the first large-scale outbreak with very strong overtones of open class warfare. Among the insurgents were men of the new industrial age—mechanics, railroad men, stevedores—as well as wine-sellers, masons, locksmiths, cabinet-makers, and other artisans who had been prominent in the capture of the Bastille in 1789. The possibility of a social revolution terrified and consolidated the propertied classes, and Tocqueville reported that "peasants, shopkeepers, landowners, and nobles" were all pouring into Paris by the new railroads to quell the uprising. The spirit of panic accounted for the severe repression of the insurgents: nearly 1,500 were killed during the fighting; others were subsequently deported, chiefly to Algeria. All socialist clubs and newspapers were padlocked, and Louis Blanc fled to England. France became a virtual military dictatorship under General Cavaignac.

The fears of the moderates were evident in the formal constitution of the Second French Republic which the National Assembly completed in November, 1848. The Assembly declared property inviolable and rejected a motion to list the right to work among the fundamental rights of French citizens. In other respects, however, the constitution was a daring venture in representative democracy and in combining a strong president and powerful legislature. The legislature was a single chamber, to be elected by universal male suffrage every three years. The president was to be chosen by popular election every four years. The French Constitution of November, 1848, thus reflected the influence of both Montesquieu's doctrine of the separation of powers and the example of the United States. Circumstances, however, did not favor the success of the Second French Republic. The military rule exercised by Cavaignac while the Assembly was drafting the constitution was one ominous sign. Another was the outcome of the presidential election in December, 1848. Fewer than half a million votes were polled by the three genuinely republican candidates, a million and a half were cast for General Cavaignac, and some five and a half million votes and the Presidency of the Republic went to Louis Napoleon Bonaparte, the nephew of the great Napoleon. President Bonaparte was to subvert the constitution in 1851 and then to proclaim himself Emperor Napoleon III (see Chapter 21). The French Revolution of 1848, like that of 1789, had established a republic that ended in a Napoleonic empire.

Italy

In 1849, President Bonaparte sent French troops to Rome to defend the pope against Italian radicals. By then the Italian revolutions were petering out. The Italian movement was ambitious, but weak and divided; it attempted to cast off the Austrian hegemony

Joseph Mazzini (1805–1872).

with only the slender military resources of the separate Italian states. Piedmont rejected the offer of assistance from revolutionary France in 1848 with the proud but unrealistic boast, *Italia farà da se*—Italy will do it alone.

Throughout the 1840's three schools of liberalism, none of them commanding really wide popular support, competed for leadership in Italy. The two moderate schools, while agreeing that political power in emancipated Italy should be limited to the nobility and the bourgeoisie, disagreed on the form that a united Italian nation should assume. One group of moderates, centered in the north, favored the domination of Piedmont. Among them was the eventual unifier of Italy, Count Cavour, a great admirer of British and French liberal ways, and the editor of the newspaper, *Il Risorgimento* (meaning resurgence or regeneration), which gave its name to the whole process of unification. The other moderate group called themselves "Neo-Guelfs" because, like the Guelf political faction of the Middle Ages, they hoped to engage the

pope in the task of freeing Italy from the control of a German emperor. The Neo-Guelf leader, the priest Gioberti, declared that the future depended on "the union of Rome and Turin" (the Piedmontese capital). The pope would head, and the army of Piedmont would defend, a federation of Italian states, each with its monarch and its cautiously liberal constitution.

The third group of liberals, "Young Italy," so named because only those under the age of forty were eligible for membership, asserted that Italy should be unified as a democratic republic. Its founder, Mazzini (1805–1872), hoped to create an organization more effective than the *Carbonari* but was frustrated by his own prolonged exile and by the frequent ineptitude of his lieutenants. Mazzini did, however, achieve an enduring reputation as the great democratic idealist of modern Italian politics. Here is a statement of his political credo:

We believe, therefore, in the Holy Alliance of the Peoples as being the vastest formula of association possible in our epoch;—in the *liberty* and *equality* of the peoples, without which no true association can exist;—in *nationality*, which is the *conscience* of the peoples, and which, by assigning to them their part in the work of association, . . . constitutes their mission upon earth, that is to say, their *individuality*, without which neither liberty nor equality are possible;—in the sacred *Fatherland*, cradle of nationality; altar and workshop of the individuals of which each nation is composed.[*]

A good European as well as an ardent Italian nationalist, Mazzini inspired the formation of Young Germany, Young Poland, and similar movements, all joined together in a federation called "Young Europe."

Revolution struck first (January, 1848) in Sicily and Naples, and King Ferdinand II was obliged to grant the Two Sicilies a constitution on the lines of the revised French Charter of 1814. During the next two months, King Charles Albert of Piedmont, the Grand Duke

*"Faith and the Future," in *Life and Writings of Joseph Mazzini* (London, 1905), III, 129.

Barricades in Milan, 1848.

of Tuscany, and Pope Pius IX (1846–1878) —whose mild reforms had already aroused great liberal expectations—all followed suit. Next it was the turn of Lombardy and Venetia, where Habsburg rule had been relatively mild and enlightened, but where the ideas of Young Italy had inspired a revolutionary movement. News of the Viennese revolution and the resignation of Metternich (see p. 173) touched off a successful insurrection in Milan, the capital of Lombardy (March 18–22), which produced some extraordinary barricades made of pianos, sentry boxes, and omnibuses in addition to the usual paving blocks. At the same time, Venice, the capital of Austria's other Italian province, proclaimed herself the independent Republic of St. Mark. The rapid collapse

of Habsburg rule in Lombardy-Venetia touched off a national crusade against the Austrians and brought the more moderate leaders of the Neo-Guelf cause to the fore. As Charles Albert of Piedmont assumed command of the Italian forces, Naples, Tuscany, and the Pope sent contingents. For the moment, it seemed likely that both nationalism and liberalism would win in Italy.

But only for the moment. During the spring and early summer of 1848, Piedmont annexed Lombardy and the two small North Italian duchies of Parma and Modena. The other Italian states, jealous of their particularist traditions, commenced to fear the imperialism of Piedmont more than they desired the unification of Italy. On April 29, 1848,

Pope Pius IX announced that his "equal affection" for all peoples obliged him to adopt a neutral position in the war with Austria and to recall his soldiers. The Pope could not be both an Italian patriot and an international spiritual leader. Moreover, Pius was alarmed by the increasingly radical political temper of the Roman population and by the threats of German bishops to create an anti-pope. The Neo-Guelf cause had received a fatal blow. In May, 1848, the King of Naples, who had scrapped his constitution, withdrew his contingents from the war. The Austrians, taking the offensive, reconquered Lombardy and crushed the forces of Charles Albert at Custozza (July, 1848). Italy had not been able to do it alone.

A few months later, the revolutionary movement got a brief second wind. Roman adherents of Young Italy, dissatisfied with the mildly liberal constitution of March, rose up in November, 1848. After Pius IX had fled to Neapolitan territory, they transformed the Papal States into a democratic Roman Republic, headed by Mazzini himself, who proved to be fairly authoritarian in a position of power. In March, 1849, radicals in Piedmont forced the reluctant Charles Albert to renew the war with Austria, but within the month Austria again overwhelmed Piedmont, at the battle of Novara. In August, 1849, the Austrians put an end to the Republic of St. Mark after a prolonged siege and bombardment of Venice, which suffered acutely from famine and cholera. Meanwhile, besieged by French troops, Mazzini's Roman Republic had surrendered (July, 1849).

Again subdivided into many sovereign states, again dominated by the Habsburgs, Italy returned almost completely to its prerevolutionary status. Both the Neo-Guelfs and Young Italy were discredited. The only bright spot in the picture was the emergence of Piedmont as the natural leader of Italian nationalism and liberalism. Despite the defeats at Custozza and Novara, despite the loss of the territories momentarily annexed in 1848, Piedmont enjoyed the prestige of having twice defied the hated Austrians.

Germany

The course of the German revolutions in 1848 roughly paralleled that of the Italian. In Germany, too, liberalism and nationalism won initial victories and then collapsed in the face of internal dissension and Austrian resistance. The failure in Germany was the more surprising—and ominous—since the revolutionary movement had begun to recruit support among industrial workers, among craftsmen who feared industrial competition, and among peasants who wished to abolish the relics of manorialism. Liberal and nationalist agitation, however, centered in the well-to-do business and professional classes, especially university professors, who enjoyed more influence and respect in Germany than anywhere else in Europe. Except for a few republicans and socialists, the German liberals were moderates. They wanted constitutional monarchies in the various German states, the strengthening of the German Confederation, and an end to the repressive hegemony of Metternich.

The hero of German liberals was King Frederick William IV of Prussia (1840–1861). Attractive and cultivated, but unstable and infatuated with Romantic concepts of divine-right kingship, Frederick William promised much and delivered little. He promised to carry out his father's unhonored pledge to give Prussia a constitution and an elected assembly; however, the meeting of representatives from the provincial diets he convoked at last in 1847 was a great disappointment.

Not this royal knight-errant, but the architects of the *Zollverein* (customs union) constituted Prussia's most solid contribution to German unification before 1848. In 1818, Prussia had abolished internal tariffs within its scattered territories and applied a uniform tariff schedule to imports. The first states to join the *Zollverein* wee small neighbors of Prussia. Membership proved so profitable that by 1844 almost all the German states, except for Austria, had joined. The *Zollverein* liberated Germany from an oppressive burden of local tolls and taxes and cleared the way for her phenomenal economic development later in the century. Although it did not exercise a decisive influence on politics, it suggested that the state which had fostered German economic unification might naturally take the initiative in politics.

Unification seemed almost a certainty in 1848. Stimulated by the example of Paris, the revolutionaries scored their first successes in the western German states at the end of February, 1848. From there, the demands for constitutions, civil liberties, and a strengthened German Confederation fanned out rapidly. By mid-March, demonstrators were throwing up barricades in Berlin. Frederick William IV accepted some of the liberals' demands and appealed for calm among "ye inhabitants of my true and beautiful Berlin." Before his appeal could be publicized, rioting broke out with redoubled violence, and more than two hundred rioters, chiefly workingmen, were killed. The mob broke into the royal palace and forced the King to go through a grotesque ceremony of saluting the corpses of the victims. Overwrought by the humiliation to himself and by the death of his subjects, Frederick

William accepted all the demands of liberals and nationalists. He summoned an assembly to draw up a constitution, declared Prussia "merged in Germany," and proclaimed himself "King of the free regenerated German nation."

Drastic reform of the German Confederation now began. In May, 1848, a constitutional convention held its first session in the Church of St. Paul at Frankfurt, the capital of the Confederation. Its 830 members, popularly elected throughout Germany, represented the flower of the German intelligentsia—18 doctors, 33 clergymen, 49 university professors, 57 schoolteachers, 223 lawyers and judges. While some 140 deputies were businessmen, there was only one dirt farmer, and not a single laboring man. The Frankfurt Assembly lacked a broad popular base, and, as events soon demonstrated, many of its members also lacked political experience and talent for practical statesmanship.

The Frankfurt Assembly had to decide the geographical limits of Germany. The Confederation included Austria proper but excluded most of the non-German Habsburg territories. Neither did it include the eastern provinces of Prussia, notably those acquired in the partitions of Poland. The Austrian issue divided the Assembly into two camps: the "Big Ger-

Barricades in Berlin, March, 1848.

mans" who favored the inclusion of Austria and Bohemia, with its large Czech population, in the projected German state, and the "Little Germans," who opposed it. Austrian objections to a "Big Germany" insured the Assembly's adoption of the "Little Germany" proposal.

On the question of Prussian Poland, the nationalism of the Frankfurt Assembly overcame its liberalism. By a large majority it voted to include some Prussian areas in which the Poles formed the majority of the population. The arguments advanced against the Poles in the debates revealed German nationalism at its most superheated. One orator declared that the minority of Germans had a natural right to rule the Poles, who had "less cultural content":

It is high time for us . . . to wake to a wholesome national egotism, to say the word right out for once, which in every question places the welfare and honour of the fatherland uppermost. . . . Our right is none other than the right of the stronger, the right of conquest.*

In contrast, the national constitution promulgated by the Frankfurt Assembly in March, 1849, was a decidedly liberal document, a combination of principles drawn from the American federal system and British parliamentary practice. The individual states were to surrender many of their powers to the German federal government. The federal legislature would consist of a lower house, elected by universal male suffrage, and an upper house, chosen by the governments and the legislatures of the constituent states. Ministers responsible to the legislature would form the federal executive. Over all would preside a constitutional monarch, the German emperor.

The Frankfurt constitution died a-borning. The Assembly elected the King of Prussia to be emperor, but Frederick William, ignoring his fine promises of March, 1848, and alarmed by Austrian opposition, rejected the offer. He called the Frankfurt constitution a "bastard" product:

*Quoted in J. G. Legge, *Rhyme and Revolution in Germany* (London, 1918), 397.

The crown is no crown. The crown which a Hohenzollern could accept . . . is not one created by an Assembly born of revolutionary seed. . . . It must be a crown set with the seal of the Almighty. . . .*

Since the major candidate for the imperial office had balked, the Frankfurt Assembly soon came to an end. It had never secured recognition from foreign governments, had never raised a penny in taxes, and had never exerted real sovereignty over Germany. The couplet mocking the plethora of academic deputies had been justified:

Hundert fünfzig Professoren!
Lieber Gott, wir sind verloren!
(A hundred and fifty professors!
Good God, we're sunk!)

German liberalism had suffered a major defeat. After the initial shock of the revolutions, the comfortably situated professional and business classes began to fear the radicalism of the workers and artisans. The German princes soon either revoked or abridged the constitutions that they had granted in 1848. In Prussia, Frederick William and his conservative advisers repeatedly doctored the work of the constitutional convention summoned in 1848. The end product, the Constitution of 1850, made Prussia relatively safe for autocracy and aristocracy down to World War I (see Chapter 22).

The Habsburg Domains

The fate of German and Italian nationalism in 1848 hinged partly on the outcome of the revolutions in the Habsburg Empire. If these revolutions had immobilized the Habsburg government for a long period, then Italian and German unification might have been realized. But Austria, though buffeted by wave after wave of revolution, rode out the storm. The success of the counter-revolution in the Habsburg Empire assured its victory in Italy and Germany.

*Ibid., 516–517.

The nature and the outcome of the Habsburg revolutions depended in turn on the complex structure of nationalities within the Austrian Empire:

NATIONALITIES
UNDER HABSBURG RULE, 1848

Nationality	Percentage of Total Population
German	23
Magyar (Hungarian)	14
Czech and Slovak	19
South (Yugo-) Slav	
Slovene	4
Croat	4
Serb	5
Pole	7
Ruthenian (Little Russian)	8
Rumanian	8
Italian	8

These national groups were not always neatly segregated geographically, each in its own compartment. For instance, in the Hungarian part of the Empire, the dominant Magyars fell slightly short of a numerical majority. Hungary contained important minorities of Slovaks, Rumanians, Croats, Serbs, and Germans. Moreover, while the bulk of the population was rural, the German element, chiefly bureaucrats and tradesmen, predominated in most of the towns and cities throughout the Empire, even in the Czech capital of Prague and the Magyar capital of Budapest.

Among the component peoples of the Habsburg realm in 1848 nationalism ran strongest among the Italians of Lombardy-Venetia, the Czechs of Bohemia, and the Magyars and Croats of Hungary. Language was an important issue with the Magyars as it was with Czechs, so that the replacement of Latin by Hungarian as the official tongue of the eastern part of the Empire in 1844 marked a victory for Magyar nationalism. Since Hungary was an overwhelmingly agricultural land, nationalism, like all other aspects of political life, was dominated by nobles and country squires who monopolized the seats in the county assemblies and the central diet. One group of Magyar nationalists aimed at the gradual modernization of Hungary's culture and economy along moderate English lines. The more extreme nationalists, however, whose spokesman was the spellbinding orator, Louis Kossuth (1802–1894), regarded the linguistic reform of 1844 as but the first in a series of revolutionary projects cutting all ties with the Vienna government. Magyar nationalists bitterly opposed the satisfaction of the growing national aspirations of their Slavic subjects. The most discontented were the Croats, whose national awakening had begun when their homeland became the Illyrian province of Napoleon's empire.

The antagonism between Croats and Magyars revealed an all-important fact about the nationalistic movements within the Habsburg Empire. Some groups—Italians, Magyars, Czechs, Poles—resented the German-dominated government in Vienna. Others, notably the Croats and Rumanians, were not so much anti-German as anti-Magyar. Here was a situation where the central government in Vienna might apply the policy of "divide and conquer," pitting the anti-Magyar elements against the anti-German Magyars, and subduing both. This was substantially what happened in 1848. A similar policy had already been used in 1846 to suppress a revolt in Galicia, the province that Austria had acquired in the partitions of Poland. When the Polish landlords revolted, their exploited Ruthenian peasants rose against them and received the backing of Vienna.

Liberalism also played a significant part in the Habsburg revolutions, especially in Austria proper. The expanding middle class desired civil liberties, a voice in government, and the lifting of mercantilist restrictions on business. In Vienna, as in Paris and Berlin, some workers went farther and demanded radical democratic reforms.

From 1815 to 1848, the Habsburg government virtually ignored the grumblings and protests that arose in almost every quarter of the Empire. If Prince Metternich had had his way, he would probably have made some concessions to liberal and nationalist aspirations. But Metternich, though he enjoyed a nearly free hand in foreign affairs, did not have his way in domestic policy. He was blocked by the emperors—the bureaucratic Francis I (1792–1835) and the feeble-minded Ferdinand I (1835–1848)—and by the vested interests of the aristocracy. The Habsburg government, though buttressed by an army of censors and spies, was at best an inefficient autocracy; Austria, Metternich accurately stated, was "administered, but not ruled."

The news of the February revolution in Paris shook the Empire to its foundations. Four separate revolutions broke out almost simultaneously in March, 1848—in Milan and Venice, in Hungary, in Vienna itself, and in Bohemia. In Hungary, Kossuth and his ardent Magyar supporters forced Emperor Ferdinand to accept the "March Laws," which gave Hungary political autonomy. The March Laws instituted parliamentary government and substituted an elected legislature for the feudal Hungarian diet. They abolished serfdom and ended the immunity of nobles and gentry from taxation. But they rode roughshod over the rights of non-Magyars by making use of the Hungarian language a requirement for election as a deputy to the legislature.

Aroused by the Hungarian revolt, workers and university students in Vienna rose on March 12. On the next day, Prince Metternich resigned from the post he had held for thirty-nine years and fled to Britain. Although the imperial government repeatedly promised reforms, rioting continued in Vienna, and by May the political atmosphere was so charged that Emperor Ferdinand and his family left the capital. Pending the meeting of a constituent assembly in July, in Vienna a revolutionary council ran affairs.

Meanwhile, in Prague, Czech nationalists were demanding rights similar to those granted the Magyars in the March Laws. Discontent mounted with the news that the "Big German" faction in the Frankfurt Assembly was contemplating the inclusion of Bohemia in a German federation. In June, 1848, the Czechs organized a Pan-Slav Congress to promote the solidarity of Slavic peoples against "Big German" encroachments. The Pan-Slav Congress set off demonstrations, in the course of which the wife of Prince Windischgrätz, the commander

of the Austrian garrison of Prague, was accidentally killed (June 12, 1848). Five days later, Windischgrätz, after bombarding Prague, dispersed the Czech revolutionaries and established a military régime in Bohemia. The counter-revolution was beginning.

A month later (July), the Austrian army in Italy defeated Piedmont at Custozza. In September, 1848, the Vienna Constituent Assembly, which represented all the provinces of the Empire except the Italian and Hungarian, passed a great reform measure that actually accelerated the counter-revolution. It emancipated the peasants from their last remaining servile obligations, notably the requirement to work for their landlords. The peasants, the core of the Habsburg population, had achieved their main goal; they now tended to withhold support from further revolutionary activities.

The time was ripe for the policy of "divide and conquer." In Hungary, the Germans, Slovaks, Rumanians, Serbs, and Croats, all outraged by the discrimination against them in the March Laws, had risen up against the Magyars. In September, 1848, the imperial government authorized Jellachich, the governor of Croatia, to invade central Hungary. While the hardfighting Magyars held off the forces of Jellachich, the radicals of Vienna revolted again, proclaiming their support of the Magyars and declaring Austria a democratic republic. But the armies of Jellachich and Windischgrätz crushed the Vienna revolution (October 31, 1848) and executed the radical leaders.

The counter-revolution was hitting its full stride. In November, 1848, the energetic and unscrupulous Prince Felix Schwarzenberg, the brother-in-law of Windischgrätz, became chief minister of the Habsburg government. Schwarzenberg arranged the abdication of the incapable Ferdinand I in December and the accession of Ferdinand's eighteen-year-old nephew, the Emperor Francis Joseph (1848–1916). Schwarzenberg declared that the promises made by the old emperor could not legally bind his successor and therefore shelved the projects of the Austrian Constituent Assembly. Schwarzenberg's high-handedness infuriated the Magyars, who fought on like tigers. In April, 1849, the parliament of Hungary declared the country an independent republic and named Kossuth its chief executive. Russia now offered Austria military assistance, for Tsar Nicholas I feared that the revolutionary contagion might spread to Russian Poland unless it was checked. Schwarzenberg accepted the Tsar's offer, and in August, 1849, Russian troops helped to subjugate the Hungarian republic.

The Lessons of 1848

The Tsar boasted in 1850 that Providence had assigned him "the mission of delivering Europe from constitutional governments." By 1850, almost the whole Continent was in the process of being delivered from the regimes of 1848. In France, the Second Republic faced a very uncertain future under an ambitious president and a conservative assembly, both very much concerned with preserving order against liberty. In Prussia, Frederick William IV, and in Austria and Italy, Prince Schwarzenberg, guided the triumphant course of the counter-revolution. Kossuth, Mazzini, and other revolutionaries went into exile. In the early months of 1848, enthusiastic liberals had hailed the arrival of the "peoples' springtime." It had been a false spring.

Mazzini undertook to explain why. In 1850, he wrote from London:

Why, then, has *reaction* triumphed?
Yes: the cause is in ourselves; in our want of organisation; . . . in our ceaseless distrust, in our miserable little vanities, in our absolute want of that spirit of discipline which alone can achieve great results; in the scattering and dispersing of our forces in a multitude of small centres and sects, powerful to dissolve, impotent to found.
The cause is in the gradual substitution of the worship of material interests . . . for the grand problem of education, which alone can legitimatise our efforts. . . . It is in the narrow spirit of *Nationalism* substituted for the spirit of Nationality; in the stupid presumption on the part of each people that they are capable of solving the political, social, and economical problem alone; in their forgetfulness of the great truths that the cause of the

peoples is one; that the cause of the Fatherland must lean upon Humanity. . . . The language of narrow nationalism held at Frankfort destroyed the German Revolution; as the fatal idea of aggrandisement of the House of Savoy [Piedmont] destroyed the Italian Revolution.*

The revolutionaries of 1848 had not fully learned the lessons of 1830. They relied on moral exhortation and pinned their hopes on spontaneous uprisings when they would have done better to concentrate on discipline and organization. Many of them were either too doctrinaire or too idealistic to make practical politicians. The strength of the revolutionary forces was sapped by the tensions between artisans and industrial workers, between radicals and moderates, between the followers of Mazzini and those of Gioberti, between "Big" and "Little" Germans, and between Magyars and Slavs.

"The narrow spirit of nationalism" deplored by Mazzini was to grow ever more intense after 1848. It was to haunt the Habsburg Empire for the rest of its days and eventually destory it. The failure of the liberals to unify Italy and Germany in 1848 transferred the leadership of the nationalist movements from the amateur revolutionaries to the professional politicians of Piedmont and Prussia. In the case of Italy, the transfer augured well; Piedmont, alone among the Italian states, retained the moderate constitution it had secured in 1848; in the case of Germany, the anti-liberal Bismarck was to achieve through "blood and iron" what the Frankfurt Assembly had not accomplished by peaceful means.

Equally prophetic were the first signals of class warfare, especially in the June Days in Paris. Europe was beginning to experience the challenge of the forces released by the industrial revolution, and new demands for drastic social and economic improvements were arising alongside the older demands for political liberties and constitutions. The year 1848 was not only the year of revolution but also the year when Marx and Engels published *The Communist Manifesto.*

Life and Writings of Joseph Mazzini (London, 1905), III, 76–77.

Reading Suggestions on Revolution and Counter-Revolution, 1815–1850

(Asterisk indicates paperbound edition.)

General Accounts

F. B. Artz, *Reaction & Revolution, 1814–1832* (*Torch). A painstaking survey of all aspects of Europe in the post-Napoleonic period; with very full bibliography.

The Cambridge Modern History, Vols. IX and X (Cambridge Univ. Press, 1965, 1960). Comprehensive account from 1793 to 1870; useful for reference.

A. J. May, *The Age of Metternich, 1814–1848,* rev. ed. (*Holt, Rinehart & Winston). Helpful brief introduction.

E. J. Hobsbawm, *The Age of Revolution, 1789–1848* (*Mentor). Stimulating analysis, stressing the social impact of the French Revolution and industrialism.

The Romantic Protest

J. B. Halsted, ed., *Romanticism: Problem of Definition, Explanation, Evaluation* (*Heath). Introductory exploration.

G. Brandes, *Main Currents in Nineteenth-Century Literature,* 6 vols. (Heinemann, 1901–1905). A monumental detailed study.

I. Babbitt, *Rousseau & Romanticism* (*Meridian). A hostile evaluation.

C. Brinton, *Political Ideas of the English Romanticists* (*Ann Arbor). A perceptive analysis.

G. Boas, *French Philosophies of the Romantic Period* (Johns Hopkins Univ. Press, 1934). Very helpful study.

K. Francke, *A History of German Literature as Determined by Social Forces,* 4th ed. (Holt, 1931). An older study, fully living up to the promise of the title.

A. N. Whitehead, *Science & the Modern World* (*Mentor). Includes a sympathetic and influential re-evaluation of Romanticism.

J. Bronowski and B. Mazlish, *The Western Intellectual Tradition from Leonardo to Hegel* (*Torch). Stresses the links between economics, politics, and intellectual history.

M. Raynal, *The Nineteenth Century: Goya to Gauguin* (Skira, 1951). Handsome volume.

K. Clark, *The Gothic Revival,* (*Penguin). Good on the neo-Gothic vogue in England.

H. R. Hitchcock, *Architecture: Nineteenth and Twentieth Centuries* (Pelican, 1958). Encyclopaedic study, giving full attention to both Europe and America.

A. Einstein, *Music in the Romantic Era* (Norton, 1947). Helpful and suggestive survey.

J. Barzun, *Berlioz and His Century* (*Meridian). Exhaustive study of Berlioz.

Conservatism and the Vienna Settlement

E. L. Woodward, *Three Studies in European Conservatism* (Constable, 1929). Thoughtful essays on Metternich, Guizot, and the Catholic Church.

H. F. Schwarz, ed., *Metternich, the Coachman of Europe: Statesman or Evil Genius?* (*Heath). Good introduction to the variety of opinions on the man.

P. Viereck, *Conservatism Revisited* (*Free Press). Brief and sympathetic reappraisal.

H. Nicolson, *The Congress of Vienna* (*Compass). Analyzed by an expert on diplomacy.

C. Webster, *The Congress of Vienna* (*Barnes & Noble). Excellent manual.

G. Ferrero, *The Reconstruction of Europe* (*Norton). Detailed study of Talleyrand and the Congress of Vienna.

C. Brinton, *The Lives of Talleyrand* (*Norton). Sympathetic biographical study.

The Revolutions: Studies of Particular Countries

J. Lucas-Dubreton, *The Restoration & the July Monarchy* (Putnam, 1929). Perhaps the most detailed account in English; conservative in tone.

A. Cobban, *A History of Modern France* Vol. II (*Penguin). A briefer and more up-to-date account.

F. B. Artz, *France under the Bourbon Restoration, 1814–1830* (Harvard Univ. Press, 1931). Monograph written from the liberal point of view.

T. E. B. Howarth, *Citizen-King* (Eyre & Spottiswoode, 1961). Biography of Louis Philippe.

D. C. McKay, *The National Workshops* (Harvard Univ. Press, 1933). Monograph on an often-misinterpreted facet of the Paris Revolution of 1848.

G. F. H. Berkeley, *Italy in the Making,* 3 vols. (Cambridge Univ. Press, 1932–1940). Very detailed study from 1815 through 1848.

A. J. Whyte, *The Evolution of Modern Italy* (*Norton). Sound introduction.

G. Salvemini, *Mazzini* (*Collier). Sympathetic scholarly analysis.

H. Treitschke, *History of Germany in the Nineteenth Century,* 7 vols. (McBride, Nast, 1915–1919). Colorful detailed narrative; strongly Prussian and nationalistic in sympathy.

A. J. P. Taylor, *The Course of German History* (*Capricorn). A lively essay on the period since 1815; a good antidote to Treitschke.

T. S. Hamerow, *Restoration, Revolution, Reaction* (*Princeton Univ. Press). Scholarly re-evaluation of German economics and politics, 1815–1871.

P. H. Noyes, *Organization & Revolution* (Princeton Univ. Press, 1966). Enlightening study of the disunity of the German working class in 1848.

A. J. P. Taylor, *The Habsburg Monarchy, 1809–1918,* 2nd ed. (Hamish Hamilton, 1948). Spirited brief treatment.

R. J. Rath, *The Viennese Revolution of 1848* (Univ. of Texas Press, 1957). Detailed monograph.

C. M. Woodhouse, *The Greek War of Independence* (Hutchinson). Readable short account.

A. G. Mazour, *The First Russian Revolution* (*Stanford Univ. Press). Excellent monograph on the Decembrists.

The Revolutions: Other Studies

P. Robertson, *Revolutions of 1848: A Social History* (*Torch). Stresses colorful details.

R. Postgate, *Story of a Year: 1848* (Oxford Univ. Press, 1956). A lively chronicle; well-illustrated.

G. Rudé, *The Crowd in History, 1730–1848* (*Wiley). Includes a chapter analyzing the make-up of the demonstrators in the Paris Revolution of 1848.

L. B. Namier, *1848: The Revolution of the Intellectuals* (*Anchor). An influential essay castigating some of the liberals for their illiberal attitudes.

H. Ausubel, ed., *The Making of Modern Europe,* Vol. II (Dryden, 1951). Includes several useful essays on the material covered in this chapter, notably a reappraisal of the German Revolution of 1848 by F. Meinecke.

Sources

H. E. Hugo, ed., *The Romantic Reader* (*Viking, 1957). Excellent cross-section of early nineteenth-century literature, with a very helpful introduction.

I. Silone, ed., *The Living Thoughts of Mazzini* (Longmans, Green, 1939). Good selection from the prolific writings of the democratic nationalist.

J. C. Legge, ed., *Rhyme and Revolution in Germany: A Study in German History, Life, Literature, and Character, 1813–1850* (Constable, 1918). An admirable collection, doing full justice to its title.

Note: Virtually all the landmarks in Romantic literature mentioned in the text of this chapter are available in inexpensive paperbound editions.

The Impact
of the Economic Revolutions

I The Industrial Revolution

On May 1, 1851, in London, Queen Victoria opened the "Great Exhibition of the Works of Industry of All Nations." The first of many "world's fairs," this international exposition displayed the latest mechanical marvels in a setting that was itself a marvel of engineering—the Crystal Palace, a structure of iron and glass stretching like a mammoth greenhouse for more than a third of a mile in Hyde Park. To the visitors who thronged the Crystal Palace it was evident that Britain was the workshop of the world. To succeeding generations the London exhibition marked the heyday of British leadership in the industrial revolution. Machines and factories had already begun to change the face of Britain in the late eighteenth century (see Chapter 16), and in the century since 1851 they have transformed not only Britain and other western nations but also many other countries on the globe.

By the mid-nineteenth century revolutionary changes in technology and business organization were exerting a revolutionary impact on society and politics. Industrialism bound nations closer together by stimulating international trade and by lowering the barriers of distance through improved transport and communication. Yet it heightened international tensions by fortifying nationalism with economic appetite and by inspiring a bloodless war for markets and raw materials. Businessmen demanded that governments pursue policies that would foster economic development, and they sought the political rights that would give them a voice in determining those policies. By making goods cheaper and more plentiful, industrialism raised standards of living and enabled increasing numbers of men to enjoy the decencies and comforts of existence. Yet it created problems of unemployment, low wages, and bad living and working conditions. Laborers clamored for the right to work, the right to organize, to strike, and to vote.

The rise of industry and labor inspired divergent schools of economic and social thought. The classical economists advocated laissez-faire, preaching that the state should let the economy regulate itself, and that what was good for business was bound to be good for labor, too. If a worker wanted economic security and political status, he should win them through his own efforts, by getting rich, as Guizot had advised the citizens of the July Monarchy. Another school of liberals, however, believed that state intervention in economic life might sometimes be justified to protect or assist the working class. The prospect of moderate reform and of gradual advance toward democracy offered by these liberals satisfied some workers. Others, however, hoping for swifter achievement of their goals, favored the more drastic but still peaceful changes of the type recommended by Louis Blanc and his fellow advocates of Utopian socialism. Still others accepted revolutionary socialism, the violent and inevitable class war predicted by Marx and Engels.

The industrial revolution thus brought to the fore economic and political issues that are still very much alive today. It created a new labor problem and intensified the older farm problem. It sharpened the differences between the champions of relatively free international trade and the economic nationalists who demanded protective tariffs. It divided liberals into the opponents and the defenders of the benevolent or welfare state. It created a radical wing of the working class, soon to be split between the rival schools of Utopian and Marxian socialism. It altered the course of human history even more radically than did a great political upheaval like the French Revolution of 1789. The forces that produced these momentous changes fully deserve to be recognized by history as the industrial revolution.

Preparation and Take-off

What has made some historians shy away from the term "industrial revolution" is the fact that economic change occurred both too slowly and too peacefully to be called truly revolutionary. The American economic historian, W. W. Rostow, has suggested that three stages may be discerned in a given country's emergence into the industrial age—preparation, take-off, and the final phase when the economy is self-sustaining and self-renewing and is, so to speak, in orbit. In Britain the crucial take-off stage was reached in the latter half of the eighteenth century as a result of the steam engine, the spinning jenny, and other inventions. While the take-off came relatively abruptly, it had been preceded by a preparatory stage lasting hundreds of years. This stage has been traced all the way back to the monasteries of the early Middle Ages, which, by their insistence on discipline and on the performance of specified tasks at specified times, have been likened to a model for the organization of the laboring force in a mine or mill.

The factors that prepared Europe and America for industrialism included, obviously, the capitalism of medieval and Renaissance bankers and merchants, and the colonialism and mercantilism of the sixteenth and subsequent centuries. Less obviously, they also included most of the forces that shaped the early modern world. The rise of the competitive state system, the Protestant stress on hard work, the brushing aside of tradition by the scientists of the seventeenth century and by the *philosophes* of the eighteenth—all played their part in creating a society ready for sweeping economic changes. Although the ultimate causes of the industrial revolution involved political, religious, and intellectual activities, its immediate causes were largely economic. Four interlocking developments, beginning in the eighteenth century, directly produced the industrial revolution of the nineteenth: (1) the increasing application of power-driven machinery to the processes of production; (2) the more efficient production of coal, iron, and steel; (3) the construction of railroads and other swift methods of transport and communication; and (4) the expansion of banking and credit facilities.

In the mid-nineteenth century, cotton was the king of mechanized industries. Beginning with the spinning jenny in the 1760's, the use of machinery gradually spread to many phases of cotton manufacturing. In 1793, the American Eli Whitney devised the cotton "gin," an engine that separated the fibers of the raw cotton from the seeds and enabled a single slave to do what had previously required the hand labor of fifty slaves. Meanwhile, British inventors perfected a power-driven loom for weaving cotton thread into cloth. By 1830, Britain operated more than 50,000 power looms, and cotton goods accounted for half of her exports. The British census of 1851 listed more than half a million workers employed in cotton manufacturing alone.

Advances in mechanical engineering made this rapid expansion possible. Earlier, for instance, the difficulty of securing exactly fitting parts had hampered the use of machines like Watt's steam engine. Then British engineers studied the precision techniques used by watchmakers. They devised a lathe that turned screws of almost perfect regularity, and they developed machines for sawing, boring, and turning the pulley blocks used by British vessels in the Napoleonic Wars. Eli Whitney, meantime, was undertaking important experiments at his arms factory in Connecticut. He explained that he planned to "make the same parts of different guns, as the locks, for exam-

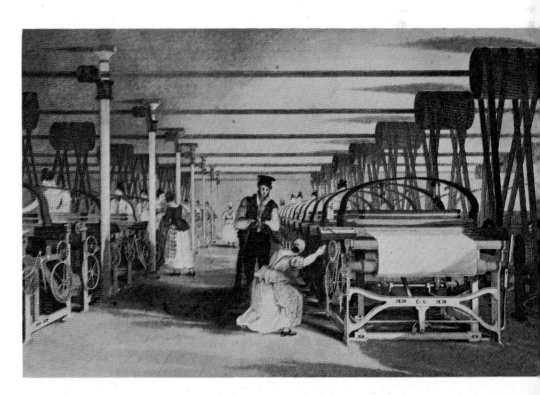

Power looms in a factory, about 1820.

ple, as much like each other as the successive impressions of a copperplate engraving." In other words, Whitney was utilizing the concept of standardized parts, one of the basic principles of mass production.

Many American and British manufacturers, however, ignored the revolutionary implications of Whitney's experiments. The tempo of mechanization, though quickening, was held back by the survival of handicraft techniques. Even in cotton, weaving on the hand loom long continued in districts with a large reservoir of cheap labor, like Ireland and Central Europe, where peasants could produce cloth in their cottages. In the woolen and clothing industries mechanization did not come until the 1850's, when Britain produced a machine for wool-combing and the American, Isaac Singer, popularized the sewing-machine.

Coal and Iron

Coal ranked with cotton as an industry that pioneered in the solution of technical problems. Steam engines pumped water from the mines; ventilating shafts and power fans supplied them with fresh air; and safety lamps gave miners protection against dangerous underground gases. The coal output of Britain, then the world's leading producer, rose steadily from about 16,000,000 tons in 1816, to 30,000,000 in 1836, and 65,000,000 in 1856. The increased consumption of coal resulted from its growing use as a household fuel in wood-short Britain, from its importance in producing steam power, and from its contribution to the expanding iron industry, which consumed large quantities of coal to make the coke needed in smelting.

The efficiency of smelting advanced rapidly after the development of the blast furnace (1828), in which fans provided a blast of hot air to intensify the action of the hot coke on the iron. Thanks to the blast furnace, Britain produced iron strong enough for use in bridges and in factory buildings. Yet the best grade of iron lacked the tremendous strength of steel, which is iron purified of all but a

minute fraction of carbon by a process of prolonged, intensive heating. Steel for industrial purposes could be made in the early 1800's, but only by ruinously expensive methods. Then in 1856 Bessemer, an Englishman of French extraction, invented the converter, which accelerated the removal of impurities by shooting jets of compressed air into the molten metal. A decade later, Siemens, a German living in England, devised the "open-hearth" process, which utilized scrap as well as new iron, and which handled larger amounts of metal than the converter could. The inventions of Bessemer and Siemens lowered the cost of making steel so substantially that the world output increased tenfold between 1865 and 1880.

Transport and Communication

The railroad consumed large amounts of iron and steel (on the average, 300 tons were required for a single mile of track). The revolution in transport began early in the nineteenth century with the growth of canals and hard-surfaced roads. During the century's first three decades many hundreds of miles of canals were dug in Europe and in North America, and highway construction was improved by the Scot, McAdam, who devised the durable road surface of broken stones that still bears his name. Shippers, however, also required a means to convey overland heavy items like coal and iron; the railroad furnished the solution. In the 1820's, methods of rolling rails and constructing solid roadbeds were already known, and only mechanization remained to be accomplished. Then George Stephenson and others put the steam engine on wheels and created the locomotive. In 1830, Stephenson's "Rocket" demonstrated its power by running twelve miles in fifty-three minutes on the new Liverpool and Manchester Railway, the first line to be operated entirely by steam. The railroad building boom was soon in full swing: Britain had 500 miles of track in 1838, 6,600 miles in 1850, and 15,500 in 1870.

Steam also revolutionized water transport,

though more gradually. Fulton's steamboat, the "Clermont," made a successful trip on the Hudson River in 1807, and soon paddle-wheel steamers plied the inland waterways of the United States and Europe. Ocean-going steamships, by contrast, long proved uneconomical to operate because of the inefficiency of the marine engine for long trips. When the Scot, Samuel Cunard, inaugurated the first regular transatlantic steamer service (between Liverpool and Boston in 1840), the coal required for the voyage took up almost half of the space on his vessels. Consequently, only passengers and mails went by steamship; most freight was still handled in sailing ships, like the beautiful and efficient American clippers. Finally, in the 1860's, the development of improved marine engines and the substitution of the screw propeller for the cumbersome paddle wheel forecast the eventual doom of the commercial sailing vessel. All these improvements in transport by sea and land greatly aided industry by facilitating shipments of raw materials and finished products and by opening up almost the whole world as a potential market.

Meanwhile, communications were also experiencing radical improvements. A beginning was made in 1840, when Great Britain inaugurated the penny post: to send a letter from London to Edinburgh, for instance, now cost only a penny, less than one-tenth of the old rate. More dramatic was the utilization of electricity for instantaneous communication. An impressive series of "firsts" started with the first telegraph message, from Baltimore to Washington in 1844. Then came the first submarine cable, under the English Channel in 1851; the first transatlantic cable, 1866; and the first telephone, 1876.

Banking and Capital

The exploitation of all these new inventions and discoveries required a constant flow of fresh capital. From the first, the older commercial community supported the young industrial community. The slave traders of Liverpool financed the cotton mills of Manchester and other nearby towns in Lancashire, thereby increasing the demand for American raw cotton and for slaves to grow the cotton. Tobacco merchants of Glasgow provided the funds that made their city the foremost industrial center of Scotland, and tea merchants in London and Bristol aided the ironmasters of South Wales. Bankers played such an important role that Disraeli, the British politician, listed the Barings of London and the international house of Rothschild among the great powers of Europe. In the early nineteenth century each of the five Rothschild brothers, sons of a German Jewish banker, established himself in an important economic center—London, Paris, Frankfurt, Naples, and Vienna. The Rothschilds prospered because, in an age of frequent speculation, they avoided unduly risky undertakings, and because they facilitated investment by residents of one state in the projects of other states. The Paris Rothschild, for instance, negotiated the investment of British capital in the construction of French railroads during the 1840's.

Banks further assisted economic expansion by promoting the use of checks and banknotes in place of specie. During the Napoleonic Wars the shortage of coins forced some British mill-owners to pay their workers in goods; the British government empowered local banks to issue paper notes supplementing the meager supply of coins. But whenever financial crises occurred—and they came frequently before 1850—dozens of local banks failed and their notes became valueless. Parliament therefore encouraged the absorption of small shaky banks by the larger and more solid institutions, and in 1844 it gave the Bank of England a virtual monopoly of the issuing of banknotes, thus providing a very reliable paper currency. It also applied, first to railroads and then to other companies, the principle of limited liability, indicated by the familiar "Ltd." after the names of British firms. Earlier, the shareholders in most British companies had unlimited liability: they might find their personal fortunes appropriated to satisfy the creditors of an unsuccessful company. The practice of limiting each shareholder's liability to the value of his shares encouraged investors by diminishing their risks.

The Timetable of Industrialization

The ready availability of capital was only one factor among many accounting for Britain's head start in industrial development. She possessed large and easily available deposits of coal and iron; the geographical compactness of the British Isles made shipments from mine to smelter and from mill to seaport short and cheap. Britain had a large reservoir of potential factory labor in the marginal farmers, driven off the land by the enclosure movement, and in the Irish, emigrating from their poverty-ridden and overcrowded island. The commercial and naval leadership gained by Britain in the eighteenth century and fortified by the Napoleonic Wars paved the way for her industrial leadership. It facilitated the search for raw materials and markets, and the profits from overseas trade

and the empire swelled investment in industry. The Napoleonic Wars themselves stimulated demand for metal goods and the invention of new machines. And the construction of great docks along the lower Thames during the wars entrenched London in its position as the greatest economic center in Europe.

Finally, it has also been argued, the fact that Britain did not have the rigid and elaborate centralized administrative structure found in France and other continental countries permitted more flexibility in accepting new enterprises. If, for example, a capitalist who wanted to set up a factory found himself blocked by vested interests in one locality, he simply went to another, where the local authorities were more agreeable. Thus it was that Manchester, which had the barest minimum of governmental apparatus in the eighteenth century, became the textile capital not only of Lancashire but also of the world.

In the mid-nineteenth century, the tangible signs of Britain's economic predominance were evident on every hand—in the teeming London docks, in the thriving financial houses of the City, in the exhibits at the Crystal Palace, in the mushrooming factory and mining towns of the Midlands, the North of England, and Scotland, and in other quarters of the globe as well. British capital and thousands of skilled British workers participated in the construction of French railroads. American trains ran on rails rolled in British mills and on the capital from British investors. Cotton goods made in Lancashire clothed a sizable part of the world's population, and British entrepreneurs and inventors brought the industrial revolution to Belgium and parts of Germany.

Britain, even in the heyday of her leadership, did not monopolize inventive skill. Frenchmen, for example, devised the chlorine process of bleaching cloth and the Jacquard loom for weaving intricate patterns. German technicians led the world in agricultural chemistry and in the utilization of the valuable by-products of coal. And from the United States came Eli Whitney and the cotton gin, Morse and the telegraph, Singer and the sewing machine, and Cyrus McCormick, whose

Industrial United States, 1860

Coal fields

Iron ore deposits

Principal manufacturing cities

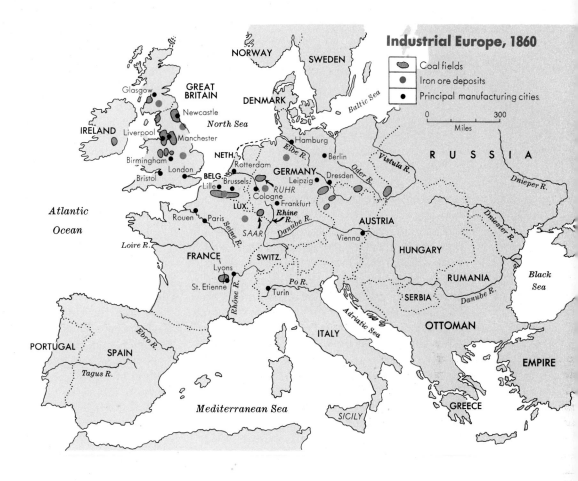

Industrial Europe, 1860

Coal fields
Iron ore deposits
Principal manufacturing cities

0   300
Miles

reaper (1831) was the first of many agricultural machines developed in America.

The timetable of industrialization depended on much besides inventions; factories required raw materials, large amounts of capital and skilled labor, and a favorable political climate. The presence of all these elements made Britain the workshop of the world in the nineteenth century. But when other countries, notably the United States and Germany, began to enjoy a favorable combination of industrial requisites, Britain lost the advantage of her head start. Although the textiles of New England had been flourishing since the early 1800's, the exploitation of rich agricultural resources dominated the American economy until the time of the Civil War. Then the United States reached the stage of industrial "take-off." Germany followed suit under the stimulus of the successful completion of political unification in 1871.

Since the turn of the century the industrial revolution has continued: Japan, Russia, and others have joined the ranks of those whose economies have "taken off." Oil and electricity have ended the dominance of coal; aluminum and the alloys have challenged that of steel; rayon and other synthetic fibers have partly displaced cotton and wool; automobiles, trucks, and airplanes have partly superseded the railroad. Industry has created great corporations, which are virtually powers in their own right; it has made possible the newspaper, television, and other media of mass communication; it has devised assembly-line methods of mass production applicable to many fields of human endeavor. The full implications of industrialization, especially since 1900, will become more evident in later chapters of this book. In this chapter, we shall stress its economic and social consequences in the nineteenth century.

II Economic and Social Consequences of Industrialization

The Agricultural Revolution

The industrial and agricultural revolutions have always been interdependent. Industry relies on a more efficient agriculture for raw materials and for additions to its labor force, recruited from surplus workers no longer needed on mechanized farms; agriculture depends on industry for the tools and short-cuts that enable fewer and fewer men to produce more and more. In the nineteenth century, factory-made implements like the steel plow and the reaper improved the cultivation of old farmlands and permitted the opening of vast new areas, like the North American prairies, that could scarcely have been touched if the pioneers had had to rely on hand labor. The mechanical cream-separator raised the dairy industry to a big business, and railroads and steamers sped the transport of produce from farm to market. The processes of canning, refrigeration, and freezing, all industrial in origin and all first applied on a wide scale during the last third of the century, permitted the preservation of many perishable commodities.

Farmers found a steadily growing market both in the industrial demand for raw materials and in the food needs of the mining and factory towns. International trade in farm products increased rapidly during the second half of the nineteenth century. The annual export of wheat from the United States and Canada rose from 22,000,000 bushels in the 1850's to 150,000,000 in 1880. Imported flour accounted for one-quarter of the bread consumed in Britain during the 1850's and for one-half in the 1870's. Denmark and the Netherlands increasingly furnished the British table with bacon, butter, eggs, and cheese; Australia supplied its mutton and Argentina its beef.

Germany now partly assumed Britain's old role as the pioneer of scientific agriculture. German experimenters, shortly after 1800, extracted sugar from beets in commercially important quantities, thus ending Europe's dependence on the cane sugar of the West Indies. In the 1840's the German chemist, Liebig, published a series of influential works on the agricultural applications of organic chemistry. Plant growth, Liebig argued, depended on three basic elements—nitrogen, potassium, and phosphorus. But the production of crops and fodder leached these elements from the soil; unless they could be returned to it, fertile lands might go the way of "the once prolific soil of Virginia, now in many parts no longer able to grow its former staple productions—wheat and tobacco." Liebig's warnings promoted the wide use of fertilizers—guano from the nesting islands of sea-birds off the west coast of South America, nitrate from Chile, and potash from European mines.

Farming progressed and prospered in the nineteenth century as never before. Yet the agricultural revolution exacted a price, sometimes a very high price. Faced with the competition of beet sugar, the sugar-cane islands of the West Indies went into a permanent depression, from which some of them have never fully recovered. In the highly industrialized countries the social and political importance of agricultural interests began to decline. Farming was no longer the principal occupation of Englishmen in the nineteenth century, and land was no longer the almost universal yardstick of wealth and power. The manufacturers and merchants of Britain scored a decisive victory over the landed gentry in the campaign to repeal the Corn Laws, the tariffs on the importation of the wheat and other cereals which the English term collectively "corn." The powerful Anti-Corn Law

League protested that the tariffs "artificially enhance the price of food," and "prevent the exchange of the products of industry for the food of other countries." Free trade was the remedy prescribed by the Anti-Corn Law League, and free trade came when Parliament repealed the Corn Laws in 1846. The decisive factor was the disastrous attack of black rot that ruined the Irish potato crop two years running and made the importation of cheap grain imperative to prevent the worsening of an already disastrous famine in Ireland, as the next chapter will show in more detail. Great Britain thus abandoned the attempt to be self-sustaining in food.

Changes in Population

As a matter of fact, the population of the British Isles was growing so rapidly that self-sufficiency was virtually impossible. Despite substantial emigration, the number of inhabitants in England and Wales more than tripled during the course of the nineteenth century, from about 9,000,000 in 1800 to 32,500,000 in 1900. Demographers tend to believe that the increase may be attributed not to an increased birth rate but to the lowered death rate resulting from the improved standard of living brought by the economic revolutions. In a predominantly agrarian country like Russia, which also experienced a steady rise in population (36,000,000 in 1800, about 100,000,000 in 1900), the experts attribute the growth also to a high birth rate.

In any event, the most important social change flowing from the industrial revolution was not the increase of the population but the alteration of its structure and balance. Wherever mines and factories were opened, towns and cities appeared. Large areas of once-rural England became urban England, and a similar transformation was beginning in the lowlands of Scotland around Glasgow, in the northern French plain around Lille, in the German Rhineland, and along the rivers of the northeastern United States. The growth of an urban population caused a rise in the numbers and influence of the two social classes that form the backbone of an industrial society. These are the businessmen and the workingmen. Industrialists, bankers, managers, and promoters of every sort joined the already established capitalists to form the modern middle class or bourgeoisie, Millhands, railwaymen, miners, clerks, and a host of other recruits swelled the ranks of wage-earning laborers.

The impact of capital and labor upon the life of industrial nations was becoming increasingly evident by the middle of the nineteenth century. Some of the signs pointed to steady material progress—the wonders of the Crystal Palace, or the conquest of space by the railroad, the steamship, and the telegraph. Other signs, however, portended serious dislocation and violent change. The repeal of the Corn Laws buried an old agrarian way of life

Conservative politicians defending the Corn Laws: The Earl of Derby says, "Now Gents, give us only a little encouragement—say a 5-shilling duty, and up goes the Quartern loaf."

"Work," by Ford Madox Brown, 1852.

in Britain. The collapse of the French railroad boom in the late 1840's suggested that in an industrial society economic slumps might have alarming consequences, for the hundreds of thousands thrown out of work aggravated the political unrest in Paris and, as we have seen, formed part of the background of the June Days of 1848.

Now it is essential for the student of history to fix his attention on both the disruptive social effects of the industrial revolution and the peaceful improvements it made possible in society. Unemployment and the other miseries of industrial labor have produced some of the most sordid pages of modern history, but they do not tell the whole story. The slums of the ugly new factory towns were often horrible indeed, yet they sometimes represented a

positive improvement over the rural slums in which the grandparents of the millhands had lived. Too often, white-washed or vine-covered country cottages concealed behind their picturesque exteriors a contaminated water supply, a total lack of sanitary facilities, and an appalling incidence of infant mortality and tuberculosis. In the cities, infant mortality dropped because of improvements in medicine and sanitation. Adults lived longer because they had better medical facilities, ate a more balanced and nourishing diet, and observed a higher standard of personal cleanliness. The economic revolutions increased the supply of fresh food and permitted the use of cheap and washable cotton clothing in place of woolens which were seldom, if ever, laundered.

The Aspirations of the Middle Class

Both the businessmen and the workingmen nourished grievances — and aspirations. A revealing view of middle-class complaints and hopes is given in a famous parable published in 1819 by the French social planner, Saint-Simon. Saint-Simon supposed that France suddenly lost fifty of her best mechanical engineers, of her finest architects, doctors, bankers — and so on through a long list comprising the three thousand leading men in business, science, and the arts. These men, Saint-Simon stated, are "the most useful to their country"; "the nation would become a lifeless corpse as soon as it lost them."

Let us pass on to another assumption. Suppose that France preserves all the men of genius that she possesses in the sciences, fine arts and professions, but has the misfortune to lose in the same day Monsieur the King's brother [and many other members of the royal family]. Suppose that France loses at the same time all the great officers of the royal household, all the ministers (with or without portfolio), all the councillors of state, all the chief magistrates, marshals, cardinals, archbishops, bishops, vicars-general, judges, and, in addition, ten thousand of the richest proprietors who live in the style of nobles.

This mischance would certainly distress the French, because they are kind-hearted, and could not see with indifference the sudden disappearance of such a large number of their compatriots. But this loss of thirty thousand individuals, considered to be the most important in the State, would only grieve them for purely sentimental reasons and would result in no political evil for the State.

These suppositions underline the most important fact of present politics: . . . that our social organization is seriously defective. . . .

The scientists, artists, and artisans, the only men whose work is of positive utility to society, and cost it practically nothing, are kept down by the princes and other rulers who are simply more or less incapable bureaucrats. Those who control honours and other national awards owe, in general, the supremacy they enjoy, to the accident of birth, to flattery, intrigue and other dubious methods. . . .

These suppositions show that society is a world which is upside down.*

To the men of the middle class, society indeed seemed upside down. In the Britain of the 1820's the new industrialists had small opportunity to mold national policy. Booming industrial cities like Manchester and Birmingham sent not a single representative to the House of Commons. A high proportion of businessmen belonged not to the Church of England but to non-Anglican Protestant chapels; nonconformists, as these dissenters were now termed, still suffered discrimination when it came to holding public office or sending their sons to Oxford or Cambridge. Even in France, despite the gains made since 1789, the bourgeois enjoyed as yet only the second-class status sketched by Saint-Simon.

The middle classes very soon won the place in the sun which they felt they deserved. In Britain, the gradual process of reform gave them substantially all they wanted. The high spot, higher even than the repeal of the Corn Laws, was the Reform Bill of 1832, which extended the suffrage to the middle class (for details, see Chapter 21). In France, as we have already seen, the bourgeois had their revolution in 1830 and got their citizen-king. In Belgium, the revolution of 1830 marked a very great advance in the power of the middle class. Elsewhere the movements of 1830 and 1848 had less favorable results, yet even at their most disappointing they represented a step forward in the political evolution of the middle class.

The Grievances
of the Working Class

The grievances of workingmen were more numerous than those of their masters, and they were more difficult to satisfy. The difficulties may be illustrated by the long struggle of laborers to secure the vote and the right to organize and to carry on union activities. In Britain, substantial numbers of workers first

*Saint-Simon, *Selected Writings,* F.M.H. Markham, ed. (New York, 1952), 72 – 74.

secured the vote in 1867, a generation after the enfranchisement of the wealthier middle class. In France, universal male suffrage was tried for a brief period starting in 1848; it became permanent only with the establishment of the Third Republic after 1870. The unified German Empire had a democratic suffrage from its inception in 1871, but without some other institutions of democracy. Elsewhere, universal manhood suffrage came slowly — in Belgium (1893), and not until the twentieth century in Italy, Austria, Russia and, more surprisingly in the light of their subsequent reputation for progressive democracy, in Sweden, Denmark, and the Netherlands as well.

During most of the nineteenth century, labor unions and strikes were regarded as improper restraints on the free operation of natural economic laws. Hence the specific ban on such combinations, as they were termed, imposed by the British Combination Acts at the close of the eighteenth century. Continental governments imposed similar restrictions, as in the Le Chapelier Law passed by the French National Assembly in 1791. It took labor a long time to win legal recognition of union activities — until 1890 in Germany, for instance, 1867 in Austria, and 1872 in the Netherlands. In France, the July Monarchy repressed strikes with great brutality; the Le Chapelier Law was relaxed in the 1860's and finally repealed outright in 1884. In Britain, Parliament modified the Combination Acts early, in the 1820's but did not repeal them until 1876.

Labor's drive for political and legal rights, however, was only a side issue during the early days of the industrial revolution. Many workmen faced more pressing problems: they had to find jobs and to make ends meet on inadequate wages. The modern western world had long experienced the business cycle, with its alternations of full employment and substantial unemployment. The industrial revolution intensified the cycle. Boom periods became more hectic, and general depressions, like that of the late 1840's, became more frequent and more severe. Factories at first made little attempt to provide a fairly steady level of employment in both boom times and slack times. When a batch of orders came in, machines and men were worked to capacity until the orders were filled. Then the factory simply shut down to await the next batch.

A century and more ago labor sometimes got such low wages that a family man might have to put both his children and his wife to work as a matter of sheer economic necessity. Humanitarian tradition probably exaggerates the extent to which industry exploited and degraded women and children, probably tends to view the exceptional instance of extreme hardship as the average situation. Nevertheless, exploitation and degradation did occur. Here is the testimony of a factory worker, Samuel Coulson, before a British parliamentary committee in 1831–1832:

At what time in the morning, in the brisk time, did those girls go to the mills?
In the brisk time, for about six weeks, they have gone at 3 o'clock in the morning, and ended at 10, or nearly half-past, at night.

What intervals were allowed for rest or refreshment during those nineteen hours of labour?
Breakfast a quarter of an hour, and dinner half an hour, and drinking a quarter of an hour.

Was any of that time taken up in cleaning the machinery?
They generally had to do what they call dry down; sometimes this took the whole of the time at breakfast or drinking, and they were to get their dinner or breakfast as they could; if not, it was brought home.

Had you not great difficulty in awakening your children to this excessive labour?
Yes, in the early time we had them to take up asleep and shake them when we got them on the floor to dress them, before we could get them off to their work; but not so in the common hours.

What was the length of time they could be in bed during those long hours?
It was near 11 o'clock before we could get them into bed after getting a little victuals, and then at morning my mistress used to stop up all night, for fear that we could not get them ready for the time. . . .

So that they had not above four hours' sleep at this time?
No, they had not.

For how long together was it?
About six weeks it held; it was only done when the throng was very much on; it was not often that.

The common hours of labour were from 6 in the morning till half-past eight at night?
Yes.

With the same intervals for food?
Yes, just the same.

Were the children excessively fatigued by this labour?
Many times; we have cried often when we have given them the little victualling we had to give them; we had to shake them, and they have fallen to sleep with the victuals in their mouths many a time.

Did this excessive term of labour occasion much cruelty also?
Yes, with being so very much fatigued the strap was very frequently used.

. . .

What was the wages in the short hours?
Three shillings a week each.

When they wrought those very long hours what did they get?
Three shillings and sevenpence halfpenny.

For all that additional labour they had only sevenpence halfpenny a week additional?
No more.*

Excessively long hours, low pay, rigorous discipline, and subhuman working conditions were the most general grievances of early industrial workers. Many plants neglected hazards to their employees, few had safety devices to guard dangerous machinery, and cotton mills maintained both the heat and the humidity at an uncomfortable level because threads broke less often in a hot, damp atmosphere. Many workers could not afford decent housing, and if they could afford it, they could not always find it. Some of the new factory towns were reasonably well planned, with wide streets and space for yards and parks. Some even had a copious supply of good water and arrangements for disposing of sewage. But many had none of these necessities, and in rapidly growing London the Thames soon became an open sewer so foul that riverside

*Bland, Brown, and Tawney, *English Economic History: Select Documents* (London, 1915), 510–513.

Child laborers in a textile factory, about 1840.

dwellers were reluctant to open their windows. Fantastic numbers of human beings were jammed into the over-crowded slums of Lille in France and of Liverpool and Manchester in Lancashire.

Lord Shaftesbury, an English reformer of the 1840's, predicted that, unless conditions were improved, Lancashire would soon become a "province of pigmies." It was estimated that the life expectancy of a boy born to a working-class family in Manchester was only half that of one born to rural laborers. The industrial nations also threatened to remain nations of semi-literates. Until they made provisions for free public schools, during the

last third of the nineteenth century, educational facilities were grossly inadequate. In England, as often as not, only the Sunday school gave the millhand's child a chance to learn his abc's. The millhand himself, if he had great ambition and fortitude, might attend one of the adult schools known as "mechanics' institutes." No wonder that in the 1840's one-third of the men and one-half of the woman married in England could not sign their names on the marriage register and simply made their mark. And no wonder that Disraeli, the Tory reformer, in his novel, *Sybil,* called Britain "two nations"—the rich and the poor.

III   The Responses of Liberalism

The Classical Economists

Faced with the widening cleavage between rich and poor, nineteenth-century liberals at first held to the doctrine of laissez-faire.

> Suffering and evil are nature's admonitions; they cannot be got rid of; and the impatient attempts of benevolence to banish them from the world by legislation . . . have always been productive of more evil than good.*

Such was the argument advanced by liberals in the British Parliament against the first piece of legislation proposed to safeguard public health. The thinkers who advanced these ideas in the early nineteenth century are known to history as the classical economists; to their enemies they were the architects of the "dismal science." The most famous of them were two Englishmen, Thomas Malthus (1766–1834) and David Ricardo (1772–1823).

"Dismal science" is hardly too strong a term for the theories of Malthus. Though educated for the ministry, Malthus became perhaps the very first professional economist in

*The Economist, May 13, 1848.

history. In 1798, he published the famous *Essay on the Principles of Population,* a dramatic warning that the human species would breed itself into starvation. In the *Essay,* Malthus formulated a series of natural laws:

> The power of population is indefinitely greater than the power in earth to produce subsistence for man.
>
> Population, when unchecked, increases in a geometrical ratio. Subsistence only increases in an arithmetical ratio. . . . Through the animal and vegetable kingdoms, nature has scattered the seeds of life abroad with the most profuse and liberal hands. She has been comparatively sparing in the room and the nourishment necessary to rear them. . . . Necessity, that imperious, all-pervading law of nature, restrains them within the prescribed bounds. Among plants and animals its effects are waste of seed, sickness, and premature death. Among mankind, misery and vice.*

Misery and vice would spread, Malthus believed, because the unchecked increase in human numbers would lower the demand for labor and therefore lower the wages of labor.

> When the wages of labour are hardly sufficient to maintain two children, a man marries and has

*Essay on the Principles of Population, Bk. I, Ch. 1.

five or six. He of course finds himself miserably distressed. He accuses the insufficiency of the price of labour to maintain a family. . . . He accuses the partial and unjust institutions of society, which have awarded him an inadequate share of the produce of the earth. He accuses perhaps the dispensations of Providence, which have assigned to him a place in society so beset with unavoidable distress and dependence. In searching for objects of accusation, he never adverts to the quarter from which his misfortunes originate. The last person that he would think of accusing is himself, on whom in fact the whole of the blame lies. . . .*

The reduction of the human birth rate was the only hope that this prophet of gloom held out to suffering humanity. It was to be achieved by "moral restraint," specifically by late marriage and by "chastity till that period arrives."

Ricardo, too, was a prophet of gloom. He attributed economic activity to three main forces: there was rent, paid to the owners of great natural resources like farmland and mines; there was profit, accruing to the enterprising individuals who exploited these resources; and there were wages, paid to the workers who performed the actual labor of exploitation. Of the three, rent was in the long run the most important. Farms and mines would become depleted and exhausted, but their produce would continue in great demand. Rent, accordingly, would consume an ever larger share of the "economic pie," leaving smaller and smaller portions for profit-making capitalists and wage-earning workers.

Ricardo tempered his pessimistic forecasts with many qualifications and reservations. He did not, for instance, believe that the size of the economic pie was altogether fixed, in other words, that the total wealth of mankind was irrevocably "frozen." Still, he did sketch a picture of eventual stagnation, and of man as the exploiter, the depleter, the wastrel. Adam Smith had cheerfully predicted an increasing division of labor, accompanied by steadily rising wages. Ricardo, in contrast, brought labor and wages under the Malthusian formula:

The market price of labour is the price which is

*Ibid., Bk. IV, Ch. 3.

really paid for it, from the natural operation of the proportion of the supply to the demand; labour is dear when it is scarce, and cheap when it is plentiful. . . . It is when the market price of labour exceeds its natural price, that the condition of the labourer is flourishing and happy. . . . When, however, by the encouragement which high wages give to the increase of population, the number of labourers is increased, wages again fall to their natural price, and indeed . . . sometimes fall below it.*

Ricardo's disciples hardened this principle into the "Iron Law of Wages," which bound workmen to an everlasting cycle of high wages and large families, followed by an increase in the labor supply, a corresponding increase in the competition for jobs, and an inevitable slump in wages. Ricardo himself, however, regarded the cycle not as an "iron law" but simply as a probability. Unforeseen factors might in the future modify its course and might even permit a gradual improvement of the worker's lot.

While it is easy to see why Malthus and Ricardo were regarded as great exponents of laissez-faire, it is more difficult to understand why they were also ranked among liberals. Yet the classical economists were indeed liberals in a sense; like the *philosophes,* they did not doubt that natural laws were superior to man-made laws. What distinguished the classical economists from their eighteenth-century predecessors was their pessimism. Adherents of the "dismal science" no longer viewed nature as the creation of the beneficent God of the deists; she was at best a neutral force and at worst a sinister one. Man himself—wasteful, careless, improvident—seemed once more afflicted with a kind of original sin. The classical economists supplied a needed corrective to the naive optimism of the *philosophes.*

Yet the classical economists, too, had their naive faith. They viewed the economy as a world-machine governed by a few simple, almost unalterable laws—Malthusian laws of population, Ricardian laws of rent and wages. The history of the last century has demon-

*On the Principles of Political Economy, Ch. V, in The Works and Correspondence of David Ricardo, P. Sraffa, ed. (Cambridge, England, 1951), I, 94.

strated the inadequacy of their view. The size of the economic pie has expanded far beyond the expectations of Ricardo, and so have the portions allotted to rent, to profit, and to wages. Malthus did not foresee that scientific advances would make the output of agriculture expand at a nearly geometrical ratio. He did not foresee that the perils of increasing birthrates would sometimes be averted by the use of contraceptives, first popularized during the nineteenth century, or by recourse to emigration. Many millions of people moved from crowded Europe to lightly populated America during the nineteenth century. The exodus from overcrowded Ireland, in particular, continued so briskly after the famine of the 1840's that by 1900 the Irish population was little more than half what it had been fifty years earlier.

Although the classical economists did not take sufficient account of the immense changes being worked by the agricultural and industrial revolutions, the laissez-faire liberalism that they championed won particular approval from the new industrial magnates. The captains of industry were perhaps disturbed by Ricardo's prediction that profits would inevitably shrink; but they could take comfort from the theory that "suffering and evil" were "nature's admonitions." It was consoling to the rich to be told, in effect, that the poor deserved to be poor because they had indulged their appetites to excess, that whatever was, was right, or at any rate ordained by nature. To the working class, however, the vaunted freedom of laissez-faire often meant freedom to be undernourished, ill-housed, and alternately overworked and unemployed. The poor did not like to hear that they deserved to be poor, and they sometimes felt that whatever was, was wrong and needed to be remedied, if necessary by interference with supposedly sacred natural laws.

To sum up: in the face of positive social evils, the classical economists offered only the essentially negative policy of laissez-faire. They were often very earnest men, honestly convinced that letting nature take her course was the only thing to do. Yet they were open to the accusation of acting without heart and without conscience, and of advancing economic theories that were only rationalizations of their economic interests. It is not surprising that, as a practical and social political philosophy, strict laissez-faire liberalism today is almost extinct.

Utilitarianism: Bentham

The retreat from laissez-faire originated with a man who was himself the friend and patron of the classical economists—Jeremy Bentham (1748–1832). Bentham behaved as popular opinion expects an eccentric philosopher to behave, astonishing his guests by trotting and bobbing about the garden before dinner, or, as he put it, performing his "anteprandial circumgyrations." In death, he directed that his body be mummified and kept at the University College of London, which he had helped to found. In life, he projected dozens of schemes for the improvement of the human race, among them a model prison and reformatory which he called the "Panopticon," because guards stationed in a central block could survey the activities of all the inmates. He coined new words by the dozen, too; some of them have been happily forgotten but others have made valuable contributions to the language, like "minimize," "codify," and "international." Bentham founded his social teachings on the concept of utility, a modern form of the old Epicurean doctrine that morality should be based on the search for pleasure and the avoidance of pain:

Nature has placed mankind under the governance of two sovereign masters, *pain* and *pleasure*. It is for them alone to point out what we ought to do. . . . They govern us in all we can do, in all we say, in all we think: every effort we can make to throw off our subjection, will serve but to demonstrate and confirm it. In words a man may pretend to abjure their empire: but in reality he will remain subject to it all the while. The *principle of utility* recognizes this subjection, and assumes it for the foundation of that system, the object of which is to rear the fabric of felicity by the hands of reason and of law.

.   .   .

The interest of the community is one of the most general expressions that can occur in the phraseology of morals: no wonder that the meaning of it is often lost. . . . The community is a fictitious *body*, composed of the individual persons who are considered as constituting as it were its *members*. The interest of the community then is, what?—the sum of the interests of the several members who compose it.

It is in vain to talk of the interest of the community without understanding what is the interest of the individual. A thing is said to promote the interest, or to be *for* the interest of an individual, when it tends to add to the sum total of his pleasures: or, what comes to the same thing, to diminish the sum total of his pains.*

Bentham listed a dozen or so simple pleasures and pains—the pleasures of the senses and the corresponding pains, the pleasure of wealth and the pain of privation, the pleasure of skill and the pain of awkwardness, and so on. Each category was subdivided, the pleasures of the senses, for instance, into those of taste, intoxication, smelling, touch, hearing, seeing, sex, health, and novelty. And each pleasure or pain could be evaluated according to its intensity, its duration, its certainty or uncertainty, its propinquity or remoteness, its fecundity, and its purity. This "felicific calculus," as Bentham termed it, was a good example of the Enlightenment's attempts to measure the immeasurable and to apply the exact methods of natural science to the subtleties of human behavior.

Nevertheless, Bentham was no doctrinaire *philosophe* and had no patience with attempts to equate principles with nature's laws. He made short work of the French revolutionaries' Declaration of the Rights of Man: *"Natural rights* is simple nonsense: natural and imprescriptible rights, rhetorical nonsense, —nonsense upon stilts." He dismissed the eighteenth-century theory of political con-

An Introduction to the Principles of Morals and Legislation, Wilfrid Harrison, ed. (New York, 1948), Ch. I, 125–127.

tracts as a mere fiction. Ordinarily, he believed, governments could best safeguard the security of their subjects by following a hands-off policy. In social and economic matters, they should act as "passive policemen," and give private initiative a generally free hand. Hence the close and sympathetic relationship between Bentham and the classical economists. Yet Bentham realized that the state might become a more active policeman when the pursuit of self-interest by some individuals worked against the best interest of other individuals. If the pains endured by the many exceeded the pleasures enjoyed by the few, then the state should step in. In such a situation Bentham believed the state to be, in a word of his own devising, "omnicompetent," fit to undertake anything for the general welfare. Twentieth-century theories of the welfare state owe a considerable debt to his utilitarianism.

By the time of his death, Bentham was already gaining an international reputation. He had advised reformers in Portugal, Russia, Greece, and Egypt, and his writings were to exert a broad influence, particularly in France, Spain, and the Spanish-American republics. As late as 1920, his "Panopticon" provided the plan for an American prison (in Joliet, Illinois). Naturally, his most important disciples were English. The middle-class group called the Philosophic Radicals pressed for parliamentary legislation to reform and simplify court procedures and local government. Their aims, however, were sometimes so narrowly utilitarian that critics claimed they wanted to drain life of all its savor and variety. Dickens lambasted them and the laissez-faire liberals to boot in his novel, *Hard Times*, with its famous description of Coketown:

. . . .It contained several large streets all very like one another, and many small streets still more like one another, inhabited by people equally like one another, who all went in and out at the same hours, with the same sound upon the same pavements, to do the same work, and to whom every day was the same as yesterday and to-morrow, and every year the counterpart of the last and the next.

You saw nothing in Coketown but what was

severely workful. If the members of a religious persuasion built a chapel there—as the members of eighteen religious persuasions had done—they made it a pious warehouse of red brick. . . . All the public inscriptions in the town were painted alike, in severe characters of black and white. The jail might have been the infirmary, the infirmary might have been the jail, the town-hall might have been either, or both, or anything else, for anything that appeared to the contrary in the graces of their construction. Fact, fact, fact everywhere in the material aspect of the town; fact, fact, fact everywhere in the immaterial. The M'Choakumchild school was all fact, and the relations between master and man were all fact, and everything was fact between the lying-in hospital and the cemetery, and what you couldn't state in figures, or show to be purchaseable in the cheapest market and saleable in the dearest, was not, and never should be, world without end, Amen.*

Democratic Liberalism: Mill

The man who injected a new note of democracy and humanity into nineteenth-century liberal teachings was John Stuart Mill (1806–1873). Mill grew up in an atmosphere dense with the teachings of utilitarianism and classical economics. From his father, who worked closely with Bentham and was a good friend of Ricardo, he received an education almost without parallel for intensity and speed. He began the study of Greek at three, was writing history at twelve, and at sixteen organized an active "Utilitarian Society." At the age of twenty the overworked youth suffered a breakdown; as Mill relates in his *Autobiography,* he had become "a mere reasoning machine." So Mill turned for renewal to music and to the poetry of Wordsworth and Coleridge; presently he fell in love with Mrs. Taylor, a woman of warm personality, to whom he assigned the major credit for his later writings. They remained friends for twenty years until the death of Mr. Taylor at length enabled them to marry. Mill's personal history is important, for it goes far to explain why he endowed the liberal creed with the warmth

*Book I, Ch. V.

and compassion it lacked in the hands of the classical economists and utilitarians.

Mill's humane liberalism was expressed most clearly in his essay *On Liberty* (1859) and his *Autobiography* (1873). But it is evident, too, in his more technical works, notably *The Principles of Political Economy.* He first published this enormously successful textbook in 1848 and later revised it several times, each revision departing more and more from the "dismal science" of Ricardo and Malthus. The first edition of the *Principles* rejected the gloomy implications of the "iron law" of wages:

By what means, then, is poverty to be contended against? How is the evil of low wages to be remedied? If the expedients usually recommended for the purpose are not adapted to it, can no others be thought of? Is the problem incapable of solution? Can political economy do nothing, but only object to everything, and demonstrate that nothing can be done?*

*J. S. Mill, *Principles of Political Economy,* Bk. II, Ch. xiii (Boston, 1848).

John Stuart Mill (1806–1873).

Of course something could be done, and Mill proceeded to outline schemes for curbing overpopulation by promoting emigration to the colonies and by "elevating the habits of the labouring people through education."

This one example is typical of the way in which Mill's quest for positive remedies led him to modify the laissez-faire attitude so long associated with liberalism. Although he did not accept the socialistic solution of abolishing private property, he sympathized with the French "National Workshops" of 1848 (see Chapter 19) and with some of the moderate socialistic projects that we shall examine shortly. He asserted that the workers should be allowed to organize trade unions, form co-operatives, obtain higher wages, and even receive a share of profits. These changes could best be secured within the framework of private enterprise, Mill believed, and not by public intervention. But he also believed that there were some matters so pressing that the state would have to step in. He read the reports of parliamentary investigating committees, like that on child labor cited earlier in this chapter, and he was shocked by their accounts of human degradation. So he recommended legislation to protect children and to improve intolerable living and working conditions.

Whereas Bentham had accepted universal suffrage and universal education only as ultimate goals for the distant future, Mill made them immediate objectives. All men, he believed, should have the right to vote; all should be prepared for it by receiving a basic minimum of schooling, if need be at state expense. Moreover, women should have the same rights—for Mill was a pioneer in the movement for feminine emancipation, thanks in part to the influence of Mrs. Taylor. He also proposed the introduction of proportional representation in the House of Commons, so that political minorities might be sure of a voice and might not be overwhelmed by the tyranny of the majority. The proposal and the fears that actuated it are particularly characteristic of Mill. He made protection of the individual's rights the basis of his famous essay *On Liberty:*

A government cannot have too much of the kind of activity which does not impede, but aids and stimulates, individual exertion and development. The mischief begins when, instead of calling forth the activity and powers of individuals and bodies, it substitutes its own activity for theirs; when, instead of informing, advising, and, upon occasion, denouncing, it makes them work in fetters, or bids them stand aside and does their work instead of them. The worth of a State, in the long run, is the worth of the individuals composing it . . . a State which dwarfs its men, in order that they may be more docile instruments in its hands even for beneficial purposes—will find that with small men no great thing can really be accomplished. . . .*

Critics have claimed that Mill's eloquent defense of the dissenting individual had undemocratic implications, for he seemed to mistrust the opinions of the majority to favor those of the intellectual and moral élite. At any rate, Mill did not so much reject as transform the liberalism of the classical economists. He had a more tender conscience than Adam Smith, Ricardo or Bentham, and he lived at a later age, when the defects of industrialism were plainer. Therefore he found the exceptions to the rule of laissez-faire more numerous and urgent than his predecessors had ever imagined them to be. Liberalism, as we understand the term today, is the legacy not of the "dismal scientists" but of Mill and of the enlightened politicians who have shaped the western democracies over the past century.

Utilitarianism, Liberty, and Representative Government, Everyman ed. (New York, 1910), 169 f.

IV   The Socialist Response — the Utopians

In his later years, Mill referred to himself as a "socialist"; by his standard, however, most of us are socialists today. Universal suffrage for men and for women, universal free education, the curbing of laissez-faire in the interests of the general welfare, the use of the taxing power to limit the accumulation of masses of private property — all these major reforms foreseen by Mill are now widely accepted. But they are not authentically socialistic. The authentic socialist does not stop, as Mill did, with changes in the *distribution* of wealth; he goes on to propose a radical change in arrangements for the *production* of goods. The means of production are to be transferred from the control of individuals to the control of the community as a whole.

Socialism — like fascism, liberalism, democracy — is one of those words in the political vocabulary so laden with moral connotations and personal conviction that their real meaning is often obscured. Everyone uses the word, yet mostly to indicate emphatic approval or disapproval of a given policy. The historian, however, attempts to use the word neutrally, for purposes of description and not of passing judgment. Historically, socialism denotes any political or economic philosophy that advocates the vesting of production in the hands of society and not those of private individuals. In practice, it usually means that the state, acting as the trustee of the community, owns major industries like coal, railroads, and steel. Socialism in its most complete form involves public ownership of almost all the instruments of production including the land itself.

Today we tend to call this complete form "communism"; a century ago, however, the terms "socialism" and "communism" were used almost interchangeably. A hundred years of history have gone into making the distinction now usually drawn between the two, which is not simply a matter of more and less complete versions of the same thing. Especially since the Bolshevik Revolution in Russia in 1917, a communist has come to mean someone who believes that the collectivization of property can only be accomplished swiftly and violently, by revolution and outright seizure, while a socialist has come to mean someone who believes that it should be accomplished gradually and peacefully through normal political procedures and with at least some compensation for private owners. Though the ends have their similarities, the means are worlds apart. This highly significant difference started to appear long before 1917, with the development of two divergent schools of socialist thought in the mid-nineteenth century, the Utopian and the Marxian.

The Utopian socialists were essentially good sons of the Enlightenment. If only men would apply their reason to solving the problems of an industrial economy, if only they would wipe out man-made inequalities by letting the great natural law of brotherhood operate freely — then utopia would be within their grasp, and social and economic progress would come about almost automatically. This is the common belief linking together the four chief Utopians of the early nineteenth century — Saint-Simon, Fourier, Robert Owen, and Louis Blanc.

Saint-Simon and Fourier

Henri, Count of Saint-Simon (1760–1825), belonged to a French noble family so old and aristocratic that it claimed direct descent from Charlemagne. Educated by *philosophes,* Saint-Simon fought with the French army in the American War of Independence. During the

French Revolution he won a large fortune by speculating in lands expropriated from the Church and the *émigrés*, then lost most of it through the trickery of an unscrupulous partner. Despite his own reverses, he never lost his enthusiasm for the industrial age, which reached a high pitch in the parable of the old and the new leaders of France, already quoted above, p. 187.

In accord with the parable, Saint-Simon would have given supreme political authority to a Parliament of Improvements, composed of 10 industrialists and 5 each of artists, philosophers, chemists, physiologists, physicists, astronomers, and mathematicians, and presided over by one of the mathematicians. He admonished the members of the new elite: "Christianity commands you to use all your powers to increase as rapidly as possible the social welfare of the poor!"* Saint-Simon combined the Enlightenment's respect for science with Romanticism's zeal for the community. So he proclaimed the one science transcending all others to be the application of the Golden Rule. Reform should come peacefully, through "persuasion and demonstration," and it should affect particularly the idlers, the rich drones of existing society. Since all men were brothers, even men of different nations, Saint-Simon envisaged a federation of European states. It would start with a union of the most advanced countries, France and Britain, under the "Council of Newton," and would culminate in the establishment of a European parliament when all states had been "organized" to the point where they could live together in "harmony."

"Organization," "harmony," and "industry" were three of Saint-Simon's catchwords. When all three elements were co-ordinated, he believed, mankind could achieve some of the major improvements he proposed, among them great networks of highways and waterways, including inter-oceanic canals. After Saint-Simon's death, his followers focused on the strain of social Christianity in his teaching and formed a fantastic religious cult. Later followers shared his enthusiasm for public improvements. One of them combined local lines into a great trunk railroad, the Paris-Lyons-Mediterranean; another was Ferdinand de Lesseps, who built the Suez Canal and made an abortive start at digging across the Isthmus of Panama. The very vagueness of Saint-Simon's concepts, and his failure to define them precisely, permitted almost every kind of social thinker, from laissez-faire liberal to communist, to cite him with approval. What was socialistic about Saint-Simon was his goal of achieving the reorganization and harmony of society as a whole, rather than the welfare of its individual members.

Saint-Simon's compatriot and contemporary, Fourier (1772–1837), also extolled harmony, and to achieve it drew up an elaborate blueprint. At the French textile center of Lyons, Fourier was shocked by the wealth of the silk manufacturers and the misery of their workmen. At Paris, he was shocked when he found that a single apple cost a sum that would have bought a hundred apples in the countryside. Clearly, he concluded, something was amiss in a society and economy that permitted such fantastic divergences. He compared the historical importance of his apple with that of Newton, and honestly believed himself to be the Newton of the social sciences. Just as Newton had found the force holding the heavenly bodies in a state of mutual attraction, so Fourier claimed discovery of the force holding the individuals of human society in a state of mutual attraction.

This force was *l'attraction passionnelle:* human beings are drawn to one another by their passions. Fourier drew up a list of passions, rather like the list of pleasures in Bentham's "felicific calculus"—sex, companionship, food, luxury, variety, and so on, to a total of 810. Since existing society thwarted their satisfaction, Fourier proposed its remodeling into units that he called *phalanges*, "phalanxes," each containing 400 acres of land and accommodating 500 to 2,000 human beings. Volunteers would form a phalanx by setting up a community company, agreeing to split its profits three ways—five-twelfths to those who did the work, four-twelfths to those who un-

---

*Saint-Simon, *Selected Writings*, F.M.H. Markham, ed. (New York, 1952), 116.

dertook the management, and three-twelfths to those who supplied the capital.

Fourier's phalanx, with its relatively generous rewards to managers and capitalists, fell short of complete equality. However, it gave labor the largest share of the profits, and it foreshadowed many other features of socialist planning. Each phalanx would be nearly self-sufficient, producing on the spot most of the things required by its inhabitants. Adult workers who performed the most dangerous or unpleasant tasks would receive the highest remuneration. The inhabitants of the phalanx were to live in one large building, a sort of apartment hotel, which Fourier called a *phalanstère*. The *phalanstère* would provide the maximum opportunity for the satisfaction of man's sociable passions, and it would also make the routine of daily living more efficient by substituting one central kitchen for hundreds of separate ones. The sordid features of housekeeping could be left to little boys, who loved dirt anyway and would cheerfully form special squads to dispose of garbage and refuse.

Other details of the phalanx bore witness to Fourier's reaction against the kind of monotony pictured in Dickens' Coketown. Places of work would be made as pleasant as possible by frequent, colorful redecoration. Members of the phalanx would change their jobs eight times a day because of the human predisposition to the *passion papillonne* (butterfly passion)—"enthusiasm cannot be sustained for more than an hour and a half or two hours in the performance of one particular operation." They would work from four to five in the morning to eight or nine at night, enjoying five meals, plus snacks, needing only five hours of sleep, since the delightful variety of work would not tire them and the days would not be long enough to permit them to taste all the pleasures of life. It would all be so healthy that physicians would be superfluous and everyone would live to 140.

Fourier carried the principle of uninhibited human association to the point of advocating sexual promiscuity, and recommending marriage only for the elderly whose passions had cooled, thus identifying Utopian socialism with "free love" in the popular mind. Yet Fourier cannot be dismissed as a mere crackpot, for he made substantial contributions to socialist theory and to social psychology. Some of his recommendations, like higher pay for dangerous jobs and devices for relieving the tedium of work, have become common practice in the modern business world.

Owen

One of the greatest Utopians was a self-made British businessman, Robert Owen (1772–1858). When he was still in his twenties, Owen took over the large cotton mills at New Lanark in Scotland. Although the former owner of the mills had been accounted benevolent by the standards of the day, conditions there shook Owen to the core. A large part of the working force consisted of children who had been recruited from institutions in Edinburgh when they were between six and eight years old. Although the youngsters did get a little schooling after hours, Owen found many of them "dwarfs in body and mind." Adult laborers at New Lanark fared little better.

Owen set out to show that he could increase his profits and increase the welfare of his laborers at the same time. He made New Lanark over into a model industrial village. For the adults he provided better working conditions, a ten-and-a-half-hour day, higher pay, and cleaner and roomier housing. He restrained the traditional Scottish Saturday night brawl by closing down the worst drinking places, making good liquor available at cheap prices, and punishing offenders who made themselves a public nuisance. As for the children, he raised the minimum age for employment to ten, hoping ultimately to put it at twelve, and he gave his child laborers time for some real schooling. His educational preferences followed Rousseau; advanced bookish subjects were avoided, while crafts, nature study, and other utilitarian subjects received much attention. A properly educated nation, Owen believed, would confute the gloomy predictions of Malthus, who "has not told us how much more food an intelligent and industrious people will create from the same soil, than will be produced by one ignorant and ill-governed."*

Owen inherited much of the optimism of the *philosophes;* he also inherited some of their failures and disappointments. Despite his own success as a philanthropic capitalist, few businessmen followed his example. Disappointed but not disheartened, Owen drew up plans for an idealized version of New Lanark, very much like Fourier's phalanx. He called his utopia a "parallelogram," for the buildings were to be arranged in that geometrical pattern. It was to be a voluntary organization,

*Robert Owen, *A New View of Society* (Glencoe, Illinois, 1948), 174–175.

relatively small in size, neatly balanced between farming and industry, and decidedly advanced in Owen's recommendation for the partial abandonment of conventional ties of marriage and the family. In the 1820's, Owen visited America to finance an abortive effort to set up a parallelogram at New Harmony, Indiana. Undaunted by this failure, he spent the rest of his career publishing and supporting projects for social reform. He advocated the association of all labor in one big union—an experiment that failed; and he sought to reduce the expenditures of workingmen by promoting the formation of consumers' cooperatives—an experiment that succeeded. He also offended many of his contemporaries by his advocacy of sexual freedom, by his Voltairean attacks on established religion, and by his enthusiasm for spiritualism.

Parallelogram projected by Robert Owen for New Harmony, Indiana.

The Early Utopians Appraised

Both Owen and Fourier attracted followers not only in their native lands but also in the United States, where religious sects were already launching ventures in communal living. The American Fourierists included many intellectuals, among them the crusading editor, Horace Greeley, and the poet, John Greenleaf Whittier. They sponsored more than thirty attempts to set up phalanxes; two celebrated ones were Brook Farm, near Boston, and Phalanx, in New Jersey. America also witnessed more than half a dozen Owenite experiments in addition to New Harmony. Like New Harmony itself, however, most of these utopias did not prosper very long; and the few that were firmly established returned to conventional ways of individual profit-taking and family life.

Owen and Fourier relied on private initiative to build the model communities that they so hopefully expected to become widely copied examples for the reconstruction of society. Expecting some millionaire to finance his phalanxes, Fourier vainly kept a daily office hour for ten years to receive him. Saint-Simon, with his stress on "organization," presumably meant to give government a larger role; his follower, Louis Blanc, explicitly advocated intervention by the state to achieve utopia.

Author of a pioneering history of the French Revolution from the socialist standpoint, and implacable critic of the bourgeois policies of the July Monarchy, Louis Blanc (1811–1882) projected the scheme that led to the controversial national workshops of 1848. He outlined the scheme first in a pamphlet, *The Organization of Labor* (1839). "What proletarians need," he wrote, "is the instruments of labor; it is the function of govern-

Louis Blanc (1811–1882).

ment to supply these. If we were to define our conception of the state, our answer would be, that the state is the banker of the poor."* The government would finance and supervise the purchase of productive equipment and the formation of "social workshops"; it would withdraw its support and supervision once the workshops were on their feet. As the workshops gradually spread throughout France, socialistic enterprise would replace private enterprise, profits as such would vanish, and labor would be the only class in society. Much of Louis Blanc's socialism is typically Utopian; he, too, relies on the workers to make their own arrangements for communal living. The real novelty of his plan lies in the role assigned to the state. With Blanc, socialism is beginning to move away from the realm of philanthropy and into the realm of politics.

*"L'Organisation du Travail," in *The French Revolution of 1848*, J. A. R. Marriott, ed. (Oxford, 1913), I, 14. Our translation.

V   The Socialist Response — Marx

With Karl Marx (1818–1883) socialism assumed its most intense form — revolutionary communism. Whereas the early socialists had anticipated a gradual and peaceful evolution toward utopia, Marx forecast a sudden and violent proletarian uprising, by which the workers would capture governments and make them the instruments for securing proletarian welfare. Dogmatic and cocksure, Marx was certain that he alone knew the answers and that the future of mankind would develop inevitably according to the pattern which he found in human history. His self-confidence, his truculence, and the fact that he was born at Trier, in the Prussian Rhineland, have earned him the label of the "Red Prussian."

Basic Principles

Marx found three laws in the pattern of history. First, *economic determinism:* he believed that economic conditions largely determined all other human institutions — society and government, religion and art. Second, the *class struggle:* he believed that history was a dialectical process, a series of conflicts between antagonistic economic groups. In his own day the antagonists were the "haves" and the "have-nots" — the propertied bourgeois and the propertyless proletarians, who, possessing nothing but their working skills, had nothing to fall back on in bad times and were thus at the mercy of their masters. Third, the *inevitability of communism:* he believed that the class struggle was bound to produce one final upheaval that would raise the victorious proletariat over the prostrate bourgeoisie in eternal triumph.

The Marxian philosophy of history derived from many older schools of thought. Although Marx himself was born and died in the nineteenth century, he belonged in spirit partly to the eighteenth. Both his grandfathers were rabbis, but his father was a deist and a skeptic who trained him in the rationalism of the Enlightenment. Marx early acquired the kind of faith in natural law that had characterized the *philosophes.* In his case it was faith in the natural laws of economic determinism and the class struggle, fortified by the crude materialistic teaching of Feuerbach, famous for proclaiming that *"Man ist was er isst"* (one is what one eats). From this followed the boast made by Marx and his disciples that their socialism alone was "scientific," as opposed to the Romantic doctrines of the Utopians.

The Romantic philosophy of Hegel, however, provided the intellectual scaffolding of Marxism. Although Hegel had died in 1831, his influence permeated the University of Berlin during Marx's student days (1836–1841). Marx translated the Hegelian dialectic into the language of economic determinism and the class struggle. In his own day he believed that capitalistic production and the bourgeoisie comprised the thesis; the antithesis was the proletariat; and the synthesis, issuing from the communist revolution, would be true socialism. In later years Marx summarized his relation to Hegel:

My dialectic method is not only different from the Hegelian but is its direct opposite. To Hegel, the life-process of the human brain, . . . which, under the name of 'the Idea,' he even transforms into an independent subject, is the demiurgos of the real world, and the real world is only the external, phenomenal form of 'the Idea.' With me, on the contrary, the ideal is nothing else than the material world reflected by the human mind, and translated into forms of thought.

. . .

The mystification which dialectic suffers in Hegel's hands, by no means prevents him from being the first to present its general form of working in a comprehensive and conscious manner. *With him it is standing on its head. It must be turned right again,* if you would discover the rational kernel within the mystical shell.*

By the time Marx was thirty, he had completed the outlines of his theory of scientific, revolutionary socialism. He had also become a permanent exile from his native Germany. On leaving the University of Berlin, he worked for a newspaper at Cologne in the Prussian Rhineland, then moved to Paris in 1843 after his atheistic articles had aroused the authorities against him. Exiled again, because the government of Louis Philippe feared his anti-bourgeois propaganda, he went to Brussels in 1845. Wherever he happened to be, he read widely in the economists of the past and talked with the socialists and other radicals of his own generation.

Everything Marx read and everyone he met strengthened his conviction that the capitalistic order was unjust, rotten, doomed to fall. From Adam Smith's labor theory of value he concluded that only the worker should receive the profits from the sale of a commodity, since the value of the commodity should be determined by the labor of the man who produced it. The "iron law of wages," however, confirmed Marx's belief that capitalism would never permit the worker to receive this just reward. And from reading other economists and observing the depression of the late 1840's, he concluded that economic crises were bound to occur again and again under a system that allowed capital to produce too much and labor to consume too little.

Meanwhile, Marx began his long friendship and collaboration with Friedrich Engels (1820–1895). In many ways, the two men made a striking contrast. Marx was poor and quarrelsome, a man of few friends; except for his devotion to his wife and children, he was utterly preoccupied by his economic studies.

*Preface to the second edition of *Capital,* Modern Library ed. (New York, n.d.), 25. (Italics ours).

Engels, on the other hand, was the son of a well-to-do German manufacturer and represented the family textile business in Liverpool and Manchester. He loved sports, women, and high living in general. But he also hated the iniquities of industrialism and, when he met Marx, had already written a bitter study, *The Condition of the Working Class in England.* Both Engels and Marx took an interest in the Communist League, a small international organization of radical workingmen. In 1847, the London office of the Communist League requested them to draw up a program. Engels wrote the first draft, which Marx revised from start to finish; the result, published in January, 1848, was *The Manifesto of the Communist Party.*

The Communist Manifesto

Today, more than a century after its original publication, the *Manifesto* remains the classic statement of Marxian socialism. It opens with the dramatic announcement that "A spectre is haunting Europe — the spectre of Communism." It closes with a stirring and confident appeal:

Let the ruling classes tremble at a Communist revolution. The proletarians have nothing to lose but their chains. They have a world to win.
Workingmen of all countries, unite!

In the few dozen pages of the *Manifesto,* Marx and Engels rapidly block in the main outlines of their theory. "The history of all hitherto existing society," they affirm, "is the history of class struggle." Changing economic conditions determined that the struggle should develop successively between "freeman and slave, patrician and plebeian, lord and serf, guild-master and journeyman." The guild system gave way first to manufacture by large numbers of small capitalists and then to "the giant, modern industry."

Modern industry will inevitably destroy bourgeois society. It creates a mounting economic pressure by producing more goods than it can sell; it creates a mounting social pressure by narrowing the circle of capitalists to fewer and fewer individuals and depriving more and more people of their property and forcing them down to the proletariat. These pressures increase to the point where a revolutionary explosion occurs, a massive assault on private property. Landed property will be abolished outright; other forms of property are to be liquidated more gradually through the imposition of severe income taxes and the abolition of inherited wealth. Eventually, social classes and tensions will vanish, and "we shall have an association in which the free development of each is the condition for the free development of all."

"The free development of each is the condition for the free development of all"—the *Manifesto* provides only this vague description of the society that would exist after the revolution. Since Marx defined political authority as "the organized power of one class for oppressing another," he apparently expected that, in the famous phrase, "the state would wither away" once it had created a classless regime. He also apparently assumed that the great dialectical process of history, having achieved its final synthesis, would then cease to operate in its traditional form. But, readers of the *Manifesto* may inquire how is this possible? Will not the dialectic continue forever creating economic and political theses and antitheses? Will not the state always be with us? To these questions Marx offered no satisfactory answer beyond the implication that somehow the liquidation of bourgeois capitalism would radically alter the course of history and transform humanity.

Marx oversimplified the complexities of human nature by trying to force it into the rigid mold of economic determinism and ignoring the non-material motives and interests of men. Neither proletarians nor bourgeois have proved to be the simple economic stereotypes Marx supposed them to be. Labor has often behaved in scandalously un-Marxian fashion and assumed a markedly bourgeois outlook and mentality. Capital has put its own house in better order—and eliminated the worst injustices of the factory system. No more than Malthus did Marx foresee the notable rise in the standard of living that would take place between the mid-nineteenth and mid-twentieth centuries.

Marx never made a greater mistake than when he failed to observe the growing strength of nationalism. The *Manifesto* confidently expected the class struggle to transcend national boundaries. In social and economic warfare, nation would not be pitted against nation, nor state against state; the proletariat everywhere would fight the bourgeoisie. "Workingmen have no country" and "national differences and antagonisms are vanishing gradually from day to day." In Marx's own lifetime, however, national differences and

Friedrich Engels (1820–1895).

antagonisms were increasing rapidly from day to day. Within a few months of the publication of the *Manifesto,* the revolutions of 1848 disclosed the antagonism between Italians and Austrians, Austrians and Hungarians, Hungarians and Slavs, Slavs and Germans.

The *Communist Manifesto* anticipated the strengths as well as the weaknesses of the communist movement. First, it foreshadowed the very important role to be played by propaganda, supplying the earliest of those effective catch-phrases that have become the mark of Marxism — the constant sneering at bourgeois morality, bourgeois law, and bourgeois property, and the dramatic references to the "spectre haunting Europe" and to the proletarians who "have nothing to lose but their chains." Second, the *Manifesto* anticipated the emphasis to be placed on the role of the party in forging the proletarian revolution. The communists, Marx declared in 1848, were a spearhead, "the most advanced section of the working class parties of every country." In matters of theory, "they have over the great mass of the proletariat the advantage of clearly understanding the line of march, the conditions, and the ultimate general results of the proletarian movement."

Third, the *Manifesto* assigned the state a great role in the revolution. Among the policies recommended by Marx were "centralization of credit in the hands of the state," and "extension of factories and instruments of production owned by the state." Thus, despite the supposition that the state would wither away, the *Manifesto* faintly foreshadowed the totalitarian regime of the Soviet Union. And, finally, it clearly established the line dividing communism from the other forms of socialism. Marx's dogmatism, his philosophy of history, and his belief in the necessity for a "total" revolution made his brand of socialism a thing apart. Like a religious prophet granted a revelation, Marx expected his gospel to supplant all other. He scorned and pitied the Utopian socialists. They were about as futile, he wrote, as "organizers of charity, members of societies for the prevention of cruelty to animals, temperance fanatics, hole-and-corner reformers of every kind."

The Later Career of Marx

Age neither mellowed Marx nor greatly altered his views. From 1849 until his death in 1883, he lived in London. There, partly because of his own financial mismanagement, the Marx family experienced at first hand the misery of a proletarian existence in the slums of Soho; poverty and near-starvation caused the death of three of the Marx children. Eventually, Marx obtained a modest income from the generosity of Engels and from his own writings.

Throughout the 1850's Marx contributed a weekly article on British politics or international affairs to Horace Greeley's radical paper, *The New York Tribune.* He produced a series of pamphlets, of which the most famous was *The Eighteenth Brumaire of Louis Napoleon,* a study of the fall of the short-lived Second French Republic. Meantime, he spent his days in the British Museum, reading the reports of parliamentary investigating committees and piling up evidence of the conditions of miners and factory hands. Thus Marx accumulated the material for his full-dress economic study, *Das Kapital.* The first volume of this massive analysis of capitalism appeared in 1867; two further volumes, pieced together from his notes, were published after his death.

In *Das Kapital,* Marx elaborated, but did not substantially revise, the doctrines of the *Communist Manifesto.* He spelled out his labor theory of value, according to which the worker created the total value of the commodity that he produced yet received in the form of wages only a part of the price for the item. The difference between the sale price and the worker's wages constituted *surplus value,* something actually created by labor but appropriated by capital as profit. *Das Kapital* goes on to relate surplus value to the ultimate doom of capitalism. It is the nature of capitalism, Marx insists, to diminish its own profits by replacing human labor with machines and thus gradually choking off the source of surplus value. Hence will arise the mounting crises of overproduction and underconsumption predicted by the *Manifesto*. In a famous passage toward the close of Volume I of *Das Kapital*, Marx compared capitalism to an integument, a skin or shell, increasingly stretched and strained from within. One day these internal pressures would prove irresistible:

This integument is burst asunder. The knell of capitalist private property sounds. The expropriators are expropriated.*

In 1864, three years before the first volume of *Das Kapital* was published, Marx joined in the formation of the First International Workingmen's Association. This was an ambitious attempt to organize workers of every country and of every variety of radical belief. A loose federation rather than a coherent political party, the First International soon began to disintegrate, and expired in 1876. Increasing persecution by hostile governments helped to bring on its end; but so, too, did the internal quarrels that repeatedly engaged both its leaders and the rank and file of its members. Marx himself set the example by his intolerance of disagreement and his incapacity for practical politics.

In 1889, the Second International was organized; it lasted down to the time of World War I and the Bolshevik revolution in Russia.

Capital, Modern Library, ed., 837.

The Second International was more coherently organized and more political in character than the First International had been. It represented the Marxian socialist parties, which, as we shall see in later chapters, were becoming important forces in the major countries of continental Europe. Among its leaders were men more adept than Marx himself at the political game. Yet the old spirit of factionalism continued to weaken the International. Some of its leaders tenaciously defended laws handed down by the master and forbade any co-operation between socialists and the bourgeois political parties; these were the orthodox Marxists. Other leaders of the Second International, however, were from the orthodox standpoint heretics. They, too, called themselves disciples of Marx; yet they revised his doctrines in the direction of moderation and of harmonization with the views of the Utopians. These "revisionists" believed in co-operation between classes rather than in a struggle to the death, and they trusted that human decency and intelligence, working through the machinery of democratic government, could avert the horrors of outright class war. Though the precise connotations have varied with the shifts of the party line, "orthodox" and "heretical" communists have persisted. The factionalism that had split the First International lived on to plague the Second and its successors in twentieth-century communism.

VI Other Responses

Socialism, both Marxian and Utopian, and liberalism, both bourgeois and democratic, were the most important responses to the economic and social problems of the nineteenth century. But they were not the only responses. As later chapters will show, nationalists gave new life to the old ideas of mercantilism, not only advocating

tariffs to protect agriculture and industry but also demanding empires abroad to provide new markets for surplus products, new fields for the investment of surplus capital, and new settlements for surplus citizens. Two very different types of response came from the anarchists and the reformers known as Christian socialists or Christian democrats.

The Anarchists

An anarchist believes that the best government is no government at all. Most of the recipes for socialism contained at least a dash of anarchism: witness the withering-away of the state promised by the Marxists and the Utopians' mistrust of governments. For a few of Marx's contemporaries, however, it was not enough that the state should wither at some distant time; such an instrument of oppression should be annihilated at once. The means to this end was terrorism, especially assassination of heads of state. These terrorists provided the stereotype of the bearded, wild-eyed, bomb-carrying radical. At the turn of the century, their assassinations levied an impressive toll—the French President Carnot in 1894, King Humbert of Italy in 1900, and the American President McKinley in 1901. Otherwise the terrorists accomplished little except to drive the governments they hated to more vigorous measures of retaliation.

Though negative and destructive in practice, anarchism exerted an important doctrinal influence on the proletarian movement. The Russian scientist and thinker, Prince Peter Kropotkin (1842–1921), made the most complete statement of its theory and ideals in his book, *Mutual Aid: A Factor in Evolution* (1902). Kropotkin foresaw a revolution that would abolish the state as well as private property and that would lead to a new society of autonomous groups whereby the individual would achieve greater self-realization and would need to labor only four to five hours a day. The most famous anarchist was Kropotkin's countryman, Bakunin (1814–1876), who helped to shape the Russian revolutionary movement (see Chapter 22) and won the attention of workers from many countries by his participation in the First International. Although Bakunin drew only a vague sketch of his utopia, he made it clear that the millennium was to be achieved through an international rebellion set off by small groups of anarchist conspirators.

Bakunin contributed to the formation of the program known as *anarcho-syndicalism* (from the French word *syndicat,* which means an economic grouping, particularly a trade union). The anarcho-syndicalists disbelieved in political parties, even Marxist ones; they believed in direct action by the workers to culminate in a spontaneous general strike that would free labor from the capitalistic yoke. Meantime, workers could rehearse for the great day by forming unions and by engaging in acts of anti-capitalist sabotage. These theories received forceful expression in *Reflections on Violence* published early in the twentieth century by the French exponent of anarcho-syndicalism, Georges Sorel.

Proudhon

The writer most frequently cited by the anarcho-syndicalists was the French publicist, Proudhon (1809–1865). "What is property?" Proudhon asked in a famous pamphlet of 1840; "property is theft." Marx praised the pamphlet for its "scientific" socialism and predicted it would rank in importance with Siéyès' *What Is the Third Estate?* Within a few years Marx's praise had turned to contempt, since Proudhon refused to accept the correctness of all of his own views. A second pamphlet by Proudhon, *The Philosophy of Poverty,* therefore, elicited a Marxian rebuttal tartly entitled *The Poverty of Philosophy.* The property that Proudhon called "theft" was not all property but unearned income, the revenues that men gained from investing their wealth rather than from the sweat of their brows. Of all the forms of unearned income, the worst, in Proudhon's view, was the "leprosy of interest," and the most diabolical of capitalists was the money-lender. Under existing conditions, only those who were already rich could afford to borrow, but in the utopia envisaged by Proudhon all men would be able to secure credit. Instead of private banks and the Bank of France, there would be only a "People's Bank," lending to all without interest and issuing notes that would soon replace ordinary money. The credit provided by the People's

Bank would enable each man to become a producer on his own.

Thus, where Marx foresaw a revolution in ownership of the means of production, Proudhon foresaw a "revolution of credit," a revolution in financing production. Where Marx proposed to have the proletariat liquidate the bourgeoisie, Proudhon proposed to raise the proletarians to the level of the bourgeois by making every worker an owner. Proudhon's utopia was not collectivized or socialized; it was a loose association of middle-class individualists. Because Proudhon dreaded restraints upon the individual, he opposed the social workshops of Louis Blanc and the phalanxes of Fourier as too restrictive. He projected, instead, a society founded upon "mutualism." Economically, mutualism would take the form of associations of producers in agriculture and industry, not unlike the producers' co-operatives found among farmers today. Politically, it would take the form of "federalism" — that is, a loose federation of associations would replace the centralized state rather on the model of the Swiss confederation of local cantons.

Proudhon's doctrines exerted a strong appeal in France, with its devotion to individualism and with the legacy of "federalism" bequeathed by the Girondins of the Revolution. Tens of thousands of small businessmen in France were often denied financial credit by the bankers denounced by Proudhon, and thus always stood on the edge of being displaced from the lower fringes of the middle class to the proletariat. Proudhon's attacks on the state naturally fed the anarchist strain in anarcho-syndicalism. Yet much of his teaching contradicted the syndicalist strain. Not only did he dislike trade unions as unnatural restrictions on individual liberty; he deplored all activities suggesting class strife, including the very strikes so beloved by the syndicalists. These views, together with his expressed hostility to Jewish money-lenders, have led some modern critics to call Proudhon an incipient fascist; other critics, however, have dismissed the charge as absurd because Proudhon seemed to reject the kind of totalitarian state identified with fascism.

The Christian Socialists

Like Proudhon, the Christian socialists endeavored to mitigate class antagonisms. The name was first applied, in the mid-nineteenth century, to a small group of English reformers, drawn from the clergy of the established Church, who believed that the Church of England needed to put theological problems to one side and direct its efforts to ending social abuses. One of their best known leaders was Charles Kingsley (1819–1875), who wrote earnest social novels and a stream of pamphlets against the wickedness of laissez-faire. His didactic novel, *Alton Locke,* and his bitter tract, *Cheap Clothes and Nasty,* both published in 1850, exposed the sweating of labor in the "show shops" and "slop shops" which forced tailors and seamstresses to work long hours for meager pay, often in appallingly crowded and unsanitary surroundings.

The positive doctrine of the Christian socialists was notable for its attack on materialism and its stress on brotherly love as against un-brotherly strife, on association and co-operation as against exploitation and competition. It was notable also for its optimism: if men would only act as Christians, they might solve their social problems. Indeed the Christian socialists were far more Christian than socialist and relied more on private philanthropy than on state intervention. Kingsley himself set an example for concrete improvement when he helped to launch the Working Men's College in London and promoted other activities of the type that organizations like the YMCA have made familiar.

The Catholic Response

Catholics, too, reacted against the evils of industrialism. Essentially, their program resembled that of the Anglican Christian socialists, but they called it by the more accurate name of "Christian democracy" or "social Christianity." Christian democracy formed a central part of the Catholic response to the problems of the modern world. As we shall see in later chapters, these problems bore heavily upon the Church. Anticlerical legislation threatened its position in France, Germany, Italy, and elsewhere. The Papal States and then the city of Rome itself, after more than a thousand years of papal rule, passed to the control of the newly unified Kingdom of Italy. Science, nationalism, and the materialistic doctrines issuing from the industrial revolution were all competing for the loyalties of men. In Catholic countries the working classes especially were drifting away from the Church.

The Church first tried to take refuge in the past. Pope Pius IX (1846–1878), whose experience in the revolution of 1848 (see p. 169) had ended his earlier flirtation with liberalism, issued in 1864 the *Syllabus of Errors,* condemning many social theories and institutions not consecrated by centuries of tradition. While Pius also condemned the materialism implicit in laissez-faire, socially-minded Catholics were disturbed by his apparent hostility to trade unions and democracy and by his statement that it was an error to suppose that the pope "can and ought to reconcile and harmonize himself with progress, liberalism, and modern civilization."

The successor of Pius, Leo XIII (1878–1903), recognized that the Church could hardly continue to turn its back on progress, liberalism, and modernity without suffering serious losses. Pope Leo fully recognized the rapid changes being worked by science and technology, and as a papal nuncio, he had witnessed them at first hand in the industrial regions of Belgium, France, and Germany. He knew that Catholicism was flourishing in the supposedly hostile climate of the democratic and Protestant United States. Moreover, his studies of St. Thomas Aquinas convinced him that the Church had much to gain and little to lose by following the middle-of-the-road social and economic policies recommended by that great medieval Schoolman. Accordingly, Leo XIII issued a series of famous documents, notably the encyclical letter, *Rerum Novarum* ("concerning new things," 1891).

In *Rerum Novarum,* the Pope exposed the defects of capitalism with as much vigor as any socialist. Then he attacked with equal vigor the socialist view of property and the socialist doctrine of class war. He pronounced it a "great mistake" to believe

. . . that class is naturally hostile to class, and that the wealthy and the workingmen are intended by nature to live in mutual conflict. . . . Each needs the other: Capital cannot do without Labor, nor Labor without Capital.*

Leo therefore urged the economic man to act as a Christian man of good will:

Religion teaches the laboring man . . . to carry out honestly and fairly all equitable agreements freely entered into; never to injure the property, nor to outrage the person, of an employer; never to resort to violence . . . ; and to have nothing to do with men of evil principles, who work upon the people with artful promises, and excite foolish hopes which usually end in useless regrets, followed by insolvency. Religion teaches the wealthy owner and the employer that their work-people are not to be accounted their bondsmen; that in every man they must respect his dignity and worth as a man and as a Christian; that labor is not a thing to be ashamed of, if we lend ear to right reason and to Christian philosophy, but is an honorable calling, enabling a man to sustain his life in a way upright and creditable; and that it is shameful and inhuman to treat men like chattels to make money by, or to look upon them merely as so much muscle or physical power.†

While Leo XIII believed that the state must always remain subordinate to the interests of the individuals composing it, he did not necessarily defend laissez-faire policies. On the contrary, he repeatedly cited St. Thomas to prove that the state should take measures for the general welfare. On behalf of capital, it should discourage agitators and protect property from violence. On behalf of labor, it should work to remove "the causes which lead to conflict between employer and employed." For example, it might regulate child labor, limit the hours of work, and insist that Sun-

The Great Encyclical Letters of Pope Leo XIII (New York, 1903), 218.
†*Ibid.,* 219.

days be free for religious activity and for rest. Leo also believed that the workers must help themselves, and *Rerum Novarum* concluded with a fervent appeal for the formation of Catholic trade unions.

These Catholic unions exist today, but they are only a minority in the realm of organized labor. Neither the Christian democracy of Leo XIII nor the Christian socialism of the Anglican reformers has achieved all that the founders hoped. Yet the Christian democrats eventually came to play a central part in the politics of Germany, Italy, and other European states, particularly after World War II. And in Britain both Marxism and the Christian socialist tradition helped to attract workingmen and middle-class intellectuals to the developing Labor Party at the beginning of the twentieth century. In the perspective of history, the Anglican and Catholic reformers succeeded in attracting an influential following and in arousing the conscience of prosperous industrial nations to the human problems created by the economic revolutions.

Reading Suggestions on the Impact of the Economic Revolutions

(Asterisk indicates paperbound edition.)

General Accounts

E. J. Hobsbawm, *The Age of Revolution, 1789–1848* (*Mentor). A survey doing full justice to the social impact of industrialism.

A. Birnie, *Economic History of Europe, 1760–1939* (*Dover). Helpful introduction.

R. C. Binkley, *Realism & Nationalism, 1852–1871* (*Torch), and C. J. H. Hayes, *A Generation of Materialism, 1871–1900* (*Torch). Stimulating comprehensive surveys in the "Rise of Modern Europe" series; with full bibliographies.

T. S. Ashton, *The Industrial Revolution, 1760–1830* (*Galaxy). Lucid introduction, centering on Britain.

A. Toynbee, *The Industrial Revolution* (*Beacon). Pioneering study, first published nearly a century ago, and influenced by Christian socialist ideas.

J. L. and B. Hammond, *The Rise of Modern Industry,* 8th ed. (Methuen, 1951). Seen from a doctrinaire socialist point of view.

L. Mumford, *Technics and Civilization* (*Harbinger). A sweeping survey, now somewhat outdated but still very suggestive.

Special Studies: Mainly Economic and Social

P. Mantoux, *The Industrial Revolution in the Eighteenth Century* (*Torch). Standard account of the beginnings of the factory system in England.

J. Clapham, *An Economic History of Modern Britain,* 3 vols., rev. ed. (Cambridge Univ. Press, 1930–1938). Major scholarly study of the workshop of the world.

J. Clapham, *Economic Development of France and Germany, 1815–1914* (*Cambridge Univ. Press). An older book and a very good one.

W. O. Henderson, *The Industrial Revolution in Europe, 1815–1914* (Quadrangle, 1961). Recent survey, stressing Germany and France.

A. L. Dunham, *The Industrial Revolution in France, 1815–1848* (Exposition, 1955). Scholarly monograph.

W. W. Rostow, *The Process of Economic Growth* (*Norton). Influential analysis responsible for adding the term "take-off" stage to the economic vocabulary.

M. C. Buer, *Health, Wealth, & Population in the Early Days of the Industrial Revolution* (Routledge, 1926). A balanced appraisal of the social consequences of industrial change.

Special Studies:
Mainly Ideological
and Political

C. Brinton, *English Political Thought in the 19th Century* (*Torch). Essays on Bentham, Mill, Owen, Kingsley, and other important figures.

J. S. Schapiro, *Liberalism and the Challenge of Fascism: Social Forces in England and France, 1815–1870* (McGraw-Hill, 1949). Stresses ideological consequences.

E. Halévy, *The Growth of Philosophic Radicalism* (*Beacon, 1955). The standard study of Bentham and his Utilitarian followers.

H. W. Laidler, *Social-Economic Movements: An Historical and Comparative Survey of Socialism, Communism, Coöperation, Utopianism* (Crowell, 1949). An encyclopaedic introduction to the topics enumerated.

J. C. Schumpeter, *Capitalism, Socialism, and Democracy* (*Torch). A thoughtful survey, extending down to the mid-twentieth century.

E. Wilson, *To the Finland Station* (*Anchor). A sympathetic and balanced history of socialism, Utopian and Marxian.

F. E. Manuel, *The New World of Henri Saint-Simon* (*Notre Dame). Sympathetic biography and evaluation.

F. Podmore, *Robert Owen, A Biography* (Appleton, 1924). An instructive account.

I. Berlin, *Karl Marx: His Life and Environment* (*Galaxy). Short and excellent.

L. Schwarzchild, *The Red Prussian: The Life and Legend of Karl Marx* (*Universal). A hostile interpretation.

R. Fülöp-Miller, *Leo XIII and Our Times* (Longmans, Green, 1937). A warmly sympathetic account.

Sources

J. Bowditch and C. Ramsland, eds. *Voices of the Industrial Revolution* (*Ann Arbor). Selections from the liberal economists and their critics.

T. R. Malthus, *Population: the First Essay* (*Ann Arbor). The original essay of 1798, stating Malthusianism in its starkest form.

D. Ricardo, *The Principles of Political Economy & Taxation* (*Irwin).

J. S. Mill, *Autobiography* and *On Liberty* (both in several * editions).

C. H. de Saint-Simon, *Social Organization, the Science of Man, & Other Writings* (*Torch).

The Life of Robert Owen, by Himself (Knopf, 1920).

K. Marx and F. Engels, *Basic Writings on Politics & Philosophy* (*Anchor).

The Great Encyclical Letters of Pope Leo XIII (Benziger, 1903). Fundamental to the understanding of modern Catholic social thought.

Historical Fiction

C. Dickens, *Hard Times* (*several editions). The shortest of Dickens' social novels; first-rate descriptions of "Coketown" and its citizens.

Mrs. E. Gaskell, *North and South* (Dutton, 1914) and *Mary Barton* (Dutton, 1912). Most instructive social novels by a perceptive contemporary of Dickens.

E. Zola, *Germinal* (*several editions). The best French novel on industrial problems; less genteel than its English counterparts.

E. Bellamy, *Looking Backward, 2000–1887* (*several editions). A highly interesting adaptation of Utopian socialist views by an American of the late nineteenth century.

21

The Western Democracies

in the Nineteenth Century

We shall now trace the background history of the major self-governing western states: Great Britain, France, Italy, and the United States. These are now all democracies; and though they have all had, especially in wartime, lapses from democratic standards, they are all, as the twentieth-century world goes, "old" democracies.

The smaller nations of western and northern Europe—the Netherlands, Belgium, Switzerland, the Scandinavian countries—are also part of the North Atlantic community. All these smaller states have worked out their own national variants of liberalism and democracy. In particular, the Scandinavian countries, with their homogeneous populations, their common Lutheran religion, their common traditions, and their very high rate of literacy, have sometimes surpassed the larger states in making democracy function effectively. Visitors to Copenhagen or Stockholm are impressed not only by their tidiness but also by the absence of slums and other signs of poverty. And the co-operatives of Denmark and Sweden have received much praise as the "middle way" between welfare socialism and uncontrolled economic individualism.

Nor should the histories of these smaller states be considered uninteresting or unimportant. They too underwent most of the stresses and strains of the rest of Europe. Belgium, notably, was divided—and still is—between French-speaking and Flemish-speaking areas, often in conflict. Switzerland in the nineteenth century underwent a real if not very long and bloody war, that of the Sonderbund, between the more conservative and rural Catholic counties and liberal urban ones. Sweden and Norway, yoked together in 1815, parted company peacefully in 1907, after nearly a century of restive partnership. But we simply cannot include these histories in a work of this scope.

These smaller states have also helped to maintain the balance of international politics and to shape European opinion, a role for which they are particularly well suited by their relative detachment from ambitious nationalist aspirations. They have collaborated effectively in many forms of internation activity. In many fields their citizens have contributed proportionately more heavily to our modern western culture than their numbers would suggest. To cite a few examples: Switzerland supplied the great historian of the Renaissance, Burckhardt, and Belgium the poet and playwright, Maeterlinck. From Finland came the composer Sibelius; from Norway, Ibsen and his modern social dramas; from Holland, the physicist Lorentz, winner of the Nobel Prize in 1902; and from Sweden, Nobel himself, the munitions king who endowed the Nobel prizes for peaceful achievement, and the novelist and playwright Strindberg.

Spain, too, had a varied and interesting history in the nineteenth century, swinging between conservative monarchy and radical republicanism. But Spain was now a minor power and, though especially in the novel, she had a distinguished cultural achievement, we must postpone longer consideration of Spanish history until in the Civil War of the 1930's Spain once more enters the mainstream of events. We must now turn to the states that fate, or history, has assigned the major roles in our story. Of these in the nineteenth century, Britain was unquestionably the first, the leading power.

I   Britain, 1815-1914

The Process of Reform

In the years immediately after Waterloo, Britain went through a typical postwar economic crisis. Unsold goods accumulated, and the working classes experienced widespread unemployment and suffering. Although trade unions were forbidden by the Combination Acts, the workers none the less asserted themselves in strikes and in popular agitation that helped prepare the way for the parliamentary Reform Bill of 1832. But by the 1820's, economic conditions had improved, and Britain had embarked on the first stage of those political reforms that were to make of her a democratic state.

Into this process, of course, there went economic and social drives, and the Britain of our mid-twentieth century was to be not only a very complete political democracy but also in part an economic and a social democracy. But the process of reform focused always on concrete political action. It is a process of which the British are very proud, for it was achieved without revolution and almost without vi-

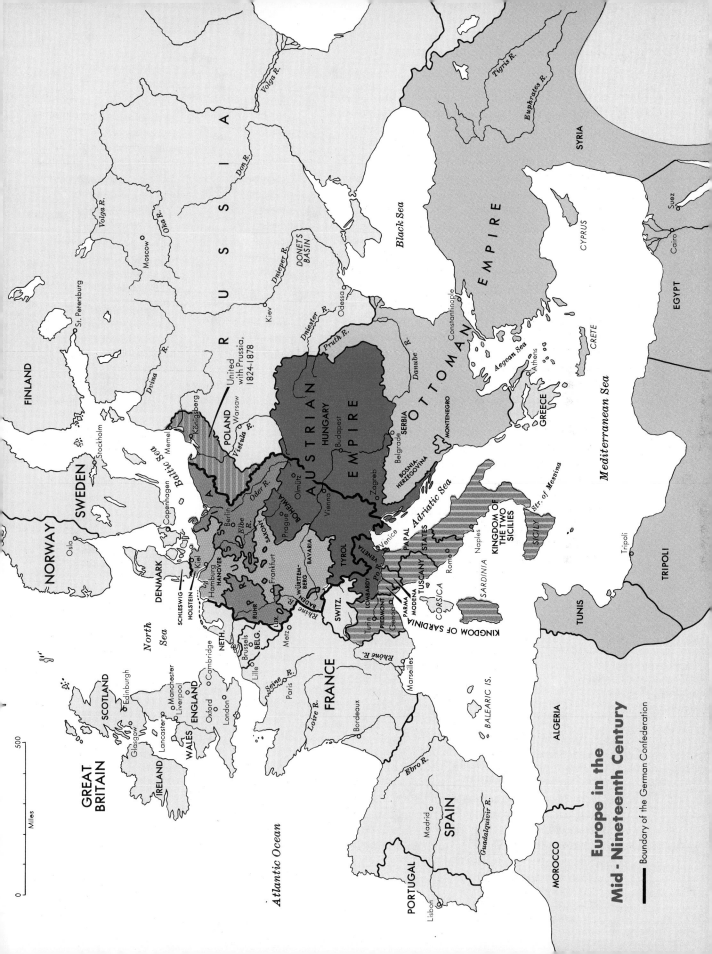

Europe in the
Mid - Nineteenth Century

— Boundary of the German Confederation

GREAT
BRITAIN

SCOTLAND
Edinburgh
Glasgow

IRELAND
Manchester
Liverpool
Lancaster

WALES
ENGLAND
Oxford Cambridge
London

NORWAY
Oslo

SWEDEN
Stockholm

FINLAND

DENMARK
Copenhagen

NORTH SEA
North Sea

Atlantic Ocean

Paris
Seine R.
Loire R.
Bordeaux
FRANCE
Rhône R.
Marseilles

Ebro R.
SPAIN
Madrid

PORTUGAL
Lisbon

Guadalquivir R.

MOROCCO

ALGERIA

BALEARIC IS.

SARDINIA

CORSICA

TUNIS

TRIPOLI
Tripoli

St. Petersburg

R U S S I A

Moscow

Volga R.
Oka R.
Don R.
Drina
Dnieper R.
DONETS BASIN
Kiev
Odessa
Dniester R.
Prut R.

POLAND
United with Prussia,
1824-1878
Warsaw
Vistula R.
Königsberg
Memel

Baltic Sea

P R U S S I A
Berlin
Elbe R.
Oder R.
Hamburg
HANOVER
Kiel
SCHLESWIG
HOLSTEIN
SAXONY
Frankfurt
BOHEMIA
Prague
Olmütz
BAVARIA
WÜRTTEM-
BERG
BADEN
Rhine R.
RUHR
LUX.
Meiz
NETH.
BELG.
Brussels
Lille

AUSTRIAN
EMPIRE
HUNGARY
Budapest
Vienna
TYROL
Zagreb
CARNIOLA
VENETIA
Venice

SWITZ.

LOMBARDY
Po R.
PIEDMONT
Turin
Genoa
PARMA
MODENA
TUSCANY
PAPAL
STATES
Rome

KINGDOM OF SARDINIA

KINGDOM OF
THE TWO
SICILIES
Naples
SICILY
Str. of Messina

Adriatic Sea

SERBIA
Belgrade
BOSNIA-
HERZEGOVINA
MONTENEGRO

OTTOMAN EMPIRE

Constantinople

Black Sea

Danube

GREECE
Athens
Aegean Sea

CRETE

Mediterranean Sea

CYPRUS

SYRIA

Tigris R.
Euphrates R.

EGYPT
Cairo
Suez

Miles
0   500

olence or indeed any serious civil disturbance. The fruits of discussion, education, and propaganda were consolidated in a specific "reform bill," followed by another stage of preparatory work and another reform bill.

Parliamentary Reform

The process is most clearly marked in the great milestones of parliamentary reform that transformed the government of Britain from an oligarchy into a political democracy. Britain emerged from the Napoleonic Wars with its executive, a cabinet of ministers presided over by a prime minister, wholly under the control of Parliament. The Crown was now, as the nineteenth-century political writer Bagehot was to put it, largely "decorative." On that decorative post, held for most of the century (1837–1901) by Queen Victoria, who has given her name to an age and a culture, were centered the patriotic emotions of loyal British subjects. Victoria never thought of herself as a mere figurehead; she was a determined, sensible, emotional, conventional, and intellectually unsophisticated Victorian lady.

Real power lay in the legislative branch, in the early nineteenth century by no means directly representative of the masses. The House of Lords, which for all save money bills had equal power with the lower house, was composed of the small, privileged class of peers born to their seats in the Lords, with the addition of a relatively few new peers created by the Crown from time to time. The House of Commons, its members unpaid, was recruited wholly from the gentry, the professional classes, and very successful businessmen, with a sprinkling of sons of peers (who were for electoral purposes commoners) and was chosen by less than one-sixth of the adult male population. Both the working classes in town and country and the run of prosperous but not spectacularly successful middle-class people were excluded from the franchise. Moreover, the largely rural South, once the most populous area of the kingdom, now had more representatives than it deserved, including a large contingent from the "rotten boroughs," towns

of very small population, or, as in the notorious Old Sarum, once a lively medieval town, none at all. The teeming new industrial centers of the North, such as Manchester, Liverpool, Sheffield, were grossly under-represented.

Projects to begin modernizing the structure of representation came close to being adopted in the late eighteenth century. But the wars with Revolutionary and Napoleonic France made reform impossible; in wartime and in the immediate postwar years, even moderate reformers were denounced as Jacobins. In 1819, a nervous Tory government permitted the soldiery to break up a large and peaceful mass meeting assembled at St. Peter's Field near Manchester to hear speeches on parliamentary reform. Soon after this "Peterloo" with its echo of "Waterloo," however, moderation prevailed, and the peaceful campaign of agitation which produced the parliamentary reform of 1832 was resumed.

In this campaign the middle class did not hesitate to appeal to the lower classes for aid by using freely the language of popular rights, and even of universal suffrage. Many popular leaders talked as if the Reform Bill would bring political democracy to England at once. Yet much of the preparation for reform was actually the work, not of liberal agitators, but of conservatives. Guided by enlightened individuals such as Canning and Robert Peel, the Tory governments of the 1820's lifted the various restrictions on civil rights imposed during the war period and the postwar crisis. They partially repealed the Combination Acts against trade unions; reformed the antiquated criminal code, so that, for example, the theft of a sheep no longer carried with it in theory a death penalty; and began the reduction in protective tariffs that was to lead to free trade. The seventeenth-century Test Act, which, though not observed, legally excluded nonconformists from public life, was repealed. So, under the name of "Catholic emancipation," were the laws that really did exclude Catholics from public life. In international politics, Canning lined Britain up as a "liberal" power against the conservative monarchies of central and eastern Europe (see Chapter 19).

The Reform Bill itself was enacted under

the leadership of the Whig Lord Grey, backed by a full apparatus of agitation and pressure groups. Tory opponents of parliamentary reform were won over—even the very Tory Duke of Wellington was converted at the last moment—until only the Tory House of Lords blocked the measure. At this climax, Lord Grey persuaded King William IV (1830–1837) to threaten the creation by royal prerogative of enough new Whig peers to put the reform through the Lords. This threat, combined with the real, or perhaps merely widely feared danger of popular violence, put the bill through on June 4, 1832.

This First Reform Bill did not bring political democracy to England. It did diminish the great irregularities of electoral districts, wiping out more than fifty rotten boroughs and giving seats in the Commons to more than forty hitherto unrepresented industrial towns. The number of voters was increased by about 50 per cent so that virtually all the middle class got the vote, but the bill by no means enfranchised the "lower" classes in urban or rural areas.

From the new ground of the partly reformed Parliament, the agitation for a still wider suffrage went on. The middle class had won its gains, not in the name of its own admission to an oligarchy, but in the name of the right of all competent men to have the vote. With the gradual spread of literacy to the lower classes, with their gradual political awakening, the middle classes could not find very good arguments for refusing to extend the franchise; moreover, a good many of the British middle classes sincerely believed in a gradual widening of the franchise.

The Second Reform Bill came in 1867, by one of the ironies of history put through by that Tory party that traditionally stood for resistance to the widening of the suffrage. But the three decades after 1832 had produced a ground swell of agitation for more parliamentary reform, a ground swell with many cross-currents from down-right radical republicanism to a resigned belief that democracy was irresistibly the wave of the future. Disraeli (1804–1881), the Tory leader in the Commons, almost certainly thought that if one party did not put through reform the other one would. With a politician's sense of reality, he decided his party might as well get the credit. Disraeli also thought that the newly enfranchised urban working class, hostile to their middle-class employers, would vote for the Tories, who were country gentlemen, good responsible caretakers of the lower classes, not exploiters like the middle-class businessmen. He was proved wrong by the very first general election after the reform, for in 1868 the Tories were turned out of office.

The Second Reform Bill did not introduce full manhood suffrage. Like the first, it was a piecemeal change that brought the electoral districts into more uniformity and equality,

Caricature of Disraeli, 1869.

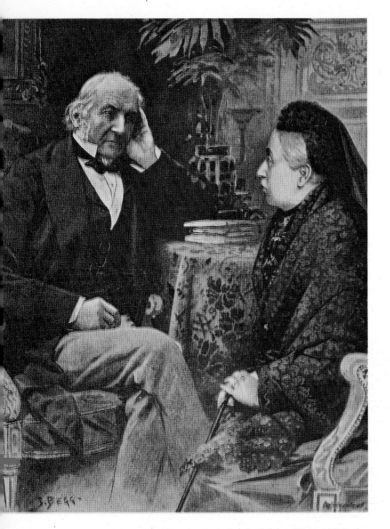

Gladstone advising Queen Victoria.

former Whigs under the leadership of Gladstone (1809–1898). Even these reforms of 1884 and 1885 did not introduce universal manhood suffrage or a neat democratic uniformity. They still tinkered with medieval forms, which were now pretty completely modernized. Lodgers and a few "floaters" (people whose specific "home" was hard to define in settled Victorian terms), and women were still without the vote; districts were not quite equalized; a few thousand voters with business property in one district and a home in another could vote twice; and graduates of Oxford and Cambridge could vote a second time for special university members; indeed, a university man with scattered property could, if he could get around to the polls fast enough, cast a dozen votes. Only in 1918, in a major Reform Act, was plural voting limited to two votes—a property and a university vote. Still, by 1885 Britain was clearly a political democracy, in which the majority of the people, through their representatives in the House of Commons, were politically "sovereign." Perhaps not quite, for the hereditary House of Lords had still a veto power over legislation that did not specifically appropriate money. This last limitation was removed in 1911, in a kind of codicil to the reforms of the nineteenth century, when the Parliament Act of that year ended the real power of the Lords, leaving them with no more than a delaying or suspensive veto.

The Two-Party System: Liberals and Conservatives

We have outlined above the legislative landmarks in the nineteenth-century democratization of the British constitution. Now the dynamics of that process are certainly in part explicable in terms of the "class struggle." Broadly speaking, over the century the "have nots"—perhaps better, the "have littles"—gained a voice in the politics of Britain they did not have in 1815. But the central human institution of the dynamics, the *party*, clearly does not present a neat alignment of the "have littles" against the "have much." That

but left them still divided into boroughs and shires as in the Middle Ages. It about doubled the number of voters in Britain by giving the vote to householders—that is, settled men owning or paying rent on their dwellings—in the boroughs. But the Reform Bill of 1867 did not give the vote in rural areas to men without the "stake" of property—that is, men who did not own a piece of real estate or even a bank account, men who were therefore felt by many upper-class Victorians to be irresponsible, willing to vote away other people's property. It did, however, give the vote to several millions of wage-earners without other sources of income.

The next reforms in the series were, more logically, put through by the Liberal party, the should be clear even from the very summary account of the reform bills we have given. The Disraeli who took the "leap in the dark" of 1867 was a conservative, not a radical leader, and he hoped that the newly enfranchised workingmen would vote conservative, not radical. He was wrong in 1868, but in the longer run not wholly wrong, for after his death his party was returned to power triumphantly under the even wider franchise of 1885 for a whole decade, 1895–1905. Some British poor and middling men obviously still continued to vote for the party of their "betters."

The fact is that the nineteenth-century British party system was not clearly based on an opposition between a possessing class and a non-possessing class. The eighteenth-century oligarchic factions of Whigs and Tories were transformed in the course of the nineteenth century into the modern mass parties of Liberals and Conservatives, both organized on a national basis, with local committees at the bottom, and making full use of party machinery for getting out the vote. The Whigs, in broadening into the Liberals, sought an electoral base ranging from the old great families, still represented in the early and middle part of the century by men like Grey and Palmerston, to the little and big businessmen, the nonconformists, the radical white-collar men, and the politically conscious workingmen. The Tories, in broadening into Conservatives, sought a base, first under Peel and then under Disraeli, from the country gentlemen, army and navy officers, and Anglican clergymen down to the agricultural laborers, the small townspeople, and even some of the urban white-collar and working classes. Both parties frankly appealed to the "people"; and the Conservatives, with their "Primrose League" in memory of Disraeli's favorite flower, their appeal to love of Queen and country, their record of social legislation against the worst evils of the new factory system, did at least as good a job in building a party machine as did the Liberals. In the Victorian heyday, the librettist Gilbert was quite justified in having his guardsman sing in the operetta "Iolanthe":

> That every boy and every gal
> That's born into the world alive
> Is either a little Liberal
> Or else a little Conservative.

The Two-Party System: An Explanation

The two-party system was almost wholly confined to the English-speaking lands, to Britain, the United States, and the British Commonwealth countries. On the Continent, not only in France, Italy, and pre-Hitler Germany, but also in the little democracies of Scandinavia, Switzerland, Holland, and Belgium, the multi-party system usually prevailed, and governments were generally coalitions of parties with separate organizations. English-speaking opinion probably exaggerates the defects and dangers of multi-party democracy. But it is clear that a two-party democracy does have distinct advantages in the way of stability and continuity of policy, if only because a given group can enjoy a longer, more assured tenure of power. The historian must attempt somehow to explain why the English-speaking peoples developed this unique institution. He must seek somewhat different explanations for Britain and for the United States, for though both have two-party systems, their total political situations and traditions are far from alike.

In terms of political psychology, the two-party system means that the millions of individual voters who make up each party are in greater agreement than disagreement over what the party stands for; or at least that when they vote for a candidate they feel he stands more for what they want than for what they don't want. Each voter makes some kind of compromise *within himself*, takes something less in practice than he would ideally like. This sort of compromise the French voter of the 1880's for instance did not need to make, at any rate not to anything like the same degree as the British voter. The Frenchman could choose, from among a dozen or more platforms and candidates, the one tailored closest to his desires.

We must still ask why Englishmen made these compromises, why they agreed more than they disagreed. The answer must be sought in the long working out of British history. One part of it lies in the relative security of the islands from external foes, in the long years in which British political habits of moderation and compromise could mature without the constant pressure of foreign wars. The immediate crisis of war may indeed promote a temporary unity in a threatened nation, like the France of 1792–1794. But long, steady exposure to war danger—and all continental states were so exposed—seems to promote psychological tendencies to seek final and extreme solutions.

This same relative isolation of Britain also contributed to the relatively mild form that the universal western struggle between feudalism and the new-model centralized state took there. In France, and on the Continent generally, the new model triumphed only in the seventeenth century, and in the form of divine-right monarchy. Continental states in the nineteenth century had only just gone through—or were still going through—the popular revolutionary modification of absolutism, and were still torn by major class antagonisms between a noble privileged class, backed usually by orthodox religion, and a middle class. In England, as we have seen in earlier chapters, that struggle had occurred a full century and a half earlier and had never been quite as bitter as on the Continent. It had left England in charge of a ruling class that was itself the product of a compromise between the old landed gentry and the new commercial classes, a ruling class that could develop within itself habits of moderation and compromise. The deep abyss the French Revolution had dug between nineteenth-century royalists and republicans and between "clericals" and "anticlericals" on the Continent did not exist in nineteenth-century England.

Thus, even more important than the fact that the Liberals and Conservatives each held together as parties whose members could sink differences in a common party action is the fact that both parties had a wide area of mutual agreement above and beyond party. To put it quite baldly, there wasn't much difference between the Conservatives and the Liberals. When one went out of power and the other came in, the ship of state tacked a bit, but it did not change direction. The Conservative Disraeli and the Liberal Gladstone were perhaps not quite shadowboxing in their heated parliamentary exchanges, but they clearly were not fighting to kill, nor perhaps even for the knockout.

To sum up, government by discussion, Her Majesty's Government and Her Majesty's Opposition equally loyal to established ways, under the shelter of the English Channel and the British navy, in a prosperous land without deep-seated class antagonisms or insuperable class barriers and rigidities—all this had developed in the British people habits of compromise, of law-abidingness, a sort of political sportsmanship. And these habits survive even in the mid-twentieth century, when Victorian geographical security has gone with the airplane and Victorian economic preponderance has gone with the rise of competing industrial nations. The British, who once cut off a king's head and drove another king into exile, have for nearly two centuries enjoyed remarkable political stability. Why these people, once thought hard to govern, have had so stable a government, is still by no means wholly understood.

Reforms of the Utilitarians

The Reform Bill of 1832 was soon followed by a series of major reforms that helped make over, not merely British political life, but British economic and social life as well. The inspiration of these reforms came in large part from a small but influential middle-class group, the "Philosophic Radicals" or Utilitarians (see Chapter 20). These disciples of Bentham and of the Enlightenment believed that men are, if once properly educated, impelled by rational self-interest and thus automatically do what is best for themselves and all their fellows. Under the influence of the Philosophic Radicals, English local government and the English legal system were made simpler and were cleansed of some of the impediments to efficient government action left by the long accumulation of traditional forms, now become "red-tape." Legal procedures, for instance, which had been so complicated that the Chancery Court was many years behind its backlog of cases, were gradually speeded up. In local government, though many medieval offices remained at least in name, the essential work was done by an elective council and by elective officers with supervisory powers over the professional civil servants—including now for the first time professional "policemen." Indeed, London policemen are still occasionally called "Bobbies," after Robert Peel's innovation of the late 1820's.

The middle-class radicals, however, believed firmly that that government governs best which governs least, and they sought rather to expedite that minimum of government than to add to its tasks. They believed in education, but not in compulsory public education; private initiative would in their opinion do well what the government would do poorly and tyrannically. Large-scale government reform of British popular education had therefore to wait until 1870. Meanwhile, the private initiative preached by the Utilitarians sponsored mechanics' institutes and other means of adult and "practical" education. It also sponsored all sorts of private schools, and universities in London, Manchester, and some other British cities. These universities, resembling in many ways our American urban universities, first broke into the centuries-old monopoly of Oxford and Cambridge.

The typical Utilitarian reform, the one that stirred up public opinion most thoroughly, was the New Poor Law of 1834. This bill codified, centralized, and made more coherent a complicated system of public relief that had orignated in the Elizabethan Poor Law of 1601 and earlier Tudor legislation. But it did more. It shifted the base of this relief. The old methods of home relief, "outdoor relief," had gradually come to permit supplementary payments from the parishes to able-bodied poor working on low wages, supplements for children, and in general by no means generous but still easy-going "doles" direct to families in their homes. The new system would have none of this laxness, this encouragement of men in what the Utilitarian, in spite of his belief in human rationality, rather feared was their "natural" laziness. Poor Law Unions united parishes for greater efficiency, permitted greater supervision by the central government in London, and supplied in formidable poorhouses in which the sexes were firmly separated, the "indoor relief" by which able-bodied paupers were made as uncomfortable as decency would allow. These pains, it was held, would encourage them to try to become self-supporting outside. The New Poor Law offended humanitarians in the upper classes, but from the point of view of middle-class business interests it had the decided merit of making poor relief both more efficient and more economical. The poor at least managed to survive in the workhouses.

Free Trade

Greatest of these Utilitarian reforms in its long-run consequences was the repeal of the Corn Laws in 1846, after a long campaign headed by the Anti-Corn-Law League (see p. 185). What these pressure-group agitators wanted, and ultimately got, was a political economy in which food and other raw materials were imported from abroad without tariffs, and the new efficiently produced manufactured goods were exported to pay for the imports. In the long run—in another century—the difficulty for Britain would lie in the fact that other parts of the world too would become industrial workshops. In the short run, in the early and middle nineteenth century, the difficulty was that protective tariffs in favor of English agriculture made importation of the cheapest possible foodstuffs from abroad impossible. To this difficulty the English industrialists addressed themselves in the campaign against the Corn Laws. Their victory was achieved in 1846 by the conversion of the Conservative leader Peel to their cause, and by the alliance of Peelites and Liberals that put the bill through. Britain was now a free-trade nation, the only major free-trade nation in a world that never quite lost its mercantilist preconceptions and habits. The repeal of the Corn Laws had, however, temporarily split the Conservative party into two groups, one the "Peelites," who accepted the repeal; the other, soon led by a brillant young man named Disraeli, who continued to support high tariffs on wheat. Within a decade the Conservatives were once more united in a single party under Disraeli's leadership.

Labor and Factory Legislation

Still another series of reforms helped make the prosperous England of Gladstone and Disraeli. These were the Factory Acts, begun in 1802 and 1819 with bills sponsored by Peel's father. Addicts of the economic interpretation of history hold that middle-class people put through reforms like those of the Poor Law and the repeal of the Corn Laws, but that the landed gentry and upper-class intellectuals, jealous of the new city wealth and outraged by the ugliness of the new industrial towns, put through reforms like those of the Factory Acts regulating hours of labor, sanitation, and the labor of women and children. It is true that many leaders of the movement to use the power of the state to regulate some part of economic life were not themselves businessmen or industrialists. They were either members of the Tory ruling class, like the Peels, or intellectuals, like Coleridge, Disraeli, Carlyle, Ruskin, and Matthew Arnold, who preached against the horrors of working-class life in prosperous Victorian England. And it is true that the formal philosophy of the British business class was laissez-faire. But the practice was a different matter. None of the Factory Acts and similar reforms of the nineteenth century could really have gone through Parliament successfully without some support from both political parties. Moreover, neither landed gentry nor industrialists and businessmen were mutually exclusive "classes" in a neat Marxist sense. Rather, they were thoroughly mingled in education, marriage, and even in economic interests, since the gentry

invested in stocks and bonds and the industrialists invested in landed estates. The elder Peel, father of the Factory Acts, was a self-made industrialist.

The Factory Acts followed a sequence not unlike the sequence of acts that reformed the suffrage. The first acts were very modest indeed; they underlined the frightful conditions they were designed to remedy. That of 1819, for instance, applied only to the cotton industry, forbade night work for children, and limited day work to twelve hours. Even so, it provided for no really effective inspection, and was violated with impunity by many employers. The Act of 1833, forbidding child labor entirely below the age of nine, and restricting it to nine hours for those below thirteen, and twelve for those below eighteen, marked an important stage by setting up salaried inspectors to enforce the law.

By the end of the nineteenth century, there was on the books a whole code of labor legislation, regulating hours of labor for everyone, giving special protection to women and children, and including provisions that made the employer responsible for workmen's compensation in industrial accidents. Then in 1911 came the great National Insurance Act, which provided through combined payments from the state, from employers and from employees, compulsory health and unemployment insurance. The "welfare state" was firmly established in Britain well before the Labour party of our own day had come to power.

Education

The same story of piecemeal but cumulative reform holds true in education. The commonly held Victorian idea that education is not properly a function of the state postponed a general education act until 1870. The issue was complicated by the wrangling of Anglicans and nonconformists, for many existing schools were controlled by a private society that made instruction in the doctrines of the Church of England compulsory. But even before 1870 a government committee had been supplementing local education boards by making grants from the national treasury (in 1860 these grants reached nearly a million pounds), by providing an inspection service, and by helping to organize teacher training. School attendance, however, was not compulsory, and the average age for leaving school was eleven years. After most workingmen got the vote in 1867, worried Tories—and Liberals—began to urge the slogan, "Educate your masters." The bill of 1870, put through under Gladstone's Minister of Education, William Forster, did not quite set up compulsory national education at the elementary level. It did permit the local school boards to compel attendance, and it did extend national aid and supervision. Church schools continued to get aid from taxes levied by the central government, however—an offense to radicals who wanted complete separation of Church and State. Non-sectarian religious instruction was given even in the equivalent of our public schools supported by local taxes, but it was not compulsory.

Beginnings were made in publicly supported schools at the secondary level, though the British "public school," which in American terms is a "private school," continued until our own day to maintain a privileged position in the British social system. In comparison with the public school systems in Germany, France, and the United States, British education on the eve of World War I was administratively complex and full of anomalies. On the whole, though, it got the job done, and the general level of popular education in the British Isles was at least as high as in the other liberal democracies at the time.

Chartism

The most radical of major organized reform movements in nineteenth-century England was Chartism, which played an important part in the political excitements of the 1830's and 1840's, and greatly alarmed the conservative classes. The Chartists were the closest English equivalent of the radical parties which on the Continent carried on the Jacobin tradition of the French Revolution, mingled with the elements of nascent socialism. The Chartists had a formal program drawn up in a "People's Charter," calling for universal manhood suffrage, the secret ballot, abolition of property requirements for members of Parliament, payment of members, equal electoral districts, and annually elected Parliaments. Their strength lay in the new urban industrial proletariat, supported by many intellectuals of varied social origins, men who clearly believed that if they got the political democracy they wanted the masses would vote themselves the kind of institutions —those of the "welfare state"—that, though maintaining free enterprize, would promote greater economic equality. The movement petered out in a monster petition to Parliament which was never even considered, and in the rising prosperity of the 1850's and 1860's it was effectively stifled. Yet of the original Chartist program all but the demand for annually elected Parliaments, which soon seemed pointless even to radicals, was achieved by act of Parliament in 1918.

Foreign Policy

Nowhere does the basic unity that underlies the party strife of nineteenth-century Britain come out more clearly than in foreign relations. The strife is real enough on hundreds of concrete matters of detail; but so is the unity in the broad lines of British policy. Almost all Englishmen (an unavoidable term, which, though offensive to many of them, has to include Scottish, Welsh, and Ulstermen) were agreed on the fundamental position of Britain: maintain the European state-system in balance, preferably by diplomatic rather than military action, but seek no new territories in Europe; police the seas with the British navy; open world markets to British goods; maintain—and in Africa extend—the vast network of the British Empire, made up of self-governing, English-speaking lands and colonial "possessions" in lands inhabited by the darker-skinned peoples. It is certainly true that the Liberals verbally and emotionally sided in Europe with the liberal nationalist movements, that they sympathized with the struggling Italians, Greeks, and Poles, and that they disliked the old Metternichian powers, especially Russia. It is even true that a Liberal—or better, a belated Whig—foreign minister like Palmerston in mid-century pursued an active policy of near-intervention in behalf of oppressed nationalities, and that British benevolence was a factor in the attainment of Italian unity.

Yet the only European war in which Britain became involved between 1815 and 1914 was the Crimean War of 1854–1856, in which France and England went to war as allies against Russia to protect Turkey and their own Near Eastern interests from what they held to be Russian aggression (see Chapter 22). This was a blundering war on both sides. But it at least checked Russian advances for a time and made the ultimate disposition of the Balkan regions of the decaying Turkish Empire unavoidably a matter for joint action by all the great powers. It was, in fact, a typical balance-of-power war in which Britain played its traditional role of taking arms against a major power (Russia) that seemed about to add unduly to its lands or its "spheres of influence."

Imperial Policy

On imperial policy, it seems at first glance as though British public opinion really was deeply divided. Disraeli and Gladstone were never so gladiatorially fierce as when the Conservative defended the greatness of the Empire and the Liberal attacked imperialism at home and abroad as un-Christian, illiberal, and unprofitable. And it would be absurd to maintain that in action there was no real difference between the two. Disraeli, on the one side, bought up the financially embarrassed Khedive of Egypt's controlling shares in the French-built Suez Canal (1875), thus initiating the British control of Egypt, and triumphantly made Queen Victoria Empress of India (1876). On the other side, Gladstone, in his succeeding ministry, withdrew British troops from Afghanistan in 1880, conceded virtual independence to the Boer Republics in South

Africa by the Pretoria Convention of 1881, and in 1884–1885 neglected General Gordon surrounded by rebels in the Sudan. Yet Gladstone kept British armies on the northwest frontier of India. It was under his administration in 1882 that the British actually bombarded Alexandria and monopolized control of Egypt. Gladstone did send troops to rescue Gordon, though they arrived too late, and even in South Africa the Boer Republics were freed only under the "suzerainty" of Britain. In short, Gladstone regretted and no doubt even neglected the Empire; but he kept it (for details, see Chapter 24).

The Irish Problem

Much nearer home, a nationality problem grew more acute as the nineteenth century came to a close, and did draw something more than a verbal line between Conservatives and Liberals. This was the Irish problem, a problem that had beset the English in one form or another, now acute and now mild, ever since the Norman-English conquest of Ireland in the twelfth century. The English, and the Scots who came to settle in the north of Ireland province of Ulster in the sixteenth and seventeenth centuries, had remained as a privileged Protestant landowning group in the midst of a subject population of Catholic Irish peasants. There were indeed native Irish among the ruling classes, but many if not most of them had been Anglicized and had turned Protestant. For three centuries, religious, political, and economic problems in Ireland had remained unsolved. As the nineteenth century opened, the English attempted to solve the political problem by a formal union of the two kingdoms, with Irish members admitted to the British Parliament, in which they were of course a minority. On January 1, 1801, began the United Kingdom of Great Britain and Ireland. In the prevailing temper of nineteenth-century Britain, it was quite impossible to deny the Irish natives all political rights; and indeed, beginning with the Catholic Emancipation Act of 1829, which allowed Irish voters to elect Catholics to office, most of the various reforms we have outlined above were extended to Ireland. The Irish, led by Daniel O'Connell, the "Great Emancipator," organized politically to press for more thoroughgoing reforms and, eventually, for home rule of the kind the overseas dominions were to achieve (see Chapter 24). They sought not only for political home rule, but also for land reforms, and for disestablishment of the Anglican Church in Ireland—that is, abolition of a state church supported by taxes levied on both members and nonmembers of the church.

Irish hatred for the English was fanned by the disastrous potato famine of the 1840's, when blight ruined a crop essential to the Irish food supply. Although the beginnings of modern transportation by railway and steamship existed, the British government was not organized for prompt and efficient relief measures, nor was the kind of international organization for such relief afforded nowadays by the Red Cross yet in existence. The result was a medieval famine in the heart of modern western civilization, in which tens of thousands died of starvation, and other tens of thousands were forced to migrate, mostly to the United States. The immigrants added to British difficulties, for they carried their inevitable hatreds with them, and formed pressure groups, like the Fenian Brotherhood organized in New York in 1858 to raise funds to aid Irish resistance and to make trouble generally for the British wherever they could. Indeed, the existence of these British-hating Irish-Americans was to be for nearly a century a serious problem for those directing American foreign policy, notably in the first World War.

British governments made piecemeal reforms. The Anglican Church in Ireland was disestablished in 1869, and in the next year an Irish Land Act began a series of agrarian reforms that were designed to protect the tenant from "rack-renting"—the extraction by the landlord, often an absentee member of the British "garrison," of as high a rent as the tenants could pay. The reforms were neither far-reaching nor rapid enough to satisfy the Irish. Moreover, the emotional strength of Irish nationalism grew with the spread of elementary education and the usual literary and cultural forms of national self-consciousness. The Irish question was not just a matter of land, or of religion, but also of a peculiarly intense form of underdog awareness of cultural differences and of nationality. Then in the 1870's a brilliant Irish leader arose, Charles Parnell, himself a Protestant descendant of the "garrison," but a firm Irish patriot. Under the leadership of Parnell in the British Parliament, the Irish nationalists were welded into a firm, well-disciplined party which, though it held less than a hundred seats in the House of Commons of the now United Kingdom, could often swing the balance between Liberals and Conservatives.

The critical step came when in 1885 Gladstone was converted to Home Rule, and introduced his first Home Rule Bill. This bill provided for a separate Irish parliament with some restrictions on its sovereignty, and of course under the Crown. Gladstone's decision split his own Liberal party in something like the way Peel's conversion to Free Trade had split the Conservatives in 1846 (see p. 219). A group led by Joseph Chamberlain, who had begun political life as the reform leader of the great city of Birmingham, seceded under the name of "Liberal Unionists." In effect, they joined the Conservative party, which was often known in the next few decades, so great were the passions aroused in Great Britain by this proposed cutting loose of Ireland, simply as the "Unionist" party. Gladstone lost the election brought on by the split, and Home Rule was dropped for the moment.

Agitation continued in Ireland. It became more bitter when Parnell, involved in a divorce scandal, was dropped by the virtuous Gladstone and by some of his own, equally virtuous Irish followers. In 1892, however, Gladstone won a close election on the Irish issue—or, rather, he obtained enough English seats to get a Second Home Rule Bill through the Commons with the aid of eighty-one Irish nationalists. The bill was defeated, however, in the Conservative House of Lords, and was dropped once more. The Conservatives, when they came in for their ten-year reign in 1895, sought to "kill Home Rule by kindness," carrying several land reform bills that furthered the process of making Ireland a land of small peasant proprietors.

But Ireland was now beyond the reach of kindness, and Irish problems were no longer—if they ever had been—largely economic and administrative. Irish nationalism was now a full cult, nourished by a remarkable literary revival in English and in Gaelic which produced writers like W. B. Yeats, John Synge, and Lady Augusta Gregory. Irish men and women everywhere—including definitely the Irish-Americans—were keyed to a pitch of emotional excitement. They would be satisfied with nothing less than an independent Irish nation.

The Liberals, back in power after 1905, found they needed the votes of the Irish nationalists to carry through their proposal for ending the veto power of the Lords. After some soul-searching, the Liberals struck the bargain: Home Rule in return for the Parliament Act. They introduced in 1912 a Home Rule Bill which—the Parliament Act in 1911 having destroyed the veto power of the Lords—was placed on the books as a law. It never went into force, however, for as Home Rule seemed about to become a fact the predominantly Protestant north of Ireland, the province of Ulster, bitterly opposed to separation from Great Britain, was organized to resist by force of arms. The Home Rule Bill as passed carried the rider that it was not to go into effect until the Ulster question was settled. The outbreak of war in 1914 made such a settlement out of the question, and the stage was set for the Irish Revolution of the 1920's (see Chapter 28).

The Threat to Free Trade

As Great Britain approached the twentieth century, then, new problems arose to disturb the underlying serenity and assurance of the Victorian Age. The Boer War in South Africa (see Chapter 24), Irish troubles, the rising international tensions that were to lead to World War I (see Chapter 25), and the difficulties of securing by taxation and adjusting the distribution of the new government income made necessary by the rise of the "welfare state," confronted the British people all at once. Though here as always in history we must avoid the temptation to seek a single underlying cause, there was undoubtedly one major factor at work. The long lead Britain had gained in the industrial revolution was being lost as other nations acquired the technical skills of large-scale production. Germany, the Low Countries, Switzerland, the United States, and in a measure all the West, were competing with Britain on the world market.

Under such conditions, it was natural that some Britishers should come to doubt the wisdom of the free trade policies that had won the day in 1846. For the Germans and others were not only underselling the British abroad; they were actually invading the British home market. Why not protect that market by a tariff system? Few Britishers were foolish enough to believe that the home islands, already by the 1880's too densely populated to feed themselves and constitute a self-sufficient economy, could surround themselves with a simple tariff wall. But the Empire was world-wide, with abundant resources, with thousands of square miles of agricultural lands. Within it the classical mercantilist interchange of manufactures for raw materials could still in theory provide a balanced economic system. Britain could still be, if not the workshop of the world, at least the workshop of the quarter of the world that composed the British Commonwealth and Empire.

The same Joseph Chamberlain who led the secession from the Liberals on the question of Home Rule for Ireland also led a secession on an issue of even more fundamental importance. He became a protectionist and imperialist. He gave special importance to the establishment of a system of imperial preference through which the whole complex of lands under the Crown would be knit together in a tariff union. Many Conservatives, never wholly reconciled to free trade, welcomed the issue, and the new Unionist party made protection a major plank in its program. Liberal opposition, however, was still much too strong, and there was opposition also in Conservative ranks. Chamberlain, reversing the aims but imitating the methods of Cobden and the Anti-Corn Law League of the 1840's, organized a Tariff Reform League. In 1903, he made in cabinet sweeping proposals that would have restored moderate duties on foodstuffs and raw materials (largely to give a basis for negotiating with the dominions, which already had tariff systems of their own) and on foreign manufactured goods. But the Conservative leader, Balfour, did not dare go so far, and Chamberlain resigned with his bill unpassed. Indeed, Chamberlain, who had already split the Liberal party on Home Rule, now split the Conservatives on tariff-reform. The new Liberal government after 1905 continued the policy of free trade. The rift Chamberlain had made in the old Liberal party was, however, never really repaired. Its right wing was driven to Toryism; its left wing to the Labour party.

The Welfare State

The Liberals were, however, committed to another policy as contrary to the classical philosophy of laissez-faire as was protectionism. This was the welfare state—social security through compulsory insurance managed by the state, and in part financed by the state, minimum-wage laws, progressive taxation on incomes and inheritances, compulsory free public education, public works and services of all kinds. The dramatic point in the working out of the program was the "People's Budget" of 1909, introduced by a new figure on the political stage, a Welshman, the Liberal Chancellor of the Exchequer, Lloyd George (1863–1945). This budget, which frankly proposed to tax the rich to finance the new welfare measures, and also the rising naval costs brought on by the aramament race with Germany (see Chapter 25), was clearly no ordinary tax measure. It was a means of altering the social and economic structure of Britain. Its opponents not unjustly called it "not a budget, but a revolution." It passed the Commons, but was thrown out by the Lords, even though it was a "money bill." The Liberals went to the country for the second time in 1910 and after a close and exciting election were able to put through the Parliament Act of 1911, which took away from the Lords all power to alter a money bill, and left them with no more than a delaying power of not more than two years over all other legislation. The Liberal program of social legislation was saved. It was saved under conditions strongly reminiscent of 1832 (see p. 215), for the new king, George V (1910–1936), had promised Prime Minister Asquith that if necessary he would create enough new peerages—which might have meant several hundred—to put the Parliament Act through the House of Lords. As in 1832, the threat was enough, and the Peers yielded.

David Lloyd George, 1898.

But was it a *Liberal* program? The dissenting Liberals who had followed Joseph Chamberlain out of the party in the 1880's thought not, and it was normal enough for Chamberlain's two sons, Austen and Neville, who played an important part in twentieth-century politics, to think of themselves as Conservatives. For what happened in the generation after 1880 was a major change in the political orientation of British parties. The Liberals, who had believed that that government governs best which governs least, and least expensively, had come to believe that the state must interfere in economic life to help the underdog, and had come to adopt Lloyd George's plan for redistributing the national wealth by social insurance financed by taxation of the rich and well-to-do. And the Conservatives, who in the mid-nineteenth century had stood for factory acts and at least mild forms of the welfare state, were now in large part committed to a laissez-faire program against government "intervention," a program astonishingly like that of the Liberals of 1850. Whatever the future verdict of historians on the "welfare state" of the twentieth century, they will note that Great Britain was the first great democratic society to institute such a state.

The Labour Party

One factor in this change had been the growth of the British Labour party, which originated in a number of groups formed in the late nineteenth century. Labour, though not yet unified, had developed by 1905 into a party able to command fifty-three seats in the Commons. The political ideas that went into the making of the British Labour Party antedate by a good deal its formal organization. Basically these are the common democratic drives and principles of the Western world, first clearly shaped and disseminated in the Enlightenment of the eighteenth century (see Volume I, Chapter 17). It wanted the welfare state, and indeed some Labourites wanted a socialist state in which at least the major industries were nationalized. Part of the motivation for the Liberal program of social legislation was a desire to forestall Labour. Just as in 1867 the Tories had "walked away with the Whigs' clothes" and had given the workingman the vote, so in 1911 the Liberals stole Labour's clothes and gave the workingman social security. But these tactics worked no better in the twentieth century than in the nineteenth, and the workingmen on the whole stuck by the Labour party. The party could not, of course, in a country like Britain have attained national power from a base limited to workingmen. It has had from the start support from many "intellectuals" as well as from many upper and middle class people who sympathized with the cause of social justice. The Liberal party began a long decline, hastened by the upsetting effects of World War I, by the addition of many new working-class voters by the Reform Act of 1918, and no doubt by many other factors.

Not all the motivation of the Liberals in these early years of the twentieth century was, however, mere fear of Labour. In part, their conversion from laissez-faire to social security was a positive one, a sincere belief that the logic of their democratic assumptions must drive them to raise the general standard of living in Britain by state action. Something broadly analogous was happening throughout the democratic West—in France, in the smaller democracies, and, a few decades later, in the United States. An important part of the bourgeoisie in all these countries swung over, not to doctrinaire socialism, but to programs of social legislation put through by the usual machinery of change under a wide democratic suffrage. The English Chartists back in the early nineteenth century had had the apparently naive belief that universal suffrage would pave the way to greater social and economic equality. In the long run, events were to prove that the Chartists were far from being entirely wrong. The welfare state began in a democracy, although in Bismarck's Germany there was also early social legislation. (see pp. 262–263).

II   France—Second Empire and Third Republic

The Coup d'État of 1851

A century ago France seemed to many English-speaking critics, as she seems to many today, a rather uncertain member of the community of nations ruled by the democratic decencies—that is, government by discussion, peaceful alternation of "ins" and "outs" through the working of the party system, and the usual freedoms of "civil rights." The democratic revolution, so optimistically begun in 1848 (see Chapter 19), had by 1852 brought still another Bonaparte to the throne of France in the person of Napoleon III, nephew of the first Napoleon. (Note that "Napoleon II," son of the first Napoleon by Marie Louise, never really ruled, any more than did the son of Louis XVI, the "Louis XVII" who died in prison during the great French Revolution.) As President of the Second Republic, Prince Louis Napoleon had soon quarreled with the National Assembly, which refused to amend the Constitution of 1848 to allow him a second term of office. Fearful of radicals and socialists, the Assembly also whittled down the universal male suffrage of 1848 and thus enabled the Prince President to maintain that he was acting as the champion of persecuted popular democracy.

The *coup d'état* of December 2, 1851, artfully timed for the sacred Bonapartist day of the coronation of Napoleon I (December 2, 1804) and the greatest Napoleonic victory, the battle of Austerlitz (December 2, 1805), was a sterotyped affair. Controlling the army, Louis Napoleon and his fellow conspirators found it easy to purge the Assembly and make way for a popular vote on a new constitution. Even the expected street fighting on the barricades of Paris, which broke out on December 3, proved to be no wholesale bloodletting. It left victims enough as martyrs, however, and, po-litically more important, it enabled the President to pose as the champion of order against a largely imaginary socialist plot. Napoleon quickly got himself approved by a plebiscite, which by 7,500,000 votes to 640,000 gave him the right to draw up a new constitution. Napoleon III's use of his strong presidential office to destroy the Second Republic left its mark on the Third and Fourth Republics; French republicans came to fear a strong president of the American type, and devised institutions which, until De Gaulle in 1958 apparently overcame this fear in many (see Chapter 31), tended to keep the French executive weak and divided.

The plebiscite was accompanied by skillful propaganda, but it was not crudely a work of force. Though many opponents of Napoleon simply did not vote, it seems that at least a very substantial majority of Frenchmen over twenty-one really were willing to try another dictator. There were many reasons why men voted "yes." Almost all were weary of the struggles of the last three years. Many were frightened by the specter of socialism, now for the first time under that name a definite factor in western politics. For nearly three decades the full force of fashionable French literature had been at work making the Napoleonic legend and identifying the name of Napoleon with the "pooled self-esteem" of French patriotism. Many a man voted "yes" not to Louis Napoleon, nor to any approval of dictatorship for itself, but to the music of the "Marseillaise," the cannon of Austerlitz, to all the glories of France.

The Second Empire, 1852–1870: Domestic Developments

The new constitution set up a lightly veiled dictatorship very much like that of Napoleon I.

The "chief of state" (he became formally "emperor" on the sacred date, December 2, in 1852) had full authority; he was responsible only to the nation. He governed through ministers, judges, and a whole bureaucracy, in the appointment of which he had the final voice. The popularly elected assembly, the *Corps Législatif,* was filled with "official" candidates sent up by influence of the efficient appointed officials in the provinces. It had no power to initiate or amend legislation; it had only a veto, which in the first few years it rarely used. Yet Napoleon III insisted that he was no mere tool of the possessing classes, no conservative, but an agent of real reform, an emperor of the masses, a kind of continental equivalent of the "Tory democrat" that Disraeli in England was claiming to be. This claim indeed has been made by almost all our recent dictators, Communist or Fascist; they all claim to be *real* democrats, real protectors of ordinary men who in the classical western democracies, they insist, are actually victims of capitalist exploitation. Napoleon III has sometimes been seen as the first of these modern dictators, as a "proto-fascist"; and the careful student of his career can learn much that throws light on our own problems today.

Certainly by comparison with later social legislation in Germany, Britain, or Scandinavia, Napoleon's concrete achievements in direct benefit of the workers were slight. He did carry through a great program of public works, notably in Paris, where his prefect Haussmann cut through the medieval mazes of streets, those broad straight avenues which all the world knows so well, and which, incidentally, could be easily swept by gunfire and made street fighting that much more difficult. And he did help with housing and encourage workers' mutual aid societies. But the legal code of labor in France in 1860 was less "modern" than that of England. The standard of living of French labor in the growing cities was well behind that of Britain, and behind that of Germany and the smaller democracies. French labor did indeed benefit from the general prosperity that came to France in the 1850's, as it came to Great Britain, but the gains in wages were at least partly counter-balanced by

rising prices. France lagged as a welfare state.

It was the bourgeoisie that made most out of the Second Empire. Napoleon's government encouraged improvement in banking facilities, helped the great growth of French railways by state guaranties, and in general furthered the rise of industry in the two decades after 1850. That rise was, especially in large-scale heavy industries, definitely inferior to that of the British and to the already growing German industry. But it was in absolute terms a very real rise. Paris grew into a major metropolitan area, and centers like Lyons and Rouen in textiles, Clermont-Ferrand and St. Etienne in metallurgy, and many other cities came to have genuine industrial economies, with all the problems of slums, trade unions, and other signs of modernity. Yet there remained then as under later French governments an adhesion to older methods of doing business, to small firms often under family control, to luxury trades in which handicraft skills remained im-

Napoleon III (1808–1873).

portant in spite of the machine, all of which meant that in quantitative terms of actual production France fell behind the industrial West. In the '60's she lost her Continental leadership in iron and steel production to the new Germany, and was subsequently far outdistanced by the burgeoning economy of the United States. Her growth in population, too, fell well behind that of the others. At the end of the nineteenth century, she was not much more than 50 per cent more populous than at the beginning—and this with almost no emigration. Britain, in spite of a large emigration, had about tripled her population, and Germany, too, was growing rapidly. Even Italy, with slender natural resources and less industry than France, was growing in population faster than France, and was to outstrip her in our own times (in 1966 Italy about 52,000,000, France about 49,000,000). It must be confessed that the reasons for this demographic weakness of nineteenth- and early twentieth-century France remain a problem for the sociological historian. In view of the actual fecundity of the kindred French-Canadian stock, it would seem that "race" factors depending on biological inheritance must be ruled out; moreover, the striking increase in the French birth rate since 1946 took place in the same "race" that had fallen behind in the nineteenth and early twentieth centuries.

The Second Empire: Foreign Policy

Yet the France of the Second Empire was still a very great power, and the extent of her comparative decline was by no means clear to contemporaries. Although the French gained little from the Crimean War, they did at least have the satisfaction of playing host to the postwar congress at Paris in 1856. And the Paris Exposition of 1855, a counterpart of the famous London exhibition of 1851, was a great success that showed Napoleon III at the height of his power. He had pledged himself to use that power for peace, but he allowed himself, partly through a romantic interest in "oppressed nationalities," partly from age-old motives of prestige, to become involved in a war

against Austria for the liberation of Italy. French armies won victories in this war of 1859; characteristically, in these modern times of "publicity," the names of the French victories of Magenta and Solferino were taken up into dressmaking, cookery, and urban real estate.

In 1860 the Italians took things into their own hands and set about organizing the whole peninsula, including papal Rome, into an Italian kingdom. Napoleon depended too much on Catholic support at home to be able to permit the extinction of papal territorial power; moreover, the too great success of his plans was threatening the European balance of power. He therefore temporized, permitting the union of most of Italy under the house of Savoy, but protecting the Pope's temporal power with a French garrison in Rome, leaving Venetia still in Austrian hands, and taking the city and region of Nice and the French-speaking part of Alpine Savoy away from Piedmont as a reward for his services. He thus managed to offend most Italians, and liberals everywhere, as well as most of his own Catholic supporters at home.

To make matters worse, in 1861 Napoleon began a wild adventure in Mexico, supporting with French arms and men an expedition to put the Austrian prince Maximilian on an imperial throne. The Europeanized Mexican upper classes were in part willing to support this venture, for like most Latin Americans of the nineteenth century, their cultural ideal was France. But from the start the Mexican people resented the foreign intruder, and Maximilian had to rely heavily on French support to penetrate to Mexico City, where he was proclaimed Emperor in June, 1863. The United States, engaged in the Civil War, could do nothing at the time against what Americans regarded as an infraction of the Monroe Doctrine. But after peace had been restored in the United States, the American government protested strongly. The rival of Maximilian, the republican leader Juarez, had no difficulty in defeating the Mexican supporters of Maximilian, once Napoleon under American pressure had abandoned them. The unfortunate Maximilian fell before a firing squad in 1867. This unsuccessful venture was the last direct attempt made by a European power to install a new government in any of the Americas in defiance of the Monroe Doctrine. Soviet support of Castro's Cuba did not quite constitute such direct interference.

The "Liberal Empire"

Napoleon had come to power, as we have seen, on a platform of national unity against the extreme demands of the social revolutionists of 1848. But in spite of the plebiscite, it became more and more clear that if France had a national unity, it was not of the monolithic, totalitarian sort, but a unity that had to be worked out in the open competition of modern western political life with parties, parliamentary debate, newspapers, in short, with government by discussion. Napoleon could not in fact be a symbolic head of state, above the struggle, nor even a final umpire. He could not be a republican; he could not be a legitimate monarchist, though much of France, and particularly the conservative France which held authoritarian views, was loyal to the legitimacy of the Bourbons, or the somewhat dubious legitimacy of the Orléanists. He could not even be a good devout Catholic, in spite of the orthodoxy of his wife, the Empress Eugénie, for his Bonapartist background was heavily tinged with the anticlericalism of the eighteenth century, and his bungling of the Italian problem had deeply offended clericals. He could only head an "official" party, relying on the manipulative skills of his bureaucrats to work the cumbersome machinery of a parliamentary system designed, like that of Napoleon I, as a disguise for dictatorship.

As the pressure of genuine party differences rose, in reflection of genuine moral, social and economic group interests, Napoleon slowly abandoned the measures of repression he had begun with and sought to establish himself in something like the position of a constitutional monarch. An act of 1860 gave the Legislative Assembly power to discuss freely a reply to the address from the throne, and throughout the 1860's these powers were extended in the

name of the "Liberal Empire." Gradually, political life in France took on a pattern of parliamentary government, with a Right, Left, and Center. As a result of the general election of 1869, the government was faced with a strong legal opposition, thirty of whom were declared republicans. On July 12, 1869, Napoleon capitulated and granted the Legislative Assembly the right to propose laws, and to criticize and vote the budget. Partial ministerial responsibility seemed just around the corner as Napoleon entrusted the government to the head of the moderates, Emile Ollivier. A plebiscite in May, 1870, overwhelmingly ratified these changes.

It is at least possible that the Second empire might thus have been converted into a constitutional monarchy. The changes had indeed been wrung from the Emperor by popular agitation, not merely political but also economic in the form of strikes. It is quite as possible that a radical republican ground swell would have gone on to submerge the Empire in any case. But the disastrous defeats of the French armies in the Franco-Prussian War into which Napoleon was maneuvered by the skill of Bismarck (see Chapter 22) put an end to the experiment of the Liberal Empire. On September 4, 1870, after the humiliating capitulation of Sedan, a Parisian mob forced a rump Legislative Assembly to decree the fall of the Empire, and at the classic center of French republicanism, the Paris City Hall, the Third Republic was proclaimed.

The Birth of the Third Republic

The government of the new Republic was too good a child of 1792 to give up the war against the national enemy. A government of national defense tried to continue the struggle, but the miracle of Valmy (see p. 104) was not to be repeated. In October, General Bazaine surrendered a large French force at Metz, and the disorganized elements of other French armies were helpless before the powerful German forces. An exhausted nation, sick of the war, chose in February a National Assembly that met at Bordeaux and sued for peace. The special circumstances of that election, however, placed on the new Republic an additional handicap. For meanwhile Paris, besieged by the Germans, had resisted desperately until starvation forced its surrender in January, 1871. Even under pressure of the siege, Parisian radicals tried to seize power and revive the old Paris Commune, or city government, of 1792. These radicals could not stomach the capitulation that the rest of the country seemed to be preparing. In the elections to the National Assembly, their intransigence helped to turn the provincial voters toward conservative candidates pledged to make peace—and to restore, not the Republic, but the old monarchy.

This new Assembly, on March 1, 1871, voted to accept a peace ceding Alsace and a substantial part of Lorraine to Germany and paying an indemnity of five billion francs (about $1,000,000,000). Then the Paris National Guard, which had not been disarmed by the Germans, went over to the radicals, and the Paris Commune was set up. Marxist legend has consecrated the Parisian Commune of 1871 as the first major socialist government. The Communards were in fact rather Jacobins, radical anticlericals and highly patriotic republicans who wanted a society of small independent shopkeepers and artisans, not the abolition of private property. In any case, they had no chance in the besieged city to introduce sweeping social reforms. But their revolutionary aspect alarmed the rest of France, and their refusal to accept the peace was a challenge the National Assembly had to meet. To the horrors of the first siege by the Germans

Barricades in Paris during the Commune, 1871.

were added the horrors of a new siege by the government of the National Assembly, which gathered its troops at Versailles and in the "Bloody Week" of May 21–28 advanced through the barricades to clear the city.

The Third French Republic was thus born in foreign and in civil war and began with a heritage of unresolved cleavages. Indeed, it was not at all clear in 1871 that there was a Third Republic at all. More than half the members of the new National Assembly were monarchists, anxious to undo the formal declaration of a republic made in republican Paris right after Sedan. But now we encounter one of those concrete events that are the despair of those who seek the clue to history in vast impersonal forces beyond the play of human personality. About half the monarchist deputies were pledged to the elder "legitimate" Bourbon line represented by the Count of Chambord, grandson of Charles X, and the other half to the younger Orléanist line that had come to the throne in 1830, represented by the Count of Paris, grandson of Louis Philippe. Chambord might have become in fact what he was to his supporters, King Henry V, had he been willing to make the slightest concession to Orléanist sentiments and accept the revolutionary blue, white, and red tricolor flag that Louis Philippe had himself accepted as the flag of France. But he insisted on the white flag and gold lilies of Bourbon, which for millions of Frenchmen meant complete repudiation of all that had happened since 1789. Chambord did not, of course, act *just* for a white flag and against a tricolor one; behind these symbols lay real motives tied up with all French history. He meant to be not just a Victorian symbol, a purely "decorative" monarch, but a real king. No one, however, could be that sort of king in France at that moment.

In the resulting stalemate, the republican minority was able to maintain itself, and slowly gather strength. Thiers, the elder statesman of the Orléanist monarchy, who had been a leader in the opposition to Napoleon III, was recognized as "President of the Republic" and carried through the final settlement with Germany. He was succeeded in 1873 by Marshal MacMahon, a soldier and a monarchist, who was elected to hold the government together while the monarchist majority sought to unite in some kind of compromise Bourbons and Orléanists. That compromise was never achieved, as Chambord continued to insist on the white flag, and in 1875 a series of constitutional measures formally established the Third Republic.

The Constitution of 1875

These laws, known collectively as the Constitution of 1875, provided for a president elected by an absolute majority of Senate and Chamber of Deputies sitting together as a National Assembly, the usual ministers, and a bicameral legislature elected by universal manhood suffrage. The Senate was chosen by indirect election, the Chamber of Deputies by direct election; all legislation had to pass both houses, though only the lower could initiate finance bills. The critical point was that of the responsibility of the ministers. Had the president been able to dismiss them, a new Napoleon III might easily have arisen to destroy the Republic. MacMahon attempted to exercise this power when on May 16, 1877, he dismissed the anticlerical premier, Jules Simon, and got the conservative Duke of Broglie to form a cabinet. But the Chamber was now really republican—or at least anti-monarchist—and voted "no confidence" in Broglie by a big majority. MacMahon was thus forced to dissolve the Chamber and call for a new national election—which he could do constitutionally. In the new elections the republicans, though losing some seats, still retained a good majority in the Chamber, and could now force the president to name a republican premier. Disgruntled, MacMahon resigned in 1879 and was succeeded by a conservative republican, Jules Grévy. This crisis of the *Seize Mai* (May 16) set a precedent for the Third Republic. No president thereafter dared to dissolve the Chamber, and the presidency became a ceremonial office, made fun of in the press and on the stage. But at any rate, nine years after its establishment in name, the Third Republic had at last become a fact.

It was in form a kind of republican transposition of constitutional monarchy, with an ornamental president instead of an ornamental king. The real executive, as in England, was the ministry, in effect a committee responsible to the legislature—indeed to the Chamber of Deputies, which soon became the focus of political action, leaving the Senate little real power. The Chamber, reflecting the political habits of the ideologically divided country, was composed not of two, but of a dozen or more parties, so that any ministry had to be supported by a coalition subject to constant shifting in the play of personalities and principles. The result was a marked instability of ministries. The "life expectancy" of a ministry under the Third Republic was hardly a year.

Yet such a figure is misleading. A French ministry under the Third Republic—and indeed under the Fourth Republic—did not usually resign and give way to a totally different ministry with totally different policies. Instead, its personnel was shifted a bit, a compromise or so was made with certain parliamentary groups, and the new ministry carried on much as did the old. For instance, Briand, the great champion of collective security (after the war of 1914–1918), headed ten different cabinets at various times between 1909 and 1926; Delcassé, the architect of France's entente with England, served as foreign minister continuously through several cabinets and seven years (1898–1905). And in our own day two individuals from the same party, Schuman and Bidault, alternated in the foreign ministry through a dozen cabinets of the Fourth Republic. Moreover, the day-to-day task of governing was carried on by a civil service, by experts in the law courts and in the educational system as well as in the executive department. This permanent personnel, or "bureaucracy" subject only to broad policy control from above, preserved a basic continuity in French political action, especially in foreign policy, which if not always successful, was at least as consistent and persistent under the Third Republic as that of any western democracy.

The system was highly democratic, for it could work only by means of constant and subtle compromises. These, the essence of democratic government, were made in France

—and in most of the democratic world outside the English-speaking countries—by the several parties in open debate and voting in the legislature *after* an election. In the English-speaking countries, these compromises are

Cartoon of 1873, illustrating the National Assembly's division into competing Bourbon, Orléanist, and Bonapartist choruses. The sculptor depicting the Republic looks down from the scaffold, and Thiers leaves the scene in despair.

made *before* an election, *within* each of the two major parties, often in the privacy of the famous smoke-filled room. Probably the English-speaking method both conceals antagonisms and encourages the habit of willing compromise more effectively than does the continental method. But neither method will work if

Help Keep the City Clean
AND BE A
PUBLIC BENEFACTOR

TWENTY-FOUR PAGES.

The Galveston Daily News.

58TH YEAR—NO. 170. GALVESTON, TEXAS, SUNDAY, SEPTEMBER 10, 1899. ESTABLISHED 1842.

USE ONLY
TEXAS MADE BAGGING.
MADE BY
GALVESTON BAGGING MILLS
MANUFACTURERS OF JUTE BAGGING.
Brands, { "Texas" 2-lb Bagging, "Star" 2¼-lb Bagging.
DEALERS IN COTTON TIES.
Write us for Prices.
GALVESTON BAGGING AND CORDAGE CO.,
GALVESTON, TEX.

GRAND OPERA HOUSE.
Nine Days, Beginning To-day Matinee.
MATINEES DAILY.
THE MANHATTAN STOCK CO.
25-PEOPLE-25
Band and Orchestra. Special Scenery.
Double Company—Dramatic and Vaudeville.
Matinee Prices............10c, 20c.
Night Prices.......10c, 20c, 30c.
To-day Matinee } "Lightning Rod Agent," at 2:30 p. m.
To-Night } "A Chain of Evidence."
SEATS ON SALE TO-DAY.

THE TELEPHONE
Is recognized by the ADJUTANT GENERAL of Texas, as an important AID to the STATE MILITIA. Every COMPANY OFFICER, every SOLDIER and EVERYBODY ELSE should have one. CHEAP RATES. Call us up.
Southwestern Telegraph & Telephone Co.

COTTON.
We are prepared to make liberal advances in COTTON shipped to us for prompt sale or to be held, and our charges are as low as can be offered by any reputable house. If you have never shipped cotton to us, give us a trial and you will be pleased with the results. Stencil and daily quotations furnished free.
GROCERIES.
Interview our traveling salesmen or send us your open orders, and note what prompt and satisfactory service and courteous treatment you will receive.
CARSON, SEWALL & CO.
Wholesale Grocers and Cotton Factors
HOUSTON, TEX.

Bagging AND Ties
We are prepared to make prompt shipment of BAGGING and TIES. Ask us for prices.
F. Cannon Commission Co.,
Galveston, Tex.

Prof. L. G. de la Canal,
Instructor on the Piano.
For terms apply to the Mexican Consul.
Phone 1091. The best of references given.

WE OFFER
For Shipment Monday.
Fancy Colorado Cabbage,
Fancy Ben Davis Apples,
Assorted California Fruits,
Grapes, Peaches and Pears.
T. H. Thompson & Co.,
HOUSTON, - - - TEXAS.

RECEIVING THE VERDICT.

Imprisonment of Dreyfus for Ten Years in Corte Fortress, Corsica.

He Must Serve His Time From Day of Second Degradation.

Scenes in the Rennes Court Room When the Verdict in the Dreyfus Case

Was Delivered by the President of the Court-Martial.

CAPTAIN DREYFUS, FROM HIS LATEST PHOTOGRAPH.

Words Can Not Describe the Painful, Tremendous Shock of the Verdict.

There Was No Outbreak, No Threat, No Passion.

Reporting the Verdict to the Prisoner by the Court-Martial Usher

And Conveying the Information to Madame Dreyfus.

(Copyright by New York Journal and Advertiser.)

Special to The News.

RENNES, Sept. 9.—The judges returned at a quarter to five, the audience all standing, not sitting down. All ears were strained to catch the vital word, the president's voice being low and rapid.

Jouaust read rapidly in a low monotone till he came to the word "guilty." A strange sound rose all over the court, a general gasp, a curse, a stamp of the foot, then breathless silence. Confusion was caused by a man fainting. He was held up by his friends, who kept their eyes fixed on the judges. The end of the judgment was awaited with anxiety. All the gendarmes turned and faced the audience, expecting an outbreak. But there was no manifestation whatever. The audience filed out in good order without a word.

After judgment had been read to Dreyfus, I interviewed Coupois, who said:

"Dreyfus showed no sign whatever of hearing his sentence."

The sentence is ten years' imprisonment in the fortress of Corte, in Corsica. The five years he has already served do not count; he must serve ten years from the day of degradation, which must take place within fifteen days if there be no appeal to the court of revision within eight days.

The judges took one ballot on retiring—is Dreyfus guilty or not? Two judges voted no. The judges then discussed the penalty. The two judges in favor of Dreyfus pressed for a low penalty on account of his sufferings, and induced the others to fix it at ten years, which is the very lowest possible penalty for the crime of which he was found guilty. In fact the judges have lowered the penalty by two degrees less than ever known in the French army before for a conviction of this kind.

Dreyfus was waiting, with feelings which can only be imagined, in a room back of the stage.

When word was given to the audience to disperse, M. Hild, Labori's assistant, at a sign from Labori, went to tell him.

Labori sat in a chair as if paralyzed. A moment before, as the judges came in, he had been pulling the end of his beard in quiet satisfaction, confident that after Demange's speech the verdict would be four to three. The result stupefied him.

Demange sat collapsed, saddened to the last degree. It was evident in the heat and fervor and feeling of the close of his speech that his whole heart was set in securing the freedom of his client. His voice was deeply hoarse, worn down by his long speech; his face as solemn as tragedy. When the verdict came he sat silent, like a man collapsed; like a man who has just heard news of death.

Hild stepped along the corridor to the room where Dreyfus was, went in and closed the door. Dreyfus looked at him and saw from his face he had bad news. Dreyfus said:

"Tell me."

"Ten years in a French fortress."

Dreyfus turned white, sank into a chair and covered his face with his hands. He sat a long time, neither Hild nor the gendarme saying anything. Then an usher came to Dreyfus. He said:

"One moment."

He rose like a drunken man, his eyes unsteady, and passed his hand over his brow. The color was all gone out of his face, which was the color of ashes. The usher gave him a moment to pull himself together. Then he went into court to hear the decision read again. Dreyfus listened stupidly, facing Coupois, who read it. He said nothing, went out and was taken over to prison like a man under the influence of morphine.

Words can not describe the painful, tremendous shock of the verdict. When the judges came in, their faces were eagerly scanned. They gave everybody hope. Jouaust looked gentle and genial; even Brogniart looked quietly pleased. All the court looked like men who had done a kindly act and felt better. The curse which went up from the audience was so bitter, so strange, that those who heard it will never forget it. Then men turned their heads away and took no further notice of the penalty.

Hope was gone. The audience went out absolutely quietly. Not a word was said. There was no demonstration, not even a single cry. The Dreyfusards were depressed, busy with their own thoughts. The anti-Dreyfus men were maliciously satisfied. Their lips curled in contemptuous triumph. The police and gendarmes hurried everybody away from the Lycee, and absolutely barred return.

Outside the court, in the squares and cafes, there was a sharp silence. A sort of spell seemed to be over men, over the whole city. There was no outbreak, no threat, no anger, no passion. Everybody seemed to be in a state of shock. This shows how very general was the conviction that the verdict would be at least four to three. It was fully an hour before bitterness began to manifest itself, beginning with fiery, caustic dispatches which socialists and Dreyfusards began to place on the wires.

Meanwhile, the sickening news was being conveyed to Madame Dreyfus by George Hadamard, her brother. Hadamard is a gentle-natured fellow, slender, about 35, with pale and small blonde mustache. Yesterday he rode up the Rue with confidence and joy, and left his bicycle just inside the gate of the Lycee. He fully expected acquittal, as did Madame Dreyfus up to yesterday. To-day, however, he did not take his bicycle, but walked slowly up the avenue de la Gare to the house, about three blocks away. His father, impatient, came out of the gate to meet him. When he heard the news he stopped a moment to realize it. Then both went in together. Madame Hadamard, the mother of Madame Dreyfus, was on the steps of the house crying. She did not need to be told. Then all went in together. George told the news to the old people, who tried to comfort their daughter.

Madame Dreyfus took it calmly, as if prepared for it. The only agony she seemed to experience was dread of the second degradation, from which she recoils in horror.

It was a time of strange, sickening suspense, that wait in the courtyard for the verdict. It seemed to affect everybody in the same way. Men would place their hands on their hearts and say, "I am ill." Two men said this in my hearing in court, five in the courtyard, when we went out to wait for the verdict. Three men were so ill they had to leave and be driven to hotels in cabs.

When the verdict was announced one man fainted, but was held erect, unconscious, by the men next to him in the packed crowd, while they looked not at him, but at the judges.

HARRY J. W. DAM.

DISTURBANCES IN RENNES

BEGUN BY THE ANTI-DREYFUSARDS, TWO MEN ENTERED THE HOTEL MODERNE AND

INSULTED LADIES IN THE GARDEN

La Dame Blanche the Special Object of Their Ire—Raised Trouble Elsewhere.

Rennes, Sept. 9.—Scenes of great excitement occurred at Rennes to-night. The anti-Dreyfusards broke loose and started a demonstration which, but for prompt and rigorous measures by the police, would undoubtedly have developed into serious disorders.

The first sign of trouble manifested itself immediately after the verdict became known. The streets leading to the Lycee were at that time filled with crowds of people awaiting news from the court room. The announcement of the prisoner's condemnation was agreeable to a majority of those, and cheers and cries of "Vive l'armee" were raised, the gendarmes and the troops looking on without making any attempt at interference. The terrace in front of the Cafe de la Paix, the leading cafe in Rennes, was filled with people taking their afternoon drinks and aperitives. When the verdict of the court was announced the customers rose to their feet and demanded that the string band should give "The Marseillaise." The band struck up the air and the crowds, both inside and out, joined in the national song.

Colonel Jouaust passed by a little later on foot and in full uniform on his way from the Lycee to his home. The crowd, with bared heads, cheered him, crying: "Vive l'armee."

Colonel Jouaust, in reply to their cheers, saluted with his hand to his kepi.

As dinner time approached the streets became empty, but about 8 o'clock the crowds again gathered. Just then an incident occurred at the Hotel Moderne, which is known as the Dreyfusard center. Two men, notorious anti-Dreyfusard, entered the winter garden, inside the hotel, and sat down at one of the little marble tables under the palm trees and ordered coffee. At an adjoining table sat La Dame Blanche, with a companion, while at other tables were seated MM. Bernard, Lazare and Gorzinetti, with other Dreyfusards. The two newcomers at once began to make offensive remarks about Dreyfus and Jews generally. One of them, turning to La Dame Blanche, said: "Oh, these dirty Jews; these dirty Dreyfusards."

La Dame Blanche replied, telling him not to address her. The men, however, persisted and added personal insults, whereupon La Dame Blanche became greatly excited and called them cowards to insult a woman. The man retorted offensively and in a moment La Dame Blanche clutched a menu card in a heavy metal frame and threw it at the head of her insulter, narrowly missing him. The other diners, seeing the trouble, rose en masse and threatened to throw the men out of the garden. In an instant the place became a perfect Babel, every one shouting at the top of his voice, calling the men cowards and "canaille."

The ladies present hastily withdrew, Madame Lazare being carried away in a fainting condition. Just as the threatened free fight was at the point of breaking out a detachment of gendarmes arrived and after a scene of intense excitement put the men who had caused the row into the street.

This, however, was but the beginning. The men proceeded to the terrace of the Cafe de la Paix, which was now crammed with anti-Dreyfusards, and there gave their own version of the row, and in a few moments an anti-Dreyfus demonstration was in full swing.

The people sitting at the tables rose with shouts of "Down with the Jews!" and "Vive l'armee!" and demanding that the band play the "Marseillaise." The band was compelled to comply with the demand and the crowd bawled the air at the top of their voices, altering the words to "March on, march on, against the Jews."

Sticks, canes and hats were waved and then the crowd chanted "Vive l'armee! Vive l'armee! Conspuez les Juifs!"

Finally one man waved his hat and shouted, "Let us march on the Hotel Moderne." The crowd showed a strong disposition to take this advice, and as the hotel is within a hundred yards of the cafe the situation began to look ugly. Two Englishmen who were sitting in the cafe were recognized as foreigners and the crowd hustled them out.

At this moment the cry "Police!" was raised, and in an instant a strong body of gendarmes and police, headed by a detective, rushed into the cafe and cleared every one out, demonstrators or not. At the same time several squadrons of mounted gendarmes and dragoons, with carbines slung across their backs, galloped up and threw themselves across the road leading to the Hotel Moderne. Other detachments of cavalry cordoned all the approaches to the cafe, and then gradually closed in on the crowd, which was now rather large and extremely threatening, and drove them like cattle across the bridge over the river and into the upper part of the town, which was filled with shouts of "Vive l'armee!" and "Down with the Jews!"

A number of the most noisy of the demonstrators were arrested, and the cavalry at a quick trot broke up every group and forced the participants in the demonstration out of the center of the town, around which was formed a cordon through which no one was allowed to pass except he was provided with a pass from the police authorities.

The demonstrations dwindled from this time until this evening, when only a few noisy bands were left, parading the smaller streets, but running at the first sight of a man in blue.

Strong repressive measures, however, alone can prevent serious disturbance. The cafes in the neighborhood have been closed, some of them by the police and others through panic, and tranquillity is now practically restored, though to-night's trouble may be only the prelude to a bigger demonstration to-morrow.

INDEX OF TO-DAY'S IMPORTANT NEWS

FIRST PAGE—
Disturbances in Rennes.
Reviewing the Verdict.
Views of Zangwill.

SECOND PAGE—
The Trial of Dreyfus.
Transvaal Situation—Foreign News.
Reports on Yellow Fever.

THIRD PAGE—
General War News.
Cable Letter From Berlin.
London Cable Letter.

FOURTH PAGE—
Pecos Valley Facts.
General Sporting News.
Austin News.

FIFTH PAGE—
The Houston Budget.
State Truck Farmers.
Religious News.

SIXTH PAGE—
Marine Matters.
Growing American Exports.

SEVENTH PAGE—
Canadian Pacific Railway—General Railroad News.

EIGHTH PAGE—
Galveston Military Company.
Police Jobs and Franchises.

NINTH PAGE—
New Military Sensation.
The Hero of the Railroad.

TENTH PAGE—
Confederate Veterans' Department.

ELEVENTH PAGE—
London Now Has a Sorosis.

TWELFTH PAGE—
Our Splendid Artillery at Work.
Questions and Answers.
Knots to Untie.
Casey Has His Fortune Told.

THIRTEENTH PAGE—
Unique Mail Service.

FOURTEENTH PAGE—
Houston Society News.
Sons of the Confederacy.

FIFTEENTH PAGE—
Theatrical Mention.

SIXTEENTH PAGE—
Editorial.
Cost of Living Increased.

SEVENTEENTH PAGE—
New Life Discovered in Our Lakes.
The Extravagant Dressing of Canine Pets Surpasses All Limits.
The Greatest Moving Feat Ever Accomplished.

EIGHTEENTH PAGE—
The Travelers' Protective Association.
Some Discord Up in Maine.
Classified Advertising.

NINETEENTH PAGE—
Classified Advertising.
Displayed Advertising.

TWENTIETH PAGE—
Children's Page.

TWENTY-FIRST PAGE—
Woman's Page.

TWENTY-SECOND PAGE—
An Object Lesson in Our Tariff System.
General Financial News.

TWENTY-THIRD PAGE—
Cotton Markets.
General Markets Abroad.

TWENTY-FOURTH PAGE—
Local Society News.
Books and Magazines.

Bridge Building Trust.

New York, Sept. 9.—The first steps in the consolidation of 90 per cent of the bridge building concerns of the United States under the name of the American bridge company are completed, the representatives of the thirty companies that have formed the combination having concluded their work here to-day. The capital will be in the neighborhood of $65,000,000.

Train Wrecked in Mexico.

City of Mexico, Sept. 9.—The south bound express and mail train on the Mexican National road was wrecked last night south of Acambaro. The passengers escaped unhurt, but Engineer Rafferty received severe injuries.

Lieutenant Appointed.

Washington, D. C., Sept. 9.—Among the army appointments announced to-day was that of Fred Dingley, late first lieutenant of the First Arkansas volunteers, to be a second lieutenant in the Forty-fourth regiment.

Venezuelan Revolution.

Caracas, Venezuela, Sept. 8.—(Delayed in transmission.)—The revolution under the leadership of General Castro is gaining ground. The insurgents now occupy Nirgua, three days' march from Valencia.

TEXANS ABROAD.

In New York.

Special to The News.

New York, Sept. 9.—The following Texans are registered at New York hotels:

Paris—H. D. Bettes, St. Denis.
Dallas—J. J. Orchard, Fifth Avenue.

FINE ARTS AT THE EXPOSITION.

Juries on Painting and Sculpture to Be Announced Shortly.

New York, Sept. 9.—John B. Caldwell, director of fine arts of the commission to the Paris exposition in 1900, in an interview said that the juries for painting and sculpture will be announced in about ten days. The personnel of these juries, which will be composed entirely of professional painters and sculptors, with the exception that Mr. Caldwell will probably act ex-officio on all juries, has naturally been a matter of lively speculation in art circles. The interest in fact has been so keen that Mr. Caldwell has been unnecessarily blamed in some quarters for not making the appointments last summer. But he has had excellent reasons for his delay, which he does not think will cause any material inconvenience to painters, as the scope of the exhibition is in one sense retrospective.

The French authorities having decided that it shall cover the period of eleven years since the exposition of 1889, most of the work to be exhibited will have been already completed, and it would be prejudicial to the interests of the exhibit that any work should be specially created with the view of appealing to any given jury. A general circular to be issued from the department of fine arts in a few days besides announcing the names of the various juries of selection in the United States, will state the date in November when they will convene, and a great deal of information of interest to all intending exhibitors. Two of the juries of selection of paintings in the United States, an eastern and a western jury, will meet respectively in New York and Chicago. Artists of the eastern and western cities will be associated on each jury and many of the same artists will be enabled to serve on both juries, thereby establishing a uniform standard of selection. There will be a similar jury in Paris, which will have representatives from London and other European cities.

James B. Eustis Dead.

Newport, R. I., Sept. 9.—James B. Eustis, ambassador to France during the second Cleveland administration, and formerly a senator from Louisiana, died at his summer home in this city at 8 o'clock to-night of pneumonia. Mr. Eustis was taken ill on Wednesday, but the local physician, after an examination, thought the trouble to be heart failure. The patient grew worse on Thursday, developing symptoms of pneumonia, and on Friday there was a consultation of physicians, who stated that there was scarcely any hope of recovery. The end came to-night very peacefully. Mr. Eustis' son, James B. Eustis, jr., and his daughter, Miss Celeste, were at the bedside.

No arrangements have yet been made for the funeral, but it is thought the body will be taken to Louisiana.

The Letter Carriers.

Scranton, Pa., Sept. 8.—The letter carriers to-day elected the following officers: President, J. W. Parsons, New York, re-elected; vice president, Charles D. Duffy, Chicago; secretary, X. W. Cantwell, Brooklyn, re-elected; treasurer, Alex. McDonald, Grand Rapids, Mich.; executive committee, John M. McElroy, Bridgeport; A. K. Young, Cincinnati; W. J. Mizner, St. Louis; H. B. Seaton, Denver; William B. Moynsham, Rochester. The various standing committees were also chosen. Detroit was selected as the place for the next convention.

PAPERS IN GERMANY

Lie Ready for Publication Which Will Prove Henry and Esterhazy Guilty of Treason and the Condemnation of Dreyfus a Brutal Judicial Crime.

(Copyright by the New York Journal and Advertiser.)

Special to The News.

BERLIN, Sept. 9.—In the safe keeping of the military staff of the German empire all the documents, which positively and unmistakably will prove that Major Esterhazy and Colonel Henry are guilty of high treason, lie ready for publication.

It is confidently expected that after the judicial outrage at Rennes to-day that the kaiser will give the magic word that will reveal the truth to the whole world.

These documents will brand the condemnation of Dreyfus as a brutal judicial crime. That France will be in the throes of another revolution in a short time is not doubted here.

The Ereisninge Zeitung says that the generals who secured the condemnation of Dreyfus stand condemned before the moral court of the world.

THE SENTIMENT IN WASHINGTON

Special to The News.

WASHINGTON, D. C., Sept. 9.—The news of the verdict in the Dreyfus case was received in Washington with a feeling of astonishment in official quarters, notwithstanding the general opinion that, regardless of the evidence, the court-martial would find him guilty.

The liveliest interest had been manifested in this case among army officers and others in official life. The president, himself, has watched it closely and has carefully followed the evidence adduced before the court. Mr. McKinley was in his office this afternoon when a bulletin announcing the verdict was carried to him. What the president may have said is maintained as a profound secret at the white house, but no effort was made to disguise the fact that the president was full of sympathy for the prisoner and was much depressed at the verdict of the court-martial.

Every member of the cabinet in the city discussed the case privately and expressed regret that Dreyfus should have been made the victim of circumstances that made it impossible to clear him of the charges. One member of the cabinet who has never been heard to utter an oath used a vigorous expletive when told of the verdict and denounced it as an outrage.

THE VIEWS OF ZANGWILL, THE FAMOUS JEWISH AUTHOR.

Special to The News.

NEW YORK, Sept. 9.—Israel Zangwill, the famous Jew author, speaking of the Dreyfus case in to-morrow's Journal, says:

"The idea said to be simmering in Chicago of a boycott of the Paris exposition by the Jews of America because of the conviction of Dreyfus does not seem to me entirely well advised, although I sympathize very strongly with the moral indignation that lies behind it. But this attempt to meet force by force seems to me the wrong way for the Jews to assert their place and mission in history.

"What I suggest myself is that every Jew who feels an injustice has been committed should of himself stay away from the exposition, and I fully expect that this course will be followed by thousands of Christians. Instead of a specific Jewish protest, I should prefer a protest in the name of the human brotherhood. Let Jews, if they will, take the lead in stimulating this protest if nobody else is found to initiate it, but let the protest be that of humanity and civilization, not of a scattered race, a member of which has been wronged.

Dreyfus himself places France first and Israel second. He in no way pretends to be part of a Jewish nation working for common aims. His greatest desire is to die, not for Israel, but for France. If ever ethics is to rule international relations, as it already does in private relations, then a beginning must be made somewhere, and France certainly should be made to feel that she has offended against the moral code and shocked the conscience of civilization, and, I repeat, the protest of Jews should be a protest on behalf of civilization and humanity, and not on behalf of a brother Jew—a protest on behalf of these great ideals which France was the first to express for the modern world."

ROYAL BAKING POWDER
ABSOLUTELY PURE
Makes the food more delicious and wholesome
ROYAL BAKING POWDER CO., NEW YORK.

no longer to pay the clergy, and private corporations organized by the faithful were to take over the expenses of worship and the ownership and maintenance of the churches. The Catholics refused to accept this settlement, and the churches remained technically government property.

But, though the separation had been carried out amid great bitterness, though the debates had revived the ferocious language of the 1790's, there was no recourse to the violence of the past. Catholicism was not proscribed, and somehow or other worship continued in churches that were not the full legal property of the faithful. Catholic education was indeed severely hindered, but there was no formal persecution. The separation did not really alter the fundamental social position of the Church in France. The upper classes, and the peasantry of the north, northeast and west, remained for the most part loyal Catholics; many of the urban middle and working classes, and many peasants in parts of the south, southwest, and center remained what they had become over the last few centuries, indifferent Catholics or outright and determined secularists.

The indifferent Catholics and the anticlericals formed the backbone of the central supporting party of the Republic, the Radical Socialists, who were not socialists at all but petty bourgeois, French Jeffersonians. Indeed, the French Republic of the early twentieth century was a typically bourgeois state. It made certain concessions to demands from the workers for social security and better living conditions, but not nearly so many as the British constitutional monarchy was then making, nor indeed so many as the only partly constitutional German monarchy had made already. Trade unions in France were legal, but they had hard sledding against the reluctance of French workers to pay dues and accept union discipline. Moreover, good democrats, like Clemenceau and Briand, had no scruples about using force against strikers.

France remained fundamentally in the early

Opposite: The Dreyfus case as covered in the American press.

twentieth century what she had been since 1789, a land of small farm-owning peasants, very conservative in their farming methods, and of relatively small family-controlled industries, very conservative in their business methods. There were some elements of big industry by the early 1900's, and French steel production at that time was actually growing faster than that of Britain, Germany, and the United States. None the less, great industry was not typical of the French economic scene, which was backward in comparison with the achievements of the industrial giants just mentioned, but at the same time well balanced by old-fashioned standards of the nearly self-sufficient national economy. But the whole question as to why France, in 1800 their equal or superior, fell so far behind Britain, Germany, and the United States in the nineteenth and early twentieth centuries as regards general economic growth remains a puzzle to the historian. The one sure thing is that there was no single, simple cause, but a whole complex set of causes.

The Third Republic had weathered the storms of domestic differences at bottom because, though some Frenchmen disliked it intensely, and though many Frenchmen felt toward it that distrust of the "government" not unknown in the American democracy, most Frenchmen felt it somehow to be the embodiment of *la patrie,* the fatherland. Differences did arise among them, notably on questions of colonial policy. The great expansion of French power in Africa, Indo-China, and Oceania which made the world empire of France second only to Britain's was the work of a determined minority (see Chapter 25). Many Frenchmen viewed their colonies with antagonism or apathy.

France since 1870 had often seemed dangerously divided on matters of domestic and imperial concern; yet on foreign policy the Third Republic was essentially united. Disagreement on the big question of foreign policy concerned details of timing, not ultimate aims. France wanted revenge for 1870, wanted Alsace-Lorraine back. In the complex workings of international politics from 1870 to 1914, the foreign ministries of the Third in the twentieth century there than in the other parts of the western world.

This belief was reinforced by the Fourteenth Amendment to the Constitution, passed in 1866 and aimed to protect the freed Negroes in the South from state action to deprive them of civil rights. The Amendment contained the famous "due process" clause: "nor shall any state deprive any person of life, liberty, or property without due process of law." In the great era of free enterprise that followed the Civil War, the Supreme Court of the United States interpreted the celebrated clause to mean that state governments should not deprive businessmen—including corporations as "persons"—of property by regulating wages, prices, conditions of labor, and the like.

Immigration since the 1890's had brought in millions of aliens from eastern and southern Europe, men and women ignorant of American ways, and readily exploited by unscrupulous or merely conventional employers. These immigrants were hard to organize in labor unions; moreover, they and their children, uprooted, scorned, though they might be, readily absorbed the American beliefs that no man is a proletarian by nature, that there is always room on top. Yet even at the height of this "Gilded Age" or "Age of the Robber Barons" there was a movement toward the welfare state. Apparently there never was a time when laissez-faire was a universally accepted principle (except for the tariff), and wistful businessmen who nowadays look back to the nineteenth century in America as free from the curse of government interference are simply inventing a myth.

Much the same forces that had produced the Factory Acts in Britain gradually brought to the United States minimum-wage acts, limitation of child labor and women's labor, sanitary regulation, control of hours of labor, and workmen's compensation. Characteristically, and in spite of the Fourteenth Amendment, these measures were taken at the state rather than at the national level, and they varied greatly in the different states. The state of Wisconsin early established a reputation for advanced social legislation, but many of the older northeastern states played an important

Honest Money

Cartoon of Marcus A. Hanna, businessman adviser of President McKinley.

part in the movement. By the early twentieth century, public opinion was ready for increased participation of the national government in the regulation of economic life.

Theodore Roosevelt, a Republican, president from 1901 to 1909, promised to give labor a "square deal" and to proceed vigorously with "trust-busting," attacks on the great trusts or combinations that had come to monopolize important sectors of the American economy. Although Roosevelt did not always fulfill his promises, his administration did assail the trusts in railroads and tobacco and did press the federal regulation of great corporations. A federal prosecution of the Standard Oil Company begun in 1906 resulted in 1911 in a Supreme Court decision dissolving the great holding company. Some of the separated parts familiar today, such as Esso (Standard of New Jersey), Socony-Vacuum (Standard of New York), and Calso (Standard of California), are in fact "bigger" than was the dissolved parent company of John D. Rockefeller. Yet the work of the radicals of 1900, particularly the "muckrakers" who wrote exposés of questionable business practices for popular magazines, was clearly not in vain. American "big business" was in the 1950's bigger than it was in the days of Theodore Roosevelt. But, to put the matter nicely and in good terms, it was aware of its responsibilities to the public—or, to put it not so nicely, it was afraid of what might happen to it if it followed the advice of one of the great nineteenth-century "robber barons," Cornelius Vanderbilt: "The public be damned!" In short, big business in the United States is ultimately, as in democratic theory it must be, under the control of public opinion. This is a "realistic," not an "idealistic" statement: American public opinion is not at bottom hostile to the existence of wealthy individuals, but it does resent excessive exploitation by big corporations.

During the first administration of Woodrow Wilson (1913–1917), a Democrat, the process of regulation gained momentum. The Federal Reserve Act of 1913, for example, gave federal officials more control over banking, credit, and currency. Approval of such measures was not, of course, unanimous, since Americans differ loudly and widely about almost everything from metaphysics to sports. But, save for the Civil War, they have usually been willing in the end to differ no more than vocally, to accept varieties of belief and action where they appeared harmless or unavoidable, to conform to the law with no more than occasional violence. To outsiders, and to many native critics, American life in the decades between the Civil War and 1917 often seemed one great brawl, a more-than-Darwinian struggle for wealth and power. Yet this apparently anarchistic society achieved extraordinary material things—bridges, dams, railroads, great cities—which required the co-operation of millions of men and women disciplined to a common task. This paradox of the co-existence in the United States of "rugged individualism" and social cohesion still disturbs and puzzles many commentators on the American scene.

In spite of the more than usual dose of distrust of "government" common in western —perhaps in human—tradition, government has in the United States come to play a larger and larger part in the lives of all. Although this is true of local and state governments too, it holds more especially of the federal government. The gradually increasing importance of the federal government, and the gradually decreasing initiative of state governments, are as objectively clear in the period 1789–1917 as is the material growth of the United States in population and wealth.

The Myth of Isolation

Quite as objectively clear, though still the subject of infinite debate among Americans, is the emergence of the United States as a great international power. The United States was never literally "isolated." From the very beginning, this country had a Department of State, our senior department, and the proper apparatus of ministers, consuls, and, later, ambassadors. The United States was involved in the world war of the Napoleonic era, and by the Monroe Doctrine of the 1820's took the firm position that European powers were not to extend their existing territories in the Western Hemisphere. This was no mere negation, but an active extension of American claims to a far wider sphere of influence than the continental United States. Although Americans took no direct part in the complex nineteenth-century balance-of-power politics in Europe, they showed an increasing concern with a balance of power in the Far East, where they had long traded. After the brief war of 1898 with Spain, a war that broke out in Cuba, always a close concern of the United States, Americans found themselves directly involved with the newly annexed territories of the Philippine Islands, Hawaii, Puerto Rico—in short, with what looked to outsiders, and to many Americans, like an American empire.

Theodore Roosevelt, who owed his rapid political rise partly to his military leadership of the "Rough Riders" in the Spanish War, was a vigorous imperialist. He pressed the building of the Panama Canal, upheld the Far Eastern interests of the United States, and advocated a larger navy. This new "navalism," which also had assertive spokesmen in Britain and Germany, derived many of its doctrines from the writings of an American officer, Captain Alfred T. Mahan. Mahan's book, *The Influence of Sea Power upon History* (1890), and his later works assigned navies a place of preeminent importance in determining power status and found an influential audience both at home and abroad. Americans as individuals had long been active in work for better international organization, world peace, a world court.

Furthermore, over these many decades of expanding wealth and trade, the United States had come to take full part in international commercial relations. In these relations she had, save when the federal government was blockading the Confederacy, stood out firmly for rights to trade even though there was a war on somewhere, stood out for the "rights of neutrals." This fact alone would probably have brought the United States into the world war of 1914–1918, as it had brought her eventually into the world war of 1792–1815. But in 1917 America was, as she had not been in 1812, a great and active participant in the world state-system, though in formal alliance with no state.

Reading Suggestions on the Western Democracies in the Nineteenth Century

(Asterisk indicates paperbound edition.)

Britain

E. Halévy, *A History of the English People in the Nineteenth Century,* 2nd rev. ed., 5 vols. (P. Smith 1949–1951; *Barnes & Noble). The classic detailed study; does not cover the entire period.

E. L. Woodward, *The Age of Reform* (Clarendon, 1938), and R. C. K. Ensor, *England, 1870–1914* (Clarendon, 1936). Two full and very useful volumes in the *Oxford History of England.*

D. Thomson, *England in the Nineteenth Century* (*Penguin, 1950). Excellent account.

A. Wood, *Nineteenth Century Britain* (Longmans, Green, 1960). Excellent survey.

M. Cole, *The Story of Fabian Socialism* (Heinemann, 1961). Excellent account, important for understanding the contemporary British Labor party.

P. Magnus, *Gladstone: A Biography* (Dutton, 1955). A sound study of the great Victorian liberal.

Roy Jenkins, *Asquith* (Collins, 1964). A good biography of a main figure.

A. Briggs, *The Age of Improvements* (Longmans, Green, 1959). A general history of England, 1783–1867, which lives up to its apt, and not wholly ironical title.

M. Bruce, *The Coming of the Welfare State* (Batsford, 1961). A good general study for Britain.

R. E. Barry, *Nationalisation in British Politics: The Historical Background* (Stanford Univ. Press, 1965). A useful monograph.

David Owen, *English Philanthropy 1660–1960* (Harvard Univ. Press, 1964). A major work, important throughout its period, perhaps most so for the nineteenth century.

Note: See also titles cited for Chapter 20.

France

D. W. Brogan, *The French Nation from Napoleon to Pétain, 1814–1940* (Harper, 1957; *Colophon). A brilliant essay by a writer who knows first-hand the great Western democracies of Britain, France, and the United States. A bit severe on the Third Republic as a political structure.

G. Duby and R. Mandrou, *A History of French Civilization* (Random House, 1964). An admirable general history. See reading suggestions for Volume I, Chapter 15.

G. Wright, *France in Modern Times* (Rand McNally, 1960). The best single volume on the subject, with good reading suggestions.

A. Maurois, *The Miracle of France* (Harper, 1948). A general survey by a Frenchman with great literary gifts.

Adrien Dansette, *The Religious History of Modern France*, 2 Vols. (Herder and Herder, 1961). Major study from French Revolution to the present. Well translated from the French.

A. Guérard, *Reflections on the Napoleonic Legend* (Scribner's, 1924). Interesting study of the magnetic attraction exerted by Bonaparte after his death.

F. A. Simpson, *The Rise of Louis Napoleon*, 3rd ed. (Longmans, Green, 1950), and *Louis Napoleon and the Recovery of France*, 3rd ed. (Longmans, Green, 1951). The most detailed study in English; goes only to 1856.

J. M. Thompson, *Louis Napoleon and the Second Empire* (Blackwell, 1954). A useful synthesis, based on detailed scholarly works.

A. Guérard, *Napoleon III* (Harvard Univ. Press, 1943). A spirited attempt to picture the emperor in the attractive role of "Caesarean democrat."

D. W. Brogan, *France under the Republic* (Harper, 1940). A witty, perceptive, but allusive history of the Third Republic.

D. Thomson, *Democracy in France: The Third and Fourth Republics*, 3rd ed. (Oxford Univ. Press, 1958). A brilliant essay of interpretation; assumes basic factual knowledge.

R. Soltau, *French Political Thought in the Nineteenth Century*, new ed. (Russell & Russell, 1959). A good survey, though perhaps unfair to the conservative thinkers.

G. Chapman, *The Dreyfus Case: A Re-assessment* (Viking, 1956). The most searching treatment of the "Affair" available in English; neglects the historical results of the case.

H. Goldberg, *Life of Jean Jaurès* (Univ. of Wisconsin Press, 1962). Best treatment in English. Very favorable to Jaurès.

G. Bruun, *Clemenceau* (Harvard Univ. Press, 1943). A first-rate biography of the redoutable politician of the Third Republic.

S. B. Clough, *France: A History of National Economics, 1789–1939* (Scribner's, 1939). A valuable treatment of topics often hard to find information on; the notes are most helpful.

C. P. Kindleberger, *Economic Growth in France & Britain 1881–1950.* (Harvard Univ. Press, 1964). A stimulating study by a professional economist.

Italy

D. Mack Smith, *Italy: A Modern History* (Univ. of Michigan Press, 1959). A sound and detailed study, actually confined to "modern" history. Good reading suggestions.

A. J. B. Whyte, *The Making of Modern Italy* (Blackwell, 1944). One of the very few good accounts in English.

B. King, *A History of Italian Unity*, 2 vols., rev. ed. (Nisbet, 1924). An old account, but still informative.

R. A. Webster, *The Cross and the Fasces: Christian Democracy and Fascism in Italy* (Stanford Univ. Press, 1960). Goes back to 1870; good general study of the background of twentieth-century Italy.

R. Grew, *A Sterner Plan for Italian Unity: The Italian National Society in the Risorgimento* (Princeton Univ. Press, 1963). Good study of the important place of Italian parties, 1848-1870.

D. Mack Smith, *Garibaldi* (Knopf, 1956). Brief and up-to-date; the best biography available in English.

D. Mack Smith, *Cavour and Garibaldi, 1860: A Study in Political Conflict* (Cambridge Univ. Press, 1954). Important monograph.

B. Croce, *A History of Italy, 1871–1915* (Clarendon, 1929). By a distinguished thinker.

S. B. Clough, *The Economic History of Modern Italy* (Columbia Univ. Press, 1964). Authoritative; useful for the nineteenth and twentieth centuries.

United States

R. Hofstadter, W. Miller, D. Aaron, *The United States: The History of a Republic,* 2nd ed. (Prentice-Hall, 1967). A readable account, well illustrated.

R. B. Morris, ed., *Encyclopaedia of American History* (Harper, 1961). A standard reference work.

C. A. and M. A. Beard, *The Rise of American Civilization* (Macmillan, 1936). A famous popular account, written from the standpoint of the economic interpretation of history.

O. Handlin, *Chance or Destiny: Turning Points in American History* (Little, Brown, 1955). Most readable general essay by a distinguished scholar.

L. Hartz, *The Liberal Tradition in America: An Interpretation of American Political Thought since the Revolution* (Harcourt, Brace, 1955). Provocative survey that has stirred up considerable controversy.

S. E. Morison, *The Oxford History of the American People,* new ed. (Oxford Univ. Press, 1965). A complete re-working of an earlier book. Most readable and authoritative.

R. Hofstadter, *The American Political Tradition* (*Vintage), and C. Rossiter, *Conservatism in America* (Knopf, 1955). Complementary studies; liberal and conservative, respectively.

The Smaller Democracies

The following is a list of brief national histories which will enable the student to go further with the history of any one of these countries.

R. Carr, *Spain, 1808–1939* (Oxford Univ. Press, 1966).

E. Bonjour and others, *A Short History of Switzerland* (Oxford Univ. Press, 1950).

H. van der Linden, *Belgium: The Making of a Nation* (Oxford Univ. Press, 1920).

G. Edmundson, *A History of Holland* (Cambridge Univ. Press, 1922).

J. Danstrup, *A History of Denmark* (Wivel, Copenhagen, 1949).

K. Larsen, *A History of Norway* (Princeton Univ. Press. 1948).

I. Andersson, *A History of Sweden* (Praeger, 1956).

J. H. Wuorinen, *A History of Finland* (Columbia Univ. Press, 1965).

Historical Fiction

B. Disraeli, *Coningsby* (Dutton, 1911, Everyman ed.). Significant for Tory democracy.

A. Trollope, *The Prime Minister* (Oxford Univ. Press, 1951, World's Classics ed.). Probably the best novel on Victorian politics.

E. Zola, *The Downfall* ("La Débacle") (Appleton, 1902). Good novel of War of 1870.

A. Bennett, *Old Wives' Tale* (Modern Library). Contains a superb account of life in Paris under the siege of 1870–1871.

A France, *Penguin Island* (A Bantam paperback, also Modern Library, 1934). A satirical history of France.

R. Martin du Gard, *Jean Barois* (Viking, 1949). Sound novel of Dreyfus affair.

W. D. Howells, *The Rise of Silas Lapham* (many editions). Typical realistic novel.

U. Sinclair, *The Jungle* (Viking, 1946). A famous exposé of the atrocious conditions in the meat-packing industry of Chicago about 1900.

M. Kantor, *Andersonville* (*Signet, 1957). Grim and realistic novel of the Civil War.

M. Mitchell, *Gone with the Wind* (Macmillan, 1936; *Pocket Permabooks).

22

Central and Eastern Europe

To the Outbreak of World War I

I   Introduction

In this chapter we shall deal with Germany (1850–1914), the Habsburg Monarchy (1850–1914), and Russia (1825–1914). These three empires were partners in crime in the partitions of Poland of the late eighteenth century, and firm allies in the Metternich system of European balance after 1815. After 1850, they passed through periods of mutual affection and hatred. In 1914 all went to war, with Germany and Austria-Hungary as allies against Russia. Internally they had much in common, although each followed its own peculiar development. In contrast with the countries of western Europe, these were the lands of autocratic monarchy and relatively powerless parliaments appearing on the scene relatively late; all were still "empires," a title that only the tottering Ottoman state also claimed in Europe.

II   Germany, 1850-1914

In 1914, the militarist and nationalist German Empire was a powerful, unified industrial state with a highly educated, obedient, and competent population. By supporting the Balkan policies of its ally, Austria-Hungary, it helped to plunge the entire world into the first of the twentieth century's wars of mass slaughter. Germany had emerged as a great continental power only after 1850, although for more than 1,400 years millions of Germans had been living in the heart of Europe under a variety of political regimes. The militarism, the authoritarianism, the whole social and cultural tone of the Germany of 1914, were determined by the fact that it was the Kingdom of Prussia that had achieved German unification. Characteristic Prussian attitudes had overcome other German ways of looking at society and had imposed themselves on non-Prussians. The Prussian triumph was complete by 1871.

Between 1850 and 1871, and especially after 1862, Prussia moved with ever-accelerating speed from triumph to triumph. Doubters and protesters were silenced or dazzled by the glitter of each new achievement; moral objections were regarded as unpatriotic. Otto von Bismarck, who directed policy, spoke of respect for legality and decency as "humanitarian twaddle" and proclaimed an era when "blood and iron" alone would decide. The ends seemed so desirable and were being gained so rapidly that even stern moralists could tell themselves that this time they need not examine the means. They shook their heads and voted the government new subsidies.

The creation of imperial Germany was above all the work of Bismarck (1815–1898). Brilliant, unscrupulous, ruthless, a genius at maneuver and at concealing his real intentions, Bismarck was often bewilderingly inconsistent in his policies. Sometimes he pursued two apparently contradictory policies at the same time, until the moment came when he had to make a final decision on which policy to follow. His intense loyalty to the Prussian Crown, however, did not falter during his long years in office, although after his dismissal by William II in 1890 he felt that his work was being undone, and he often tried to embarrass the Emperor and his own successors in the government. He could not endure criticism of himself. At different periods, he loathed liberals, Catholics, and socialists. And he despised his intellectual inferiors even when they belonged to his own class, the Prussian landed nobility: the Junkers, who believed firmly in their own privileges, monopolized commissions in the Prussian army, and dominated the administrative services of the Prussian state. Whatever Bismarck's policy of the moment, force lay at its roots. Influential before 1862, he towered over Prussia from 1862 to 1871, and over the German Empire thereafter until 1890. Yet his efforts could not have succeeded had they not met with general approval from the German people, who had hungered for unity since before 1848.

Prussia and the German Confederation, 1850–1859

The first major question facing the statesmen of Central Europe after the revolutions of 1848 was whether Prussia or Austria would dominate the German Confederation. A creation of the Congress of Vienna (see Chapter 19), it had been temporarily shaken and split by the developments of 1848, and now needed to be rebuilt. The "Big German" solution called for federation with Austria; the "Small German" solution called for separation from Austria or even from South Germany. The "Small German" program meant Prussian

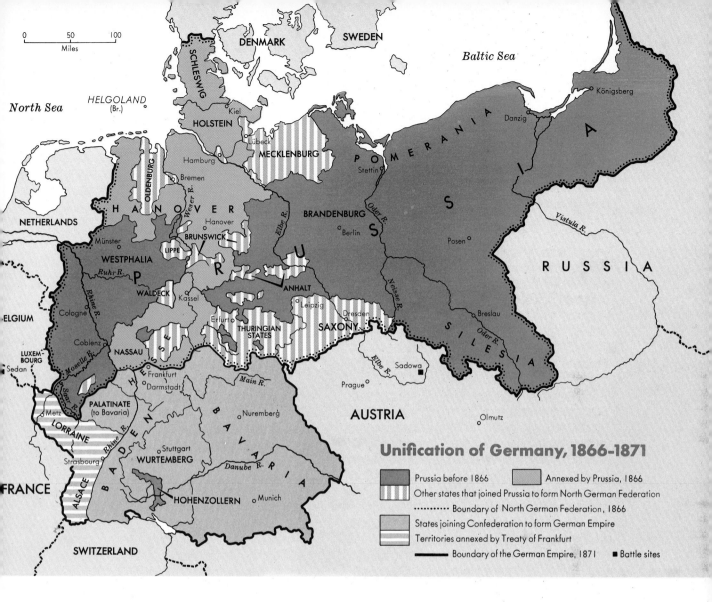

Unification of Germany, 1866-1871

- ▨ Prussia before 1866
- ▨ Annexed by Prussia, 1866
- ▥ Other states that joined Prussia to form North German Federation
- ········ Boundary of North German Federation, 1866
- ▤ States joining Confederation to form German Empire
- ▦ Territories annexed by Treaty of Frankfurt
- ━━━ Boundary of the German Empire, 1871   ▪ Battle sites

domination of the non-Austrian German states, and therefore became Bismarck's goal.

The period after 1848 opened with a defeat for a Prussian "Small German" solution. King Frederick William IV, who had refused to accept the imperial crown "from the gutter" when it was offered by the Frankfurt Assembly (see Chapter 19), none the less cherished the hope that the German princes might offer it to him. Taking advantage of Austria's preoccupation with the remnants of the Revolution of 1848, and overriding his own Prussian conservatives, who wished simply to strengthen their own state, Frederick William IV formed the Erfurt Union of Princes, an agreement to pool military resources. This

union was designed to lead to Prussian political as well as military dominance.

The Austrians managed to bring Russian pressure to bear on Prussia. The Tsar opposed the unification of the Germans no matter under whose auspices. At Olmütz, in November, 1850, the Prussians renounced the Erfurt Union and reluctantly agreed to the revival of the Confederation. This episode is known as the "humiliation" of Olmütz, a term that shows how bitterly many Prussians resented it. Yet Bismarck himself defended the treaty, and as a result was sent as Prussian representative to the Diet of the Confederation.

At the Diet Bismarck took every occasion to work against Austria, and to thwart

Austrian designs. As one facet of his policy, he favored Prussian neutrality in the Crimean War (1854–56), in which England and France fought with Turkey against Russia, and Austria harassed rather than helped the Russians (see p. 281). Realizing that Austrian behavior was alienating Russia, and that Russian friendship would be valuable later when Prussia came to grips with Austria, Bismarck frustrated those Prussians who hoped that Prussia would enter the war against Russia and thus line up with the West. He was counting on a military showdown with Austria. With this purpose in mind, he also wooed the French Emperor Napoleon III, despite the horror that many Prussians felt over dealings with a Bonaparte, whom they regarded as the heir of the French Revolution.

Both the constitutional and economic foundations of future Prussian development were laid during the 1850's. The Prussian Constitution of 1850, which lasted down to the end of World War I, provided for a bicameral legislature: a hereditary upper house including the nobles and royal appointees, and an elected lower house. But the method of electing this lower house made it certain that the popular will would be frustrated. Electors were divided into three classes, according to the amount of taxes they paid. The 4 per cent of the electorate who paid high taxes selected one-third of the representatives. The 14 per cent of middle taxpayers selected another third, and the remaining 82 per cent of low taxpayers selected the last third. The preponderant power of the wealthy is clear.

Even so, the lower house had very little to do beyond approving the budget. Policy questions were decided in the upper house, or still more often by the king and his personal circle of military and political advisers. The king appointed his ministers, could veto any bill he disapproved, and had a fixed sum of money at his disposal for expenses. He had a special "military cabinet" for army affairs that reported neither to the ministers nor to the legislature. Practically speaking, the king and the Junkers ran Prussia.

With its possessions in western Germany, including the Ruhr, Prussia had the richest coal deposits in Europe. The iron and steel industry, without which her future political and military triumphs would have been impossible, now began its phenomenal growth. Alone among the continental nations, the Prussians turned over the planning of their new railway system to the army general staff, which laid out the lines with an eye to rapid and efficient mobilization and transportation of troops and military supplies in time of war.

Bismarck Comes to Power

Indeed these military concerns led directly to the beginning of Bismarck's undisputed domination of Prussian policies. King William I, who succeeded Frederick William IV in 1861, was above all a soldier. His minister of war, Roon, a friend of Bismarck's, easily persuaded the King that an army reorganization was necessary. He wanted to increase the number of conscripts drafted each year from 40,000 to 63,000, and to lengthen the term of their service from two to three years. Roon hoped that a big conservative army might serve as counter-weight to any liberal or revolutionary tendencies in the state. A prolonged political crisis arose over these aims in 1861 and 1862, when the Prussian parliament refused to vote the budget. At the very height of the crisis, the King, convinced that Bismarck could outwit the parliament, appointed him to the key posts of prime minister of Prussia and minister of foreign affairs.

On the fallacious principle that there was a "gap" in the constitution that permitted the government to collect taxes even when the budget had not been approved by parliament, Bismarck now collected and spent revenue quite illegally. Again and again he dissolved the parliament, called new elections, faced another hostile house, and then repeated the process. He suppressed opposition newspapers in defiance of a constitutional provision that the press should be free. He indicted an opposition deputy, himself a judge and a loyal Prussian, in spite of the constitutional provision that deputies could not be indicted for anything they said on the floor of the house. Yet

after four years of this illegal behavior (1862 –
1866), he got away with everything in the end
because of the glittering successes he scored
by his unorthodox daring in foreign policy.

Since Bismarck intended to overthrow the
German Confederation as it was then constituted, he opposed Austrian efforts to reform
it. Austria wished to create an assembly of
delegates chosen by the parliaments of the
member states, in addition to those named by
the princes, and a directorate of six monarchs.
Bismarck prevented William I from attending
a congress of princes called by Austria to discuss these proposals, and thus wrecked the
congress (1862). In 1863, he kept Austria out
of the *Zollverein*, the German Customs Union
(Chapter 19). He also consolidated his good
relations with Russia during the Polish revolt
(see p. 263) by concluding the Alvensleben
convention, which allowed the Russians to
pursue fleeing Poles onto Prussian territory
and capture them there. Thus Bismarck wooed
the Russians a second time, as he had during
the Crimean War.

Bismarck in 1859.

The Schleswig-Holstein
Question, 1863–1865

When the King of Denmark died in late
1863, the celebrated Schleswig-Holstein
question gave Bismarck further opportunities.
The prime minister of England once remarked
that only three men had ever understood this
complex problem, and that one was dead and
one insane, while he himself, the third, had
forgotten all about it. In brief, the duchies of
Schleswig and Holstein at the southern base
of the Danish peninsula had been ruled by the
King of Denmark, but not as part of Denmark.
A fifteenth-century guarantee assured the duchies that they could never be separated from
one another. Yet Holstein to the south was a
member of the German Confederation;
Schleswig to the north was not. Holstein was
mostly German in population; Schleswig was
mixed German and Danish. In 1852, Prussia
had agreed in an international conference on
an heir who would succeed both to the Danish
throne and to the duchies. At the same time,
Prussia had joined the other powers in recommending that Denmark and the duchies
should be united by a constitution. But, when
the constitutional union of Denmark and the
duchies was attempted, the duchies resisted,
and the Danes tried to incorporate Schleswig.
German patriots objected. The Prussians and
Austrians wanted the duchies to have special
representation inside the Danish parliament
and insisted that Schleswig should *not* be
incorporated into Denmark. None the less, the
King of Denmark in 1863 followed a policy
that supported annexation.

Into this situation Bismarck now moved to
win the duchies for Prussia. He wanted both
the prestige that Prussia would gain and the
valuable commercial port of Kiel in Holstein. First he maneuvered Prussia and Austria
together into a victorious war against Denmark (1864), although Austria had no real
interest in the duchies. Then he quarreled
with the Austrians over the administration of
the duchies. At the Convention of Gastein,

1865, it was decided that Prussia was to administer Schleswig and that Austria was to administer Holstein. But this arrangement provided only a temporary halt in Bismarck's drive against Austria.

War with Austria, 1866

Bismarck kept nagging Vienna about Austrian behavior in Holstein. He tried and failed to tempt France into an alliance. But he did succeed in lining up the Italians, who secretly obliged themselves to go to war on the side of Prussia if Prussia fought Austria within three months. This was contrary to the constitution of the German Confederation, which forbade members to ally themselves with a foreign power against other members. So distressed was William I at this illegality that he lied flatly when the Austrian emperor asked him if such a treaty existed. Finally, Bismarck suddenly proposed that the German Confederation be reformed, and that an all-German parliament be elected by universal suffrage, which everybody knew he hated.

Bismarck probably advanced this proposal for universal suffrage in order to make it appear that his quarrel with Austria rested on a less sordid ground than the mere Schleswig-Holstein question. Yet the proposal also reflected his calculation that enfranchisement of all Germans would weaken the Progressive party, heir to the liberalism of 1848, and would produce many conservative and royalist votes from the peasantry. He had seen how Napoleon III had risen to imperial power in France on the strength of universal suffrage. And he had been influenced by conversations with Ferdinand Lassalle, a German socialist, who argued that universal suffrage would weaken the middle classes. Bismarck had hoped that the Austrians might try to throw his plan out, but the other members of the Confederation asked Prussia to propose a full plan of reform. Austria now laid the Schleswig-Holstein question before the Diet of the Confederation. Bismarck ordered Prussian troops into Holstein and declared that Austrian motions in the Diet were unconstitutional.

He succeeded in provoking war with Austria. It was an all-German civil war, since Bavaria, Württemberg, Saxony, Hanover (the four other German kingdoms), and most of the lesser German states sided with Austria.

The war lasted seven weeks and was virtually decided in less than three. The Austrians had to commit a substantial part of their forces against Italy. Skillfully using their railway network, the telegraph, and superior armaments, the Prussians quickly overran northern Germany, invaded Bohemia and defeated the Austrians at Königgrätz (Sadowa), defeated the Bavarians, and entered Frankfurt, seat of the German Confederation. The states of Hanover, Hesse-Cassel, and Nassau were all annexed to Prussia and their dynasties expelled. Schleswig-Holstein and the free city of Frankfurt were also taken over.

Bismarck successfully opposed the generals, and even his king, who wished to punish Austria severely. Except for the cession of Venetia to Italy, Austria suffered no territorial losses as a result of the Peace of Prague (1866), but she did pay a small indemnity. Most important from Bismarck's point of view, Austria had to withdraw forever from the German Confederation, which now ceased to exist. Germany north of the Main River was to join a new North German Confederation to be organized by Prussia. However, it was stipulated that the German states south of the Main were to be free to form an independent union of their own. But Bismarck had previously concluded secret treaties of alliance with the most important South German states —Bavaria, Württemberg, and Baden—who promised to put their armies at the disposal of the king of Prussia in case of war. So the proposed South German union could never come into existence. Bismarck thus broke the Peace of Prague before it had been concluded, a real piece of diplomatic skill. Bismarck's gentle treatment of Austria was not just a matter of generosity. He was convinced that Prussia would need Austrian help in the future. Now that he had expelled Austria from Germany, imposed a "Small German" solution, and elevated Prussia to the position of dominance, he had scored his point.

Now Bismarck was free to turn to the Prussian parliament, with which he had been feuding for four years. He asked for an "indemnity"—that is, a certification that all the revenue he had illegally collected and illegally spent, ever since the parliament had refused to pass the budget in 1861, had in fact been legally collected and legally spent. The deputies were so dazzled by the feats of arms against Denmark and Austria, and by the enormous new acquisitions of power and territory, that they voted the indemnity and awarded Bismarck personally a cash gift of roughly $300,000.

The North German Confederation

An assembly elected by universal manhood suffrage now debated and adopted a constitution for the new North German Confederation, of which the Prussian king was president. The draft that Bismarck submitted is eloquent testimony to his determination to "kill parliamentarism through parliament." The future parliament (*Reichstag*) was to have no power over the budget, and the ministers were not to be responsible to it. Instead, a Federal Council (*Bundesrat*), consisting of delegates from the member states and voting according to instructions from their sovereigns, would reach all key policy decisions in secret and would have veto power over any enactment of the Reichstag. A chancellor would preside over the Bundesrat, but would not have to explain or defend its decisions before the Reichstag. Since Prussia now had not only its own votes in the Bundesrat but also those of the newly annexed states, Bismarck's plan in effect made it possible for the king of Prussia to run Germany.

This plan was only slightly modified so that the future chancellor would have to sign every act undertaken by the king of Prussia as president of the Confederation. But the executive was in no way made "responsible" to the Reichstag. Bismarck's plan also specified that, beginning five years later in 1872, the size of the army would be fixed by law and that the Reichstag would have a vote on the budget. However, Bismarck, who became chancellor, saw to it that the debate on the military budget did not take place every year, but that sums were appropriated for long periods in advance.

Showdown with France

As long as Bismarck needed the benevolent neutrality of Napoleon III, he had hinted that he might not object if Napoleon took Belgium. Now the gullible Napoleon found that Bismarck no longer remembered the matter. Hoping to be compensated for his assistance in making peace between Prussia and Austria, Napoleon III tried to acquire Luxemburg by purchase from the king of Holland. Again he was frustrated by Bismarck. Suddenly confronted with the new Germany, many members of the French public and press hoped to get "revenge for Sadowa," and became strongly anti-German. The German press responded in kind. Napoleon III tried to obtain an alliance with Austria and Italy in order to thwart further Prussian expansion. But the Austrians shied away from a true commitment, and the Italians were unable to reach an agreement with the French because of the Roman question (see Chapter 21).

When the Spaniards ousted their queen in 1868, one of the candidates for the throne was a Hohenzollern prince, whom Bismarck secretly backed by discreetly bribing influential Spaniards. Because of family dynastic practice, it was necessary to secure the consent of the reluctant King William I of Prussia, and this Bismarck finally extracted without hinting that war with France might result. Napoleon III, also deep in Spanish intrigue, feared that a Hohenzollern on the Spanish throne would expose France to a two-front attack. French diplomatic pressure was exerted directly on King William, and the Hohenzollern candidate withdrew. At this moment, Bismarck seemed to be defeated.

But the French, overstimulated by their success, now demanded that William publicly endorse the withdrawal of the candidacy, and promise never to allow it to be renewed. William, who was at Ems, courteously refused, and sent a telegram to Bismarck describing his interchange with the French ambassador. Bismarck then abridged this famous Ems telegram, and released his doctored version to the press and all the European chanceries. He made it seem that William had thoroughly snubbed the French ambassador, and that the ambassador had been "provocative" to the King. Public opinion in Germany was now inflamed, and Bismarck set out to bait the French still further by unleashing a violent campaign against them in the German press, and boasting of his prowess in editing the Ems despatch. The French reacted as Bismarck had hoped. They declared war on July 19, 1870.

Within six weeks the Germans had advanced into France, bottled up one French army inside the fortress of Metz, defeated another at Sedan, and captured Napoleon III himself. The protracted siege of Paris followed, ending in surrender early in 1871. A new French government had to sign the treaty of Frankfurt. Bismarck forced the French to pay a billion-dollar indemnity, to cede the rich province of Alsace and about two-fifths of Lorraine (which the German military wanted as a defense against possible future French attack), and to support German occupying forces until the indemnity had been paid.

The German Empire

Even before this peace had been imposed, King William of Prussia was proclaimed Emperor of Germany in the great Hall of Mirrors in Louis XIV's palace at Versailles. Bismarck had to make a few unimportant concessions to the rulers of the South German states to secure their entry into the new empire, but he never had to consult the Reichstag, which simply hastened to send its own deputation begging the King to accept the Crown. The proclamation took place in a ceremony of princes and soldiers. When a constitution for the new empire was adopted, it was simply an extension of the constitution of the North German Confederation of 1867.

As Chancellor of the German Empire from 1871 to 1890, Bismarck became the leading statesman in all Europe. He felt that Germany had no further need for territory or for war. As a nineteenth-century realist with no dream of world-empire, he felt that his limited goals had been attained. As diplomat, he henceforth worked for the preservation of Germany's gains against threats from abroad, especially the threat that haunted him most: foreign coalition against Germany (see Chapter 25). As politician, he worked for the preservation of the Prussian system against all opposing currents.

Bismarck's chancellorship falls naturally into two periods: (1) a period of free trade, co-operation with the Liberals, and opposition to the Catholics (1871–1878); and (2) a period of protective tariffs, co-operation with the Catholics, and opposition to the socialists (1878–1890).

Domestic Developments, 1871–1878

At home, a multitude of economic and legal questions arose as a result of the creation of the new empire. Working with the moderate Liberal party in the Reichstag, Bismarck put through a common coinage and a central bank, co-ordinated and unified the railroads and postal systems, and regularized the legal and judicial systems. In 1871, the Reichstag voted to maintain 1 per cent of the population under arms for three years. In 1874, Bismarck, simply by threatening to resign, forced the Reichstag to fix the size of the army at 401,000 for a seven-year period, until 1881. In 1880, a year before the period expired, he forced an increase to 427,000 for another seven years, to 1888. The privileged position of the army made a military career ever more attractive and served as a constant spur to German militarism.

But the great drama of the 1870's in Germany was furnished by Bismarck's attack on the Roman Catholic Church, the *Kulturkampf* ("battle for civilization"). The "Syllabus of Errors," published by the Vatican in 1864 (see Chapter 20), had denounced the toleration of other religions, secular education, and state participation in church affairs. Then in 1870 the Vatican Council, the first general council of the Church to meet since the Council of Trent in the Reformation period, adopted the dogma of papal infallibility. This dogma asserted that the judgments of the pope on faith and morals were infallible. To many non-Catholics, this seemed to say that no state could count on the absolute loyalty of its Catholic citizens.

In Germany, the Catholics were a large minority of the population. They had formed a political party, the Center, that quickly became the second strongest party in the Empire. The Center defended papal infallibility, and wished to restore the pope's temporal power, which had been ended by the unification of Italy. The Center not only had many sympathizers in the Catholic Polish provinces of Germany but also sponsored a labor movement of its own, which seemed to pose a social threat. Catholic peasant and workman, priest and nobleman, all opposed the Protestant urban middle class and the Prussian military predominance in the state. Bismarck identified his clerical opponents with France and Austria, the two nations he had defeated in making the new Germany.

In collaboration with the Liberals, Bismarck put through laws expelling the Jesuits from Germany, forbidding the clergy to criticize the government, and closing the schools of religious orders. In Prussia, civil marriage was now required, appropriations for the Catholic Church were stopped, and priests were forced to study at secular universities. The Pope declared these laws null and void, and summoned all good Catholics to disobey them. Catholic services stopped in towns and villages, and many Catholics were deprived of their sacraments.

Bismarck never appreciated that the Church thrives on persecution. By declaring that he would not "go to Canossa," he summoned up for Protestant Germans the picture of the German Emperor Henry IV humbling himself before the Pope in 1077. But Bismarck in the end had to go to Canossa, and repealed in the eighties most of the anti-Catholic measures he had passed in the seventies. By then he needed the support of the Center party against his former allies the Liberals, whose demands for power he found exorbitant, and against the growing menace of the Social Democrats. Moreover, the Protestant Church itself and many of the conservative Prussian nobility had grown alarmed over the excesses of the anti-Catholic campaign.

Domestic Developments, 1878–1890

Indeed, in 1877 and 1878, Bismarck had begun a gradual shift in policy, dictated in the first place by the need for more revenue. The Empire got its money in part from indirect taxes imposed by the Reichstag on tobacco, alcohol, sugar, and the like. The rest came from the individual states, which controlled all direct taxation and made contributions to the imperial budget. As military costs mounted, the government's income became insufficient, and Bismarck did not want to increase the Empire's dependence on the states by repeatedly asking them to increase their contributions. He wanted the Reichstag to vote higher indirect taxes, but its Liberal members suspected that if they acceded he might do to them what he had formerly done to the Prussian parliament: govern without them if a dispute arose, and depend on the money he would collect from the higher taxes they had granted him. Therefore they wanted some sort of guarantee before they untied Bismarck's hands.

Basically, German tariff policy had been one of free trade, with little protection for German goods. But after a financial panic in 1873, the iron and textile industries put pressure on Bismarck to shift to a policy of protection that would help them compete with England. Moreover, an agricultural crisis led conservatives to abandon their previous support of free trade, and to demand protection against cheap grain from eastern Europe. In 1879, Bismarck put through a general protective tariff on all imports, a move on which his former allies, the Liberals, were split.

In order to avoid granting the constitutional guarantees demanded by the Liberals, Bismarck gradually abandoned the *Kulturkampf*. The Catholic Center favored his protectionist policy; moreover, the lessening of the clerical threat in France and the conclusion of a firm German alliance with Austria in 1879 (see Chapter 25) removed the foreign causes for the attack on the Church. Bismarck therefore secured the support of the Center as well as that of the conservatives. Thus he was able to avoid making concessions to the Reichstag, and thus he launched Germany on an era of protection. The protectionist policy spurred still further the rapid and efficient growth of industry, especially heavy industry. Politically, the conservative Protestant agrarian forces now grew stronger, and gained many urban votes. But Bismarck never entirely trusted the Center, and strove successfully to remodel the Liberals into a stanchly conservative industrialist group.

While he was easing the *Kulturkampf* and swinging to protection in 1878–1879, Bismarck also began to proceed against the Social Democratic party. The Marxists Liebknecht and Bebel had founded this small party in 1869; in 1875, they enlarged it, much to Marx's own disgust, by accepting the followers of Lassalle, an apostle of non-violence. The German Social Democrats were not nearly so revolutionary as their own Marxist phraseology suggested, and had no doubt inherited some of Lassalle's willingness to make a deal with the existing regime. They had many supporters among intellectuals and former liberals, and a substantial trade-union following, polling half a million votes in 1877, about 10 per cent of the total electorate. They were prepared to concentrate their efforts on improving working conditions rather than on revolution. But Bismarck always needed an enemy against whom he could unify his supporters; besides, he had been deeply impressed by the Paris Commune (see Chapter 21), and believed that something similar might occur in Germany.

Using as a pretext two attempts by alleged Social Democrats to assassinate William I, Bismarck called a general election in 1878

and rammed through the Reichstag a bill making the Social Democratic party illegal, forbidding its meetings, and suppressing its newspapers. Individual socialists could even be expelled from their domiciles by the police. Abandoning their alleged principles, the Liberals supported this law, but they would not allow Bismarck to make it a permanent statute. He had to apply to the Reichstag for its renewal every two or three years; it was renewed each time, until just before Bismarck's own downfall in 1890. Interestingly enough, Social Democrats were still allowed to run for the Reichstag, and their votes increased during the years when they were suffering legal disabilities.

But Bismarck felt that "a remedy cannot be sought merely in repression of Socialist excesses—there must be simultaneously a positive advancement of the welfare of the working classes." As a result, all during the 1880's, the government put forward a series of bills in favor of the workers: in 1882 compulsory insurance against illness, and in 1884 against accidents. The sickness insurance funds were raised by contributions from both workers and employers; the accident insurance funds were contributed altogether by the employers. In 1889, old-age and invalidism insurance followed, with employers and employees contributing equally, and with an additional subsidy from the state. The German system of social security as developed initially under Bismarck did not reduce the Social Democratic vote, but it did provide much that the worker desired.

William II

Bismarck's faithful William I died at the age of ninety in 1888, and William's son, Frederick III, already mortally ill, ruled for only about three months. The next emperor was Frederick's son, William II, a young man of twenty-nine whose advent his father had greatly feared because of his immaturity, impulsiveness, and conceit. William I had allowed Bismarck to act for him, but William II was determined to act for himself. This determination underlay the subsequent controversy between him and Bismarck.

On his accession, William loudly proclaimed his sympathy with the workingman. When the anti-socialist law came up for renewal, the Emperor supported a modified version that would have taken away the power of the police to expel Social Democrats from their residences. Bismarck opposed the measure, hoping that the Social Democrats would indulge in excesses which would give him the excuse to suppress them by armed force. As a result, there was no anti-socialist law after 1890. Other differences arose between the Chancellor and the Emperor over relations with Russia, and over procedure in reaching policy decisions. Finally, in March, 1890, William commanded Bismarck to resign.

Although four chancellors succeeded him during the years before the outbreak of war in 1914, none of them can be compared with Bismarck in ability and influence. The years 1890–1914 are truly the years of William II. Energetic but unsteady, pompous and menacing but without the intention or the courage to back up his threats, emotional and vacillating, William was ill-suited to govern any country, much less the militaristic, highly industrialized, imperial Germany with its social tensions and its lack of political balance.

Domestic Tensions, 1890–1914

Party structure reflected the strains in German society. The Liberals, a party of big business, usually had little strength in the Reichstag, although many industrialists were on intimate terms with the Emperor personally. The great landowners banded together in protest against a reduction in agricultural duties which was included in a series of trade treaties concluded between Germany and other continental European countries between 1892 and 1894. In 1894, they organized the Agrarian League, which spearheaded all conservative measures and became enormously powerful

in German politics. In 1902, they forced a return to protection.

The electoral strength of the Social Democrats increased during William's reign from 1,500,000 to 4,250,000, and embraced one-third of the voting population by 1914. Freed from interference by the removal of the anti-socialist law, they organized trade unions, circulated newspapers, and successfully brought pressure on the regime for more social legislation. The party had no immediate plan for a revolution, although its radical wing expected, especially after the Russian Revolution of 1905 (see pp. 289–290), that a revolution would come. The moderate or "revisionist" wing, which expected no open conflict between capital and labor, felt that, by allying them-

Emperor William II (1859–1941).

selves with the middle class to attain a majority in the Reichstag, the Social Democrats might eventually overthrow the militarist regime. This the radical wing scornfully dismissed as mere temporizing.

As the Social Democrats became more powerful, the government allied itself more closely with the Catholic Center. Between 1895 and 1906, and again between 1909 and 1914, a coalition of conservatives and the Center formed the majority group in the Reichstag. The coalition did not wish to see any increase in the powers of parliament. Yet left-wingers within the Center party occasionally called for a liberalization of the system, and for tactical purposes would even ally themselves with the Social Democrats.

Meanwhile, issues of military, colonial, and foreign policy began to complicate the internal politics of Germany. The size of the army rose from 479,000 in 1892 to 870,000 in 1913. And for the first time Germany sought a big navy, after Admiral Tirpitz became minister of the navy in 1897. The Emperor issued a series of warlike and grandiose statements hailing Germany's "future on the waters," and he and Tirpitz planned a high-seas fleet to supersede the naval forces that had been designed for coastal defense and for the defense of commerce. The navy boom was at least partly intended to supply a market for the expanding steel industry. A Navy League, ostensibly a private organization but constantly hand in glove with the regime, spread propaganda on behalf of the new fleet. The first rather modest naval law of 1898 provided for a navy that was doubled by the second law of 1900.

But the army and navy were only the most obvious weapons of world power. Bismarck's satisfied country seemed satisfied no longer. The Colonial Society thrived, as Germany seized lands in the Far East and in Africa (see Chapter 24), despite the drain on the budget (for the colonies were never profitable), and despite scandal after scandal (for the Germans were often brutal colonial administrators). "Pan-Germans" planned the great Berlin-Baghdad railway to the Near East and cried shrilly for more and more adventure and conquest.

William's naval and colonial policies embittered Germany's relations with Great Britain. In 1896, the Emperor himself sent the Boer President Kruger a telegram congratulating him on his having repelled the Jameson Raid (Chapter 24) and hinting that Germany would have been willing to intervene on the side of the Boers against Britain. Again in 1908, he gave an interview to a London newspaper, the *Daily Telegraph*, in which, with monumental indiscretion, he protested his friendship for Britain, yet at the same time declared that the English had been ungrateful to him in not acknowledging that his own military plans, sent to them in secrecy, had enabled them to win the Boer War. Of course there was nothing in his claim.

The *Daily Telegraph* affair aroused a storm of protest against William in Germany itself, and the Emperor had to apologize and promise to do better in the future. This episode illustrates the dangerous instability of the man who was all-powerful in a mighty military state. Moreover, it also reveals the general uneasiness that underlay the apparently smooth and prosperous surface of William's Germany. The protest against the anachronistic system under which Germans lived and labored, and against the external bombast and internal insecurity of the regime, was expressed in the enormous vote of the Social Democrats in 1912.

In 1913–1914, a German army officer in the Alsatian town of Saverne (Zabern) wounded a lame shoemaker with his sword, and the commanding officer of the German garrison illegally arrested and jailed townspeople who protested. The bitter resentment of the Alastians was echoed by a tremendous number of Germans who had become resentful over the outrageous and unrestrained behavior of their military. By a vote of 293 to 54, the Reichstag passed a resolution of censure against the government. Even more interesting is the sequel, for William decorated the guilty officer, who was acquitted by a court-martial. The Saverne affair proved that the German public was still capable of feeling discomfort over the excesses of their Prussian masters, but it also proved tht even a public expression of disapproval had little effect on these masters—the Emperor, the Junkers, and the military.

III   The Habsburg Monarchy, 1850-1914

Character of the Empire

The extraordinary empire of the Habsburgs has been called ramshackle, heterogeneous, and anachronistic. And much scorn has been poured upon it for its incompetence, its smugness, its stupidity, and its failure to keep up with modern times. No doubt these charges are largely justified. But in recent years voices have been raised mourning the Empire's disappearance, and regretfully echoing a nineteenth-century Czech patriot's celebrated remark that if the Empire did not exist it would be necessary to invent it. These expressions of longing come not only from monarchists and clericals lamenting a past hopelessly beyond recovery, but from many who have experienced the far more oppressive nationalist or Fascist regimes that governed much former Habsburg territory in the 1920's and 1930's, or the Communist régimes of the period since 1945. By contrast, even the Habsburgs seem preferable.

For sixty-four mortal years from 1850 to 1914, the Emperor Francis Joseph sat on the Habsburg throne. Simple in his personal life and immensely conscientious, he worked hard at his desk, reading and signing state papers for hours every day. But he was without fire or imagination, uninterested in books dealing with current problems, or even in newspapers, devoted to the rigid court etiquette prescribed for Habsburgs, inflexibly old-fashioned and conservative. He was intensely pious. He loved to hunt. His mere longevity inspired loyalty, but it must be admitted that he was a dull fellow, in every sense of the term. His decisions usually came too late, and conceded too little. His responsibility for the course of events is large.

Political Experiments, 1850–1867

Habsburg history between 1850 and 1914 divides naturally into unequal portions at the convenient date 1867, when the Empire became the dual monarchy of Austria-Hungary. After the suppression of the Revolution of 1848, there was a decade of repression usually called the "Bach period," from the name of the Minister of the Interior, ending in 1859 with the war against Piedmont and France (see Chapter 21). Then came eight years of political experimentation, from 1859 to 1867, punctuated by the war of 1866 with Prussia.

In 1849, all parts of the Empire were for the first time unified and directly ruled from Vienna by German-speaking officials. In 1855, the state signed a concordat with the Catholic Church, giving clerics a greater influence in education and in other fields than they had enjoyed since the reforms of Joseph II. The repressive domestic policies of the Bach period required expensive armies and policemen. Instead of investing in railroads and industry, Austria went into debt by enforcing the Bach system. These expenditures left it at a disadvantage compared with Prussia. Then, during the Crimean War, instead of repaying Tsar Nicholas I for Russia's aid in subduing the Hungarian revolution, Austria "astonished the world by her ingratitude." Not only did Francis Joseph fail to assist the Russians, he actually kept them in fear of an attack by occupying the Danubian principalities (modern

Rumania). In 1857, Austria experienced a severe financial crisis partly as a result of this long mobilization.

The defeat of 1859 at the hands of the French and Italians, and the loss of Lombardy with its great city of Milan, brought about the end of the Bach system. War continued to threaten, and the nationalities inside the Empire, especially the Magyars, could not be kept in a state of smoldering discontent which would render their troops unreliable. Several solutions were now tried in an effort to create a structure that would withstand the domestic and foreign strains, but that would not jeopardize the Emperor's position. Francis Joseph made no effort to consult the people. Instead, he listened first to the nobles, who favored a loose federalism, and then to the bureaucrats, who favored a tight centralism.

The "October Diploma" (1860) set up a central legislature to deal with economic and military problems. To it the provincial assemblies (diets) throughout the Empire would send delegates. All other problems were left to the provincial diets, elected by a system that worked to disfranchise the peasants, and to benefit the rich, and (in Bohemia) the German townspeople rather than the Czech farmers. But the October Diploma did not satisfy the most important non-German province: Hungary. The Magyars continued to press for autonomy, as they had in 1848. Francis Joseph, who really preferred the Bach system, opposed Magyar wishes for special treatment, and hoped that the nobles could stave off further liberalization.

On the other hand, the German liberals and bureaucrats of Austria felt that the October Diploma went too far and gave the Magyars too much. To them it seemed that the Empire was being dismembered on behalf of the nobility, who dominated the provincial assemblies. The "February Patent" of 1861 was actually a new constitution in line with their views. It proclaimed a more centralized scheme. The imperial legislature took over most of the powers the October Diploma had reserved for the provincial assemblies or diets.

Naturally, the Magyars objected to this second solution even more than to the first, and flatly refused to participate. To the applause of the Germans in Vienna, including the liberals, Hungary was returned to authoritarian rule. Czechs and Poles also eventually withdrew from the central parliament and left only a German rump. Disturbed, the Emperor suspended the February Patent; he began to negotiate with the Magyars, who were represented by the intelligent and moderate Francis Deák, but the negotiations were interrupted by the war with Prussia in 1866. The Austrian defeat at Sadowa (see above), the expulsion of Austria from Germany, and the loss of Venetia seemed to threaten the entire Habsburg system. Francis Joseph resumed negotiations with the Magyars, with the help of the great Magyar noble, Andrássy, and of Beust, who had become Austrian foreign minister. In 1867, a formula was found which was to govern and preserve the Habsburg domains down to the World War of 1914–1918.

The Dual Monarchy, 1867

This formula was the famous *Ausgleich,* or "compromise," which created the "dual monarchy" of Austria-Hungary. The Hungarian constitution of 1848 was restored, and the entire Empire was reorganized on a strict partnership basis. Austria and Hungary were united in the person of the emperor, who was always to be a Catholic legitimate Habsburg, and who was to be crowned King of Hungary in a special ceremony in Budapest. For foreign policy, military affairs, and finance, the two states had joint ministers appointed by the emperor. A customs union subject to renewal every ten years also united them. Every ten years the quota of common expenditure to be borne by each partner was to be settled. A unique body, the "delegations," made up of sixty members from the Austrian parliament and sixty members from the Hungarian parliament, meeting alternately in Vienna and in Budapest, was to decide on the common budget. After the budget had been approved, it had to be ratified by the full

Emperor Francis Joseph (1830–1916).

parliaments of both countries, and signed by the emperor-king. The delgations also had supervisory authority over the three joint ministers, and might summon them to give an account of their activities. In practice, the delegations seldom met, and were almost never consulted on questions of policy. The system favored Hungary, which had 40 per cent of the population but never paid more than one-third of the expenses. Every ten years, when the quota of expenses and the customs union needed joint consideration, a new crisis arose.

Otherwise, Hungary and Austria were separate states. As King of Hungary, Francis Joseph appointed cabinet ministers, professors, bishops, civil servants, and other officials. He was obliged at least once a year to summon the Hungarian legislature, which had an upper house of hereditary peers and a lower house elected by an elaborate system with more than fifty types of voters. However, qualifications regarding economic status and nationality made the Hungarian lower house entirely undemocratic; the voters never totaled more than 6 per cent of the population. For its part, Austria retained the parliament and the seventeen provincial assemblies provided by the February Patent of 1861. According to the new Austrian constitution of 1867, the authority of the emperor somewhat resembled that of other constitutional monarchs, with the fundamental exception that he could legislate by himself when parliament was not in session. Since he could dissolve parliament at will, he enjoyed a very large discretion and was potentially a strong personal ruler.

The dual structure of Austria-Hungary was unique in Europe, and indeed in history. Because of it, many domestic developments in the two parts of the monarchy may be considered quite separately. Yet one overwhelmingly important and complicated problem remained common to both halves of the monarchy: the problem of the national minorities that had not received their autonomy. Some of these minorities (Czechs, Poles, Ruthenes) were largely in Austria; others (Slovaks, Rumanians) were largely in Hungary; the rest (Croats, Serbs, Slovenes, all of them south Slavs) were in both states. These nationalities were at different stages of development and of national self-consciousness. Some of them were subject to pressures from fellow-nationals living in states outside the dual monarchy.

The Austrian constitution of 1867 provided that all nationalities enjoy equal rights, and guaranteed that each might use its own language in education, administration, and public life. Even the Hungarians in 1868 abandoned on paper the fierce Magyar chauvinism of Kossuth and the superpatriots of 1848 (Chapter 19), and put on the statute books a law that allowed the minorities to conduct local government in their own language, to hold the chief posts in their counties, and to have their own schools. But in practice, neither the Austrian nor the Hungarian statute was respected. The nationalities suffered varying degrees of discrimination and even persecution. Since the nationality problem was common to Austria and to Hungary, and since it ruined the entire dual monarchy in the end, after the disastrous defeats of World War I, we must examine it in some detail.

The Czechs

After 1867, many Czechs felt that they were entitled to an *Ausgleich* on the model which the Magyars had obtained. They argued that the lands of the Crown of St. Wenceslaus (d. 929)—the provinces of Bohemia, Moravia, and Austrian Silesia—possessed rights comparable to those that the Magyars had successfully claimed for the lands of the Crown of St. Stephen (997–1038). But the Czechs never had the power or the opportunity that the Magyars had to bring pressure on the Austrians, although Czech deputies boycotted the Austrian parliament in the hope that Francis Joseph would consent to become King of Bohemia in Prague as he had become King of Hungary in Budapest.

In 1871, the Emperor did indeed offer to be crowned as King of Bohemia. The Bohemian diet, from which all Germans had withdrawn in a fury, drew up proposals that would have produced a triple instead of a dual monarchy. The rage of Austrian and Bohemian Germans, the opposition of Magyar politicians, who predicted chaos, and a Slavic uprising in southern Austria forced Francis Joseph to change his mind. Deeply disappointed, the Czech nationalist leaders returned to passive resistance.

By 1879, when the Czech deputies returned to the Vienna parliament, they were divided into moderate "old Czechs" and radical and impetuous "young Czechs." In the 1880's and 1890's, each time the Czechs won cultural or political gains, the German extremists bitterly opposed them, strengthening the Czech extremists and weakening the moderates. A statute requiring all judges in Czech lands to conduct trials in the language of the petitioner led to the development of an experienced body of Czech civil servants, since many Czechs knew German already, while Germans usually had to learn Czech. In 1890, the gov-

ernment and the old Czechs had tentatively agreed on an administrative division of Bohemia between Germans and Czechs, but the young Czechs rioted in the Bohemian diet, and Prague was put under martial law, which lasted until 1897. When a new law was passed requiring that all civil servants would have to be bilingual after 1901, the Germans in the Vienna parliament threw inkwells, blew whistles, and forced out the ministry, while Czech extremists began to talk ominously about a future Russian-led Slavic showdown with the Germans. All moderation vanished in the waves of noise and hatred. No Austrian parliament could stay in session, and the government had to be conducted by decree.

Under the stress of prolonged agitation, and influenced by the apparent triumph of constitutionalism in Russia (see p. 291), Francis Joseph finally decided to reform the franchise. In 1907, all male citizens of the Austrian lands were now enfranchised and could vote for deputies on their own nationality. Of the 516 deputies in the new parliament, 233 would be German and 107 Czech, a figure almost proportional to the census figures.

Yet in 1913 the Bohemian diet was dissolved by a *coup*, and in 1914 Czech deputies in the Austrian parliament refused to allow national business to proceed. Thus World War I began with both parliament and the Bohemian diet dissolved, and with the Emperor and ministers ruling by themselves. Perhaps chief among the many causes for this general parliamentary breakdown was the failure to give the Czech provinces the self-government they had vainly sought since 1867. Most Czechs did not wish to cut loose from the Empire and establish a separate state of their own. Amounting to about 23 per cent of the Austrian population, the Czechs formed a hard core of discontent.

Yet, from the economic and cultural points of view, the Czechs were by far the most advanced of the Slavic peoples in the dual monarchy. By 1900, the famous Skoda armament works had become the largest in the Empire, and the rival of Krupp in Germany. Porcelain and glassware, lace and beer, sugar and the tourist trade, made the Czech middle class

NORWEGIANS

FINNS

SWEDES

SWEDES

North Sea

ESTONIANS

Baltic Sea

FINNS

GREAT RUSSIANS

DANES

LETTS

GERMANS

LITHUANIANS

DUTCH

WHITE RUSSIANS

GERMANS

FLEMINGS

POLES

WALLOONS

LUX.

ALSATIANS

CZECHS

LITTLE RUSSIANS

KALMUKS

FRENCH

SLOVAKS

RUTHENIANS

(UKRAINIANS)

SWISS

SLOVENES

MAGYARS

MAG.

CROATS

RUMANIANS

Black Sea

GEORGIANS

SERBS

CROATS

GREEKS

ITALIANS

Adriatic Sea

BULGARS

GREEKS

ARMENIANS

ALBANIANS

Aegean GREEKS

TURKS

KURDS

Sea

ARABS

Mediterranean Sea

GREEKS

GREEKS

Nationalities in
Central and Eastern
Europe
— About 1914 —

——— Political boundaries, 1914

- - - - Boundary between Austria
and Hungary

ARABS

ARABS

rich and Czech craftsmen famous. Laboring conditions were bad, however, and the Czech Social Democrats were weakened by their refusal to work with their German opposite numbers.

Czech nationalism was fostered by an active Czech-language press, by patriotic societies, by Czech schools, and by the famous *sokols* ("hawks"), a physical-training society with strong nationalist leanings. At the ancient Prague University, learned Czech scholars taught, of whom Thomas Masaryk, married to an American, became the most famous. Professor of philosophy and student of Slavic culture, but a lover of the West, Masaryk deeply influenced generations of students, and upheld democratic ideals in politics. Historians studied the heroic past of the Czechs, and poets, novelists, and musicians glorified it for the popular audience. Deprived of their national autonomy and exposed to German bias though the Czechs were, they can hardly be regarded as a persecuted minority. They had their language and their freedom to develop under Austrian domination.

Poles and Ruthenians

Of all the minorities in Austria, the Poles (18 per cent of the population) were the most satisfied, the only contented Poles in Europe. Most of them lived in Galicia, where they formed the landlord class and generally oppressed their peasants, especially the backward Ruthenians (Ukrainians). Like the Czechs, the Galician Poles asked for provincial self-government on the Magyar model, and like the Czechs, they were denied. But they had their own schools, and Polish was the language of administration and the courts. The Poles enjoyed favorable financial arrangements, and after 1871 there was a special ministry for Galicia in Vienna. Since they hated Russia, Pan-Slavism never tempted them as it did the Czechs; they were not even very much interested in a future independent Poland.

The contrast between this generous treatment and the brutality suffered by the Poles living in Prussian and Russian Poland led Poles everywhere to look to Austrian Galicia as the center of national life and culture. Polish refugees from tyranny elsewhere took refuge in the cities of Cracow and Lemberg. Here were splendid Polish universities, noble families living grandly as they always had in Poland, and opportunities to serve the Crown in the provincial administration. The universities trained generations of Poles who were available later for service in independent Poland. Polish literature and the study of Polish history flourished. Though slowly, industrialization began, and a promising petroleum industry was launched. Only the Ruthenians and the Jews suffered discrimination and hardship.

The Poles eliminated Ruthenians from the Galician diet, and until 1907 kept them from the imperial parliament. The Ruthenians themselves were divided into an older pro-Russian generation, and a younger generation of Ukrainian nationalists, often fanatical, who hated Poles and Russians alike, and who hoped for their own autonomous status within the monarchy. In 1908, a Ukrainian assassinated the Polish governor of Galicia after a horrible instance of Polish police brutality.

Other Minorities in Austria

The other minorities in Austria were far less numerous. Less than 3 per cent of the population was Italian in 1910; about $4\frac{1}{2}$ per cent was Slovene; and less than 3 per cent was Serb and Croat. The Italians of the south Tyrol and Istria, where their center was the seaport of Trieste, were far more important than their numbers warranted, however, because of the existence of the Kingdom of Italy across the monarchy's frontier. Almost all of them wanted to belong to Italy, and Italy regarded their lands as *Italia Irredenta* (see Chapter 21). Of all the Austrian minorities, the Italian steadily proved itself the most anxious to get out of the Habsburg Monarchy altogether.

Among the south Slavs in Austria proper, the Slovenes were the most contented. Scattered in six provinces, and often living at odds with their German or Italian neighbors, they usually made only local demands, like that for lecture courses in Slovene at Graz university. The Croats in Austria (mostly in Dalmatia) were fewer and less disaffected than those in Hungary, and the Serbs in Austria were far fewer and less disaffected than the Serbs in Hungary and in the separate province of Bosnia. Yet both Serbs and Croats in Austria were divided: some preferred autonomy within the Empire and others hoped one day to join a still hypothetical south Slav state.

Minorities in Hungary: Slovaks, Rumanians, South Slavs

In Hungary, minority problems were even more acute. Magyar behavior toward other national groups grew increasingly outrageous as moderate counsels vanished in the face of short-sighted demagoguery. The Slovaks, the Rumanians, and the Serbs and Croats living in Hungary proper were the worst victims of a deliberate policy of Magyarization, but even the Croatians of Croatia, whose province had its own constitutional special status, suffered. The Magyar aim was actually to destroy the national identity of the minorities, and to transform them into Magyars. The weapon used was language.

It is difficult to understand the passionate attachment felt by the backward peasant peoples of southeastern Europe for their own languages. Yet, deprived of economic opportunity and sometimes of complete religious freedom, these peoples in the nineteenth century found in the languages they talked a living proof of national identity. The Magyars too, who made up only 55 per cent of the population of their own country exclusive of Croatia, had a fanatical devotion to their own language, an Asian tongue quite unrelated to the German, Slavic, or Rumanian languages of the minorities. They tried to force it upon the subject peoples, particularly in education. All state-supported schools, from kindergartens to universities, had to give instruction in Magyar. The state postal, telegraph, and railroad services used only Magyar.

The Slovaks, numbering about 11 per cent of the population of Hungary, were perhaps the most Magyarized. Poor peasants for the most part, the more ambitious of them often became Magyars simply by adopting the Magyar language as their own. As time passed, a few Slovaks came to feel a sense of unity with the closely related but far more advanced Czechs across the border in Austria. The pro-Czechs among the Slovaks were usually liberals and Protestants. Catholic and conservative Slovaks toward the end on the century found their leader in a priest, Father Hlinka, who advocated Slovak autonomy. After Czechoslovakia had been formed in 1918, the Hlinka movement continued to be anti-Czech, and became pro-Hitler in the 1930's.

The Rumanians, who lived in Transylvania, amounted in 1910 to $16\frac{1}{2}$ per cent of the population of Hungary, and possessed a majority in Transylvania itself. For centuries they had been downtrodden by the Magyars, and had had to fight to achieve recognition of their Orthodox religion. Indeed, largely in the hope of receiving better treatment, many of them had become "Uniates," accepting the supremacy of Rome but otherwise preserving their own liturgy. Despite laws designed to eliminate the use of the Rumanian language, and a great deal of petty persecution, the Rumanians stoutly resisted assimilation. For redress of grievances, many looked to Vienna, which before the *Ausgleich* had often been a source of assistance against the Magyars, but which was now committed to give the Magyars a free hand. These Rumanians hoped that Transylvania might again be made autonomous, as it had once been in the past. They pressed for the enforcement of the liberal Hungarian nationalities law of 1868. They wanted their language and their church to have equal standing with other languages and other churches.

But when in 1892 the Rumanians petitioned Vienna on these points, their petition was returned unopened and unread. When they circulated the petition widely abroad, their leaders were tried and jailed. It was little wonder that many Transylvanian Rumanians ceased to look west to Vienna for help that never came, and began to look south and east across the Carpathians to Rumania, where their fellow-nationals had a kingdom of their own and a strong wish to annex the whole of Transylvania.

Under Magyar rule, some Serbs and Croats lived in Hungary proper and others in Croatia. In 1910, those in Hungary totaled about 600,000, of whom two-thirds were Serbs. Living in a compact mass in the southern and western frontier regions, these were the inhabitants of the old Habsburg "military frontier" against the Turks. They were transferred to Magyar rule in 1869, and they resented it. The Serbs especially disliked Hungarian administration and looked to the independent kingdom of Serbia to the south. But a far greater menace to Hungarian unity was provided by Croatia proper.

Croatia

The Croats, though connected since the eleventh century with the Crown of Hungary, had become strongly nationalistic under the impact of the Napoleonic occupation, and had fought on the side of the monarchy against the Magyar revolutionaries of 1848. None the less, Francis Joseph, as part of the *Ausgleich* settlement, handed them back to the Magyars. Croatian nationalists were deeply disappointed. Led by the Roman Catholic Bishop Strossmayer, a man of deep intelligence, high culture, and liberal views, they had hoped for an autonomous Croatia and Dalmatia inside the Empire, which would serve as a nucleus to attract all the other southern Slavs. But instead, the Magyar moderates, led by Deák, worked out in 1868 an *Ausgleich* of their own between Hungary and Croatia.

All military and economic affairs were to be handled in Budapest by a special cabinet minister for Croatian affairs. Representatives from the Croatian parliament at the Croatian capital of Zagreb would sit in Budapest whenever Croatian affairs were under discussion. Croatian delegates would be part of the Hungarian "delegation" of the dual monarchy. The Croatian language could be spoken by Croat representatives at the sessions of any body they attended, and the language of command in the Croatian territorial army would be Croatian. The Croats would control their own educational system, their church, their courts and police, but all taxes would be voted by Budapest and collected by agents of Budapest. Although the Croats were far better off than any national minority in Hungary, this "compromise" did not satisfy them.

The "Party of the Right," the ancestor of Croat extremism in our own day, wanted a completely autonomous Croatia, and scorned as inferior the Serbs and other non-Catholic south Slavs, whom Strossmayer had hoped to attract. Further problems were created in Catholic Croatia by the existence of a Serb Orthodox minority (more than a quarter of the population), which spoke the same language as the Croats, and which was racially indistinguishable from them. But the Orthodox minority worshipped in different churches, and was therefore subject to religious discrimination.

For twenty years at the close of the nineteenth century, the Hungarian-appointed governor cleverly fostered this Serb-Croat antagonism by using the Serbs for local offices. He received the support only of those Croats who had become Magyar-speaking, usually great landowners or government officials.

By 1903, Serbs and Croats were beginning to co-operate against Hungarian rule, and to spread pro-Slav propaganda in Dalmatia. In 1905, Croats asked Vienna for Dalmatia and for electoral reforms, but professed that they wanted to observe faithfully the arrangement of 1868 with Hungary. Serbians endorsed these Croatian demands, though some Serbs hoped for union with independent Serbia, and some Croats still hoped for complete independence.

In spite of these hopeful signs, the hopes of the moderates were dashed by the fearfully unpopular Railway Servants Act (1907), which forced all railroad workers to speak Magyar. Croats began to boycott Hungarian-made goods; the Croatian diet refused to collaborate with the new governor, who in 1909 arrested fifty-odd Croats and Serbs and charged them with plotting to unite Croatia and Bosnia with Serbia. The evidence was ridiculously inadequate, and the defendants, though condemned, obtained a reversal of the sentences on appeal to a higher court. But these Zagreb trials gave the Slavic press a splendid opportunity to denounce the policy of the dual monarchy.

In the same year, 1909, a celebrated Austrian historian, Friedjung, charged in the Vienna press that the Croatian and Serbian politicians in Croatia were plotting with Serbians in Serbia. Friedjung was eventually forced to admit that his documentary sources, which in all probability had been fed to him by the Vienna foreign office, were forgeries. The Zagreb trials and the Friedjung case, coming only five years before the assassination of Francis Ferdinand by a Bosnian Serb and the outbreak of war, demonstrated the incompetence of the dual monarchy in dealing with its own loyal south Slav inhabitants. In 1912, 1913, and 1914, Bosnian students tried to assassinate the Hungarian governor of Croatia. These were ominous rehearsals for the crime of June 28, 1914, which led not merely to internal crisis but to world war.

Bosnia-Herzegovina

In the dual monarchy, the region of Bosnia-Herzegovina had a special status. By the 1870's, these two provinces had been part of the Ottoman Empire for about four centuries. Although ethnically south Slavic, the population included in 1879 about half a million Moslems, half a million members of the Orthodox Church, and perhaps 150,000 Catholics. Under Turkish rule, those who accepted Islam had enjoyed economic advantages. Most of the Orthodox Christian population consisted of peasants working on the estates of Moslem landlords, and looking across the frontiers to Serbia in hope of liberation. Some of the Catholics were educated in Strossmayer's seminary, and leaned toward eventual absorption in his south-Slav state, but almost nobody wanted to join the Habsburg monarchy as it was then constituted.

The Herzegovinian uprising of 1875 against the Turks precipitated a general Balkan Slavic attack on the Turks. Russia too went to war against the Turks, but first the Austrian and Russian foreign ministers reached an agreement on the future status of the two provinces. But they later disagreed on what the agreement had been. At the Congress of Berlin in 1878 (see p. 286), the Austrians obtained the right to occupy the provinces, but not to annex them.

From 1878 to 1908, the forces of the monarchy occupied Bosnia and Herzegovina. The sovereignty of the Turkish sultan was recognized throughout this period, but in fact the provinces were ruled from Vienna, though not as part of either Austria or Hungary. Instead, they were put under the common Austro-Hungarian minister of finance.

The discontent of the Orthodox Serbs of Bosnia was fanned by propaganda from Serbia itself. Patriotic Serbs considered that the first logical step toward creating a greater Serbia would be to incorporate these provinces inside their own frontiers, and they resented the decision of the Congress of Berlin that had allowed Habsburg occupation. However, so long as the occupation was not turned into annexation, the Serbs preserved the hope that the provinces might some day become theirs, and meanwhile flooded them with agents and plotters. The Moslems, though favored by the Habsburg authorities, never reconciled themselves to the ending of Turkish rule, and the Catholics hoped to join Croatia.

Thus these provinces perpetually threatened to create an explosion. The more intelligent observers in Vienna pressed for some sort of an all-south-Slav solution, not unlike that of Strossmayer. This would have put Dalmatia, Croatia, and Bosnia-Herzegovina together into a south-Slav kingdom under Francis Joseph, with the same status as Hungary—a triple rather than a dual monarchy. The advocates of this solution, known as "trialists," met with violent Magyar opposition.

However, the Young Turk Revolution of 1908 caused the adventurous Austrian foreign minister Aehrenthal to fear that the status of the provinces might be changed. Fortified by a prior secret agreement with Russia, Aehrenthal simply annexed the two provinces in October, 1908, and announced that they would be given a diet of their own. This move precipitated a major European crisis (Chapter 25), which threatened world war, but eventually subsided, leaving the Serbs bitterly resentful. Serbian ambition to acquire the provinces now seemed permanently checked. The humiliation of Serbia, the disappointment of Russia, the solidarity of Germany with Austria-Hungary as revealed by the crisis, helped set the stage for the catastrophe of 1914. The discontent of the population of Bosnia, when added to the discontent of the Czechs and Italians in Austria, and of the Slovaks, Rumanians, Croats, and other south Slavs in Hungary, goes far to account for the wartime weaknesses and postwar disintegration of the dual monarchy.

Yet the minority question, critical though it was, does not provide the entire answer. We must now briefly consider the Austrian-German and Hungarian majorities, both in their separate development and in their critical relationship to each other. Only then can we see that even the two ruling groups were subject to divisive forces that crippled them individually and together.

Austrian Society and Politics, 1867–1914

From the earliest days of the *Ausgleich*, the Austrian liberals fought the clerical conservatives. They legalized civil marriages, secularized all but religious instruction, canceled the concordat of 1855 after the proclamation of papal infallibility in 1870, and taxed church property (1873). These measures were the Austrian counterpart of the German *Kulturkampf*, but they were much milder, since Austria was 90 per cent Catholic, and did not share the Protestant Prussian suspicion of the Vatican. The liberals were discredited by the financial crash of 1873, during which it was revealed that some of them had accepted bribes in return for voting in favor of charters for shady and unstable new companies. From this period dates the earliest political anti-Semitism in Austria, since some Jewish liberals were involved in the scandals and served as convenient scapegoats. Economic advance during the early years

of the monarchy had brought the usual increase in the working class, which after the crash turned toward socialism in both its Marxist and its milder forms.

The Austrian nobles, who often owned great estates which they ruled almost like independent potentates, were on the whole frivolous in their tastes, and took little interest in the problems of the nineteenth and twentieth centuries. They squandered their incomes on high living and gambling. Yet they supplied almost all the political leadership that the nation got. The large size of their estates was one fundamental reason for the small size of the average peasant holding, and made it necessary even for landowning peasants to try to obtain part-time employment on a noble's property. The peasants' standard of living and level of literacy were extremely low, yet the influence of the clergy kept them subservient to their masters, loyal to the dynasty, and almost contented with their lot.

The middle class of town-dwellers and men of business, so familiar in western Europe, came later and was smaller in number in Austria. The wealthier tried to imitate the aristocracy's mode of life and to buy their way into the charmed circle. Others joined the professions, which they found overcrowded and badly paid. The unemployment of intellectuals is an extremely dangerous matter politically.

Among the bourgeoisie there were many Jews. Numbering 5 per cent of the total population of Austria, the Jews (except for very few) could not be nobles, peasants, members of the clergy, bureaucrats, or army officers. So they were forced to enter trade, the professions, and the arts, where they often prospered and distinguished themselves. What we mean when we refer loosely to pre-war "Viennese" life, with its charm and gaiety, its cultivation, its music, its cafés, its high reputation in medicine and science, was the life of a society very largely Jewish or part-Jewish. Conversion, intermarriage, and assimilation were not uncommon among the upper-middle-class Jews.

Anti-Semitism, fanned by the continued migration of poorer Jews from regions of eastern Europe where oppression had rendered them squalid and uncouth, was general among the non-Jews of Austria. But we must distinguish between the social anti-Semitism of most aristocrats, which was often simply a form of snobbery, and the serious political anti-Semitism of the lower middle classes, often the unsuccessful competitors of the Jews in the world of small shop-keeping. Partly out of religious prejudice, partly out of distaste for the liberal politics usually preferred by the middle-class Jews, the clericals inveighed against them. One response among the Jews to the swelling chorus of anti-Semitism was Zionism (sponsorship of a Jewish state in Palestine), which originated in the dual monarchy.

The stresses and strains inherent in this social structure, aggravated by the problems of the national minorities, produced in the late nineteenth century two important new political movements among the Germans of Austria: Pan-Germanism and Christian Socialism. In the early 1880's, even moderate Austrian Germans wanted to hand over the Slavic lands of Austria to the Hungarians to rule, and then, stripped to the German core, to unite economically with Germany. The Pan-Germans were more radical and more violent. They opposed the Habsburg dynasty. They opposed the Catholic Church and led a noisy movement called "Away from Rome" (*Los von Rom*). They demanded that Austria become Protestant, and unite politically with Germany. They were furiously anti-Slav and anti-Semitic. They adored Bismarck and Wotan, but Bismarck did not encourage them. Their leader, Schönerer, himself a convert to Protestantism, was elected to the Austrian parliament in 1873 from the same district that later gave birth to Adolf Hitler. But the Pan-Germans never managed to become more than an extreme vocal minority.

The Christian Socialists, on the other hand, became the most important Austrian political party. Strongly Catholic and loyal to the Habsburgs, they appealed at the same time to the peasant and the small businessman by favoring social legislation and by opposing big business. They too were violently anti-Semitic. At first skeptical of the value of Christian Socialism, the clergy later made the movement its own, and especially in the country prevailed on the people to vote for its candidates. The most

famous single Christian Socialist was the perennial Mayor of Vienna after 1895, Karl Lueger, the idol of the lower middle classes of the capital. For years he sponsored public ownership of city utilities, parks, playgrounds, free milk for schoolchildren, and other welfare services. Lueger always catered to his followers' hatred of Jews, Marxian socialists, and Magyars. Hitler, who saw Lueger's funeral procession in 1910, hailed him in *Mein Kampf* as the greatest statesman of his times. It is impossible to understand the doctrines of German Nazism in this century without understanding the social and racial structure of the Habsburg monarchy in which Hitler grew up, and especially the doctrines and the appeal of Pan-Germanism and Christian Socialism.

To the Pan-Germans and the Christian Socialists, the Austrian Social Democrats, founded in 1888, responded with a Marxist program calling for government ownership of the means of production and for political action organized by class rather than by nationality. But the Austrian Social Democrats were not revolutionaries, and set as their goals such political and social gains as universal suffrage, secular education, welfare legislation, and the eight-hour day. They were usually led by intellectuals, many of them Jewish, but they were followed by an ever-increasing number of workers.

On the nationality question, Social Democratic leaders strongly urged a reform in the direction of democratic federalism. Each nationality should have control of its own affairs in its own territory; in mixed territories, minorities should be protected; and a central parliament should decide matters of common interest. Cultural autonomy for the nationalities of a multi-national state was by no means an impractical or doctrinaire Marxist idea. Its practicality was later attested by the Soviet Russians, faced as they were with a similar problem and much influenced by the thinking of Austrian Social Democrats on the question. Otto Bauer, a doctrinaire Marxist, tried to explain away national antagonisms in the Empire as a manifestation of class warfare. But the program of another Social Democrat, Karl Renner, who lived to be chancellor of the Austrian Re-

Reading Suggestions on Central and Eastern Europe

(Asterisk indicates paperbound edition.)

General Accounts

R. C. Binkley, *Realism and Nationalism, 1852–1871* (Harper, 1935). Though this volume, in the "Rise of Modern Europe" series, develops a somewhat implausible thesis about the possibilities of "federative polity," it provides an often illuminating discussion of the period indicated.

C. J. H. Hayes, *A Generation of Materialism, 1871–1900* (Harper, 1941). Another volume in the "Rise of Modern Europe" series, this does some penetrating probing beneath the surface on an apparently successful era, particularly in Germany.

A. J. P. Taylor, *The Struggle for Mastery in Europe, 1848–1918* (Clarendon, 1954). A volume in "The Oxford History of Modern Europe"; crisp and provocative.

Special Studies:
Germany

R. Flenley, *Modern German History* (Dutton, 1953), and K. S. Pinson, *Modern Germany, Its History and Civilization* (Macmillan, 1954). Two textbooks, of which Pinson's is the longer and Flenley's perhaps the more useful.

A. J. P. Taylor, *The Course of German History* (Coward-McCann, 1946). A lively essay on the period since 1815, with strong, but not unreasonable, anti-German overtones.

F. Meinecke, *The German Catastrophe* (Harvard Univ. Press, 1950). A useful antidote to Taylor, by a very great German historian.

T. Veblen, *Imperial Germany and the Industrial Revolution,* new ed. (Viking, 1954). An old, brilliant, and still very important analysis by a great American sociologist.

J. H. Clapham, *The Economic Development of France and Germany, 1815–1914,* 4th ed. (Cambridge Univ. Press, 1936; reprinted 1955). A somewhat out-of-date but still instructive introduction to the subject.

F. Darmstaedter, *Bismarck and the Creation of the Second Reich* (Methuen, 1948). A valuable study.

E. Eyck, *Bismarck and the German Empire* (Allen and Unwin, 1950). Translation and condensation of a large standard work in German.

A. J. P. Taylor, *Bismarck: The Man and the Statesman* (Knopf, 1955). A provocative and often hostile re-evaluation.

E. J. Passant, *A Short History of Germany, 1850–1945* (Cambridge Univ. Press, 1959). An up-to-date general survey.

H. von Treitschke, *History of Germany in the 19th Century,* 7 vols. (Humanities Press, 1915–1919), and *Origins of Prussianism,* ed. by E. and C. Paul (Humanities Press, 1942). Celebrated detailed studies emphasizing the period before 1870; strongly Prussian in tone and sympathy.

Special Studies:
The Habsburg
Monarchy

A. J. May, *The Hapsburg Monarchy, 1867–1914* (Harvard Univ. Press, 1951). Concise general account.

A. J. P. Taylor, *The Habsburg Monarchy, 1809–1918,* 2nd ed. (Hamish Hamilton, 1948). A spirited brief treatment.

R. A. Kann, *The Multinational Empire,* 2 vols. (Columbia Univ. Press, 1950). A monograph, arranged nationality by nationality, and discussing national sentiments and the government's efforts to deal with them.

O. Jászi, *The Dissolution of the Habsburg Monarchy* (Univ. of Chicago Press, 1929). From a rare point of view, that of the liberal Magyar.

R. W. Seton-Watson, *German, Slav, and Magyar* (Williams and Norgate, 1916). By the greatest British authority on southeast Europe, the author of many other valuable studies of the area.

E. Wiskemann, *Czechs and Germans* (Oxford Univ. Press, 1938). A good case history of national antagonisms.

Special Studies: Russia

H. Seton-Watson, *The Decline of Imperial Russia, 1855–1914* (Praeger, 1952). The only sound work in English covering virtually all the period dealt with in this chapter.

G. T. Robinson, *Rural Russia under the Old Regime,* 2nd ed. (Macmillan, 1949). A splendid monograph on the peasant question.

A. Herzen, *My Past and Thoughts,* 6 vols. (Chatto and Windus, 1924–1927). The classic picture of nineteenth-century Russia, by its most distinguished rebel.

Martin Malia, *Alexander Herzen and the Birth of Russian Socialism* (*Grosset and Dunlap, Universal Library, 1965). Excellent monograph on Herzen's life and thought, considered in the framework of contemporary European ideas.

N. V. Riasanovsky, *Russia and the West in the Teaching of the Slavophiles* (Harvard Univ. Press, 1953). A useful study of one side of the chief intellectual controversy of the period.

Sidney Monas, *The Third Section: Police and Society in Russia Under Nicholas I* (Harvard Univ. Press, 1961). Pioneering study of the repressive machinery and its impact.

D. Footman, *Red Prelude* (Yale Univ. Press, 1945). A good biography of Zhelyabov, populist and terrorist.

Peter Kropotkin, *Memoirs of a Revolutionist,* ed. James A. Rogers (*Anchor, 1962). A delightful anarchist's story of his own life and times.

James Joll, *The Anarchists* (*Grosset and Dunlap, Universal Library, 1964). Excellent chapters on Bakunin and Kropotkin, and a fine study of the movement.

B. Pares, *The Fall of the Russian Monarchy* (Jonathan Cape, 1939). An excellent study of the period 1905–1917; by an authority who was frequently on the spot.

S. Witte, *Memoirs* (Doubleday, 1921). The somewhat apologetic memoirs of the man who did most to industrialize imperial Russia.

B. D. Wolfe, *Three Who Made a Revolution* (Dial Press, 1948; *Beacon). A fine triple study of Lenin, Trotsky, and Stalin; with emphasis on the period before 1914.

A. Lobanov-Rostovsky, *Russia and Asia,* rev. ed. (G. Wahr, 1951). A useful introductory survey.

B. H. Sumner, *Russia and the Balkans, 1870–1880* (Clarendon, 1937). A monograph including a helpful discussion of Panslavism.

Historical Fiction

T. Mann, *Buddenbrooks* (*Pocket Books). Inexpensive reprint of a long novel about a family in imperial Germany.

G. Hauptmann, *The Weavers, Hannele, The Beaver Coat* (*Rinehart, 1951). Three plays that convey some of the flavor of nineteenth-century Germany.

R. Musil. *The Man without Qualities* (Coward-McCann, 1953). A novel steeped in the atmosphere of pre-1914 Vienna.

M. Jókai, *Eyes Like the Sea* (Putnam, 1901). Fictionalized autobiography of a romantic Hungarian novelist, the author of many novels that give insights into Magyar nationalism.

N. Gogol, *The Inspector General* (many editions), and *Dead Souls,* George Reavey trans. (Oxford Univ. Press, 1957–The World's Classics; *Rinehart Editions). Brilliant satirical play and novel.

I. Turgenev, *Fathers and Sons* (sometimes called *Fathers and Children*—many editions), and *Smoke* (Dutton, 1949; *Everyman). Superb contemporary realistic fiction reflecting Russian intellectual and political life.

F. Dostoevsky, *The Brothers Karamazov* (*Modern Library, 1937), and *Crime and Punishment* (*Modern Library, 1932). Famous novels depicting the turbulent life of Russian intellectuals in the mid-nineteenth century; more romantic in tone than Turgenev's works.

The Portable Chekhov (*Viking, 1947). A selection from the short stories and plays of A. Chekhov, a skillful portraitist of the upper classes in tsarist Russia.

L. Tolstoy, *Anna Karenina* (*Modern Library). A celebrated novel set in late nineteenth-century St. Petersburg and the countryside.

The Intellectual Revolution

The sources for the intellectual history of the nineteenth century—the great books and the ephemeral books, the articles, stories, advertisements, sermons, paintings, sculptures, all the accumulated symbols of culture—have been preserved in bewildering quantity. The last century seems, in our present retrospect, to have presented samples of almost all varieties of human thought and feeling, of all western "styles." A detailed catalogue of these varieties would be dull and confusing. Here we shall center on one main theme—the qualifications, emendations, even repudiations, made by the late nineteenth century in the western heritage of the Enlightenment, that heritage of optimistic faith in simple, static, reformist "reason" and a simple "natural law", largely divorced from its Roman and Christian meanings, which rules men and matter. The most striking of these emendations was made by Darwin.

I Darwinism

The Origin of Species

Darwin's *On the Origin of Species by Means of Natural Selection* (1859) is one of the books that mark a revolution in intellectual history. Like all important revolutions, the Darwinian was no bolt from the blue. Into Darwin's work had gone long years of preparation, not merely those of Darwin's own life, but those of his predecessors and colleagues in the scientific study of what was then called natural history and is now called biology or ethology. Before him was the long record of the hundreds of thousands of years of organic life on earth. Already well established by geologists like Sir Charles Lyell and by paleontologists, this record told of the rise, development, sometimes of the disappearance, of thousands of different forms of plant and animal organisms, or *species*. The record contradicted an important part of the commonly accepted theory men of the West had about the past of organic life. The Bible in the Book of Genesis described all forms of life as begun in the space of a single week by a Creator about 6,000 years ago. And this same religious account furthermore stated explicitly that all existing men and animals were descended from single pairs of each species preserved in Noah's ark during a great universal flood that took place some time after the Creation.

Now Darwin was by no means the first to find a discrepancy between the historical and scientific record and the accepted Biblical explanation. The men of the Enlightenment had felt compelled by the facts of the record to give up the Biblical explanation. Some of them had gone so far as to conceive the record as a very long evolutionary process in which no God, at least no personal, Christian God, had a hand, but only the impersonal forces of Nature or the deist's "watchmaker God" (see Chapter 27). But they had arrived at no satisfactory explanation of how Nature or the watchmaker God had done the job; they had no satisfactory theory of how organisms had evolved. This Darwin gave the world.

Darwin's Theories

One of his clues he found in the work of the economist Malthus (see Chapter 20). In his *Essay on Population,* Malthus had maintained that organisms—including man—tended to multiply to a point where there simply was not food enough for them all. In the intense competition for food, some of these organisms did not get enough, and died. This was the germ of the conception Darwin phrased as the *struggle for existence.* He next asked himself what determined that certain individuals would survive and that others would die. Obviously the surviving ones got more food, better shelter, better living conditions of all sorts. If they were all identical organisms, the only explanation—apart from the intervention of a supernatural being or force—would have to be accidental variations in their environment. But it was clear from observation that individual organisms of a given species are not identical. Variations appear even at birth. Thus in a single litter of pigs there may be sturdy, aggressive piglets and a runt. The runt, even if a sentimental farmer tries to protect it, is likely to get shoved aside in suckling by his sturdier brothers, and starve. In the wild state, in free competition, the runt is almost certain to die. In the struggle for existence, the runt is proved "unfit."

Here is the second of Darwin's key phrases, the *survival of the fittest.* The organism best endowed in its variations to get food and shelter lives to procreate young that will tend to inherit these favorable variations. The variations are slight indeed, but over generation after generation they are cumulative; finally an organism so different from the long-distant ancestor is produced that we can speak of a new species. This new species has *evolved*. It has evolved by the working of *natural selection*. Man as a plant and animal breeder has long made use of this process and has hastened and indeed guided it for his own purposes by *artificial selection*, by breeding only the best strains—"best," of course, from a human point of view. But man has been doing this with domesticated plants and animals for but a tiny period of geological time, and with but few species. Over the eons, *natural selection has* been the working force; *and for man himself,* according to the Darwinian system, natural selection alone has been at work, since man has yet to breed his own kind as he breeds his domestic plants and animals.

Darwin held that the variations in individuals of the same species at birth are accidental, and that they are generally transmitted through inheritance. Those biologists who developed his doctrine, notably the German Weismann, did not—and this is a very important point—believe that the evidence showed that variations produced in an individual organism in the course of its life could be transmitted to its offspring. Thus, orthodox Darwinism denies the inheritance of "acquired characteristics." Obviously, a man with an amputated leg will not produce one-legged children. Experimenters have docked the tails of generations of laboratory rats, but the rats are still born with long tails. Efforts by such Russian geneticists as Lysenko to show that environmental changes can be transmitted to offspring have not yet convinced most scientists.

Today, more than a century after the publication of the *Origin of Species,* Darwin's work as a biologist is still accepted in most of its larger outlines. Later work, however, has found that variations of importance in the evolutionary process are probably not so much the numerous tiny ones Darwin emphasized, but rather bigger and much rarer ones now known as "mutations." Scientists have begun to study the effect of various forms of radiation on such mutations. A still much-disputed geological theory holds that catastrophic crustal movements in the past have so radically altered environment as to wipe out whole species and speed up the evolution of others. Emphasis on either mutations or on extensive crustal movements tends also to be emphasis on the sudden and catastrophic rather than on the gradual. Such emphasis may well reflect the violent character of our twentieth century in contrast with the relatively peaceful nineteenth. For, though many scientists would deny this, it would seem that even science is to a degree affected by human "attitudes."

Darwin believed that what he called "sexual selection"—that is, the ability of the fittest individual to attract and mate with fittest individuals of the opposite sex and thus produce the fittest offspring—was a very important factor in natural selection. Although sexual selection is by no means wholly discarded by geneticists today, many of them do not accept Darwin's version of it. The actual mechanism of heredity we know much better than Darwin did, thanks to the work of an Austrian monk, Gregor Mendel, in the late nineteenth century, and many, many successors up to the present day.

The Effect on Theology

The *Origin of Species* stirred up a most heated theological controversy. It added fuel to a fire kindled earlier by historical and linguistic scholarship with its practice of applying the same standards to the Bible that the scholar would apply to Homer, or to the old Norse and Germanic epics. Fundamentalists, both Protestant and Catholic, simply stuck by Genesis and damned Darwin and all his work. But the Catholic Church and many Protestant bodies eventually took at least a neutral attitude toward Darwinism, which they viewed as a scientific biological hypothesis neither necessarily correct nor necessarily incorrect. The great majority of Christians tacitly or openly accepted sufficient modification of Genesis to accommodate themselves to the scientist's

An 1871 anti-Darwinian cartoon by Thomas Nast. The defrauded gorilla, pointing to Darwin at right: "That man wants to claim my pedigree. He says he is one of my descendants." Mr. Bergh (founder of the Society for the Prevention of Cruelty to Animals): "Now, Mr. Darwin, how could you insult him so?"

The Effect on Social and Economic Attitudes

This theological conflict had pretty well run its course by the beginning of the twentieth century. More important in the long run was the use men made of some of Darwin's basic concepts—or at least, of his more smoothly coined phrases—in debates on matters moral, economic, and political. The blanket term, "Social Darwinism," which covers all these transfers of ideas from biology to the social sciences and human relations, takes in a very wide range of persons and ideas. Darwin himself was a biologist, not a "Social Darwinist." He did not write as a social scientist. It must be noted, however, that in a free and literate society, ideas produced by scientists invariably spread to many people not trained in science, and that such ideas are modified in the process of spreading. Not all professional scientists are reconciled to this fact.

The central idea that social and political thinkers took over from Darwin was that of competition among individuals and groups of individuals. This was of course a conception already central in their thinking, but Darwin buttressed it with the prestige of the natural sciences. The majority of these late nineteenth-century thinkers interpreted the human struggle as a struggle for the means of livelihood. There is, they were sure, among men a human "struggle for life." The variations that counted here were the variations that brought success in economic competition—the variations that produced inventors, business organizers, even perhaps political, artistic, and professional leaders. Darwin's work in natural history came to confirm the economist's doctrine of laissez-faire and the nineteenth-century liberal's doctrine of individual freedom for a man to do what his capacities permitted.

Formal economists did not indeed make much use of, or have much need for, Darwin. The classical economists had already brought

time-scale, and adjusted the classic theological arguments from first cause, design, and the like to a God who worked his will in accordance with organic evolution; and they accepted the assimilation of the Biblical account, at least in part, with other fallible histories. In short, they were willing to grant that the *men* who wrote the Bible were not infallible. Moreover, it was quite clear to reflective men that nothing Darwin or any other scientist or scholar could produce would give ultimate answers to the kind of problem set by the existence of God. It was quite clear to them that since God's eye is now on the sparrow, it must once have been on the dinosaur. Christians can be Darwinians: millions of them are. But Darwinism, if taken over wholesale into a philosophy of life, remains a denial of any supernatural intervention in the planning and running of the universe, remains a support for secularism.

the arguments for laissez-faire to their height (see Chapter 20). On the whole, for the rest of the century, the economists were to temper somewhat the rigor of the doctrine of competition among individuals. But the average successful middle-class person in the West took Darwin to heart. Here was scientific confirmation of the middle-class notions that the universe was designed to reward hard work, thrift, intelligence, and self-help and to punish laziness, waste, stupidity, and reliance on charity. Above all, the middle-class person of the time took Darwin to confirm the notion that the poor were poor because they were unfit, badly designed for living. The work of Darwin confirmed the complementary notion that attempts by private charity or by state action to take from the rich and moderately well-to-do and give to the poor were useless and quite contrary to nature, shocking efforts to reverse the course of evolution. If a man cannot earn enough to feed himself, it was argued, he had better die; lowlier organisms too incompetent to feed themselves certainly die off, to the greater good of the species. Herbert Spencer (1820–1903), an ardent British evolutionist, summed it up neatly:

Of man, as of all inferior creatures, the law by conformity to which the species is preserved, is that among adults the individuals best adapted to the conditions of their existence shall prosper most, and the individuals least adapted to the conditions of their existence shall prosper least. . . . Pervading all Nature we may see at work a stern discipline which is often a little cruel that it may be very kind. . . . The ultimate result of shielding men from folly is to fill the world with fools.*

Spencer himself, if it came to that, could not have stood by while the unemployed and their families starved to death, for he was a kindly man. But he had an almost maniacal hatred of the state, of local government as well as national; he held out even against laws requiring houseowners to connect their houses with sewers in cities. But even Spencer

*Herbert Spencer, *Principles of Ethics* (London, 1879–1893), section 257; *Social Statics* (London, 1851), p. 149; *Autobiography* (London, 1904), II, 5.

could not transfer to the struggle for existence among human beings the fine ruthless freedom of the jungle, of what Tennyson called "Nature red in tooth and claw." He was against all forms of government provision for what we now call social security. But what government may not do he believed the ethically sound individual will do as charity. The rich and well-to-do will take care of the poor voluntarily—not enough to spoil them, not enough to frustrate the designs of evolution by letting them prosper and propagate their kind, but enough to prevent their starving or freezing to death.

In his *Principles of Ethics,* Spencer discovered that the softer emotions promoted by Christianity and the other higher religions —kindness, dislike of cruelty, love—were also in accord with the intentions of the laws of the universe as summed up in evolution. Mutual extermination might be the law for tigers, but not for human beings. Indeed, Spencer and many other Social Darwinists held that the altruistic moral sentiments that impel us toward charity are the highest achievement of the evolutionary process, and that a society with many altruists is thereby shown to be the fittest for survival.

Eugenics

The Social Darwinists were, then, faced with this primary difficulty. Darwin seemed to have shown that the unmitigated struggle for life within a given species, and among rival species, was the law of the universe; but human history, and human feelings, showed that men could not in practice look on with indifference while their fellow men starved to death. One way out of the dilemma was that recommended by Spencer, a sort of humanized and mitigated struggle in which the incompetent were shelved but not destroyed. Many who held this view accompanied it with a faith in what came to be called eugenics.

Eugenicists sought to encourage child-bearing by the fit and to discourage ever present child-bearing by the unfit. Darwin had begun his *Origin of Species* with a consideration of the extraordinary success men had had with artificial selection in the breeding of plants and animals. Why not do the same thing with human beings? Since, according to strict Darwinian theory, acquired characteristics were not transmitted by heredity, no amount of manipulation of the social environment, no amount of wise planning of institutions, would alter human beings. Therefore, the only way to secure permanent improvement of the race was by deliberate mating of the fit with the fit.

The eugenicists, however, ran at once against the fact that man, though he domesticates plants and animals, is still himself in this respect a "wild" animal. The individual human being in choosing a mate is no doubt influenced by a great variety of motives, which the social scientist or even the practical man in human relations still understands only imperfectly. But no master human breeder, not even an understandable master principle or idea, decides who shall mate with whom. So far, the eugenicists have had little success with the positive side of their program. On the negative side, they have urged that the obviously unfit, the idiots, the feeble-minded, the insane, be prevented, even if necessary by compulsory sterilization, from having children. Some few American states have passed laws for such compulsory sterilization, but only a tiny handful of human beings, not enough to affect in the slightest the general course of human physical evolution, have undergone this treatment. Moreover, the eugenicists have aroused the opposition of many Christians who believe that it is wrong to tamper with God's human creations.

"Racism"

By far the commonest way out of the dilemma facing the Social Darwinists lay in the obvious notion that it is not so much among individual human beings that the struggle for existence really goes on, as it is among human beings organized in groups, as tribes, "races," or national states. The struggle that counts is not the struggle, say, among individual Englishmen to survive, but the struggle between the entity England—or Great Britain—and its rivals. The struggle for existence among men is now lifted from the biology of the individual to the politics of the group. And for the nineteenth century the group had to be the nation-state, perhaps kindred nation-states that could be organized for the struggle as one bloc of states, such as the "Nordic" or the "Latin," or perhaps at the very widest the Caucasian or white peoples in competition with the colored peoples, yellow, brown, or black. This struggle had an ultimate form: war. The group that defeated another group in war had thereby shown itself, *these* social Darwinists maintained, to be fitter than the beaten group. It had a right—indeed in evolutionary terms, which usually have moral overtones, a *duty*—to eliminate the beaten group, seize its lands, and people them with its own fitter human beings. The English imperialist Cecil Rhodes held that a world wholly and exclusively peopled with Anglo-Saxons would be the best possible world.

The idea of a Chosen People was of course not a new one in Darwin's time. But there is no doubt that Darwin's work, however little he may have meant it to be, was a most important element in the special forms that competition among organized states took in the latter half of the nineteenth century, and right on to our own day. Darwinism came too late to do more than prop up the philosophy of laissez-faire in economics. But Darwinism came at just the right time to intensify the struggle among organized human groups in international politics.

The particular groups or states that were to benefit as the elect of evolution in this special political sense varied with the aims, sympathies, and actual citizenship of the individual who was seeking to promote an ultimate evolutionary victory. Britain, Germany, the United States, the Latins, the Slavs, were all defended as the true elect of evolution. Most of the writers who preached this kind of political evolution proceeded from the assumption that at bottom the men of a given group had certain physical and therefore intellectual

—at least, of the "re
lar vision. He prop
with the classic, flo
by the academics 1
blocks, chunks of
that is after all rea
stemmed in a sense
painting. Cubism, v
Cézanne's insisten
sionality, is most o
too are Abstractio
Cézanne's work an
poraries, the Dut
Frenchman Gaugui
private, and unpr
they are now po
countless inexpens
the artist nor the
process by which
tion becomes an
enough to be sure
rary work will or v
purchase of *conter*
public collections
speculative of hun
heavily against the
seurship, includin
terms of economic
as there is, though
our culture, the
collector wins grea

The Other Arts

The nineteenth
riod for sculpture
the industrial art
mental statues ap
Americans is the
York harbor, the
Bartholdi, a gift f
public to the A
statues of statesm
public places ever
conventionally rea
them as human be
at least would app
designed for the p
Its nineteenth-cen

litical
The d
cally

II

The Vict

It i
ture
centur
to be
has n
can fin
ly or
Victor
Mélan
by wh
Landse
fellow
forte.
ing ro
worke
letters
been
writer
would
toevsk
not ha
For
formal
teenth
it was
of this
rious"
before
vated
agains
nomic
is, the
were
they
years
torian

and spiritual traits in common, traits that gave them their superiority, and that could not possibly be transmitted to men of another group. Most of these writers, in short, were "racists" who believed that in fact *homo sapiens* had already evolved into what were really separate species. A black skin, for instance, was for them a sign of innate inferiority. The blacks would simply have to go the way of the dinosaurs, into extinction. Evolution had spoken.

There were indeed all sorts of half-way stations proposed by these writers. Few of them quite dared to preach what has in our own day been christened *genocide*—that is, the actual wholesale murder of those held to be of inferior race. We had to wait for Hitler for this. Most of them, though perhaps they held that in the long run the inferior peoples would in fact die out, were willing to see the inferiors duly subjected to the superiors, to have the less fit peoples serve as hewers of wood and drawers of water for their masters.

Indeed, some Social Darwinists applied their theories to a new form of caste organization, which came to be known as "élitism." The fit were not limited to any one race, but they were still marked out by the rigid hand of biological inheritance. They were the master group, the élite, the "supermen;" and they should everywhere band together against the dull average men, and dutifully exploit them. The German, Friedrich Nietzsche (1844–1900), who gave currency to the phrase "superman," was a subtle and difficult thinker, who disliked Darwin as a grubbing Englishman, and who was certainly no racist, no Social Darwinian. Still Nietzsche's influence among the half-educated who admired him in the late nineteenth and early twentieth centuries was to further racist and élitist causes.

Theories of the evolution-guided superiority of certain groups were not limited to Europe. In the United States, the innate, unchangeable superiority of whites to blacks was an article of faith among many whites in the North and almost universally in the South. This faith was greatly bolstered by Darwinian anthropologists and biologists. The notion that the degree of blondness, and other readily visible traits, such as long-headedness and

tallness, measured suitableness for citizenship in a great democracy helped dictate the American immigration act of 1924, which encouraged immigrants from northwestern Europe, and almost barred those from southern and eastern Europe. The American, Madison Grant, in his *The Passing of the Great Race,* published in 1916, asserted that the Nordics—the tall, long-headed, light-haired peoples of northern Europe—were "a race of soldiers, sailors, adventurers and explorers, but above all, of rulers, organizers and aristocrats." Grant continued confidently and picturesquely:

Before leaving this interesting subject of the correlation of spiritual and moral traits with physical characters we may note that these influences are so deeply rooted in everyday consciousness that the modern novelist or playwright does not fail to make his hero a tall, blond, honest and somewhat stupid youth and his villain a small, dark and exceptionally intelligent individual of warped moral character.*

The title of Madison Grant's book, however, betrays an anxiety that is never far from the surface even in the most confident of these Social Darwinists. Grant feared that his "great race," gifted summit of evolution though it was, was paradoxically not going to survive. The lower races were breeding faster; democratic equalitarianism was lopping off the best and encouraging the worst. Somehow evolution was going wrong. Degeneration, not progress, was the mark of the times. Like those other "scientific" determinists, the Marxists, the Social Darwinists believed that men of good will had to set to work with pen and tongue to help along the predetermined process and keep it on the right track.

A New
Historical Determinism

Darwinian science no more than Newtonian science really answered the great questions about good and evil, about the ends of human life, that men have been asking and

*Madison Grant, *The Passing of the Great Race,* 4th rev. ed. (New York, 1921), 229.

Mane
pletel
specti
top o
ing t
(whic
uses
occas
which
poses
the re
ought
the la
sense.
way:
truer,
whose
spoile
or "r
artist
any r
with
or ju
mode

among the creative writers, artists, intellectuals, than among ordinary educated men and women. This was an intensification of the revolt against "reason" already initiated by the Romantics earlier in the century; it may be called "anti-intellectualism," "irrationalism," or, more exactly, "anti-rationalism." Even this last term is somewhat misleading, for it stresses negation, whereas the attitude it describes is also an affirmation. There seems, however, to be no better term for the attitude than anti-rationalism.

One further caution. This anti-rationalism is one of the "roots" of contemporary totalitarianism, and especially of fascist and Nazi totalitarianism (see Chapter 27). But it is by no means a simple synonym for totalitarianism. It is a much broader and more inclusive term. It is quite possible to have been influenced by anti-rational currents and remain a good, if not altogether orthodox, democrat and individualist. It is quite possible to be a Marxist totalitarian and reject a great deal, especially in its psychological core, of modern anti-rationalism. Indeed, the conventional Marxist is in an important sense a naive, almost an eighteenth-century, rationalist. Get the economy to work perfectly, he says, and men will behave themselves perfectly.

The basic position of anti-rationalism, and one for which it is heavily indebted to the Romantic movement, is a rejection of the eighteenth-century Enlightenment's belief that the ordinary human being is naturally reasonable. To the extent that it rejects the Enlightenment, anti-rationalism is indeed a negation, as the "anti" implies. But it has its positive side—the belief that if men can accept their true nature as human beings they can lead richer lives than any rationalist ever planned for them; but what they must accept is the radical limitation of their thinking mind, or brain, to which so much of their experience never penetrates.

The Chastened Rationalists

Broadly speaking, there are two kinds of anti-rationalism, which shade into one another:

the moderate and the extreme. Moderate anti-rationalism at bottom is trying to salvage as much as possible of the eighteenth-century belief in human rationality. Such on the whole is the attitude of modern psychology from Freud (see Chapter 32) and William James on. This psychology seeks to aid human reason by pointing out the difficulties under which it must work. Reason, these thinkers maintain, is limited by men's instincts or "drives," by their biological inheritance of animality, so much emphasized by the evolutionists, and by their sociological inheritance of custom and tradition so much emphasized by historians and by the school of Edmund Burke (see Chapter 19).

To use a metaphor from John Locke, which he in turn derived from the slogan of the Cambridge Platonists, "the mind of man is the light of God," moderate anti-rationalists regard human reason as a flickering candle, not as the great white universal light it appeared to be to *philosophes* like Condorcet. *But they do not wish to extinguish this candle.* On the contrary, they wish to keep it alive, to nurse it along into greater and greater brightness. This process, in keeping again with the views of the evolutionist, they regard as inevitably long and slow, likely to be hindered rather than helped by ambitious plans to hasten it. These moderate thinkers are not so much anti-rationalists as they are disillusioned or chastened rationalists.

The Extreme Anti-Rationalists

By contrast, the second kind of anti-rationalism would actually put out the candle of human reason. For the extreme anti-rationalists reason is not just feeble; it is bad. It is for them, so to speak, a mistake evolution has made—a wrong turning, from which the human race must somehow retrace its steps to a sounder life of pure unsullied instinct, emotion, and faith. Thomas Hardy, the English novelist, put the position clearly in the remark, "Thought is a disease of the flesh." There was a strong dose of this extreme anti-rationalism in the Nazi movement. Hitler himself distrusted reason as a degenerate French invention. Good Germans, he hoped, would come to think with their blood, with their German folk inheritance. This is the attitude reflected in the cry of a Spanish falangist general in 1936: "Down with intelligence and long live death!" Extreme anti-rationalism may also be found at the bottom of some of the wilder movements in modern art, which want to do away with all the rules of grammar or harmony or perspective, and write or compose music or paint from the heart—or the guts—without regard for "meaningless forms."

The position of these extremists is strongly rooted in the Romantic movement, with its emphasis on the heart as against the head, on fresh instinct as against stale logic, on "the desire of the moth for the star," on the impossibility of the impossible, on always wanting more, more, more (see Chapter 19).

IV   Political and Social Thought

Many of the extreme anti-rationalists turned violently against democracy, which seemed to them to rest on an altogether false estimate of what human beings were really like. The democrat believes at bottom that the ordinary man can be freed from the weight of erroneous traditions, habits, and prejudices. Once he has the real facts before him, he can attain by free discussion among his fellows a series of decisions that will be incorporated in acts and institutions under which all men can live more happily. But if you hold that most, or even many, men are by nature incapable of fair, dispassionate thinking and discussion, if you hold that men are by nature hopelessly irrational, you will at least have to revise drastically your notions of democracy, or reject them.

The extreme anti-rationalist rejected the notions of democracy. The German philosopher Nietzsche, who did most of his work in the 1880's, will do as a sample of such political thinkers in this period. Nietzsche wrote mostly in short aphoristic passages, which are hard to systematize and are often quite contradictory. But the central line of his thinking led to the concept of a new aristocracy, to the "superman",—better, perhaps because of the vulgarization of that word, the "overman"—(in German, *Uebermensch*). Nietzsche's followers, who were numerous throughout the West in the two decades before 1914, insisted that he meant a new *spiritual* aristocracy. The overmen would be above the petty materialism and national patriotism of the middle classes. Nietzsche's opponents, who were also many, held that he was just another preacher of Nordic superiority, that his overmen were, as he put it in one of his famous passages, "the blond beasts" who had so often terrorized Europe. Certainly some of his German followers held that he meant the real live Germans to be his overmen.

At any rate, Nietzsche was clearly an enemy of democracy, which he held to be second only to its child, socialism, as a society in which the weak unjustly and unnaturally ruled the strong. Here are some of his aphorisms, from which the reader can judge for himself:

Democracy represents the disbelief in all great men and in all élite societies. everybody is everybody else's equal. 'At bottom we are all herd and mob.'

I am opposed to Socialism because it dreams ingenuously of 'goodness, truth, beauty, and equal rights' (anarchy pursues the same ideal, but in a more brutal fashion).

I am opposed to parliamentary government and the power of the press, because they are the means whereby cattle become masters.*

Nietzsche may have hoped that the herd, the slaves, the masses would, in spite of their crass materialism, somehow recognize the true mas-

*Friedrich Nietzsche, *The Will to Power,* A. M. Ludovici, trans. (London, 1910), II, 206.

ters, the new enlightened despots; or he may have thought of himself as the prophet of a vast moral and religious revolution which would in his own phrase, achieve a "transvaluation of all values," a new world for a new species of man. At any rate, it is—or should be—safe to say that he was no good conventional democrat.

Nietzsche is frankly attacking, from what he thought was a fundamental position, the values associated with the democratic inheritance of the eighteenth-century Enlightenment. But even those thinkers we have already noted (see Chapters 19 and 20) as defenders of that inheritance were in the nineteenth century influenced by romantic and anti-rationalist doubts as to the natural goodness and reasonableness of ordinary men and women, as to the beneficent workings of a free market, the "invisible hand" of laissez-faire economics, and much else of conventional, established, no longer innovating liberalism. John Stuart Mill in the mid-century had worried over the "tyranny of the majority." Walter Bagehot, a good English liberal much influenced by Darwin, pointed out in his *Physics and Politics* (1872) how strong was the accumulated force of habit and tradition, which he called the "cake of custom," how hard it was to persuade men to rational action. By the end of the century, liberals throughout the West were facing the problem of revising their attitudes toward life to conform with the new emphasis on the tough network of habit, custom, and prejudice.

Already by 1914 the broad lines of the social attitudes of our own time were being laid out. One line went toward some kind of revolutionary élitism, toward the seizure of power by a minority that believes itself to have the formula whereby the gifted few can put order into a society threatened with chaos because of attempts to make decisions democratically by counting heads, no matter what is inside them. The variety of these specific formulas was, however, very great, for the late nineteenth century was in its political and ethical ideas at least as eclectic as it was in architecture. Some made race the mark of the élite, and went so far as to preach world rule for their chosen race. Others made class the mark of the

élite, and sought to achieve the "dictatorship of the proletariat." Indeed, as Marxian socialism developed in Lenin's hands, the élitist implications of Marx's thought came out openly as the doctrine often called the Leninist corollary—that the enlightened minority must seize power and rule dictatorially in the name and in the "true" interest of the proletarian masses. Others dreamed of a brand-new élite, such as Nietzsche's overmen, to be created by a kind of new religion. Others looked to eugenics to make possible the breeding of such a new élite.

A second line went toward a more flexible form of élitism, one that tried to conserve as much as possible of democratic values. On the whole, English Fabianism and continental revisionist socialism deserve this classification. The leaders of these movements wanted no violent overturns, no seizure of power. They believed in gradualness, even in the basic democratic counting of heads. But there was in all of them a strong touch of doubt as to the

Friedrich Nietzsche, 1892.

political capacity of the ordinary man. They were not for the extension of New England town-meeting democracy to the millions of the modern state. They hoped they could persuade the millions to elect legislators who would listen to the wise planners who had studied the social sciences, who could devise the wise new institutions that would make human life so much better. Above all, the planners themselves would by no means disdain what the anti-rationalists had taught them about the irrationality of ordinary men; they would make full use for good ends of what they could learn from the "practical" politician, the advertising man, the skilled professional manipulator of human beings; they would be Machiavellians, but Machiavellians on the side of the angels.

A third line sought to preserve and protect what they considered a good, or at any rate an existing, élite from democratic drives toward equality, especially in the form of state intervention in economic and social life to promote security for all. This was substantially the line followed by men like the American sociologist William Graham Sumner, by the English philosopher Herbert Spencer, and by many others throughout the West. They are not unfairly labeled conservatives, for they sought to preserve in its broad lines an established order. But they were not simply routine, unphilosophical conservatives who opposed any changes at all. They had a definite philosophy, strongly influenced by the spirit of the times, by the anti-rationalism we have here outlined. Their basic position was a distrust of the instrument of thought applied unsparingly to human society, and in this they go back to Burke and indeed to philosophical conservatives throughout the western tradition.

But they were clearly children of their age, above all in their concrete fears of "socialism." Most of them believed in progress, and most of them prized material plenty, peace, industrial society. They held, however, that on the whole the existing middle classes, the existing leaders of a business world, the existing—or rather, the recently existing—network of Victorian habits and morals, were the best insurance that progress would continue. Above all, they feared planners and planning, at least in political positions. They distrusted the state. At bottom, they were good Darwinians, who believed that the evolutionary process depended on the struggle for life among competing individuals fettered as little as possible by planned human attempts to "rig" the struggle. They believed that social evolution could not be hastened, and that attempts to hasten it, no matter how well meant, would in fact retard it by limiting actual human variation and initiative. They are by no means altogether without sympathizers among us today, but it must be admitted that theirs has not, so far, been the "wave of the future." The Herbert Spencer who thought compulsory sewage disposal in cities was an interference with the "right" of the individual to conduct his own private struggle against typhoid fever would be even more uncomfortable in the mid-twentieth century than he was in the late nineteenth. Indeed, though there are signs of a Spencer revival, he is little read today.

V   The Century of Hope

It would, however, be a great mistake to dismiss the whole nineteenth century as something altogether outlived. On the contrary, we are all, and not merely those of us brought up in western civilization, living with problems as well as with achievements the nineteenth century brought to us, its heirs. The achievements are obvious and we have noted them in earlier chapters. They add up above all to an extraordinary command over natural forces, a command attained by the collaboration, usually by no means wholly conscious and "planned," of pure scientists, applied scientists and engineers, businessmen—yes even those abused individuals, the bureaucrats and the politicians—right on down to ordinary men and women, who had somehow to want and work for all this material progress.

The problems are also obvious and have perhaps been dwelled on at too great length in the preceding pages. There was above all the widespread feeling, obvious especially among the intellectual classes as early as the beginning of the nineteenth century, that "something went wrong," that the promised new and better world ushered in by the American and French revolutions had proved an illusion. It is easy to point out how many nineteenth-century writers—the youthful Marx, Flaubert, Kierkegaard, Nietzsche—were "alienated" from the ways of their world. It is even easier to see how many more, indeed how most of those now studied in formal courses in literature, from genteel Victorians like Matthew Arnold and John Ruskin through stormy prophets like Carlyle, worried liberals like Mill and Tocqueville, deeply concerned critics of their own culture like all the great Russian novelists of the century, even to those supposedly optimistic children of the Enlightenment, the Americans—think of James Fenimore Cooper the bitter critic of our American democracy, Mark Twain who despaired of "the damned human race," Henry Thoreau who believed that even in gentle Concord most men led lives of quite desperation—it is easy to see how all these and many more can be labeled, if not "alienated," at least pessimistic. Yet an interesting and competent American publicist of the last generation, Everett Dean Martin, could entitle a brief survey of the cultural history of the nineteenth century "The Century of Hope."

The difficulty of reconciling Martin's title with the record of nineteenth-century intellectual history cannot be wholly—though it can be partly—solved by insisting that although many if not most of the thinkers of the century tended to pessimism about their own time, the great majority of Europeans and Americans, especially the dominant middle classes, the Babbitts if you like, the Bouvards

and Pécuchets (see p. 308) were on the contrary optimists, believers in Progress, capable of singing Pippa's song:

> The year's at the spring,
> The day's at the morn;
> Morning's at seven;
> The hill-side's dew-pearled;
> The lark's on the wing;
> The snail's on the thorn:
>   God's in his heaven—
> All's right with the world!*

The bulk of newspaper and magazine writing, the testimony of informal letters, much other evidence would indeed support the social historian in an assertion that Victorian non-intellectuals, in contrast with Victorian intellectuals, were on the whole contented, hopeful, if a bit self-righteous. The gap between the state of mind, the tastes, of the intellectuals and those of the rest of mankind continues in mid-twentieth century in a somewhat different form, as we shall see.

Yet we must not take leave of nineteenth-century culture with quite so simple a dichotomy. There is even among the serious writers and artists of the time an attitude hard to pin down, impossible to put into a fine "scientific" formula, which goes far to justify even for them that phrase "the century of hope." For almost all of them, bitter and indignant though they may have been about their times, doubtful though they were about the goodness and reasonableness of "ordinary human nature," nevertheless rarely displayed a cosmic despair, rarely whined or whimpered, but shared with their grandfathers of the eighteenth century a kind of gusto, an energy, a conviction that what they wrote and said would have results, a belief in the future, even, perhaps above all, a belief in progress. The twentieth-century French royalist Leon Daudet once wrote a book entitled *The Stupid Nineteenth-Century*. But not even Daudet, who hated the century for its democratic and egalitarian aims, would have called the nineteenth

*Browning, *Pippa Passes,* Part I.

century dull, despairing, disoriented, beaten. The writers and artists we have written about in this chapter did not think and feel with T. S. Eliot's "hollow men":

This is the way the world ends
Not with a bang but a whimper.

They did not think it would, or ought to, end.

Reading Suggestions on the Intellectual Revolution

(Asterisk indicates paperbound edition.)

General Accounts

C. Brinton, *Ideas and Men* (Prentice-Hall, 1950). The later chapters of this general survey of intellectual history are also available in an inexpensive reprint: *The Shaping of the Modern Mind* (*Mentor).

R. C. Binkley, *Realism and Nationalism, 1852–1871* (Harper, 1935), and C. J. H. Hayes, *A Generation of Materialism, 1871–1900* (Harper, 1941). These two volumes provide fairly full coverage of the topics treated in this chapter.

J. T. Merz, *A History of European Thought in the 19th Century*. 4 vols. (Blackwood, 1912–1928). Misleadingly named, for it deals with philosophy and scientific thought only.

F. S. Marvin, *The Century of Hope*, 2nd ed. (Oxford Univ. Press, 1927). A bird's-eye view of general cultural history, somewhat old-fashioned now.

Morse Peckham, *Beyond Tragic Vision: The Quest for Identity in the Nineteenth Century* (Braziller, 1962). A very modern psychological treatment. Striking contrast with the Marvin book above.

G. H. Sabine, *A History of Political Theory*, rev. ed. (Holt, 1955). The nineteenth-century portions of this general account are the best in this field. For more on socialism in the nineteenth century, see reading suggestions for Chapter 20.

K. S. Latourette, *Christianity in a Revolutionary Age: A History of Christianity in the 19th and 20th Centuries*, 5 vols. (Harper, 1958–1962). Very detailed; covers whole world.

G. D. Charlton, *Secular Religions in France, 1815–1870* (Oxford Univ. Press, 1963). An interesting and scholarly survey of "substitute religions."

F. E. Manuel, *Prophets of Paris* (Harvard Univ. Press, 1962). From Turgot to Comte, history of ideas in the best sense.

K. Löwith, *From Hegel to Nietzsche: The Revolution in 19th Century Thought* (Holt, Rinehart and Winston, 1964). A good study with emphasis on German thought.

Melvin Richter. *The Politics of Conscience: T. H. Green and His Age* (Harvard Univ. Press, 1964). Good study of a leading British exponent of German idealism.

H. D. Aiken, *The Age of Ideology: The 19th Century Philosophers* (*Mentor, 1957). A volume of selections with introduction and interpretations in the useful series "Great Ages of Western Philosophy."

Special Studies: Darwinism

C. Darwin, *On the Origin of Species by Natural Selection* (Modern Library, 1936, *New American Library), and *Journal of Researches into the Geology and Natural History of the Various Countries Visited during the Voyage of H.M.S.* Beagle *round the World* (Dutton, 1908. Everyman ed.; *Bantam). Darwin's classic expositions.

J. Barzun, *Darwin, Marx, Wagner* (Little, Brown, 1941; *2nd ed., Anchor). An interesting study; finds common denominators in men usually catalogued as quite different.

H. Spencer, *The Man versus the State,* A. J. Nock, ed. (Caxton, 1940). A representative work by a whole-hearted Social Darwinist.

M. R. Davie, ed., *Sumner Today* (Yale Univ. Press, 1940). Selected essays by William Graham Sumner, the most famous American Social Darwinist.

W. Bagehot, *Physics and Politics* (*Beacon, 1956). An early and suggestive adaptation of Darwinism to the political realm; very good reading.

B. Kidd, *Social Evolution* (Macmillan, 1898). Typical social Darwinism.

R. Hofstadter, *Social Darwinism in American Thought* (*Beacon, 1955). Interesting study of the ultimate impact of Darwin's theories.

C. Zirkle, *Evolution, Marxian Biology, and the Social Scene* (Univ. of Pennsylvania Press, 1959). A controversial treatment of a controversial subject.

Special Studies: Literature and the Arts

G. M. Young, *Victorian England: Portrait of an Age* (Doubleday, 1954; *Anchor). A brilliant evocation.

E. Wilson, *Axel's Castle. A Study in the Imaginative Literature of 1870–1930* (Scribner's, 1931; *same publisher). A suggestive study.

G. Brandes, *Main Currents in Nineteenth-Century Literature,* 6 vols. (Heinemann, 1901–1905). A valuable detailed study.

J. C. Sloane, *French Painting between the Past and the Present: Artists, Critics, and Traditions from 1848 to 1870* (Princeton Univ. Press, 1951).

C. Graña, *Bohemian vs. Bourgeois: French Society and the French Man of Letters in the 19th Century* (Basic Books, 1964). Interesting socio-economic history.

W. L. Burn, *The Age of Equipoise: A Study of the Mid-Victorian Generation* (Norton, 1964). Stimulating study in British intellectual history.

M. Raynal, *The Nineteenth Century: Goya to Gauguin* (Skira, 1951). Superbly illustrated.

S. Giedion, *Mechanization Takes Command* (Oxford Univ. Press, 1948). Interesting account of the effects of industrialism on the arts.

P. H. Lang, *Music in Western Civilization* (Norton, 1941), and C. Gray, *History of Music,* 2nd ed. (Knopf, 1947). Two very different and helpful histories of music.

H. R. Hitchcock, *Architecture: Nineteenth and Twentieth Centuries* (Pelican, 1958). A massive detailed study.

Novels and Dramas

G. Flaubert, *Madame Bovary* (many editions). The classic novel of French realism.

E. Zola, *Germinal* (many editions) and *L'Assommoir* (translated under several titles). Two characteristic novels by the great French exponent of naturalism.

S. Butler, *The Way of All Flesh* (many editions). A good example of gloomy naturalism in the novel, English-style.

S. Lewis, *Babbitt* (Harcourt, Brace, 1949), and *Main Street* (Harcourt, Brace, 1950). Novels that are important documents of American social history.

E. Bellamy, *Looking Backward, 2000–1887* (*Modern Library, 1951); H. G. Wells *A Modern Utopia* (Scribner's, 1905); and W. Morris, *News from Nowhere* (Longmans, Green, 1901). Three contrasting visions of Utopia in the light of science and industrialism.

H. Ibsen, *Six Plays: A Doll's House, Ghosts, An Enemy of the People, Rosmersholm, Hedda Gabler, The Master Builder* (*Modern Library). Six pioneering dramas by a master.

E. Brieux, *Damaged Goods*, preface by G. B. Shaw (Fifield, 1914). On venereal disease.

G. B. Shaw, *Man and Superman* (*Penguin), and *Back to Methuselah* (Oxford Univ. Press, 1947. World's Classics). Plays on aspects of the modern intellectual revolution.

24

Nineteenth-Century Imperialism

I The Movement in General

In the *Oxford English Dictionary*, which tries to find the earliest possible example of a definition, the editors can go no further back than 1881 for "imperialism: the principle of the spirit of empire; advocacy of what are held to be imperial interests." The word is new; what it stands for is in part very old indeed—as old as human war and conquest. Yet there were some important new elements in the imperialism of western peoples in the nineteenth century. Nineteenth-century imperialism was in almost every country a major part of political life, with goals, methods, and advocates known to all who were concerned with politics. And since by 1900 almost all of western and central Europe, the United States, and indeed all the outposts of European culture enjoyed high

327

literacy and widespread public discussion, imperialism took its place with liberalism, conservatism, nationalism, socialism, and a host of other "isms" as a subject of universal debate. Perhaps no important "ism" seems to us now, a mere half-century after the heyday of this imperialism, to be quite so outdated. Indeed, we now use as a smear word the term "colonialism" rather than "imperialism."

The Economic Aspect

Carefully defined, another element, the economic, may be said to distinguish nineteenth-century imperialism from early forms of imperialism. No doubt the material, acquisitive motive runs through all forms of territorial expansion from prehistoric times to the present. It is clear in the earliest days of Spanish and Portuguese expansion in the quest for gold, silver, and profits. But, as the nineteenth century wore on, imperialist nations were responding to economic pressures in a new form. Liberal, and especially Marxist, economists and sociologists no doubt exaggerated this new element, but there is a basis of truth in their arguments.

According to these economic critics of imperialism, capitalists and industrialists in the older countries began to discover in the nineteenth century that they were unable to market at home all they could produce. But, being capitalists, they could not bring themselves to solve their difficulties by paying proportionately *less* of the total product of society in interest, dividends, and other payments to their own kind of people, the upper classes, and paying *more* in wages, pensions, bonuses, and the like to their workmen. Instead of sharing the wealth and creating at home the mass purchasing power and the mass market they needed, they preferred to turn to the non-western world, to markets abroad, to the exploitation of dependent peoples. This attempt to bolster the capitalist system meant competition among the great western industrial powers for land and peoples to exploit. Lenin, in his *Imperialism as the Latest Stage of Capitalism*

(1917), stressed the need to use the finance-capital that was rapidly accumulating, rather than the need for markets. The great bankers, according to Lenin, drove the willing politicians into the search for dependencies in which this available capital could be profitably invested, a search that marked what he termed the inevitable "last stage of capitalism."

A non-Marxist would of course call attention to the fact that the "nineteenth-century colonial" world produced raw materials and little else; the exchange of these for European and American manufactured goods was easy, "natural," and not yet held to be wicked or unfair to the colonial areas. Furthermore, as we have already seen, leading industrial powers in both America and Europe were experiencing an increasing demand for higher tariffs by the late 1800's. In the United States and Germany, and even in free-trading Britain, industrialists wanted protection against foreign competitors. This was an era of neo-mercantilism, reviving and "streamlining" the older mercantilist doctrines of Colbert and others. Colonies as well as tariffs entered into the strategy of the neo-mercantilists, as they had done in the case of the old.

The Powers Involved

The year 1870 is a convenient dividing line between the more active age of imperialism that was to come and the less active age that had preceded. The period from 1815 to 1870 saw a partial decline in imperialist fortunes, as most of Spain's American colonies gained their independence, and as Britain took the first steps leading to the virtual independence of Canada (see p. 350). In this same period, however, the French established themselves in Algeria, and the British extended their rule in India. The dividing line of 1870 does not mark a sharp break in the history of imperialism, but rather the acceleration of a movement that had never ceased.

The successful competitors in nineteenth-century imperialism, those who brought new lands under their flags, were Great Britain,

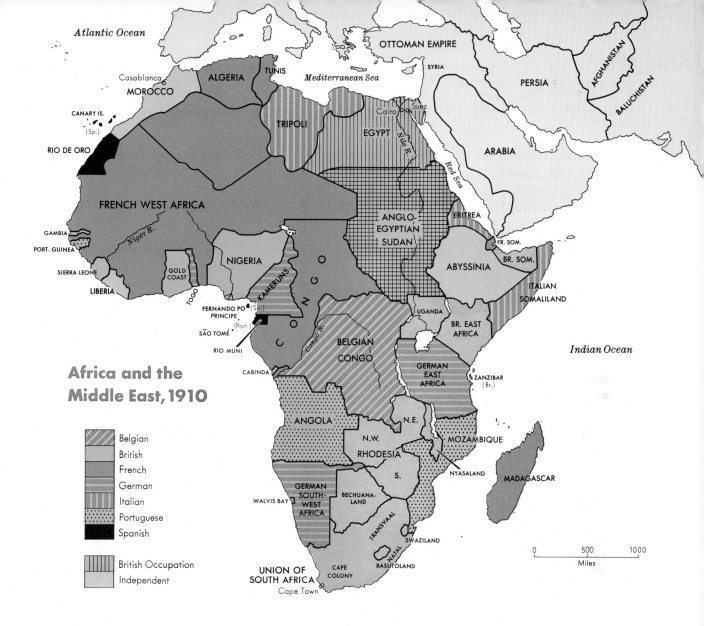

Africa and the Middle East, 1910

Legend:
- Belgian
- British
- French
- German
- Italian
- Portuguese
- Spanish
- British Occupation
- Independent

which already in 1815 had a great empire, France, Germany, Italy, and the United States. Even little Belgium, itself a "new" nation in 1830, acquired a tremendous piece of tropical Africa, the Congo, 900,000 square miles in area in comparison to the homeland's 11,775 square miles. Russia did not expand overseas, and indeed parted with her vast but thinly inhabited possession in North America when the tsarist government sold Alaska to the United States in 1867. But she began the effective settlement of the great areas east of the Urals and began to push into the borderlands of the Middle and Far East, toward Persia, India, and China.

In the process of expansion, the expanding nations inevitably rubbed up against one another in all sorts of competition, from the economic to actual shooting war. Almost every great international conflict of the nineteenth century, save for the mid-century duels between Prussia and Austria and between Prussia and France, had a direct concern in imperialist rivalries outside Europe. Imperial competition is a complicated story, then, woven into the whole fabric of international relations in the nineteenth century. We shall note briefly the major areas of inter-European rivalries and then summarize the growth of the major empires over the century.

The Areas Involved

The Monroe Doctrine (see Chapter 19), toward which European nations were increasingly respectful as the strength of the United States increased, helped to keep both American continents free from further actual annexation by outside powers. So, too, did the British navy, for British policy was there to support the *status quo*. Toward the fateful year 1914, the competition between Britain and Germany for markets and for fields of invest-

Chinese painting of the arrival of one of the first English steamers and her passengers at Canton, about 1840.

ment in South America grew intense and was one of the many factors that brought these powers to war. Since no state was strong enough to take from Britain her older colonies, throughout the nineteenth century British problems in both colonies of settlement and colonies of exploitation were limited to the British system itself. The Americas and the lands of the British Empire were then, on the whole, outside the scramble.

A major field of imperialist rivalry and penetration was the Near or Middle East, essentially the widespread lands under varying degrees of Turkish control, and Persia. In earlier chapters (19 and 22) we saw how the Balkans and the Straits became major issues in nineteenth-century diplomatic history. The whole "Eastern Question," as it used to be called, revolved around the problem of what was to be done with these old lands, which were peopled almost wholly by Moslems. They were backward lands by nineteenth-century western standards, mostly with poor rainfall, farm lands exhausted by centuries of primitive agriculture, and their ancient irrigation systems long since in disrepair. They were poor also in natural resources, for their great wealth in petroleum was not really known or very important until the twentieth century. England, France, and Russia were in active competition over the Near East early in the nineteenth century, and they were later joined by Italy and Germany.

Africa was the scene of the most spectacular imperial rivalry. In 1815, except for the nominally Turkish lands of North Africa, the little Dutch settlement at the Cape of Good Hope (taken over by the British in 1815), and a string of Portuguese, Spanish, French, and British "factories" or trading posts along the old Portuguese exploration route that went back to the fifteenth century, Africa was untenanted by Europeans and, in the interior, almost unexplored. It was peopled by Negro races, long subjected to the horrors of the slave trade and often living at the level of primitive tribesmen. The slave trade was almost abolished in many areas by mid-century, and exploration was well under way. Then in the latter half of the century the great powers

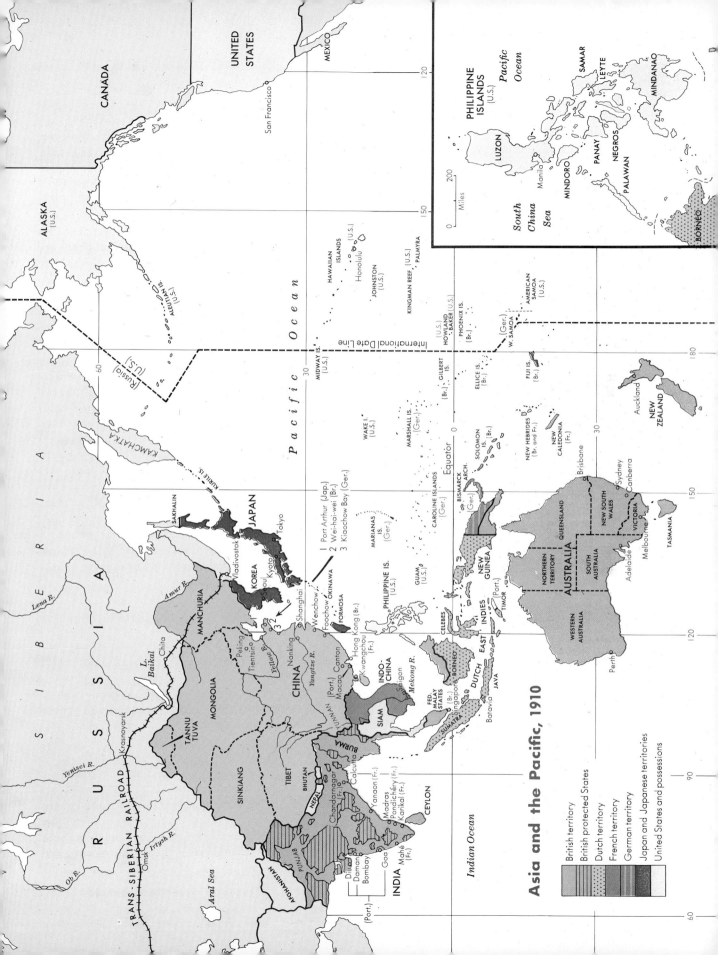

Asia and the Pacific, 1910

Legend:
- British territory
- British protected States
- Dutch territory
- French territory
- German territory
- Japan and Japanese territories
- United States and possessions

1 Port Arthur (Jap.)
2 Wei-hai-wei (Br.)
3 Kiaochow Bay (Ger.)

—Britain, France, and Germany—with Portugal, Italy, and Belgium tagging along, succeeded in blocking out in territorial units under their respective flags almost the whole of the continent. The only exceptions were the small Republic of Liberia, which had been set up by American anti-slavery groups as a land for emancipated American Negro slaves (though very few of them went there), and the mountainous and backward inland state of Abyssinia (now known as Ethiopia). Abyssinia, coveted by Italy, had a very narrow escape. In 1896, the Abyssinians, under their Emperor Menelek and with French help, defeated an Italian army at Adowa and secured a respite in independence until the Italians tried again under Mussolini in 1935.

The Far East, too, was a major scene of imperialist rivalries. European powers strengthened their hold on older colonies and acquired new ones in Southeast Asia—the mainland areas of Burma, Indo-China, and Malaya, and the island groups of Melanesia and Polynesia. But the ancient, thickly populated, highly civilized Chinese Empire was never subjected, as was Africa, to actual partition and direct annexation. China was, however, not well enough organized politically or industrially to stand up against European penetration and was by the end of the century subjected to a rough, *de facto* partitioning among Britain, France, Germany, and Russia. Each power, operating from certain "treaty ports" as centers, was able to exercise a degree of control—basically economic—over considerable areas, typical "spheres of influence" as they were called. Rivalry among these European powers, and the rising power of the United States, which was exercised in favor of the "Open Door" policy of permitting as much free trade in China as was possible and of preserving Chinese sovereignty, served to counterbalance Chinese weakness and kept China throughout this period on the list of independent nations.

Finally, Japan kept herself isolated from the rest of the world for two centuries, from the mid-seventeenth to the mid-nineteenth. This compact island empire was closed to foreigners during the period when the European powers slowly strengthened their small holds in China. Then in 1853 the American naval officer, Perry, induced Japan to open her ports to outside trade. By adopting some western ways, particularly economic ways, Japan was able not merely to preserve her real independence during the late nineteenth century but actually to begin her own imperial expansion on the mainland of Asia after winning a brief war with China in 1894–1895 (see p. 346). Japan was thus the first modern nation-state in the Far East.

II   The British Empire

We may now move on through the imperial record, country by country. Nineteenth-century Britain retained and, with the help of emigrants from the mother country, developed the great areas that were suitable to white colonization—Canada, Australia and New Zealand, and South Africa. This section focuses on Britain's imperial possessions in Africa and Asia. The development of self-government in Canada, Australia, and New Zealand will come more appropriately at the close of this chapter, in our survey of the results of nineteenth-century imperialism.

South Africa

In 1815, Britain had just acquired Cape Colony at the southern tip of Africa from the Netherlands. Cape Colony was inhabited by a few Dutch and French Huguenot colonists and was suited, in spite of a relatively low rainfall, to European living. As Britishers moved in, the older colonists, known in their own Dutch vernacular as Boers, grew more and more discontented. The adoption of English as the sole official language, the abolition of slavery throughout the Empire in 1834, the attempts of the government at London to protect the native blacks, and other measures of Victorian liberalism went against the grain of the patriarchal Boers, who were fundamentalist Christians for whom slavery was ordained of God and for whom liberalism was the work of the devil. Between 1835 and 1837, some ten thousand Boers moved north overland into country sparsely settled by primitive Negro tribes in the "Great Trek," a heroic folk migration that bulks even larger in contemporary nationalist South African feeling than do the comparable sagas of covered-wagon days in American tradition. After some confused three-cornered fighting among Boers, British, and native Zulus, the Boers established two virtually independent South African states — the Transvaal and the Orange Free State. Well inland, on territory suitable for grazing but not for intensive agriculture, these thinly populated states lived on for a time hardly noticed by the outside world.

The British in South Africa noticed them, of course, and many of the British wished to add these lands directly to the Empire. They settled from the sea another British province to the east, along the Indian Ocean side, known as Natal. In the course of the century, Cape Colony and Natal, which together had a black population heavily outnumbering the British and remaining Boers combined, acquired the self-governing rights that British colonies of settlement in Canada, Australia, and New Zealand were also acquiring. British South African leaders for the most part wanted to bring the Boer Republics under the British flag. But as the London home government swung between Tory and Liberal domination, it also swung between a policy of imperialist expansion and the "Little Englander" policy of leaving the Trekkers alone. In 1852, by the Sand River Convention, the British acknowledged the independence of Transvaal.

But in 1877 they reversed themselves and annexed it as a step toward the federation of all South Africa under the British Crown. The Boers revolted in 1880 and the Liberal Gladstone, then in power, lived up to his principles by making at Pretoria in 1881 a treaty with the Boers which re-established Transvaal as independent, though under the "suzerainty" of Great Britain.

The British were already filtering up through the semi-desert country to the west of the Boer Republics when the discovery of gold and the development of the diamond industry in these republics undid Gladstone's work. The Transvaal was no longer just a poor and isolated grazing country; it offered a great source of wealth that tempted quite different kinds of settlers. The region about Johannesburg, the famous Rand, filled up with adventurers and entrepreneurs of a dozen nations, all looking to Britain to protect them from the conservative Boers, to whom they were undesirable *Uitlanders* (outlanders, foreigners).

The Boer War and After

The inevitable conflict came to a head with the Jameson Raid of December 29, 1895 — midsummer in South Africa. The British in South Africa were now under the leadership of Cecil Rhodes, prime minister of Cape Colony, a determined and articulate imperialist who had made a quick fortune consolidating the chaotic diamond industry. The raid itself, under a follower of Rhodes, Dr. Jameson, was an invasion of Transvaal from British territory to the west, and was planned to coincide with a rising of Uitlanders in Johannesburg. But the rising did not take place, and the President of Transvaal, Kruger, had no trouble in defeating Jameson's handful of invaders. The famous "Kruger telegram," in which the German Kaiser congratulated the Boer President, was one of the critical steps in sharpening the Anglo-German rivalry that helped lead to world war in 1914 (see Chapter 25). Its immediate effect in South Africa was to harden Boer resistance and bring about in 1899 open war between Britain and the two Boer Republics.

The war, following the pattern of British wars in modern times, went badly at first for the British, who did not have enough troops immediately available to put down determined men who had been brought up in outdoor life and who were fighting on their own ground. Western opinion, including opinion in the United States, generally sided with the underdog Boers, and in Britain itself many Liberals and Laborites strongly opposed the war as rank imperialism. But in the long run the overwhelming strength of the British prevailed. By the middle of 1900 the British had won in the field, but they needed another eighteen months to subdue the desperate guerrilla bands into which Boer opposition dissolved. In 1902, by the Treaty of Vereeniging, the Boers accepted British rule, with

the promise of ultimate self-government. This promise the British fulfilled speedily. In 1910 there came into being a Union of South Africa, uniting Cape Colony, Transvaal, Orange Free State, and Natal in a state in which the central government was stronger than the provinces. English and Afrikaans, as the South African Dutch dialect had come to be called, were set up as equally official languages.

On the eve of World War I, South Africa was among the self-governing British dominions. British and Boer seemed to be well on the way to composing their long quarrel and to be ready to collaborate in setting up a new outpost of the West. But there were ominous signs even then. The Boers had by no means been Anglicized, and they were still fundamentally opposed to their partners in empire. And the two European elements together were in a minority of one to four as

The Boer War: British advance toward Johannesburg, 1901.

compared with the non-Europeans—the native blacks, the East Indians (who had come in numbers as immigrants, especially to Natal), and the "colored" peoples of mixed blood. The seeds of the current troubles in South Africa were clearly present even in the hopeful days immediately after the establishment of the Union.

Egypt

At the opposite end of Africa, Britain during the last half of the nineteenth century took over from the French the control of Egypt, nominally a vassal state of the crumbling Ottoman Empire. French influence there, already strong in the eighteenth century, was increased by Napoleon's expedition (see Chapter 18); indeed, a degree of French cultural influence persists among the Egyptian upper classes and intellectuals to this day. Under French supervision, a private company built between 1859 and 1869 the Suez Canal, which united the Mediterranean with the Red Sea and shortened the sea trip from Europe to India and the Far East by thousands of miles. The British had bitterly opposed the building of this canal under French patronage; but now that it was finished, the canal came to be considered an essential part of the "lifeline" of the British Empire.

Accordingly, the British took over Egypt and with it Suez. They carried out this action skillfully and slowly, threatening at crucial moments to use force, but not using it on any large scale. The decisive step in the process was the purchase by the British under Disraeli of 176,000 shares of stock in the Suez Canal Company. These shares had originally been assigned to the ruler of Egypt, the Khedive, as the price of his co-operation in the canal project. The Khedive, a great and unwise spender, was heavily in debt to European financiers by 1875, and he sold his shares for a good price. The largest block of Suez stock was now in British hands.

By the eve of World War I, Britain exercised virtual sovereignty over Egypt. The

PUNCH, OR THE LONDON CHARIVARI.—December 11, 1875.

"MOSÉ IN EGITTO!!!"

Khedive and his government remained. Legally Egypt was still a separate state. But a British Resident was always at hand to exercise firm control, especially over foreign relations. Under this British regime—the word "protectorate" is the usual term—much was done to modernize Egypt. The standard of living of the masses in Egypt was by no means raised to anything like that of the European masses. But the great dam at Aswan on the Nile, finished in 1902, was the first of a series of public works that added to the total productive power of the country, improved public health, lowered the mortality rate, and strengthened the numbers and prosperity of the middle class. Modernization also meant the beginnings of a wider literacy, of an educated middle class, and indeed of an intellectual class that earned its living by the written or spoken word. Most of these people responded by hating the British and by nursing

335

a constantly growing nationalism — "Egypt for the Egyptians." We shall encounter this pattern again elsewhere.

The Rest of British Africa

In between South Africa and Egypt the British pieced out their African possessions throughout the century. At its end, they had the lion's share of the continent. They had only 4,000,000 square miles out of over 11,000,000, but they controlled 61,000,000 people out of some 100,000,000. A mere listing of these holdings would be a dull and unenlightening catalogue. They can be found, usually colored red, in any good atlas of the turn of the century and, also with British possessions colored in red, on a famous Canadian postage stamp of 1898 (see map, Chapter 31). A good sample of these colonies is Nigeria, in which the great administrator Sir Frederick (later Lord) Lugard worked out the characteristic British method of colonial government in tropical Africa that was known as "indirect rule."

The colony and protectorate of Nigeria, centering around the great river Niger, was formally put together from earlier West African colonies in 1914. Northern Nigeria was ruled by Moslem emirs of the Fulani race whose culture was superior to that of the subject and exploited Negroes; southern Nigeria was inhabited by numerous heathen tribes that had long been harassed by slave raids. The British had first to subject the Fulani by force, a process that was completed late in the nineteenth century.

They then applied, as a French statesman put it, "with method but not with system," what came to be called indirect rule. Emirs and chieftains were confirmed in their separate rules, subject to the banning of internal warfare, the abolition of slavery, and similar measures imposed from above. A British Resident supervised the rule of the leading chiefs, with district Residents (later Commissioners) to supplement the work in the local subdivisions. But native law, native religion, and native traditions, in so far as they did not conflict violently with western standards, were carefully maintained. The British staff was never large; Lugard complained that in 1903 he had only one British administrator on the average for every 400,000 natives. But somehow the handful of imperial officials were able to ensure the peace. Slowly, much too slowly for impatient idealists, railroads, roads, improved agriculture, commerce, and education — the externals at least of western civilization — began to appear in Nigeria. Early in this century the first African Negro students began to appear in British universities. By mid-century, there was already a small western-educated group of native Nigerians using English as their chief language.

Other British Spheres

In the Americas, Britain maintained her colonial dependencies in the Caribbean, in Bermuda and the Bahamas, and, on the mainland, in British Honduras and British Guiana. Limited self-government of the seventeenth-century kind, which some of them had lost in the mid-nineteenth century, was only gradually granted them in the twentieth. These were all tropical or semitropical lands, with a relatively small planter class and with large Negro or mixed lower classes. These lands suffered gradual impoverishment as a result of certain economic developments, notably the great competition offered to the staple cane sugar of the region by the growth in temperate climates of the beet-sugar industry, together with an increase in population beyond the limited resources of the region. By 1914, the British West Indies had already become a "problem area."

In the Pacific and in Southeast Asia, Britain in the nineteenth century added some red dots on the map of her empire, and especially in Malaya she developed the great industries of rubber and tin that were to be major factors in her economy after World War I. She took an important part in the process of opening China to western trade by means of treaty-port concessions and spheres of influence. Indeed, Britain took one of the great steps in breaking

German view of British imperialism in Africa.

down Chinese attempts to keep off the foreigner, for in 1841 she waged what has come to be called invidiously but not unjustly the "Opium War." This war was brought on by a Chinese attempt to control the opium trade in which British merchants had an important stake. By the Treaty of Nanking in 1842, Britain acquired Hong Kong and secured the opening of five ports, including Canton and Shanghai.

India: Political Organization

In China, however, Britain was but one, though the most important, of the Great Powers scrambling for empire in that densely peopled land. In India her victory over France in 1763, confirmed by her victory in 1815, left her in sole control over a subcontinent of Asia, for the remnants of French and Portuguese possessions there hardly counted. India was the richest of Britain's overseas possessions, the center and symbol of empire, as the imaginative Disraeli realized when in 1876 he had Queen Victoria proclaimed Empress of India.

In 1763, India was already a great and well-peopled land, but not, in the western sense, a single *nation*. It was a vast congeries of races and religions, ranging from the most cultivated and philosophic Brahmins to the most primitive tribesmen, still in the Stone Age. As the nineteenth century began, the two

main methods of British control had already become clear. The richest and most densely populated regions, centering on the cities of Calcutta, Madras, Bombay, and on the Punjab, were maintained under direct British control. The British government did not originally annex these lands; they were first administered as the property, so to speak, of the English East India Company, a chartered enterprise surviving from the great days of mercantilism in the seventeenth and eighteenth centuries. The company in its heyday, led by empire-makers like Clive and Warren Hastings, had taken on enormous territories and made treaties like a sovereign power. Hastings was prosecuted for "high crimes and misdemeanors" in a famous trial of the late eighteenth century. But what he acquired the British kept.

In the nineteenth century, the company was regarded by most economists and political thinkers as a shocking anomaly, and the India Office of the central government in London gradually took over the real control and administration of British India. The trading monopoly of the company had long since been undermined. In 1857, the company's native army of Sepoys rebelled. As usual in such major uprisings, the rebellion was brought on by a number of causes. But the basic cause was that the soldiers, Hindu, Moslem, and others, all had come to fear that British ways were being imposed on them to the destruction of their own ways. The Sepoy Rebellion was put down, but not before several massacres of Europeans had occurred, and not without a serious military effort by the British. The mutiny meant the end of the English East India Company. In 1858, the British Crown took over the company's lands and obligations, announcing that no further annexations were sought in India.

The rest of India—roughly a third of its area and a fourth or a fifth of its population—came to be known as the "feudal" or "native" states. These were left nominally under the rule of their own princes, who might be the fabulously rich Sultan of Hyderabad or the Gaekwar of Baroda, or merely a kind of local chieftain. The "native" states were actually governed by a system of British Residents somewhat like the system we have just seen in Nigeria. The India Office never hesitated to interfere with the succession, or to disallow acts of princes, who were frequently irresponsible and extravagant, or even to assume direct rule for a time when it was thought necessary. The "native" states add many picturesque notes to a detailed history of India, but in the long run the distinction between direct and indirect rule in India did not mean very much in practice.

India: "The Meeting of East and West"

The years between 1763 and 1919 in India are a fascinating record of what Arnold Toynbee, the philosopher of history, calls "contacts between civilizations." Indeed, anyone who wants to understand the great contemporary problem of relations between the West and the rest of the world—to use clear terms, between white peoples and colored peoples—will do well to learn all he can of this great meeting of East and West in the subcontinent of India.

In material terms, many phases of the British rule in India are readily measurable. In 1864, the British *Statesman's Year Book* gave the population of India as about 136,000,000, and in 1904 close to 300,000,000. Although the latter figure includes additional territories, in Burma and elsewhere, it is clear that

nineteen-century India experienced a significant increase in total population. In 1901, one male out of ten could read and write, a low rate of literacy by western standards, but already a high one by contemporary Asian standards. It is characteristic of Indian society that the comparable figures for women in the same census of 1901 show that only one out of one hundred and fifty could read and write.

Such statistics are plentiful, and what they show is an India on the eve of World War I with thousands of miles of railroads, telegraph lines, universities (teaching in English), hospitals, factories, and great and busy seaports. But, in proportion to the total population, India did not have these advantages to anything like the extent that even the poorest of European countries had them. Statistics show a native ruling class sometimes fantastically rich, and an immense peasant class for the most part living as their ancestors had lived, on the edge of starvation. A middle class was just beginning to form, and, like all the middle classes formed in non-European lands under European penetration, it had proportionately far more aspirants to genteel white-collar posts in the older "liberal" professions than to posts in commerce, engineering, and industry, to say nothing of scientific research.

The total wealth of India certainly increased under British rule in this century and a half, and in 1914 it was spread more widely among the Indian populations, save for the most primitive areas, than it had been in 1763. Proportionately less and less wealth went directly from an "exploited" India to an "exploiting" Britain. The familiar Englishman of the seventeenth and eighteenth centuries, the "nabob" who made a fortune in India and retired with it to comfort, and perhaps to a peerage, in England, almost ceased to exist as the nineteenth century wore on. Anglo-Indian economic relations took on more and more the form of trade between a developed industrial and financial society in Britain and a society geared to the production of raw materials—we should now call it an "underdeveloped" society—in India. In this trade, native Indians took an increasing part if only as middlemen, and toward the end of the century native industries, notably textile manufacturing, financed for the most part with British capital, began to arise in India.

Throughout the century, of course, a large number of British—small in proportion to the total population, but numbering in the thousands—were basically supported by the Indian economy; they "lived off India." Some of them were private businessmen, but the greater number were military and civilian workers, the latter the celebrated Indian Civil Service who "ran" India. Yet natives were gradually working their way into positions of greater responsibility, into both private and public posts at the policy-making level.

Of this British ruling class in India one very important fact is now plain. It did not, like the English and Scots who went to Ireland in early modern times, really take root in India. Britain—one must be careful not to say "England," for the Scots played a conspicuous role in India as they did throughout the Empire—was always "Home," always the place where one hoped to end one's days. Though son not infrequently followed father in the Indian army or civil service, or even in business, these "Sahibs" as a whole never became fully adjusted to life in India. The spiritual climate was perhaps an even greater barrier than the physical climate. Here is a letter from an Englishwoman in Madras in 1837:

It is wonderful how little interested most of the English ladies seem by all the strange habits and ways of the natives. . . .

I asked one lady what she had seen of the country and the natives since she had been in India. 'Oh, nothing!' said she: 'thank goodness, I know nothing at all about them, nor I don't wish to: really I think the less one sees and knows of them the better!'*

The natives, too, often found the gap between East and West too great to be bridged. Another Englishwoman writes in 1913:

Coming home we saw a native cooking his dinner on a little charcoal fire, and as I passed he threw the contents of the pot away. Surprised, I asked why. 'Because,' I was told, 'your shadow fell on it and defiled it!'†

Yet the work of raising the economic basis of Indian life was in large part the work of the British. They were often overbearing, insensitive, white men at their worst in their dealings with the natives. But they were, more often than the doctrinaire liberal will admit, men devoted to the task of bettering the lot of their charges, men who made a real effort to understand them. Some of them studied with western scholarly methods the past and present of Indian culture and society, thus laying the foundations on which Indian scholars now build.

*Hilton Brown, ed., *The Sahibs* (London, 1948), 225.
†*Ibid.,* 230.

III   The Other Empires

The French: North Africa

The British victory in the "Second Hundred Years' War," capped by their defeat of Napoleon in 1815, had stripped France of all but insignificant remnants of her former empire. Yet during the nineteenth century France succeeded in building up a new colonial empire second in area only to that of the British. France, despite her frequent revolutionary changes in government, maintained an imperialist policy that added between 1824 and 1914 close to three and a half million square miles to the lands under the French flag, and some fifty million people, almost all non-European. The figures for area are indeed somewhat misleading, for a million and a half square miles are included in the Sahara Desert, which is almost uninhabited.

Africa had by no means been modernized even in material conditions by 1914, everywhere a beginning had been made. Everywhere the tricolor went, there also went the beginnings of medicine and hygiene, modern methods of communication, industry, and agriculture, and formal education for at least a few natives. In justifying the policy of assimilation, the French claimed for themselves, in contrast with the British, a lack of race prejudice, a willingness to accept the blacks as equals. This contrast is underlined by the English author whose figures we have just quoted:

Of course, it is true that the French also attempt to understand the native and in the main to give him freedom to produce as he pleases. The Frenchman actually tends much more to be a 'good fellow' with the natives than does the Briton, who is much more aloof. But this greater democracy does not seem to inspire a greater degree of confidence. Somehow, the Briton is more apt to succeed in instilling in the native confidence in the results of producing by the system that he recommends.*

Although there is some truth in the claim for greater French toleration, the deed is not quite up to the word. The French in Africa did not often marry Negroes; but intermarriage is in this real world an unreal test of racial equality. Negroes very rarely *commanded* white Frenchmen in military or civilian activity. Both at home and in Africa, on the other hand, once the Negroes seemed firmly under control, the French went a long way toward encouraging Negro art and folkways, in keeping with a policy very close to the ideal delineated by Lugard for Nigeria. The British, however, especially in the twentieth century, edged toward some kind of assimilation; African Negro undergraduates in British universities took on a lot more of Britishness than just their fine standard English accent. The contrast between British and French African policies was far from complete—there were many similarities.

*Ibid., 193

The French: Asia

In Asia, the French took over in the nineteenth century lands that came to be called French Indo-China. These lands included two rich rice-growing deltas (around Hanoi in the north and Saigon in the south), inhabited by peoples culturally and in part racially related to the Chinese. They also included Cambodia, culturally related to India, and the primitive mountain peoples of Laos. French experience here on the whole ran parallel to imperialist experience elsewhere in Southeast Asia, though the Anglo-Saxon fondness for nagging the French has tended to create the impression that the French did far worse in Indo-China than did the Dutch in Java or the British in Malaya. Slow but real material progress was made, though the basic problem of poverty among the masses remained unsolved. Native nationalist movements, nourished by educated natives with jobs of less dignity and authority than they believed should be theirs, rose in strength as the years went on. France also took part, from her base in Indo-China, in the struggle for control of China proper. The French sphere of influence was southern China, in particular the province of Yunnan adjoining Indo-China, and in 1898 the French got a lease on a port in Kwangchou Bay.

The Germans

We can be brief in listing the colonial acquisitions of the other powers. Germany and Italy came late to the imperial scramble, as they came late to national unity. Nevertheless, Germany was clearly a great power, and Italy aspired to be one; hence, both sought to acquire the token colonies, at least, that seemed necessary to that dignified status—the familiar policy of "keeping up with the Joneses." Germany in 1914 had three really large pieces of tropical and subtropical Africa—the Kameruns (Cameroons), German Southwest

Africa, and German East Africa—and the smaller Togoland, close to a million square miles in all, nearly four times the size of Texas. These were not rich or well-developed areas, and their total contribution to the German economy was almost negligible. The German achievement on the whole was not greatly different from that of other European powers in Africa; it was neither morally nor economically much better or much worse. In the Pacific, the Germans picked up some small islands, and a large, primitive territory on the island of New Guinea. Germany took part in the attempted partition of China; *her* ninety-nine-year lease was on Kiaochow Bay.

The German drive for colonies was quite self-conscious; it was well organized in a pressure group with all the fixings of modern propaganda. Bismarck himself, who cared little for the prestige of colonies, was obliged to give way and consent to African ventures. His successors went farther, and William II helped Germany to enter one of the most confused and dangerous fields of imperialist expansion, the Near East. On the eve of World War I, the German "Berlin to Baghdad" push was well under way, and the Germans had supplanted the British as patrons of the Turks.

The Italians and Belgians

Italy, condemned to the role of weakest of the great powers, got very little even out of the partition of Africa. Tunis, which she coveted, went instead to France. Italy's major effort centered on the African lands at the southern end of the Red Sea, but after her defeat by the Abyssinians under Menelek in 1896 she had to content herself with a few thousand square miles, most of it desert, in Eritrea and Somaliland. Italian efforts to add to this inadequate empire by taking Tripoli from its nominal Turkish suzerains succeeded, but these same efforts led to the Italo-Turkish war of 1911, which was in a sense the real beginning of World War I (see Chapter 25). The Italians had so little to work with it is hard to assess their success or failure.

President Theodore Roosevelt on a steam shovel in Panama during the construction of the canal.

Little Belgium, largely through the enterprise of her King Leopold II (1865–1909), managed to acquire a large piece of equatorial Africa. This project began as the Congo Free State, with all sorts of noble ideals of co-operative European civilizing missions in Africa; but it ended up in 1908 as simply the Belgian Congo. Nineteenth-century scandal about forced labor and native exploitation in the Congo called Leopold's experiment to the attention of the world and provided liberal anti-imperialists with fresh arguments. But the Belgians, who had long since moderated Leopold's policies, retained until 1960 a legal hold on a restive Congo seeking independence (see Chapter 31).

The Americans

To the horror and indignation of many Americans, to the delight of others, the United States at the very end of the century joined the great powers and acquired overseas lands. In 1898, we waged a brief and success-

North America and the Caribbean, 1910

Dates indicate year of admittance into Dominion of Canada

Map labels:

RUSSIA

GREENLAND

0   500   1000
Miles

ALASKA

YUKON

NORTH WEST TERRITORIES

Hudson's Bay

NEWFOUNDLAND

C A N A D A

BRITISH COLUMBIA 1871

ALBERTA 1905

SASKATCH-EWAN 1905

MANITOBA 1870

ONTARIO 1867

QUEBEC 1867

ST. PIERRE AND MIQUELON (Fr.)

1867 P.E.I.

1867 NOVA SCOTIA

NEW BRUNSWICK 1867

Vancouver

Winnipeg

L. Superior

Quebec

Montreal

Ottawa

St. Lawrence R.

Pacific Ocean

Missouri R.

L. Michigan

L. Huron

L. Ontario

L. Erie

Detroit

Chicago

Boston

New York

Philadelphia

Washington, D. C.

San Francisco

U N I T E D   S T A T E S

St. Louis

Ohio R.

Atlantic Ocean

Los Angeles

Colorado R.

Mississippi R.

New Orleans

BERMUDA (Br.)

Rio Grande

Platt Amendment, 1901

BAHAMAS (Br.)

PUERTO RICO (U.S. 1898)

VIRGIN ISLANDS (Den.)

Gulf of Mexico

Havana

CUBA

Santiago

DOM. REP.

BARBUDA (Br.)

ANTIGUA (Br.)

GUADELOUPE (Fr.)

DOMINICA (Br.)

MARTINIQUE (Fr.)

ST. KITTS (Br.)

MEXICO

Tampico

JAMAICA (Br.)

HAITI

ST. LUCIA (Br.)

BARBADOS (Br.)

ST. VINCENT (Br.)

Mexico City

Vera Cruz

BR. HONDURAS

Caribbean Sea

(Dutch) CURAÇAO

ARUBA

BONAIRE

GRENADA (Br.)

TOBAGO (Br.)

TRINIDAD (Br.)

HONDURAS

GUATEMALA

Guatemala

NICARAGUA

EL SALVADOR

Managua

COSTA RICA

San José

PANAMA

VENEZUELA

COLOMBIA

GUIANAS

BR.

DU.

FR.

Legend:

- British
- Danish
- Dutch
- French
- Independent
- United States and possessions

---

ful war with Spain, for which the immediate cause was the still mysterious sinking of the American battleship *Maine* in the harbor of Havana, Cuba. The Spanish-American War left the United States in control of the remnants of the Spanish Empire in America (the Caribbean islands of Cuba and Puerto Rico) and the large archipelago of the Philippines (about the size of Montana) off the coast of Asia. Mean-

time, the United States also acquired Hawaii (1898) and part of the Samoan Islands in the Pacific (1899). Then in 1903 American support of a revolution in Panama, then a part of Colombia, assured the independence of a new republic and direct American control of the zone of the projected Panama Canal.

The Americans withdrew from Cuba, leaving her as an independent republic, though subject under the Platt Amendment of 1901 to what in foreign eyes always seemed American "protection." The Platt Amendment, named from its proposer, Senator Orville Platt of Connecticut, limited Cuban control of its foreign policy and its national debt and gave the United States the formal right to intervene to preserve Cuban independence. It was resented bitterly by Cuban patriots as an infringement of Cuban sovereignty and was given up by the United States in 1934. The rest of her acquisitions the United States kept for the time, though in the Philippines she had to put down an armed rising by Filipinos who wanted immediate independence. American anti-imperialists attempted to upset the somewhat anomalous arrangement under which their government kept lands without strict authorization from the American Constitution. But a Supreme Court decision in the so-called "Insular Cases" (1901) held that territory might be subject to American jurisdiction without being incorporated constitutionally in the United States of America. Under this decision, Americans began the process of training the Filipinos for eventual independence. Meanwhile, the United States, too, had an empire, which on the maps was duly colored as an American "possession."

The Japanese

One more empire was being formed during the decades before World War I, the only empire to be created by a people of non-European stock — the Japanese. Even during their isolation (see Volume I, Chapter 14), the Japanese had maintained an interest in western developments through the trading station that the Dutch were allowed at Nagasaki. When Japan was opened to the world in 1853, its basic political and economic structure had long needed overhauling. An oligarchy of the feudal type ruled, but its ineffective government made it widely unpopular. Discontent was growing, especially among two important social classes. One was the urban middle class of merchants and craftsmen. Although the industrial revolution had not yet reached Japan,

the country already had populous cities, notably Tokyo (then called Yedo or Edo). The urban middle class, somewhat like the French bourgeoisie on the eve of 1789, wanted political rights to match their increasing economic power. The other discontented class may be compared roughly with the poorer gentry and lesser nobility of Europe under the Old Régime. These were the *samurai* or feudal retainers, a military caste now threatened with impoverishment and political eclipse. The *samurai* dreaded the growth of cities and the subsequent threat to the traditional domination of agriculture and the landlords; many of them also resented the fact that they were largely excluded from positions of power by the prevailing oligarchical regime. These social pressures, more than any outside western influence, forced the modernization of Japan.

The American Commodore Perry, who "opened" Japan; Japanese woodblock print, 1853.

Economically, the transformation proceeded rapidly. By 1914, much of Japan resembled an advanced western country. She, too, had railroads, fleets of merchant vessels, a large textile industry, big cities, and big business firms. The industrialization of Japan was the more remarkable in view of her meager supplies of many essential raw materials. But she had many important assets. As a glance at the map will show, her geographical position with respect to Asia is very like that of the British Isles with respect to Europe. Japan, too, found markets for her exports on the continent nearby and used the income to pay for imports. The ambitious Japanese middle class, supplemented by recruits from the *samurai,* furnished aggressive business leadership. A great reservoir of cheap labor existed in the peasantry, a large and submissive class. The peasants, who needed to find jobs away from the overcrowded farms, were inured to a very low standard of living and were ready to work long and hard in factories for what seemed by western standards indecently low wages.

Politically, Japan appeared to undergo a major revolution in the late nineteenth century and to remodel her government along western lines. Actually, however, the change was by no means so great as it seemed. A revolution did indeed occur, beginning in 1868 when the old feudal oligarchy crumbled under the pressure of the discontented elements. Authority and prestige were restored to the position of emperor ("mikado"), a largely forgotten office whose incumbents had for years had no real power. In 1889, the emperor bestowed a constitution on his subjects, with a bicameral diet composed of a noble House of Peers and an elected House of Representatives. The architects of these changes, however,

were not democrats. They were aristocrats, ambitious young *samurai*, supported by allies from the business world and determined to make Japan over from above as they wished. The result was to substitute a new oligarchy for the old; a small group of aristocrats dominated the emperor and the state. The constitution of 1889, rather like that of the German Empire, provided only the outward appearances of liberal parliamentary government. The ministry was responsible not to the diet but to the emperor, and hence to the dominant ruling class. The diet itself was scarcely representative; the right to vote for members of its lower house was limited to a narrow electorate, including the middle class but excluding the peasants and industrial workers. As Sir George Sansom, a British expert on Japan, has observed, she had no trouble in accepting western "things" but a great deal in handling western "ideas."

Japan began her expansion by taking from China, after a brief war in 1894–1895, the island of Formosa, which she annexed, and the piece of Asiatic mainland closest to Japan, the peninsula of Korea, whose independence China was forced to recognize as a preliminary to eventual Japanese annexation. But Russia, too, had designs on Korea; the results of this rivalry were the Russo-Japanese War of 1904–1905 and a second great Japanese victory (see Chapter 22). Japan now secured unchallenged preponderance in Korea, which she annexed in 1910, special concessions in the Chinese province of Manchuria, and the cession by Russia of the southern half of the island of Sakhalin, to the north of the main Japanese islands. She had expanded in the classic European way; that is, she now had an empire.

IV   The Debate Over Imperialism

In the nineteenth century all the western countries, even monarchical states like Germany, had a wide range of free public

opinion and some kind of parliamentary government by discussion. The kind of expansion we call imperialism, therefore, had to be de-

Cecil Rhodes (1853–1902).

already begun to worry a bit. White men, this argument insisted, are simply better specimens of *homo sapiens* than are colored men; Anglo-Saxons (or Germans, or Slavs, or Latins, depending on the writer's origins) are simply better specimens than other white men.

An imperialist like Cecil Rhodes, to judge from much that he wrote and said, very likely dreamed of a world which in the fullness of time and evolution would be peopled entirely by Anglo-Saxons. Their breed would actually be improved over their ancestors of 1900, after the inferior peoples had died out—or had been killed off. But these were very distant views indeed. The prospect of ruddy Kentish farmers actually established in freeholds along the Congo simply was unrealistic. More fashionable imperialistic doctrine held that throughout the tropical world, the superior white men would put order and prosperity into the lives of colored men, would as trustees of civilization give up the comforts of Europe to rule in discomfort in the hot countries. Some imperialists thought that this benevolent rule of white men in the tropics would last indefinitely, since in their opinion non-whites were totally unable to undertake tasks of leadership and to assume moral responsibility.

fended articulately, since it was attacked articulately. The defense and attack are both important parts of the intellectual history of our times.

Pro: The Argument from Social Darwinism

One central argument for the defense borrowed heavily from the Social Darwinists (see Chapter 23). Europeans both in Europe and in their "colonies of settlement," so ran the argument, were able to beat non-Europeans in war. By this very fact they had shown that they were in terms of evolution and progress more fit to survive than were the non-Europeans. Eternal competition is the price of survival and the best always survive—or *ought* to survive, for these theorists of imperialism had

Pro: The Argument of Duty

Other European imperialists, however, took the attitude that, though the non-whites could not run their own affairs then, they could ultimately learn to do so. For the present and for a good many years to come, whites would have to educate them on the spot; someday—the length of time judged necessary varied with the temperament of the judge—these non-whites would have matured sufficiently to take over responsibilities now confined to whites. These whites will not be *owners,* merely *trustees.* Kipling put the case comfortably enough—for white men—in his famous poem:

> Take up the White Man's Burden—
> Send forth the best ye breed—
> Go bind your sons to exile

> To serve your captives' need;
> To wait in heavy harness,
>   On fluttered folk and wild—
> Your new-caught, sullen peoples,
>   Half-devil and half-child.*

This argument of trusteeship was by all odds the most popular defense of imperialism, particularly among Anglo-Saxon peoples.

Yet the historian, aware of the complexities of human nature, will be wary of the notion that the ethical arguments of the imperialists were insincere. Many a European both in and out of the colonies of exploitation really believed in the trusteeship theory, and really did his best to live up to it. The Christian missionary is a major factor in the nineteenth-century expansion of the West. Indeed, Kenneth Latourette's long and thorough history of the expansion of Christianity has a final volume entitled *The Great Century* for the nineteenth century. More formal converts to Christianity were made all over the world in this century, so often labeled the century of materialism, than ever before.

The reality of the conversion of the colored peoples presents a difficult problem. In areas of primitive culture, whole tribes nominally accepted Christianity but continued many of the immemorial ways of their heathen past. In India, China, and Japan, old civilized countries with deep-rooted religious faiths of their own, Christianity did not win over anything like a majority of the people. Nevertheless, the missions did succeed in the course of the century in building up devoted native followers, of whom the most intelligent or most enterprising were often sent to Europe or the United States to complete their education.

Pro: The Defensive Argument

Finally, the imperialist philosophy of 1900 was by no means based on an unworried sense of white supremacy. Western civilization is

*"The White Man's Burden," from "The Five Nations," *Rudyard Kipling's Verse, 1885–1932* (London, 1933), 320.

one of the most worrying of all civilizations. Many publicists regarded imperialism as essentially defensive. The whites, outnumbered in a harsh world, had to organize themselves and hold the non-whites off. There was talk of the "yellow peril" and of white "race suicide." The writings and speeches of such apparently confident imperialists as Rhodes, Kipling, the German Emperor Wilhelm II, and Theodore Roosevelt sounded this curious note of fear and uncertainty. We are the best, but really we are a little too good for this world; we cannot breed fast enough.

One further aspect, or variation, of the defensive argument involved the importance of naval bases and coaling stations. Here the appetite tended to grow by eating. First, the French could argue that security of the homeland required control of North Africa, but presently the far-off holdings in Indo-China demanded a string of bases along which the navy could operate to protect the empire.

Con: Anti-Imperialist Arguments

Against imperialism, opponents marshaled a great many arguments. To the Social Darwinists the anti-imperialists replied by denying that the struggle for existence applied to human groups in the way it applied to plants and animals. It is precisely by sublimating the crude conflict of kill-or-be-killed into the higher rivalry for cultural excellence, they argued, that human societies transcend the struggle for life. Each group, each race, has something to contribute to the total of civilization, and the deliberate destruction or suppression of any group lames and lessens the others, prevents the true working out of evolution—that is, *cultural* evolution—among human beings as contrasted with mere animals. The anti-imperialists also brought forward very prominently the economic argument we have already noted (p. 341). They worked hard to show that in fact, especially in Africa, colonies did not "pay," that the imperialist appeal to self-interest in the homeland was a delusion, the dishonest work of propagandists for the privileged minority in the homeland and in the colonies who *did* profit personally from imperialist ventures.

From this point the anti-imperialists went on to maintain that support at home for colonial expansion rested therefore on the ordinary man's vicarious satisfactions from national achievements. The ordinary man liked to see his country figure in the world atlas as an imperial power. He liked to think of Britain's empire on which the sun never set; or, if he was a Frenchman, of the tangible evidence that France was still a great power, still carrying on her *mission civilisatrice;* or, if he was an Italian, that at last Italy too was a nation, and behaving as nations should. The anti-imperialists were on the whole not very successful in their attempts to use ridicule and irony against behavior that they found irrational. But their conviction that human action ought to be rational and devoted to the greatest good of the greatest number placed them firmly in the liberal tradition.

So strong was the anti-imperialists' belief that they were right—in spite of the growth of empires all about them—that in Britain the school of "Little Englanders," much influenced by laissez-faire economics, came to the comforting assurance that imperialism was impossible. The colonies, they held, must inevitably drop away from the mother country—to use their favorite stereotype—like ripe fruit from a tree. Why not then avoid getting into the futile process further by *not* taking any more of Africa or China? Why not hasten the inevitable by giving up the empire?

In fairness, we must add that much liberal opposition to imperialism was motivated by humanitarian sympathy for the colored peoples under imperial rule.

Not all the anti-imperialists were liberals or idealists. Indeed in France some of the most vehement were the extreme nationalists who wanted *revanche* (revenge) on Prussia for the French defeat in the war of 1870. These *revanchards* were not sorry for the Negroes; they opposed French colonialism because it distracted French energies from what they thought was the sole proper national business—getting ready to beat the Germans.

What sank into the mind and feelings of the ordinary westerner as a result of the anti-imperialist arguments was an uneasy awareness that somehow the practice of imperial expansion did not square with the best avowed intentions of democracy. Particularly in the United States, the feeling grew that imperialism and colonialism were contrary to the ideas of liberty and equality, even if the imperialists honestly claimed to be following the "trusteeship" principle. America took over an empire in 1898, but not without vigorous protests from numerous groups of anti-imperialists, and not without specific promises from the government that it would "free" dependents the moment they were capable of self-rule. This opposition of Americans to colonialism, especially when practiced by themselves, is one of the important factors in the world situation of the mid-twentieth century, and we shall return to it in later chapters, for it played a large part in our foreign policy.

V   The Colonies of White Settlement

Thus far our account of the nineteenth-century expansion of Europe has been limited largely to the "colonies of exploitation," the protectorates, and the spheres of influence held by Europeans. No such account is at all complete, for the most striking thing about this expansion was that it involved an actual transplantation of Europeans to "colonies of settlement" on a scale incomparably greater than in the previous three centuries since Henry the Navigator and Columbus.

The colonies of settlement were originally

very thinly inhabited lands. Australia, indeed, was almost empty; and the whole native Red Indian population of America north of the Rio Grande was almost certainly in 1800 not over a million, perhaps less. The European settlers simply overwhelmed these primitive peoples. In Tasmania, a large island to the south of the Australian mainland, the natives were totally wiped out, and in Australia itself they were very nearly wiped out. In the United States the Red Indians were so far eliminated that many an American grew up in the later nineteenth century without ever seeing a redman except in a Wild West show.

In most of Latin America, however, the native Indian stock, far from being wiped out, persisted; the upper class, politically and economically, was drawn from European "creole" stock; and a great many people of mixed European and Indian and Negro blood filled the lower social ranks. In the far south of the continent, in the Argentine, Uruguay, and Chile, conditions resembled more nearly those in the United States, and these twentieth-century nations are now almost wholly European in stock, largely from the Iberian peninsula and Italy.

The expansion of Europe into the Americas was also an expansion of Africa. By 1850 the leading European powers had pretty generally got the slave trade under control; but the nucleus of Negroes brought into both North and South America by the trade in the earlier centuries continued to grow. Despite handicaps of race barriers, strongest in the United States, the Negroes multiplied; by 1900, for example, there were some 9,000,000 of them in the United States.

Canada: Background of Revolt

Apart from the extraordinary growth of the United States, the most important phase of the nineteenth-century movement of Europeans overseas is the growth of what is now called the British Commonwealth of Nations, or, more correctly, simply the Commonwealth. Doubtless it is an oversimplification to claim that the British learned their lesson from the

American Revolution, and that consequently in Canada, Australia, and South Africa they were wise enough to abandon the policies of George III and Lord North. But the formula is fundamentally sound. The first laboratory for this experiment in a new kind of "colonialism" was Canada (see map on p. 344).

The rebellious thirteen colonies of North America had wanted to add a fourteenth, and had tried hard to win Canada. But a complex of causes all contributed to leaving Canada in British hands at the peace in 1783. The French Canadians in Quebec distrusted the new Protestant power growing up to the south; the American rebels had grave difficulties keeping up an army to cope with the British in the United States itself; America's French ally did not wish the new country to be too strong. Later, as we have seen in Chapter 22, the United States failed in the War of 1812 to reverse the verdict of 1783.

Upper Canada (Ontario), which was mainly British in stock, and Lower Canada (Quebec), which was mainly French, and the Maritime Provinces of Nova Scotia, New Brunswick, and Prince Edward Island were at first quite separate British "colonies," as the American thirteen had once been. Each had an apparatus quite like the old American one—a royal governor appointed by the Crown, a council appointed by the governor, and an elected assembly based on a more or less popular franchise. But just as in the thirteen colonies during the preceding century, the arrangement bred conflicts between the assemblies and the royal government. In 1837, revolts broke out in both Upper and Lower Canada, with popular leaders like Mackenzie and Papineau arrayed against the governor and his followers, and with essentially the same kind of constitutional and financial grievances that the thirteen colonies had had sixty years before.

Canada: Durham and a New Status

The revolt of 1837 was a military fiasco, and it is probable that public opinion in both provinces was against the rebels; there was a fear that too close an imitation of the American Revolution would lead to absorption by the United States. But the British government was alarmed and sent out as governor-in-chief of all the British North American provinces the Earl of Durham, a young lord of Whig antecedents and Utilitarian leanings. Durham, feeling that he was not properly supported from London, resigned after less than a year in Canada. But the famous report he made to the British Parliament on his return in 1839 became the cornerstone of the new British imperial structure of dominions, a constitutional document that Durham's admirers have sometimes ranked with Magna Carta.

The Durham Report proposed the union of Upper and Lower Canada and the establishment of responsible government—that is, a popularly elected legislature with ultimate authority—for both the union and each of the separate provinces. The report is still of great interest. Durham had all the average Englishman's insensitivity to things French, and it is an understatement to say that he never understood the Québecois of Lower Canada. But he was true to his principles—even these French Canadian Catholics must have their own responsible government. As he wrote, with prescience:

The maintenance of an absolute form of government on any part of the North American Continent can never continue for any long time, without exciting a general feeling in the United States against a power of which the existence is secured by means so odious to the people; and as I rate the preservation of the present general sympathy of the United States with the policy of our Government in Lower Canada as a matter of the greatest importance, I should be sorry that the feeling should be changed for one which, if prevalent among the people, must extend over the surrounding Provinces. The influence of such an opinion would not only act very strongly on the entire French population, and keep up among them a sense of injury and a determination of resistance to the Government, but would lead to just as great discontent among the English. . . .*

The actual realization of Durham's recommendations was achieved with due British slowness. The first step, the Union Act of

*Sir Reginald Coupland, *The Durham Report* (Oxford, 1954), 155–156.

1840 passed by the British Parliament, though it did unite Upper and Lower Canada, was at the very least unspecific on the critical point of responsibility—that is, on whether an administration defeated in the legislature had to resign or not. Nearly a decade later, under the governorship of Lord Elgin, the principle was quietly established in practice, never to be withdrawn. Nor was the next step unduly hurried. The British North America Act of 1867 achieved in principle the union of all the British provinces in North America, except Newfoundland, oldest of all, whose separatist tendencies were so strong that it did not join Canada until 1949. The act of 1867, itself basically due to formal Canadian initiative at a meeting of the "Fathers of Confederation" at Charlottetown, set up the Dominion of Canada by the union of Ontario, Quebec, and the Maritime Provinces, with provision for the admission of territories in the west as provinces on something like the pattern for admission of the western states in the United States. There were still many survivals of the former "colonial" status of Canada, from the bestowal of titles, especially knighthood with its unrepublican and undemocratic "Sir," to the possibility of judicial appeal from Canadian courts to the Privy Council in Westminster. Above all, the relation of Canada to Britain in terms of international affairs, armed forces, right of secession, and much else was not yet spelled out, and was not to be spelled out formally until the Statute of Westminster in 1931 (see Chapter 28).

The Extension of Dominion Status

The individual provinces of Australia had common British origins and had relatively short lives as separate territorial units—the oldest, New South Wales, dates only from 1788. But, in spite of these facts, these provinces developed their local differences and separateness, symbolized by the fact that they used differing gauges for their railroads. They gained the essentials of self-government in the Australian Colonies Government Act of 1850, but federal union of New South Wales,

Victoria, Queensland, and the others was not achieved until the Commonwealth of Australia was formed in 1901. The influence of the American example is clear in the constitution of the Commonwealth, which provides for a senate with equal membership for each of the six states, a house of representatives apportioned on the basis of population, and a supreme court with something close to the American power of judicial review. But in Australia as in the other British dominions, the parliamentary system of an executive (prime minister and cabinet) dismissible by vote of the legislative body was retained; the American "presidential" system was deliberately rejected.

Australia, like Canada, was essentially an empty country in 1800, and like Canada it filled gradually with immigrants, mostly from Britain. Perhaps the head start of the United States, with its great attraction for British and European immigration, slowed down the growth of these British dominions. But the process, though slow, was steady, and by 1914 all the dominions, including the quiet islands of New Zealand, traditionally most "English" of them all, were prosperous, democratic societies just settling down from the last of the pioneer stage. Their narrative history is most interesting, but we cannot go into it here, nor into the fascinating and illuminating subject—insufficiently pursued—of the likenesses and unlikenesses of the corporate personalities of these new countries and the United States, all offsprings of the "frontier."

The Commonwealth in Review

In the nineteenth century, Americans pushing west and Russians pushing east added millions of square miles to their respective lands as colonies of settlement. Although in both, and especially in America, this process of the "frontier" had important effects on their national character, it did not create great immediate problems concerning the "independence" of the settlers. The British, however, went thousands of miles overseas for their colonies of settlement. They found very soon that these colonies could not be treated as the long tradition since Columbus prescribed —that is, as mere outposts of the mother land with no political self-rule, held in strict mercantilist economic leading strings. Nor could they be, if only because of the separating seas, simply added as they filled up as a territorial continuation of the mother land, as Siberia was added to Russia and the territories of the American West to the federal Union. By 1914, the British at home and the citizens of their overseas colonies of settlement had worked out something new in political configurations, unprecedented in man's brief history.

Canada, Australia, New Zealand, and South Africa were indeed by 1914 wholly self-governing. They could and did even levy customs dues on imports from Britain. They had the beginnings of military forces of their own, and of course complete control of that clear attribute of "sovereignty"—their own internal police. Men were even beginning to speculate about whether they were not in possession of that other clear attribute of sovereignty—the right to conduct foreign relations, both diplomatic and military. For example, could Canada be at peace with a country with which Great Britain was at war?

The first test came in 1914. All the dominions went to war against Germany and her allies. Even the dubiously loyal Union of South Africa went to war against the sender of the Kruger telegram; we are bound to record that the always land-hungry Boers had their eyes on the German colonies in Africa, and especially on the big empty colony of German Southwest Africa, right adjacent to the Union. The government of each dominion, however, went through the formal process of declaring war, just as "sovereign" countries do. Yet the relation between Canada, for instance, and Great Britain was something different from the relation between two such sovereign countries as the Argentine and Spain. The dominions had not quite set up wholly for themselves, nor, to revert to the favorite cliché of the nineteenth-century Little Englander, had they dropped off like ripe fruit. The nature of the tie between the dominions and Britain was not clear then, and it must be admitted it is not fully clear even now. But it still exists, though greatly weak-

ened, and to it also we shall return in a chapter on imperialism in our own day. (See Chapter 31.)

VI   The Results of Imperialism

The broad general results of this long phase of European expansion down to 1914 may now be summarized.

First and most obviously, in the nineteenth century almost the whole planet was affected by the process. The white man was almost everywhere by 1914, and white explorers not infrequently found that the tin can, that ubiquitous symbol of the West, had got there ahead of them.

Second, the expansion of Europe was accompanied by a numerical expansion of the whole human race. Between 1800 and 1900, the population of the world just about doubled, from some 800,000,000 in 1800 to some 1,600,000,000 in 1900. European white stock did indeed account for the most spectacular part of the rise, but non-whites in Asia and elsewhere also increased. We do not sufficiently understand human population growth to say flatly that the expansion of Europe *caused* the growth of population among non-European peoples in the nineteenth century. But it did bring to many areas of the world some increase of law and order, some increase in material production and improvements in transportation and distribution, health and sanitation—factors that probably contribute to population growth. And, with such exceptions as the native Australian "Blackfellows" and some North American Indians, European expansion did not usually mean the physical extermination of non-European peoples.

Third, we may say with no reservations whatever that by 1914 it was quite clear that "natives" were beginning to reject the claims of white supremacy. Among the more civilized and long-established peoples in the Near East and Asia, the educated classes were already developing a sense of nationalism. They

took over from the West that particular form of group consciousness that is attached to a territorial political unit and that is shared, in principle at least, by all who live within the unit. This nationalism was a new thing outside Europe, and a very important one for us today, for it has gone on increasing and developing. In the early twentieth century, it was most evident in Japan and, to some extent, China, and in advanced "colonial" nations like Egypt and India, though there were signs of it almost everywhere.

This new phenomenon was not the same thing as simple hostility to whites, or to particular nations among the whites. It was an organized political faith—in short, modern "patriotism." Naturally, Egyptian, Indian, and Chinese patriots were first of all concerned with getting rid of their European imperial masters; their attitudes were those of oppressed nationalistic groups everywhere, even in Europe itself. After all, the most striking and most successful rebellion of early twentieth-century nationalist movements against an imperial "master" was that of very European and very white Ireland against the British. These "colonial" peoples were touchy, addicted to nursing grievances imaginary as well as real, eager to seize on any national trait that could be glorified, admiring, hating, and envying their masters. Above all, they were organized on a new principle taken from the West, a principle that is ultimately perhaps more destructive of their own traditional cultures than anything else that has come to them from the West. This is the equalitarian and leveling, if not democratic, spirit inherent in the secular religion of nationalism. In theory at least nationality transcends the dividing lines of profession, social class, and even caste. The fellah, the Egyptian peasant whose ancestry reaches back through the centuries, could claim to be as good an Egyptian as the aristocratic pasha —indeed a better one, since he was uncorrupted by European culture. People began to talk and write of "Arab" nationalism; yet the "Arabs" were not exactly a race, nor a people, nor any specific political-territorial entity—at most, "Arab" referred to a language, a culture, and to a part of those who held the Moslem faith.

Fourth, and in spite of the gloomy economic conclusions of anti-imperialists, there seems no doubt that over the century the homelands of Europe gained in total wealth from their expansion overseas. Indeed, raw materials from overseas were necessary to maintain the standard of living in thickly populated countries like Britain, Germany, Belgium, and the Netherlands. Theoretically, these raw materials could have come into European lands in free trade with free countries overseas; actually they came in part from imperial expansion. In purely empirical terms, the imperialism of the nineteenth century does seem to confirm Professor Webb's analysis (see Volume I, Chapter 14): The expansion of Europe was a great demographic and economic bonanza, a dynamic material growth never before attained by man.

Finally, imperialist rivalries, especially after 1870, exacerbated the normal rivalries among the European great powers and were thus a major factor in the complex of causes that brought on general war in 1914. This is particularly true of the Anglo-German rivalry, which, unlike that of France and England or of Austria and Russia, had no long historical background. This Anglo-German rivalry was everywhere by 1900—among commercial travelers of both nations, trying to sell machinery in Peru; among missionaries trying to convert the heathen in Africa; among army officers, naval officers, editors, organizers, all seeking to make German influence more important than British somewhere or to keep British influence more important than German. The rivalry extended even to the academic world and to that world in the United States. There were those who regarded the Rhodes Scholarships for study at Oxford (1904) as a British attempt to counterbalance the great prestige that the German universities, and especially their degree of Ph.D., had acquired in America during the latter nineteenth century.

Reading Suggestions on Nineteenth-Century Imperialism

(Asterisk indicates paperbound edition.)

General Accounts

W. L. Langer, *The Diplomacy of Imperialism, 1890–1902,* 2nd ed. (Knopf, 1951). Study of a hectic period of the imperial scramble; includes a discussion of forces making for imperialism.

J. A. Hobson, *Imperialism. A Study* (Nisbet, 1902). Famous attack on imperialism.

V. I. Lenin, *Imperialism, The Highest Stage of Capitalism* (International Publishers, 1939). The classic expression of the communist interpretation of imperialism.

R. Koebner and H. D. Schmidt, *Imperialism: The Story and Significance of a Political Word, 1840–1960* (Cambridge Univ. Press, 1964). Important sequel to Dr. Koebner's *Empire.*

B. Kidd, *The Control of the Tropics* (Macmillan, 1898). A defense of imperialism.

J. A. Schumpeter, *Imperialism and Social Classes* (Noonday, 1955; *Meridian). A valuable essay on imperialism from the standpoint of the economist and sociologist.

D. K. Fieldhouse, *The Colonial Empires: A Comparative Survey from the Eighteenth Century* (Delacorte Press, 1967). Authoritative and complete.

K. S. Latourette, *A History of the Expansion of Christianity,* 7 vols. (Harper, 1937–1945). Volumes 5 and 6 concern the expansion of Christianity into the non-European world.

Special Studies:
Africa

L. Woolf, *Empire and Commerce in Africa* (Allen & Unwin, 1919). A left-wing critique.

H. H. Johnston, *The Opening Up of Africa* (Holt, 1911. Home University Library). Sympathetic popular account by the author of many other works on Africa.

H. L. Hoskins, *European Imperialism in Africa* (Holt, 1930. A Berkshire Study). Handy introductory manual.

James Duffy, *Portugal in Africa* (Harvard Univ. Press, 1962). The best account.

R. L. Buell, *The Native Problem in Africa* (Macmillan, 1928), and H. A. Wieschoff, *Colonial Policies in Africa* (Univ. of Pennsylvania Press, 1944). Two solid and helpful studies.

R. Robinson and others, *Africa and the Victorians: The Climax of Imperialism in the Dark Continent* (St. Martin's Press, 1961). Excellent study from archival material.

C. W. de Kiewiet, *A History of South Africa, Social and Economic* (Clarendon, 1941), and E. A. Walker, *A History of South Africa*, 2nd ed. (Longmans, Green, 1940). Two good studies.

B. Williams, *Cecil Rhodes* (Constable, 1921). Probably the best book on the famous empire-builder. But for a different estimate, see G. S. Millin, *Cecil Rhodes* (Harper, 1933).

W. H. Hancock, *Smuts: The Sanguine Years* (Cambridge Univ. Press, 1962). A final volume is promised in this definitive biography of a major South African leader.

B. Williams, *Botha, Smuts, and South Africa* (Macmillan, 1948. Teach Yourself History series). Introduction to the period following the Boer War.

F. D. Lugard, *The Dual Mandate in British Tropical Africa,* 3rd ed. (Blackwood, 1926). Significant detailed account of British colonial policy in action.

H. R. Rudin, *Germans in the Cameroons, 1884–1914: A Case Study in Imperialism* (Yale Univ. Press, 1938). Good study of the topic indicated.

L. de Lichtervelde, *Léopold of the Belgians* (Century, 1929), and L. Bauer, *Leopold the Unloved, King of the Belgians and of Wealth* (Little, Brown, 1935). Vindicating and attacking, respectively, the great exploiter of the Congo.

Special Studies:
Asia

J. T. Pratt, *The Expansion of Europe into the Far East* (Sylvan Press, 1947). Excellent introduction to the subject.

D. E. Owen, *Imperialism and Nationalism in the Far East* (Holt, 1929. A Berkshire Study). Handy brief introductory manual.

K. S. Latourette, *The Development of China,* new ed. (Houghton, Mifflin, 1956). A good survey.

A. C. Lyall, *The Rise and Expansion of British Dominion in India,* 5th ed. (Murray, 1914). Sympathetic account.

R. Coupland, *Britain and India, 1600–1941* (Longmans, Green, 1941). Very brief introduction by an authority on imperial questions.

G. Sansom, *The Western World and Japan, A Study in the Interaction of European and Asiatic Cultures* (Knopf, 1950), and *Japan, A Short Cultural History*, rev. ed. (Appleton-Century, 1943). Two indispensable works by a great authority on Japan.

S. N. Fisher, *The Middle East: A History* (Knopf, 1959). A solid detailed account, emphasizing the nineteenth and twentieth centuries.

K. S. Latourette, *A History of Modern China* (*Penguin). Sound reliable survey.

E. O. Reischauer, *Japan, Past and Present* (Knopf, 1946). Reliable introduction.

B. H. Sumner, *Tsardom and Imperialism in the Far East and Middle East, 1880–1914* (British Academy, 1944). Good short account.

R. E. M. Wheeler, *Cambridge History of India,* Vols. V and VI (Cambridge Univ. Press, 1929). A new edition of these standard detailed volumes is in preparation.

V. H. Smith, *The Oxford History of India*, 3rd ed. (Oxford Univ. Press, 1958). Brief detailed account of the history of India, edited by Percival Spear.

H. Brown, ed., *The Sahibs: The Life and Ways of the British in India as Recorded by Themselves* (Hodge, 1948). An illuminating compilation.

Special Studies: British Empire and Dominions

J. H. Rose and others, eds., *The Cambridge History of the British Empire*, 7 vols. (Macmillan, 1929–1940). Separate volumes on India, Canada, and Australia and New Zealand.

P. Knaplund, *The British Empire, 1815–1939* (Harper, 1941). An authoritative work.

C. E. Carrington, *The British Overseas: Exploits of a Nation of Shopkeepers* (Cambridge Univ. Press, 1950). An advanced and detailed study from a British point of view.

R. Anstey, *Britain and the Congo in the Nineteenth Century* (Oxford Univ. Press, 1962). A good special study.

M. Perham and M. Bull, eds., Diaries of Lord Leyard, 4 vols. (Northwestern Univ. Press, 1959–1963). Useful source material for the state of mind of a superior "imperialist."

C. P. de T. Glazebrook, *Canada: A Short History* (Oxford Univ. Press, 1950). A good brief survey.

C. F. Wittke, *A History of Canada,* 3rd ed. (Crofts, 1941). Emphasis on recent history.

R. Coupland, ed., *The Durham Report* (Clarendon, 1946). The famous document that in a sense marks the beginning of the development of the British Commonwealth.

G. Greenwood, ed., *Australia: A Social and Political History* (Praeger, 1955). Good collaborative work, with bibliographies.

M. Barnard, *A History of Australia* (Praeger, 1963). A readable brief history.

H. Belshaw, ed., *New Zealand* (Univ. of California Press, 1947). An informative volume.

J. B. Condliffe, *New Zealand in the Making,* and *The Welfare State in New Zealand* (both Macmillan, 1959). These books provide a good economic history of 1792–1957.

Special Studies: Other Subjects

S. H. Roberts, *History of French Colonial Policy, 1870–1925,* 2 vols. (King, 1929). Detailed.

M. E. Townsend, *The Rise and Fall of Germany's Colonial Empire, 1884–1918* (Macmillan, 1930). A useful account.

J. W. Pratt, *America's Colonial Experiment* (Prentice-Hall, 1950). A valuable survey.

D. Perkins, *Hands Off: A History of the Monroe Doctrine* (Little, Brown, 1941). A useful popular account by a leading specialist.

Historical Fiction

R. Kipling, *Kim* (many editions) and *Soldiers Three* (many editions). Famous works by the even more famous champion of imperialism.

N. Coward, *Cavalcade,* in *Play Parade* (Garden City Publishing, 1933). A patriotic play and a sentimental tribute to old imperial glories.

S. Cloete, *The Turning Wheels* (Houghton, Mifflin, 1937). A novel about nineteenth-century Boers.

A. Gide, *The Immoralist* (*Vintage). European hero corrupted by North Africa.

E. M. Forster, *A Passage to India* (many editions). A celebrated and astringent novel.

L. Hémon, *Maria Chapdelaine* (Macmillan, 1940; *Image). The best-known novel about rural French Canada.

Hugh McLennan, *The Precipice* (Duell, Sloan & Pearce, 1948). One of the few good psychological studies of relations between English-speaking and French-speaking Canadians.

H. H. Richardson, *The Fortunes of Richard Mahony* (Readers Club, 1941). A series of novels about modern Australia by an Australian.

H. Rider Haggard, *King Solomon's Mines* (Longmans, Green, 1926). A splendid example of the rousing novel of imperialist adventure.

25

The First World War

I Introduction

On June 28, 1914, the Habsburg Archduke Francis Ferdinand, heir to the throne of Austria-Hungary, and his wife were assassinated in the streets of Sarajevo, capital of the recently (1908) annexed provinces of Bosnia and Herzegovina, which had been occupied by Austria-Hungary since 1878 (see Chapter 22). The assassin, Princip, was a Serbian nationalist. Bosnia had long been coveted by the Serbs. The Austro-Hungarian government, alarmed by the ambitions of Serbian nationalists, took the occasion of the assassination to send a severe ultimatum to Serbia. The Serbian government's refusal to accept the ultimatum in its entirety led to an Austrian declaration of war on Serbia, on July 28. Within the week, the great states of Europe were engaged in a general war—the Central Powers (Austria-

Hungary and Germany) against the Allies (Serbia, Russia, France, and Britain). Princip's revolver shot was eventually to kill some ten million men.

This was the first general war, the first war to involve most of the members of the world state-system, since the wars of the French Revolution and Napoleon a century earlier. There had indeed been wars enough, foreign and civil, in the century between. They were, however, save for relatively minor wars like the Crimean War of 1853, wars between two parties, like the Franco-Prussian War of 1870, the bloody American war between North and South in 1861–1865, and a whole series of colonial wars against rebellious natives.

In 1914 a great many people in Europe and America felt that this sort of general war was all but impossible. These people, predominantly liberal intellectuals, had been alarmed by the series of crises we shall shortly describe, crises that showed how close a general war might be. But they had followed hopefully the movements for international peace and cooperation—the Red Cross, the international labor movements, and the Hague conferences of 1899 and 1907, which, though they failed to achieve their avowed purpose of limiting armaments, did set up a tribunal for the arbitration of international disputes, the "world court." And many intellectuals simply refused to believe that a world war, should it break out, could last more than a few months. The cost of such a war, they maintained, would be so great it would bankrupt any government. Such was the thesis of a best seller, Norman Angell's *The Great Illusion* (1910).

World War I was long, bloody, and destructive. The shock of its outbreak, vastly increased by the strains of the war itself, and above all by the failure of the postwar peace settlement, brought on in the 1920's a most extraordinary discussion of the causes of the war. This discussion was by no means limited to profes-

sional historians. It was carried on in the press and on the platforms by all the agencies that touched public opinion. Most of it was designed to "revise" the verdict of the Versailles Treaty of 1919, in which the victorious Allies declared Germany and Austria-Hungary solely responsible for precipitating the war of 1914. The beaten Germans, penalized in the peace, had obvious reasons for trying to prove themselves innocent of war guilt. But important currents in public opinion in Great Britain, the United States, and even in France also flowed into this "revisionist" movement. So far did revisionism go in the 1920's that some American historians parceled out varying portions of the guilt among the victors and the vanquished alike, with the confidence of schoolmasters handing out merits and demerits.

We cannot be so confident today. From our further perspective, the question of war guilt in 1914 fades out into a question of historical causation, and into the fact of historical tragedy. We can say with the English writer, George Meredith:

> In tragic life, God wot,
> No villain need be! Passions spin the plot.
> We are betrayed by what is false within.*

No one power or group of powers "caused" the war of 1914. Its causes lie deep in the history of the state-system of western civilization, and, more particularly, in its history since 1870. They lie deep also in that fundamental form of group-consciousness we call "nationalism" and in the very structure of the modern nation-state. The dramatic date of the assassination of Francis Ferdinand, June 28, 1914, serves as a dividing line between the ultimate, or long-term, factors and the proximate, or short-term, factors.

*Modern Love, XLIII.

II Causes of the War

The Shift
in the Balance of Power

In the long term, an obvious factor that made war more likely was the unification of Germany and Italy. The creation of these two new major states in the 1860's and 1870's altered the always delicate balance of power in the European state-system. The efforts of statesmen during the next forty years to adjust the system and to take account of the two new powers and their claims proved ultimately unsuccessful. The older established powers were by no means willing to give up their own claims. We have seen that ever since the modern European—or, better, the western—state-system developed out of medieval fragmentation, the separate units, the states, have tried to grow. They have tried to grow in wealth, in prestige, and, most conspicuously of all, in territory. In the second half of the nineteenth century, with the principle of national sovereignty well established, with even the smaller states like Switzerland and Sweden generally accepted as not to be swallowed, there was little territory in Europe that could be easily disposed of for the purpose of making adjustments. Unification had closed off Germany and Italy, which as recently as 1815 had been classic areas for "compensation." Only southeastern Europe, the Balkan lands of the obviously weakening Turkish Empire, remained in the late nineteenth century as possible pickings for ambitious powers. Even there, the growth of national feeling in states like Rumania, Serbia, Bulgaria, and Greece made sheer annexation difficult. Nevertheless, Russia and Austria-Hungary both had ambitions in the Balkans; behind them, aiming rather at domination of Turkey and the Near East, came Germany and Great Britain. Finally, as we have noted in Chapter 24, much of

Africa, Asia, and Oceania had been partitioned among the great powers amid intense rivalry. It seemed always possible to re-do this partitioning.

Meantime, influenced by their rivalries in Europe and abroad, the great powers were also choosing sides in a series of alliances and agreements. By the early years of the twentieth century two camps existed—the Triple Alliance of Germany, Austria-Hungary, and Italy, and the Triple Entente of France, Britain, and Russia. The system, as many people at the time saw clearly, had grown so tightly organized that there was almost no free play left, and with the wisdom of hindsight we can now see that after 1900 almost any crisis might have led to war. Sarajevo was the one that did.

This state of international politics was christened by an English liberal, Lowes Dickinson, "the international anarchy." It was, however, no chaos, but a highly organized rivalry, "anarchical" only in the sense that there was no higher authority to put a stop to the rivalry. In concrete instances, two or more powers wanted the same piece of land, as a territorial addition or as a sphere of influence. France and Great Britain both wanted Egypt; France and Germany both wanted Morocco; Russia and Austria-Hungary both wanted control over the Balkans; Russia and Japan both wanted Manchuria; and so on around the map. Compromises were made, lands and spheres of influence were shared, but in the long run there simply wasn't enough to go around.

The Role of Public Opinion

We have in this outline used the shorthand of names like "Great Britain" or "Germany." But these are mere symbols, as colored blobs on a map are symbols, for millions of human beings whose desires somehow do add up into the actions of states, did add up to the war of 1914. In no state were the millions all in agreement. There were Germans who wanted no bit of Africa or any other piece of land. There were Englishmen who, far from being content with Britain's place in the world, wanted more, wanted Britain to be for the whole round world what Rome had been for the Mediterranean world in the first centuries of the Christian Era, hoped eventually to eliminate all but Englishmen (and perhaps Scotsmen) in a fine Darwinian struggle. There were everywhere in Europe at least a few absolute pacifists, men who were determined under any conditions to refuse to fight, men who once war broke out became "conscientious objectors." We must not think of the war and the events that led up to it as simply the work of a few men at the top in each nation, the professional soldiers, the villainous diplomats in frock coats and striped trousers. In all the countries, there was a spectrum that ran from militarist to pacifist, through all shades of opinion.

But the outbreak of the war saw in each belligerent nation a broad national public opinion in support of the government. In 1914, a good many men marched to war convinced that war was a beneficial thing; the bands played, the crowds shouted, and war, perhaps for the last time in our day, seemed romantic as well as necessary. Here is the account of a young German on the last train out of Switzerland before the outbreak of war:

> An elderly gentleman was sitting in our compartment. He began to talk to us at once, as if we were intimate acquaintances. On the back of his hotel bill he had added up the numerical strength of the European armies and balanced them against each other. He compared the two totals and assured my mother that the spiritual qualities of the German troops compensated for the numerical superiority of the Russians. For in this war spiritual qualities alone would decide the day, and Germany's spiritual qualities were the best in Europe. As a university professor he knew that our youth were ready for the fray, and full of ideals. At last the hour had come when our people could enter on its great world mission. . . .*

*Ernst Glaeser, *Class of 1902*, Willa and Edwin Muir, trans. (London, 1929), 171–172.

"European Balance," viewed by Daumier after 1870.

German Aspirations

The Germans were led by their Kaiser, William II, who had come to the throne in 1888. The "revisionist" historians have been able to show that in the hectic five weeks after the assassination at Sarajevo the Kaiser, contrary to world opinion at the time, did not work steadily for war, that toward the end he tried to avoid a general war. But he cannot be even partially absolved for the long-term, for the ultimate, causes of the war. In the decisive years between 1888 and 1914 he was the posturing, aggressive leader of patriotic expansion, the "White Knight" leading his people to glory (see also Chapter 22). He was perhaps more of a figurehead, less of an actual maker of policy, than the world took him to be, but still a willing and effective figurehead for expansionists and violent nationalists.

German ambitions and German fears produced an intense hatred of Britain, a hatred mixed with envy and a sense of inferiority, a hatred that focused on the English upper classes, perfectly tailored, serene in effortless superiority, the favorite children of fortune. Many a German tourist, perhaps quite accidentally given an Italian hotel room inferior to that given a traveling Englishman, would come home burning with indignation at this personal evidence that Germany was being denied its place in the sun. In the German navy, in the years just before the war, there was a simple toast in the officers' mess: *Der Tag* (The Day). Everyone knew that this was the day of the declaration of war between Germany and Britain. These feelings are all condensed in the famous "Hymn of Hate" of the German poet Ernst Lissauer:

> We will never forego our hate,
> Hate by water and hate by land,
> Hate of the head and hate of the hand,
> Hate of the hammer and hate of the Crown.
> Hate of the seventy millions choking down.
> We love as one, we hate as one,
> We have one foe and one alone:
>   England!*

*Ernst Lissauer, "A Chant of Hate Against England," trans. by Barbara Henderson, in Burton E. Stevenson, comp., *The Home Book of Verse,* 3rd ed. (New York, 1918), II, 2549–2550.

British Aspirations

Few Englishmen returned this hate; the English were still on top. Yet as the years wore on, the expensive race between Britain and Germany in naval armaments continued; in incident after incident German and British diplomats took opposite sides; and—this seemed especially important to the hardheaded—German wares of all sorts undersold British wares in Europe, in North and South America, and in Asia. Englishmen began to think that someone ought to teach these ill-mannered Germans a lesson. Moreover, they had begun to worry about their own position of prosperity and leadership. In India, the greatest possession of the English, it was clear already that great concessions toward self-government would have to be made to the natives. Close at home the Irish crisis was in one of its most acute phases, with Protestant Ulster in arms against the proposed Home Rule. British officers were indeed guilty of planning actual mutiny, much as did French officers in

Soldiers leaving Berlin for the front.

1961 during the Algerian crisis. Englishmen were worried about their obsolescent industrial plants, their apparent inability to produce goods as cheaply and as efficiently as the Germans; they were self-critical about their failures as salesmen abroad, their stodgy self-satisfaction.

A great many Britishers thought of themselves as good liberals and good internationalists, anxious to preserve the peace and the decencies of international life. Many were radicals and Labor party men committed to pacifism. The coming of war in 1914 was to show how thoroughly almost all these men identified Great Britain and righteousness. As for the bulk of the conservatives, they were as nationalist as in any other great country. In Britain, their nationalism attached itself to the Empire, to the "White Man's Burden," to a whole set of symbols that the Germans found intolerable.

The Other Belligerents

In democratic France as in democratic England there was a wide spread of opinion on international politics. A numerous socialist Left was committed to pacifism and to the concept of an international general strike of workers at the threat of actual war. A more moderate group also opposed conventional patriotic aggressiveness toward the foreigner. Both among the men who conducted French foreign relations and among the general public, however, there remained right down to the eve of the Great War the embittered patriotism of the beaten. Frenchmen wanted *revanche*, revenge for the defeat of 1870. They wanted Alsace-Lorraine back. For all these years, the statue representing Strasbourg among the cities of France in the Place de la Concorde in Paris was draped in black. With the warmest patriots, the organizers of patriotic societies, the editors of patriotic journals, this feeling for revenge was an obsession.

By the opening decade of the 1900's many observers thought that the new generation was losing its desire for revenge, that Frenchmen had at last decided to accept the verdict of 1870. But French diplomatists continued to preserve and strengthen the system of alliances against Germany, and in the excited weeks of July, 1914, it was clear that the French were ready for war.

Among the other major belligerents, too, the ultimate decisions of governments won much popular support. Russians were filled with the "pooled self-esteem" of nationalism, were convinced that God and the right were on their side. Italians saw in war the chance to get *Italia Irredenta* (Trent, Trieste, and their surrounding lands) and still more territory from the Habsburg Monarchy. In the dual monarchy, as we have seen (see Chapter 22), the loyalty of subject nationalities could scarcely be counted on; but the dominant Germans of Austria and Magyars of Hungary welcomed the opportunity to put the troublesome Slavs in their place for good and all.

The Era of Bismarck, 1871–1890

The road to Sarajevo starts in 1871, at the Treaty of Frankfurt, where France was obliged to cede Alsace and Lorraine to the new German Empire. It was no straight road, but one of many twists and turnings, and few historians would now maintain that 1871 made 1914 inevitable. We cannot follow the road in detail, but we must map its main course.

For some twenty years Bismarck was its chief engineer. In fairness to the Iron Chancellor, it must be said that during his last twenty years in office he sought peace, and indeed obtained it. Powerful elements in the new empire made it impossible for him to grant to France the same kind of generous peace he had given Austria in 1866. Yet Bismarck did try to salve the wound he knew France had suffered; he encouraged her to expand her empire in North Africa by the acquisition of Tunisia in 1881, even though this offended the Italians, who also coveted Tunisia. But he feared a French attempt at revenge and sought to isolate her diplomatically by building a series of alliances from which she was excluded. Germany, he insisted, was now a "saturated" power, and wanted nothing more in Europe; and in a famous phrase he insisted that all the Balkans were not worth "the bones of a single Pomeranian grenadier." Above all, he sought to keep on good terms with *both* Austria and Russia, and, what was much more difficult, to keep both these powers on good terms with each other. Since both wanted predominance in the Balkans, Bismarck's task was formidable.

He laid the cornerstone of his diplomatic system by a defensive alliance with Austria-Hungary in 1879, an alliance that held right down to 1918. And he was able to make a not-so-secret treaty, the so-called League of the Three Emperors, which bound Germany, Russia, and Austria together. The three powers agreed to act together in dealings with Turkey and to maintain friendly neutrality should any one of them be at war with a fourth power other than Turkey. Next, working skillfully on Italian annoyance over the French expansion in Tunis, Bismarck secured an alliance among Germany, Austria-Hungary, and Italy, directed chiefly against France. This was the famous Triple Alliance of 1882, often renewed, which still existed on paper in 1914.

On this series of tightropes Bismarck maintained a precarious balance through the 1880's. Chief in his mind was the danger that the Russians, always fearful of Austrian schemes in the Balkans, would desert him and ally themselves with France, still a great power and anxious to escape from the isolation that Bismarck had designed for her. In 1887, Russia did refuse to renew the League of the Three Emperors, but Bismarck was able to repair the breach for the moment by a secret Russo-German agreement known as the Reinsurance Treaty. The two promised each other neutrality in case either was involved in a war against a third power; but this neutrality was not to hold if Germany made an "aggressive" war against France or if Russia made an "aggressive" war against Austria. Since Russian nationalist agitation continued against both Austria and Germany, Bismarck in 1888 made public as a warning to Russia the terms of the Austro-German alliance and allowed the main terms of the Triple Alliance to be known informally.

Formation of the Triple Entente, 1890–1907

Then in 1890 the young Emperor William II dismissed Bismarck. The Emperor's advisers, headed by Baron von Holstein, persuaded him not to renew the Reinsurance Treaty with Russia, in spite of Russian desire for such renewal. Shortly afterward, what Bismarck had worked so hard to prevent came about. After lengthy negotiations, Russia and France in 1894 came together in an alliance that ended French isolation. It was formally a defensive alliance, in which each was to come to the aid of the other if Germany or Austria made "aggressive" war against either, and it was accompanied by the necessary military agreements between the two general staffs. Against the Triple Alliance there now stood, quite openly, a Dual Alliance of France and Russia. Great Britain as yet remained technically uninvolved by any formal treaty with a European ally and indeed never did make a full legal commitment even with France.

The next great stage in the tightening network of alliances was to bring Great Britain in against the Central Powers, at least by informal "entente" or agreement. In the two decades after the accession of William II, Britain made a formal alliance with Japan and informal "understandings" (*ententes*) with France and Russia. What chiefly drove Britain to these actions was the naval race with Germany and the rapid worsening of Anglo-German relations, a worsening even more evident perhaps at the level of public opinion than at the level of formal diplomacy.

A good concrete instance of this rising hostility is the Kruger telegram of 1896, in which the Kaiser congratulated President Kruger of the Boer Republic of Transvaal on the defeat of the Jameson raid (see p. 333). It may be that the Kaiser and his circle hoped at bottom that this gesture would be taken by the English government as a kind of polite and permissible diplomatic blackmail, an evidence of how great a nuisance the German government could be

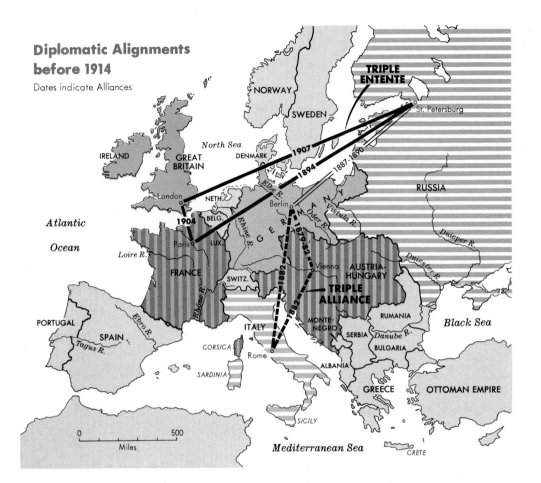

Diplomatic Alignments before 1914

Dates indicate Alliances

to the British if it were not on their side. But the British press took the telegram as an unbearable insult, and the German press replied angrily to British anger.

It was fear of Russia rather than fear of Germany, however, that inspired Britain to make the first break with formal isolationism, the alliance with Japan in 1902. The outbreak of war between Russia and Japan hastened negotiations between Britain and France. In the Anglo-French Entente of 1904, France gave England a free hand in Egypt, England gave France a free hand in Morocco, and various outstanding difficulties between the two in other parts of the world were ironed out. More important, the base was laid for general collaboration between the two in international affairs. Only six years previously, in 1898, there had been a grave flareup of the traditional colonial rivalry between France and England when a French column was met by a British column at Fashoda in the disputed Sudan

territory of the upper Nile Valley. Fashoda caused quite as big an outbreak of fury in the French and the British press as the Kruger telegram only two years before had caused in the German and the British press. Yet Fashoda left wounds much less deep than the Kruger telegram; the contemporary press is not always a faithful guide to the climate of public opinion, let alone to that of professional diplomacy.

The final stage in aligning the two camps came in 1907 when Russia, chastened by her defeat at the hand of Japan and encouraged by the French, came to an understanding with Great Britain. Both countries made concessions in regions where they had been imperialist rivals—Persia, Afghanistan, Tibet—and the British at last made some concessions toward the Russian desire to open up the Straits. The agreement was scarcely based on any genuine sympathy between the two peoples, for the British, notably, had been

Russophobic for well over a century. Nevertheless, it did round out the Triple Entente against the Triple Alliance.

A Decade of Crises, 1905–1914

The last decade before 1914 was a series of crises and local wars, any one of which might have spread into a world war. First came a deliberate theatrical gesture from the Kaiser, when in 1905 he made a ceremonial visit to Tangier in Morocco as a way of telling the world that the Germans would not accept the Anglo-French assignment of Morocco to France. The net effect of this blustering was to *tighten* the entente between France and Britain, for the British indicated clearly to the French that they would support them. Indeed at this time there began the informal military and naval conferences between the British and the French that the French, at least, believed "committed" the British to armed support if the Germans attacked. Although the French Foreign Minister, Delcassé, a partisan of firm policy toward the Germans, was forced out of office, even this partial victory did the Germans no good. French public opinion was infuriated by this intervention in their domestic politics. In the end, a general international conference at Algeciras in Spain (1906) backed up the French, who went ahead with their plans for a protectorate in Morocco. At Algeciras American diplomatic influence was used on the side of France; the United States, too, was beginning to emerge from its own variety of isolationism.

A "second Moroccan crisis" in 1911 heightened tensions and brought the possibility of a general war home to most Frenchmen. The Kaiser sent a German gunboat, the *Panther*, to the Moroccan port of Agadir as a protest against French occupation of the old city of Fez. In ensuing negotiations, well-publicized in the press, the Germans finally agreed to leave the French a free hand in Morocco, but only at a price the French considered blackmail: part of French Congo was ceded to Germany.

In the Balkans, a decisive turn of the road toward Sarajevo came in 1908. Austria formally proclaimed the annexation of the old Turkish provinces of Bosnia-Herzegovina, which she had occupied since 1878. Austria's decisive act infuriated the Serbs, who wanted to add Bosnia to their state. It also infuriated the Russians, all the more since few Russians knew that their diplomat Izvolski had in fact made an informal agreement with the Austrian minister Aehrenthal in September, 1908, to accept the annexation of Bosnia-Herzegovina in return for Austrian support of an agreement permitting Russian warships to use the Straits. In the event, Austria did the annexing, but Russia did not get her use of the Straits. This wound to Russian pride was profound.

War now broke out on the edges of Europe. In 1911, the Italians sent troops to Tripoli, the poorest part of North Africa, but at least a part that had not yet been taken from the Turks by other Europeans. Then in 1912 war spread to the Balkans. Nationalist revolutionaries called the "Young Turks" had risen successfully against the Sultan in 1908. The Young Turks wanted the modern industrial achievements of the West, they wanted its political apparatus of representative government, and they wanted above all to have Turks respected, admired, and feared as members of a thoroughly modern *nation*. Some of their intellectuals followed the nineteenth-century Romantic pattern back into the past, where they found, not the nomad Turks of history, but fine sturdy "Turanians" from the inspiring steppes of Central Asia. There was even a "Pan-Turanian" movement, strangest of the "Pan" movements, which sought to group Magyars, Turks, and the Turkish peoples of Central Asia, who were all only distantly related to each other, as children of a common destiny. No wonder the Habsburgs were alarmed! It began to look as if those who hoped to divide up Turkey had better hurry while the dividing was good. In the hurry, the world got swept into the War of 1914, the preliminary stages of which were the Balkan Wars.

In the first of these wars, in 1912, an alliance of Bulgaria, Serbia, and Greece beat the Turks, and started the process of dividing up most of European Turkey. But here Austria imposed an absolute veto on granting Serbia territories that would give her access to the Adriatic Sea. Meanwhile, the victors quarreled among themselves, and in the Second Balkan War (1913) the Greeks and Serbs, joined by the Rumanians and the all-but-beaten Turks, readily defeated the Bulgarians. Turkey got back some of her territory in Europe. But the Balkans were in a state of uncertainty and bad blood when Francis Ferdinand was assassinated; and Bulgaria was ready to ally with Austria and Germany against her former allies.

The Final Crisis, July-August, 1914

There are millions of words in print about the proximate causes of World War I in the six weeks between the assassination on June 28 and the general spread of war on August 4, when Britain came in against Germany. Thanks to the end of the rule of Hohenzollern, Habsburg, and Romanov houses as a result of the

"Disturbing the Peace," 1897: the Great Powers (France and Britain on the left) chorus "Scat!"

war, the secret archives were thrown open much sooner than would be normal. And in the pressure of debate in the 1920's over the question of war guilt, even the victorious countries, Britain, France, and the United States, opened their archives to a surprising extent. These are weeks for which documents, often telegrams, can be dated by the hour and minute. These are weeks in which messages are constantly crossing each other, confusing things hopelessly. These are weeks in which professional diplomatists and statesmen, egged on by an excited—and it must be said often *irresponsible*—press, nevertheless tried for the most part to master the crisis without recourse to war.

The diplomats and statesmen were drawn into war because almost all of them believed that they faced an alternative worse than war, a defeat or loss of face for their nation. Austria believed correctly, though without positive proof, that the Serbian government had some foreknowledge or at least suspicion of Princip's plot and should therefore have given her warning. For this reason, and also because she wished to check the Serb agitation that had long been unsettling the Yugoslav peoples living in the dual monarchy, Austria-Hungary decided to make stiff demands on Serbia after the assassination of Francis Ferdinand. Before doing so, however, she consulted her German ally, who promised to support whatever policy Austria might adopt toward Serbia. This German response has become famous as a diplomatic "blank check," duly signed by Germany in advance with the precise amount to be filled in later by Austria.

Thus encouraged, the Austrian government, on July 23, sent Serbia an ultimatum to be answered within forty-eight hours. The ultimatum made many separate demands, which added up to an insistence that Serbia and Serb propagandists keep their hands off Habsburg territories and populations, now and in the future. Most of the demands the Serbs accepted, at least in principle; but they refused to accept two of them, which would have permitted Austrian police or military men to take, on Serbian soil, an actual part in a Serbian investigation of Princip's plot. Probably Serbia

Princip, immediately after the assassination at Sarajevo, June 28, 1914.

had some assurance that Russia was willing to give her a kind of "blank check," and would assist her if the partial refusal of the ultimatum led to war. The Serbian reply, therefore, was a little less virtuously honest than it seemed to be to most of the world in July, 1914. Still, the Austrian ultimatum appears to have been couched in terms deliberately unacceptable to the Serbs, and the Serb reply seems to have been a base for more consideration than it got from the Austrians. Because the Serbs had not accepted the whole of the ultimatum, Austria declared war on July 28, after turning down as inconsistent with national honor a European conference proposed by the British foreign minister, Sir Edward Grey, on July 26.

From this declaration of war on, the German diplomatists, backed by William II and actually resisting the German military men, tried to hold back their Austrian ally. It is impossible to clear William from responsibility for the German "blank check," which had emboldened Austria and had perhaps been designed by Germany to do just that. Now, however, the Germans certainly tried to revoke the check and made a last effort to stop the spread of the war. Since Russia was beginning the full mobilization of her armies, the Kaiser, on July 29, told Tsar Nicholas II in a personal telegram of the German attempt to get the Austrians to compromise. Apparently this telegram served to get full Russian mobilization modified into partial mobilization and to get direct Austro-Russian talks resumed on July 30. For a brief moment it looked as if the crisis might be overcome.

But mobilization was not easy in Russia, a country of long distances, poor communications, and bureaucratic red tape; and the Russian military feared that their enemies would get the jump on them. In perhaps the most crucial decision of this hectic last week, the Russian government, probably against the deeper inclinations of the Tsar himself, decided to renew general mobilization. Germany at once insisted that all Russian mobilization cease, and, when it continued, ordered her own at 4:00 P.M. on August 1, and declared war on Russia at 7:00 P.M. the same day. France, meantime, had determined to stand by her Russian ally, now evidently about to be attacked, and also mobilized at 3:55 P.M. on August 1. Germany declared war on France on August 3.

Britain was still wavering. Although her entente with France did not legally bind the two nations together, it had led, as we have just seen, to the very close co-ordination of defense plans by the French and British military and naval staffs. Perhaps, then, Britain would have come into the war anyway. What made her entry certain was the German violation of the neutrality of Belgium, which both Britain and Prussia (now Germany) had joined with other powers to guarantee in 1839. The German military were determined to take decisive action in the West and to knock France out of the war before the Russians could get their vast but slow-moving armies into action. Accordingly, German plans called for a sweep through a corner of Belgium to avoid the heavily fortified and hilly terrain in northeastern France. On August 2, the Germans had notified Belgium that they intended to march through her territory, though they promised to respect her territorial integrity in the peace to come.

Belgium rejected this demand and appealed to the other guaranteeing powers. Sir Edward Grey, though opposed in the British cabinet by the Liberals, Lord Morley and John Burns, who did not believe defense of the neutrality of Belgium worth a war, seized firmly on this ground of action. On August 4 Britain declared war on Germany. The German chancellor, Bethmann-Hollweg, informed of this action, let slip the phrase that Britain had gone to war just for a "scrap of paper"—the treaty of 1839 that established Belgian neutrality. This unhappy phrase, seized upon by the press of the world, not only solidified British opinion in favor of the war but was responsible more than any other single factor for the charge of war guilt laid against Germany.

The Entry of Other Powers

By August 6, when Austria declared war on Russia, all the members of the Triple Alliance and the Triple Entente had come to blows, with the exception of Italy, who, however, had never really been a good ally of Austria because of the Irredentist issue. Italy, refusing to consider herself bound by the Triple Alliance, declared her neutrality. The Central Powers of Germany and Austria-Hungary, then, stood against the Allies—Russia, France, Britain,

and Serbia. Japan came in on the side of the Allies late in August, and Turkey came in on the Austro-German side in November, 1914. After competing territorial offers from both Allies and Central Powers, Italy finally joined the Allies in May, 1915. Bulgaria came in on the side of the Central Powers in 1915, Rumania on the side of the Allies in 1916.

As the war turned into a stalemate, on both Western and Eastern fronts in the winter of 1916–1917, the Germans made the desperate decision to try to get at Great Britain by the only way that seemed available. They would use their submarines to cut off the food and raw materials that came to the British Isles from overseas, and without which their peoples would have starved. This unrestricted submarine warfare meant sinking American ships that Americans held were quite legally bringing such supplies, *not* contraband of war, to England and France. On April 6, 1917, the United States completed the roster of great powers involved in the conflict by declaring war on Germany. Lesser powers all over the world joined in, mostly against Germany, so that all told there were 53 declarations of war before the end in 1918.

Dissident Americans, then and since, have declared that the United States was enticed into the war by the wicked few—by sentimental lovers of England or France; by bankers who had lent money to the Allies and wanted to protect their investments; by silly idealists who agreed with President Wilson in wishing to "make the world safe for democracy"; and, of course, by scheming Allied diplomatists, corrupt Europeans who held a strange fascination over American "babes in the wood."

Deep-seated sentiments among many good Americans in 1916–1917 rebelled against our jeopardizing American ideals by involving ourselves in the conventional—and wicked —European struggle for power. Even today, after a second general or world war in which American participation aroused much less opposition at home (see Chapter 29), it is difficult for the historian to discuss objectively the causes of our entrance into this so-called First World War. The historian must indeed note that ever since what Americans call King

William's War and Europeans usually call the War of the League of Augsburg (1688–1697) (see Volume I, Chapter 15), we as colonists or as an independent nation have sooner or later been drawn into every major general war in the western state-system. In purely empirical terms, it may be argued that the normal expectation is for the United States to enter into any great world war. And in more disputable general terms, such as we have brought out in Volume I, Chapter 13, it may be argued that in the western (now world) state-system a general or world war never breaks out unless there is an aggressor nation whose activities in the opinion of their leaders threaten the independent existence of all other nations. The United States, in this view, went to war in 1917 for a very deep-seated reason indeed. The possible victory of Germany threatened our very existence as an independent, but committed and co-operating, participant in an international order.

More specifically, in 1917 the United States insisted that the existing international order gave Americans the right to travel and to trade freely with neutrals and, in dealings with belligerents, to be limited only by well-known principles of international law forbidding actual transport of munitions, or other *direct* forms of aid to belligerents. This is the doctrine of "freedom of the seas," which would indeed have allowed Germans to search American vessels, but which quite clearly did not permit German submarines to sink American vessels on sight and without notice. The German decision to undertake unrestricted submarine warfare was in western historical precedent a completely adequate and normal justification of, and explanation for, our declaration of war. But, we must repeat, behind this reason lay a widespread though by no means universal feeling among many Americans, a feeling especially strong in those persons most concerned with our foreign relations, that a German victory would mean a world order in which the kind of America we wanted could not be secure.

Jefferson had indeed in 1807 abandoned the doctrine of freedom of the seas and had in the Embargo Act simply forbidden American vessels to trade either with the French or the British side. In 1917, we should have had to put an embargo on all American shipping to most foreign ports, or else put up with German torpedoing of American ships, and the drowning of American citizens. Neither course would seem to have been acceptable to a majority of Americans in 1917.

III   The Course of the War

Resources of the Belligerents

As the opposing nations lined up in 1914, the Allies (British, French, Russians, and others) had an overwhelming superiority in total population and resources. The Central Powers (Germany, Austria-Hungary and Turkey) had in their own continental lands not over 150,000,000 people; Britain, France, Russia, and Italy in their own continental lands had at least 125,000,000 more people than their enemies. Moreover, in their overseas possessions, which included the 315,000,000 people of India, the Allies had many millions more. As for material resources, the Central Powers had, especially in Germany, admirably organized industries and enough coal and iron to fight a long war. But here too the statistics were overwhelmingly in favor of the Allies. Moreover, though German submarines and, in the early days, surface raiders were able to interrupt seriously Allied lines of communication overseas, on the whole the Allies were still able to get from these overseas sources indispensable food and other supplies. And when in 1917 a beaten Russia, in the throes of a revolution, ceased to be of aid, the Allies gained the great resources of the United States.

In the long run, much as in the American Civil War, the side with the most men and materials wore down its enemies and won the war. But it was by no means the uneven struggle that the statistics of total population and material resources would indicate. Again as in our Civil War, the weaker side had initially important advantages, won great victories, seemed indeed at critical moments on the point of final victory.

Geography gave Germany and Austria the advantages of being side by side, and of having interior lines of communication, which enabled them to make rapid transfers of troops from one threatened front to another. Though the Germans and Austrians did not always see eye to eye, they did speak the same language and had for long been firmly allied. Most important of all, Germany in particular was more ready for war than were her enemies. She had an efficiently organized military machine and a good stock of munitions, her industry could be readily geared to war, her plans were complete, her people were united in support of the war, and they enjoyed the great psychological advantage of being on the offensive, of carrying the war to the enemy. Indeed, no important part of the war was ever fought on German soil; it ended, with important results for later history, with the German army still in being, with the soil of the German Fatherland still uninvaded.

By contrast, geography separated the western Allies from Russia. German control of the Baltic and Turkish control of the Straits proved throughout the war a serious obstacle to communication between Russia and her allies, who had to take roundabout and difficult routes through Archangel in Arctic waters and even through Vladivostok on the Pacific at the end of the long, slow, single-track Trans-Siberian railway. For the Allies, transfer of troops between eastern and western fronts was militarily almost impossible, even had it been politically possible. It was not, however, politically possible, and here is one of the greatest weaknesses of the Allies.

Russia, Britain, and France had only recently come together, as "friendly" powers and not as close allies. Each of them was a strongly marked nationality, having many sources of conflict with the others. They had no long tradition of mutual co-operation, no common language. France and England were democracies, and though the peoples of both rallied firmly to the national cause in 1914, they were of recent years unused to the kind of firm, centralized, political and military control that is necessary in war. As for unified military planning and administration, it was never achieved between Russia and the western Allies. Even among Britain, France, and the United States on the Western Front, it was not achieved until the French General Foch was appointed commander-in-chief in 1918, and then only imperfectly, for full merging of staffs was not achieved.

Finally, of the three great Allied powers in 1914, only France was ready with a good big land force, and France, with only 39 millions of people against Germany's 65 millions, was the weakest of the Allies in manpower. Britain was indeed prepared on the sea, and her navy was an invaluable asset; but it could not be of direct use against the German army. Russia had universal military service and an army great in numbers. But she had vast distances to overcome, an inadequate railway system, a relatively undeveloped heavy industry, an army whose morale had been shaken by the recent defeat at the hands of the Japanese, a people whose morale had been shaken by the recent abortive revolution, a military and a political organization riddled with inefficiency and corruption.

The Western Front: German Offensive

The Germans had a plan, the so-called Schlieffen plan, which they immediately put into execution. It called for a holding operation on the left, with a strong right wing that was to advance swiftly through Belgium, take Paris, and then fall on the rear of the French armies. While this great enveloping movement in the west swiftly eliminated France, relatively weaker German forces, it was planned, would hold down the slow-moving Russians. With France beaten, the Germans could turn their full force against the Russians and beat them. Then there would be only the British left, and the future would take care of them.

The German plan almost succeeded. It failed for two reasons, to which a great number of separate tactical factors contributed. In the first place, the German chief of staff, Moltke, had seriously modified the Schlieffen plan by weakening the critical right wing, partly in order to send divisions to the east, which, ironically, arrived there too late to participate in the defeat of the Russians. By the time the German right wing neared Paris, it had too few divisions to take the capital and then roll up the French army to the eastward. In the second place, the French, though at first they rashly developed the offensive eastward, shifted their armies northward and westward to meet the invading Germans. With the help of the British they exploited a gap that developed between the German First and Second armies. The Germans lost this first great battle, known as the Battle of the Marne.

The German advance, which had been almost continuous since August 2, had been stopped. In the next few weeks the opposing forces engaged in what came to be called the "race for the Channel," with the Germans trying to outflank the Allies and get the Channel ports, thus shutting the short sea passage to future British reinforcements. They failed here, too, and throughout the war the ports of Calais and Boulogne, and indeed a small southwestern corner of Belgium, were to remain in Allied hands—a valuable military advantage.

By the autumn of 1914 the Western Front was thus stabilized. For over three hundred airline miles between the Channel and the Swiss border of Alsace near Basel, hundreds of thousands of soldiers faced each other in a continuous line that was full of bends called "salients." Both sides "dug in" and formed a series of rough fortifications. The central feature of these fortifications was a series of parallel trenches deep enough to conceal a man standing upright. As time went on, these trenches were greatly improved; they were supplied with parapets, machine-gun nests, and an elaborate network of approach trenches and strong points, until the whole front became one immense fortification. Thousands of local actions in the four years of trench warfare shifted the lines here and there, and a series of partial break-throughs occurred on both sides. But on the whole the lines held, and the actual fighting in the west was confined to an extraordinarily narrow, though very long, field.

On this Western Front the ultimate decision was reached; but there were many other fronts. Some of them were disparagingly called "the side-shows" by those who advocated concentrating in the west. Yet in perspective we can now see that they all played a part in determining the final result. Since, over the long pull, the Germans had fewer men and resources, the dispersal of energies that these "side-shows" called for, and the continuous need to bolster their Austrian, Turkish, and Bulgarian allies, were major factors in their defeat. For the sake of clarity, we shall here take up these other fronts separately and briefly, but the reader must never forget that for the belligerents the war was a whole; its wide-flung theaters were mutually dependent, with each one influencing the others.

The Eastern Front

The Eastern Front, where the Russians faced both the Germans and the Austrians, was certainly no mere side-show. Millions of men were involved on both sides, and had the Russians not held out, as they did, until the end of 1917, the Allies in the west could hardly have withstood the reinforcements that the Germans and Austrians would have been able to send to France and Italy. The war in the east was more a war of movement than the war in the west. But even in the east there were long periods of stalemate, especially during the winters, periods when the opposing armies faced each other in long lines of improvised fortifications in trench warfare much like that in the west.

The Russians began well. Against the exposed Austrian salient of Galicia (Austria's share of the eighteenth-century partitions of Poland), the Russians threw in vast masses of men. They pushed the Austrians out of Lemberg (later the Polish Lwów, now the Soviet Lvov), and by the end of September, 1914, they had reached the northern ends of some of the passes leading into Hungary through the Carpathian Mountains. Against the Germans, who also had to defend in East Prussia a salient surrounded on the east and south by Russian territory, the Russians won the Battle of Gumbinnen, in August, 1914, and so alarmed the German general staff that the Germans felt obliged to reorganize their eastern command. General von Ludendorff, under the nominal command of his senior, Von Hindenburg, and aided by a brilliant junior, Von Hoffmann, turned successfully against the two Russian armies, which were attempting a pincers movement. Late in August, at Tannenberg, the Germans decisively defeated a Russian army under Samsonov, who committed suicide. And early in September they won another decisive victory against the Russians at the Masurian lakes, thus clearing East Prussia of Russians.

The Germans' hard-pressed Austrian allies to the south were by now clamoring for help, and the Western Front was still demanding

Allied soldiers trying to keep warm, near Ypres in Flanders, 1914.

men. Hindenburg and his aides had to do their best with what they had. In a series of hard-fought battles in Poland, they succeeded in relieving the pressure on the Austrians. The end of the year 1914 found the Austrians still hanging on in Galicia and found the Germans in a good position to push eastward from East Prussian and Polish bases. In two great joint offensives in May and July, 1915, the Central Powers won substantial successes; they inflicted severe losses on the Russians from which the Russians never really recovered. At the end of the year 1915 the battle line ran roughly from near Riga, deep in the Baltic provinces of Russia, to the eastern edge of Galicia at Tarnopol and Czernowitz.

In 1916, the Russians, with a new commander, General Brusilov, undertook a great new offensive against the Austrians in the south. The Russian need to bolster their failing morale would probably have made some action necessary, but the Russians were also being pressed by the Western Allies to do something to help the Italians, who were threatened by the Austrians in the region of Trent. It seems likely that the Brusilov offensive was begun too soon, without adequate preparation. It scored a striking success at first; in places, the Russians drove the Austrians back some eighty miles, and they took large numbers of prisoners. But once more the Germans came to the rescue; with fresh troops transferred from the west, they halted Brusilov before he had won a decisive success.

It was from the backwash of this defeat that the Russian Revolution, which began early in March, 1917, was born. In the moderate phase of that uprising, before the Bolshevik revolution of November, 1917, Brusilov undertook one last desperate offensive. But he was soon checked, and the way was open for the Bolsheviks to carry out their promise to make peace. By the end of 1917, Russia was out of the war. She was forced by the Central Powers to sign the extraordinarily punitive Peace of Brest-Litovsk (March, 1918), by which she lost her Polish territories, her Baltic provinces, the entire Ukraine, Finland, and some lands in the Caucasus. The Caucasian lands went to Turkey; most of the others came under what

proved to be the temporary domination of Austria and Germany.

The Italian Front

In April, 1915, Italy concluded with Britain, France and Russia the secret Treaty of London, which promised the Italians their long-sought-for Trent and Trieste, and other lands at Austro-Hungarian and Turkish expense. In May, the Italians formally declared war on Austria-Hungary (they did not declare war on Germany until August, 1916), and a new front was added along the Austro-Italian frontier at the head of the Adriatic. Much of this front was too mountainous for effective action, and it was pretty much confined to some sixty miles along the Isonzo River. For two years there was a series of bloody but indecisive actions along this river that at least pinned down several hundred thousand Austrian troops. Then in the late autumn of 1917, with Russia already beaten, came the blow that very nearly knocked Italy out. Once again the Germans supplied the propulsive force. Ludendorff, now in supreme command, sent six German divisions to the Isonzo. The Germans and Austrians broke through at Caporetto and sent the Italians into a retreat across the Venetian plains, a retreat that was really a rout. French and British reinforcements were hastily rushed across the Alps, but what did most to stop the Austro-Germans was probably the grave difficulty, under modern conditions of warfare, of supplying mass armies of infantry in rapid advance. The Italians were finally able to hold along the line of the Piave River, almost at the Po.

The Dardanelles

One of the most important of the "sideshows," the Dardanelles campaign of 1915, not only proved in its failure to be a bad blow to the morale of the Allies, but was to have important repercussions in World War II. With the entry of Turkey into the war in November, 1914, and with the Western Front capable for the moment of being held against the Germans by the French alone, a group of British military and political leaders advanced the idea that British strength should be put into amphibious operations somewhere in the Aegean area. A steady drive could also be made overland toward Vienna and Berlin through territory where the Central Powers were not expecting an attack in force. The great exponent of this "Eastern Plan" was Winston Churchill, First Lord of the Admiralty. The British decided to try the plan. The point of attack chosen was the Dardanelles, the more westerly of the two straits that separate the Black Sea from the Aegean. The campaign is sometimes known as the "Gallipoli campaign" from the long narrow peninsula on the European side of the Straits which was one of the keys to the whole action. Here Allied victory would have had the additional advantage of opening communication with Russia via the Black Sea.

In March, 1915, the British and French fleets tried to force the Straits, but they abandoned the attempt somewhat prematurely when several ships struck mines. Later landings of British, Australian, New Zealand, and French troops at various points on both Asian and European shores of the Dardanelles were poorly co-ordinated and badly backed up. They met with fierce and effective resistance from the Turks—a junior officer named Mustafa Kemal greatly distinguishing himself —and in the end they had to be abandoned. Russia remained sealed in by the Straits all during the war. But Churchill continued to believe that the Dardanelles plan had failed, not because it was a bad plan, but because it had not been carried out with determination. And in the Second World War he was to revive, against American military opinion, something of his old plan, which became known as the plan to strike at the "soft underbelly" of the Axis.

The Balkan Fronts

Serbia's part in the crisis that produced the war meant that from the start there would be a Balkan front. In the end there were several such fronts, and no Balkan state remained uninvolved. The Austrians failed here also, and although in December, 1914, they did manage to take the Serbian capital, Belgrade, they were driven out again. Bulgaria, wooed by both sides, finally came in with the Central Powers in the autumn of 1915. The Germans sent troops and a general, von Mackensen, under whom the Serbs were finally beaten. The remnant of their armies was driven to take refuge on the island of Corfu in neutral Greece.

To counter this blow in the Balkans, the Allies had already landed a few divisions in the Greek city of Salonika and had established a front in Macedonia. The Greeks themselves were divided into two groups. One was headed by King Constantine, who at bottom was sympathetic with the Central Powers, but who for the moment was seeking only to maintain Greek neutrality. The other was a pro-Ally group headed by the able old politician Venizelos. Although the Allies rode roughshod over formal notions of Greek neutrality, Venizelos did not get firmly into the saddle until June, 1917, when Allied pressure compelled King Constantine to abdicate in favor of his second son, Alexander.

Meanwhile Rumania, whom the Russians had been trying to lure into the war, finally yielded to promises of great territorial gains at the expense of Austria-Hungary and came in on the Allied side late in August, 1916, at a time most inopportune for the Rumanians. Stiffened by German help, the Austrians swept through Rumania and by January, 1917, held most of the country. When the Russians made the separate Peace of Brest-Litovsk with the Germans in March, 1918, the Rumanians were obliged to make cessions of territory to Bulgaria, and to grant a lease of oil lands to Germany.

In spite of the formal accession of Greece to the Allied side in June 1917, the Macedonian front remained in a stalemate until the summer of 1918, when, with American troops pouring rapidly into France, the Allied military leaders decided they could afford to build up their forces in Salonika. The investment

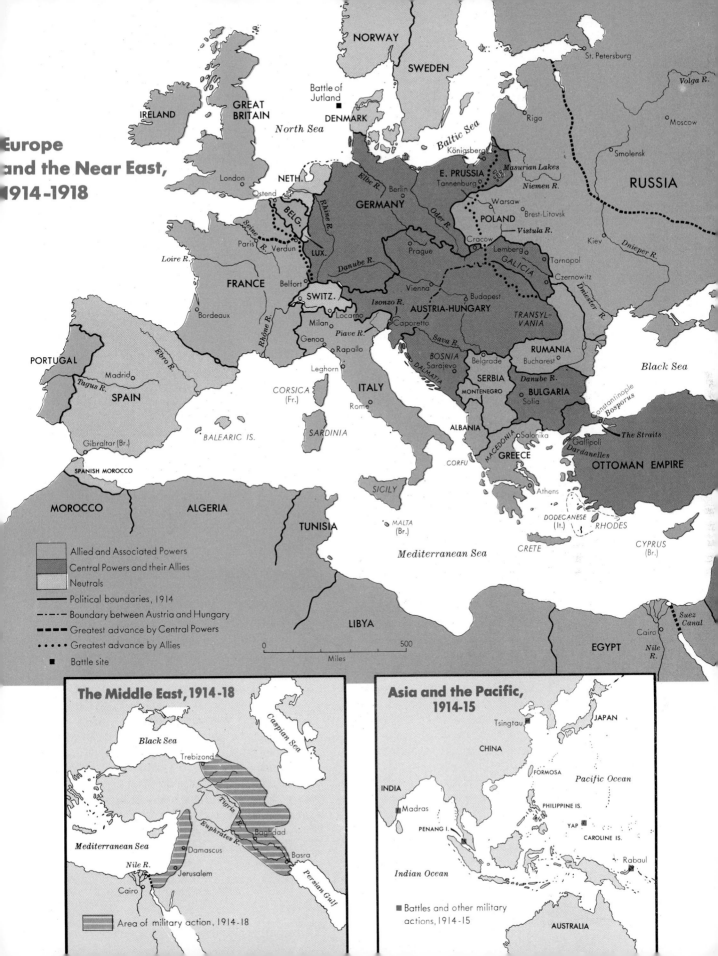

Europe and the Near East, 1914-1918

NORWAY

SWEDEN

IRELAND

GREAT BRITAIN

North Sea

DENMARK

Battle of Jutland ■

Baltic Sea

St. Petersburg

Volga R.

Riga

Moscow

Smolensk

RUSSIA

Königsberg

E. PRUSSIA

Masurian Lakes

Tannenberg

Niemen R.

London

NETH.

Berlin

GERMANY

Elbe R.

Warsaw

Brest-Litovsk

Kiev

Dnieper R.

Ostend

BELG.

Rhine R.

Oder R.

POLAND

Vistula R.

Paris

Seine R.

Verdun

LUX.

Cracow

Lemberg

GALICIA

Tarnopol

Czernowitz

Loire R.

FRANCE

Belfort

Danube R.

Prague

Vienna

Budapest

Dniester R.

SWITZ.

AUSTRIA-HUNGARY

TRANSYL-VANIA

Bordeaux

Rhône R.

Isonzo R.

Locarno

Milan

Caporetto

Sava R.

RUMANIA

Bucharest

Black Sea

PORTUGAL

Ebro R.

Genoa

Piave R.

BOSNIA

Sarajevo

Belgrade

Danube R.

Rapallo

DALMATIA

SERBIA

Constantinople

Madrid

Tagus R.

SPAIN

Leghorn

ITALY

MONTENEGRO

BULGARIA

Sofia

Bosporus

Gibraltar (Br.)

CORSICA (Fr.)

Rome

ALBANIA

MACEDONIA

Salonika

Gallipoli

The Straits

Dardanelles

SPANISH MOROCCO

BALEARIC IS.

SARDINIA

CORFU

GREECE

OTTOMAN EMPIRE

MOROCCO

ALGERIA

TUNISIA

SICILY

■ *MALTA (Br.)*

Athens

DODECANESE (It.)

RHODES

CYPRUS (Br.)

CRETE

Mediterranean Sea

LIBYA

Cairo

EGYPT

Nile R.

Suez Canal

	Allied and Associated Powers
	Central Powers and their Allies
	Neutrals
——	Political boundaries, 1914
—·—·—	Boundary between Austria and Hungary
—— ——	Greatest advance by Central Powers
• • • •	Greatest advance by Allies
■	Battle site

0   500

Miles

The Middle East, 1914-18

Black Sea

Caspian Sea

Trebizond

Tigris R.

Euphrates R.

Baghdad

Mediterranean Sea

Damascus

Basra

Nile R.

Jerusalem

Persian Gulf

Cairo

	Area of military action, 1914-18

Asia and the Pacific, 1914-15

JAPAN

Tsingtau ■

CHINA

FORMOSA

Pacific Ocean

INDIA

Madras ■

PHILIPPINE IS.

YAP ■

Penang I. ■

CAROLINE IS.

Rabaul ■

Indian Ocean

AUSTRALIA

	Battles and other military actions, 1914-15

paid well, for under the leadership of the French general, Franchet d'Esperey, the Allied armies on this front were the first to break the enemy completely. The French, British, Serbs, and Greeks began a great advance on September 15, 1918, all along the line from the Adriatic to the Bulgarian frontier. They forced the Bulgarians to conclude an armistice on September 30, and by early November they had crossed the Danube in several places. The armistice in the west on November 11 found the tricolor of France, with the flags of many allies, well on its way to Vienna. This hark-back to Napoleon helped inspire in the French a somewhat unfounded confidence that they were once more the dominant nation on the continent of Europe.

The Near East and the Colonies

A whole series of fronts throughout the world was involved in what we may call the colonial "clean-up," the subduing of the German overseas empire and of the outlying parts of the Turkish Empire. The Turks, trained and in part officered by German experts, often resisted effectively. In Mesopotamia, in April, 1916, in a blow to British prestige as bad as the Dardanelles defeat, they forced the surrender of the British general, Townshend, who had landed at Basra from India in 1915 and had marched up the Tigris-Euphrates Valley. But the Turks were never able to take the Suez Canal, nor to advance far into Russian Armenia. Moreover, the British were able to play on the Arabs' dislike for their Turkish suzerains. In a series of desert campaigns the romantic Colonel T. E. Lawrence, an Englishman who knew the Arabs intimately, played a leading part. By the end of 1917, the British held Baghdad and Jerusalem. In September, 1918, a great British offensive in Palestine was so successful that on September 30 the Turks concluded an armistice which took them out of the war.

These campaigns, fought in the lands that had been the cradles of western civilization, were of great importance in making the world we live in today. For from them came not only the independent Arab nations (Syria, Lebanon, Iraq, Jordan, Saudi Arabia, Egypt) but also the Jewish national state of Israel, to which these Arab states are so hostile. In November, 1917, in the Balfour Declaration, the British promised "the establishment in Palestine of a national home for the Jewish people." This promise bore fruit in the mandate of 1922 from the League of Nations, by which such a state was set up under British protection under the name of Palestine.

In the overseas colonies the Germans, though cut off from the homeland by the British navy, fought well. In German East Africa they actually managed to hold out to the bitter end in a series of skillful campaigns, so that they still had forces in the field in East Africa on Armistice Day, November 11, 1918. But elsewhere they were fighting from inadequate bases and with inadequate forces, so that by the end of 1914 the British, Australians, South Africans, French, and Japanese had pretty well taken over the German overseas possessions. The Allies had won the "colonial war." Only years later, however, did the most important result of that war become clear. The subject races had learned that their rulers were by no means invulnerable.

The War at Sea

This brings us to a most important front —the war at sea. In the long pull, British sea power, reinforced by the French and later by the Italian and the American navies, once more proved decisive. The Allied command of the sea made it possible to draw on the resources of the rest of the world, and in particular to transfer with surprisingly few losses large numbers of British and American troops to the crucial Western Front. Quite as important, sea power enabled the Allies to shut Germany and her allies off from overseas resources. The Allied blockade slowly but surely constricted Germany, limiting not merely military supplies for her armies, but food supplies for her civilian population. At the end of 1918, many Germans were suffering from malnutrition, an important factor in the German willingness to surrender without fighting to the bitter end.

Yet the war at sea was not easy for the Allies. The submarine proved every bit as dangerous as British alarmists before the war had feared. When the Germans launched their unrestricted submarine warfare, they made dangerous inroads on the merchant ships that were essential to the very life of Britain. By the end of 1917, some 8,000,000 tons of shipping had been sunk by the Germans, most of it by submarines. And at one point in 1917, the British had barely enough food reserves to last a month. The submarine menace was eventually overcome by a series of measures co-ordinated between the Allies and the Americans—extensive use of the convoy system, attack on the submarines by depth bombs, constant anti-submarine patrols, and development of small, fast "subchasers." But we might wonder what would have happened in 1916–1917 (and again in 1942–1943) if the Germans had contented themselves with holding actions on land and had put all their productive and fighting energies into the submarine. This they did not do in either war. Temptation for quick and obvious land success was too great.

The navy of surface vessels that the Germans had built up since the 1890's—and that, as we have seen, was so important in the growth of Anglo-German hostility—never played a really decisive part in the war itself. German surface-raiders caused severe damage in the first year, but they were finally swept off the seas. Once, however, the main German fleet threw a very bad scare into the British. This was the famous Battle of Jutland, which has been refought over and over again by naval historians. This running battle, fought in the North Sea on May 31 and June 1, 1916, resulted in the sinking of twice as much British as German tonnage, and showed how good the German navy was. But the German admiral, Scheer, was forced to run into port before the British capital ships, for which he was no match. Although Jutland was a tactical victory for the Germans, the strategic victory remained with the British, for never again did the German surface navy seriously threaten British command of the sea in European waters. At the war's end the German high command attempted to get the fleet out in a heroic last stand. It was the German sailors' refusal to take the ships out—their mutiny, in fact—that gave a critical push to the German revolution which led to the Armistice of 1918.

The Western Front: Allied Victory

This war also saw the beginnings of air warfare. German lighter-than-air machines, the Zeppelins, raided London many times in 1916–1917, and both sides made airplane bombing raids on nearby towns. But the total damage was relatively light and had no decisive effect on the final result. The airplane was of more importance in scouting, and especially in spotting for artillery; in spite of its short range in those days, it also proved useful as a means of locating submarines. The fighter plane was greatly improved during the war, and the base was laid for the development of the air forces we now know. Indeed, the airplane made greater technical strides in these four years of war than it had made since the Wrights first flew at Kitty Hawk in 1903.

Although the great new invention of the airplane did not itself alter traditional warfare, a new type of warfare was indeed developed, especially on the great Western Front, the warfare of the trenches. The machine gun, the repeating rifle, and fast-firing artillery, with the guidance of spotter planes, could pour in such deadly fire that it was almost impossible for either side to break through the opposing trench systems on a wide front. Both sides tried to break through in the two years after the Marne, and both sides suffered losses of a kind that had never been suffered before.

Two new weapons almost broke the deadlock. The first was poison gas, which was first used by the Germans in shells in October, 1914, with disappointing results. Then in April, 1915, the Germans used chlorine gas discharged from cylinders. The overwhelmed French broke in a line five miles wide, leaving the line completely undefended. But the Germans had not prepared to follow through,

Aerial combat in World War I.

and the gap was closed once the gas had dispersed. Meanwhile the experts developed a simple countermeasure, the gas mask, which became part of the equipment of every soldier on both sides. The age-old balance of attack and defense was once again reestablished.

The second new weapon came much nearer to producing decisive success. This was the tank, a sort of armored land battleship for which plans had been made back in the Renaissance by the fertile Leonardo da Vinci. But da Vinci's tank remained a mere sketch for lack of propulsive power. In the second decade of the twentieth century, however, the internal-combustion engine was ready to do what horses could not do. The tank was a British invention that had been nursed along in its infancy by the always adventurous Winston Churchill. But the new weapon was used too soon, in inadequate numbers and before adequate mechanical tests had been made, in the British Somme offensive of 1916. Even so, nine tanks led or accompanied the infantry triumphantly through the German lines to the capture of Flers. Had the tanks been withheld for a few more months and been backed up with careful planning, they might have broken

the German lines on a wide front. The Germans naturally took up the tank at once, and were soon producing their own.

The technique of attack in the west gradually developed over the years and in the end broke the defensive stalemate. Long and careful artillery preparation, known as a "barrage," literally flattened out a section of the enemy defenses and the "no man's land" in front of them and forced the enemy to retire to rear trenches. Then, accompanied or preceded by tanks, the infantry edged in while the artillery barrage was lifted and focused on the next enemy line. It was a slow and costly process which did not work on a wide scale until 1918. Then the Germans, with the Russians out of the fight, made a last and almost successful effort to break through, trying to separate the British from the French where their lines joined near Amiens. With the failure of this last German push in the summer, Foch ordered a general attack. French, British, and American armies had all broken the German lines by early autumn and were just gaining freedom of action in the open country when the Germans surrendered. The Germans later maintained that they were not beaten decisively in the field. Most experts, however, now think that had the war gone on the Germans could not have stopped an Allied invasion of Germany in 1919.

Morale on the Fighting Fronts

The long narrow battle lines of the four-year trench war were the scene of a concentrated destruction hardly equaled in the war of 1939–1945, except by the atomic bomb at Hiroshima; at some points in France the top soil was blown completely away by shellfire, producing a desert that is still visible today. The war, however, was not unique, unprecedented, or unlike all other wars, as many an excited publicist at the time declared. It produced military heroes and military scapegoats, great generals and generals who failed. As with the Confederacy in the American Civil War, the defeated Germans seem to have had the most-praised generals, the Ludendorffs, the Mackensens, the Hoffmanns. The old traditional chivalrous warfare, the warfare of athletic heroes, was continued, and even heightened in the air, where the "aces" of the highly individualistic duels between planes were the Rolands of a machine age. And in many of the fronts on land, and in the war at sea, the age-old and for many males not altogether unhappy melodrama of war lost none of its reality. Lawrence in Arabia was no disgrace to the tradition of Sir Walter Scott or even, in the eyes of good patriotic Englishmen, to the tradition of Homer.

Yet especially on the Western Front, this war seemed to many of its participants an unheroic nightmare of blood and filth. Sensitive young intellectuals, who in earlier times would never have had to fight, survived to write bitterly about their experiences—in war novels like *Under Fire,* by the Frenchman Barbusse, or *All Quiet on the Western Front* by the German Remarque, and in war poems like those of Siegfried Sassoon and Wilfred Owen. But this literature cannot be trusted fully as an accurate reflection of what the millions of common soldiers who were not intellectuals felt about the war. We know simply that for

four years they bore up under it in stints in the front lines separated by rest leaves. For most of them the dullness, the discomforts, and the brief terror of battle must have tested their patriotism and worn out their sense of adventure.

The Home Fronts

These soldiers and sailors were, for the most part, not professionals; they were civilians, "drafted," lifted from civilian families unused to the ways of the military. Behind the front, on the production lines, subject to the unheroic but harassing strains of rationing and all sorts of limitations in daily living, subject also to the constant prodding of war propaganda, the families too were part of this great "total war." They too bore up under it, though in France in 1917, after the bloody failure of a great offensive under General Nivelle, civilian and military discontent, fanned by politicians, came almost to the point of breaking French morale. And in Germany, the collapse that resulted in the armistice of November 11, 1918, though it obviously had many complex causes, looks like a general failure of morale,

Allied tank going "over the top" on the Western front.

English policewomen hurrying to spread the news of an impending Zeppelin raid.

a psychological collapse under intolerable spiritual and material pressures.

For the Germans, still influenced by nineteenth-century ideas about the rights of the individual and laissez-faire economics, were slow to organize their society for total war. They failed notably to ensure the proper and equitable distribution of food supplies, so that as 1918 wore on whole sectors of the urban population began to suffer from malnutrition. Nor were finances and war production managed with that perfection of techniques that most of the world had already come to expect of the Germans. Rationing, strict control of production, price control, systematic use of the resources of conquered countries, these and many other measures were employed by the Germans, but not with the care, decisiveness, and long preparation that were to characterize them in the conflict of 1939–1945.

All countries engaged in the war, the democratic western Allies as well as the autocratic Central Powers, sooner or later felt obliged to introduce drastic wartime economic planning, which anticipated in some sense the more collectivistic economy of today. Everywhere there was compulsory military service. Even in Britain, proud of its long devotion to the rights of the individual, the famous Defense of the Realm Act—known with wry affection

as DORA—clamped down severely on the Englishman's sacred right to say and do what he liked, even if he did not seem to be giving aid and comfort to the enemy. In the United States, all sorts of men, including the famous "dollar-a-year men," business executives who were working for the government for the first time, flocked to Washington and helped build up an enormous new central government, which regulated the economy as it had never been regulated before. And of course all the belligerents engaged in the war of propaganda, or, as it came to be called in the next great war, in psychological warfare.

The Allies won the battle of the production lines, in which the United States played a major if not a decisive part. We have already noted that in material resources the Allies had a marked potential superiority over the Central Powers; this superiority they were eventually able to realize to the full. Allied production was slow in getting started. There were mistakes, bottlenecks, and experiments like that of the tanks which failed at first because of undue haste. At the beginning the Allies were often at cross-purposes in production as well as in actual military strategy. Nevertheless, by the end of 1917 the Allied military machine was adequately, indeed in some ways wastefully, supplied.

The Role of Propaganda

The Allies also won the most critical phase of the war of propaganda. They sought to convince the neutral world, especially the neutrals of western civilization, the United States, Latin America, and the Swiss, Dutch, Scandinavians, and Spanish, that the Allies were fighting for the right and the Central Powers for the wrong. It was not a complete victory, for important groups in all these countries remained "pro-German" to the end, and Spain on the whole was probably throughout the war pro-German, or at least anti-French and anti-English. Still, it seems that a majority of the neutral West was early convinced that the cause of the Allies was just. This conviction was strengthened from the very start by the traditional liberalism of France and Britain in contrast with the traditional autocracy of the German and the Austrian empires, though the presence of the autocratic Russian Empire on the Allied side somewhat handicapped Allied propagandists. In the early days of the crisis of 1914, the intransigence of the Austrians toward the Serbs, and in particular the blundering phrase of Bethmann-Hollweg, that Britain had gone to war for a mere "scrap of paper," got the Central Powers off to a bad start in world opinion.

The sense of Allied rightness was strengthened by early Allied propaganda, which was often one-sided and unfair. Notably, it accused the Germans of frightful atrocities in Belgium. The Germans did indeed impose rigorous military controls on conquered populations, but little in their record was worse than is usual, and perhaps inevitable, in all warfare. Allied propaganda also simplified and falsified the complex chain of causation that produced the war, making it appear that the Germans and the Austrians were wholly responsible for the outbreak of the war, that the "predatory Potsdam gang" had planned the whole thing from the beginning, and that Serbs, French, Russians, and British had been wholly innocent of deed or word that might have brought on the war. This propaganda backfired shortly after the war; revulsion against its unfairness had much to do with the widespread acceptance of the extreme—and false—revisionist thesis that on the whole Germany, in particular, had been quite guiltless of starting the war.

World War I poster.

Political Repercussions

Except in Russia, the four years of war saw no major changes in political structure. The Central Empires retained until their collapse their incompletely responsible parliamentary governments, and the parliaments on the whole were reasonably submissive. And in spite of the inevitable strengthening of the executive in wartime, France, Britain, and the United States carried on their democratic institutions. In the United States the critical presidential election of 1916 came just before American entrance into the war, and resulted by a narrow margin in the return of the incumbent, Woodrow Wilson. In Britain and France the democratic process brought to power in the midst of wartime crisis two strong men—Lloyd George and Clemenceau—who carried through with great vigor the prosecution of the war, and who, though their fame was dimmed in the troubled years after the war, remain in historic memory as great national heroes of their respective countries.

In Britain the skillful but indecisive Liberal leader Asquith proved unable to master events, even though he widened his government into a coalition in May, 1915. In December of that year he was succeeded by another Liberal, Lloyd George, the architect of Britain's social insurance system (see Chapter 21), who had also proven himself an admirable organizer of war production. Under Lloyd George the coalition really worked, and his position as war leader was to remain unchallenged. We shall meet him again at the peace negotiations, as we shall meet his French counterpart, Clemenceau. The "Tiger," as Clemenceau was known to his friends and enemies alike, came to power at the end of 1917, at a time when defeatism threatened both the military and the civilian strength of France. Clemenceau took firm command of the war effort and disposed summarily of the disaffected politicians with the decisiveness—and disregard for the peacetime "rights of man"—of an old Jacobin.

IV   The Peace Settlements

As in Westphalia in 1648, at Utrecht in 1713, and at Vienna in 1815, the warring powers gathered in a great meeting to make the peace settlement. This time they met at Paris—or, rather, in suburban Paris. They met at Versailles to settle with the Germans, and at other suburban *châteaux* to settle with the rest. Peace congresses almost never meet in a world that is really at peace. There are always aftermaths, local wars and disturbances. The aftermaths of 1918–1919 were particularly numerous and acute and conditioned the whole work of the peace congresses. To them we must turn briefly before we consider the actual settlements.

The Aftermath of World War

The sorest spot was Russia, then in 1919 in the throes of civil war and foreign invasion. No sooner had the Germans been forced to withdraw from the regions they had gained at Brest-Litovsk (see p. 373) than the Allies sent detachments to various points along the rim of Russia—on the Black Sea, on the White Sea in the far north, and on the Pacific (for details see Chapter 26). The Allies still hoped to restore in Russia, if not the monarchy, at least a moderate democratic republic. Their dread of final Bolshevik success (the term "Bolshevism" was then almost universally used, instead of communism) and of the possible spread of Bolshevism westward, added to the tensions at Versailles and confirmed the conservative position Clemenceau and Lloyd George were taking.

Bolshevism was indeed spreading westward. The German revolution of November, 1918, had been carried out under socialist auspices. But all through the winter of 1918–1919 there were communist riots and uprisings, and in Bavaria in April a soviet republic was proclaimed. The government of the new republic of Germany put these communist uprisings down, but only by an appeal to the remnants of the old army and to officers thoroughly hostile to any form of republic. In the break-up of the Austro-Hungarian monarchy in the autumn of 1918, the successor states—Czechoslovakia, Austria, Hungary, Yugoslavia, Rumania—which had been formed in whole or in part out of the former Habsburg lands, were disturbed by all sorts of social and economic troubles. In Hungary, Bela Kun, who had worked with Lenin in Moscow, won power by means of a socialist-communist coalition, and then elbowed out his socialist colleagues and set up a communist dictatorship. In August, a Rumanian army that had invaded Hungary forced Bela Kun to flee. Finally, all through the Germanies groups of ex-soldiers, the *Freikorps,* were roving about, stirring up trouble, and threatening the overthrow of the German Republic (for details, see Chapter 27).

In the Near East the Allies had even worse troubles to face. Greece, which had been so hard to drag into the war, was now in full cry against the Turks. Her nationalists had revived the old hope of a restored Byzantine Empire, with the Greeks once more in command of the Straits. Her armies, not without Allied encouragement, landed at Smyrna in Asia Minor in the spring of 1919 and marched off in the track of Alexander the Great. The French and the British, to whom control over different parts of the former Turkish Empire had been assigned, began at once having trouble with their new Arab wards. The Jews were already pressing for the establishment of a national home in Palestine in accordance with the Balfour Declaration, and the Arabs were already opposing them.

In India the aftermath of war was bad indeed. The universal epidemic of influenza—actually a pandemic—in 1918 (which most public-health experts believed killed more people than were killed in battle) had been especially disastrous in India. Indians had fought well as professional soldiers during the war on the Allied side; educated Indians thought their country was ripe for much more self-rule. The disorders of 1918–1919 culminated in the Amritsar massacre of April, 1919, in which a British general, reverting to old-time methods, ordered his soldiers to fire on an unarmed crowd, killing or wounding some 1,600 people. Amritsar shocked world opinion, added to the odium the Allies were al-

ready acquiring among liberals everywhere, and knitted India more closely together in opposition to the British. In China, the weakening of Russia had been taken by the Japanese as a signal to renew their ambitious plans in the north of China, and indeed the American troops sent to Vladivostok in Siberia (see Chapter 26) were there less to oppose the Bolsheviks than to oppose the Japanese.

So the world was in turmoil and disorder when the Allies, great, small, and middle-sized, assembled in and near Paris to make the peace. The problems that faced the peacemakers were world-wide, complex, and often insoluble—insoluble in the sense that no decision on a given problem, say the disposition of the Adriatic port of Fiume which was claimed by Italians and Yugoslavs, could possibly satisfy all the major groups concerned, to say nothing of the minorities. Yet the world hoped, and indeed expected, from the peacemakers more than it had in any previous crisis. Public opinion in the eighteenth and nineteenth centuries had built up a tremendous faith in the possibility of a peaceful, just, and happy world. This war had been a war to "make the world safe for democracy," a "war to end war." It had produced in the American President Wilson a man who could phrase skillfully the hopes of men, and who as he journeyed to Paris after the Armistice appeared to be the heroic savior and hope of mankind.

These liberal dreams and expectations were, however, by no means the sole tenants of men's minds. All men were not Wilsonians. There were, inevitably, the selfish, the disillusioned, the narrow, the jingoists, and the professionals who had made promises to the Italians and the Rumanians, who had planned all sorts of compensations and adjustments. There were, more important, the plain ordinary men and women who wanted peace and security but who also wanted national glory and the punishment of the wicked Germans who, they believed, had put them through those four years of hell. There were, in short, thousands of conflicting hopes and fears, all of them embodied in living human flesh, not just the abstractions they must seem to be on the printed page.

of them were quite articulate they did much to discredit the work of the conference, especially among liberal intellectuals everywhere.

Wilson and his experts were gradually badgered into accepting harsher peace terms. The reparations bill against Germany was lengthened; Poland, Italy, and Japan made claims to lands that clearly would not be theirs by self-determination of their peoples; the victors more and more openly showed that they proposed to behave as victors in war habitually have behaved. Wilson gave way or compromised on a dozen points and then chose to stand fast against the weakest of the Allies. He would not let the Italians have the Adriatic seaport of Fiume, which had once been the sole seaport of Hungary. They might have neighboring Trieste and their coveted Trentino, where they could rule over German or Slavic-speaking minorities, indeed, in some areas, majorities; but Fiume they might not have. Fiume was indeed a difficult case. It was Italian-speaking and historically was linked with the great past of Venice; but it had never been part of modern Italy, and it had *not* been promised to Italy in the secret treaties of 1915. The Italian delegation left the conference in anger, but Wilson was immovable. The fate of Fiume was not settled at the conference; only in 1924, by treaty with Yugoslavia, did the city go to Italy in return for Susak, a port right next door that served the Yugoslavs quite adequately for the next two decades.

But Wilson did get his new international organization, the cornerstone of his plans for a better world. The covenant of the League of Nations was an integral part of the Treaty of Versailles. The League was no true supranational state, but a kind of permanent consultative system composed of the victors and a few neutrals. The way was left open for the Germans and the Russians to join the League, as they later did. But in 1919–1920, Wilson's League looked to many liberals a lot like Metternich's and Castlereagh's old Congress system of 1815, by no means worth the sacrifices Wilson had made to obtain it. The League had an assembly in which each member-state had one vote, and a council in which the five great powers (Britain, France, Italy, the United States, and Japan) had permanent seats, and to which four other member-states were chosen by the assembly for specific terms. A permanent secretariat, to be located at Geneva, was charged with administering the affairs of the League. In its working out, as we shall see (Chapter 29), the League never fulfilled the hopes of the liberals. It did not achieve disarmament, nor did its machinery of peacemaking prove capable of preventing aggression. The great powers simply went on their usual ways, using the League only as their policy-makers —their heads of state rather than their diplomatists—saw fit.

The Territorial Settlement

Central to all the work in Paris was the problem of territorial changes. Here, peacemakers were confronted not merely, as at most peace conferences in our western society, with the claims of the victorious Allies but also with the claims of the new nations that had sprung up from the disintegrating Austrian, Russian, and Turkish empires. They had to try to satisfy the eternal land hunger of those who run nations, without violating too obviously the great Wilsonian principle of "self-determination of peoples." This principle was hard indeed to apply in much of Central Europe, where peoples of different language and national self-consciousness were mixed together in an incredible mosaic of unassimilated minorities (see map on p. 389). The result was to multiply the number of "sovereign" nations in this world. Nationalism, which some hopeful people had thought was on the wane, was now fanned to intense new life in a dozen states.

France received Alsace-Lorraine back from Germany. Clemenceau also hoped both to annex the small but coal-rich Saar Basin of Germany as compensation for French coal mines destroyed by the Germans during the war, and to detach from Germany the territory on the left (or west) bank of the Rhine, thereby strengthening French security and setting up a Rhineland republic that might become a French satellite. Both French hopes, opposed

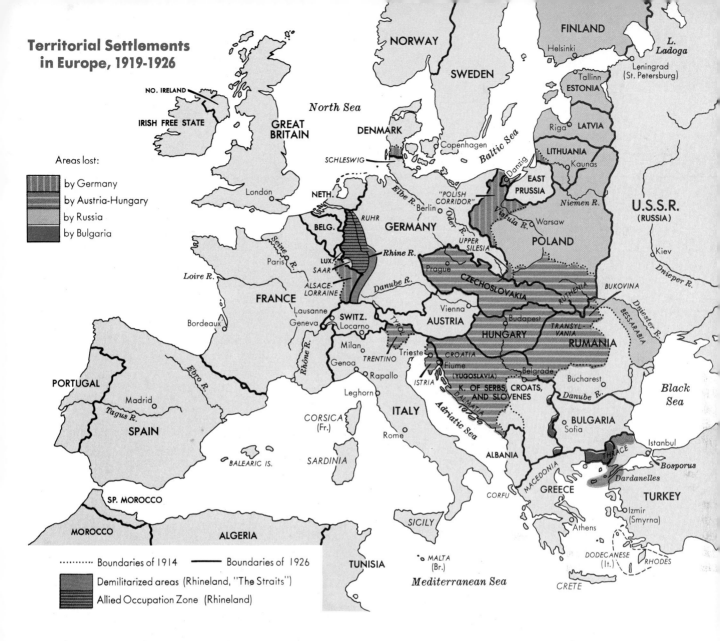

Areas lost:

by Germany
by Austria-Hungary
by Russia
by Bulgaria

·········· Boundaries of 1914   —— Boundaries of 1926

Demilitarized areas (Rhineland, "The Straits")

Allied Occupation Zone (Rhineland)

by Wilson and Lloyd George, went unrealized. The Saar was to be separated from Germany for fifteen years as an international ward supervised by the League of Nations. At the end of the fifteen-year period a plebiscite would determine its future status; meanwhile, its coal output was to go to France. The Rhineland remained part of the German Republic, though it was to be demilitarized and occupied for a time by Allied soldiers.

Belgium was given some small towns on her German border. Italy gained her Irredenta of Trent and Trieste, indeed in generous measure, for thousands of German and Slavic-speaking peoples were included within her new boundaries. Poland, erased from the map as an independent state in 1795, was now restored and given lands that she had had before the partitions of the eighteenth century and that contained important minorities of Germans and other non-Polish peoples. The old Habsburg Empire was entirely dismembered. The heart of its German-speaking area was constituted as the truncated Republic of Austria, which was forbidden to join itself to Germany, and the heart of its Magyar-speaking area became a diminished Kingdom of Hungary. The Czech-inhabited lands of Bohemia and Mo-

389

ravia were joined with Slovakia and the Ruthenian lands of the Carpatho-Ukraine further east in the brand-new "succession state" of Czechoslovakia. This new state faced the problem of a large and discontented Sudeten German minority.

Another "succession state" was Yugoslavia, officially the Kingdom of Serbs, Croats, and Slovenes, which, as its full name suggests, represented a great expansion of pre-war Serbia to include the south Slav territories of the Habsburgs. Rumania, too, profited by the break-up of the old dual monarchy by receiving the former Hungarian lands of Transylvania. Rewarded also with Bessarabia, a Russian province that the Bolsheviks could not defend, Rumania emerged with doubled territory, and some restive non-Rumanian minorities. In the southern Balkan Peninsula, Greece received all of Thrace, at the expense of Turkey and Bulgaria.

Out of the former tsarist domains held at the end of the war by the Germans there were set up, in addition to Poland, the "Baltic republics" of Estonia, Latvia, and Lithuania. Once Europe had settled down, plebiscites were provided for to determine certain other territorial adjustments, notably whether certain parts of East Prussia and Silesia should go to Poland or remain German. The new Polish state had been granted access to the Baltic Sea through the so-called "Polish corridor," a narrow strip of land which had once been Polish, and which terminated in the almost wholly German city and port of Danzig. The Poles wanted Danzig, but the Allies compromised by setting up a Free City of Danzig and by giving the Poles free trade with the city. Even so, the Polish corridor now separated East Prussia from the rest of Germany, and Germans had to cross it in sealed trains.

Outside Europe, the Near East presented the most acute problems. By the Treaty of Sèvres the Turks were left in Europe with no more than Constantinople and a small strip of land around it, and in Asia with only their homeland of Anatolia. Mesopotamia and Palestine were given as mandates—a term we shall shortly explain—to Britain, while Syria and Lebanon were given as mandates to France. The

Greeks were to hold Smyrna and nearby regions in Asia Minor for five years and then submit to a plebiscite. But the Treaty of Sèvres never went into effect, though it was duly signed by the Sultan. In Anatolia a group of army officers led by Mustafa Kemal revolted against the government at Constantinople and galvanized the Turkish people into a new national life. The Turks drove the Greek army out of their country and set up a Turkish republic with its capital not at Constantinople but at Ankara in the heart of Anatolia. With this new government the Allies were finally obliged to conclude the Treaty of Lausanne in 1923. The new peace transferred the Smyrna area and eastern Thrace from Greek to Turkish control and was in general more advantageous to the Turks than the Treaty of Sèvres had been.

The treaty of Lausanne embodied in dramatic form a principle new in part in the West —the formal transfer of populations. True, peoples had been evicted by conquers before; witness among other instances the eviction of the French Acadians from Nova Scotia by the British in the eighteenth century, or the settling of our Indians in Indian Territory, now part of the state of Oklahoma. But here was an almost complete exchange: Greeks in Turkey were moved to Greece. Turks in Greece were moved to Turkey. No very significant discontented national minorities were left. Each government was to take care of the transferred populations, and though much hardship occurred, on the whole the plan worked. There was no such exchange of populations in the then British-held island of Cyprus, on which mutually hostile Greek and Turkish towns and villages continued to exist.

The Mandates

For the rest of the world the old straightforward policy of annexing overseas territories of defeated powers, as practiced in 1713, 1763, and 1815, seemed no longer possible in 1919. Liberal opinion both in Europe and in America had already been offended to the bursting point, and Wilson himself would never have permitted outright annexations. The consequence was the mandate system, whereby control over a given territory was assigned to a particular power by the League of Nations, which undertook periodic inspections to see that the terms of the mandate were being fulfilled. This system was designed by its proponents as a means of educating colonial peoples, leading them into the ways of democratic self-government, and preparing them for eventual independence. Under it the former German overseas territories and the non-Turkish parts of the Ottoman Empire were now distributed. Of Germany's African possessions East Africa (rechristened Tanganyika, and in 1964 merged with Zanzibar as independent Tanzania) went to Britain; Southwest Africa went to the Union of South Africa; and both the Cameroons and Togoland were divided between Britain and France. In the Pacific, the German portion of New Guinea was given to Australia, western Samoa to New Zealand, and the Caroline, Marshall, and Mariana island groups to Japan. In the Near East, as we have seen, France thus secured Syria and Lebanon, while Britain took Palestine and Mesopotamia.

The mandate system may seem to have been a way of disguising annexation, the hypocritical tribute of reactionary vice to progressive virtue. And so to a man like Clemenceau it probably was. The Japanese quite openly annexed and fortified their new Pacific islands in defiance of the terms of their mandate. But to many of the men who put through the idea of mandates the system really was what it professed to be, a nursery for eventual nationhood. For the most part the mandatory powers did make some show at least of treating mandated territories in a way that would prepare them for eventual freedom. Most of them are now indeed "free," or at least independent, nations.

The Punishment of Germany

After land transfers, the most important business of the Peace Conference was reparations, which were imposed on Austria, Hungary, Bulgaria, and Turkey as well as on Germany. It was, however, the German reparations that so long disturbed the peace and the economy of the world. The Germans were made to promise to pay for all the damage done to civilian property during the war, and to pay at the rate of five billion dollars a year until 1921, when the final bill would be presented to them. They would then be given thirty years in which to pay the full amount. The amount was left indefinite at Versailles, for the Allies could not agree on a figure. But the totals suggested were astronomical. It was clear from the first that the payments would ultimately have to be in goods—German goods in competition with the goods of the Allies. A Germany prosperous enough to pay reparations could not be the weak and divided nation that men like Clemenceau really wanted. Thus from the very start the "realists" at Versailles—Lloyd George and Clemenceau—cherished quite inconsistent hopes for the future.

The Versailles settlement also required Germany to hand over many of her merchant ships to the Allies and to make large deliveries of coal to France, Italy, and Belgium for a ten-year period. Furthermore, a whole miscellany of articles in the treaty was directed toward the disarmament of Germany on land, on sea, and in the air. The German army was to be limited in size to 100,000 men, and the western frontier zone, extending to a line 50 kilometers (about 30 miles) east of the Rhine, was to be completely "demilitarized"—that is, to contain neither fortifications nor soldiers. In addition, the Allies could maintain armies of occupation on the left bank of the Rhine for fifteen years, and perhaps longer. The treaty forbade Germany to have either submarines or military planes and severely limited the number and size of surface vessels in her navy.

Last, and by no means least important, Article 231 of the Treaty of Versailles obliged Germany to admit that the Central Powers bore sole responsibility for starting the war in 1914. Here is the article that was to cause so much history to be written—and made:

The Allied and Associated Governments affirm, and Germany accepts, the responsibility of Germany and her allies for causing all the loss and damage to which the Allied and Associated Governments and their nationals have been subjected as a conse-

AUSTRIA-HUNGARY

Vienna

Budapest

Drava R.

Karlovitz

Sava R.

Passarovitz

BOSNIA

Belgrade

HERZEGOVINA

SERBIA
(Ind. 1878)

MONTE-
NEGRO

Vardar R.

ITALY   *CORFU*

CRIMEA

MOLDAVIA

Dniester R.

Pruth R.

Dnieper R.

RUSSIAN   EMPIRE

Rostov

Don R.

Volga R.

Sea of Azov

Odessa

RUMANIA
Bucharest   (Ind. 1878)

Danube R.

Sofia   (Ind. 1878) BULGARIA

E. RUMELIA   Ottoman Occupied

Adrianople

Constantinople

Unkiar Skelessi

San Stefano

Salonika

Aegean

CHIOS *Sea*

Athens

GREECE
(Ind. 1830)

RHODES

CRETE

Mediterranean Sea

Sevastopol

Black Sea

Sinope

Angora

OTTOMAN EMPIRE

ANATOLIA

CYPRUS
(to Britain, 1878)

Beirut

Damascus

Jerusalem

Batum

CAUCASUS

*Caspian
Sea*

ARMENIA

Mosul

PERSIA

Baghdad

Tigris R.

Euphrates R.

Basra

TRIPOLI

EGYPT   Cairo

Alexandria

Port Said

Suez Canal
(1859-69)

Nile R.

Red Sea

ARABIA

Persian Gulf

**The Balkans and the Middle East
1878**

0   500
                    Miles

quence of the war imposed upon them by the aggression of Germany and her allies.

The Settlement Evaluated

To the Germans, Versailles was of course a cruel and humiliating peace, the *Diktat*, the great national grievance on which Hitler was to play so skillfully. To liberals of the time and later it seemed an unsound, revengeful peace, above all disastrous in its unrealistic reparations policy. In our present world of cold and hot wars, Versailles almost arouses nostalgia. It was at least a settlement, and one that in the best moments of the 1920's seemed a basis for slow improvement in international relations (see Chapter 29).

The League it set up was potentially a means by which a new generation of international administrators might mitigate the old rivalries of nations. The reparations could be, and indeed were, scaled down to something more reasonable. The new succession states were based on a modern popular national consciousness that had been developing for at least a hundred years. Though the theorist might protest at the "Balkanization of Europe," the creation of more weak and discontented little states like those in the Balkans, the fact remains that it would have been hard to deny national independence, or at least autonomy, to the Czechs, the Poles, the Baltic peoples, and the south Slavs. Germany, though she certainly was not treated generously, was at least not wiped off the map, as Poland had been in

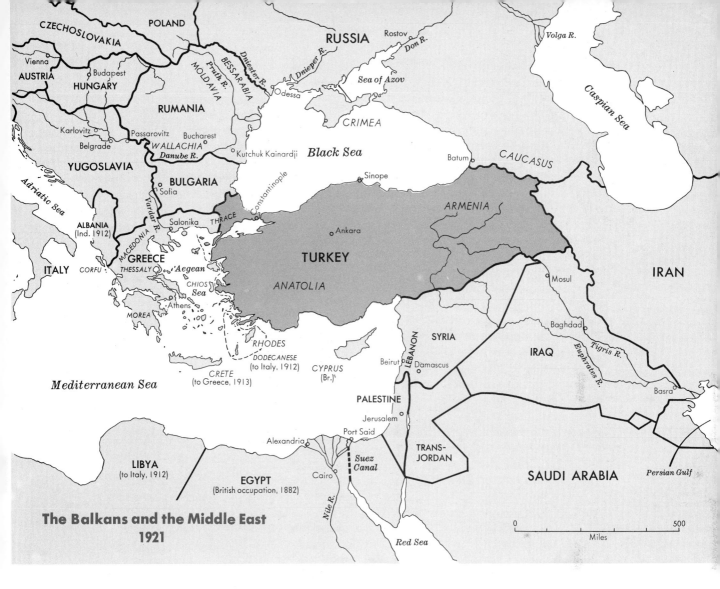

**The Balkans and the Middle East
1921**

the eighteenth century. She was not even actually demoted to a second-rate position in the world. She remained, as she was shortly to prove, a first-rate power. In the long series of settlements under our modern western state-system, which goes back to the Italian wars of the fifteenth century, Versailles looks nowadays like neither the worst nor the best, but like a typical compromise peace.

It was, however, too much for the American people, who were not used to the harsh needs of international compromise. But it is an over-simplification to argue that this was solely a matter of American idealism turning away in disgust from a settlement that was all too spotted with unpleasant realities. The final American refusal to ratify the Treaty of Versailles, like all great collective decisions, was

the result of many forces. Politics certainly played an important part, for the Republicans had won control of both the Senate and the House of Representatives in the congressional elections of November, 1918. The President of course was still Wilson, a Democrat, and Wilson made no concessions to the Republicans either by taking a bipartisan delegation of Democrats and Republicans to Paris with him or by accepting modifications in the treaty which would have satisfied some of his Republican opponents. The Senate thereupon refused to ratify the treaty.

It is, however, extremely unlikely that even a much more pliable and diplomatic American president than Wilson could have secured from the Senate ratification of another important treaty involved in the proposed settlement.

This was the project of a defensive alliance among France, Britain, and the United States into which Wilson had been pushed as part of the price of getting France to give up her proposals for a separate Rhineland republic and for annexation of the Saar. With the United States out, Britain refused a mere dual alliance with France against a German attack. France, still seeking to bolster her security, patched up a series of alliances with the new nations to the east and south of Germany — Polland, and the "Little Entente" of Yugoslavia, Czechoslovakia, and Rumania, a rather unsatisfactory substitute for Britain and the United States as allies.

The peace thus left France with an uneasy hegemony in Europe, a hegemony dependent on the continued disarmament and economic weakening of Germany, on the continued isolation of Russia, and on the uncertain support of her new allies. Moreover, France had been disastrously weakened by the human and material losses of the war, and her position of leadership, though it alarmed the British with their long memories of French rivalry in the past, was an unreal thing. In reality, Germany was the strongest nation in Europe, and the Great War had checked, but not halted, her attempt to dominate the Continent and indeed the world. The next German attempt was to draw both Britain and America back from the isolation into which they attempted to withdraw after the collapse of the system planned at Paris in 1919.

A most important matter, however, was not directly touched by the Versailles settlement: Russia, or the Union of Soviet Socialist Republics (U.S.S.R.), the formal name of the new communist state, did not figure in the great treaties. Yet in many senses the most important result of World War I was the emergence of this new-old Russia, her strength and capabilities in the long run increased by the stimulus of successful revolution.

Reading Suggestions on the First World War

(Asterisk indicates paperbound edition.)

The Background: General Accounts

A. J. P. Taylor, *The Struggle for Mastery in Europe, 1848–1918* (Clarendon, 1954). A crisp and suggestive survey.

S. B. Fay, *The Origins of the World War,* 2nd ed. (Macmillan, 1932). A fully documented account by an American scholar; somewhat sympathetic to Germany.

B. E. Schmitt, *The Coming of the War, 1914,* 2 vols. (Scribner's, 1930). Another well-documented scholarly account; somewhat sympathetic to Britain.

H. E. Barnes, *The Genesis of the World War: An Introduction to the Problem of War Guilt* (Knopf, 1926). An extreme statement on the "revisionist" position on war guilt.

M. von Montgelas, *The Case for the Central Powers, An Impeachment of the Versailles Verdict* (Knopf, 1925). Representative of the German "revisionist" school.

L. Albertini, *The Origins of the War of 1914,* 2 vols. (Oxford Univ. Press, 1952–1953). By an Italian scholar; stresses the role of Italy.

N. Mansergh, *The Coming of the First World War* (Longmans, Green, 1949). A brief popular survey from 1878 to 1914.

Barbara Tuchman, *The Proud Tower* (Macmillan, 1966). A very good and most readable account of the European society out of which the "Great War" came.

The Background: Special Studies

W. L. Langer, *European Alliances and Alignments, 1871–1890.* 2nd ed. (Knopf, 1950). A detailed scholarly survey, favorable to Bismarckian diplomacy.

W. L. Langer, *The Diplomacy of Imperialism, 1890–1902,* 2nd ed. (Knopf, 1951). Includes much material pertaining to the shifting alliances of the European powers.

L. C. B. Seaman, *From Vienna to Versailles* (Coward-McCann, 1956). Interesting essay in interpretation by a young British scholar.

E. M. Carroll, *French Public Opinion and Foreign Affairs, 1870–1914* (Century, 1931), and *Germany and the Great Powers, 1866–1914: A Study in Public Opinion and Foreign Policy* (Prentice-Hall, 1938). Scholarly studies in a significant area of research.

R. J. S. Hoffman, *Great Britain and the German Trade Rivalry, 1875–1914* (Univ. of Pennsylvania Press, 1933). A helpful monograph.

E. L. Woodward, *Great Britain and the German Navy* (Clarendon, 1935); A. J. Marder, *The Anatomy of British Sea Power* (Knopf, 1940); and B. Brodie, *Sea Power in the Machine Age* (Princeton Univ. Press, 1943). Three useful studies of the important question of naval power.

E. N. Anderson, *The First Moroccan Crisis, 1904–1906* (Univ. of Chicago Press, 1930), and I. C. Barlow, *The Agadir Crisis* (Univ. of North Carolina Press, 1940). Two useful monographs on the issue of Morocco in pre-war diplomacy.

E. M. Earle, *Turkey, The Great Powers, and the Bagdad Railway* (Macmillan, 1923). Scholarly account of another major issue of pre-war diplomacy.

A. F. Pribram, *Austrian Foreign Policy, 1908–1918* (Allen & Unwin, 1923). Balanced statement from the Austrian standpoint.

P. Renouvin, *The Immediate Origins of the War* (Yale Univ. Press, 1928). Scholarly account from the French point of view.

G. P. Gooch and H. Temperley, eds., *British Documents on the Origins of the War, 1898–1914,* 12 vols. (His Majesty's Stationery Office, 1926–1938). Representative of the great collections of diplomatic documents published by the governments of the major belligerents after World War I.

Outbreak of the World War: German Documents Collected by Karl Kautsky (Oxford Univ. Press, 1924), and *German Diplomatic Documents, 1871–1914,* 4 vols. (Methuen, 1928–1931). English translations of some of the vast number of German diplomatic documents.

The Background of the War: American Policy

T. A. Bailey, *A Diplomatic History of the American People,* 4th ed. (Appleton-Century-Crofts, 1950), and S. F. Bemis, *A Diplomatic History of the United States,* 3rd ed. (Holt, 1950). Two standard surveys.

W. Millis, *The Road to War: America, 1914–1917* (Houghton, Mifflin, 1935). Readable journalistic account, highly critical of Wilson's policy.

C. C. Tansill, *America Goes to War* (Little, Brown, 1938). Scholarly treatment, also critical of Wilson's policy.

C. Seymour, *American Diplomacy during the World War,* 2nd ed. (Johns Hopkins Univ. Press, 1942). Sympathetic toward Wilson's policy.

The War

W. S. Churchill, *The World Crisis,* 6 vols. (Scribner's, 1923–1931). Detailed survey by the famous British statesman.

C. R. M. Cruttwell, *History of the Great War,* 2nd ed. (Oxford Univ. Press, 1936), and B. H. Liddell Hart, *The Real War, 1914–1918.* Remain the best single-volume histories. The Liddell Hart book was re-issued as a paperback (*Atlantic; Little, Brown, 1964).

H. W. Baldwin, *World War I: An Outline History* (Harper, 1962), also paperback. Most recent survey by a good military historian.

J. E. Edmonds, *A Short History of World War I* (Oxford Univ. Press, 1951). A brief account by an official British military historian.

Barbara Tuchman, *The Guns of August* (Macmillan, 1962; *Dell). A fascinating account of the immediate background and the first critical month of the war.

Alan Moorhead, *Gallipoli* (Harper, 1956), also a paperback. By a skillful writer and trained historian.

A. Horne, *The Price of Glory: Verdun 1916* (St. Martin's Press, 1964), also a paperback. An excellent narrative of a most important battle.

Note: There are many detailed military histories of World War I. The problems that arose on the home front have been the subject of a large number of special studies published under the auspices of the Carnegie Endowment for International Peace. Some idea of their scope may be had by consulting *Economic and Social History of the World War: Outline of Plan, European Series* (Carnegie Endowment for International Peace, 1924). Another useful collection of special studies has been published by the Hoover Institute of War, Revolution, and Peace at Stanford University.

The Peace

H. R. Rudin, *Armistice, 1918* (Yale Univ. Press, 1944). The standard monograph.

H. W. V. Temperley, *A History of the Peace Conference of Paris,* 6 vols. (Frowde, Hodder and Stoughton, 1920–1924). The standard detailed account; by a British scholar.

H. G. Nicolson, *Peacemaking, 1919* (Constable, 1933). A good shorter account; by a British expert on diplomacy.

P. Birdsall, *Versailles Twenty Years After* (Reynal & Hitchcock, 1941). Balanced reappraisal by an American scholar.

T. A. Bailey, *Wilson and the Peacemakers* (Macmillan, 1947). Sound study of America's role.

J. M. Keynes, *The Economic Consequences of the Peace* (Harcourt, Brace, 1920), and E. Mantoux, *The Carthaginian Peace; or, the Economic Consequences of Mr. Keynes* (Scribner's, 1952). Respectively, the most famous attack on the Versailles settlement and a thoughtful study of the results of that attack.

Historical Fiction

E. Childers, *The Riddle of the Sands* (Nelson, 1913), and H. H. Munro ("Saki"), *When William Came* (Lane, 1914). Two unusual novels, written before the outbreak of the war and predicting what it might be like. Childers' is a story of intrigue and adventure, and "Saki's" is a forecast of the German occupation of Britain.

J. Romains, *Verdun* (Knopf, 1939). Excellent and balanced novel about French troops on the western front, 1914–1916.

H. Barbusse, *Under Fire* (Dutton, 1917), and E. M. Remarque, *All Quiet on the Western Front* (Lion Books). Two famous novels, by a Frenchman and a German, respectively, reflect the horror aroused in intellectuals by trench warfare.

J. Dos Passos, *Three Soldiers* (Modern Library, 1941), and E. Hemingway, *A Farewell to Arms* (many editions). Two American novels about the war, indicative of the post-war disillusionment of the "lost generation."

E. E. Cummings, *The Enormous Room* (Modern Library, 1941), and A. Zweig, *The Case of Sergeant Grischa* (Viking, 1928). Novels about prisoners of war and the eastern front, respectively.

C. S. Forester, *The General* (Little, Brown, 1947). Astringent novel about the "brass" in World War I.

J. Buchan, *Greenmantle* (Nelson, many eds.). A novel of espionage indicating that the war contained its ingredient of high adventure in addition to blood and guts.

What Price Glory? in M. Anderson and L. Stallings, *Three American Plays* (Harcourt, Brace, 1926). A famous play showing that the war had its rowdy side.

26

Communist Russia, 1917 – 1941

I Introduction

On June 22, 1941, Adolf Hitler's German armies poured over the frontier of his Russian ally and began a rapid advance toward Moscow, toward the major Russian industrial centers, and toward the most productive Russian agricultural centers. The Russia Hitler invaded was no longer the Russia into which Napoleon had sent the *grande armée* a hundred and twenty-nine years before, or the Russia whose millions of embattled soldiers had perished in the First World War against the Germany of William II and his Habsburg allies. It was no longer the Russia of the tsars. Since 1917 it had been the Russia of the Bolsheviks. Yet it was still Russia.

Along with the tsars, the nobility and the bourgeoisie had gone down to ruin after the communist revolution of 1917, and the clergy

397

as a class had suffered almost as much. A small, tightly knit, conspiratorial group of fanatical Marxist revolutionaries had seized power and for the next twenty-four years had striven to make Russia over. Drawn mostly from the peculiarly Russian class of the intelligentsia, and declaring themselves to be the representatives of the industrial proletariat, the Bolsheviks had worked gigantic changes, especially in the years after 1928. Industry, proceeding under forced draft, had expanded enormously, and the proportion of the population employed in industry had risen to almost 50 per cent; the proportion engaged in agriculture had fallen correspondingly.

The peasant had been a victim of serfdom until 1861, had been subject to the initiative-destroying domination of the commune until 1906, and had then been encouraged by Stolypin to make himself a free farmer (see Chapter 22). Now, under the Bolsheviks, he found himself subjected to new and grievous pressure. Agriculture had been collectivized, and the age-old longing of the peasant for private property in land had been ruthlessly suppressed.

These staggering social and economic changes had not been accomplished without internal friction. Inside the government, personal rivalries, plots, counter-plots, fake plots, and charges of plots had produced repeated purges extending down through the ranks of the population. The choking conspiratorial atmosphere which the Bolshevik rulers had breathed during their long years of underground preparation for a seizure of power now enveloped the citadels of power. Personal rivalries for domination of the machinery of the state were cloaked beneath the Byzantine theological language of doctrinal controversy over fine points in the sacred writings of Marx and Lenin. Yet the controversies had immediate significance in the formulation and choice of government policies. The Communist party, the secret police, and the army had become the interlocking agencies which ran the state at the bidding of the dictator. The dictator himself, Stalin, had made his own career possible chiefly through the ruthless use of his position as Secretary of the Communist party.

The foreign policy of the communist state had passed through a brief period in which ideological considerations had seemed occasionally to outweigh national interest in the old sense. It had then returned to the pursuit of traditional Russian ends, coupled with the objective of promoting eventual world-revolution. But in furthering Russian aims abroad, the Bolshevik leaders were now in possession of an instrument more flexible than any the tsars had ever commanded. This was the Communist International, or Comintern, a federation of the Communist parties in the individual countries of the world. These parties could often be used as promoters of purely Russian ends rather than strictly communist ends. With the shifting stresses and strains of international politics during the late 1920's and 1930's, the "line" of the Comintern shifted often and bewilderingly, but always in accordance with the aims of the Soviet foreign office. Usually the majority of communists elsewhere in the world fell meekly into position and loudly proclaimed when necessary the opposite of what they had proclaimed the day before.

Yet the changes during the first twenty-four years of the Soviet period, vast though they were, could not conceal the continuities between the new Russian system and the old. The dictator of 1941, the revered leader of his people, for whom his followers made increasingly grandiose claims, was not unlike the tsar of 1917 in his assumption of autocratic power. The individual Russian of 1941, despite his sufferings under the new system, had remained deeply patriotic, ready to sacrifice himself for his country, even under a government he hated. The peasant of 1941 still yearned hopelessly for his land; the worker struggled for economic advancement and social security. Bureaucrats, managers, intellectuals, and artists, all in the service of the state, formed in 1941 a new élite which replaced but did not differ greatly from the old privileged class. A police force superior in efficiency to those of Ivan the Terrible, Peter the

Great, and Nicholas I, but not different in kind, in 1941 exercised thought control over all citizens and terrorized even prominent members of the system itself.

More and more, Stalinist communism had taken on the trappings of a religion, with its sacred books, its heresies, its places of pilgrimage, its doctrinal quarrels. Thus the old Russian orthodoxy had by 1941 not been replaced but rather modified. Russian nationalism, too, asserted itself ever more insistently and crudely, until finally, in the war that Hitler began, the government encouraged the cult of traditional heroes of earlier times, and even glorified Ivan the Terrible himself, a symbol no longer of "feudal" domination but of the Russian national spirit. The early revolutionary departures from accepted standards in Russian marriage, family life, and education, had by 1941 all been abandoned in favor of a return to conventional bourgeois behavior. This chapter will trace in some detail the series of vast changes here summarized and will attempt to demonstrate the continued survival of the old Russia beneath the veneer of the new.

II The Russian Revolution of 1917

The Immediate Background

Ridden by domestic crisis though Russia was in 1914 (see Chapter 22), the country greeted the outbreak of World War I with demonstrations of national patriotism. The Duma supported the war and did yeoman service in organizing Red Cross activities. The left-wing parties—the radical agrarian SR's (Social Revolutionaries) and the Marxist SD's (Social Democrats)—abstained from voting war credits, but offered to assist the national defense. By 1917, more than 15,000,000 Russians had been drafted into the armies. Losses in battle were staggering from the first; the Russians suffered more than 3,800,000 casualties during the first year of war. On the home front, criticism was aroused by the inadequate handling of the supply of munitions, and by mid-1915 the Center and Left groups in the Duma were urging moderate reforms, such as the end of discrimination against minority nationalities and an increase in the powers of the *zemstvos,* the local assemblies. The Empress Alexandra took the lead in opposing all such measures, and kept urging her weak husband, Tsar Nicholas II, to act more autocratically. When Nicholas took personal command of the armies in the field and prorogued the Duma (autumn, 1915), she became virtually supreme at home. The supremacy of the Empress meant also the supremacy of her favorite, the unscrupulous adventurer Rasputin.

With the Empress and Rasputin in control, a gang of shady adventurers, blackmailers, and profiteers bought and sold offices, speculated in military supplies, put in their own puppets as ministers, and created a series of shocking scandals. Confusion, strikes, and defeatism mounted at home during 1916, while the armies slowly bled to death at the front. Even the conservatives began to denounce Rasputin publicly, and in December, 1916, he was poisoned, shot several times, and ultimately drowned, all in one nightmare evening, by a group of conspirators closely related to the imperial family. Despite repeated warnings from moderates in the Duma that the government itself was preparing a revolution by its failure to create a responsible ministry and to clean up the mess, the Tsar remained apathetic. Relatives of the imperial family and members of the Duma began independently to plot for his abdication. In the early months of 1917, all conditions favored a revolution, but the revolutionaries were not prepared.

The March Revolution

On March 8, strikes and bread-riots broke out in the capital, and four days later Romanov rule, which had governed Russia since 1613, was doomed. Yet this revolution of March, 1917, has been well called leaderless, spontaneous, and anonymous. SR's and both Bolshevik and Menshevik factions of SD's (Chapter 22) were genuinely surprised at what happened. Indeed, the Bolshevik leaders were either abroad in exile, or under arrest in Siberia. The determining factor in the overthrow of the Tsar was the disloyalty of the garrison of Petrograd (the new Russian name given to St. Petersburg during the war). Inefficiency had led to a food shortage in the capital, though actual starvation had not set in. When the Tsar ordered troops to fire on striking workers, only a few obeyed, and on March 12, in revulsion against the order, the troops joined the strikers, broke into the arsenals,

Rasputin (1871?–1916).

and began to hunt the police, who quickly disappeared from the scene. The Duma lagged behind the revolting troops and workers in estimating the situation, and the Tsar lagged behind the Duma. By March 14, when the Tsar had finally decided to appoint a responsible ministry, it was too late; the cabinet had vanished. Troops ordered to put down the revolt simply melted away and joined the rebels.

Leftists, released from prison by the mobs, formed a Soviet of workers and soldiers, modeled on the 1905 Soviet of workers (Chapter 22), but now including soldiers as well. The Soviet proceeded to organize a workers' militia, to create a food-supply commission, and to issue newspapers. Its fifteen-man executive committee became the policy-makers of the revolution. The Soviet located its headquarters across the hall from the Duma, which did not obey the Tsar's order to dissolve, but remained in session.

The Marxists among the Soviet leaders still believed in the necessity of a preliminary bourgeois revolution, and did not yet regard the Soviet itself as an organ of power. They favored the creation of a provisional government, in which they would not participate, but to which they would offer limited support. They put themselves at the disposition of the Duma, and asked that it temporarily run the country. Thus the Duma, a limited assembly elected by a restricted franchise, was literally forced by the Soviet into the position of leading the revolution.

Negotiations between the Soviet and a Duma committee brought a provisional government into existence. Despite the widely differing social and economic aims of Soviet and Duma, both agreed to grant political liberties immediately, and to summon a constituent assembly, which was to establish the future form of government by giving Russia a constitution. The provisional government was composed mainly of Kadets (Constitutional Democrats) and other moderates, and was headed by the liberal Prince Lvov, chairman of the union of *zemstvos* and of the Red Cross. It included also one radical member of the Soviet, Alexander Kerensky, Minister of Jus-

Soldier delegates to the Petrograd Soviet meeting in the Duma building.

tice, a clever labor lawyer and member of the Duma also, who accepted office despite the understanding that members of the Soviet would not do so.

After some abortive efforts to save the dynasty in the person of the Tsar's brother, Nicholas finally abdicated, and his brother refused the throne because of the popular hatred of the family. Under pressure from the Soviet, the provisional government arrested Nicholas II and the Empress on March 20. The Duma had thus accepted the mandate given it by the revolutionaries. Had it accepted instead its dismissal at the hands of the Tsar and gone home, it seems probable that the monarchy would have been preserved at the cost of some liberal concessions. But moderate reformers were now in power, and Russia embarked on the troubled months between March and October, 1917.

The Provisional Government

The provisional government is usually regarded as having been a total failure. Measured by the final results, such a view is perhaps justified. But the judgment of history must take into consideration the dreadful difficulties that faced the provisional government. These were not only immediate and specific, but general and underlying. Russian moderates had had no experience of authority. They were separated by a great cultural gulf from the lower classes. Their opportunity to rule now came to them in the midst of a fearful war, which they felt they had to pursue while reconstructing and democratizing the enormous and unwieldy Russian Empire.

Moreover, the Soviet possessed many of the instruments of power, yet refused to accept any responsibility. Workers and soldiers in the capital supported the Soviet, while in the provinces the new governors appointed by the provisional government had no weapon except persuasion to employ against the local peasant-elected soviets, which multiplied rapidly. Present-day critics of the provisional government often denounce its failure to suppress its revolutionary opponents, but they overlook the fact that the provisional government did not possess the tools of suppression. The Petrograd garrison, for instance, by agreement with the Soviet, could not be removed or disarmed. The support given by the Soviet to the provisional government has been com-

401

pared to the kind of support that is given by a hangman's noose.

The two great specific issues facing the provisional government were agrarian discontent and the continuation of the war. The peasants wanted land, and they wanted it immediately. The provisional government, however, made up as it was of responsible liberals, believed in acting with deliberation and according to law. It refused to sanction peasant seizure of land, despite increasing disorder in the countryside. Instead, it appointed a commission to collect material on which future agrarian legislation was to be based—an act totally inadequate to the emergency.

As to the war, the members of the government felt in honor bound to their allies not to make a separate peace. Moreover, most of them still unrealistically hoped that Russia might win, and gain the territories which the Allies had promised. But the Soviet subverted discipline in the armies at the front by issuing a "declaration of the rights of soldiers," which virtually put an end to the authority of officers over enlisted men. Although the Soviet made it as hard as possible for the government to pursue the war, it did not sponsor a separate peace. Even the Bolshevik members of the Soviet, who now began to return from exile, demanded only that Russia participate in general peace negotiations, which, they urged, should begin at once.

Lenin and Bolshevism

The most important of the returning Bolshevik exiles was Lenin. His real name was Valdimir Ilyich Ulianov, but in his writings he used the pen-name Lenin, to which he sometimes prefixed the initial N., a Russian abbreviation for "nobody," in order to tell his readers that he was using a pseudonym. This "N." has given rise to the mistaken but still widely held idea that Lenin's first name was Nikolai (Nicholas). Son of a provincial official and intellectual, Lenin became a revolutionary in the late 1880's and, as we have seen (Chapter 22), took a chief role in the early years of the SD's as the leader of the party's Bolshevik

wing. He had returned to Russia from abroad for the Revolution of 1905, but he left Russia once more in 1908, and stayed abroad until 1917.

When the news of the March Revolution reached Lenin in Switzerland, he made desperate efforts to get back home. Finally, through the Swiss Social Democrats, he made contact with the German general staff, which felt that it would be a good investment to see that Lenin reached Russia, where he might disrupt the Russian war effort against Germany. Thus it was that the German military transported Lenin across Germany from Switzerland to the Baltic in the famous sealed railroad car. He arrived at the Finland Station in Petrograd on April 16, 1917, a little more than a month after the March Revolution.

Most Russian Social Democrats had long regarded a bourgeois parliamentary republic as a necessary preliminary to an eventual socialist revolution and socialist society. For this reason, they were prepared to help in transforming Russia into a capitalist society, though not without grave doubts that the bourgeois capitalists might be as bad as the tsar and the landlords, or that the masses might be "deluded" into accepting the new system. They favored the creation of a democratic republic, at the same time believing that complete political freedom was absolutely essential for their own future rise to power. Despite the Marxist emphasis upon the industrial laboring class as the only proper vehicle for revolution, Lenin early realized that in Russia, where the "proletariat" embraced only about 1 per cent of the population, the SD's must seek other allies. At the time of the Revolution of 1905, he began to preach the need for limited alliances for tactical purposes between the Bolsheviks and the SR's, who commanded the support of the peasantry. When the alliance had served its purpose, the SD's were to turn on their allies and destroy them. Then would come the socialist triumph.

Instead of a preliminary bourgeois democratic republic, Lenin called in 1905 and later for an immediate "revolutionary-democratic dictatorship of the proletariat and the peasantry," a concept that seems to us self-contradictory and is surely vague. Lenin's view, however, was not adopted by most Bolsheviks. Together with the Mensheviks, they continued to believe and urge that a bourgeois revolution and a parliamentary democracy were necessary first steps.

Because Lenin did not trust the masses to make a revolution (by themselves, he felt, they were capable only of "trade-union consciousness"), he favored a dictatorship of the Bolshevik party over the working class. Because he did not trust the rank and file of Bolshevik party workers, he favored a dictatorship of a small élite over the Bolshevik party. And in the end, because he really trusted nobody's views but his own, he favored, though never explicitly, his own dictatorship over this élite. Another future Russian leader, the brilliant intellectual Leon Trotsky, early warned that in Lenin's views one-man dictatorship was implicit.

Trotsky, for his part, voiced an opinion of his own, held by neither Mensheviks nor Bolsheviks. The bourgeoisie in Russia, he argued, was so weak that the working class could telescope the bourgeois and socialist revolutions into one continuous movement. After the proletariat had helped the bourgeoisie achieve its revolution, he felt that the workers could move immediately to power. They could nationalize industry and collectivize agriculture, and, although foreign intervention and civil war were doubtless to be expected, the Russian proletariat would soon be joined by the proletariats of other countries, which would make their own revolutions. Except for this last point, Trotsky's analysis accurately forecast the course of events. Between 1905 and 1917, Lenin himself accepted Trotsky's view from time to time, but warned that it endangered political democracy.

Lenin had been deeply depressed by the failure of 1905, and by the threat posed by Stolypin's agrarian reforms. He almost despaired when the socialist parties of Europe went along with their governments in 1914 and supported the war. To him this meant the end of the second socialist International, for the Social Democrats had failed to recognize the war as the "bourgeois-imperialist" venture that it appeared to Lenin to be. He preached defeatism as the only possible view for a Russian SD to follow.

Lenin's greatest talent was not as an original thinker but as a skillful tactician. He often seemed able to judge with accuracy just what was politically possible in a given situation, and he was not afraid to gamble. Thus, even before he returned to Russia in April, 1917, he had assessed some of the difficulties facing the provisional government and decided that the masses could take over at once. Immediately upon his arrival, he hailed the worldwide revolution, proclaiming that the end of imperialism, "the last stage of capitalism," was at hand. Ignoring the positions previously taken by Bolsheviks and Mensheviks alike, he demanded now that all power immediately be given to the soviets. His speeches sounded to the SD's themselves like the ravings of a madman.

Almost nobody but Lenin felt that the losely organized soviets could govern the country, or that the war would bring down the capitalist world in chaos. In April 1917, Lenin called not only for the abandonment of the provisional government and the establishment of a republic of soviets but for the confiscation of estates, the nationalization of land, and the abolition of the army, of government officials, and of the police. He was offering land at once to the impatient peasants, peace at once to the war-weary populace. This program fitted the mood of the people far better than the cautious and well-meant efforts of the provisional government to bring about reform by legal means. Dogmatic, furiously impatient of compromise, entirely convinced that he alone had the truth, Lenin galvanized the Bolsheviks into a truly revolutionary group waiting only the moment to seize power.

The Coming
of the November Revolution

The months from March to November, 1917, before the Bolsheviks came to power, can be divided into a period between March and July, during which revolution deepened, a feeble reaction from July to September, and a new quickening of the revolutionary current from September to the final uprising in November. In the first period, the government faced a crisis, because the Kadet ministers wished to maintain the Russian war aim of annexing the Straits, while the Soviet wanted a peace "without annexations or indemnities." Out of the crisis Kerensky, now war minister, emerged as the dominant leader. He failed to realize that it was no longer possible to restore the morale of the armies, which were dissolving under the impact of Bolshevik propaganda. A new offensive ordered on July 1 collapsed, as soldiers refused to obey orders, deserted their units, and rushed home to their native villages, eager to seize the land. Ukrainian separatism also plagued the officials of the government. The soviets became gradually more and more Bolshevik, as Lenin and Trotsky worked tirelessly at recruitment and organization. Although the June congress of soviets in Petrograd was less than 10 per cent Bolshevik in make-up, the Bolshevik slogans of peace, bread, and freedom won overwhelming support.

Yet an armed outbreak by troops who had accepted the Bolshevik slogans found the Petrograd Soviet unwilling and unable to assume power. While the mob roared outside, the Soviet voted to discuss the matter two weeks later, and meanwhile to keep the provisional government in power. A regiment loyal to the Soviet protected it against the working class! The government declared that Lenin was a German agent, and, as his supporters wavered, raided the newspaper offices of *Pravda* ("Truth," the Bolshevik paper); Lenin had to go into hiding to avoid arrest. This episode of mid-July is what is known among Bolsheviks as "playing at insurrection." Though shots had been exchanged and overt action had been embarked upon, there had been no revolutionary follow-through. Power had not been seized, probably because Lenin felt that the Bolsheviks did not have enough support in the provinces.

Now Kerensky became premier. The government hardened its attitude toward the Ukrainians, but could not come to a popular decision on either land or peace. General Kornilov, chosen by Kerensky as the new commander-in-chief of the armies, quickly became the white hope of all conservative groups, and in August plotted a *coup*, intended to disperse the Soviet. His attitude toward the provisional government was uncertain, but, had he succeeded, he would probably have demanded a purge of its more radical elements. The plot, however, was a failure, because railroad and telegraph workers sabotaged Kornilov's movements, and because his troops simply would not obey him. The Bolsheviks, adopting the slogan "We will fight against Kornilov, but will not support Kerensky," threw themselves into preparations for the defense of Petrograd, which proved to be unnecessary. By September 14, Kornilov had been arrested, and the affair ended without bloodshed. The threat from the Right helped the Bolsheviks greatly, and sentiment in the Petrograd and Moscow soviets now for the first time became predominantly Bolshevik.

The Kornilov affair turned the army mutiny into a widespread revolt. Instances of violence multiplied. No longer satisfied with merely disobeying their officers, more and more soldiers murdered them instead. No longer satisfied with merely refusing to pay their rent or pasturing their animals on their landlords' land, more and more peasants burned the manor house and killed the owner. It was true that the nobility owned only a quarter as much land as the peasants, but the peasants no longer listened to statistics or to arguments that rash action retarded progress. As disorder mounted in the countryside, the Bolsheviks tightened their hold over the soviets in the cities.

Lenin returned to Petrograd on October 20. Soon thereafter the Bolsheviks got control over a Military Revolutionary Committee, originally chosen to help defend Petrograd against the advancing Germans, and now transformed, under the guidance of Trotsky, into a general staff for the revolution. Beginning on November 4, huge demonstrations and mass meetings were addressed by Trotsky, and on November 7 the insurrection broke out.

In Petrograd, the revolution had been well prepared, and proceeded with little bloodshed. Kerensky escaped in a car belonging to the American Embassy. The Military Revolutionary Committee, as an organ of the Petrograd Soviet, simply took over. The Bolsheviks called a second congress of soviets, and when the Mensheviks and right-wing SR's walked out, Trotsky called them the refuse that would be swept into the garbage-can of history. Co-operating with the left-wing SR's, and adopting their land program, Lenin abolished all property rights of landlords, and transferred the land thus affected to local land committees and soviets of peasant deputies. Though Lenin did not in the least approve of the system of individual small-holdings which this decree put into effect, he recognized the psychological advantage which the adoption of the SR program would gain him. He also urged an immediate peace without annexations or indemnities, and appealed to the workers of Germany, France, and England to support him in this demand. Finally, a new cabinet, called a

"Under the snug wing of Kerensky," a cartoon attacking Kerensky's alleged affection for the generals.

Council of People's Commissars, was chosen, with Lenin as President, and Trotsky as Foreign Commissar.

As Commissar of Nationalities the Bolsheviks installed a younger man, a Georgian, named Joseph Djugashvili, who had been a successful organizer of bank robberies in the days when the party treasury was filled in this way, but whose role had otherwise been relatively obscure. He had taken the name Stalin, which suggests a steel-like hardness. Under

Moscow at the time of the November revolution, 1917.

Lenin's coaching, Stalin had also become the party authority on questions of minority nationalities, and had published a pamphlet on the subject in 1913.

Outside Petrograd, the revolution moved more slowly. In Moscow there was a week of street-fighting between Bolshevik Reds and Whites, as anti-Bolshevik forces were already known. Elsewhere in factory towns, the Bolsheviks usually won speedily; in non-industrial centers it took them longer. Most of Siberia and of Central Asia came over, but Tiflis, the capital of Georgia, went Menshevik, and passed resolutions calling for a constituent assembly and the continuation of the war. The reason for the rapid and smooth success of the Bolsheviks was that the provincial garrisons opposed the war, and willingly allied themselves with the workers. Local Military Revolutionary Committees were created in most places, and held elections for new local soviets. Naturally there was much confusion at first, but surprisingly little resistance to the consolidation of the authority of the new regime. Gradually the town of Rostov-on-Don, near the Sea of Azov, became the main center of resistance, as Kornilov and other generals, together with a number of the leading politicians of the Duma, made their way there.

This initial triumph of the revolution did not mean that the population of Russia had been converted to Bolshevism. By cleverly sensing the mood of the people, Lenin had opportunistically given the Bolsheviks a set of slogans around which the people could rally, although some of the slogans did not at all correspond with the true Bolshevik views. As we shall shortly see, the Russian people were in fact strongly anti-Bolshevik. But the Bolsheviks had triumphed, and the democratic hopes for freedom of the press and other freedoms were now doomed to disappointment.

Deprived of competent civil servants, the new regime worried along through an atmosphere of continued crisis. Late in November, 1917, an agreement was reached with the Left-Wing SR's, three of whom entered the government, and peace negotiations were begun with the Germans. The revolution proper was over. Lenin was in power.

The Constituent Assembly

It is of great interest to record that the Bolsheviks now permitted elections for a constituent assembly. Lenin had no use for this sort of democratically chosen parliament, which he considered "inferior" to the soviet. Yet, probably because he had so long taunted the provisional government with delaying the elections, he seems to have felt compelled to hold them. The Russian people for the first and last time in their history had a completely free election, under universal suffrage. Lenin himself accepted as accurate figures showing that the Bolsheviks polled about one-quarter of the vote. The other socialist parties, chiefly the SR's, polled 62 per cent. As was to be expected, the Bolshevik vote was heaviest in the cities, especially Moscow and Petrograd, while the SR vote was largely rural.

Disregarding the majority cast for his opponents, Lenin maintained that "the most advanced" elements had voted for him. It was of course only his opinion that made those who had voted Bolshevik more "advanced" than those who had voted SR or Kadet. The constituent assembly met only once, on January 18, 1918. Lenin dissolved it the next day by decree, and sent guards with rifles to prevent its ever meeting again. The anti-Bolshevik majority was naturally deeply indignant at this pure act of force against the popular will, but there was no public outburst, and the delegates disbanded. In part, this was because the Bolsheviks had already taken action on the things that interested the people most—peace and land—and in part because of the lack of a democratic parliamentary tradition among the masses of the Russian people.

In spite of the many years of agitation by intellectuals and liberals for just such a popular assembly, Russia did not have the large middle class, the widespread literacy, the tradition of debate, and the respect for the rights of the individual which seem to be an essential part of constitutionalism. Yet it is surely extreme to decide that there was no chance for constitutional government in Russia in 1917–1918. Was the constituent assembly "an attempt to transplant an alien concept of government to a soil where it could never flourish"? Or was it "a noble experiment incorporating a sound principle but doomed by the crisis into which it was born"? The fact that Lenin had the rifles to prevent the constituent assembly from fulfilling the function which the popular will had assigned to it does not answer the question either way.

III War Communism and NEP, 1917–1928

War Communism

The first period of Soviet history, which runs from the end of 1917 to the end of 1920, is usually called the period of "war communism," or "military communism." The term itself of course implies that the main features of the period were determined by military events. Civil war raged, and foreign powers intervened on Russian soil. But the term is also somewhat misleading. This was a period of militant as well as military communism, symbolized early in 1918 by the change of the party's name from Bolshevik to Communist. At the same time, the capital was shifted from Petrograd, with its exposed location on the western fringe of Russia, to the greater security of Moscow, in the heart of the country.

Flushed with victory in Russia, the Bolsheviks firmly believed that world revolution was about to begin, probably first in Germany, but surely spreading to Britain and even to the United States. This view led the Bolsheviks to hasten the construction of a socialist state in Russia and to take a casual attitude toward their international affairs, since they expected that relations with capitalist states would be very temporary. Although the actions of the Russian government during this period were later described almost apologetically as emergency measures, this is only partly true. Many of the decisions that were taken in part under the spur of military pressure were also regarded as leading to a new society.

A supreme economic council directed the gradual nationalization of industry. Sugar and petroleum came first, and then in June, 1918, a large group including mines, metallurgy, and textiles. By 1920, the state had taken over all enterprises employing more than ten workers (more than five, if motor power was used). The state organized a system of barter, which replaced the free market. Internal trade was illegal; only the government food commissary could buy and sell; money disappeared, as the state took over distribution as well as production. It expropriated the banks, repudiated the tsarist foreign debt, and in effect wiped out savings. Church and State were separated by decree, and judges were removed from office and replaced by appointees of the local soviets.

The government subjected the peasantry to ever more arbitrary and severe requisitioning. It mobilized the poorer peasants against those who were better off, called *kulaks* (from the word meaning "fist" and used to apply to usurers, as if to say "hardfisted"). By calling for a union of the hungry against the well-fed, the regime deliberately, and not for the last time, sowed class hatred in the villages, and stimulated civil war in the countryside. It should be remembered that by western European standards even a Russian *kulak* was often wretchedly poor. The decree forming the first secret police, the "Cheka" (from the initials of the words meaning "extraordinary commission"), was issued in December, 1917, only a few weeks after the revolution and long before any intervention from abroad. Terror became a weapon in the civil war.

Before the communist government could function at all, peace was necessary, as the army had virtually ceased to exist. Negotiations between the Russians and the Germans and Austro-Hungarians at Brest-Litovsk dragged on into 1918, the Russians hoping that revolution would break out in Germany, and the Germans demanding enormous territorial cessions, which they increased as the Russians delayed. Finally, on March 3, 1918, the Russians signed the Peace of Brest-Litovsk, which deprived them of the entire Ukraine, the Baltic provinces, Finland, and some Caucasian lands. It cost Russia one-third of its population, 80 per cent of its iron, and 90 per cent of its coal. Many communists resigned rather than accept the peace, and the Left SR's quit the government. The Germans overran the Ukraine and the Crimea and installed a highly authoritarian regime, against which the communists continued to agitate. The Whites, with German help, put down the Reds in Finland.

Civil War

During the months following Brest-Litovsk, disorder in the countryside as a result of requisitioning and class warfare was swelled by the outbreak of open civil strife. During the war, a brigade had been formed inside Russia of Czechs resident in the country and of deserters from the Habsburg armies. When Russia withdrew from the war, it was decided to send the Czech brigade east across Siberia by rail, and then by ship across the Pacific, through the Panama Canal, and finally west across the Atlantic to France, to fight the Germans there. On the rail trip across Siberia, the Czechs got into a brawl with a trainload of Hungarian prisoners, and one of the Hungarians was killed. This obscure quarrel on a Siberian railway siding between members of the unfriendly races of the Habsburg Empire touched off civil war in Russia. When the Soviet government tried to take reprisals against the Czechs, who numbered fewer than 35,000 men, the Czechs seized a number of towns in western Siberia. The local Soviets were un-

prepared, and the SR's were sympathetic to the Czechs. Local anti-Bolshevik armies came into being. It was under threat from one of them in July, 1918, that a local soviet decided to execute the Tsar and his entire family rather than lose possession of them. All were murdered.

By late June, 1918, the Allies had decided to intervene in Russia on behalf of the opponents of Bolshevism. The withdrawal of Russia from the war had been a heavy blow to them, and they now hoped to re-create a second front against the Germans in the east. The idea of a capitalist "crusade" against Bolshevism, later popularized by Soviet and pro-Soviet historians as the sole motive for the intervention, was in fact much less significant. Yet the Allies had been at war a long time, and their populations were war-weary. So they naturally were apprehensive at the communist efforts to stimulate revolution in all the capitalist nations of the world.

Out at the eastern end of the Trans-Siberian Railroad in Vladivostok, the Czechs overthrew the local soviet in June, 1918, and by early August British, French, Japanese, and American forces had landed. The assignment of the Americans was to occupy Vladivostok and to safeguard railroad communications in the rear of the Czechs. Of the Allies, only the Japanese had long-range territorial ambitions in the area. In effect, the Bolshevik regime had now been displaced in Siberia; the SR's disbanded the soviets and re-established the *zemstvos*, calling for "all power to the constituent assembly." There were three anti-Red governments of varying complexions in three different Siberian centers. Elsewhere, in August, 1918, a small British and American force landed at the White Sea port of Archangel. An SR assassin killed the chief of the Petrograd Cheka, and Lenin himself was wounded.

The regime now sped its military preparations. As Minister of War, Trotsky imposed conscription, and, by a mixture of cajolery and threats of reprisals against their families, secured the services of about 50,000 tsarist officers. The Red Army, which was Trotsky's creation, grew to over 3,000,000 strong by 1920. Its recapture of Kazan and Samara on the Volga in the autumn of 1918 temporarily

Russian territorial losses, Brest-Litovsk, 1918

Boundaries as of 1914

Curzon Line

Boundary between Poland and the U.S.S.R., 1920-1939

Russia in Revolution, 1917-1921

turned the tide in the crisis that seemed about to engulf the Soviet state.

The German collapse on the Western Front permitted the Bolsheviks to repudiate the Treaty of Brest-Litovsk, and to move back into parts of the Ukraine, where they faced the opposition of a variety of local forces. Elsewhere, the opposition consisted of three main armies. General Denikin led an army of Whites, which moved from Rostov-on-Don south across the Caucasus, and received French and British aid. Admiral Kolchak's forces in

409

Trotsky and his staff in Red Square, Moscow.

western Siberia overthrew the SR regime in Omsk, and Kolchak became a virtual dictator. General Yudenich's army, including many former members of the German forces, operated in the Baltic region and threatened Petrograd from the west. Allied unwillingness to negotiate with the Bolsheviks was heightened by the successful Red *coup* of Bela Kun in Hungary (see Chapter 27), which seemed to foreshadow the further spread of revolution.

In the spring of 1919, the Reds defeated Kolchak, and by winter took Omsk. In 1920, the Admiral was arrested and executed. Though the Reds also reconquered the Ukraine, mutinies in their own forces prevented them from consolidating their victories and from moving, as they had hoped to do, across the Russian frontiers and linking up with Bela

Lenin addressing a throng in Moscow's Red Square, 1919.

Kun in Hungary. In the summer of 1919, Denikin took Kiev and struck north, advancing to within two hundred and fifty miles of Moscow itself. But his position was weakened by the repressive character of the regime he brought with him and by his recognition of Kolchak as his superior officer, together with the poor discipline of his troops and his own rivalry with one of his generals, Baron Wrangel. Yudenich advanced to the suburbs of Petrograd, but the Reds by the end of 1919 were able to defeat the White threat everywhere, though Wrangel retained an army in the Crimea. Trotsky now called for the militarization of labor to reconstruct the ravaged country; labor battalions were formed, but recovery was long delayed.

Even after the defeat of the Whites, the Reds in 1920 had to face a new war with the Poles, who hoped to keep Russia weak, and to create an independent Ukraine. After an initial retreat, the Red armies nearly took Warsaw, failing only because the French chief of staff, General Weygand, assisted the Poles. The Reds, eager to finish off the Whites, and persuaded that there was after all no hope for the establishment of a communist regime in Poland, concluded peace in October, 1920. The Poles obtained a large area of territory in White Russia and the western Ukraine. This area was not inhabited by Poles, but had been controlled by Poland down to the eighteenth-century partitions. It lay far to the east of the "Curzon line," the ethnic frontier earlier proposed by the British foreign minister, Lord Curzon. The Reds then turned on Wrangel, who had marched northward from the Crimea and had established a moderate regime in the territory he occupied. He was forced to evacuate, assisted by a French fleet, in November, 1920. The White movement had virtually come to an end.

Why the Counter-Revolution Failed

Many factors accounted for the Whites' failure and the Reds' victory. The Whites could not get together on any political program beyond the mere overthrow of the Reds. They adopted a policy of "non-anticipation," which meant that some future constituent assembly would settle the governmental structure of Russia. Their numbers included everybody from tsarists to SR's, and they disagreed so violently on the proper course for Russia to follow that they could agree only to postpone discussion of these critical problems.

Moreover, their movement was located on the geographical periphery of Russia—in Siberia, in the Crimea, in the Ukraine, in the Caucasus, and in the Baltic. But the Whites never reached an understanding with the non-Russian minorities who lived in these regions. Thus they ignored the highly developed separatist sentiments of the Ukrainians and others, to which the Bolsheviks were temporarily willing to cater.

Furthermore, the Whites could not command the support of the peasantry. Instead of guaranteeing the results of the land division already carried out with Bolshevik sanction, the Whites often restored the landlords and undid the land division. During the civil war, the peasantry on the whole grew sick of both sides. This attitude explains the appearance of anarchist bands, especially in the south. Then too, the Whites simply did not command as much military strength as the Reds, who outnumbered them in manpower, and who had inherited much of the equipment manufactured for the tsarist armies. Holding the central position, the Reds had a unified and skillful command, which could use the railroad network to shift troops rapidly. The Whites, moving in from the periphery, were divided into at least four main groups, and were denied effective use of the railroads.

Finally, the intervention of the Allies on the side of the Whites was ineffectual and amateurish. It may even have harmed the White cause, since the Reds could pose as the national defenders of the country, and could portray the Whites as the hirelings of foreigners. In the light of hindsight, it seems safe to say that either the Allies should have mounted a full-fledged military operation against the Reds, or, if this was impossible (as it probably was, in view of the condition of their own armies after the end of the First World War), they should have stayed out of Russia and allowed the civil war to burn itself out. It is still sometimes argued, however, that, although the Reds won the civil war, the Allied intervention helped keep them so heavily engaged inside Russia that they could not sponsor successful revolutions in other countries. This point of view may well have some justification.

NEP ("The New Economic Policy")

Since 1914, Russia had been deeply involved in fighting and turmoil. By early 1921, with the end of the civil war, famine was raging and sanitation had broken down. Family ties were disrupted, human beings brutalized, and class hatreds released on an unparalleled scale. Industry was producing at a level of about one-eighth of its pre-war output, and agricultural output had decreased by at least 30 per cent. Distribution approached a breakdown. The communist regime appeared to be facing its most serious trial of all: the loss of support in Russia.

A large-scale anarchist peasant revolt broke out in early 1921 and lasted until mid-1922. Lenin remarked that this revolt frightened him more than all the Whites' resistance. But the decisive factor in bringing about a change in policy was the mutiny at the Kronstadt naval base near Petrograd in March, 1921. Formerly a stronghold of Bolshevism, Kronstadt now produced a movement of rebellious anarchists who called for "soviets without communists" to be chosen by universal suffrage and secret ballot, for free speech and free assembly, for the liberation of political prisoners, and for the abolition of requisitioning. Except for the last item and for the phraseology of the first, the program was ironically similar to that of all liberals and socialists in tsarist Russia. The Kronstadt movement seems to have expressed the sentiments of most Russian workers and peasants. Had the government been conciliatory, there might have been no bloodshed; but Trotsky went to war against the rebels, and defeated them after a bloody fight.

This episode led directly to the adoption of the "New Economic Policy," always referred to by its initials as NEP. But the underlying reason for the shift was the need for reconstruction, which seemed attainable only if militant communism were at least temporarily abandoned. Lenin himself referred to "premature" attempts at socialization. It was also necessary to appease the peasants and to ward off any further major uprisings. Finally, the expected world revolution had not come off, and the resources of capitalist states were badly needed to assist Russian reconstruction. The adoption of NEP coincided with the conclusion of an Anglo-Russian trade treaty. Abroad, NEP was hailed as the beginning of a Russian "Thermidor," a return to normality like that following the end of the Terror in the French Revolution (see Chapter 18).

Under NEP the government stopped requisitioning the whole of the peasant's crop above a minimum necessary for subsistence. The peasant had still to pay a very heavy tax in kind, but he was allowed to sell the remainder of his crop and keep the money. The peasant could sell his surplus to the state if he wished, but he could also choose to sell it to a private purchaser. Peasant agriculture became in essence capitalist once more, and the profit motive had reappeared. Lenin imitated Stolypin by guaranteeing the peasant permanency of tenure. The whole system tended to help the *kulak* grow richer and to transform the poor peasant into a hired, landless laborer.

Elsewhere in the economy, under NEP the state retained what Lenin called "the commanding heights" — heavy industry, banking, transportation, and foreign trade. In domestic trade and in light industry, however, private enterprise was once more permitted. This was the so-called "private capital sector" of the economy, in which workers could be paid according to their output, and factory managers could swap some of their products in return for raw materials.

Lenin himself described NEP as a partial return to capitalism, and urged the communists to become good businessmen. Yet NEP was never intended as more than a temporary expedient. Lenin believed that it would take a couple of decades before the Russian peasant could be convinced that co-operative agriculture would be the most efficient. He also argued that a temporary relaxation of government intervention would increase industrial production and give the Russians a useful lesson in entrepreneurship.

Economic recovery was indeed obtained. By 1926–1927, industrial production was back at pre-war levels, although agriculture had not kept pace. But NEP was bitterly disliked by leading communists, who were shocked at the reversal of all the doctrines they believed in. By 1924, private business accounted for 40 per cent of Russian domestic trade, but thereafter the figure fell off. Those who took advantage of the opportunities presented by the NEP were known as NEPmen. They were often persecuted in a petty way by hostile officials, who tried to limit their profits, tax them heavily, and drag them into court on charges of speculation. The *kulak* had essentially the same experience. Thus the government often seemed to be encouraging private enterprise for economic reasons and simultaneously to be discouraging it for political reasons.

Within the Communist party, one group favored the increase of the private sector and the extension of NEP, as a new road toward the socialist goal. These were the so-called "Right deviationists." Their opponents favored the ending of concessions, the liquidation of NEPmen and *kulaks*, and a return to Marxist principles at home and the fostering of world revolution abroad—in short, the pressing of the "socialist offensive." These were the "Left deviationists," who included Trotsky. In the Center stood men who attacked both deviations, the Right as an abandonment of communism, the Left as likely to lead to a disruption of the worker-peasant alliance.

The Struggle for Power: Stalin versus Trotsky

But the NEP question was not the only one to agitate the communist leaders in the early twenties. Lenin suffered two strokes in 1922, and another in 1923, and finally died in January, 1924. During the last two years of his life, he played an ever-lessening role. Involved in the controversy over NEP and the other controversies was the question of the successor to Lenin. Thus an individual communist's answer to the question of how to organize industry, what role to give organized labor, and what relations to maintain with the capitalist world depended not only upon his estimate of the actual situation but also upon his guess as to what answer was likely to be politically advantageous. From this maneuvering the Secretary of the Communist party, Joseph Stalin, was to emerge victorious by 1928.

The years between 1922 and 1928, especially after Lenin's death, were years of a desperate struggle for power between Stalin and Trotsky. Lenin foresaw this struggle with great anxiety. He felt that Trotsky was abler, but feared that he was overconfident, and inclined to make decisions on his own. He felt that Stalin had concentrated enormous power in his hands, in his role as party secretary, and feared that he did not know how to use it. When he learned that Stalin had gone counter to his orders in smashing the Menshevik Republic of Georgia instead of reaching an accommodation with its leaders, he wrote angrily in his testament that Stalin was too rude, and that his fellows should remove him from his post as general secretary. At the moment of his death, Lenin had published a scathing attack on Stalin, had broken off relations with him, and was about to try to relegate him to the scrapheap. Trotsky's suggestion that Stalin poisoned Lenin is not based on any evidence, but it is clear that Lenin's death rescued Stalin's career, and that, far from being the chosen heir, as he later claimed, he did not enjoy Lenin's confidence at the end.

During these years, Trotsky argued for a more highly trained managerial force in industry, and for economic planning as an instrument that the state could use to control and direct social change. He favored the mechanization of agriculture and the weakening of peasant individualism by encouraging rural co-operatives, with even a hint of the collective farms where groups of peasants, in theory, would own everything collectively, rather than individually. As Trotsky progressively lost power, he championed the right of individual communists to criticize the regime. He referred to the policies of Stalin and his other increasingly powerful enemies as "bureaucratic degeneration," and came to the conclusion that only through the outbreak of revolutions in other countries could the Russian socialist revolution be carried to its proper conclusion. Only if the industrial output and technical skills of the advanced western countries could be put at the disposal of communism could Russia hope to achieve its own socialist revolution. This is the famous theory that socialism cannot succeed within the boundaries of one country. Either world revolution must break out, or Russian socialism is doomed to inevitable failure.

The opponents of Trotsky's "left deviation" found their chief spokesman in Nikolai Bukharin. A man who never held such responsible administrative posts as Lenin or Trotsky or Stalin, and who had often shifted his position on major questions, Bukharin none the less took a consistent line during these years; as editor of *Pravda*, he was extremely influential. A strong defender of NEP, Bukharin softened the rigorous Marxist doctrine of the class struggle by arguing that, since the proletarian state controlled the commanding heights of big capital, socialism was sure of success. This view is not unlike the "gradualist" position taken by western European Social Democrats. Bukharin did not believe in an ambitious program of rapid industrialization; he favored co-operatives, but opposed collectives. In foreign affairs he was eager to co-operate abroad with non-communist groups who might be useful to Russia. Thus he sponsored Soviet collaboration with Chiang Kai-shek in China and with the German Social Democrats.

In his rise to power, Stalin used Bukharin's arguments to discredit Trotsky and to eliminate him. Then, partly because Bukharin's policies were failing, Stalin adopted many of Trotsky's policies, and eliminated Bukharin. Original Stalinist ideas, however, developed during this process. Stalin was not basically an intellectual or a theoretician; he

was a party organization stalwart. He adopted theoretical positions partly because they seemed to him the ones most likely to work, and partly because he was charting his own course to supreme power. He came to favor rapid industrialization, and to understand that this meant an unprecedentedly heavy capital investment. At the end of 1927, he suddenly shifted from his previous position on the peasantry, and openly sponsored collectivization. This shift arose because of his concern that agricultural production was not keeping pace with industry. He declared that the balance could be redressed only if agriculture, like industry, was transformed into a series of large-scale unified enterprises.

In answer to Trotsky's argument that socialism in one country was impossible, Stalin maintained that an independent socialist state could exist. This view did not at all imply the abandonment of the goal of world revolution, as has often been thought. Stalin always maintained that the socialist state (Russia) should be the center of inspiration and assistance to

Lenin and Stalin in 1923.

communist movements everywhere; Russia would help them and they would help Russia. But, in his view, during the interim period before the communists had won elsewhere, it was perfectly possible for Russia to exist as the only socialist state, and indeed to grow more socialist all the time. In international relations, this doctrine of Stalin made it possible for the Soviet Union to pursue either a policy of "peaceful coexistence" with capitalist states, when that seemed most profitable, or a policy of militant support of communist revolution everywhere, when that seemed most profitable. Stalin's "socialism in one country" also struck a responsive chord in the rank and file of Russian communists, who were disappointed in the failure of revolutions elsewhere. It also meant that Russia, not the West, was to be the center of the new society. Stalin's doctrine reflected his own Russian nationalism rather than the more cosmopolitan and more western views of Trotsky.

The Struggle for Power: Stalin's Victory

Analysis of the rival theories competing for acceptance in Russia in the twenties helps explain the alternatives before the communist leadership. It does not explain how Stalin won. To understand this, we must move from the realm of theory and political platforms to the realm of practice and political power. At the end of the civil war, Stalin was Commissar of Nationalities. In this post, he dealt with the affairs of 65,000,000 of the 140,000,000 inhabitants of the new Russian Soviet Republic. He managed the destiny of the Asians, whom he, as one of them, understood. Their local Bolshevik leaders became his men; where they did not, as in his native Georgia, he ruthlessly crushed them. Though a Georgian, he identified himself with Russian nationalism in the interests of a centralized Bolshevik state.

It was Stalin who took charge of creating the new Asian "republics," which enjoyed the appearance of local self-government, programs of economic and educational improvement,

and a chance to use their local languages and develop their own cultures. It was he who in 1922 proposed and guided the adoption of a new Union of Socialist Soviet Republics as a substitute for the existing federation of republics. In the U.S.S.R., Moscow would control war, foreign policy, trade, and transport, and would co-ordinate finance, economy, food, and labor. And on paper it would leave to the republics home affairs, justice, education, and agriculture. A Council of Nationalities, with an equal number of delegates from each ethnic group, would join the Supreme Soviet as a second chamber, thus forming the Central Executive Committee, which would appoint the Council of People's Commissars —the Government. Stalin regarded this reform as an achievement equal to Trotsky's military organizational work during the civil war.

Stalin was also Commissar of the Workers' and Peasants' Inspectorate. Here his duties were to eliminate inefficiency and corruption from every branch of the civil service, and to train a new corps of civil servants. His teams moved freely through all the offices of the government, observing and recommending changes, inspecting and criticizing. In creating this post, Lenin had hoped to clean house, but the ignorance and the lack of tradition that rendered the tsarist and Bolshevik civil service incompetent and corrupt operated in Stalin's Inspectorate as well. Although the Inspectorate could not do what it was established to do, it did perform another role. It gave Stalin control over the machinery of government. Lenin attacked Stalin's work in the Inspectorate just before he died, but by then it was too late.

Stalin was also a member of the Politbureau, the tight little group of party bosses elected by the Central Committee, which included only five men throughout the civil war. Here his job was day-to-day management of the party. He was the only permanent liaison officer between the Politbureau and the Orgbureau, which allocated party personnel to their various duties, in factory, office, or army unit. In addition to these posts, Stalin became general secretary of the party's Central Committee in 1922. Here he prepared the agenda

The exiled Trotsky and his wife arriving in Mexico, 1937.

for Politbureau meetings, supplied the documentation for points under debate, and passed the decisions down to the lower levels. He controlled party patronage—that is to say, all party appointments, promotions, and demotions. He saw to it that local trade unions, co-operatives, and army units were put under communist bosses responsible to him. He had files on the loyalty and achievement of all managers of industry and other party members. In 1921, a Central Control Commission, which could expel party members for unsatisfactory conduct, was created; Stalin, as liaison between this commission and the Central Committee, now virtually controlled the purges, which were designed to keep the party pure.

In a centralized one-party state, a man of Stalin's ambitions who held so many key positions had an enormous advantage in the struggle for power. Yet the state was so new, the positions were so much less conspicuous and so much more humdrum than the Ministry of War, for instance, held by Trotsky, and Stalin's manner was so generally conciliatory, that the likelihood of Stalin's success did not become evident until it was too late to stop him. Inside the Politbureau he formed a

three-man team with two other prominent Bolshevik leaders, the demagogue, Zinoviev, and the expert on doctrine, Kamenev. Zinoviev was chairman of the Petrograd Soviet and boss of the Communist International; Kamenev was Lenin's deputy and president of the Moscow Soviet. All three were old Bolsheviks, in contrast to Trotsky, who had been a Menshevik and an independent member of the intelligentsia.

The combination of Stalin, Zinoviev, and Kamenev proved unbeatable. The three put down all real and imagined plots against them by the use of the secret police. They resisted Trotsky's demands for "reform," which would have democratized the party to some degree, and would have strengthened his position while weakening Stalin's. They initiated the cult of Lenin immediately before his death, and kept it burning fiercely thereafter, so that any suggestion for change coming from Trotsky seemed almost an act of impiety. They dispersed Trotsky's followers by sending them to posts abroad. They prevented the publication of Lenin's "testament," so that the rank and file of the party would not know about Lenin's doubts concerning Stalin. They publicized all Trotsky's earlier statements in opposition to Lenin, and did not hesitate to "revise" history in order to belittle Trotsky. They were confident, and rightly so, that Trotsky was too good a communist to rally around him such anti-Bolshevik groups as old Mensheviks, SR's, and NEPmen.

Early in 1925, Stalin and his allies were able to force the resignation of Trotsky as Minister of War. Soon thereafter the three-man team dissolved; Stalin moved into alliance with Bukharin and other right-wing members of the Politbureau, to which he began to appoint some of his own followers. Using all his accumulated power, he beat his former allies on all questions of policy, and in 1926 they moved into a new but powerless alliance with Trotsky. Stalin now (1926) deposed Zinoviev from the Politbureau, charging him with intriguing in the army. Trotsky was the next one to be expelled from the Politbureau, and Zinoviev was ousted as president of the Comintern.

In 1927, differences of opinion over Stalin's foreign policy in England and in China (see p. 429) led to public protests by the opposition. And these in turn led to the expulsion of the opposition from the party itself. Refusing to renounce his views, Trotsky was deported to Siberia, the first stage in a long exile that took him to Turkey, Norway, and Mexico, where he died in 1940 at the hands of an assassin armed with an ice-axe. The others recanted and obtained a new lease on life. Stalin's victory was virtually complete.

IV   Stalin's Supremacy: Russian Internal Affairs, 1928–1941

The Communist party congress that expelled Trotsky in December, 1927, also brought NEP to an end, and proclaimed that the new "socialist offensive" would begin in 1928. The thirteen years between 1928 and 1941 were to see almost incredible changes in the domestic life of Russia—collectivized agriculture, speedy industrialization, forced labor, the great purges and the extermination of all political opposition, the building of an authoritarian state apparatus, and a "retreat" to bourgeois standards in almost every department of social and intellectual life.

Collectivized Agriculture

In 1928, the failure of the peasants to deliver to the cities as much grain as had been required seemed to underline the dangers inherent in the land divisions of 1917 and in the concessions of NEP. Farm productivity on the small individual holdings was not high enough to feed the city population. Food prices for the workers were high, yet the *kulaks* wanted further concessions. Grain was hoarded. Stalin had often inveighed against "fanning the class struggle in the countryside," and had denied the intention of collectivizing agriculture rapidly or on a mass scale. The government economic plan issued during 1928 set a figure of 20 per cent of Russian farms as the *maximum* to be collectivized by 1933. Yet during 1929, Stalin embarked on immediate full-scale collectivization, declared war on the *kulaks*, and virtually put an end to individual farming in Russia.

The government did not have the money or the credit to import food. Furthermore, no governmental machinery is adequate to force peasants to disgorge crops that they are hiding. Therefore, the government enlisted on its side the small peasants; in exchange for their assistance in locating and turning over the *kulaks'* crops, they promised them a place on a collective farm, to be made up of the *kulaks'* land and equipped with the *kulaks'* implements. Probably a good many of the subsistence farmers (about 20 per cent of the number of private farms, possibly 5,000,000 households) more or less welcomed this opportunity. Initial encouraging reports led Stalin to go full speed ahead. The *kulaks,* he declared in late 1929, were to be liquidated as a class. There were about 2,000,000 households of them, perhaps as many as 10,000,000 people in all. They were now to be totally expropriated, and at the same time barred from the new collectives. Since no provision was made for them, this move turned collectivization into a nightmare.

Peasants now were machine-gunned into submission; *kulaks* were deported to forced labor camps or to desolate regions in Siberia. In desperate revolt against the command to join collectives, the peasants burned crops, broke plows, and killed their cattle rather than turn them over to the state. More than half the horses in all Russia, 45 per cent of the cattle, and two-thirds of the sheep and goats were slaughtered. Russian livestock has never since caught up with the losses it suffered because of the excesses of collectivization. Land lay uncultivated, and over the next few years famine took a toll of millions of lives. As early as March, 1930, Stalin showed that he was aware of the ghastly mistakes he had made. In a famous statement on "dizziness with success," he put the blame on local officials who had been too eager to rush through the program. By contradicting his own orders of a few months before, he managed to escape some of the hatred that would otherwise have been directed at him. As usual, many Russian peasants disliked the man they could see, the local official, and were willing to exculpate the "little father" in the capital.

Fifty per cent of Russian farms had been hastily thrown together into collectives during this frightful year. Only an additional 10 per cent were added during the next three years, so that by 1933 60 per cent in all had been collectivized. The number rose again later in the 1930's, until by 1939 more than 96 per cent of Russian farms were collectivized. In 1941, there were 250,000 collectives, 900,000,000 acres in extent, supporting 19,000,000 families. Yet the excesses of the early "dizziness with success" were never repeated.

The 1930's also brought a modification of the original rules governing collectives. Originally, collectives had been of two main types: the *sovkhoz*, or soviet farm, not strictly a collective at all but a state-owned enterprise, operated by the government and worked by hired laborers who were government employees; and the *kolkhoz*, or collective farm proper. The *sovkhozes* were designed as centers of government research and development in agriculture, and were often very large in size. But they were mostly brought to an end by Stalin in the 1930's, when he ordered some forty million acres originally allotted to them to be distributed among the *kolkhozes*. As of 1941, the *sovkhozes* occupied no significant area of land.

The *kolkhoz* itself was also originally of two types: the commune, in which all the resources of the members without exception were owned together, and the *artel*, or co-operative, in which a certain amount of private property was permitted to the members. After Stalin's modifications of the system in the thirties, the *artel* became the overwhelmingly predominant

form of collective farm. In an *artel*, each family owned its homestead, some livestock, and minor implements; these could be left by will to the owner's descendants. But most of the work was done on the collectively operated land. Each collective had its own managing board, responsible to the government, which supervised the work of the peasants, who were organized in brigades, each under a brigadier. Like factory laborers paid on a "piece-work" basis, peasants were remunerated according to their output, which was measured by the artificial unit of the "labor day." One day's work in managing a farm might be, for example, assessed at three labor days, while one day's work weeding a vegetable patch might be assessed at only half a labor day.

Each *kolkhoz* turned over to the government a fixed amount of produce at fixed rates, and the total of all these amounts was designed to guarantee the feeding of the urban population, especially workers in heavy industry and members of the Red Army. In addition, the *kolkhoz* paid further taxes to cover government expenses for local construction and education. Any surplus might be sold by the peasant directly to the consumer, without the participation of any middleman. Private resale was regarded as speculation, and was subject to punishment. After 1934, the government obtained at least two-thirds of its revenue by the resale on the markets at a large profit of farm produce bought at low fixed prices from the *kolkhoz*. This government profit was known as the "turnover tax."

The government assisted and controlled the *kolkhoz* through the supply of mechanical equipment furnished by the Machine Tractor Stations. The collectives could not own their own tractors, but rented them from the stations, paying in exchange a fee ranging up to perhaps 20 per cent of the crop. The stations became important centers for political surveillance. By the decision when and to whom to allot tractors, and how many tractors to allot, administrators of the Machine Tractor Stations could directly affect the success of a collective; their good will was therefore of the utmost importance to the management.

In general, the aim of collectivization was to reorganize farming so as to ensure food for the industrial labor force, which was being increased by recruitment from the farms themselves. Collectivization certainly increased the total food supplies at the disposal of the government, and released farmers for work in industry. But it seems certain that the over-all rise in agricultural production was small, and that in many cases the yield per unit decreased.

Industrialization

Intimately related to the drive in agriculture was the drive in industry. Here, too, Stalin originally had viewed with scorn the grandiose plans of the "superindustrializers," and as late as 1927 had proposed an annual increase rate in industrial production of only 15 per cent. But just as he shifted to the frantic pace of col-lectivizing agriculture, so he first gradually, then suddenly, shifted to forced draft in industry also.

In 1928 began the era of the Five-Year Plans, each setting ambitious goals for production over the next five years. In 1929 and 1930, Stalin appropriated ever higher sums for capital investment, and in June, 1930, he declared that industrial production must rise by 50 per cent in the current year, a fantastic and impossible figure. Under the First Five-Year Plan, adopted in 1928, annual pig-iron production was scheduled to rise from 3,500,000 tons to 10,000,000 tons by 1932, but in that year Stalin demanded 17,000,000 tons instead. It was not forthcoming, of course, but Stalin's demand for it was symptomatic of the pace at which he was striving to transform Russia from an agricultural to an industrial country.

Part of the reason for this rapid pace lay precisely in the collectivization drive itself.

Charcoal-burning or wood-burning tractors at a Machine Tractor Station, 1939.

Large-scale farming, to which Stalin was committing Russia, must be mechanized farming. Yet there were only 7,000 tractors in all Russia at the end of 1928. Stalin secured 30,000 more during 1929, but this was nowhere near a beginning. Industry had to produce millions of machines, and the gasoline to run them. Since the countryside had to be electrified, power stations were needed by the thousands. And literally millions and millions of peasants had to be taught how to handle machinery. But there was nobody to teach them, and no factories to produce the machinery. The output of raw materials was inadequate, and the plants to process them were not there.

Another part of the reason for the drive to industrialize lay in the tenets of Marxism itself. Russia had defied all Marx's predictions by staging a proletarian revolution in a country almost without a proletariat. Yet despite the communists' initial political successes, Stalin felt that "capitalism had a firmer basis than communism in Russia, so long as it remained a country of small peasants." The communists felt that the world proletariat expected them to industrialize Russia, but even more they were determined to create as a support for themselves the massive Russian proletariat which as yet did not exist. Furthermore, Stalin was determined to make Russia as nearly self-sufficient as possible, in line with his theory of socialism in one country. Underlying this was a motive at least as intense as any dictated by Marxist doctrine—Russian nationalism.

The strength of this motive is revealed in a speech that Stalin made in 1931:

To slacken the pace means to lag behind, and those who lag behind are beaten. We do not want to be beaten. No, we don't want to. . . . Old Russia . . . was ceaselessly beaten for her backwardness. She was beaten by the Mongol Khans, she was beaten by Turkish Beys, she was beaten by Swedish feudal lords, she was beaten by Polish-Lithuanian gentry, she was beaten by Anglo-French capitalists, she was beaten by Japanese barons; she was beaten by all—for her backwardness. For military backwardness, for cultural backwardness, for political backwardness, for industrial backwardness, for agricultural backwardness. She was beaten because to beat her was profitable and went unpunished. . . . We are fifty or a hundred years behind the advanced countries. We must make good this lag in ten years. Either we do it or they crush us.*

Whatever one may think of this quotation as history (and it omits all Russia's *victorious* wars), it reveals that Russian national self-interest as interpreted by Stalin required the most rapid possible industrialization. And it is of interest that ten years afterward the Germans did attack, something Stalin could of course not have predicted so accurately, but something that he seems to have sensed.

Stalin seems also to have felt that he had only to keep a fierce pressure on the management of industry, and the desired commodities and finished goods would be forthcoming in the desired quantities. The goals of the First Five-Year Plan were not attained, although fulfillment was announced in 1932. Immediately, the second plan, prepared by the state planning commission, went into effect, and ran until 1937; the third was interrupted only by Hitler's invasion. Each time the emphasis was on the elements of heavy industry—steel, electric power, cement, coal, oil. Between 1928 and 1940, steel production was multiplied by four and one-half, electric power by eight, cement by more than two, coal by four, and oil by almost three. Similar developments took place in chemicals and in machine production. Railroad construction was greatly increased, and the volume of freight carried quadrupled with the production of new rolling stock.

By 1940, Russian output was approaching that of Germany, although Russian efficiency and the Russian standard of living were far lower. What the rest of Europe had done in about seventy-five years Russia had done in about twelve. Enthusiasm was artificially whipped up by wide publicizing of the high output of individual workers called "Stakhanovites," after a coal miner who had set production records. "Stakhanovites" and "heroes of labor" were richly rewarded, and

---

*Quoted in Isaac Deutscher, *Stalin* (New York, 1950), 328.

the others were urged to imitate them in "socialist competition."

All this was achieved at the expense of dreadful hardships, yet eyewitnesses report that many of the workers were as enthusiastic as if they had been soldiers in battle, as indeed in a sense they were. Valuable machinery was often damaged or destroyed by inexperienced workers right off the farm. The problems of repair, of replacement, of achieving balance between the output and consumption of raw materials, of housing workers in the new centers, of moving entire industries thousands of miles into the Ural region and Siberia, were unending and cost untold numbers of lives. An American eyewitness estimates that Russia's "battle of ferrous metallurgy alone involved more casualties than the battle of the Marne."

Administratively, the Russian economy was directly run by the state. The Gosplan, or state planning commission, drew up the Five-Year Plans and supervised their fulfillment at the management level. The Gosbank, or state bank, regulated the investment of capital. An economic council administered the work of various agencies. Its major divisions were metallurgy and chemistry (iron and steel, non-ferrous metals, chemicals, rubber, alcohol); defense (aviation, armaments, munitions, tanks, ships); machinery (heavy machines, medium machines, machine tools, electrical industry); fuel and power (coal, oil, electric power); agriculture and procurement; and consumer's goods (grain, meat and dairy products, fisheries, textiles, light industry). Under iron and steel, for example, there functioned the production trusts controlling their own mines as well as blast furnaces and rolling mills. These were the so-called "combinats," or great production complexes like that at Magnitogorsk in the Urals. In each plant, as in each collective, the manager was responsible for producing the quota set for him within the maximum cost allowed him. He was consulted on production targets, and had considerable leeway in selecting his staff and allocating labor and raw materials. He was bound to render a rigid accounting to the government, which of course fixed the price he must pay for his raw materials.

The Social Impact

The social effects of the economic program were dramatic. Urban population rose from about 18 per cent in 1926 to about 33 per cent in 1940. The number of cities with a population between 50,000 and 100,000 doubled, and the number of cities with a population exceeding 100,000 more than quadrupled. The largest cities, Moscow and Leningrad (the new name for Petersburg-Petrograd after the death of Lenin), almost doubled in size, and among smaller cities, to take just one example, Alma Ata in Siberia grew from 45,000 to 230,000 between 1928 and 1939. The entire social picture was radically altered.

The relative freedom to choose one's job which had characterized the NEP period disappeared. Individual industrial enterprises signed labor contracts with the *kolkhozes* by which the *kolkhoz* was obliged to send a given number of farm workers to the factories, often against their will. Peasants who had resisted collectivization were drafted into labor camps. In the factories, the trade unions became simply another organ of the state. The chief role of the unions was to achieve maximum production and efficiency, to discourage absenteeism and poor work. Trade unions might not strike, or engage in conflict with management. All they could do was administer the social insurance laws and seek improvements in workers' living conditions by negotiation.

Thus in the U.S.S.R. the old privileged classes of noble landlords, already weak at the time of the revolution, ceased to exist. The industrial, commercial, and financial bourgeoisie, which was just coming into its own at the time of the revolution, was destroyed after 1928, despite the temporary reprieve it had experienced under NEP. Most of the old intelligentsia, who had favored a revolution, could not in the end stomach Stalin's dictatorship, and many of them emigrated. Of the million and a half émigrés from Russia after the revolution, only a very small number (contrary to the general view in the West) were cousins of the Tsar. Those of the old intelligentsia who remained were forced into line with the new Soviet intelligentsia, which Stalin felt to be a very important class. All were compelled to accept the new Stalinist dogma and to drop their interest in the outside world. The new intelligentsia was expected to concentrate on technical advance, and on new administrative devices for speeding up the transformation of the country.

Although the effect of these social changes would presumably have been to level all ranks, Stalin set himself against the old Bolshevik principles of equality. The Marxist slogan, "From each according to his capacity, to each according to his needs," was shelved in favor of a new one, "From each according to his capacity, to each according to his work." Where Lenin had allowed none of the members of the government to earn more than a skilled laborer, Stalin set up a new system of incentives. A small minority of bureaucrats and skilled laborers, factory managers, and successful *kolkhoz* bosses earned vastly more than the great majority of unskilled laborers and peasants. Together with the writers, artists, musicians, and entertainers who were willing to lend their talents to the services of the régime, these men became a new élite, separated by a wide economic and social gulf from the toiling masses. They had a vested interest in furthering a regime to which they owed everything, and without which they would be nothing.

Soviet propagandists declared that this was a temporary situation. They described the present society in the Soviet Union as "socialist," while regarding "communism," not yet achieved, as the goal toward which the U.S.S.R. was still moving. Yet, just as the "withering away" of the state, which the Marxists predicted, was instead replaced under Stalin by the enormous swelling of state power and state machinery, so the equality predicted by the Marxists was replaced by a new caste system. The means of production were publicly owned in the Soviet Union, as the Marxists had urged. But the power of the state, the birth of a new élite, the brutalization of millions of human beings, and the ruthless use of force after the

revolution had been achieved were all the contributions of Stalin.

The Purge Trials

Stalin's program was not achieved without opposition. The crisis of 1931 and 1932, when industrial goals were not being met, and starvation swept the countryside, created discontent inside the regime as well as outside. A small number of officials circulated memoranda advocating Stalin's deposition as General Secretary, an act which the party had every right to perform. Stalin jailed them for conspiracy, and one leading Bolshevik committed suicide. It is widely believed that Stalin's own wife reproached him at this time with the ravages that the terror was working, and that she too committed suicide. At one moment, but only at one, we are told, Stalin's self-confidence wavered and he offered to resign, but nobody in the Politbureau dared accept the offer, and the moment quickly passed. His attack against those he believed to be his enemies took the form of the famous purges, which began in 1934 and continued at intervals until 1938.

These purges remain the most mysterious episode in Soviet history. They are often compared with the Jacobin Terror of the French Revolution, when the revolution "devoured its children." But, in contrast to the rapid appearance of the Terror in France, the purges did not begin for seventeen years after the Russian Revolution. Members of the opposition had been demoted, expelled from the party, and even exiled, as in the case of Trotsky, but nobody had been executed. There is an entirely credible story that the Bolshevik leaders had agreed among themselves early in their career never to start guillotining each other. Yet, when the terror began in Russia, it was even more drastic than it had been in France. Moreover, unlike Robespierre, Stalin managed to survive.

From exile, Trotsky continued to attack Stalin in a journal called *The Bulletin of the Opposition*. Clever as always, he scored telling points against Stalin, and his words were carefully read by Soviet officials. Yet the older generation of communists, though they may have hated Stalin, made no move against him. A younger group, however, seemingly more restless and convinced that Stalin had abandoned Lenin's program, found the model for conspiracy in the heroes of the terrorist movement who had assassinated Alexander II (see Chapter 22). They were apparently prepared to use terrorism against Stalin and his henchmen. Even within the Politbureau men loyal to Stalin grew restless at his ruthlessness, and urged him to relax the pressure; Sergei Kirov, boss of Leningrad, took the lead.

Stalin at times seemed to yield to this urging, as when he ordered more gentle treatment for rebellious *kulaks* in June, 1932, and limited the powers of the political police. But at other times he seemed to be taking the opposite course, as when he issued a decree making an entire family responsible for the treason of any of its members. On the whole, however, tension relaxed during 1932–1934. Kirov proclaimed a new era of lenience at a party conference, and former leaders of the opposition, including Bukharin, were appointed to help draft a new and liberal constitution.

Then on December 1, 1934, Kirov was assassinated by a young terrorist communist in Leningrad. Although the story that Stalin himself had plotted the assassination cannot be confirmed, it is clear that Stalin now determined to strike at the opposition. The assassin was executed. Accused of complicity, Zinoviev and Kamenev were jailed, and forced to admit that they had plotted to restore capitalism. Yet the drafting of the new "democratic" constitution went on. Stalin became ever more withdrawn, ever more autocratic, ever more resolved to destroy the old Bolsheviks, as Ivan the Terrible had destroyed the old nobility. After an interlude during 1935 and early 1936, during which Stalin said that "life had become more joyous," the purges proper began.

The official story was that Trotskyite agitation abroad was linked with the murder of Kirov, and with the alleged plans for the murder of Stalin. A series of public political trials took place. In the first (1936), Zinoviev, Kamenev, and fourteen others admitted these charges and were executed. In the second (1937), seventeen other leading Bolsheviks declared that they had knowledge of a conspiracy between Trotsky and the German and Japanese intelligence service, by which Russian territory was to be transferred to Germany and Japan. All were executed. Then (June 1937) came the secret liquidation of the top commanders in the Red Army, who were ac-

Factory workers listening to an engineer read the charge made by Vishinsky against the "Anti-Soviet right-Trotskyist bloc" during the purge trials of 1937.

cused of conspiring with "an unfriendly foreign power" (Germany) with a view to sabotage. All were executed after an announcement that they had confessed. The last of the public trials took place in March, 1938, as twenty-one leading Bolsheviks, including Bukharin, confessed to similar charges and were executed.

But these public trials and the secret trial of the generals give only a faint idea of the extent of the purge. Every member of Lenin's Politbureau except Stalin and Trotsky was either killed or committed suicide to avoid execution. Two vice-commissars of foreign affairs and most of the ambassadors of the diplomatic corps, fifty of the seventy-one members of the Central Committee of the Communist party, almost all the military judges who had sat in judgment and had condemned the generals, two successive heads of the secret police, themselves the leaders in the previous purges, the prime ministers and chief officials of all the non-Russian Soviet Republics—all were killed or vanished. A list of those who disappeared reads like a "who's who" of high officialdom in state and party throughout the twenties and thirties. Literally thousands were executed or disappeared without a trace. The public trials probably included only those who were willing to confess, whether guilty or not. The rest were condemned privately and quite without due process of law.

Although it is clear that many of those who were executed opposed Stalin, the charges against them were certainly not true. Had they been true, the great conspiracy involving almost everybody but Stalin himself would surely have accomplished more than the assassination of Kirov. It is altogether unlikely that any of the top communists conspired with Hitler, little though they loved Stalin. Some who confessed may have felt so great a loyalty to the cause of communism, however perverted, that they sacrificed themselves for Stalin's soviet state. Some doubtless hoped to save their families, or even themselves, and a few leaders were spared the death penalty to encourage confessions from the others. Many may have hoped that the confessions were so ridiculous that nobody could believe them.

What Stalin apparently wanted was to destroy utterly all possibility of future conspiracies. So he trumped up charges against anybody who conceivably could become a member of a regime that might replace his own. Despite the enormous upheaval of the purges, no breakdown took place in the state. New bureaucrats were found to take the places of the old. The new Stalin-trained officials, uncultivated but competent, now manned all top-level positions.

The Authoritarian State

In the midst of the purges, in 1936, Stalin proclaimed the new constitution, the "most democratic in the world." By its provisions nobody was disfranchised, as priests and members of the former nobility and bourgeoisie had previously been. Civil liberties were extended, but even on paper these were never more than a sham, since the constitution provided that they could be modified in the "interest of the toilers." The fact that the U.S.S.R. was a one-party state prevented elections from being anything but an expression of unanimity. The right to nominate candidates for the Supreme Soviet belonged to Communist party organizations, trade unions, co-operatives, youth groups, and cultural societies; but all were completely dominated by the party. The party picked the candidates, and no more than one for each post was ever presented to the voters. The party controlled the soviets, and the party hierarchy and government hierarchy overlapped and interlocked.

Every citizen was eligible for membership in the party on application to a local branch, which voted on his application after a year of trial. Communist children's organizations fed the youth groups, which in turn fed the party. The party was organized both territorially and functionally in pyramidal form, with organizations at the bottom level in factory, farm, and government office. These were grouped together by rural or urban local units, and these in turn by regional and territorial conferences and congresses. The party organizations elected the All-Union party congress, which selected the Central Committee of the party, and which was in theory the highest policy-making organ, though actually no party congress was held between 1939 and 1954. The Central Committee selected the Politbureau. At each level of the party pyramid there were organizations for agitation and propaganda, for organization and instruction, for military and political training. The party exercised full control over the government, which simply enacted formally what the party had decided upon. The Five-Year Plans, for example, were party programs that went into effect even before they were formally adopted by the government.

The highest organ of the government was the Supreme Soviet, made up of two houses — a Soviet of the Union, based on population, and a Soviet of Nationalities, elected according to national administrative divisions. In theory, the Supreme Soviet was elected for a term of four years. The Supreme Soviet itself did little; it appointed a presidium which issued the decrees and carried on the work of the Supreme Soviet between sessions. It also appointed the Council of Ministers (long called the Council of People's Commissars). This cabinet, rather than the Supreme Soviet or its presidium, enacted most of the legislation, and was thus the legislative as well as the executive organ of the Russian state. The chairmanship of the Council of People's Commissars, the chairmanship of the Politbureau, and the General Secretariat of the Communist party were all posts held by Stalin, who in addition served as Commissar of Defense, chief of the State Defense Council, which ran the country during wartime, and Generalissimo. Similar overlapping of party and government posts was the regular practice.

In 1924, Stalin's constitutional reform had created the new Union of Soviet Socialist Republics, including the enormously large Russian Federative Republic, the Ukraine, White Russia, Georgia, Armenia, and Azerbaidjan, and three central Asian Soviet Socialist republics: Uzbekistan, Turkmenistan, and Tadjikistan. In 1936, Kazakh and Kirghiz republics were added, making a total of eleven. As a result of the annexations of the Baltic states and

of Finnish and Rumanian territory in 1940, five more republics were created: Lithuania, Latvia, Estonia, Karelia, and Moldavia. These sixteen "Union" republics differed widely in population. Within the huge Russian republic were sixteen "autonomous" republics, and numerous other subdivisions, all called "autonomous." The larger SSR's had similar subdivisions.

Each of the Union republics and autonomous republics had a government patterned exactly on that of the Soviet Union, except that the supreme soviet of each republic was unicameral and not bicameral, since it lacked a chamber of nationalities. Many complaints have been heard in recent years about the way in which "Great-Russian chauvinism" has permeated official policy toward the individual minority republics. Although this soviet descendant of tsarist Russification policy has always been a menace, it is widely believed that in the years before World War II, the chief objective was not to try to Russify the nationalities but to communize them. With this end in view, the party permitted and encouraged local nationalities to revive their culture, study their past traditions, and use their own language. Like every other cultural manifestation permitted in the U.S.S.R., these national cultural achievements were "managed." Not only was it impossible for anti-Soviet or anti-communist material to appear in print or in any of the plastic arts, but, as everywhere, all artistic effort was closely supervised and had to serve the regime positively. The value of "cultural autonomy" under these circumstances is of course highly debatable.

Although the Stalin constitution specifically gave each republic the right to secede, this provision was pure window-dressing. The central government was overpoweringly stronger than the government of any one republic, which in any case was often not even made up of natives. Although each of the sixteen republics was in 1944 given its own foreign office by an amendment to the constitution, this amendment was never intended to give them autonomy in this critically important field. Actually, it seems simply to have been a device for securing representation of the Ukraine and White Russia in the United Nations. The representatives of these two republics to the United Nations have never been anything but extra Soviet delegates; the first Ukrainian delegate to the U.N. was not even a Ukrainian, but a Russian who was once Soviet ambassador to the independent Ukraine of the revolutionary era.

The Russian Thermidor?

The period between 1934 and 1941, notable for the purges and for the constitutional development of Stalin's one-party state, is also called by many shrewd observers of revolutions the true Russian "Thermidor," as distinct from NEP. The term "Thermidor" has come to mean a period in which a revolution has burnt itself out, and the prevailing mood shifts from messianic enthusiasm to one of desire for normality. In revolutionary France, the shift was signalized by the fall of Robespierre and the Jacobin régime, and the advent of the Directory, a different government with different objectives, policies, and personnel, which was in turn succeeded by Napoleon's dictatorship (see Chapter 18). In the U.S.S.R., the striking fact was that Stalin stayed in office throughout. He was in effect the Russian Robespierre, Directory, and Napoleon all rolled into one. If we accept the parallel, the Russian Thermidor was a managed and manipulated Thermidor, involving no real liberalization of the regime or relaxation of controls. Yet perhaps the parallel is not entirely valid, since Stalin resembled Napoleon far more than he did the weak Directory.

In any case, the period of the late 1930's saw a wholesale retreat from many ideas of the revolution. Simultaneously with the purges and the new constitution, the bread ration was raised; the *kolkhoz* was reformed to permit the individual farmer to own his homestead; new medals and titles were awarded to leading workers in plants, and to scientists, engineers, and military men. In the Red Army, traditional tsarist distinctions between officers and men were restored, and marshals were named for

the first time. Thus, without relaxing political control, Stalin introduced an element of relaxation into the daily life of the rank and file, at the very height of his Terror. The standard of living went up, as the production of consumer's goods was encouraged, and as workers were invited to spend their earnings on little luxuries previously unavailable.

Simultaneously, the state rediscovered Russia's great past. The standard communist teaching had been that proletarians have no fatherland; the very name of Russia had almost been abandoned. Now, in contrast, officially controlled organs of opinion editorialized that one should love one's own country, and hailed the heroes of the tsarist era. Alexander Nevsky, who had defeated the Teutonic knights; Dmitri Donskoi, who had defeated the Tartars; Peter the Great; Kutuzov, who had defeated Napoleon; even Ivan the Terrible—all were praised to the skies. The reputations of the great literary figures of the nineteenth century underwent a similar rehabilitation. This retreat to Russian nationalism reached its climax during World War II, when the Marxist *Internationale* itself was dropped as the national anthem.

The old Bolsheviks had attacked the family as the backbone of the old order, had made marriage difficult and divorce easy, had drawn no distinction between legitimate and illegitimate children, and had encouraged promiscuity and abortions. Stalin's state now rehabilitated the sanctity of marriage, denounced the seducer, made divorces very hard to get, declared the family essential to the state, and encouraged children to obey their parents. Doubtless the shift came in part as a result of the falling birthrate and increasing juvenile delinquency, but it was none the less part of the abandonment of radicalism.

The early Bolsheviks had destroyed the old school system, abolished homework and examinations, and allowed children to administer the schools collectively with their teachers. Attendance fell off, the schools became revolutionary clubs of youngsters, and the training of teachers was neglected. The universities deteriorated, since anybody aged sixteen could

tion the
unwilling
of capital
the revol
lation, an
edge to
permitted
armamen
soil in d
In 192
with Bri
the Strai
arose ove
the Sovie
descriptic
Donald
country
that illus
getting a
in the sar
letter" w
to instruc
techniqu
certainly
ter" influ
a Conser
the treat
offices of
don proc
agitation
ment no
gether.
unions s
when the
tion in t
the Unit
with the
it until l
Durin
tern cor
Russians
the Itali
1921, an
success
failed in
agrarian
right-wir
they fail
actually
French

enroll in them. Degrees were abolished, and technical training was stressed to the exclusion of other subjects. Under NEP, this chaotic situation was modified, and the basic problem of increasing literacy was seriously tackled. But the subjects of ordinary school curricula were replaced by the so-called "project" system with heavy emphasis on labor problems and Marxist theory. The teachers had little to do except memorize texts, and quiz the children to test their mastery of them. The Communist party itself took over the universities, purged the faculties, and compelled the students to spend one week in three at work in factories—a system that helped neither the student nor the university, and cannot have increased industrial production by very much.

The "thermidorean reaction," as might have been expected, changed this system drastically. Training of teachers improved, their salaries were raised, and regular ranks in the civil service were established for them. The old pre-revolutionary system of admissions and degrees in the universities was restored, as was the pre-revolutionary school curriculum. Examinations and homework re-appeared; discipline was enforced on school children. The emphasis on political education was reduced, and co-education was abandoned. Fees for tuition were restored for secondary schools, the Russian counterpart of the American high school or the French *lycée*. These tuition fees made higher education difficult to obtain except for children of the new élite or unusually talented students who were able to win state scholarships. Literacy rose to about 90 per cent, if we may believe Soviet figures.

The educational reforms certainly made books, theaters, museums, and libraries available to many more Russians than ever before. Newspapers and periodicals multiplied, and the regime's respect for science and learning was genuine. But the regime's attitude was narrowly utilitarian and thoroughly intolerant. All cultural activities were measured by their positive contribution to the state. Education became indoctrination. Systems of ideas that might rival communism were not allowed to compete, since the government could always

silence those who might be their spokesmen. In this respect the Soviet regime was even more authoritarian than that of a ruler like Tsar Nicholas I (see Chapter 22).

Under Nicholas I, censorship prevented the writer from saying certain things, but it did not positively prescribe what he must say. It was a negative, not a positive censorship, and it left a margin of personal freedom that permitted some of the greatest works of all literature to be written in Russia. The Soviet censorship, on the other hand, was positive, and required of all artists that they constantly praise the new system and devote their talents to publicizing its merits. The party line extended into all cultural fields, even music, where talented composers had to apologize abjectly for failing to produce communist symphonies, whatever they may be. The creative artist, the scientist, the scholar did not know from day to day whether his efforts would win him a Stalin prize or a sentence to a Siberian labor camp.

The Russian Thermidor came last of all, and doubtless very reluctantly, to modify the traditional communist position on religion. Here militant atheism had been the policy of the early Bolsheviks. They jailed and sometimes executed bishops and priests; they sponsored an atheist society and a museum of anti-religious propaganda. Behind this attitude lay more than the standard Marxist feeling that religion was the opium of the masses; in Russia, the Orthodox Church had always been a pillar of tsarism, and had held back the intellectual advance of the country. Many years of attacks on religion, however, failed to eradicate Orthodoxy from among the people. When in 1937 Hitler built a Russian church in Berlin, and took every occasion to speak kindly of the Orthodox Church, Stalin moved in the religious field also. Declaring that Christianity had contributed to past Russian progress, the government called off its anti-religious propaganda and enlisted its own atheist society to rehabilitate the Church. Church-going became respectable once more, although members of the party were not encouraged to profess religion. As a result, when war came, the leading church dignitaries supported the regime

of the only successful revolutionary country it enjoyed great prestige. Successively, the Comintern was influenced to denounce the enemies of Stalin: Trotsky and the Left in 1924, Bukharin and the Right in 1928. Thereafter there was no divergence between the Comintern and the Foreign Office.

Stalin and the West, 1928– 1939

Simultaneously with the adoption of the "new socialist offensive" at home, Stalin swung the Comintern leftward into a new period of militant revolutionary activity. The Social Democrats of western countries were denounced now as "social fascists" and as the most dangerous enemies of communism. The communists were going to bring about revolutions by themselves. Yet Stalin's personal belief in the possibility of revolution elsewhere seems to have been small. "One Soviet tractor is worth more than ten good foreign communists" is a remark quoted as typical of the views of Stalin's entourage in the days of the First Five-Year Plan; it reflects his real contempt for the rest of the world and his deep-rooted Russian nationalism.

This lack of real interest in the behavior of communists abroad and the failure to understand the true play of forces inside other countries led directly to the triumph of Hitler in Germany in 1933 (see Chapter 27). The communists in Germany, who had been instructed by the Comintern that the Social Democrats and not the Nazis were their worst enemies, fought the Nazis in the streets, but allied themselves with them in the Reichstag. They believed that a Nazi triumph would very soon be followed by a communist revolution. Thus even after Hitler came to power, the Russians renewed their nonaggression pact with Germany.

Yet the shock of realization that Hitler had meant precisely what he said about liquidating communists, and the fear that the U.S.S.R. itself might be in danger, soon led Stalin to modify Russian policy in the direction of collective security. After Hitler had refused to guarantee the Baltic states jointly with Stalin, Russia entered the League of Nations in September, 1934. The Soviet delegate, Litvinov, now became the most eloquent defender of universal disarmament and of punishment for aggressors. Soon afterward, the Russians began to negotiate for an "eastern Locarno" security pact to balance the agreement reached by the western European nations at Locarno in 1925 (see p. 457). Although no such structure could be created because of Polish and German hostility to the U.S.S.R., Russia did sign pacts with France and Czechoslovakia in 1935 providing for consultation, under the terms of the League, in the event of aggression, and for mutual aid, if the League certified that aggression had occurred. Soviet aid to Czechoslovakia, if the Czechs became victims of aggression, was to be delivered only if the French, who were bound to the Czechs by a long-standing alliance, honored their obligations first.

In view of the shift in Soviet foreign policy, the Comintern also shifted its line. In 1935, their recent deadly enemies, the Social Democrats and bourgeois liberals of the West, were suddenly embraced as allies against the fascist menace. Communists were to take the lead in forming "popular fronts" against fascism, and might properly welcome anybody, no matter how conservative in other ways, who would stand together with them on this principle. Revolutionary propaganda and anti-capitalist agitation were to be soft-pedaled. The communists in all the countries of the world led the fight for the defense budgets that they had previously sabotaged. Georgi Dimitrov, the Bulgarian communist, hero of the Reichstag fire trial (Chapter 27) and a symbol of antifascist courage and wit, was made boss of the Comintern. Inside the Soviet Union, the adoption of the "popular front" strategy was probably not unrelated to the purges, since the "Right deviationists" were anxious to reach an accommodation with the fascist states, and the "Left deviationists" insisted on the steady pursuit of world revolution.

This was the period when popular front governments came to power in France and Spain, and when some people in the West naively accepted the communists as their true brothers in arms against the menace of Hitler. However effective the "popular front" may have been as a tactic with western individuals, the purges inside Russia disillusioned western governments. A state that had to exterminate its top civil and military personnel for the crime of collaborating with the enemy did not make an attractive ally. If one believed the purge charges, one regarded a Soviet alliance as of doubtful value; if one did not believe them, how could one trust Stalin? On Stalin's side, western appeasement of Hitler and Mussolini (see Chapter 29) doubtless increased his disillusionment with the West.

Russia and the western European bloc each assumed that the chief purpose of the other was to turn the full force of Hitler's forthcoming attack away from itself and in the opposite direction. That Hitler intended to attack nobody could doubt. On September 12, 1936, in a speech at Nuremberg, he specifically declared once more that

if I had the Ural mountains with their incalculable store of treasures in raw materials, Siberia with its vast forests, and the Ukraine with its tremendous wheatfields, Germany under National Socialist leadership would swim in plenty.[*]

There was, then, much reason for the West to hope that the attack would be directed against the U.S.S.R.; this Stalin was determined to avert.

Soviet intervention in the Spanish Civil War (see Chapter 27) is an interesting demonstration of Stalin's real position. General Francisco Franco, who led an army revolt against the republican government of Spain in 1936, soon obtained aid from Mussolini and Hitler. The Russians, though reluctant to intervene in Spain at all because of their anxiety to prove their respectability to the western powers, realized that a failure to help the Spanish republic would cost them support all over the world. But their aid was too little and came too late, and consisted largely of police agents who devoted themselves to fighting Spanish anarchists and Trotskyites. The Russians hoped

that the western powers would intervene also, feeling that if they did so they would be irrevocably committed to continue the fight against Hitler on other battlefields. But western neutrality in Spain helped convince Stalin that a western alliance could not be counted upon.

A still more important factor here was the western appeasement of Hitler, which reached its climax in the Munich agreement of Britain, France, Germany, and Italy in September, 1938 (see also Chapter 29). From the Russian point of view, the Munich cession of Czech lands to Hitler, and the French failure to support Czechoslovakia and thus make operative the Russo-Czech alliance, could have only one purpose—to drive Hitler east. Stalin was apparently ready to support the Czechs if the French did too; when they did not, he seems to have decided that he had better sound out Hitler for an understanding. Thus a truly operative alliance between Stalin and the West proved impossible between 1935 and 1939.

When the British and French realized that appeasement had failed to stop Hitler, they sought reluctantly for a firmer alliance with the U.S.S.R. From March to August, 1939, Stalin kept open both his negotiations with the West and his slowly ripening negotiations with the Germans, which at first seemed to be concerned only with a trade agreement. The British and French mission, when it finally arrived in Moscow, was not composed of sufficiently high-ranking men to inspire Russian confidence. Moreover, the western powers naturally refused to turn over to Stalin the territories that he wanted as a bulwark against Germany—Finland and the Baltic republics of Estonia, Latvia, and Lithuania.

The growing eagerness of the Germans to secure a nonaggression pact gave Stalin the opportunity he sought to divert the war from Russia. In May, 1939, Litvinov was dismissed as foreign minister because he was Jewish and could therefore not negotiate with Germans; he was replaced by Molotov. In the pact Molotov eventually reached with Hitler late in August, 1939, each power undertook to remain neutral toward the other in the event of war. A secret additional protocol provided

[*]A Hitler, *My New Order*, R. de Sales, ed. (New York, 1941), 400.

for a division between Germany and Russia of Poland, which Hitler was about to attack. At worst, this put Russia's frontier farther west in the event of a subsequent German attack. The Russians lived up to the economic clauses of the agreement to the letter, although the Germans did not. The publication of the Hitler-Stalin pact necessitated an abrupt shift in the world communist line, which had remained staunchly "popular front." Now it was once more necessary for puzzled communists to denounce liberals and Social Democrats as enemies. They had to call the war that Hitler launched against Poland within a few days an "imperialist war," in which there was no difference between the two sides and in which communists should not get involved.

Stalin
and the Second World War

Stalin overrated the military power of the Poles to resist Hitler, and thus miscalculated the course of the first weeks of war. Faced with the complete collapse of Poland, he marched into the eastern portion. Disturbed by the lull ("the phony war") on the western fronts, he probably feared that Hitler would turn against him at once. This might well have happened

had Hitler been able to secure peace with France and England, as he strove to do. During the lull, in December, 1939, came Stalin's attack on Finland, which, unlike the Baltic states, had refused to grant him strategic bases. The attack on the Finns by Stalin aroused a storm of anti-Russian sentiment in the West. Both Britain and France supported the recruitment of armies of volunteers, and considered air raids against Russian targets in support of the Finns. The League of Nations expelled Russia. Despite severe setbacks to the Russian troops, the war against the Finns was won by the spring of 1940, before the western allies had been able to give them effective aid.

And in the spring of 1940, Stalin's second major calculation went awry. Like many observers, he apparently expected France to hold out a long time, and believed that, even if Hitler eventually defeated the French, Germany would be greatly weakened. Now instead came the lightning German operations in the west, and the war on the Continent seemed to be over. Only the British held out (see Chapter 29). Preoccupied with the security of his western frontiers, Stalin simply seized the three Baltic republics, and staged rigged plebiscites in which the Latvians, Estonians, and Lithuanians asked to be included in the Soviet Union. He demanded of Rumania in June, 1940, the

Rendezvous. Hitler-Stalin pact, August, 1939.

province of Bessarabia, whose loss after World War I the U.S.S.R. had never recognized, and also northern Bukovina, which had formerly been Habsburg, not Russian, territory, but which had a large Ukrainian population and was strategically valuable. Parts of these territories were annexed to existing SSR's and parts were incorporated into the new Moldavian SSR. The Germans had expected Russian seizure of Bessarabia, but not of northern Bukovina; they permitted the seizure, however, telling the Rumanians that they could expect no help from Hitler. But that was as far as Hitler's co-operation with Stalin in eastern Europe went. The re-annexation of Bessarabia had given the U.S.S.R. the mouths of the Danube, controlling an important artery. The Russians seemed to be moving into southeast Europe, a region in which the Germans were not prepared to let them operate alone.

Only a few weeks after the Russian seizure of Rumanian territory, Hitler asserted his own southeastern interests by forcing the Rumanians to cede territory to Hungary (August, 1940) and then guaranteeing the new Rumanian frontiers, a guarantee that could apply only against the U.S.S.R. Soon afterward, German troops appeared in Finland, "to reinforce the German armies in Norway," Hitler explained. And in the autumn of 1940, German troops entered Rumania proper, "to guard the Rumanian oil-fields against British sabotage." These maneuvers on his new frontiers deeply disquieted Stalin, as well they might have.

In October, 1940, Italy attacked Greece, and open war had spread to the Balkans. In November, when Molotov went to Berlin, Hitler tried to dazzle him with grandiose offers of an enormous future Soviet sphere of influence extending through Persia to the Persian Gulf and Indian Ocean, and including India, after the British Empire was destroyed. Each time this luscious bait was held out, Molotov tried to bring the discussion back to southeast Europe and Finland, and to establish Russia's sole rights in this sphere. This the Germans would not allow. After the failure of the conversations, Hitler ordered preparations for an attack on the U.S.S.R.

In the spring of 1941, the Germans had to rescue the Italians from the Greek campaign, which had bogged down in Albania. This rescue was preceded by the movement of German troops into Bulgaria, which the U.S.S.R. regarded as essential to its own defense. Then came an unsuccessful German effort to win Yugoslavia without war, and swift victorious German campaigns in Yugoslavia and Greece (March-May, 1941). Germany alone ruled supreme in the Balkan region, and, though the Yugoslav and Greek resistance had delayed the German timetable, Hitler was able to launch the invasion of the U.S.S.R. on June 22, 1941. Stalin must have known it was coming; indeed the western powers had warned him. But he seems to have hoped against hope to the end. A few weeks before it came, Stalin, proudly calling himself an Asiatic, had secured a neutrality pact with Japan, Hitler's ally. The Japanese, deeply engaged in China, and intending to go to war with the United States, wished as much as did the Russians for insurance against a war on two fronts.

VI   Conclusion

Karl Marx, who scorned and disliked Russia, would have been utterly dumbfounded had he lived to see that backward agricultural land, almost without a proletariat, produce the only successful European communist revolution. Although much ink has been spilled in an effort to discover why a Marxist revolution took place in the country where, in theory, the conditions were least favorable, the problem is not really so difficult. Two possible general solutions suggest themselves. Either Marx was wrong, or what happened in Russia was not a Marxist revolution at all. Or perhaps both these answers are partly right. It seems clear that Marx did not correctly estimate the revolutionary force latent in the Russian peasantry; since Marx died in 1883, he could not foresee the full inadequacy of the tsarist regime, the extent of the tensions created by World War I, or the feebleness of the provisional government of 1917. But it also seems clear that to bring the Bolsheviks to power it took Lenin's appreciation of the importance of the peasantry, his grasp of the immediate situation, his willingness to risk everything, and his luck at being in the right place at the right time with the right weapons.

On the other hand, the revolution was not wholly Marxist. Once the Bolsheviks were in power, of course, it was inevitable that the succession of real situations they faced should modify their Marxist-Leninist theories. Thus civil war and foreign intervention brought chaos, from which NEP provided a necessary respite. And in Stalin there came to power an amalgam of Marxist, Russian nationalist, and power-hungry politician such as nobody could have foreseen. Moved by a combination of motives, Stalin proceeded hastily and brutally to make over Russia in a decade. Although he fell short of his goal, his program had created an industrial state not totally unprepared for the blows that Hitler was to deal it. Slaves of the state though they were, collectivized by force, industrialized by force, purged, terrorized, and struggling by the million to exist in forced labor camps, the Russians in World War II succeeded, with much help from the United States, in defeating Hitler and his allies.

How much the loyalty of Russians to Stalin was due to the failure of the German invaders to treat them well, and how far Hitler with a different policy might have won their support are questions with which we cannot deal here. The Russians were facing a coalition of fascist states — Germany, Hungary, Rumania, and others grouped together in an alliance called "the Axis powers" (from the German-Italian "Axis"), a coalition pledged to the utter destruction of communism. We turn now to the history of these powers and of the fascist form of totalitarian doctrine they embraced.

Reading Suggestions on Communist Russia, 1917-1941

(Asterisk indicates paperbound edition.)

General Accounts

E. H. Carr, *A History of Soviet Russia*. Eight volumes of this work, still in progress, have so far appeared (Macmillan, 1950–1964). The only attempt at a complete history of the Soviet Union from original sources; Carr is a somewhat uncritical admirer of Lenin, and his work must be used with care.

B. Moore, Jr., *Soviet Politics: The Dilemma of Power* (Harvard Univ. Press, 1950). An illuminating analysis of the relationship between the communist ideology and Soviet practice.

R. N. Carew Hunt, *The Theory and Practice of Communism* (Macmillan, 1951). An excellent introduction to the subject.

M. Fainsod, *How Russia Is Ruled* (Harvard Univ. Press, 1953). An analysis of the Soviet system in 1953, firmly rooted in the historical background. Second edition, up to date, 1963.

W. W. Rostow and others, *The Dynamics of Soviet Society* (*Mentor, 1954). Attempt by a group of scholars to determine why the Russians behave as they do.

Robert V. Daniels, *The Nature of Communism* (*Vintage). A valuable study of totalitarianism.

Special Studies

W. H. Chamberlin, *The Russian Revolution, 1917–1921,* 2 vols. (*Grosset's Universal Library). Still the standard work on the subject.

L. Trotsky, *The History of the Russian Revolution*, 3 vols. (Simon and Schuster, 1932). A brilliant but biased study by one of the leading participants.

B. D. Wolfe, *Three Who Made a Revolution* (Dial, 1948; *Beacon). Excellent triple study of the careers of Lenin, Trotsky, and Stalin down to 1914.

D. Shub, *Lenin* (Doubleday, 1948; *abridgment available, Mentor). The best biography of Lenin in English.

I. Deutscher, *The Prophet Armed, The Prophet Unarmed, The Prophet Outcast* (Oxford Univ. Press, 1954, 1959, 1963; *Vintage). Biography of Trotsky, written by an admirer of the man.

I. Deutscher, *Stalin: A Political Biography* (Oxford Univ. Press, 1949). The most complete account in English.

J. Maynard, *Russia in Flux* (Macmillan, 1948). Enlightening though sometimes farfetched attempts to show basic continuities between the old and new régimes in Russia, written by a British civil servant stationed in India who made the study of Russia his avocation.

C. Brinton, *The Anatomy of Revolution,* 2nd ed. (Prentice-Hall, 1952; *Vintage). Comparison of the Russian revolution with the French revolution of 1789 and the English seventeenth-century revolution.

M. Fainsod, *Smolensk Under Soviet Rule* (Harvard Univ. Press, 1959). A uniquely important study, based on a huge collection of captured documents, of the actual workings of the communist system in Smolensk in the 1930's.

R. C. Tucker and S. F. Cohen, eds. *The Great Purge Trials* (*Grosset's Universal Library). A translation of the major portion of the actual text of the 1938 trial.

H. Schwartz, *Russia's Soviet Economy,* 2nd ed. (Prentice-Hall, 1954). Good introduction to the subject.

N. Timasheff, *The Great Retreat* (Dutton, 1946). An account of the "Russian Thermidor."

R. Pipes, *The Formation of the Soviet Union* (Harvard Univ. Press, 1954). Excellent monograph on the question of national minorities in Russia, 1917–1923.

J. L. Wheeler-Bennett, *Brest-Litovsk, The Forgotten Peace* (Macmillan, 1938). Excellent monograph.

L. Fischer, *The Soviets in World Affairs,* 2nd ed. (Princeton Univ. Press, 1951). The only study of Soviet foreign policies up to 1929.

M. Beloff, *The Foreign Policy of Soviet Russia*, 2 vols. (Oxford Univ. Press, 1947, 1952). A solid study covering the years 1929–1941.

E. Lyons, *Assignment in Utopia* (Harcourt, Brace, 1937). An American journalist records his disillusionment with Soviet communism.

R. H. Crossman, ed., *The God That Failed* (Harper, 1959). Brief statements by Arthur Koestler, Stephen Spender, Ignazio Silone, and other intellectuals recording their disenchantment with communism.

V. A. Kravchenko, *I Chose Freedom* (Scribner's, 1946). The most celebrated of many works written by ex-Soviet officials and citizens who preferred life in the West to the U.S.S.R.

Historical Fiction

A. Koestler, *Darkness at Noon* (Modern Library, 1956; *New American Library). A famous novel, presenting in fictional form a keen analysis of the attitudes of the Old Bolsheviks whom Stalin purged.

V. Serge, *The Case of Comrade Tulayev* (Doubleday, 1950). Another excellent novel of the purges.

G. Blunden, *The Room on the Route* (Lippincott, 1947). Perhaps the most vivid fictional portrayal of the impact of terror on the ordinary person.

A. Tolstoy, *Road to Calvary* (Knopf, 1946). Translation of a Stalin Prize Novel about the revolution and civil war.

27

The Rise of Fascism, 1918-1939

I Introduction

In this chapter we shall deal with the rise of fascism in Europe in the period between the two great wars. By 1939, authoritarian governments of the Right had taken firm control of Italy, Germany, Spain, and all the countries of eastern and southeastern Europe except Russia. The process by which these regimes came to power differed widely from country to country, as did some of the external features of the regimes. At first glance, fascism is more complex and more difficult to understand than communism, whose development as a doctrine can be traced from Marx through Lenin before its followers were able to put it, or something like it, into practice in Russia. Unlike communism, fascism has no such line of theoretical development. Its proponents often seem to have acted first and worried about doctrine later, devising theories to meet the needs of the moment.

Fascism has been called the revolution of the classes of order. Political parties on the Continent have often represented the interests of the various social classes; when those interests have seemed to be about evenly balanced in a parliamentary state, a long and indecisive political tug-of-war has often ensued. For example, let us assume that a revolution from the Left threatens or can be made to seem to threaten. Then the middle classes, so the theory runs, seize power and take refuge in their own form of extremism—fascism, that is, nationalism tricked out with a few radical phrases to win mass support, and draped in mystical garments. This formula can be applied to Mussolini's rise to power in Italy in 1922, to Hitler's rise to power in Germany in 1933, to Franco's rise to power in Spain in 1936–1939, and to many of the eastern European dictators. Yet the formula takes us only so far. Only a study of the different circumstances in each of the different countries can give it body and meaning.

Economic depressions played a role in the rise of almost every dictator—in Italy the post-war depression, and elsewhere the world-wide depression of 1929 and later. We notice, moreover, a certain similarity in the externals of fascism everywhere—colored shirts, private armies, mass hypnotism, special salutes, special war cries and ceremonies, mystical glorification of the nation, and a vast program of conquest. The dictator justifies his program by references to "have" and "have-not" nations; his own nation is always a "have-not," always oppressed.

Fascism is just as violent in its hatred of democracy, liberalism, and parliamentary institutions as in its professed dislike of communism. Indeed fascism shares communism's abhorrence of constitutional procedure, its disregard of the individual human being, and its insistence that the state is supreme. Fascism persecutes its enemies, both real and fancied, with the same ruthlessness we have observed in Stalin's Russia. Censorship, political police, concentration camps, the rule of the bludgeon, the end of legal protection—all these practices are common to both fascism and communism.

When Mussolini ruled in Rome, public buildings everywhere carried the admonition to loyal Italians, "Believe, fight, obey" (*Credere, combattere, obbedire*). Presumably this was intended to be inspiring. Yet all it really means is: Believe (what Mussolini tells you), fight (for Mussolini and his backers), obey (Mussolini). When put this way, the formula is seen to subvert all religion and all human decency. Yet, under the stress of the unbearable pressures on individuals generated by the tension of the years between the wars many an idealist was taken in, surrendering his right to think and to make his own decisions.

II   Italy and Fascism

The Setting

Although Italy was a member of the victorious Allied coalition, she finished the First World War with a sense of defeat. Six hundred and fifty thousand of her men had been killed and one million wounded. Industry slumped immediately after the war, and within a few months 10 per cent of the industrial workers were unemployed. Prices rose rapidly, and wages failed to keep up. The promised pensions for wounded veterans and families of the killed were long delayed. Strikes and disorders became frequent. Many of the young men released from the armies with no trade but war and no job to go to drifted restlessly and discontentedly, fit prey for leaders with glittering promises.

Perhaps most important, the Italian government itself, hoping to influence the peace negotiations, began to spread propaganda among the Italian people to the effect that their wartime allies were robbing them of the Slavic lands in Dalmatia, across the Adriatic, promised to Italy by the secret Treaty of London (see Chapter 25) in exchange for Italy's entrance into the war. This arrangement the United States had never agreed to, and now would not accept. Although the Allied leaders at the Paris Peace Conference remained unaffected by the storms of protest arising from Italy, the Italian people did come to believe that they had shed their blood in vain. Popular sentiment in Italy, especially in the army, swung toward extremists of one sort or another.

Some Italians hysterically supported Gabriele d'Annunzio, a short, bald nationalist poet and romantic novelist who formed a band of volunteers. They seized the city of Fiume, the Adriatic seaport over which Croatians and Hungarians had long disagreed (Chapter 25). Referring to the "stench of peace," and denouncing Woodrow Wilson, d'Annunzio declared that the time for heroic individual action was at hand. Fiume had actually not been awarded to Italy even by the Secret Treaty of London, but d'Annunzio felt that Italy must have it, and that was enough. He ran his own government in Fiume until the end of 1920.

D'Annunzio patterned his régime there upon that of an imaginary medieval commune in a poem by Italy's romantic poet Carducci (1835–1907). Modeling himself consciously upon the governor of the commune in the poem, d'Annunzio would appear on the balcony of the city hall, address an inspirational harangue to the crowd, and ask for its unanimous consent for whatever he wished to do. This his listeners would grant, raising their right hands high, as the imaginary citizens of Carducci's commune had done. Some of d'Annunzio's followers wore black shirts. When d'Annunzio asked them to whom Fiume belonged they would shout *A noi*, "to us," and when he asked them to whom Italy belonged, they would give the same answer. Indeed, he planned to lead his followers from Fiume to Rome, and thence out into the world to conquer it, presumably with daggers, which he preferred to mechanized weapons. He drafted the Statutes of Fiume, a constitution in which he made a conscious attempt to organize society along the lines he imagined to have existed in the guilds and artisans' corporations of the Middle Ages.

In November, 1920, the Italian government signed the Treaty of Rapallo with Yugoslavia, by which Fiume was to become a free city. Italian forces drove d'Annunzio out, and into retirement in a villa on the Italian lakes. But the techniques of force, the haranguing of the mob from the balcony, the straight-arm salute, the black shirts, the rhythmic cries, the plans for conquest, and the "corporative" scheme of the Statutes of Fiume served as precedent and inspiration for Benito Mussolini, founder of Italian fascism.

In the first four years after the end of the war, Mussolini created and brought to power a new political force in Italy. In October, 1922, he was summoned to office by King Victor

Gabriele D'Annunzio.

Emmanuel III (1900–1947); from then on he gradually created a totalitarian state of which he was the sole, undisputed ruler. Suppressing all opposition at home, and threatening the peace abroad, the fascist state in Italy served in some degree as model for the Nazis in Germany, for the Falangists in Spain, and for totalitarian regimes in virtually all the European successor states of the Habsburg and Ottoman empires. Eventually, Mussolini was forced, largely by his own propaganda, into an alliance with Hitler. In 1940, this alliance took Italy into World War II, and in 1945 it brought Mussolini himself to an ignominious death, upside down on a communist partisan gallows, with his mistress beside him.

Mussolini: Early Career

Mussolini was born in 1883, in the Romagna, a province of central Italy famous for its political extremists, and for the violence with which they express themselves. His father was an ardent socialist who had begun his career as an anarchist under the influence of Bakunin (Chapter 22). Trained as an elementary-school teacher, Mussolini was already a passionate socialist by the time he was eighteen. He spent some time as an agitator among Italian emigrant laborers in Switzerland (1902–1904) and in Austria (1909) but was expelled by the police. Back in Italy, he was imprisoned for opposing the war against Turkey over Tripoli (1911). In 1912, he became editor of the most important Italian socialist newspaper, *Forward (Avanti)*.

When World War I began, Mussolini at first vigorously opposed Italy's entry. But then, during 1914, he changed his mind. First he favored "relative neutrality," meaning that socialists should leave themselves free to support Italian entry if such a course seemed likely to prove favorable to them. When the Italian Socialist party refused to follow this idea, he resigned as editor of *Avanti*. Soon afterward (November, 1914), he founded his own newspaper, *The People of Italy (Il Popolo d'Italia)*, in Milan, and began to advocate an immediate Italian declaration of war on the side of the Al-

lies. For this the Socialist party expelled him.

But these bare bones of a biography reveal only the externals. As a socialist, Mussolini before 1914 was a passionate left-winger. He was an apostle of violent social revolution and a bitter opponent of milder evolutionary and reformist doctrine. He urged that a small, well-knit armed minority should seize power and establish a dictatorship. He loathed militarism, was himself a draft-dodger, and urged soldiers to desert the army. He hated monarchy, and savagely attacked in his writings all the crowned heads of Europe, especially the Italian House of Savoy. He was a vigorous atheist, urged workers to stay away from church, and scorned the teachings of Christ. As an international revolutionary, he opposed nationalism, and even referred to the Italian flag as "a rag to be planted on a dunghill."

Yet he was to repudiate almost all these positions, and as fascist chieftain to substitute almost the exact opposites. As a fascist, he attacked bolshevism and all left-wing movements; he made his peace with the monarchy and the Church; he became a militant nationalist, a mystic patriot, and a rabid militarist. The repudiation of the views he had held so long and advocated so skillfully is not nearly so astonishing as it seems. From the first, Mussolini did not much care for programs; what he wanted was to rule.

A complete opportunist, he could shift his line on any question at a moment's notice if it seemed advantageous. For example, after the war, though he was now a fascist, he at first supported a radical program of social change, indistinguishable from the program he would have advocated had he still been a socialist. He favored the action of the Italian workers in the fall of 1920 when they occupied the factories in a kind of sit-down strike. Yet, within a year, he was using the fears which this strike had aroused in the middle classes to argue that he was the only possible bulwark against "bolshevism." About certain matters, however, he was consistent. He always hated parliaments and he always loved violence.

Mussolini's switch from isolationism to interventionism in the war in 1914 was the first of his important shifts. After his expulsion from the Socialist party, he agitated furiously for war, speaking to groups of similarly minded young men called *fasci* or groups (the image is of a bundle of rods, a symbol of office in the Roman Republic of antiquity). Soon after Italy did enter the war in 1915, Mussolini was conscripted and sent to the front. He was wounded in 1917 by an Italian mortar shell that exploded during practice. When he got out of the hospital, he continued to edit his newspaper, spewing forth a mixture of extreme revolutionary and extreme nationalist propaganda.

Mussolini: Rise to Power

In March, 1919, Mussolini founded the first *fasci di combattimento* ("groups for combat"). There was no sign as yet to indicate that by October, 1922, the leader of this small movement would become the most powerful man in Italy. In 1919, he called for every kind of revolutionary violence—seizure of the land, attacks on the factories, shooting of storekeepers who charged high prices, expropriation of mines and transports, and war by the vanquished "proletarian" nations against the victorious capitalists who had kept Italy from annexing Dalmatia. He now maintained that socialism was too conservative; his movement, far from setting itself against a revolution, was in the vanguard of those who were crying for one.

Yet in Italy a revolution along Bolshevik patterns was most unlikely, if not impossible. The peasants were not very revolutionary, for they already held much of the land except in the extreme south. And the industrial workers, though often discontented, knew that a revolution could be starved out because the country needed to import most of its raw materials. The Socialist party was overwhelmingly in the hands of moderates, and in 1919 Catholics founded the Popular party *(Partito Populare Italiano)*, designed to compete with the Socialists for the votes of the lower classes, who now had universal suffrage.

In the postwar disorders the peasants seized without consent of the landowners less than one-tenth of 1 per cent of the arable land in Italy. The leaders of the Socialist party and the General Confederation of Labor voted down the proposals of anarchist and communist extremists to turn the workers' occupation of the factories into a revolution. The government waited for the workers to grow tired. This they did in less than a month (September, 1920); then they left the occupied factories and went home.

Yet, although the danger of revolution was small, the fear of revolution was great. During 1920 and 1921, the industrialists and landowners, squeezed by taxation and inflation, became bitter. Shopkeepers and tradesmen wanted street disorders to end, food prices to be regulated, and the co-operative food stores of the Socialist and Catholic parties to be put out of business as competitors. Professional men and others with fixed incomes suffered as prices and wages went up and salaries lagged behind. The police grew tired of suppressing local disorders and of being repaid with insults. Ex-servicemen, insulted by anarchists and communists for their war records, naturally grew more patriotic.

All these groups identified the forces they did not like as Bolshevik, and accepted as an article of faith the myth of an impending Bolshevik revolution. After a series of fascist-socialists street fights and riots, these "anti-Bolsheviks" began to look to Mussolini's fascist bands as the defenders of their interests. D'Annunzio's defeat left Mussolini as his natural heir. The Left opposition to Mussolini was weakened when the communists split off from the Socialist party in 1921. The *fasci* grew enormously, from 30,000 in May, 1920, to 100,000 in February, 1921, to more than 300,000 at the time of the "March on Rome" in October, 1922. No longer were they merely squads of discontented and idle youths with vaguely revolutionary and nationalist ideas. Now, says one fascist of the period, "the sons and hangers-on of the bigwigs" poured into the organization.

They had come into the Fascio for their own ends. . . . If they met men in working clothes, they fell on them and began beating them. Their mentality was on a par with that of the Communists, who had beaten and murdered anybody who was decently dressed. One saw . . . the well-known surly and rapacious faces of war profiteers . . . and we were obliged to accept their money because we needed it to stifle an evil worse than they.*

The liberal parliamentary leaders of Italy felt that the fascist bands were teaching the Left a useful lesson. They encouraged the commanding officers of the army to issue rifles and army trucks and gasoline to the fascists, and even assigned army officers to command their operations. The police were encouraged to look the other way during disorders started by the fascists, and local judges were urged to help by releasing arrested fascists. Mussolini's newspaper was circulated free to the soldiers in the army as a "patriotic" sheet.

A campaign of terror now began against the socialists and Christian Democrats, as the fascist squadrons cruised around Italy in trucks, burning down labor-union offices, newspaper offices, and local Socialist party headquarters, and beating up and sometimes murdering labor leaders or local anti-fascist politicians. The *fasci* forced duly elected officials to resign. The torch, the cudgel, and the famous castor-oil treatment were all characteristic weapons. It is estimated that 2,000 people, anti-fascist and fascist, policemen and innocent bystanders, died by violence between October, 1920, and October, 1922.

The "March" on Rome

In the elections of May, 1921, Mussolini and thirty-four other fascists were elected to Parliament, along with ten Nationalists, their political allies. The momentum of the fascist movement was now too great to be slowed down. Mussolini abandoned his anti-monarchical views, and fascism became a political party (November, 1921) as a necessary step in the drive for power. Too late, the government became alarmed, and tried to take measures against the fascists, but the squads

*Umberto Banchelli, *Memorie di un Fascista,* quoted by G. Salvemini in *The Fascist Dictatorship* (New York, 1927), 67–68.

were too strong, the police too accustomed to collaborating with them, and the politicians themselves as yet unaware that a tightly directed armed mob could really take over the state. Inside the royal family, the King's cousin, the Duke of Aosta, had become a fascist sympathizer, as had many army generals, the entire Nationalist party, and the leading industrialists.

In the fall of 1922, it was clear that the army would not resist a fascist *coup* in Rome itself. When a decree of martial law was presented to the King, he refused to sign it, probably influenced by his knowledge that the army would not fight the fascists, and that the Duke of Aosta would gladly take his crown. The refusal of the King to declare martial law greatly heartened the fascists. Now, as the fascists "marched" on Rome, mostly by storming railroad trains and stealing free rides, the King (October 29, 1922) telegraphed Mussolini in Milan to come to Rome and form a cabinet. Mussolini arrived by sleeping-car the next morning.

Fascism, which had begun as a patriotic anti-Bolshevik movement, and had then turned into an anti-labor movement in the service of the industrialists and landowners, had finally come to power as a conspiracy against parliamentary government in the service of a military clique. Just before taking office, Mussolini announced:

Our program is simple: we wish to govern Italy. They ask us for programs, but there are already too many. It is not programs that are wanting for the salvation of Italy but men and will-power.*

The Fascist Dictatorship

Mussolini now moved gradually to turn his premiership into a dictatorship. A month after coming to office, he obtained dictatorial powers that were to last only until the end of 1923. Although the constitution theoretically remained in force, Mussolini proceeded to take over the administration. He created a Fascist Militia almost 200,000 strong, which owed complete allegiance to him. He en-

*Quoted by H. Finer, *Mussolini's Italy* (New York, 1935), 152.

larged the regular army, and required its members to take an oath of personal loyalty to him. Before his dictatorial powers expired, he secured from Parliament by pressure a new electoral law. This law provided that the political party which received the largest number of votes in a general election, if that number amounted to at least one-quarter of the vote, should automatically receive two-thirds of the seats in Parliament. The rest of the seats would be divided proportionately. This law made certain the fascists' domination of future parliaments. Indeed, in the election of April, 1924, the fascists actually polled 65 per cent of the vote cast; but this figure reflects a widespread use of intimidation and terrorism at the polls. The first all-fascist cabinet was now appointed. Meanwhile, local administration was made secure by the appointment of fascist prefects and subprefects in the provinces; these officials pursued the enemies of fascism with the same weapons of murder and mayhem that had been used before Mussolini's March on Rome.

Early in 1924, the leader of the opposition to Mussolini, the socialist Giacomo Matteotti, published a book called *The Fascists Exposed*, in which he detailed many of the outrages the fascists had committed on their way to power. It seemed probable that further revelations were in store, exposing some of Mussolini's cabinet members as corrupt. On June 10, 1924, Matteotti was "taken for a ride" in true gangster style and murdered. The crime was traced to members of Mussolini's immediate circle. This scandal rocked Italy, and for a moment it even seemed possible that Mussolini would fall. But he dismissed from office those who were involved, and pledged himself to restore law and order. Actually, he delayed trying the guilty men until March, 1926, and even then they all got off lightly.

What really helped Mussolini over the crisis, ironically enough, was the departure of most of the opposition deputies from Parliament. They declared that they would not return until the Matteotti murder had been solved and the government had been shown to be innocent. Far from making things harder for Mussolini, as they had intended, their departure actually made things easier. Mussolini denied his own guilt, imposed a rigid press censorship, and forbade the opposition to meet. Most of the deputies never did return to Parliament, and in 1926 their seats were declared forfeit.

Mussolini during the fascist "March" on Rome, 1922.

Next, a series of laws called the "most fascist laws" (*legge fascistissime*) tightened control over the press, abolished secret societies like the Freemasons, whom Mussolini had loathed ever since his socialist youth, and replaced all elected local officials by men appointed from Rome. Opponents of the regime were arrested and exiled to desolate islands off the Italian coast. Early in 1926, Mussolini was empowered to govern by decree. Three attempts on his life led to a new law providing the death penalty for action against the King, the Queen, or Mussolini. All opposition political parties were abolished in the same year, and the Fascist party was left as the only legal political party in Italy.

More and more the Italian state and the Fascist party were brought into co-ordination. Mussolini was both the *Duce* (leader) of the fascists and the *capo di governo*, the chief of state. At one moment he also held eight cabinet posts simultaneously. The members of the Fascist Grand Council, a "politbureau" numbering roughly twenty of the highest party functionaries, all appointed by Mussolini, held all the important posts in the administration not held by Mussolini himself. In 1928, the Grand Council was given important constitutional duties: preparing the lists of candidates for election of the Chamber, advising Mussolini, and proposing changes in the constitution or the succession to the throne. The Grand Council thus became a kind of third house, above the other two houses of Parliament, the Senate and the Chamber.

The Corporative State

Mussolini believed that the interests of labor and capital could and must be made to harmonize with the over-riding interests of the state. Instead of a political system as we understand it, he accepted the idea that representation should be based on economic interests organized in "syndicates." Such an idea was not new: the French syndicalist, Georges Sorel (Chapter 20), had already argued in this vein. But Sorel believed in class warfare, and in government by syndicates of workers only.

Mussolini, following the Italian nationalist syndicalist, Rossoni, believed in capitalism, class-collaboration, and producers' syndicates as well as workers' syndicates.

In 1925, fascist labor unions were recognized by employers as having the sole right to negotiate labor contracts. Then, in April, 1926, the state officially recognized producers' and workers' syndicates in each of six areas —industry, agriculture, commerce, sea and air transport, land and inland waterway transport, and banking—plus a syndicate of intellectuals, making thirteen syndicates in all. Each syndicate could bargain and reach contracts and could assess dues upon everyone engaged in its own economic field, irrespective of membership in the syndicate. Strikes and lockouts were both forbidden. When labor conditions did not improve, a "charter of labor," promising insurance and other benefits, was issued in 1927. In 1926, the syndicates were put under the control of a special Ministry of Corporations; Mussolini was the minister.

In 1928, the system of parliamentary representation was changed in accordance with fascist syndicalism. A new electoral law provided for a new Chamber of Deputies (400 instead of 560 members). The national councils of the thirteen syndicates could nominate a total of 800 candidates. Each syndicate had a quota, half to be selected by the employers and half by the employees. Cultural and charitable foundations could nominate 200 more candidates. When the total list of 1,000 was completed, the Fascist Grand Council could either select 400 of them, or strike out names and add names of its own, or even substitute an entire new list. The voters would then vote in answer to the question: "Do you approve of the list of deputies selected by the Fascist Grand Council?" They could vote "Yes" or "No" on the entire list, but they could not choose from among the candidates. If a majority voted "Yes," the list was elected; if not, the procedure was to be repeated. Despite the highly touted role of the syndicate, all the power obviously lay with the Fascist Grand Council. Universal suffrage was abolished even for this very limited form of election. Payment of a minimum tax or dues to a syndicate was required of each voter; women could not vote. In 1929, the elections under this system produced a "yes" vote of 8,519,559 and a "no" vote of 137,761.

Between 1930 and 1938, several constitutional steps were taken which seemed to move the syndicates into the center of the stage. Representatives from the syndicates and the government were now formed into a Council of Corporations, which was to act as a coordinating committee, settle disputes between syndicates, assist production, and establish the fascist corporations themselves, which had not yet been created. The Council was divided into seven sections corresponding to the seven syndicate areas, and in 1931 each of these sections of the Council was simply declared to be a corporation. In 1933, it was announced that the whole corporate system would be revised; and in 1934 the new elections (which of course returned the Fascist Grand Council's list of candidates) produced a "suicide" Chamber of Deputies, which was expected eventually to put an end to its own existence. Its replacement was to be a new "revolutionary assembly," which Mussolini called into existence in the fall of 1934. The assembly, also called the Central Committee of Corporations, contained 824 members, representing twenty-two newly created corporations. The Fascist party, as well as employers and employees, was represented on each corporation.

Finally, in 1938 the "suicide chamber" replaced itself with the Central Committee of Corporations, now called the Chamber of Fasces and Corporations. Nothing remained of the old parliamentary constitution that had been set up by Cavour except the Senate, nominally appointed by the King but actually subservient to Mussolini, who on one occasion had the King appoint forty fascist senators all at once. This new structure, the corporative state, was influenced by d'Annunzio's strange medieval ideas, and by Mussolini's own wish to produce new political and economic forms. But in spite of much oratory by fascist sympathizers about the corporative state and its virtues, it does not appear that the new bodies ever had very much to do with running the economic or political life of Italy, which remained firmly under the direction of the fascist bureaucracy.

Other Fascist Domestic Policies

During the thirties, the fascist version of the planned economy made its appearance in Italy. The government issued or withheld permits for factory construction. In agriculture, a concerted effort was launched to make Italy more nearly self-sufficient. This effort was dramatized with the "Battle of Wheat," in which the Italians were treated to contests, prizes, and personal appearances by Mussolini. In 1932, official figures reported that wheat production had risen to a point where it could supply 92 per cent of the nation's normal needs, and the drive was enlarged to include other cereal products. The government subsidized steamship and air lines, encouraged the tourist trade, and protected Italian industries by means of high tariffs on foreign products. Marshes were drained and land was reclaimed; the incidence of malaria was reduced. Enormous sums were spent on public works, and great strides were made in the development of hydroelectric power. The trains, at least so thousands of tourists reported, ran on time; many argued that "there must be something in this man Mussolini." Yet Italy's weakness in essential raw materials proved to be insuperable.

The state reached into the life of the individual at almost every point. Though Italy was overpopulated, and had for decades relieved the situation only by mass emigration, Mussolini made emigration a crime. He encouraged people to marry and have the largest possible families. He reduced their taxes, extended special loans, taxed bachelors, and extended legal equality to illegitimate children. He hoped in this way to swell the ranks of his armies, and to strengthen his claim that Italy must expand abroad. Children, the future party members, were enrolled in a series of youth movements, beginning at the age of six. The textbooks in the schools, the books in the libraries, the professors in the universities, the plays on the stage and the movies on the screen were all made vehicles of fascist propaganda. The secret police, OVRA (from the initials of the Italian words for "Vigilance Organization against Anti-Fascist Crimes"), endeavored to discover and suppress all opposition movements.

In 1929, Mussolini settled the Roman question (see Chapter 21) by entering into the Lateran Treaty with the papacy. This treaty recognized the independent state of Vatican City, and thus restored the temporal power of the pope, though on a greatly reduced scale. Mussolini also recognized Catholicism as the state religion, and promised to halt anti-papal propaganda. He gave up the right to tax contributions to the Church or the salaries of the clergy, and paid $105,000,000 to compensate the papacy for the Italian occupation of papal territories since 1870. A further concordat legalized religious marriages and extended religious instruction in the schools. The Church agreed not to engage in politics in its newspapers and periodicals.

Yet, despite the fact that many church officials viewed the fascist movement sympathetically, difficulties arose after these agreements had been concluded. In an encyclical, Pope Pius XI (1922–1939) indicated his disapproval of Mussolini's "relentless" economic policies and of the corporations as "serving special political aims rather than contributing to the initiation of a better social order." Mussolini now charged that the Church's "Catholic Action" clubs were engaged in politics, and dissolved them. The Pope denied the charges and denounced the Fascist party's practice of monopolizing the time and education of the young. In 1931, however, a further agreement was reached, and the clubs were re-opened.

Fascist Foreign Policy and Its Consequences

Since Mussolini's foreign policies form an integral part of the international relations leading up to World War II, we shall discuss them more fully in Chapter 29. Here we may simply point out that his extreme nationalism, his love of panoply and parades, and his militarism were the logical extensions of his domestic ideas and accomplishments. Mussolini's wish to re-create the glories of ancient Rome impelled him to undertake a policy of adventure in the Mediterranean, which he called *Mare Nostrum* (Latin for "our sea") as a sign that he was the heir to the Caesars. This policy began in 1923, when five Italians working for the League of Nations were assassinated as they marked out the new frontier between Albania and Greece. Mussolini bombarded and occupied the Greek island of Corfu and refused to recognize the League's right to intervene. Only British pressure led to a settlement of the matter.

Later, Mussolini's policy of adventure led him to military aggression in Ethiopia, in Spain, and in Albania (which he dominated during the 1920's and occupied in April, 1939). It drove him into an alliance with his fellow-fascist, Hitler, and led him to voice loud claims against the French for Corsica, Tunisia, Nice, and Savoy. And it alienated Italy from her natural allies, France and Britain. Thus, Mussolini's grandiose fascist ideology first spurred Italy to win self-sufficiency, to rebuild her seaports, and to create a merchant fleet and navy. But the same ideology ultimately separated her from the only powers who might have saved her from the disaster toward which Mussolini was driving.

The German alliance was also responsible for a striking new departure in fascist domestic policy. This was the official adoption of anti-Semitism, which took place in 1938. With only 70,000 Jews, most of whom had long been resident, Italy had no "Jewish problem." Italian Jews were entirely Italian in their language and sentiments, and could be distinguished from other Italians only by their religion. Many of them were prominent in the fascist movement, and many were anti-fascist. There was no widespread sympathy in Italy for the government's adoption of Hitler's racial policies. Yet Hitler's dominating influence led Mussolini to expel Jews from the Fascist party, and to forbit them to teach or attend school, to intermarry with non-Jews, and to obtain new licenses to conduct businesses.

In summing up Mussolini's career, we may turn to a quotation from an article that he himself wrote in 1920 to denounce Lenin. In reading it, substitute Italy for Russia and Mussolini for Lenin, and you will have a clear idea of fascism:

Russia is a state . . . composed of men who exercise power, imposing an iron discipline upon individuals and groups and practicing 'reaction' whenever necessary. . . . In the Russia of Lenin there is only one authority: his authority. There is only one liberty: his liberty. There is only one opinion: his opinion. There is only one law: his law. One might either submit or perish. . . . Russia . . . swallows up and crushes the individual and governs his entire life. . . . Whoever says state necessarily says the army, the police, the judiciary, and the bureaucracy. The Russian state is the state *par excellence*. . . . It has *statized* economic life . . . and formed a huge army of bureaucrats. At the base of the pyramid, . . . there is the proletariat which, as in the old bourgeois regimes, obeys, works, and eats little or allows itself to be massacred. . . .*

*Mussolini on Lenin in 1920, quoted by G. Megaro, *Mussolini in the Making* (Boston, 1938), 325–326.

III   Germany and the Weimar Republic, 1918-1933

Whereas Mussolini took over in Italy less than four years after World War I ended, the Germans experimented with democracy for fifteen years before succumbing to Adolf Hitler. Two days before the armistice of November 11, 1918, the German Social Democrats proclaimed a republic. On July 31, 1919, this republic adopted a constitution drawn up by a national assembly at Weimar; it is therefore known as the "Weimar Republic." The Weimar Constitution was never formally abandoned, but after Hitler became chancellor on January 30, 1933, Germany was in fact a dictatorship.

The history of the Weimar Republic divides itself naturally into three periods: a period of political threats from Left and Right and of mounting economic chaos, from 1918 to the end of 1923; a period of political stability, fulfillment of the Versailles Treaty requirements, and seeming economic prosperity, from 1924 to late 1929; and a period of economic depression and mounting right-wing power, from late 1929 to January, 1933.

The Impact of Defeat

For the overwhelming majority of the German people, defeat in 1918 came as a great shock. The military authorities who ran the German Empire during the last years of the war had failed to report to the public German reverses on the battlefield. No fighting had ever taken place on German soil, and the Germans had got used to thinking of their armies as in firm possession of the foreign territories they had overrun. Now these armies came home. It is often argued that the Allies committed a grave blunder by their failure to march to Berlin and demonstrate to the German people that they had actually been defeated. Schooled in reverence for their military forces, the Germans could not grasp the fact that their armies had lost the war. Moreover, the Allies, under the leadership of Wilson, simply refused to deal with the Supreme Command of the German armies. Field Marshal von Hindenburg, as supreme commander, was never required to hand over his sword to Marshal Foch, or to sign the armistice. Rather, it was the civilian politicians who had to bear the odium. In this way, the Allies unintentionally did the German military caste a great favor.

Before the ink was dry on the armistice agreement, the generals, led by Hindenburg himself, were explaining that the German armies had never really been defeated. This was exactly what the public wanted to believe, and the harsh facts—that Ludendorff and Hindenburg had insisted on surrender because the armies could no longer fight—were never effectively publicized. So the legend that Germany had somehow been "stabbed in the back" by civilians, by liberals, socialists, communists, and Jews, took deep root, and became almost an article of faith among many Germans. This legend was widely disseminated by politicians, especially by those who had a stake in the old Prussian system—the monarchists, agrarians, industrialists, and militarists. All through the period of the Weimar Republic, these groups remained hostile toward it; their hostility ranged from political opposition to conspiracies to overthow the government.

The Allies added another error by including the celebrated "war-guilt" clause in the Treaty of Versailles. The German signatories were obliged to acknowledge what none of them believed, and what subsequent historians would disprove: that Germany alone had been responsible for the outbreak of the war. The war-guilt clause made it harder for the German public to acknowledge defeat and the evils of the past system, to sweep away the militarists, and to bend to the task of creating a virile republic. Instead, it led many Germans to dissipate their energies in denying war-guilt, in hating the enemies who had saddled them with the charge, in bewailing the sell-out of their generals, and in waiting for a chance to show by force that they had been right all the time.

Postwar Political Alignments and Activities

Threats to stability from the Left further strengthened the anti-republican forces of the Right. Responsibility for launching the republic and for preventing disorder fell upon the "majority socialists," made up of Social Democrats and right-wing Independent Socialists, and led by the Social Democrat, Ebert. The Social Democrats were a moderate group. They made no attack on agrarian property, and they allowed the Junkers to maintain intact their estates and the social and political posi-

tion that went with them. True to their reformist tradition, the Social Democrats concluded with the industrialists collective bargaining agreements that guaranteed the eight-hour day, rather than trying to launch a serious movement for nationalizing German industry.

But to the left of the Social Democrats the left wing of the Independent Socialists and the communist "Spartacists" (named for Spartacus, the leader of a slave revolt in ancient Rome) agitated for a proletarian revolution on the Russian pattern. Unable to operate effectively through soviets, the Left tried to stage a revolution in the winter of 1918–1919, but Ebert called in the army to stop it. The generals used not only regular units but also newly formed volunteer units, or "Free Corps," made up mostly of professional soldiers, who were embittered by Germany's recent military defeat and were violently opposed to democracy.

Now the right wing of the Independent Socialists withdrew from the government, and sole responsibility thenceforth rested with the Social Democrats, who put their man, Noske, into the war ministry. As the civil strife continued, the communists attempted a *coup*, which Ebert, Noske, and the troops put down. Cavalry officers murdered the two chief leaders of the communists after peace had been restored, at the cost of more than a thousand casualties. Meanwhile, in Catholic Bavaria, disorders led to the brief emergence of a Soviet republic, which was liquidated in May, leaving Bavaria the home of a sort of permanent red-scare. The Bavarian local authorities, throughout the entire life of the Weimar Republic, encouraged the intrigues of monarchists, militarists, and nationalists. It was in Bavaria that Free Corps assassinations were planned, and it was there that Hitler got his start.

In this way the forces of the German Right, ostensibly crushed by the war, were given a powerful new lease on life by the Allies. Meantime, Germany still had an army, the *Reichswehr,* limited in size to 100,000 men, consisting chiefly of officer cadres, magnificently trained and able to take over the command of far larger numbers if and when troops became available.

The political constellation of the new Germany did not consist solely of Social Democrats and extremists of Right and Left. The old parties of imperial Germany (see Chapter 22) reappeared, often with new labels. The right wing of the old Liberals now emerged as the People's party, including the more moderate industrialists, with a platform of private property and opposition to socialism. Its leader was Gustav Stresemann. Former Progressives and left-wing Liberals now formed the new Democratic party, a genuine middle-class republican and democratic group, including many of Germany's most distinguished intellectuals. The Catholic Center party reemerged with its name and program unchanged. It accepted the Republic, rejected socialism, and favored social legislation under pressure from its left wing of trade-union members, but it opposed far-reaching reform under pressure from its right wing of aristocrats and industrialists. The Social Democrats, the Democrats, the Center, and the People's party represented those groups which, though not all enthusiastic, were willing to try to make the new state work. On the Right, the former Conservatives reemerged as the National People's party or Nationalists, dominated by the Junkers as before. The Nationalists had the support of some great industrialists, of most of the bureaucrats, and of a substantial section of the lower middle class, which hoped to return to the good old

days of the monarchy. The Nationalists did not accept the Republic.

The Weimar Constitution, 1919

When the Germans voted for a national constituent assembly in January, 1919, the parties supporting the Republic won more than 75 per cent of the seats (see table below), with the Social Democrats alone obtaining nearly 40 per cent. The assembly met in Weimar, elected Ebert President of Germany, and formed a government that reluctantly signed the Treaty of Versailles after a delay of some months. The assembly then adopted the new constitution. The new Germany was still a federative state, but the central government had great authority to legislate for the entire country. The president might use armed force to coerce any of the states that failed to obey the constitution or national laws. The cabinet was responsible to the lower house, or *Reichstag,* which was to be chosen by universal suffrage of all citizens (including women) over twenty.

The president, who was to be elected every seven years by the entire people, was given considerable authority. He was empowered to make treaties, appoint and remove the cabinet, command the armed forces and appoint or remove all officers, dissolve the Reichstag, and

German Elections to the Weimar Assembly and Reichstag, 1919–1933

(Number of seats obtained by the major parties, arranged with the Left at the top, the Right at the bottom)

	Jan. 1919	June 1920	May 1924	Dec. 1924	May 1928	Sept. 1930	July 1932	Nov. 1932	Mar. 1933
Communists	—[a]	2	62	45	54	77	89	100	81
Independent Socialists	22	81	—[b]						
Social Democrats	163	112	100	131	152	143	133	121	125
Democrats	74	45	28	32	25	14	4	2	5
Center	71	68	65	69	61	68	75	70	74
People's party	22	62	44	51	45	30	7	11	2
Nationalists	42	66	96	103	78	41	40	51	52
Nazis			38	20	12	107	230	196	288

[a]The Communist party boycotted the elections to the Weimar constituent assembly.
[b]In these and succeeding elections the Independent Socialists had merged with the Social Democrats.

call new elections. Furthermore, he could take any measure he deemed necessary to restore order when it was threatened, and might temporarily suspend the civil liberties that the constitution granted. Yet the Reichstag could order such measures repealed. Inside the cabinet, the chancellor was a real prime minister, with responsibility for planning policy. The constitution also provided for popular initiative. One-tenth of the electorate could bring in a bill or propose an amendment to the constitution. On the economic side, the constitution provided that the government might socialize suitable enterprises, but guaranteed private property and the right of inheritance.

Several other contradictions reflected the conflict of interest between the Social Democrats and the middle-class parties. But the powers of the president and the introduction of proportional representation were perhaps the two chief weaknesses. The powers of the president made dictatorship a real possibility. Proportional representation required that votes be cast for entire party lists of candidates, and thus prevented independent voters from "splitting the ticket," and independent politicians from obtaining office. This system encouraged small splinter parties to multiply.

Right and Left Extremism, 1920–1922

In 1920, pressure from the Right loomed as the most serious threat to the Republic. In March, 1920, a *coup* (in German, *putsch*) drove the government from Berlin for several days. The commander of the Berlin military district, supported by Ludendorff and the Free Corps leaders, hoped to bring to power an East Prussian reactionary official named Kapp. Ebert managed to defeat this "Kapp *putsch*" by calling a general strike that paralyzed Germany. Because the old monarchical judicial system still existed, the men arrested and tried for the Kapp *putsch* all got off with extremely light sentences, whereas left-wingers brought before the courts were very harshly punished.

As an immediate outgrowth of the strike called by the government, a communist revolt took place in the Ruhr. In pursuit of the communists, German troops entered the area, which had been demilitarized by the Versailles Treaty; this action in turn led to French military intervention and a brief occupation of the Ruhr and Frankfurt (April-May, 1920). In the elections of June, 1920, the electorate began to support the extremists of Right and Left. The Democrats and Social Democrats lost strength.

In April, 1921, when the Allies presented the bill for reparations, which totaled 132 billion gold marks, the politicians of the Right favored simple rejection of the terms, while the Weimar parties realistically decided that the threat of invasion made this course impossible. Again, the moderates had to take responsibility for a necessary decision that was sure to prove unpopular, and that they themselves did not approve. The minister for reconstruction, Walter Rathenau, a Democrat and a successful industrialist, hoped that a policy of "fulfillment" might convince the Allies that Germany was acting in good faith, and might in the long run lead to concessions. An intensely patriotic German, Rathenau was also a Jew, and drew the particular venom of the anti-Semitic nationalist orators.

The secret terrorist groups of the Right began a campaign of assassination. They began (August, 1921) by murdering Matthias Erzberger, the Catholic Center politician who had signed the armistice, and a leading moderate. His assassins escaped through Bavaria. When one of them was caught, the courts acquitted him. When the League of Nations awarded to Poland a substantial area of the rich province of Upper Silesia, containing many German inhabitants, the Right grew still angrier. Rathenau was killed in June, 1922, by men who believed in the "stab-in-the-back" theory, and thought that by murdering a Jew they could avenge the "betrayal" of the German army.

Hitler: Early Career

During the months between the assassinations of Erzberger and Rathenau, a new and ominous element had emerged among the wel-

perial regime had expected
make the losers pay German
imposing huge indemnities.
only about 4 per cent of th
means of taxation. As defeat
ernment borrowed more an
from the banks. When the loar
government repaid them wit
that was not backed by gold.
happened, more paper mone
circulation, and prices rose; ea
naturally led to a demand for
which had to be paid with mo
The inflationary spiral was un
of cutting purchasing powe
heavy taxes, the government p
to compete with each othe
short supply, thus speeding
process of inflation.

Many other forces helped
For several reasons, Germany
back its currency. Germany h
for goods bought abroad dur
rich sent great sums out of C
that the government would at
reparations. Raw materials w
ply; industry was disorganizec
curtailed. The armies of occu
maintained at German expens
payments had to be made.
mans maintained that these
cially reparations, were the c
but, though reparations certa
process, they were by no mea
sible for it. The total sums i
rations were never great eno
German currency until long a
was under way. Indeed, the in
due to the industrialists' wish
reparations, and to clear thei
ness by letting the currency b

The following timetable sh
situation had become by th
When the war was over, the
valued at 4.2 to a dollar, had
January, 1921, it was 45; by
By September, 1922, it was
end of the year it was 7,000.
the government begged for
reparations payments and fo

Officer addressing a Berlin
crowd during the Kapp
Putsch of 1920.

ter of right-wing organizations in Bavaria. This
was the "National Socialist Party of the German Workers" (called "Nazi" as an abbreviation of the word *National*) led by Adolf Hitler,
the son of an obscure, illegitimate Austrian
customs official, whose real name had been
Schicklgruber. Born in 1889, Hitler early
quarreled with his father, and seems always to
have felt bitter and frustrated. In 1907, he was
rejected by the Vienna Academy of Fine Arts,
where he wished to study painting. He became
an odd-job man, selling an occasional watercolor, but always hovering on the edge of starvation. It was during these years that his hatred
of the Jews began. As we know (see Chapter
22), lower-middle-class Vienna at the time was
deeply devoted to its anti-Semitic Mayor Lueger, whom Hitler admired. Because Karl Marx
himself had been of Jewish origin and because
many Viennese Jews were socialists, Hitler
associated socialism with the Jews and lumped
both together as somehow responsible for his
own personal troubles and for the ills of
the world.

Hitler drew support for his anti-Semitism
from several nineteenth-century theorists. The
French Count Joseph Arthur de Gobineau
(1816–1882) had laid the pseudo-scientific
foundation for modern theories of "Nordic"
and "Aryan" supremacy. One of Gobineau's
most influential readers was the great German
composer, Richard Wagner (see Chapter 23).

Wagner's son-in-law, the Englishman Houston
Stewart Chamberlain (1855–1927), wrote a
long and turgid book called *The Foundations
of the Nineteenth Century,* which glorified the
Germans and assailed the Jews; one section
was devoted to a "demonstration" that Christ
had not been of Jewish origin. Chamberlain
furiously opposed democratic government
and, interestingly enough, capitalism. Thus he
provided Hitler with a congenial mixture of
racism, nationalism, anti-democratic thought,
and radicalism.

Hitler came to hate Vienna as a cosmopolitan and Jewish community, and moved to Munich in 1913. In 1914, he enlisted in the German army, and fought through the war as a
corporal. He won the iron cross for bravery,
but was regarded by his commanding officer
as too "hysterical" to deserve a commission.
After the war, he went back to Munich, where,
as might have been expected, he loathed
the new republic and the "Bolsheviks," admired the Free Corps, and decided to become
a politician.

Ludendorff had moved to Munich, and had
become the center of the reaction. Hitler was
employed as a political education officer for
the troops. While engaged in this work, he discovered a small political group that called
itself the "German Workers' Party." This group
combined nationalism and militarism with a
generous amount of radicalism. Hitler joined

Watercolo[...]
in Vienna[...]

the party in 191[...]
be a far abler p[...]
leagues. He urg[...]
the union of al[...]
many, for the e[...]
political life, a s[...]
ment, the confis[...]
tionalization of[...]
small business, [...]
antry. The seem[...]
program caused[...]
sympathetic to [...]
money. As earl[...]
assure them by[...]
dustrial capital" [...]
loan capital."

Hitler was an[...]
with almost hy[...]
crowd. By 1921[...]
absolute leader, [...]
duce) of the Naz[...]

republic in 1924, and for a monarchy again in 1935, always by enormous majorities. Economic dislocation brought strength to communism among the refugees and in labor groups. The political exuberance for which Greece is celebrated made the regular conduct of parliamentary government impossible. The inter-war period was punctuated by a whole series of *coups* by generals, some republican, some monarchist, all more or less authoritarian, but most of them ineffective and none especially bloodthirsty. The last of these was the most fascist, General John Metaxas, who became dictator in August, 1936. Metaxas abolished political parties, instituted censorship and political persecution of his opponents, launched a program of public works, and imitated the Nazis in other ways. But when the Italian invasion came from Albania in October, 1940, Metaxas ordered resistance, which was the beginning of Greece's heroic showing in World War II.

Fascism in Review

None of these regimes in eastern Europe was fascist in the full sense of the term. In Italy and Germany the regimes rested, at least initially, upon the popular support of a substantial proportion of the people, even though that support was kept alive by the technique of artificial stimulation. In eastern Europe, on the other hand, the dictatorships rested on the police, the bureaucracy, and the army, and not on the support of the peasant masses. To an eastern European politician of almost any complexion, an election was an occasion for bribery, intimidation, and promises that he had no intention of trying to fulfill. The hope placed by some western liberals in peasant parties proved in the end illusory.

Thus the growth of anti-democratic governments of the Right in Europe during the period between the wars strikingly reveals the difficulties in the way of moderate parliamentary regimes in countries without parliamentary traditions. This does not mean that the western liberal tradition cannot be exported. But a liberal constitution on paper and a liberal franchise are in themselves no guarantee that a regime on western models can become stabilized. The postwar economic agony had scarcely disappeared before the depression of the late twenties and early thirties struck. Under these circumstances, men turned to extremists of the Left and Right. But the fear of communism, combined with the seductive nationalist propaganda of the Right, brought about fascist victories in Italy and Germany. Mussolini's and Hitler's successes helped to tip the scale: the triumph of the Right elsewhere was assured, and a new world war was inevitable.

Reading Suggestions on the Rise of Fascism

(Asterisk indicates paperbound edition.)

The Roots
of Fascism

A. Cobban, *Dictatorship: Its History and Theory* (Scribner's, 1939). Highly suggestive survey, reaching well back into history.

P. Viereck, *Metapolitics: From the Romantics to Hitler* (Knopf, 1941). A survey of the background in German political thought.

C. J. Hayes, *A Generation of Materialism, 1871–1900* (Harper, 1941). Contains a concise and corrosive section on the seedtime of fascism.

Note: The titles listed above present differing views on the origins of fascism, a subject still much debated by historians. Further titles bearing on the subject may be found in the reading suggestions for Chapter 23.

Italy

G. Magaro, *Mussolini in the Making* (Houghton Mifflin, 1938). An unequaled study of Mussolini's early career.

H. Finer, *Mussolini's Italy* (Holt, 1935), and H. A. Steiner, *Government in Fascist Italy* (McGraw-Hill, 1938). Two very solid studies by expert political scientists.

G. A. Borgese, *Goliath: The March of Fascism* (Viking, 1938), and G. Salvemini, *Under the Axe of Fascism* (Viking, 1936). Lively works by important anti-fascist Italians.

G. Salvemini, *Prelude to World War II* (Doubleday, 1954). A survey of Mussolini's foreign policy, by one of his most implacable enemies.

Germany

A. Hitler, *Mein Kampf* (Reynal and Hitchcock, 1939). A complete English translation of the Nazi bible, the basic work to be read for an understanding of the movement.

A. Hitler, *My New Order,* R. de Sales, ed. (Reynal and Hitchcock, 1941). Speeches after the Führer's coming to power.

A. L. C. Bullock, *Hitler: A Study in Tyranny* (Oxham's, 1952; *abridgment, Bantam). The best biography.

S. W. Halperin, *Germany Tried Democracy* (Crowell, 1946). A reliable history of the Weimar Republic, 1918–1933.

R. G. L. Waite, *Vanguard of Nazism* (Harvard Univ. Press, 1952). A good study of the "Free Corps" movement.

J. W. Wheeler-Bennett, *Wooden Titan* (Morrow, 1936), and *Nemesis of Power* (St. Martin's Press, 1954). Two first-rate studies, the first dealing with Hindenburg, and the second with the role of the German army in politics from 1918 to 1945.

F. L. Neumann, *Behemoth: The Structure and Practice of National Socialism* (Oxford Univ. Press, 1944). The best work on the subject.

K. Heiden, *History of National Socialism* (Knopf, 1935), and S. H. Roberts, *The House That Hitler Built* (Harper, 1938). Two older and still useful studies of the Nazis.

F. von Papen, *Memoirs* (Dutton, 1953). An apologetic autobiography by the scheming right-wing politician.

E. Wiskemann, *The Rome-Berlin Axis* (Oxford Univ. Press, 1949). A study of the formation and history of the Hitler-Mussolini partnership.

R. Fischer, *Stalin and German Communism* (Harvard Univ. Press, 1948). A study of the role played by the communist movement in the history of Germany between the wars.

Note: Some of the titles listed under the reading suggestions for Chapter 28 deal with international relations during the inter-war period and will illuminate Nazi foreign policy.

Other Countries

G. Brenan, *The Spanish Labyrinth* (Macmillan, 1943). A useful study of the Spanish Civil War against its historical and economic background.

C. Bowers, *My Mission to Spain* (Simon & Schuster, 1954); C. J. Hayes, *Wartime Mission to Spain, 1942–1945* (Macmillan, 1945); and Lord Templewood (Sir Samuel Hoare), *Complacent Dictator* (Knopf, 1947). Three differing views of Franco and the Spanish problem, by three ambassadors, the first two American, the last British.

Hugh Thomas, *The Spanish Civil War* (Harper, 1961; rev. ed., *Penguin, 1965). The best single work on the subject.

G. E. R. Gedye, *Betrayal in Central Europe* (Harper, 1939). A careful journalist's account of Austria and Czechoslovakia.

H. Seton-Watson, *Eastern Europe between the Wars, 1918–1941* (Cambridge Univ. Press, 1946). A useful account dealing with all the eastern European countries except Greece and Albania.

R. L. Buell, *Poland: Key to Europe* (Knopf, 1939). A helpful survey.

R. West, *Black Lamb and Grey Falcon* (Viking, 1941). A highly subjective account of Yugoslavia, loaded with political bias, but fascinating and informative reading.

Historical Fiction

I. Silone, *Bread and Wine* (*Penguin, 1946; *New American Library), and *Fontamara* (Smith and Haas, 1934). Two good novels on rural Italy under fascism; by a distinguished anti-fascist writer.

C. Levi, *Christ Stopped at Eboli* (Farrar, Straus, 1947; *Universal Library). An anti-fascist Italian doctor and painter writes movingly of his exile in a remote and poverty-striken southern Italian village.

H. Fallada, *Little Man What Now?* (Simon & Schuster, 1933; *Ungar), and E. Remarque, *Three Comrades* (Little, Brown, 1937; *Popular Library). Two touching novels of depression-ridden Germany.

E. von Salomon, *"Der Fragebogen" (The Questionnaire)* (Doubleday, 1955). One of the plotters against Rathenau, a strong sympathizer with authoritarian movements, tells his life story satirically, against the background of American military government in post-1945 Germany.

E. Hemingway, *For Whom the Bell Tolls* (Scribner's, 1940). A characteristic Hemingway novel, set in the Spain of the Civil War.

28

The Democracies

and the Colonial World

Domestic and Imperial Problems, 1919–1939

I   Introduction

The central fact—or irony—of politics between the two world wars is that the war "to make the world safe for democracy" seemed to have made it in effect a difficult and dangerous place for democracy. Idealists like President Wilson had expected that the collapse of the old Romanov, Habsburg, and Hohenzollern empires would automatically ensure an increase in the number of democratic states. But instead, as we have just seen, much of Europe came under régimes that were hostile to liberal democracy. Even Italy, which had appeared to be evolving toward a democratic constitutional monarchy, turned fascist. In the 1920's and 1930's, then, the core of democracy remained in the great North Atlantic powers—Britain, France, and the United States—and in the smaller states of the Low Countries, Switzerland, and Scandinavia.

The upsurge of communism and fascism created grave problems in international relations for the three great democracies. At times in the 1920's it looked as if they might successfully overcome these problems and bring the world back to peaceful habits. But in the 1930's the great world-wide depression, the advent of Hitler, and the aggressions of fascist states in the West and of an expansionist Japan in the Far East rapidly darkened the international scene. With the outbreak of another general war in 1939, it was clear that the two decades since 1919 had been at best a twenty year's truce, a truce broken with increasing frequency by international troublemakers.

Certainly the totalitarian aggressors bore the major responsibility for the unleashing of a second world war. Yet a far from minor factor in the deterioriation of the twenty years' truce was the failure of the peaceful democracies to present a unified front against those who threatened world peace. In the 1920's Britain, France, and the United States became preoccupied with their own domestic problems. In the early 1930's their preoccupation increased as a result of the urgent crisis of the depression. But this was the very time when international problems demanded equally urgent attention. International trade was steadily shrinking in the face of the depression and of mounting tariff barriers; the prospects for peace were steadily fading before the saber-rattling and actual saber-wielding of the enemies of democracy. Faced with two equally urgent sets of problems, the democracies turned first to the domestic ones and then discovered that the international situation was rapidly moving toward war.

Nor was this all. During the twenty years' truce, the democracies faced a third set of problems, not as yet so urgent as the other two, but of very great potential importance. This third set involved imperial issues—the relationship between the great democracies and the non-western peoples, many of whom were still under colonial rule or some other form of control by democratic mother countries. Particularly in Asia and the Middle East, the non-western peoples were beginning to assert their nationalism and to demand the loosening of old imperial ties. This formidable political movement did not reach full intensity until the years following World War II when a long procession of former colonies, protectorates, and mandates began to join the ranks of independent states (see Chapter 31). But the nationalist movements that have brought these newcomers into the family of nations since 1945 grew steadily in the 1920's and 1930's.

The three sets of problems—domestic, foreign, and imperial—faced by the democracies during the twenty years' truce were interconnected and interrelated in countless ways. We shall underline some of these interrelations, as we have shown the links between the internal and external policies of the communist and fascist states. But, in order to point up the main issues, we shall also separate national, international, and colonial problems in a fashion that must oversimplify the complexities of real life. Our survey emphasizes first the chief domestic problems of the democracies in the inter-war years and then considers the growing conflict between their colonialism and the nationalism of the non-western world; in Chapter 29 we shall analyze their foreign policies, as distinguished from their imperial policies. We begin here with an examination of the crisis confronting Britain on the home front after November, 1918.

II   Great Britain

The Postwar Depression

Save for trifling losses from German Zeppelin raids and coastal bombardments, the British Isles suffered no direct material damage in World War I. But the British armed forces lost about seven hundred and fifty thousand men killed in action, and about a million and a half wounded. The casualties of the Empire and the Commonwealth as a whole came to nearly a million killed and over two million wounded. The economic losses of the mother country had been grave indeed—the almost incalculable difference between the actual cost of destructive war and what might otherwise have been productive effort.

The national debt after the war was ten times that of 1914. Many British investments abroad, returns on which had been a major factor in Victorian prosperity, had had to be liquidated to get purchasing power abroad for food and war materials. Forty per cent of the great British merchant fleet, the income from which had helped to balance Britain's international accounts and pay for her imports, had been destroyed by enemy action. The whole fabric of international trade on which Britain depended was torn in a thousand places in 1918 and could not be rapidly restored in the unsettled conditions that prevailed in the postwar world. And, finally, to supplement the war production of Britain and France, the industrial plants of the United States, of Canada, and even of India had been called on, and had received a stimulus that made them in peacetime more effective competitors of the British. In the 1920's, the industrial plant of the Germans, nourished in part by loans from America, once more took up the rivalry that had so alarmed the British before the war.

In short, victorious Britain faced in an ag-gravated form the basic economic difficulty that we analyzed in Chapter 21. The country that had been in Victorian days the "workshop of the world" had now lost its head start and could no longer give full employment to its millions of workers. And yet those workers were in no mood to accept a lower standard of living. They had made great gains in social security before the war, and they had fought the war in the hope of still better things to come. They had been promised that the defeated enemy would through reparations pay the costs of the war and give Britain a new start.

This hope was very early disappointed. No substantial reparations came through, economic difficulties soon began to accumulate, and by 1921 there were already almost a million unemployed. In that same year the British government, faced with the rising cost of living, increased the very meager unemployment payments. These payments, soon given the derogatory name of the "dole," were strictly speaking not old-fashioned poor relief, but payments on unemployment insurance policies that had been part of Lloyd George's social legislation of prewar days. However, large-scale unemployment continued, and some young workers never acquired employment status. Unemployment insurance could not be maintained on a sound actuarial basis, and the payments became in fact a form of poor relief.

The Great Britain of the 1920's experienced no equivalent of the "Coolidge prosperity" that the United States was to enjoy. We must not exaggerate: The British economic decline was not catastrophic. London, Manchester, and Liverpool did not become ghost cities, though some of the gravely depressed areas, like the coal-mining regions of South Wales, did begin to show real signs of decay. What happened was rather a *relative* decline, the comparative slowing up of an economy geared to dynamic growth, with a working population conditioned psychologically to a slowly rising standard of living and a middle class similarly conditioned to traditional comforts. Moreover, this was the twentieth century, the century of the newspaper, the movie, the radio. The British were well aware, for instance, that Americans had automobiles, radios, and a lot else; they, too, wanted those things.

Britain was, then, suffering from ills characteristic of economic old age. The coal industry is a good concrete illustration of these ills. There was still a lot of coal in Britain; but much of it was costly to mine, since the most easily and cheaply worked seams were being exhausted. The industry was badly organized, with many small and inefficient mines running at a loss, and with machinery and methods that were antiquated in comparison with American and the best continental standards. Productivity per man-hour over the whole industry was low. Worst of all, perhaps, the 1920's saw the rapid rise all over the industrialized world of major competitors of coal — oil, and electricity based on water power — and the consequent decline of British coal exports. Since the British Isles had no petroleum, and no very great potential in hydroelectric power, coal, the historic basis of British industrial power, simply had to be mined. The workers were unionized and were in no mood to accept cuts in wages; the owners did not want to run their business at a loss. A strike in March, 1921, after the government had rejected Labor party proposals for making permanent the wartime nationalization of the industry, focused national attention on this critical problem. The strike was settled in July, but only by the government's consenting to pay subsidies to cover increased wages.

The Conservative and Labor Programs

Against the background of economic depression, British domestic politics during the twenty years' truce displayed a fairly clear class basis. The Conservatives, still often called Tories, tended to get the support of aristocrats and of middle-class people who wanted to attack new problems with traditional methods and with a minimum of government intervention. The Labor party tended to get the support of trade unionists and of intellectuals from all classes who demanded that the government intervene more vigorously in the economic field. We must not oversimplify, however; not every reformer necessarily voted Labor nor every stand-patter Tory. Yet economic issues did sharpen the differences between the two major British parties.

The first casualty in the struggle between Labor and the Conservatives was the old Liberal party, which was ground to a mere husk between the two contending groups. The Conservatives, who had won the lion's share of seats in the election of 1918, held immediately after the armistice, and known as the "khaki election," decided in 1922 to withdraw their support from the coalition government headed by the Liberal Lloyd George. In the ensuing elections the Conservatives won, and the Liberals, split between the followers of Lloyd George and those of the more orthodox Asquith, lost heavily. Labor won 142 seats — more than the Liberals did — and became for the first time His Majesty's Opposition.

Both Conservatives and Labor realized the underlying difficulties of Britain's position. Both were fully aware that twentieth-century Britain had to sell enough goods and services abroad — enough manufactured goods and shipping, insurance, banking, and tourist services — so that the income from them would buy food for her people and much of the raw materials for her factories. But the parties were not agreed on how to achieve this necessary task. Broadly speaking, the Conservatives wanted to retain private industry, with government and other technical experts helping to make it efficient. But they were thwarted by high tariffs in the United States and elsewhere, by the drive to economic self-sufficiency all over the world, and by the difficulties of trade with communist Russia.

The state of world trade drove the Conservatives more and more to the solution Joseph Chamberlain (see Chapter 21) had advocated earlier: protective tariffs against competing foreign goods, and the knitting of the Empire and Commonwealth, with their vast variety of resources, into a largely self-sufficient trade area by "imperial preference" agreements. Such agreements would give raw materials from the colonies and dominions preferred treatment in the British market in return for preferred treatment of British manufactures in the colonial and dominion markets. In theory, at least, the scheme could have worked, for the Commonwealth and Empire of the nineteen-twenties—one-quarter of the world's land and people—had the requisite natural resources and offered a potential market capable of supporting the British Isles in the style to which they were accustomed. In practice, however, the great snag was the unwillingness of the constituent parts of the Empire and Commonwealth to accept for themselves the role of producers of raw materials in exchange for British manufactured goods and British services. The self-governing dominions, loyal though they had been during the war, were in no mood to assume a role essentially like that of colonies in the old mercantilistic days. They were looking toward independent nationhood, and they wanted what seems to go with nationhood in our world—their own industries. This was also true of what was potentially the richest unit in the Empire, India.

The Labor solution was nationalization —that is, government purchase and operation of key industries with just compensation to their private owners, rather than seizure without compensation as in Soviet Russia. The key industries were transportation, power, coal, steel, perhaps even textiles, cutlery, pottery, machine tools—all the industries that seem to thrive best on large-scale organization. A good many Laborites wanted nationalization simply because, as socialists, they believed that profits, rent, and interest paid to "capitalist" private owners were forms of worker-exploitation, and that under nationalization these forms of exploitation would cease. But many of their leaders knew that even nationalized

industries would still face the fundamental problem of selling enough goods abroad to keep the economy going. They argued, therefore, that nationalization would enable British industries to produce more cheaply and efficiently. It would do away with wasteful competition and with the inefficient firms so conspicuous in the coal industry, for instance. It would, they fondly believed, force into productive work both unnecessary managerial and selling staffs, and stockholders and other investors who lived without working.

Moreover, Labor supporters believed that, once nationalization had been achieved, the British workmen would take a new attitude toward their work. Knowing that they were now the *real* owners of their own industries, they would put their hearts into their work, abstain from feather-bedding, absenteeism, and similar practices, and raise production to a point where the goods of Britain could undersell those of her capitalist rivals in world markets. This belief was reinforced by the somewhat paradoxical faith in free trade that the Labor party had inherited from the Liberals, and by its high hopes for improved international relations. Consequently, Labor was hostile to the Conservative policies of protective tariffs and imperial preference.

Postwar Politics

In the twenty years between the wars, neither the Tories nor the Laborites were able to carry out their full platforms. Labor itself, though it came to power briefly in 1924 and in 1929, with its leader Ramsay MacDonald as prime minister, never had a parliamentary position firm enough to nationalize any industry. The Conservatives, by no means unanimous on the degree of economic self-sufficiency they wanted for the Empire, were decisively held up by the refusal of the Commonwealth countries to go much further than to accept certain limited imperial preferences.

Despite the wider cleavage between the two parties, British politics still retained many of the amenities of Victorian parlia-

Emergency transport conveying London office workers during the general strike of 1926.

In 1928, almost unnoticed, the last step was taken in the *political* democratization of Britain that had begun in 1832. In 1918, in preparation for the "khaki election," the government had put through a reform bill which eliminated all the old exceptions to universal male suffrage and gave the vote to all men over twenty-one. Culminating a long and spectacular campaign in which "suffragettes" had demonstrated, marched, orated, and even chained themselves to lamp posts, destroyed property, and gone to jail in behalf of women's rights, the bill also gave the vote to women. But, with almost a caricature of British caution, it set the voting age for women at thirty years, thus insuring that there would always be more male than female voters. The distinction was too irrational to stand up, especially after experience had demonstrated—as it also did in the United States—that women divide politically about the way men do. In 1928, a measure known irreverently as the "bill for flapper suffrage" gave women the vote at twenty-one.

Although the dole, depressed industries, and other signs of economic ill-health persisted, Britain did experience a measure of recovery in the late 1920's. But then the great depression, the signal for which was given by the New York stockmarket crash in October, 1929, began its spread around the world. Britain, already weakened, was one of the first to be engulfed. Faced by a serious deficit, and unwilling to try to meet it by cutting the dole and other social services, the second Labor government of Ramsay MacDonald resigned in August, 1931.

It gave way to a coalition of Conservatives, Liberals, and right-wing Laborites headed by the same MacDonald. This coalition cabinet put through reductions in the dole and the social services. Late in 1931, it took the decisive step, a hard one in view of Britain's traditional financial leadership and devotion to the gold standard, of going off the gold standard and letting the pound fall in value. In 1932, it made the first move away from free trade by enacting protective tariffs, and in the same year Britain ceased payment on her war

mentary life. The House of Commons, even though it now included workingmen and others who by no means spoke with an upper-class "Oxford accent," was still one of the best clubs in the world. For a few weeks in 1926 some 2,500,000 trade-union members attempted a general strike in support of the coal-miners, who were already on strike in protest against a cut in their wages. The general strike failed, but during its brief course fundamental British attitudes were revealed. Thousands of men from the middle and upper classes volunteered to keep essential services operating, and in Plymouth a soccer team of strikers played a team of police. Britain, despite mounting tensions, remained a land of general law-abidingness, where the class struggle that the Marxists talked so much about seemed to have come thoroughly under the control of the parliamentary decencies.

De Valera taking the salute of the Irish Republic Army, Western Division, in County Clare, autumn, 1921.

debts to the United States, except for a few "token" payments. These measures did little to help the unemployed or to strike at the roots of British economic troubles. But they did stem the depression sufficiently to enable the coalition to win two general elections in 1931 and 1935.

Yet the coalition government was in fact dominated by Conservatives, and after the 1935 election the Conservative leader, Stanley Baldwin, took over the post of prime minister. Gradually the British economy pulled out of the worst of the depression, although—some economic theorists might say *because*—Baldwin did nothing beyond keeping the budget in balance. By 1936, however, Mussolini's and Hitler's aggressions were beginning to demand British attention. The economic question and the social question, by no means solved, faded before the threat of another war.

Settlement of the Irish Question

The years between the wars were of great importance for Ireland. The outbreak of war in 1914 put off the threatened revolt against Home Rule in Ulster (see Chapter 21), but the Irish were hardly reliable partners in the war. In 1916, the faction furthest removed

from the Ulster rebels, the Irish nationalists, got some German help in guns and ammunition and staged an armed rising in Dublin. The British put down this "Easter rebellion," but not before they had created a fresh and effective set of Irish political martyrs. The British government did not dare extend conscription to Ireland until April, 1918, and the attempt made then led the Irish nationalists to boycott the British Parliament and to cease attending its sessions.

By 1919, Home Rule as decreed in 1914 was not enough for the nationalists of Ireland. The Home Rulers of prewar days had yielded to more extreme rebels, the Sinn Fein (meaning in Gaelic, "ourselves alone"), who wanted complete independence. The years 1919–1921 were filled with violence, ambushes, arson, and guerrilla warfare, as the Irish, who now had their own illegal parliament, the Dail Ereann, moved into full revolution. The British, tired from their long war, were not in a state of mind to use force effectively; the Irish, on the other hand, were admirably organized and full of fight.

Yet the immediate upshot of the violent phase of the revolution was a compromise, for the Sinn Fein split in two. A moderate wing, led by Arthur Griffith and Michael Collins, was willing to accept a compromise in which Protestant Ulster would remain under direct British rule and the Catholic counties

485

would be given dominion status. A radical wing, led by Eamon De Valera—exceedingly Irish in spite of his Spanish surname—insisted that the whole island achieve complete independence as a unified republic. The moderates negotiated with the British, and in 1921 obtained for the twenty-six counties of southern Ireland dominion status under the name of the Irish Free State. The Free State had its own parliament, the Dail, and was completely self-governing with its own army and its own diplomatic services; it merely accepted the British Crown as symbolic head. The six Protestant counties of Ulster maintained their old relationship with Britain, which now became officially the United Kingdom of Great Britain and Northern Ireland. Ulster had, however, its own parliament at Belfast, and considerable local autonomy.

This settlement was unacceptable to De Valera and the more extreme revolutionaries, and the Irish revolution now became a civil war between partisans of the Free State and partisans of a republic, with the old round of burning, ambush, and murder. But the Irish, too, were beginning to tire of violence. When the moderate leader, Michael Collins, a man much closer to earth than De Valera, was assassinated by a republican, public opinion turned away from the extremists. Meantime the Free State was gradually settling down. De Valera, after refusing to sit in the Dail because he would have had to take an oath of loyalty to the king, changed his mind and decided to bring his fellow republicans into the national parliament in 1927.

From then on, almost in the manner of illogical and compromise-loving England, the Irish Free State gradually and peacefully got what the extremists had been killing and burning for. De Valera's party won a plurality in the Dail in 1932, and a majority in 1933; thereupon it proceeded to abolish the oath of loyalty to the Crown and to cut most of the slender threads that still tied the Free State to England. In 1939, Catholic Ireland was so free from British domination that she could declare and maintain her neutrality throughout World War II. In 1949, the final step was taken when Britain recognized her as the fully independent Republic of Eire (Gaelic for "Ireland").

The Commonwealth of Nations

No such secession took place elsewhere among the British possessions in the years between the two world wars. On the contrary, definite constitutional recognition of the essential independence of the dominions seemed to make them more loyal, though at the cost of any central British authority over their economic policies, and, at least in law, over their foreign policies. The capstone of a long process that had begun with the Durham Report nearly a century before (see Chapter 24) was the Statute of Westminster of 1931. This spelled out the new relations between the dominions and the mother country that had been negotiated in an imperial conference five years earlier. The preparatory report of 1926 anticipated the gist of the Statute of Westminster by declaring that Britain and the dominions

. . . are autonomous communities within the British Empire, equal in status, in no way subordinate one to another in any aspect of their domestic or external affairs, though united by a common allegiance to the crown and freely associated as members of the British Commonwealth of Nations.

That phrase "freely associated" means also "able freely to choose to be dis-associated." In other words, the right of a state to secede, which Americans fought a great civil war to decide is *not* a part of the United States Constitution, *is* a part of the constitution of the British Commonwealth of Nations. And the twenty-six counties of Southern Ireland in effect took advantage of this right to set up their republic quite outside the Commonwealth. South Africa dis-associated itself in 1961 and became an independent republic, and in 1965 the Rhodesian government made a unilateral declaration of independence (for details see Chapter 31).

The new status acquired by the dominions in 1931 was symbolized by a change in terminology. Henceforward they were no longer to be considered parts of the British Empire but free members of the British Commonwealth of Nations. In this new relationship, Britain would have to *negotiate* with Canada or Australia about tariffs, trade conditions, immigration, and the like, just as if they were foreign countries. Although Britain was unable to build a self-sufficient economic unity out of her dominions, still in 1939, as in 1914, the dominions all came into the war on Britain's side. They made this decision even though they had the legal right to follow the example of Ireland and remain neutral.

III France

The Impact of the War

In France, both World War I and the postwar difficulties caused more serious dislocation than they did in Britain. In the war itself, France lost proportionately more in human lives and in material damage than did any other major belligerent. Two million Frenchmen in the prime of life were either killed or so seriously mutilated as to be incapable of normal living. In a land of only 39,000,000, and with an already low birth rate, it is likely that this human loss impaired the French potentiality for achievement in all phases of civilization. Many of the men who would have been statesmen, industrialists, scientists, and artists in the 1930's were killed off in 1914–1918. Three hundred thousand houses and twenty thousand factories or shops were destroyed. In a land of conservative economic organization, where work was done slowly and for the most part without large-scale automatic machinery, this material setback would be long felt. Psychologically, the feeling of victory by no means compensated for the traumatic losses of the four years of struggle.

France set as her goal the laming of her re-

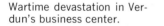

Wartime devastation in Verdun's business center.

cent enemy, Germany, in every possible way. She tried to extract reparations to the last possible sum, undeterred by the arguments of economic theorists that Germany could not pay. But she insisted even more on keeping Germany down, isolated in international relations, and without the physical means of fighting. In a pinch, most Frenchmen would probably have been willing to forego reparations in order to deprive Germany of the economic plant necessary for modern war. They would have preferred this to collecting reparations from a rich and productive Germany.

In the postwar years, however, French statesmen attempted to follow both policies simultaneously and of course failed. The culmination came in January, 1923, under the premiership of the conservative Raymond Poincaré, when French and Belgian troops occupied the great German industrial region of the Ruhr in an effort to make Germany pay full reparations. The Germans replied by passive resistance (see Chapter 27). By 1925, it was clear that the Ruhr occupation had brought no gains to France, and the new French government, chosen after the failure of Poincaré's policy, withdrew the troops.

Meanwhile, the French were undergoing inflation. The inflation resulted in part from the cost of rebuilding the devastated areas—a cost that drained government finances and that was only partly covered by German payments. It resulted also from the high cost of maintaining armed forces—for the French dared not disarm, from the general disorder of international trade, and from the staggering debts piled up during the war by the French government, which, like the imperial German government, had preferred loans to taxes. By the mid-1920's, the franc had slipped from its prewar value of 20 cents to a dangerous low of about 2 cents. In the crisis, Poincaré was recalled to power to "save the franc." In 1926, he initiated new taxes and stern measures of economy which, together with the gradual restoration of normal international trade after the French withdrawal from the Ruhr, stemmed the decline of the franc. In 1928, it was officially revalued at 3.92 cents.

The French inflation, though mild compared with the German, nevertheless caused economic and social dislocation. Frenchmen who had lent their government francs worth 20 cents now found themselves deprived of four-fifths of their loans. This very considerable repudiation fell with particular severity on the middle class, especially the lower middle class, the *petite bourgeoisie*. The greatest sufferers were those living on their savings or on relatively fixed incomes—on pensions, for example, or on the return from bonds, or even on the contents of the wool sock in which the suspicious French peasant traditionally hoarded his cash. Bourgeois people naturally fear pauperization, fear being pushed down into the ranks of the proletariat, and the French were no exceptions. Inflation thus weakened a social class that had long been a mainstay of republicanism in France and added to the social tensions that form the central theme of French domestic history in the period between the two world wars.

Social and Political Tensions

During World War I, the French had temporarily put aside the great political and social conflict they had inherited from 1789. After the war, the "sacred union" of political parties that had carried France through the struggle soon dissolved, and the traditional conflict was resumed. This is sometimes termed the conflict between the "two Frances"—the republican France of the Left, and the royalist, or authoritarian France of the Right. The conflict was not quite a simple Marxian class struggle between rich and poor, capitalist and proletarian, though it was certainly in part such a struggle. On the Right were the wealthier classes, many of them openly hostile to the very existence of the parliamentary state. They were reinforced by conservative peasants and by small businessmen and investors, who were not hostile to the Third Republic as such but who were determined to resist any attempt to extend the social services of the "welfare state." As a result of this right-wing resistance,

France lagged behind Britain, Germany, Sweden, and other European states in providing measures of social security.

On the Left were the champions of the welfare state, the Socialists and the Communists, backed by the more radical workers, by many white-collar people, especially in the government service, and by some intellectuals. The effectiveness of the Left was hampered by the postwar split between the Communists, who followed the Moscow line, and the Socialists, who did not, and by a comparable schism within the major trade-union organization, the C.G.T. (*Confédération Générale du Travail*—General Confederation of Labor). Still nominally part of the Left, but actually in the political middle and not anxious to go far toward the welfare state, was the misleadingly named Radical-Socialist Party, long the political bulwark of the Third Republic. The Radicals were strong among the peasants of southern France, and among white-collar workers and smaller professional men.

Religious difficulties further embittered French politics. French Leftists, including the Radicals, were anticlerical by tradition. After the war they rashly attempted to introduce anticlerical measures into strongly Catholic Alsace. Alsace had not been affected by the separation of Church and State carried through in France after the Dreyfus crisis (see Chapter 21), since it had then belonged to Germany. In the long run, the government was obliged to make compromises on the Alsatian question and on other clerical issues. After bitter public debate, it finally decided in the mid-1920's to resume diplomatic relations with the Vatican, which had been broken off at the time of the separation.

In the late 1920's, the years of increased prosperity that followed the revaluation of the franc, the Third Republic seemed to be getting the better of its internal difficulties. Indeed, the world economic crisis that began in 1929 was late in striking France, and for a while in 1930 it looked as though the French economy, less devoted to large-scale industry than that of the United States, Britain, or Germany, might weather the crisis much more easily. But France, too, depended on international trade, particularly on the export of perfumes, wines and brandies, Paris gowns, and other luxuries. By 1932, the depression had struck, and the government was in serious economic and political difficulties.

The Stavisky Case and the Popular Front

The political crisis came to a head in February, 1934, as a result of the Stavisky case, a financial scandal reminiscent of the Panama scandal of the 1890's (see p. 234). Stavisky, a shady promoter and swindler who had all sorts of connections with important public figures of the Third Republic, was caught at last in a fraudulent bond issue of the municipal pawnshop of Bayonne. The full details have never emerged, but Stavisky's suicide—or murder—in December, 1933, rocked France. On the extreme Right, royalists, enjoying the freedom of a democratic society, had long been organized, notably in a pressure group known as the *Action Française*, and were gaining recruits among upper-class youth. The *Camelots du Roi* ("The King's Henchmen"), strong-armed squads of the *Action Française*, went about beating up Communists, who in turn responded with violence. Less fascist in character, yet also supporting the Right, was a veterans' organization, the *Croix de Feu* ("cross of fire"—the reference is to war), organized by Colonel de la Rocque. During the agitation following the Stavisky case, the *Camelots du Roi* and the *Croix de Feu* took part in riots against the government that broke out in Paris in February, 1934. The Left countered with a brief general strike; France seemed to be on the eve of revolution.

Once more, however, as in the time of Dreyfus, the republican forces rallied to meet the threat, and once more after the crisis had been surmounted France moved to the Left. The February crisis itself was overcome by a coalition of all parties save royalists, Socialists, and Communists. But the franc was again falling in value. The conservative premier,

Demonstrators in the Stavisky riots, Paris, February, 1934.

Flandin, attempted to cut back government expenditures by measures similar to those that had worked a decade earlier under Poincaré; this time they did not work. The forces of the Left responded by forming the so-called Popular Front, made up of the Radical-Socialist, Socialist, and Communist parties, and backed by the C.G.T., which had temporarily healed the schism between Communists and non-Communists. Their victory in a general election in May, 1936, led to the formation of a Popular Front ministry under the leadership of the Socialist Léon Blum.

The Popular Front came to power in part as a kind of French equivalent of the American New Deal. The workers, the white-collar men, the government employees, even many of the peasants and shopkeepers, were now convinced that the classical formulas of economic retrenchment were not the remedy for the ills of France. They wanted a direct attack on the stronghold of retrenchment, the Bank of France, still a private institution dominated by the "two hundred families" alleged to control the French economy. They wanted more equal distribution of wealth by government spending; in short, they wanted the "welfare state."

Other factors entered into the victory of the Popular Front. Mussolini had begun his Ethiopian adventure, and Hitler his rearmament; many a Frenchman in 1936 voted Left as a protest against the compromises that French politicians had been making with the dictators. Finally, these were the years when Russia, just admitted to the League of Nations, seemed to be pursuing a course of collaboration with the West against the threat of Nazi Germany. Moscow therefore urged the French Communists to give up their old policy of constant opposition and to co-operate with their hated enemies, the Socialists.

It was a bad time for a French New Deal. The nation was bitterly divided between partisans and enemies of the Popular Front; business and farming classes were traditionally reluctant to pay income taxes, which would have to be raised to meet the costs of social services; the economy was not geared to labor-saving devices. The Blum cabinet had an ambitious program—a maximum work week of 40 hours; paid vacations and the like; partial nationalization of the Bank of France, the railroads, and the munitions industry; compulsory arbitration of labor disputes; and other measures of social welfare. Although Blum achieved most of this program on paper, everything conspired to block its successful execution. The Communists did not really co-operate, for they refused to participate in the Blum cabinet and sniped at it from the sidelines in the Chamber and in the press. Businessmen took fright at the mushrooming membership of the C.G.T. and at the "sit-down" or "stay-in" strikes of French industrial workers in June, 1936.

Moreover, as the anti-democratic régimes in Germany, Italy, and Spain went on to new victories, France was driven to expensive rearmament. Capital, however, was rapidly leaving the country to be invested or deposited abroad, and the monied class would not subscribe to the huge defense loans that were essential if the French armed forces were to be put in shape to face the war that began to seem inevitable. Blum was obliged to call a halt in March, 1937. The Popular Front now disintegrated, and the C.G.T. lost millions of its newly recruited members and suffered a new schism between Communists and anti-Communists.

Divided France

The morale of the French sagged badly after the collapse of the Popular Front. Under the mounting tensions of 1938 and 1939, the Radical-Socialist premier, Daladier, kept France on the side of Britain in opposition to the Rome-Berlin axis, and various measures of retrenchment — including virtual abandonment of the 40-hour week — kept the French economy from collapse. But the workers took very badly the failure of the Popular Front, and as late as November, 1938, a general strike almost came off, and was combated by putting the railway workers under military orders. The "have" classes, on the other hand, were outraged by the fact that Blum's experiment had been made at all; many of them were convinced that their salvation lay in a French totalitarian state — "better Hitler than Blum,"

as their despairing slogan went. The France that was confronted with war in 1939 was not only inadequately prepared in terms of materials; it was psychologically and spiritually divided, uncertain of what it was fighting for.

Many Frenchmen before 1940 relied on their great empire to restore the flagging morale and material capabilities of the mother country. Colonial troops, particularly from Senegal and North Africa, had helped to replenish the diminished ranks of the army during World War I. Enthusiasts spoke of France as a nation not of just the 40,000,000 at home but of 100,000,000 Frenchmen, including the population of the colonial territories. But this was stretching the facts too far. Economically, the Empire as a whole did advance in the 1920's and 1930's, yet only small native elite groups — only a relative handful of Indo-Chinese or Senegalese or Algerian Arabs, for instance — were assimilated as Frenchmen or desired such assimilation. What the colonial populations were beginning to desire was some sort of home rule or independence. Although some leaders of the French Left urged concessions to native aspirations, little was in fact conceded, and French imperial policy in the 1920's, and 1930's continued along traditional lines. Perhaps no policy pursued then could have prevented the disintegration of the French Empire that occurred after World War II, but the old-fashioned policy that prevailed did nothing to reconcile native nationalists to the French overlords.

Yet we must not here give way to the American fondness for lecturing the French on their weaknesses, and especially on their social and political divisions. The fact remains that in the years between the two World Wars France did not take the totalitarian path, did not go the way of Italy, Germany or Russia. She remained a democracy, with a parliamentary government, and the essential freedoms of speech, press and association.

IV   The United States

Neither the human nor the material losses of the United States in World War I were at all comparable with those of Britain and France. American casualties were 115,000 dead and 206,000 wounded; the comparable French figures were 1,385,000 dead and 3,044,000 wounded *in a population one-third as large.* Moreover, in purely material terms, the United States probably gained from the war. Heavy industries were greatly stimulated by Allied war orders; the war put the growing financial center of New York at least on equal terms with that of London; the dollar had begun to dethrone the monarch of the nineteenth century, the pound sterling. The Allies had borrowed from the American government, but until 1933 some interest came in on these loans. Moreover, the stimulation of American industry resulting from these loans exceeded the loss from the final repudiation of war debts in the early 1930's. The United States, then, came out of the war almost unscathed, victorious, and prosperous.

Isolationism

Yet in some ways the American revulsion against the war in 1919 and the years following was as marked as that of Britain, France, and defeated Germany. On the level of party politics, that revulsion helped to unseat the Democrats, who, under President Wilson, had controlled the federal government since 1913. The Republicans won the presidential elections of 1920, 1924, and 1928. Three successive Republicans occupied the White House —Harding (1921–1923), Coolidge (1923–1929), and Herbert Hoover (1929–1933). The elections were uneventful and not very close; the election of 1928 was, however, notable for the bitterness aroused in many quarters by the unsuccessful candidacy of the Democrat Alfred E. Smith, a Roman Catholic. Many sound observers felt that Smith's religion had been largely instrumental in his defeat and that the American people simply would not elect a Roman Catholic to the highest office of state.

On the level of policy and public attitudes, American revulsion against war took the form of *isolationism,* the desire to withdraw from international politics. This isolationism was by no means universal among Americans. Some historians feel that the drives and attitudes of millions of men had already made isolationism certain in 1919. Others feel that a slight shift in the words and deeds of men in high places could have changed the final decision and could at least have brought America into the League of Nations. If, as we have already seen, the Democratic President Wilson had been willing to meet Republican opposition in the Senate by a few concessions, then perhaps the Treaty of Versailles, League of Nations and all, might have achieved the two-thirds majority in the Senate the Constitution requires for treaties. Or if someone on the Republican side, with skill and prestige, had been able to put through the notion of a bipartisan foreign policy, then with patience and good will the United States might have been brought into the League. Public opinion, say those who take this view, was not against our carrying on the task we had begun in 1917; only a noisy minority in the country as a whole, and the little group of obstinate senators at the top, wanted us to withdraw.

Yet those who remember the years right after 1918 find it hard to deny that the country was swept by a wave of desire to get back to "normalcy," as President Harding later termed it. A great many Americans felt that they had done all they needed to do in beating the Germans and that further direct participation in the complexities of European politics would simply involve American innocence and virtue that much more disastrously in European sophistication and vice. The not uncommon American reaction against its "strong" presidents took the form of repudiating all of Wilson's work at Paris as unAmerican. Furthermore, as the months of negotiation went on with no final decisions reached, Americans, always an impatient people, began to feel that sheer withdrawal was about the only effective action they could take.

The Treaty of Versailles, containing at Wilson's insistence the League of Nations, was finally rejected in the Senate on March 19, 1920. The United States remained technically at war with Germany until July, 1921, when a resolution making a separate peace was passed by Congress and signed under the presidency of Harding. American isolationism was expressed in these years in other concrete measures. The Fordney-McCumber Tariff of 1922 and the Smoot-Hawley Tariff of 1930 set successively higher duties on foreign goods and emphasized America's belief that her high wage scales needed to be protected from cheap foreign labor.

Yet the United States continued all through the 1920's to insist that the debts owed to her by the Allied powers be repaid. It is true that these were refunded in a series of agreements, and that in the closely related problem of German reparations Americans on the whole cast their weight on the side of a general scaling-down of German obligations. But Congress paid little heed to the argument, so convincing to most economists, that European nations could not repay save through dollars gained by sales of their goods in the American market, and that American tariffs continued to make such repayment impossible. Congressmen tended to reduce the complexities of international debts to President Coolidge's simple dictum: "They hired the money, didn't they?"

The spirit of isolationism also lay behind the immigration restrictions of the 1920's, which reversed the former American policy of almost free immigration. The act of 1924 set an annual quota limit for each country of 2 per cent of the number of nationals from that country resident in the United States in 1890. Since the heavy immigration from eastern and southern Europe had come after 1890, the choice of that date reduced the flow from these areas to a mere trickle. Northern countries like Britain, Germany, and Scandinavia, on the other hand did not use up their quotas.

The Road to Internationalism

Yet during this era of partial isolationism the United States by no means withdrew entirely from international politics. Rather, as an independent without formal alliances, she continued to pursue policies that seemed to most Americans traditional, but that in their totality gradually lined her up against the chief perturbing nations of the years between the two world wars. Even before the drift of her commitments against Germany, Italy, and Japan became clear in the 1930's, Americans had in fact engaged themselves. In 1928, the Republican Secretary of State Kellogg submitted to the great European powers a proposal for a renunciation of war. Incorporated with similar proposals from the French Foreign Minister Briand, it was formally adopted in August of that year as the Pact of Paris, commonly known as the Kellogg-Briand Pact. It was eventually signed by twenty-three nations, including the United States. It is now the fashion to decry the Pact as futile, and it is certainly true that it did not prevent World War II. Yet by this action the United States expressed a concrete concern over the peace of the world.

In a hundred ways the United States was at work laying the foundations for the position of world leadership it reached after World War II. American businessmen were everywhere; American loans were making possible the revival of German industrial greatness; American motors, refrigerators, typewriters, telephones, and other products of the assembly line were being sold the world over. In the Far East, the United States as early as 1922 took the lead in the Nine-Power Treaty that committed her and the other great powers, including Japan, to respect the sovereignty and integrity of China. If President Roosevelt in 1941 resisted the Japanese attempt to swallow China and other Far Eastern territory, he was simply following a line laid down under President Harding.

Boom—and Bust

In domestic affairs, the Coolidge era (1923–1929) has now become legendary. These were years of frantic prosperity; nearly everybody played the stock market and the market value of stocks rose to fantastic heights. They were the years of "prohibition," the ban on the manufacture and sale of alcoholic beverages, enforced, in theory, by the Volstead Act of 1919 under the Eighteenth Amendment to the Constitution. And so they were also the years of the speakeasy and the bootlegger. They were the years of the short skirt (it was not nearly as short as the skirt of 1966), of sex appeal (abbreviated as "SA"), the Charleston, and other forms of "sin." They were years which, like the "naughty nineties" of the nineteenth century, we look back on with a sort of reproving envy, years that now look colorful and romantic.

But the Coolidge era was by no means completely summed up in novels of the jazz age, like *The Great Gatsby* of F. Scott Fitzgerald, or even in Sinclair Lewis' half-satirical *Babbitt* and *Main Street*. It was an era of marked industrial progress, of solid advancement of the national plant and productive capabilities. It was an era of the steady spreading in the United States of standards of living heretofore limited to the relatively few, standards of living that seemed to intellectuals vulgar and inadequate, but that were nevertheless a new thing in the world. These were the years when, if you had a servant, you could no longer take her for granted, but had to take some pains to keep her satisfied. They were years for which, at their best, the right symbol is no Hollywood character, no intellectual, no great pioneer of industry, nor even a gangster, but rather President Coolidge himself, sober,

plodding, insensitive, who said that "the business of America is business."

At its most glamorous, the era ended with the onset of the great depression in the autumn of 1929. During the preceding year, Wall Street had enjoyed an unprecedented boom. Speculators by the millions were playing the market in the hope of quick resale of stocks at huge profits; they bought shares "on margin," paying only a fraction of their cost in cash, and often borrowing the money to pay that small fraction. Not only stocks but many other purchases were financed on borrowed money. Credit had swollen to the point where it was no longer on a sound basis in a largely unregulated economy. Eventually, shrewd investors began to sell their holdings in the belief that the bubble soon would burst. The result was a disastrous drop in stock values, beginning in October, 1929, and continuing almost without let-up to 1933. Both the speculators and the lenders from whom they had borrowed money were ruined.

The immediate cause of the depression, then, was the stock-market crash. About the more deep-seated causes the economic physicians are not even today wholly agreed. Some of them believe that a capitalist society inevitably produces business cycles oscillating from the highs of prosperity to the lows of depression; that these cycles are of various lengths, short, medium, and long; and that an unusual number of cyclical lows coincided in the late 1920's to make the depression particularly serious. Others, not uninfluenced by Marx, hold that under American capitalism the troughs of a depression are bound to be deeper each time, if only because of the great scale of the American economy.

This much seems certain: Coolidge prosperity was very unevenly distributed among the various parts of the American economy and American society. Agriculture, notably, suffered a kind of permanent depression throughout the 1920's. At the close of World War I, farmers commanded very high prices for their produce and enjoyed an apparently insatiable market at home and abroad. They expanded their production—and borrowed to finance the expansion — often at a reckless rate. Then, as "normalcy" returned in the early 1920's, the foreign market dried up, the home market shrank, farm prices fell rapidly, and the inevitable foreclosure of farm mortgages began. Wage-earning workers, though not hard hit like the farmers, gained comparatively little increase in their purchasing power during the 1920's. The worker did often raise his standard of living, by purchasing a house or a car, but he did it on credit, by assuming the burden of a heavy mortgage or by financing a purchase on installments to be paid over a long period. The "big money" of the Coolidge era went chiefly to business, above all to big business.

The great depression was very severe in many countries throughout the world, but nowhere was it worse than in the United States. Its effects may be measured by the round figure of 16,000,000 Americans unemployed at the low point in the early 1930's — something like one-third of the national labor force. In terms of what economists call the "gross national product" (GNP), the United States Department of Commerce sets for 1929 the figure of $103,828,000,000; for 1933, however, the same department sets a figure of only $55,760,000,000.

The most remarkable thing about this grave crisis in the American economy is that it produced almost no organized movements of revolt, no threat of revolution. The intellectuals of the 1930's did indeed turn to "social consciousness," and Marxism made some converts among writers and artists. But the bulk of the population showed no serious signs of abandoning their fundamental belief that the way out lay through the legal means provided by existing American institutions. Even before the election of Franklin D. Roosevelt in 1932, local authorities and private charities, helped out by the establishment early in 1932 of the federal R.F.C. (Reconstruction Finance Corporation) to release frozen assets, did a good deal to soften the worst sufferings of the unemployed. The Republican administration of President Hoover, however, was generally committed to the philosophy of laissez-faire;

aside from the R.F.C., it did little to cushion the effects of the depression. People who wanted a more vigorous attack on economic problems voted for the Democrats in 1932; most significantly, they did not vote in very important numbers for the socialist or communist presidential candidates. In the crisis of a great depression, the American two-party system evidently continued to meet basic political needs.

The New Deal

The victory of the Democrats in 1932 seemed to give them a clear mandate to marshal all the resources of the federal government against the depression. The Democratic president, Franklin Roosevelt (1933–1945), took office on March 4, 1933, in the midst of a financial crisis that had closed the banks all over the country. He at once summoned Congress to an emergency session and declared a bank holiday. Gradually the sound banks reopened, and the New Deal began. Subsequently, under improving economic conditions, the American business community mostly turned with great bitterness against Roosevelt and all his works. But in those early months of 1933 the mere fact that a national administration was trying to do something about the situation was a powerful restorative to national morale. The nation emerged from the bank holiday with a new confidence, echoing the phrase from Roosevelt's inaugural address that there was nothing to fear "but fear itself."

The New Deal was in part a series of measures aimed at immediate difficulties and in part a series of measures aimed at permanent changes in the structure of American society. The distinction between its short-term and its long-term measures is in a sense arbitrary, for the men who carried both through were never quite clear in their own minds exactly what they were trying to do. What must chiefly interest us is the implications of their work. In the perspective of western history, the New Deal was the coming to the United States, under the special pressures of

VANITY FAIR

Cartoon on a magazine cover, 1934: the blue eagle was the symbol of the NRA, an ambitious effort by the New Deal to bolster the industrial recovery and the welfare of labor; the Supreme Court declared it unconstitutional in 1935.

the great depression, of those measures—"socialist" to some of their opponents—that we have already seen in European countries like Great Britain and imperial Germany. They are best summed up in that value-charged term, the "welfare state."

The short-term measures of the New Deal aimed by releasing the dollar from its tie with gold to lower the price of American goods in a world that was abandoning the gold standard. They aimed to thaw out credit by extending the activities of the R.F.C. and by creating such new governmental lending agencies as the Home Owners' Loan Corporation. They aimed to relieve unemployment by public works on a large scale, to safeguard bank deposits by the Federal Deposit Insurance Corporation, and to regulate speculation and other stockmarket activities by the Securities

and Exchange Commission. The historical significance of many of these innovations rested in the fact that they were undertaken not by private business or by state or local authorities but by the federal government. There was one exception to the rule of widening federal activity. The Twenty-first Amendment to the Constitution repealed the Eighteenth and abandoned the increasingly unsuccessful federal efforts to enforce prohibition.

The long-term measures of the New Deal were, of course, more important. The Social Security Act of 1935 introduced to the United States on a national scale the unemployment insurance, old-age pensions, and other benefits of the kind that Lloyd George had brought into Britain. Somewhat more equal distribution of the national wealth resulted from increased federal taxation, especially taxes on individual and corporate incomes. Congress passed a whole series of acts on labor relations, the net effect of which has been to strengthen and extend the role of organized labor in American economic life. A series of acts on agriculture, though leaving the business of farming still in the hands of several million individual farmers producing for sale in a cash market, nevertheless regulated crops and prices to a degree that would have been incomprehensible to a nineteenth-century farmer. And finally—the showpiece of the New Deal—a great regional planning board, the Tennessee Valley Authority, used government power to make over the economic and social life of a relatively backward area by checking the erosion of farmlands, by instituting flood control, and by providing cheap electric power generated at government-built dams.

Nearly thirty-five years after the bank holiday of 1933, Americans were still debating the New Deal. It unquestionably left the United States a society very different from that pictured by the classical economists. No real society has ever quite corresponded to the theoretical extreme of free enterprise, in which every man sells and buys what he wants—or can—and in which the man who cannot "earn" a living quite simply dies. But in the sense in which the United States of, say, 1870 was close to such a society, the United

States of the New Deal and after has been quite far from such a society. The rush of free competition has been tempered by government regulation, because it has become clear that in such competition much that men prize would in fact be competed out of existence. Most Americans have come to see the need for government regulation in the conservation of natural resources. Even here, however, when it comes to the overgrazing of pasture lands or the farming methods that lead to soil erosion, some Americans are still reluctant to have the government interfere with their "rights."

When the question at stake is the distribution of wealth, rather than its actual exhaustion, Americans are often unwilling to accept limitations on free enterprise. On this issue, even after the New Deal, the champions of government regulation and private initiative still do battle. The Marxist indictment of a competitive society, that under it the rich tend to become richer and the poor to become poorer, is not wholly true. But the last two hundred years of western history suggest that without some government regulation the modern scramble for wealth tends to produce a society pyramidal in structure. With a few men of great wealth at the top, the pyramid spreads out through the well-to-do to a broad base of human beings just able to scrape along. In our western society, however, the political power democracy gives to that numerous broad base has over the years been used to alter the very shape of the social pyramid. "Soak-the-rich" taxation and government aid to the poor have flattened it out, cutting it down at the top and pushing it up from the bottom. Indeed, the figure is almost certainly no longer a pyramid, but somewhere approaching a diamond shape, widest in the middle. It is not yet in any human society a straight line, representing absolute social and economic equality.

There is, then, in modern America a leveling, both up and down. The great baronial mansions of the Hudson Valley, of Newport, even of California, are too expensive to maintain, and are being turned into museums or put to institutional use. There are still a number of very rich men, but they no longer build themselves palaces, and in general they try to lead inconspicuous lives. The worst of the urban slums are being slowly demolished to make way for modern housing projects. The number of the very poor is diminishing. Meanwhile, the total national product has increased. It is not merely that a fixed national income is being more evenly distributed; despite the complaints of conservatives that the leveling process is destroying incentives to hard work and invention, the gross national product has increased greatly since the depth of the depression in 1932–1933. There is more to be shared.

It must be noted that the American society that emerged from the New Deal can by no means be accurately described as "socialistic." The United States of the mid-twentieth century is rather a "mixed economy," in which individual economic activity—that of the worker as well as that of the entrepreneur or manager—is indeed regulated and restricted, but not entirely controlled, by government. The United States still displays an extraordinary range of economic activity, from the "socialistic" Post Office to enormous private industries that are themselves societies, almost governments, with administrative problems and bureaucracies of their own, and on down to small independent businessmen, who are often the best examples of almost pure free enterprise.

Confident America

Although Americans still argue about the New Deal, it seems evident that the measures taken by the Roosevelt administration, combined with the strength of American institutions and culture, pulled the United States at least part way out of the depression. These measures also restored a high degree of confidence to Americans. The intellectuals, whose role in modern America has generally been in opposition to the men of business, in the 1920's had found the United States a hopelessly crass and vulgar society. But in the 1930's, though some intellectuals flirted with

Marxism, many of them turned to support the new American way marked out by the New Deal.

The onset of war in Europe found Americans, as we shall see in the next chapter, anxious not to jeopardize in war their still precarious prosperity, anxious to remain neutral if Europe should persist in going to war. Roosevelt and his Republican opponents had been for some time exchanging insults: the "economic royalists" fought back at "that man in the White House." Yet in the pinch of the international crisis of 1939–1941 it became clear that, although the nation was not completely united, at any rate it was not pathologically divided. As so often in American history, the violence of verbal politics masked a very basic unity. When the war came to the United States in 1941, Americans were largely ready for it psychologically and—what is really remarkable in a western democracy—not too unready for it militarily.

When the war came, moreover, the United States had already made many efforts to enlist the support of the Latin-American states. In 1930, before the so-called "Roosevelt Revolution" in American diplomacy, President Hoover's State Department issued the Clark Memorandum, specifically stating that the Monroe Doctrine does not concern itself with inter-American relations but is directed against outside intervention in the affairs of the Western Hemisphere. The United States was no longer to land the Marines in some Central American republic at the drop of a hat but was trying to strengthen hemispheric solidarity. And so, on the foundations of the Clark Memorandum, President Roosevelt built his celebrated "Good Neighbor" policy toward the other American nations (for details on Latin America, see Chapter 31).

Meantime, what may be called American imperial policy was likewise undergoing some liberalization, notably with respect to the Philippines. When the United States had annexed the islands at the close of the Spanish-American War (see Chapter 24), a stubborn Filipino insurrection broke out in protest, and it took American forces three years (1899–1902) to subdue the rebels. Filipino nationalists, though partially disarmed by the conciliatory measures taken by the United States after the suppression of the rebellion, none the less continued to advocate eventual freedom. In the 1930's, American officials negotiated with Filipino leaders with the aim at first of bestowing a rather dilute kind of dominion status on the islands. But by the outbreak of World War II the negotiations had advanced to the point where it was evident that the Philippines would soon gain at least nominal independence.

V   The Loosening of Imperial Ties

The Filipino insurrection of 1899 was a portent. Even before 1914, there were signs that many of the more advanced "colonial" peoples were already chafing under imperialism. Native nationalist movements were creating trouble for the British in Egypt and India, for the French in Morocco and Algeria, and for all the imperial powers in China. The First World War itself speeded up the process of rousing national consciousness among the "natives" of the various empires, and at its end there was no doubt that the hold of the West had been loosened. Psychologically, the experience of the war gave a lift to non-western peoples; they had often rendered important services to their white masters, and their leaders had widened their knowledge of the West. The Arab peoples of the old Ottoman Empire had raised armies of their own and had fought with European aid for their own freedom from Turkish rule. French colonial troops and British India troops had taken part in the conflict, sometimes in Europe itself.

The very spectacle of the masters quarreling among themselves did something to lower the prestige of the West among subject peoples. Moreover, the Allies had fought the war in the name of democratic ideals of self-determination for all peoples, and in their propaganda against the Central Powers they had stressed their opposition to imperialism. The fifth of Wilson's Fourteen Points asserted that in disputed claims to colonial territories "the interests of the populations concerned must have equal weight" with the interests of the colonial powers. It is true that the Allies did not give up any of their territories in 1919, and did indeed add to them under the mandate system (see Chapter 25). To many of the subject races, as to liberals in the West itself, the mandate was simply a disguise for the old imperialism; but it is surely significant that a disguise seemed necessary to the imperialist powers. The West now appeared to be committed to a process of at least gradual emancipation of the colonial dependencies.

It was in the Far East that old imperial ties were most clearly loosened during the interwar years. China, as we shall soon see in more detail, was engaged in a great struggle to free herself from the tutelage of the western colonial powers. The conflict in China, however, was much more than a simple conflict between oriental nationalists and occidental imperialists. Almost from the start it was complicated by two additional elements—increasing communist intervention in Chinese politics, and the increasing threat to Chinese independence from an expansionist Japan. It is scarcely an exaggeration to say that China faced the prospect of simply exchanging one set of imperial overlords for another.

Japan

Alone among non-western peoples, the Japanese experienced the industrial revolution and were able to maintain themselves as a fully independent major political entity during the great age of imperialism (see Chapter 24). More than that, as the twentieth century opened, Japan was clearly a great power, a full but somewhat unwelcome participant in the struggle for imperial position. As we have seen, the Japanese made these impressive accomplishments without radically altering their traditional oligarchical and absolutist political structure.

In the decade after World War I, it looked as though Japan might achieve a gradual liberalization of her political institutions. The cabinets of the 1920's included many men from the business class who favored vigorous expansion abroad but who also granted some measures of cautious liberalism at home. The suffrage was gradually extended, and in 1925 all men received the right to vote. For the first time, political parties, western-style, began to put down roots, especially in the urban population, and seemed likely to give new vitality to the Diet, the not very powerful central representative assembly of Japan. Trade unions also took shape and began to win a following.

Japan, however, did not evolve into a parliamentary democracy on the western model during the twenty years' truce. By the early 1930's, political power was falling more and more into the hands of army and navy officers, many of whom were descended from the feudal *samurai* class (see p. 345). This officer clique hated the prospect of liberal civilian government and envied and mistrusted the business class. They found a potent political weapon in the institution of the emperor, who was supposed to possess the kind of political infallibility that westerners associate with a divine-right monarch. Putting their own words into the emperor's mouth, the admirals and generals used his pronouncements to further their own ends. And, to make doubly sure, they assassinated or terrorized the chief spokesmen of nascent Japanese liberalism.

The consequence was the progressive clamping of a military dictatorship on Japan during the 1930's. Although popular elections continued to be held, their results were disregarded, and the Diet lost its recently acquired vitality. Businessmen supported the new régime out of fear or out of anticipation of the

policies in Iraq and in Transjordan, the half-desert area east of Palestine. Until World War II, it looked as though Britain might have found a way of leading the Arabs gradually to independence and retaining their friendship. But the exacerbation of the Palestine problem after the war and the rapid intensification of Arab nationalism were to blast any hope that the Arabs would remain grateful and loyal "old boys" of the British imperial school.

In the meantime, Turkey was undergoing a political renaissance. The losses suffered by Turkey as a result of World War I reduced her territory for the first time to a cohesive national unit, the largely Turkish-populated lands of Anatolia (or Asia Minor). To defend this Anatolian core against threatened additional losses to the Greeks and to the victorious Allies, the Turks at once launched an ardent nationalist revival extending considerably the reforms begun by the Young Turks before 1914 (see p. 365). The leader of this new political revolution was a highly gifted army officer, Mustafa Kemal (1881–1938), who forced the expulsion of the Greek forces from Anatolia and negotiated more favorable terms with the Allies at Lausanne in 1923 (see p. 390). Under his guidance, the old Ottoman Empire was abolished in 1922, and in its stead the Republic of Turkey was proclaimed, with a constitution modeled on western parliamentary lines. To point up the new orientation of the republic, Kemal moved its capital from cosmopolitan Istanbul, on the western edge of Turkish territory, to Ankara in the heart of Anatolia.

Kemal also imposed rapid, wholesale, and sometimes ruthless measures of westernization. Women received the vote and, at least in theory, were emancipated from traditional Moslem restraints, including the wearing of a veil in public. The whole fabric of social and political life was removed from the highly conservative influence of Islam, again in theory at least. An advanced European law code was introduced; Sunday, not the Moslem Friday, was made the weekly day of rest; even the Turkish language was drastically reformed by the requirement that it employ a western alphabet—a move of major importance, for

only a fraction of the Turkish people had ever been able to master the old Ottoman Turkish, with its heavy content of Persian and Arabic words, and with its difficult Arabic script. All Turks were now required to take surnames in the western manner, and Kemal himself appropriately took that of Atatürk, "Father of the Turks." By the time of his death in 1938, Atatürk had indeed revolutionized his country, even though westernization was only just beginning to trickle down to the grass roots of Turkish society. And he had insured its independence of the West as Turkish neutrality during World War II was soon to demonstrate.

The example of Turkey was followed, though less sweepingly and less effectively, by the other traditionally independent major state of the Middle East—Persia, or, as it has been officially styled since 1935, Iran ("Land of the Aryans"). The Iranian revolution began in 1906 in response to the imperialist encroachments by Britain and Russia that were making Persia a kind of Middle Eastern China. The political structure inherited from the Middle Ages was gradually altered in the direction of limited monarchy, with an elected parliament and with the Shah as a constitutional ruler. Since the political transition was far from smooth, the Iranian revolution proved to be an arrested or abortive one. The country, with its highly powerful class of wealthy landlords and its millions of poor peasants and restless tribesmen, did not adapt itself readily to modern western political institutions. The nearest Iranian equivalent of Atatürk was Reza Shah, an able army officer and a feverish but erratic modernizer who lacked Kemal's sense of the possible. Reza Shah seized the Iranian throne after World War I and lost it in 1941 when his pro-Nazi sympathies led Britain and Russia to send in troops and force his abdication. The fate of Reza Shah served as a reminder that the British and the Russians still kept some of their old interests in Iran, where they had often competed for concessions and for spheres of influence in the past. It also showed that some of the seemingly sovereign states of the nonwestern world were not yet strong enough to maintain their independence against the might of the great powers. By the time of World War II, imperial ties had been loosened, but they were by no means severed or dissolved; the revolution against imperialism was yet to come (see Chapters 30 and 31).

Reading Suggestions on the Democracies, 1919–1939: Domestic and Imperial Problems

(Asterisk indicates paperbound edition.)

Britain and France

R. Graves and A. Hodge, *The Long Weekend* (Faber & Faber, 1940). A lively social history of Britain during the inter-war years.

G. E. Elton, *The Life of James Ramsay MacDonald* (Collins, 1939); G. M. Young, *Stanley Baldwin* (Hart-Davis, 1952); and K. Feiling, *The Life of Neville Chamberlain* (Macmillan, 1946). Biographies of three important British statesmen.

A. Bullock, *Life and Loves of Ernest Bevin, Vol I. 1881– 1940* (Heinemann, 1960). A second volume is promised of this major work.

J. P. Mackintosh, *The British Cabinet* (Univ. of Toronto Press, 1962). From Charles II to the present, an important study of a key institution.

Richard W. Lyman, *The First Labour Government, 1924* (Dresser, Chapman & Grimes, 1957). An important monograph.

C. R. Attlee, *The Labour Party in Perspective,* 2nd ed. (Gollancz, 1949). A review of the inter-war period in Britain by the Labor leader.

E. Weber, *Action Francaise: Royalism and Reaction in 20th Century France* (Stanford Univ. Press, 1962). Covers the period 1898 to 1939; thorough, readable.

R. Albrecht-Carré, *France, Europe and the Two World Wars* (Harper, 1961). An admirable account of French difficulties in these years.

D. Brogan, *France under the Republic* (Harper, 1940). Still one of the most informative introductions to French history in the 1920's and 1930's. See also Brogan's *The French Nation: From Napoleon to Pétain, 1814–1940* (Harper, 1958).

D. Thomson, *Democracy in France,* 3rd ed. (Oxford Univ. Press, 1958). A most stimulating essay in interpretation for those already acquainted with the basic facts.

E. J. Knapton, *France since Versailles* (*Holt, 1952, A Berkshire Study). Handy little manual.

A. Werth, *The Twilight of France, 1933–1940* (Harper, 1942). Condensation of several longer studies by an able foreign correspondent.

The United States

Four volumes in the "Chronicles of America Series" (Yale Univ. Press) provide good coverage of the period: H. U. Faulkner, *From Versailles to the New Deal* (1950); D. Brogan, *The Era of Franklin D. Roosevelt* (1951); A. Nevins, *The United States in a Chaotic World* (1950); and A. Nevins, *The New Deal and World Affairs* (1950).

D. Perkins, *The New Age of Franklin Roosevelt, 1932–1945* (Univ. of Chicago Press, 1957). A sympathetic but by no means uncritical survey.

F. L. Allen, *Only Yesterday* (*Bantam Books), and *Since Yesterday* (Harper, 1940). Lively social histories of the 1920's and 1930's, respectively.

F. Perkins, *The Roosevelt I Knew* (Viking, 1946), and R. E. Sherwood, *Roosevelt and Hopkins,* 2 vols. (*Bantam Books). Perhaps the best of the books about Franklin Roosevelt by the people who worked with him.

F. Freidel, *Franklin D. Roosevelt* (Little, Brown, 1952–1956), 3 vols. A detailed and careful biographical study.

A. M. Schlesinger, Jr., *The Crisis of the Old Order, 1919–1933,* and *The Coming of the New Deal* (Houghton Mifflin, 1957, 1959). The first two volumes in "The Age of Roosevelt" by an historian favorable to the New deal but objective in his judgments.

J. M. Burns, *Roosevelt: The Lion and the Fox* (Harcourt, Brace, 1956). A stimulating though rather limited estimate of Roosevelt the politician.

Economic
Developments

J. K. Galbraith, *The Great Crash, 1929* (Houghton Mifflin, 1955; *Sentry). A well-written study of the Wall Street slump by a prominent American economist.

P. Einzig, *The World Economic Crisis, 1929–1932* (Macmillan, 1932); H. V. Hodson, *Slump and Recovery, 1929–1937* (Oxford Univ. Press, 1938); H. W. Arndt, *The Economic Lessons of the Nineteen-Thirties* (Oxford Univ. Press, 1944). Other useful books on the great depression.

J. Schumpeter, *Capitalism, Socialism, and Democracy,* 3rd ed. (Harper, 1950; *Torchbooks); J. M. Keynes, *The End of Laissez-Faire* (Woolf, 1926). Incisive essays by economists.

D. A. Shannon, ed., *The Great Depression* (*Spectrum). A useful collection of source readings, stressing the social consequences of economic ills in the United States.

Other Topics

E. Fischer, *The Passing of the European Age* (Harvard Univ. Press, 1943). Defense of the thesis that leadership in western civilization has passed from Europe to other continents.

E. O. Reischauer, *Japan, Past and Present,* 2nd ed., rev. (Knopf, 1956). An excellent introductory account. See also Reischauer's *United States and Japan,* 3rd ed. (Harvard Univ. Press, 1965).

L. Fischer, *Gandhi* (*New American Library, 1954). A sympathetic biography.

P. Spear, *India, Pakistan, and the West,* 3rd ed. (Oxford Univ. Press, 1958). Illuminating.

W. N. Brown, *The United States and India and Pakistan,* rev. ed. (Harvard Univ. Press, 1963). An excellent introduction. This edition has a very good reading list.

J. K. Fairbank, *The United States and China,* rev. ed. (Harvard Univ. Press, 1958). Reliable, informative introduction to the controversial subject of recent Chinese history.

K. S. Latourette, *A History of Modern China* (*Penguin). A good brief account.

S. N. Fisher, *The Middle East: A History* (Knopf, 1959). Well-balanced survey.

G. L. Lewis, *Turkey* (Praeger, 1955). Summary and results of Atatürk revolution.

Sir Harry Luke, *The Old Turkey and the New* (Bles, 1955). Perceptive essay on the contrasts between the Ottoman Empire and the Turkey of Atatürk.

S. H. Longrigg, *Syria and Lebanon under French Mandate* (Oxford Univ. Press, 1958). Detailed study of the very mixed record of French rule in the Levant.

Note: Many titles useful for the history of the non-western world during the twenty years' truce will also be found in the reading suggestions for Chapter 30; for background and more information on the twenty years, see also some of the titles in Chapter 24.

Fiction

E. Waugh, *A Handful of Dust* (New Directions, 1945). Corrosive novel satirizing English society in the inter-war years.

H. Spring, *Fame Is the Spur* (Viking, 1940). A politician is corrupted by ambition; largely parallels the career of Ramsay MacDonald.

W. Holtby, *South Riding* (Macmillan, 1936). Good social novel of industrial England.

A. Gide, *The Counterfeiters* (Knopf, 1927). Mordant study of the French middle class by an eminent novelist.

29

The Second World War

General or world wars in our state-system are usually born of a previous war, or, perhaps better, of a previous peace settlement that fails to solve certain important problems. We have already been obliged in seeking the origins of the First World War to go back to 1870, to Bismarck, to the "rape of Alsace-Lorraine" and the consequent rise of the spirit of revenge among Frenchmen. We shall now have to go back to 1919 and the grave difficulties that arose in the attempt to carry out the settlement of Versailles. So troubled were international relations for the twenty years after 1919, so closely in time did the Second World War follow on the First, that the interval between the two has been christened the "twenty years' truce." And it is not impossible that historians in the future will actually consider the two wars really one war, as they now consider the wars of the French Revolution and Napoleon essentially one war. Though to the purist historian the first world wars were perhaps those of Louis XIV, if not those of Charles V and Philip II, for the present we must use the accepted terms, World War I (1914–1918) and World War II (1939–1945). Such usage has at least the advantage of pointing up by the use of roman numerals the close relationship of these two wars. In both wars Germany appears as the perturber.

I   International Politics, 1919–1932

During the first part of the twenty years' truce, international leadership of the democratic world rested with Britain and France. Though supported in principle and often in practice by the United States, they were increasingly unable to stem the rise of powers hostile to liberal democracy—Italy, Germany, Spain, Russia, Japan. In the end, the beaten perturber of 1918, Germany, waged aggressive warfare against the major Allies of 1918. This time Germany allied with two of its former enemies, Italy and Japan, each disappointed with its share of the spoils of victory in 1918.

Why was the peace settlement of 1919 followed in twenty years by a second great war? Why was it so unlike the last great settlement, that of 1815 following the Napoleonic wars, which had inaugurated a long period of general peace, interrupted only by localized wars? Nazi Germany maintained that the second war was the direct and inevitable result of the *Diktat,* the dictated peace of Versailles that ended the first war. Supported by most Germans and many German sympathizers, the Nazis claimed that Germany was humiliated by the war-guilt clause, stripped of territories and colonies that were rightfully hers, saddled with an astronomical and unpayable reparations bill, denied the normal rights of a sovereign state in armaments—in short, so badly treated that simple human dignity made revolt against the *Dikat* and its makers a necessity. Now this is partly true. The settlement of Versailles did saddle the new German Republic with a heavy burden in part dictated by revenge and fear. A wiser Allied policy would perhaps have tried to start the new government off without too great a burden, as the Allies in 1815 did with the France of Louis XVIII (see Chapter 19).

The "Era of Fulfillment"

But the *Diktat* thesis is very far from containing the whole truth. What breaks down the argument that the iniquities of Versailles alone explain the second war is the "era of fulfillment." In spite of the Treaty of Versailles, the Germans and their former enemies did manage to come together in the 1920's.

The great landmark of the "era of fulfillment" was a general treaty negotiated in October, 1925, at Locarno in Switzerland. Germany there agreed with France and Belgium on a mutual guarantee of their common frontiers; Britain and Italy agreed to act as guarantors—that is, to provide military aid against the violator if a violation of the frontiers occurred. Germany affirmed her acceptance of the western frontier drawn for her at Versailles, and France, for her part, affirmed the new moderate direction that her German policy had taken since the failure of her occupation of the Ruhr.

The "Locarno spirit" of reconciliation endured for the next several years. It was nourished by the general prosperity of both the French and the Germans and by the constructive policies of their respective foreign ministers, Briand and Stresemann. In 1926, Germany was admitted to the League of Nations, an event that seemed to signify not only

Signing of the Locarno Pact, October, 1925.

the restoration of Germany to international respectability but also German acceptance of the peaceful purposes and duties of League membership. These hopeful impressions received confirmation when Germany signed the Kellogg-Briand Peace Pact of 1928 (see p. 493). In 1929, the French consented to withdraw the last of their occupation troops from the Rhineland during the forthcoming year, thus ending the Allied occupation of Germany at a date considerably in advance of the one stipulated in the Versailles Treaty.

Meantime, other international developments were bolstering the "Locarno spirit." The great world-wide organization planned by Wilson, the League of Nations, began its operations in 1920. We shall soon see that the League was never able to impose its will on a determined and defiant aggressor. Yet the record of the League during the 1920's was by no means one of unmitigated failure. In the first place, the League became a going concern. Its Council, dominated by the great powers, and its Assembly, representing all its members, met regularly at the League's "capital," the Swiss city of Geneva. Second, the League played a direct part in the peaceful resolution of two crises that, had they not been resolved, might well have led to little wars—in 1920 a dispute between Sweden and Finland over some Baltic islands, and in 1925 a frontier incident in the Balkans involving Greece and Bulgaria.

The United States, though not a member of the League, took a leading part in furthering one of the League's chief objectives—disarm-

ament. Soon after the first war, the United States invited the other principal sea powers to consider the limitation of naval armaments. Meeting in Washington during the winter of 1921–1922, the naval conference achieved an agreement establishing a ten-year "holiday" in the construction of capital ships (battleships and heavy cruisers). The agreement also set the allowed tonnages of capital ships at a ratio of 5 for the United States, 5 for Britain, 3 for Japan, and 1.67 each for France and Italy.

A conference at London in 1930, however, had less success in limiting "non-capital" ships, including submarines. The partial failure of the London naval conference was a portent. Two years later, after long preparation, the League itself convoked a meeting to address the still more pressing problem of limiting military armaments. Not only the League members, but also the United States and the Soviet Union, sent representatives to Geneva. The Geneva disarmament conference of 1932, however, accomplished nothing. It was wrecked above all by a renewal of Franco-German antagonism, by the German demand for equality in armaments with France, and by the French refusal to grant the demand.

The Failure of "Fulfillment"

In 1932, then, the "Locarno spirit" was dead, and the "era of fulfillment" had ended. There is one very obvious factor in any explanation for the failure of the hopes aroused in the 1920's—the world depression that began in 1929. In Germany itself the depression was a last straw, a decisive factor in putting Hitler in power. In the democracies, too, it had heavy consequences for the peace of the world, for the depression sapped their morale and made them less confident. But the great world-wide depression is no more in itself a *sole* explanation of World War II than is the *Diktat* of Versailles.

Another factor that was unsettling to international politics was Soviet Russia. In the eyes of the western nations, Russia was a revolutionary power that could not really be trusted, that could not be fully integrated into the international state-system. The Soviet Union was the center of a revolutionary faith hated and distrusted by the politicians of the West, who feared, by no means without justification, communist agitation among their own peoples. Westerners simply could not trust a Marxist government which was based on the belief that all western "capitalist" democracies were destined to collapse and become communist after a violent class war.

Still another basic factor that led to the second war was the continuing failure of the three great western democracies, Britain, France, and the United States, to present anything like a united front. Americans of internationalist sympathies have probably exaggerated the results of the sudden American withdrawal into isolationism in 1919. It is hard to believe, especially in light of the rivalry and cross-purposes that Britain and France displayed *within* the League of Nations, that formal American membership in the League would have helped the situation greatly. Still, the isolation of the United States undoubtedly exacerbated French fears and the French sense of weakness, and pushed France toward the sort of intransigence that was illustrated by her disastrous intervention in the Ruhr in the mid-1920's (see p. 488).

More serious was the failure of France and Britain to work together effectively. France, exhausted and in this decade with a declining population, endeavoring to play the part of a first-rate power but supported only by second-rate resources, lived in perpetual fear of a revived Germany. She sought not only to carry out to the full the economic and political measures of the Versailles Treaty that aimed at weakening Germany and keeping Germany weak, but also to make up for Russia's defection as her eastern ally against Germany. This she did by making alliances, beginning in 1921, with the smaller states to the east of Germany—Poland, Czechoslovakia, Rumania, and Yugoslavia. All of them wanted French protection against the possible restoration of the Habsburg Empire, from which they had gained so much territory, and all of them except Poland were informally linked together as the "Little Entente."

To a Britain whose statesmen knew well the long story of Anglo-French conflicts from the Hundred Years' War to Napoleon, the France of the 1920's seemed once more aiming at European supremacy, seemed once more an active threat to the traditional British policy of preventing any such supremacy. Although it is now plain that the French were animated rather by fear than by ambition, and that they could never again be major aggressors, it is true enough that many of their statesmen seemed to be falling into old ways, or at least old words, of aggression. The mistaken British diagnosis was at least understandable.

Finally, something of the old British isolationism had survived the war, and made the British—and especially their dominions—unwilling to commit themselves firmly to guarantees to intervene with force in continental Europe. Britain did indeed accept Locarno, but in the previous year the dominions had played a large part in her rejection of the more sweeping "Geneva protocol" urged upon her by France, which would have committed its signatories to compulsory arbitration of international disputes.

The difficulties of the Anglo-French partnership also go far to explain the weakness of the League of Nations. The effectiveness of any piece of machinery is bound to hinge on the skill and co-ordination of the mechanics who operate it. The League lacked a means of enforcing its decisions. And it was somewhat top-heavy, since the fully representative Assembly counted for less than did the smaller

Council, where Britain and France took a preponderant role. When these two mechanics disagreed, therefore, the machinery scarcely operated at all. One example of the way in which the grand purposes of the League suffered from Anglo-French friction is the rejection of the Geneva protocol. Another is the Corfu incident of 1923, when Mussolini for a time defied the League and set a sinister precedent for the later use of gangster tactics by the dictators (see Chapter 27). In the midst of the Corfu crisis, the League was crippled by Anglo-French discord over the Ruhr policy of France.

The Aggressors

The Corfu incident underlines the presence of one more element, the most important of all, in the rapid deterioration of the twenty years' truce. This, of course, was the fact of aggressions by Italy, Germany, and Japan. In Chapter 27, we saw how the ruthlessly ambitious programs of fascism and Nazism steadily led Mussolini and Hitler to a foreign policy of adventure and aggression. In Chapter 28, we saw how the somewhat similar totalitarian policies of the Japanese militarists led them to begin the seizure of China by their occupation of Manchuria in 1931. With this background of underlying tensions—the punitive features of the Versailles settlement, the disastrous effects of the depression on the Locarno spirit, the continuance of the revolutionary focus in Russia, the defensive attitude of the western democracies and their mutual mistrust, the new aggressive faiths of fascism and Nazism, and the rise of imperialist Japan—we may now proceed to turn our attention to the actual steps taken by the nations along the road to a second world war.

II The Road to War, 1931-1939

The First Step: Manchuria, 1931

It is now clear that the first step along the road to war was the Japanese seizure of Manchuria in 1931. Stimson, President Hoover's Secretary of State, responded to the seizure by announcing that the United States would recognize no gains made by armed force. Stimson hoped that Britain and the other democracies might follow this American lead, but his hopes were largely disappointed. The League of Nations did send out a commission headed by the British Earl of Lytton, and the subsequent Lytton Report condemned the Japanese act as aggression. Neither the United States nor the League, however, fortified verbal protests by effective action; force was not met by force. Japan, refusing to accept the Lytton Report, withdrew from the League of Nations in March, 1933, making the first formal breach in the League's structure.

The Second Step: German Rearmament, 1935–1936

The next breach in the League's structure, and the next step toward war, was made by Germany. In October, 1933, Hitler withdrew from the League, thereby virtually serving notice on the world of his aggressive intentions. On March 16, 1935, he denounced the clauses of the Treaty of Versailles that limited German armanents and set about the open rebuilding of the German armed forces.

The response to this unilateral and hence illegal act set the pattern for the next few years. On April 17, 1935, the League of Nations formally condemned Germany's repudiation of treaty obligations—and Germany continued to rearm. In May, 1935, France hastily concluded with the Soviet Union a treaty of alliance against German aggression—and Germany continued to rearm. In June, 1935, the British, realistically and short-sightedly

Emperor Haile Selassie protesting to the League of Nations (1935) after the Italian invasion of Ethiopia.

—for their action seemed like desertion to the French—signed with rearming Germany a naval agreement limiting the German navy to one-third the size of the British, and German submarines to 60 per cent of those of Britain.

It is hardly surprising that Hitler's next act drew no more than the customary protests from the signatories of Locarno. This was the "reoccupation" of the Rhineland in March, 1936—that is, the sending of German troops into the western German zone that had been demilitarized by the Treaty of Versailles. Britain and France once more did nothing, although many military critics thought then—and still think—that united British-French military action in 1936 could have nipped Hitler's career of aggression in the bud. Such action would have been fully legal in terms of existing treaties and might well have succeeded, for German re-armament was far from complete.

The Third Step: Ethiopia, 1935

Meanwhile the Italians struck in Ethiopia. In that pocket of old Africa an independent state had precariously maintained itself, largely because its imperial neighbors, Britain, France, and Italy, would neither agree to divide it nor let any one of the three swallow it whole. The Italians, who wanted it most, had lost the disastrous battle of Adowa to the native Ethiopians in 1896. This humiliation rankled with the fascists, who felt they had to show the world that there was more than rhetoric in their talk about a revived Roman Empire.

In 1934, a frontier incident at Ualual, a desert post in Italian Somaliland—or in Ethiopia, for both sides claimed the place—put the matter before the international politicians. France and Britain were characteristically quite ready for appeasement of Italy, partly because they hoped to align Mussolini with them against Hitler. They offered him almost everything in Ethiopia, including those concrete economic concessions naive people think are the essence of imperialism—and wars, and indeed everything in human events. But since Ethiopia was a member of the League, the French and the British insisted that its formal independence be observed. This Mussolini would not accept, and in October, 1935, his troops began the invasion of Ethiopia. Airplanes, artillery, and tanks made the difference between 1896 and 1935. This time the underdog was not the winner. Poison gas finished the task early in 1936, and the King of Italy acquired the coveted title of Emperor of Ethiopia. Once more there was an emperor—of sorts—in Rome!

The League of Nations had already formally condemned the Japanese aggression in Manchuria and the German denunciation of the disarmament clauses of the Treaty of Versailles. In 1935, it at once declared that Italy, by invading Ethiopia, a League member, had violated her obligations under the Covenant of the League. Now the League made the momentous decision to test its power to move from words to deeds. This action had the accord of most of its members, and was urged on by the British, less vocally by the French, and strongly by Haile Selassie, the rightful Emperor of Ethiopia. On October 11, 1935, fifty-one member nations of the League voted to invoke against Italy the famous Article 16 of the League Covenant, which provided for economic sanctions against a member resorting to war in disregard of its covenants.

The sanctions thus invoked failed. There were loopholes; oil, for instance, was not included in the list of articles barred from commerce with Italy, which had only meager stockpiles of this vital war material. There was much mutual recrimination among members of the League over what articles should be placed on the prohibited list and over the fact that Britain and France did nothing to check Italian movements of troops and munitions through the Suez Canal, which Britain then in fact controlled. Germany was no longer in the League, and was wholly unbound by its decision. No major power applied these sanctions rigorously. To that extent, it is true that the method of economic sanctions was not really tried.

The Ethiopian fiasco was a disastrous blow to the League, which from now on was helpless in high international politics. Its special services as a group of trained international civil servants, its "functional groups," dealing with labor problems, international police matters like the drug traffic and prostitution, and much else, persisted, however, to be absorbed after World War II by the United Nations. But for the rest of the 1930's, the League was hardly even a formal factor in the increasing tensions. No one was surprised or greatly concerned when Italy, copying Japan and Germany, withdrew from the League in December, 1937.

The Fourth Step:
The Spanish Civil War, 1936–1939

The next step after Ethiopia on the road to war is of great psychological and moral interest. No doubt the later direct aggressions of Hitler in Czechoslovakia and Poland were the politically decisive steps. But the Spanish Civil War (for details, see Chapter 27), which broke out in July, 1936, was the emotional catalyst that divided millions of men and women all over the western world. It is still, in spite of the passing of years, a kind of great

collective Dreyfus case, a test of conscience and loyalty for our time.

The Spanish Civil War was fought between a Right and a Left. On the Right were fascists, monarchists, and just plain conservatives; on the Left were socialists, communists, anarchists, and a few liberals or just plain democrats. As in most great civil wars, there was really no Center. It was a quasi-religious war, waged with the great violence and with the consecrated devotion that mark wars of principle. No one can say for sure how the struggle would have ended if it had remained a purely Spanish one, as the American Civil War had remained a purely American one. Certainly the Loyalists of the Left would have been in a much stronger position if the democratic powers had followed the usual practice in international law of sending arms to the *de jure* government of Spain. Such speculation, however, is useless. Almost from the very start the Spanish Civil War engaged, not merely the vicarious emotional participation of the West, not merely individual foreign enlistments, but the active though never wholly open intervention of other nations. This intervention was decisive and effective on the part of the fascist powers, Italy and Germany; it was less determined and effective on the part of communist Russia; and feeblest of all on the part of Britain and France. Early in 1939, with the fall of Barcelona, the Civil War was in effect over. Once more a fascist group had won.

Meantime, dizzy with success, Mussolini was going on to other adventures. In October, 1936, he signed a pact with Hitler, thereby formally establishing the Rome-Berlin "Axis" and committing fascist Italy to alliance with Nazi Germany. Mussolini gave strong support to Franco's rebellion in Spain. And, late in 1938, he orchestrated a public outcry in Italy for the French to hand over certain territories. He wanted not only Nice and Savoy, which had been ceded to Napoleon III during Italian unification negotiations almost a century earlier (see Chapter 21, p. 239), but also the Mediterranean island of Corsica, which had been French since the days of Louis XV in the eighteenth century, and Tunisia, which had never been under Italian rule and had been a French protectorate since 1881. These demands came to nothing, but they did not exactly improve relations between France and Italy. Finally, on Good Friday (April 7), 1939, Mussolini attacked Albania, long coveted by the Italians, and quickly subjugated this backward little Balkan state. For a few years, Victor Emmanuel was to be King of Albania as well as Emperor of Ethiopia.

The Fifth Step: "Anschluss," 1938

The immediate origins of World War II lie, however, neither in Italian nor in Spanish fascist aggression, but in the mounting series of German aggressions. Hitler had begun the open rebuilding of German armed forces in 1935. Three years later, he felt strong enough to undertake the first enterprise of expansion, an enterprise which, like all he undertook, he insisted was no more than a restoration to Germany of what the *Diktat* of Versailles had deprived her. Austria, German in language

and tradition, had been left a mere fragment by the disruption of the Habsburg Empire. Ever since 1918 there had been a strong movement among Austrians for annexation ("*Anschluss*") to Germany proper. This movement had been strenuously opposed by the victors of the first war, and especially by France, but agitation for *Anschluss* kept on, nourished by Nazi propaganda and, in 1934, an attempted *Putsch*.

Hitler carefully laid the ground for the success of the next Nazi attempt. The pact with Italy that formally established the Rome-Berlin "Axis" (October, 1936) disarmed Mussolini's opposition to *Anschluss*. Early in 1938 Hitler began what turned out to be his standard technique of softening his victims for the final blow. He unleashed a violent propaganda campaign by press, radio, and platform against the alleged misdeeds of the government of independent Austria. In February, 1938, he summoned the Austrian Chancellor Schuschnigg to his Bavarian retreat at Berchtesgaden. There he let loose a bullying

"Honest, Mister, there's nobody here but us Spaniards." — Franco's explanation to Chamberlain and Daladier.

tirade against the hapless Schuschnigg. In March, he moved his troops into Austria and made *Anschluss* a fact.

Hitler now had six million more German-speaking nationals in the fold; and in the union of Austria and Germany he had achieved something that no Habsburg and no Hohenzollern had been able to do in modern times. But he showed no signs at all of being content with what he had gained. Almost at once he went to work on the acquisition of the Sudeten Germans of Czechoslovakia.

The Sixth Step: Czechoslovakia Dismembered, 1938–1939

The Czechoslovak republic was the only state in central or eastern Europe where parliamentary democracy had achieved a real success after World War I. The republic faced a difficult problem of national minorities, but it had the good fortune to inherit some of the most highly developed industrial regions of the old Habsburg Empire. Its economy, consequently, was far better balanced between industry and agriculture than was that of the other states of eastern Europe. This healthy economy was mirrored in the social structure, where a working balance was maintained among peasants, middle classes, and industrial workers. The period immediately after the war, as well as the great depression of the 1930's, times of great suffering elsewhere, affected Czechoslovakia very lightly. Yet these advantages could hardly have preserved democracy in the republic had it not been for the enlightened policies of Thomas Masaryk, liberator and president of his country until his resignation at the age of 85 in 1935.

Even the enlightened Czech regime, however, could not keep the country from ultimately being smashed by outside pressures working on its sensitive minorities. The Sudeten German minority of 3¼ millions, feeling, as Germans, superior to Slavs, resisted the new republic at every turn, even when the Prague government made concessions to satisfy their just grievances. Sudeten extremists early turned to Hitler, but even moderates

and socialists among the Sudetens were more or less pan-German in their views. From 1933 on, Nazi agitation, supported by Hitler with men and money, became increasingly serious in Czechoslovakia. Early in 1938, having secured Austria, Hitler decided to push the Czech affair next. Henlein, his Sudeten agent, made demands on the Prague government for what amounted to complete Sudeten autonomy. The summer of 1938 was spent in negotiations and in mutual propaganda blasts. The Czechs relied heavily on their French allies and on the friendly, though not formally allied, British. But by the spring of 1938, it seems clear now, Britain and France had agreed not to defend the territorial integrity of Czechoslovakia.

By the autumn of 1938, Hitler was ready for action. On September 12 he made a violent speech at Nuremberg, insisting on self-determination for the Sudeten Germans. This was the signal for widespread disorders in Czechoslovakia and for the proclamation of martial law by its government. The situation was now a full-fledged European crisis that called for the personal intervention of heads of state. The British Prime Minister, Neville Chamberlain, made two preliminary visits to Hitler in Germany in an effort to moderate German demands, and finally—with the help of Mussolini—persuaded Hitler to call a full conference of the four great western powers. This conference—Hitler, Mussolini, Chamberlain, with Daladier for France—met in Munich on September 29, 1938. Russia was not invited; her exclusion was to complete her abandonment of the "Popular Front" policy (see Chapter 26).

Munich was a sweeping victory for Hitler. Czechoslovakia was partially dismembered; her Sudeten rim-lands were turned over to Germany; the Czechs were obliged to hand over Teschen and certain other areas to the Poles; the whole economy and transportation system were lamed; the defense of her frontiers was made impossible by the loss of the border mountains and their fortifications; and Slovakia was given autonomy within a federal state, emphasized by the official change in spelling from Czechoslovakia to Czecho-Slovakia. The Czech leaders had felt it impossible to resist the Germans without the aid of the French and British; their people acquiesced bitterly in the settlement of Munich. The Germans had played fully on the differences between the more industrialized Czechs and the still largely agricultural Slovaks. But even had the country been strongly united, the laming blow of Munich would have ruined its morale. Hitler acted quickly. In the very next spring, before the final lines of demarcation set at Munich had actually been drawn, he summoned the Czech President, Hacha, to Germany for another of those ghastly interviews, in which he announced that the fate of the Czech people "must be placed trustingly in the hands of the *Fuhrer.*" In March, 1939, Hitler sent his army into the remaining fragments of Czechoslovakia, meeting no real resistance.

The most respectable defense that can be made of Munich and "appeasement" rests on the argument that the West was buying time to prepare for a war which it knew to be inevitable but for which it was not yet ready.

Chamberlain and Hitler during the negotiations preceding the Munich agreement of 1938.

Chamberlain may have thought so; but Winston Churchill and others have pointed out most cogently that the democracies were in a stronger military position relative to that of Germany in September, 1938, than in September, 1939. It also seems likely that Chamberlain and Daladier, as well as millions all over the world, believed or hoped that the acquisition of Sudeten Germans would satisfy Hitler, that after Munich he would behave as Bismarck had behaved after Sedan, and that he would settle down and try to preserve the balance of power. Some westerners even hoped that Hitler would perhaps ally with them against communist Russia or obligingly get himself so entangled in eastern Europe that he would bring on a Russo-German war. Hitler's words and deeds, however, had given no real foundation for the belief that he would now "play ball" with the West. And we now know that he had as early as November 5, 1937, announced to his close advisers his unalterable intention of destroying Czechoslovakia and moving on into Poland and the Ukraine.

The actual destruction of old Czechoslovakia in March, 1939, seems not to have surprised anyone. Indeed the curious mixture of resignation, condemnation, and resolution with which this action was greeted in the West marks a turning point. The days of appeasement were over. Munich had proved to be an epoch-making event, a catalyst for both professional western diplomatists and statesmen and for western opinion generally. Hitler's next aggression would not lead to a Munich. We can never be quite sure whether Hitler and his aides thought they could take their next step without bringing on a general war. In public and semi-public, Hitler, Goering, and the other leaders made no secret of their feeling that the British and French were decadent, spineless, inefficient societies, quite unable to summon the courage needed to resist an inspired and rejuvenated Germany. Yet there is good evidence that Hitler expected at least a local war with Poland this time, and that he was quite prepared to face involvement with the French and the British. "Whom the gods would destroy, they first make mad."

The Final Step: Poland, 1939

Poland was inexorably Hitler's next victim. The Polish corridor dividing East Prussia from the rest of Germany was an affront to great-power psychology. So, too, was the separation from Germany of the Free City of Danzig, on the edge of the Polish corridor. Danzig was thoroughly German in language and tradition. Germans, even quite enlightened Germans, thought of the Poles, as indeed of all Slavs, as inferior people who would benefit from capable German supervision. Hitler began his Baltic adventure in March, 1939, when he took the port town of Memel from Poland's northern neighbor, Lithuania.

The critical issue in the tense half-year that led up to the outbreak of war on September 1, 1939, was not at all the possibility that Poland, unsupported by Britain and France, would undergo the same fate as Czechoslovakia. The British government publicly supported Poland by signing a pact of mutual assistance with her in April. Indeed, in the midst of the final week of crisis, Chamberlain's foreign minister, Lord Halifax, sent a telegram to Hitler himself in which he made a pathetic appeal to the lessons of history:

> It has been alleged that if His Majesty's Government had made their position more clear in 1914 the great catastrophe would have been avoided. Whether or not there is any force in that allegation, His Majesty's Government are resolved that on this occasion there shall be no such tragic misunderstanding. If the need should arise, they are resolved and prepared to employ without delay all the forces at their command. . . . I trust that Your Excellency will weigh with the utmost deliberation the considerations which I have put before you.*

The real critical point at issue was the attitude of Russia. Hitler had a for once sensible fear of a war on two fronts, a war against major powers to the east and to the west of the kind

*Documents on British Foreign Policy, 1919-1939, E. L Woodward and R. Butler, eds. (London, 1954), 3rd series, Vol. II, No. 145.

on which Germany had embarked in 1914. He was in fact to be drawn within two years into just such a war. Even if he had been faced in 1939 by the united front of Britain, France, and Russia in support of Poland, it is perfectly possible that he could not have restrained himself and his followers. One is tempted to see the Nazi top command as driven on by some abnormal and obsessive motivation and quite oblivious to ordinary considerations of self-interest. Hitler perhaps could no more keep his hands off Poland than an alcoholic can keep his hands off liquor. But, as events developed, Hitler was able to seize Poland without fear of Russian intervention. Indeed, he was able to arrange with Stalin a partition of Poland quite recognizably on the model of the eighteenth-century partitions.

Why did the Russians make their about-face? They had been deeply hurt by their exclusion from the negotiations over the Czechoslovakian crisis of the year before, an exclusion that they blamed primarily on the British and the French. From the failure of the western powers to stand up to German violations of the Versailles Treaty ever since 1934, the Russians had drawn conclusions at least as disparaging to the western will to fight as those drawn by Hitler. In particular, they deeply distrusted the British Tories under Neville Chamberlain, for they believed that in many ways Tory Britain was more fundamentally hostile to communist Russia than even Nazi Germany was.

The Russians' mistrust of the West was not dispelled by the diplomatic mission that Britain and France sent, belatedly and grudgingly, to negotiate with Russia in this critical summer of 1939. The western powers proposed a mutual assistance pact, but the efforts of their negotiators were inept and halfhearted. Moreover, Chamberlain's government made a tactless choice of negotiators. One of them, Ironside, had been involved in the British intervention against the Reds at Archangel in the early beleaguered days of the Bolshevik state—he had, indeed, been made a peer under the title "Baron of Archangel and of Ironside"; another was a mere functionary of the Foreign Office. The Russians like to

Europe on the Eve, August 1939

Atlantic Ocean

NORWAY
Oslo

SWEDEN
Stockholm

FINLAND
Helsinki
Leningrad

NO. IRELAND

UNITED
KINGDOM

DENMARK

North Sea

Baltic Sea

ESTONIA

LATVIA

EIRE
(IRISH FREE STATE)
Dublin

ENGLAND
London

NETH.

Memel
1939

LITHUANIA

Danzig

English Channel

BELG.

Brunswick
Elbe R.

G E R M A N Y

Berlin

Warsaw
Bug R.

POLAND

U.S.S.R.

Kiev

Dnieper R.

Neutral countries

0   300
Miles

FRANCE

LUX.

SAAR
1935

Weimar

Frankfurt
Nuremberg

1936

Rhine R.

CZECHOSLOVAKIA

Vistula R.

Dniester R.

Seine R.
Paris

Loire R.

Munich

AUSTRIA
1938

Vienna

Budapest

HUNGARY

Pruth R.

BESSARABIA

SWITZ.

BASQUE
PROV.
Bayonne

Rhône R.

SAVOY

Geneva

Locarno

Po R.

SLOVENIA

CROATIA

R U M A N I A

ASTURIAS

NAVARRE

Nice

Belgrade

Bucharest

Danube R.

*Black
Sea*

PORTUGAL

Madrid

Ebro R.

CORSICA
(Fr.)

ITALY

Rome

YUGOSLAVIA

BULGARIA
Sofia

Lisbon

Tagus R.

SPAIN
CASTILE

Barcelona

Istanbul

ANDALUSIA

BALEARIC IS.

SARDINIA

ALBANIA

GREECE

*Aegean
Sea*

TURKEY

Gibraltar
(Br.)

SICILY

to Italy, 1939

Athens

DODECANESE
(It.)

RHODES

MOROCCO

ALGERIA

TUNISIA

MALTA
(Br.)

The Axis Powers

Areas annexed by Germany, 1935-39

Areas made "protectorates" of Germany, 1939

Annexed by Italy, 1939

Mediterranean Sea

CRETE

LIBYA

---

deal with top people; they like to be made to feel important. Significantly, Hitler, who was also negotiating with Russia at the time, put Foreign Minister Ribbentrop himself on the job. So the Anglo-French overture to Moscow came to nothing. The Russian leaders had apparently reached the conclusion that the West was a broken reed, that if they themselves did not come to terms with Hitler he would attack them anyway.

Finally, the Russians were quite as distrustful of the Polish government as of anyone else. The western, especially the French, policy of encouraging the smaller powers of eastern Europe to act as counterweights to *both* Germany and Russia now bore its natural fruit. The Polish government would not accept Russia as protector; it would not, in these hectic months of negotiations, consent to the passage through Polish territory of Russian troops in case of war with Germany. The Russians were tempted by the opportunity to recover lands in eastern Poland that they had lost in World War I and its aftermath. To the horror of the West, they signed at Moscow on August 23, 1939, a nonaggression pact with Germany, the "Hitler-Stalin" or "Ribbentrop-Molotov pact," a cynical about-face of two supposedly irreconcilable ideological enemies (see the Low cartoon, p. 432). A week later, the German army marched into Poland. On September 3, Britain and France honored their obligations and declared war on Germany. The twenty years' truce was at an end.

Democratic Policy in Review

It is not really difficult to understand why the democracies behaved as they did in these years. Britain, France, and the United States were the victors of 1918, and by the very fact of their victory they were on the defensive. Wisdom and luck might have made their defense more effective than it was, but nothing could have altered the fact that they were on the defensive. In the long past of our state system, the defensive has always proved a difficult position, has always been—perhaps from the very nature of western culture with its drives toward change—at a disadvantage against aggression. This disadvantage seems by no means associated with democracies as such. Absolute monarchies have suffered quite as much from the difficulties of the defensive, as the failure of Metternich shows (see Chapter 19).

In the years between the two world wars, the normal tendency of the victors to relax was no doubt increased by some of the facts of democratic life. The western democracies were committed to an effort to secure for every citizen some minimum of material comforts; they were committed to the pursuit of happiness. Their normal tendency was to produce butter rather than guns. Their totalitarian opponents may well have been quite as "materialistic" as they, but for them the butter was to be attained in the future, and by means of the guns. In short, the German, Japanese, and Italian governments were able to get their societies to tighten their belts in order to make military preparation possible. On the other hand, it was exceedingly difficult for democratic governments to get such sacrifices from their citizens until war actually broke out.

III   The Nature of the War

The first world war of our century had, in its main theater, the Western Front, been one long siege. Since the military experts tended to fight it over and over again in their planning, both France and Germany in the 1930's built two confronting lines of fortifications on their common frontier. The Maginot Line, on the French side, and the Siegfried Line, on the German, were far more formidable than the improvised trenches of the war of 1914–1918. So it is not surprising that on the outbreak of hostilities in September, 1939, most people expected first, that the war would be decided primarily in the area between France and Germany, and second, that it would be a closely confined war of siege in the West, with at most diversional activity in other parts of the world.

But the war itself showed once more the perils of prediction in great human affairs. As Germany was joined by her Axis partners, Italy and Japan, and as the United States entered it, this second world war became much more truly a world war than the first had been. It was decided in Russia, in the Pacific, even in the Mediterranean, quite as much as in the West. And it turned out to be one of the most extraordinarily open wars of movement in history. Indeed, the armies of the British Montgomery and the German Rommel in

North Africa moved through the desert with the freedom of nomad hordes of old; but the gasoline engine had replaced the horse and camel.

It was also a war in which for the first time the airplane played a major role, a role foreshadowed in the fighting waged in Ethiopia and Spain during the 1930's. Over the water, the airplane, both land-based and carrier-based, soon established itself as a central factor in naval warfare; in the opinion of many experts, it had made the great warship obsolete. Over the land, the airplane soon established itself as an essential arm of the fire power of land armies, an arm that needed and in the end got careful integration with the ground forces. But even in this war the airplane did not live up to the advanced billing given it by its more imaginative proponents; it did not become the *sole* means of warfare, superseding all others. Air power by itself alone proved inadequate in the great test of 1940, when the Germans tried to reduce Britain from the air.

Aerial bombardment—toward the end of the war carried on by German pilotless aircraft and rocket missiles—did indeed bring the horrors of warfare back to the civilians of the cities. Military experts had been inclined to believe that civilians could not possibly stand aerial bombardment, and that any country whose cities were subject to a few such bombardments would be obliged to sue for peace. Yet European and Asian civilian populations proved able to stand up to months of bombardment. German civilian deaths from air bombardment have been estimated at about 500,000. Organized systems of shelter, partial dispersal of populations, the obvious but not previously noted fact that much of the space of modern cities is made up of streets, parks, gardens, churches, and other public buildings not used at night (when much of the bombing was done)—all combined to make it possible for the people of heavily bombed cities like Berlin and Tokyo to endure what were in effect front-line conditions.

Yet at the very end of the war a technical innovation was introduced that may have altered radically the character of war, may indeed make any future war so unendurably destructive that it will at least be brief. This was the atomic bomb, developed in secrecy by American, Canadian, and British experts, and first used on the Japanese city of Hiroshima on August 6, 1945. A single bomb destroyed something over half the city. Somewhat less material damage was done by a second and somewhat different bomb dropped on Nagsaki, a hilly city, three days later. But over a hundred thousand people were killed in the two cities by the two bombs, an incidence of death that seems to justify fully the fears that the atomic bomb and its still more frightful hydrogen bomb successors have aroused in our own generation.

IV Early Successes of the Axis

Polish and Finnish Campaigns

The first campaign of World War II reached a by no means unexpected conclusion. No one had seriously supposed that isolated Poland could possibly stand up for long against the German armed forces, or that Britain and France could possibly get into action rapidly enough to help their Polish ally decisively. Yet the speed of the German conquest surprised almost everyone. The German air force, the *Luftwaffe,* soon gained absolute command of the air, and used it to disrupt Polish communications and to spread terror with its dive bombers. Special German task forces, fully motorized, swept through and around the more primitively armed Poles. This was what the Germans called a *Blitzkrieg,* or lightning war. The German word was later simplified by the English into "blitz," and was used by them to apply to the German air bombardment of Britain in the years 1940–1941.

Anxious to get his share of Poland, Hitler's new collaborator, Stalin, hastened to push the Russian armies in from the east on the hapless Poles. He also established Russian military bases in the Baltic republics of Estonia, Latvia, and Lithuania, which had been created out of Russian provinces at the close of World War I. "Mutual assistance" pacts between giant Russia and the tiny Baltic states were to be the entering wedge for their full occupation by Russia in 1940 and their amalgamation, as constituent republics, into the Union of Soviet Socialist Republics—a title officially without the word "Russia."

Fear of Germany, or an imperialistic desire to expand, or both, also drove the Russian leaders into a war with neighboring Finland for bases in the Baltic (November, 1939). The Russians, who had perhaps miscalculated the strength of their little opponent, did rather badly at first. By March, 1940, however, they had worn down the Finns; they secured their bases and annexed Finnish lands very close to the great Russian city of Leningrad. It seems quite possible that this "winter war" with Finland had a major effect in encouraging Hitler to his fateful decision of 1941 to make war on Russia. The German military experts drew from Russian difficulties in this war conclusions extremely disparaging to Russian capabilities.

"Phony War" and Blitzkrieg in the West

Meanwhile in the West what the British called the "phony war" was pursuing its uneventful course. The French and the British duly mobilized as in 1914, and as in 1914 the British sent a few divisions to the Continent. But the Germans refused to repeat the pattern of 1914. Occupied in Poland, they did nothing in the West. Occasionally a French patrol from the Maginot Line would exchange shots with a German patrol, but for the most part the troops exercised, ate, slept, and went on leave as though they were merely in training.

The Germans, however, had no intention of sitting out a defensive war in the West. But not even modern warfare is wholly emancipated from the weather. The German general staff was not prepared to begin a decisive campaign in the West with the winter ahead. They waited until spring, and in April they made sure of their northern flank, as they had not in 1914, by making without declaration of war a sea and air invasion of neutral Denmark and Norway. Denmark, totally unprepared, was occupied almost without resistance. Norway, also unprepared, made a brave showing. But neither the British nor the French were able to help her with more than token forces, and by the end of April important Norwegian resistance was broken. The Germans now had admirable bases for air and submarine action against the British.

The great blow was struck, without warning, on May 10, 1940, when the German armies, brilliantly supported in the air, invaded the Low Countries. Holland, spared in 1914, was this time invaded so that the Germans might make doubly sure of their northern flank. A carefully planned attack on the key Belgian fort of Eben Emael, an attack that had been rehearsed on a dummy of the fort set up inside Germany, was at once successful, and opened the way into the Low Countries.

In the era of weakness among western democracies in the 1930's, both the Belgians and the Dutch had been extremely anxious to avoid compromising themselves by planning for joint resistance with Britain and France against a possible German attack. They were now to suffer the full consequences of their own policy of attempting to appease Hitler. For the crucial failure to hold the Germans in actual battle was in the Low Countries. We cannot be sure that a carefully co-ordinated plan among French, British, Belgians, and Dutch would have stopped Hitler. But clearly the lack of such co-ordination was a major factor in the German success. Indeed, though much has since been written against the "Maginot mentality," it is a fact that the Germans did not take the French Maginot Line by frontal assault, but outflanked it at the critical

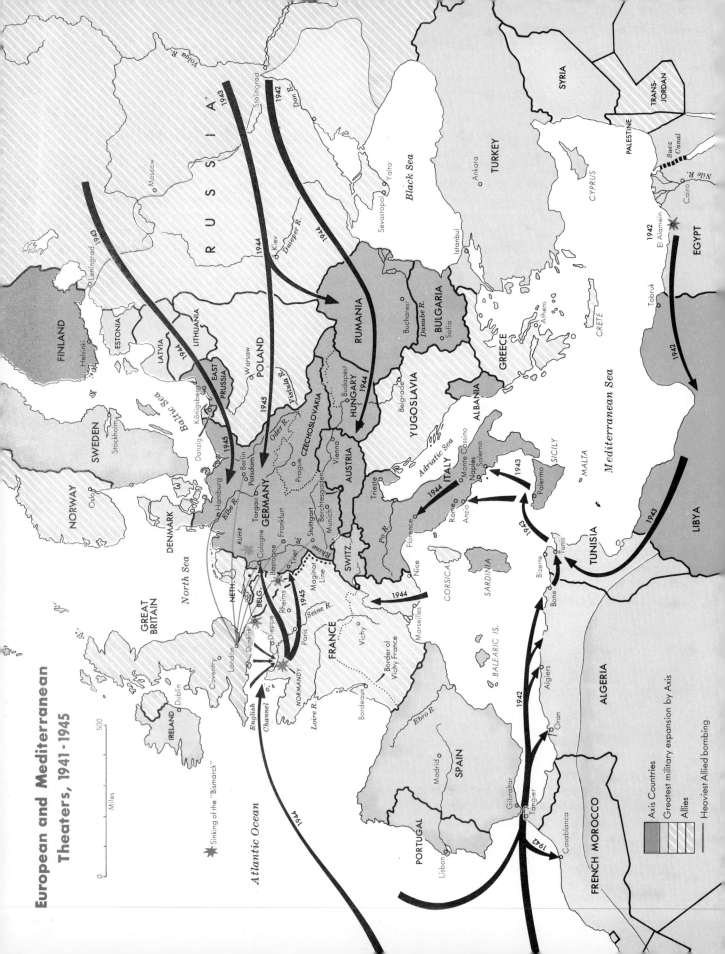

European and Mediterranean Theaters, 1941-1945

Atlantic Ocean

Miles
500

⚹ Sinking of the "Bismarck"

RUSSIA

Volga R.
1943 Stalingrad 1942 Don R.
Moscow
Leningrad 1943
1944 Dnieper R. Kiev
1944

FINLAND
Helsinki

ESTONIA
LATVIA
LITHUANIA
Baltic Sea

NORWAY
Oslo

SWEDEN
Stockholm

DENMARK
North Sea

GREAT BRITAIN
London
Coventry
Dublin
IRELAND
English Channel

NETH.
Dunkirk Dieppe
BELG. Rheims 1945
NORMANDY
Seine R. Paris
FRANCE Vichy
Loire R.
Bordeaux
Border of Vichy France
1944

Hamburg Elbe R.
Berlin Potsdam
EAST PRUSSIA Königsberg Danzig
1945 Warsaw Vistula R. **POLAND**
1945 Oder R.
GERMANY Torgau Prague **CZECHOSLOVAKIA**
RUHR Cologne
Bastogne Frankfurt
Trier Stuttgart Berchtesgaden Munich
Rhine Maginot Line **SWITZ.**
AUSTRIA Vienna
HUNGARY Budapest 1944
1944

Trieste
YUGOSLAVIA Belgrade
Po R. Adriatic Sea
Florence **ITALY** 1944
Nice Rome Anzio Monte Cassino
Marseilles Naples Salerno 1943
CORSICA
SARDINIA
BALEARIC IS.
Ebro R.
Madrid
SPAIN
Lisbon
PORTUGAL

RUMANIA Bucharest Danube R.
Sofia **BULGARIA**
ALBANIA
GREECE Athens

Black Sea
Sevastopol Yalta
Ankara **TURKEY**
Istanbul
CYPRUS
CRETE

SYRIA
PALESTINE
TRANS-JORDAN
Suez Canal
Nile R. Cairo
EGYPT
1942 El Alamein
1942

Mediterranean Sea
SICILY Palermo 1943
MALTA
Tobruk 1943
LIBYA

Bizerte Tunis 1943
Bone **TUNISIA**
Algiers 1943
Oran 1942
Gibraltar Tangier
Casablanca 1942
FRENCH MOROCCO **ALGERIA**

Legend:
Axis Countries
Greatest military expansion by Axis
Allies
Heaviest Allied bombing

point where it tapered off along the Franco-Belgian border in the hilly region of the Ardennes.

Through the Ardennes the Germans poured their best motorized troops into France. In a blitzkrieg that once more capitalized on the "lessons of 1914," the Germans resisted the temptation to turn at once on the prize of Paris, but instead drove straight through northern France to the Channel, where the port of Boulogne fell on May 26, a little over two weeks after the start of the campaign. By this stroke the Germans separated the British, Belgian, and part of the French troops from the bulk of the French armies to the south. Shortly afterward the French replaced General Gamelin with General Weygand as commander-in-chief. Meanwhile in Britain Neville Chamberlain had resigned after an adverse vote in the Commons on May 8 as a result of failure in Norway. He was succeeded as prime minister by Winston Churchill. The British act was of major importance, comparable to the replacing of Asquith by Lloyd George in World War I. Chamberlain was neither a man of action nor an appealing or heroic figure; Churchill was to prove himself all this and more. Under him the British made a united front in the crisis.

The new leaders, in a desperate last moment, attempted to work out a plan for pinching off the adventurous German motorized thrust by a concerted attack from north and south. But the Belgians, badly disorganized, decided to capitulate, and neither the French nor the British could rally themselves to carry out the movement. In the last days of May and the first days of June the British did indeed achieve the miracle of the successful withdrawal of some 215,000 British and 120,000 French soldiers by sea from the beaches around Dunkirk at the northern tip of France. With useful protection from the Royal Air Force, an extraordinary flotilla of all sorts of vessels, including private yachts and motorboats, got the men off, though almost all their equipment had to be abandoned. Dunkirk was a courageous action, and one that did much to help British morale. But from German documents that fell to the Allies after the final de-

feat of Germany it is pretty clear (though the point is still controversial) that the miracle of Dunkirk was possible largely because Hitler himself decided not to press home the destruction of the British forces penned on the coast, on the ground that Britain was no longer a real threat. At the last moment, Hitler too gave in to the lure of Paris, and decided to push the attack on the French homeland at once. Here he was wholly and rapidly successful. The French under Weygand could not rally, and the Germans marched southward almost unopposed. The clear signal to the world that the rally of 1914 at the Marne would not be repeated was given on June 13, when the French declared Paris an "open city" and evacuated it without fighting.

"The Fall of France"

The battle of France was thus decided by mid-June. But the French might yet try to defend the south, or, failing that, use their navy and merchant marine to get as many men as possible across the Mediterranean into French North Africa. There, based on their great empire overseas, they might have continued with British aid the fight against the Germans. Some of the French leaders wished to do this, and in the crisis Winston Churchill made to the French the extraordinary offer of a complete governmental union of the two countries to continue the struggle. His offer was not accepted.

On June 16, Reynaud was supplanted by Marshal Pétain as prime minister, in what amounted to a kind of *coup d'état*. Pétain and his colleagues were determined on peace at any price, and this they got. On June 22, 1940, an armistice was signed at Compiègne at the spot where the armistice of November 11, 1918 had been signed. By this armistice, the French withdrew from the war, handed over three-fifths of France, including the whole Atlantic and Channel coasts, to German occupation, and retained under strict German supervision no more than the central and Mediterranean regions. This "unoccupied France" was ruled from the little resort city of

Civilians in Marseilles watching historic French battle flags being evacuated from the country, 1940.

Vichy, where Pétain set up a French form of authoritarian, anti-democratic state of which he was "chief." History has labeled his government simply "Vichy France." To most Frenchmen it was a German-imposed rule.

Some few of Pétain's collaborators were pro-German, convinced that totalitarianism was inevitable. But it is now clear that for most of them, even for men like the "collaborator" Laval, a dominant figure at Vichy, and indeed for Pétain himself, the important motive in those bewildering June days of 1940 was simply a desire to make terms with the inevitable. They were absolutely sure that Hitler had won the war. They did not believe that Britain had any chance of successfully resisting the German war machine that had crushed France. In this belief they were followed at first by the great majority of Frenchmen.

The new Vichy government attempted to remake France along conservative, indeed monarchist, lines that had not been practical politics since the *Seize Mai* of 1877 (see Chapter 21). Symbolic of why the Vichy régime failed is its attempt to substitute for the great slogan "Liberty, Equality, Fraternity" a new trinity of "Labor, Family, Fatherland." Even an outsider can see that the new slogan lacked fire. More concretely, the Vichy régime from the start was compromised by its association with the hated Germans; born of defeat, it could do little in the few years it had to live before it died in the Allied victory.

Even in the dark days of June, 1940, a few Frenchmen, led by General Charles de Gaulle, who was flown out to London at the last moment, refused to give up the fight. De Gaulle, with British aid, set up a French National Committee with headquarters in London. A nucleus of French soldiers taken off the beach at Dunkirk, and a stream of refugees who came out of France by all sorts of means in the next few years, made up the "Free French" or "Fighting French." At home in France the "Resistance movement" gradually formed underground to prepare for eventual liberation. North Africa, strongest of the French colonies, remained under the control of Vichy. But some parts of the colonies rallied to the Free French from the start. Notably in Equatorial Africa, under the leadership of the great Negro governor, Félix Eboué, a most useful base for Allied operations was secured from the first. Weak as these fighting French groups were in the early days, they were at least a rallying point. They were able to set up an effective radio center in England from which they conducted a skillful propaganda campaign against Vichy and the Germans, beamed across the Channel to the homeland, where, we now know, it achieved a large audience.

On June 10, Hitler's ally Mussolini had brought the Italians into the war against France and Britain, too late to affect the outcome of the battle of France. But this "stab in the back" as Franklin Roosevelt called it, further outraged American opinion, already alarmed by the Nazi successes. And Italy was now irrevocably engaged in the struggle, anxious to secure some kind of success that would offset the great gains of her German ally. The war, up to this time confined to northern and western Europe, now spread to the Mediterranean.

The Battle of Britain

The Germans, for all their miracles of planning and execution, had not really worked out a way to deal with Britain. Hitler seems to have believed that with France out of the war Britain would see the light and make a separate peace, a peace of compromise in which Germany would dominate the continent of Europe and Britain would continue satisfied with her overseas empire. This division of the spoils, Hitler reiterated in public and private, should be eminently satisfactory; he did not threaten the British Empire. Yet for over four centuries Britain had gone to war rather than accept the kind of one-power domination over western and central Europe that Hitler exercised after the fall of France. The British, therefore, paid no attention at all to his peace feelers.

Hitler was counting heavily on the possibility that German submarines could eventually cut off British supplies of food and raw materials from overseas, and thus starve her into submission. But at best this must take a long time. Hitler and his colleagues were impatient. The obvious thing to do was to attempt a landing in England. But the Germans had made no real preparation for amphibious warfare; they had no specially designed landing craft. Moreover, the German air force and the German navy were at odds over the best way of combining for an invasion across the Channel. A hastily assembled flotilla of miscellaneous vessels was badly damaged by British aircraft, and early in August, 1940, Hitler and Goering, his air marshal, made the fateful decision to try to do the job solely with air power.

The Battle of Britain that followed had two main phases. First, in August and September the Luftwaffe attempted in daylight bombing attacks to wipe out British airports and fighter planes. The Royal Air Force, admirably organized and directed, and using the new detection apparatus called radar to spot the attackers early, proved just barely strong enough to check the Germans. In the critical actions of September 15–21, German official records now available show 120 planes lost (the British at the time claimed 268). This was, however, a rate of loss Goering, head of the Luftwaffe, felt the Germans could not stand. This phase of the blitz was called off. In one of his imperishable phrases, Churchill said of the small group of British fighter pilots who had saved Britain, "Never . . . was so much owed by so many to so few."

The second phase began in the autumn of 1940. The Germans sought by night bombing of major British industrial centers to destroy British production and to terrify the civilian population so that the government would be obliged to sue for peace. Neither aim was successful. Even at Coventry, an important center of the automotive industry, though

Collapse of a building near St. Paul's during the London "blitz."

grave damage was done, the industry was by no means knocked out. Indeed, more damage was done to the cathedral and other buildings in the center of the city than to the great factories on the outskirts. As for civilian morale, it is clear that these bombings strengthened the British will to resist. Civilian defense measures proved adequate to protect both persons and property from that extreme of destruction which might indeed have broken the will to resist. By winter, when the weather gave the British some respite, the Battle of Britain had been won.

Mediterranean and Balkan Campaigns

Hitler now faced the possibility of a long stalemate, something that conquerors like Napoleon in the past have rarely been able to face. Like Napoleon turning to Egypt in 1798, Hitler turned at first to the obvious strategy of getting at Britain through her Mediterranean lifeline to India and the East. His ally Mussolini, already itching to expand in the Mediterranean, invaded Greece from Albania in October, 1940, with no success. The Greeks held on valiantly and even pushed the Italians back. But, just as the Germans came in the first world war to the rescue of their Austrian ally, so they now came successfully to the rescue of Mussolini.

Just how far Hitler himself wanted to invest in action in this theater is not clear. Certainly he toyed with the idea of a campaign against the British fortress of Gibraltar through Spain, to be co-ordinated with Axis attacks in the eastern Mediterranean to clear that sea of the British. But the Spanish dictator Franco wanted too high a price from the French for his consent to a German march through Spain, and Hitler was unwilling to risk driving Vichy France, which still controlled French North Africa, too far. In the upshot, the Germans had to be content with backing up Mussolini in Greece and with an attack on Egypt from the Italian colony of Libya. Efforts to rouse native action against the British and French in the Near East were suppressed without grave difficulty by British and Free French action, and Turkey stood obstinately neutral.

Nevertheless, the German commitment to help the Italians in Greece took valuable German divisions away from another task in the spring of 1941, and as the Germans attempted to move overland through Yugoslavia they were involved in a costly guerrilla war. The British did their best to back up their Greek allies, but once more they were not strong enough. German air power crippled British naval power in the waters around Crete, and by June the Axis had conquered the Greek mainland and the islands.

The Invasion of Russia

The other task for which the German forces were to be used in the spring of 1941 was the conquest of Russia. Hitler had firmly resolved not to repeat what he thought was the fateful mistake of Germany in 1914; he would not engage in a war on two fronts. Yet by his invasion of Russia in June, 1941 — an invasion delayed for a perhaps decisive two months by the Balkan adventure — he committed himself to just such a war. Russia was indeed a tempting goal. The Nazi plan had always looked to the fertile areas of Poland and South Russia as the natural goal of German expansion, the *Lebensraum* (see p. 462) of German destiny. With the precedents of successful blitzkrieg in Poland, western Europe, and now Greece, Hitler and his military experts believed that they could beat the Russians in a single campaign before winter set in. It was quite clear that neither Britain nor the United States — even though the latter should enter the war — could land armies in Europe in 1941. An attack on Russia, then, Hitler seems to have told himself, would not *really* create two fronts. Indeed, once Russia was conquered, as in Hitler's mind it was sure to be, the Germans would have no trouble disposing of Britain, and, if necessary, the United States.

Russia was not conquered in 1941. But it was very close, closer perhaps than the Battle of Britain. Hitler's plan almost worked. There really was a successful blitzkrieg. Within two months the Germans were at the gates of Leningrad, and in the south they had conquered the Ukraine by the end of October. Hundreds of thousands of Russian troops had been killed or taken prisoner. In sheer distance, the German armies had pushed more than twice as far as they had in France.

Yet, as the Russian winter closed in, the Germans had taken neither Moscow nor Leningrad. Russian heavy industry had been in part transferred to the remote Urals, and existing plants there and in Siberia had been strengthened. The United States was beginning to send in supplies. The vast resources of Russian manpower were still adequate for Russian needs. The government had not collapsed, and national spirit was high. Moreover, the Germans had shown once more, as they had in the Battle of Britain, that their boasted planning was far from perfect. Their troops were not sufficiently equipped to stand the rigors of a Russian winter. Confident that one summer and autumn would be enough to finish the business, the German planners had left the winter to take care of itself. Indeed, in winter fighting between December, 1941, and May, 1942, the Russians regained much useful ground.

American Policy

Meanwhile, the Germans had fallen into a second fatal involvement. Impressed with what he thought were the disastrous failures of German policy in World War I, Hitler had sought to keep out of war with the United States. Although the United States had a strong isolationist element and even a handful of Axis sympathizers, American opinion had from the very beginning of the attack on Poland in 1939 been far more nearly unanimous against the Germans and Italians than it had been against the Central Powers in 1914. With the fall of France in 1940, anti-Axis sentiment grew stronger, reinforced by a feeling that if Hitler had his way in Europe the United States would be marked out as his next victim.

Between June, 1940 and December, 1941, the Roosevelt administration, with the consent of the Congress and with the general —though not unanimous—backing of American public opinion, took a series of steps "short of war" in aid of Britain and later Russia. By conventional nineteenth-century standards of international relations, these steps were far from being in accord with America's technical status as a neutral; they would have given Hitler ample legal justification for declaring war against the United States. The American government transferred to the British fifty "over-age" destroyers in exchange for Atlantic naval bases in British colonies, supplied the British with all sorts of arms, and used the American navy to help get these supplies across the Atlantic. Above all, in March, 1941, by the so-called "Lend-Lease Act," the United States agreed to supply materials needed for defense, including foodstuffs, to "any country whose defense the President deems vital to the defense of the United States." Supplies at once began rolling into England, and later to other allies in the struggle against the Axis, without the unfortunate complications produced by the war-debt methods employed during World War I.

This help went, as we have just noted, even to communist Russia, The "cold war" of the 1950's between Russia and the United States produced currents of opinion in this country which held that we should never have helped Russia in 1942–1945. But the historian knows that in great wars of coalition the wise rule is: help your allies even if you don't like them, even, indeed, if you don't trust them. Strict adherence to this doctrine by Roosevelt and Churchill clearly helped prevent among Britain, the United States, Russia, and the Free French the kind of actual back-stabbing and desertion that characterized the failure of Europe to defeat, or even contain, the revolutionary French and Napoleon between 1792 and 1812 (see Chapter 18).

Yet Hitler still did not let himself get involved in war against the United States. He had, however, firm commitments to aid Japan. And Japan, controlled by a militarist group, had taken advantage of the fall of France and

Part of the destruction at Pearl Harbor, December 7, 1941.

the Netherlands and the weakness of Britain to speed up vastly the policy of expansion in Asia that she had begun in Manchuria as far back as 1931. She early took advantage of the fall of France to penetrate into French Indo-China. She continued to press her campaign on the mainland of China. The American government, which had never in the days of technical peace in the 1930's been willing to accept Japanese conquests in China, did not now abandon its policy of opposition to what it considered Japanese aggression. It is indeed highly likely that had the American government been willing to allow Japan a free hand to do what she liked in the Far East there would have been no Pearl Harbor. But short of such complete abandonment of the previous American policy in the Far East, it is unlikely that the United States could have kept out of war with Japan.

Pearl Harbor and After

In the summer and autumn of 1941, the American government took steps to freeze Japanese credits in the United States, to close Japanese access to raw materials, and to get the Japanese to withdraw from China and Indo-China. Negotiations toward these ends were going on between the Japanese and the Americans when on December 7, 1941, the Japanese without warning struck with carrier-based airplanes at the American naval base at Pearl Harbor in Hawaii. Grave damage was done to ships and installations, but American power in the Pacific was by no means destroyed. Moreover, the psychological effect of the "day of infamy" on American public opinion was to produce in a nation of many millions an almost unanimous support for war against Japan. And the consequence was the immediate declaration of war against Japan by the United States. Germany and Italy honored their obligations to their Axis partner by declaring war against the United States on December 11. As the year 1942 began, the war was literally and fully a world war.

Although the United States was incomparably better prepared than she had been in 1917, she was still at a disadvantage. Against Germany she could for the moment do no more than continue, indeed increase, aid to Britain and Russia by Lend-Lease and take full part in the struggle against the German submarines. Against Japan she was almost as powerless. Her Pacific outposts of Guam, Wake Island, and the Philippines fell in rapid succession to Japanese arms. Nor could the British and the exiled Dutch governments

532

protect their colonies in Southeast Asia. By the spring of 1942, the Japanese had taken Malaya from the British and Indonesia from the Dutch, and had virtual control of Siam (Thailand) and Burma. They seemed poised for an attack on Australia.

V   The Victory of the United Nations

The Turning Points

There were several turning points in the struggle. The earliest was a series of naval actions in which Japanese expansion was stopped. In these actions, carrier-based airplanes played a decisive role. On May 7, 1942, in the battle of the Coral Sea in the southwest Pacific, Allied sea and air power halted a possible Japanese invasion of Australia and its protecting islands. In June, American sea and air power dispersed a Japanese fleet that was aiming at the conquest of Midway Island. Although the Japanese landed on American territory in the Aleutians, they never seriously threatened Hawaii or mainland Alaska.

In the West, the Americans and the British were as yet unwilling to respond to Russian pressure for a "second front" on the European mainland. But they were able in November, 1942, to effect a series of landings in French North Africa. Secret negotiations with anti-Axis elements among the French in North Africa were not completely successful, and the landings in Morocco were sharply though briefly resisted by the Vichy French. None the less, the Allies were rapidly established in force in Morocco and Algeria.

The Libyan segment of the long North African coast had been held by the Germans and their Italian allies since the beginning of the war in the Mediterranean, and there had been seesaw campaigns in these desert areas, campaigns that recaptured some of the adventure, even romance, of wars of old. At the time of the North African landings, the British under General Montgomery were holding a defensive line inside the Egyptian frontier; but on October 23, 1942, the British started on an offensive which was planned to co-ordinate with that of General Eisenhower, commander of the Allied forces in French North Africa, in the classic maneuver of catching the enemy in a vise. The Germans responded quickly to the threat, and succeeded in reinforcing their African armies through Tunis, which was delivered to them by the Vichy authorities. The planned expulsion of the Germans and Italians from North Africa was thus delayed, but the vise closed slowly. In May, 1943, Free French, British, and American troops took the last Axis strongholds of Tunis and Bizerte, and accepted the surrender of some three hundred thousand Axis troops.

The North African campaign had clearly been a turning point. The Allies had successfully made large-scale amphibious landings, and they had annihilated one of the most renowned of Axis forces, commanded by one of the few German generals in this war to strike the imagination of the world, Rommel, the "desert fox." North Africa was by no means a great central operation, but it was nevertheless a major campaign in which the Allies gained confidence and prestige.

The great turning point on land was, however, the successful Russian defense of Stalingrad, (now Volgograd), a defense that turned into an attack in the same month (November, 1942) that saw the Allied landing in North Africa. After their check in the winter of 1941–1942, the Germans had turned their Russian summer offensive of 1942 away from Leningrad and Moscow and toward the oil-rich regions of southeastern European Russia. The Germans were already beginning to suffer oil shortages, partly because of Allied bombing, but even more because, though they held the oil fields of Rumania, they simply did not have oil enough for the ravenous demands of mechanical warfare. This push toward the Russian oil fields carried the Germans a prodigious distance inside Russia, over a thousand miles from their original starting point. But again it failed, falling just short of the really rich oil fields of Grozny and Baku. Russian distance and Russian manpower, and the Russian ability to take punishment, were too much for these overextended Germans. Their armies were pinched off at Stalingrad, and early in 1943 the Russians started the long march that was to take them to Berlin two years later.

The Battle of Supply

A much less spectacular turning point than the engagements in the Coral Sea, in North Africa, and at Stalingrad was the Allied victory in the battle of supply. Yet this victory was of even greater importance, since naval and military successes ultimately depend on supplies. Even for Russia, an important source of supplies was the United States. But the United States was separated from its allies — and its enemies — by water, and all but the most precious and least bulky supplies, which could go by air, had to move across the seas. If the Germans could stop this movement, or even reduce it greatly, they might still be able to win in spite of the overwhelming resources of the Allies. They made important improvements in their submarines, notably the schnorkel, a device that enabled submarines to travel submerged for great distances. Submarine crews and commanders were well trained and resourceful. But there were not enough submarines, and the countermeasures of the Allies — radar, co-ordination of naval vessels and aircraft, the convoy system, and others — slowly reduced the proportion of sinkings.

Early in 1942, after Pearl Harbor, the rate of sinkings had been really dangerous, and German submarines had operated close to the Atlantic coast of the United States. But by the

end of 1942, the statistics showed a turn of the tide, and in the summer of 1943 the Allies were confident enough to announce publicly that the number of sinkings from U-boat action in the first half of 1943 was only a quarter of what it had been in the first half of 1942.

The Axis on the Defensive

In the last two years of the war, the Axis powers were on the defensive. Both in Europe and in Asia the Allies attacked with land forces along definite lines of march; these were "campaigns" of the traditional kind. But the way for these armies was made easier by two new factors in warfare, air power and modern propaganda, or "psychological warfare." These new methods did not "win" the war by themselves, but they were useful adjuncts, and they undoubtedly hastened the process. Air bombardment, at least until the atomic bomb at Hiroshima, was never quite the perfect annihilation that the prophets of air power had preached. The Germans put some of their key production underground. Allied "precision" bombing rarely reached perfection. But as the superior Allied air power grew, as it was used systematically to destroy enemy capabilities in critical materials like ball bearings, machine tools, and oil, and as American airplanes dropped incendiary bombs on the relatively flimsy Japanese cities, it did much to destroy the Axis will and power to resist.

On Germany and Italy, the attack by land was pressed in three directions — by the Russians from the east, and by the British, French, Americans, and the other Allies from the south and from the west. In the south, the Allies moved over to Sicily in a successful amphibious operation (July, 1943) within two months of their final victory in North Africa, and from Sicily they moved in another six weeks across the Straits of Messina to the mainland of Italy. Yet the Italian campaign was never quite the great success the Allies hoped it would be in these earlier days. The Allied victories of the summer of 1943 were, however, sufficient to put Italy itself for the most part out of the war. High officers of the Italian army and others close to the king, helped by dissident fascist leaders, engineered a *coup* in July which brought about the fall and imprisonment of Mussolini and the beginnings of negotiations between the Allies and the new government headed by Marshal Badoglio.

But the Germans were quite unwilling to abandon the peninsula, perhaps as much for reasons of prestige as for military reasons. A detachment of German troops rescued Mussolini from his Apennine prison (September, 1943), and set him up as the head of a "Fascist Republic." The former *Duce* continued in this post until he was executed by partisans in April, 1945. Meantime, Italy had a civil as well as a foreign war on her hands. The majority of the Italian people, never really taken in by Mussolini's posturing as an imperial Roman, had never liked the war and were now heartily sick of it. Still, many were politically active in Italy in 1943–1945, and of these the fascist-Axis group was far less strong than the pro-Allied group. Italy came naturally enough into the United Nations. The war in Italy went on. In June, 1944, the Allies succeeded,

after particularly severe fighting around Cassino, in breaking through to Rome, and by August they were in Florence. They did not really penetrate any farther until the final collapse of the Germans in the early months of 1945.

The Defeat of Germany

The great Allied push in the west, it was finally decided at the Teheran conference of Churchill, Roosevelt, and Stalin (December, 1943), would be in France. After meticulous preparation, the long-awaited landings in France began on June 6, 1944. The Allies had chosen the Norman coast at the base of the Cotentin (Cherbourg) peninsula, and seem thereby to have gained some initial advantage of surprise, for the German high command believed the landings would come farther north and east along the Channel coast. The Germans had in their four years of occupancy fortified the French coastline with great thoroughness. But the Allies had also had those four years for study, invention, and planning. In the test, Allied landing craft, amphibious

American troops landing in Normandy, June, 1944.

trucks, called "ducks," naval and air support—by now the Luftwaffe had almost been driven from the skies—artificial harbors, and a well-organized supply system proved sufficient to gain a beachhead for the land forces. From this beachhead, a little over a month after "D-Day," they were able to break out at Avranches and sweep the Germans back across the Seine in a great flanking movement led by the American General Patton's Third Army.

A long-planned auxiliary landing on the French Mediterranean coast and a march north up the Rhone-Saône valleys was launched on August 15, 1944, and met very little resistance. Everywhere the French, by now well organized for resistance, welcomed the liberating forces, some of whom were French and French colonials fighting as heirs of the Free French of 1940. Paris, a symbol rather than a mere place, was liberated toward the end of August after its inhabitants had staged an uprising, barricades and all, in the style of 1848, against the German garrison.

The Germans were beaten, but not disorganized. In July, 1944, an attempt to assassinate Hitler and to pave the way for negotiations was made by conservative elements, both military and civilian. But Hitler survived the bomb intended for him, and the Nazis retained their firm grip on the German state. The Allies were encouraged by their rapid successes in July and August to try to destroy the German armies before winter, or to cut them off from their homeland. Patton's mechanized troops, however, ran out of fuel; the new German pilotless planes and rocked-propelled missiles delayed the full use of Antwerp as a port of supply; and by late autumn it was clear that the Germans had retired in good order to their own Siegfried Line.

From the east, the Russians had been pushing on relentlessly ever since the turning of the tide at Stalingrad. In the campaign of 1943, while the western Allies were busy in Italy, the Russians won back most of their own territories that had been lost in 1941 and 1942. They kept up the pressure during the winter and started an early spring campaign in the south. By the autumn of 1944, the Russians had been able to sweep through half-hearted resistance from Hitler's Balkan satellite governments to a juncture with the Yugoslav communist guerrillas under Tito, and were ready for the attack on Hungary. In the center and north, they had recovered all their own territory and were ready to attack Germany itself from the east.

This year 1945 saw the rapid conclusion of the Battle of Germany. The Russians had not stopped for winter, but had pressed on through Poland to menace Berlin early in March. The western Allies broke through the Siegfried Line in February, crossed the Rhine, and entered the heart of Germany. Early in February, 1945, the leaders of the three great Allied powers, Stalin, Churchill, and Roosevelt, met at Yalta in the Crimea and confirmed final plans for the conquest of Germany. It was plain that the Germans, whose key industries had been so riddled from the air that they no longer could support their armies adequately, and whose manpower had been reduced to the very bottom, could not hold out for long. But the Allied planners were anxious to prevent, or at least to check, the race to be the first to arrive in Berlin, and they wanted to arrange peacefully for demarcations between the parts of Germany that each ally was to occupy. The decision to give the Russians the honor of taking Berlin is one that, with many other decisions reached in the conference at Yalta, has since been severely criticized in the West. At the time, however, it seemed a natural decision, a legitimate recognition of the fact that during the two years of successful offensive against the Germans the Russians had worn down many more German divisions than had the western Allies.

The Russians fought their way into a Berlin already pulverized by the air power of the western Allies. Hitler went down to his death, as he had long promised, in a Germanic funeral pyre at his Berlin headquarters.

The Allied advance into Germany revealed for the first time the full ghastliness of Nazi treatment of slave laborers from conquered lands, of political opponents and of Jews, Poles, and other German-styled "inferior" peoples. One after another, the concentration camps were liberated—Auschwitz, Belsen,

Buchenwald, Dachau, Nordhausen, and others. And the world was appalled at the gas ovens that had claimed so many victims, at the piles of emaciated corpses not yet cremated, and at the pitiful state of the prisoners who had survived. This was one of the horrors of war whose reality exceeded the grimmest expectations of Allied opinion.

By May 8, 1945, Churchill and Truman (who had become the American president on Roosevelt's death in April) were able to announce the end of German resistance, the day of victory in Europe, V-E Day. It was symbolic of difficulties to come that Stalin was offended because the western Allies had accepted from some of the German army leaders a formal surrender at Rheims in France. He chose to announce separately, on Russia's part, the final victory over Germany, and not until the next day.

The Defeat of Japan

V-J Day, the day of victory in Japan, was now the great goal of Allied effort. Russia had carefully refrained from adding Japan to its formal enemies as long as Germany was still a threat. Britain and the United States, on the other hand, were anxious to win Russia as a formal fighting ally against the Japanese. This natural desire—natural in the sense of historical precedent, for coalitions in the past have usually sought to rally as many allies as possi-

Corpses of Gestapo victims, Nordhausen concentration camp, 1945.

ble—was responsible for many of the concessions made to Russia in the last months of the German war.

The two years of Allied successes against Germany had also been two years of Allied successes against Japan. The attack on Japan had been pressed home in three main directions. First, in a process that the American press soon christened "island-hopping," the American navy drove straight toward Japan from the central Pacific. One after another, the small island bases that stood in the way were reduced by American naval forces, which used both air support and the amphibious methods that were being worked out simultaneously in Europe and North Africa. The names of these islands are now a part of the litany of American arms—Tarawa, Eniwetok, Kwajalein, Iwo Jima, Okinawa.

Second, in a series of operations calling for the close co-operation of air, sea, and land forces, the Americans and Australians, with help from other Commonwealth elements, worked their way up the southwest Pacific through the much larger islands of the Solomons, New Guinea, and the Philippines. The base for this campaign, which was under the command of the American General MacArthur, was Australia and such outlying islands as New Caledonia and the New Hebrides. The start of the campaign goes back to the first major offensive step in the Far East, the dramatic and difficult seizure of Guadalcanal in the Solomons by the United States Marines on August 7, 1942. These campaigns involved jungle fighting of the hardest sort, slow and painful work. But by October, 1944, the sea forces had won the great battle of the Philippine Sea and had made possible the successful landing of MacArthur's troops on Leyte and the reconquest of the Philippine Islands themselves from the Japanese.

The third attack on the "Greater East Asia Co-Prosperity Sphere" as the Japanese, imitating the West, as propagandists, called their conquered land, came from the south, in the "CBI"—the China-Burma-India Theater. No brief narrative can do justice to the complex interweaving of events in this theater, where the main effort of the Allies was to get ma-

terial support to Chiang Kai-shek and the Chinese Nationalists at Chungking (see Chapter 30) and, if possible, to damage the Japanese position in Burma, Thailand, and Indo-China. After Pearl Harbor, when the Japanese seized and shut the famous "Burma Road," the only way for the Allies to communicate with Chiang's Nationalists was by air. It is perhaps true that the western Allies did not invest an overwhelming proportion of their resources in this CBI Theater, but they did help keep the Chinese formally in the fight. And, as the final campaign of 1945 drew on, the British, with Chinese and American aid, were holding down three Japanese field armies in this CBI Theater.

The end came in Japan with a suddenness that the Allied peoples, perhaps even the Allied governments, hardly expected. From Pacific island bases, American airplanes inflicted crippling damage on Japanese industry in the spring and summer of 1945; the Japanese fleet had been almost destroyed; submarine warfare had brought the Japanese economy near to strangulation; and there was impressive evidence of the declining morale of Japanese soldiers. None the less, American decision-makers were convinced that only the use of their recently invented atomic bomb could bring a quick decision and avert the very heavy casualties likely in the proposed amphibious invasion of the Japanese home islands. The result was the dropping of the first atomic bomb, on Hiroshima, August 6, 1945. On August 8, the Russians, who had agreed to come into the war against Japan once Germany was beaten, began an invasion of Manchuria in full force. Faced with what they felt was certain defeat, the Japanese government, unlike the German, decided not to make a last-ditch stand in their own country. On September 2, after brief negotiations, the Japanese made formal surrender at Tokyo. Japan gave up its conquests abroad and submitted to American military occupation. Contrary to the desires of part of Allied opinion, however, the Emperor of Japan was not dethroned. Purged of most of its militarists, the Japanese government continued to rule under Allied—actually American—supervision.

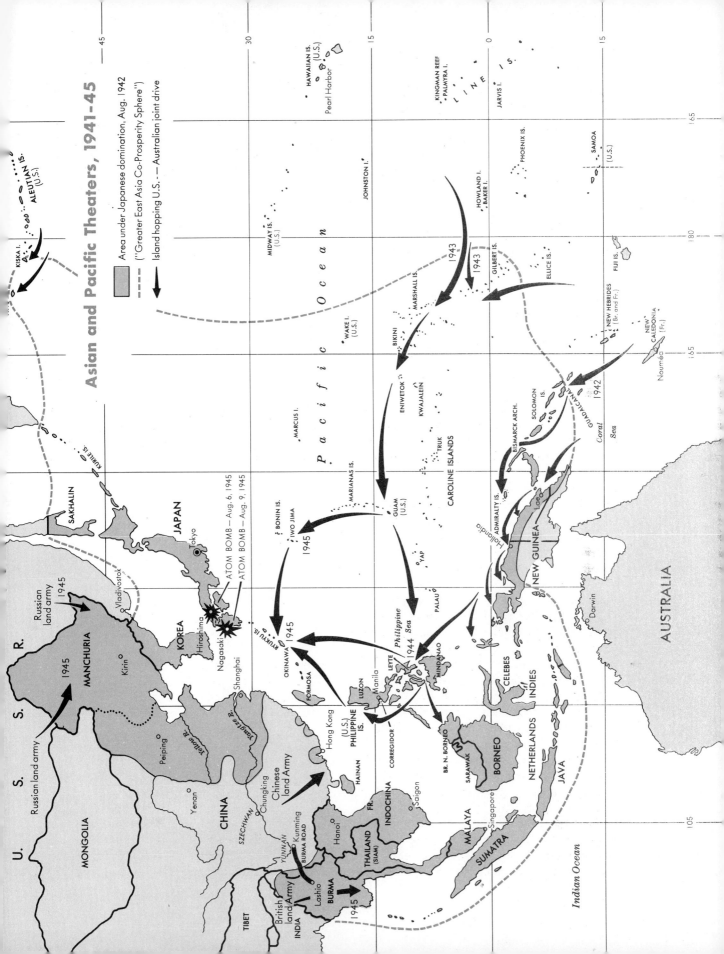

Asian and Pacific Theaters, 1941-45

Area under Japanese domination, Aug. 1942 ("Greater East Asia Co-Prosperity Sphere")

Island hopping U.S. — Australian joint drive

U. S. S. R.

MONGOLIA

TIBET

INDIA

British land Army

BURMA
Lashio
1945

YUNNAN
BURMA ROAD
Kunming

SZECHWAN
Chungking
Yenan

CHINA

Peiping

Yellow R.

Kirin
MANCHURIA
1945

Russian land army
1945

Vladivostok

Russian land army
1945

SAKHALIN

KURILE IS.

JAPAN
Tokyo

KOREA
Hiroshima
ATOM BOMB — Aug. 6, 1945
Nagasaki
ATOM BOMB — Aug. 9, 1945

Shanghai

Yangtze R.

Chinese land Army

Hanoi
THAILAND (SIAM)
Saigon
FR. INDOCHINA

Hong Kong
HAINAN

FORMOSA

RYUKYU IS.
OKINAWA 1945

BONIN IS.
IWO JIMA
1945

MALAYA
Singapore

SUMATRA

NETHERLANDS INDIES

BORNEO
SARAWAK
BR. N. BORNEO

CELEBES

JAVA

LUZON
Manila
CORREGIDOR
PHILIPPINE IS. (U.S.)

Philippine Sea
1944

LEYTE
MINDANAO

PALAU
YAP

CAROLINE ISLANDS
TRUK

MARIANAS IS.
GUAM (U.S.)

MARCUS I.

WAKE I. (U.S.)

BIKINI
ENIWETOK
KWAJALEIN
MARSHALL IS.
1943

GILBERT IS.
1943

ELLICE IS.

MIDWAY IS. (U.S.)

JOHNSTON I.

HAWAIIAN IS. (U.S.)
Pearl Harbor

KINGMAN REEF
PALMYRA I.
LINE IS.

JARVIS I.

PHOENIX IS.

HOWLAND I.
BAKER I.

SAMOA (U.S.)

FIJI IS.

NEW HEBRIDES (Br. and Fr.)
NEW CALEDONIA (Fr.)
Nouméa

Coral Sea
GUADALCANAL
1942

SOLOMON IS.
BISMARCK ARCH.

ADMIRALTY IS.

Hollandia
NEW GUINEA
Lae

Darwin

AUSTRALIA

Pacific Ocean

Indian Ocean

45

30

15

0

15

165

180

165

105

The Allied Coalition

The "Grand Alliance," as the historian Churchill liked to call it, but mostly known in its last years as the "United Nations," had mustered overpowering strength against Germany, Japan, Italy, and such collaborators as the Axis powers could secure in the Balkans, Southeast Asia, and western Europe. Britain, Russia, and the United States were the heart of the Allied coalition. But Nationalist China, for all its inefficiencies, had occupied the attention of hundreds of thousands of Japanese soldiers, and the resources of the French Empire and the French resistance movements at home and abroad had been most useful. The United Nations had been able to count on the resources of Latin America, and Brazil had been an active member of the alliance. In this truly global war, Brazilian troops had fought in Italy, which at the end had been the most cosmopolitan of theaters. There American (including Japanese-American, or Nisei), French imperial, British imperial, pro-Allied Italian,

Polish, and other troops had fought, in addition to the Brazilians. At the very end of the war, even Argentina was brought into the United Nations coalition, when she declared war on Germany and Japan on March 27, 1945.

The instruments of continuing Allied union were the conferences of the "Big Three"—Churchill, Roosevelt, and Stalin—with their political and military advisers and experts, and the more frequent Anglo-American conferences. Even before the United States entered the shooting war, Roosevelt and Churchill met off Newfoundland and issued the Atlantic Charter, on August 14, 1941, in which they declared for the freedom of the seas, equality of access to economic opportunity, abandonment of aggression, and the restoration of rights to conquered peoples. The Atlantic Charter had been attacked as no more than another empty assertion of impossible ideals, but the true realist sees in it an important step in rallying world opinion against the Axis. Later, formal conferences —between Roosevelt and Churchill at Casablanca (January, 1943) and Quebec (August, 1943), and among the "Big Three" at Teheran (December, 1943) and Yalta (February,

Scene in Hiroshima a few hours after the bomb hit, August 6, 1945.

1945)—brought to a head consultations that had been steadily carried on at lower political and military levels. From July 17 to August 17, 1945, a final great conference at Potsdam near conquered Berlin brought Britain, Russia, and the United States, with two new figures, President Truman and Prime Minister Attlee, together to confirm in general the Yalta decisions.

There were always grave military and political matters to be ironed out. It was not easy to maintain even the Anglo-American collaboration, which was perhaps the closest military collaboration between two major sovereign powers ever achieved. For the actual direction of operations in the field, the British and Americans decided to set up, not just the sort of supreme command the Allies painfully achieved late in World War I under Foch (Chapter 25), but a complete intermeshing of staffs. All down the line, an American in command always had a Britisher as his second, and a Britisher in command always had an American as his second. In the pinch, and in spite of normal national jealousies, the arrangement worked. An anecdote about General Eisenhower from North African days relates that he sent an American officer home, not because he called his immediate superior a so-and-so, but because he called him an *English* so-and-so. At the highest level, the Combined Chiefs of Staff, in close touch with top American and British government officials, did the over-all planning. The Russians were never brought into such close military co-operation, and in the field the Russians always fought on their own.

Political Issues

A political issue that bulked large at the time with liberals seems not to have seriously divided the Allies during the war itself. This was the issue of "unconditional surrender." Here recent history had an overpowering influence on the policy adopted. Hitler had simply followed widespread German opinion in insisting that in World War I Germany had not really been defeated in the field but had

Giraud, Roosevelt, de Gaulle, and Churchill at Casablanca, January, 1943.

been betrayed by the false promises of Wilson's Fourteen Points into surrendering while still undefeated. This time the Allied leaders were determined to give the Germans no excuse for a future rallying point of this sort. The Germans must be beaten unmistakably, and Allied troops must enter Berlin as conquerors. There must be no political negotiation at all, simply unconditional military surrender. There was some opposition to this policy during the war, at least in lands of free political expression like Britain and the United States. This opposition rested partly on humanitarian grounds, but also on the belief that the prospect of unconditional surrender would inevitably stiffen the German will to resist, and would unite the nation behind Hitler instead of allowing Allied psychological warfare its full effect by promising anti-Nazi elements some reward for deserting the Nazi cause. In retrospect, it does not seem that Hitler would ever have negotiated with the Allies; and after the failure of the attempt to kill him with a bomb in July, 1944, there was little chance that the Germans themselves would overthrow the Nazi government.

Another political problem made a much clearer rift between the British and the Americans. The underlying issue was just how far anti-German elements in France, Italy, and other occupied lands must go in proving that they were good honest democrats in order to secure the backing of the democratic western powers. Here the difference in the underlying tone of American and British policies was evident in the views of Roosevelt and Churchill. Roosevelt was convinced that if the Allies did not interfere to support scheming conservatives and reactionaries in the occupied lands, but instead allowed their peoples to choose their form of government freely, then they would choose democracy. Churchill was much less idealistic. He was eager to use any elements that were hostile to the Germans, even if their hostility was quite recent, and he had little faith in the capacity or desire of peoples like the Italians for Anglo-Saxon democracy. Therefore he was quite willing to back Badoglio and the monarchists in Italy; Roosevelt kept insisting that the Italians wanted and needed a republic. Yet the opposition between American support of democratic or Leftist elements and British support of conservative, monarchist, Rightist elements was not a clear one. We were hard on Badoglio and soft on Vichy; the British were hard on Vichy, soft on Badoglio.

In French politics the issue was further complicated by Roosevelt's suspicions of de Gaulle, whose firm resistance in June, 1940, had made him the inevitable leader of the French movement for liberation. To Roosevelt, de Gaulle seemed a potential man on horseback, no better than Boulanger or Napoleon III. To Churchill, de Gaulle seemed indeed difficult, a man obsessed with the need to restore the greatness of France, but an indispensable ally. As it turned out, the Gaullists, in collaboration with the organized French resistance in the homeland, did take over the civilian administration of French territory as it was liberated, and France by free popular vote restored in the Fourth Republic a form of government essentially like that of the Third. In Italy, the liberated people voted the establishment of a republic. What had threatened at one time to be a serious difficulty between American policy and British policy was resolved by the action of the liberated people themselves.

The anger aroused in de Gaulle himself, and in many other French leaders, by Roosevelt's policy of refusing solid support to de Gaulle and the Fighting French has embittered Franco-American relations to this day. In particular, Roosevelt's intention to "occupy" France under AMGOT (Allied Military Government in Occupied Territory) wounded the French, who thought of themselves as allies, not enemies, of the democracies.

But the political issue that has bulked largest since World War II was by no means so clear an issue during the war itself. This is the problem of Russian domination in eastern and southeastern Europe. It is easy to say that at Yalta the western powers took much too soft a line with the Russians, allowed them to push their armies much too far westward, and relied foolishly on Russian promises to permit free elections in Poland, Hungary, Czechoslovakia, and the Balkans. This criticism may be supplemented by the old British motif of the "soft under-belly," by maintaining that the western powers should have struck as soon as possible, perhaps in 1943, from the Mediterranean into the Danube Valley in order to get there ahead of the Russians. Proponents of these criticisms present us with an Iron Curtain that would then have been drawn far to the east of where it now is, with an eastern and a southeastern Europe that would now be democratic and on the side of the West rather than on the side of the Russians.

The chief trouble with this argument is that it fails to take into account two basic facts. First, most of the small eastern European countries had no real tradition of western-style democracy; most of them had moved toward fascist totalitarianism before World War II (see Chapter 27). Their transition to communist totalitarianism was easy. Second, during the war itself it was by no means clear to western leaders, or to western public opinion, that the Germans and the Japanese would be beaten so readily. Even leaders like Churchill, who seems never really to have trusted the Russians and who was to coin the phrase "the Iron Curtain" soon after the war, did not dare risk losing the aid of Russian manpower and material resources during the war itself. Even in 1945, at Yalta, with Japan still very much in the fight, appeasement of the Russians seemed absolutely essential, not only to Roosevelt, who hoped the Russians would collaborate with us in the post-war world, but also to Churchill, who seems to have had little if any hope of such collaboration from the Russians.

In the Far East, political problems seemed less serious — at least in wartime. There was general agreement that the Chinese Nationalists, however corrupt and inefficient their government was, had to be supported against the Japanese. Nor did the final decision to accept the continuance on the throne of the Japanese emperor arouse serious opposition in the West. The critical decisions on the Far East were rather the work of the troubled period after V-E and V-J days, when to the bitter disappointment of most western peoples it became clear that the peace was likely for some time to be no more than a continuation of war. Indeed, there was no peace, and these years deserve a term that was soon coined, the years of "cold war." The once "colonial" peoples throughout the world were now roused against "imperialism."

In sum, as we all know now, and as we shall see in more detail in the next three chapters, the great war of 1939–1945 ended indeed, but there was no peace. From our own western point of view, and in plain language, the defeat of the perturbers, the aggressors, the villains, Germany and Japan, was *almost immedi-ately* followed by the rise of a new perturber, a new villain, Russia, which had already given clear indications of its perturbing power. And indeed, it is easy to go on to the conclusion that just because the Germans and Japanese were beaten in the way they actually were, the present menace of Russia — pretty clearly a greater menace than the old German menace — was helped, was in fact made possible, by that defeat; from there it is a fatally easy step to the dangerous conclusion that Russia, not Germany, was our enemy all along.

Yet the wise student of history will not readily jump to the conclusion that any other Allied policy, and in particular a different American policy at Yalta and Potsdam, could have either prevented the rise of Russia, or produced a virtuous, co-operative, democratic Russia. We are still far too close to World War II to understand its many ramifications. The historian who sticks to his last can do no more than conclude that in the perspective of modern western history the sorely tried western statesmen at Yalta and Potsdam, in the midst of a hot war, were using time-honored methods to win that war as quickly and as decisively as possible: and in particular, with the long record of failures of coalitions in the past before them, they were determined to hold together their extraordinary and by no means "natural" coalition, known hopefully as the United Nations, until *both* the mainstay powers of the Axis coalition were beaten. This they did.

Reading Suggestions on the Second World War

(Asterisk indicates paperbound edition.)

General Accounts

W. S. Churchill, *The Second World War*, 6 vols. (Houghton Mifflin, 1948–1953). Magisterial account by a chief architect of Allied victory; the first volume reviews international affairs between the wars.

E. H. Carr, *The Twenty Years' Crisis* (Macmillan, 1946). A stimulating review of interwar diplomacy by a capable and opinionated Englishman. Now a Beacon paperback.

F. L. Snyder, *The War: A Concise History 1939–1945* (Messner, 1960), and K. S. Davis, *Experience of War: The U. S. in World War II* (Doubleday, 1965). These two books with notes and bibliography are good guides to the already enormous literature of the war.

J. F. C. Fuller, *The Second World War* (Duell, Sloane, and Pearce, 1949), and C. Falls, *The Second World War,* 2nd ed. (Methuen, 1948). Two succinct and very useful military accounts. Both are written from a British viewpoint.

D. Flower and J. Reeves, eds., *The Taste of Courage: The War, 1939–1945* (Harper, 1960). A good anthology of "war pieces."

F. Pratt, *War for the World: A Chronicle of our Fighting Forces in World War II* (Yale Univ. Press, 1950). A good succinct American account.

United States Army in World War II (Dept. of the Army, 1947). The official history, in many detailed volumes, to be found in library catalogues under the general title above, or under "United States: Department of the Army."

S. E. Morison, *History of United States Naval Operations in World War II* (Little, Brown, 1947–1962). 15 vols. Official but detached and professional history, with full attention to political and diplomatic problems, and to the work of other branches of the armed forces.

C. Wilmot, *The Struggle for Europe* (Harper, 1952). Highly controversial study, critical of the American high command.

Special Studies

F. Gilbert and G. A. Craig, eds., *The Diplomats, 1919–1939* (Princeton Univ. Press, 1953). A helpful symposium.

A. Wolfers, *Britain and France between Two Wars* (Harcourt, Brace, 1940). A solid analysis of the foreign policies of the two powers.

S. R. Smith, *The Manchurian Crisis, 1931–1932* (Columbia Univ. Press, 1948). Monograph on the crisis that marked the watershed between post-war and pre-war periods.

J. W. Wheeler-Bennett, *Munich: Prologue to Tragedy* (Macmillan, 1948), and L. B. Namier, *Diplomatic Prelude, 1938–1939* (Macmillan, 1948). Good studies of the last international crises before World War II.

W. L. Langer and S. E. Gleason, *The Challenge to Isolation, 1937–1940* (Harper, 1952), and *The Undeclared War, 1940–1941* (Harper, 1953). Solid studies of America's role.

C. C. Tansill, *Back Door to War: The Roosevelt Foreign Policy* (Regnery, 1952). Representative work of the "new revisionists," a school of writers who castigate Roosevelt for allegedly pushing America into war.

H. F. Armstrong, *Chronology of Failure* (Macmillan, 1940); "Pertinax" (André Géraud), *The Gravediggers of France* (Doubleday, 1944); M. Bloch, *Strange Defeat* (Oxford Univ. Press, 1949). Three perceptive studies of the French defeat in 1940.

A. J. Liebling, ed., *The Republic of Silence* (Harcourt, Brace, 1947). Excellent collection of materials pertaining to the French resistance movement.

L. Collins and D. LaPierre, *Is Paris Burning?* (Simon and Schuster, 1965). Deservedly best-selling account of the liberation of Paris.

R. Wohlstetter, *Pearl Harbor: Warning and Decision* (Stanford Univ. Press, 1962). First-rate monograph.

A. Weber, *Farewell to European History; or, the Conquest of Nihilism* (Kegan Paul, Trench, Trubner, 1947). A German sociologist reviews—and regrets—his country's part in the crises of World War II.

D. L. Gordon and R. Dangerfield, *The Hidden Weapon: The Story of Economic Warfare* (Harper, 1947). A very good popular account by trained experts.

H. Feis, *Churchill, Roosevelt, Stalin* (Princeton Univ. Press, 1957). A fascinating and very fair-minded account of the relations among these three leaders during the war.

There are many memoirs of actors in this great war. The following make a good beginning: D. D. Eisenhower, *Crusade in Europe* (Doubleday, 1948); H. Truman, *Memoirs,* 2 Vols. (Doubleday, 1958); B. L. Montgomery, *Memoirs* (World, 1958); C. de Gaulle, *War Memories,* English translation, 3 Vols. in one (Simon and Schuster, 1964).

30

The Post-War World, 1945-1953

I   The Cold War

During World War II, most people expected that when the shooting stopped there would be a general peace conference, as there had been after all the major general wars of modern times. As we have abundantly seen, even a general peace conference (Westphalia, Utrecht, Vienna, Versailles) leaves many problems unsolved or solves them in a way that proves unsatisfactory. As it turned out, however, the tensions that arose between the Soviet Union and its western Allies during the war itself made it impossible to plan for, much less convoke, a Peace Conference. So World War II bequeathed to mankind a legacy of problems to be solved one by one if at all.

The damage done by World War II greatly exceeded even that done by World War I. The total number of human deaths resulting from the war has been estimated at 22 million, more than half of them civilians, who died by mass executions in concentration camps, or in air attacks, or by starvation or disease. Material damages have been estimated at more than $2,000 billion. Despite a sharply rising birth rate and vast programs of economic reconstruction, such losses could never be fully repaired, and it took the first decade after the war to launch effectively the necessary programs of modernization.

Atomic Weapons

After the defeat of the Axis powers, new and terrifying problems faced the statesmen of the world. Atomic weapons—before very long, hydrogen bombs, the possibility— and soon the development—of guided missiles, made concrete and plausible the threat that a new general war might wipe out the human race or so terribly shatter the physical and moral bases of modern civilization as to reduce what was left of mankind to something like another Stone Age. At the same time, the war had so limited the war-making potential of all other states that the United States and the Soviet Union emerged as super-powers, the only powers capable of initiating or pursuing the new warfare. Given the ideology of the U.S.S.R. and the suspicious and vengeful character of its supreme dictator, Stalin, it was inevitable that the Russians would regard the Americans as their rivals for control of the world, and that the Americans should quickly have been forced to accept the same estimate of the situation. The post-war history of international politics became in large part a history of Soviet-American rivalry.

In 1945 enemy attack and occupation had caused incalculable devastation inside the Russian borders, and left millions of survivors destitute, while Russia's capitalist ally, the United States, had invented and used a weapon so decisive as to make war against its possessor impossible for any power that did not possess it. Stalin, who liked nothing so much as the destruction of an enemy, and who regarded the whole capitalist world as his enemy, knew that if he had been the sole possessor of the atomic bomb, he would have used it. He attributed to his rival the strategy that he himself would have pursued. It seemed to him that all the technological advance of the Soviet period, undertaken precisely to bring the U.S.S.R. up to the industrialized West, had now been wiped out by the American development of the atomic bomb. It took Stalin four years (1945–1949) to catch up once again, by making his own atomic bomb. No doubt scientific information given the Russians by agents and spies made some contribution to this achievement, but only the high level of Russian science and technology and the Soviet capacity to concentrate their investments made it possible at all.

A Divided World: Germany and China

Even before the U.S.S.R. could join the United States as an atomic power in 1949, the two had engaged in a series of tests of will, in Europe and in Asia, that determined where the increasingly clear boundary between a Russian sphere of influence and an American sphere of influence would run. And the confrontation continued after 1949. In Iran, in Greece, in Berlin, in Korea the lines were drawn, tested, and re-drawn, sometimes after bloodshed. Though the Soviet Union and its former western allies were able to reach agreement on peace treaties with Italy and with three of the Axis powers' former European satellites—Hungary, Rumania, and Bulgaria—no such treaty could ever be concluded with Germany itself or with Japan.

But whereas the American occupation of Japan rendered a Russian presence there impossible, defeated Germany was divided into four zones—American, British, French, and Russian. The U.S.S.R. obtained the eastern regions of Germany, bordering on Poland, but extending considerably west of Berlin, which as the former capital, was also divided into four occupation zones. This arrangement, designed for temporary military occupation, continued in effect because no treaty could be reached. It proved dangerous in the extreme, since it left Berlin as an island surrounded by Soviet-dominated territory, yet an island including zones to which the western allies were entitled to access. The failure to reach any settlement over Germany left the most serious problem in Europe without a solution.

As time passed, the three western powers allowed their zones to unite in the "Federal Republic of Germany" (1949), called West Germany, with its capital at Bonn, and the Russians responded by creating the "German Democratic Republic"—East Germany—with its capital at Pankow outside Berlin. Many if not most West Germans were naturally eager for reunion with their fellow-Germans in the Soviet zone. Yet a reunion of Germany under western capitalist auspices was precisely what the Russians feared the most, believing that it would portend a revival of aggression, while an all-communist Germany was equally intolerable to the western powers. Indeed, few Frenchmen or Englishmen looked with any enthusiasm upon the idea of a reunified Germany, and if there were more Americans who sympathized with reunion as an ultimate goal, there were no responsible men in high places who failed to understand the dangers of trying to bring it about unilaterally. The German question would no doubt have baffled any hypothetical peace conference that had been convoked to find a solution; in the absence of any such international conference, it continued to baffle everybody.

In Asia—with Japan under American occupation—the most grievous problem remained that of China. The communists, who had challenged Chiang Kai-shek's ruling Kuomintang (nationalist) party for power in a struggle which had developed into a virtual civil war by the late 1930's, kept their forces in being during the years of Japanese occupation. The United States, having backed Chiang during the war, tried in 1946 to bring about an agreement between Chinese nationalists and Chinese communists that would end the civil war and leave China a democratic state, in which the communists, though a legal party, as in Italy or France, would not dominate the country. The American negotiator, General George C. Marshall, failed to bring the two parties into a working agreement, and after he returned to the United States early in 1947, the civil war in China continued.

Supported by Soviet aid, including former Japanese war material in Manchuria that had been surrendered to the U.S.S.R. by Japan, the communists were able by 1949 to expel the forces of Chiang Kai-shek, who took refuge on the off-shore island of Formosa (Taiwan), where the communists could not follow because they lacked the naval strength. In the last years of the struggle, Chiang had lost his hold over the Chinese people; the morale of his own forces was low, and an ever-mounting inflation ravaged the economy, already ruined by the long Japanese occupation. By 1950, mainland China had gone communist, and formed part of the Soviet bloc. Only Chiang's government in Taiwan, where it ruled ruthlessly and absolutely, remained a part of the American bloc. American foreign policy had suffered a major defeat. Though some Americans were quick to blame the failure on a conspiracy by a few evil men, the magnitude of the change, the huge numbers of Chinese involved, rendered this answer unsatisfactory.

As the case of China shows, the Soviet Union pursued its goal of turning the whole world communist through the agencies of individual Communist parties. In virtually every country a Communist party existed, sometimes strong—as in France or Italy—sometimes weak—as in Britain or the United States—often varying in its precise degree of subservience to the Communist party of the Soviet Union (CPSU) and the Soviet government, but virtually always prepared to act as the domestic agent for Soviet interests and policies. The United States in most of the world had no such disciplined and reliable supporters; it could not give orders and expect French or Italian politicians to follow them; it had to conduct its rivalry with the U.S.S.R. on other terms. Often the existence of a local

Communist party gave the Soviet Union an advantage in the Cold War.

The Two Coalitions

The situation, then, after World War II, though familiar enough in one way (after a war the victorious allies had found themselves unable to agree on a settlement and had become rivals) contained many brand new elements. There were only two super-powers. Neither of them had ever in history taken one of the leading roles in international affairs, although of course Russia since Peter the Great had played an important part in both Europe and Asia, and the United States had in the twentieth century made the decisive contribution to the Allied victory in World War I, but had then withdrawn into relative isolation. Yet at no time did the United States and the Soviet Union, taken together, possess as much productive capacity as the rest of the world combined, or more than an eighth of the population of the globe. The Cold War consisted in part of a great competition between the two for the allegiance and support of the rest of the world. And each became the leader of a great coalition, whose members were attached more or less tightly by bonds of self-interest to the senior partner.

The members of the loose American coalition, often in these years called the "free world," included in 1945 Japan, the Philippines, Australia and New Zealand, the Western Hemisphere, Great Britain, and western Europe. The Soviet coalition included the countries of eastern Europe, and by 1949 China. The border between the two coalitions in Europe—called the "Iron Curtain" for the first time by Winston Churchill in 1946—ran along a north-south line extending from Stettin on the Baltic (formerly German and now Polish) to Trieste on the Adriatic. Yugoslavia lay in the Soviet sphere, and the frontier resumed again with the border between northern Greece and the three Soviet satellites of Albania, Yugoslavia, and Bulgaria. Turkey belonged to the western coalition, and portions of the Middle East and of Southeast Asia

were linked to it by a network of pacts, often impressive chiefly on paper. India remained neutral. The dividing line between North and South Korea, with the U.S.S.R. occupying the north, and the United States the south, represented a kind of Asian extension of the long frontier between the two coalitions. Along the frontier came the aggressive Soviet probing operations that led to crises and in several cases to wars.

Repeatedly the United States sought in vain to ease the relationships between the two coalitions. In 1946, Stalin refused to join in a United Nations atomic energy commission, or to have anything to do with international control of atomic weapons. In 1947, the United States proposed an international plan of massive American economic aid to accelerate recovery from the ruin of the war, the Marshall Plan, so-called for George C. Marshall, then Secretary of State. The Soviet Union refused to accept the aid for itself, and would not let its satellites participate. The Marshall Plan nations subsequently formed the nucleus of the North Atlantic Treaty Organization (NATO: 1949). The Soviet coalition founded the Cominform ("Communist Information Bureau") in 1947, as a successor to the former Comintern, "abolished" during the war (see Chapter 26), and created the Warsaw Pact (1955), binding eastern Europe together, as an answer to NATO.

Within every country attached to either coalition there were many individuals who preferred the leader of the other coalition: thus there were pro-Soviet Frenchmen, not necessarily communists, and pro-American Bulgarians. But in addition, a good many individual human beings in the West disliked both powers, regarding them as aggressive, as vulgarly materialistic. We shall meet these alienated intellectuals again (see Chapter 32). Needless to say, many individuals neither knew nor cared about power politics at all. Others, remembering the time when their own countries (France, Britain, Germany) had shared more largely in the leadership of the world, scorned the United States and the U.S.S.R. as newcomers. But these individual neutrals did not, between 1945 and 1953, anywhere command a share of public opinion sufficiently strong to weaken their countries' memberships in one of the great coalitions.

Outside the coalitions remained the neutral nations. Some, like Switzerland or Sweden, were simply maintaining their traditional legal policies of not aligning themselves with any grouping of powers. But most belonged to the new nations that were now emerging as independent, having discarded their former colonial status. During the years between 1945 and 1953, India under Nehru (Chapter 31) was the most influential. Nehru certainly hoped by taking a lofty position above the battle to retain the confidence of both sides and to act as mediator if necessary; he also took from both the assistance that India so badly needed. As economic aid became an instrument in the Cold War, neutral nations tried, often with success, to play the Americans off against the Russians, raising the not too subtle threat that if Washington saw fit to deprive them of something they wanted, they might regretfully have to go communist. It was not until the 1960's that the United States learned to regard neutrality as often positively helpful to its interests.

The United Nations

Through the years of Cold War, and the occasional outbreaks of something hotter, the United Nations—formed during World War II from among the opponents of the Axis and chartered in 1945 at San Francisco—served as an international organization where members of both coalitions and neutrals alike could meet in peaceful discussion. As direct successor to the League of Nations, it inherited the League's duty of keeping the peace, but like the League it lacked independent sovereignty or authority over its members. Its charter created a Security Council, to deal with threats to the peace, with eleven member-states, five of which—the United States, the Soviet Union, Great Britain, France, and Nationalist China —held permanent memberships. The other six were elected to rotating two-year terms by the General Assembly. In the General Assembly,

to which all member states belonged, each had an equal voice. The Secretary General, elected by the Security Council, could exert great personal influence in international affairs. But each of the five permanent members of the Security Council had a veto over any substantive question. All five had to be unanimous before action could go forward. Both the U.S.S.R. and the United States insisted on this provision in the Charter. As a result, the Security Council often found itself unable to act because of a veto: of the eighty vetoes cast between 1945 and 1955 the U.S.S.R. cast seventy-seven.

Looking beyond the strict chronological limits of this chapter, we should note that in the mid-fifties new nations joined the U.N.: some pro-western, like Austria and Italy (both former Axis states and so originally excluded), some pro-Soviet like Albania, Bulgaria, and the other former Axis satellites in eastern Europe, and some neutral and mostly former colonies, like Ceylon or Libya. Japan joined in 1956. As former colonies obtained their independence during the late fifties and early sixties, each joined the United Nations, where the "Afro-Asian bloc" commanded a majority in the General Assembly (Chapter 31). Germany remained outside the U.N., but both East and West Germany had their observers there. The United States resisted all efforts of the Chinese communists to join, which left the permanent Chinese seat on the Security Council in the possession of Chiang Kai-shek's representative, although as we have seen, Chiang now governed only Taiwan (Formosa). Chinese aggression in Korea and elsewhere had hardened American policy against any attempt of the Chinese communists to "shoot their way into the U.N.," while by the mid-sixties, the Chinese communists often denounced the body, and seemed no longer much interested in membership.

The three successive Secretaries-General, Trygve Lie of Norway, Dag Hammarskjöld of Sweden, and U Thant of Burma, commanded universal international respect as men who served the cause of world peace. Though the U.N. could not "settle" the Cold War, or bring about the international control of atomic

GREENLAND

ALASKA

CANADA

UNITED STATES

Atlantic Ocean

HAWAIIAN ISLANDS

MEXICO

BR. HOND.
HONDURAS

CUBA
DOM. REP.
HAITI
PUERTO RICO

GUATEMALA
EL SALVADOR
NICARAGUA
COSTA RICA
PANAMA

Pacific Ocean

VENEZUELA

BR. GUIANA
DUTCH GUIANA
FR. GUIANA

COLOMBIA

Equator

ECUADOR

PERU

BRAZIL

BOLIVIA

PARAGUAY

The World, 1953

Communist nations
Neutral nations
Western nations
★ Trouble spots through 1967

CHILE

URUGUAY

NEW ZEALAND

ARGENTINA

NATO   WARSAW PACT

ICELAND

NORWAY
SWEDEN
FINLAND

UNITED
KINGDOM

EIRE
DEN.
NETH.
E.
GER. POLAND
BEL
L.
W.
GER. CZECH.
FRANCE
AUST. HUN.
SW.
RUM.
ITALY
YUG.
BUL.
ALB.

PORTUGAL
SPAIN

U.S.S.R.

MONGOLIA

KOREA

JAPAN

MOROCCO
IFNI
O DE ORO

ALGERIA

TUNISIA

LIBYA

EGYPT

TURKEY

LEBANON
ISRAEL
SYRIA
IRAQ
JORDAN

IRAN

AFGHAN.

KASHMIR

W. PAKISTAN

TIBET

NEPAL
BHUTAN

CHINA

FORMOSA

SAUDI
ARABIA

OMAN

YEMEN

INDIA

E. PAK.

BURMA

THAI.
FR.
INDO-
CHINA

PHILIPPINE IS.

MBIA
PORT.
GUINEA
RRA LEONE
LIBERIA

FRENCH WEST AFRICA

NIGERIA

CAM.

SUDAN

FR.
EQUAT.
AFRICA

FR.
SOM.

ETHIOPIA

BR. SOMALILAND

SOMALIA

CEYLON

BRUNEI
SARAWAK
MALAYA
BR. N. BORNEO

NORTHEAST
NEW GUINEA

NETH.
NEW GUINEA

RIO MUNI
TOGO
GOLD COAST

CABINDA

UGANDA

BELGIAN
CONGO

KENYA

RUANDA-
URUNDI
TANGANYIKA

ZANZIBAR

NYASALAND

Indian Ocean

INDONESIA

PAPUA

ANGOLA
NO.
RHOD.

MOZAMBIQUE

Atlantic Ocean

SOUTH-
WEST
AFRICA

BECH.

SO.
RHOD.

MADAGASCAR

SWAZILAND

AUSTRALIA

UNION OF
SOUTH AFRICA

BASUTOLAND

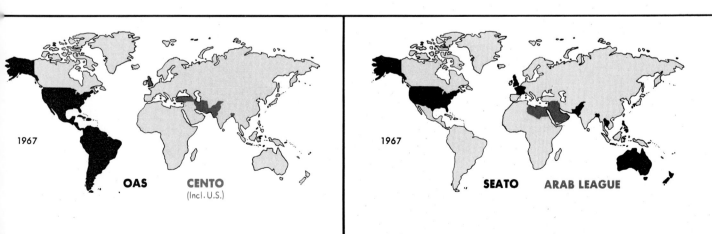

1967

OAS   CENTO
(Incl. U.S.)

1967

SEATO   ARAB LEAGUE

weapons, it did repeatedly manage to prevent small wars from becoming big ones: in Palestine, in Korea (where, because of the absence of the Soviet representative from the Security Council, the Russians failed to veto the Council's decision to intervene, and the American army fought under the sponsorship of the U.N.), and in other parts of the world (see Chapter 31).

Through its functional councils and special agencies—for example, the Economic and Social Council, the Educational, Scientific, and Cultural Organization (UNESCO), the World Health Organization, the Food and Agricultural Organization, and the World Bank—the U.N. advanced loans to governments to initiate new development plans, controlled epidemics, and provided experts on modern farming techniques. The U.N.'s international civil servants deserved well of mankind by promoting "social progress and better standards of living" as its Charter undertook to do. Occasional critics leveled their shafts at its striking new buildings in New York and wished that it had never left Switzerland because it might now be mistakenly taken for an instrument of American imperialism. Occasional isolationist Americans demanded that "the U.S. get out of the U.N. and the U.N. out of the U.S.," while their opposites could be heard asking that the U.N. be given more "teeth" and that the nations abandon more of their sovereignty to it. Yet with its successes and its faults it reflected both the diversity and the elements of unity in the world of which it was the spokesman, and perhaps it would have been unreasonable to demand more of it than that.

II   The Major Free-World States: 1945 - 1953

The United States

The most obvious fact about the post-war United States was its prosperity. But perhaps the most important, and to some observers the most surprising, development was the way in which the American people proved willing to assume the responsibilities that came their way in international politics. At the end of World War I we had cut ourselves as free of "foreign entanglements" as we could, and some of our European allies feared at the end of World War II that we might do so once more. But on the contrary we continued, after a rather abrupt cutting off of Lend-Lease in 1945, to render substantial economic aid to our allies. And when we joined NATO, we became a party to what was basically an old-fashioned alliance. In 1919 we had refused to join the League of Nations; in 1945 we were the heart and soul, the organizers, of its successor, the United Nations. Isolationists still existed and commanded great newspapers and a solid representation in Congress. But they were now a minority that was unable to block a single measure of foreign policy.

A major step in realizing this new American foreign policy was announced by General George Marshall, then Secretary of State, in a Harvard commencement address in 1947. The "Marshall Plan," of course the work of many hands in our government, promised American economic and technological help to war-stricken nations. The promise was carried out over the last two decades in many ways, commonly lumped together as "foreign aid," and was most strikingly successful in its original purpose of starting the remarkable economic recovery and indeed "boom" in western Europe during these years. Help was later extended to many neutral nations, and in particular to the "emerging" nations of the old colonial world. Some of it was direct military aid, but most of it was aid for economic development. Stalin's Russia and its allied states refused from the very start to accept the aid the Marshall Plan offered them. The Marshall Plan was in part an instrument of traditional international power politics; that is, like the subventions dominant powers in a coalition —France under Richelieu, Britain under Pitt —have extended to needy allies. But it had many new elements, notably that it was meant to be used, and to a large degree was used, to promote the material prosperity of the peoples of those states to which it was given, and not merely to add to our own military capabilities.

A well-organized movement against any of our numerous treaty commitments from the Marshall Plan of 1947 on to the present, *if it had had the majority of the American people behind it*, could have succeeded in spite of the fact that since the end of World War II official Republican and Democratic party policies were on the whole in "bipartisan" agreement on the role we were playing in international politics.

Indeed, the political history of the United

The first Marshall Plan shipment for Greece being loaded, May, 1948.

States since 1945 provided another illustration of what we have already said about the basic agreement that must be shared by both parties in the two-party system that prevails in the English-speaking countries (see Chapter 21). Harry Truman, Democrat, who as Vice-President had succeeded to the office on the death of Franklin Roosevelt in 1945, was elected over the Republican Thomas Dewey in 1948 in an election that caught the experts by surprise, for the advance polls indicated the opposite result. In 1952, however, General Eisenhower, Republican, with his immense personal popularity, was elected president over the Democratic candidate, Adlai Stevenson, and carried his party to a majority in Congress. Now by tradition the Republicans were (comparatively) conservative, the party of business and the solid prosperous farmers; and the Democrats were (comparatively) liberal or radical, the party of the working man, the "little fellow." Those parentheses were important. In fact, the victorious Republicans after 1952 left intact the essentials of Democratic legislation since Franklin Roosevelt's victory in 1932: the system of social security, which the Republicans actually extended; the Tennessee Valley Authority; and a whole complex set of federal agencies, the main task of which was to "intervene" in the economic life of the nation, as for instance, the federal purchase of farm surpluses to keep up the income of farmers. The Republicans did this, even though their official philosophy stressed free enterprise and condemned government regulation. And they also retained the great armed forces that we had had to build up since 1940, and the foreign policy we have already outlined.

The economy of the United States, which had proved more than equal to the task of carrying on the Second World War, continued its upward course in the years after 1945. There were mild "recessions" in 1948 and 1953, but nothing the most pessimistic commentator could call a real depression. Indeed, by the mid-fifties even a few Marxists were beginning to express their doubts about the inevitable "bust" their theories told them must always follow a capitalist "boom." And on the other side, orthodox western economists were beginning to assert that the United States had in fact licked the problem of the business cycle, that we had so many "built-in safe-guards" in our social insurance, our banking and corporation laws, our ability—and willingness—to undertake public works at the first sign of depression, that though we should have recessions, we should never have a depression like that of the thirties.

Socially, the American drive toward some very concrete forms of equality continued after the Second World War. It was not quite true that in the traditional sense of the word there were no "classes" in the United States in the mid-twentieth century, but it was almost true. In the polls, the overwhelming majority of Americans refused to call themselves "upper class" or "lower" or "working class"; forced to use a label, something like 90 per cent chose "middle class." In terms of sheer income, we had some very rich men in spite of graduated income taxes and inheritance taxes. And we still had, in part but not wholly because of the low economic status of many Negroes, some very poor, who were not well fed or well housed. Indeed, in terms of actual average real income, some nations of western Europe were closer to rough equality than we. And yet both in terms of the career open to talents—the absence of barriers to social mobility—and in terms of what we may loosely call the social atmosphere, the United States remained the land where the social ideals of democracy were most nearly realized. The Negroes were indeed an exception, though not wholly so; in the arts, in the fields of entertainment and sports, and within their own community in all fields, the gifted Negro could and did rise.

The most common complaint against the atmosphere, the "style" set by mid-twentieth-century democracy in the United States, was foreshadowed in the fears of men like Alexis de Tocqueville and J. S. Mill (see Chapter 20) concerning the "tyranny of the majority." Americans, so it is claimed, tended to be conformists instead of equals; they tended to eat the same frozen and packaged foods,

to look at the same television programs, ride in the same cars, and live in the same ranch houses. French or English travelers could write that if you had seen one American city you had seen them all. Americans, the argument continued, tried to keep down individuals and groups who did not conform to the general standards of mediocrity, and American society might become a kind of democratic totalitarianism of equal, average, conforming individuals. In response, the historian, trying to be objective, could point to the rich and varied group life in contemporary America. The very intellectuals who so disliked the "average" American were wholly free to attack him, wholly free to avoid him—with a little effort, perhaps—wholly free to eat their own unfrozen foods, and read their own "little magazines," attend their own "little theaters," and never look at television.

The historian must also record in the 1950's one of the occasional periods when America temporarily gave way to fear in crisis, and partly repressed civil rights. The Cold War had inevitably made difficult the existence of believers in communism in the United States. Under the leadership of the late Senator Joseph McCarthy of Wisconsin, what opponents of the process called "witch-hunts," and proponents called "security measures," were undertaken often on the flimsiest evidence, or none at all, against individuals in responsible positions, especially in education, defense in dustries, and government, who might be pro-communist—that is, pro-Russian. The fact that some genuine American pro-communists actually had obtained posts in positions where they could and did pass valuable information to Russian agents clouded the issue and helped make McCarthy's performances possible.

When the gifted and irresponsible English publicist Bertrand Russell wrote of a "reign of terror" in the United States in the early 1950's he was grossly exaggerating, despite the grave injustices done to many individuals. McCarthy himself was an unscrupulous demagogue. But if one compares the French reign of terror in 1792–1794 or the Russian "purge" trials of the 1930's, one is struck with the really enormous differences. No blood was shed, the prisons were not filled, and the ordinary citizen went on his way just as he always had. The beginning of the end of McCarthy's influence was his formal condemnation in the Senate in 1954, 67 to 22, for misuse of his investigative powers. Public opinion was much influenced, in one of the earliest proofs of the power of television, by the televised spectacle of McCarthy's bullying of witnesses. Even many who had thought him right were disgusted by seeing him in action. Americans did not like a bully even in a "patriotic cause."

Canada

As in the First World War, Canadian troops fought in the Second World War from the start, and proved a most important factor in the great coalition against the Axis. After 1945, Canada enjoyed an economic growth and prosperity proportionately even greater than that of the United States. A great deal of capital from the United States poured in, and much was raised at home and in Britain. Canada, though still producing vast amounts of raw materials from farm, mine, and forest, came now to be a great industrial nation, exploiting her remarkable hydroelectric resources and her oil and mineral wealth. In the mid-fifties Canada took the lead in carrying out a long-discussed plan for a canal from the Great Lakes to the lower St. Lawrence, a canal deep enough to accommodate ocean-going ships, and producing in addition important hydroelectric power. In the United States, vested interests along the Atlantic seaboard, foreseeing competition from the new seaway in the lucrative Midwest trade, had long succeeded by typical pressure-group lobbying methods in preventing American participation in the scheme. It is indicative of Canada's independent nationhood that she was able to announce her intention of going ahead with the scheme—which could be done, though imperfectly, entirely on Canadian territory —without the United States if necessary.

Faced with this prospect, the United States joined Canada in a collaborative development; work began in 1954, and the canal was opened in 1959.

Politically, post-war Canada was one of the stablest of western nations. Although in the provinces other parties at times held power, in the federal government the Liberals, first under Mackenzie King, who died in 1948, and then under Louis St. Laurent, remained in power from 1935 to 1957. The Liberals depended for their support on an effective collaboration between the English-speaking provinces and the French-speaking province of Quebec. Already in the mid-fifties there were signs that Quebec might desert the Liberals, as strong French-Canadian nationalist sentiments, accompanied by no doubt exaggerated threats of secession, had begun to manifest themselves.

The Dominion conformed to the general western pattern; it preserved freedom of the press, the "career open to talents," and a "mixed economy," in which private enterprise was perhaps somewhat stronger than government participation and regulation. Many Canadians in the immediate post-war world had begun to worry over what they felt was undue cultural and economic dependence on the United States. But relations of all sorts continued to tie the two countries closely together, and the three-thousand-mile frontier without a fort remained wholly peaceful.

Western Europe

The Cold War turned the old geographical term "western Europe" into a political, indeed a cultural, term for those nations of Europe outside Russian domination. Some of these, like Greece and Turkey, were certainly not geographically part of western Europe.

The nations of "western Europe" preserved the form of the "sovereign" state, and many of the sentiments we call "nationalism" or "patriotism," but after 1945 made real attempts to transcend the limitations of narrow nationalism to organize a "free Europe" on a level above and beyond that of the national state. The first step was the successful establishment of the European Coal and Steel Community (1952), named for the man who did much to organize it as the "Schuman Plan." (Schuman, appropriately enough, was a Frenchman with a German name). Under this plan France, West Germany, Italy, Belgium, the Netherlands, and Luxembourg ("Benelux") created for their coal and iron industries a free market area of all six nations in which a joint administrative body could make certain final and binding decisions without the participation of any government officials of any one of the six na- tions—and of course, without their veto power. This Coal and Iron Union meant that each nation give up some part of its "sover- eignty." In spite of some pessimistic predic- tions, the plan was a success, and paved the way for the creation of the "Common Market" (see Chapter 31).

In military affairs, the North Atlantic Treaty Organization included the United States and indeed was led by the United States. But it was also an attempt to organize western European military capabilities more tightly than in the old-fashioned alliance system. In economic affairs the Organization for Euro- pean Economic Cooperation (OEEC), also under American patronage, but none the less manned by Europeans, put into effect the American Marshal Plan for recovery. In gen- eral European politics, the Council for Europe (1949), had indeed no "teeth," no binding powers over the separate nations making it up, but acted as a kind of semi-official federal consultative parliament for western Europe, to which governments sent official representatives. It met in Strasbourg, a city delicately poised between France and Germany.

Started as they were in the immediate post-war years in a Europe keenly aware of the danger from the Soviets, and also of the need for economic cooperation in the work of re- storing war damages, these attempts to organ- ize Europe on a scale beyond its nation-states were bound to run into difficulties once the crisis that gave impetus to them was past (see Chapter 31).

Great Britain

In the United Kingdom of Great Britain and Northern Ireland (no longer "Ireland," for the South had gained its independence of the Crown) a general election held in July, 1945, after war had ended in Europe gave results opposite to those of the famous "khaki elec- tion" of 1918 (see Chapter 28). Though Churchill was even more of a national hero than Lloyd George had been in 1918, a nation clearly determined to make radical changes, not just to congratulate itself on winning the war, threw out Churchill and his Conservative party, and returned a Labour party pledged to a measure of social reform. For the first time in its half-century of existence the Labour party now secured an absolute majority of the House of Commons, 393 out of 640 seats. The Liberal party was practically extinguished; former Liberal voters had for the most part voted Labour. The new Prime Minister was Clement Attlee, himself no laboring man, (and certainly no revolutionist or communist), but a middle-class British gentleman and high-minded social worker. Under the Labour cabinet, the government proceeded to take over, with due compensation to the owners, the coal industry, the railroads, and some parts of commercial road transportation, and began to nationalize the steel industry. Britain al- ready had a well-developed system of various social insurances; this was now capped by a system of socialized medical care for all who wished it, a system strongly opposed at first by the medical profession. The educational sys- tem was partly reformed in an effort to make education more democratic, and to lengthen the required period of compulsory education. In accordance with Labour party philosophy, various parts of the old empire were given independence, like Burma, and others were granted dominion status—that is, national independence within the extraordinary British multi-national system.

Yet the nature and extent of this British "revolution by consent" were greatly misunderstood, especially by American conservatives. We can now see clearly that the new Britain was more like than unlike the old one and the rest of the free West. What came out of the changes after the Labour party victory of 1945 was an economy pushed a little more toward collectivism than before, but still very much indeed a "mixed" economy. Coal and railroads, nationalized, did not become great state trusts run by bureaucrats on the Russian model, but rather public corporations with a structure not unlike that of great private industries in the West, run by a board not by any means wholly under either bureaucratic or political thumbs. Great sectors of the economy remained in private hands, under no more than the kind of government regulation common even in the United States, which itself had a "mixed economy."

Proof of the essential moderation of this British revolution is afforded by the conduct of the Conservatives, who with Churchill still at their head were returned to power once more in 1951. The nationalization of steel, which had begun, was indeed stopped; but otherwise the victorious Conservatives kept intact the "socialism" of their opponents, including the national health scheme of socialized medicine, to which most of the medical profession had become reconciled.

In American—and, it must be added, in German—eyes, the British were not in the post-war years resilient enough to keep up with the extraordinary pace of economic improvements through technological innovation. A symptom: the British motor-car industry, which immediately after the war was in a good position to gain a big share of the world market, in the 1950's saw its lead reduced, until the Germans, especially with their inexpensive, standardized light car, the *Volkswagen,* took over the lead. In all the various indices of production, the British were definitely behind the Germans and the Americans. But they were still a great industrial people, suffering from the fact that just because they were the *first* to industrialize in the modern manner their plant tended toward obsolescence (see p. 224) and, more important, their ways tended to be set, hard to change rapidly.

The British, for instance, were usually, in the opinion of Americans who are used to high-pressure methods, ineffective salesmen. But it must be admitted that by the mid-fifties the British economy had begun to improve, had in fact statistically outstripped its pre-war totals.

The British were the last of the major western nations to feel themselves able to give up rationing and other belt-tightening measures the war had made necessary. Britain, more than any other great nation, had completely outgrown its ability to raise enough food to supply its inhabitants. The British had to export manufactured goods to get money to import the food they needed; but they also had to limit those imports, to raise all they possibly could on home lands. The British people therefore put up with many restrictions in what they rather mildly called an "austerity program." By the mid-fifties most of these restrictions had been lifted, and the British consumer could buy whatever he could afford.

To all these troubles was added a widespread awareness of the fact that Britain, which only a long lifetime ago was the leading nation of the world, now saw herself stripped of most of her empire, with the rest uncertain, playing what American editorial writers liked to call "second fiddle" to her former colonial possession, the United States. No wonder the British felt they were suffering undeservedly, and had what a witty commentator called a "Job complex." British leaders could hardly forget their former supremacy, and still, quite naturally, could not readily adjust to their new position of comparative inferiority. Yet in spite of all these real difficulties, both material and psychological, the British remained true, often under much strain, to the American alliance. No doubt they were a "practical" people, less worried than others over prestige and "grandeur."

France

On the French the war years inflicted what the psychologists call a trauma. Complete defeat by the Germans; occupation by the hated

Europe, 1953

foe; economic exploitation by the Germans to the point where the French government was almost bankrupt; liberation which, in spite of the admirable part played in it by the Fighting French and the French Resistance movement, was still clearly the work of American and British and indirectly, of Russian arms; the grave post-war difficulties of trying to hold together an empire whose peoples were in revolt — all these were elements in a picture of drastic decline. To complete the picture must be added the fact that France had not since the early nineteenth century kept pace with the leading industrial nations in production, in finance, above all in population.

The French government in exile, led by General de Gaulle, very easily re-established in 1944 in liberated France the old republican forms of government. Frenchmen called this state the Fourth Republic; but after de Gaulle, disappointed by his failure to attain real power in a state still ruled by unstable parliamentary coalitions of "splinter parties," retired from politics in 1946, the Fourth Republic began to look exactly like the Third. Cabinets lasted on an average only a few months; to the old splinter parties was added a Communist party of renewed strength, openly dedicated to revolutionary change; the problems of the old empire, now known as the French Union, seemed insoluble. Indo-China was lost in 1954 in a great defeat at Dienbienphu at the hands of the Vietnamese rebels under the Communist Ho Chi Minh. In the same year an active rebellion against the French began in Algeria.

Thus to many, post-war France seemed sunk in a slough of despond at least as deep as that in which Britain was mired. But one fact, little noted at the time, hardly jibed with this analysis. The French birth rate began to rise. Already lower than that of France's competitors in the nineteenth century, it had by the 1930's sunk to the point where, without the immigration from neighboring countries which actually did take place, the total French population would have declined. In France in 1942 the "net reproduction rate" for 100 women had sunk to 85 — that is, fifteen less than the figure needed to maintain without immigration

the existing population; by 1949 it had risen to 133 — that is, 33 above mere stability. The rate continued at 124 or higher through 1955. In a land where birth-control methods were in spite of legal restrictions fully understood and fully available to all classes of the population, this could mean only that hundreds of thousands of French men and women deliberately decided to have children, a clear sign of the recovery, the optimism, that lay just ahead.

West Germany

West Germany was in many ways the success story of the post-war world. Strengthened by refugees from the East, its population of some 50 million was nearly three times that of East Germany. The great material destruction of much of Germany's industrial plant paradoxically soon proved beneficial: the new plant was built with the latest technological equipment. The Allied High Commission, never very severe, gradually abolished controls over German industry, save for atomic energy and a few other military restrictions. They advanced economic aid, and scaled down pre-war German debts. By the early 1950's West Germany had a favorable balance of trade and was achieving industrial growth as high as 10 per cent a year. To a degree, this prosperity was shared even by the working classes, though in the first crucial years there was much plowing back into capital goods used for further production.

Politically, the independent West German state proved a workable democracy. It was endowed with a constitution providing for a bicameral legislature, with a lower house representing the people directly and an upper house representing the states (Länder), and a president elected by a special assembly for a five-year term, in practice largely a ceremonial figure. Real executive leadership was vested in a chancellor, a prime minister dependent on a parliamentary majority. One obvious fact of German political stability was soon established: the old splinter-party system, though it was not replaced by a neat two-party one, did not return to plague the new republic. Under the leadership of Konrad Adenauer, the Christian Democrats, distant heirs of the old Centrist party (see Chapter 27), maintained in the post-war decade a sufficient majority to insure steady rule. The chief opposition came from the Social Democrats. These "gradualist" socialists, firmly anti-communist, were strong in the industrial cities, and in free Berlin, but were unable to attain federal power.

"De-nazification" was of course on the Allied program, and at the Nuremberg trials in 1946 seventy-four top Nazi leaders indicted in the autumn of 1945 were convicted of war crimes. Ten were hanged, after two had committed suicide; one was sentenced to life imprisonment, others to shorter terms; and three were acquitted. Such trials were an innovation in international law and practice; as such they were condemned by many conscientious conservatives in the West as mere revenge, as punishment for "crimes" not established as such and therefore wholly *ex post facto*. But most of the free world, and perhaps most West Germans, approved the innovation.

To have dismissed all civil servants who had held posts under the Nazi regime would have dismantled German administration altogether. A moderate weeding-out of the most compromised Nazis was achieved, though not sufficiently to satisfy many western anti-Nazis. The new republic had its nationalist groups, but in the first decade after the war they were not very vocal. Skeptics remained doubtful about the extent of German conversion to the habits of democracy as practiced in the West, and there were sporadic outbreaks of antisemitism in West Germany, where, however, there were only a few thousand Jews left alive.

The Other Western Countries

In Italy a plebiscite in 1946 showed 54.3 per cent of the voters in favor of a republic. In spite of the comparative narrowness of the margin by which it was established, the new Italian republic proved a viable state. There were monarchists who regretted the forced departure of the House of Savoy, and there were even those who regretted the end of the fascist régime. But neither group was able to influence greatly parliamentary politics. A strong Christian Democratic party under an able leader, Alcide de Gasperi, with support from other centrist and right centrist groups, was able to hold power for seven years. The Christian Democratic party was a Catholic party with a relatively liberal reform program. It took positive measures to break up the large landed estates in the South with a view to redistributing the land. But Italian politics still were splinter-party politics; the necessary coalitions were assembled without much difficulty. Indeed in the post-war decade there was an approximation to two-party politics, with de Gasperi in power challenged chiefly by a very strong Communist party, the most numerous in the West, with whom the larger faction of the Socialists—that led by Pietro Nenni—was allied. The firmly anti-communist socialist faction led by Guisppe Saragat, participated in the government.

Italy shared in the post-war economic resurgence. Economic growth was strongest in the northern and central areas, but, as mentioned, the efforts to improve the conditions in the backward South were seriously undertaken and some progress was made. Italy enjoyed a cultural upswing, especially marked in the novel and in motion pictures, and Italian names like Silone, Moravia, de Sica, Rossellini were familiar throughout the West. Notably for those Americans who felt the need for a European love, Italy often supplanted France as an object of affection. Certainly among American and British intellectuals there was a sharp turn away from Paris toward Rome and Florence and Venice. Most Italians seem relieved that they no longer had to aspire to imperial greatness.

III   The Communist Bloc, 1945 to 1953

Soviet Government and the Economy

Alone among the leaders of the "Big Three" throughout the war years, Stalin remained in power after the war, the British elections having ousted Churchill, and Roosevelt having died in April, 1945. Facing the devastation caused by the war, and what he regarded as the immediate threat of American atomic weapons, Stalin felt obliged to decree a contination of austerity into the post-war years, at just the moment when the Russian people most yearned for new housing and a few creature comforts. The party, still his docile instrument, and experiencing regular purges to prevent any relaxation, dominated political life with the constant assistance of the secret police; while the army, still mobilized at high strength and performing a variety of occupation duties abroad, remained the third Soviet institution with power of its own. Elections, held in 1946 and 1950, returned the usual government-and-party-sponsored lists of candidates to office.

Few important administrative changes took place: the "people's commissariats" became ministries (1946), and not long before he died Stalin in 1952 abolished both Politburo and Orgburo, and combined them into a new Presidium. This he planned as a larger body than the Politburo, to include the ten Politburo members and fifteen additional high-ranking Soviet officials. But he did not live to announce the membership of the new body or to summon a meeting of it. After his death, the new "Presidium" remained at ten members, and simply replaced the old Politburo. Krushchev later declared that, in enlarging the membership and changing the name of the Politburo, Stalin had been taking the first step toward the complete purge and liquida-

tion of its ten existing members; so it is perhaps no wonder that, having survived this first step, they declined to take a second.

The fourth Five-Year Plan (1946–50) and its successor the fifth (1951–55) continued to emphasize investment in heavy industry at the expense of consumer goods. Though Stalin promised that the U.S.S.R. would now soon overtake America, sheer economic statistics made this a vain dream: the United States would have had to stand still industrially for twenty years to enable the Russians to come near to realizing such an ambition. Financial measures: the raising of prices, the wiping out of savings by the establishment of a new currency, kept the severest sort of economic pressure on the population. Reparations exacted from Germany and industrial loot from the eastern European countries gave massive stimulus to Soviet reconstruction. The fourth Five-Year Plan saw the first Soviet atomic bomb completed; the fifth saw further advances in armaments and the building of the Volga-Don canal. In agriculture, the regime embarked on a policy of reducing the number and increasing the size of collective farms. In 1951, Nikita Khrushchev, now appearing as a leading party agricultural expert, proposed a plan to create great agricultural cities (*agrogoroda*), in order to concentrate farm labor, and abolish rural backwardness.

Soviet Intellectual Life

The cultural policy of the régime was in keeping with the bleak austerity and terror of these years. In the first years after the war the authoritarian Andrei Zhdanov, boss of the Leningrad party organization and a leading member of the Politburo, made the arts his special concern. Maintaining that Soviet literature had to take an active role in the "engineering" of human souls, and that the official school of "socialist realism" was the only permissible line for a writer to follow, Zhdanov denounced in particular Mikhail Zoshchenko, writer of witty and satirical short stories, whose *Adventures of a Monkey* accidentally set free by a bomb suggested strongly that life in a cage in a zoo was more agreeable than life at large among the Soviet people; and Anna Akhmatova, a sensitive lyric poet, who had had the unpatriotic ill-judgment to lament in verse her feeling of loneliness, which no proper Soviet citizen would do. Both were expelled from the Union of Soviet Writers and thus silenced. Though Zhdanov died suddenly in 1948, his principles continued to reign. Violent anti-western propaganda filled Soviet books and resounded from the Soviet stage, as in the play called *The Unfortunate Haberdasher,* in which President Truman was cast as Hitler.

With the attack on the western nations went a constant drumbeat of new (and sometimes comic) claims for Soviet, or at least Russian "firsts" in every field of intellectual and artistic endeavor. No scholar could safely investigate a topic in the social sciences or humanities without denigrating the achievements of any non-Russian predecessors in the field or without paying respects to the supreme authorities on everything: Marx, Lenin, and, chiefly, Stalin. Archaeologists, historians, students of literature began their work with a compulsory quotation from Stalin, and a genuflection before him as the great teacher, the "Choryphaeus of the sciences."

Stalin emerged as an authority on biology, when the régime supported the geneticist Trofim Lysenko, who maintained—contrary to all accepted biological doctrine—that acquired characteristics were hereditary, strongly implying that "new Soviet man" would emerge as a biological phenomenon, and giving support to the political argument that communism would change the human species. Lysenko also denounced traditional western genetics, and the leading rival Soviet biologists, whose careers were now destroyed. In

linguistics too, Stalin personally intervened in 1950 to denounce the prevailing theories originated by Nikolai Marr, then sixteen years dead, who had implied that the world's languages corresponded to the degree of social development reached by their speakers, and so had at first attracted Soviet scholars. In the case of Lysenko, Stalin supported quackery (not finally denounced as mad until early 1966); in the case of Marr, Stalin supported common sense. Neither biologist nor linguist, Stalin fearlessly laid down the law for both. In the U.S.S.R. in these years, it was prudent to withhold one's views on any subject until Stalin had pronounced on it first.

As Stalin grew older, the secrecy, censorship, and conspiratorial miasma at the top of the Soviet state and society all intensified. Catering to ancient prejudices and violating Leninist precepts, Stalin now, in his fear of the West, moved against that group of Soviet citizens who had the closest contacts with the western world, the Jews. The press began to denounce long lists of "rootless, homeless cosmopolitans," who always proved to have Jewish names, thus fanning the strong traditional anti-Semitism of the Russians and Ukrainians. The government closed Jewish cultural organizations, and stopped publications in Yiddish, imposed religious restrictions, and eventually began a series of arrests and purges and deportations of prominent Jews, often those who had been active in the régime itself. Government service, the army, the professions, the universities, all experienced purges. Propaganda reached its peak with the publicity given an alleged "Doctors' Plot," in which Jewish doctors were accused of plotting to poison Stalin. When Stalin died, the stage seemed set for a full-scale anti-Semitic drive reminiscent of Hitler. Fear of the West, and detestation of Zionism—many Soviet Jews wanted to live in Israel—did not alone explain Soviet anti-Semitism. Despite their long years of preaching cultural autonomy for nationalities, many Soviet leaders were anti-Semitic, and recognized that the population at large could be expected to welcome anti-Semitism at a moment when there

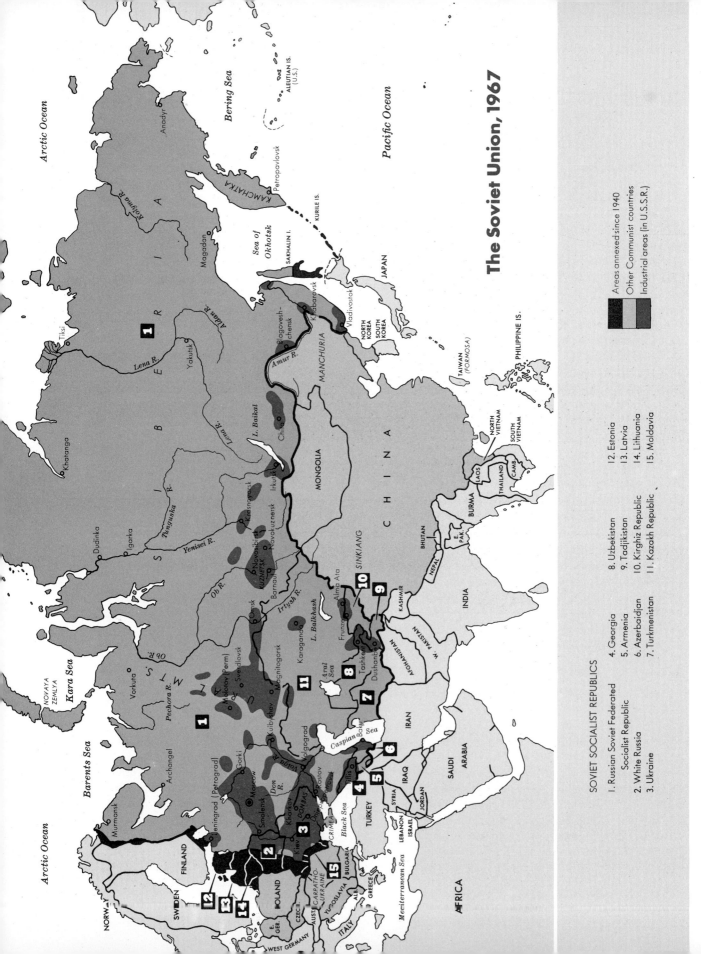

The Soviet Union, 1967

Areas annexed since 1940
Other Communist countries
Industrial areas (in U.S.S.R.)

SOVIET SOCIALIST REPUBLICS

1. Russian Soviet Federated
   Socialist Republic
2. White Russia
3. Ukraine

4. Georgia
5. Armenia
6. Azerbaidjan
7. Turkmenistan

8. Uzbekistan
9. Tadjikistan
10. Kirghiz Republic
11. Kazakh Republic

12. Estonia
13. Latvia
14. Lithuania
15. Moldavia

was little else in the government's policies that they could endorse.

Soviet Foreign Policy: Europe

When the war ended, the Soviet Union did not immediately terminate all forms of co-operation with its allies. The joint plan for dividing and ruling Germany went through. The four occupying powers together tried the chief surviving Nazi leaders at Nuremberg in 1946. In February, 1947, came the peace treaties with Italy, Rumania, Bulgaria, Hungary, and (for the U.S.S.R.) Finland. These confirmed Soviet territorial gains: from Rumania, Bessarabia and northern Bukovina; from Finland, portions of Karelia and a long lease on the naval base at Porkkala. In addition, the U.S.S.R. annexed part of former East Prussia, including the capital, Königsberg, home of the great philosopher, Kant, which the Russians renamed Kaliningrad after a high Soviet official. They also annexed the extreme easternmost portion of Czechoslovakia, inhabited largely by the Ukrainian-speaking Ruthenian people (see Chapter 22), who had not, however, for almost a thousand years been subject to any Russian state.

Elsewhere in eastern Europe — in Poland, Czechoslovakia, Rumania, Hungary, and Bulgaria — the U.S.S.R. sponsored the creation of new "people's republics" under communist governments, while Yugoslavia organized its own communist state, and had Albania as its own satellite. Soviet troops formally occupied about one-third of Germany, roughly between the Elbe and the Oder rivers, where they organized a satellite communist-ruled East Germany. The parts of Germany lying east of the line formed by the Oder and Neisse rivers, save for the sections of East Prussia directly annexed to the U.S.S.R., the Russians handed over to their Polish satellite. Here a wholesale transfer of population removed the Germans, and replaced them with Poles. Finland became part of the Russian security system, but enjoyed distinctly more autonomy than the satellites, and retained its pre-war political institutions. The four Allied powers detached Austria from Germany, thus undoing Hitler's *Anschluss* of 1938; and divided it, like Germany, into four occupation zones. The presence of Soviet troops in Hungary and Rumania was specifically guaranteed, in order to "protect" the communication lines between the Soviet Union and its occupying forces in Austria.

The presence of the Red Army alone made it possible for the U.S.S.R. to install satellite régimes in Poland, Hungary, Rumania, and Bulgaria. Following slightly different time tables in each country, the Russians none the less used the same methods: the elimination of all political groups that could be claimed to have collaborated with the Germans; the formation of "progressive" coalitions of parties; the destruction of all non-communist elements in these coalitions by splitting off from each of the component political parties a small fragment that would collaborate unquestioningly with the communists; and the denunciation and persecution of the remainder. Elections, despite the promises at Yalta, were accompanied by intimidation and atrocity. Western protest uniformly failed. Most disturbing of all was the communist take-over in Czechoslovakia, delayed until 1948, and directed against the government of Edward Beneš, brave enemy of Hitler in 1938 (see Chapter 29), betrayed now for a second time. Within each satellite the communists aped Soviet policies, moving with all speed to collectivize agriculture, impose forced-draft industrialization, control religious and cultural life, and govern by police terror.

As early as 1946 the U.S.S.R. refused to withdraw its forces from northwest Iran, and yielded only to pressure from the United Nations. But a more alarming probe of the Soviet perimeter came in Greece. Here, during World War II, a communist-dominated guerrilla movement had already once (December 1944 – February 1945) attempted to seize control, and had been thwarted only by British troops and Winston Churchill's determination not to allow Greece to go communist. In 1946, the Greek communists tried again, backed this time by the Soviet-dominated governments of their northern Balkan neigh-

Blockaded Berliners watch the arrival of airlift supplies, July, 1948.

bors. Simultaneously, Stalin exerted pressure on the Turks for concessions in the Straits area. Now President Truman proclaimed that countries facing the threat of communist aggression could count on help from the United States. Under this "Truman Doctrine," he sent American military aid to Greece and Turkey. The threat to the Turks evaporated, and by 1949, after severe fighting, the Greeks had put down the communist rebellion with the help of American advisers.

In Germany, on April 1, 1948, the Russians began one of the most bitter phases of the Cold War. By shutting off the land routes from the West into Berlin, they attempted to force the western Allies to turn Berlin wholly over to them. The Allies stood firm, however, and achieved the almost incredible feat of supplying a great metropolitan area wholly by air. In the six months of the blockade, Allied aircraft flew over 2,300,000 tons of coal, food, and other necessities into west Berlin. They also set up their own counter-blockade of Russian-occupied east Berlin. On September 1, the Russians gave up, and Berlin returned to its sufficiently abnormal status of joint occupation. But Soviet determination to oust the western powers from Berlin remained unaltered, and would be reiterated in 1958–1961 (see Chapter 31).

The Yugoslav Rebellion

In addition to their defeats in Greece and Berlin, the Russians found themselves, in 1948, faced with rebellion from a country that had seemed the most loyal of all their newly acquired European satellites; and this rebellion, Stalin felt, threatened their whole European position. Yugoslavia, which had overthrown a pro-German government in 1941, had remained throughout World War II a theater of intense guerrilla action against the Germans and Italians. There were two main groups of guerrillas, the Chetniks, led by General Mikhailovich, representing the Serb royalist domination over the south Slav kingdom, and the Partisans, led by the communist Joseph Broz, better known by his underground nickname, Tito. As the war continued, the communist-dominated Partisans gained ground against the Chetniks, who preferred to compromise with the German and Italian occupying forces rather than continue a war in alliance with communists. By 1943, Britain and the United States, with their eyes fixed on the paramount need to beat Hitler, decided to support Tito with supplies. When the Russians entered Belgrade in October 1944, they helped put their fellow-communist Tito in control.

Once in power, Tito installed his own communist government, abolished the Yugoslav monarchy, and in governing Yugoslavia and remaking its economy followed standard Soviet policies even more slavishly than any of the Russians' subordinates in satellite Europe. Yet in June, 1948, the world learned with surprise that the U.S.S.R. had quarreled with Yugoslavia, and expelled Tito's régime from the Cominform (see p. 565). The Soviet satellites swung into line, including Yugoslavia's own special puppet, Albania. All these east-European communist states broke their economic agreement with Yugoslavia, unloosed great barrages of anti-Tito propaganda, and stirred up border incidents. The Yugoslavs published the secret correspondence with Moscow that had led to the break, from which we learn that Soviet arrogance and insistence on penetrating the Yugoslav army and security organizations had aroused Yugoslav national feeling, never very far below the surface. Stalin, for his part, suffered from the misapprehension that he could bully the Yugoslovs into submission. "I will shake my little finger," he said, "and there will be no more Tito."

But Tito remained in power, accepting the aid that was quickly offered him by the United States. Washington saw that a communist régime hostile to Stalin was a new phenomenon that could not help embarrassing the Russians. Gradually Yugoslav communism evolved a modified ideology of its own, declaring that Stalin was a heretic and Tito and his followers the only true Leninists. Tito decentralized the economy, beginning in the factories, where workers' committees now began to participate actively in the planning. From the economy, decentralization spread to the local government apparatus, then to the central government, and finally to the Yugoslav Communist party, now rechristened "League of Yugoslav Communists." Though the régime admitted its past outrageous excesses, the police continued to be a powerful force. Tito gradually abandoned agricultural collectivization, which, as always, was most unpopular with the peasants.

The Yugoslav régime, however, remained a communist régime, suspicious of the western capitalists who were helping it, and including many men who hoped for an eventual reconciliation with the U.S.S.R. So long as Stalin lived, that proved impossible. In their fear of the spread of the new "national" communism to the other satellites, the Soviets directed the other east-European régimes in a series of ferocious purges, executing leading communists for "Titoism," and thus terrorizing anyone who might hope to establish any sort of autonomy within the communist bloc. When Stalin died in 1953, his heirs gave high priority to healing the breach with Yugoslavia, and eliminating the weakness it had created in their European position (see Chapter 31).

Soviet Foreign Policy: Asia

When balked in Europe, Tsarist Russian governments had often turned to Asia in pursuit of expansionist policies. Similarly, the Soviet Union, after the failures in Greece and Berlin, kept the pressure on its former allies by new adventures in Asia. Here, communists had tried and failed to win power in Indone-

Tito (right) and fellow partisans in a mountain retreat during World War II.

American infantrymen entering an evacuated Korean town, February, 1951.

sia, Burma, Malaya, and the Philippines, and had succeeded in China. The Korean War, which broke out in June, 1950, was in some measure a Soviet-sponsored operation, although the Russians themselves limited their contribution to support and sympathy, and allowed their Chinese ally to take the military lead. Korea, a peninsula at the eastern extremity of Asia, bordering on Manchuria and Siberia and close to Japan had been a target of Russian interest in the late-nineteenth and early-twentieth centuries, but the Japanese defeat of the Russians in 1905 (see Chapter 22) had led instead to Japanese annexation in 1910. In 1945, at the close of World War II, Russian troops occupied the northern part of Korea, and American troops occupied the southern part. The country was divided in the middle by a line along the 38th parallel of latitude; a communist-inspired North Korean People's Republic was set up on one side, and an American-inspired South Korean Republic on the other. When all American forces except for a few specialists were withdrawn from South Korea, the North Koreans marched South to unite the nation under communist control.

It is probable that the communists thought the operation was safe, since American pronouncements had stated that Korea was outside the American "defense perimeter." But when the invasion began, the United States — with U.N. approval, as the vote was taken in the absence of the Russians — at once moved troops into Korea. They got there barely soon enough to halt the North Korean drive, and then to push the enemy back well north of the 38th parallel, almost to the Yalu River, the frontier of China. At this point, Communist China entered the war, and Chinese troops joined the North Koreans in pushing the Americans southward again. By 1951, the line of battle had been stabilized roughly along the old boundary between North and South Korea. After prolonged negotiations, an armistice was finally concluded in July, 1953.

The United States carried on its defense of South Korea in the name of the United Nations and received small but valuable detachments of troops from some of its allies. Although President Truman and his advisers in Washington wanted to limit the war to the defense of South Korea, the United Nations commander on the spot, the American General, MacArthur, wanted to press the war into Communist China. American officials, and in particular America's allies, feared that such a step would bring Russia actively in on the Chinese side and might precipitate World War III. President Truman therefore recalled General MacArthur in April, 1951.

The Korean settlement by no means ended the tension between Communist China and the United States. The American government continued its refusal to recognize Red China, and serious friction developed over Formosa and the smaller off-shore islands, Quemoy and Matsu, now in the hands of Chiang Kai-shek, which the communists seemed determined to

capture and the United States seemed equally determined to keep out of communist hands. The Korean settlement of course brought understanding between the U.S.S.R. and the United States no closer. It was at best a compromise: after all the bloody fighting, the United States had managed to hang on to the devastated southern portion of the country, and the communists had been driven back to the north, which they governed undisturbed. Neither side could call it a victory. By the time it was reached, Stalin had been dead for more than three months. He had remained to the end the suspicious, ruthless dictator that he had been since the late 1920's, but his paranoia had grown so mightily over the years that his closest aides lived in constant fear of their lives. Now a transfer of power had to be made; any change seemed likely to be an improvement for the Russians and for the world at large.

IV   The Revolt against Imperialism

The First World War had brought a gradual loosening of the imperial ties binding non-western peoples to the great colonial powers of the West. The Second World War greatly accelerated and intensified this process. Not only were the empires of vanquished Italy and Japan dismantled after 1945; the imperial possessions of the victors and the nominal victors—the British, Americans, French, Belgians, and Dutch—experienced major amputations. Moreover, states like China, Iran, and Egypt, that had long been sovereign in name but that in practice were often subject to political or economic tutelage by the imperial powers, vigorously asserted their independence. The nationalism of the non-western world was coming of age. It scored its first victories, in the immediate post-war years, chiefly in areas of Asia and the Middle East where anti-colonial sentiments and movements had been developing before 1939. Later, after 1953, as the next chapter

will show, it spread to Africa and within a few years revolutionized the political status of the continent that had long been dominated by European empire-builders.

Causes of the Revolt

The immediate reasons for the anti-imperialist revolution may be found in the Second World War itself. In this war, as in World War I, the western democracies often relied on colonial troops, with a consequent boost to the self-esteem of the peoples providing the troops. In both wars the propaganda of the democracies to show the justness of their cause fostered ambitions for the basic democratic rights of self-government and self-determination. In both wars inflation and other economic dislocations such as shortages, conscription of labor, and the enjoyment of war profits by the few rather than the many, heightened these ambitions and swelled the sense of grievance.

The second war, unlike the first, destroyed the magic invulnerability of the West, for the western possessions in the Far East fell before the attacks of non-western conquerors, the Japanese. The final defeat of Japan apparently did little to offset the immense damage done to western prestige. Moreover, two of the great imperial powers, the French and the Dutch, were only by courtesy numbered among the victors of World War II, with almost fatal consequences for their prestige. Nationalist leaders in the non-western world also knew that British power had been seriously weakened by the tremendous drain of the war, and that the defeat of the resolutely imperialist Conservatives by the rather anti-imperial Labour Party in the election of 1945 promised liberalization of British policy. Nationalist leaders further knew that the real victors in the war were the United States and the Soviet Union, each in its very different way outspokenly anti-colonial.

While the Second World War touched off the colonial revolt, the deeper causes of the revolt must be sought in the five-hundred-year record of western expansion, and in the western tradition itself. The mainsprings of western culture—Christianity and the secular faiths of progress, democracy, and nationalism—provided little nourishment for imperialist policies. The West could not conceal from the educated natives its own great ethical and political writings. Indeed, it often laid before them with pride the Christian Bible, the American Declaration of Independence, the French Declaration of the Rights of Man, even the Communist Manifesto. It was hardly possible to keep on insisting that "all men are created equal" really meant that "white men are created the superiors of colored men." In terms of ideals and ideology, western imperialism carried within itself the seeds of its own failure—or, more positively, its own transfiguration into self-determination for all peoples.

The great instrument for the spread of western ideas was the education, both formal and informal, provided to non-western peoples by the West itself. In the nineteenth cen-

tury, this education owed a great deal to the efforts of Christian missions, though toward the end of the century it became more secular as a result of increasing participation by the governing powers themselves. Almost everywhere formal education was limited to a comparatively small number of natives. From India, the sons of rajahs went to Oxford, and so too did bright boys from the slowly rising middle classes; by the twentieth century western education in India itself was beginning to assume the western form of "careers open to talents." Some non-Europeans turned against this western education and took refuge in a reaffirmation of the values of their traditional culture, of Hinduism or Islam, for example. But for the most part, the educated natives came to feel that independence could be won only by imitating the West, by learning its industrial, technological, and military skills.

The educated classes throughout the world of western imperialism emphatically wanted independence. Many were by the twentieth century revolutionaries; some became great admirers of the Bolshevik revolution in Russia, and a few received training in the techniques of revolution in Moscow itself. A great many westerners made the mistake of assuming that these nationalist revolutionaries were an unrepresentative minority of the native populations, and that the great colonial masses, illiterate and poor, did not really follow their own native educated class but asked nothing better than to be ruled by the kindly whites. Of course the subject races have always had their share of "Uncle Toms" (a term used in scorn by American Negroes for their fellows who appear too submissive toward the whites). But the "Uncle Toms" have not given their stamp to non-western populations. The urban masses, and then, more gradually, the peasant masses, began to share the feelings of nationalism and to demand that the foreigner must go.

The imperialist powers themselves followed policies that greatly aided the ripening of nationalism. Almost everywhere they penetrated they brought enough sanitary engineering, enough medicine, enough law and order to lower the death rate and to enable the native population to grow as it had never grown before. But that very growth made more mouths to feed, and the fact of population pressure became increasingly obvious to the educated and uneducated alike. Furthermore, education gave the natives some of the white man's special magic, his control over material things and over the elaborate machines of the modern world; the natives began to acquire scientific knowledge and engineering skills. Thereby, they came to feel more and more the white man's equal, less and less willing to accept a subordinate social and political position now that, in material things, they seemed to be drawing even.

The Far East

The Second World War produced a major shift in the balance of power in the Far East. While China turned communist and grew increasingly antagonistic to the West, as we have already seen, Japan went down to defeat. The Japanese, who were the first non-western people to be recognized as equals by the West, had conquered an empire rivaling those of the West. Their "Greater East Asia Co-Prosperity Sphere" showed at its peak many obvious analogies with Napoleon's system of satellite states, and even more with that of Hitler. The Japanese employed methods of rule that were directly patterned on western precedent; they relied chiefly on the time-honored device of setting up puppet native governments, and exploiting for their own benefit the economic resources of the conquered lands. Their empire disintegrated in the atomic blast over Hiroshima, for it had never been cemented by the loyalty of its component parts.

Yet the Japanese started with at least one very great asset: they were an Asian people, a colored people, not westerners with the burden of white supremacy to carry. They could come as the emancipators of Asians and Pacific islanders, and their propaganda sounded this note most vigorously. Yet, Asians though they were, they did not endear themselves to their fellow Asians. Their armies looted and committed atrocities; the Japanese abroad behaved like any other master race, and did not conceal their feelings of superiority over the natives. Time might have taught the Japanese a lesson in social psychology, and they might have been able with time to consolidate their grandiloquently named "co-prosperity sphere"; but time they did not have.

The end of World War II saw Japan reduced to her own islands, stripped of her overseas possessions. The overwhelming part played by the United States in the defeat of Japan insured that the military occupation and the subsequent peace of 1952, whereby Japan regained formal independence, would be almost wholly an American concern. Though there was a strong current in American opinion that demanded the deposition of the Emperor, he was left on his throne, deprived of his divine status, and subjected to the close control of General MacArthur and the forces of occupation. Americans found to their astonishment that on the surface at least the Japanese people, far from taking the occupation with hostility, seemed almost to admire their occupiers. They seemed not to understand what democracy meant—apart from baseball and some other American folkways—but they appeared very anxious to learn. Their behavior roused a good deal of speculation about national psychology; some scholars called attention to the rigorous early toilet-training of Japanese children in order to explain the national willingness to obey a master.

In the past, the Japanese had not had a democratic society or a democratic political organization. It was by no means certain at the time of the peace treaty in 1952 that they would firmly establish a democracy of the western type, although they had made a promising start since 1945. If a well-developed industrial economy is an indispensable base for the development of democracy, the Japanese already had a great advantage over all other non-western peoples. It remained to be seen whether Japan, because she took over industrialism from the West, would automatically become thoroughly westernized. It also remained to be seen whether the Japanese would be able to secure the markets abroad that their export-centered industry required.

Southeast Asia

In Southeast Asia, too, the Second World War upset the traditional balance of power, and set off a really major political explosion. The Japanese conquest and occupation destroyed belief in the invincibility of the white nations, and in 1945 the western powers were by no means able to pick up where they had left off. Moreover, the United States was in the process of granting independence to its own imperial wards, the Filipinos. In 1949, consequently, the Dutch abandoned the attempt to retain a stake in their former colony, the Netherlands East Indies, and recognized its independence as the Republic of Indonesia. Britain gave Burma independence outside the Commonwealth (1948) and the Federation of Malaya independence within the Commonwealth (1957); the great port of Singapore at the tip of Malaya, with its largely Chinese population, secured a special autonomous status (1958). When Malaya joined with the former British protectorates on the great island of Borneo in the Federation of Malaysia (1963), Singapore at first participated, then withdrew (1965).

France, meanwhile, made rather more limited concessions to the component states of Indo-China—Vietnam, which included the populous and fairly prosperous coastal areas, and Cambodia and Laos in the more primitive hinterland. But the French did not go far enough or fast enough to prevent their involvement in a lengthy war (1945–1954), during which Indo-Chinese communist rebels called the Viet Minh received support from Communist China. Increasingly hard-pressed, the French agreed in 1954 to partition Vietnam into a communist north and a south under a rather weak anti-communist government. The sequel was the outbreak of communist guerrilla activity in South Vietnam and more prolonged warfare.

In the Philippine Republic and Malaya the communists had already launched stubborn guerrilla campaigns, which were finally checked in the late 1950's. To counter the threat of communist penetration, the West sponsored the Southeast Asia Treaty Organization (SEATO) in 1954, but only two states in the area—the Philippines and Thailand (Siam)—joined with Pakistan and the western powers in participating. By the 1960's, as we shall find in the next chapter, the communist threat was focused on South Vietnam and on Indonesia, the most populous state in Southeast Asia, and perhaps the most unstable. The whole area, moreover, faced formidable economic problems. Southeast Asia, so long cast in the colonial role of producing rice, spices, rubber, tin, and other raw materials, found it hard to achieve economic independence without western assistance. Many of its peoples regarded with suspicion the aid offered by their former masters; yet, if they did not take it, they might drift into economic chaos and possibly into the communist orbit.

India and Pakistan

At the end of World War II, the victory of the British Labour party, pledged to grant India self-government, made Indian emancipation a certainty. But the deep-seated tension between Moslems and Hindus now assumed critical importance. When the Hindus' Congress party and the All-India Moslem League faced the need to make a working constitution for India, they found themselves in complete disagreement. The Moslems had long been working for a partition into separate Hindu and Moslem states, and this was in the end reluctantly accepted by the Hindus. In 1947, Hindu India and Moslem Pakistan were set up as self-governing dominions within the British Commonwealth.

Pakistan ("land of the pure," a name coined by Moslem students in Britain in the 1930's) is a state divided into two parts, widely separated by intervening Indian territory—the larger, West Pakistan, in the northwest, and the smaller and more densely populated, East Pakistan, in East Bengal. The rest of the former British Indian Empire and four-fifths of its inhabitants became the Republic of India by virtue of its constitution of 1950. Pakistan, with its smaller population and its relatively poorly developed industry, was weaker than India and at first kept closer political ties with the British Commonwealth.

The partition was not achieved without violence. In view of the way races and religions are geographically mingled in the subcontinent, it could not result in a complete separation of Hindus in one state and Moslems in another. The line of partition between India and West Pakistan evoked bitter fighting between members of the two communities, and many thousands of lives were lost. It resulted in a wholesale transfer of populations as Hindus moved from Pakistani territory into India and Moslems moved from Indian territory into Pakistan. A particular source of trouble was the mountainous region of Kashmir, an important tourist center. Though mainly Moslem in population, it was at the time of partition ruled by a Hindu princely house which turned it over to India. India has continued to occupy most of Kashmir, to the great economic disadvantage of Pakistan. The United Nations sought to determine the fate of Kashmir by arranging a plebiscite, but failed to secure the needed approval of both parties. Generally, however, despite the passions aroused by Kashmir and despite periodic rioting between Hindus and Moslems, both India and Pakistan came to accept partition as a normal state of affairs.

In domestic politics the two states went through sharply contrasting experiences. The chief architect of Pakistani independence, Mohammed Ali Jinnah, (head of the Moslem League), died in 1948. Deprived of its leader, the young state floundered in its attempts to make parliamentary government work and to attack pressing economic difficulties. Newly emancipated India also suffered a grievous loss when Gandhi was assassinated by an anti-Moslem Hindu fanatic in 1948. But Nehru, Gandhi's "younger brother," as he was termed, at once assumed full leadership. Under the guidance of Nehru, who was already a seasoned politician, and aided also by the long experience of British administration, India accomplished a feat almost without precedent in the non-western world. It successfully inaugurated a genuine parliamentary democracy of the western type and conducted free and hotly fought elections, based on universal suffrage, among voters who were in the main illiterate and rural. Understandably, Indians have been very proud of their accomplishment.

Both countries had to cope with formidable economic problems — Pakistan with poverty and lack of industry, and India with poverty and lack of sufficient agricultural output to sustain her enormous population. India has faced in an acute form the population pressure that bears so heavily on many other non-western countries. By the 1950's there were over 400,000,000 people in the Republic of India, with approximately 8,000,000 added annually, and the threat of famine and actual death through starvation was always present. In 1950, the government launched the first in a series of Five-Year Plans for economic development. While permitting the expansion of private industry, the Five-Year Plans stressed government projects. Irrigation and flood control works were started, transport and communications improved, and a beginning made

Nehru, as Prime Minister, receiving symbolic golden mace on the eve of Indian independence.

on the enormously difficult and significant task of educating hundreds of millions of peasants in new and more efficient ways of working the land. The West helped by furnishing technical experts, money, and the surplus grain needed to avert the threat of famine. Experts estimated, however, that even with a modernized economy India would find it hard to support a population growing so rapidly. Although birth control is abhorrent to the traditional ways of Hinduism, the government sponsored a campaign for its practice.

The traditions of Hinduism have exerted manifold influences on the Republic of India, throwing much light on the whole problem of the essential differences between East and West. Hinduism is an immensely complex and ancient way of life for which the word "religion," in its western connotation, is not adequate. It has no church organization in the Christian sense, no clear-cut theology, no established Bible. Of the three major developed cultures that the West has encountered in expanding over the world, Hinduism is farthest from ours. In comparison, Islam is actually a relative of Christianity, and Chinese society, in spite of its traditional un-western family structure, has affinities with the utilitarian or worldly strain in the West.

For Hinduism, this world of sense-experience is an illusion, but an illusion that has somehow to be overcome. Death is essential to the overcoming, but death is not enough. Each living man, indeed each living thing, is a soul alienated by the very fact of living from the ultimate, universal soul which is peace, absence of struggle and desire, ineffable non-being. The holiest of men by turning away entirely from the world, by living without desire—but not by any such simple solution as suicide—can perhaps attain this nonbeing in the end. But most human beings are now living out in this world the consequences of a sinful life as another personality in the past. Indeed, the most sinful of men who have lived in the past have been punished by reincarnation as animals or even as insects (which is why the most orthodox of Hindus will harm no living thing, even wearing gauze masks so that no minute insect can be breathed in or swallowed inadvertently).

Among men, their sins in past incarnations are reflected by their status, their *caste*. The poor, the humblest, are such because their sins have been greater; they cannot improve their lot in the western sense, for they can only slowly in subsequent incarnations redeem their wickedness by living as holy a life as possible. The lowest Hindu group, actually below and outside the caste system, were called "untouchables," because even their shadow would corrupt a caste-Hindu. Yet no one can keep untouchable in a railroad car, and the Indian Constitution of 1950 abolished the outcast status of the untouchables as undemocratic. The legal change, however, penetrated Indian custom only very slowly.

Hindu society, then, with its caste system, its innumerable tabus, and its lack of any basis for belief in material progress, found grave difficulties in the way of adopting western culture. That the Hindus adopted as much as they did was testimony to the penetrating power of the West. Many Hindu intellectuals were so far westernized that they had no real basis for calling themselves Hindus. But even for them, and much more for the uneducated, the long accumulation of habits, feelings, and ingrained attitudes could not be quickly altered.

The Middle East: Three Crises

In the Middle East, the mandates obtained by France and Britain after World War I collapsed after World War II. Syria and Lebanon won their full independence from the French, and the British withdrew from Palestine. The new state of Israel took over western Palestine, and the eastern part was annexed by Transjordan, which now styled itself, after its ruling dynasty, the Hashimite Kingdom of Jordan. Still other imperial ties were severed after World War II, notably those linking Egypt and Iran to Britain.

The first major crisis in the Middle East after World War II arose over the question of

Palestine. For half a century, Zionism, with its goal of creating a new Jewish state on the site of the ancient Jewish homeland, had been attracting support among Jews, especially in the often-persecuted Jewish communities of Russia and eastern Europe. Zionist hopes of creating a new state on the site of the ancient Jewish homeland received a great lift from the Balfour Declaration of 1917 and the subsequent British policy of admitting Jewish immigrants into Palestine. Hitler's persecutions and World War II made the problem of increased immigration to Palestine critical. At the same time, Britain, the mandatory power, wished to protect its great interest in the Middle East by cultivating the friendship of the Arabs. But in Palestine itself the flooding Jewish tide was submerging the Arabs, who had long been settled there and felt that this was *their* homeland.

Worn out after a decade of fruitless efforts to secure a compromise between Arabs and Jews, the British turned the problem over to the General Assembly of the United Nations, which proposed to partition the country into an Arab state and a Jewish state. When the British withdrew their forces from Palestine in 1948, the Jews at once proclaimed their state of Israel and secured its recognition by the U.N.; the Arabs declared the proclamation illegal and at once invaded the new state. In the ensuing war, the total resources in manpower of the Arab states were far greater than those of Israel, but the dissensions among the various Arab states, their military inefficiency, and the better technical equipment and morale of the Israelis resulted in a victory for the Jews. A truce, but not a formal peace, was patched up under the auspices of the United Nations (1949). Israel secured more of Palestine than had been allotted to her under the U.N. partition plan, and took over the western part of Jerusalem, the spiritual capital of Judaism, a city which the U.N. had proposed to neutralize. The "old city" of Jerusalem, however, including the Wailing Wall and the site of Solomon's temple, remained in the hands of Jordan and thus under the control of the Arab enemy.

In the course of the Arab-Israeli struggle, most of the Palestinian Arabs, numbering nearly a million, fled from Israel to the surrounding Arab states. The United Nations organized a special agency to extend relief to the refugees and to arrange for their permanent resettlement. The Arab states, however, were either unable or unwilling to absorb them, and many refugees insisted on remaining in depressing camps, for they viewed resettlement as an abandonment of their cherished conviction that the Israelis would soon "be pushed into the sea" and that they themselves would return to their old homes. This acute problem of the Palestinian refugees sharpened the hostility between Arab and Israeli and made the truce of 1948 a most uneasy affair, frequently broken in frontier incidents by both sides.

The new state of Israel faced not only a grave problem in external relations but also grave internal problems. It could not trust its Arab minority, numbering about 200,000, approximately one-tenth of the population. It continued to admit as many Jewish immigrants as possible, some of them of advanced western culture, but others, from North Africa and Yemen, still largely living in the Middle Ages. The welding of these disparate human elements into a single nationality was a formidable task. Immigration also swelled the total population of Israel, which soon contained about a million more people than Palestine had before World War II, and in an area not much bigger than Connecticut. Much of that area is mountainous, with a thin rocky soil and inadequate rainfall, and some of it is sheer desert. The Israelis applied talents and training derived from the West to make the best use of their limited resources, but they depended on outside aid, especially from their many sympathizers in the United States.

The dependence of Israel on western support, indeed the very existence of Israel, profoundly affected relations between the Arabs and the West. To most Arabs Israel appeared to be a new outpost of western imperialism, set up in their midst to spite them. They claimed that American policy had been unduly influenced by Jewish financiers, Jewish journalists, and Jewish voters. In such an atmosphere it was difficult for the United States and other western nations to retain cordial relations with the Arabs, who were in any case very sensitive nationalists.

A second major post-war crisis in the Middle East concerned Iranian oil. The oil was extracted, refined, and marketed by the Anglo-Iranian Oil Company, in which the British government had a large stake. Since the 1930's the Iranian government had been pressing the company to make larger royalty payments, and the issue became acute after World War II when Aramco (the Arabian-American Oil Company) set a new and more generous pattern for royalty agreements by making a 50:50 split with the monarchy of Saudi Arabia. More than economics was involved here, for Iranian nationalists resented Anglo-Iranian's policy of reserving managerial and technical posts for westerners, who lived almost entirely segregated lives in the company's towns in Iran, with their own clubs, schools, and cinemas. Memories of Britain's military occupation of parts of Iran during both world wars further embittered the nationalists.

In 1951, therefore, after a campaign led by the ardent nationalist politician, Mossadeq, the Iranian legislature nationalized the properties of Anglo-Iranian. Mossadeq, who now became Prime Minister, at first won wide support among his countrymen for his bold defiance of the West in highly emotional speeches at home and at the United Nations. But a world-wide boycott of nationalized Iranian oil caused a disastrous drop in the revenues of the Iranian government and a severe economic crisis. The issue was finally resolved after a *coup* in Tehran, the Iranian capital, in which United States intelligence agents were said to be involved, had driven Mossadeq from office and into jail (1953). Although Iranian oil remained nationalized, the government now paid western companies, including the successor to Anglo-Iranian, to assist in exploiting and marketing the oil.

The third major Middle Eastern crisis was the revolution that broke out in Egypt in 1952, directed both against the British and against the traditional ruling groups among the Egyptians themselves. Although Britain had taken real steps toward freeing Egypt from her tutelage before World War II (see Chapter 28), she did not move fast enough to satisfy Egyptian nationalists. During the war, furthermore, she offended them deeply by mobilizing tanks to force King Farouk to dismiss a pro-Axis cabinet. After the war, Farouk, once a very popular monarch, lost prestige both because of his well-publicized appetite for high living and because of his involvement in a scandal concerning the provision of defective supplies to the Egyptian army in the Palestinian War. From Farouk and his palace clique the odor of corruption and scandal spread through the upper levels of the government.

The virtually bloodless revolution of July 23, 1952, was the work of a group of young army officers, who were greatly chagrined by Israel's defeat of Egypt. In some policies the new government of Egypt's strong man, Gamal Abdul Nasser, followed a path paralleling that marked out by Turkey's strong man, Atatürk, a generation earlier. (see Chapter 28). It abolished the monarchy and drew up a republican constitution. It encouraged the emancipation of women and pared down the traditionally large role of the conservative courts of religious law without, however, making the kind of frontal assault on Islam that Atatürk had attempted. In practice, the régime was rather markedly dictatorial: only one party was tolerated, elections were closely supervised, and press campaigns were orchestrated by the Ministry of National Guidance. Nasser justified this absolutism in this way:

Before July 23rd, I had imagined that the whole nation was ready and prepared, waiting for nothing but a vanguard to lead the charge against the battlements, whereupon it would fall in behind in serried ranks, ready for the sacred advance towards the great objective. And I had imagined that our role was to be this commando vanguard.

Then suddenly came reality after July 23rd. The vanguard performed its task and charged the battlements of tyranny. It threw out Farouk and then paused, waiting for the serried ranks to come up. . . .

For a long time it waited. Crowds did eventually come, and they came in endless droves—but how different is reality from the dream! The masses that came were disunited, divided groups of stragglers. . . . At this moment I felt, with sorrow and bitterness, that the task of the vanguard, far from being complete, had only begun.

We needed order, but we found nothing but chaos. We needed unity, but we found nothing behind us but dissension. We needed work but we found behind us only indolence and sloth. . . .

In addition to all this, there was a confirmed individual egotism. The word "I" was on every tongue. It was the solution to every difficulty, the cure for every ill. I had many times met eminent men—or so they were called by the press—of every political tendency and color, but when I would ask any of them about a problem in the hope he could supply a solution, I would never hear anything but "I."

Economic problems? He alone could understand them; as for the others, their knowledge on the subject was that of a crawling infant. Political issues? He alone was expert. No one else had gotten beyond the a-b-c's of politics. After meeting one of these people, I would go back in sorrow to my comrades and say, "It is no use. . . ."*

This passage nevertheless reveals much about the difficulty of establishing stable and responsible régimes in the new world of non-western nationalism. Nasser's pressing domestic problems and his need for economic and military assistance led him into further adventures after 1953 (see Chapter 31).

Latin America

At first glance it may seem odd to include parts of the Western Hemisphere in a survey of the revolution against imperialism. While remnants of old colonial empires lingered in the Caribbean after World War II, most of the Latin American republics had already enjoyed independence for a century or more and re-

*Gamal Abdul Nasser, *Egypt's Liberation* (Washington: Public Affairs Press, 1955), 32–36.

tained close bonds of language, religion, and culture with the great nations of western Europe. Populated by a mixture of Indian, Negro, and white Creole stock, many of them had advanced substantially toward the establishment of multi-racial societies. Yet a second look shows that the peoples of Latin America and the Caribbean have long been struggling with the kinds of problems we have found in Asia and the Middle East. Especially since 1945, they have been trying to go beyond their traditional and essentially colonial role as suppliers of such foodstuffs as bananas, sugar, coffee, and beef, and such raw materials as oil, nitrates, and minerals. They have sought to end their almost total dependence on commodities that fluctuate widely in price on the world market, and to lay a more stable economic base on which to raise the standard of living of their still impoverished masses. Politically, the parallels with the non-western world are often striking. There have been the same denunciations of western colonialism (in this case usually "Yankee imperialism"), the same emergence of military dictators, the same round of *coups* and revolutions, the same promises of utopia so easy to make and so hard to fulfill.

Many Latin American revolutions have actually been no more than shifts of power from one ruling strong man or clique to another; in a book of this kind we cannot survey them all, and must be content with a sample. Immediately after World War II, for example, democracy seemed to be making notable progress in several Latin American states, only to lose ground after 1948, so that by 1955, eleven of the twenty republics were ruled by dictators, most of them military men. We shall consider two case histories—those of Mexico and of Argentina.

In Mexico the overthrow of Napoleon III's puppet emperor, Maximilian, in 1867 (see Chapter 21) marked an apparent victory not only for the Monroe Doctrine but also for Mexican nationalism and liberalism. In 1876, however, power was seized by Porfirio Díaz, a leading specimen of the *caudillo* or military hero, who dominated the country for the next thirty-five years. Díaz enforced law and order, punctually met payments on foreign debts (non-payment of which had occasioned the venture of Napoleon III), won high respect abroad, and attracted the investment of much foreign capital in his country. But he also catered almost exclusively to the interests of foreign investors and the large Mexican land-owners; agitation by laborers for redress of legitimate grievances was suppressed; many peasants lost their stake in the land and were reduced to being peons, hardly better than serfs, on large agricultural estates.

Popular discontent with the Díaz régime finally boiled over in 1910, and the dictator fled abroad in the next year. The acute phase of the revolution thus begun continued for thirty years, marked by intermittent violence and insurrection, by revolutionary reformers who turned into wealthy dictators, and by radical social and economic experimentation. The Catholic Church, long regarded by many Mexicans as opposed to economic and political reform and indifferent to the welfare of the masses, was the target of extreme anticlerical measures. The foreign oil companies, American and British, suffered expropriation of valuable concessions. All this did not make for harmonious relations with the United States, and at one point early in the revolution (1916) President Wilson sent troops into Mexico to retaliate for a Mexican incursion into the American state of New Mexico. The revolutionary governments gave labor unions extensive privileges and power, expropriated great estates to emancipate the peons, and began a vigorous program of educating the large and neglected population of native Indians. A remarkable cultural awakening took place, based on native traditions and crafts, and Mexican painters like Rivera and Orozco won international fame.

The Mexican revolution, however, stopped short of installing a fully socialistic régime, and by World War II seemed to be entering the Thermidorean stage. The course of Mexican history after 1945 confirmed this impression. Like many revolutions, the Mexican appeared to have lost much of its extremism, its radical dogmatism, its determination to realize for all the promises of Liberty, Equality, and Fraternity. Post-revolutionary Mexico was in part at least reconciled to the need for foreign capital, for the good opinion of North Americans, and above all for patience in the long task of raising the standards of her masses.

At the other extremity of Latin America, the Argentine Republic has not faced Mexico's problem of a large and backward Indian population, since it is peopled almost entirely by European immigrants and their descendants. Although independent for over 150 years (since 1810), Argentina had until the middle of the twentieth century a typical colonial economy, exporting beef and grain and other raw materials to Europe and importing manufactured goods. The economy was based on a social system that gave power to a small landlord class. The beginnings of industrialization, and especially the growth of the Argentine capital, Buenos Aires, into a great metropolis of nearly 5 million increased the numbers of working-class and middle-class people and increased also popular dissatisfaction with the aristocratic régime. Mussolini and Hitler won admirers in many circles in Argentina; democratic elements generally looked to France and to the radical French republican tradition. The United States, to phrase it mildly, was rather envied than admired. Argentina sat out World War II, coming in on the Allied side only at the very end.

After the war, in the national election of 1946, a newcomer to Argentine politics rose to prominence, Colonel Juan Perón. Perón became a dictator on the fascist European model—that is, he contrived to hold power by the kind of appeal and by the methods that we have analyzed for Mussolini, Hitler, and Franco. Perón, however, never established himself quite as firmly as did his European counterparts, and in 1955 he went down before a characteristic Latin-American military *coup d'état*. Many factors accounted for his fall. In searching for support, Perón was driven more and more to appeal to the poorer masses, the *descamisados* ("shirtless ones"), and thus lost much of his following in the conservative upper classes. Moreover, after the death of his actress wife Eva, who seems to have been much brighter than her husband, he quarreled with the Roman Catholic Church and put through anticlerical measures that cost him further support. Finally, Perón never solved the grave economic and financial problems arising out of his country's essentially colonial position; indeed, his extravagant spending on public works and welfare projects virtually bankrupted Argentina. Although it is hazardous to generalize on the basis of Latin-American experience, his fall suggests two tentative conclusions. First, a great weakness of the Nazi-fascist formula was its attempt to solve social problems by a modern form of the old Roman "bread and circuses," which simply would not work in the twentieth century. Second, the overthrow of Perón without outside interference showed that dictators could be unseated from within, even in modern times of mass propaganda, if they lost the support of the military. We shall encounter other examples in the next chapter.

Reading Suggestions on the Post-War World, 1945–1953

(Asterisk indicates paperbound edition.)

The Democracies

S. P. Graubard, ed., *A New Europe?* (Houghton Mifflin, 1964). Stimulating essays by specialists, analytical rather than narrative.

S. Kuznets, *Post War Economic Growth* (Harvard Univ. Press, 1964). Good analytical study of this important phase of recent history.

C. E. Black, *Dynamics of Modernization* (Harper and Row, 1966). An important essay in comparative contemporary history.

J. Freymond, *Western Europe since the War* (Praeger, 1964). Good brief manual.

A. M. Schlesinger, Jr., *A Thousand Days* (Houghton Mifflin, 1965). Fascinating account of the Kennedy years by a member of his team.

I. F. Stone, *The Haunted Fifties* (Random House, 1963). Selections from his Washington newsletter; most readable.

A. Sampson, *Anatomy of Britain Today* (Harper and Row, 1965). Lively and readable.

F. Boyd, *British Politics in Transition, 1945–1963* (Praeger, 1964). A good up-to-date account.

F. S. Northedge, *British Foreign Policy: The Process of Readjustment, 1945–1961* (Praeger, 1962). A similar up-to-date manual of foreign policy.

H. S. Hughes, *The United States and Italy,* rev. ed. (Harvard Univ. Press, 1965). This revised edition has an excellent chapter on current history and a bibliography brought up to date.

E. McInnis, *Shaping of Postwar Germany* (Praeger, 1961). A good brief survey.

D. M. Pickles, *The Fifth French Republic,* 3rd ed. (Praeger, 1966). A well-known treatment.

R. Aron, *France Steadfast and Changing* (Harvard Univ. Press, 1960). Thoughtful study by a very fair-minded Frenchman.

R. M. and J. Brace, *Ordeal in Algeria* (Van Nostrand, 1960). Objective study by two Americans.

Communism and the Cold War

D. J. Dallin, *The New Soviet Empire* (Yale Univ. Press, 1951). An anti-Soviet survey.

G. A. Almond, ed., *The Appeals of Communism* (Princeton Univ. Press, 1954). An interesting symposium.

W. Leonhard, *Child of the Revolution* (Regnery, 1958; *Gateway). Revealing account by a defecting East German Communist official.

M. Einaudi and others, *Communism in Western Europe* (Cornell Univ. Press, 1951). A very illuminating examination of French and Italian communists.

R. L. Wolff, *The Balkans in Our Time* (Harvard Univ. Press, 1956). An informed account.

H. L. Roberts, *Russia and America: Dangers and Prospects* (Harper, 1956; *New American Library). A valuable summary.

C. J. Friedrich and Z. K. Brzezinski, *Totalitarian Dictatorship and Autocracy* (Harvard Univ. Press, 1956). Systematic examination of totalitarian institutions.

W. Z. Laqueur, *The Soviet Union and the Middle East* (Praeger, 1959). A pioneering investigation of a new and important subject.

R. Walker, *China Under Communism* (Yale Univ. Press, 1955). See also books recommended in Chapters 26 and 31.

The Revolt against Imperialism

S. C. Easton, *Rise and Fall of Modern Colonialism* (Praeger, 1962). Informative survey.

V. M. Dean, *The Nature of the Non-Western World* (*Mentor). Sympathetic general appraisal.

J. Strachey, *The End of Empire* (*Praeger), Viewed by a British leftist.

F. S. C. Northrop, *The Meeting of East and West* (*Collier); B. Ward, *The Interplay of East & West* (*Norton). Two general interpretations of the confrontations of cultures.

B. Rowland, *Art in East and West* (*Beacon). A valuable comparative study.

E. O. Reischauer, *The United States & Japan* (*Compass). Admirable survey by a leading authority on Japan.

C. Dubois, *Social Forces in Southeast Asia* (Harvard Univ. Press, 1959). Valuable analysis of a basic aspect of non-Western culture.

P. Spear, *History of India,* Vol. II (*Penguin), and *India, Pakistan, and the West* (*Galaxy). Useful introductions by an expert.

W. N. Brown, *The United States and India and Pakistan,* rev. ed. (Harvard Univ. Press, 1963). Another good introduction.

W. C. Smith, *Islam in Modern History* (*Mentor). Instructive discussion of a difficult topic.

G. Lenczowski, *The Middle East in World Affairs,* 3rd ed. (Cornell Univ. Press, 1962), and *Oil and State in the Middle East* (Cornell Univ. Press, 1960). Respectively, a general review emphasizing the diplomatic aspects, and a particular study, stressing the impact of oil on the host countries.

W. R. Polk and others, *Backdrop to Tragedy: The Struggle for Palestine* (Taplinger, 1959), and D. Peretz, *Israel and the Palestine Arabs* (Middle East Institute, 1958), Balanced accounts of the controversial Arab-Israeli conflict.

D. N. Wilber, *Contemporary Iran* (Praeger, 1963), and P. Avery, *Modern Iran* (Praeger, 1965). Informative introductions to a fascinating and bewildering country.

T. Little, *Egypt* (Praeger, 1958); C. Issawi, *Egypt in Revolution* (Oxford Univ. Press, 1963); G. G. Stevens, *Egypt Yesterday & Today* (*Holt). Three helpful surveys; Issawi's is the most scholarly, Stevens' the most popular.

A. P. Whitaker, *Argentina* (*Spectrum). General introduction by a leading expert on Latin America.

H. F. Cline, *Mexico* (*Oxford). Broad survey by a specialist.

Novels

See titles listed in Chapter 31.

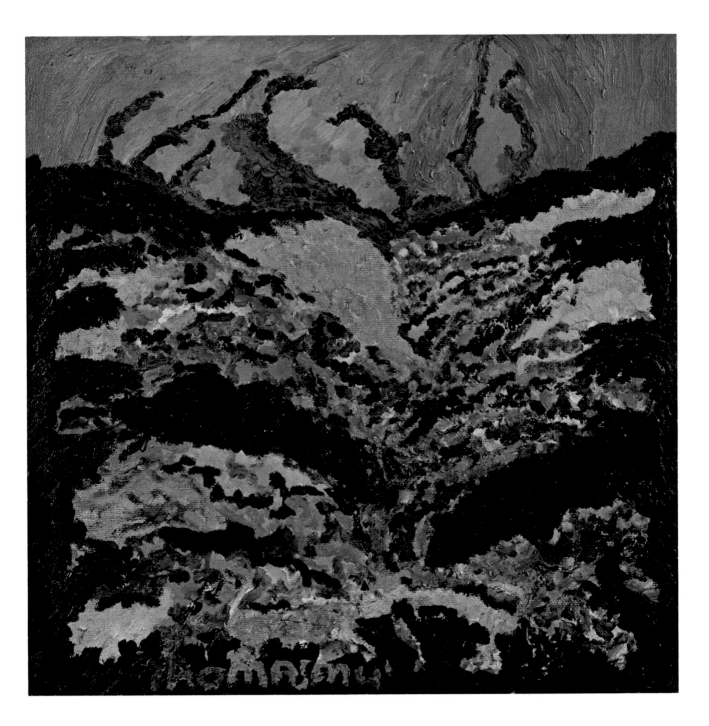

31

The Contemporary World

since 1953

In this chapter we are dealing largely with what most historians would consider "current events," questions on which we cannot pass even temporary judgments because time has not permitted us to view them in proper perspective. Yet we must and do try to reach tentative conclusions about them in the pages of this book, as we do in our daily lives. Two important points deserve consideration here.

In recent years, the world has seemed increasingly to divide itself into a bloc generally pro-communist, a bloc generally pro-western, and a bloc generally uncommitted. Yet at the same time it has become harder and harder to deal with any event in any one of the three blocs without discussing its impact on the other two. The Soviet Union's policies in India have implications for the United States;

a domestic Algerian or Indonesian upheaval affects both Peking and Washington; the death of Mao Tse-tung, when it occurs, will have repercussions in Tanzania and in London. Although this chapter includes sections on each of the three blocs, each section intimately involves members of all three.

Second, the murder of President Kennedy has led to the publication for the Kennedy years, 1960–1963, of a mass of detailed information of the kind ordinarily kept confidential for many years. To fail to take advantage of this information would be absurd. But to use it no doubt creates inevitable distortions: we simply do not know anything like as much about the way American decisions were reached or what other powers said before 1960 or after 1963.

I   The Communist World since the Death of Stalin: The U.S.S.R. at Home

The Soviet Succession

As Josef Stalin grew older, it had become a favorite occupation in the West to speculate on his succession, and on the forces that would be released at the moment of his death. Would it be the Communist party, or the secret police, or the army—the three agencies in the U.S.S.R. that had power of their own—that would emerge supreme? Would it be some combination of two of these against the third? Was this or that member of the Politburo identified with one or another of these three chief agencies? Would the world see ensue a bitter personal rivalry comparable to the struggle between Stalin and Trotsky for the succession to Lenin? If so, would the resulting instability go so far as to disrupt the machinery of Soviet government?

When the moment actually came, in March, 1953, there was at first no evidence of disunity or personal rivalry within the Presidium. Georgi Malenkov, personally close to Stalin, succeeded him as Premier, but surrendered his Communist party secretaryship to Nikita Khrushchev. It was thus clear from the beginning that nobody would immediately inherit all of Stalin's power, and the fact that it would be shared was underlined almost at once by the pronouncements that came from the régime, denouncing the "cult of personality" (i.e., Stalin's former one-man rule), and proclaiming a "collegial" system (i.e., government by committee). But before the end of 1953 there came the official announcement that the dreaded chief of the secret police, and Presidium-member, Beria, always regarded as a potential heir of Stalin, had been executed for treason. The observer might interpret this move, so reminiscent of the purges of Stalin's own era, as an indication that the members of the Presidium were circling around each other with their knives out, or that the Communist party and the army had indeed united to thwart a bid for power on the part of the secret police. The emergence of the war hero, Marshal Zhukov, into positions of some political importance gave color to this view as, perhaps, did the rise to even higher eminence of the "political" general, Bulganin.

But all expectation that a "free-for-all" among the remaining members of the inner circle would ensue, or that the régime might be shaken by personal rivalries, was in error. True, Malenkov vanished from the top post of Premier, to be succeeded by Bulganin; but Malenkov, though he admitted grievous errors, was at first simply demoted to a lower cabinet post, and remained in the Presidium. Some indication of the real locus of power might perhaps be found in the fact that the errors confessed by Malenkov (especially the effort to concentrate collective farms into enormous *agrogorods* or agricultural towns, see p. 562, which had indeed failed) were actually Khrushchev's errors, for which Malenkov now had to take responsibility. Yet, though Khrushchev was certainly very powerful, his fellow-members on the Politburo had great influence, and showed no outward signs of fearing him as all had feared Stalin. On the whole, it appeared that the transfer of power had actually gone quite smoothly in the U.S.S.R. and that among the rulers, in the happy phrase from George Orwell's *Animal Farm* "all were equal, but some were more equal than others."

The Denunciation of Stalin and its Consequences

At a Party Congress, held early in 1956, Khrushchev made a speech in which he not only carried the attack on the "cult of personality" to new heights, but openly denounced Stalin by name, emotionally detailing the ghastly acts of personal cruelty to which the psychopathically suspicious nature of the late dictator had given rise. Khrushchev thus echoed what western observers of the U.S.S.R. had been saying for years. As the details of the speech were leaked out to the Soviet public, there was of course some distress at the smashing of the idol they had worshiped so long; but a good many of them no doubt had all along suspected that Stalin was something less than god-like. So the widespread disorders that some observers were predicting failed to materialize.

But outside the U.S.S.R., the sudden deflation of Stalin and the admission of so many past injustices proved far too strong a brew for the citizens of some of the European satellites to swallow. Anti-communist riots by workers— supposedly the pillars of any communist state—in Poznan, Poland, in June, 1956, were followed by severe strikes, demonstrations, and upheavals in the rest of Poland a few months later. Polish national sentiment was declaring itself, but the uprising remained within the grip of one wing of the Communist party, that led by Wladislaw Gomulka, who

had been purged for alleged Titoism in 1951. Not even the presence in Warsaw of Khrushchev himself and other members of the Soviet Presidium prevented the rise of Gomulka to power, although at one moment the Russians seem to have contemplated using their army to impose their will by force. Yet because the new government in Poland was, after all, a communist government, they allowed it to remain in power.

In Hungary, however, the movement went farther. Starting, like the Polish uprising, as a movement within the Communist party, and spurred by the outspoken writings of many communists who loathed the restraints of Stalinism, the Hungarian movement brought Imre Nagy, a communist like Gomulka, into office as Premier. But then the popular hatred for communism and for the Russians got out of hand, and heroic young men and women flew to arms in Budapest in the hope of ousting the communists and of taking Hungary altogether out of the Soviet sphere. They even denounced the Warsaw Pact, the Russian alliance of eastern European satellites set up by Moscow to oppose NATO. It was then that Khrushchev ordered full-fledged military action. In November, 1956, Soviet tanks and troops, violating an armistice, swept back into Budapest and put down the revolution in blood and fire. A puppet government led by

The Hungarian Revolt: head of the statue of Stalin toppled in downtown Budapest.

Janos Kadar was installed. More than 150,000 Hungarian refugees fled to Austria, to be resettled in various western countries. Despite the Soviet charges that the uprising had been trumped up by the western "imperialists" and "fascists," the West in fact had played no part at all, not daring to help the Hungarians for fear of starting the world war that everybody knew must be avoided.

These momentous events of 1956 in eastern Europe gave Khrushchev's opponents at home an opportunity to unite against his policies. Within the Presidium they had a majority. But Khrushchev was able to rally to his support the larger body of which the Presidium was the inner core, the Central Committee of the Communist Party of the U.S.S.R. A veteran party worker, he had installed his own loyal supporters in all key party posts, repeating Stalin's performance after the death of Lenin (see above, Chapter 26), and emerged from this greatest test not only unscathed, but with his powers immeasurably enhanced (June, 1957). Now the Soviet press denounced the "anti-party group" of Malenkov, Molotov, and Kaganovich, three of the members of Stalin's own entourage. In Stalin's own day, this would have led them to the execution-block, or would have been reported only after they were safely dead. Khrushchev, however, acted differently. All three were expelled from the Presidium and removed from their high posts, but all three were given minor positions at a safe distance from Moscow. Molotov, for example, became ambassador to Outer Mongolia.

Late in 1957, Marshal Zhukov, who had helped Khrushchev win his struggle, and had in return received what looked like valuable concessions limiting the role of party representatives in army affairs, found himself ousted from all his political posts as a "politically deficient figure." During 1958, Bulganin followed him into the discard: he had sided against Khrushchev, and took the consequences. Men of Khrushchev's own choosing replaced them at the top level of the hierarchy. Khrushchev's succession to Stalin's position of undisputed power seemed complete.

The Khrushchev Era:
The Bureaucratic Problems

Yet there were certain differences. Already in his sixties, Khrushchev could hardly hope for a quarter century of dictatorship such as Stalin had had. Moreover, in the very course of making himself supreme, he had deprived himself of some of the instruments available to Stalin. After 1953 he had released millions of captives from prisons and slave-labor camps. Almost everybody in Russia had a relative or friend now freed. These men and women now took jobs, some of them even government jobs. Within a year or two Soviet society at every level except at the very top of the bureaucracy had absorbed these sufferers from tyranny, who would be the first to oppose its reimposition. Khrushchev's own government had severely curbed the secret police. Beria, its chief, was the only major figure to have been executed after Stalin's death. It no longer enjoyed a power almost independent in the state, such as might challenge the party or the army. It no longer was the largest single "employer of labor." Khrushchev himself had emotionally denounced its terror. Though it was still possible to prosecute and even persecute individuals by terrorist means, Stalin's mass terror as a system of government had disappeared. Khrushchev's denunciation of the "cult of personality" required him to protest against the adulatory references to him that came from the Party Congress in 1959, if only because they sounded too much like the old lavish hymns of praise for Stalin.

Instead of terror, Khrushchev embarked on a series of bureaucratic changes within government and party, especially in the organs that controlled the economy. By creating for the Russian Republic, by far the largest and most populous of the republics, a special branch of the Central Committee Secretariat and a set of bureaucratic departments parallel to those that existed for the U.S.S.R. as a whole, he gave this large territory virtually a separate administration, and took complete control of its personnel. In 1963 he took parallel measures for Central Asia and the Transcaucasus. He began a whole series of moves to decentralize party activity; but in 1962, when these were considered to have failed, he re-centralized once more, and then reorganized the party on a production basis: all regional parties at every level below the republic were to be divided into industrial and agricultural wings, receiving coordination only at the level of the republic and the All-Union Central Committees. These efforts within the party were more easily understood in the light of developments within the Soviet economy during these years.

With his eye always upon production, Khrushchev wrestled with the problems of efficiency, output, and morale. Under Stalin, centralization had reached an intolerable tightness. But how far could one decentralize so huge an operation as the Soviet economy and still retain control over local operations? How far could one centralize and still obtain local co-operation, loyalty, and, especially production? Between 1953 and 1957, responsibility for many heavy industries was transferred from the ministries of the central government to those of the individual republics. In May, 1957, a decree abolished many central ministries, and transferred their duties to 105 newly created regional economic councils (sovnarkhoz), in the hope of giving full play to informed on-the-spot decisions, of improving the use of local resources, of consolidating overlapping services, and of reassigning experts from the central government to the grass-roots. Though many regarded the change as an improvement, some factory managers still complained of being bound in a strait-jacket imposed by bureaucrats closer to home than before but still bureaucrats; and many experts lamented or evaded the need to move from the capital to the provinces. "Regionalism"—devotion to regional interests as against national ones—replaced what might be called devotion to one industry ahead of others. But patriots for Armenian industry (to the detriment of other regions) were no more

helpful to the national economy than patriots for the cement industry (to the detriment of other industries).

By 1960 a process of re-centralizing had begun, as republic-level councils appeared in the Russian Republic and two of the other major republics; and in 1961 nineteen new large "natural" regions, cutting across republic lines, were set up to ensure integrated economic development for each region. By the end of 1962, the sovnarkhozes were reduced from 105 to about 40, and new state committees appeared to oversee their work. These committees greatly resembled the old ministries, and were before long reorganized as ministries. The pendulum had swung back almost the entire distance. It was then that all lower levels of the party were reorganized along agricultural-industrial lines, in the apparent effort to make the political functionaries serve the economy more efficiently.

The Khrushchev Era and Beyond: Industry and Agriculture

Khrushchev faced the same problem that had faced all Soviet leaders: how much emphasis could be put on consumer goods, and how much still must be devoted to heavy industry? Though temperamentally more interested in providing consumer goods than Stalin or Malenkov, Khrushchev, who acceded to power during the Fifth Five-Year Plan (1951–1955), made the same choice as they: continued emphasis on the means of production. The sixth plan (1956–1960), setting more ambitious goals than ever before, aimed specifically at catching up with the United States. But the huge expenses involved in the Polish and Hungarian outbreaks ($1 billion worth of credits to eastern Europe alone) forced the Soviet government to shelve the plan. By the end of 1958 they announced a new Seven Year Plan, to run until 1965. Starting from base figures of 500 million tons of coal, 55 million tons of steel, and 113 million tons of oil, output by 1964 had reached 554 million tons of coal, 85 million tons of

Crisscross sowing of wheat on virgin land in the Altai Territory, U.S.S.R.

steel, and 224 million tons of oil. A return to the system of Five-Year Plans was announced for 1966.

Most spectacular were the successes achieved in the field of rocketry and space. It was the U.S.S.R. that successfully launched the first earth-satellite (Sputnik—1957) and that first reached the moon with a rocket (1959). Heavy payloads soared aloft before American engineers could get their lighter ones off the ground. Though inter-continental missiles were apparently more readily available to Moscow earlier than to Washington, American bases in Europe and Africa made our own shorter-range weapons equally dangerous to the U.S.S.R. Each power had enough nuclear weapons and means of delivering them to destroy the other and itself at the same time. Spurred to some degree by the Soviet technical advance, the United States itself embarked in the late fifties on an intensive program of research and development in space. Though the U.S.S.R. got the first man into space, and for some time held the lead in technical

achievements, by the mid-sixties the United States had logged more hours of flight by spaceships with one-man and two-man crews, and had virtually solved the problem of rendezvous in space, while the successful Mars-probe operation of 1965 overshadowed comparable Soviet exploration of the solar system.

Agriculture continued to present the Soviet planners with some of its seemingly most insoluble problems. In 1953 Khrushchev embarked on the "virgin lands" scheme, a crash program to plow under more than 100,000, acres of prairie in the Urals region, Kazakhstan, and Siberia. Although weather favored the operation during its first few years, drought and poor planning and performance led to a clear failure by 1963. Khrushchev then called for an all-out crash program for the production of chemical fertilizers. After the death of Stalin, the régime had continued to amalgamate collective farms. By 1964, their number was down to about 40,000 from an original quarter of a million; and the average size of the new units was far larger, perhaps about 5,000 acres. By 1965, the government recognized that many collectives were now too big.

To increase incentives, the regime in 1958 abolished compulsory deliveries of farm products, the most onerous of the peasant's burdens, and raised agricultural prices. Simultaneously, the government decreed the gradual abolition of the MTS (Machine Tractor Stations, see p. 418) and the sale of the tractors to the individual collective, which the government undertook to subsidize in part. In 1964, for the first time, the government extended its system of old-age and disability pensions to agricultural laborers: men might claim them at age sixty-five after twenty-five years of labor, and women at age sixty after twenty years of labor, in amounts calculated according to earnings. In 1964, the régime removed the ceilings on the size of the private allotment of land allowed to the individual peasant in a collective and on the number of cattle that he might own privately. Yet yields continued low; each year the U.S.S.R. had to buy many millions of tons of grain abroad; animal husbandry in particular caused grave concern, and the régime's agencies thundered against inefficiency and "fascination with administration by fiat."

In the two years after Khrushchev's fall from power in 1964, the Soviet authorities engaged in an open debate about the best way to revise the statutes governing the collective farm (artel) in view of the immense changes since they were used in 1936. Late in 1966 the new statute had not yet been promulgated. But the party and the government ordered the collective farms to guarantee the individual farmers a monthly sum in cash for their work, and to pay in addition for the produce actually received. The state bank would advance the farms the credit where necessary. Some economists were arguing for the introduction of a free market economy; others vigorously defended centralized planning (with improvements). It seemed improbable that the Soviet authorities would abandon their centralized control over the farms to any great degree, but it was clear that they also were recognizing

the importance of incentives and of the individual in the field of agriculture as in many others. Fighting a wordy rear-guard defense of traditional communist economic practices, they were quietly retreating toward certain tested principles associated with capitalism. The Minister of Agriculture in 1966 proclaimed his hope that by constantly raising rural standards of life and education, the new Five-Year Plan would greatly diminish the "intrinsic differences between town and countryside."

Education and the Arts

In 1958 Khrushchev introduced an important change in the Soviet educational system: "polytechnization," which emphasized vocational training and on-the-job experience. This represented in some respects a reversion to the immediate post-revolutionary educational experiments of 1919 and later (see Chapter 26), and a retreat from the 1931 program setting a goal of a ten-year general educational program for all. The régime wanted to avoid producing a "white-handed elite" — young men and young women who had had no practical labor experience, and whose schooling made them feel entitled to continue their education in universities in the hope of pursuing professional careers. Since the universities could accept roughly only one-fifth of school graduates, the remainder found themselves unable to continue, and yet without experience in labor or training in technology, were unwilling to become workers. Khrushchev ordered the universities now to favor applicants who had had practical experience, and also intended to make available evening and extension classes for those whose formal education had stopped.

By the mid-sixties, almost all children in the U.S.S.R. finished the first four years of school (ages seven to eleven), and illiteracy had virtually disappeared. Almost as many finished the second four years (ages eleven to fifteen), which was now combined with "polytechnization." In August, 1964, the conventional next course of three-years (ages fifteen to eighteen) usually taken by only about 40 per cent of Soviet youth, was reduced to two years, and the heavy proportion of time now given to outside industrial work—from one third to one half—was somewhat reduced. Students received pay for their work, which was assigned them in accordance with the requirements of their native region. Soviet universities regularly reserved 20 per cent of their places for the ablest graduates of secondary schools; and the four "physicomathematical" high schools conducted a nation-wide "Olympiad" or talent contest to discover the most promising candidates in these fields.

Khrushchev extended to the field of arts and letters the same partial relaxation that accompanied de-Stalinization in other fields. It took Soviet writers some time to accustom themselves to the idea that it might now be possible to voice dissent: too many had vanished forever at Stalin's whim to make the risk an attractive one. Moreover, convinced Stalinists or party hacks who had grown up under Stalinism lay in wait to attack the innovator. They regarded as heresy all literary experiment or deviation from the old rules of "socialist realism." Khrushchev himself, though eager to destroy the cult of Stalin's personality, was himself opinionated and autocratic, declaring on one occasion that an exhibition of abstract art—entirely forbidden under Stalin—must have been painted by donkey's tails, and keeping artists and writers in constant uncertainty lest new purges break forth. The dangers of self-expression continued great indeed.

In a few individual books and authors we may find indices of the new policies. Ilya Ehrenburg, veteran propagandist for the régime, in *The Thaw* (1955) hailed the relaxation of coercive measures over artists. Vladimir Dudintsev's novel, *Not By Bread Alone* (1956), had as its hero a competent and enthusiastic engineer, whose invention of a new pipe-casting machine was thwarted at every turn by the entrenched bureaucrats. Government-controlled writers' agencies denounced Dudintsev, who retracted his views, and for six or seven years was forced to earn his living by translation only. Boris Pasternak's *Dr. Zhivago* (1958) became a *cause célèbre* throughout the world. Pasternak, a brilliant poet, who had for years confined himself to translating Shakespeare, took advantage of the "thaw" to offer for publication his novel about a doctor who, through all the agonies of the first World War and the Russian Revolution, affirms the freedom of the human soul. Accepted for publication in the U.S.S.R., the novel was sent to Italy to be published. Then the Soviet censors changed their minds, and forced Pasternak to ask that the manuscript in Italy be returned to him. The Italian publisher refused, and versions in Russian, Italian, English, and other languages appeared abroad, and aroused great admiration. In 1958 the Nobel Prize Committee selected Pasternak as the winner of the prize for literature. He accepted. But then the Khrushchev régime reverted to Stalinism: Pasternak's fellow-writers reviled him as a pig and a traitor, and the government threatened him with exile if he accepted the prize. As a patriotic Russian he then declined it.

In the same week that a Soviet physicist accepted the Nobel prize for physics, the régime called the Nobel prize for literature a capitalist invention. And a few years later, Michael Sholokhov, author of the famous Cossack trilogy, *The Quiet Don,* and a personal friend of Khrushchev, accepted the Nobel prize in literature. Pasternak's persecution revealed the limits of the thaw as of 1958. His Jewish origins, his intellectualism, his proclamation of individualism touched hostile chords in Khrushchev himself and in other Soviet officials and writers that made it impossible to publish *Dr. Zhivago* in the U.S.S.R.

But the spirit of individualism, slow to express itself even when liberated in the older generation, found in the 1960's new and more vigorous expression among the younger poets and novelists who had grown up since the Second World War, and for whom the heroic age of the revolution and the early Bolshevik struggles were ancient history. The young Ukrainian poet, Yevtushenko, bitterly denounced Soviet anti-Semitism in his *Babi Yar* (the name of the ravine near Kiev in which the Nazis had massacred thousands of Jews), and declared his identity with the murdered human beings. In another poem he begged the government to double and triple the guard over Stalin's tomb

"So that Stalin may not rise
And, with Stalin
the past.
. . . the ignoring of the people's welfare
The calumnies
The arrests of the innocent."

Former supporters of Stalin, he went on,

"Do not like these times
When the camps are empty
And the halls where people listen to poetry
Are crowded."*

When Yevtushenko recited his verse, the halls were indeed always crowded with eager excited contentious young people, claiming the right to think for themselves. "We've found out," said another young poet, "what it leads to when somebody else does our thinking for us." Often in trouble with the régime, leading a stormy life recorded in an autobiography published first in France without permission, Yevtushenko hailed Fidel Castro and all true Leninists, but constantly needled the Soviet

*Pravda, Oct. 21, 1962.

authorities. Severely disciplined in 1963, he was publicly on the attack again in 1965.

Yevtushenko's mention of "the camps" suggests another new phenomenon in the Soviet writing of the early sixties, the deep interest in the terrible days of Stalin's labor camps and in the suffering of their inmates, reflected in the novel by Solzhenitsyn, *A Day in the Life of Ivan Denisov;* in the sensational memoirs of a Soviet General, Gorbatov, who described the horrible tortures to which he, like many others, had been subjected on mere suspicion; and in the songs of the camps that the students at the universities had begun now to sing to their guitars—bitter, mocking, cynical, and often deeply moving. Khrushchev viewed with some apprehension the flood of fiction about the camps that came pouring into the publishing houses, and only a few novels and stories were published, but even these marked an astonishing new trend. Often the anxious Khrushchev would try to remind the younger generation of the glorious revolutionary past through which their elders had triumphantly lived. He declared—as if in answer to their demands for full freedom—that even under full communism it would not be possible to give complete liberty to the individual, who would continue "like a bee in a hive" to make his contribution to society.

After Khrushchev's ouster in October, 1964 (see p. 602), his successors denounced him for

Left: Yevgeny Yevtushenko photographed at his home in Moscow; *right:* Andrei Sinyavsky (foreground) and Yuli Daniel at their trial in Moscow, February, 1966.

interfering in intellectual life, but here, as elsewhere, they did not depart very far from his policies. Writers of the Stalinist type kept on the offensive; for example, a novel called *The Plant Louse* violently denounced modern painters and painting. It received a harsh review from a critic named Andrei Sinyavsky. And in September, 1965, Sinyavsky was arrested along with another writer named Yuli Daniel. Sinyavsky, said the government, had written under the pseudonym of Abram Tertz and smuggled abroad for publication anti-Soviet fiction and an essay that had been creating a sensation for over a year; and Daniel, under the pseudonym of Nikolai Arzhak, had committed the same crime.

Indeed, Tertz's *The Trial Begins,* dealing with the purges, gave a candid and revolting picture of the life of the Soviet leaders under Stalin; his novel *Lyubimov* (translated into English as *The Makepeace Experiment*) dealt with a one-man revolt against communism in a small Russian town; and his essay *On Socialist Realism* damned what was still the official literary doctrine of the régime. Arzhak's *Moscow Calling* was a fantasy in which the Soviet government set aside one day on which murder was allowed. Foreign readers, who had been hailing Tertz for his irony, subtlety, and love of freedom had been wondering who he could be. It came as a surprise that Sinyavsky, not a Jew, but descendant of a family of Old Be-lievers (Volume I, p. 379), had chosen a Jewish pseudonym. But this too was explained in January, 1966, when an American periodical, *The New Leader*, published an English translation of a popular Russian song about a thief named Abram Tertz and his girl Sonka, a prostitute. From this ballad, apparently, Sinyavsky had chosen the name. In 1966 Sinyavsky and Daniel went on trial. Soviet officialdom railed at them for publishing abroad, for suggesting the prevalence of anti-Semitism in the U.S.S.R., and for their frankness in treating sexual matters, which ran counter to the prevailing Soviet literary prudery. Their sentences served as a warning to other Soviet writers, and aroused much protest inside the U.S.S.R. and out.

When students demonstrated on behalf of the arrested writers, the régime reverted to a practice sometimes followed by Tsar Nicholas I (Chapter 22), who had confined rebellious intellectuals to insane asylums on the pretext that they must be crazy. It was clear that the "intelligentsia," now about 20 per cent of the Soviet working population, posed for its masters a continuing problem whose dimensions, during the continued thaw and occasional light freeze, grew clearer than ever. To an American observer, Soviet youth in 1967—the "new right" in the U.S.S.R.—showed signs of resembling its American opposite numbers, the "new left" in the United States.

II   Soviet Confrontation with the West

Stalin's heirs inherited formidable powers, but they also inherited formidable problems. Any attack that threatened the vital interests of the United States, with its thermonuclear arsenal and its superior industrial resources, might well touch off the ultimate disaster. A policy of probing to see just which interests the United States considered vital had already led to the Korean War. Continued tension between the two super-powers required the U.S.S.R. to continue to devote its resources to guns rather than to butter. To relax the tension would theoretically have meant more butter, but would in turn raise the danger that the U.S.S.R. would lose its position as leader of the world communist movement. China, with its determination to seize Taiwan and to expand in Asia, might seize the leadership of revolutionary forces at least in Asia, and would represent the Russians as old and tired, no longer true Leninists. In the end it proved to be impossible for Krushchev to hold all these threats in balance, and the choices he eventually was forced to make led to a major split in the communist world.

In the years immediately following Stalin's death, Soviet foreign policy continued along Stalinist lines. The Russians moved into the Middle East with new vigor. Here they had the advantage of being able to deal with Gamal Abdel Nasser, the new ruler of Egypt and an inveterate enemy of the West, which he associated not only with past colonialism but with support for Israel. Czechoslovak and Russian arms flowed to Egypt, and Russian technicians followed. Perhaps the high point of Soviet influence was reached during the Suez affair in 1956 (Section IV). When the United States joined the U.S.S.R. in denouncing the British and French attack, however, it became impossible for Nasser to lump all the western powers together. Soon Nasser began to learn that Russian influence usually followed Russian favors. He experienced some disillusion during the summer of 1958, when revolution broke out in Iraq, where Soviet-sponsored communists were opposing Nasser's own pan-Arab aims. Prompt American intervention in Lebanon and British intervention in Jordan in 1958 may have temporarily countered the threat of the spread of Soviet influence beyond Iraq. It was the Russians who provided the aid that made possible the high dam at Aswan and much armament for the Egyptian armies, but Nasser remained unaligned with either major bloc. In the Middle East and in other "undeveloped" areas, notably Africa, the U.S.S.R. had begun to challenge the West as the supplier of economic and technological aid. A new chapter in the Cold War had opened.

In eastern Europe, Soviet influence continued stable until Khrushchev's policies of de-Stalinization at home touched off the Polish and Hungarian uprisings (see p. 583). But even before this, Khrushchev had departed from Stalinism by making a great effort to heal the breach with Tito. In May, 1955, he went in person to Belgrade, and not only publicly apologized for the quarrel, taking the blame upon the U.S.S.R., but openly agreed that "differences in the concrete forms of developing socialism are exclusively matters for the people of the country concerned," which seemed to echo Tito's own views. Relations between Tito and Moscow were temporarily improved, although the Yugoslavs never abandoned their ties to the West. Khrushchev even went so far as to declare that many prominent victims of the "Titoist" purges had been executed wrongly, and abolished the Cominform, the body that ostensibly had started the qurrel with Tito. But in making these admissions and healing the quarrel Stalin had started, Khrushchev had opened the door to the Polish and Hungarian troubles that soon began; Soviet military intervention in Hungary showed Tito and the rest of the world how limited was Khrushchev's willingness and ability to permit free choices to other communist states. Tito denounced the Soviet intervention against Nagy, though he was frightened by the wholly anti-communist character that the Hungarian revolt subsequently took on, and failed to oppose the decisive Soviet operations that put an end to the uprising.

For a second time, relations between Moscow and Tito were strained. They were patched up again in the summer of 1957; the Soviets once more hoped that Tito would again accept Moscow's leadership of the world communist movement. But when in November the Russians invited representatives of all the world's Communist parties to Moscow to celebrate the fortieth anniversary of the Russian Revolution, and produced a declaration of twelve Communist parties denouncing "revisionism"—as Tito's views had come to be known—Tito flatly refused to sign. Indeed he published his own counter-program declaring that each communist nation should make its own decisions freely. The old quarrel was renewed for the third time. Tito would not re-enter a world communist union led by Russia. Khrushchev's efforts had failed. Moreover, the Poles signed the declaration with obvious reluctance, and Gomulka continued to insist on autonomy for his government in internal and party affairs.

The harshness of the onslaught against revisionism and Khrushchev's acceptance of defeat in his efforts to win the Yugoslavs by softness reflected Chinese influence. After the Polish and Hungarian revolts, the Chinese communist leaders had been invited to visit those countries, and lay down the line; they now appeared very eager to play a role in formulating world communist ideology, and displayed a strong preference (probably for internal reasons) for Stalinist orthodoxy and repression. By the spring of 1958, the Chinese and Khrushchev himself had declared that Stalin's original denunciation of the Yugoslavs back in 1948 has been correct after all. In June, 1958, the Soviet government underlined this decision in grim fashion when it announced the executions of Imre Nagy and other leaders of the Hungarian uprising, in violation of solemn promises of safe-conduct. The executions probably were intended also to serve as a warning to Gomulka not to try to push Polish independence too far. Soon afterward, Gomulka did denounce revisionism, and criticized both Nagy and the Yugoslavs, but in a tone far milder than that employed by the Russians and Chinese.

All the eastern European satellites were bound together in the "Council for Mutual Economic Aid" (Comecon) established in 1949, which took measures to standardize machinery and coordinate economic policies, and issued blasts against western European efforts at cooperation like the Common Market and Euratom. The Asian communist régimes also collaborated. Yugoslavia never was a member, and after 1958 was no longer invited to send observers. Khrushchev had not solved a problem that indeed seemed essentially insoluble: how to maintain totalitarian authority over the European satellites while simultaneously trying to relax Stalinist methods.

Berlin

But the central concern of Soviet foreign policy in Europe remained Germany. In East Germany (DDR, *Deutsche Demokratische Republik*) it had created its most industrially productive European satellite, now fully geared into the Comecon, and expected to make a long-term contribution to the development of the communist world. Except for a brief but violent workers' riot in East Berlin in 1953, the German communist puppets had succeeded in repressing the population's aversion to Soviet and communist rule. Moreover, strategically the DDR was of great importance to the U.S.S.R.: control over East Germany enabled the Russians to keep Poland surrounded, and helpless to achieve more than a token autonomy. Yet full domination over this important satellite was impeded by the fact that the United States, Britain, and France each retained a zone of occupation in Berlin, deep in the heart of the DDR, and accessible by subway from East Berlin. Every year, thousands of East Germans showed how they felt about communism by escaping into West Berlin. The East German population actually declined by 2,000,000 between 1949 and 1961. For those who stayed behind in the DDR, West Berlin provided an example of prosperity and free democratic government that acted more effectively on their minds than any mere propaganda.

This situation accounted for Khrushchev's determination to get the western powers out of Berlin. The method he proposed in 1958 and later years was thoroughly Stalinist: he threatened to sign a peace treaty with the puppet government of East Germany, never recognized by the West; to turn over to it the communications to Berlin; and to support it in any effort it might then make to cut these communications and force the western powers out. Western refusal to accept this highhanded and unilateral abrogation of agreements concluded during World War II led to a prolonged diplomatic crisis during 1959, in which the U.S.S.R. several times postponed a final date of decision, but made no real concession to the western view.

All the powers had come to realize that no problem was more critical. The West could hardly permit the U.S.S.R. to recreate the conditions it had fought during the airlift of 1948 (see Chapter 30). Nor could it accept the suggestion that, once western troops were removed, Berlin would be a "free city." Defenseless and surrounded by communist territory, Berlin and its 2,000,000 "free" citizens, it feared, would soon be swallowed up. Moreover, the negotiations proposed by the U.S.S.R., whereby the DDR would thereafter "confederate" with the West German Federal Republic, aroused the gravest doubts. How could a state that was a full member of the western system of NATO federate with one that belonged to the Soviet system's Warsaw Pact? How could a state that stood for free capitalist development federate with one completely communized? How could a parliamentary state responsibly governed by a multi-party system with checks and balances federate with a communist totalitarian state? It seemed probable that Khrushchev did not believe in the possibility of the confederation he was proposing, and hoped instead that any possible union of the Germanies would be discredited, and that the DDR, with full control over Berlin, would emerge as a permanent Soviet satellite. But even a Soviet success in Berlin short of this complete victory would have meant that the West had in some measure at least recognized East Germany, which in turn would have severely disturbed West German stability, and disrupted NATO.

U-2, The Wall, Testing, Cuba

While the Berlin threat persisted, exchanges continued between Moscow and Washington. Khrushchev's two deputies, Mikoyan and Kozlov, visited the United States, and Vice-President Nixon visited the U.S.S.R., where he and Khrushchev had a famous confrontation in a model kitchen that was part of an American exhibit. President Eisenhower and Khrushchev agreed to exchange visits, and Khrushchev actually made a dramatic, unprecedented, and highly publicized tour of the United States. When the leaders of the great powers met at the "Summit" in Paris (May 1960), tensions, however, were once again inflamed by the U-2 incident: a Soviet missile brought down a light-weight extremely fast American plane which had been taking high altitude photographs of Soviet territory, and the Russians had captured the pilot unharmed.

After an initial denial, President Eisenhower found himself obliged to acknowledge the truth of the charge and to accept responsibility for the episode; and this ended both the summit meeting and the plans for his own visit to the U.S.S.R.

Khrushchev's next move against Berlin came early in the administration of Eisenhower's successor, John F. Kennedy. In June, 1961, when the two leaders met in Vienna, Kennedy found Khrushchev adamant in insisting that the U.S.S.R. would unilaterally abrogate the agreements on Berlin and sign the treaty with East Germany before the end of the year. As the tension mounted during the summer, with Kennedy and Khrushchev both unyielding on the basic position, the number of refugees fleeing East Berlin rose to a thousand a day. On August 13, East German forces cut the communications between East and West Berlin and began to build a barrier—the Berlin Wall—to prevent further departures. Taken by surprise, the United States yet realized that it could not legitimately resort to arms to prevent the closing of the East Germans' own border, and confined its response to protests, to a military build-up, and to the mission of Vice-President Lyndon Johnson to Berlin, where he reassured the West Berliners of America's unshaken resolve to preserve their status unchanged. The wall itself became the symbol of repression, of a government that had to imprison its own people to keep them at home. Occasional hair-raising escapes and poignant recaptures or shootings continued to take place along the wall's length. But the crisis proved to be over. Khrushchev had backed away from unilateral abrogation of the Berlin treaty.

As if to warn the world not to underestimate Soviet belligerence, however, Khrushchev announced on August 30, 1961, that the U.S.S.R. would resume atomic testing in the atmosphere, which had been stopped by both powers in 1958. In the two months that followed, the Russians exploded 30 huge bombs, whose total force considerably exceeded all previous American, British, and French explosions. After months of agonizing scientific and political review of the problem,

President Kennedy decided that the United States too had to conduct a new round of tests, unless Khrushchev would agree to a treaty banning all tests. When Khrushchev refused, the new American tests began late in April, 1962. All during the months that followed, conversations on disarmament, including of course arrangements for the banning of future tests, continued with the Russians at Geneva.

During the summer of 1962, Khrushchev also decided to place Soviet missiles with nuclear warheads in Cuba, where American foreign policy had failed dismally in the Bay of Pigs fiasco of the year before. The increasingly pro-communist Castro Cuban government may not have asked for them, but in any case accepted them. Soviet officers were to retain control over their use. Their installation would effectively have doubled the Soviet capacity to strike directly at the United States, but the chief threat was political: when known, the mere presence of these weapons ninety miles from Florida would shake the confidence of all other nations in the American capacity to protect even the United States. It would enable Khrushchev to blackmail America on the question of Berlin. American military intelligence discovered the sites and photographed them from the air. Khrushchev tried to deceive Kennedy into thinking the Soviet pur-

pose was simply to help the Cubans resist a new invasion from the United States, which he professed to believe threatened.

Once he knew certainly that the missiles were in Cuba, Kennedy could not allow their installation to continue. The only course of action at first seemed an air strike, which might well have touched off the world war that both sides wished to avert but that Khrushchev seemed to be courting. Kennedy instead found a measure that would prevent the further delivery of missiles: a sea blockade ("quarantine") of the island, and combined it with the demand that the missiles already in Cuba be removed. He thus gave Khrushchev a way to avoid world war, and a chance to save face. Adlai Stevenson at the United Nations put the American case impressively. The President ordered that troops be massed in Florida ready to invade Cuba if necessary, but continued to correspond with Khrushchev, emphasizing the American eagerness for a peaceful solution. After several days of almost unbearable tension, Khrushchev backed down, agreed to halt work on the missile sites in Cuba and to remove the offensive weapons there, while reaffirming the Soviet wish to continue discussions about disarmament. Soviet ships at sea with new missiles turned back to home ports.

Berlin: the historic Brandenburg gate behind the new wall.

The Test-Ban Treaty

President Kennedy did not crow or allow American officials to crow. Khrushchev had moved aggressively in an area close to the United States, where Soviet national security was not threatened. By lying about the missiles, he had destroyed whatever case he might otherwise have had in world opinion. Kennedy did not misread the event by concluding that the U.S.S.R. would back down if Soviet vital interests were affected or if the U.S.S.R. had what it regarded as a good case. He made the American victory as little painful as possible by exploiting it only to push for a further relaxation in tensions. In November, 1962, only a month after the Cuban crisis, Khrushchev in Moscow called for a return to concentration on Soviet domestic economic problems.

Months of preparatory and often discouraging interchanges led in July, 1963, to the signing by the United States, the U.S.S.R., and Great Britain of a treaty banning nuclear weapons tests in the atmosphere, in outer space, or under water. Ratified by the Senate in September, the treaty subsequently received the adherence of more than seventy nations, though France and China—a fledgeling and a prospective nuclear power—would not sign it. Hailed as a "first step" toward reducing the likelihood of a new world war, the treaty none the less aroused the unhappiness of the West Germans: the East Germans would surely adhere to it, and the very presence of their official signature on the same document seemed to Bonn to be elevating the prestige of East Germany.

As a next step toward peace Khrushchev proposed a non-aggression pact to be signed between NATO and the Warsaw Pact nations. This would have effectively put an end to the American plan for a Multilateral Force (MLF), a naval force armed with nuclear weapons and manned by mixed crews from the NATO countries, which in turn meant that, however international the force, some Ger-

man officers and men would have obtained access to nuclear weapons. The plan appealed to the Germans, and frightened the Russians. A non-aggression pact would also have tended to weaken NATO and enabled the U.S.S.R. to hope that the French and Italian Communist parties might emerge once more to neutralize western Europe. West German apprehension at the possibility of a non-aggression pact no doubt contributed to the failure of that Soviet plan, while Soviet apprehension at the possibility of MLF no doubt contributed to the eventual failure (1965) of that American plan.

The installation of the "hot line" communications system between the White House and the Kremlin so that the leaders of the two countries might talk to each other in case of need, the sale of surplus American wheat to the Russians, and President Kennedy's proposal that the United States and the U.S.S.R. might combine their efforts for a moon-shot, which was not accepted, marked the final few months of the Kennedy administration. Despite these limited gains, Khrushchev in this period was proclaiming that "peaceful coexistence" would be impossible in the field of ideology: i.e., that the communists expected to continue their campaign against the capitalist world by words at least, and by aiding "progressive" revolutionary forces everywhere. The assassination of President Kennedy in November, 1963, by a psychopathic young American who had lived in the U.S.S.R., married a Russian, and flirted with Castroism, certainly alarmed the Soviet authorities, who took great pains to assist the American agencies investigating the murder; the act proved to be that of an individual madman and not a plot.

Rumania Disengages

In the years between 1959 and 1964, while Khrushchev was failing to win the struggle over Berlin or to redeem his failure there by blackmail in Cuba, his policies had also led to new trouble within his own eastern European bloc. In 1958–1959, Comecon called for a "specialization" plan, in accordance with which the more developed countries would concentrate on heavy industry, and Rumania in particular on the production of raw materials (chiefly food and oil). The Rumanian government, communist though it was, protested, pointing to its already considerable achievements in heavy industry, and in December, 1961, openly refused to accept the "principles" of the "international socialist division of labor," issued at the twenty-second Congress of the CPSU. All through 1962 the disagreement persisted, with Khrushchev trying and failing to force the Rumanians into line. Emphasizing the need for equal treatment and for the observance of national sovereignty, the Rumanians assumed an independent position within the communist bloc. They increased their trade with the non-communist world, and they remained neutral in the Soviet-Chinese quarrel (see p. 597). In July, 1963, the Russians gave in on the economic question, and sanctioned Rumania's continued efforts to build a steel industry, while postponing the economic integration of the bloc until 1966, by which time Rumania would be entitled to the same status as Czechoslovakia and Poland.

Though the disagreement arose in the field of economic planning, it eventually extended much farther. Soviet propaganda called for integrating the lower Danube region — which would have meant taking territory from Rumania — and denied that the Rumanians had contributed to the Allied cause in World War II. The Rumanians claimed full credit for their own "liberation from fascism," and — most important — even dared to demand the return to Rumania of the provinces of Bessarabia and northern Bukovina, annexed by the U.S.S.R. in 1940 (Chapter 26). Yugoslav-Rumanian co-operation became an important part of Rumanian policy. The signs that old-fashioned territorial nationalism still throve in Rumania raised the possibility that Hungary might one day revive against the Rumanians its old demands for Transylvania.

The "Bloc" in 1966

Rumanian "disengagement" provided certainly the most dramatic episodes in eastern Europe in the early 1960's, but it was accompanied almost everywhere else by a liberalizing trend. In Hungary a milder criminal code (1961) and a general amnesty for political prisoners (1963) preceeded acts (1963 and 1964), enabling those who had fled from the country between 1945 and 1963 to return to Hungary to visit, and to realize money on property they had had to leave behind. Increased tourism, wider trade with the West, better living conditions, even a notable success with agricultural collectivization, a new agreement with the Vatican concerning the Hungarian Church, and improved education all spoke of a combination of relaxed terror and general improvement under Premier Kadar, in 1956 a Soviet puppet but by 1966 apparently a genuinely popular figure.

In Czechoslovakia, most Stalinist of the satellites except for East Germany, the winds of change began to blow in 1963–1964, largely because of economic failure and discontent. Economic decentralization and liberalization were the first steps, despite considerable entrenched opposition. In Poland, however, which had after Gomulka's success in 1957 enjoyed more freedom of discussion and contact with the West than any other communist country, the trend was reversed. In economic planning, in agriculture, in education, in religious policies, the government tightened the strings somewhat, probably to appease hardliners within the party.

Yugoslavia, on the other hand, freed from Stalinist control five years before Stalin died, continued (in the Constitution of 1963) to give more powers of decision to local organizations of workers and producers, strengthening the judiciary, limiting the terms of office of each of the new specialized five chambers (!) of the federal assembly, and providing that the successor of Tito, (President for life but 73 years old in 1966) should serve no more than two consecutive four year terms. The Communist party (League of Yugoslav Communists) retained its hold on all branches of the national life, but life in Yugoslavia was freeer than anywhere else in the communist world. A sensational purge of the secret police in 1966, in which Aleksandar Ranković, widely regarded as Tito's most probable heir, fell from power, opened what would probably be a new period of serious further reform and of increased efforts to arrange a succession agreeable to Tito before Tito himself should actually die.

III   The U.S.S.R., China, and America in Asia

During the years between Stalin's death in 1953 and Khrushchev's denunciation of Stalin in 1956, Chinese-Soviet relations were basically amicable, and Chinese influence rose in the communist world. The Russians returned Port Arthur and Dairen to China in 1955. But when Khrushchev denounced Stalin without consulting Mao, the Chinese disapproved of the new emphasis on peaceful co-existence. They also wanted far more economic aid than the U.S.S.R. had been able or willing to provide, and especially aid in developing nuclear weapons. In 1957 Mao experimented briefly with a liberated public opinion ("let one hundred flowers bloom"), but soon returned to, and remained on, a thoroughly "leftist" and militant course at home and abroad.

Chinese intervention in eastern Europe in 1956 and 1957, though indecisive, gave them their first role in European communist affairs. They continued to denounce Tito and the Yugoslavs as "revisionists," and to try to block Khrushchev's reconciliation with them. At home, doubtful of increased Soviet aid, they embarked on forced-draft industrialization, the "great leap forward," with its backyard blast-furnaces, and its mass collectivization of the "people's communes," with disastrous results to both industry and agriculture. The Russians disapproved of their policies, and the latent disagreement between the two communist giants now began to emerge.

While the Chinese communists strove to win influence within the Communist parties of the world and to use it against the U.S.S.R., Khrushchev in 1959 told Peking that the U.S.S.R would not furnish China with atomic weapons, and launched what proved to be an unsuccessful intrigue against Mao with some dissident members of the Chinese communist leadership. The Chinese bombardment of Quemoy and Matsu (1958), the savage conquest of Tibet, and—as a result—the first invasion of Indian territory in Ladakh (September, 1959) were apparently undertaken without consultation between China and the U.S.S.R.; and the Russians publicly declared themselves to be neutral as between the Chinese and the Indians. Though the Chinese-Russian quarrel was not yet completely out in the open, and though the Chinese tactic was to avoid a complete and public rupture, western observers had already begun to take note of it, but many wondered whether it might not be a deceptive tactic of some sort.

It was not. In a series of articles ("Long Live Leninism") in April, 1960, the Chinese attacked the Russian ideological position. Khrushchev replied at a secret session of the Rumanian Party Congress (June), and withdrew all Soviet technicians from China. In November, 1960, the quarrel grew worse (privately) at the Congress of eighty-one Communist parties held in Moscow. The Chinese refused to call a halt to their efforts to take over other parties, and the Russians refused to allow the Chinese to share in the leadership of the world communist movement.

Along the way, the Chinese picked up a European satellite: Albania, smallest and poorest of the Balkan countries, with a population well under two million people, and a long historic tradition of heroism, but suffering from all forms of backwardness in a modern industrialized world. The Albanian Communist party, trained and marshaled by emissaries of Tito during World War II into a guerrilla movement, had taken power in the country after the war, and had thrown off Yugoslav domination after Tito's rebellion from Stalin in 1948. More than anything else the Albanian communists feared a renewed subjection to the Yugoslavs. When Khrushchev made his repeated efforts to conciliate Tito, the Albanians looked for a counterweight to the U.S.S.R., and found it in the Chinese. Though Khrushchev apparently tried to instigate a coup against the Albanian government, he failed, and from 1960 on, Albania belonged to the Chinese camp, and took the lead in praising Stalin's memory and denouncing Khrushchev at every turn. By the end of 1961 Khrushchev broke relations with the Albanian régime. The Chinese Foreign Minister, in Moscow, countered by defending Albania and placing a wreath on Stalin's tomb. Though to have Albania as a satellite was an economic liability, the Chinese could rejoice in having subtracted a European communist state from the Russian orbit. As Tito continued to play the role, for the Chinese, of chief traitor to the communist cause, Khrushchev's own relations with Tito grew correspondingly warmer.

In the very midst of the 1962 crisis over Soviet missiles in Cuba, the Chinese chose to attack India. At the time, it was difficult to interpret this move as anything but brutal opportunism designed to show the world that the Chinese were supreme in Asia. In retrospect it seems to have been intended as a limited operation undertaken chiefly to enable the Chinese to seize the border regions in Ladakh, including important road communications. The Chinese had long maintained that the Indian frontier in this area actually included territory that belonged to them. After smashing through the Indian defenses, the Chinese withdrew when they had what they wanted; but the U.S.S.R., though ostensibly neutral, was clearly, like the United States, pro-Indian.

By 1963, pro-Soviet delegates at communist congresses were publicly shouting down Chinese speeches. The Chinese intensified their disruptive activities within world communist bodies; built up their own organizations in Africa and Asia; and began to make threatening remarks about their boundary with the U.S.S.R. When the test-ban treaty was signed (see p. 595), the Chinese called the Russians traitors to the international communist movement. Though Khrushchev tried to arrange for a general public excommunication of the Chinese by other communist parties, he was unable to bring it off, because the Rumanian, Polish, and Italian Communist parties refused to go along, not so much because they were pro-Chinese—they were not—as because they feared the precedent: if the Soviet Union could rally the communist parties of the world to discipline the Chinese in 1963, might they not in some later year try in the same way to discipline Rumanians, Poles, or Italians? During 1964, Mao not only called for Khrushchev's removal, but accused the Russians of illegally occupying eastern European and Japanese territory. By the time of Khrushchev's fall in October, 1964, the breach between China and the U.S.S.R. seemed irreparable.

The Soviet-Chinese Quarrel: Ideology

Behind the series of incidents that revealed the mounting quarrel to the world there lay profound theoretical disagreements between the Russian and the Chinese communist leaders about the best way to impose communist control over the peoples of Africa, Asia, and Latin America. The Chinese favored direct sponsorship of local communist revolutionary movements, the Russians "peaceful" economic competition with the capitalist world for the loyalty and admiration of the emerging peoples. Khrushchev believed that undeveloped countries would be attracted by the magnitude of Soviet economic achievement, and that the Russians could then support indigenous revolutionary movements, in which the communists might at first, play a subordinate role, but could then be helped to take over. He argued that the existence of nuclear weapons and the fear of general war would inhibit the "imperialists" from resisting these efforts. The communists would win the competition without world war, while helping along local wars of national liberation—i.e., revolutions at least partly under communist control. The

Chinese refused to grant that nuclear weapons had changed war or imperialism, and regarded war as inevitable. "The bourgeoisie," they maintained, "will never step down from the stage of history of its own accord."

The disagreement, then, centered not on ends but on means. Khrushchev maintained that the U.S.S.R. would continue to support any Communist party that had decided the time was ripe for war; but he emphasized the need for correct analysis of all situations and the dangers of premature wars. He also argued that the neutralist countries were actually an asset for communism: they deprived the imperialists of support they would otherwise have had. Soviet help to their economies struck new blows at imperialism: though Nasser was no communist, Soviet aid to him in building the Aswan dam would outlast Nasser and redound to the advantage of communism by showing the Egyptian masses what it could do. Khrushchev compared the economic competition between the U.S.S.R. and the United States to an "international class struggle." The December, 1960, conference of 81 Communist parties issued a Soviet-sponsored statement recognizing the existence of "national democracies," an intermediate form of society between capitalism and socialism, a society which has already had its "anti-feudal bourgeois democratic revolution," but not yet its proletarian revolution. No state had by 1966 yet earned the classification of a national democracy, although Indonesia, Guinea, Ghana, and Mali were considered prime prospects. Castro's Cuba declined the title.

The Chinese insisted that communists alone must take charge of all revolutionary movements from the beginning, and claimed that aid to non communist countries was a delusion. They particularly objected to Soviet aid to India, their own enemy. They opposed disarmament. They had expected Khrushchev to freeze Soviet living standards at a low level and to invest the savings in helping the Chinese catch up, but of course Khrushchev preferred to let his own people enjoy some of the fruits of their own labors. Remembering their own success as a guerrilla operation that first came to control the countryside and then moved in on the cities, Chinese theoreticians extended this lesson to the whole globe, regarding Asia, Africa, and Latin America—the underdeveloped areas—as the countryside, and Europe and North America as the cities. From the massed peoples of the backward continents the communists would mount an offensive against the peoples of the developed industrial world and conquer them. How seriously even the authors of this startling theory believed what they said we cannot know.

One additional factor, seldom mentioned, but extremely important in the Chinese-Russian quarrel, was simply that of race. The Russians—though they would deny the charge—disliked and feared the Chinese, the yellow peril on their borders. The huge masses of Chinese—soon inexorably to number one billion people—crowded into territory adjacent to the vast sparsely populated regions of the U.S.S.R., to some of which they were already laying claim—would frighten any reasonable government even if the threat came from fellow whites; but since it came from yellow men, the fear increased. Despite their protestations to the contrary, the Russians were extremely race-conscious, as the experiences of many African students in Moscow testified, and they reserved for the Chinese the deepest dislike of all. The Chinese used race openly as a weapon in their efforts to win support among other Asians, Africans, and Latin Americans, lumping the Soviet Union with the United States as symbols of the evil white intention to continue dominating the world. Convinced of their own superiority to the rest of mankind, the Chinese were racists too.

Southeast Asia: Vietnam and Laos

A special problem for the Chinese, Russians, and Americans arose in Southeast Asia as the result of the revolt of the Viet Minh communist forces against France that broke out in French Indo-China with the end of World War II in 1945 (Chapter 30). During the Korean War, the United States, fearing that the Chinese communists would strike across the border into northern Indo-China, gave substantial assistance to the French, but the French did not permit any American share in political and military policy-making. In 1954, with the French defeated after the fall of their stronghold of Dienbienphu, a conference of powers at Geneva gave independence to the Indochinese provinces of Cambodia and Laos. Vietnam, the third and largest portion of the former French colony, was divided along the seventeenth parallel into a northern section with its capital at Hanoi under the government of the Communist Viet Minh party, whose leader was the veteran communist Ho Chi Minh, and a southern portion with its capital at Saigon under a nationalist leader, Ngo Dinh Diem, who was a Catholic. The Geneva agreements guaranteed free elections. The United States did not sign the agreements, but endorsed their purport, and retained the hope that the area, in which it had already invested more than four billion dollars, might not fall to the communists.

Between 1954 and 1959 Ngo Dinh Diem struggled with problems of fantastic difficulty: creating the bureaucratic machinery for a new régime, restoring order in territory that had long been held by communist guerrillas and was now held by dissident sects, providing for almost a million refugees from the communist north, resettling in the countryside millions of peasants who had fled to the cities. After the departure of the French in 1956, the Americans assumed the responsibility for assisting in the solution of these problems with financial aid and technical advice. Diem put down the dissident sects. New agencies accomplished much in dealing with the refugees, and in building new railroads, increasing rice, rubber, and electric-power production, and distributing land to 300,000 peasant families. American aid helped triple the number of trained teachers and quadruple the number of children enrolled in the schools, while drastically reducing malaria.

But Diem failed politically. He and his immediate family governed despotically and could not command widespread political support. He cancelled the scheduled elections.

In 1958 and 1959, communist-led guerrilla activity broke out again. Now known as the Viet Cong, the guerrillas set up a National Liberation Front. In September, 1960, Ho Chi Minh, no doubt convinced that Diem's economic successes had rendered South Vietnam secure except from war, endorsed the Viet Cong movement, which he was already supplying with arms and training. Using terror in the villages as a weapon, the guerrillas by 1961 were moving almost at will in South Vietnam, overrunning much of the countryside, murdering, looting, and burning.

Meanwhile, in neighboring Laos, strategically important but nationally a mere collection of unwarlike Buddhist tribes, where traditionally a small clique of families alone indulged in politics, one faction, communist-oriented, supported by Ho Chi Minh, and calling itself Pathet Lao, seized the northeastern portion of the country in 1953. The United States tried with massive financial and military aid to build a national Laotian army and establish a firm régime, but succeeded largely in creating corruption and factionalism. The head of the government, Souvanna Phouma (who was the brother-in-law of the head of the Pathet Lao), reached agreement with him in 1957 to set up a coalition government and neutralize the country, absorbing the Pathet Lao into the army. This the United States resisted, ousting Souvanna, and introducing the right-wing Phoumi Nousavan. By 1960, Souvanna was working with the Russians, and a portion of the army under the neutralist Kong Le (not a communist) was working with the Pathet Lao. Soviet airlifts of supplies to their side enhanced the possibility that the little country would be lost to the communists, and that Thailand and Burma—to say nothing of South Vietnam—would be endangered also.

President Kennedy sought for ways to neutralize Laos, and to convince the U.S.S.R. that if his efforts failed, American military intervention would follow. In April, 1961, the U.S.S.R. agreed to neutralization, but fighting in Laos itself between Soviet-backed and American-backed forces continued until mid-May, when Khrushchev apparently realized the full implications of American intentions to send marines from Okinawa to Laos. A conference at Geneva followed the cease-fire, but before an agreement was reached in July, 1962, Kennedy had to send marines to Thailand in order to stop the Pathet Lao from continuing to violate the truce. And when the decision to neutralize the country was reached—many years too late—the Pathet Lao, now a strong force armed with Russian weapons and still supported by Ho Chi Minh, withdrew from the coalition and maintained control over its own portion of the country, which bordered on South Vietnam, and included the "Ho Chi Minh trail," a road down which came supplies from Hanoi for the Viet Cong guerrillas. But a form of stability had been created in Laos itself. Souvanna and Kong Le, who had all along been neutralist, were now no longer pro-communist but anti-communist, since it now was the Pathet Lao, (and not Phoumi —who had fled the country—or the United States—which now helped Souvanna) that was keeping Laos divided and in turmoil.

Incomplete and unsatisfactory as the Laos solution was, it far surpassed any arrangement that could be reached for South Vietnam. There guerrilla warfare continued. Effective opposition required political reform as well as counter-guerrilla activity. But American efforts—including those of Vice-President Johnson—to get Ngo Dinh Diem moving politically—all failed. All that emerged was the "strategic hamlet" plan: a program to create fortified villages and "relocate" peasants in them in the hope that this would provide protection against the guerrillas and make the enemy campaigns first expensive and then impossible. More American forces arrived, and in late 1962 and early 1963 optimism rose in Washington, but was not shared by American reporters in Saigon. In May, 1963, when Diem's troops fired on a crowd of Buddhists in the city of Hue, protesting against Diem's edict that they might not display flags in honor of Buddha's birthday, riots followed, and several Buddhists soaked themselves in gasoline and set themselves afire. Though the United States tried to persuade Diem to abandon his course, in August he staged a mass arrest of Buddhists, and in November he and his brother were ousted and murdered in a coup led by dissident generals.

Between the end of 1963 and the beginning of 1966, the South Vietnamese government changed hands several times, each time by military coup. The latest and longest-lived régime, that of General Cao Ky, had more stability than its predecessors, and successfully conducted elections in September 1966. But between 1963 and 1965, the hamlet program was a failure; insurgency increased: North Vietnamese regular troops appeared in South Vietnam in support of the guerrillas; more than half a million peasant families were made refugees once more by floods and by terrorism. During 1965 and 1966, the United States stepped up the number of its troops from fewer than a single division to almost 400,000, and initiated a policy of bombing certain selected North Vietnamese installations, sparing Hanoi and other cities, but hitting transport and some industrial targets, as well as missile sites supplied by the Russians. Fleets of heavy bombers based as far away as Guam bombed the jungle refuges of the Viet Cong in South Vietnam.

Massive American intervention made it impossible for the Viet Cong to conquer the entire country, and assured the United States of certain bases along the coast; but by October, 1966, it had not induced Hanoi to negotiate the issues involved, which was what America wanted. It led to ever fiercer denunciations of the United States by Communist China, which were designed as a warning that the Chinese might intervene, as they had in Korea, something the North Vietnamese wished as little as anybody. It elicited repeated denunciations also, though in a somewhat milder key, from the U.S.S.R., pledged to support Ho Chi Minh. On this issue the communist rivals agreed, though the Russians accused the Chinese of delaying in China munitions sent from Russia to North Vietnam, in order to arouse North Vietnamese suspicions of the good faith or efficiency of their Soviet allies.

Having increased the American commitment to such a level that none could doubt his earnestness, President Johnson then began a thoroughgoing world-wide exploration of ways to bring Ho Chi Minh to the conference table. In early 1966, before such talks had begun, he was ready to assure the enemy that the United States had no long-range intention of remaining in the country, and sought no military bases there. To lend point to his overture he suspended the bombing. When this failed, he undertook many other approaches, culminating in a Conference at Manila in October, 1966, in which Asian nations participated. But while this conference sat, the enemy was still insisting that there could be no negotiations until all American troops had left the country. And the very act of offering to negotiate with the North aroused uneasiness in the South.

Much articulate public opinion in the United States itself disliked the war or professed not to understand it. Opposing public opinion urged that it be intensified and "won." Its prospective costs perhaps endangered the President's widely-hailed domestic programs. On the one hand, continued intensification ("escalation," as it was lamentably called) threatened a land-war in Asia of unprecedented difficulty and unpredictable length and severity. On the other hand, withdrawal threatened loss of the aims for which the United States had fought the Asian portion of World War II: the Chinese communists of the 1960's, like the Japanese militarists of the 1940's, would dominate the entire Asian continent in a spirit of intense hostility to the United States. In 1967, the Vietnam War presented the United States with its most grievous immediate problems.

Khrushchev's Fall:
Kosygin and Brezhnev

In mid-October, 1964, the world learned to its astonishment that Khrushchev had been removed from power, and succeeded by two members of the Presidium. L. I. Brezhnev replaced him as First Secretary of the Central Committee of the Communist party, and A. N. Kosygin as Premier (Chairman of the U.S.S.R. Council of Ministers). Both were "Khrushchev

men": Brezhnev, aged 58, a metallurgist by training, had held posts in the Ukrainian, Moldavian, and Kazakhstan Communist parties, entering the Presidium in 1957; Kosygin, aged 50, an engineer, Commissar of the Textile Industry in 1938, Premier of the Russian Republic throughout World War II, member of the Politburo from 1949 to 1952 and Minister for Light Industry, went into eclipse shortly before Stalin died and re-emerged as a member of the Presidium only in 1957. The published communiqués spoke of Khrushchev's ill health and advanced age, but it was clear that he had not acquiesced in his own removal. How had Brezhnev and Kosygin managed it? And why? And what did they stand for?

Khrushchev had grown overconfident. He made frequent trips away from Moscow, and did not practice the kind of constant vigilance over his associates that alone could have ensured him security in office. The plotters acted in his absence, and took careful steps to line up the members of the Central Committee in support of their action so that Khrushchev could not appeal to the Central Committee over the head of the Presidium as he had done in 1957 (see p. 562). It was soon clear that Khrushchev had been disgraced but not punished. He continued to live in retirement in Moscow and in his country house. No large-scale purge followed his removal, though some officials close to him personally, including his son-in-law, who was editor of one of the two official newspapers, lost their jobs.

Khrushchev was responsible for major failures, at home and abroad. Corn had refused to grow above the Arctic Circle at his bidding, the western powers remained in Berlin, and the missiles he had sneaked into Cuba he had to withdraw in the full glare of world publicity, while the Chinese were compiling an astonishing record of success in the face of his opposition. Yet he had relaxed the terror, and his rockets had greater thrust than anybody else's. Probably he might have continued in office had it not been for his personality and style of rule. He was rough, tough, and nasty, pounding the table with his shoe, not only before the world in the United Nations but no doubt with even more earthy emphasis when laying down the law to his colleagues and subordinates. The very communiqué that announced his replacement referred to his *prozhekterstvo* ("hare-brained scheming"), no doubt in reference to the virgin lands fiasco, and to "half-baked conclusions and hasty decisions and actions, divorced from reality; bragging and bluster; attraction to rule by fiat (literally 'commandism')." Caustic and crude, Khrushchev had apparently tried his former supporters too far.

Unprepared, the Communist parties of many other countries protested against the manner of the ouster. Startled, the West wondered whether perhaps a "pro-Chinese" faction had taken over the U.S.S.R. and what might happen next. But, during the first two years of the new administration, it seemed that only the boss had changed, and that bossism—now divided between two men—perhaps had been diluted. No major changes took place on the domestic scene. Foreign policy also followed the same course: there was no reconciliation with the Chinese, who continued to pose for the U.S.S.R. a problem that had come to equal in importance their confrontation with the United States.

Implacably hostile to America, the Chinese did not seem to mind having the U.S.S.R. as an enemy at the same time. By the time of Khrushchev's ouster in October, 1964, they had won the support of the North Korean and North Vietnamese Communist parties, and enjoyed a special position of strength in Indonesia and Algeria. In Europe, Albania continued as a Chinese satellite. In Africa the Chinese had established a predominant influence in the former French colony of the Congo (Brazzaville), and in the former French colony of Burundi, and took the lead in sponsoring a major rebellion in the tormented former Belgian Congo (Leopoldville) that bordered on both. In South America they had supported Castroites within the pro-Soviet Latin-American parties in the hope of starting active revolutionary movements. In the United States, Chinese propagandists won the support of some American Negroes. They had defeated India. They had exploded an atomic bomb. They were actively supporting, as were the Russians, the communist efforts in South Vietnam.

Brezhnev and Kosygin took the problem in hand. Kosygin visited North Korea and North Vietnam. The U.S.S.R. successfully countered Chinese efforts to subvert the pro-Soviet régime in Outer Mongolia. Events elsewhere also contributed notably to Chinese setbacks during 1965. A congress scheduled for Algiers, in which they had expected to condemn the Russians, had been canceled, in part because of the Algerian coup against Premier Ben Bella; the Congo revolt had been put down, and the Chinese actually expelled from Burundi. An attempted communist *coup* in Indonesia had failed after the assassination of numerous leading army officers, and the army had virtually taken power and revenged itself heavily, with the help of the Moslem population, upon the Chinese minority and upon the native communists, of whom 250,000 or more were reported killed.

The Chinese threat to renew the attack on India during the Indian-Pakistan conflict of 1965 evaporated as the United States and the U.S.S.R. tacitly co-operated in the United Nations to force a temporary cease-fire. Early in 1966, Premier Kosygin at Tashkent acted as mediator between India and Pakistan, achieving an agreement to seek a peaceful solution, and thus depriving the Chinese of a pretext for intervention, while reasserting Soviet influence in Asia. It was no accident that simultaneously Brezhnev went to Outer Mongolia and strengthened the bonds between that state and Moscow, while Alexander Shelepin, former chief of the secret police (KGB) and present member of the Presidium, visited Hanoi and reiterated past declarations of Soviet support for the North Vietnamese.

Perhaps in part as the result of successive setbacks abroad, the Chinese in 1966 began to behave at home in ways suggesting that the régime was undergoing almost unbearable tensions. Denunciations and removals of important figures at the top of the government and party were accompanied by a new wave of adulation for Chairman Mao, who—as if to disprove rumors about his ill-health—plunged

A young Red Guardsman shouts his support of "Maoism" during a demonstration in a Peking Street.

into the Yangtze River for refreshment, and —to believe the Chinese press—set a new world's record for a nine-mile swim. One of his military entourage, who dived in to emulate the leader, later reported that the water had acquired a heavenly new taste. Youngsters in their teens, the "Red Guards," erupted into the streets of the cities of China, beating and sometimes killing older people whose loyalty they professed to suspect, destroying works of art and other memorials of China's pre-communist past, and rioting against foreigners and foreign influences. It seemed possible that the Chinese leadership was trying to solve its succession-crisis while Mao was still alive, and to cow the population and the party so completely that when Mao, in his seventies, should actually die, the transfer of power to the leaders of his choice might proceed smoothly. When his government in October, 1966, successfully fired a guided missile with a nuclear warhead—the third Chinese nuclear explosion in two years—it served further notice that the political turmoil was not interfering with unbelievably rapid progress in military hardware.

The U.S.S.R. could not publicly let down the cause of the Vietnamese communist revolution and the North Vietnamese communist government. But the mood of the Chinese, and the Soviet quarrel with China, indicated that the continuation of the Vietnamese war held dangers for the Soviet Union as well as for the West. As 1966 wore on, and Foreign Minister Gromyko conferred with President Johnson, some observers thought that the Russians would be as relieved as anyone if the American efforts to negotiate the issues at stake in Vietnam should meet with success.

IV   The Emerging Nations

The Asian and African states which thus became the arena for the competition of the western powers and the rival communist giants form part of the former colonial preserve of the West. It had taken the great imperialist nations four centuries to assemble the world-wide possessions over which they presided on the eve of World War I. It took only the two decades following World War II to liquidate the empires of Britain, France, Belgium, and the Netherlands, none of which retained more than small outposts by the mid–1960's. By then only Portugal still held on to its major possessions overseas—Angola, on the west coast of Africa, and Mozambique, on the east coast. Though the smallest and weakest of the empire-building nations, Portugal was able to hang on largely because it was a conservative dictatorship which would not yield to the kinds of political pressures by native peoples that had often influenced the other imperial powers. The Portuguese bowed only to force, when India, for example, used its army to dislodge them from Goa in 1962.

Britain, to be sure, continued to head her Commonwealth of Nations, whose membership now included some of the new non-white nations as well as the older white-controlled dominions. Economically, the Commonwealth continued to have great significance as an association of trading partners, the nucleus of the "sterling bloc." Politically, however, the importance of the Commonwealth began to fade, in part because of the conflicting interests of its western and non-western members and in part because of the further loosening of the ties between the white dominions and the mother country. Indeed, South Africa severed its bonds with the Commonwealth in 1961 and declared itself a wholly independent republic. Australia and New Zealand, while still calling Britain "home," looked more and more to the United States as the potential defender of their security.

Altogether, then, by the 1960's it seemed old-fashioned to speak of the revolt or revolution against imperialism, as had seemed natural enough in the 1950's (see Chapter 30). With the revolt an accomplished fact, states that achieved effective independence only after 1944 now constitute about half the membership of the United Nations. It seems appropriate therefore to look to the future, not the past, and speak of the "emerging nations." We use the rubric in this chapter to cover not only the new states of the Middle East, Asia, and Africa but also the older independent states in those areas together with those in Latin America. Many of the South and Central American republics, though their independence dates back a hundred years or more, face problems not unlike those confronting the newer states on other continents. They, too, have their political life chronically punctuated by military *coups* and are still in search of stable governmental institutions. They, too, feel the pressure of a rapidly increasing population, with the consequent movement of many peasants to the squalid shantytowns of overcrowded cities. They, too, want to end their semi-colonial status of suppliers of food and raw materials to the advanced industrial powers and hope to reach the "take-off" stage of economic growth (see Chapter 20). Other common denominators will become evident in the course of this rapid survey of the emerging nations, beginning with East and Southeast Asia.

East Asia

In the Far East—East Asia and Southeast Asia, according to the more exact contemporary terminology—the headline events after 1953 were, as we have seen earlier in the chapter, the increasingly bitter war in Vietnam and the increasingly bitter rivalry between Communist China and Communist Russia. Almost equally significant was the continued recovery of Japan. The Japanese economy grew so rapidly in the late 1950's and the 1960's that experts began to predict that it would soon overtake France and West Germany and rank third among the world's industrial powers, after the U.S.A. and the U.S.S.R. Despite the strained relations between Japan and Communist China, fears that the Japanese would be unable to find adequate markets for their products proved unfounded, as sales of Japanese goods in other quarters of the world continued to mount, and as the domestic market underwent a phenomenal expansion. Signs of change and of affluence multiplied. The birth rate dropped, to become one of the lowest in the world; peasants emigrated to the cities, especially to Tokyo, which surpassed London and New York to rank as the most populous city in the world; Tokyo and Osaka, Japan's second city, were linked by a new high-speed rail line, the fastest in the world, while weekend traffic jams resulted from the rush of Tokyo residents to the beaches in the summer and the ski slopes in winter. As of the late 1960's, inflation appeared to be the main threat to Japan's continued prosperity and to her social and economic westernization.

Politically, Japanese developments were perhaps less promising. The democratic parliamentary institutions so carefully fostered by

Asia, 1967

Communist bloc nations

Miles
0   500   1000

Pacific Ocean

Indian Ocean

Arabian Sea

Bay of Bengal

South China Sea

Sea of Japan

U. S. S. R.

TRANS-SIBERIAN RAILROAD

SAKHALIN
KURILE IS. (U.S.S.R.)
JAPAN
Tokyo
Osaka
Nagasaki
Khabarovsk
Vladivostok
Amur R.
Lena R.
L. Baikal
Chita
Harbin
MANCHURIA
Mukden
Dairen
N. KOREA
Seoul
S. KOREA
38°
Yalu R.
Irkutsk
Ulan Bator
MONGOLIA
GOBI DESERT
Peking
Yellow R.
Nanking
Shanghai
Changsha
Hong Kong (Br.)
Canton
HAINAN
Sverdlovsk
Omsk
KUZNETSK BASIN
Novosibirsk
Stalinsk
Barnaul
Semipalatinsk
Krasnoyarsk
Yenisei R.
Ob R.
Karaganda
L. Balkhash
Alma Ata
Urumchi
Qomul
Lanchow
SINKIANG
Siking
Chungking
Yangtze R.
Kunming
CHINA
NORTH VIETNAM
Hanoi
SOUTH VIETNAM
Saigon
Mekong R.
Tashkent
Shalinabad
AFGHANISTAN
Herat
Kabul
Kandahar
KASHMIR
Srinagar
Lahore
W. PAKISTAN
Karachi
Indus R.
TIBET
MT. EVEREST
Lhasa
HIMALAYAS
NEPAL
BHUTAN
E. PAK.
Ganges R.
Benares
Calcutta
Chittagong
New Delhi
Ahmedabad
Hyderabad
Bombay
Madras
INDIA
CEYLON
Colombo
LACCADIVE IS. (Br.)
MALDIVE IS. (Br.)
ANDAMAN IS. (India)
NICOBAR IS. (India)
BURMA
Mandalay
Rangoon
Irrawaddy R.
Tavoy
Salween R.
LAOS
Vientiane
THAILAND
Bangkok
CAMBODIA
Pnom Penh
Tovoy
MALAYSIA
MALAYA
Kuala Lumpur
Singapore
SUMATRA
Medan
Palembang
Djakarta
JAVA
Surabaja
REPUBLIC OF INDONESIA
BORNEO
Balikpapan
Kuching
SARAWAK
BRUNEI (Br.)
SABAH (N. BORNEO)
Jesselton
Makassar
CELEBES
Makassar
CERAM
AMBOINA
TIMOR (Port.)
Darwin
AUSTRALIA
NEW GUINEA
IRIAN BARAT
PHILIPPINE IS.
Manila
Tacloban
Davao
Zamboanga
TAIWAN (FORMOSA)
OKINAWA (U.S. Administration)
RYUKYU IS.
GUAM (U.S.)
MARIANAS IS.
CAROLINE IS. (U.S. Trust Territory)

IRAN

THAILAND
CHINA
FRENCH INDO-CHINA
TONKIN
ANNAM
COCHIN CHINA
Saigon
Mekong R.

the American occupation forces flourished under the perennial cabinets of the essentially conservative Liberal Democratic Party. The left-wing opposition, including both socialists and communists, objected to the mutual security pact binding Japan and the United States following the official restoration of full Japanese sovereignty in 1952. The opposition staged demonstrations, which caused the last-minute cancellation of President Eisenhower's planned visit to Japan in 1960. Anti-Americanism, though not the dominant force in Japanese politics, was nurtured by resentment over the continued United States occupation of Okinawa, to the south of the main Japanese islands, by the residue of bitterness left by the defeat of 1945 and the atomic blasts over Hiroshima and Nagasaki, and by mistrust of American policy and aims in Vietnam. In addition, despite the claim of the Japanese to have the highest rate of literacy in the world, the extreme insularity of many Japanese and their ignorance of the world outside their islands combined to make Japan seem at times more nationalist and neutralist than pro-western. The cautious historian is bound to suggest that it may take more than two decades to cure the Japanese of the aggressive expansionism of the recent past or to give up their deference to traditional authority which makes it hard for them to accept the give-and-take of democracy.

The Republic of Korea, in the southern half of the former Japanese imperial possession on the Asian mainland, also attempted constitutional government in the western manner but ran into serious difficulties. Following the long and disruptive Korean War of the early 1950's, the government of Syngman Rhee, the perennial South Korean president, came under mounting criticism for its corruption and its arbitrary actions. In 1960, massive protests by students forced the 85-year-old Rhee out of office and inaugurated a hectic period of several years, marked by the political intervention of the army and then by another attempt at constitutional rule. Meantime, the political future of the Republic of Korea continued to be clouded by its ailing economy, which depended heavily on American assistance.

Southeast Asia

In Southeast Asia, too, mixed results flowed from the efforts to transplant western political institutions. The Republic of the Philippines achieved some success with a congressional-presidential régime of the American type, and the component states of the Federation of Malaysia did likewise with a constitutional monarchy fashioned on the British model. The largest state of the area, however, the Republic of Indonesia, with a population of about 100,000,000, furnished a spectacular case history of transplantation that failed.

The former Netherlands East Indies were scarcely prepared at all for eventual self-government by their former Dutch rulers — another common denominator of the difficulties facing emerging nations — for Holland was not the only imperial power to neglect the political education of its subjects. Nevertheless, the Indonesians attempted to run their government along the lines of a parliamentary democracy. Almost everything went wrong. The economy was crippled by inflation and shortages, by administrative corruption and the black market, and by the expulsion of experienced Dutch businessmen. The Moslems, who comprised the bulk of the population, were unable to form coherent, responsible political parties. The outlying islands of the archipelago, resentful of domination by the island of Java, which contained the capital (Djakarta, the former Batavia) and two-thirds of the population, rebelled against the central government. As the high expectations raised by the achievement of independence were disappointed, President Soekarno, the hero of the Indonesian struggle for independence, began to speak of the need for "guided democracy" and for the operation of indigenous rather than borrowed political institutions.

In 1959 and 1960, Soekarno suspended the ineffectual parliamentary regime and vested authority in himself and in the army and an appointive council. In practice, "guided democracy" created still more turmoil. Inflation ran wild, necessities vanished from the market, pretentious new government buildings were left unfinished for lack of funds, and all foreign enterprises were confiscated. In external policy, Indonesia pursued an increasingly hysterical course. Soekarno denounced the new Federation of Malaysia as a lackey of the western imperialists and initiated an alternating hot and cold war with Malaysia for control of the large island of Borneo, where both states had territory. When the United Nations recognized Malaysia, Soekarno withdrew Indonesia from membership early in 1965; he also told the United States "to go to hell with their aid" and provoked a series of violent anti-American demonstrations in Djakarta and other centers. Meantime, Indonesia was being propelled rapidly into the communist orbit, as it received aid from the Soviet Union and also drew closer and closer to Red China.

As we have already seen (above, p. 603), however, a *coup* planned by Indonesian communists misfired at the last moment in the autumn of 1965, and the result was a wholesale slaughter of local communists. The anticommunist forces who came to power included Moslem leaders, members of the army, and students. They appeared to resent the mounting influence of the Chinese Communists, particularly as Chinese, a people identified by

the Indonesians with an often grasping minority of traders and storekeepers. Since President Soekarno still commanded a wide loyalty, especially among the people of Java, the new regime allowed him to remain in office but reduced his authority, brought some of his pro-communist associates to trial, and reversed his policies by reaching a settlement with Malaysia and rejoining the United Nations. As of early 1967, it was still problematical whether the new régime would be able to establish viable institutions in a country exceptionally hard to govern because of its geographical and political fragmentation and because of the desperate overcrowding of the island of Java, where 65,000,000 people live in an area about the same as that of New York State, with its 17,000,000.

South Asia

In South Asia—the Indian sub-continent—the building of the new nations of India and Pakistan has continued to battle against the handicaps of economic underdevelopment, population pressure, and the residues of religious hostility. In the Republic of India the democratic régime negotiated with ease two crises in leadership—when its "founding

President Soekarno (center) and his Cabinet, October, 1965.

father," Prime Minister Nehru, died suddenly in 1964, and again, early in 1966, when his successor, Shastri, fell victim to a heart attack. In both instances the new prime minister was chosen by due constitutional process; the choice in 1966 devolved upon Nehru's daughter, Mrs. Indira Gandhi. The Congress Party, long the spearhead of Hindu nationalism, continued to dominate the parliament and to provide a fairly effective rule, although its policies provoked a good deal of grumbling and occasional violent protests.

One center of political controversy was the question of language, for India contains ten major linguistic regions, each with its own distinctive tongue. Believing that a common language would be essential to a common sense of national identity, the government promoted a new national language, Hindi, to which it gave official status in 1965. It also recognized English as an associate language, though ardent nationalists deplore this "ignoble concession" to colonialism. In fact, English is indispensable both because of its modern scientific and technical vocabulary, which Hindi cannot provide, and also because it is the only common language of educated Indians, who cannot understand one another's native tongues. The elevation of Hindi to official status aroused strong opposition in some regions as an instrument of Hindu persecution of religious minorities and likewise as an instrument of the central government's hostility to regional or provincial pride in language and political home rule. The government met the problem by making some concessions to regional sensibilities, but without abandoning its aim of promoting national loyalties in every possible way. No doubt it will take a long time to forge the disparate peoples of India into a nation, as the West understands the term, but the Republic of India, in its first two decades of existence, made a notable beginning on this formidable undertaking.

Some observers believe that India's preoccupation with national political goals has created a disposition to make concessions which has weakened the government's attack on urgent economic problems by fostering compromise where bold new initiatives are required. Expert opinion also holds that India, in her planning, has put too much stress on industrial growth and invested too little in the agricultural sector. India's capacity to "take off" economically may well hinge on her ability to provide more and more of the food needed by her enormous population, which increases by about 15,000,000 annually and, at the end of 1966, was estimated to total about 500,000,000. Whenever, as frequently happens, the monsoon rains fail, India must import huge amounts of wheat from abroad, especially from the United States, to avert a famine that would cause many thousands of deaths from starvation. Paying for this wheat reduces investment in more constructive projects.

What can India do in the face of this discouraging situation? Hindu tradition does not look favorably on birth control or on measures to reduce the number of sacred cattle competing with humans for food. The government has made a modest start on the staggering task of educating the population in the benefits of contraception; as of 1966, any proposals for curbing cattle touched off storms of protest by the devout. On the other hand, western agricultural technicians believe that the low yields on much of India's crop land could be improved if the government invests more in fertilizers, promotes small local irrigation projects to supplement the showy large ones, encourages the use of modern tools and equipment, and in general convinces the Indian peasant of the desirability of changing inefficient ways of doing things.

One other major problem facing India is the question of relations with the Moslems, especially with the Islamic Republic of Pakistan. Ever since the partition of the sub-continent after World War II, sporadic outbreaks of religious persecution have taken place, especially near the line dividing overcrowded Bengal between India and East Pakistan. Deeply troubling the frontier between India and West Pakistan is the still unresolved question of Kashmir (see Chapter 30). Pakistanis have found it hard to accept permanent Indian control of Kashmir because the majority of the

Moslem refugees, driven out of India-held Kashmir during the fighting between India and Pakistan, seek shelter in refugee camps.

coup d'état in 1958. The Army commander, Ayub Khan, took full powers, attacked administrative corruption and the black market, and instituted a program of "basic democracies" to train the population in self-government at the local level and thence gradually upward through a pyramid of advisory councils. Ayub's "basic democracies" proved more workable than Soekarno's "guided democracy" and led to the proclamation of a new constitution in 1962, which provided for a national assembly and also for a strengthened president, an office that Ayub continued to fill.

The Middle East

Despite the vagueness about the geographical limits of the Middle East, the alternative label of Southwest Asia, to match up with East, Southeast, and South Asia, has never caught on. This area also exemplifies the oscillation between democratic and authoritarian régimes and between western and indigenous political institutions. Other guideposts to follow through the jungle of Middle Eastern developments after 1953 are the continued hostility between Israel and the Arab states, the continued frustration of Arab yearnings for political togetherness, and continued world concern over Middle Eastern oil, which reached a peak during the Suez crisis of 1956.

After World War II, the Republic of Turkey, fortified against Russian designs on her eastern provinces or the Straits, settled down to work out the full consequences of the revolution launched by Atatürk in the 1920's (see Chapter 28). The Republican People's Party, the only political formation allowed in Atatürk's day, permitted the activities of an opposition, and in the election of 1950 went down to defeat at the hands of the young Democrat party. Western opinion saluted this peaceful shift of power as the coming of age of Turkish parliamentary democracy. The Democrat government of Prime Minister Menderes proceeded to promote both state and private industry, to build roads and schools, and in other ways to bring the spirit of modernization to the villages, which had been neglected in

population is Moslem, while Indian nationalists believe that giving up Kashmir would be a deadly blow to national pride and to a lucrative income from tourists. In 1965 war seemed likely to break out over the issue until the Soviet Union invited leaders of both countries to a conference, where they agreed on a mutual withdrawal of troops from their common frontier but not to a permanent settlement. Unsolved and seemingly insoluble problems like Kashmir, where intensely felt religious or nationalist convictions are at stake, furnish yet another common denominator in the non-western world.

Pakistan itself had a full roster of domestic problems, resulting in part from the untimely death of its "founding father," Jinnah, in 1948, and in part from the division of the country into two widely separated regions, the large but arid West and the small, fertile, but over-populated East. Even more than India, Pakistan has depended on American wheat and aid to overcome the inadequacies of its own economy. The inability of the government to cope with economic problems was a major reason for the liquidation of the parliamentary régime by a

Atatürk's day but contained three-quarters of the population. To propitiate Moslem opinion, some of Atatürk's secularist policies were moderated, religious instruction was restored in the schools, and the call to prayer sounded once more in Arabic from the minarets (sometimes on amplified tape-recordings made in Mecca).

As the 1950's wore on, Menderes' régime became increasingly arbitrary, muzzling the press, persecuting the Republican opposition both in and out of the Grand National Assembly, and restricting more and more the free conduct of elections. In May, 1960, student riots following the precedent set in South Korea a few weeks earlier, touched off a *coup* by the Turkish army, which overthrew the government, outlawed the Democrat party, and brought Menderes to trial and execution. A new constitution, in 1961, sought to avert a repetition of the experience with Menderes by strengthening the legislature and judiciary against the executive. The victory for parliamentary democracy was at best a precarious one, since the army continued to exert ultimate control, and since the new Justice party, to which followers of Menderes gravitated, soon established itself as the most popular political formation, winning a majority of the seats in the parliamentary election of 1965. Thus tensions persisted between the urban champions of secularization and westernization, represented by army leaders and by Atatürk's old Republican People's party, and the defenders of the conservative Moslem way of life in Turkish towns and villages, who tended to support the Justice party.

Meantime, low wages and the lack of employment opportunities at home were impelling tens of thousands of Turks to take jobs abroad, especially in West Germany, and the marginal quality of much Anatolian farmland, with its thin soil and scanty rainfall, promoted an even greater exodus from the villages to the towns and cities. Turkey appeared to be suffering a sharp attack of social and economic growing pains. Its hopes for achieving a quick "take off" were thwarted by the country's meager resources, by its chronic difficulty in paying for needed imports, especially oil, and by the government's slowness in fashioning an effective organization for economic planning.

The most developed and the most westernized country in the Middle East is the young State of Israel. Though without a formal constitution, it functions in practice as a multi-party parliamentary democracy on the European model. By employing compromise and tact, the Israeli government has eased, though it has not solved, the problems of absorbing large numbers of immigrants, of accommodating western ways to tradition-bound "oriental" Jews from other parts of the non-western world, and of conciliating the clashing views of orthodox Jews and secular Israelis on such issues as strict observance of the sabbath and of dietary laws. The two difficulties that Israel had scarcely begun to resolve by 1967 were its continued dependence on outside aid to subsidize its economic growth and its chronic cold war with the Arabs. Tension along Israeli frontiers reached a peak in the months before and during the Suez crisis of 1956 and mounted again in the mid–1960's, as Israel began to siphon off more water from the River Jordon for irrigation, and the Arabs retaliated by threatening to divert the Jordan tributaries rising in Syria and Lebanon; also, a militant organization of Palestinian Arab refugees stepped up its terrorist campaign in Israel, and Israel retaliated by an armed raid into the Kingdom of Jordan, which brought a censure from the United Nations late in 1966.

Israeli nervousness over Egyptian command of a possible Arab attack, the intensification of Egyptian nationalism under Nasser's leadership after the revolution of 1952 (see Chapter 30), and the determination of Britain and France to teach Nasser a forceful lesson in the old imperialist manner combined to produce the crisis over Suez in 1956. In June of that year, by prior agreement, the last British soldiers withdrew from the Suez Canal zone. In July, Nasser was told by Eisenhower's Secretary of State, John Foster Dulles, that American aid and contingent help from Britain and the United Nations would not be available to assist the building of the showpiece of Egyptian revolutionary planning—the High Dam at Aswan to impound more of the Nile's water

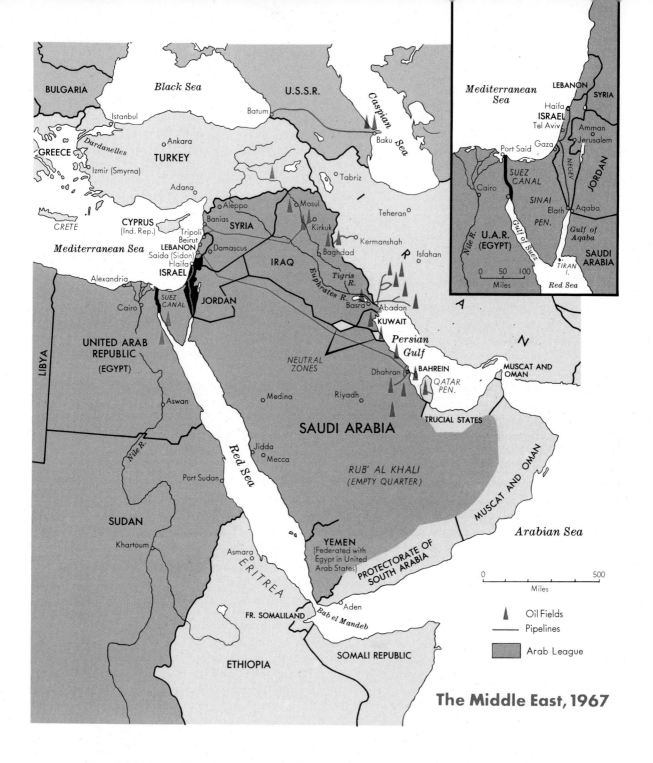

The Middle East, 1967

Inset map labels:
Mediterranean Sea, LEBANON, SYRIA, Haifa, ISRAEL, Tel Aviv, Amman, Gaza, Jerusalem, Port Said, NEGEV, JORDAN, SUEZ CANAL, Cairo, SINAI PEN., U.A.R. (EGYPT), Nile R., Gulf of Suez, Elath, Aqaba, Gulf of Aqaba, TIRAN I., SAUDI ARABIA, Red Sea

Scale: 0 50 100 Miles

Main map labels:
BULGARIA, Black Sea, U.S.S.R., Caspian Sea, Istanbul, Batum, Baku, GREECE, Dardanelles, Ankara, TURKEY, Izmir (Smyrna), Adana, Tabriz, CYPRUS (Ind. Rep.), Aleppo, Mosul, Kirkuk, Teheran, CRETE, Banias, SYRIA, Kermanshah, Mediterranean Sea, Tripoli, Beirut, Damascus, Isfahan, LEBANON, Saida (Sidon), Haifa, ISRAEL, IRAQ, Baghdad, Tigris, Alexandria, Euphrates R., Basra, Abadan, Cairo, SUEZ CANAL, JORDAN, KUWAIT, Persian Gulf, LIBYA, UNITED ARAB REPUBLIC (EGYPT), NEUTRAL ZONES, BAHREIN, MUSCAT AND OMAN, Dhahran, QATAR PEN., Aswan, Medina, Riyadh, TRUCIAL STATES, SAUDI ARABIA, Nile R., Jidda, Mecca, RUB' AL KHALI (EMPTY QUARTER), MUSCAT AND OMAN, Arabian Sea, Port Sudan, Red Sea, SUDAN, Khartoum, Asmara, YEMEN (Federated with Egypt in United Arab States), PROTECTORATE OF SOUTH ARABIA, ERITREA, FR. SOMALILAND, Aden, Bab el Mandeb, ETHIOPIA, SOMALI REPUBLIC

Scale: 0 500 Miles

Legend:
Oil Fields
Pipelines
Arab League

for irrigation. Nasser countered almost at once by announcing that the dam would be financed by the revenues received as a result of nationalizing the Suez Canal, until that moment operated by a Franco-British company. The new Egyptian management kept canal traffic moving smoothly, thus refuting western predictions that the "wogs" could never manage to operate a facility which required constant dredging and expert piloting.

In the autumn, a major international crisis resulted, made to seem still more critical because it took place at the time of the revolt in communist Hungary (pp. 583–584). Israel invaded Egyptian territory in the Sinai Peninsula, to the east of the canal, and Britain and

France began to land troops in the zone of the canal itself. As Egypt seemed to face certain defeat, the war was nipped in the bud when the Soviet Union threatened to send "volunteers" to defend Egypt, and when both the United States and a majority of United Nations members vigorously disapproved the invasion. In due course, a United Nations Emergency Force was established and moved into the troubled areas, the canal was reopened after it was cleared of sunken vessels and wrecked bridges, and the canal company accepted Egypt's offer of a financial settlement.

In 1958 Nasser pulled another surprise by proclaiming the merger of Egypt and Syria into the United Arab Republic. The two components of the U.A.R. were separated by territories of Israel, Lebanon, and Jordan; their rather unlikely union seems to have been dictated by the fear, both on Nasser's part and on that of moderate Syrian leaders, that the chronic instability of Syrian politics might precipitate a *coup* by Communists or fellow travelers. Nasser soon regretted his experiment in trying to govern the almost ungovernable Syrians, and when they revolted in 1961 announced that he could never fire on "brother Arabs" and permitted them to regain their independence as the Syrian Arab Republic. Yet after the secession, Egypt continued to style itself the U.A.R.—an ironic commentary on the difficulties of translating into action the Arabs' devotion to the ideal of Pan-Arab unity. The Arab League, a loose association of the Arabic-speaking states of the Middle East and North Africa, has often proved to be little more than a forum for expressing the conflicts of views and personalities that keep the Arab world disunited.

After the Suez crisis, Nasser continued to act the role of the leader of a "vanguard" waiting for the nation to "fall in behind in serried ranks" (see above, p. 577). Only very slowly did the Egyptians fall in, and Nasser tried one experiment after another to create a party and other institutions that would gain support for his régime at the grass roots. His economic policy has been governed by the grim struggle to support a fast-growing population (the birth-rate in Egypt is double that in the United States) in a country that is 95 per cent desert. In addition to building the High Dam, the revolutionary government undertook programs to reclaim land from the desert by exploiting underground water, and to limit the size of an individual's landholdings, so that the surplus might be redistributed to landshort peasants. To provide more jobs—and to bolster national pride—it also accelerated the pace of industrialization, often at very high cost. Following the example of the Suez Canal Company, most foreign enterprises were nationalized. As of 1966, most Egyptians seemed to accept their revolutionary government as a permanent régime, although with a good deal of grumbling over its high-handed methods and the sacrifices and shortages that its policies entailed.

Two other Arab states presently acquired revolutionary regimes—Iraq and Yemen. After World War II, the tough Iraqi politician, Nuri Sa'id, brought his country into close alignment with the West, particularly Britain, and initiated a development program of dams, oil refineries, and other public works, financed

Nasser receiving the plaudits of fellow Egyptians after announcing the nationalization of the Suez Canal, 1956.

by royalties from the western-controlled Iraq Petroleum Company. Iraqi nationalists agitated against Nuri's pro-Western policies and his harsh repression of political opponents. On July 14, 1958, a conspiracy of nationalistic officers overthrew the régime, and executed both Nuri and the inoffensive young king. The revolutionary government of Iraq has had a much more hectic time than its Egyptian counterpart. Beset by the factionalism of pro-Nasser and anti-Nasser nationalists and of fellow-travelers and anti-communists, shaken by repeated *coups* and abortive *coups*, and distracted by a stubborn rebellion of the fierce non-Arab Kurdish tribes in the mountainous north, the administration did little more than tread water in the eight years following the revolution.

In remote Yemen, in the highlands of southwestern Arabia, republican rebels overthrew the very old-fashioned monarchy of the Imam in 1962. A civil war with international ramifications ensued, as Nasser sent Egyptian troops to help the republicans, and Saudi Arabia, Yemen's northern neighbor, aided forces loyal to the deposed Imam. The situation in Yemen's southern neighbor—the British colony and protectorate of Aden, from which Britain was scheduled to withdraw in 1968—apparently involved conflicting Egyptian and Saudi aspirations for an eventual sphere of influence and contributed to the failure of the cease fire arranged for Yemen in 1965.

Involved in almost all the strategic issues affecting the Middle East is the question of oil. The Middle East is the second largest oil-producing area in the world (North America is first), its reserves of petroleum are the largest, and costs of production are very low because of the immense size of individual pools and the presence of natural gas to pump the oil. The main fields are in the southeastern quadrant of the Middle East—in Iraq, in the adjacent region of southwestern Iran, and along the Persian Gulf in Saudi Arabia and Kuwait. They have been prospected and developed by European and American companies, which have not simply taken the oil, as the Spaniards took

the precious metals of the New World, but have paid for it with mounting royalty payments to the Middle Eastern states. Dissatisfaction over the amount of royalties and related issues was one of the problems accompanying the mushrooming expansion of Middle Eastern oil after World War II; it caused an acute crisis in Iran (see Chapter 30), and under the threat of possible nationalization the oil companies have granted the other Middle Eastern producing states more generous terms. A second problem was the dependence of non-communist Europe on the Middle East to supply its fast-growing demand for cheap crude. Whence the alarm of Britain and France, during the Suez crisis, over Syrian sabotage of the pipeline from Iraq to the Mediterranean and the temporary blocking of the canal to the passage of tankers. Whence also the interest of the West in alternative cheap sources of supply, especially in Libya and the Algerian Sahara, which emerged as significant competitors of the Middle East in the 1960's.

A third problem has centered on the utilization of oil revenues by the producing countries and the pressures exerted on them by their less fortunate neighbors to share their wealth. At one extreme is Saudi Arabia, where much of the income went to support conspicuous consumption on the part of the very large royal family until more moderate reforming members of the family gained the upper hand in the 1960's. At the other is Kuwait, where the ruler has used his immense wealth to make his little country a welfare state, with elaborate facilities for free education and medical care, and has also made large sums available for development projects in other Arab states. In Iran, after the fall of Mossadeq and the resumption of oil payments, the Shah and his advisers used some of the revenue to assist much-needed land reform and promote an overall economic renewal of the oil-producing province of Khuzistan on the model of the American Tennessee Valley Authority. As the Iraqi revolution of 1958 demonstrated, however, oil-financed development schemes did not necessarily insure the popularity of a government.

Africa

When the revolution against imperialism reached Africa, in the 1950's, it moved with astonishing speed. In the space of a dozen years some three dozen European colonies, protectorates, and mandates became sovereign states, a process made the more bewildering because countries with names that were barely familiar in the West took new names that were totally unfamiliar. The Gold Coast became Ghana; the French Sudan became the Republic of Mali; Tanganyika merged with Zanzibar to become Tanzania; Nyassaland became Malawi; Northern Rhodesia, Zambia; Urundi, Burundi; Basutoland, Lesotho — and so on and on. It seemed almost as if there were not enough names to go around, for the world outside had to distinguish between the Federation of Nigeria, formerly part of the British Empire, and its northern neighbor, the Republic of Niger, formerly part of the French, and also between the Democratic Republic of the Congo, the former Belgian Congo, and its neighbor, the Republic of the Congo, the former French Congo. By the close of 1966, the tradition of white domination over Negro majorities persisted only in the southern quarter of the continent — in the Portuguese territories of Angola and Mozambique, in the Republic of South Africa, and in adjacent Southern Rhodesia.

In a book like this it is impossible to list all the separate steps leading to the liberation of the African states and all the many crises that have beset their struggles to make themselves viable nations. We can, however, suggest both the causes and some of the results of a revolution that has swept over more than three-quarters of a continent. The explanation of Africa's sudden leap forward may be found in the operation of forces that we have encountered elsewhere in the non-western world. The white rulers brought with them at least a little sanitation, engineering, law and order, and economic development. Above

Sekou Touré of Guinea addresses the United Nations, October, 1960.

all, they brought the schooling which kindled in the minority of educated natives the inevitable aspirations for self-rule. Some of the future leaders of African states received their training in the West itself — Habib Bourguiba of Tunisia at the Sorbonne, Julius Nyerere of Tanzania at the University of Edinburgh, Kwame Nkrumah of Ghana at Lincoln University in Pennsylvania. The explanation may also be found in the rigors of tropical life, for only a relative handful of Europeans settled in the vast steaming areas which include most of the western half of the continent and some of the eastern. It has been easier for the colonial powers to drop their imperial reins in tropical Africa than in areas of more temperate climate, where the white man came in larger numbers, put down deeper roots, and acquired more vested interests.

A case in point is South Africa, where, beginning with the Boers' great trek of the 1830's (see Chapter 24), the Europeans began to push north from the Cape of Good Hope, establishing themselves as farmers, grazers, businessmen, and professional men, much as their contemporaries were doing in North America and in Australia. But there was one great difference. The South African whites did not push aside a relatively small group of Red Indians or Australian Blackfellows; on the contrary, they have remained a minority, dependent on the Negro Bantus for laborers on their farms and mines and for domestic servants. The consequence is that today, for every European South African, there are more than three non-Europeans—mainly Bantus but also including Asians (chiefly Indian shopkeepers) and Coloreds, the designation for those of mixed European and Negro blood. The whites, too, are divided, between the English-speaking "British" and the larger group of "Afrikaners" (the new name for the Boers), who speak a dialect of Dutch.

During World War II the Afrikaners, who often sympathized with Hitler and the Nazis, came close to preventing their country's fighting at Britain's side. In 1948, they won a national election, and ever since they have shaped South Africa's policies along lines that have produced increasing tension with Great Britain, the United Nations, and the other African states. In 1949, under Afrikaner influence, South Africa annexed the former German colony of Southwest Africa in defiance of the United Nations, which wanted South Africa to change its mandate under the League of Nations for a U.N. trusteeship. Above all, South Africa enacted increasingly stringent measures to ensure white supremacy, cutting down the rights of the Colored, and all but liquidating those of the Bantu. This was the policy called *Apartheid*, which involved a separation of the races more rigorous than that applied in the United States during the heyday of segregation. The Bantu must use separate post offices, must live where they are ordered to—in slummy "townships" outside the cities, on the poorest farmland, or in barracks near the mines, where the laborers are usually at a great distance from their families. They must not expect to advance much beyond an elementary education, and must carry passbooks to permit the police to enforce these and all other requirements of *Apartheid*.

How has it been possible for the bonds of *Apartheid* to tighten in South Africa, just as those of segregation have been loosened in the United States, and most of the rest of Africa has cast off white control? In the first place, the Afrikaners, who are mainly Calvinists, have very strong convictions that the total separation of the races is the will of God. The "British" South Africans at first often opposed very strongly the extremes of *Apartheid*, but many of them rallied to support the Afrikaners as a result of the fears aroused by the chaos in the Congo and by the uncertain future of Rhodesia. The Afrikaners met criticism from the British Commonwealth by seceding in 1961 and proclaiming the Union of South Africa an independent republic, though one that remained part of Britain's sterling bloc. At home they have silenced critics and potential opponents by censorship, internment, violent repression of demonstrations, and other acts suggesting a police state. Ultimately, the Afrikaners must rely on force, but, since they continue to rely on Bantu manpower to maintain their booming economy, the oppressed Negroes have the potential weapon of the strike at their command, if they can find a way to use it. The "if" is a very big one, for as of 1967 the Bantus were kept largely without leadership, since potential leaders were all interned.

In neighboring Rhodesia (the "Southern" was dropped when Northern Rhodesia became independent Zambia) the whites, many of them immigrants from South Africa, also seemed determined to fight on in the cause of white supremacy until some more-than-Wagnerian twilight of the gods. Though outnumbered by the Negroes by more than 10:1, they rejected the condition for independence laid down by Britain—that some step must be taken to insure the natives' participation in politics—and declared their independence unilaterally in 1965. Supplied through South Africa and Mozambique, the rebel Rhodesian régime appeared to be weathering a boycott imposed by Britain, though facing another imposed by the United Nations early in 1967. In the face of these developments at the southern end of the continent, one can understand the intensely hostile reaction of other Africans, and their determination to liquidate the last outposts of

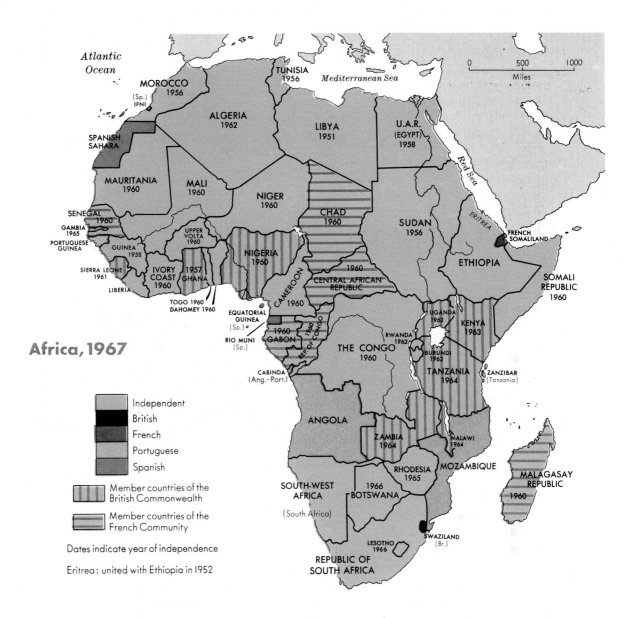

Africa, 1967

Legend:
- Independent
- British
- French
- Portuguese
- Spanish

Member countries of the British Commonwealth

Member countries of the French Community

Dates indicate year of independence

Eritrea: united with Ethiopia in 1952

Map labels:

Atlantic Ocean

Mediterranean Sea

MOROCCO 1956
(Sp.) IFNI
TUNISIA 1956
ALGERIA 1962
LIBYA 1951
U.A.R. (EGYPT) 1958
SPANISH SAHARA
Red Sea
MAURITANIA 1960
MALI 1960
NIGER 1960
CHAD 1960
SUDAN 1956
ERITREA
FRENCH SOMALILAND
SENEGAL 1960
GAMBIA 1965
PORTUGUESE GUINEA
GUINEA 1958
UPPER VOLTA 1960
NIGERIA 1960
CENTRAL AFRICAN REPUBLIC 1960
ETHIOPIA
SOMALI REPUBLIC 1960
SIERRA LEONE 1961
IVORY COAST 1960
1957 GHANA
LIBERIA
TOGO 1960
DAHOMEY 1960
EQUATORIAL GUINEA (Sp.)
RIO MUNI (Sp.)
GABON 1960
CAMEROON 1960
REP. OF CONGO 1960
UGANDA 1962
KENYA 1963
RWANDA 1962
BURUNDI 1962
THE CONGO 1960
TANZANIA 1964
ZANZIBAR (Tanzania)
CABINDA (Ang.-Port.)
ANGOLA
ZAMBIA 1964
MALAWI 1964
MOZAMBIQUE
MALAGASAY REPUBLIC 1960
SOUTH-WEST AFRICA (South Africa)
RHODESIA 1965
BOTSWANA 1966
LESOTHO 1966
SWAZILAND (Br.)
REPUBLIC OF SOUTH AFRICA

colonialism and white supremacy. This is one of the major pieces of unfinished business left by the African revolution.

For a time, in the 1950's, it looked as though the Europeans might try to hold on at all costs in two other areas. One was Algeria, where *colons* (as the settlers were called) were attracted to the pleasant regions near the Mediterranean and came to number more than a million, over ten per cent of the population. Algerian nationalists, who were not Negroes but Berbers and Arabs, had to stage a war of rebellion for eight bloody years before France gave in and granted Algeria independence in 1962. The other area was Kenya, in East Africa, lying across the Equator but with high, rolling plateaus suitable for Europeans. White settlers came and developed large farms, which used native labor, on the five million acres of Kenya reserved for white settlement. But the native tribe, the Kikuyu, living in the highland areas adjacent to the white preserve and growing in numbers, felt the pinch of land hunger and unemployment. Within the tribe a secret society was formed, the Mau Mau, which aimed at the extermination or expulsion of the whites and spread terror by murdering isolated white farmers and also the more peaceful Kikuyu.

617

Police disperse African women after a demonstration in Durban, South Africa, June, 1959.

The Mau Mau gained particular notoriety for the method they used to safeguard the secrecy of their operations—a solemn oath forced on reluctant tribesmen, and backed by the tribal fear of gods who would take vengeance on any backsliders and their families. After eight years of civil war (1952-1960) the British authorities finally broke the power of the Mau Mau, yet they also gave up the struggle to keep the highlands for the whites and granted Kenya independence in 1963. The whole Mau Mau experience, which had terrified westerners all over Africa, was a dramatic example of the power of pagan customs and tribal folkways.

It is a power which may be found elsewhere in the emerging nations—in the voodoo of Haiti, for example—and it is another item in the unfinished business of the African revolution.

Primitive customs can assume a particularly savage aspect when they survive in a large country, populated by mutually hostile tribes, ruled after a fashion by rival political leaders, and virtually devoid of experience in self-government. The country is the former Belgian Congo, which Belgium emancipated in 1960, with no prior effort to train native administrators to take over from Europeans. The attempt to transplant into the heart of tropical

Nationalist terrorist suspects in Algerian prison compound, December, 1956.

Africa a western political structure, with parliament, president, and prime minister, at once produced a situation to which the overworked words "anarchy" and "chaos" really do apply. The army mutinied; prominent politicians were assassinated; major provinces rebelled and for a time seceded, notably copper-rich Katanga; thousands of whites were held as hostages by rebels, and many were slain; many thousands of Congolese also died. Outside powers—Belgium, India, Ghana, Communist China, South Africa, among others —took sides in the Congolese free-for-all and actively assisted their favorites. By the mid-1960's, after prolonged assistance by the United Nations, a central government emerged which began to restore a minimum of law and order and bring mutineers and rebels under control.

Perhaps more ominous than the difficulties of the Congo were those of Nigeria, in West Africa, the most populous state on the continent (one out of every five or six Africans is a Nigerian). Endowed with diverse economic resources, carefully groomed for independence by its British overlords, and made into a federation of semi-autonomous regions to ease the tensions among its various peoples, Nigeria was widely expected to serve as a model for the smaller and less favored states of Africa. Yet it soon became doubtful whether the Nigerian Federation could survive at all because of the mounting tensions between the conservative Moslems of the inland northern region and the more aggressive peoples of the coastal regions. In 1966, attempts to end Moslem domination of the federation government precipitated the assassination of the federal prime minister, a takeover by the army, and a massacre of non-Moslems living in the Moslem northern region.

The years 1965 and 1966 were marked by political upheavals in many other young African states, with *coups* by the military occurring at an average of nearly one per month. One celebrated victim was the President of Algeria, Ahmed Ben Bella, ousted in 1965 in part because of his growing flirtation with the

A student from the Cameroon speaks at a protest meeting in Moscow against foreign interference in the Congo, November, 1964.

Chinese communists. Another was Kwame Nkrumah, the pioneer of post-war African emancipation, who had headed the government of Ghana since 1957. He had become increasingly high-handed (to put it mildly) at home, increasingly erratic in economic policy, and increasingly obsessed by schemes for a Pan African union dominated by himself. He was in China courting communist support when he learned of his ouster in 1966.

Here, then, are more matters of unfinished business for Africans. They need to find ways of engaging the loyalty of the masses, for in many states only a tiny educated elite have an allegiance to an entity transcending the tribe. They need to work out their own forms of government, not carbon copies of western models, and if the military strong man becomes the characteristic African leader, it is well to remember that historically such men have sometimes proved to be enlightened despots. The Africans also need to replace, or recall, the European experts, political, technical, and economic, who often vanished at the time of emancipation, and not only from the Congo. In the West African Republic of Guinea, for instance, the utilities ceased to function when the French withdrew abruptly in 1958 out of pique at Guinea's opting for immediate independence, and in Algeria, the precipitate departure of three-fourths of the *colons* in 1962 crippled the economy. The dismantling of empire has often proved a harsh experience.

Perhaps the most inhibiting legacy of colonialism has been the Balkanization of Africa, its division into dozens of political units, large, small, and minute. Whereas the several Balkan states of Europe before 1914 had an ethnic or religious justification for their separateness, no such rationale exists for many African entities, which are the accidental end-product of the piecemeal partitioning of the continent over the centuries by the European powers. Most experts feel that the African states must form larger entities if they are to achieve the political and economic advances they seek. A few beginnings have been made. Most of the former French colonies in Equatorial and West Africa have agreed to operate a joint airline and to co-ordinate their postal

and telecommunications services; the United Nations has a single Economic Commission for Africa, based in Ethiopia; also based in Ethiopia is the Organization of African Unity, formed in 1963 and including nearly all the African states, which had little to show, however, for its first years beyond the fact of its existence.

In 1966 one of the most moderate and successful leaders of the new Africa, President Bourguiba of Tunisia, concluded that:

African unity will be a long, hard pull. It took more than twenty years to cement the ranks of the Tunisian people. What can one expect, then, from a whole continent, as diverse, balkanized and so long subservient as Africa?[*]

It is very difficult, Bourguiba continued, to bring together even the three former French North African possessions of the Maghreb (Arabic for "West") — Tunisia, Algeria, and Morocco:

. . . .This region constitutes a distinct geographical bloc; we speak the same language, have the same beliefs, the same culture, and the same past. Ethnically we are homogeneous; the frontiers separating us are artificial. In spite of all this, we step gingerly. Why? Simply because we must take into account that newly independent countries are still very jealous of their sovereignty. . . .Even in purely economic matters the pace is still very slow.[†]

As for the rest of Africa, Bourguiba recommended:

. . . .It will be necessary for the poor countries to rid themselves of demagogues, of verbalism and the sterile conflicts engendered by power complexes or the will to dominate. Let them recognize their true problems, which are essentially domestic and, more precisely, economic.[**]

The achievement of a greater degree of political realism and stability may well be the essential precondition for economic growth, and thus the topmost item on Africa's agenda of unfinished business.

[*]Habib Bourguiba, "The Tunisian Way," *Foreign Affairs,* Vol. 44 (1966), 487.
[†]*Ibid.*
[**]*Ibid.,* 488.

Latin America and the West Indies

In the Western Hemisphere, too, colonialism has left its residue of Balkanization. After World War II, Great Britain hoped to foster a federation of her separate island colonies in the West Indies as a stepping stone to their independence. But, after a brief trial demonstrated the incompatibility of the members, Britain decided to emancipate the most important islands one by one. In Latin America, the legacy of Spanish rule coupled with the geographical barriers of high mountains and tropical jungle goes far to explain its fragmentation into twenty separate republics. In the 1960's the little states of Central America, following European precedent, sought to counter the economic effects of Balkanization by joining together in a common market. A more ambitious project sponsored by the United States to help the Latin Americans to help themselves toward social and economic advance—the Alliance for Progress—has run into difficulties, because of the widely differing views on reform taken by the various Latin American régimes and also because of the wide-spread mistrust of "Yankee imperialism."

This mistrust increased because of the Dominican crisis of 1965. For thirty one years, 1930-1961, the Dominican Republic was ruled by General Trujillo, a particularly unsavory representative of the *caudillo,* the Latin military hero or dictator. After his assassination, the first freely elected government in a generation took office in Santo Domingo, but increasing tension between conservative and reforming elements led to military *coups* and finally to a civil war in 1965. Fearing that communist elements supporting the reformers might soon take over, the United States sent in troops, then tried to internationalize the intervention by appealing to the Organization of American States, the inter-American grouping for collective security formed after World War II. By a narrow margin, the OAS responded, and five of its member states, all with conservative military régimes, sent troops to join the Americans. The Dominican Republic was pacified sufficiently for constitutional

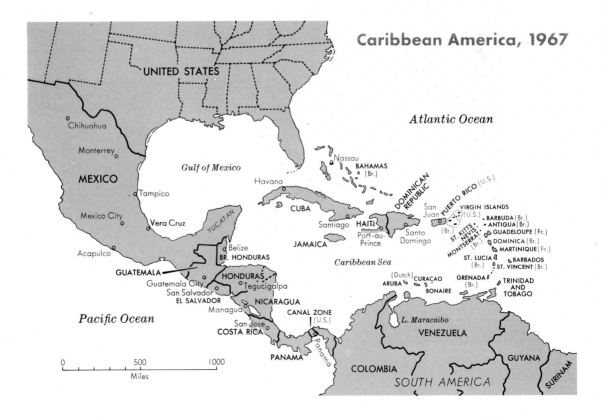

Caribbean America, 1967

elections to be held in 1966; a moderate, who had once been a lieutenant of Trujillo, became President. The oscillation between the *caudillo* and the constitutional president is a very characteristic Latin American political rhythm.

By 1966 the threat of communist penetration appeared to be subsiding not only in Santo Domingo but in many other parts of Latin America. Even in Cuba itself the dictatorship of Fidel Castro seemed to be developing more according to the usual Latin pattern of the *caudillo* and his personal following rather than along the lines of a carefully structured Marxist party and state, although Castro himself in a New Year's day speech in 1967, condemned such a trend. Castro had seized power in Havana on New Year's Day, 1959, overthrowing a particularly corrupt dictatorship after a long guerrilla struggle. Castro promised that the sweeping reforms he initiated would release the Cuban economy from its traditional—and in the eyes of patriots, humiliating—dependence on the United States and would also raise the standard of living, especially for the poor. In fact, the Cuban economy soon depended on sales of sugar to the communist world, and its productivity declined because of inept administration and because Cuban machines could not function without spare parts from the United States. After the missile crisis of 1962 (see p. 594), moreover, even the communist world seemed to weary of Castro's interminable speeches and his endless requests for assistance.

On the Latin American mainland the chief target of Castro's hopes for successful communist penetration was Venezuela, endowed with rich oil deposits but also with a very high cost of living and a social structure that permitted little of the revenues from the oil to trickle down to the average Venezuelan. In 1959, however, the last in a line of Venezuelan *caudillos* was supplanted by a constitutional President, Betancourt, who headed a moderate reforming government of civilians. Betancourt's firmness defeated a long campaign of intimidation and violence by Castro's sympathizers, who hoped to disrupt the presidential elections of 1963. In Chile, the presidential election of 1964 brought defeat to the popular Marxist candidate and victory to Eduardo Frei, a Christian Democrat committed to a program of vigorous but constitutional reform. Also in 1964, the Brazilian army turned out an erratic president, Goulart, who was unable or unwilling to check either the country's runaway inflation or the alleged penetration of its administration by pro-communists. In British Guiana, meantime, a very tense situation had developed between the two main elements in the population—the East Indians, led by the communist Cheddi Jagan, and the Negroes. The British postponed the scheduled emancipation of the colony until an effective anti-communist coalition government was in office, and in 1966 the state of Guyana joined the ranks of free nations.

Containing communism is only one element in shaping the future of Latin America; the really crucial factor is the success of other states in advancing the kind of social and political revolution begun by Mexico in the 1910's (see Chapter 30). Will Mexico's sister republics be able to equal her record in achieving a reasonably stable and democratic government, promoting a healthy economic growth, and curbing the privileges of the few, notably the landowners and the Catholic Church, for the benefit of the many? As of 1966, the answer was far from clear, and we may take as a representative sample of Latin American problems and prospects the situation in the "ABC powers"—Argentina, Brazil, and Chile.

During the eleven years after Perón's overthrow in 1955 (see Chapter 30), Argentina was still struggling to recover from the experience of his dictatorship. The economy floundered, Perónist sentiment continued strong among workers and some other groups, and on two occasions (1962 and 1966) a weak, elected government was overthrown by a military *coup*. The army régime installed in 1966 promised to purge Argentina of corruption but aroused much opposition by its pro-Catholic policies and by its repression of academic freedom. In Brazil the military régime that ousted President Goulart in 1964 seemed to dig in for a long tenure of power. It endeavored with some success to curb inflation, but it also

Caribbean Sea

PANAMA
CANAL
Cartagena

Caracas

TRINIDAD AND TOBAGO

VENEZUELA

GUYANA

SURINAM

Medellin

Orinoco R.

Bogotá

Georgetown

Paramaribo

DEVIL'S ISLAND

COLOMBIA

Cayenne

GUIANAS

FRENCH GUIANA

ECUADOR

Quito

(1966) (1954) (1626)

Guayaquil

Negro R.

Iquitos

Manaos

Amazon R.

Belem
(Pará)

Amazon R.

Fortaleza

PERU

R.

Purus

Madeira R.

Tapajos R.

B   R   A   Z   I   L

Natal

Recife
(Pernambuco)

Callao

Lima

Cuzco

L. Titicaca

La Paz

BOLIVIA

Sucre

Arequipa

Tacna

Arica

GRAN CHACO

Paraguay R.

Araguaia R.

Tocantins R.

São Francisco R.

FEDERAL
DISTRICT

Brasilia

Salvador
(Bahia)

Parana R.

Belo
Horizonte

Pacific Ocean

Antofagasta

PARAGUAY

São Paulo

Tucuman

Asunción

Santos

Rio de Janeiro

Atlantic Ocean

Cordoba

Parana R.

Pôrto Alegre

CHILE

Valparaiso

Mendoza

URUGUAY

Santiago

Buenos Aires

Montevideo

ARGENTINA

Rio de la Plata

Colorado R.

Bahia Blanca

0   500
Miles

◉ Capital cities

FALKLAND IS.
(Br.)

South America, 1967

Str. of Magellan

Punta Arenas
(Magallanes)

CAPE HORN

strengthened the executive arm of the government at the expense of elective institutions. Brazil was one of two South American states (the other was Paraguay, a dictatorship) to send a contingent to Santo Domingo under the OAS mandate in 1965. In Chile, on the other hand, the duly elected Christian Democratic government of Eduardo Frei made good on its campaign promises by enacting a bold program of land reform, expanding oppor-

tunities for the unemployed, and in general trying to modernize and democratize a society described as composed 20 per cent of "haves" and 80 per cent of "have nots." The Latin American states, then, like their counterparts all over the world, exemplify the political uncertainties accompanying the quest of the emerging nations for the kinds of economic and social progress achieved by the western powers half a century and more ago.

V   The Free World System

It was a peculiarity of the years between 1953 and 1966 that the efforts of the nations of the free world were designed essentially to *prevent* a take-over by the communists of further territory and human beings. Accompanying and supporting this generally negative major aim, of course, were many policies and many more actions wholly positive in character: to assist in the development of the emerging nations, to strengthen and spread prosperity and contentment within the borders of the free world itself, to control the weapons of mass destruction. Yet the free world was not aggressively striving to take over territories and people already in the hands of the other side. It is hard to judge the successes of an essentially preventive policy, since these successes depend on one's worst fears *not* being realized, on Armageddon *not* happening; and who can say at any given moment that Armageddon is now beyond the bounds of possibility? Yet in 1967 one could say at least that it had not yet happened, and to this degree—a very high degree indeed —the policies of the free world had so far been successful.

NATO and the other American Alliance-Systems

To accomplish these ends, the United States had already helped to form a series of international coalitions.

The North Atlantic Treaty Organization (NATO) formed in 1949 (see Chapter 30) was the keystone. Somewhat similar treaty arrangements were formed in the Middle East, the Far East, and Latin America. Most of these arrangements survived in the mid-sixties, though all of them underwent stresses and strains. NATO in particular encountered hard sledding, since it alone was designed as a tight military force with inter-leaved staffs from various nationalities: to some degree at least a supra-national organization. Past coalitions have usually fallen apart when their members have ceased to feel immediately threatened. And the fear of Russia felt to be acute while Stalin was alive, gradually but surely diminished among Europeans after 1953. Perhaps the real marvel was not that NATO continued to have its troubles, but that nearly two decades after its foundation it continued to exist.

As the German Federal Republic formally achieved independence, the question of its future armies posed a problem for NATO. The French first proposed and then in 1954 refused to accept a plan that would have tightly integrated the new German forces in a European Defense Community (EDC). But in 1955 the West Germans became full-fledged members of NATO. Within the alliance, the Suez crisis of 1956—in which the British and French acted without informing the United States in advance—created less strain than might have been expected. But the quarrel between the Greek majority (80 per cent) and the Turkish minority (20 per cent) on the island of Cyprus severely strained the relations between Greece and Turkey, both members of NATO, especially after the island became independent of Great Britain in 1960. Its constitution made provison for representation of the Turkish minority, but the struggle over its application led to open warfare between the two peoples. The United Nations sent a force which was still present on the island in 1967.

The continuing liquidation of the British and French colonial empires, a process which American opinion and to a degree American governmental policy applauded, certainly angered many in both France and England, but in itself proved no serious challenge to NATO. Perhaps this American attitude, and the memories of American quarrels with de Gaulle during the war, sharpened official French intransigence toward the tight supranational organization of NATO. At any rate, from about 1960 on, de Gaulle, now firmly in power, began to insist that NATO be turned more and more into an old-fashioned alliance system, in which each partner had, subject to actual war needs, complete independence, with no more interleaving of staffs, no more "foreigners" commanding French soldiers and sailors. France achieved, though on a small scale, her own atomic bomb in an explosion in the Sahara desert in 1960, thus whetting the desires of other powers to join the "atomic club."

The United States and Britain, charter members of the club, sought by a variety of means to prevent the spread of atomic weapons: the chief device was the plan for the joint Multilateral (nuclear) Force in which the Germans would participate. The French rejected MLF, and in 1966 the whole problem—a grave one indeed—remained unsolved. In February, 1966, de Gaulle gave notice that at the expiration in 1969 of the treaty establishing NATO he would not renew it in its present form. By the end of 1966, NATO was planning to move its headquarters to Belgium. Despite the manifold difficulties the alliance had encountered, it was very much in being, and even de Gaulle, whatever he might say, in fact depended for French security upon its continuance.

In the Near East, the Baghdad Pact and its successor, the Central Treaty Organization (CENTO), proved no more than a series of agreements among the United States, Britain, Turkey, Iran, and Pakistan. With the withdrawal of Iraq from the Baghdad Pact in 1959, no direct alliances linked the Arab world with the West. In the Far East, SEATO still existed (see p. 572) and the United States could count solidly on Australia and New Zealand. Despite the presence in South Korea and the Philippines of elements who disapproved of the ties with the United States, both governments helped us actively in the Vietnam war, while Thailand supplied the base for many American troops. President Johnson's trip to the area in October, 1966, helped to strengthen these ties.

The United Nations

The United Nations Organization, twenty-two years old in 1967, had already outlived the League of Nations (1919–1939). More important, the United Nations had shown possibilities of adapting to changed conditions in ways the old League never did. Yet it made little progress toward the supranational state that world-government enthusiasts aimed at. It was still no more than a league of "sovereign" states not subject to any "laws" enforceable by the agents of the United Nations. Moreover, it encountered serious opposition; it experienced financial difficulties which it could not have survived without American aid; and it probably grew too fast. Numbering 76 in 1956, its membership rose rapidly to 122 in 1966. The problem of the Chinese Nationalists' permanent seat and the exclusion of the Chinese Communists (see Chapter 30) continued to arise at every session of the Assembly.

In the old League of Nations, and almost certainly in the intention of *both* the U.S. and the U.S.S.R. in the Charter of the United Nations, a council of great powers was supposed to have sole power in important matters, such as admission of members: and in this Security Council each of the permanent members (U.S., U.S.S.R., Britain, France, Nationalist China) had a veto on all save merely procedural problems. There was a still untested provision that a permanent member of the Security Council that was party to an actual dispute being adjudicated must simply abstain from voting on that dispute. The Assembly of the U.N. in which each of the member states, big or little has one vote, played a far more important role in elections for membership than the Assembly of the old League had ever played. Moreover, the United Nations put its own military forces in the field in Israel, in Korea, in the Congo, and in Cyprus, something the old League never came close to attempting. Even though Russia and France refused to pay their assessments for the cost of the Congo operation, the organization managed to keep its head above water financially. Finally, the various social, economic, and cultural services performed by agencies of the U.N., noted earlier in Chapter 30 (see p. 552), continued to grow in scope and effectiveness. If the U.N. remained essentially a great international debating center, a place for open propaganda, it also made some real progress toward true governmental power, especially in the development of an international civil service devoted to the practical affairs of administration.

Between 1953 and 1967 the very great material progress of the free world continued apace. If we take the number 100 to represent industrial production in the year 1958, the figure for such production five years later, in 1963, is as follows:*

France	127
Italy	165
West Germany	137
United Kingdom (Great Britain)	119
United States	133

*Figures from the *Statistical Yearbook* of the United Nations for 1964 (New York, 1965). The high figure for Italy is to be explained partly by the comparatively low base from which her industrial production started. Similarly, the low figure for Britain is in part a reflection of her long head start in industry.

Though experience with the so-called "business cycle" made many Europeans and Americans feel that perhaps this prosperity could not last forever, nevertheless, as of 1967 we must record that in the midst of all kinds of real difficulties, from general welfare to juvenile delinquency that justifiably worried almost everyone everywhere, the "advanced" areas of the world were still enjoying material prosperity.

The United States

The year 1954, which saw Senator McCarthy condemned by his colleagues in the Senate, also saw one of those critical decisions of the Supreme Court which mark a turning point in our history. The existence of compulsory separate public schools for whites and Negroes was declared unconstitutional by a unanimous decision of the nine judges, led by Chief Justice Earl Warren of California. Notably in the District of Columbia, in Maryland, Kentucky, Missouri, and in a few districts elsewhere, steps were taken at once to implement this decision. In the rest of the South, the decision evoked serious opposition. Not even the bitterest southern opponent of desegregation talked about secession; but there was much talk about what amounted to nullification (the right claimed by South Carolina in 1832, when it declared unconstitutional the tariff acts of Congress). The majority of southerners were clearly determined to "get around" the decision somehow or other. Thirteen years after the original decision of the Supreme Court, there was at least "token" desegregation in the public schools of all fifty states. In the border states and in some of the states of the old Confederacy, and some of the big cities of the Deep South, such as Atlanta, fairly large numbers of Negro children were being taught in classes with white children. But in most of the south only a few Negro children were so taught. In both North and South, in fact more particularly in the big cities of the North, the existence of Negro "ghettos" and the deliberate policy of school committees and administrators in drawing district lines, meant that thousands of Negro schoolchildren were still segregated.

The decision of the Supreme Court on school desegregation was merely the starting point for a whole series of efforts to elevate the American Negro to the status of full citizenship, a movement known commonly as the "civil rights" movement. In this movement predominantly Negro organizations such as the National Association for the Advancement of Colored People (N.A.A.C.P.) as well as many with mixed white and Negro membership made use of the whole gamut of methods permissible in a modern western democracy, from propaganda in the various mass media to boycott, street demonstrations, "freedom marches," and pressure-group work at local, state, and federal levels.

There was indeed violence. But as such movements go, this was certainly a comparatively peaceful one, exemplified by such Negro leaders as Martin Luther King, who insisted on the "non-violent" character of their movement. By the mid-sixties some more intransigent Negro groups were angrily calling for "Black Power," and urging that the Negroes alone take control of the movement.

Pressure began with efforts to do away with "Jim Crow," the relegation of Negroes to separate and usually inferior treatment by law and custom in public accommodations of all sorts, in transportation, railroad and bus stations, airports, restaurants, hotels, golf courses, swimming pools, and churches. It is symbolic of the relative ease of changing new and modern habits and of urban as contrasted with rural ways that in general airports were the earliest and easiest to desegregate. Custom proved firmer than most Americans imagined; though the symbolism is subtler, it is a fact that churches were among the most difficult to desegregate. Even the legal changes at the heart of the movement—registration of Negro voters in particular—ran up against firm opposition. Equal employment opportunity, and its essential condition, equal educational opportunity, found hard going, and by no means solely in the South. With the passage of a fed-

eral Civil Rights Bill in 1965, the capstone of legal enactments had been placed. There remained for the future a long process of realizing in actual political and social life for Negroes the equality Jefferson held in his Declaration of Independence to be self-evident for all men.

Relatively unnoticed, another innovation took place in the structure of the American political society. The United States, regretting its experiment in "imperialism" after the Spanish-American War of 1898, had taken up a firm position in foreign policy in favor of the emancipation of dependent peoples. We ourselves freed the Philippines, which on July 4, 1946, became a sovereign state, though still clearly in the American orbit. Our relatively small Pacific island possessions we could justify on the grounds of military necessity. Alaska in 1958 and Hawaii in 1959 became full-fledged states, raising the number of states to fifty.

There remained the large and populous island of Puerto Rico, which was in fact a colonial dependency, in a singularly anomalous relation to the United States. Only a minority

Dr. Martin Luther King leads parade of civil rights marchers in Washington, D.C., August, 1965.

of its inhabitants really wanted independence on the Philippine model, because the economic advantages of free trade with and free immigration to the United States were so great for the island, which had a very high birth rate. We arrived at a compromise that probably owed something to British precedents in their Commonwealth. Puerto Rico in 1952 became an *Estado Libre Asociado,* or *Commonwealth,* with its own constitution, its own self-government, but still a part of, or "associated with," the United States. Puerto Rican emigration to the mainland raised its own problems of assimilation, notably in New York City, which had over 600,000 Puerto Ricans in 1966.

As a by-product of the presidential election of 1960, another customary barrier fell. The successful Democratic candidate, John Fitzgerald Kennedy, was the first Roman Catholic to be elected to the presidency, ending the prejudice, evident as recently as 1928 (see Chapter 28, p. 492), against a Roman Catholic in the president's office. Kennedy's presidency marked a renewed push toward the welfare state. Under his "New Frontier," plans were made, and in some cases bills were introduced in Congress, to provide hospital and medical aid for older people ("Medicare"), tax reform, civil rights, and measures against unemployment and poverty. For all his great personal charm, Kennedy had a good deal of trouble with Congress, and the actual achievement in formal legislation of most of the program of the New Frontier was the work of his Vice-President and successor, Lyndon Johnson, former Democratic leader in the Senate, and a man with rare skills in handling his fellow congressmen.

Kennedy's assassination at the hands of Lee Harvey Oswald in Dallas on November 22, 1963, shook the United States and indeed the world. The assassin was himself shot by a night-club proprietor two days later in the confusion of a public arraignment. A later inquiry headed by Chief Justice Warren concluded that Oswald was an unbalanced person, who had been involved in communist causes, but perhaps at bottom was chiefly motivated by an insane desire to attract public attention and go down in history. Though the Warren Commission Report was later attacked by certain students both sober and sensational, it seemed unlikely that the murders involved a conspiracy of any sort.

Lyndon Johnson, who was at once sworn into office as president, made no break with Kennedy's basic policies. In 1964 he was elected president by a sweeping majority over the conservative Republican candidate Barry Goldwater, Senator from Arizona. With a comfortable Democratic majority in both houses, Johnson set about carrying out many of Kennedy's projects and others of his own, such as a national campaign to eliminate poverty and a renewed national effort to conserve our natural resources. Johnson's "Great Society" thus took its place as a democratic slogan in the long line begun with Woodrow Wilson's "New Freedom." The worsening of the international situation in 1966, however, and in particular the Vietnam war, seemed to threaten the financial underpinning of Johnson's domestic program.

The fundamental basis of American foreign policy,—containment of communist expansion—did not alter substantially under three presidents of very different personality, the Republican Dwight Eisenhower, and the Democrats John Kennedy and Lyndon Johnson. Substantially successful and substantially supported by American public opinion, many specific phases of this policy met with opposition at home and among our many allies and sympathizers in the free world. Perhaps the strongest single current in such opposition, strong among "intellectuals" here and abroad, insisted that in our opposition to communism we had in many parts of the world allowed ourselves to be maneuvered into a position of supporting the ruling classes, often a small minority of wealthy people, against all attempts to achieve a better distribution of wealth. It may well be that history will ultimately decide that this accusation was unfair. Certainly the United States sought to take firmly a position against "colonialism" and in support of the new nations of Africa and Asia in their drive to attain freedom and prosperity; and it continued to give economic aid to many of them.

Canada

A prosperous Canada, subject to occasional mild recessions and specific difficulties in world market prices for her agricultural and mineral production, changed between 1953 and 1967 for chiefly political and psychological reasons. In 1958 John Diefenbaker, a Conservative, won a close victory, ending a twenty-two year Liberal tenure of power. In 1959 a new election gave the Conservatives a landslide majority. In 1963, the Liberals returned to power, but with only 130 seats, which meant that they had to govern as the principal party in a coalition. Still another election in 1965 failed to give the Liberals a solid majority. In addition to Conservatives and Liberals there were minority parties — New Democrats, definitely to the left; Social Credit, based on some unorthodox economic ideas, not however, socialist; and a French-Canadian

variant of this last. It seemed possible that Canada was beginning to develop a splinter-party system like those of many European democracies.

One reason for this, though by no means the only one, was the rise of French-Canadian nationalist feeling in the province of Quebec and the French-speaking regions of adjoining provinces. The few thousands of French left in Canada in 1763 had multiplied by the 1960's to some seven million. Since World War II they had for the first time enjoyed a vigorous economic growth and increasingly high standards of living, after lagging for decades, in this respect, behind the rest of Canada. Their unrest was not therefore due to absolute economic deprivation, though in part it was a demand for a greater share in the Canadian managerial and financial worlds. It was also a demand for greater cultural participation in Dominion life, and especially for true bilingualism after the Swiss pattern. Many people in the rest of Canada, who long felt culturally superior to the French, resisted their demands. By 1967, the French extremists who actually proposed to secede and set up an in-

President John F. Kennedy addresses officers and civilians at NATO headquarters outside Paris, June 2, 1961.

dependent nation, were probably no more than a noisy few young people addicted to violent rejection of any kind of "establishment." A federal commission on biculturalism was set up, and Canadians were at least well alerted to the problem. Any tolerable solution they might reach would be useful for the rest of a world troubled in many regions by problems of minorities.

Western Europe

In 1957, after careful preparation, France, West Germany, Italy, Belgium, the Netherlands, Luxembourg—the six countries of the Coal and Steel Community—set up, by the Treaty of Rome, the European Economic Community (EEC), better known as the Common Market, or sometimes as just "the Six." This was the beginning of true economic union under a central administration composed of delegates from each partner nation; its administration had certain rights independent of any member government. The treaty also provided for increasing powers over trade, production, immigration, and other matters for the Common Market, according to a carefully worked-out schedule. By the 1970's, it was planned that there would be in effect one common trading and producing society, a single market free from internal tariffs, and a population of some 180 million or more, substantially equal to that of the United States and equipped with equal economic skills and experience, and with similar "mixed" economies —free enterprise under government regulation.

The decade 1956–1966 saw substantial progress toward this goal. The tourist by car or rail, who remembered pre-war travel in the six countries and the delays at frontiers, was atonished to be able to pass from one country to another almost as easily as he crossed state lines in the United States, and quite as easily as he crossed the Canadian-American frontier. Yet difficulties arose in the orderly carrying out of the schedule. In 1963, for example, France vetoed Britain's proposed entry, and insisted on specific provisions favoring French farmers in the Common Market. But the dif-

ficulty about a British part in any European supra-national arrangement was real. Many of the British regard themselves as primarily part of the Commonwealth and not as Europeans. The British set up in 1959 the European Free Trade Association, often called the "Outer Seven," with Britain, Sweden, Norway, Denmark, Austria, Switzerland, and Portugal as members. This was a much looser arrangement than the Common Market, an arrangement which allowed each member to set its own external tariffs as it wished, thus protecting British "imperial preference" in favor of Commonwealth countries.

The Council for Europe (Chapter 30, p. 556) on the whole marked time between 1953 and 1966. Yet the Council, the Common Market, the Outer Seven, and the U.N. all helped preserve the idea of supra-national grouping in Europe. There were even those who dreamed of a United States of Europe that would ultimately include Russia and her present satellites. A united Europe would not necessarily be favorable to American leadership in world politics and might indeed set itself up as definitely a rival of ours. It is perhaps a tribute to American unwillingness to look at international politics with Machiavellian eyes that, on the whole, American opinion since World War II—including the opinion of men very high in our government —generally favored 'movements for greater European unity.

Great Britain

During the period 1953–1967 Great Britain enjoyed virtually full employment. Her growth rate was considerably greater than in the decades between 1919 and 1939, but not equal to those of her continental neighbors. She continued as leader of the "sterling-bloc" to be a financial power in the world. An American traveler in Britain who remembered the "austerity" of the immediate postwar years was bound to be struck on his return in the 1960's by the evidence of renewed prosperity—traffic jams, new housing, modern factories, especially in the area of Greater

London, attractive window displays in the stores, even the return of "the roast beef of old England."

Yet even in purely economic terms, there was always a threat to this prosperity. The pound, a currency still used as standard along with the dollar in the "free world," was always in danger. Its exchange value, already reduced from its nineteenth-century stable equivalence to $5.00, had after 1949 been pegged at $2.80. But continued pressure on the pound in the 1960's repeatedly required help from Britain's allies in the form of rather complex financial measures to maintain this value. This weakness of the pound signaled an unfavorable "balance of trade": the British people were buying more from the rest of the world than they could sell to it.

Behind this imbalance lay a condition evident even before World War I: Britain, the first nation to industrialize, was, in part as a result of the very size of her early industrial plant, suffering from its inefficiency and its obsolescence, in comparison with that of the United States, Germany, and Japan. Observers felt that Britain's managers lacked enterprise, were unwilling to adapt new ways, or to invest sufficiently in research; and found her workers suspicious of any change in methods, regarding management as the perpetual enemy, more interested in the tea-break than in the quality of the product. Many of Britain's distinguished scientists and engineers left home to migrate to the United States, Canada, or Australia. This was what the British called the "brain drain." Finally, the loss of much of the nineteenth-century empire meant that Britain had to pay more *relatively* for the raw materials she had to import for her food and her industrial use than she did in the nineteenth century; and also, that she certainly had to face even in her old "colonies" the competition of new and more efficient industries as well as new tariff barriers. These old "colonies" now were making some of the things they had had to buy in England in the old days.

This fundamental economic difficulty, thoroughly aired in press, radio, and television, was not reflected in any threat of political instability. Certainly the Britain of the mid-

1960's showed no signs of intense class or ideological warfare. The basic two-party state prevailed. The Conservatives in the general election of 1964 gave way to the Labor party, which had only a tiny majority of three in a House of Commons of 630 members. The new Prime Minister, Harold Wilson, skillfully held on until a new election in 1966, when he emerged with a greatly increased majority. Thus strengthened, he proposed in the late summer of 1966 measures to cope with the by-then menacing danger to the pound. These measures were essentially old-fashioned economic orthodoxy: a freeze of wages and prices in an effort to restore the balance between what British workmen—and managers—spent and what they produced. Put in moral rather than in economic terms, Wilson was proposing to the British that they tighten their belts, give up some of their recently acquired good things of life, and work harder for less cash return.

Wilson insisted that this renewed "austerity" would apply to everybody—managers, businessmen, upper and middle classes generally, as well as to the working classes. But his proposals threatened to split his own party down the middle, with the more radical half insisting that what he was doing was playing the capitalists' game, exploiting the poor to support the rich. At the critical Trades Union Congress of September, 1966, he won a precarious victory. The future, however, remained most uncertain. A new general election might bring in a Conservative government. But the Conservatives were no more willing than Labor to take drastic measures. The two great British parties continued not very different in fundamentals: Tories have not proposed real laissez-faire or "capitalism," and Liberals or Laborites have not proposed real "socialism," let alone totalitarian communism.

Britain, again under both Conservative and Labor party governments, remained a firm if at times somewhat critical, ally of the United States. In the difficulties encountered by NATO (see p. 624) she consistently supported American policy, though much English public opinion opposed the war in Vietnam. Anti-Americanism was a reality in many quarters in

Britain: on the left, which regarded us as too rich; on the right, which regarded us as too pushing; and among "intellectuals," who found us too immature for our power. Much of this was sheer jealousy. Prime Minister Wilson largely disregarded it, and consistently sought to play the honest broker, and to bring about a settlement at the conference table.

Thus Britain in 1967 was in real trouble. Part of that trouble was the marginal costs of preserving something of her great past as a world power; costs of relatively large armed forces; costs of her "presence east of Suez," which we very much wished her to continue; costs of an elaborate diplomatic and intelligence network; costs of a whole way of life. Perhaps the British could solve their basic problem if they accepted a small-power status somewhat like that of Sweden today; perhaps they could solve it by membership in a more united European community, or even in the existing Common Market.

West Germany

The central fact about Germany in 1967 was that there was still no Germany, but two separate Germanies. The Federal Republic of Germany (West Germany) and the German Democratic Republic had no formal diplomatic relations, neither recognizing the other as legitimate. After long years, during which East Germans attracted by better West German living conditions both material and spiritual simply crossed the border, the East German government in August, 1961, began building the "wall of infamy" between the two parts of the city (see p. 593). This wall still stood in 1967, though on special holidays, families in West Berlin were allowed to cross into East Berlin briefly to visit relatives and friends. As European tensions relaxed somewhat, West and East German teams were both entering general sports competitions, such as the World Cup in soccer, though they did not directly compete against each other. The press in West Germany and, less freely in East Germany, now at least occasionally hinted

at possible improvements in relations between the two.

In West Germany, gross national product (GNP) rose from $23 billion in 1950 to $103 billion in 1964, with no serious monetary inflation. As elsewhere in the western world, this prosperity was to a large degree well spread through all classes of society. The working man in West Germany had begun to enjoy the kind of things—even a car of his own—that his opposite number in the United States had had for some time. New buildings, not by any means just replacements for those damaged by Allied air attacks, rose everywhere. Notably in the Ruhr and the Rhineland, the divided superhighways Hitler built for largely military purposes were now fearfully overcrowded, and were gradually being widened and extended.

To this economic prosperity was added an apparent political stability surprising in a society that had undergone three revolutionary changes of régime between 1918 and 1945. West Germany from 1949 to 1961 was governed federally by the moderate Christian Democrats under Konrad Adenauer (see Chapter 30) and, after he retired late in his 80's, by his successor, Ludwig Ehrhard. This long continuance in office was one supported by the voters, not the result of one-party totalitarian politics. West Germany seemed to be approaching two-party democratic politics, with the Christian Democrats challenged chiefly by the Social Democrats, roughly similar to the British Labor party. The Social Democrats held power in some of the states and cities of the federal union, and notably in West Berlin, whose popular mayor, Willy Brandt, ran unsuccessfully for the federal chancellorship against Ehrhard in 1964. A neo-Nazi minority existed in West Germany, but by 1966 it had achieved no very alarming successes at the polls, and was conspicuous largely in newspaper accounts of occasional antisemitic activities. Militant organizations of war veterans and of refugees from the "lost" eastern territories now included in Poland, the U.S.S.R., or Czechoslovakia, perhaps posed more of a possible threat to stability.

West Germany of course owed its present

position in part to the Cold War. It was allowed to re-arm early in the 1950's and to join NATO. Military conscription was introduced in 1957, and in 1967 West Germany had a relatively large and very modern army, navy, and air force. Government and people supported the armed forces as a necessity, but the old Wilhelmine and Nazi militarism did not revive among the people at large. In the autumn of 1966 a crisis arose between the military top brass and the civilian administration, in which the civilians apparently won. Access to the atom bomb was not included in this re-armament, but German public opinion apparently was not greatly exercised over this exclusion, though there were occasional ominous rumbles of discontent.

Between 1953 and 1967 the German Federal Republic maintained good relations with its hereditary foe, France, in part a product of the friendship between Adenauer and de Gaulle, both moderate conservatives, both good Catholics. Without such Franco-German cooperation, the successes of the Common Market could hardly have been achieved. In the mid-sixties a number of difficulties arose between the two. Adenauer's successor, Ehrhard — a Protestant and much disliked by Adenauer himself — got on much less well with de Gaulle than Adenauer had. Within the Common Market, difficulties arose over agricultural tariffs. Within NATO, de Gaulle's break with the closely knit military alliance confronted the West Germans with what seemed to many of them a choice between the United States and France, a choice they did not wish to make but which mere prudence dictated should be in favor of the United States. Nevertheless, Franco-German relations, diplomatic, commercial and above all, cultural, continued better than they had been for centuries.

In the late autumn of 1966 there arose in West Germany a political crisis which could perhaps indicate that her long political stability was threatened. Neither the Christian Democrats nor the Social Democrats had a secure majority in the Reichstag. Chancellor Erhard was governing in coalition with a small right-wing party, the Free Democrats, basically non-Nazi conservatives opposed to "socialism". Mounting difficulties with some of the high command in the armed forces, diplomatic difficulties of trying to support American policies in Europe and yet not breaking entirely with France, and no doubt some underlying fears that the clear slowing down of West German economic growth in 1966 might presage a real recession, all contributed to Erhard's political difficulties. In November 1966, the Free Democrats brought his government down by refusing to support his proposals for higher taxes. But the Christian Democrats came forward with Christian Georg Kiesinger, a Catholic, who succeeded in forming a "grand coalition" with the Social Democrats. Willy Brandt became Vice-Chancellor and Foreign Minister. Though some members of both parties disapproved, and though Kiesinger's past membership in the Nazi Party aroused some alarm abroad, the new coalition, if stable, would command overwhelming popular support. It was designed to last until the next scheduled elections in 1969.

A prosperous West Germany seemed, as 1967 began, to have lived down its past as an aggressor, as a perturbing factor in the world, as a totalitarian society capable of the genocide of the 1940's (see Chapter 29). Yet the twenty-year postwar prosperity, particularly great in West Germany, might not, in spite of the optimism of many economists, prove to be depression-proof. Anything like the worldwide depression of the 1930's might well destroy the social stability on which West German democracy rests. Moreover, the sepparation of West from East Germany was unprecedented, yet after two decades there were no signs that a United Germany was possible. Then too, the loss of much of pre-war Germany to the Slavic powers of Poland and Russia (see Chapter 30, p. 565) was traumatic for German nationalists. If German nationalism should in the future prove anything like as strong a collective emotion as it clearly has been in the past, the unfortunate division of Germany might confront the next generation with a grave potential source of that next world war that mankind knows must not take place.

France

In France, the year 1958 saw the Fifth Republic replace the Fourth, as General de Gaulle took power in the midst of a crisis provoked largely by the revolt in Algeria. Governmental financial instability, inflation resulting from war costs in Indo-China, and a rising popular disgust with the "politicians" combined to bring about the fall of the Fourth Republic in 1958. A military and rightist *coup d'état* in Algeria, headed by General Massu, a tough veteran, took place on May 13, 1958. On May 15, de Gaulle, who must have known what was brewing, but who was in no sense part of a conspiracy, announced that he was willing to come out of retirement and take power. The army officers in revolt and their supporters wrongly assumed that he would carry out their policies for keeping Algeria French.

The change was in France itself accompanied by comparatively little violence, was confirmed by a plebiscite, and all in all looked more like a *coup d'état* than a revolution. The Constitution of 1958 substituted for *parliamentary* government of the British type, *presidential* government of something approximating the American type. The president was, after an amendment of 1962, elected for a seven-year term by direct popular vote rather than by an electoral college. An absolute majority was required, and if not achieved in a first election, was to be obtained in a run-off between the two candidates with the greatest number of votes. In the general election of 1965, de Gaulle, running for re-election, in the first round got only a plurality among four major candidates, but won in the final election against the leftist Mitterand. The president appointed the premier, who could dissolve the legislature and order new elections any time after the first year of the life of the legislature. Thus the new Constitution gave the executive more power, the legislature much less. Those who disliked the new constitution complained that it made the legislature a mere rubber stamp.

But France had still a basically democratic and not a totalitarian constitution. De Gaulle's enemies called him a dictator, and likened him to Napoleon III. Cartoonists everywhere enjoyed drawing him as Louis XIV, the *roi soleil*, with wig and silk stockings, the personification of French haughtiness and superiority. He was certainly an obstinate, opinionated man, by no means a Jeffersonian democrat; but though a general and personally authoritarian, he was no Boulanger or Pétain. He used convincingly and with conviction the vocabulary of conventional middle-class democracy. During a decade in power he never once gave even a hint of dropping that sacred word *république*; a century earlier the elected "Prince-president" Louis Napoleon had become within two years the Emperor Napoleon III.

Between 1953 and 1967 France did undergo a revolution in the daily life of the ordinary Frenchman. Once addicted to hoarding money in a sock under the mattress, he now bought cars, televisions sets, and hi-fi sets on the installment plan. Once reluctant to travel abroad, explaining that France itself had everything, he now flocked in droves to Spain, Italy, Germany, to Britain, that land of barbarous *cuisine*, and even, at bargain off-season airplane rates, to the United States. Once insistent on freshly-baked bread twice a day from the bakery around the corner, he now tentatively experimented with bread produced on a large scale, wrapped in waxed-paper, and kept—incredibly—for several days, and in a refrigerator at that. Most French intellectuals objected vainly to this "Americanization."

All this was based upon, and in turn sustained, economic growth in a thoroughly modern, large-scale industrial society. In France, the economic growth of the period was particularly striking because, unlike Britain, Germany, and the United States, it had hitherto preserved much of the older, small-scale, conservative individualistic economy. A few statistics of September 1966: growth rate, about 6 per cent annually, slightly greater than that of West Germany at the time, and well ahead of that of Britain; index of industrial production, 123, with a 1962 base of 100; consumer price level, 114 on a 1962 base of 100.* This last meant an "inflation" of a little over 3 per cent annually, which is about that of the American economy at present, a rate which many economists think is probably inevitable in a free society enjoying economic growth. The ordinary Frenchman, like the ordinary American, was having a "love affair with the automobile." It is true that relatively many more Frenchmen than Americans could not yet really express that love, but at least they could roll along on some vehicle, if only a *motovélo* (very light motorcycle) run by an internal combustion engine. One result, even in provincial cities, was a parking problem worse, if possible, than our own; another was the steadily increasing rate of fatal accidents on the roads; still another, the virtual disappearance of the peasant's horse or ox in favor of the tractor.

All these socio-economic changes in their beginnings antedated the accession of de Gaulle to power in 1958. They had their beginnings in American Marshall Plan aid in 1947, and their critical initial growth, the "take-off," came during the last years of the much maligned Fourth Republic. Yet the continuance and increase of economic growth no doubt owed much to the political stability achieved so far under the Fifth Republic. France in 1967 still enjoyed freedom of speech, of the press, of public assembly. French journalists could and did say as nasty things about their president as American journalists could and did say about ours. A best-selling phonograph record was a hilarious and most irreverent parody of de Gaulle's pontifical style of oratory. The cartoonists had great fun with his height (6' 3") and his prominent nose. The régime did control radio and television (though not the newspaper and magazine press) and monopolized these important organs of opinion between 1958 and 1965. But in the general election of 1965 it

*See the French news weekly, L'Express, No. 794, 5–11 September, 1966, pp. 10–11.

yielded to the pressure of public opinion, and consented to give de Gaulle's opposition candidates some time if not quite "equal time" on the air. One of the candidates, the centrist Lecanuet, proved to have the sort of TV appeal associated with J. F. Kennedy, and de Gaulle's failure to obtain an absolute majority in the first election was usually attributed to this fact.

In foreign policy de Gaulle was certainly a deeply committed French nationalist. His insistence on developing a French atomic bomb and the *force de frappe* (striking force) needed to deliver it reflected his determination to make France capable of making its own international decisions. In order to do this, he refused to sign the Test-Ban Treaty, and France continued in 1966 to test atomic weapons in the atmosphere, much to the distress of the United States, which indeed found de Gaulle's policies in general illogical, dangerous, irritating, and hard to understand. Yet it was not at all clear that he was an aggressive, romantic nationalist, intent on achieving an impossible French world leadership. He did oppose any attempt to achieve a United States of Europe, or even a closely integrated supra-national NATO; instead, he wanted what he called a *Europe des patries,* the Europe of the Fatherlands. He held that for Europe federal union was impossible, and preferred an old-fashioned "balance of power." Striking predominance of *either* American or Russian power in Europe, he argued, upset the balance of power; Russia was the danger in 1947, the United States in 1967.

De Gaulle succeeded, against his upbringing and traditions, in the task of liquidating the French colonial empire. The French, or at least the French ruling classes, believed that their colonial subjects wanted, or at least could be persuaded to want, to become real Frenchmen, the empire to become a true federal union. This feeling was strongest as regards Algeria, which was politically a part of France, organized in *départements* and represented in the legislature at Paris. But most of the Moslem nine-tenths of the Algerian population disagreed. De Gaulle had come to power in 1958 with conservative support during a series of disorders between extremists who wanted the Algerians suppressed and extremists who wanted the French to get out of Algeria at any cost. He it was who in 1962 worked out the compromises of Algerian independence, leaving France some "influence," and some rights over Saharan oil. For this "treason" the rightists never forgave him. Most of the leftists on the other hand never gave him even grudging credit for it. He remained a leader supported mostly by the moderates.

Indeed the "new France" appeared to be politically moderate. The communists on the far left were far stronger than what was left of the old rightists, who hardly any longer even claimed to be royalists. This, and not de Gaulle's claims for French "grandeur," was the striking thing about recent French history. But could this new political stability and apparent lessening of class conflict withstand a serious depression? What would happen when the aging de Gaulle died or retired? Would France revert to splinter parties, frequent cabinet changes, and *coups d'état?* These were the large unanswerable questions.

Italy

Italy's economic growth, between 1953 and 1966, was so remarkable that the Italians themselves refer to it as their *"miracolo economico."* As in France, this was achieved with some government ownership, and with much government regulation and planning. Italy was a "mixed" economy, but a free society. Milan, long a busy and active city, began to look like another Chicago. Rome had perhaps the most desperate traffic problem of any great city in the world. Membership in the Common Market, and freedom from the troubles of imperial liquidation, gave Italian enterprise opportunities it had never had before.

Politically, Italy was surprisingly stable, and that without any "strong man" like de Gaulle. Since World War II, three Christian Democrats, Alcide de Gasperi, Amintore Fan-

fani, and Aldo Moro, have somehow managed most of the time to command adequate parliamentary majorities in a multi-party state. The Italian Communist party was the strongest in the free world, and communists governed a number of important cities. But they have never attained national power. In a series of complicated negotiations in the 1960's the major political group, the Christian Democrats, in themselves a complex and by no means united group, with its own right and left, began a process the Italians called the "apertura a sinistra," the opening to the left. In this process they won over some Socialist support without altogether losing rightist support. Thus, although in the elections of 1963 the Christian Democrats had only 41 per cent of the Chamber of Deputies and 38 per cent of the popular vote (communists, 26 per cent of the Chamber, 25 per cent of the popular vote) they were able to govern by coalition with other groups without marked difficulties. A further weakening of the extreme left was achieved in 1966, when the Socialists—long split between an anti-communist wing and a wing that often collaborated with the communists—reunited as one party.

The grave problems of the "mezzogiorno," the southern part of the peninsula, and the islands of Sardinia and Sicily, were attacked by programs of investments, by providing jobs in the north or in Germany or Switzerland for the surplus workers of the south, and by old-age pensions. Italy had in the last decade made extremely effective use of one of her major assets, her natural beauty and her historic and artistic heritage. In her balance of payments, an income of about $1 billion annually from tourists brought in a useful item on the "export" side.

Among the smaller states of "free" Europe, all of which shared in the general economic prosperity, Spain—still in Franco's control almost thirty years after the Civil War—had taken major steps toward modernization and a few mild measures to relax political tyranny. In Belgium, which enjoyed great material well-being, the chronic difficulties between the French-speaking Walloons and the

Dutch-speaking Flemish continued to worsen and to threaten the stability of the country.

In 1967, a pessimist could argue that we were no nearer to a peaceful world than we were in 1946. Yet even a pessimist would have to admit that the United States, most of Europe, the former British self-governing colonies, Japan, and the Soviet Union have had plenty if not peace; that Asia, Africa, and Latin America have gained — if unevenly — in material wealth; and even that the civil wars, guerrilla wars, revolutions, and other disturbances of our day were in no way comparable to the holocausts of World War I and World War II. As the simple confrontation of the late 1940's between the American coalition and the Soviet coalition grew more complicated and more dispersed, and as Communist China rose in power and menace, the Russians lost some of their earlier fervor to make the formerly colonial world communist immediately and by force, and the sharpest edges of the tensions between the two super-powers, the United States and the Soviet Union, seemed to grow duller. Though the mid-sixties could rightly be regarded as a "Time of Troubles," the worst was not happening: the world continued to exist, to progress rapidly in material terms, and to grow in population. Here indeed, perhaps, lay the best excuse for pessimism: in the likelihood that mankind was breeding faster than its food supplies could be increased, despite the miracles in agricultural science, and the possibilities of exploiting the food supplies till hidden in the ocean depths. Compared with this threat, the continued lack of concord in international politics seemed almost bearable.

Reading Suggestions for the Contemporary World since 1953

(Asterisk indicates paperbound edition.)

Note: For the most recent materials in this chapter, the only sources are current newspapers and periodicals, both domestic and foreign.

General

Arthur M. Schlesinger, Jr., *A Thousand Days, John F. Kennedy in the White House* (Houghton, Mifflin, 1965), and Theodore C. Sorensen, *Kennedy* (Harper & Row, 1965). Extraordinarily full accounts of American foreign relations during the Kennedy era by close confidants of the President.

Dwight D. Eisenhower, *The White House Years,* 2 vols. (Doubleday, 1963–1965). Former President Eisenhower's account of his years in office, 1952–1960.

D. Donnelly, *Struggle for the World: The Cold War, 1917–1965* (St. Martin's Press, 1965. Good general account.

C. Quigley, *Tragedy and Hope: A History of the World in Our Time* (Macmillan, 1966). A long, thoughtful attempt to understand what we can learn from recent history.

U.S.S.R.

Leonard Schapiro, *The Government and Politics of the Soviet Union* (Hutchinson, 1965). Excellent short treatment by a leading authority.

Alfred G. Meyer, *The Soviet Political System. An Interpretation* (Random House, 1965). Sound recent study by a political scientist.

Randolph L. Braham, ed., *Soviet Politics and Government: A Reader* (*Knopf). Useful collection of source materials and scholarly short studies.

Donald S. Zagoria, *The Sino-Soviet Conflict, 1956–1961* (Atheneum, 1964), and William E. Griffith, *Albania and the Sino-Soviet Rift* (M.I.T. Press, 1963), and his *The Sino-Soviet Rift, Analysed and Documented* (M.I.T. Press, 1964). Three useful studies on the quarrel between the U.S.S.R. and China.

Zbigniew K. Brzezinski, *The Soviet Bloc: Unity and Conflict* (Harvard Univ. Press, 1960). A solid study by a leading political scientist.

Emerging Nations

Note: the following are all supplemental to those cited for the Revolution against Imperialism (p. 580).

V. M. Dean and H. Harootunian, *West and Non-West: New Perspectives* (*Holt). An anthology covering many aspects of the relations between the developed and the emerging nations.

E. Demig, *Modern Japan* (Praeger, 1961). Helpful general view; in the series, "Nations of the Modern world."

P. Langer, *Japan Yesterday & Today* (*Holt). Popular introduction; in the series, "Contemporary Civilizations."

K. S. Latourette, *China;* O. D. Corpuz, *The Philippines;* J. D. Legge, *Indonesia;* S. Wolpert, *India.* Informative volumes in the series, "Modern Nations in Historical Perspective" (*Spectrum).

D. N. Wilber, *Pakistan Yesterday & Today* (*Holt). Excellent popular introduction; in the "Contemporary Civilizations" series.

H. Tinker, *India & Pakistan* (*Praeger). Useful political analysis.

G. Lewis, *Turkey,* 3rd ed. (Praeger, 1965). Competent general introduction; in the series, "Nations of the Modern World."

P. Stirling, *Turkish Village* (*Wiley). Valuable insights into an essential aspect of emerging societies.

N. Safran, *The United States & Israel* (Harvard Univ. Press, 1963); W. R. Polk, *The United States & the Arab World* (Harvard Univ. Press, 1965). Detailed volumes, stressing the background of the Middle Eastern nations; in the series, "American Foreign Policy Library."

H. B. Sharabi, *Nationalism and Revolution in the Arab World* (*Van Nostrand). Valuable reflections by an expert on the subject.

J. Hatch, *A History of Postwar Africa* (Praeger, 1965). Clear and helpful guide to a complex subject.

B. Ward, *Africa in the Making* (Norton, 1966). Discussion by a well-informed publicist.

G. M. Carter, *National Unity and Regionalism in Eight African States* (Cornell Univ. Press, 1966), and G. M. Carter, ed., *Politics in Africa: Seven Cases* (*Harcourt, Brace & World). Two recent works by a ranking expert on Africa.

J. Cope, *South Africa* (Praeger, 1965). General survey; in the series, "Nations of the Modern World."

J. F. Gallagher, *The United States and North Africa* (Harvard Univ., 1963). Valuable introduction to Morocco, Algeria, and Tunisia.

J. E. Flint, *Nigeria and Ghana* (*Spectrum). Study of two states that have made more than their share of recent history; in the series, "Modern Nations in Historical Perspective."

R. J. Alexander, *Today's Latin America* (*Anchor), and T. Szulc, *Latin America* (*Atheneum). Suggestive general introductions.

M. Rodriguez, *Central America;* J. E. Fagg, *Cuba, Haiti & the Dominican Republic;* H. Bernstein, *Venezuela & Colombia.* Handy volumes in the series, "Modern Nations in Historical Perspective" (*Spectrum).

K. Silvert, *Chile Yesterday & Today* (*Holt). In the informative popular series, "Contemporary Civilizations."

Western
Democracies

S. R. Graubard, ed., *A New Europe?* (Houghton Mifflin, 1964). Essays, mostly analytical, by various hands. Stimulating.

S. Kuznets, *Postwar Economic Growth* (Harvard Univ. Prss, 1964). An important synthesis of a major topic, by a distinguished economist.

T. H. White, *The Making of the President, 1960* (*Pocket Books), and *The Making of the President, 1964* (Atheneum, 1965). Two most readable books illuminating many phases of our recent history.

D. E. Butler and A. King, *The British General Election of 1964* (St. Martin's Press, 1965). Fine example of current political scientific studies.

J. Lacouture, *De Gaulle* (*New American Library, 1966). The best short life, somewhat too allusive for American consumption.

S. Hoffmann and others, *In Search of France* (Harvard Univ. Press, 1963). Fine analytical studies of various phases of contemporary France.

L. Wylie, *Village in the Vaucluse* (*Harper Colophon), and L. Wylie, ed., *Chanzeaux* (Harvard Univ. Press, 1966). Two complementary studies of French villages today, based on field work.

M. Salvadori, *Italy* (*Spectrum). A valuable final chapter on contemporary Italy.

A. Grosser, *The Federal Republic of Germany,* (Praeger, 1964; *Praeger). Best short account.

Germany Reports, 4th ed., (Press and Information Office, West Germany, 1966). A mine of information, to be used with knowledge; it is an official government publication.

Bernard B. Fall, *The Two Viet-Nams: a Political and Military Analysis,* rev. ed. (Praeger, 1965), and Robert Shaplen, *The Lost Revolution; the U.S. in Vietnam, 1946–1966,* rev. ed. (Harper & Row, 1966). Two interesting studies of the Vietnam war.

Fiction

Note: The following books are all discussed in the text.

Ilya Ehrenburg, *The Thaw,* trans. Manya Harari (Harvil, 1955).

V. Dudintsev, *Not by Bread Alone,* trans. E. Bone (Dutton, 1957).

B. Pasternak, *Dr. Zhivago,* trans. Max Hayward and Manya Harari (Pantheon, 1958; *Signet).

Michael Sholokhov, *And Quiet Flows the Don,* trans., S. Garry (L. Putnam, 1953; *Vintage, 1966), *The Don Flows Home to the Sea,* trans. S. Garry (*Vintage, 1966), and *Harvest on the Don* (*Signet).

A. I. Solzhenitsyn, *A Day in the Life of Ivan Denisovitch,* trans., Max Hayward and R. Hingley (Praeger, 1963; *Bantam, 1963).

Abram Tertz, pseud., *The Makepeace Experiment,* trans., Manya Harari (Pantheon, 1965); and, in one volume, his *Socialist Realism,* trans., G. Dennis, and *The Trial Begins,* trans. Max Hayward (*Vintage, 1965).

Yevgeny Yevtushenko, *A Precocious Autobiography,* trans., A. R. MacAndrew (*Dutton, 1963), and his *Selected Poetry,* trans. Robin Milner-Gulland and Peter Levi (*Penguin, 1962).

32

Man's Fate

in the Twentieth Century

I The Intellectual
Revolution Continues

The old truism about the difficulty of seeing the whole forest when attention is fixed on the separate trees holds especially for contemporary intellectual history. Among the countless "ideas" that come to our attention through the printed or the spoken word, through symbols, diagrams, pictures, even through musical sounds, it is almost impossible to distinguish those ideas which are characteristic of our age, which give it its flavor or style, which establish its "climate of opinion." Indeed, it is tempting to conclude that this very *variety* of ideas, spread abroad among countless millions through all the channels of mass communications, is the distinguishing mark of our time. There is, moreover, a further difficulty confronting the historian of contemporary thought and feeling. As we shall note later in this chapter, the gap between the culture of the few, the "highbrows," and the culture of the many, who are not necessarily "lowbrows," just not highbrows—this gap seems nowadays especially wide and deep. The historian who relied wholly on evidence from the work of "serious" modern poets or artists would come to quite different conclusions from one who rested on evidence from "comic" strips, popular music, conventional artists and illustrators, and what goes out over the air on television and radio.

Yet a historian writing in the twenty-first century and using only the evidence from "popular" culture would see and sense great differences from the popular culture of Victorian days. Our hot jazz would not sound to him much like a Viennese waltz, the violent and sexy "whodunits" would not be to him much like the Sherlock Holmes stories, the picture magazines would not remind him of Currier and Ives prints, and even in the so-called comic strips the frustrations, the inferiority complexes, and pathetic illusions, even the horrors that fill many strips would seem worlds apart from the naive buffoonery of the first such strips of about 1900, "Happy Hooligan," for instance, or "Buster Brown," or the "Yellow Kid."

Nor were such a twenty-first-century historian to concentrate on the high culture would he be any less struck with the great changes since 1890, perhaps in fact he would be more struck with the changes. It is true that he would readily see in the *avant garde* writers and artists and in the "anti-intellectual" philosophers of the late nineteenth century (see Chapter 23) precursors of twentieth-century philosophical and artistic movements. Yet he would surely be struck by the way the twentieth century has gone beyond its precursors. He would not confuse contemporary abstractionists with Monet or Cézanne, nor atonal music, let alone "concrete" music, with the music of Brahms, nor James Joyce's *Ulysses,* let alone some modern French "anti-novels," with the novels of Henry James or even Sinclair Lewis.

We shall slowly return to some of these specific representatives of contemporary high culture. Here let us note that our hypothetical twenty-first century historian, though he would have to note the differences between the highbrow and the popular culture of our time, would not conclude that they were wholly separate and wholly different cultures. He would see that they have much in common, that both have strong elements of contrast with the culture of the nineteenth century. We cannot of course begin to guess how he would feel toward us and our culture, nor with what terms he would try and tell his readers about us. But he would surely have to call attention to the notes of violence and despair, the unprecedented frankness with which the Anglo-Saxon four-letter words are printed as well as uttered, the repudiation of conventional representational art, the preoccupation with such psychological difficulties as are indicated by "alienation," "identity-crisis," "commitment," the great premium set upon originality, novelty, youth against age, the rise of a popular slick urban cynicism, the doubts about even so ingrained a belief, in the United States at least, as the belief in inevitable progress with a capital P. We shall in conclusion consider how far all this is in fact a repudiation of, a resistance to, our democratic inheritance from the eighteenth-century Enlightenment. Meanwhile, we must essay some more specific analysis of the attitudes, the tastes, the "ideas" of our confused and confusing age. We shall not attempt a detailed "coverage," but rather attempt by concentrating on representative figures to illustrate the characteristics of our "high" culture and how it differs from that of the nineteenth century.

Psychology: Freud

Following leads from the biological sciences, the nineteenth century came to put particular emphasis on *process,* on the dynamics of change in time. The twentieth century, taking its cue from psychology, has come to put particular emphasis on the role of the unconscious in human thought and action, on the irrationality—or at least non-rationality—of much human behavior. Foremost among the

Freud, as interpreted by Cocteau, the French surrealist.

thinkers responsible for this emphasis was Sigmund Freud (1856–1939). Freud was a physician, trained in Vienna in the rationalist medical tradition of the late nineteenth century. His interest was early drawn to mental illness, where he soon found cases in which patients exhibited symptoms of very real organic disturbances, but for which no obvious organic causes could be found. Under analysis, as Freud's therapeutic treatment came to be called, the patient, relaxed on a couch, is urged to pour out what he can remember of his earliest childhood, or indeed infancy. After many such treatments the analyst can hope to find what is disturbing the patient, and by making him aware of what that is, hope to help him.

Had Freud merely contented himself with this kind of therapy, few of us would have heard of him. But from all this clinical expe-rience he worked out a system of psychology that has had a very great influence, not only on psychiatry and psychology, but on some of our basic conceptions of human relations. Freud starts with the concept of a set of "drives" with which each person is born. These drives, which arise in the unconscious, are expressions of the "id." Freud never tried to locate the id physiologically; he used the term, which in Latin means "this [thing]," to avoid the moralistic overtones in words like "desires." These drives try to get satisfaction and pleasure, to express themselves in action. The infant, notably, is "uninhibited"—that is, his drives well up into action from the id without restraint from his conscious mind. But by no means without restraint from his parents or nurse—and there's the difficulty. The infant finds himself frustrated. As he grows, as his mind is formed, he comes to be conscious of the fact that some of the things he wants to do are objectionable to those closest to him, and on whom he is so dependent. He himself therefore begins to repress these drives from his id.

With his dawning consciousness of the world outside himself, the child has in fact developed another part of his psyche, which Freud at first called the "censor," and later divided into two phases which he called the "ego" and the "superego." The ego is the individual's private censor, his awareness that in accordance with what Freudians call the "reality principle" certain drives from his id simply cannot succeed. The superego in a way is what common language calls "conscience"; it is the individual's response as part of a social system in which certain actions are proper and certain actions improper. Now these drives of the id, and indeed in most of its phases the dictates of the superego, are for Freud a sort of great reservoir of which the individual is not normally aware—that is, they are part of his "unconscious.'" In a mentally healthy individual, enough of the drives of the id succeed so that he feels contented. But even the healthiest of individuals has had to repress a great deal of his drives from the id. This successful repression the Freudians account for in part at least by a process they call "sublimation." They think that the healthy individual somehow finds for a drive suppressed by ego or superego, or by both working together, a new and socially approved outlet or expression. Thus a drive toward sexual relations not approved in one's circle might be sublimated into the writing of poetry or music or even into athletics.

With the neurotic person, however, Freud held that drives, having been suppressed, driven back down into the unconscious, find no suitable other outlet or sublimation, and continue, so to speak, festering in the id, trying to find some outlet. They find all sorts of outlets of an abnormal sort, symptoms of illness in great variety. They display themselves in all sorts of neuroses and phobias, which have in common a failure to conform to the "reality principle." The neurotic individual is "maladjusted." And if the failure to meet the reality principle is really complete, the individual is insane, "psychotic," and lives in an utterly unreal private world of his own.

Freud's therapy rested on the belief that if the individual neurotic could come to understand why he behaved as he did he could frequently make a proper adjustment and lead a normal life. But here Freud parted company with the rationalist tradition of the eighteenth century. He held that there was no use preaching at the individual, reasoning simply with him, telling him the error of his ways, pointing out what was unreasonable in his behavior. Reason could not get directly at the unconscious, where the source of his trouble lay. Only by the long slow process of psychoanalysis, in which the individual day after day sought in memories of his earliest childhood for concrete details, could the listening analyst pick from this stream of consciousness the significant details that pointed to the hidden repression, the "blocking" that came out in neurotic behavior. Freud gave special importance to the dreams of the patient, which he must patiently describe to the analyst; for in dreams, Freud thought, the unconscious wells up out of control, or but partly controlled, by the ego. Once the patient, however, got beneath the surface of his conscious life, and became aware of what had gone wrong

with his hitherto unconscious life, he might then adjust himself to society.

The Implications of Freudianism

What is important for us in the wider implications of Freud's work, his part in the broad current of contemporary modifications of eighteenth-century rationalism, is first this concept of the very great role of the unconscious drives—that is, the unthinking, the non-rational, in our lives. Ordinary reflective thinking is for the Freudian a very small part of our existence. We are back at the metaphor of reason as a flickering candle, or to use another well-worn metaphor, of reason as simply the small part of the iceberg that shows above the water, while submerged down below is the great mass of the unconscious. Much even of our conscious thinking is, according to the Freudian, what psychologists call "rationalization," thinking dictated, not by an awareness of the reality principle, but by the desires of our id. One can get a good measure of the difference between eighteenth-century rationalism and Freudian psychology by contrasting the older belief in the innocence and natural goodness of the child, Wordsworth's "mighty prophet, seer blest," with the Freudian view of the child as a bundle of unsocial or antisocial drives, as in fact a little untamed savage.

But second, and most important, note that the Freudians do not wish to blow out the candle of human reason. They are moderate, not extreme, anti-rationalists; they are chastened rationalists. Their whole therapy is based on the concept, which has Christian as well as eighteenth-century roots, that "ye shall know the truth, and the truth shall make you free." Only, for the Freudian, truth is not easily found, cannot be distilled into a few simple rules of conduct which all men, being reasonable and good, can use as guides to individual and collective happiness. It is on the contrary very hard to establish, and can be reached only by a long and precarious struggle. Many will not reach it, and will have to put up with all sorts of maladjustments and frustrations. The Freudian is at bottom a pessimist, in that he does not believe in the perfectibility of man. Indeed, there are those who see in the Freudian concept of human nature something like a return to the Christian concept of original sin. They continue the parallel, which many others find absurd or offensive, by maintaining that for the Freudian too there is, though difficult to find, a way out, a form of salvation, in the full self-knowledge that comes from successful psychoanalysis.

Freud, to whom religion was an "illusion," was himself a cult-leader. His faithful disciples still form an orthodox nucleus of strict Freudian psychoanalysts. Other disciples parted with the master, notably the Swiss Jung (1875–1961) who did believe in religion, and whose great popular phrase was the "collective unconscious," and the Austrian Adler (1870–1937) who rejected the master's emphasis on the sexual, and coined the familiar phrase, "inferiority complex."

Full psychoanalysis remains an extremely expensive process limited to those who can afford it or can receive it through charity. There are, however, modified forms of analytical therapy, such as "group therapy" and the like, which are much less expensive. The Freudian influence on imaginative writing, indeed on philosophy and the arts generally, was and remains very great indeed, though usually dispersed, vague, indirect, and very hard to summarize. Negatively, the life work of this nineteenth-century-trained scientist went in these "humanistic" fields to reinforce the reaction against nineteenth-century scientific and rationalistic materialism; positively, Freud's work helped all sorts of modernisms, strengthened the revival of intuition, "hunch," sensibility, and, perhaps paradoxically, a Stoic or existentialist rejection of bourgeois optimism.

Psychology: Behaviorism

It need hardly be said that in this multanimous century of ours the Freudians hold no monopoly of the field of psychology. Indeed, the eighteenth-century tendency to regard human nature, if not as wholly rational, at

Pavlov watching an experiment with a dog.

least as wholly malleable by those who could manipulate the human and non-human environment, still had representatives in the mid-twentieth century. Yet at least one of these "behaviorist" tendencies in psychology had its own flareback to reinforce pessimism over the possibilities of immediate reform of the human condition. The Russian psychologist Pavlov (1849–1936), Nobel prize-winner in 1904, has given us the now familiar term "conditioned reflex." Pavlov's laboratory dogs, after being fed at a given signal, came to water at the mouth at this signal, though no food was within sight or smell. The "natural"—that is, inborn—response of watering at the mouth would ordinarily come only when the dog's senses showed him actual food; Pavlov got the same response artificially by a signal that certainly did not smell or look like food to the dog. The upshot was clear evidence that training or conditioning can produce automatic responses in the animal that are essentially similar to the kind of automatic responses the animal is born with.

Pavlov's experiments had important implications for the social scientist. They confirmed eighteenth-century notions about the power of environment, of training and education, in the sense that environment can be manipulated to produce specific responses from organisms.

645

But—and this is a bitter blow to eighteenth-century optimism—they suggested that once such training has taken hold, the organism has, so to speak, incorporated the results almost as if they had been the product of heredity, not environment, and further change becomes very difficult, in some instances impossible. Pavlov, after having trained some of his dogs, tried mixing his signals, frustrating and confusing the dogs by withholding food at the signal that had always produced food for them. He succeeded in producing symptoms of a kind close to what in human beings would be neurosis.

Still another lead, this time from biologists interested not in the most fashionable "microbiology" but rather in the behavior of individuals (the old-fashioned name for it was natural history), came from such scientists as the Austrian Konrad Lorenz (1903–   ) and the Dutchman Nikolaas Tinbergen (1907–   ), founders of what is called "ethology." Their key phrase is "species-specific behavior." This behavior does indeed depend on hereditary constitutional features of the organism, but especially at key moments when development of the organism must be triggered by specific normal features of the environment. Thus, for instance, newly hatched goslings normally see first and attach themselves to the mother goose; but if she is removed before they hatch, they will attach themselves to a foster mother, even to a human being. Modern ethology thus *reinforces* the notion that neither heredity nor environment alone "determine" behavior, including human behavior, but rather a complex and subtle interaction of the two. There is room for accident, and even for "will," if not quite free will.

Socio-political Thought

We have in the foregoing already edged over naturally enough from psychology to the wider field of man's behavior as a political animal. In what are sometimes optimistically called the social or behavioral sciences, the twentieth century has continued to develop the critique of our eighteenth-century inheri-

tance of belief in the basic reasonableness and goodness of "human nature." In fact, the very term "human nature" seems to some social scientists to be so all-embracing as to make no sense. Once more, let us re-emphasize, first, that this "revolt against reason" is better and more fully to be described as a revolt against reason as exemplified in popular concepts of what science is and does. Second, that many thinkers in this revolt did not attack scientific reason as such in its own fields of established sciences, but simply urged that there are other valuable ways of using the human mind. And third, that though many of these thinkers were anti-rationalists, and almost always "élitists," fascists, racists, reactionaries hostile to the democratic tradition, others were what we have called "chastened rationalists," thinkers who wished to salvage what they could of the eighteenth-century basis of the democratic tradition (see Chapter 23).

The specific programs, the emotional allegiances, the "values" of twentieth-century thinkers in this broad field we may hesitantly call "sociological" were varied indeed. And yet most of them, certainly the great ones, do have in common a sense of the subtlety, the complexities, the delicacy—and the toughness and durability—of the ties that bind human beings together—and hold them apart—in society. Indeed, that last sentence of ours, with its coupling of opposites in tension, is typical of this twentieth-century approach to problems of man in society; compare an incidental and therefore significant remark tossed off by Arthur Koestler, "for we are moving here through strata that are held together by the cement of contradiction."[*] Or, as the Swiss writer Denis de Rougemont puts the same kind of challenge to our conventional notions of what makes sense, tensions between two terms that are *"true, contradictory, and essential."*[†] The distinguished American sociologist, Talcott Parsons, in his *The Structure of Social Action* (1937) finds in the work of many different thinkers, such

[*]A. Koestler, *The Invisible Writing* (Boston, 1954), 349.
[†]D. de Rougemont, *Man's Western Quest* (New York, 1957), 116.

as the German Max Weber, the Frenchman Durkheim, the Englishman Alfred Marshal, the Italian Pareto, and others, a common aim to put the study of man in society on a basis that takes full account of the difficulties of "objectivity" in such study, and gives full place to our contemporary awareness of the place of the subjective and non-rational in human life.

Pareto

We may here speak for a moment about Pareto (1848–1923), not because he was the greatest or the most influential thinker, for he was not, but because the work of this scientifically trained engineer is such a clear example of the difficulties of thinking about men as we think about things. Pareto tried hard to establish a genuine *science* of sociology; but it was a sociology very different from that of his only slightly older contemporary Herbert Spencer (see Chapter 23). Pareto in his *The Mind and Society* (original Italian edition, 1916) is concerned chiefly with the problem of separating in human actions the rational from the non-rational. What interests Pareto is the kind of action that is expressed in words, ritual, symbolism of some kind. Buying wool socks for cold weather is one such action. If they are bought deliberately to get the best socks at a price the buyer can afford, this is rational action in accord with the doer's interests; it is the kind of action the economist can study statistically. If, however, they are bought because the buyer thinks wool is "natural" (as compared with synthetic fibers) or because he finds snob value in improved English socks, or because he wants to help bring sheep-raising back to Vermont, we are in a field less "rational" than price. The practical economist will still study marketing and consumer demand, but he will have to cope with many complex psychological variables.

It is these that Pareto studies under the name of "derivations," which are close to what most of us know as rationalizations. These are the explanations and accompanying ritualistic acts associated with our religion, our patriotism, our feelings for groups of all kinds. Prayer, for instance, is for Pareto a derivation; he was, like so many of this period, a materialist, at bottom hostile to Christianity, though he approved of it as means of social concord, and was fascinated by its hold over men. It is irrational, or non-rational, to pray for rain, because we know as meteorologists that rain has purely material causes quite beyond the reach of prayer. These derivations are indeed a factor in human social life, but they do not really move men to social action.

What does move men in society, and keeps them together in society, says Pareto, are the *residues*. These are expressions of relatively permanent, abiding sentiments in men, expressions that usually have to be separated from the part that is actually a derivation, which may change greatly and even quickly. Pagan Greek sailors sacrificed to Poseidon, god of the sea, before setting out on a voyage; a few centuries later, Christian Greek sailors prayed, lighted candles, and made vows to the Virgin Mary just before sailing. The derivations are the explanations of what Poseidon and the Virgin respectively do. They vary. The believer in the Virgin thinks his pagan predecessor was dead wrong. The residues are the needs to secure divine aid and comfort in a difficult undertaking, and to perform certain ritual acts that give the performer assurance of such aid and comfort. The residues are nearly the same for our two sets of sailors. Both the pagans and the Christians have the same social and psychological needs and satisfy them in much the same ways, though with very different "explanations" of what they are doing.

Two of the major classes of "residues" Pareto distinguishes stand out, and help form his philosophy of history. These are first the "residues" of persistent aggregates, the sentiments that mark men who like regular ways, solid discipline, tradition and habit, men like the Spartans, the Prussians, or any rigorously disciplined military class. Second, there are the residues of the instinct for combinations, the sentiments that mark men who like novelty and adventure, who invent new ways of doing things, who like to cut loose from the old and the tried, men not easily shocked, men who hate discipline, men like most intellectuals and inventors—and many entrepreneurs and businessmen. In societies of many individual members, men influenced largely by one or the other of these major residues tend to predominate and to characterize that society. Like most philosophers of history, Pareto is far from clear on just how a conservative society where the residues of persistent aggregates predominate changes into another kind of society. But he does have this conception of a pendulum swing, even a struggle of thesis and antithesis.

The nineteenth century in the West was in Pareto's mind a society in which the residues of instinct for combinations played perhaps the greatest role of which they are capable in a human society. The nineteenth century was a century of competition among individuals full of new ideas, inventions, enterprises, convinced that the old ways were bad, that novelty was the great thing to strive for at the expense of everything else. It was a society notably out of equilibrium. It had to run toward the other kind of residues, toward the persistent aggregates, toward a society with more security and less competition, more discipline and less freedom, more equality and less inequality, more uniformity and less variety. It had to go the way some writers hold that we are going in the twentieth century, toward the welfare state, even toward the totalitarian state.

The Planners and Persuaders

Yet the abiding influence of the newer psychological and sociological approach to the study of man in society has by no means been in the Paretan and conservative direction. Those who want to influence human behavior, all the way from the microcosmic field of personal consumer-choices to the macrocosmic field of international relations, have been willing to make use of the new psychological insights. From the latest piece of "motivational research" to show the cigarette manufacturer how to overcome the effects on his customers of recent medical research on the causes of lung cancer to the high-minded efforts of proponents of world-government to devise some symbol, visual, musical, concrete, that will supplant nationalist symbols, such as patriotic hymns, flags, and the like, hard-working planners are busily engaged in trying, often successfully, to change our habits, even our prejudices. To use Pareto's now little-used terminology, they are seeking, not to ·change our behavior by appealing to our "reason" in the plain sense of that word; they are trying to "activate" certain of our sentiments, our residues, or "de-activate" others, or both.

In the field of serious political and social thought, this characteristic twentieth-century emphasis on the psychology of motivation has been appealed to not only by conservatives or "reactionaries" like Pareto and others, including both Mussolini and Hitler, who had pretensions to philosophy, but also by many who were democrats, or at least "progressives," at heart. An early example of this latter type of political thinker is Graham Wallas, a British leftist, whose *Human Nature in Politics* (1908) was a most influential book. Wallas, campaigning as a Progressive for a seat in the London County Council, discovered by experience that the voters he canvassed were more pleased and influenced by little tricks of baby-kissing, chit-chat, and personal flattery than by appeals to reason or even to self-interest. Something of the same emphasis on the need to go beyond abstractions to practical psychology in politics appears in the earlier writings of the American Walter Lippmann, whose *Preface to Politics* appeared in 1913. It has, of course, always been known to politicians.

There remains, especially among American intellectuals, a strong current of thought-feeling that refuses to descend into Machiavellian strategy, even—indeed most of all—in a righteous cause. It still seems to these good children of the eighteenth-century Enlightenment that reason and high ethical principles must and will prevail together, and that to appeal to the "lower" elements in nature so emphasized by modern psychology is no way to rise above the evils of existing society. Such opinions are by no means commonly held, or, at any rate, not commonly put into practice, by active politicians, and one of the many gaps that seem in our society to widen rather than to narrow in these days is the old gap between the idealistic "theorist" and the "practical man" who wants to get things done.

Yet the intellectual leaders of mid-twentieth century progressive political thought are increasingly forced to the conclusion that more has to be done in the way of planning. Notably, they urge, we must plan in the whole sector of our economy which deals with such essentials as education, social service, housing, hospital care, scientific research, public transportation, and the means of preservation of fast-vanishing natural resources, especially our scenic wildernesses, as well as means for the prevention of air- and water-pollution. All these are expensive. The planners know that in a democracy plans cannot simply be imposed on those planned for, as to a great degree they can in a totalitarian state like Russia. They are paying great attention to the problems, on which modern thinking in the field of the social sciences does throw some light, of how to get the many to want and ask for—and pay for—what the planners think the people really need, and *ought* to want. A representative writer who is concerned with such matters is the persuasive American economist J. K. Galbraith (1908–), author of *The Affluent Society*.

Philosophy

In the field of formal—which nowadays tends to mean also university-supported—philosophy the mid-twentieth century displays once more its variety. It is safe to say that in the West at least there are today representatives of almost every philosophical system, from extreme idealism to extreme materialism and complete skepticism, that has ever existed; and even in the communist countries, one suspects that there are lurking idealists ready to come out in the open if official Marxist

materialist metaphysics are ever relaxed. The currents of voluntarism, pragmatism, and psychologism we noted earlier (see Chapter 23) still flow, no doubt a bit diminished.

From such nineteenth-century sources as Nietzsche and the gravely disturbed and disturbing Danish theologian, Kierkegaard (1813–1885), there has developed a philosophy known as "existentialism." The existentialists are somewhat harried Stoics (see Volume I, p. 90) who find this existing reality of mid-twentieth century all there is, and pretty depressing, but are determined to face this reality as heroically as possible. They are sometimes divided into Christian existentialists, who retain a concept of God, and free-thinking or atheistic existentialists. The central theme of existentialism has been stated by the French writer Sartre (1905–) as "existence precedes essence." This cryptic pronouncement seems to mean that human awareness of living, of being, precedes in time, and is therefore somehow more important than our thinking, or than our mental ticketing of "reality" by means of words. Clearly existentialism does at bottom belong in the current of anti-intellectualism of our time.

We have certainly not done the existentialists justice in this brief description. They are sensitive artists and intellectuals, by no means simple anti-intellectuals who want us to "think with our blood"—or our hormones. They respect the instrument of thought, and use it themselves. But they do not quite trust it, and they do not trust its chief representatives in our time, the conventional scientists. Their noblest representative, though not formally one of the existentialist group, the French novelist and philosopher, Albert Camus (1913–1960) is perhaps destined to be remembered as a classic of our age. Finally, formal philosophical idealism, which a generation ago seemed, save for Croce, to be languishing everywhere, has proved of recent years to have considerable vitality, perhaps basically in forms we may call Neo-Kantian, as with the late German philosopher, Ernst Cassirer (1874–1945).

The most original, and in a sense most typical and vital, philosophic movement of our century bears clearly and paradoxically the stamp of the "revolt against reason." It looks to an outsider as if the movement called variously logical analysis, logical positivism, the linguistic philosophy, and, in one of its phases, symbolic logic, accepted most of the strictures the new psychology made on old-fashioned rationalism and then went ahead to insist that, although only a tiny bit of human experience could be brought under rubrics of rational thought, that tiny bit was indeed to be protected and explored carefully. This somewhat varied school can be considered as beginning early in the twentieth century in Vienna, the city of Freud. But such distinguished pioneers of the school as Ludwig Wittgenstein (1889–1951) and Rudolf Carnap (1891–   ) emigrated, the first to England, the second to the United States. Logical analysis could hardly flourish in Hitler's Germany or in Stalin's Russia. It is skeptical of too much to flourish in any but a very free and many-minded society.

The American physicist, P. W. Bridgman, put one of the school's basic positions clearly in various writings. Where, on the pattern of scientific practice, a problem can be answered by the performance of an "operation" and the answer validated by logical and empirical tests or observations, knowledge can be achieved; where, however, as in such problems as whether democracy is the best form of government, whether a lie is ever justifiable, or whether a given poem is a good one or a bad one—in short, almost all the great questions of philosophy, art, literature, history—no such "operation" is possible, the problem is *for the logician* "meaningless."

Most of these logical positivists would admit that non-logical or pseudo-logical methods for getting at such problems, though they could not result in the kind of finally accepted answers the scientists expect to get, are nonetheless for normal human living, useful and indeed necessary. Some of the *popularizers* of this philosophy, however, pretty explicitly held that all mental activity save logical analysis and empirical verification is at best inferior mental activity, or more likely, nonsense,

a waste of time, or worse. A distinguished American popularizer, Stuart Chase, in his *Tyranny of Words* (1938) proposed to clarify our thinking by substituting "blah-blah" for terms that have no such good logical or "operational" clearance. Thus the famous French revolutionary slogan, "Liberty, equality, fraternity" would come out simply as "Blah-blah, blah-blah, blah-blah." Approaching their problems very differently from the way Freud and Pareto did, these logical analysts nevertheless came to a similar conclusion about the reasoning capacity of most human beings. Most human beings, they conclude, are at present incapable of thorough, persistent, successful logical thinking, and they cannot be taught to do this kind of thinking in any foreseeable future. Of course, just as there are radical Freudians who hold that if everybody could be psychoanalyzed all would be well, there are radical positivists, usually labeled "semanticists" who hold that semantics, the study of meaning, if available to everyone would cure all our troubles. The leading expert of this rather naive semantic therapy was the Polish-American scientist Alfred Korzybski (1879–1950), author of *Science and Sanity* (1933).

Once more we encounter the sharp tensions of modern intellectual life. Since these logical analysts seemed to set up the practices of science, as they understood them, as the sole right way of thinking, many of those devoted to the arts and the humanistic studies generally turned in revenge to the denunciation of science as a narrowing, dangerous, use of the mind. Anti-scientism is as characteristic of our age as scientism.

Probably the most widespread philosophical movement of our century developed outside of, or on the margin of, formal professional philosophy. This movement may be called "historicism," the attempt to find in history an answer to those ultimate questions of the structure of the universe and of man's fate the philosopher has always asked. At bottom, the transfer of Darwinian concepts of organic evolution from biology to this great, sweeping field of philosophical questions contains the essence of twentieth-century historicism. Once the traditional Judaeo-Christian concepts of a single creation in time, a God above nature, and the rest of the traditional world-view were abandoned, men in search of answers to their questions about these ultimates had to fall back on the historical record. Man is not made by God, but by nature, which amounts to saying that *man makes himself* in the course of history. We get our only clues as to man's capacities here on earth, clues as to how he ought to behave, clues as to that future that so concerns him, from the record of the past.

But "clues" is a modest and misleading word here. Many of the thinkers who appealed to history found much more than indications of what *might* be, much more than the always tentative, never dogmatic or absolute "theories" the scientist produces in answer to the less-than-ultimate questions he asks. Many of these philosophers of history, to simplify a bit, found in what they held to be the course of history a substitute for the concepts of God or Providence. They found in the record of the past substantially the equivalent of what Christians found in revelation—the explanation of man's nature and destiny, his *end* in the sense of a teleology or an eschatology. Paradoxically, they found in history something quite outside and beyond history, a substitute for a theology.

Of these historicisms, the most important and the most obviously a substitute for Christianity is of course Marxism, which we have dealt with elsewhere (see Chapter 22). The theological parallels are plain, and have been frequently noted by non-Marxists: for God, absolute and omnipotent, the Marxist substitutes the absolutely determined course of Dialectical Materialism; for the Bible, he substitutes the canonical writings of Marx-Engels, with the addition, for the orthodox of the Soviet Union and its satellites, of those of Lenin; for the Church, the Party; for the Christian eschatology of divine judgment and heaven or hell, the revolution and the "classless society."

But Marxism, if the most rigorous, is only one of the historicisms of our time. The German, Oswald Spengler (1880–1936), produced in his *Decline of the West,* published just at the end of World War I, a characteristic specimen. Spengler found from the historical record that societies or civilizations have, like human beings, an average life-span, a thousand years or so for a civilization being the equivalent of seventy years or so for the individual human being. He traced several non-western civilizations, but in the West he found three main ones, a Hellenic from 1000 B.C. to about the birth of Christ, a Levantine or Middle Eastern from the birth of Christ to about 1000 A.D., and our own modern western, which began (according to him) about 1000 A.D. and was, therefore, due to end about 2000 A.D. We cannot here analyze his work at length. Spengler had real insights, but his work as a whole, most historians would say, is simply not history—it is metaphysics, or if you like a coined word, meta-history. There are critics who explain Spengler simply; he saw Germany was about to be defeated, and he therefore consoled himself by believing western civilization was about to end.

Better known nowadays than Spengler's is the work of the English historian, Arnold Toynbee (1889–   ), whose many-volumed *Study of History* (1934–1954) has been neatly condensed by D. C. Somervell into two manageable volumes. Toynbee is worth studying as a symptom of the intellectual difficulties of historicism and of our age. He has a Christian background, a careful training in historical scholarship, and a strong family tradition of kindly humanitarian social service. World War I marked him with a great hatred for war, and a conviction that nationalism, which he once declared to be the real if unavowed religion of our western society, is the villain of the piece. His great system is an attempt to trace the causes of the rise and fall of societies in the past, and owes a good deal to Spengler. But Toynbee is a gentle English Christian humanist, not a German romantic racist brought up on what is no doubt a perversion of Nietzsche. He does, like the majority of contemporary philosophers of history, conclude that our western society is facing a very serious challenge, that in terms of the cyclical rise and fall of societies he has traced it looks as if we were about to give ourselves the "knockout blow." But he refuses to abandon hope. The facts of historical development may, he holds, indicate destruction for us; but we may transcend history, and under the influence of a revived, or new, or Buddhist-influenced Christianity of gentleness and love, pull ourselves out of the hole.

Historicism has, again quite characteristically in our culture, given rise to bitter protests and to its opposite. Almost all professional historians, in the West nowadays mostly conventionally democratic in their values, simply give these philosophers of history the cold shoulder. Independent existentialists like Camus (who did not consider himself an existentialist) are firm in their contention that, though we may not neglect history as a record of human experience, we must find in ourselves something—salvation, perhaps—quite beyond history. And as for the logical analysts, history is far too lacking in precise data to make it a subject worth their while.

The Sciences

No general history can readily deal substantively with the history of science and technology in the twentieth century. Each science, each branch of each science, has continued in this century its cumulative course. The co-operation (not without rivalry) among "pure" scientists, applied scientists, engineers, bankers, businessmen, and government officials has produced in all phases of human control over material things the kind of exponential increases that send the lines of our graphs quite off the paper. Man's attained rate of travel is no doubt an extreme example, one not achieved in the same degree for instance in such fields as those of medicine and genetics. But in 1820 the fastest rate was still 12 to 15 miles an hour; railroads made it 100 miles or so by 1880; piston-engined airplanes made it 300 miles or so by 1940; jet planes broke the sound barrier only yesterday in 1947, making speeds of close to 1,000 miles per hour possible; and now in the 1960's rockets have propelled living men in space free of our

atmosphere at speeds of thousands of miles an hour.

Each science is of course highly specialized, and the active scientist usually is supreme master of only part of a given science. Indeed, one of the great worries of our numerous contemporary worriers is well expressed in the old tag that has modern specialists knowing more and more about less and less. But the tag really is an old one—and, like most such tags, partly true and worth our attention, yet not quite borne out by any catastrophic break in our culture. For the fact is that at a broad, non-specialist's level of understanding many educated men in the West have a very good idea of what modern science is trying to do, and how it does it.

The wider implications of modern science as its ways of work and its general concepts affect our world-views is a subject no general history can neglect. In the broadest sense, there can be no doubt that, though many practicing scientists are good Christians, scientific attitudes toward nature and natural laws, and scientific skepticism toward the supernatural, have added powerfully to the modern drive toward rationalism, positivism, materialism. Science continues to promote the world-view we have seen arising in early modern times, and culminating in the Enlightenment of the eighteenth century (see Chapter 17). Indeed, many scientists have managed to make of the pursuit of scientific knowledge itself a kind of religion.

More particularly, the great event of the twentieth century has been the revolution in physics symbolized for the public in the figure of Albert Einstein (1879–1955). The concepts of relativity, a space-time continuum, and quantum mechanics freed physics from the "Newtonian world-machine" and helped the very great modern innovations in the field, innovations that worked together with the late nineteenth-century discoveries of the phenomena of radiation (X-rays, the researches of the Curies, Roentgen, and others) to make possible our contemporary developments in fields like electronics. Einstein's theories on the equivalence of mass and mechanical energy, his concept of time as the fourth dimension and the representation of gravitation as a field (compare "magnetic field") rather than a force secured wide public attention, if not always comprehension. From all this a few laymen came to the conclusion that since the apparently rigid world of mechanical causation of classic physics had broken down, since there was associated with the name of the distinguished German physicist Werner Heisenberg an "indeterminacy principle" familiar to practicing scientists, the common-sense law of cause-and-effect had in fact been repealed, and the universe was once more a fine free space in which anything could happen. This of course is not true, and the work of Newton has not been so much contradicted by modern physics as supplemented. Heisenberg's principle resulted from close work on the particle called an electron. An *individual* electron observably can jump from one orbit to another without evident and predictable sequence. Yet *statistically* the behavior of many, many electrons together is predictable, as predictable as it was in Newton's day. It is quite likely that misunderstood doctrines of "relativity" in physics, misapplied to ethics and aesthetics, did have a part in the fashionable doctrines of moral and aesthetic relativism of only yesterday.

The development of astronomy has been largely influenced by that of physics. To the layman, such modern astronomical concepts as that of a finite but expanding universe, of curved space, and perhaps above all the almost inconceivable distances and quantities, light years, galaxies, and the like, have made astronomy the most romantic of sciences. And these distances and quantities *are* almost inconceivable. A light year is the distance traversed by light in one year, or roughly 5,880,000,000,000 miles; our own Milky Way Galaxy has some thirty thousand million stars and nebulae, in the form of a disk with a diameter of about 100,000 light years. Recent developments in rocketry have made our moon seem attainable by actual human flight instead of merely by flight of the science-fiction imagination. Chemistry, on the other hand, in

spite of the marvels of synthesis it produces, has less attraction for the imagination. Yet in our daily living it is surely the science of chemistry that touches us most closely, in our foods, our medicines, our clothing, almost all the material objects we use.

Chemistry has also aided the very great gains that have been made in the twentieth century in the biological sciences and in their applications to medicine and public health as well. Not only in the United States and the rest of the West, but all over the world, infant mortality, many contagious diseases, even undernourishment, have been so far conquered that the average expectancy of life at birth has gone up as much as twenty years in advanced nations since 1900. In the economically backward areas of the globe, more children are born and more live, so that the population problem has become acute, and is still unsolved. Yet even in this matter of food supply, astonishing achievements by plant-breeders, as with hybrid corn (maize), the development of fertilizers, the use of irrigation, the possibilities of food from the sea opened up by marine biology and other scientific advances promise some considerable alleviation in a foreseeable future. It is significant, however, that the actual extreme limits of the human life span have not yet been significantly affected. It does not seem that a limit of something like 110 to 120 years for human life, historically known to have prevailed for centuries, has yet been exceeded.

There remains one more major problem which the progress of twentieth-century science has sharpened, a problem closely related to that of specialization in science and learning. There is in some senses a widening gap today between those who pursue what we call "humanistic" studies and those who pursue scientific studies. It is by no means difficult philosophically to reconcile these two pursuits; the poet and the physicist have, as creative human beings, more in common than we others usually can see. But the fact remains that from the point of view of the sociologist the two groups in our cultural life do clash, the scientists finding the humanists fuzzy-

minded, sloppy intellectually, and clearly inferior, the humanists finding the scientists
limited, pedestrian, cold, inhuman, and quite
unable to manage the Frankenstein monster of
modern technology they have created. Fortunately, there are good men who are at work
mediating between these two sides, men who
incline to the belief that the opposition is by
no means one rooted in the facts of life and
human nature, but merely in present-cultural
fashion.

In sum, the very great achievements of
modern science and technology have raised
many problems for our western democracy:
the overriding problem presented by the fact
that hydrogen bombs, missiles, and biological
warfare have made the destruction of the human race no mere bit of rhetoric, nor a theological doctrine like that of Judgment Day,
but a possible situation confronting even common sense; the problem of humanizing
science; the problem of overpopulation; the
problems of educating scientists and endow-
ing scientific research; and many other problems. Yet the fact remains that science and
technology seem to be the deciding factors
that have raised the masses far enough beyond
misery and near-starvation to make possible
what we Americans call democracy. And perhaps even more important, the continuing
very great vitality of western civilization—a
vitality as real in the arts as in the sciences—is
at its clearest in the magnificent achievements
of modern science. Modern science rightly
worries the worriers, but it should also con-
sole them, for it shows man still in a light reflected long ago by the Greek Sophocles:

> What a thing is man! Among all wonders
> The wonder of the world is man himself
> . . .
> Man the Contriver! Man the Master-mind.*

Literature and the Arts

In the field of imaginative literature, music,
painting, the fine arts, and the arts generally,

*Sophocles, *Antigone,* John Jay Chapman, trans. (Boston, 1930), lines 332–340.

we invent new styles and attitudes yet by no
means wholly destroy what the past has left us.
Here, as for all our culture, the contemporary
historian has to note the great variety of tastes
and standards that have piled up. But he must
also note that there appears in mid-twentieth
century with special sharpness another characteristic of our time on which we have already briefly touched, the wide and deep gap
between the art—in the broad sense of "art" to
include letters, music, architecture—of the
few, or "highbrow" art, and the art of the
many, or popular art. Bridges between the two
there are, usually built on highbrow initiative
from the highbrow side toward the lowbrow
side. A good example is the fashion among the
cultivated few for some phases, at least, of
American popular music, or jazz. For many
French intellectuals, as difficult, as refined, as
remote from the masses as any intellectuals
have ever been, "le jazz hot" is the only cultural achievement of the United States. Every
now and then, if only briefly, some contribu-
tor to that most popular form of popular art,
the American comic strip, gains a following
among the highbrows or, at least, among
undergraduates.

High Art: Literature

Once more, imaginative writing in the
twentieth century makes no striking break
with that of the late nineteenth. Poetry and
literary criticism remain, as they had begun to
be in the 1890's or even earlier (see Chapter
23), difficult, cerebral, and addressed to a very
small, if fit, audience. An occasional poet, like
the American, Robert Frost, breaks from the
privacy of the little magazines and the limited
editions to wide popularity and a place enshrined in old-fashioned anthologies. But
Frost is no more esoteric in form or substance
than Wordsworth. More remarkable and more
symptomatic, there are signs that T. S. Eliot,
born in St. Louis, but as an adult wholly Anglicized, an abstruse and allusive poet, an intellectual of intellectuals, is also attaining a
wider audience. The figure of speech with
which he began "The Love Song of J. Alfred

Prufrock" in 1917, which once seemed strange, "advanced," is now tame enough for any anthology:

> Let us go then, you and I
> When the evening is spread out against the sky
> Like a patient etherised upon a table.*

The novel remains the most important form of contemporary imaginative writing. Critics have long bemoaned its exhaustion as an art-form, and the French have even invented what they call the "anti-novel," but the novel does not die. It is quite impossible here for us to give even a thumb-nail sketch of the contemporary novel. It is not even wise of us to attempt to indicate writers likely to be read in the twenty-first century. It may be that a social novelist like the American, J. P. Marquand (1893–1960), disliked by the pure highbrow because he wrote best sellers, will survive better than such a favorite of the pure as William Faulkner (1897–1962), who wrote existentialist novels about darkest Mississippi. The late Thomas Mann (1875–1945) seems already enshrined as a classic; but Mann, who began with a traditionally realistic novel of life in his birthplace, the old Hanseatic town of Lübeck, never really belonged to the *avant garde.* He is typical of the sensitive, worrying, class-conscious (his class was that of the artist-intellectual, no mere Marxist class) artist of the age of psychology.

More useful for us here, since it illustrates one of the problems of all contemporary art, is the career of the Irishman, James Joyce (1882–1941). Joyce began with a subtle, outspoken, but formally conventional series of sketches of life in the Dublin of his youth, *Dubliners* (1914), and the novelist's inevitable, and with Joyce undisguised, autobiography, *Portrait of the Artist as a Young Man* (1916). Then, mostly in exile on the Continent, he wrote what may well prove a classic, the experimental novel *Ulysses* (1922). This novel is an account, rather than a narrative, of twenty-four hours in the life of Leopold Bloom, a Dublin Jew. It is full of difficult allusions,

*T. S. Eliot, *Complete Poems & Plays* (New York, 1952), 3.

parallels with Homer, puns, rapidly shifting scenes and episodes, and is written without regard for the conventional notions of plot and orderly development. Above all, it makes full use of the then recently developed psychologies of the unconscious as displayed in an individual's "stream of consciousness." The last chapter, printed entirely without punctuation marks, is the record of what went on in the mind of Bloom's Irish wife as she lay in bed waiting for him to come home. What went on in her mind was in large part too shocking for the early century, and *Ulysses,* published in Paris, long had to be smuggled into English-speaking countries. It is now freely available everywhere.

Ulysses, though it took attentive reading, and even for those most fully abreast of the *avant garde* culture was often puzzling, is still a novel in English. Joyce's final big work, long known as simply "Work in Progress," but finally published as *Finnegans Wake* (1939), is

James Joyce (1882–1941).

one of those works of radical experimentation about which, like many modern paintings, the ordinary educated layman simply has to say that it means nothing, or very little, to him. The continuities and conventions of narration and "plain English," not wholly flouted in *Ulysses,* are here quite abandoned. There are words, and even sentences; but *meaning* has to be quarried out by the reader and may when quarried turn out to be quite different from what Joyce intended. But there are keys to *Finnegans Wake*—we cite one in our reading list for this chapter—and the reader who wants to try to get at this interesting experiment in modern art can get his start there. Here is the beginning and ending of *Finnegans Wake:*

rivverrun, past Eve and Adam's, from swerve of shore to bend of bay, brings us by a commodius vicus of recirculation back to Howth Castle and Environs.

. . . A gull. Gulls. Far calls. Coming, far! End here. Us then. Finn, again! Take. Bussoftlhee, mememormee! Till thousendsthee. Lps. The keys to. Given! A way a lone a last a loved a long the*

Note once more: such writing may well be a blind alley, but the traditions of western invention—we use that word in a very broad sense—insist that it may not be declared a blind alley until it has been well explored.

High Art: The Fine Arts

It is, however, the fine arts, painting perhaps in first rank, but with sculpture, architecture, and the minor decorative arts all included, that confront the ordinary cultivated westerner with the problem of "modernism" in its most clear form. The process of getting beyond the camera eye and Renaissance ideas of perspective—in general, "realism"—which we began to trace in Chapter 23 has gone on right to this day. Indeed, painting done today can be almost—not quite—sharply divided into two groups: that done traditionally,

*J. Joyce, *Finnegans Wake* (New York, 1959), 3, 628.

academically, representational painting of the kind that surprises and puzzles no one though it still pleases many; and the many kinds of experimental or non-representational, or simply "modern," painting. The variety of these experiments is great indeed. Most of them have been made by the great figure of contemporary painting, Pablo Picasso (1880–   ).

A native Spaniard, and an adopted Frenchman, Picasso has in his long life painted in many "styles" or "periods." The paintings of his "Blue Period," for instance, executed in the first years of our century, exemplify Expressionism, the attempt to express in art such highly subjective emotional states as grief and despair. These pictures are said to have been influenced by the work of El Greco, the sixteenth-century master (see Volume I, p. 608); certainly, both artists convey a sense of concentrated emotion by exaggerating human proportions. Around 1905, Picasso, stimulated in part by primitive art, turned to more daring innovations, striving, as Cézanne had striven (see p. 312), to transfer to the two dimensions of a picture the three dimensions of the real world but, so to speak, their dimensions *in motion.* Sometimes he used the techniques of Abstractionism, the reduction of figures to a kind of plane geometry, all angles and lines. Sometimes he used those of Cubism, the reduction of figures to a kind of solid geometry, all cubes, spheres, and cones. Sometimes he even glued onto a picture bits of real objects—paper or the caning from a chair—in the process called *collage* ("paste-up"). In the range and inventiveness of his work Picasso calls to mind the masters of the Renaissance. On the one hand, he has done many portraits that are almost classical in style, as in the work of his "White Period" following World War I. On the other hand, he has continued radical experimentation not only on canvas but also in sculpture, in ceramics, and in "constructions" of wood and other materials that might be called the sculptor's counterpart of *collage.* Most disturbing to the ordinary viewer, perhaps, are Picasso's recurrent efforts, stemming from Cubism, to show the human figure from two or more angles simultaneously—whence the apparently misplaced eyes and the anatomical distortions and rearrangements in many of Picasso's pictures.

Most remote from this world of sense experience as organized by common sense is the work of various kinds of abstract painters, paintings which are sometimes elaborate patterns of lines and colors, sometimes geometrical, sometimes apparently mere random daubs. It all means something, if only to the painter; but that meaning cannot be seized by the uninitiated.

The conservative worried by modern art can perhaps take some comfort in the fact that the most extreme manifestation of this art is now nearly fifty years past, and has never been quite equaled in its extraordinary defiance of all conventions, all rules, all forms. This extreme manifestation, perhaps more important sociologically than artistically, was the protest made by a very alienated group of intellectuals, the Dadaists, the "angry young men" of World War I and its aftermath. They reacted against a world so much sillier than their Dada that it could slaughter millions in warfare. Here are some characteristic passages from an account of Dada written by a sympathetic observer:

In Berlin as elsewhere we notice the persistent desire to destroy art, the deliberate intent to wipe out existing notions of beauty, the insistence upon the greatest possible obliteration of individuality. Heartfield works under the direction of Grosz while Max Ernst and Arp sign each other's paintings at random.

. . .

In the first New York Independents' exhibition, 1917, he [Marcel Duchamp] entered a procelain urinal with the title *Fontaine* and signed it R. Mutt to test the impartiality of the executive committee of which he himself was a member. By this symbol Duchamp wished to signify his disgust for art and his admiration for ready-made objects.

. . .

At an exhibition in Paris among the most remarkable entries sent by the poets was a mirror of Soupault's entitled *Portrait of an unknown.* . . . Certain paintings by Duchamp supposed to be in this exhibition were replaced by sheets of paper marked with numbers which corresponded to the Duchamp entries in the catalog. Duchamp, who had

been asked to take part in the exhibition, had just cabled from New York: "Nuts."*

Again we must repeat what we have said before: it is perfectly possible that in the long run of history the directions taken in the contemporary fine arts by those we now think of as leaders, pioneers, will prove stale and unprofitable. But no one who has not made an effort to understand these arts is justified in condemning them out of hand. And one hostile position the disgruntled conservatives in these fields often take seems quite untenable: this is the labeling of such modern art as "pedantic," "decadent," as a sign of exhaustion, death, lack of creative power. Quite the contrary, this art is alive, inventive, dynamic, an attempt to extend the confines of human experience, an attempt quite as remarkable, though in its results not so readily assessed, as that of modern science and technology. The historian must note that the extreme traditionalists, doing exactly what their forefathers have done, are much more vulnerable to the accusation that their work is a sign of exhaustion and decay.

*Georges Huguet in *Fantastic Art, Dada, Surrealism,* A. H. Barr, Jr., ed. (New York, 1936), 23, 19, 33.

"Op" Art: "Current," by Bridget Riley.

The arch in design: the IBM Building in Seattle and the Gateway Arch in St. Louis.

This remark holds even more strikingly true in architecture. The twentieth century has seen the growth of the first truly original style in architecture since the end of the eighteenth century. "Modern" or "functional" architecture is no revival of a past style, no pastiche of elements of such past styles, no living museum of eclectic choice, like most of nineteenth-century architecture. It prides itself on its honest use of modern materials, its adaptation to modern living, its dislike of waste space and over-display. There is in modern architecture a certain touch of austerity, even puritanism, that should confound those who think that our age is sunk in lush sensuality. In the long run, mid-century modern architecture will probably seem to have carried its dislike for ornamentation, especially external ornamentation, rather too far. There are already signs that architects are beginning to

tire of vast expanses of plain glass and steel.

"Modern" music, unlike "modern" painting or architecture, has never quite crystallized into a distinctive style. The twentieth century has produced a great many attempts to get beyond classical music and its rules of harmony—by using scales other than the conventional one, by stressing dissonance and discord, by borrowing the insistent rhythms of popular jazz, and in extreme forms, by abolishing any formal notation and allowing the performer to bang away at will, even on pipes or tin pans. A generation ago, the general public came to identify musical innovation most closely with the Russian, Igor Stravinsky (1882–   ), who on the eve of World War I composed two ballet scores, *Petrouchka* and *The Rite of Spring,* that were far removed from the polite and formalized ballet of tradition. Stravinsky may prove to be the musical coun-

An unsentimental approach to design: the Central Technical School, Toronto, Canada.

terpart of the successful artistic pioneer Picasso; significantly, however, although Stravinsky has continued experimental compositions, none of his later works has equaled his great ballets in impact or popularity, and in fact, one of his phases was a return to the eighteenth century.

In sum: all the "creative" modern arts are complex and difficult, and as of this moment far from being "understanded of the people." The very evident gulf between the tastes of the many and the tastes of the few may be an indication of a dangerous side of our democratic society. Certainly this is a subject on which no one is justified in taking an attitude of "holier than thou." But here the complete prevalence of the popular side, the elimination of the art of the few, seems most unlikely.

Left: Alexander Calder: an untitled stabile-mobile of painted aluminum. Henry Moore: "Family Group," a bronze sculpture.

It would seem that contrasting sets of standards and tastes, and the consequent great variety of works of art of all kinds, are one of the marks of our democratic society.

For it is fact that the two great attempts to put across a really totalitarian society in this century, that of Stalin in Russia and that of Hitler in Germany, were marked by very successful efforts to suppress highbrow culture, especially in art and in philosophy. Science, as we now know, flourished in Nazi Germany, and continues to flourish in a Russia which bans Boris Pasternak's novel, *Dr. Zhivago*, and in 1966 sends to prison for literary "treason" two writers, Andrei Sinyavsky and Yuli Daniel, who had smuggled out of Russia mildly "modern" works under the pseudonyms of "Abram Tertz" and "Nikolai Arzhak". Russia was in most ways the most extreme example. This great socio-economic experiment, it may seem somewhat paradoxically, banned experiment in the arts and in the whole range of humanistic culture, at least after the accession of Stalin to power. Soviet architecture was even more atrociously monumental than the worst of nineteenth-century commercial architecture. Until Pasternak's novel, sent out of Russia in manuscript for translation into Italian under communist patronage, came in 1958 to widespread attention, no piece of Soviet writing really struck the imagination of the West. This failure cannot justly be laid to western censorship or banning; it is simply that the crude propaganda literature of Communist Russia did not greatly interest even fellow-traveling western highbrows. Things got worse under Stalin, when such promising beginnings as Soviet movies—those of Eisenstein, for instance—and the more daring music of Russian composers like Shostakovich, came under what one has to call censorship by bourgeois taste. For it is quite clear from the Russian experience that when the proletariat gets power, it wants, and in the arts at least gets, about what the conventional bourgeois of an earlier generation thought desirable and lovely. The Nazis, too, were all against any of the kinds of art and literature we have discussed in this chapter, all in favor of popular art in the taste of a century ago.

II The Temper of Our Times

Modern western man is acutely conscious of what may be called, a trifle imprecisely, the spirit of the age, the temper of the time, the climate of opinion. In the United States we incline to believe that each recent decade has had a character of its own, from the naughty 'nineties to the fearful 'fifties. For the present, and the immediate past, we have a number of popular phrases—The Age of Anxiety, The Aspirin Age, The Age of Longing, The Age of Conformity, The Age of Suspicion, even The Age of Tranquilizers.

These phrases all have in common a tone of pessimism, mildly seasoned with the shrug-it-off, laugh-that-we-may-not-weep, not very profound cynicism which is a mark of our urban democratic culture. And it surely is also a mark of our age that its serious, its highbrow, culture is to an extraordinary degree pessimistic about the present state of man, gloomy and fearsome about the future, though by no means in agreement either on diagnosis of what is wrong with our culture or in prognosis of its development. Here is a dignified and eloquent sample from the late Albert Camus' speech of acceptance of his Nobel Prize in 1958:

. . . As the heir of a corrupt history that blends blighted revolutions, misguided techniques, dead gods, and worn out ideologies, in which second-rate powers can destroy everything today, but are unable to win anyone over; in which intelligence has stooped to becoming the servant of hatred and oppression, that generation [Camus' own], starting from nothing but its own negations, has had to re-establish both within and without itself a little of what constitutes the dignity of life and death. Faced with a world threatened with disintegration, in which our grand inquisitors may set up once and for all the kingdoms of death, that generation knows that, in a sort of mad race against time, it ought to re-establish among nations a peace not based on slavery, to reconcile labor and culture again, and to reconstruct with all men an Ark of the Covenant. Perhaps it can never accomplish that vast undertaking, but most certainly throughout the world it has already accepted the double challenge of truth and liberty, and, on occasion, has shown that it can lay down its life without hatred. That generation deserves to be acclaimed wherever it happens to be, and especially wherever it is sacrificing itself.*

This is not, of course, sheer pessimism, but it is a kind of unhappy faith, a Stoic determination to fight against the way things are.

Let us note that, although from Plato, even from Ikhnaton on, our serious literary and artistic culture has always shown a strain of pessimism, our own intellectual leaders are, first, more than usually apprehensive and censorious and second, more than usually aware of the gulf between their way of living, their standards of value, and those of their fellow citizens. Just one sample—here in a recent work is a well-known American writer complaining that most Americans confuse "normal" with "average," and suggesting that we need a genuine synonym for "average":

Fortunately, such a genuine and familiar synonym does exist. That which is "average" is also properly described as "mediocre." And if we were accustomed to call the average man, not "the common man" or still less "the normal man," but "the mediocre man" we should not be so easily hypnotized into believing that mediocrity is an ideal to be aimed at.†

This passage is hardly fair to American democratic beliefs; we Americans do not aim at mediocrity as an ideal, but on the contrary

admire greatly the record-breaker, the outstanding personality. But, unlike Mr. Krutch, we are not indignant over the failure of everybody to measure up to highbrow standards and we do not think "common" a synonym of "mediocre."

Now the historian, in attempting by comparative study of similar phenomena in different times and places to arrive at workable generalizations, has great difficulty with this problem of what is the "normal" or "usual" relation between intellectual classes—the writers, artists, scholars, teachers, preachers, and their followers—and other classes, even within our western culture. Such study simply isn't well enough developed to permit measurement, graphs, quantitative generalization. Qualitatively, we may risk the assertion that the gravity and extent of the gap between the way American intellectuals, and to a degree western intellectuals generally, think and feel and the way the rest of western society thinks and feels—the phenomenon we may call in shorthand "the alienation of the intellectuals"—this phenomenon may well be a grave symptom of weakness in our society.

Yet the degree of alienation of the intellectuals is hard to measure, and we may have exaggerated it in the passage above. American intellectuals complain bitterly about the impossibility of the good life in the machine age, but they for the most part use the machines with apparent satisfaction. They find fault with our business civilization, but a great many of them do a very good business in it, and the rank-and-file are not in terms of income as badly off as they think they are. They often regard themselves as a scorned and victimized minority in a hostile society of Babbitts, but a distinguished American sociologist has recently argued that they are in fact well regarded:

While he [the American intellectual] may feel himself neglected and scorned, his work poorly valued by the community, the community places him fairly high when polled on the relative status of occupations. In one such study of the ranks of ninety-six occupations, conducted in 1947 by the National Opinion Research Center of the Univer-

*Reprinted with the permission of Alfred A. Knopf, Inc., from Albert Camus' Speech of Acceptance upon the award of the Nobel Prize for Literature, December 10th, 1957, translated by Justin O'Brien. Copyright © 1958 by Alfred A. Knopf, Inc.

†J. W. Krutch, *Human Nature and the Human Condition* (Random House, (New York, 1959), 93.

sity of Chicago, college professors ranked above every non-political position except that of physician; artists, musicians in a symphony orchestra, and authors ranked almost as high. . . . [In another poll in 1950] professors came out fourth among twenty-four categories, and thirty-eight per cent of those polled placed them definitely in the "upper class."*

At any rate, it is clear that the great majority of Americans, and even the great majority of Europeans, are not as cosmically worried, not as pessimistic about man's fate, as are the intellectuals. Indeed, it seems likely that the many in western society still adhere basically to the eighteenth-century belief in progress, moral as well as material. A recent candidate for the American presidency could say in a campaign speech, which by its very nature must be what hearers want to hear, "It is an article of the democratic faith that progress is a basic law of life."† In fact, one of the reproaches the intellectuals make to the many in the West is that the many appear on the whole quite contented with their material prosperity, their gadgets, their amusements, their American-style "classless society," a society where one man can be said to be as good as another, where all have a high level of consumption, but where there are inequalities, "status seekers", failures, tragedies, not the Utopian, theoretical Marxist heaven of an unrealized "classless society."

Yet the pessimism of the intellectuals is understandable. The almost-Utopia which many of the thinkers of the Enlightenment believed was just around the corner in the eighteenth century is not here yet. Let us, in conclusion, briefly review that eighteenth-century basis of our western democratic faith, and see what our intellectual guides are making of that faith now, two hundred years later.

The Optimism
of the Enlightenment

As we have pointed out (Chapters 17, 20 and 23), there grew up among western men

*S. M. Lipset, *Political Man* (New York, 1960).
†Adlai Stevenson, quoted in C. A. Chambers, "Belief in Progress in Twentieth Century America," *Journal of the History of Ideas* (April, 1958), 221.

in the early modern centuries, and there came to full bloom in the eighteenth and nineteenth centuries, a view of man's fate here on earth which was essentially new. This is the view that all men may rightly expect to be happy here on earth. As St. Just, the youthful colleague of Robespierre in the French Revolution, put it, "Happiness is a new idea in Europe"; or as Jefferson, with his gift for phrasing, put it, one of the unalienable rights of man is the "pursuit of happiness." Of course men have presumably always sought happiness here on earth. In historic Christianity, however, they did not really expect it here on earth, but only in an afterlife in heaven; indeed, Christianity had an overtone of belief that happiness in heaven was in part at least a reward for suffering here on earth.

The *philosophes,* the eighteenth-century thinkers who set the broad terms of this modern optimistic world-view, meant by happiness a condition or state in which each man had at any given moment what he wanted, a state in which each man—each woman, and, incredibly, even each baby—was not aware of being thwarted, frustrated. To the inner state of this happiness there would conform an outer state of material plenty in which everyone would have what he wanted to eat, would be well housed, would have a satisfactory sex life, and would of course enjoy good health, both mental and physical. The matter may indeed be put in terms of modern psychology. Man can rightfully expect in this world, certainly before very long, a society in which everyone would have a life of perfect adjustment, a life without conflict, aggression, insecurity.

Broadly speaking, the *philosophes* held that such perfect happiness had not yet been attained on earth—an obvious fact—because there had grown up a whole set of institutions, habits, and beliefs that had brought evil into human life. Men in 1750, the *philosophes* believed, were not following the natural laws that would make them happy, but the unnatural laws that made them unhappy. The formulators of the new idea of happiness believed that the unhappy state of the world could be traced to a combination of the privileges unnaturally acquired over the centuries by the few rich and powerful (the leaders in church and state), together with the unnatural ignorance and prejudices these few had imposed on the many. They therefore concluded that the solution lay first in depriving the few of their unnatural privileges and, second, in disclosing to the many by a natural system of education and government the key to their own happiness. In short, they believed that men are *by nature* good not evil, reasonable not foolish, intelligent not stupid, certainly improvable. Though it is perhaps unfair to say that they believed in the "natural goodness of man," at a very minimum most of the philosophers held that men as they are now, but under the rule of "cultural engineers," "engineers of the soul," instead of under their present rulers, could all be happy, certainly again at a minimum, much, much happier. Something close to Utopia was to them just around the corner.

This, then, though put oversimply, is the essence of what may be called the democratic dream of the eighteenth-century *philosophes,* the dream of a heavenly city here on earth. But two hundred years later the dream has not come true. Some men still persist in it, holding that we have not yet conquered the privileged classes, not yet opened men's minds, not yet really tried full democracy or not yet allowed free play to the kindly cultural engineers. We must insist: many are now alive who think and feel about man's destiny in essentially eighteenth-century ways. Marxism, for example, in its simplest outline, is the eighteenth-century formula all over again: the bad institutional environment under which men cannot help being miserable is capitalism; the good institutional environment under which men cannot help being happy is socialism. In fact, it seems that Stalin invented that phrase "engineer of the soul." It is, however, quite unfair to limit these believers in what is essentially eighteenth-century rationalist empiricism to the Marxists. There are many respected and influential Americans—and a few such Europeans—who preserve intact a belief in the "principles of 1776 and 1789." They may concede that some men are irrational, but they hold that man is rational. Needless to say, the Soviet Russian experiment has not yet brought this kind of socialism to earth.

But the failure of the dream has caused many more men, at least in the free world, to question its very basis, the doctrine of the basic rationality of man, or at least to question man's complete pliability to the best-intentioned cultural engineering. Such men hold that something profoundly rooted in human nature, and not merely in man's institutions, or in his environment, makes a measure of unhappiness the natural lot of mankind. The modern western world, in consequence, has witnessed a process of reaction and adjustment to the contrast between the high hopes of the Enlightenment and the continuing evils of the world. We may distinguish three broad classifications of these reactions and adjustments, which we may compare with the reactions and adjustments that faced early Christianity once the promise of an *immediate* Second Coming of Christ had to be abandoned.

Repudiation or Revision of the Enlightenment

First, there is the reaction of complete repudiation of all the Enlightenment stood for. This reaction takes many forms. One of them, limited largely to some emotional intellectuals, is the sense of doom we have just discussed, the feeling that in trying to make this earth a heaven man has in fact made it a hell. More commonly, this reaction takes the form of denying all the premises of democracy. It is maintained that most men are wicked or stupid or foolish, or at any rate not up to the burden a democratic society sets on them, that they need to be ruled by their betters, who are always few in number, and that therefore we must return to divine-right monarchy or to the feudal-clerical aristocracy of the Middle Ages, or follow the "new conservatism," or devise some new authoritarianism of the Right or Left. Such views are not commonly held, or at any rate not commonly expressed in the United States. Not even our extreme Rightists quite repudiate the *language* of Jefferson, however much at bottom they disagree with his democratic ideals.

Second, there is the Christian view that men must return to the basic Christian concept of an unavoidable mixture of good and evil in humanity. In this view, life on earth must always demonstrate the conflict between the divine and the animal in man, a conflict tragic and profound, not mean, vile, and hopeless as the mere pessimist sees it, and, above all, not for the individual a ceaseless "existentialist" conflict, but a conflict that has an end in heaven or hell, and that takes place in a universe dominated by *purpose,* not by *accident* or the *merely natural.* For some of these Christians, the desirable earthly society is indeed rather an aristocracy than a democracy. But many of them, like the American theologian and moralist, Reinhold Niebuhr, may be described as moderate democrats. Though they believe that the democratic dream in its radical eighteenth-century form is impious nonsense, they none the less hold that a balanced democratic society is the best way of attaining justice on earth, that such a society is the best, or least bad, earthly reflection of man's dual nature.

Third, there are those who accept the aims of the *philosophes* and even in part the eighteenth-century estimate of human nature. But they find that the Enlightenment of the eighteenth century went wrong in its time-sense, wrong in its hope that its claims could be attained in a generation or two. These thinkers are essentially chastened children of the Enlightenment. They share the view that men are made to be happy, but are convinced by the events of the last two generations that wickedness and unreason are not, as the *philosophes* believed, rooted shallowly in a few bad institutions. On the contrary, they believe that evil, prejudice, and stupidity are deeply rooted in very complex institutions, in tradition, and perhaps even in man as a biological organism.

These thinkers have been greatly influenced by the emphasis that modern psychology has put on the irrational character of the human personality, on the subconscious and the unconscious, and on the consequent difficulty of the actual task of "enlightenment." They now think the task of making the world better will be long and difficult. But it is a task they believe can and must be continued. And they differ basically from the Christians in that they refuse to accept the Christian tension between this world and the next one, or any other one. They do not subscribe necessarily to naive scientific "reductionism" which holds that all productive thinking will end up by accepting simple scientific materialism—or in the popular language of the cliché, that "it's all physics or chemistry." But they do hold that man is a product of nature, that the supernatural does not exist, and that individual immortality is impossible.

The important thing for us to note at the end of this long historic record is that between the second and the third groups we have been discussing, between the Christians and the chastened children of the Enlightenment, a practical accord is possible, and necessary. It is indeed being worked out in the West. In this accord lies the possibility that the men of the first group, the enemies of democracy, may be defeated, and that democracy may live on to give the lie to the prophets of doom. In such an accord we may preserve the willingness to put up with restraints, with imperfections, with frustration, and with suffering without losing the hope, the dream, that is still alive for us in "liberty, equality, fraternity," in "life, liberty, and the pursuit of happiness," in the "principles of 1776 and 1789." Perhaps, above all, those of us called to intellectual pursuits can re-learn the great Christian lesson of humility, can cease in our pride to berate our fellow men as mediocre men. We may thus avoid the illusions and retain the ideals of our historic heritage.

Reading Suggestions on Man's Fate in the Twentieth Century

(Asterisk indicates paperbound edition.)

General

There is not yet a good full intellectual history of the twentieth century; but the chapters dealing with ideas in H. Stuart Hughes, *Contemporary Europe*, 2nd ed. (Prentice-Hall, 1966) are an admirable survey.

Philosophy
and Psychology

E. Jones, *The Life and Work of Freud*, 3 vols. (Basic Books, 1953–1957). The standard work.

R. L. Schoenwald, *Freud: The Man and His Mind* (Knopf, 1956), and P. Rieff, *Freud: The Mind of the Moralist* (Viking, 1959). Two good modern studies emphasizing Freud's place in our contemporary culture.

B. F. Skinner, *Science and Human Behavior* (Macmillan, 1956). A clear and extreme statement of contemporary behavioristic psychology.

M. G. White, *The Age of Analysis: Twentieth-Century Philosophers* (*Mentor, 1955). Excerpts and comments, very well chosen.

M. G. White, *Foundations of Historical Knowledge* (Harper & Row, 1965). A difficult but rewarding book which seeks to rescue historical knowledge from the skeptical position some modern analytical philosophers take toward the subject.

R. Harper, *Existentialism: A Theory of Man* (Harvard Univ. Press, 1949). A sympathetic introduction to a "movement" not quite philosophically respectable but still very fashionable.

W. Kaufman, ed., *Existentialism from Dostoevsky to Sartre* (*Meridian, 1956). Instructive selections from the existentialists, together with helpful critical comment.

P. W. Bridgman, *The Way Things Are* (Harvard Univ. Press, 1959). A distinguished physicist sets down a chastened statement of a contemporary positivist's point of view.

Politics and Sociology

H. S. Hughes, *Consciousness and Society: The Reorientation of European Social Thought, 1890–1930* (Knopf, 1958). A superb and unique study of the intellectual history of the early twentieth century, broader than its title might indicate.

T. Parsons, *The Structure of Social Action,* 2nd ed. (Free Press, 1949). A landmark in American sociological thinking.

R. D. Humphrey, *Georges Sorel: Prophet Without Honor* (Harvard Univ. Press, 1951). A suggestive study of an anti-intellectual.

V. Pareto, *The Mind and Society,* 4 vols. (Harcourt, Brace, 1935). A major work in general sociology, hardly to be read quickly. A good though difficult brief exposition of Pareto's thought is L. J. Henderson, *Pareto's General Sociology* (Harvard Univ. Press, 1937).

J. H. Meisel, *The Myth of the Ruling Class: Gaetano Mosca and the 'Elite'* (Univ. of Michigan Press, 1958). An illuminating study of an important thinker too little known in this country.

G. Wallas, *Human Nature in Politics* (Constable, 1908; *Bison). A pioneer study in political psychology. See also his *The Great Society* (Macmillan, 1915, and later editions).

K. R. Popper, *The Open Society and Its Enemies* (Princeton Univ. Press, 1950). A major work on the problems of modern democracy.

K. E. Boulding, *The Meaning of The Twentieth Century: The Great Tradition* (Harper & Row, 1964). A discerning study. See also Professor Boulding's *Social Justice* (*Spectrum).

Sciences and Arts

I. Asimov, *The New Intelligent Man's Guide to Science* (Basic Books, 1965). A good survey, with a fine bibliography, pp. 815–823).

C. T. Chase, *The Evolution of Modern Physics* (Van Nostrand, 1947), and L. Barnett, *The Universe and Dr. Einstein* (*Mentor, 1952). Two useful popular accounts of a difficult and important subject.

E. C. Berkeley, *Giant Brains* (Wiley, 1949), and N. Wiener, *Cybernetics; or Control and Communication in the Animal and the Machine,* new ed. (Wiley, 1957). Two by no means easy studies of another important related aspect of our world.

Editors of the "Scientific American," *Atomic Power* and ten other volumes covering various fields of science (Simon and Schuster, 1953–1957). These paperback volumes are admirable examples of sophisticated scientific popularization. The parent magazine, *Scientific American,* gives a fine running account of the whole range of contemporary science, including the more "scientific" of the behavioral or social sciences.

B. Barber, *Science and the Social Order* (Free Press, 1952). A suggestive study in a little-cultivated field.

M. McLuhan, *Understanding Media* (*McGraw-Hill). Controversial appraisal of communications in the present-day world.

L. Mumford and others, *The Arts in Renewal* (Univ. of Pennsylvania Press, 1951), and R. Richman, *The Arts at Mid-Century* (Horizon Press, 1954). Two wide-ranging collections of essays by Americans, touching critically on all the arts.

C. Mauriac, *The New Literature* (Braziller, 1959). Interesting essays translated from the French, mostly but not wholly dealing with French writers.

E. Wilson, *Axel's Castle: A Study in the Imaginative Literature of 1870–1930* (*Scribners, 1957). Already a classic of criticism, ranging in subject matter from French nineteenth-century symbolism to Joyce and Gertrude Stein.

F. J. Hoffmann, *Freudianism and the Literary Mind,* 2nd ed. (Louisiana State Univ. Press, 1957; *Evergreen Books). A suggestive study. See also the somewhat wider treatment of "moderns" in H. Slochower, *Literature and Philosophy between Two World Wars: No Voice Is Wholly Lost* (*Citadel).

W. P. Jones, *James Joyce and The Common Reader* (Univ. of Oklahoma Press, 1955). The simplest introduction, with good bibliographies leading to more advanced critical work.

A. H. Barr, Jr. *What Is Modern Painting?* (*Museum of Modern Art—Doubleday). Good, brief introduction, with helpful bibliography.

J. Canaday, *Embattled Critic: Views on Modern Art* (*Noonday). By the respected art critic of the *New York Times.*

T. H. Robsjohn-Gibbings, *Mona Lisa's Mustache: A Dissection of Modern Art* (Knopf, 1947). Amusing debunking.

A. H. Barr, Jr., ed., *Picasso: 75th Anniversary Exhibition* (*Museum of Modern Art-Doubleday). Illustrated review of the productions of the best-known modern artist.

D. Herzka, *Pop Art* (*George Wittenborn). Introduction to one of the most recent and most baffling *genres* of modern art.

Frank Lloyd Wright on Architecture, F. Guttheim, ed. (*Universal). Views of a great pioneer in modern architecture.

A. Copland, *Our New Music* (McGraw-Hill, 1941). A good introduction by a leading modern American composer.

P. H. Lang, ed., *Stravinsky: A New Appraisal of His Music* (*Norton). Evaluations of a characteristic modern composer.

Our Present
Discontents:
Hopes and Fears
for the Future

D. Riesman and others, *The Lonely Crowd,* abridged ed. (Doubleday, 1953; *Anchor). One of the outstanding current books in the behavioral sciences field.

W. H. Whyte, *The Organization Man* (Doubleday, 1957; *Anchor) and V. O. Packard,

The Status Seekers (McKay, 1959). Two recent best sellers of popular sociology, interesting as indications of problems we are very aware of.

L. Mumford, *Technics and Civilization* (Harcourt, Brace, 1934). A still influential work by a leading intellectual of the just-past generation.

F. E. Manuel, ed., *Utopias and Utopian Thought* (Houghton, Mifflin, 1966). An interesting symposium on an eternal theme of man's fate.

R. Williams, *Culture and Society, 1780–1950* (Columbia Univ. Press, 1958). An important book that sets in historical background the problem we here call "the alienation of the intellectuals." For other contemporary aspects of this problem, consult C. Brinton, "Reflections on the Alienation of the Intellectuals" in A. V. Riasanovsky and B. Riznik, eds., *Generalizations in Historical Writing* (Univ. of Penn. Press, 1963), with bibliographical footnotes; Lewis A. Coser *Men of Ideals* (Free Press, 1965); G. B. de Huszar. *The Intellectuals: A Controversial Portrait* (Free Press, 1960); the older classic, J. Benda. *The Betrayal of the Intellectuals,* translated from the French, *La Trahison des Clercs* (*Beacon); and R. Hofstadter, *Anti-Intellectualism in American Life* (Knopf, 1963).

L. Mumford, *The Transformations of Man* (Harper, 1956), C. G. Darwin, *The Next Million Years* (Doubleday, 1953), R. Seidenberg, *Post-historic Man* (Univ. of North Carolina Press, 1950; *Beacon), H. Brown, *The Challenge of Man's Future* (*Viking, 1956). Four brief, diverse attempts to chart the future of the human race. For guidance in this important contemporary literature of "Whither Mankind" consult also C. Brinton, *The Fate of Man* (Braziller, 1961), with bibliography.

R. Niebuhr, *The Structure of Nations and Empires* (Scribner's, 1959). A wise book that uses history as servant, not master.

A. J. Toynbee, *A Study of History,* abridged ed. by D. C. Somervell, 2 vols. (Oxford Univ. Press, 1947–1957). A faithful condensation of a ten-volume work.

I. Berlin, *Historical Inevitability* (Oxford Univ. Press, 1954). A brief, difficult book attacking historicism. For a wide range of critics of Toynbee in particular, see M. F. Ashley-Montagu, *Toynbee and History* (Porter Sargent, 1956); and for good leads into many phases of the problem of history today, see P. Zagorin, "Historical Knowledge: A Review Article on the Philosophy of History," *Journal of Modern History,* Sept. 1959, Vol. XXXI, No. 3, pp. 243–255.

F. E. Manuel, *The Shapes of Philosophical History* (Stanford Univ. Press, 1965). An admirable summing up of western thought on history as a guide to present and future.

A. H. Leighton, *The Governing of Men,* new ed. (Princeton Univ. Press, 1955), and C. Kluckhohn, *Mirror for Man* (McGraw-Hill, 1949; *Premier Books). Two good examples of the uses of the newer concepts in the social sciences.

J. Barzun, *The House of Intellect* (Harper, 1959). A brilliant American intellectual on the present state of our intellectual life.

A. C. Valentine, *The Age of Conformity* (Regnery, 1954). A good example of the criticism of modern American democracy from the worried conservative standpoint.

C. Frankel, *The Case for Modern Man* (Harper, 1956; *Beacon). An admirable restatement of hopeful belief in democracy; antidote to the prophets of gloom.

R. L. Heilbroner, *The Future as History* (Harper, 1960). Interesting "revisionism" applied to the traditions of democratic optimism.

R. Niebuhr, *The Children of Light and the Children of Darkness* (Scribner's, 1944), and *The Irony of American History* (Scribner's, 1952). An important American theologian argues that Christian pessimism offers a good working basis for democracy.

P. Geyl, "The Vitality of Western Civilization," *Delta: A Review of Life and Thought in the Netherlands,* Spring, 1959, pp. 5–19. A splendid reply to the prophets of doom, by an esteemed intellectual.

Illustrations

London during South Sea Bubble, *The Bettmann Archive,* 7

Eighteenth-century grinders, *The Bettmann Archive,* 9

House of Commons, by Hogarth, *The New York Public Library,* 12

Marquise de Pompadour, by de la Tour, 16

Giant soldier of Prussia, *The Granger Collection,* 20

Peter I, by Serov, 29

Battle of Culloden, *The Bettmann Archive,* 35

Frederick the Great, *The Granger Collection,* 37

Table talk with Voltaire, *The Granger Collection,* 51

Frederick the Great playing the flute, *The Bettmann Archive,* 57

Joseph II, *Austrian Information Center,* 60

Charles III, *The Metropolitan Museum Reference Collection,* 61

Catherine the Great, *The Granger Collection,* 66

Alexander I, *The Granger Collection,* 69

English commentary on Boston Tea Party, *The Metropolitan Museum of Art,* 75

Samuel Johnson, by Reynolds, *The Granger Collection,* 81

Library at Ken Wood, London, 82

Gallery at Strawberry Hill, 82

Mozart, *The Granger Collection,* 84

Paris City Hall, July 14, 1789, *French Cultural Services,* 97

Marie Antoinette and children, 99

Danton, by David, *The Bettmann Archive,* 104

Louis XVI, *The Granger Collection,* 106

Robespierre, *The Granger Collection,* 108

Marie Antoinette on way to guillotine, by David, *The New York Public Library Picture Collection,* 109

Napoleon, by David, 114

Napoleonic scheme for invasion of England, *The Bettmann Archive,* 121

Napoleon's bivouac preceding Battle of Austerlitz, *The Granger Collection,* 122

Gillray, British comment on Napoleon's imperialism, *The Granger Collection,* 127

"The Third of May," by Goya, *Prado, Madrid,* 129

Delacroix, self-portrait, *French Cultural Services,* 142

Houses of Parliament, *British Travel Association,* 142

Monticello, *The Granger Collection,* 143

Talleyrand, *French Embassy Press and Information Service,* 146

Statesmen at Congress of Vienna, *The Bettmann Archive,* 147

"The Massacre of Scio," by Delacroix, 156

"The Fight of the Citizens of France against the Oppression of Louis-Philippe," by Daumier, *The Bettmann Archive,* 164

"The Uprising, 1848," by Daumier, *Phillips Memorial Gallery,* 166

Joseph Mazzini, *Istituto Italiano di Cultura,* 167

Barricades in Milan, 1848, *The Granger Collection,* 168

Barricades in Berlin, 1848, *The Granger Collection,* 170

Power looms, about 1820, *The Bettmann Archive,* 179

Corn Laws, *The Bettmann Archive,* 185

"Work," by Ford Madox Brown, 186

Child laborers, about 1840, *The Bettmann Archive,* 189

John Stuart Mill, *The Bettmann Archive,* 194

Parallelogram for New Harmony, *The Bettmann Archive,* 199

Louis Blanc, *French Embassy Press and Information Division,* 200

Friedrich Engels, *The Bettmann Archive,* 203

Disraeli, *The Granger Collection,* 215

Gladstone advising Queen Victoria, *The Bettmann Archive,* 216

David Lloyd George, *The Granger Collection,* 225

Napoleon III, *The Bettmann Archive,* 228

Barricades in Paris, *The Bettmann Archive,* 231

Division into choruses of France's National Assembly, cartoon, *The Bettmann Archive,* 233

Dreyfus case, covered by American press, *The Bettmann Archive,* 236

Cavour, *The Bettmann Archive,* 238

Garibaldi, *Istituto Italiano di Cultura,* 239

Marcus A. Hanna, *The Granger Collection,* 248

Bismarck, *The Bettmann Archive,* 257

William II, *The Granger Collection,* 263

Francis Joseph, *The Granger Collection,* 266

Nicholas I, by Landseer, *The Bettmann Archive,* 279

Bursting of the Russian Bubble, *The Bettmann Archive,* 281

Alexander II, *The Granger Collection,* 282

Alexander III, *Brown Brothers,* 287

"Bloody Sunday," *Sovfoto,* 290

Anti-Darwinian cartoon, by Nast, *The Granger Collection,* 300

Bernard Shaw, by Beerbohm, *The Bettmann Archive,* 308

Cabaret scene, by Seurat, *Otterloo Museum,* 310

"The Starry Night," by van Gogh, *The Art Institute of Chicago,* 311

"La Montagne Sainte Victoire," by Cézanne, *The Home House Trustees, London,* 312

Fifth Avenue, in 1898, *The Granger Collection,* 314

Auditorium Hotel and Theater, Chicago, *The Bettmann Archive,* 315

The public and music by Wagner, Daumier caricature, *The Bettmann Archive,* 317

Friedrich Nietzsche, *The Bettmann Archive,* 322

Arrival of one of the first English steamers, *The Bettmann Archive,* 330

British advance toward Johannesburg, *The Bettmann Archive,* 334

"Mosé in Egitto!", *The Granger Collection,* 335

British imperialism in Africa, German view, *The Bettmann Archive,* 337

Entry of French into Algiers, *The Bettmann Archive,* 341

Theodore Roosevelt in Panama, *The Granger Collection,* 343

Commodore Perry, *The Granger Collection,* 345

Cecil Rhodes, *The Granger Collection,* 347

"European Balance," by Daumier, *The Bettmann Archive,* 360

Soldiers leaving Berlin for front, *Wide World Photos,* 361

"Disturbing the Peace," *The Bettmann Archive,* 366

Princip, after assassination, *The Granger Collection,* 367

Allied soldiers keeping warm, *Wide World Photos,* 372

Aerial combat, World War I, *The Granger Collection,* 378

Allied tank on Western front, *Wide World Photos,* 379

English policewomen spreading news of Zeppelin raid, *The Bettmann Archive,* 380

Halt the Hun!, *Brown Brothers,* 381

American soldiers celebrate Armistice, *The Granger Collection,* 384

Paris greets Armistice, *The Granger Collection,* 384

The Big Four at Paris, 1919, *The Bettmann Archive,* 387

Rasputin, *The Granger Collection,* 400

Soldier delegates to Petrograd Soviet meeting, *Sovfoto,* 401

"Under the snug wing of Kerensky," *The Bettmann Archive,* 405

Moscow, 1917, *Sovfoto,* 405

Trotsky and staff, *The Bettmann Archive,* 410

Lenin addressing a throng, *Brown Brothers,* 410

Lenin and Stalin, *The Granger Collection,* 414

Trotsky and wife, *Wide World Photos,* 416

Tractors at a Machine-Tractor Station, *Sovfoto,* 419

Factory workers listening to charge made by Vishinsky, *Sovfoto,* 423

"Rendezvous," *The London Express,* 432

D'Annunzio, *Brown Brothers,* 439

Mussolini during "March" on Rome, *Brown Brothers,* 443

Officer addressing crowd during Kapp *putsch, The Granger Collection,* 451

Hitler watercolor and pencil drawing, *Wide World Photos,* 452

German inflation, *Wide World Photos,* 453

Ludendorff and Hitler, *The Bettmann Archive,* 455

Berliners hailing Hitler, *The Granger Collection,* 459

"Jews not wanted in this place," *Wide World Photos,* 462

Franco inspecting trenches during Spanish Civil War, *Brown Brothers,* 469

Dollfuss poster, *United Press International,* 470

King Alexander and loyal Croats, *Wide World Photos,* 473

Emergency transport carrying London office workers, *Wide World Photos,* 484

De Valera taking salute of Irish Republican army, *Brown Brothers,* 485

Wartime devastation in Verdun, *The Bettmann Archive,* 487

Demonstrators in Stavisky riots, *United Press International,* 490

NRA cartoon, *The Granger Collection,* 496

"Rule, Japannia," cartoon by Low, *The London Express,* 500

Chinese prisoners during Boxer rebellion, *The Bettmann Archive,* 501

Gandhi, *Wide World Photos,* 506

Signing of Locarno Pact, *Wide World Photos,* 513

Haile Selassie protesting to League of Nations, *The Granger Collection,* 516

"Honest, Mister, there's nobody here but us Spaniards," cartoon by Low, *The London Express,* 518

Chamberlain and Hitler, *Wide World Photos,* 520

Civilians in Marseilles watching flags being evacuated, *United Press International,* 528

Collapse of building during London "blitz," *Brown Brothers,* 529

Pearl Harbor, *United Press International,* 532

American troops landing in Normandy, *Wide World Photos,* 535

Corpses of Gestapo victims, *United Press International,* 537

Hiroshima after the bomb hit, *Wide World Photos,* 540

Casablanca conference, *United Press International,* 541

Marshall Plan operation, *Wide World Photos,* 553

Berliners watching airlift during Berlin Blockade, *The Granger Collection,* 566

Tito and fellow partisans, *The Granger Collection,* 567

American infantrymen in evacuated Korean town, *Wide World Photos,* 568

Nehru receiving golden mace, *Wide World Photos,* 573

Stalin statue toppled in Budapest, *Wide World Photos,* 583

Crisscross sowing of wheat, U.S.S.R., *Sovfoto,* 586

Yevgeny Yevtushenko, *Sovfoto,* 589

Syniavsky and Daniel trial, *Sovfoto,* 589

Brandenburg gate, *Wide World Photos,* 594

Red Guardsman shouting support of Maoism, *Wide World Photos,* 604

President Soekarno and Cabinet, *Wide World Photos,* 608

Moslem refugees, *Wide World Photos,* 610

Nasser receiving plaudits, *Wide World Photos,* 613

Sekou Touré, *United Nations,* 615

Police dispersing demonstrating African women, *Wide World Photos,* 618

Nationalist terrorist suspects, *Wide World Photos,* 618

Student from the Cameroon speaking at Moscow protest meeting, *Wide World Photos,* 619

Dr. Martin Luther King, *Wide World Photos,* 627

President John F. Kennedy at NATO headquarters, *Wide World Photos,* 629

Freud, by Cocteau, *The Bettmann Archive,* 643

Pavlov watching experiment, *Sovfoto,* 645

James Joyce, *Monkmeyer Press Photo Service,* 655

"Current," by Bridget Riley, *The Museum of Modern Art,* 657

IBM Building, Seattle, *University Properties, Inc.,* 658

Gateway Arch, St. Louis, *Arteaga Photos, St. Louis,* 658

Central Technical School, Toronto, *Panda Associates,* 659

Untitled stabile-mobile, by Calder, *The Museum of Modern Art,* 659

"Family Group," by Moore. *The Museum of Modern Art,* 659

Acknowledgments

Grateful acknowledgment is made to the following publishers for granting permission to use the material quoted on the pages indicated: Allen & Unwin, Ltd., 321; Doubleday & Company, Inc., 662; E. P. Dutton & Company, Inc., 15, 44, 50, 54, 55, 79, 86, 136, 137, 138, 143, 145, 190, 195; Faber & Faber, Ltd., 655; Hafner Publishing Company, 52, 53; Harcourt, Brace & World, 526, 655; William Hodge & Company, Ltd., 339; Houghton Mifflin Company, 126, 447; The Macmillan Company, 187, 197; The Museum of Modern Art, 657; Oxford University Press (London), 309, 506; Oxford University Press (New York), 420; Random House, 202, 205, 661; Charles Scribner's Sons, 303; The Society of Authors, 656; Viking Press, Inc., 656.

"The White Man's Burden" on page 348 is from "The Five Nations" by Rudyard Kipling. Copyright 1903 by Rudyard Kipling, reprinted by permission of Mrs. George Bambridge, Doubleday & Company, Inc., and Methuen & Company, Ltd.

Index

A

Abstractionism, 656
Abukir Bay, battle of, 115
Abyssinia (*see* Ethiopia)
Action Française, 489
Adam, Robert; *illus.,* 82
Addresses to the German Nation (Fichte), 128
Aden, 614
Adenauer, Konrad, 561, 632, 633
Adler, Alfred, 645
Adowa, battle of, 242, 516
Adrianople, Treaty of, 155
Adventures of a Monkey (Zoshchenko), 563
Aehrenthal, Count Aloys von, 273, 365
Affluent Society, The (Galbraith), 649
Afghanistan, 222, 364
Africa (*see also individual countries*); 1900, *map,* 329; imperialism in, 330-331, 336, 339-343; independence problems, 615-620, *maps,* 887
Agrarian League (Germany), 263, 458
Agriculture; Canadian, 184; French, 4, 8, 92-93, 95, 163, 237; German, 184, 463; Irish land reforms, 223-224; Prussian, 56-57; Russian tsarist, 281-283, 291-292; Russian Soviet, 398, 402, 405, 407, 412-413, 417-419, 426, 562, 582, 585-587; scientific advances in, 8-9, 184-185; Spanish, 62; U. S., 184, 494-496; Yugoslavian, 567

Aix-la-Chapelle, Treaty of, 34-35
Akhmatova, Anna, 563
Alaska, 153, 329, 627
Albania, 433; Chinese satellite, 597, 603; Italian conquest, 446, 518; U.S.S.R. satellite, 548, 567
Alberoni, Cardinal Giulio, 15
Alexander, King (Greece), 374
Alexander, King (Yugoslavia), 473; *illus.,* 473
Alexander I (Russia), 68-70, 120, 122-123, 129-130, 146, 148, 153, 156-157, 161
Alexander II (Russia), 281-283, 286; *illus.,* 282
Alexander III (Russia), 286-287
Alexandra, Empress (Russia), 399, 401
Alexis (son of Peter the Great), 62-63
Alfonso XIII (Spain), 466-467
Algeciras Conference (*1906*), 365
Algeria, 328, 340, 603, 620, 634
All Quiet on the Western Front (Remarque), 379
Alsace-Lorraine, 231, 237, 260, 264, 362, 385, 388, 489
Alton Locke (Kingsley), 207
American War of Independence, 94; background, 74-76; political implications, 76-78
Amiens, Peace of, 120
Amritsar massacre, 383, 505
Anarchism, 206-207, 466-468
Anarcho-syndicalism, 206, 466
Andrassy, Count Gyula, 266
Angola, 615
Annals of Agriculture (Young), 73
Anne, Empress (Russia), 62-64

Anschluss, 470-471, 518-519
Anticlericalism; Austria, 59, 274; France, 51-52, 91, 100, 118, 235, 237, 489; Mexico, 578; Portugal, 61; Spain, 62, 152-153
Anti-Corn Law League, 184-185, 219
Anti-Machiavel (Frederick the Great), 56
Anti-semitism; Austria, 59, 274-275; Dreyfus case, 234-235; Germany, 461-462, 536-537; Hungary, 276, 471; Italy, 446; Prussia, 57; Rumania, 474; Russia, 287, 290, 563, 565; theorists, 451; Yugoslavia, 474
Antonescu, Marshal Ion, 474
Apartheid, 616
Arab League, 611
Arakcheev, Count Aleksei, 70, 156-157
Architecture; eclectic, 313-314, *illus.,* 314-315; Gothic revival, 141-142, *illus.,* 82, 142; modern, 314-315, 658, *illus.,* 658-659; neoclassic, 81, *illus.,* 82
Argentina, 184, 578-579, 622
Armenia, 425
Arnold, Matthew, 220, 309, 324
Arp, Jean, 657
Art (*see* Painting; Sculpture)
Artois, Count of (*see* Charles X)
Arzhak, Nikolai (*see* Daniel, Yuli)
Asbury, Francis, 80
Asia (*see also individual countries*); in Cold War, 597-604; imperialism in, 332, 337-339, 342-346, *map,* 331, *1967, map,* 876
Asiento privilege, 7, 33-34
Asquith, Herbert H., 225, 382, 482

Assignats, 99-100, 103, 108, 111
Asturias uprising, 467-468
Aswan Dam, 611
Atatürk (*see* Kemal, Mustafa)
Atlantic Charter, 540
Atomic weapons; China, 595, 604; France, 625, 635; test ban agreement, 595; U. S., 524, 538; U.S.S.R., 546, 548, 552
Attlee, Clement, 541, 556
Auerstädt, battle of, 122
Augustus III (Poland), 32, 70
Augustus the Strong (Poland), 24-25, 32
Austerlitz, battle of, 121-122; *illus.,* 122
Australia, 184, 350-352, 548, 625
Australian Colonies Government Act, 351-352
Austria, 31, 70, 73, 188, 229, 280-281, 383, 630; *Anschluss,* 518-519; anti-semitism, 274-275; anti-clericalism, 59, 274; Charles VI, 17-18; Congress of Vienna, 145-149; dual monarchy, 267-268; economy, 59, 61, 469; education, 59; European revolutions, 153, 161, 166-169; fascism in, 469-471; French Revolution, 102, 106, 112-113; Italy and, 17, 166-169, 239-241; Maria Theresa, 58-59; minorities in, 268-271, 275-276, *map,* 269; Napoleonic Wars, 114-115, 119-123, 128-129; occupation status, 565; politics *1867-1914,* 274-276; politics, inter-war, 469-471; "Potato War," 60; *pre-Ausgleich,* 265-266; Prussian war, 258-259; revolution of 1848, 171-174; social classes, 274-275; Troppau Protocol, 153; Turkish wars, 32-33; Versailles settlement, 385, 389; War of Austrian Succession, 34, 71; War of Polish Succession, 32-33; World War I, 357-359, 362-363, 365-368, 370-374
Austrian succession, War of the, 11, 34, 58, 71
Autobiography (Mill), 194
Aviation; in World War I, 377; in World War II, 524-525, 529-530, 534, 536
Ayub Khan, 610
Azaña, Manuel, 468
Azerbaidjan, 425
Azov, 71

B

Babbitt (Lewis), 308, 494
Babeuf, Gracchus, 111
Babi Yar (Yevtushenko), 588
Bach, Johann Sebastian, 83, 85, 140
Bach system (Austria), 265-266

Baden, 5, 120, 258
Badoglio, Marshal Pietro, 535, 542
Bagehot, Walter, 214, 322
Baghdad Pact, 625
Bahamas, 336
Bakunin, Michael, 206, 284-285, 440, 466
Balfour Declaration, 376, 383, 507, 575
Balkans, 32-33, 59; in World War I, 359, 363, 365-366, 374-376
Baldwin, Stanley, 485
Balearic Islands, 37
Baltic provinces, 15, 24-26
Balzac, Honoré de, 306
Bank of England, 6-8, 181
Bank of France, 119, 490
Banking, 5-8, 94, 119, 490; and Industrial Revolution, 181; Russian Gosbank, 421
Barbary pirates, 159
Barbusse, Henri, 379
Barings of London, 181
Baroja, Pio, 308
Basel, Treaty of, 113
Bastille, fall of, 96-98
Battle of Arminius (Kleist), 139
Battle of Britain, 529-531
"Battle of the Nations," 130
Bavaria, 34, 60, 120, 258, 382, 448
Bazaine, General Achille François, 230
Beauharnais, Eugène de, 126
Beauharnais, Josephine de, 112, 123
Beaumarchais, Pierre, 92
Bebel, August, 262
Beccaria, Cesare, 49, 59, 61, 66
Beerbohm, Max, *illus.,* 308
Beethoven, Ludwig van, 139-140
Beggar's Opera (Gay), 83
Behaviorism, 645-646
Belgium, 211-212, 449; Austrian control, 15, 17, 36, 59; colonies, 329, 343, 603, 618-619; European union and, 630; Locarno treaty, 512; Napoleonic Wars, 112-114, 120, 123; Netherlands control, 148; revolution of 1830, 160-161, 187; suffrage, 188; World War I, 368, 370, 385, 389; World War II, 525, 527
Belgrade, Treaty of, 70
Belorussia, 72-73
Ben Bella, Ahmed, 603, 619-620
Beneš, Edward, 565
Bennett, Arnold, 308
Bentham, Jeremy, 192-195
Bergson, Henri, 319
Beria, Lavrentia, 582, 584
Berlin, 18, 20, 547; blockade, 566, *illus.,* 566; in Cold War, 592-593; Wall, 593, 632
Berlin, Congress of, 286
Berlin, University of, 128
Berlin Decree, 126
Berlioz, Louis Hector, 140

Bermuda, 336
Bernadotte, Crown Prince, 123
Berri, Duke of, 158
Bessarabia, 390, 433, 474, 565, 596
Bessemer, Sir Henry, 180
Bestuzhev-Ryumin, Mikhail, 70-71
Betancourt, Romulo, 596
Bethlen, Count István, 472
Bethmann-Hollweg, Theobald von, 368, 381
Beust, Friedrich Ferdinand, 266
Bidault, Georges, 233
"Biglow Papers" (Lowell), 309
Bill of Rights: English, 77; U. S., 77
Biology: Darwinian eugenicists, 301-302; evolutionary, 298-299; Linnaeus' contributions, 45; U.S.S.R., 563, 645-646
Bismarck, Otto von, 174; Austrian war, 258-259; colonial policy, 343; domestic policies, 256, 260-263; foreign policies, 257-260, 343, 362-363; Franco-Prussian war, 259-260; German Confederation, 254-256; League of the Three Emperors, 363; North German Confederation, 259; Pan-Germans and, 275; Roman Catholic Church, 260-262; Triple Alliance, 363; welfare measures, 262; *illus.,* 257
Black, Joseph, 45
Black Partition (Russia), 286
Black Sea, 72-73, 281, 286
Blanc, Louis, 165, 178, 200, 207
Blücher, Gebhard Leberecht von, 131
Blum, Leon, 490-491
Boer War, 264, 333-334; *illus.,* 334
Bohemia (*see also* Czechoslovakia), 18, 59, 171-172, 268, 389
Bolsheviks, 288-291, 400, 403-406
Bonaparte, Jerome, 123
Bonaparte, Joseph (Naples), 123, 152
Bonaparte, Louis (Holland), 126, 132
Bonaparte, Louis Napoleon (*see* Napoleon III)
Bonaparte, Lucien, 115
Bonaparte, Napoleon (*see* Napoleon Bonaparte)
Bonapartists; in 1848 revolution, 164, 166
Booth, John Wilkes, 246
Boris, King (Bulgaria), 474
Borodin, Mikhail, 429
Bosanquet, Bradley, 318
Bosnia-Herzogovina, 273-274, 286, 375
Boston Tea Party, 76; *illus.,* 75
Boulanger, General Georges, 234
Bourgeoisie (*see* Classes, social; Middle Classes)
Bourguiba, Habib, 615, 620
Bouvard et Pécuchet (Flaubert), 308
Boxer Rebellion, 288, 501
Boyars, 63
Bradley, Henry, 318

Brandenburg, 18
Brazil, 153, 622
Brest-Litovsk, Peace of, 373, 382, 408-409
Brezhnev, L.I., 602-603
Briand, Aristide, 233, 512-513
Bridgewater, Duke of, 5
Bridgman, P. W., 650
Brieux, Eugene, 307
British Commonwealth of Nations, 486-487, 572-573, 605, 616
British Guiana, 336, 622
British Honduras, 336
Broglie, Duke of, 232
Broz, Joseph (see Tito)
Bruening, Heinrich, 457, 459, 470
Brunswick, Duke of, 103-104, 113
Brusilov, General Aleksei Alekseevich, 373
Bukharin, Nikolai, 414, 416, 423-424, 430
Bukovina, 433, 565, 596
Bulganin, Nikolai, 582, 583, 584
Bulgaria, 286, 429, 474-475; in Soviet bloc, 548, 565; in World War I, 368, 374, 376; in World War II, 433
Bulletin of the Opposition, The (Trotsky), 422
Burckhardt, 212
Burgoyne, General John, 76
Burke, Edmund, 112, 115-116, 136, 145
Burma, 533, 556, 568, 600
Burne-Jones, Sir Edward, 310
Burns, John, 368
Burundi, 603
Business (see Economy; Industry; Industrial Revolution)
Bute, Lord, 74
Butler, Samuel, 308
Byng, Admiral, 37.
Byron, Lord, 137

C

Caballero, Largo, 468
Cahiers, 93
Calas, Jean, 51
Calder, Alexander, illus., 659
Caldwell, Erskine, 308
Calonne, Charles Alexander de, 94
Calvinism, 59, 276
Cambodia, 600
Camelots du Roi, 489
Cameroon (Kamerun), 342, 391
Campoformio, Treaty of, 114
Camus, Albert, 649, 652, 660-661
Canada, 13, 38, 74, 76, 184, 245, 328, 350-351, 555, 629-630
Candide (Voltaire), 44, 52
Canning, George, 153-154, 214
Cape Breton Island, 34
Cape Colony, 332-334

Cape of Good Hope, 148
Carbonari, 153, 161
Caribbean: British imperialism in, 336-337
Carlism (Spain), 466, 468
Carlsbad Decrees, 162
Carlyle, Thomas, 220, 324
Carnap, Rudolf, 650
Carol, King (Rumania), 474
Casablanca Conference, 540; illus., 541
Cassirer, Ernst, 649
Castlereagh, Viscount, 146-149, 153
Castro, Fidel, 589, 594, 622
Catherine I (Russia), 23, 62-63
Catherine II, the Great (Russia), 8, 63-67, 71-73
Catholic Center party (Germany), 261-262, 264, 449, 457, 459, 461
Catholic Church (see Roman Catholic Church)
Cavaignac, General, 165-166
Cavour, Count Camillo Benso di, 167, 238-240; illus., 238
Central Treaty Organization (CENTO), 625
Ceylon, 148
Cézanne, Paul, 312-313; illus., 312
Chaadaev, 283
Chamberlain, Austen, 226
Chamberlain, Houston Stewart, 451
Chamberlain, Joseph, 223-224, 226, 482-483
Chamberlain, Neville, 226, 519-520, 527; illus., 520
Charles III (Spain), 61-62; illus., 61
Charles VI (Austria), 17-18, 29-30, 32, 34
Charles VII (Bavaria), 34
Charles X (France), 158-159
Charles XII (Sweden), 24-26, 32, 61
Charles Albert (Piedmont), 167-169
Charter of 1814 (France), 130
Chartism, 221
Chase, Stuart, 650
Cheap Clothes and Nasty (Kingsley), 207
Chekhov, Anton Pavlovich, 307
Chemistry, 45, 653
Chetniks (Yugoslavia), 566
Chiang Kai-shek, 414, 429, 502-504, 538, 547, 549, 569
Chile, 622-624
China, 288, 346, 383, 429; Africa and, 619, 620; atomic weapons, 604; Boxer Rebellion, 288, 501; Civil War, 502-504, 547; Communist party, 547, 549, 592; imperialism in, 332, 336-337, 342; India invasion, 598; Indonesia and, 607-608; industry, 597; Japanese occupation, 502-504; Korean War, 568-569; Mao's succession, 603-604; Nine Power Treaty, 493-494; Revolution of 1911, 501-502; UN representation, 625; U.S.S.R. split,

592, 597-599, 603; Vietnam War, 601; World War II, 538 (see also Manchuria)
Chios, 155
Chippendale, Thomas, 82
Choiseul, Duke of, 39, 47
Christian Democratic party (Germany), 561, 632-633; (Italy), 442, 636
Christian Socialist party (Austria), 275, 469-470
Christianity (see Religion; Roman Catholic Church)
Chronometer, 5
Church of England, 79, 223
Churchill, Winston, 374, 378, 520, 527, 529, 531, 535-536, 540, 542, 548, 556-557, 565; illus., 541
Cisalpine Republic (Napoleonic), 114-115
Civil Constitution of the Clergy, 100, 118
Civil War (United States), 243-246
Civil liberties (see also Law; Religion; Suffrage); in Austria-Hungary, 267; France, nineteenth century, 117-118, 131-132, 158-159; Great Britain, nineteenth century, 214; Italy, fascist, 444-445; Japan, imperial, 499; Poland, nineteenth century, 161; Prussia, nineteenth century, 162, 171; Revolutions of 1820 and, 149; Russia, 289-290, 424-425; Spain, nineteenth century, 152; Turkey, 508; U. S. desegregation laws, 627
Civil Rights Bill of 1965 (United States), 627
Clarissa Harlowe (Richardson), 80, 137
Classes, social (see also Labor; Middle Classes); anarchist theory of, 206-207; Austrian, 274-275; British, 214-216, 225-226, 482-484; French, 90-96, 99, 164-165, 174, 488-491; Indian, 338, 574; Industrial Revolution and, 187-190; Japanese, 345-346; Marxist theory, 201-205; Russian, 66-69, 281-282, 421-422; Social Darwinists' theory of, 301, 303; United States, 554
Clemenceau, Georges, 382, 391; illus., 387
Clement XIV, Pope, 50
Cleves-Mark, 18-19
Clive, Robert, 35, 38, 337
Clough, Arthur Hugh, 309
Coal, 10, 180, 182, 256
Cocteau, Jean, illus., 643
Code Napoléon, 117, 152, 158
Colbert, Jean Baptiste, 5, 14
Cold War: atomic weapons, 546; Berlin, 592-593; Cuban crisis, 593, 622; defensive alliances, 624; "hot line," 595; Multilateral Force, 595; in Southeast Asia, 546-547, 566-

569, 600-604; test ban agreement, 593-595; U-2 incident, 593; U.S.S.R.-China split, 597-598

Coleridge, Samuel Taylor, 137-138, 140, 143, 194, 220

Collins, Michael, 485-486

Colombia, 344

Colonial Society (Germany), 264

Colonies (*see also* Imperialism): American War of Independence, 74-78; British, 11, 35-39, 222; French, 13-14, 159, 237, 491; French Union, 560; German, 264, 342-343, 391; nationalism in, 498-499, 569-577; North African, 159; Portuguese, 153, 615; Seven Years' War, 35-39; Spanish, 152

Combination Acts (England), 188, 214

Cominform, 548, 567

Comintern, 398, 428-430, 548

Committee of General Security (France), 110

Committee of Public Safety (France), 107-108, 110

Common Market, 556, 630

Communications, and the Industrial Revolution, 181

Communism: definition of, 196; Karl Marx, 201-205; revisionism, 591; U.S.S.R.-China split, 597-598

Communist League, 202

Communist parties: Chinese, 504, 592 (*see also* China); England, 429; French, 489-491; German, 448-449, 454-456, 458-459, 461; Italian, 636; Korean, North, 603; Pathet Lao, 600; Soviet bloc, 583, 591, 596; Spanish, 466, 468; U.S.S.R., 415-416, 582-585

Condition of the Working Class in England, The (Engels), 202

Condorcet, Marie Jean, 45, 47, 105-106, 110; *illus.,* 51

Confederation of the Rhine, 123

Congo, Belgium, 329, 603, 618

Congo, French, 365, 615

Congress party (India), 506, 609

Conservative party (Canada), 629

Conservative party (England), 217-218, 222-223, 225-226, 482-485, 631

"Conspiracy of the Equals," 111

Constable, John, 141

Constantine, King (Greece), 374

Constantine (brother of Alexander I), 157

Constitutional Democrats (Russia), 288-289, 291, 400, 404, 406

Continental System, 126-128

Coolidge, Calvin, 492-494

Cooper, James Fenimore, 324

Coral Sea, battle of the, 533

Corfu, 446, 515

Corn Laws, 184-185, 187, 219-220

Corsica, 113, 517

Così Fan Tutte (Mozart), 84

Cotton, and Industrial Revolution, 179-182

Coulson, Samuel, 188

Council for Europe, 556, 630

Council for Mutual Economic Aid (Comecon), 592, 595

Crane, Stephen, 307

Crimea, 72-73

Crimean War, 222, 229, 239, 256, 280-281

Croatia, 271-273, 390, 473

Croce, Benedetto, 319

Cromwell, Oliver, 67, 502

Cuba, 344-345, 595, 622

Cubism, 656-657

Culloden, battle of, 34; *illus.,* 35

Culture; European eighteenth century, 78-85; French, 109; German Nazi, 465; Prussian, 21; in review, 662-664; Russian Soviet, 427, 562-563; Russian tsarist, 21, 28, 30; twentieth century, 641-642, 654, 660-662; U. S. postwar, 554; Victorian, 305, 317-318, 323-325

Cumberland, Duke of, 38

Cunard, Samuel, 181

Curzon Line, 411

Cyprus, 390, 625

Czechoslovakia: German take-over, 472, 519-520; "Little Entente," 514; U.S.S.R. treaty, 430; Versailles settlement, 382-383, 389-390, 394; satellite status, 565, 596

D

Dacia, Kingdom of, 73

Dadaism, 657

Daily Telegraph Affair, 264

Daladier, Edouard, 491, 519-520

Daniel, Yuli, 590

D'Annunzio, Gabriele, 439, 441

Danton, George Jacques, 103; *illus.,* 104

Danzig, 390, 521

Danubian principalities (*see also* Moldavia; Rumania; Wallachia), 73, 265-266, 281

Darby family, 10

Dardanelles, 72, 280, 373-374, 385

Darwin, Charles, 298-305

Darwinism: and eugenics, 301-302; and historicism, 303-305; philosophic effect, 319; and political thought, 322-323; and racism, 302-303; Social Darwinism, 300-301; theological effect, 299-300

Das Kapital (Marx), 204-205

Daudet, Leon, 324

Daumier, Honoré, 312; *illus.,* 164

David, Jacques Louis, 140-141

Davis, Jefferson, 246

Dawes, Charles G., 456

Dawes Plan, 456

Day in the Life of Ivan Denisov, A (Solzhenitsyn), 589

Deák, Francis, 272-273, 277

Debussy, Claude, 316

Decembrist Revolution, 156-157, 279

Declaration of Independence (United States), 44, 77

Declaration of the Rights of Man, 99

Declaratory Act, 75

Decline of the West (Spengler), 651

Defense of the Realm Act, 380

Defoe, Daniel, 50

De Gasperi, Alcide, 561, 636

De Gaulle, Charles, 528, 542, 560; Fifth Republic, 625, 633-636; *illus.,* 541

Deism, 50-52, 57

Delacroix, Eugene, 141; *illus.,* 142, 156

Delcassé, Théophile, 365

De Maupassant, Guy, 307

Democratic party (Germany), 449

Democrat party (Turkey), 611

Deniken, General Anton Ivanovich, 409, 411

Denmark, 24-25, 120, 148, 188, 257, 259, 525, 630

Derby, Earl of, *illus.,* 185

Der Freischutz (Von Weber), 140

Descartes, René, 44

De Sica, Vittorio, 561

D'Esperey, Franchet, 376

De Valera, Eamon, 486

Dewey, Thomas, 553

Díaz, Porfirio, 578

Dickens, Charles, 193, 306

Dickinson, Emily, 310

Dickinson, Lowes, 359

Diderot, Denis, 47, 65; *illus.,* 51

Diefenbaker, John, 629

Dienbienphu, 600

Directory (France), 111-112, 115-116

Discourse on the Moral Effects of the Arts and Sciences (Rousseau), 53-54

Disraeli, Benjamin, 13, 190, 217-218, 220, 222, 335, 337

Dr. Zhivago (Pasternak), 588, 660

Dollfuss, Engelbert, 467, 470; *illus.,* 470

Dolgoruky family (Russia), 63

Doll's House (Ibsen), 307

Dominican Republic, 621

Don Giovanni (Mozart), 84

Dostoevski, Fëdor, 306

Dreiser, Theodore, 307

Dreyfus, Alfred, 234-236

Dubliners, The (Joyce), 655

Duchamp, Marcel, 657

Dudintsev, Vladimir, 588

Dulles, John Foster, 611

Duma (Russia), 69, 290-292, 399-401

Dumouriez, Charles François, 106

Dunkirk, 527-528

Dupleix, Marquis Joseph François, 35
Durham, Earl of, 351
Durham Report, 351, 486
Durkheim, Emile, 647

E

East India Company (British), 8, 34-35, 37, 76, 337-338
East India Company (French), 35
Eboué, Felix, 528
Ebert, Friedrich, 448-449, 456
Economic theory: classical, 190-192; Christian Socialist, 207; Marxian, 201-205; mercantilist, 47-48; J. S. Mill, 194-195; Proudhon, 206-207; Roman Catholic Church, 207-209; utilitarianism, 192-194; utopian, 196-200
Economy (see also Agriculture; Industry): agricultural revolution, 184-185; in Argentina, 578-579; in Austria, 59, 61, 469; in England, 225-226, 481, 557, 626, 630-632; Egypt, 611-613; France, 108-109, 111, 119, 126-128, 159, 163, 228-229, 237, 487-490, 560, 626, 634-635; France, Old Régime, 4, 89-96, 99-100; German, 452-458; German Nazi, 463-464; German postwar, 560, 626; German Zollverein, 169-170; imperialism and, 328, 341, 348-349; in India, 609; Industrial Revolution and, 177-183; in Italy, 438, 561, 626, 636; in Italy, fascist, 444-445; in Japan, 500, 605-607; mercantilism, 4-6, 47-48; in Prussia, 57; Russia, tsarist, 278, 287; Russia, Soviet, 407, 412-413, 421, 562; in Spain, 62, 636; in Sweden, 61; in Turkey, 610-611; United States, 247-249, 494-498, 553-554, 626-627; U.S.S.R. satellites, 592, 596; World War I European, 380
Education; Austrian, 59; British, 190, 219-221, 556; British colonial, 336, 338-339, 342, 570; French, 91, 118-119, 235, 237; French colonial, 342; Italian fascist, 445; J. S. Mill on, 195; R. Owen on, 198-199; philosophes' attitude, 49-50; Rousseau on, 49-50, 53, 55, 79; Russian tsarist, 28, 280; Russian Soviet, 426-427, 587-588; U. S. school desegregation, 627
Egypt, 164, 359, 364; British protectorate, 222, 335-336, 507; Napoleonic campaign, 114-115; Nasser, 576-577, 591, 611-613
Ehrenberg, Ilya, 588
Eighteenth Brumaire of Louis Napoleon, The (Marx), 204
Einstein, Albert, 652

Eisenhower, General Dwight D., 533, 541, 553, 593, 607
Eisenstein, Serge, 660
Elba, island of, 130, 148
Elgin, Lord Victor Alexander, 351
Eliot, T. S., 325
Elizabeth, Empress (Russia), 36-37, 63-65, 71
Emigration: from Europe, 1800s, 185, 192; from Ireland, 223; from Italy, 242, 445
Emigrés, 103, 108, 115-116, 130, 158-159
Emile (Rousseau), 49-50, 53, 55, 79
Ems telegram, 260
Enemy of the People (Ibsen), 307-308
Enabling Act (Germany), 461
Enclosure movement, 8-9
Encyclopédie, 46-47, 65
Engels, Frederick, 178, 202; illus., 203
Enghien, Duke of, 117
Eniwetok, 538
Enlightenment, Age of: art, 81-82; Catherine the Great, 65-67; economic theories, 47-48; education, 49-50; enlightened despots, 56-62; French leadership, 46-47; law, 48-49; limitations of reason, 78-79; literature, 80-81; music, 83-85; political thought, 52-56; religion, 50-52, 79-80; Romantic protest 136-144; science, 45-46
Equality (see Civil liberties)
Equatorial Africa (French), 528
Erhard, Ludwig, 632-633
Erfurt, meeting of, 129
Erfurt Union of Provinces, 255
Ernst, Max, 657
Erzberger, Matthias, 450
Essay Concerning Human Understanding (Locke), 44
Essay on Crimes and Punishments (Beccaria), 49, 66
Essay on the Principles of Population (Malthus), 190, 298
Estates General, 90, 94-96
Esterhazy, Major, 235
Estonia, 390, 425, 431-432, 525
Ethiopia, 242, 332, 343, 446, 516-517
Eugénie, Empress (France), 230
Europe (see also individual countries): 1715, map, 2-3; 1812 Napoleonic, map, 124-125; 1815, map, 150-151; 1850, map, 213; 1914-1918, map, 374-375; 1953, map, 558-559; Coal and Steel Community, 556, 630; Council for Europe, 556, 630; European Defense Community, 624; Organization for European Economic Cooperation, 556
European Coal and Steel Community, 556

European Free Trade Association, 630
Evelyn, John, 23
Existentialism, 649

F

Factory Acts (England), 220
Falange (Spain), 468
Fanfani, Amintore, 636
Farnese, Elizabeth, 16-17, 31-32, 34, 61
Farouk, King (Egypt), 576
Fascism: in Austria, 469-471; definition, 437-438; in eastern Europe, 472-475; in Hungary, 472; in Italy, 437-447, 475
Fascists Exposed, The (Matteotti), 443
Fashoda incident, 364
Fathers and Sons (Turgenev), 285
Faulhaber, Cardinal, 465
Faulkner, William, 655
Faust (Goethe), 137
February Patent (Austria), 266
Federal Deposit Insurance Corporation, 496
Federal Reserve Act (1913), 249
Fehrbellin, battle of, 18
Fenian Brotherhood, 223
Ferdinand I (Austria), 173
Ferdinand I (Two Sicilies), 153
Ferdinand II (Two Sicilies), 167
Ferdinand VII (Spain), 152, 158
Feuerbach, Ludwig Andreas, 201
Fichte, Johann Gottlieb, 128
Fielding, Henry, 80-81
Finance (see also Banking Economy): European, eighteenth century, 6-8, 10, 14, 89, 94; and Industrial Revolution, 181-182
Fine Arts (see Architecture; Culture; Music; Painting; Sculpture)
Finland, 70; Brest-Litovsk Treaty, 409; Great Northern War, 26; Russian domination, 148, 373, 525; World War II, 432-433, 565
Finnegans Wake (Joyce), 655-656
First International Workingmen's Association, 205
First International, 206
Fiume, 388, 439
Flandin, Pierre, 490
Flaubert, Gustave, 306, 308
Fleury, Cardinal, 14-15, 33
"Flying shuttle," 10
Foch, Marshal Ferdinand, 370, 378
Forain, Jean Louis, 312
Fordney-McCumber Tariff, 493
Formosa, 346, 500, 547, 569
Forster, William, 221
Fort Duquesne, 35, 38
Foster, Stephen, 316
Foundations of the Nineteenth Century, The (Chamberlain), 451

Fourier, François M. C., 197-200, 286
Fourteen Points, 385-387
Forward, 440
France (*see also* Enlightenment; French Revolution; *philosophes*), 1, 14, 16, 18, 31-34, 73, 187, 256, 258, 265-266; agriculture, 4, 8, 92-93, 95, 163, 237; Algeria and, 617, 635-636; American War of Independence, 76; anticlericalism, 51-52, 91, 100, 118, 235, 237, 489; atomic weapons, 635; Boulanger threat, 234; civil liberties, 99, 101, 107, 111, 117-118, 131-132, 152, 158-159; Congress of Vienna, 146-148; Continental system, 126-128; Crimean War, 222; Declaration of the Rights of Man, 99; de Gaulle's Fifth Republic 630, 634, 635; Directory, 111, 113-115; Dreyfus Case, 234-235; economy, nineteenth century, 119, 126-127, 237; economy, twentieth century, 487-491, 560, 626, 635; education, 101, 118-119; Ethiopian crisis, 516-517; Fashoda incident, 364; First Republic, 100-112; Fourth Republic, 557, 560; Greek War of Independence, 155; imperialism, 13-14, 237, 328-329, 339-342, 491, 507, 560, 572; Industrial Revolution, 182; July monarchy, 158-160; Little Entente, 394, 514; Locarno treaty, 456, 512; Moroccan crisis, 365; Munich agreement, 519-520; Napoleon I, 112-132; Napoleon III, 227-230; Napoleonic Europe, *map,* 124-125; painting, 310-313; Popular Front, 490-491; Prussian War, 259-260; Reign of Terror, 106-110; Revolution of 1848; 163-166; revolutions, nineteenth century European, 153, 160-162, 239-240; *map,* 152; Rhineland, 513, 516; Ruhr, 453, 514-515; Russian relations, 64, 409, 411, 430, 515; Seven Years' War, 35-39; social classes, 488-490; Stavisky case, 488; suffrage, 101, 107, 111; Third Republic, 230-238, 487-491; Triple Entente, 363-365; Versailles treaty, 387-388; World War I, 358-359; 362, 368, 370-371, 374, 376-378; World War II, 521-528, 541-542
France, Anatole, 308
Francis I (Austria), 173
Francis II (Austria), 102, 121, 123, 128
Francis II (Sicily), 239
Francis Ferdinand, Archduke of Austria, 357-358, 366
Francis Joseph, Emperor (Austria), 173, 239, 265-266, 268, 272-273, 277

Franco, Francisco, 431, 467-468, 517, 530; *illus.,* 469
Frankfurt, Treaty of, 360, 362
Frankfurt Assembly, 170-171, 173-174
Franklin, Benjamin, 45, 89
Frederick II, the Great (Prussia), 32, 34-37, 39, 56-58, 60, 62, 71-72; *illus.,* 37, 57
Frederick III, Emperor (Germany), 262
Frederick William, the Great Elector, 18-20
Frederick William I (Prussia), 20-21
Frederick William II (Prussia), 62
Frederick William III (Prussia), 123, 161
Frederick William IV (Prussia), 169-171, 174, 255
Free Democratic party (Germany), 633
Free French, 528, 530, 536, 542
Freemasonry, 70, 156
French Academy, 47
French Revolution; causes, 89-96; Civil Constitution of the Clergy, 100; civil liberties, 99, 101; Constitution of 1791, 100-101; Constitution of 1793, 107; Constitution of 1795, 111; Declaration of the Rights of Man, 99; Directory, 111, 113-115; Estates General, 94-96; European war, 112-113; Laws of Ventôse, 108-109; Legislative Assembly, 102-103; Louis XVI, 90, 94-96, 98, 100-103, 105; National Assembly, 98-102; National Convention, 104-106; Reign of Terror, 106-110; Roman Catholic Church, 90-91, 99-101, 110; September massacres, 103-104; suffrage, 101, 107, 111; Thermidorean Reaction, 110-111
Frei, Eduardo, 622
Freud, Sigmund, 320, 642-645; *illus.,* 643
Friedjung, Heinrich, 273
Friedland, battle of, 122
Frost, Robert, 654
Fuad, King (Egypt), 507
Fulton, James, 181

G

Gabelle, 93
Gainsborough, Sir Thomas, 82
Galbraith, J. K., 649
Galicia, 128-129, 172, 270, 372-373
Galitsyn family (Russia), 63
Gallipoli campaign, 373-374
Galsworthy, John, 308
Gamelin, General Maurice, 527
Gandhi, Indira, 609
Gandhi, Mahatma, 506, 573; *illus.,* 506

Garibaldi, Giuseppe, 240; *illus.,* 240
Gas, poison, in World War I, 377-378
Gastein, Convention of, 257-258
Gauguin, Paul, 313
Gay, John, 83
George I (England) 11-12
George II (England), 11-12, 34
George III (England), 8, 38, 73-74, 350
George V (England), 225
General Confederation of Labor (France), 489-491
General Confederation of Labor (Italy), 441
Geneva disarmament conference (*1932*), 513
German East Africa, 343
German Southwest Africa, 342-343, 391
Germany, 17-21, 113; agriculture, 184, 463; *Anschluss,* 470-471, 518-519; anti-semitism, 461-462, 536-537; Battle of Britain, 529-530; Bismarck era, 254, 256-263, 362-363; Boer War, 363-364; Confederation, *1850-1859,* 254-256; Congress of Vienna, 147-148; Czechoslovakia take-over, 519-520; de-nazification, 561; domestic policies *1870-1914,* 260-265; domestic policies, Hitler, 460-465; divided East and West, 546-547, 549, 561, 565-566, 592-594, 624, 630, 632-633; economy, nineteenth century, 228-229; economy, twentieth century, 452-458, 463-464, 561, economy, West, 626, 632; education under Nazis, 465; Franco-Prussian War 1871, 230-232; Greek War of Independence, 155; Hitler's Balkan policy, 472-474; imperialism, 264, 329, 342-343, 391; Industrial Revolution in, 182-183; League of Nations, 388, 512-513, 515; Locarno Pact, 457, 512; Moroccan crisis, 365; Munich agreement, 519-520; Napoleonic Wars, 120, 123, 128; Polish invasion 1939, 521-523; religion, 260-262; reparations, 450-453, 456-459, 488; revolutions, nineteenth century, 161-162, 169-171; revolution, 1918, 382; Rhineland occupation, 516; Romantic movement, 137, 139; suffrage, 188; Treaty of Rapallo, 428-429; unification, *map,* 255; Versailles treaty, 386-394; Weimar Republic, 447-460; World War I, 358-361, 366-379, 447-448; World War II, 525-527, 529-531, 533-537
Gestapo, 463
Ghana (Gold Coast), 615, 620
Ghosts (Ibsen), 307
Gibbon, Edward, 81

Gibraltar, 76, 530
Gioberti, Vincenzo, 167
Giraud, Henri Honoré, *illus.,* 541
Girondins, 102, 104-107, 110
Gladstone, William, 216, 218, 220-223, 333; *illus.,* 216
Glinka, Fëdor N., 140
Glorious Revolution, 11-12
Gluck, Christoph, 83
Gobineau, Count Joseph de, 451
Goebbels, Paul Joseph, 457, 459, 461
Goering, Hermann, 452, 464, 529
Goethe, Johann Wolfgang von, 137, 139-140
Gold Coast, 491
Goldwater, Barry, 628
Gömbös, Gyula, 472
Gomulka, Wladislaw, 583, 592, 596
Gothic revival, 141-142
Goulart, Juan, 622
Goya y Lucientes, Francisco de, 140-141
Grant, Madison, 303
Great Britain, 33-34, 71, 106, 152; agriculture, 8-9, 184-185; American War of Independence, 74-77; Boer War, 264, 333-334; Chartism, 221; classes, social, 12-13, 214-216, 225-226, 482-484; Cold War policies, 546-547, 572, 625; colonies, liquidation, 614-620; Common Market, 630; Commonwealth, 350-353, 486-487, 572-573, 605; Corn Laws, 219-220; Crimean War, 280-281; economy, 5-8, 481-485, 556-557, 626, 630-631; education, 190, 219-221, 556; education, colonial, 336, 338-339, 342; Ethiopian crisis, 516-517; Factory Acts, 220; Fashoda incident, 64; George III, 73-74; Great Northern War, 33; Greek War of Independence, 154-155; imperialism, 221-222, 332-339, 498, 506, 572, 574, 614 industry, 9-10, 177-182; Irish question, 222-224, 485-486; law, 218-219; literature, 137, 139, 306-310; Locarno treaties, 457; mercantilism, 5-6; Monroe Doctrine, 154; Moroccan crisis, 365; Munich agreement, 519-520; Napoleonic Wars, 114-115; Parliament, 11-13, 214-216; political parties, 216-218, 226; Poor Laws, 219; and revolutions, European, 153, 160-162; Russian relations, 409, 428-429; Seven Years War, 35-39; South Sea Company, 6-8; suffrage, 13, 214-216, 221, 484; test ban agreement, 595; trade policies, 126-128, 219-220, 224-225, 484-485; Triple Entente, 363-365; welfare legislation, 219-220, 225-226; World War I, 358-359, 361-362; 367-371, 373-374, 376-378;

World War II, 514-527, 530, 533-537, 540-543
Great Century, The (Latourette), 348
Great Gatsby, The (Fitzgerald), 494
Great Northern War, 1, 15, 21, 24-26
Greece, 383, 446; Balkan wars, 365-366; Cyprus question, 625; Civil War, 565-566; independence, 154-156; Metaxas dictatorship, 475; Treaty of Lausanne, 390; Versailles settlement, 390; in World War I, 374, 376; in World War II, 433, 530
Greeley, Horace, 200, 204
Green, T. H., 318
Gregory, Lady Augusta, 224
Grévy, Jules, 232, 234
Grey, Sir Edward, 367-368
Griffith, Arthur, 485
Grimm, Johann, 128, 139
Grimm, Wilhelm, 128, 139
Gromyko, Andrei, 604
Guadeloupe, 13
Guam, 532
Guest, Edgar, 310
Guinea, 493
Guizot, François, 164-165, 178
Gumbinnen, battle of, 372
Gustavus III (Sweden), 61-62
Guyana (British Guiana), 622

H

Habsburg-Valois Wars, 31
Hacha, Emil, 520
Haile Selassie, 516; *illus.,* 516
Haiti, 120
Halifax, Lord Edward, 521
Hammarskjöld, Dag, 549
Handel, George Frederick, 83, 85
Hanover, 36, 258
Hargreaves, James, 10
Hard Times (Dickens), 193
Harding, Warren, 492, 494
Hardy, Thomas, 307, 320
Hastings, Warren, 337
Haushofer, Karl, 463
Hawaii, 249, 344, 532-533, 627
Hay, John, 501
Haydn, Joseph, 83, 85, 140
Hayes, Rutherford B., 246
Hegel, George W. F., 143-144, 201-202, 318-319
Heimwehr (Austria), 470
Heine, Heinrich, 310
Heisenberg, Werner, 653
Henlein, Konrad, 519
Herder, Johann Gottfried von, 139
Herzegovina, 286, 357
Herzen, Alexander, 284-285
Hess, Rudolf, 463
Hesse-Cassel, 258
Himmler, Heinrich, 457

Hindenburg, Paul von, 372-373, 447-448, 456, 458-461
Hinduism, 505-506, 572-574
Historicism, 650-652
History of the Decline and Fall of the Roman Empire (Gibbon), 81
Hitler, Adolf, 430-431, 515, 648; *Anschluss,* 470-471, 518-519; anti-semitism, 275, 451-452, 461-462; Battle of Britain, 529; Czechoslovakia take-over, 519-520; dictatorial powers, 460-461; economic policy, 463-464; educational views, 465; *Lebensraum* theory, 462-463; legal policies, 463; Munich agreement, 519-520; Nazi party leader, 450-452, 454-455, 457-460; Poland invasion, 521-523; racist views, 461-462; Roman Catholic Church, 464-465; Rome-Berlin Axis, 517-518; Russian campaign, 530-531; World War II, 536
Hlinka, Father, 271
Ho Chi Minh, 600-601
Hoffman, General Max von, 372
Hogarth, William, 82
Hohenzollern, House of, 18-21
Holbach, Baron d', 52
Holstein, 257-258
Holstein, Baron Friedrich von, 363
Holy Alliance, 146, 148
Holy Roman Empire, 123, 147
Home Owners' Loan Corporation, 496
Homer, Winslow, 310
Hong Kong, 337
Hood, Thomas, 309
Hoover, Herbert, 458, 492, 495
Hopkins, Gerard Manley, 310
Horthy, Admiral, 471
Howells, William Dean, 306
Housman, A.E., 310
Hubertusberg, Peace of, 37, 39
Hugenberg, Alfred, 456
Hugo, Victor, 139, 309
Human Nature in Politics (Wallas), 648
Humbert I (Italy), 206, 242
Hume, David, 78-79
Hungary, 17, 58-59, 172, 276-277, 280, 383, 474, 565; anti-semitism, 276, 471; civil liberties, 267; classes, social, 276; dual monarchy, 267-268; fascism in, 471-472; minorities in, 271-274; revolt, *1956,* 583, 591; revolution of 1848, 172-174; revolution of 1918, 410-411; satellite status, 596; Versailles settlement, 389

I

Ibn Saud, 507
Ibsen, Henrik, 307-308

Idyls of the King (Tennyson), 309

Il Risorgimento, 167

Illyrian provinces, 123, 128-129, 148, 155, 172

Immigration: to Australia, 352; to Palestine, 507; Social Darwinist view, 303; to U.S., 248; U.S. restrictions, 493

Imperialism (*see also* Colonies), in Africa, 221-222, 330-336, 339-343, 498, *map,* 329; in Asia, 337-339, 342, 344-346, *map,* 331; Belgian, 343; British, 221-222, 332-339, 498, 572, 574; in the Caribbean, 336; consequences of, 353-354; definition of, 327-328; economics of, 328, 354; in the Far East, 332, 571, *map,* 331; Fourteen Points, 499; French, 339-342, 498, 574; German, 342-343; India and, 37-39, 222, 572, 574; Italian, 343; Japanese, 345-346; in Latin America, 577-579; Marxist view, 328; in Middle East, 330, 574-576, *map,* 329; pro and con views, 346-349; Social Darwinist view, 347; U.S., 343-345, 498; in Western Hemisphere, *map,* 344

Imperialism as the Latest Stage of Capitalism (Lenin), 328

India: Amritsar massacre, 383, 505; British control, 222, 287, 337-339, 361, 483; caste system, 574; China attack, 603; economy, 573-574, 609; education, 570; Hindu-Moslem conflict, 505-506; Hinduism, 574; independence drive, 506, 572-573; Kashmir question, 487, 593, 609-610; languages, 609; neutralism, 548-549; population, 609; Seven Years' War, 37-39

Independent Socialists (Germany), 448

Indo-China, 342, 532, 572

Indonesia, 533, 567-568, 572, 603, 607-608

Industrial Revolution, 9-10, 177-183; economic and social consequences, 184-190; *illus.,* 182-183

Industry (*see also* Agriculture; Economy): in France, 163, 228-229, 237; in Germany, 262, 456, 560; in Great Britain, 482, 557; in Japan, 346; in Prussia, 256; in Russia, 28, 398, 412-413, 419-421

Influence of Sea Power Upon History, The (Mahan), 250

Ingria, 25

In Memoriam (Tennyson), 309

Inquiry into the Nature and Causes of the Wealth of Nations (Smith), 48

Inquisition, 153

Insular Cases decision, 345

Intellectual Revolution: architecture, 313-315; Darwinism's effect, 298-305; literature, 305-310, 317-318; music, 316-317; painting, 310-313, 318; philosophy, 318-321; politics and social thought, 321-323

"Intolerable Acts," 76

Iran, 508, 565, 576, 625

Iraq, 507-508, 591, 613-614

Ireland; Free State, 485-486; Home Rule agitation, 222-224, 361; potato famine, 185, 223

Irish Land Act, 223

Iron, and Industrial Revolution, 180, 182

"Iron Law of Wages," 191

Israel, 574-576, 611 (*see also* Palestine)

Italy, 15-17, 32-33, 188, 229, 258-259, 266; *Anschluss* and, 470-471; anticlericalism, 241; anti-semitism, 446; Communist party, 636; Congress of Vienna, 147-148; economy, 241-242, 561, 626, 636-637; emigration from, 242, Ethiopia and, 242, 516; European union, 630; fascism in, 437-447; imperialism, 242, 329, 343, 365; Lateran Treaty, 446; Locarno treaties, 457; Munich agreement, 519; Napoleonic Wars, 114-115, 119-120, 123, 126; political parties, postwar, 561, 636-637; revolutions, nineteenth century, 161, 166-169; Rome-Berlin Axis, 517; social classes, 241; Spanish civil war, 517; Treaty of London, 373; Treaty of Rapallo, 439; Triple Alliance, 363; unification, 238-241, *map,* 240; Vatican City, 241, 446; Versailles conference, 385, 387-389; World War I, 359, 362, 368, 372-373; World War II, 433, 530, 533-535, 565

Ivan VI (Russia), 62-64

Ivanhoe (Scott), 139

Iwo Jima, 538

Izvolski, Aleksandr Petrovich, 365

J

J'Accuse (Zola), 235

Jacobins, 101-106, 111

Jacquerie, 93

Jagan, Cheddi, 622

James II (England), 11-12, 34, 44

James, William, 318-320

Jameson Raid, 333, 363

Jameson, Sir Leander Starr, 333

Janissaries, 31

Japan: British alliance, 363; China and, 502-504; in Cold War, 548; 607; economy, 499-500, 605-607; imperialism, 332, 345-346, 409; Korea and, 500-568; League with-drawal, 515; Manchuria and, 359, 503, 515; mandate islands, 391; Nine-Power Treaty, 502; occupation status, 546-547, 571-572; Russo-Japanese War, 288-289; Shintoism, 500; World War I, 368; World War II, 433, 533, 537-538

Java, 342

Jefferson, Thomas, 46, 95, 141

Jellachich, Joseph, 173

Jena, battle of, 122, 128

Jenkins' Ear, War of, 33-34, 37

Jesuits (*see* Society of Jesus)

Jews (*see also* Anti-semitism): in Austria, 59; in Austro-Hungarian empire, 270, 274-276; Dreyfus case, 234-235; in fascist Italy, 446; Hitler's Aryan theories, 451; in Nazi Germany, 461-462, 536-537; in Prussia, 57; in Russia, 287, 563, 565; in Sweden, 61

Johnson, Lyndon Baines, 593, 601-602, 604, 625, 628

Johnson, Dr. Samuel, 76, 81; *illus.,* 81

Jordan, 611

Jordan River, 611

Joseph I (Portugal), 61

Joseph II (Austria), 58-60, 62, 73, 78, 85

Journey from St. Petersburg to Moscow (Radishchev), 67

Joyce, James, 655-656; *illus.,* 655

July Ordinances, 159

Jung, Carl, 645

Junkers, 19, 21, 57, 62, 129, 256; Weimar era, 448-449, 458, 460; in Nazi Germany, 563

Justice party (Turkey), 611

Jutland, battle of, 377

K

Kadar, Janos, 584

Kadets (*see* Constitutional Democrats)

Kaganovich, Lazar, 422

Kamenev, Lev Borisovich, 416, 423

Kant, Immanuel, 79, 85, 318

Kapp, Wolfgang, 450

Karageorge, 154-155

Karelia, 425

Karlovitz, Peace of, 17, 24

Karolyi, Count Michael, 471

Kaunitz, Chancellor Anton von, 36

Kazakh Republics, 425

Keats, John, 137

Kellogg-Briand Pact, 457, 493, 513

Kemal, Mustafa, 374, 390, 508, 611

Kennedy, John F., 600-601, 628; assassination, 595; Cuban crisis, 594; and Khrushchev, 593

Kenya, 616

Kerensky, Alexander, 400-401, 404-405
Khrushchev, Nikita: atomic weapons, 593-594; Berlin policy, 592; China split, 597-599; Communist party and, 583-585; Cuban crisis, 594; educational policies, 587; removal, 602-603; rise to power, 582-583; satellite revolts, 583-584, 591-592, 595-596; Southeast Asia policy, 600-601; U-2 incident, 593; U.S. contacts, 593-594
Kiel, 257
Kierkegaard, Soren, 649
King, Mackenzie, 555
King, Martin Luther, 627
Kingsley, Charles, 207
Kipling, Rudyard, 310, 347-348
Kirghiz Republic, 425
Kirov, Sergei, 423-424
Kleist, Paul von, 139
Knights of Malta, 115, 120
Koestler, Arthur, 646
Kolchak, Admiral Aleksandr, 409-411
Kong Le, 600
Korea, 346, 500, 548-549, 552, 568-569, 603, 606, 625
Korean War, 568-569
Kornilov, General Lavr, 404,406
Korzybski, Alfred, 650
Kossuth, Louis, 172-174, 267, 277
Kosygin, A.N., 602-603
Kozlov, Frol, 593
Kredit-Anstalt, 458, 470
Kronstadt Movement, 412
Kropotkin, Prince Peter, 206
Krüdener, Madame de, 70, 146
Kruger, Stephanus, 264, 333, 363-364
Kruger telegram, 333, 363-364
Kun, Bela, 383, 410-411, 471
Kuomintang, 429, 502, 504, 538, 540, 543, 547
Kutchuk, Kainardji, treaty of, 72
Kutuzov, Prince Mikhail, 130
Kuwait, 614
Kwajalein, 538
Kwangchow Bay, 342, 501
Ky, General Cao, 601

L

La Belle Hélène (Offenbach), 316
Labor (*see also* Classes, social); and enclosure movement, 8-9; in France, 93, 95, 100, 119, 228; in Germany, 262, 454, 464; in Great Britain, 164, 220, 225-226, 484; grievances, nineteenth century, 187-190; in Hungary, 276; and Industrial Revolution, 9, 178; J. S. Mill on, 195; Mussolini's syndicates, 444; National Workshops, *1848,* 165; Russia, tsarist, 28, 287; utopian socialist views on, 196-200
Labor Front (Germany), 464
Labour party (England), 225-226, 556-557, 572, 631
Lafayette, Marquis de, 8, 92, 159-160, 162, 165
Laffitte, Jacques, 159
Lamballe, Princesse de, 104
"Land and Liberty" society (Russia), 285
Language: and Austro-Hungarian minorities, 172-173, 267-268, 270-272, 277
Laos, 599-601
Laplace, Pierre Simon, 45, 110
Lassalle, Ferdinand, 258, 262
Lateran Treaty, 446
Latin America (*see also* individual countries); *1828,* map, 154; "Good Neighbor" policy, 498; Monroe Doctrine, 153-154
Latourette, Kenneth, 348
Latvia, 390, 425, 431-432, 525
Lausanne, Treaty of, 390
Laval, Pierre, 528
Lavoisier, Antoine, 45, 110
Lavrov, Pëtr Lavrovich, 285
Law (*see also* Civil liberties): in Austria, 59; Beccaria's essay, 49, 66; *Code Napoléon,* 117, 152, 158; in fascist Italy, 444; in France, 90, 101, 107, 117, 158; in Great Britain, 218-219; in Nazi Germany, 463; *philosophes'* views, 48-49; in Prussia, 57; in Russia, 66, 280, 283
Law, John, 6-7, 14-15
Law of Hostages, 115
Laws of Ventôse, 108-109
Lawrence, Sir Thomas, 82
Lawrence, T. E., 376, 385-386
League of Nations, 388, 492-493; and Austrian recovery, 469; Ethiopian crisis, 516-517; Germany and, 457, 512-513; Hungary and, 472; Italy and, 517; Manchurian War, 503, 515; mandate system, 390-391; Poland and Upper Silesia question, 450; U.S.S.R. and, 430, 432; U.S. and, 492-493; weaknesses, 514-515, 517
League of the Three Emperors, 363
Lebanon, 390-391, 507, 574, 610
Lecanuet, Jacques, 635
Le Chapelier Law, 100, 119, 188
Lefort, Field Marshal, 23
Leipzig, battle of, 130
Lend-Lease, 531-532
Lenin, 278, 288-289, 291, 328, 402-404, 406-407, 409-410, 412-413, 415-416, 428; *illus.,* 410, 414
Leo XIII, Pope, 208-209
Leopold of Saxe-Coburg (Belgium), 160-161
Leopold II (Austria), 60-62, 102
Leopold II (Belgium), 343
Lesotho (Basutoland), 615
Lesseps, Ferdinand de, 197, 234
Lesczynski, Stanislas, 25, 32, 70
Lewis, Sinclair, 308, 494
Ley, Dr. Robert, 464
Liberal party (Canada), 555, 629
Liberal party (England), 216, 218, 221-226, 482, 556
Liberal party (Germany), 260-263
"Liberal Unionists" (England), 223
Liberia, 332
Lie, Trygve, 549
Liebknecht, Wilhelm, 262
Ligurian Republic, 114
Lincoln, Abraham, 246
Linnaeus, Carolus, 45
Lippmann, Walter, 648
Lissauer, Ernst, 361
Literature: Enlightenment era, 80-81; Freudian influences, 645, 655; Irish nationalistic, 224; modern, 654-656; Romantic period, 137-139; U.S.S.R., 563, 588-590; Victorian era, 305-310
Lithuania, 73, 161, 390, 425, 431-432, 521, 525
Little Entente, 394
Litvinov, Maxim, 428, 430-431
Lloyd, Edward, 5
Lloyd George, David, 225-226, 382, 389, 391, 481-482, 556; *illus.,* 225, 387
Lloyd's of London, 5
Locarno pact, 430, 457, 512
Locke, John, 44-45, 53-54, 77
Lombardy, 17, 148, 168-169, 172, 239, 266
London Society for the Encouragement of Arts, Manufacturers, and Commerce, 10
London, Treaty of, 373, 439
Longfellow, Henry Wadsworth, 309-310
Lorentz, Hendrik Antoon, 212
Lorenz, Konrad, 646
Lorraine, 32, 260 (*see also* Alsace-Lorraine)
Louis Napoleon (*see* Napoleon III)
Louis Philippe (Citizen King), 159-160, 164-165, 202
Louis XIV, 1, 4, 6, 14-15, 18
Louis XV, 1, 6, 13, 15, 32, 36, 47, 90
Louis XVI, 48, 90, 96, 98, 100-103, 105, 159
Louis XVII, 98
Louis XVIII, 130, 146, 158
Louisburg, 34, 37-38
Louisiana Territory, 120
L'Ouverture, Toussaint, 120
Lowell, James Russell, 309
Loyola, Ignatius, 62
Ludendorff, General Erich von, 372-373, 448, 450; in Weimar era, 450-451, 454-455; *illus.,* 455

Lueger, Karl, 275
Luftwaffe, 524-525, 529-530
Lugard, Lord Frederick, 336, 343
Lunéville, Treaty of, 120
Luther, Hans, 455
Lutherans, 59
Luxembourg, 259, 630
Lvov, Prince Georgi, 400
Lyautey, Marshal Louis Hubert, 340
Lyell, Sir Charles, 298
Lyrical Ballads (Wordsworth), 137-138
Lysenko, Trofim, 299, 563
Lytton Report, 515

M

Mably, Abbé, 78
McAdam, John Loudon, 180
MacArthur, General Douglas, 538, 569, 571
McCarthy, Joseph, 554-555
McCormick, Cyrus, 182
MacDonald, Ramsay, 429, 483-484
Mackensen, General von, 374
Mackenzie, William Lyon, 350
McKinley, President William, 206
Mackintosh, Charles Rennie, 316
MacMahon, Marshal Marie, 232
Madame Bovary (Flaubert), 306
Madras, 34
Maeterlinck, Maurice, 212
Magenta, battle of, 239
Magic Flute, The (Mozart), 85
Maginot Line, 523, 525-527
Magyars (*see also* Hungary), 172, 174, 266, 268, 271
Mahan, Captain Alfred T., 250
Maillol, Aristide, 313
Main Street (Lewis), 308, 494
Maine (battleship), 344
Makepeace Experiment, The (Tertz), 590
Malawi (Nyassaland), 615
Malaya, 336, 342, 533, 568, 572
Malaysia, 572, 608
Malenkov, Georgi, 582-583
Mali (French Sudan), 615
Mallarmé, Stéphane, 309
Malta, 115, 120, 148
Malthus, Thomas, 190-192, 194, 298
Man and Superman (Shaw), 307
Manchu Dynasty, 501
Manchuria, 288-289, 346, 359; Japanese designs, 503, 515; Russian invasion, 538
Mandate system, 390-391
Manet, Edouard, 311-312
Manifesto of the Communist Party (Engels and Marx), 202-205
Manila Conference (*1966*), 602
Mann, Thomas, 655
Mao Tse-tung, 597-598, 603-604
March Laws (Hungary), 173

March on Rome, 441-442; *illus.,* 443
Maria Theresa (Austria), 17, 32, 34; as enlightened despot, 58-60
Marie Antoinette, Queen, 90, 94, 98, 102, 104, 107; *illus.,* 99
Marie-Louise (wife of Napoleon), 125-126
Marquand, J. P., 655
Marne, First Battle of the, 371
Marr, Nikolai, 563
Marriage of Figaro, The (Mozart), 84
Marshal, Alfred, 647
Marshall, General George C., 547-548, 552
Marshall Plan, 552-553, 635
Martin, Everett Dean, 324
Martinique, 13-14
Marx, Karl, 144, 178, 201-205, 433
Marx, Wilhelm, 456
Marxism (*see also* Communism); and historicism, 651; and philosophy, 663
Marxist Socialist party (Spain), 466
Masaryk, Thomas, 270, 519
Massu, General Jacques, 634
Masurian Lakes, battle of, 372
Matsu, 569, 597
Matteotti, Giacomo, 443
Mau Mau, 617
Maximilian, Prince, 229-230
Mazepa, 25
Mazzini, Guiseppi, 163, 167, 169, 174
Mecklenburg, 36
Mehemet Ali, 155, 164, 280
Mein Kampf, 455
Mendel, Gregor, 299
Menderes, Adnan, 611
Menelek, 343
Mensheviks, 288, 400, 403, 405-406
Menshikov, Prince, 23-24, 27, 63
Mercantilism, 5, 15, 39, 47-48, 57, 59
Meredith, George, 358
Mesopotamia, 390-391
Messiah, The (Handel), 83
Metaxas, General John, 475
Methodism, 79-80
Metric system, 110
Metternich, Prince Clement, 145-147, 153, 155, 161-162, 169, 172-173
Metz, battle of, 260
Mexico, 229-230, 577-578
Middle classes (*see also* Classes, social); Austro-Hungarian, 274-276; French, 93-95; German, 454; Industrial Revolution and, 187; Japanese, 345-346; and nineteenth century literature, 308-309; Prussian, 57; Russian tsarist, 67
Middle East (*see also* individual countries): imperialism in, 330, 507-508, 574-576, *map,* 329, 392-393; oil in, 507, 576, 613-614
Mikhailovich, General, 466

Mikoyan, Anastas, 593
Milan Decrees, 126-127
Mill, John Stuart, 163, 194-195, 286, 322, 324, 554; *illus.,* 194
Minorca, 37, 76
Minorities: in Austria-Hungary, 266-276, *map,* 269; in Russia, 287, 399, 405-406, 415, 425
Mirabeau, Comte Honoré Gabriel de, 95-96
Mississippi Company, 6-7
Mitterand, Francois, 634
Modena, Duchy of, 161, 168
Mohammed Ali Jinnah, 573
Moldavia, 25, 155, 425, 433
Moldavian Republic, 433
Molotov, Vyacheslav, 431, 433, 584
Moltke, Helmuth von, 371
Monet, Claude, 311
Money: European eighteenth century, 5-7; and Industrial Revolution, 181; in Weimar Germany, 453-455
Monroe Doctrine, 230, 330
Montagu, Lady Mary, 14
Montenegro, 385
Montesquieu, Baron de, 47, 52-55, 66, 77, 166
Montgomery, Field Marshal Bernard, 533
Monticello, *illus.,* 143
Montreal, 38
Moore, Henry, *illus.,* 659
Moravia, 268
Moravia, Alberto, 561
Moravian Brethren, 79
Morea, 155
Morley, Lord, 368
Morocco, 340, 359, 364-365, 533, 620
Morris, William, 316
Morse, Samuel, 182
Moscow Calling (Azhak), 590
Moslems, 273, 505, 572-573, 609, 619
Mossadeq, Mohammed, 576
Mountain: and French Revolution, 104-107, 111
Mozambique, 615-616
Mozart, Wolfgang Amadeus, 83-85, 140; *illus.,* 84
Multilateral Force (MLF), 625
Münnich, Marshal, 64, 70-71
Murat, Joachim, 123
Music: eighteenth century, 83-85; modern, 658-659; nineteenth century, 316-317; Romantic period, 139-140
Mussolini, Benito, 241, 431, 439, 515, 648; Albania invasion, 518; and *Anschluss,* 470-471; corporative state, 444-445; death, 535; domestic policies, 445-446; early career, 440-441; Ethiopian conquest, 516; fascist dictatorship, 442-444; foreign policy, 446-447,

517-518; Greece invasion, 530; Rome-Berlin Axis, 517; *illus.,* 443
Mutual Aid: A Factor in Evolution (Kropotkin), 206

N

Nagy, Imre, 583, 591-592
Nanking, Treaty of, 337
Naples, 17, 32, 148, 153, 167-168, 239-240
Napoleon I, 70, 146-148, 155; Continental system, 126-128; *coup d'état,* 115-116; early career, 113-115; domestic rule, 116-119; European wars, 119-132; Napoleonic Europe, *illus.,* 124-125; Russian campaign, 129-130; *illus.,* 114
Napoleon II (King of Rome), 126
Napoleon III, 166, 240, 256; *coup d'état,* 227; domestic policy, 228-229; foreign policy, 229-230, 259-260; *illus.,* 228
Napoleonic Wars, 114-116
Narva, battle of, 258
Nasser, Gamal Abdel, 591, 611-614
Natal, 333-334
National Association for the Advancement of Colored People, 627
National Insurance Act (England), 220
National Liberation Front (Vietnam), 600
National People's party (Germany), 449, 452, 456
National Workshops, 165, 195, 200
Nationalism: Arab, 507-508; Balkan, 365-366; and colonial revolts, 353-354, 569-577; and Industrial Revolution, 178; and Irish Home Rule, 223-224; Marxian theory, 203-204; Mussolini's use of, 446; Napoleon's impetus to, 114, 128, 131-132, 145; and European revolutions, 154-155, 160-161, 163, 167-174, 239-241; Romantic protest and, 138-139; in World War I, 360-362
Nationalist party, Chinese (*see* Kuomintang)
Nationalists, Germany (*see* National People's Party)
Navarino, battle of, 155
Nazi party (Austria), 470-471
Nazi party (Germany), 430, 451-452, 456-461 (*see also* Hitler, Adolf)
Necker, Jacques, 96
Negroes (*see also* Slavery), 350, 554, 615-616, 626-627
Nehru, Pandit, 549, 573; 609; *illus.,* 573
Nelson, Horatio, 115, 120

Nemours, Duke of, 160-161
Neo-Guelfs, 167-169
Netherlands, 4, 15, 36, 106, 112-113, 123, 126, 148, 160-161, 184, 188, 211, 572, 630
Neutrality: and Cold War, 548-549; Napoleon's Continental System, 126-127; World War I violations, 368-369
New Deal, 495-498
New Economic Policy (NEP), 412-413, 416-417
New Guinea, 391, 538
New Harmony, 199; *illus.,* 199
New Hebrides, 538
New Lanark, 198-199
New Zealand, 352, 548, 625
Newcastle, Duke of, 13
Newfoundland, 351
Newton, Sir Isaac, 44-45, 77
Next Million Years, The (Darwin), 304
Ngo Dinh Diem, 599-600
Nibelungenlied Wagner, 139
Nicholas I (Russia), 157, 161, 174, 265, 279-281, 283-284, 286; *illus.,* 279
Nicholas II (Russia), 287, 289-290, 292, 367, 399-401
Niebuhr, Reinhold, 664
Niemoeller, Martin, 464
Nietzsche, Friedrich, 303, 319, 321, 649; *illus.,* 322
Niger, 615
Nigeria, 336, 619
Nightingale, Florence, 281
Nihilism, 285
Nine-Power Treaty, 493-494, 502
Nivelle, General Robert Georges, 379
Nixon, Richard, 593
Nkrumah, Kwame, 615, 620
Noailles, Viscount of, 98-99
Nobel, Alfred, 212
Nobility: French, 91-96, 98-99; Russian, 64-65, 67-69
Normandy landings, 535-536
North America Act of 1867, 351
North Africa: in World War II, 527-528, 533-534
North Atlantic Treaty Organization (NATO), 430, 548, 552, 556, 593, 624-625
North Briton, 74
North, Lord Frederick, 74-76, 350
Northern Society (Russia), 157
Norway, 148, 212, 525, 630
Noske, Gustav, 448
Not By Bread Alone (Dudintsev), 588
Notre Dame de Paris (Hugo), 139
Novikov, Nicholas, 67-68
Noyades, 107
Nuri Sa'id, 613
Nyerere, Julius, 615
Nystadt, Treaty of, 26

O

Obrenovich, Milosh, 155
O'Connell, Daniel, 223
October Diploma (Austria), 266
October Manifesto (Russia), 290
Octobrists (Russia), 291
Odessa, 155
Offenbach, Jacques, 316
Oil: Middle Eastern, 507, 576, 613-614
Okinawa, 538, 607
Oldenburg, state of, 129-130
Old Believers, 22, 30; Ollivier, Emile, 230; Olmütz, humiliation of, 255
On Liberty (Mill), 194-195
On the Origin of Species by Means of Natural Selection (Darwin), 298-299, 302
On the Origin of the Inequality of Mankind (Rousseau), 54
"Open hearth" process, 180
Opium War, 337
Organization for European Economic Cooperation (OEEC), 556
Organization of American States, 621, 624
Organization of Labor, The (Blanc), 200
Orgburo, 562
Orlando, Vittorio Emanuele, *illus.,* 387
Orleans, Duke of, 6, 14
Orozco, José, 578
Orthodox Church, 24, 59, 271-273, 284, 427
Ostermann, Count Andrei Ivanovich, 63-64, 70-71
Ottoman Empire (*see also* Turkey), 30-33, 123, 154-156, 273, 280-281
Outer Mongolia, 603
OVRA ("Vigilance Organization against Anti-Fascist Crimes"), 446
Owen, Robert, 198-200, 286
Owen, Wilfred, 379

P

Painting: modern, 656-657; *illus.,* 657; nineteenth century, 310-313; Romantic era, 140-141, *illus.,* 142
Pakistan, 572-573, 625, 609-610
Palestine, 376, 383, 390-391, 507-508, 552
Palmerston, Lord, 222, 239
Panama, 344
Panama Canal, 249, 344
Panama scandal, 234
Pan-German movement, 275
"Panopticon," 192-193
Pan-Slavism, 173, 270
Paoli, Pasquale, 113

Papal States, 17, 148, 169, 208, 229, 241

Papen, Franz von, 459-460

Papineau, Louis Joseph, 350

Paraguay, 624

Pareto, Vilfredo, 647-648

Paris: Commune of 1871, 231-232; in French Revolution, 96-98; in revolution of 1848, 165; in World War II, 527, 536

Paris, Peace of (1763), 38-39, 74

Paris, Peace of (1856), 281

Parlement of Paris, 94

Parliament Act of 1911, 216

Parliament Act of 1918, 221

Parma, Duchy of, 161, 168

Parnell, Charles, 223

Parsons, Talcott, 646

Parthenopean Republic, 115

Partisans (Yugoslavia), in World War II, 566

Passarowitz, Treaty of, 32-33

Passing of the Great Race, The (Grant), 303

Pasternak, Boris, 588, 660

Pathet Lao, 601

Patkul, 24-25

Patton, General George, 536

Paul (Russia), 67-69, 115, 119-120

Paul, Prince (Yugoslavia), 473

Pavelich, Ante, 473-474

Pavlov, Ivan, 645-646; *illus.,* 645

Peasants (see also Serfs): in Austria, 59, 173; in China, 503; in France, 91-98, 165; in Hungary, 276; in Prussia, 19, 57; in Russia, tsarist, 66, 68, 287, 291-292; in Russia, Soviet, 398, 402, 407, 411-413, 417-419

Peel, Robert, 214, 217, 219-220

Penn, William, 24

People's party (Germany), 449, 452, 456

People's Will (Russia), 286, 288

Perry, Commodore Matthew, 332; *illus.,* 345

Perón, Eva, 579

Perón, Juan, 579, 622

Persia (see also Iran), 364

Pestalozzi, Johann, 50

Pestel, Colonel, 157

Pétain, Marshal Philippe, 527-528

Peter I, the Great, 21-30, 32-33

Peter II (Russia), 62-63

Peter III (Russia), 37, 63-65, 71

Petrouchka (Stravinsky), 658

Philhellenic movement, 155-156

Philip II (Spain), 5

Philip V (Spain), 15-17, 31, 62

Philippine Islands, 249, 344-345, 498, 532, 548, 568, 572, 607, 625, 627

Philippine Sea, battle of, 538

Philosophes, 43, 56, 78-79, 93, 99, 136-139, 191, 201, 662-664

"Philosophic Radicals" (*see* Utilitarians)

Philosophy: eighteenth-century social, 78-79; existentialist, 649; historical review, 662-664; modern, 649-652, 660-662; nineteenth century, 318-321; of the Romantic era, 143-144; Social Darwinist, 300-305

Philosophy of Poverty, The (Proudhon), 206

Physics, 45-46, 652-653

Physics and Politics (Bagehot), 322

Physiocrats, 47-48, 55-56, 59, 61, 78

Picasso, Pablo, 656-657

Piedmont, 123, 148, 167, 169, 173-174, 229, 238-239, 265

Pietism, 70, 79-80, 136

Pilsudski, Jozef, 429, 474

Pitt, William, 32, 37-39, 74

Pitt, William, the Younger, 76

Pius VII, Pope, 118

Pius IX, Pope, 168-169, 208

Pius XI, Pope, 241, 446

Plains of Abraham, battle of, 38

Platt Amendment, 345

Plehve, Vyacheslav, 289

Poincaré, Raymond, 488

Poland, 18, 30-33, 55, 170, 174, 257, 279-280; Congress of Vienna, 146-147; Fourteen Points, 385; Great Northern War, 24-25; Little Entente, 514; partitions of, 70-73, 113, 411; Pilsudski *coup,* 429, 474; revolt of 1956, 583, 591; revolution of 1830, 161; satellite status, 565, 583, 591, 596; Upper Silesia, 450; Versailles settlement, 388-390; World War II, 432, 521-525

Police: in French Revolution, 107; in fascist Italy, 446; in Nazi Germany, 463; in U.S.S.R., 398-399, 407

Polignac, Prince of, 159

Polish Succession, War of the, 32-33, 70-71

Political thought: anarchist, 206-207; and American Revolution, 77-78; Burke, 145; élitist and anti-rationalist theories, 321-333; Enlightenment and, 52-56; Hegel's influence, 143-144; historical determinism, 303-305; and Industrial Revolution, 187; Locke, 44; Marxian, 203-205; J. S. Mill, 194-195; Mussolini, 444-445; nihilism, 285; Pareto, 647-648; racism, 302-303; Social Darwinist, 300-301; socialist utopian, 196-200; Utilitarianist ("Philosophic Radical"), 193

Pombal, Marquis of, 61-62

Pomerania, 21

Pompadour, Madame de, 36, 47

Poniatowski, Stanislas, 71

Pope, Alexander, 52

Popolo d'Italia, Il, 440

Popular Front, 490-491

Popular party (Italy), 441

Population (see also Emigration; Immigration): Austrian Empire, 172; France, 92, 229; India, 609; Industrial Revolution and, 185; Malthusian theory, 190-192; nineteenth-century world, 353; Prussia, 18, 57; Russia, 285-286

Port Arthur, 288-289

Portrait of the Artist as a Young Man (Joyce), 655

Portsmouth, Treaty of, 289

Portugal, 61, 153, 604, 630

Positivists, 650

Potato War, 60

Potemkin villages, 73

Potsdam conference, 541

Pragmatic Sanction, 17, 34

Prague, Peace of, 258

Pravda, 404, 414

Preface to Politics (Lippmann), 648

Pressburg, Treaty of, 121

Pretoria Convention, 222

"Primrose League," 217

Prince, The (Machiavelli), 56

Principles of Ethics (Spencer), 301

Principles of Political Economy, The (Mill), 194

Progress of the Human Mind, The (Condorcet), 45

Proudhon, Pierre, 206-207

Prussia (see also Bismarck; Germany), 4, 18-21, 34, 71, 128-129, 240, 280-281; *1740-1795, map,* 19; Congress of Vienna, 146-147; European revolution, 161; Frederick the Great, 56-58; and French Revolution, 103, 106, 112-113; Napoleonic Wars, 114, 120-123; Potato War, 60; Revolution of 1848, 169-171, 174

Psychology, 642-646, 655

Puerto Rico, 249, 344, 627-628

Pugachev, Emelyan Ivanovich, 66-67

Pushkin, Aleksandr Sergeyvich, 139

Pu-yi, Emperor, 502-503

Q

Quadruple Alliance, 148-149, 153

Quakers, 77

Quebec Act, 76

Quemoy, 569, 597

Quesnay, François, 47

Quiet Don, The (Sholokov), 588

R

Racine, Jean Baptiste, 46

Racism: in Nazi Germany, 461-462; Nietzsche and, 321-322; Social Darwinist view, 302-303

Radical-Socialists (France), 489-490

Radich, 473

Radischev, Alexander, 67-68

Railway Servants Act (Hungary), 272

Rankovic, Aleksandr, 596

Rapallo, Treaty of, 428-429, 439

Rasputin, Gregory, 292, 399; *illus.,* 400

Rathenau, Walter, 450, 452

Reconstruction Finance Corporation, 495-496

"Red Sunday," 289

Reflections on the Revolution in France (Burke), 112, 136, 145

Reflections on Violence (Sorel), 206

Reform Act of 1918, 216

Reform Bill of 1832, 214-215

Reform Bill of 1867, 215-216

Reign of Terror, 106-110

Reinach, Joseph, 234

Reinsurance Treaty, 363

Religion (*see also* Roman Catholic Church): in Austria, 59; and Austro-Hungarian minorities, 271-273; Bismarck and the Church, 260-262; Darwinism and, 299-300; Deism, 50-52; evangelism, eighteenth century, 79-80; in France, 110, 117-118, 158-159; in Great Britain, 222; and historicism, 650-652; imperialism and, 348; and Irish Home Rule, 222-223; in Nazi Germany, 464-465; *philosophes* and, 50-52; and philosophy, 664; in Prussia, 57; and Romantic movement, 137, 142-143; in Russia, 22, 24, 70, 427

Remarque, Erich Maria, 379

Renner, Karl, 275-276

Reparations (German), 450, 453, 456-459, 488, 493

Republican People's party (Turkey), 610

Rerum Novarum, 208-209

Resistance movement (French), 528, 542, 560

Reynaud, Paul, 527

Reynolds, Sir Joshua, 81-82; *illus.,* 81

Rhee, Syngman, 606

Rhineland, 389, 457, 510, 512

Rhodes, Cecil, 302, 333, 347-348

Rhodesia, 616

Ribbentrop, Joachim von, 457, 522

Ricardo, David, 190-192, 194-195

Richardson, Samuel, 80-81, 137

Richelieu, Cardinal, 14

Riego, Colonel, 152-153

Riley, Bridget, *illus.,* 657

Rime of the Ancient Mariner (Coleridge), 138

Ring of the Nibelungen (Wagner), 316

Ripperdá, 15

Rise of Silas Lapham (Howells), 306

Rite of Spring, The (Stravinsky), 658

Rivera, Diego, 578

Rivera, General Primo de, 466-467

Robespierre, Maximilien, 105-107, 109-110; *illus.,* 108

Robinson Crusoe (Defoe), 50

Robles, Gil, 467-468

Rockefeller, John D., 248

Roderick Random (Smollett), 80

Rodin, Auguste, 313

Roehm, Captain Ernst, 452, 461; *illus.,* 455

Roger-Ducos, 115

Roman Catholic Church: in Austria, 58-59, 265, 274-275; in Belgium, 160; Bismarck and, 260-262; Darwinism and, 299; and Dreyfus case, 235, 237; in France, 90-91, 118, 489; and French Revolution, 98-101, 110; in Great Britain, 214, 222; in Hungary, 276; and Industrial Revolution, 207-209; in Italy, 241, 446; Lateran Treaty, 446; Montesquieu on, 53; in Nazi Germany, 464; *philosophes'* attacks on, 50-52; in Portugal, 61; in Spain, 62, 152, 465-467

Roman Republic (French), 115

Romanov, Fedor, 21-22

Romanov, Ivan, 22

Romanov, Sophia, 22

Romanticism: in the fine arts, 140-142; in literature, 137-139; in music, 139-140; in philosophy, 143-144; in religion, 142-143; Romantic "Style," 144

Rome, 17, 123, 240

Rome, Treaty of, 630

Rommel, Field Marshal Erwin, 533

Romney, George, 82

Roon, Albrecht von, 256

Roosevelt, Franklin D., 495-498, 528, 531, 535-536, 540, 542-543; *illus.,* 541

Roosevelt, Theodore, 248-249, 289, 348; *illus.,* 343

Rosenberg, Alfred, 452

Rosetta Stone, 115

Rossellini, Roberto, 561

Rossoni, 444

Rostow, W. W., 178

Rothschild, House of, 181

Rougemont, Denis de, 646

Rousseau, Jean Jacques, 47, 49-50, 53, 54, 55, 58, 79, 95, 105, 113, 136

Royal Academy (England), 81

Royce, Josiah, 318

Ruhr, 450, 453-454, 456, 488, 514-515

Rumania (*see also* Moldavia; Wallachia), 271-272, 366, 368, 374, 383, 385, 390, 394, 432-433, 472, 474, 514, 534, 565, 596

Ruskin, John, 220, 324

Russell, Bertrand, 554

Russia (*after 1917 see* Union of Soviet Socialist Republics), 265-266, 273; agriculture, 281-283, 291-292; Alexander II's reforms, 281-283; anti-semitism, 287, 290; and Belgian independence, 161; civil liberties, 289-290; Congress of Vienna, 146-149; culture, 21, 28, 30; Crimean War, 222, 256, 280-281; Decembrist revolt, 156-157; domestic policies, *1881-1914,* 287-288; Dumas, *1906-1914,* 291-292; economy, 278, 287; education, 28, 280; eighteenth century, 1, 4, 21-30, 32-33, 36, 62-73; Enlightenment, 65-67; foreign policy, nineteenth century, 286-287; Greek independence, 154-155; and Hungarian 1848 revolt, 174; imperialism, 329; intellectual activity, 283-284; law, 66, 280, 283; literature, 306-307; Napoleonic Wars, 115, 119-123, 129-130; Nicholas I, 279, 281; and Poland, 113, 161, 257; Quadruple Alliance, 153; revolution of 1905, 289-291; revolutionary thought, 285-286; Russo-Japanese War, 288-289; Troppau Protocol, 153; Versailles settlement, 385-386, 388, 394; World War I, 358-359, 362-365, 367, 370-373

Russlan and Ludmilla (Glinka), 140

Russo-Japanese War, 288-289, 346, 364

Russo-Turkish Wars, 71, 73

Ruthenia, 390, 472

S

Saar Basin, 388-389

Sadowa, battle of, 258

St. Germain, Treaty of, 469

St. Helena, 131

St. Petersburg, 25, 27-28

Saint Simon, Count Claude Henri de, 187, 196-197, 200

Sakhalin Island, 289, 346

Salammbô (Flaubert), 306

Samoa, 344, 391

Samsonov, General, 372

San Stefano, Treaty of, 286

Sand River Convention, 333

Sansom, Sir George, 346

Santo Domingo, 120

Saragat, Giuseppe, 561

Saratoga, battle of, 76

Sardinia, 17, 636

Sargent, John Singer, 310
Sartre, Jean Paul, 649
Sassoon, Siegfried, 379
Saudi Arabia, 507, 576, 614
Savoy, 517
Saxony, 36, 146-147, 258
Schacht, Hjalmar, 455
Scharnhorst, General Gerhard Johann David von, 129
Schleicher, General Kurt von, 457, 459-461
Schleswig-Holstein, 257-258
Schlieffen Plan, 370-371
Schönbrunn, Treaty of, 128
Schopenhauer, Arthur, 319
Schubert, Franz, 140
Schuman, Robert, 233, 556
Schuman Plan, 556
Schuschnigg, Chancellor, 470-471, 518
Schutzbund (Austria), 470
Schwarzenberg, Prince Felix, 173-174
Schroeder, Baron Kurt von, 460
Science, 45, 46, 586, 652-654
Science and Sanity (Korzybski), 650
Scott, Sir Walter, 139
Sculpture: modern, *illus.*, 659; nineteenth century, 313
Sebastopol, 73, 281
Second International, 205
Securities and Exchange Commission, 496
Sedan, battle of, 230-231, 260
Sepoy Rebellion (India), 337-338
"September massacres," 104
Serbia: Balkan wars, 365-366; independence movement, 154-155; World War I, 357-358, 365-367, 374, 376, 385; Yugoslavia, 472-473
Serfdom (*see also* Peasantry): in Austria, 58-60, 173; Decembrist revolt, 157; in France, 92; French abolition, 99; in Poland, 55; in Prussia, 19; Prussian abolition, 129; in Russia, 27-29, 64-66, 68-69, 157, 278; Russian abolition, 281-283
Service, Robert, 310
Seurat, Georges, *illus.*, 310
Seven Years' War, 14, 34-39, 71, 74
Sèvres, Treaty of, 390
Sewing machine, 180-182
Shaftesbury, Lord, 190
Shastri, Lal Bahadur, 609
Shaw, George Bernard, 307, 319; *illus.*, 308
Shelepin, Alexander, 603
Shelley, Percy B., 137, 143
Shintoism, 500
Sholokov, Michael, 588
Shostakovich, Dmitri, 660
Siam (*see* Thailand)
Siberia, 64, 409

Sicily, 167, 239-240, 534, 636
Siegfried Line, 523, 526
Siemens, Sir William, 180
Siéyès, Abbé Emmanuel, 95-96, 115-116
Silesia, 34, 36, 56, 268
Silone, Ignazio, 561
Simon, Jules, 232
Singapore, 572
Singer, Isaac, 180
Sinn Fein, 485
Sinyavsky, Andrei, 590
Skoda armament works, 268
Slavery: Asiento agreement, 7; in British colonies, 336; French abolition, 109; U. S. civil war, 246
Slovakia, 390, 472
Slovenia, 390
Smith, Adam, 48, 191, 195
Smith, Alfred E., 492
Smollett, Tobias, 80-81
Smoot-Hawley Tariff, 493
Social Contract, The (Rousseau), 54-55, 105
Social Credit party (Canada), 629
Social Darwinism, 300-305, 347
Social Democratic party (Austria), 275-276, 469-470
Social Democratic party (Germany), 262-264, 430, 448-449, 456, 561, 632-633
Social Democratic party (Hungary), 472
Social Democrats (Russia), 288-289, 291-292, 399-400, 402-403
Social Revolutionaries (Russia), 288, 291-292, 399-400, 402, 405-406, 409-411
Social Security Act of 1935, 496
Socialism: Austrian Social Democrats, 275; British Labor party platform, 483; British welfare measures, 225-226; and French 1848 revolution, 163-165; French movement, Third Republic, 488-489; German Social Democrats, 262-264; and Industrial Revolution, 178; Marxian, 201-205; Paris Commune of 1871, 231-232; in Republican Spain, 466-467; Russian nineteenth century movement, 286, 288; utopian, 196-200
Socialist party (Italy), 440-442, 636
Socialist party (France), 489-490
Socialist Realism, On (Tertz), 590
Society of Jesus, 50, 52, 57, 61-62, 143, 152, 158
Sociology, 646-648
Soekarno, President, 607-608
Solferino, battle of, 239
Solomon Islands, 538
Solzhenitsyn, 589
Sorel, Georges, 206, 319, 444
Sorrows of Young Werther (Goethe), 137, 140
Soubise, Prince de, 91

South Sea Bubble, 6-8, 11-12
Southeast Asia Treaty Organization (SEATO), 572, 625
Southern Society (Russia), 157
Southwest Africa (German), 491
Souvanna Phouma, 600
Soviets: 1905 revolution, 289-291; 1917 revolution, 400-404
Spain, 212, 259, 446; Civil War, 431, 466-468, 517; in eighteenth century, 5, 15-17, 33-34, 39, 61, 76; economy, present day, 636; and French Revolution, 106, 112-113; Monroe Doctrine, 153-154; and Napoleonic Wars, 123; revolution of 1820, 152-153; Spanish American War, 343-344
Spanish Succession, War of, 7, 20
Spencer, Herbert, 301, 323, 647
Spengler, Oswald, 651
Speransky, Michael, 69, 280
"Spinning jenny," 10, 178-179
Spirit of the Laws, The (Montesquieu), 52-53, 66, 77
Stalin, and China, 504, 546; Cold War policies, 546; and Comintern, 429-430; death and succession, 569, 582-583; domestic policies, 426-428; intellectual life under, 562-563; Poland partition, 525; purges, 422-424; Trotsky and, 405-406, 413-417; World War II, 535-536; Yugoslav revisionism, 566-567; *illus.*, 414
Stalingrad (Volgograd), 533-534
Stamboliisky, Aleksandr, 474
Stamp Act of 1765, 75
Statute of Westminster, 351, 486-487
Stavisky case, 489, *illus.* 490
Steam engine, 10, 178
Steel, Bessemer process, 180
Stein, Baron vom und zum, 129
Stephenson, George, 180
Stevenson, Adlai, 553, 594
Stimson, Henry, 515
Stolypin, Peter, 291-292
Strauss, Johann, 316
Stravinsky, Igor, 658-659
Streltsy, 22, 24
Stresemann, Gustav, 449, 456, 512
Strike, right to, 188 (*see also* Le Chapelier Law)
Stroganov, Michael, 68
Strossmayer, Bishop, 272-273
Study of History, A (Toynbee), 651
Stupid Nineteenth Century, The (Daudet), 324
Sturm und Drang, 137
Sudan, 222
Suez Canal, 114, 197, 222, 335
Suez crisis, 611-613
Suffrage: in Austro-Hungarian Empire, 268, 276-277; British Reform Bills, 187-188, 214-216, 484; Chartism, 222; in France, 116,

158-160, 164-165; and French Revolution, 95, 101, 104-106, 111; in Germany, 170, 256, 258-259, 449; in Italy, 238, 444-445; in Japan, imperial, 346; in Poland 1815, 161; in Russia, 283, 290-292; Russian Constitution of 1936, 424; Spanish Constitution of 1812, 152

Sugar Act of 1764, 74-75
Sumner, William Graham, 323
Sun Yat-sen, 429, 502, 504
Suvorov, General Aleksandr, 115
Sweden, 1, 15, 18, 21, 24-26, 61, 120, 123, 148, 188, 212, 549, 630
Switzerland, 115, 123, 148, 211-212, 549, 630
Syllabus of Errors, 208, 260
Synge, John, 224
Syria, 390-391, 507, 574, 611-613

T

Tables Turned, The (Wordsworth), 138
Tadjikistan, 425
Taiwan, 547, 549
Talleyrand, 146-147, 159
Tanganyika, 391 (*see also* German East Africa)
Tannenberg, battle of, 372
Tarawa, 538
Tashkent Conference, 603
Tasmania, 350
Teheran Conference, 535, 540
Tertz, Abram (*see* Sinyavsky, Andrei)
Tennessee Valley Authority, 496
"Tennis-Court Oath," 96
Tennyson, Alfred, 309-310
Test Act, 214
Thailand, 533, 572, 601, 625
Thaw, The (Ehrenberg), 488
Thiers, Adolphe, 159, 164, 232
Thirty Years' War, 18
Thyssen, Fritz, 458
Tibet, 364, 597
Tilden, Samuel Jones, 246
Tilsit agreement, 123, 129, 146
Tinbergen, Nikolaas, 646
Tirpitz, Admiral Alfred von, 264
Tisza, Coloman, 277
Tisza, Stephen, 277
Tito, 536, 566-567, 591, 597, 598; *illus.,* 567
Tocqueville, Alexis de, 131-132, 164-165, 324, 554
Togoland, 343, 391
Tom Jones (Fielding), 80
Townshend, Viscount, 8
Townshend Duties, 75-76
Toynbee, Arnold, 651-652
Trade: British Commonwealth, 483; British Corn Laws, 219-220, 224-225; eighteenth-century European,

5, 11, 33-34, 38; German nineteenth century, 261, 263; and Napoleonic Wars, 120, 126-128
Trafalgar, battle of, 120-121, 130
Transjordan, 508
Trans-Siberian railway, 287-288, 370
Transvaal, 333-334, 363
Transylvania, 390, 471-472, 474, 596
Trent, 241, 362, 388-389
Trial Begins, The (Tertz), 590
Trianon, Treaty of, 471
Trieste, 241, 388-389
Triple Alliance, 359, 363
Triple Entente, 359, 363-365
Tripoli, 242, 343, 365
Tristan and Isolde (Wagner), 316
Trollope, Anthony, 306
Troppau Protocol, 153
Trotsky, Leon, 404, 429-430; civil war actions, 409, 411; exile, 422-423; NEP, 412-413; during revolution, 404-405; and Stalin, 413-417; *illus.,* 410, 416
Trujillo, Rafael, 621-622
Truman, Harry S., 537, 553, 569
Truman Doctrine, 566
Tsushima, battle of, 288
Tull, Jethro, 8
Tunisia, 340, 362, 517-518, 620
Turgenev, Ivan, 285, 306
Turgot, Anne Robert, 47-48, 90, 94
Turkmenistan, 425
Turkey (*see also* Ottoman Empire), 59, 70-72, 123, 242, 256, 286, 363; Ataturk, 508; CENTO, 625; Cyprus question, 625; Great Northern War, 23-26; Menderes crisis, 610-611; Truman Doctrine, 566; World War I, 365-366, 368, 376, 385, 390
Turner, Joseph Mallord, 311
Tuscany, 17, 32, 60, 123, 168, 239
Twain, Mark, 324
Two Sicilies, Kingdom of, 153
Two Treatises of Government, The (Locke), 44
Tyranny of Words (Chase), 650

U

U-2 Incident, 593
U Thant, 549
Ukraine, 161, 373, 408-409, 425-426; during civil war, 409-411
Ulm, battle of, 121
Ulysses (Joyce), 655-656
Under Fire (Barbusse), 379
Uniates, 271
Union Act of 1840 (Canada), 351
Union of South Africa, 352, 391, 486, 605, 615-616
Union of Soviet Socialist Republics (*see also* Russia *for pre-1917*):

1953, *map,* 564; agriculture, 562, 586-587; anti-semitism, 427, 563; atomic weapons, 593-594; bloc relations, 565-567, 583, 591-592, 596-597; Brest-Litovsk, 408-409; China split, 547, 597-599, 603-604; civil war, 409-412; Cold War policies, 546-549, 565-566; collectivization and industrialization, 417-421; Constitution of 1936, 424-426; Cuban crisis, 595; culture, 562-563, 588-590; economy, 407-409, 412-413, 562, 585-587; education, 426-427, 587-588; and Egypt, 591; Finland conquest, 525; Franco-Russian alliance, 1935, 515; Germany and, 546-547, 566, 592-593; Greek civil war, 565; Korean War, 568-569; Marxism and, 433-434; Molotov-Ribbentrop pact, 431-432; nationalizations, 407; NEP, 412-413; Poland partition, 521-523, 525; purge trials, 422-424; religion, 427-428; revolution of 1917, 399-407 *map,* 409; science in, 586; Southeast Asia policies, 567-569, 600-603; Stalin-Trotsky struggle, 413-417; Stalin's successors, 582-583; test ban agreement, 595; war communism, 407-409; in World War II, 431-433, 530-531, 533-534, 536-538, 540-543
Unionist party (England), 223-224
Unitarians, 276
United Arab Republic, 613
United Nations: China representation, 625; Cyprus crisis, 624; and Congo, 618-619; Indonesia and, 608; Israel-Arab conflict, 575, 611; and Iran, 565; Kashmir issue, 609-610; Korean War, 568-569; powers of, 548-549, 552, 626; and Union of South Africa, 615-616
United States: agricultural revolution, 184; Alliance for Progress, 621; China policy, 547, 625; civil rights, 626-627; civil war, 243-246; Cold War policies, 546, 548-549, 593-594, 625; and Dominican Republic crisis, 494; economy, 247-249, 494-498, 625; Germany occupation, 546-547, 592-593; and Greek independence, 155; imperialism, 329, 343-345; Industrial Revolution, 179-182; isolationism, 492-493, 514-515; Japan occupation, 571; Kellogg-Briand pact, 493; Korean War, 568-569; Lend-Lease, 531; literature, 307-310; Louisiana Purchase, 120; Marshall Plan, 552-553; McCarthyism, 554-555; Mexico and, 229-230; Monroe Doctrine, 153-154, 249; Napoleonic wars, 128; New Deal, 494-498; Nine Power Treaty, 493-

494; "Open Door" policy, 332; Russian civil war, 409; Southeast Asia policy, 599-600, 608; Spanish American war, 249-250; test ban agreement, 595; Truman Doctrine, 566; U-2 incident, 593; Versailles treaty, 394; Vietnam War, 600-602; War of Independence, 74-78; World War I, 368-369, 380; World War II, 531-538, 540-543
Unkiar Skelessi, Treaty of, 280-281
Ustashi (Yugoslavia), 473-474
Utilitarianism, 192-194, 218-219
Utrecht, peace of, 1, 4, 15, 17, 20, 33
Uzbekistan, 425

V

Vaihinger, Hans, 319
Van Gogh, Vincent, 313, *illus.,* 311
Vanderbilt, Cornelius, 249
Vanderlubbe, 460
Varennes, Louis XVI's flight, 102
Vatican City, 241; Lateran Treaty, 446
Vatican Council (*1870*), 261
Venetia, 168, 172, 239-240, 258
Venezuela, 622
Venizelos, 374
Vereeniging, Treaty of, 334
Versailles, Treaty of, 382-394, 448, 492-493; *Diktat* thesis, 512, 514; settlement, *map,* 389
Vichy France, 527-528
Victor Emmanuel, King, 239-240
Victor Emmanuel III, King, 242, 439-440, 442, 518
Victoria, Queen, 177, 214, 222, 337; *illus.,* 216
Vienna, Congress of, 130, 145-149
Vienna Constituent Assembly, 173
Viet Cong, 600-601
Viet Minh, 572, 600
Vietnam, 572; Vietnam War, 599-604
Villeneuve, Admiral Pierre, 120-121
Volstead Act, 494, 496
Voltaire, 7, 14, 37, 47, 50-52, 56, 58, 65, 71; *illus.,* 51
Von Weber, Carl, 140
Voting (*see* Suffrage)

W

Wagner, Richard, 316, 451
Wagram, battle of, 128
Wake Island, 532
Waldteufel, Emil, 316
Wallachia, 155
Wallas, Graham, 648

Walpole, Horace, 82
Walpole, Robert, 8, 12, 33-34, 37-38
Warren Commission Report, 628
Warren, Earl, 626, 628
Warsaw, Grand Duchy of, 73, 123, 128-129
Warsaw Pact, 548, 583
Washington, George, 8, 35, 77
Waterloo, battle of, 131
Watt, James, 10
Watts, George Frederick, 310
Way of All Flesh, The (Butler), 308
Weber, Max, 647
Wei-hai-wei, 501
Weisman, August, 299
Well-Tempered Clavichord (Bach), 316
Wellington, Duke of, 130, 215
Wells, H. G., 308
Wesley, Charles, 80
Wesley, John, 79-80, 136
West Indies, 13, 27, 38, 120, 184, 336
Westphalia, Kingdom of (Napoleonic), 123
Westphalia, Peace of, 17
Weygand, General Maxim, 411, 527
Whig party (England), 11-13, 33, 37-38, 216-217
Whistler, James M., 311
White Terror, 111, 130
Whitman, Walt, 309
Whitney, Eli, 179-180, 182
Whittier, John Greenleaf, 200, 309
Wilkes, John, 74
William I (Netherlands), 160-161
William I (Prussia), 256-257, 259-260, 262
William II, (Germany), 262-264, 343, 348, 360, 363, 365, 367
William IV (England), 215
Wilson, Daniel, 234
Wilson, Harold, 631-632
Wilson, Woodrow, 249, 382, 385-386, 388-390, 394, 439, 492-493, 578; *illus.,* 387
Windischgrätz, Prince, 173
Witte, Count Sergei, 287, 289-291
Wittgenstein, Ludwig, 650
Wordsworth, William, 137-138, 143, 194, 309
Working classes (*see* Classes, social; Labor)
World Court, 458
World War I: *map,* 375; Balkan front, 374-376; causes, 359-369; and colonies, 376; Dardanelles campaign, 373-374; eastern front, 371-373; German defeat, 447-448; Italian front, 373; morale, 379-380; naval battles, 376-377; peace settlement, 382-394; propaganda in, 381; Russia and, 399, 404-409; technological innova-

tions, 377-379; western front, 370-371
World War II: *map,* 526; *map,* Pacific, 539; Allied coalition, 540-543; Axis defeats, 533-537; Battle of Britain, 529-530; casualties, 545-546; fall of France, 527-528; Finnish campaign, 525; Greek campaign, 530; Japan conquests, 532-533; Lend-Lease, 532; "phony war" and blitzkrieg, 525-527; Polish campaign, 524-525; Russian invasion, 530-531; supply problems, 534; technological innovations, 524; unconditional surrender policy, 541; Yalta Conference, 536
Wrangel, Baron Peter N., 411
Württemberg, 120, 258

X

Xerxes (Handel), 83

Y

Yalta Conference, 536, 542-543, 565
Yeats, W. B., 224
Yemen, 575, 613
Yevtushenko, Evgenii, 588-589
Young, Arthur, 8, 73, 97
Young, Owen D., 457
Young Plan, 457, 459
Young Turks, 273
Ypsilanti, General, 155
Yuan Shih-k'ai, 502
Yudenich, General Nikolai, 410-411
Yugoslavia, 32, 383; Constitution of *1963,* 596; economy, 567; revisionism, 591; Serb and Croat extremists, 472-474; Treaty of Rapallo, 439; Tito, 548, 566-567, 591-592, 597; Versailles settlement, 390-394; World War II, 433, 530

Z

Zambia (Northern Rhodesia), 615
Zashchenko, Mikhail, 563
Zemski sobor, 22
Zhdanov, Andrei, 562-563
Zhukov, Marshal Georgi, 582, 584
Zinoviev, Grigori, 416, 423, 428-429
Zinzendorf, Count, 79
Zionism (*see also* Israel), 275, 575
Zola, Emile, 235, 306-307
Zollverein, 169-170, 257

1909	"Soak-the-rich" budget in Britain: step toward the welfare state
1911	Onset of prolonged revolution in China and Mexico
1914	(June 28) Assassination of Archduke Francis Ferdinand at Sarajevo: outbreak of First World War
1917	(March 8) Riots in Petrograd: beginning of Russian Revolution
1919	Postwar peace conference at Paris: Treaty of Versailles
1922	(October 30) Fascist "March" on Rome: Mussolini in power
1923	Turkey declared a republic: landmark in Atatürk's revolution
1925	Locarno agreements: brief era of "fulfillment" in Europe
1929	(October) "Crash" in Wall Street: beginning of Great Depression
1931	Japanese aggression in Manchuria: first step on road to World War II
	Statute of Westminster: "constitution" of British Commonwealth
1933	Hitler Chancellor of Germany: Nazi dictatorship
	Franklin D. Roosevelt President of United States: the New Deal
1936	Outbreak of Civil War in Spain
	Wholesale purge trials in Stalinist Russia
1938	(September) Munich agreements dismembering Czechoslovakia: "appeasement"
1939	(August 23) Hitler-Stalin non-aggression pact
	(September 1) Outbreak of Second World War
1941	(June) Nazi attack on Russia and (December) Japanese attack on Pearl Harbor
1945	End of World War II: Charter of United Nations drawn up at San Francisco